7TH EDITION

BUSINESS RESEARCH METHODS

WILLIAM G. ZIKMUND
Oklahoma State University

Australia · Canada · Mexico · Singapore · Spain · United Kingdom · United States

Business Research Methods, 7th Edition
William G. Zikmund

Vice President/Editor-in-Chief:
Jack Calhoun

Vice President/Team Director:
Melissa Acuña

Acquisitions Editor:
Steve Hazelwood

Developmental Editor:
Mary Draper

Marketing Manager:
Marc Callahan

Production Editor:
Robert Dreas

Manufacturing Coordinator:
Diane Lohman

Compositor:
Parkwood Composition Service, Inc.

Printer:
Quebecor World Versailles
Versailles, Kentucky

Design Project Manager
Michael H. Stratton

Internal Designer:
Ann Small Design

Production House:
Lifland et al., Bookmakers

Cover Designer:
Michael H. Stratton

Cover Photographer/Illustrator:
Humberto Calzada

Photography Manager:
Deanna Ettinger

Photo Researcher:
Susan Van Etten

Printed in the United States of America
1 2 3 4 5 05 04 03 02

For more information contact South-Western, 5191 Natorp Boulevard, Mason, Ohio 45040.
Or you can visit our Internet site at: http://www.swcollege.com

Library of Congress Cataloging-in-Publication Data

Zikmund, William G.
Business research methods/William G. Zikmund.—7th ed.
p. cm.
Includes index.
ISBN 0-03-035084-0
1. Management—Research. 2. Business—Research. I. Title

HD30.4.Z54 2002
658.4'03'072—dc21 2002020827

TO MY PARENTS

BRIEF CONTENTS

CONTENTS

PART 2 BEGINNING STAGES OF THE RESEARCH PROCESS 91

PART 3 RESEARCH METHODS FOR COLLECTING PRIMARY DATA 173

CHAPTER 25
COMMUNICATING RESEARCH RESULTS: REPORT, PRESENTATION, AND FOLLOW-UP 597

PART 7 VIDEO CASES

PART 8 CRITICAL THINKING CASES

PREFACE

Since the last edition of *Business Research Methods,* the use of the Internet for business research has come of age. I am now very certain that technological developments and social diffusion of the Internet will dramatically shape the future of business research. As the Internet becomes increasingly representative of the U.S. population, innovative techniques that can uniquely be administered online will become standard. In the 21st century, business research on the Internet has moved out of the introductory stage of its product life cycle into the growth stage.

This seventh edition of *Business Research Methods* reflects the astonishing changes in information technology that have taken place in the last few years. I have worked diligently and carefully to make this edition a book that reflects the practice of business research in our new digital age. While this seventh edition of *Business Research Methods* remains focused on time-honored, traditional business research methods, the addition of extensive coverage of Internet research is a major change in this new edition.

NEW TO *BUSINESS RESEARCH METHODS*, SEVENTH EDITION

The seventh edition of *Business Research Methods* places greater emphasis on using the power of the Internet to conduct business research. It was important to me that the new material on Internet business research not be lumped into a closing chapter at the end of the book or into a single chapter on survey research. There are unique aspects of Internet research that touch on information systems, gathering of secondary data, survey design, sample selection, questionnaire design, Web traffic monitoring, and many other topics. The placement of Internet issues was carefully thought out. These issues are integrated in the right place, surrounded by the right context. Enhancements to the chapters and expanded coverage of the Internet's impact on marketing are summarized below.

Chapter 1: The Role of Business Research includes a new, forward-looking discussion called "Business Research in the 21st Century." It examines how two trends, globalization of business and growth of the Internet as a communication medium, have changed the way we think about business research. It sets the stage for many of the changes in other chapters.

Chapter 2: Information Systems and Knowledge Management spotlights the very latest information technology in business enterprises and not-for-profit organizations. This chapter deals with the means for instantaneous and interactive access to information. It expands the discussion of decision support systems with new material on CRM (customer relationship management). A new discussion of business intelligence software explains how researchers analyze data in extensive data warehouses to discover significant patterns and relationships. The material on computerized data archives and databases, especially video databases, has been updated and revised.

Concerns about privacy have caught the attention of the public and the business research world. The impact of new technology on privacy is discussed in depth in Chapter 5: Ethical Issues in Business Research.

The use of the Internet for qualitative exploratory research is growing rapidly. Chapter 7: Exploratory Research and Qualitative Analysis discusses the use of online focus groups, videoconferencing, and streaming media technologies.

Chapter 8: Secondary Data has been substantially revised. Information technology is rapidly changing how secondary data are acquired, and this new edition is at the cutting edge in explaining how. Chapter 8 has been revised to reflect the 2000 Census and the changing face of secondary data in our Internet age.

Chapter 9: Survey Research: An Overview and Chapter 10: Survey Research: Basic Methods of Communication with Respondents have been greatly expanded to reflect the role of the Internet and other new technologies. Chapter 10 has changed more than any other chapter in this textbook. It now includes a major section on the advantages and disadvantages of Internet surveys. It explains everything from the basics (defining an Internet survey) to sophisticated topics such as security concerns. A new section at the end of the chapter explains how WebSurveyor software, available free to students with the purchase of the textbook, can be used to design Internet surveys and compute results quickly and easily.

Chapter 11: Observation Methods features a new section on monitoring Web site traffic. It uses relevant examples about companies—such as Jupiter Media Metrix and Nielsen//NetRatings—that specialize in monitoring Internet activity.

Chapter 15: Questionnaire Design has extensive new material on writing questions and formatting Web pages for Internet surveys. It discusses why the layout and physical attractiveness of a questionnaire are crucial in Internet and other self-administered questionnaires. Going beyond a mere cursory description of Internet questionnaires, this chapter explains how graphical user interfaces allow the researcher to control the background, colors, fonts, and other visual features displayed on the computer screen. It explains status bars, radio-button questions, drop-box questions, variable piping, and many other questionnaire design issues unique to Internet surveys.

Chapter 16: Sampling Designs and Sampling Procedures includes a new section that describes the best methods for drawing Internet samples. The discussion ranges from drawing samples of Web site visitors to forming panels from opt-in sampling frames. It covers sampling problems associated with surveys conducted on the Internet.

Traditional coding of open-ended responses is an expensive, labor-intensive task. Chapter 19: Editing and Coding: Beginning to Transform Raw Data into Information illustrates how Verbastat, new software by SPSS, can provide a fast, reliable way to automate as much of the coding process as possible.

Chapter 20: Basic Data Analysis: Descriptive Statistics has been updated and revised to reflect the growing use of Microsoft Excel in data analysis. Several exhibits and end-of-chapter questions show statistical menus and output from Excel.

Chapter 25: Communicating Research Results: Report, Presentation, and Follow-Up includes discussion of real-time report distribution, whereby employees can share data, executive summaries, and reports on a company intranet.

ORGANIZATION OF THE BOOK

The organization of the seventh edition of *Business Research Methods* follows the logic of the business research process. The book is organized into eight parts. Each of the first six parts presents the basic research concepts for one of the stages in the research process and discusses how these concepts relate to decisions about conducting specific projects.

Part 1: Introduction discusses the scope of business research, provides an overview of the entire business research process, and explains how the Internet and globalization are changing the nature of information systems and research methods. It also addresses theory development and ethical issues in business research.

Part 2: Beginning Stages of the Research Process covers problem definition, research proposals, exploratory research, and secondary data.

Part 3: Research Methods for Collecting Primary Data examines the concepts and issues related to designing and using surveys, observation studies, and experiments.

Part 4: Measurement Concepts discusses the logic of measurement and the practical issues involved in attitude measurement and questionnaire design.

Part 5: Sampling and Fieldwork explains why sampling is required, how to design samples, how to conduct fieldwork, and how to determine sample size. A review of basic statistical concepts appears in this part of the book.

Part 6: Data Analysis and Presentation covers editing, coding, descriptive data analysis, inferential statistical analysis, and communication of research results. It ends with a final note on the use of business research.

Part 7: Video Cases provides 13 outstanding video cases.

Part 8: Critical Thinking Cases includes 32 critical thinking cases, many with computerized databases. The computerized databases are available at http://zikmund.swcollege.com. These cases challenge students to apply and integrate the concepts they have learned.

SUPERIOR PEDAGOGY

More than other research methods textbooks, the seventh edition of *Business Research Methods* addresses students' need to comprehend all aspects of the business research process. To achieve these objectives, chapters include the following features:

- **Learning objectives** at the beginning of each chapter preview the important topics in each chapter. Students can also use the objectives to determine whether they understand the major points of the chapter.
- **Opening vignettes** describe actual business research challenges that may spark class discussion and demonstrate how chapter topics apply to the real world.
- **Research Insights** illustrate key points from the chapter and delve deeper into related business research topics. For example, a Research Insight box in Chapter 10 challenges readers to weigh the impact of Ameritech's new phone service, Privacy Manager, on the success of telephone surveys.
- **An accessible, interesting writing style** continues to be a hallmark of this textbook. With a careful balance between theory and practice and a sprinkling of interesting examples, the writing style helps clarify rather than mystify. In addition, the text offers comprehensive rather than superficial treatment of topics.

- **A review of statistical theory** in Chapter 17 provides students with an overview of the basic aspects of statistics theory. Because this managerially oriented textbook is a business research textbook and not a statistics monograph, students are given the tools needed to review and comprehend statistical theory. Even students with rusty statistical skills will benefit from a quick review of the basic statistical concepts in Chapter 17. In addition, **Statistical Tutor** boxes aid in the learning process by visually reflecting statistical concepts.
- **Key terms** within the chapter and in the margins help students recognize and retain important business research and statistical terminology. Learning the vocabulary of business research is essential to understanding the topic, and *Business Research Methods* facilitates this in three ways. First, key concepts are boldfaced and completely defined when they first appear in the text. Second, all key terms and concepts are listed at the end of each chapter, and many terms are highlighted in a marginal glossary. Third, a glossary summarizing all key terms and definitions appears at the end of the book for handy reference. A glossary of frequently used symbols is also included.
- **Questions for Review and Critical Thinking** promote student involvement in the classroom by prompting them to think about topics beyond the text's coverage. Review materials enhance students' understanding of key concepts.
- **Ethics questions,** identified by a special icon, are included in each chapter. Among the compelling issues students are asked to explore is the redefining of the right to privacy in light of new technology.
- **Exploring the Internet** activities provide considerable value for students of business research. A serious effort has been made to provide current URLs for numerous worthwhile Internet sites. These are not just a bunch of trivial sites, but educational sites that a professor will want his or her students to visit to learn more about a concept. The Internet activities range from going to the Census Bureau's Population Clock to participating in Internet surveys.
- **Extensive video cases and cases** at the end of the textbook illustrate business research concepts and build knowledge and research skills. These cases present interesting, real-life research situations that require students to make thoughtful decisions. They offer the opportunity for active participation in the decision-making process, one of the most effective forms of learning. The video cases portray actual research activities for brands and companies such as Rescue Heroes by Fisher-Price, I-Zone by Polaroid, V8, Ben and Jerry's, and Burke, Inc.

COMPREHENSIVE INSTRUCTOR RESOURCES

Materials to supplement the content of the textbook are available to help instructors perform their vital teaching function. The extensive learning package provided with *Business Research Methods* includes a Test Bank, a computerized Test Bank (ExamView Testing Software), a comprehensive Instructor's Manual and Transparency Masters, PowerPoint presentation slides, data sets for several cases, a comprehensive video library, and online business research resources (available at http://zikmund.swcollege.com).

- **The Instructor's Resource CD-ROM** (ISBN: 0-324-1182406) contains many valuable instructor resources on one easy-to-use CD-ROM:

the Test Bank, ExamView Testing Software, the Instructor's Manual, PowerPoint presentation slides, and data sets for cases.

- **The Test Bank,** written by Tom Quirk of Webster University, has been revised to provide a variety of questions covering every major concept in the textbook. The questions have all been scrutinized to eliminate ambiguity and to provide varying levels of difficulty. Each question is identified with a page number from the textbook where the answer may be located.
- **ExamView,** an easy-to-use automated testing program, allows instructors to create exams by using provided questions, modifying questions, or adding new questions.
- **The Instructor's Manual and Transparency Masters** was designed to ease lecture presentation by offering detailed and comprehensive lecture outlines, solutions to all assignments, and transparency masters. The solution to each case and video case includes the objective of the case, a brief summary of the case, and recommended questions and solutions. The Instructor's Manual is available both on the Instructor's Resource CD-ROM and at the password-protected Instructor Web site at http://zikmund.swcollege.com.
- **PowerPoint Presentation Slides** summarize and illustrate key concepts in each chapter. These slides are available both on the Instructor's Resource CD-ROM and at http://zikmund.swcollege.com, where they can be downloaded.
- **Excel and SPSS Data Sets** are available for several of the end-of-book cases. Theses cases present entire research projects and include databases useful for assignments dealing with statistical analysis. Students may download the data sets at http://zikmund.swcollege.com by clicking on the textbook and then on "Data Sets." Data sets are also available on the Instructor's Resource CD-ROM.
- **The Comprehensive Video Library** introduces students to business research challenges in a variety of interesting businesses. Video cases guide students through problem analysis, problem solving, and application of chapter concepts. Suggested solutions and teaching notes for the video cases are included in the Instructor's Manual.
- **Web Resources at http://zikmund.swcollege.com** provide the latest information about "what's new" and "what's cool" in business research. The site features links to other research-related sites, tips about using the supplemental video library, and much more.

RESOURCES FOR STUDENTS

In addition to the coverage of the latest information technology (described above), the seventh edition includes the following new student resources:

- **A partnership with WebSurveyor,** a specialist in Web-based business research, has made it possible to greatly enhance student learning by providing sample surveys, response scales, question libraries, and survey results developed specifically for *Business Research Methods.* WebSurveyor activities and quizzes, written by the textbook author, appear both in the textbook and on the companion Web site. The WebSurveyor Desktop software is available to students who purchase new textbooks that contain a WebSurveyor postcard with a serial number. Students with a serial numbers should go to http://zikmund.swcollege.com, click on the textbook, click the WebSurveyor button, and follow the steps for registering. Students who need to purchase a serial number should go to http://zikmund.swcollege.com, click on the textbook, click the WebSurveyor button, and follow the steps for purchasing access to this software.

- **The Dedicated Web Site http://zikmund.swcollege.com** has been developed especially for the new edition. Features of the Web site include chapter quizzes that allow students to test and retest their knowledge of chapter concepts. Three separate quizzes are offered for each chapter to encourage retesting. In addition, the Web site features downloadable PowerPoint slides, the very best online business and marketing research resources available, data sets for all the cases, flash cards of key terms, and much more.
- **InfoTrac—College Edition** is packaged free with each new text. This fully searchable online database gives professors and students 24-hour access to full-text articles from a variety of well-known periodicals and scholarly journals.
- **SPSS—Student Version** brings affordable, professional statistical analysis and modeling tools to a student's own PC. Based on the professional version of one of the world's leading desktop statistical software packages, *SPSS 10.0 for Windows Student Version* (ISBN: 0-324-108699) includes an easy-to-use interface and comprehensive online help that lets students learn statistics, not software.

ACKNOWLEDGMENTS

I would like to acknowledge the help of the business research muse, who came to me at odd times without any understanding of the requirements of family life. The time required to write a textbook must be paid for by family and friends.

I owe a debt of gratitude to many people who helped me finish this book. John Bush wrote the first draft of Chapter 25, and I sincerely appreciate his contribution. Lorna Daniells, for many years head of the Reference Library at the Baker Library, Harvard Business School, provided much-needed assistance with earlier drafts of Chapter 8 and Appendix 8B.

Many colleagues contributed ideas and made suggestions that greatly enhanced this book. For their insightful reviews of the manuscript for this and previous editions, I would like to thank the following people, who provided discerning comments and suggestions:

Jack B. Abbott, *University of Phoenix*
Nathan Adams, *Middle Tennessee University*
Donna M. Anderson, *University of Wisconsin–La Crosse*
J. K. Bandyopedyay, *Central Michigan University*
James D. Bell, *Southwest Texas State University*
Ralph F. Catalenello, *Northern Illinois University*
Duane S. Crowther, *Horizon Publishers*
James R. Dyprey, *Lawrence Institute of Technology*
Jud Faurer, *Metropolitan State College of Denver*
Nancie Fimbel, *San Jose State University*
Jim Grimm, *Illinois State University*
Gwenn Grondal, *University of Phoenix*
Nell Tabor Hartley, *Robert Morris College*

Alan G. Heffner, *Silver Lake College*
Kenneth B. Hunt, *University of Phoenix*
Jeffrey J. Jung, *University of Phoenix*
Burton S. Kaliski, *New Hampshire College*
Laurie Larwood, *Claremont McKenna College*
Tony Lybarger, *Friends University*
Iraj Mahdavi, *National University*
Ernie Maier, *Lawrence Institute of Technology*
E. J. Manton, *East Texas State University*
John D. Nicks, Jr., *Pepperdine University*
James Novitzki, *University of Montana*
Carl Obermiller, *University of Florida*
Marjorie Platt, *Northeastern University*
Arthur Reitsch, *East Washington University*
Gerald O. Rintala, *University of Phoenix*
William D. Terpening, *Gonzaga University*
John P. Tillman, *University of Wisconsin–La Crosse*
Gerrit Wolf, *University of Arizona*

There are many people to thank at the South-Western Publishing Company. Behind the scenes, Bob Lynch, Dave Shaut, Jack Calhoun, Melissa Acuña, and Mike Roche made the acquisition of the Dryden Press and the transition to South-Western seamless. Mark Orr and C. J. Jasieniecki cheerfully performed the necessary editorial and developmental efforts during the early stages of the book. Steve Hazelwood and Mary Draper took over in midstream. I appreciate Steve's understanding of my position and his support for this book. Mary Draper coordinated many activities to make my work easier. Marc Callahan's creative thinking and his heartfelt concern for the book's success are especially valued.

The attentive copy editing and permissions work by Quica Ostrander, Sally Lifland, and others at Lifland et al., Bookmakers is greatly appreciated. Photo research by Susan Van Etten made the book more attractive. Barbara Fuller-Jacobsen's management and Bob Dreas's execution of the production tasks related to composition and printing were key factors in the quality improvements in this edition. I appreciate working with such fine professionals. Humberto Calzada graciously allowed us to reproduce his painting "The Way It Was" for the cover. I hope the artwork brings as much joy to others as it does to me.

William G. Zikmund
March 2002

ABOUT THE AUTHOR

A native of the Chicago area, William G. Zikmund Oklahoma. He is a professor in the College of Busine Oklahoma State University. He received a Bachelor of Sci ness from the University of Colorado, a Master of Scienc ing from Southern Illinois University, and a Ph.D. in bus from the University of Colorado.

Before beginning his academic career, Professor Zikmund research for Conway/Millikin Company (a business rese Remington Arms Company (an extensive user of business Zikmund also has served as a business research consultant and nonprofit organizations. His applied business research from interviewing and coding to designing, supervising, a research programs.

During his academic career, Professor Zikmund has publish cles and papers in diverse scholarly journals ranging fr *Marketing* to the *Accounting Review* to the *Journal of Applied* tion to *Business Research Methods,* Professor Zikmund has *Marketing Research, Essentials of Marketing Research,* *Marketing,* and a work of fiction, *A Corporate Bestiary.*

PART 1

INTRODUCTION

CHAPTER

1

THE ROLE OF BUSINESS RESEARCH

What you will learn in this chapter

- To understand the importance of business research as a management decision-making tool.
- To define *business research.*
- To understand the difference between basic and applied research.
- To understand the managerial value of business research and the role it plays in the development and implementation of strategy.
- To define *total quality management* and show its relationship to business research.
- To understand when business research is needed and when it should not be conducted.
- To identify various topics for business research.
- To explain that business research is a global activity.

DuPont has 94,000 employees worldwide and 54,000 in the United States.[1] Its 2000 Work/Life Needs Assessment Survey of employees, conducted across all of DuPont's U.S. business units, is the fourth of its kind in 15 years. This business research provides the company with extensive trend data on employees' work/life behavior and their needs. A key finding of DuPont's latest survey is that, as the company's work force ages, employees' child care difficulties are diminishing, but they see elder care needs emerging on the horizon.

The survey found 88 percent of the respondents identified themselves as baby boomers. About 50 percent of respondents say they have—or expect to have—elder care responsibilities within the next 3 to 4 years, up from 40 percent in 1995.

Prior surveys uncovered that DuPont employees want very much to be able to balance work and family responsibilities, feeling deeply committed to both aspects of their lives. The latest research shows that the company's efforts along these lines have been successful. Employees perceive even greater support by management for work/life issues since the 1995 survey, and indicate that they feel less stress. Support from colleagues is rated high, and women indicated that they now have more role models. Work/life programs are clearly powerful tools that are good for employees and good for business.

The researchers concluded that the feeling of management support is directly connected to employees' discretionary efforts to make the company successful. Employees who use work/life programs reported that they are willing to "go the extra mile."

Other major findings indicate that

- DuPont's work/life programs are highly valued, even by those employees who don't personally use them.
- Flexibility, in particular, is highly valued and appears to work quite well (e.g., almost half of employees have used flexible work hours).
- Other highly valued aspects of work/life are tuition reimbursement, Dependent Care Spending Accounts (where employees can put away before-tax dollars to use on certain types of dependent care), and the company's resource and referral service.

Business research input like this has helped expand and revise work/life programs offerings at DuPont year after year. ■

In thousands of organizations, business research is an important managerial tool that exerts a major influence on decision making. The above example about DuPont's Work/Life Needs Assessment Survey illustrates how business research can provide insights into and solutions for organizational problems. The managerial value and diverse nature of business research can be illustrated by the following additional examples. As you read through these examples, imagine you are an executive considering the importance of business research in providing information essential for good decision making.

Harley-Davidson researchers had Harley owners, would-be owners, and owners of other brands create cut-and-paste collages to express their feelings about Harley-Davidson motorcycles. Whether the artwork was from longtime Harley loyalists or fresh prospects, common themes emerged: enjoyment, the great outdoors, and freedom. Subsequent surveys among customers identified seven core types: Adventure-Loving Traditionalists, Sensitive Pragmatists, Stylish Status-Seekers, Laid-Back Campers, Classy Capitalists, Cool-Headed Loners, and Cocky Misfits. While the groups differed in many aspects, they all appreciated Harley-Davidson products because they were associated with independence, freedom, and power.[2]

When Steelcase, an office furniture manufacturer, decided there was an opportunity for a new product specifically designed for work teams, researchers conducted an observation study. Steelcase placed video cameras at various companies so that they could observe firsthand how teams operate. After the recording period ended, the researchers exhaustively analyzed the tapes, looking for patterns of behavior and motion that workers don't even notice themselves. The main observation was that people in teams function best if they can do some work collaboratively and some privately. Designers used these findings to develop the Personal Harbor brand of modular office units. The units are similar in shape and size to a phone booth and can be arranged around a common space where a team works, fostering synergy but also allowing individuals to work alone when necessary.[3]

Most physicians connect to the Internet daily, and 42 percent work in practices that have Web sites, according to business research conducted in 2001.[4] The study from Harris Interactive found that doctors' use of the Internet has increased significantly since 1999. Only 7 percent of physicians do not use the Internet, compared with 11 percent in 1999. Over half (55 percent) of physicians now use e-mail to communicate with professional colleagues, while 34 percent communicate with support staff via e-mail.

Another study showed that despite the popularity of the Internet among the medical community, few physicians are using the Internet to perform work-related tasks such as communicating with patients and storing medical records.[5] Approximately one in five physicians e-mail their patients, while 4 percent prescribe medicine online. Overall, only 20 percent of doctors believe the Internet is essential to their professional practices. The study found that privacy and security concerns have deterred many physicians from using online services.

According to the Bureau of Labor Statistics (BLS), there were about 693,000 financial managers nationwide in 1998.[6] Although these managers were found in virtually every industry, more than a third were employed by services industries, including business, health, social, and management services. Nearly 3 out of 10 were employed by financial institutions, such as banks, savings institutions, finance companies, credit unions, insurance companies, securities dealers, and real estate firms. Median annual earnings of financial managers were $55,070 in 1998. The middle 50 percent earned between

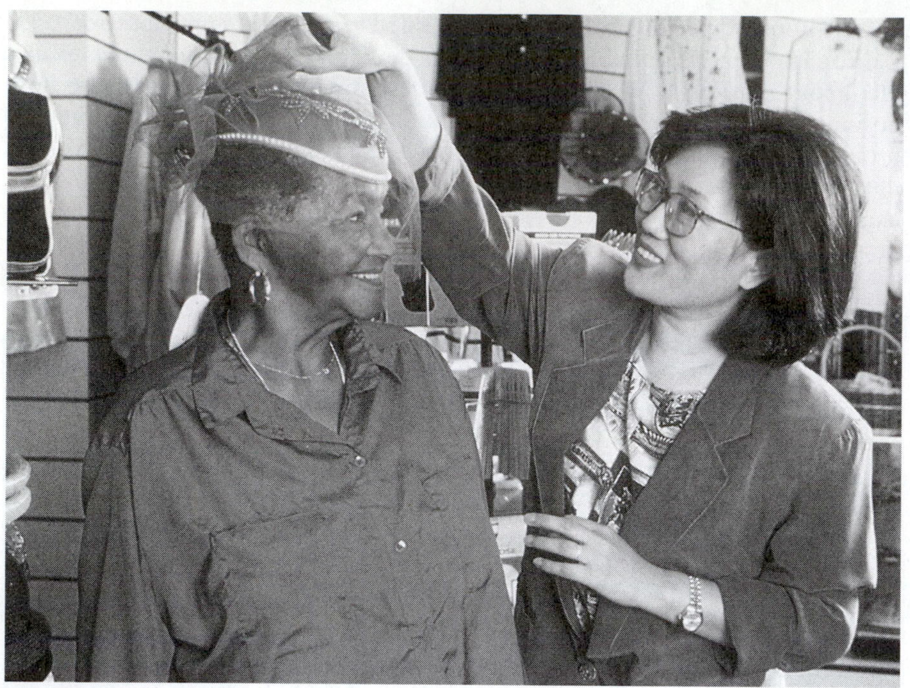

Business research evidence has indicated that customer satisfaction and employee satisfaction are closely linked.[7] *Separate research studies carried out by Ryder and Sears found a very high correlation between the way employees viewed an organization and the way its customers felt about it. Companies like these realize that business research is important to their success.*

$38,240 and $83,800. The lowest 10 percent had earnings of less than $27,680, while the top 10 percent earned over $118,950. The BLS projects that the total employment for the American work force will increase by 14 percent between 1998 and 2008. The outlook for financial managers is good, as the need for financial expertise will keep the profession growing about as fast as the average for all occupations through 2008.

An academic researcher conducted an experiment to determine whether workers whose goals are set unattainably high will perform better than workers whose goals are relatively easy to achieve. The experimenter concluded that the higher the intended level of achievement, the higher the level of performance.

Campbell Soup Company's IntelligentQuisine brand of frozen meals designed to combat high blood pressure, high cholesterol, and diabetes, never made it to national distribution, despite the company's $30 million commitment in resources from its Center for Nutrition and Wellness. Tests in limited markets indicated that demand was not great enough to warrant national marketing.[8] On the other hand, Pepsi's Storm, a caffeinated lemon-lime drink, showed promise in test markets.[9] Equally useful, however, was Pepsi's finding that its replacement for the company's Slice brand would best be marketed nationally under the name Sierra Mist rather than Storm. Pepsi also tested two new flavors of Mountain Dew, cherry-colored Code Red and electric-blue Arctic.

Each of these examples illustrates a business research problem. All of the examples relate to business research, but each illustrates a different form of research. The DuPont example illustrates how survey findings can be directly translated into business strategy. The Steelcase example points out the value of an observation study. The other examples illustrate that researchers use more than surveys. Government and trade association statistics, internal records, psychological tests, and experiments are valuable tools for business research. Because these examples illustrate only a few applications of business research, it should not surprise you to learn that business research is widespread and growing in importance.

SCOPE OF BUSINESS RESEARCH

The scope of business research is limited by one's definition of "business." Certainly research in the production, finance, marketing, or management areas of a for-profit corporation qualifies as business research. A broader definition of business, however, includes not-for-profit organizations, such as the American Heart Association, the San Diego Zoo, and the Boston Pops Orchestra. Each of these organizations exists to satisfy social needs, and each requires business skills to produce and distribute the services that people want. Business research may be conducted by organizations that are not business organizations. (The federal government, for example, performs many functions that are similar, if not identical, to those of business organizations. Federal managers may use research techniques for evaluative purposes in much the same way as managers at DuPont or Ford.) This book uses the term *business research* because all research techniques are applicable to business settings.

Business research covers a wide range of phenomena. For managers the purpose of research is to fulfill the need for knowledge of the organization, the market, the economy, or another area of uncertainty. A financial manager may ask, "Will the environment for long-term financing be better 2 years from now?" A personnel manager may ask, "What kind of training is necessary for production employees?" or "What is the reason for the company's high employee turnover?" A marketing manager may ask, "How can I monitor my retail sales and retail trade activities?" Each of these questions requires information about how the environment, employees, customers, or the economy will respond to executives' decisions. Research may be one of the principal tools for answering these practical questions.

The development and implementation of plans and strategies require information, and every day managers translate their experiences with business phenomena into tactics and strategies. Managers often rely on their own intuition and experience in making decisions because of time pressure or because a problem is minor. However, the primary task of management is effective decision making. "Flying by the seat of the pants" decision making, without systematic inquiry, is like betting on a long shot at the racetrack because the horse's name is appealing. Occasionally there are successes, but in the long run, intuition without research can lead to disappointment. Business research helps decision makers shift from intuitive information gathering to systematic and objective investigation.

A business researcher conducting research within an organization may be referred to as a "marketing researcher," an "organizational researcher," a "director of financial and economic research," or one of many other titles. Although business researchers are specialized, the term *business research* encompasses all of these functional specialties. While researchers in different functional areas may investigate different phenomena, they are comparable to one another because they use similar research methods.

Now that we have illustrated the nature and importance of business research, it is appropriate to provide a formal definition and consider its implications.

BUSINESS RESEARCH DEFINED

business research
The systematic and objective process of gathering, recording, and analyzing data for aid in making business decisions.

The task of business research is to generate accurate information for use in decision making. As we saw above, the emphasis of business research is on shifting decision makers from intuitive information gathering to systematic and objective investigation. **Business research** is defined as the systematic and objective process of gathering, recording, and analyzing data for aid in making business decisions.

This definition suggests, first, that research information is neither intuitive nor haphazardly gathered. Literally, research *(re-search)* means to "search again." It connotes patient study and scientific investigation wherein the researcher takes another, more careful look at data to discover all that can be known about the subject of study.

Second, if the information generated or data collected and analyzed are to be accurate, the business researcher must be objective. The need for objectivity was cleverly stated by the 19th-century American humorist Artemus Ward, who said, "It ain't the things we don't know that gets us in trouble. It's the things we know that ain't so." Thus, the role of the researcher is to be detached and impersonal rather than engaging in a biased attempt to prove preconceived ideas. If bias enters the research process, the value of the data is considerably reduced.

A developer who owned a large area of land on which he wished to build a high-prestige shopping center wanted a research report to demonstrate to prospective retailers that there was a large market potential for such a center. Because he conducted his survey *exclusively* in an elite neighborhood, not surprisingly his findings showed that a large percentage of respondents wanted a "high-prestige" shopping center. Results of this kind are misleading, of course, and should be disregarded. If the user of such findings discovers how they were obtained, the developer loses credibility. If the user is ignorant of the bias in the design and unaware that the researchers were not impartial, his decision may have consequences more adverse than if he had made it strictly on intuition. The importance of objectivity cannot be overemphasized. Without objectivity, research is valueless.

Third, the above definition of business research points out that its objective is to facilitate the managerial decision-making process for all aspects of a business: finance, marketing, personnel, and so on. The definition is not restricted to one aspect of business. An essential tool for management in its problem-solving and decision-making activities, business research generates and provides the necessary qualitative or quantitative information upon which

Some 700 million Sacagawea golden dollars were circulated in the first year they were issued—seven times the initial projection of 100 million coins.[10] The last dollar coin, the Susan B. Anthony, took 14 years to reach the 500 million mark. Extensive business research helped the U.S. Mint, a not-for-profit government agency, design, market, and gain popular support for the Sacagawea dollar.

to base decisions. By reducing the uncertainty of decisions, research reduces the risk of making wrong decisions. However, research should be an *aid* to managerial judgment, not a substitute for it. There is more to management than research. Applying research remains a managerial art.

BASIC RESEARCH AND APPLIED RESEARCH

basic (pure) research
Research that is intended to expand the boundaries of knowledge itself or to verify the acceptability of a given theory.

One reason for conducting research is to develop and evaluate concepts and theories, and **basic**—or **pure—research** attempts to expand the limits of knowledge. It does not directly involve the solution to a particular, pragmatic problem. It has been said that "there is nothing so practical as a good theory." Although this statement is true in the long run, *basic* research findings generally cannot be immediately implemented. Basic research is conducted to verify the acceptability of a given theory or to discover more about a certain concept.

For example, consider this basic research conducted at a university. Academic researchers investigated whether an individual's perception that he or she was doing well on a task would have any influence on future performance. Two nearly identical groups of adults were given the same set of ten puzzles to solve. After the subjects had given their solutions to the researchers, they were told "how well" they did on the test. All members of the first group were told that they had done well: 70 percent correct (regardless of the actual percent correct). The members of the other group were told that they had done poorly (30 percent correct). Then both groups were given another set of ten puzzles. Those subjects who had been told they had done well on the first set of puzzles performed better with the second set of puzzles than did those who had been told they had been relatively unsuccessful with the first puzzle solving. The results of this basic research expand scientific knowledge about theories of general performance behavior. This study was conducted because the researchers thought the theory being tested was far-reaching and applicable to a broad range of situations and circumstances.

applied research
Research undertaken to answer questions about specific problems or to make decisions about a particular course of action or policy decision.

Applied research is conducted when a decision must be made about a specific real-life problem. Applied research encompasses those studies undertaken to answer questions about specific problems or to make decisions about a particular course of action or policy. For example, an organization contemplating a paperless office and a networking system for the company's personal computers may conduct research to learn the amount of time its employees spend at personal computers in an average week.

scientific method
Techniques or procedures used to analyze empirical evidence in an attempt to confirm or disprove prior conceptions.

The procedures and techniques utilized by basic and applied researchers do not differ substantially. Both employ the **scientific method** to answer the questions at hand. Broadly characterized, the scientific method refers to techniques and procedures that help the researcher to know and understand business phenomena. The scientific method requires systematic analysis and logical interpretation of empirical evidence (facts from observation or experimentation) to confirm or disprove prior conceptions. In basic research, first testing these prior conceptions or hypotheses and then making inferences and conclusions about the phenomena lead to the establishment of general laws about the phenomena.

Use of the scientific method in applied research assures objectivity in gathering facts and testing creative ideas for alternative business strategies. The essence of research, whether basic or applied, lies in the scientific method, and much of this book deals with *scientific methodology.* The difference in the techniques of basic and applied research is largely a matter of degree rather than substance.

MANAGERIAL VALUE OF BUSINESS RESEARCH

We have argued that research facilitates effective management. At many companies research drives every aspect of major decision making. For example, at Ford Motor Company, research is so fundamental that management makes hardly any significant decision without the benefit of some kind of business research.

The prime managerial value of business research is that it reduces uncertainty by providing information that improves the decision-making process. The decision-making process associated with the development and implementation of a strategy involves four interrelated stages:

1. Identifying problems or opportunities
2. Diagnosing and assessing problems or opportunities
3. Selecting and implementing a course of action
4. Evaluating the course of action

Business research, by supplying managers with pertinent information, may play an important role by reducing managerial uncertainty in each of these stages.

Identifying Problems or Opportunities

The secret of success is to know something nobody else knows.

ARISTOTLE ONASSIS

Before any strategy can be developed, an organization must determine where it wants to go and how it will get there. Business research can help managers plan strategies by determining the nature of situations or by identifying the existence of problems or opportunities present in the organization.

Business research may be used as a scanning activity to provide information about what is occurring within an organization or in its environment. The mere description of some social or economic activity may familiarize managers with organizational and environmental occurrences and help them understand a situation. Consider two examples:

- The description of the dividend history of stocks in an industry may point to an attractive investment opportunity. Information supplied by business research may also indicate problems.
- Employee interviews undertaken to characterize the dimensions of an airline reservation clerk's job may reveal that reservation clerks emphasize competence in issuing tickets over courtesy and friendliness in customer contact.

Once business research indicates a problem or opportunity, managers may feel that the alternatives are clear enough to make a decision based on experience or intuition, or they may decide that more business research is needed to generate additional information for a better understanding of the situation.

Diagnosing and Assessing Problems or Opportunities

After an organization recognizes a problem or identifies a potential opportunity, an important aspect of business research is the provision of diagnostic information that clarifies the situation. Managers need to gain insight about the underlying factors causing the situation. If there is a problem, they need to specify what happened and why. If an opportunity exists, they may need to explore, clarify, and refine the nature of the opportunity. If multiple opportunities exist, research may be conducted to set priorities. Quantitative or qual-

A cruise line industry study shows that although 43.6 million Americans have considered taking a cruise, 88 percent of Americans have not been on a ship.[11] Further, business research suggests that consumers perceive cruising to be sedentary, regimented, and boring. Most people have the attitude that a shipboard vacation involves sitting around the pool, playing shuffleboard, and putting on pounds. Royal Caribbean Cruise Lines' assessment of these findings led to service changes and new ads showing that its ships are for the adventurous and active. Their large ships have rock climbing walls, jet skis, basketball courts, and more. In television commercials a guest may be shown snorkeling in turquoise waters among tropical fish that glimmer like jewels or riding in a helicopter over majestic seas of ice.

itative investigations may help managers better understand what alternative courses of action are practical.

Selecting and Implementing a Course of Action

After the alternative courses of action have been clearly identified, business research is often conducted to obtain specific information that will aid in evaluating the alternatives and in selecting the best course of action. For example, suppose a fax machine manufacturer must decide to build a factory either in Japan or in South Korea. In such a case, business research can be designed to supply the relevant information necessary to determine which course of action is best for the organization.

Opportunities may be evaluated through the use of various performance criteria. For example, estimates of market potential allow managers to evaluate the revenue that will be generated by each of the possible opportunities. A good forecast supplied by business researchers is among the most useful pieces of planning information a manager can have. Of course, complete accuracy in forecasting the future is not possible, because change is constantly occurring in the business environment. Nevertheless, objective information generated by business research to forecast environmental occurrences may be the foundation for selecting a particular course of action.

Even the best plan is likely to fail if it is not properly implemented. Business research may be conducted with the people who will be affected by a pending decision to indicate the specific tactics required to implement that course of action.

Evaluating the Course of Action

After a course of action has been implemented, business research may serve as a tool to inform managers whether planned activities were properly executed and whether they accomplished what they were expected to accomplish. In other words, managers may use evaluation research to provide feedback for evaluation and control of strategies and tactics.

evaluation research
The formal, objective measurement and appraisal of the extent to which a given activity, project, or program has achieved its objectives.

Evaluation research is the formal, objective measurement and appraisal of the extent to which a given activity, project, or program has achieved its objectives. In addition to measuring the extent to which completed programs achieved their objectives or whether continuing programs are presently performing as projected, evaluation research may provide information about the major factors influencing the observed performance levels.

In addition to business organizations, nonprofit organizations, such as agencies of the federal government, frequently conduct evaluation research. Every year thousands of federal evaluation studies are undertaken to systematically assess the effects of public programs. For example, the General Accounting Office has been responsible for measuring outcomes of the Employment Opportunity Act, the Job Corps program, and Occupational and Safety and Health Administration (OSHA) programs.

performance-monitoring research
Research that regularly provides feedback for evaluation and control of business activity.

Performance-monitoring research is a specific type of evaluation research that regularly, perhaps routinely, provides feedback for the evaluation and control of recurring business activity. For example, most firms continuously monitor wholesale and retail activity to ensure early detection of sales declines and other anomalies. In the grocery and retail drug industries, sales research may use the universal product code (UPC) for packages, together with computerized cash registers and electronic scanners at checkout counters, to provide valuable market-share information to store and brand managers interested in the retail sales volume of specific products.

total quality management (TQM)
A business philosophy that focuses on integrating customer-driven quality throughout the organization.

Performance-monitoring research is an integral aspect of total quality management programs. **Total quality management (TQM)** is a business philosophy that embodies the belief that the management process must focus on integrating customer-driven quality throughout the organization. Total quality management stresses continuous improvement of product quality and service. Managers improve durability and enhance features as the product ages. They strive to improve delivery and other services to keep their companies competitive.

United Airlines' Omnibus in-flight survey provides a good example of performance-monitoring research for quality management. United routinely selects sample flights and administers a questionnaire about in-flight service, food, and other aspects of air travel. The Omnibus survey is conducted quarterly to determine who is flying and for what reasons. It enables United to track demographic changes and to monitor customer ratings of its services on a continuing basis, allowing the airline to gather vast amounts of information at low cost. The information relating to customer reaction to services can be compared over time. For example, suppose United decided to change its menu for in-flight meals. The results of the Omnibus survey might indicate that, shortly after the menu changed, the customers' rating of the airline's food declined. Such information about product quality would be extremely valuable, as it would allow management to quickly spot trends among passengers in other aspects of air travel, such as airport lounges, gate-line waits, or

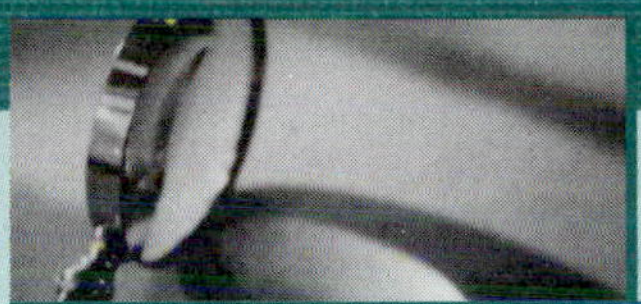

RESEARCH INSIGHT

TQM: NO SWEAT AT JEEP

Chrysler Corporation, Jeep's parent company, asked about 380 paint line workers who wash, wipe, and prepare Jeep Cherokees and Comanches for painting to stop using antiperspirants as part of the company's total quality management effort.[12] Business research on production quality indicated that falling flakes from antiperspirants leave costly blemishes on the sport utility vehicles. Chrysler's investigation showed that antiperspirants worn by workers flaked and fell onto the new paint. Antiperspirants contain chemicals, such as zinc zirconium, that can damage paint. The paint flows away from a fallen flake of these chemicals, causing a depression about the size of a baby's fingertip. George Nancarrow, a regional service manager for the paint maker BASF Corp., said the problem extends to all automakers. He heads a team that investigates cratering in auto finishes. "Craters have a thousand mothers," Nancarrow said. "It can be caused if somebody comes in with too much hand cream on and touches the vehicle, or somebody goes at lunchtime and buys a bag of microwave popcorn and eats it and wipes his hands on the coverall and leans on the car."

Chrysler looked into the matter after its quality control system reported that every vehicle coming off the line had up to 50 imperfections on the roof and hood. Such damage can be enough for an inspector to send a car back for thousands of dollars in repairs.

Because of these findings, managers are trying to persuade workers to switch to deodorants, which control odor but do not stop sweating. Jeep workers are not banned from wearing antiperspirants, but they are being educated about the problem. An awareness program that employees helped develop includes a training session that shows some of the common causes of paint flaws. "You do what you got to do," said one paint line worker. "We want to turn out the best Jeeps. If antiperspirants are causing problems, you got to give them up."

cabin cleanliness. Then managers could rapidly take action to remedy such problems.

When analysis of performance indicates that all is not going as planned, business research may be required to explain why something went wrong. Detailed information about specific mistakes or failures is frequently sought. If a general problem area is identified, breaking down industry sales volume and a firm's sales volume into different geographic areas may provide an explanation of specific problems, and exploring these problems in greater depth may indicate which managerial judgments were erroneous.

Implementing a total quality management program requires considerable measurement. It involves routinely asking customers to rate a company against its competitors, measuring employee attitudes, and monitoring company performance against benchmark standards. It uses a lot of business research. Thus, outside business research with external customers and internal business research with employees in the organization are both important components of a total quality management program.

In Chapter 9, a major section on implementing total quality management discusses planning and researching quality in detail. However, throughout this book, we will explain how business research may contribute to the achievement of customer-driven quality.

WHEN IS BUSINESS RESEARCH NEEDED?

A manager faced with two or more possible courses of action faces the initial decision of whether or not research should be conducted. The determination of the need for research centers on (1) time constraints, (2) the availability of data, (3) the nature of the decision that must be made, and (4) the value of the business research information in relation to its costs.

Time Constraints

Conducting research systematically takes time. In many instances management concludes that, because a decision must be made immediately, there will be no time for research. As a consequence, decisions are sometimes made without adequate information or thorough understanding of the situation. Although such rapid decision making is not ideal, sometimes the urgency of a situation precludes the use of research.

Availability of Data

Often managers already possess enough information to make sound decisions with no business research. When they lack adequate information, however, research must be considered. Managers must ask themselves if the research will provide the information needed to answer the basic questions about a decision. Furthermore, if a potential source of data exists, managers will want to know how much it will cost to obtain the data.

If the data cannot be obtained, research cannot be conducted. For example, many African nations have never conducted a population census. Organizations engaged in international business often find that data about business activity or population characteristics that are readily available in the United States are nonexistent or sparse in developing countries. For example, imagine the problems facing marketing researchers who wish to investigate market potential in places like Uzbekistan, Yugoslavian Macedonia, and Rwanda.

Nature of the Decision

The value of business research will depend on the nature of the managerial decision to be made. A routine tactical decision that does not require a substantial investment may not seem to warrant a substantial expenditure for research. For example, a computer company must update its operator's instruction manual when it makes minor product modifications. The research cost of determining the proper wording to use in updating the manual is likely to be too high for such a minor decision.

The nature of the decision is not totally independent of the next issue to be considered: the benefits versus the costs of the research. In general, however, the more strategically or tactically important the business decision, the more likely it is that research will be conducted.

Benefits versus Costs

Some of the managerial benefits of business research have already been discussed. Of course, conducting research activities to obtain these benefits requires an expenditure; thus, there are both costs and benefits in conducting business research. In any decision-making situation, managers must identify alternative courses of action, then weigh the value of each alternative against its cost. It is useful to think of business research as an investment alternative.

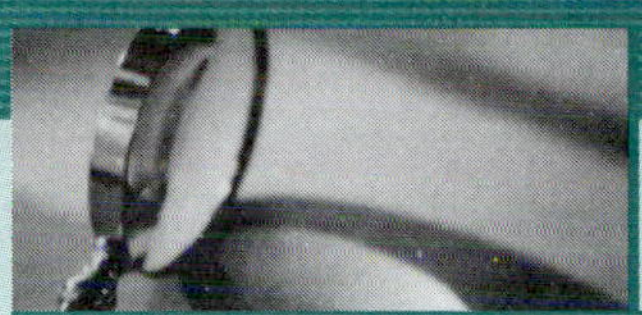

Research Insight

Rolling Rock

For many years Rolling Rock beer was a regional brand in western Pennsylvania.[13] Its signature package was a longneck green bottle with white painted label featuring icons such as a horsehead, a steeplechase fence, and the number "33," which concludes a legend about the beer being brought to you "from the glass-lined tanks of Old Latrobe." The brand, now marketed by Labatt USA, expanded nationally during the 1980s by focusing on core consumers who purchased specialty beers for on-premise consumption and were willing to pay prices higher than those of national brands such as Budweiser.

As years went by packaging options expanded to include bottles with mystique-less paper labels for take-home consumption, often packaged in 12-packs. In the mid-1990s, in response to a competitive explosion from microbrews, Rolling Rock offered a number of line extensions, such as Rock Bock and amber Rock Ice. They failed. Sales stagnated. In New York and other crucial markets price reductions to the level of Budweiser and Miller became inhibiting aspects of the marketing program. Marketing executives held the view that the longneck painted bottle was the heart of the brand. However, earlier efforts to develop a cheaper imitation of the painted-label look had not achieved success.

Rolling Rock executives decided to conduct a massive business research project, recruiting consumers at shopping malls and other venues to view "live" shelf sets of beer, not just specialty beer but beer at every price range from sub-premiums and up. Consumers given money to spend in the form of chips were exposed to "old-bundle" packages (the old graphics, and the paper-label stubbies) and "new-bundle" packages (two new graphics approaches, including the one ultimately selected, and painted-label longnecks), at a variety of price points, and asked to allocate their next ten purchases. Some were even invited to take the "new-bundle" packages home with them for followup research.

As the execs had hoped, the results did not leave any room for interpretation: not only did the new packages meet with consumers' strong approval, but consumers consistently indicated that they would be willing to pay more for the brand in those packages. In fact, not only were they *willing* to pay more, they *expected* to pay more, particularly those already in the Rock franchise. In three regions, the Northeast, Southeast, and West, purchase intent among users increased dramatically both at prices 20 cents higher per sixpack and at prices 40 cents higher. The increase in purchase intent was milder in the Midwest, but Rock there already commanded a higher price than Bud and other premium beers. The sole exception to that trend was in the brand's core markets in Pennsylvania and Ohio, where Rock has never entirely escaped its shot-and-a-beer origins, and even there, purchase intent declined by only 2 percent at each of the higher prices.

When deciding whether to make a decision without research or to postpone the decision in order to conduct research, managers should ask: (1) Will the payoff or rate of return be worth the investment? (2) Will the information gained by business research improve the quality of the decision to an extent sufficient to warrant the expenditure? and (3) Is the proposed research expenditure the best use of the available funds?

For example, *TV Cable Week* was not test-marketed before its launch. While the magazine had articles and stories about television personalities and events, its main feature was a channel-by-channel program listing showing the exact programs that a particular subscriber could receive. To produce a "custom" magazine for each individual cable television system in the country

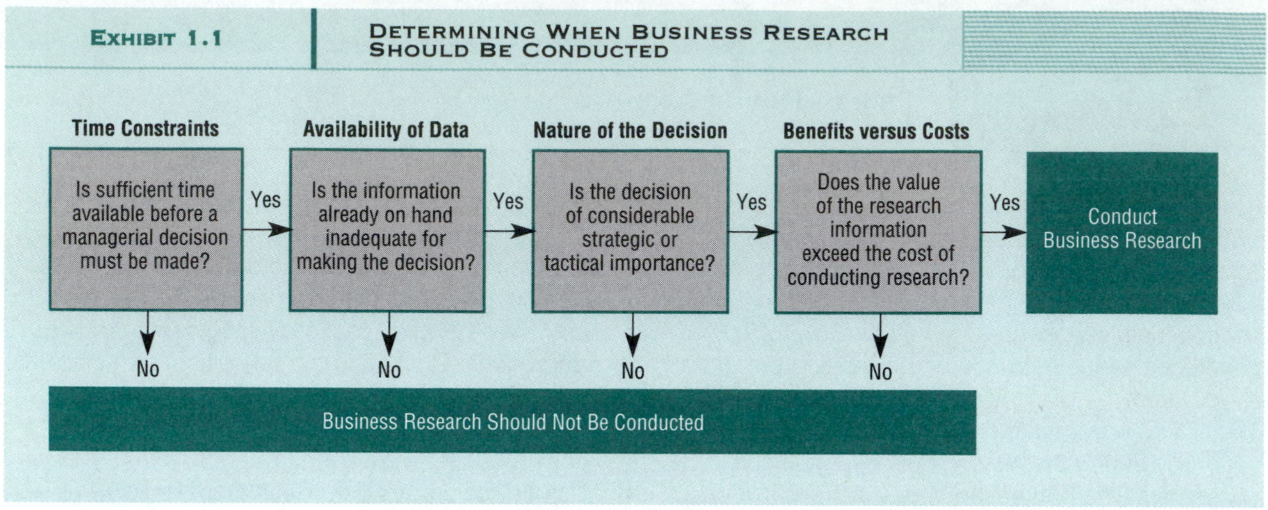

required developing a costly computer system. Because the development of the computer system required a substantial expenditure, one that could not be scaled down for research, the conducting of research was judged to be an unwise investment. The value of the research information was not positive, because the cost of the information exceeded its benefits. Unfortunately, pricing and distribution problems became so compelling after the magazine was launched that it was a business failure. Nevertheless, the publication's managers, without the luxury of hindsight, made a reasonable decision not to conduct research. They analyzed the cost of the information (i.e., the cost of business research) relative to the potential benefits. Exhibit 1.1 outlines the criteria for determining when to conduct business research.

MAJOR TOPICS FOR RESEARCH IN BUSINESS

Research is expected to improve the quality of business decisions, but what kinds of business decisions benefit most from research efforts? Exhibit 1.2 lists several major topics for research in business.

Exhibit 1.2 is arranged, to a large extent, according to the traditional business functions. However, many business efforts, such as new product development, are not neatly classified as financial projects, marketing projects, or information system projects. They are cross-functional efforts.

Cross-Functional Teams

As more companies awake to the challenge of the global information age and the need to act quickly, old forms of organizational structures are fading fast. Today, in progressive organizations, everyone from accountants to engineers engages in a unified effort to consider all issues related to the development, production, or marketing of new products.

cross-functional teams
Teams of people from various departments within a company, who work together to accomplish a common goal.

Cross-functional teams are composed of individuals from various organizational departments such as engineering, production, finance, and marketing who share a common purpose. Current management thinking suggests that cross-functional teams help organizations focus on a core business process, such as customer service or new product development. Working in teams

EXHIBIT 1.2 | **MAJOR TOPICS FOR RESEARCH IN BUSINESS**

General Business Conditions and Corporate Research

Short-range forecasting (up to 1 year)
Long-range forecasting (over 1 year)
Business and industry trends
Global environments
Inflation and pricing
Plant and warehouse location
Acquisitions

Financial and Accounting Research

Forecasts of financial interest-rate trends
Stock, bond, and commodity value predictions
Capital formation alternatives
Mergers and acquisitions
Risk–return trade-offs
Impact of taxes
Portfolio analysis
Research on financial institutions
Expected rate of return
Capital asset pricing models
Credit risk
Cost analysis

Management and Organizational Behavior Research

Total quality management
Morale and job satisfaction
Leadership style
Employee productivity
Organizational effectiveness
Structural issues
Absenteeism and turnover
Organizational climate
Organizational communication
Time and motion
Physical environment
Labor union trends

Sales and Marketing Research

Market potentials
Market share
Market segmentation
Market characteristics
Sales analysis
Establishment of sales quotas, territories
Distribution channels
New product concepts
Test markets
Advertising research
Buyer behavior
Customer satisfaction
Web site visitation rates

Information Systems Research

Knowledge and information needs assessment
Computer information system use and evaluation
Technical support satisfaction
Database analysis
Data mining
Enterprise resource planning systems
Customer relationship management systems

Corporate Responsibility Research

Ecological impact
Legal constraints on advertising and promotion
Sex, age, and racial discrimination/worker equity
Social values and ethics

reduces the tendency for employees to focus single-mindedly on an isolated functional activity. The use of cross-functional teams to help employees to improve product quality and increase customer value is a major trend in business today.

At trend-setting organizations, many business research directors are members of cross-functional teams. New product development, for example, may be done by a cross-functional team of engineers, finance executives, production personnel, marketing managers, and business researchers who take an integrated approach to solve problems or exploit opportunities. In the old days, business researchers may not have been involved in developing new products until long after many key decisions about product specifications and manufacturing had been made. Now, business researchers' input is part of an integrated team effort. Researchers act both as business consultants and as providers of technical services. Researchers working in teams are more likely to understand the broad purpose of their research and less likely to focus exclusively on research methodology.

Cross-functional teams are having a dramatic impact on how business research is viewed within the organization.

BUSINESS RESEARCH IN THE 21ST CENTURY

Business research has been strongly influenced by two major trends in business: increased globalization and the rapid growth of the Internet and other information technologies. These trends will continue, and likely accelerate, as the 21st century progresses. This section outlines their significance for business research.

Global Business Research

Business research has become increasingly global and will become more so in the 21st century. Some companies have extensive international business research operations. Upjohn conducts business research in 160 different countries. A. C. Nielsen International, with its television ratings, is the world's largest business research company. Two-thirds of its business comes from outside the United States.[14]

Companies that conduct business in foreign countries must understand the nature of those particular markets and judge whether they require customized strategies. For example, although the 15 nations of the European Union share a single formal market, business research shows that Europeans do not share identical tastes for many consumer products. Business researchers have found no such thing as a typical European consumer; language, religion, climate, and centuries of tradition divide the nations of the European Union. Scantel Research, a British firm that advises companies on color preferences, found inexplicable differences in Europeans' preferences concerning medicines. The French prefer to pop purple pills, but the English and Dutch favor white ones. Consumers in all three countries dislike bright red capsules, which are big sellers in the United States. This example illustrates that companies that do business in Europe must judge whether they need to adapt to local customs and buying habits.[15]

Although the nature of business research can differ around the globe, the need for business research is universal. Throughout this book, we will discuss the practical problems involved in conducting business research in Europe, Asia, Latin America, the Middle East, and elsewhere.

Growth of the Internet

The Internet is transforming society. Time is collapsing. Distance is no longer an obstacle. Crossing oceans requires only a mouse click. People are connected 24 hours a day, 7 days a week. "Instantaneous" has a new meaning.[16]

The Internet is a worldwide network of computers that allows users access to information and documents from distant sources. Many people believe that the Internet is the most important communications medium since television. It has certainly changed the way millions of people think about getting and distributing information. And, of course, obtaining and communicating information is the essence of business research. Consider that a researcher seeking facts and figures about a business issue may find more extensive information

The world economy has become global, and corporations market products in many countries. People think of their home culture as the normal way of life, but consumers in other cultures may have different values, beliefs, and behaviors. Business research helps marketers understand cultural differences. Colgate-Palmolive is a progressive company that conducts business research around the world. Colgate-Palmolive used business research when it introduced a new and improved toothpaste in Colombia.

on the Internet more quickly than by visiting a library. Another researcher who is questioning people from around the globe may do so almost instantaneously with an Internet survey and get responses 24 hours a day, 7 days a week. Visitors to an organization's Web site may find that online questions are personalized, because the site incorporates information technology that remembers the particular "click-stream" of the Web pages they visited. These few examples illustrate how the Internet and other information technologies are dramatically changing the face of business research.

In the 21st century, business research on the Internet is moving out of the introductory stage of its product life cycle into the growth stage. The rest of the book reflects this change. Throughout the book, we will discuss the latest information technologies and their application to business research. Business research via the Internet has come of age.

SUMMARY

Business research is a management tool that companies use to reduce uncertainty. Business research, managers' source of information about organizational and environmental conditions, covers topics ranging from long-range planning to the most ephemeral tactical decisions.

Business research is the systematic and objective process of gathering, recording, and analyzing data for decision making. The research must be systematic, not haphazard. It must be objective to avoid the distorting effects of personal bias. The objective of applied business research is to facilitate managerial decision making. Basic or pure research is used to increase knowledge about theories and concepts.

Managers can use business research in all stages of the decision-making process: to define problems, to identify opportunities, to diagnose causal factors, and to clarify alternatives. Research is also used to evaluate current programs and courses of action, to explain what went wrong with managerial efforts in the past, and to forecast future conditions.

Total quality management (TQM) is a business philosophy that embodies the belief that the management process must focus on integrating the idea of customer-driven quality throughout the organization. Total quality management stresses continuous improvement of product quality and service delivery. Business research plays a major role in total quality management programs.

A manager determines whether business research should be conducted by considering (1) time constraints, (2) the availability of data, (3) the nature of the decision to be made, and (4) the benefits of the research information in relation to its costs.

Applied research is directed at a broad variety of topics, such as general business conditions and corporate research; financial and accounting research; management and organizational behavior research; sales and marketing research; information system research; and corporate responsibility research.

The Internet and other information technologies are dramatically changing the face of business research. Business research has become increasingly global. Multinational companies must understand the particular nature of foreign markets and determine whether they require customized business strategies.

Key Terms

business research
basic (pure) research
applied research
scientific method
evaluation research
performance-monitoring research
total quality management (TQM)
cross-functional team

Questions for Review and Critical Thinking

1. What are some examples of business research in your particular field of interest?
2. In your own words, define *business research* and list its tasks.
3. How might a not-for-profit organization use business research?
4. What is the difference between applied and basic research?
5. Classify each of the following examples as basic or applied research.
   (a) A researcher investigates whether different sites in a manager's brain (e.g., right versus left hemisphere) are active during different kinds of managerial decision making.
   (b) A researcher investigates consumers' attitudes toward a prototype of an innovative home cleaning kit for use on clothes that require dry cleaning.
   (c) A researcher investigates five personality traits to see if they can explain the purchasing behavior of automobile buyers.
   (d) A new technology that nullifies the need to refrigerate fish has been invented. Heat processing and the use of flexible pouches for storage help retain the freshness of fish for 3 years. A researcher investigates how this new technology will affect the market for fish in India.
   (e) A researcher working for a candy company has children evaluate concepts and prototypes for new candies. The researchers ask children to taste the products and rate them. Sometimes, the candy company develops unique items that taste good and researchers ask children to name the product.
   (f) A researcher investigates whether introducing a "subbrand" at new-car dealerships, identified by an AutoNation USA logo below the dealership name, is an effective basic strategy that can be applied to all its dealerships.
6. Discuss how business research can be used in each stage of the decision-making process.

7. In your own words, describe the scientific method and state why it is an essential part of business research.
8. Describe a situation in which business research *is not* needed and one in which business research *is* needed. What factors differentiate the two situations?
9. In your own words, what is the role of business research in a total quality management program?
10. What is a cross-functional team? What types of projects might use business research directed by a cross-functional team?
11. Suppose you have been hired as a consultant by an American fast-food restaurant chain that plans to expand into Europe. What role would business research play, if any, in providing advice to your client?

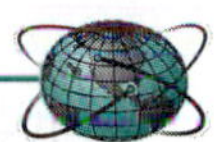

Exploring the Internet: What Is Ahead?

Exploring the Internet is a feature that will give you an opportunity to use the Internet to gain additional insights about business research. The Internet is discussed in depth in Chapter 2, and Internet exercises are included in each of the remaining chapters.

The home page for this textbook is at

http://zikmund.swcollege.com

or you may go directly to the business research supplemental materials at

http://www.swcollege.com/management/strategy_suite/strategy_suite.html

The author's home page is at

http://www2.bus.okstate.edu/mktg/zikmund/index.htm

Case Suggestions

Case 1: The Atlanta Braves
Video Case 1: Polaroid I-Zone
Video Case 2: WBRU
Video Case 3: Ben & Jerry's
Video Case 4: Fossil—A Watch for Every Wrist

CHAPTER

2

INFORMATION SYSTEMS AND KNOWLEDGE MANAGEMENT

What you will learn in this chapter

- To distinguish between data, information, and knowledge.
- To understand the importance of global information systems in international business.
- To explain the nature of decision support systems.
- To identify several computerized data archives.
- To explain the significance of the Internet.
- To understand the basics of navigating the World Wide Web.

The last things likely to come to mind when you walk into Starbucks are complex data warehouses and business intelligence software. How about insurance, then? Probably not.[1]

But Zurich U.S., a leader in business and casualty insurance, is paid to think about risk management, not caffeine rushes. And Zurich U.S. has come up with a way to use the highest-tech database technology to help Starbucks and other big-liability customers manage and minimize insurance claims.

Zurich's product, an Internet-based service called RiskIntelligence, lets its clients view insurance data in any number of ways. For a company like Starbucks, which doles out coffee all day to hundreds of thousands of possibly clumsy consumers, RiskIntelligence means a better chance to control claims.

The RiskIntelligence data management software allows users to view data from many different angles. Some use the metaphor of a Rubik's Cube, because the data can be twisted and turned in order to discern patterns. Correlations and relationships between data that are not otherwise obvious can be revealed.

Starbucks uses many different floor designs in its 3,500 North American retail locations. So, Starbucks' executives might, for example, look at its claims data to see whether there were more falls from spills in stores with a specific foot-traffic pattern. The executives might further drill down to find out that accidents were more frequent at certain times of the day. Good analytical tools could also reveal that these things happen mostly in a certain region of the country during a certain time of the year. This all could result in decisions that would help minimize those risks—and help the company handle its claims more effectively in general.

RiskIntelligence gives clients like Starbucks much more up-to-date information than did the old way, which consisted of mailing out disks with static reports to customers once a month.

Starbucks' use of RiskIntelligence, a computerized decision support system, illustrates how the management of information has changed in recent years. This chapter discusses the nature of decision support systems within the context of knowledge management and global information systems. It also investigates the dramatic implications of the Internet for business research. ■

DATA, INFORMATION, AND KNOWLEDGE MANAGEMENT

data
Recorded measures of certain phenomena

information
A body of facts that are in a format suitable for decision making.

Managers make a distinction between *data* and *information*. The primary difference between data and information is that **data** are simply facts, or recorded measures of certain phenomena, while **information** refers to a body of facts in a format that facilitates decision making or in a context that defines relationships between pieces of data. To illustrate the difference between data and information, consider Toys Я Us. The company stores records of thousands of individual transactions, which are fed into the company computer system when a retail clerk scans an item at the cash register. At the same time, the data are also entered into a computerized inventory system. These data lack any meaning until managers instruct the information system to translate the data into product sales totals by store, country, or state or into forecasts for future time periods.

knowledge
A blend of information, experience, and insights that provides a framework that can be thoughtfully applied when assessing new information or evaluating relevant situations.

knowledge management
The process of creating an inclusive, comprehensive, easily accessible organizational memory, which is often called the organization's intellectual capital.

Effective organizations make a concerted effort to capture, organize, and share what their employees know.[2] They create *knowledge,* which is broader, deeper, and richer than data or information.[3] Knowledge can be defined many ways. However, for our purposes, **knowledge** is a blend of information, experience, and insights that provides a framework that can be thoughtfully applied when assessing new information or evaluating relevant situations.

Knowledge management is the process of creating an inclusive, comprehensive, easily accessible organizational memory, which is often called the organization's intellectual capital.[4] The purpose of knowledge management is to organize the "intellectual capital" of an organization in a formally structured way for easy use. Knowledge management assumes that relevant information, intelligently and quickly communicated to the right person, can make the difference between making great decisions or making bad ones. Knowledge is presented in a way that helps employees comprehend and act on that information.[5]

New information technologies and new ways of thinking about data, information, and knowledge lie at the heart of knowledge management. Effective organizations systematically manage activities from information

Facing a public increasingly critical of logging in national forests, the U.S. Forest Service uses an information system and a technique called "seen-area analysis" to plan national forests. The information system helps foresters tuck clear-cuts behind ridges, shield them from view with "beauty strips"—veneers of trees maintained to hide bare patches—and identify areas where they can use one of several "partial cut" techniques to subtly thin the forest without ruining the view.

acquisition to the distribution of knowledge. Tools for preserving and sharing data, information, and knowledge involve global information systems, decision support systems, the Internet and intranets, as well as communication vehicles as basic as newsletters.

GLOBAL INFORMATION SYSTEMS

The well-being of multinational corporations—indeed, the health of any business organization in the 21st century—depends on information about the world economy and global competition. Contemporary managers require timely and accurate information from around the globe to maintain competitive advantages. In today's world managers can access a wealth of information instantaneously, and this has changed the way they do business.

Increased global competition and technological advances involving interactive media have promoted the development of global information systems. At any moment, on any day, United Parcel Service (UPS) can track the status of a shipment around the world. UPS drivers use handheld electronic clipboards called delivery information acquisition devices (DIADs) to record appropriate information after each pickup or delivery. The information is then entered into a larger computer for record keeping and analysis to allow UPS to track any shipment for its customers.

global information system
An organized collection of computer hardware and software, data, and personnel designed to capture, store, update, manipulate, analyze, and immediately display information about worldwide business activity.

Global information systems combine satellite communications, high-speed microcomputers, electronic data interchange, fiber optics, CD-ROM data storage, fax machines, and other advances in interactive media technology. A **global information system** is an organized collection of computer hardware and software, data, and personnel designed to capture, store, update, manipulate, analyze, and immediately display information about worldwide business activity.[6] A global information system is a tool for providing past, present, and projected information on internal operations and external activity. It organizes and integrates data from production, operations, marketing, finance, accounting, and other business functions.

Consider how global information systems are changing the nature of business. If executives at Motorola must make pricing decisions about their European markets for cellular phones, they can get immediate information about international exchange rates without leaving their desks. An investor can review information about leading economic indicators in Japan instantaneously. With a few simple keystrokes, a library researcher can generate a bibliography on a particular subject that includes hundreds of abstracts.

The information age has already begun, yet, as amazing as today's technology is, it will seem primitive as we progress through the 21st century.

DECISION SUPPORT SYSTEMS

decision support system
A computer-based system that helps decision makers confront problems through direct interaction with databases and analytical software.

An organization may have several, even many, decision support systems that are components of its larger global information system. A **decision support system** is a computer-based system that helps decision makers confront problems through direct interaction with databases and analytical software. The purpose of a decision support system is to store data and transform them into organized information that is easily accessible to a division, department, or functional area of the organization.

EXHIBIT 2.1 | **DECISION SUPPORT SYSTEM**[7]

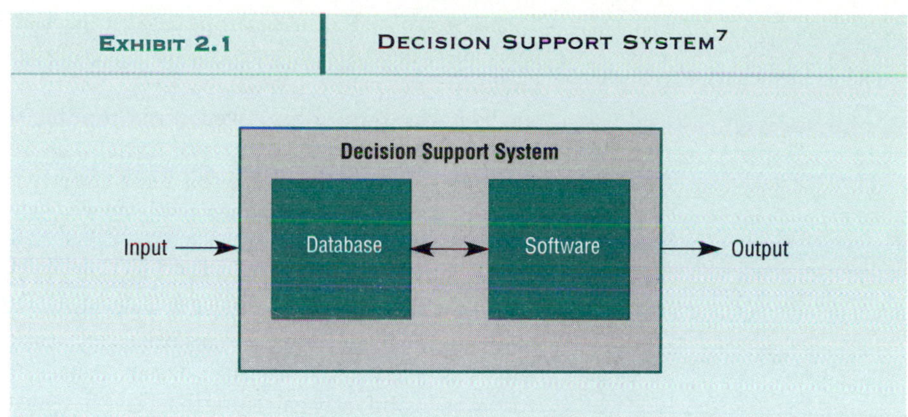

customer relationship management (CRM)
A decision support system that brings together numerous pieces of information about customers and their relationship with the company.

Most major corporations have a decision support system to facilitate **customer relationship management (CRM).** A CRM decision support system might bring together numerous pieces of information about customers, sales, market trends, marketing effectiveness, and company responsiveness.[8] The goal of the CRM system is to describe customer relationships in sufficient detail that managers, salespeople, customer service representatives, and perhaps the customers themselves can access information directly, match customer needs with satisfying product offerings, remind customers of service requirements, know what other products a customer has purchased, and so forth.[9] Once a CRM system is established, an executive might query the system to investigate demographic changes or to learn whether special efforts are needed to retain certain types of customers. An efficient CRM system should give a service representative in a call center the ability to retrieve a complete record of a customer's interactions with the company seconds after the customer provides identification information.

Decision support systems serve specific business units within a company, operating within the context of the global information system. No single decision support system is independent of the more comprehensive global information system.

A successful decision support system must continuously expedite flows of information to decision makers. Data must be timely and easily accessible if they are to be useful to a manager who must make decisions. Such a system must also be able to display nonrecurring information (e.g., special project reports) in a format that satisfies information requirements.

Exhibit 2.1 illustrates a decision support system. Raw, unsummarized data, often collected in business research, are inputs to the decision support system. Effective companies spend a great deal of time and effort collecting data to input into their decision support systems. Useful information is the output of a decision support system.

Database Systems

database
A collection of raw data or information arranged in a logical manner and organized in a form that can be stored and processed by a computer.

A **database** is a collection of raw data arranged in a logical manner and organized in a form that can be stored and processed by a computer. A mailing list of customer names is one type of database. Another database may contain employment data recorded by state, county, and city. When internal data from accounting, finance, sales, manufacturing, payroll, and other areas of the business are stored in a computer system and arranged in a logical order, they are called *internal databases.* Exhibit 2.2 illustrates the type of data that may be included in an internal database.

Databases are often saved on computer storage devices such as hard disk drives. Furthermore, vendors of information services may store other types of databases. (We will address this issue shortly.)

Because most companies compile and store many different databases, they often develop data warehousing systems. The term *data warehouse* is used by managers of information technology to refer to a comprehensive collection of data that describes the extensive operations of an organization. More specifically, a data warehouse is a multitiered computer storehouse of current and historical data. Data warehouse management involves the mechanics of selecting and using information that is relevant to decision-making tasks. Data warehouse management requires that the detailed data from operational systems be extracted, transformed, and stored (warehoused) so that the various database files (commonly referred to as *tables*) are consistent. An organization with a data warehouse may integrate databases from both inside and outside the company.

The link between the database system and a company's software is strong, because database management software provides easy access to the data, and other software allows the researcher to manipulate data for analysis.

EXHIBIT 2.2 **SPREADSHEET SOFTWARE FOR ANALYSIS OF AN INTERNAL DATABASE**

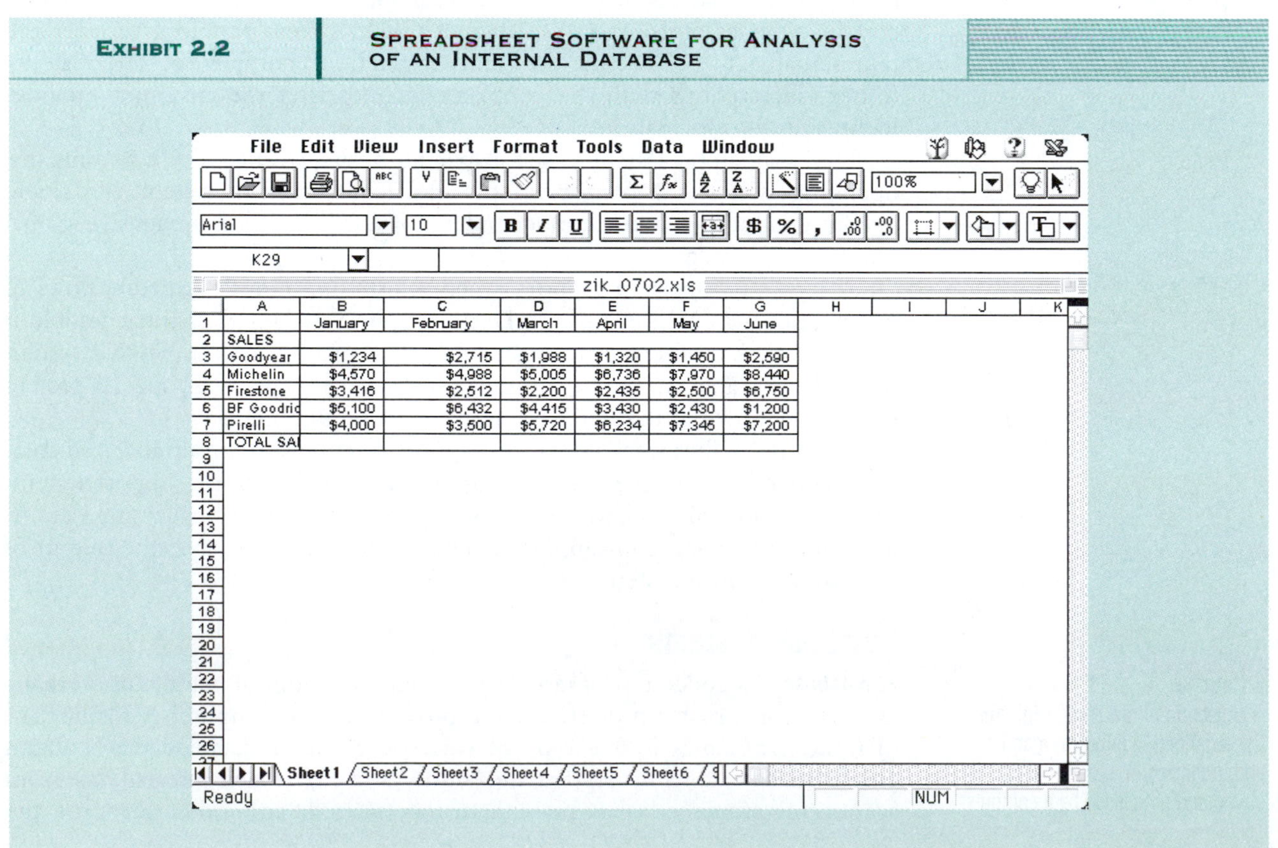

	A	B	C	D	E	F	G
1		January	February	March	April	May	June
2	SALES						
3	Goodyear	$1,234	$2,715	$1,988	$1,320	$1,450	$2,590
4	Michelin	$4,570	$4,988	$5,005	$6,736	$7,970	$8,440
5	Firestone	$3,416	$2,512	$2,200	$2,435	$2,500	$6,750
6	BF Goodric	$5,100	$6,432	$4,415	$3,430	$2,430	$1,200
7	Pirelli	$4,000	$3,500	$5,720	$6,234	$7,345	$7,200
8	TOTAL SA						

Research Insight

We Are Resetting Our Clocks to Real Time

Imagine a world in which time seems to vanish and space seems completely malleable.[10] Where the gap between need or desire and fulfillment collapses to zero. Where distance equals a microsecond in lapsed connection time. A virtual world created at your command. Imagine a world in which everything you do, from work to education, is clothed as an entertainment-like experience, veiled by technology so subtle and transparent that you have no idea it is there at all. Habits, attitudes, opinions, preferences, expectations, demands, perceptions, and needs all adapt unwittingly to an environment in which immediacy rules.

All of this may sound like material for a science fiction thriller. But it is very nearly the world we are living in today.

Technology is transforming our existence in profound ways, and the pace of change is speeding up, not slowing down. Almost all technology today is focused on compressing to zero the amount of time it takes to acquire and use information, to learn, to make decisions, to initiate action, to deploy resources, to innovate. When action and response are simultaneous, we are in *real time.*

. . . The change in our consciousness of time is the creation of ubiquitous programmable technology producing results at the click of a mouse or the touch of a button or key. Real time occurs when time and distance vanish, when action and response are simultaneous.

Software

business intelligence software Computer programs that permit managers to restructure and analyze data in extensive data warehouses to discover significant patterns and relationships.

The software portion of a decision support system consists of various types of programs that tell computers, printers, and other hardware what to do. Advances in database management, spreadsheet, and statistical software have revolutionized access to and analysis of business data. A decision support system's **business intelligence software** allows managers to combine and restructure databases, diagnose relationships, discover patterns, estimate variables, and otherwise analyze various databases. For instance, suppose a bank has a listing of all its customers in its data warehouse. Analysts can create a new database of high-volume customers using certain analytical procedures. They can also analyze the demographic structure of this group and make projections about the group's future savings behavior based on economic forecasts and other forecasted trends. The bank could then use its CRM system to build a personalized mailing list based on any customer characteristic or behavioral pattern.

Most of today's business intelligence software is so user-friendly that it is easy for nonexperts to maintain direct control over the computer's tasks and outcomes. A manager can sit at a computer terminal and instantaneously retrieve personalized data files and request special, creative analyses to refine, modify, or generate information in a tailor-made format suited specifically for evaluating particular consequences or alternatives. User-friendly graphics software enables managers to convert endless columns of numbers to colored charts, graphs, and maps almost instantaneously.

For example, most major league baseball teams have business intelligence software to analyze information from game records (e.g., how often a single advances a runner from first base to third) so that managers can make decisions about how to play against opponents. A business researcher keeps a record of every pitch on a laptop computer and, after a ball is hit, records its precise direction, the number of feet it travels, the player who fields the ball, and the outcome of the play. Computerized summaries of play-by-play activities are provided for broadcasters who cover the games. The information is also stored in a data warehouse that keeps pitch-by-pitch records for the entire season, as well as for past seasons. Managers may use this information to have the computer draw a diagram of a baseball field indicating where a particular batter has hit against a particular pitcher or a particular type of pitch. Old-time managers like Casey Stengel had to keep this sort of information on paper or in their heads. Using this research technique, modern baseball teams can see the data instantly on a computer screen, then select a pinch hitter or a relief pitcher or reposition their fielders accordingly.

Input Management

So far the discussion of decision support systems has focused on the organization and accessibility of computerized information. We have not discussed the nature of the input function in detail.

Input includes all the numerical, text, voice, and image data that enter the decision support system. Systematic accumulation of pertinent, timely, and accurate data is essential to the success of a decision support system. Clearly, the input function must be managed.

Information system managers, systems analysts, and computer programmers are responsible for the decision support system as a whole. However, the task of providing input is shared by many functions within an organization. Business researchers, accountants, corporate librarians, sales personnel, production managers, and many others within the organization collect data and provide input for the decision support system. Input data can come from sources outside the company as well. Often, data come from computerized data archives.

Computerized Data Archives

Historically, collections of organized and readily retrievable data were available in printed form at libraries. The *Statistical Abstract of the United States,* which is filled with tables of statistical facts, is a typical example. Printed copies of this book can be found in most public and corporate libraries. In recent years, the *Statistical Abstract* has become available on CD-ROM and on the Internet. The entire 2000 census is also available in print as well as on CD-ROM. Other databases can be accessed on the Internet. As the 21st century progresses, even more data will be stored in digitized form in computerized data archives.

Numerous computerized search and retrieval systems and electronic databases are available as subscription services or in libraries. A researcher can query the library computer to learn whether the library owns a particular book and whether that book is on the shelf or checked out. Today, business people can use personal computers to access online information search and retrieval services, such as Dow-Jones News Retrieval and Bloomberg Financial Markets, without leaving their offices. In fact, some information services can be accessed from remote locations via digital wireless devices.

Computerized database searches offer the most efficient and exhaustive way to find published information. Most online information services use *electronic indexing systems* that function much like the *periodic indexes* found in book form in libraries. For example, an electronic indexing system may allow a researcher to search for information by subject. A *subject index* is an information resource that contains lists of references to other database resources, categorized by subject, usually in a hierarchy. Most online information services also have software that allows a researcher to do keyword searches for information in their databases.

Modern library patrons can command a computer to search indexes and retrieve databases from a range of vendors. Major wholesalers or online vendors of *bibliographic databases* include PROQUEST, INFOTRAC, DIALOG (Dialog Information Services, Inc.), LEXIS-NEXIS, and Dow Jones News Retrieval Services. These services index information and provide access to computer-readable databases to business people and scholars.

DIALOG, for example, maintains more than 600 databases. A typical database may have a million or more records, each consisting of a one- or two-paragraph abstract that summarizes the major points of a published article along with bibliographic information. One of the DIALOG databases, ABI/INFORM, abstracts significant articles in more than 1,000 current business and management journals. Many computerized archives provide more than abstracts of published articles and journals. The *New York Times* database and the Dow Jones Text-Search Services are full-text databases that allow the retrieval of an entire article or document. ABI/INFORM offers full-text versions of the articles on CD-ROM.

Exhibit 2.3 illustrates the services provided by two popular vendors of information services that electronically index numerous databases.[11]

Several types of databases from outside vendors and external distributors are so fundamental to decision support systems that they deserve further explanation.

Statistical Databases

Statistical databases contain numerical data for market analysis and forecasting. Often demographic, sales, and other relevant marketing variables are recorded by geographical area. Geographic information systems use these *geographical databases* and powerful software to prepare computer maps of relevant variables. Companies such as Claritas, Urban Decision Systems, and CACI all offer geographic/demographic databases that are widely used in industry.

Known as *scanner data,* or single-source data, the wealth of product and brand sales information collected by optical scanners in supermarkets and other retail outlets is another example of statistical data. (The term *single-source data* refers to the ability of these systems to gather several types of interrelated data, such as purchase, sales promotion, or advertising frequency data, from a single source in a format that will facilitate integration, comparison, and analysis.) As the number of scanner-equipped stores continues to increase, scanner systems are replacing human record keeping for in-store auditing. Substituting mechanized record keeping for human record keeping results in greater accuracy and rapid feedback about store activity.

One weakness of scanner data is that the largest stores, such as supermarkets, mass merchandisers, and warehouse retailers, are the most likely to have scanner systems, causing the sampling base of stores to be less than perfectly representative. Things are changing, however. A. C. Nielsen and the National Housewares Manufacturers Association formed a partnership to provide data generated by the Universal Product Codes scanned at housewares retailers' checkouts. (The Universal Product Code, or UPC, contains information on

Exhibit 2.3 | **Two Vendors of Information Services and Electronic Indexing**

Vendor	Selected Databases	Type of Data
DIALOG	ABI/INFORM	Summaries and citations from over 1,000 academic management, marketing, and general business journals, with full text of more than 500 of these publications
	ASI (American Statistics Index)	Abstracts and indexes of federal government statistical publications
	PROMT (The Predicast Overview of Markets and Technologies)	Summaries and full text from 1,000 U.S. and international business and trade journals, industry newsletters, newspapers, and market research studies; information about industries and companies, including the products and technologies they develop and the markets in which they compete
	Investext	Full text of over 2 million company, industry, and geographic research reports written by analysts at more than 600 leading investment banks, brokerage houses, and consulting firms worldwide
Dow Jones News Retrieval	Business Newsstand	Articles from *New York Times, Los Angeles Times, Washington Post,* and other leading newspapers and magazines
	Historical Market Data Center	Historical data on securities, dividends, and exchange rates
	Web Center	Information obtained from searches of corporate, industry, government, and news Web sites

the category of goods, the manufacturer, and product identification based on size, flavor, color, and so on.) Nevertheless, if a large percentage of a product category's sales occur in small stores or in vending machines (e.g. candy), which tend not to have scanners, the scanner data may not be representative.

Financial Databases

Competitors' and customers' financial data, such as income statements and balance sheets, may interest managers. These are easy to access in financial databases. CompuStat publishes an extensive financial database on thousands of companies broken down by industry and other criteria. To illustrate the depth of this pool of information, CompuStat's Global Advantage offers extensive data on 6,650 companies in more than 30 countries in Europe, the Pacific Rim, and North America.

Video Databases

Video databases and streaming media are having a major impact on many business activities. For example, movie studios provide clips of upcoming films, and advertising agencies put television commercials on the Internet. (See http://www.adcritic.com.) McDonald's maintains a digital archive of hundreds of its television commercials and other video footage to share with its franchisers around the world. The video database enables franchisers and their advertising agencies to create local advertising without filming the same types of scenes already archived. Just imagine the value of digital video databases to advertising agencies' decision support systems.

Networks and Electronic Data Interchange

Individual personal computers can be connected through networks to other computers. Networking involves linking two or more computers to share data and software.

electronic data exchange (EDI)
The linking of two or more companies' computer systems.

Electronic data interchange (EDI) systems integrate one company's computer system directly with another company's system. Much of the input to a company's decision support system may come through networks from other companies' computers. Companies such as Computer Technology Corporation and Microelectronics market data services that allow corporations to exchange business information with suppliers or customers. For example, every evening Wal-Mart transmits millions of characters of data about the day's sales to its apparel suppliers. Wrangler, a supplier of blue jeans, for instance, shares the data and a model that interprets the data. It also shares software applications that act to replenish stocks in Wal-Mart stores. This decision support system lets Wrangler's managers know when to send specific quantities of specific sizes and colors of jeans to specific stores from specific warehouses. The result is a learning loop that lowers inventory costs and leads to fewer stockouts.

WHAT IS THE INTERNET?

Internet
A worldwide network of computers that allows access to information and documents from distant sources; a combination of a worldwide communication system and the world's largest public library, containing a seemingly endless range of information.

The **Internet** is a worldwide network of computers that supports electronic communication and gives users access to information and documents from distant sources. Because it is a combination of a worldwide communication system and the world's largest public library, containing a seemingly endless range of information, many people believe the Internet is the most important communications medium since television.

The Internet has changed the way millions of people get and distribute information. It is estimated that more than 269 million users in Europe, the Pacific Rim, and North America can access the Internet from a home computer.[13] For many years the number of users doubled annually, making the Internet the fastest-growing communication medium in history.

Computer communication and resource discovery are two central functions of the Internet. Electronic mail or messaging is the most widespread communication function. For example, users send messages on the Internet by

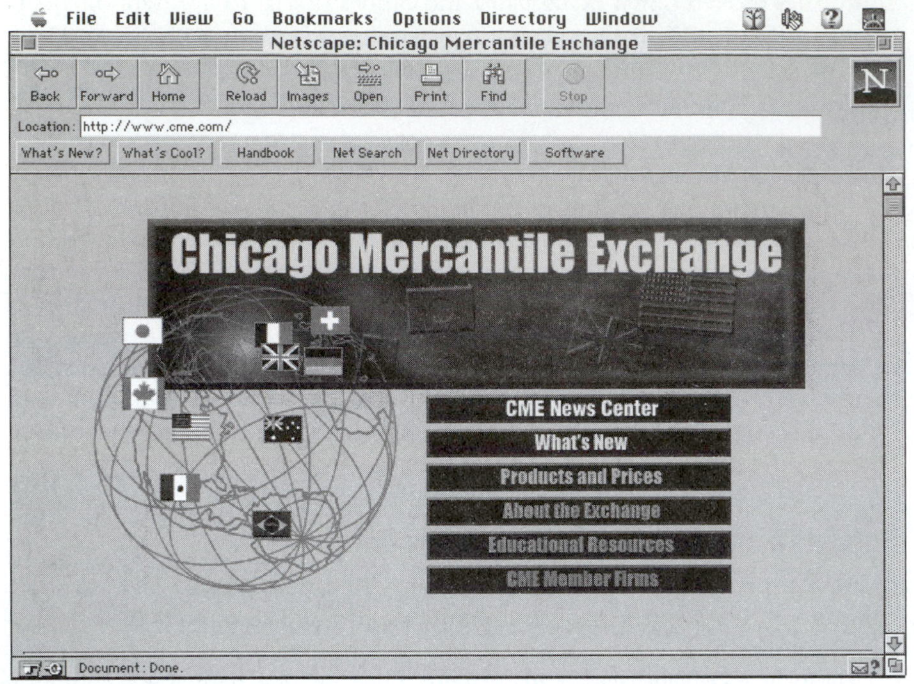

The Chicago Mercantile Exchange provides daily settlement prices, including currency, interest-rate, stock index, and agricultural contracts.

The Net is 10.5 on the Richter scale of economic change.

NICHOLAS NEGROPONTE

host
Any computer that has access to other computers on the Internet. One or more people may log on to a host computer through their personal computers.

e-mail (electronic mail) to ask questions of experts or, in other ways, communicate with individuals who share similar interests. Just as a letter delivered by a postal worker requires an address, so does e-mail. An e-mail address consists of two parts, separated by the @ symbol. The name of the user's mailbox is on the left-hand side. The name of the system on which the mailbox resides is on the right-hand side. System, or domain, names have two or more fields, separated by dots, and can follow many different naming schemes, such as by country (.uk, .jp) or by type of activity (.com, .org).

The domain is typically a company name, institutional name, or organizational name associated with the **host** computer. For example, *Forbes* magazine's Internet edition is located at forbes.com. The "com" indicates this domain is a commercial site. Educational sites end in "edu," government sites end in "gov," and other types of organizations end in "org." (Some new host names, such as "info" and "biz," have been proposed and may be in effect by the time this book is published.)

The Internet allows users instantaneous and effortless access to a great deal of information. Noncommercial and commercial organizations make a wealth of data and other resources available on the Internet. For example, the U.S. Library of Congress provides full text of all versions of House and Senate legislation and full text of the *Congressional Record*. The Internal Revenue Service makes it possible to download an income tax form. Thomson Learning (http://www.thomsonlearning.com) and its South-Western college division (http://www.swcollege.com) have online directories that allow college professors to access information about the company and its textbooks.

The Internet began in 1969 as an experimental hookup between computers at Stanford University, the University of California at Santa Barbara, the

University of California at Los Angeles, and the University of Utah, in conjunction with the Department of Defense.[14] The Defense Department was involved because it wanted to develop a communications network that could avoid being destroyed under severe battle conditions. The Internet gradually grew into a nationwide network of connected computers, and now it is a worldwide network often referred to as the "information superhighway." The Internet has no central computer; instead, each message sent bears an address code that lets the sender forward a message to a desired destination from any computer linked to the Net.[15] Many benefits of the Internet arise because it is a collection of tens of thousands of small networks, both domestic and foreign, rather than a single computer operation. These many small networks contain millions of databases that are accessible to Internet users, mostly without fees.

In the following pages we discuss the World Wide Web and how to use the Internet for research. However, keep in mind that the Internet is constantly changing. The description of the Internet, especially home page addresses, may be out of date by the time this book is published. Be aware that the Internet of today will not be the Internet of tomorrow.

Navigating the World Wide Web

Anyone with a computer and a modem can access the Internet by subscribing to a gateway company, known as an Internet service provider (ISP), such as America Online (AOL), AT&T WorldNet, Earthlink, or Cox Cable. In addition, many college and university campus networks also offer Internet access either in common user laboratories or through off-campus dial-up services.

World Wide Web (WWW)
A portion of the Internet that is a system of computer servers that organize information into documents called Web pages.

The **World Wide Web (WWW)** refers to that portion of the Internet made up of servers that support a retrieval system that organizes information into documents called Web pages. World Wide Web documents, which may include graphic images, video clips, and sound clips, are formatted in special programming languages, such as HTML (HyperText Markup Language) and XML (Extensible Markup Language), that allow for displaying, linking, and sharing of information on the Internet.

Over the past few years, many universities, government agencies, academic associations, newspapers, TV networks, libraries, and corporations have decided to provide information on the Internet. Parties that furnish information on the World Wide Web are called *content providers.* Content providers maintain Web sites. A Web site consists of one or more web pages with related information about a particular topic; for example, a university Web site might include pages about its mission, courses, and faculty. The introductory page or opening screen is called the *home page* because it provides basic information about the purpose of the document along with a menu of selections or links that lead to other screens with more specific information. Thus, each page can have connections, or *hyperlinks,* to other pages, which may be on any computer connected to the Internet. People using the World Wide Web may be viewing information that is stored on their host computer or on a machine halfway around the world. The World Wide Web allows users to point and click on where they want to go and to call up video, sound bytes, and graphics from different participating computer networks around the world.

TO THE POINT

An immense and ever-increasing wealth of knowledge is scattered about the world today; knowledge that would probably suffice to solve all the mighty difficulties of our age, but it is dispersed and unorganized. We need a sort of mental clearing house for the mind: a depot where knowledge and ideas are received, sorted, summarized, digested, clarified and compared.[12]

H. G. WELLS

To access the World Wide Web, the typical home user needs a Web browser, which is a software program with a graphical user interface that enables the

RESEARCH INSIGHT

ACTION MAN

Action Man is the European counterpart to G.I. Joe, and he has his very own Web site, courtesy of Hasbro Europe, the U.K.-based division of toy-maker Hasbro International.[16] After a design team created the site, Graphics Services Manager Julian Jones decided he needed to find out how people were using it. To do so, he installed Market Focus, a site-analysis tool, on the company's server. The first thing Jones learned from the Market Focus reports was that fully 40 percent of Action Man's visitors never even crossed the threshold. From that information, he deduced that they were literally being blown away by the time it took to load the site's snazzy graphics. "We thought people would wait," says Jones, "but we were wrong."

By making the opening image smaller, the team reduced the number of visitors who bailed before entering to 25 percent. Also in response to the data, Jones rearranged links to take visitors deeper into the site on the first click. As a result, the duration of the average visit has increased by almost 50 percent, to 11 minutes.

Jones could have tried tracking site usage himself, but analyzing the data produced by a server log is tedious, time-consuming, and often produces errors. Fortunately, the Internet industry has never been shy about offering solutions, and there now exists a whole category of tools that address the tracking problem. These products use different means, but they have in mind the same end: to tally, slice and present log data so that it yields valuable visitor information.

The companies that offer site-tracking services collect data from clients' server logs and provide regular reports. Depending on the company and the customer, these services can take readings once a day or as often as every half-hour. (Not surprisingly, frequent readings of server logs can exact a price in performance, but some site owners prefer that to the possibility of receiving outdated reports.) Once collected, the data can be massaged in a variety of ways, enabling users to answer questions such as: How many visitors came from Japan? How many visitors went straight from the home page to our order form? Or even, How many visitors from Japan went straight from the home page to our order form?

user to display Web pages as well as to navigate the Internet. Popular Web browsers, such as Netscape Navigator and Microsoft Explorer, make it easy to move from Web site to Web site on the World Wide Web (often called navigating the Net, navigation, or surfing). With these Web browsers even a novice on the Internet can search for information by simply using point-and-click graphics that resemble the familiar Windows or Macintosh interface. The links to other documents are usually highlighted in another color, underlined, or identified by a unique icon. Often, the user may be linked to a series of expanded menus or navigation buttons containing descriptions of the contents of various Web pages around the Internet. The user moves the cursor to highlighted words or colorful icons and then clicks the mouse button to immediately go to the file, regardless of what server it may be stored on. At this point the user can either read or download the material. By clicking on "US Government Information" in one electronic document, for example, a Netscape user might connect to a computer in Washington, D.C. with more information. A few more clicks, and the user could be perusing files from the U.S. Census or the Small Business Administration.

Most Web browsers also allow the user to enter a Uniform Resource Locator, or URL, into the program. The URL is really just a Web site address of a computer host that can be accessed with the browser software. Many Web sites allow any user or visitor access without previous approval. However, many commercial sites require that the user have a valid account and password before access is granted.

search engine
A computerized directory that allows anyone to search the World Wide Web for information in a particular way. Some search titles or headers of documents, others search the documents themselves, and still others search other indexes or directories.

A researcher who wants to find a particular site or document on the Internet or is just looking for a resource list on a particular subject can use one of the many Internet search engines. A **search engine** is a computerized directory that allows anyone to search the World Wide Web for information in a particular way. Some search titles or headers of documents, others search words in the documents themselves, and still others search other indexes or directories. Yahoo (http://www.yahoo.com) and Excite (http://www.excite.com) offer such a broad array of resources and services that they are also called *portals.* A person using Yahoo will find lists of broad categories on topics such as art, business, entertainment, and government. Clicking on one of these topics leads to other subdirectories or home pages. An alternative way to use a search engine is to type key words and phrases associated with the search and wait for a list of Web sites to be displayed. (See pages 34–35.)

Some of the most comprehensive and widely used search engines are

Yahoo	http://www.yahoo.com
Google	http://www.google.com
Lycos	http://www.lycos.com
Alta Vista	http://www.altavista.com
Hotbot	http://www.hotbot.com
Go	http://www.go.com
Excite	http://www.excite.com

Interactive Media and Environmental Scanning

Because people who use the Internet interact with their computers, it is an interactive medium. A user clicks a command, and the computer responds in sophisticated ways—so the user and the equipment can have a continuing conversation. Two or more people who communicate one-to-one via e-mail using an Internet service provider are also using interactive media. So are individuals who communicate with many senders and receivers via bulletin boards. Because of its vastness, the Internet is an especially useful source for scanning many types of changes in the environment.

Ford Motor Company maintains an Internet-based relationship marketing program that, among other things, helps the automaker scan its environment using the Internet. Its dealer Web site provides a centralized communication service linking dealers via an Internet connection. Its buyer Web site allows prospective buyers to visit a virtual showroom and to get price quotes and financial information. Its owner Web site allows an owner who registers and supplies pertinent vehicle information to get free e-mail and other ownership perks. A perk might be a free Hertz upgrade or an autographed photo of one of the Ford-sponsored NASCAR drivers. In return, Ford collects data at all

Doing a Category Search

As each menu comes up, the user selects from it. The search progressively narrows until a specific Web site is reached.

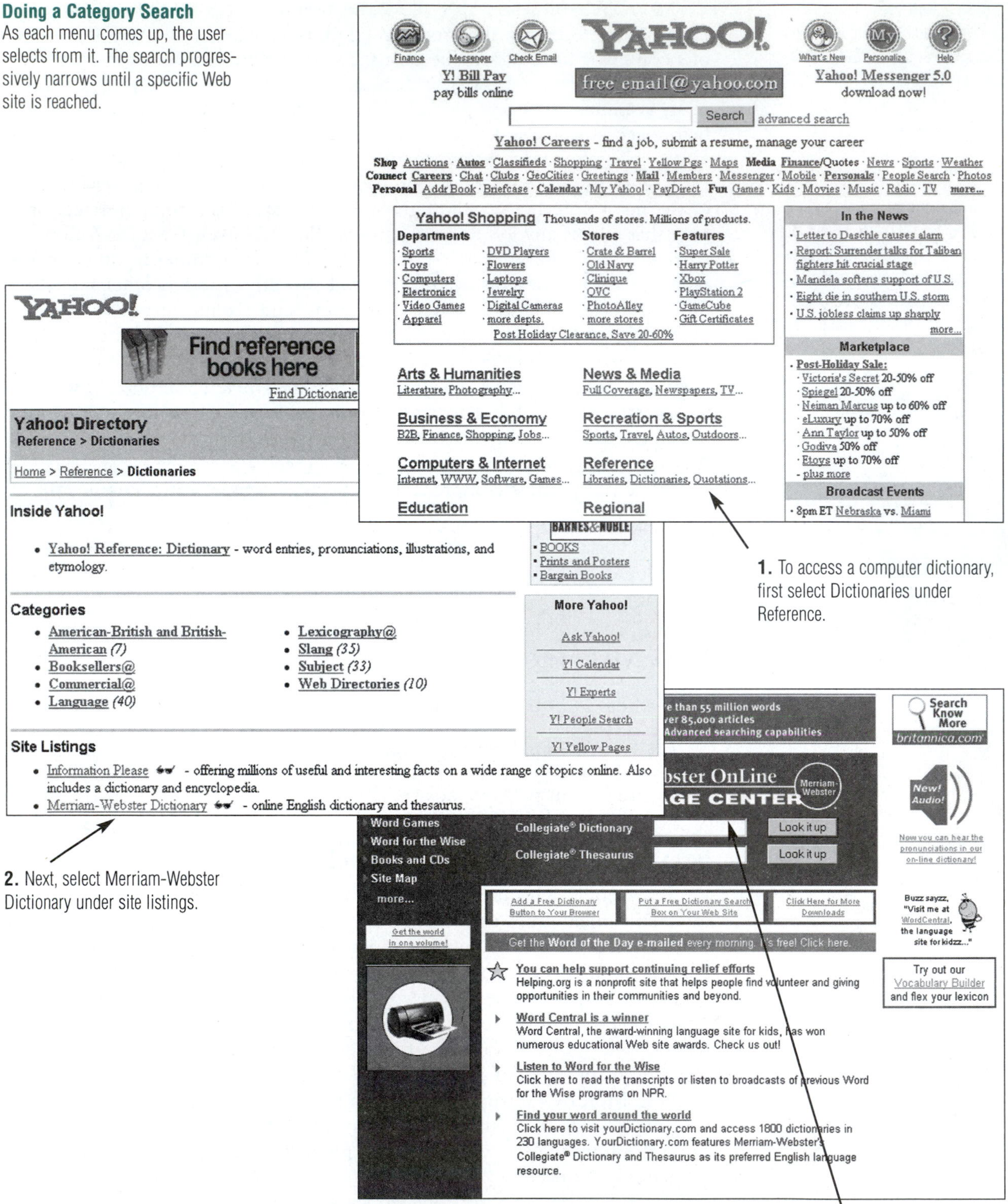

1. To access a computer dictionary, first select Dictionaries under Reference.

2. Next, select Merriam-Webster Dictionary under site listings.

3. The Merriam-Webster Online Language Center site opens and the word search option is displayed.

Doing a Search

A string search lets the user type in a keyword or phrase that relates to the topic.

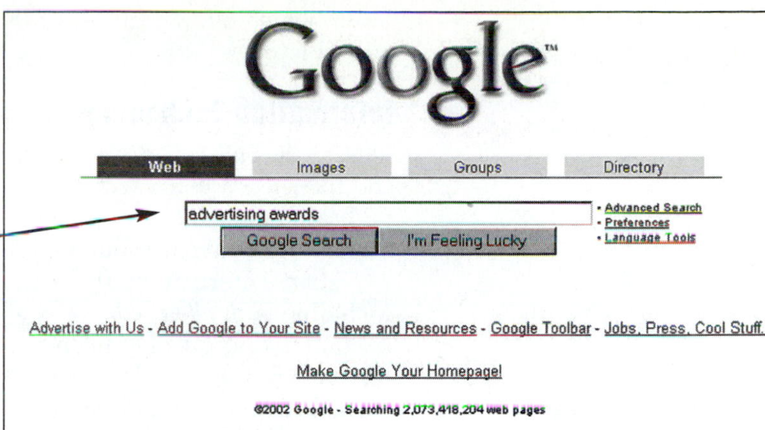

1. First, move the cursor to the text box preceding the Search button and enter a word or phrase.

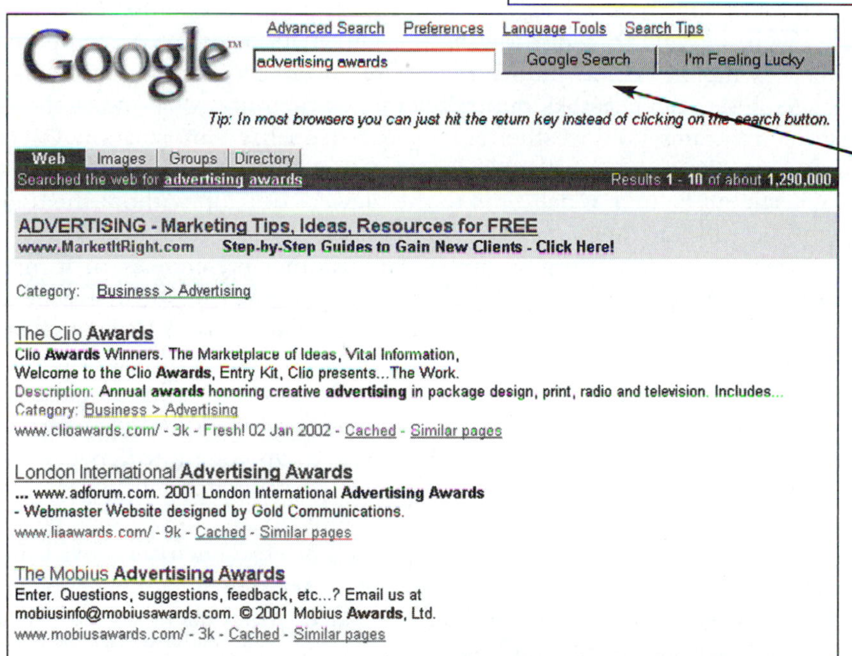

2. Clicking on the Search button causes a list of documents to appear.

CLIO AWARDS

Clio Awards | Clio Archives | Clio Entry Kit | Clio Festival | Clio Resources | Clio Store

Clio Headquarters
Press Releases
International Reps
Juries
Screening Calendar
Feedback
Site Outline

Welcome to the Clio Awards Web Site. We want to make this site your first stop for news about Clio and its 42-year history, and eventually for all relevant news about the world of creative advertising. We are very excited about our year 2002 program.

We are gearing up for the 43rd Clio Festival, to be held in May, 2002 in Miami Beach. Please refer to our Festival link for relevant information concerning dates and events, to be updated as the season progresses. For those of you who have already received our 2002 entry kit, the original event calendar has changed, so please be sure to check in at our Festival page.

Our 2002 entry kit has been mailed out. Downloadable versions of the entry kit are now available at this site in both Macintosh and Windows formats, as well as a replica of the entry kit in PDF format for reviewing on-screen or printing out as a hard copy for manual use. The Clio Rules of Entry, translated into Spanish, German and French, are also available.

Keep watching our Archives section. This file can be easily searched, so that you can look up the record an individual or an agency back through the years.

Incidentally, we are offering a special 40th Anniversary Reel, with over 100 commercials drawn from the rich, four decades of Clio. Please check the Clio Store link in the Marketplace section of this site - hosted by Brandera.com - for further details about this reel and other Clio material, including yearly winners' reels and duplicate statues.

Clio's universe is the worldwide creative community. We want to be the nerve center for this global community, and to make this web site its meeting place.

nuary 2002

Entries are nowbeing accepted for the 2002

Andrew Jaffe
Executive Director, Clio Awards

3. By selecting a document from the list, you access the Web site associated with the document.

levels, which allow managers to scan for trends and apply what they learn at a local level.

Information Technology

The terms *pull technology* and *push technology* describe how data are sent over the Internet. When a Web page isn't delivered until a browser requests it, it is said to be pulled. The opposite of pull is push. Push technology sends data to a user's computer without a request being made.

Smart information delivery (known by a variety of technical names, including *push phase technology*) allows a Web site, such as the Yahoo portal, to become a one-on-one medium for each individual user. Today's information technology uses "smart agents" or "intelligent agents" to deliver customized content to the viewer's desktop. **Smart agent software** is capable of learning an Internet user's preferences and automatically searching out information at selected Web sites and then distributing the information to a user's computer for later viewing. MyYahoo and MyExcite are portal services that personalize Web pages. Users can get stock quotes relevant to their portfolios, news about favorite sports teams, local weather, and other personalized information. Users can customize the sections of the service they want delivered. With push technology, pertinent content is delivered to the viewer's desktop without the user having to do the searching.

smart agent software
Software that learns preferences and finds information without the user's having to search for it.

Push technology may employ surveys of customer preferences, or it may use cookies. **Cookies**, or "magic cookies," are small computer files that a content provider can save onto the computer of someone who visits its Web site. The cookie allows the content provider's computer to track other Web sites visited by the user and store these Web sites in a file that uses the cookie in place of the person's name (which in most cases the content provider never knows). If a person looks up a weather report by keying in a zip code into a personalized Web page, the computer can note that. This is a clue that tells where the person lives (or maybe where he or she may be planning to visit). The computer might note whether a user looks up stock quotes. Then the next time the person visits the Web site the computer might serve up an ad for a restaurant in Seattle, Washington or an online brokerage firm, depending on what the computer's managed to learn.

cookies
Small computer files inserted by a content provider into the computer of a visitor to a Web site; a cookie allows the content provider to track the user's visits to other Web sites and store that information.

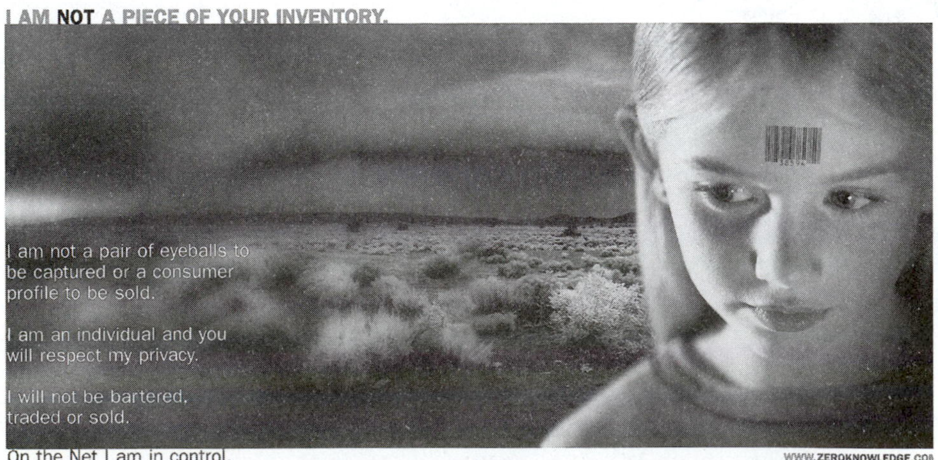

Privacy on the Internet is a growing concern for many consumers. ZeroKnowledge Systems offers software to protect the privacy of Internet users.

Information technology is having a major impact on the nature of business research. We will explore this topic in several places throughout this book.

INTRANETS

intranet
A company's private data network that uses Internet standards and technology.

An **intranet** is a company's private data network that uses Internet standards and technology. The information on an intranet—data, graphics, even video and voice—is available only inside the organization. Thus, a key difference between the Internet and an intranet is that security software programs, or "firewalls," are installed to limit access to only those employees authorized to enter the system.

A company uses Internet features, such as electronic mail, Web pages, and browsers, to create an intranet, which is a communications and data resource for that specific company. Company information is accessible using the same point-and-click technology used on the Internet. Managers and employees use links to get complete, up-to-date information. An intranet lets authorized personnel—some of whom were previously isolated on departmental local area networks—look at product drawings, employee newsletters, sales figures, and other kinds of company information. Whether the information comes from a spreadsheet or a word-processing document is not an issue to the user of an intranet. Managers and employees do not have to worry about the format of the information. Groupware such as Lotus Notes or Microsoft Exchange and other technology can facilitate the transfer of data, information, and knowledge.[17]

Knowledge from Experts—Experience and Expertise Databases

In organizations that practice knowledge management, intranets function to make the knowledge of company "experts" more accessible throughout their organizations.[18] Such companies make a well-organized and purposeful effort to retain, analyze, and organize employee expertise so that it is easily obtainable at any time from anywhere. Extracting knowledge from experts and putting it into document databases may not be easy because experts often are unforthcoming, busy, or otherwise uncooperative. To collect and organize expert knowledge, many companies have hired journalists, librarians, and business researchers to work with their experts. These "knowledge workers" interview the experts, write relevant documents, update experience and expertise databases, and make sure white papers, reports, and related databases are put in a database that is accessible across the organization.

INTERNET2

As we mentioned earlier, information technology changes rapidly. As sophisticated as the Internet and intranets are today, new technologies, such as Internet2, will dramatically enhance researchers' ability to answer business questions in the future.

Internet2 (http://www.internet2.edu) is a collaborative effort involving over 100 universities, industrial organizations, and governmental affiliates in the United States. The goal of those working to create Internet2 is to build and operate a research network with more than 100 times the bandwidth of the current Internet.

SUMMARY

The primary difference between data and information is that data are simply facts or recorded measures of certain phenomena, while information refers to a body of facts in a format that facilitates decision making or that defines relationships between pieces of data.

Knowledge is a blend of information, experience, and insights that provides a framework that can be thoughtfully applied when assessing new information or evaluating relevant situations. Knowledge management is the process of creating an inclusive, comprehensive, easily accessible organizational memory, which is often called the organization's intellectual capital.

Increased global competition and technological advances involving interactive media have stimulated development of global information systems. A global information system is an organized collection of computer hardware, software, data, and personnel designed to capture, store, update, manipulate, analyze, and immediately display information about worldwide business activity.

A decision support system is a computer-based system that helps decision makers confront problems through direct interaction with databases and software. The purpose of a decision support system is to store data and transform them into organized information that is easily accessible to business managers. Effective companies spend a great deal of time and effort collecting information to input into their decision support systems.

A database is a collection of raw data arranged logically and organized in a form that can be stored and processed by a computer. Because most companies compile and store many different databases, they often develop data warehousing systems. A data warehouse is a comprehensive collection of data that describes the extensive operations of an organization. Data warehouse management requires that the detailed data from operational systems be extracted, transformed, and stored (warehoused) so that the various database files, from both inside and outside the company, are consistent.

Numerous database search and retrieval systems are available by subscription or in libraries. Computer-assisted database searching has made the collection of external data faster and easier. Business researchers refer to many different types of databases.

Although personal computers work independently, they can connect to other computers in networks to share data and software. Electronic data interchange (EDI) joins one company's computer system directly to another's.

The Internet is a worldwide network of computers that allows users access to information and documents from distant sources. It is a combination of a worldwide communication system and the world's largest public library. This system of thousands of interconnected pages, or documents, called the World Wide Web (WWW) can be easily accessed with Web browsers and search engines. It has changed the way business researchers think about distributing and accessing information.

Key Terms

data
information
knowledge
knowledge management
global information system
decision support system
customer relationship management (CRM)
database
business intelligence
electronic data interchange (EDI)
Internet

host
server
World Wide Web (WWW)
search engine
smart agent software
cookies
intranet

Questions for Review and Critical Thinking

1. What is the difference between data and information? Provide examples.
2. What are the characteristics of useful information?
3. Define *knowledge management*. What is its purpose?
4. What are the major sources of input for a decision support system?
5. In your own words, describe the Internet. What is its purpose?
6. Define *intranet*.
7. Give three examples of computerized databases that are available at your college or university library.

Exploring the Internet

1. Go to your school's computer center to learn how to obtain an e-mail address and how to establish an account that allows you to access the Internet. Get instructions on how to access the Internet using your local computer system.
2. The Spider's Apprentice is a Web site that provides many useful tips about using search engines. Go to http://www.monash.com/spidap.html, then click on The Spider's Apprentice to learn the ins and outs of search engines.
3. Use a Web browser to visit Yahoo at http://www.yahoo.com. You will see a list of the major search categories. Click on Business and Economics. What additional search categories become available to you?
4. CEO Express (http://www.ceoexpress.com), Brint.com (http://www.brint.com/), and WorldOpinion (http://www.worldopinion. com) provide information about research topics and links to other Web pages. These pages will be extremely useful in your study of many business research topics. Visit these sites often during your study of business research.
5. For a useful business and personal tool, go to http://www.mapblast.com. Describe the site.
6. To learn more about data warehousing, go to http://www.knowledgecenters.org/ or to http://www.datawarehousing.org.
7. Use the Internet to see if you can find information to answer the following questions:
   a. What is the weather in Denver today?
   b. What are four restaurants in the French Quarter in New Orleans?
   c. What is the population of Brazil?

Case Suggestions

Case 2: Harvard Cooperative Society
Video Case 4: Fossil—A Watch for Every Wrist
Video Case 5: IBM: Enterprise Resource Planning

CHAPTER

3

THEORY BUILDING

What you will learn in this chapter

- To understand the goals of theory.
- To define the meaning of *theory.*
- To understand the terms *concept, proposition, variable,* and *hypothesis.*
- To understand that because concepts abstract reality, it is possible to discuss concepts at various levels of abstraction.
- To understand the scientific method.
- To discuss how theories are generated.

The purpose of science concerns the expansion of knowledge and the discovery of truth. Theory building is the means by which basic researchers hope to achieve this purpose. ■

WHAT ARE THE GOALS OF THEORY?

A scientist investigating business phenomena wants to know what produces inflation. Another person wants to know if organizational structure influences leadership style. Both want to be able to predict behavior, to be able to say that if we do such and such, then so and so will happen.[1]

Prediction and understanding are the two purposes of theory.[2] Accomplishing the first goal allows the theorist to predict the behavior or characteristics of one phenomenon from the knowledge of another phenomenon's characteristics. A business researcher may theorize that older investors tend to be more interested in investment income than younger investors. This theory, once verified, should allow researchers to predict the importance of expected dividend yield on the basis of investors' ages. The ability to anticipate future conditions in the environment or in an organization may be extremely valuable, yet prediction alone may not satisfy the scientific researcher's goals. Successfully forecasting an election outcome does not satisfy one's curiosity about the reason *why* a candidate won the election. A researcher also wants to gain understanding. In most situations, of course, prediction and understanding go hand in hand. To predict phenomena, we must have an explanation of why variables behave as they do. Theories provide these explanations.

TO THE POINT

Theories are nets cast to catch what we call "the world": to rationalize, to explain, and to master it. We endeavour to make the mesh ever finer and finer.

—KARL R. POPPER, THE LOGIC OF SCIENTIFIC DISCOVERY

THE MEANING OF THEORY

> Like all abstractions, the word "theory" has been used in many different ways, in many different contexts, at times so broadly as to include almost all descriptive statements about a class of phenomena, and at other times so narrowly as to exclude everything but a series of terms and their relationships that satisfies certain logical requirements.[3]

For our purposes, a **theory** is a coherent set of general propositions, used as principles of explanation of the apparent relationships of certain observed phenomena. A key element in our definition is the term *proposition*. Before we can see what a proposition is, however, we must discuss the nature of *theoretical concepts.*

theory
A coherent set of general propositions used to explain the apparent relationships among certain observed phenomena. Theories allow generalizations beyond individual facts or situations.

CONCEPTS

Theory development is essentially a process of describing phenomena at increasingly higher levels of abstraction. Things that we observe can be described as concepts. A **concept** (or construct) is a generalized idea about a class of objects, attributes, occurrences, or processes that has been given a name. If you, as an organizational theorist, were to describe phenomena such as supervisory behavior, you would categorize empirical events or real things into concepts. Concepts are building blocks, and in organizational theory, "leadership," "productivity," and "morale" are concepts. In the theory of finance, "gross national product," "asset," and "inflation" are frequently used concepts.

concept
A generalized idea about a class of objects; an abstraction of reality that is the basic unit for theory development.

Concepts abstract reality. That is, concepts are expressed in words that refer to various events or objects. For example, the concept "asset" is an abstract term that may, in the concrete world of reality, refer to a specific punch press machine. Concepts, however, may vary in degree of abstraction. The abstraction

Exhibit 3.1 | **A Ladder of Abstraction for Concepts**

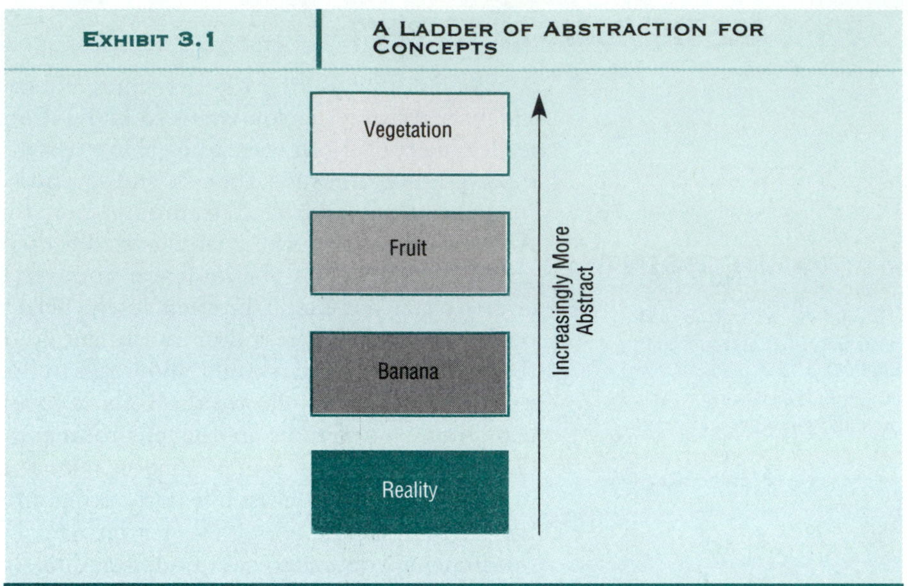

ladder in Exhibit 3.1 indicates that it is possible to discuss concepts at various levels of abstraction. Moving up the **ladder of abstraction,** the basic concept becomes more abstract, wider in scope, and less amenable to measurement. The basic or scientific business researcher operates at two levels: on the **abstract level** of concepts (and propositions) and on the empirical level of variables (and hypotheses). At the **empirical level,** we "experience" reality—that is, we observe or manipulate objects or events (see Exhibit 3.2).[4]

ladder of abstraction
Organization of concepts in sequence from the most concrete and individual to the most general.

abstract level
In theory development, the level of knowledge expressing a concept that exists only as an idea or a quality apart from an object.

empirical level
Level of knowledge that is verifiable by experience or observation.

If the organizational researcher says "Older workers prefer different rewards than younger workers," two concepts—age of worker and reward preference—are the subjects of this abstract statement. If the researcher wishes to test this hypothesis, John, age 19, Chuck, age 45, and Mary, age 62—along with other workers—may be questioned about their preferences for salary, retirement plans, intrinsic job satisfaction, and the like. Recording their ages and observing their stated preferences are activities that occur at the empirical level.

Researchers are concerned with the observable world, or what we shall loosely term "reality." Theorists translate their conceptualization of reality into

Exhibit 3.2 | **Concepts Are Abstractions of Reality**

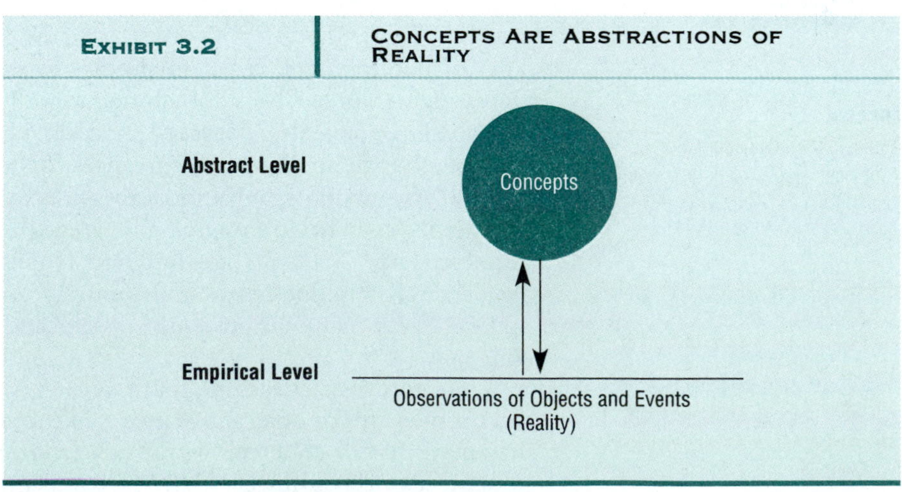

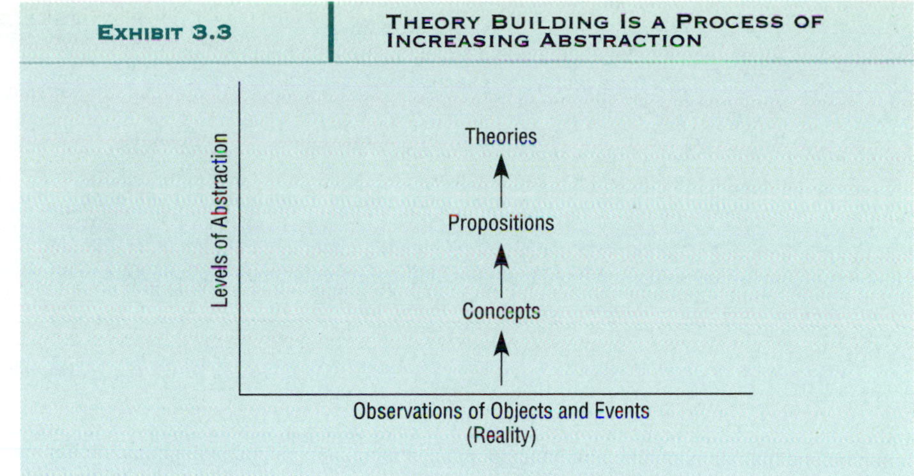

Reality is merely an illusion, albeit a very persistent one.

ALBERT EINSTEIN

abstract ideas. Thus, theory deals with abstraction. Things are not the essence of theory; ideas are.[5] Concepts in isolation are not theories. Only when we explain how concepts relate to other concepts do we begin to construct theories.

NATURE OF PROPOSITIONS

proposition
A statement concerned with the relationships among concepts; an assertion of a universal connection between events that have certain properties.

Concepts are the basic units of theory development. However, theories require an understanding of the relationship among concepts. Thus, once reality is abstracted into concepts, the scientist is interested in the relationship among various concepts. **Propositions** are statements concerned with the relationships among concepts. A proposition explains the *logical* linkage among certain concepts by asserting a universal connection between concepts. A proposition states that every concept about an event or thing either has a certain property or stands in a certain relationship to other concepts about the event or thing.[6]

Consider the following behavioral science proposition that permeates many business theories: If reinforcements follow each other at evenly distributed intervals, and everything else is held constant, the resulting habit will increase in strength as a positive growth function of the number of trials.[7] This proposition identifies theoretical relationships between the concepts "reinforcements" and "habit." It identifies the direction and magnitude of these relationships.

We have indicated that a theory is an abstraction from observed reality. Concepts are at one level of abstraction (see Exhibit 3.3). Investigating propositions requires that we increase our level of abstract thinking. When we think about theories, we are at the highest level of abstraction because we are investigating the relationship between propositions. Theories are networks of propositions.

THE SCIENTIFIC METHOD

scientific method
Techniques or procedures used to analyze empirical evidence in an attempt to confirm or disprove prior conceptions.

The **scientific method** is a set of prescribed procedures for establishing and connecting theoretical statements about events, for analyzing empirical evidence, and for predicting events yet unknown. There is no consensus concerning exact procedures for the scientific method, but most discussions of the scientific method include references to "empirical testability." *Empirical* means verifiable

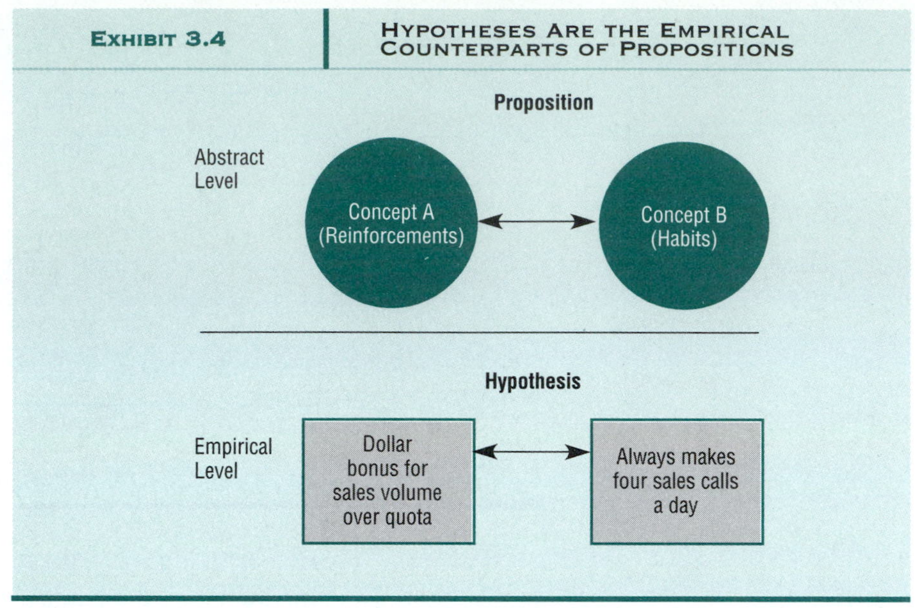

by observation, experimentation, or experience. The process of empirical verification cannot be divorced from the process of theory development.

hypothesis
An unproven proposition or supposition that tentatively explains certain facts or phenomena; a proposition that is empirically testable.

variable
Anything that may assume different numerical values.

A **hypothesis** is a proposition that is empirically testable. It is an empirical statement concerned with the relationship among variables. The abstract proposition "Reinforcements will increase habit strength" may be tested empirically with a hypothesis. Exhibit 3.4 shows that the hypothesis "Bonus pay given for sales volume consistently above quota will be associated with the number of sales calls a day" is an empirical counterpart of the proposition. Bonus pay and sales calls are **variables,** reflecting the concepts of reinforcement and habits. Because variables are at the empirical level, variables may be measured. Thus, the scientific method has two basic levels:

> . . . the empirical and the abstract, conceptual. The empirical aspect is primarily concerned with the facts of the science as revealed by observation and experiments. The abstract or theoretical aspect, on the other hand, consists in a serious attempt to understand the facts of the science, and to integrate them into a coherent, i.e., a logical, system. From these observations and integrations are derived, directly or indirectly, the basic laws of the science.[8]

AN EXAMPLE OF A THEORY

Exhibit 3.5 is a simplified portrayal of a theory to explain voluntary job turnover—that is, the movement of employees to other organizations. Two concepts—(1) the *perceived desirability of movement* to another organization and (2) the *perceived ease of movement* from the present job—are expected to be the primary determinants of *intention to quit*. This is a proposition. Further, the concept *intention to quit* is expected to be a necessary condition for the actual *voluntary job turnover behavior* to occur. This is a second proposition that links concepts together in this theory. In the more elaborate theory, *job performance* is another concept considered to be the primary determinant influencing

Exhibit 3.5 | **A Basic Theory Explaining Voluntary Job Turnover**[9]

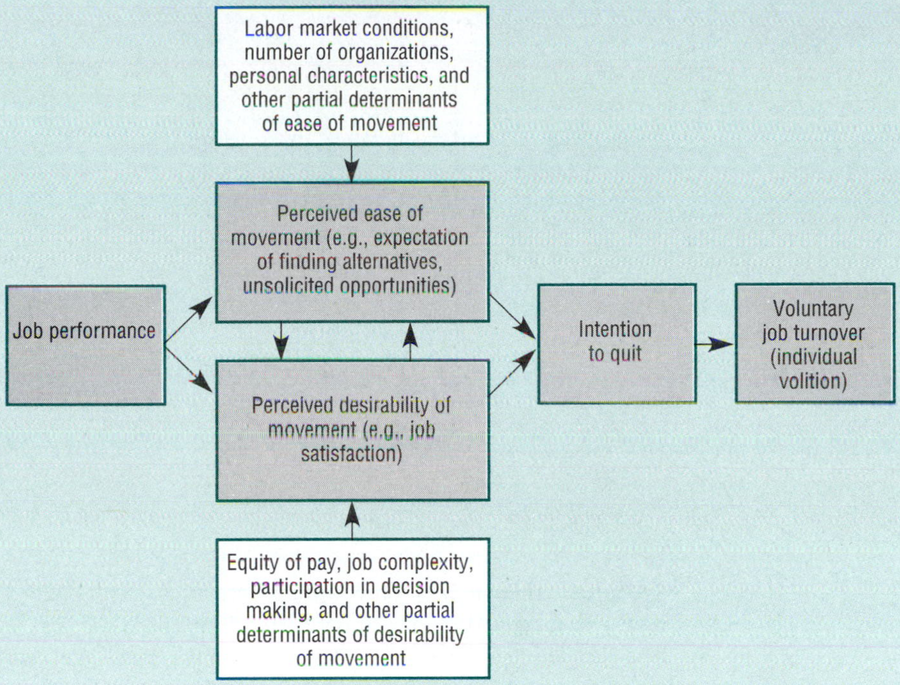

Labor market conditions, number of organizations, personal characteristics, and other partial determinants of ease of movement

Perceived ease of movement (e.g., expectation of finding alternatives, unsolicited opportunities)

Job performance

Intention to quit

Voluntary job turnover (individual volition)

Perceived desirability of movement (e.g., job satisfaction)

Equity of pay, job complexity, participation in decision making, and other partial determinants of desirability of movement

both *perceived ease of movement* and *perceived desirability of movement*. Moreover, perceived ease of movement is related to other concepts such as *labor market conditions, number of organizations visible* to the individual, and *personal characteristics*. Perceived desirability of movement is influenced by concepts such as *equity of pay, job complexity,* and *participation in decision making*.

A complete explanation of this theory is not possible; however, this example should help you understand the terminology used by theory builders.

VERIFYING THEORY

If facts conflict with a theory, either the theory must be changed or the facts.

BENEDICT SPINOZA

In most scientific situations there are alternative theories to explain certain phenomena. To determine which is the better theory, researchers gather empirical data or make observations to verify the theories.

Maslow's hierarchical theory of motivation offers one explanation of human behavior. For example, Maslow theorizes that individuals will attempt to satisfy physiological needs before self-esteem needs. An alternative view of motivation is provided by Freudian (psychoanalytic) theory, which suggests that unconscious, emotional impulses are the basic influences on behavior. One task of science is to determine if a given theoretical proposition is false or if there are inconsistencies between competing theories. Just as records are made to be broken, theories are made to be tested.

> It must be possible to demonstrate that a given proposition or theory is false. This may at first glance appear strange. Why "false" rather than "true"?

RESEARCH INSIGHT

THEORY AND SONG

This song (attributed to George Schultz, a former U.S. Secretary of State) is sung to the lively tune *Silver Dollar.*[10]

A fact without a theory
Is like a ship without a sail,
Is like a boat without a rudder,
Is like a kite without a tail.
A fact without a figure
Is a tragic final act,
But one thing worse
In this universe
Is a theory without a fact.

> Technically, there may be other untested theories which could account for the results we obtained in our study of a proposition. At the very least, there may be a competing explanation which could be the "real" explanation for a given set of research findings. Thus, we can never be certain that our proposition or theory is the correct one. The scientist can only say, "I have a theory which I have objectively tested with data and the data are consistent with my theory." If the possibility of proving an idea false or wrong is not inherent in our test of an idea, then we cannot put much faith in the evidence that suggests it to be true. No other evidence was allowed to manifest itself.[11]

Business research gathers facts to verify theories. However, the researcher who wishes to identify inconsistency within a particular theory must understand the difference between facts and theories:

> Facts and theories are different things, not rungs in a hierarchy of increasing certainty. Facts are the world's data. Theories are structures of ideas that explain and interpret facts. Facts do not go away when scientists debate rival theories to explain them. Einstein's theory of gravitation replaced Newton's, but apples did not suspend themselves in midair pending the outcome.[12]

HOW ARE THEORIES GENERATED?

Many students ask, "Where do theories come from?" Although this is not an easy question to answer in a short chapter on theory in business research, we shall nevertheless explore this topic briefly.

In this chapter, theory has been explained at the abstract, conceptual level and at the empirical level. Theory generation may occur at either level.

deductive reasoning
The logical process of deriving a conclusion about a specific instance based on a known general premise or something known to be true.

At the abstract, conceptual level, a theory may be developed with deductive reasoning by going from a general statement to a specific assertion. **Deductive reasoning** is the logical process of deriving a conclusion about a specific instance based on a known general premise or something known to be

RESEARCH INSIGHT

BALLISTIC THEORY

Ballistic theory is a theory because it deals with measurable factors, because it states their relationships in detail, and because any one factor can be fairly completely determined by a knowledge of all the others.[13] Given all of the factors except the initial speed of the projectile, an engineer can determine what that speed was. Asked to change the point of impact, he can suggest several ways in which this can be accomplished—all of which will work.

It is common knowledge that the behavioral sciences are not as advanced as the physical sciences. What this means, in effect, is that no one has yet defined all of the factors in human behavior or determined the influence that each has on events. In fact, no one has really done a very good job of determining what an event is, that is, how to measure it or what to consider relevant about it.

Again, an example may help explain the dilemma. It is irrelevant to ballistic theory that John Gingrich is standing beside the 155 mm rifle when it is fired. It may not be irrelevant to consumer behavior theory that he is standing beside the person who selects a necktie. It is not relevant to ballistic theory that the gunner's father once carried an M-1. It may be relevant to consumer behavior theory that the automobile purchaser's grandfather once owned a Ford.

true. For example, we know that *all managers are human beings.* If we also know that *Steve Hazelwood is a manager,* then we can deduce that *Steve Hazelwood is a human being.*

inductive reasoning
The logical process of establishing a general proposition on the basis of observation of particular facts.

At the empirical level, a theory may be developed with inductive reasoning. **Inductive reasoning** is the logical process of establishing a general proposition on the basis of observation of particular facts. All managers that have ever been seen are human beings; therefore, all managers are human beings.

Suppose a stockbroker with 15 years' experience trading on the New York Stock Exchange repeatedly notices that the price of gold and the price of gold stocks rise whenever there is a hijacking, terrorist bombing, or military skirmish. In other words, similar patterns occur whenever a certain type of event occurs. The stockbroker may induce from these empirical observations the more general situation that the price of gold is related to political stability. Thus, the stockbroker states a proposition based on his or her experience or specific observations.

Over the course of time, theory construction is often the result of a combination of deductive and inductive reasoning. Our experiences lead us to draw conclusions that we then try to verify empirically by using the scientific method.

OVERVIEW OF THE SCIENTIFIC METHOD

It is useful to look at the analytic process of scientific theory building as a series of stages. Seven operations may be viewed as the steps involved in the application of the scientific method:

1. Assessment of relevant existing knowledge of a phenomenon
2. Formulation of concepts and propositions

3. Statement of hypotheses
4. Design of research to test the hypotheses
5. Acquisition of meaningful empirical data
6. Analysis and evaluation of data
7. Proposal of an explanation of the phenomenon and statement of new problems raised by the research[14]

An excellent overview of the scientific method is presented in Robert Pirsig's book *Zen and the Art of Motorcycle Maintenance:*

> Actually I've never seen a cycle-maintenance problem complex enough really to require full-scale formal scientific method. Repair problems are not that hard. When I think of formal scientific method an image sometimes comes to mind of an enormous juggernaut, a huge bulldozer—slow, tedious, lumbering, laborious, but invincible. It takes twice as long, five times as long, maybe a dozen times as long as informal mechanic's techniques, but you know in the end you're going to get it. There's no fault isolation problem in motorcycle maintenance that can stand up to it. When you've hit a really tough one, tried everything, racked your brain and nothing works, and you know that this time Nature has really decided to be difficult, you say, "Okay, Nature, that's the end of the nice guy," and you crank up the formal scientific method.
>
> For this you keep a lab notebook. Everything gets written down, formally, so that you know at all times where you are, where you've been, where you're going and where you want to get. In scientific work and electronics technology this is necessary because otherwise the problems get so complex you get lost in them and confused and forget what you know and what you don't know and have to give up. In cycle maintenance things are not that involved, but when confusion starts it's a good idea to hold it down by making everything formal and exact. Sometimes just the act of writing down the problems straightens out your head as to what they really are.
>
> The logical statements entered into the notebook are broken down into six categories: (1) statement of the problem, (2) hypotheses as to the cause of the problem, (3) experiments designed to test each hypothesis, (4) predicted results of the experiments, (5) observed results of the experiments and (6) conclusions from the results of the experiments. This is not different from the formal arrangement of many college and high-school lab notebooks but the purpose here is no longer just busywork. The purpose now is precise guidance of thoughts that will fail if they are not accurate.
>
> The real purpose of scientific method is to make sure Nature hasn't misled you into thinking you know something you don't actually know. There's not a mechanic or scientist or technician alive who hasn't suffered from that one so much that he's not instinctively on guard. That's the main reason why so much scientific and mechanical information sounds so dull and so cautious. If you get careless or go romanticizing scientific information, giving it a flourish here and there, Nature will soon make a complete fool out of you. It does it often enough anyway even when you don't give it opportunities. One must be extremely careful and rigidly logical when dealing with Nature: one logical slip and an entire scientific edifice comes tumbling down. One false deduction about the machine and you can get hung up indefinitely.
>
> In Part One of formal scientific method, which is the statement of the problem, the main skill is in stating absolutely no more than you are positive you know. It is much better to enter a statement "Solve Problem: Why doesn't

cycle work?" which sounds dumb but is correct, than it is to enter a statement "Solve Problem: What is wrong with the electrical system?" when you don't absolutely know the trouble is in the electrical system. What you should state is "Solve Problem: What is wrong with cycle?" and then state as the first entry of Part Two: "Hypothesis Number One: The trouble is in the electrical system." You think of as many hypotheses as you can, then you design experiments to test them to see which are true and which are false.

This careful approach to the beginning questions keeps you from taking a major wrong turn which might cause you weeks of extra work or can even hang you up completely. Scientific questions often have a surface appearance of dumbness for this reason. They are asked in order to prevent dumb mistakes later on.

Part Three, that part of formal scientific method called experimentation, is sometimes thought of by romantics as all of science itself because that's the only part with much visual surface. They see lots of test tubes and bizarre equipment and people running around making discoveries. They do not see the experiment as part of a larger intellectual process and so they often confuse experiments with demonstrations, which look the same. A man conducting a gee-whiz science show with fifty thousand dollars' worth of Frankenstein equipment is not doing anything scientific if he knows beforehand what the results of his efforts are going to be. A motorcycle mechanic, on the other hand, who honks the horn to see if the battery works is informally conducting a true scientific experiment. He is testing a hypothesis by putting the question to nature. The TV scientist who mutters sadly, "The experiment is a failure; we have failed to achieve what we had hoped for," is suffering mainly from a bad scriptwriter. An experiment is never a failure solely because it fails to achieve predicted results. An experiment is a failure only when it also fails adequately to test the hypothesis in question, when the data it produces don't prove anything one way or another.

TO THE POINT

A motorcycle mechanic . . . who honks the horn to see if the battery works is informally conducting a true scientific experiment. He is testing a hypothesis by putting the question to nature.

ROBERT M. PIRSIG

Skill at this point consists of using experiments that test only the hypothesis in question, nothing less, nothing more. If the horn honks, and the mechanic concludes that the whole electrical system is working, he is in deep trouble. He has reached an illogical conclusion. The honking horn only tells him that the battery and horn are working. To design an experiment properly he has to think very rigidly in terms of what directly causes what. This you know from the hierarchy. The horn doesn't make the cycle go. Neither does the battery, except in a very indirect way. The point at which the electrical system directly causes the engine to fire is at the spark plugs, and if you don't test here, at the output of the electrical system, you will never really know whether the failure is electrical or not.

To test properly the mechanic removes the plug and lays it against the engine so that the base around the plug is electrically grounded, kicks the starter lever and watches the spark-plug gap for a blue spark. If there isn't any he can conclude one of two things: (a) there is an electrical failure or (b) his experiment is sloppy. If he is experienced he will try it a few more times, checking connections, trying every way he can think of to get that plug to fire. Then, if he can't get it to fire, he finally concludes that (a) is correct, there's an electrical failure, and the experiment is over. He has proved that his hypothesis is correct.

In the final category, conclusions, skill comes in stating no more than the experiment has proved. It hasn't proved that when he fixes the electrical system the motorcycle will start. There may be other things wrong. But he does know that the motorcycle isn't going to run until the electrical system is working and he sets up the next formal question: "Solve problem: What is wrong with the electrical system?"

He then sets up hypotheses for these and tests them. By asking the right questions and choosing the right tests and drawing the right conclusions the mechanic works his way down the echelons of the motorcycle hierarchy until he has found the exact specific cause or causes of the engine failure, and then he changes them so that they no longer cause the failure.

An untrained observer will see only physical labor and often get the idea that physical labor is mainly what the mechanic does. Actually the physical labor is the smallest and easiest part of what the mechanic does. By far the greatest part of his work is careful observation and precise thinking. That is why mechanics sometimes seem so taciturn and withdrawn when performing tests. They don't like it when you talk to them because they are concentrating on mental images, hierarchies, and not really looking at you or the physical motorcycle at all. They are using the experiment as part of a program to expand their hierarchy of knowledge of the faulty motorcycle and compare it to the correct hierarchy in their mind. They are looking at underlying form.[15]

PRACTICAL VALUE OF THEORIES

As the above excerpt makes evident, theories allow us to generalize beyond individual facts or isolated situations. Theories provide a framework that can guide managerial strategy by providing insights into general rules of behavior. When different incidents may be theoretically comparable in some way, the scientific knowledge gained from theory development may have practical value. A good theory allows us to generalize beyond individual facts so that general patterns may be predicted and understood. For this reason it is often said there is nothing so practical as a good theory.

SUMMARY

Prediction and understanding are the two purposes of theory. A theory is a coherent set of general propositions used as principles of explanation of the apparent relationships of certain observed phenomena. Concepts and propositions are the elements of theory at the abstract level. At the empirical level, theory is concerned with variables and testable hypotheses, the empirical counterparts of concepts and propositions. The scientific method is a series of stages utilized to develop and refine theory.

Key Terms

theory
concept
ladder of abstraction
abstract level
empirical level
proposition
scientific method
hypothesis
variable
deductive reasoning
inductive reasoning

Questions for Review and Critical Thinking

1. What are some theories offered to explain aspects of your field of business?
2. How do propositions and hypotheses differ?
3. How do concepts differ from variables?
4. Comment on this statement: "There is nothing so practical as a good theory."
5. The 17th-century Dutch philosopher Benedict Spinoza said, "If the facts conflict with a theory, either the theory must be changed or the facts." What is the practical meaning of this statement?
6. Find another definition of *theory*. How is the definition you found similar to this book's definition? How is it different?

Exploring the Internet

1. The *American Heritage Dictionary of the English Language* can be found at http://www.bartleby.com/am/. What is the definition of *theory* given at this site? How does it compare to the definition given in this chapter?
2. Go to http://www.utm.edu/research/iep/ to find the Internet Encyclopedia of Philosophy. Look up the term *logical positivism*. Is empirical verification important in this field of philosophy?
3. The *Logic of Scientific Discovery* is an important theoretical work. Visit The Karl Popper Web site at http://www.eeng.dcu.ie/~tkpw/ to learn about its author and his work.

Case Suggestion

Case 27: Old School versus New School Sports Fans

CHAPTER

4

THE RESEARCH PROCESS: An Overview

What you will learn in this chapter

- To classify business research as exploratory research, descriptive research, or causal research.
- To list the stages in the business research process.
- To identify and briefly discuss the various decision alternatives available to the researcher during each stage of the research process.
- To explain the difference between a research project and a research program.

Two contrasting models dominate the way managers think about the design of the work process.[1] On the one hand, a task may require the input of several highly interdependent people. One example of a design to accomplish such a task is a team responsible for creating a new advertising campaign. The team might include copywriters, graphic artists, and project managers, all of whose contributions are necessary for completing the task, and all of whom are held collectively accountable for the quality of the new promotion strategy. Alternatively, work can be structured to be performed by highly independent individuals. The reward system in that case must be designed to reinforce individual excellence. An example is a sales team in which each member is given responsibility for sales in one specific territory and is paid a commission based solely on his or her individual sales performance.

A third model has received relatively little attention: a "hybrid" design that combines elements of interdependent and independent work. One example of such a design is a group of researchers in a development laboratory, each of whom pursues independent research projects and, in addition, collaborates on some larger shared enterprise. Members of such hybrid groups sometimes operate entirely independently and sometimes work as a team.

Suppose a manager wanted to determine how important interdependence is for accomplishing a particular task. Suppose the manager was also interested in knowing how to assess and reward both independent performance and interdependent teamwork performance. Should a survey of employees be taken? Should employees be observed on the job? Should an experiment be designed to evaluate the distinct forms of interdependence? Should a survey of managers be part of the research strategy?

This chapter discusses how managers make decisions about planning research strategies and tactics. ■

DECISION MAKING

Formally defined, *decision making* is the process of resolving a problem or choosing among alternative opportunities. The keys to decision making are recognizing the nature of the problem/opportunity, identifying how much information is available, and determining what information is needed. Every business problem or decision-making situation can be classified on a continuum ranging from complete certainty to absolute ambiguity. To facilitate discussion, the scale in Exhibit 4.1 shows three categories: certainty, uncertainty, and ambiguity.[2]

Certainty

Complete certainty means that the decision maker has all the information that he or she needs. The decision maker knows the exact nature of the business problem or opportunity. For example, an airline may need to know the demographic characteristics of its pilots. The firm knows exactly what information it needs and where to find it. If a manager is completely certain about both the problem/opportunity and future outcomes, then research may not be needed at all. However, perfect certainty, especially about the future, is rare.

Uncertainty

Uncertainty means that managers grasp the general nature of the objectives they wish to achieve, but the information about alternatives is incomplete. Predictions about the forces that will shape future events are educated guesses. Under conditions of uncertainty, effective managers recognize potential value in spending additional time gathering information to clarify the nature of the decision.

Ambiguity

Ambiguity means that the nature of the problem to be solved is unclear. The objectives are vague and the alternatives are difficult to define. This is by far the most difficult decision situation.

Business managers face a variety of decision-making situations. Under conditions of complete certainty, when future outcomes are predictable, business research may be a waste of time. However, under conditions of uncertainty or ambiguity, business research becomes more attractive to decision makers. The more ambiguous a situation is, the more likely it is that additional time and money must be spent on business research.

EXHIBIT 4.1 DECISIONS ARE NOT ALL THE SAME: A CONTINUUM OF DECISION MAKING

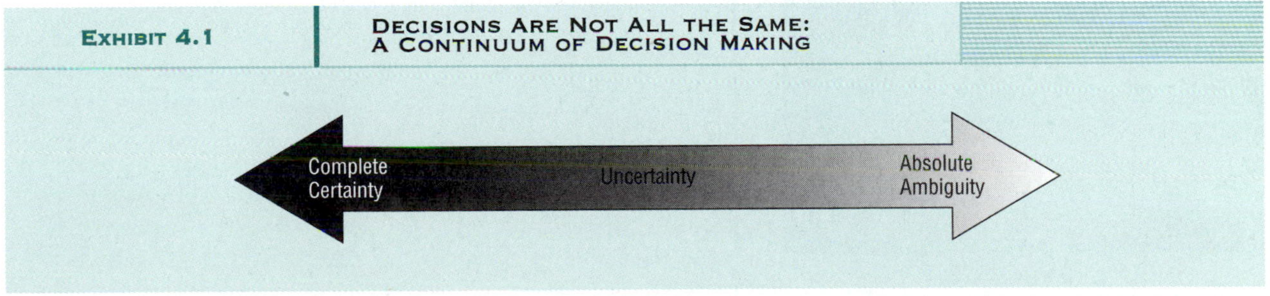

TYPES OF BUSINESS RESEARCH

Business research produces information to reduce uncertainty. It helps focus decision making. In a number of situations business researchers know exactly what their business problems are and design studies to test specific hypotheses. For example, a soft drink company introducing a new iced coffee might want to know whether a gold or a silver label would make the packaging more effective. This problem is fully defined and an experiment may be designed to answer the business question with little preliminary investigation. In other, more ambiguous circumstances management may be totally unaware of a business problem. For example, a plant manager may notice when employee turnover increases dramatically but be totally ignorant of the reason for the increase. Some exploratory research may be necessary to gain insights into the nature of such a problem.

Because of the variety of research activity, it will be helpful to categorize the types of business research. Business research can be classified on the basis of either technique or function. Experiments, surveys, and observational studies are just a few common research *techniques.* Classifying business research on the basis of purpose or *function* allows us to understand how the nature of the problem influences the choice of research method. The nature of the problem will determine whether the research is (1) exploratory, (2) descriptive, or (3) causal.

Exploratory Studies

exploratory research
Initial research conducted to clarify and define the nature of a problem.

Exploratory research is conducted to clarify ambiguous problems. Management may have discovered general problems, but research is needed to gain better understanding of the dimensions of the problems. Exploratory studies provide

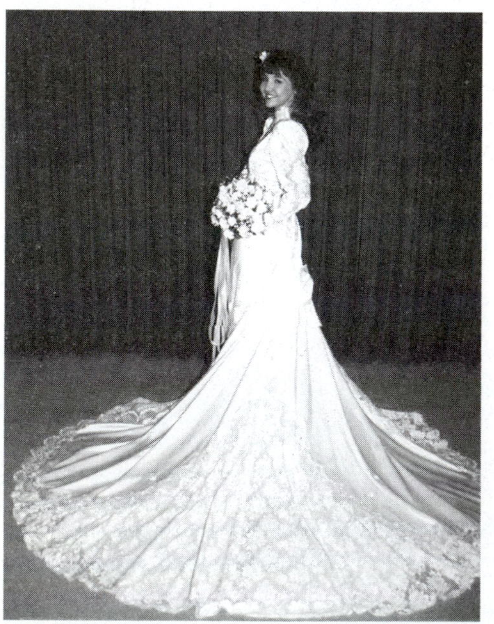

Descriptive research often is used to reveal the nature of shopping or other consumer behavior. Bride *magazine's descriptive research revealed that the average bride tries on 12 wedding gowns; one in five considers more than 21 dresses before choosing the right one; and 20 percent cry when they find it.*[3]

information to use in analyzing a situation, but uncovering conclusive evidence to determine a particular course of action is *not* the purpose of exploratory research. Usually, exploratory research is conducted with the expectation that *subsequent* research will be required to provide conclusive evidence. It is a serious mistake to rush into detailed surveys before less expensive and more readily available sources of information have been exhausted.

In an organization considering a program to help employees with child-care needs, for example, exploratory research with a small number of employees who have children might determine that many of them have spouses who also work and that these employees have positive reactions to the possibility of an on-site child-care program. In such a case exploratory research helps to crystallize a problem and identify information needs for future research.

Descriptive Research

descriptive research
Research designed to describe characteristics of a population or a phenomenon.

The major purpose of **descriptive research**, as the term implies, is to describe characteristics of a population or phenomenon. Descriptive research seeks to determine the answers to *who, what, when, where,* and *how* questions. Every month the Bureau of Labor Statistics (BLS) conducts descriptive research in the form of the *Current Population Survey.* Official statistics on unemployment and other characteristics of the labor force are derived from this survey.

Descriptive research often helps segment and target markets. For example, business researchers conducted descriptive surveys to identify the characteristics of consumers who purchase organic food products. Such consumers tend to live in larger cities, those with populations over 500,000. More than half live on the coasts, with the majority residing on the West Coast. The most frequent buyers of organic foods are affluent men and women ages 45–54 (36 percent) and 18–34 (35 percent).[4] Interestingly, consumers who buy organic foods are not very brand-oriented—81 percent of them cannot name a single organic brand.

Consider another example of descriptive research. A university career placement service may want to determine if its facilities and services are adequate. A descriptive study might be initiated to determine how many interviews each student wants to schedule, whether students are able to schedule appointments with certain desirable organizations, and if there are any problems with physical facilities. It should be clear that simply describing a situation may provide important information and that in many situations descriptive information is all that is needed to solve business problems—even though such research may not answer the *why* question.

Accuracy is of paramount importance in descriptive research. Although errors cannot be completely eliminated, good researchers strive for descriptive precision. Suppose the purpose of a study is to describe the market potential of portable digital music players for MP3 formats. If the study does not present a precise measurement of sales volume, it will mislead the managers who are making production scheduling, budgeting, and other decisions based on that study.

Unlike exploratory research, descriptive studies are based on some previous understanding of the nature of the research problem. For example, state societies of certified public accountants (CPAs) conduct annual practice management surveys that ask questions such as "Do you charge clients for travel time at regular rates?" "Do you have a program of continuing education on a regular basis for professional employees?" "Do you pay incentive bonuses to professional staff?" Although the researcher may have a general understanding

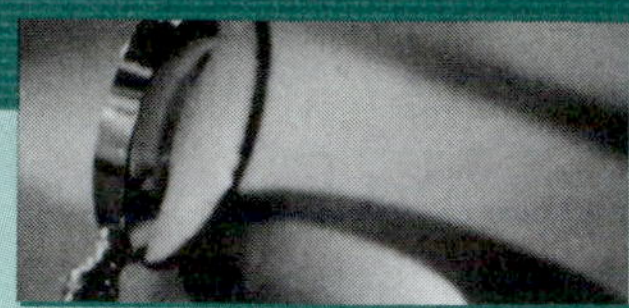

RESEARCH INSIGHT

POETRY AND RESEARCH: AN ODD COUPLE?

I keep six honest serving men,
(they taught me all I knew).
Their names are What, and Why, and When,
and How, and Where, and Who.

—Rudyard Kipling, *Just So Stories*

Kipling's words can be helpful to the business researcher. Those who ask the *what, why, when, how, where,* and *who* questions will be started on the right road to solving their business research problems.

of the business practices of CPAs, conclusive evidence in the form of answers to questions of fact must be collected. Frequently, descriptive research will attempt to determine the extent of differences in the needs, perceptions, attitudes, and characteristics of subgroups.

diagnostic analysis
Analysis used to clarify research findings, such as explanations respondents give for a behavior or attitude.

The purpose of many organizational behavior studies, for example, is to describe the reasons employees give for their explanations of the nature of things. In other words, a **diagnostic analysis** is performed when employees in the various subgroups are asked questions such as "Why do you feel that way?" Although the reasons employees feel a certain way are described, the findings of descriptive studies such as this, sometimes called *diagnostics,* do not provide evidence of a causal nature.

Causal Research

causal research
Research conducted to identify cause-and-effect relationships among variables when the research problem has already been narrowly defined.

The main goal of **causal research** is to identify cause-and-effect relationships among variables. (Exploratory and descriptive research normally precede cause-and-effect relationship studies.) In causal studies it is typical to have an expectation of the relationship to be explained, such as a prediction about the influence of price, packaging, advertising, and the like on sales. Thus, researchers must be knowledgeable about the research subject. Ideally, a manager would like to establish that one factor (say, a new package) is the means for producing another event (an increase in sales).

Causal research attempts to establish that when we do one thing, another thing will follow. The word *cause* is frequently used in everyday conversation, but from a scientific research perspective, a causal relationship is impossible to prove. Nevertheless, researchers seek certain types of evidence to help them understand and predict relationships.

A typical causal study has management change one variable (e.g., training) and then observe the effect on another variable (e.g., productivity). In this situation there is evidence for establishing causality because it appears that the cause precedes the effect. In other words, having an appropriate causal order of events, or temporal sequence, is one criterion that must be met to establish a causal relationship. If an organizational behavior theorist wishes to show that attitude change *causes* behavior change, one criterion that must be established is that attitude change *precedes* behavior change.

Further, there is some evidence of concomitant variation in that, in our example, increased training and increased productivity appear to be associated.

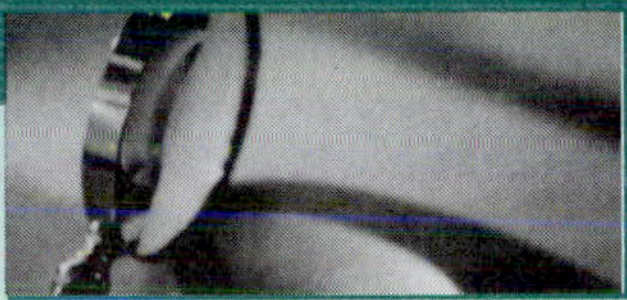

RESEARCH INSIGHT

LAY'S NEW GLOBAL PACKAGE DESIGN

PepsiCo Foods International, marketer of Lay's potato chips, the number one potato chip in the United States, unified its market-leading potato chip brands, such as Walkers Crisps in the United Kingdom, Papas Sabritas in Mexico, and Matutano chips in Spain, with the Lay's name and a new global package design highlighted by a bold red and yellow color scheme and centered on a new icon called the "Banner Sun."[5]

This global initiative followed the most comprehensive business research program in food products history. More than 100,000 consumers were interviewed in over 30 countries to describe, understand, and develop the worldwide potato chip market. From its global research program, PepsiCo learned that potato chips are "the cola of snacks." The descriptive research showed that in country after country, potato chips are consumers' favorite snack, ranked ahead of chocolate bars, ice cream and candy, and all other salty snacks. The company's new worldwide marketing approach enables Lay's to communicate and enhance the concept of potato chips as a timeless, simple pleasure to consumers around the world.

Concomitant variation is the occurrence of two phenomena or events that vary together. When the criterion of concomitant variation is not met—that is, when there is no association between variables—reason suggests that no causal relationship exists. If two events vary together, one *may* be the cause. However, concomitant variation by itself is not sufficient evidence for causality, because the two events may have a common cause—that is, both may be influenced by a third variable.

For instance, one morning at Atlantic City's beach a large number of ice cream cones are sold, and that afternoon there are a large number of drownings. Most of us would not conclude that eating ice cream cones causes drownings. More likely, the large number of people at the beach probably influenced both ice cream cone sales and drownings. It may be that the "effect" was produced in other ways. Just because there is concomitant variation and a proper time sequence between the occurrence of Event A and Event B, causation is not certain. There may be plausible alternative explanations for an observed relationship.[6] A plurality of causes is possible.

Consider a presidential candidate who reduces advertising expenditures near the end of the primary campaign and wins many more delegates in the remaining primaries. To infer causality—that reducing advertising increases the number of delegates—might be inappropriate, because the *presumed* cause of the increase may not be the real cause. It is likely that, near the end of a race, marginal candidates withdraw. Thus, the real cause may be unrelated to advertising.

In these examples, the third variable that is the source of the spurious association is a very salient factor readily identified as the more likely influence on change. However, within the complex environment in which managers operate, it is difficult to identify alternative or complex causal factors.

In summary, research with the purpose of inferring causality should do the following:

1. Establish the appropriate causal order or sequence of events

2. Measure the concomitant variation between the presumed cause and the presumed effect
3. Recognize the presence or absence of alternative plausible explanations or causal factors[7]

Even when these three criteria for causation are present, the researcher can never be certain that the causal explanation is adequate.

Most basic scientific studies in business (e.g., the development of organizational behavior theory) ultimately seek to identify cause-and-effect relationships. When one thinks of science, one often associates it with experiments. Thus, to predict a relationship between, say, price and perceived quality of a product, causal studies often create statistical experimental controls to establish "contrast groups." A number of business experiments are conducted by both theory developers and pragmatic business people. (More will be said about experiments and causal research in Chapter 12.)

INFLUENCE OF UNCERTAINTY OF TYPE OF RESEARCH

The uncertainty of the research problem is related to the type of research project. Exhibit 4.2 illustrates that exploratory research is conducted during the early stages of decision making when the decision situation is ambiguous and management is very uncertain about the nature of the problem. When management is aware of the problem but not completely knowledgeable about the situation, descriptive research is usually conducted. Causal studies can only be conducted when a problem is sharply defined.

Exhibit 4.2 RELATIONSHIP OF UNCERTAINTY TO TYPE OF BUSINESS RESEARCH

	Exploratory Research (Ambiguous Problem)	Descriptive Research (Aware of Partially Defined Problem)	Causal Research (Clearly Defined Problem)
Examples of Business Problems	"Absenteeism is increasing and we don't know why." "Would people be interested in our new product idea?" "What task conditions influence the leadership process in our organization?"	"What kind of people favor trade protectionism?" "Did last year's product recall have an impact on our company's stock price?" "Has the average merger rate for savings and loans increased in the past decade?"	"Which of two training programs is more effective?" "Can I predict the value of energy stocks if I know the current dividends and growth rates of dividends?" "Will buyers purchase more of our product in a new package?"

Note: The degree of uncertainty about the research problem determines the research methodology.

STAGES IN THE RESEARCH PROCESS

As previously noted, business research can take many forms, but systematic inquiry is a common thread. Systematic inquiry requires careful planning of an orderly investigation. Business research, like other forms of scientific inquiry, is a sequence of highly interrelated activities. The stages in the research process overlap continuously, and it is somewhat of an oversimplification to state that every research project has exactly the same ordered sequence of activities. Nevertheless, business research often follows a general pattern. The stages are (1) defining the problem, (2) planning a research design, (3) planning a sample, (4) collecting data, (5) analyzing the data, and (6) formulating the conclusions and preparing the report. These six stages are portrayed in Exhibit 4.3 as a cyclical, or circular-flow process, because conclusions from research studies usually generate new ideas and problems that need to be further investigated.

In practice, the stages overlap chronologically and are functionally interrelated. Sometimes the later stages are completed before the earlier ones. The terms *forward* and *backward linkage* reflect the interrelatedness of the various stages.[8] The term **forward linkage** implies that the earlier stages of research will influence the design of the later stages. Thus, the objectives of the research outlined in the problem definition will have an impact on the selection of the sample and the way in which the data will be collected. The decision concerning who will be sampled will affect the wording of questionnaire items. For example, if the research concentrates on respondents who have low educational levels, the wording of the questionnaire will be simpler than it would be if the respondents were college graduates. The notion of **backward linkage** implies that the later steps have an influence on the earlier stages in the research process. If it is known that the data will be analyzed by computer, then computer coding requirements are included in the questionnaire design.

forward linkage
A term implying that the early stages of the research process will influence the design of the later stages.

backward linkage
A term implying that the late stages of the research process will have an influence on the early stages.

EXHIBIT 4.3 PHASES OF THE RESEARCH PROCESS

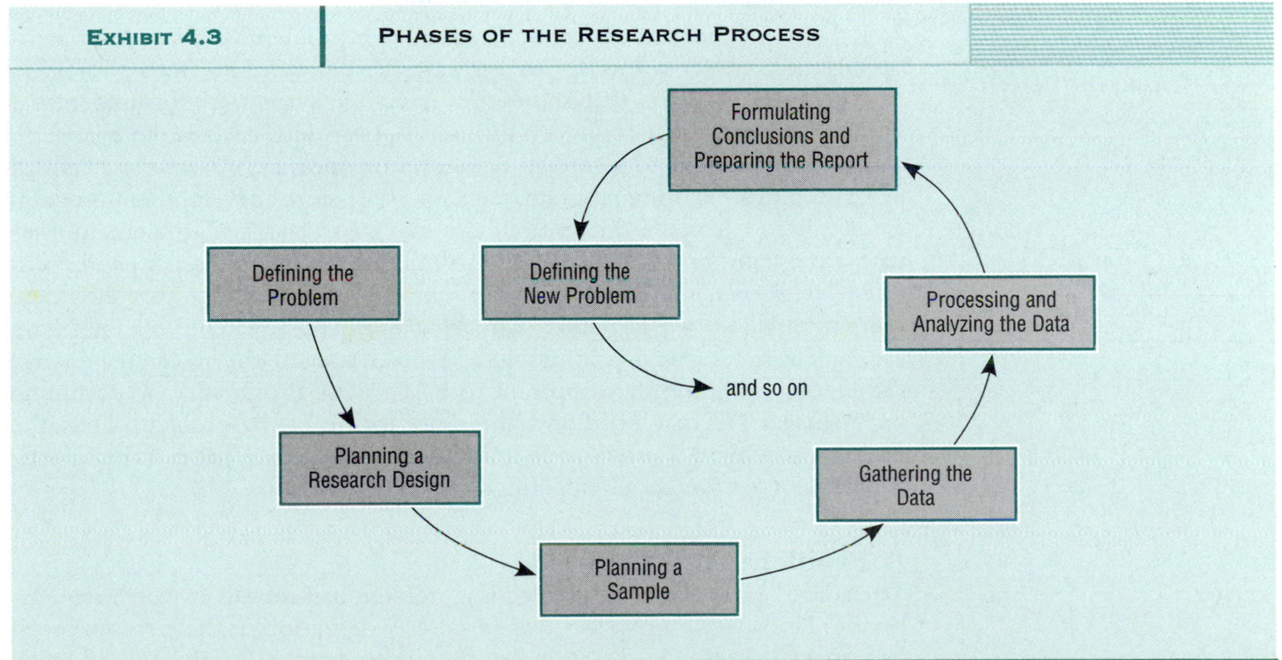

Perhaps the most important example of backward linkage is the knowledge that the executives who will read the research report need certain information. The professional researcher anticipates executives' needs for information in the planning process and considers these needs during the analysis and tabulation stages.

Decision Alternatives in the Research Process

A number of alternatives are available to the researcher during each of the six stages of the research process. The research process can be compared with a guide or a map.[9] On a map some paths are better charted than others. Some are difficult to travel, and some are more interesting and scenic than others. Rewarding experiences may be gained during the journey. It is important to remember there is no single right path or best path for all journeys. The road one takes depends on where one wants to go and the resources (money, time, labor, and so on) one has available for the trip. The map analogy is useful for the business researcher because at each stage of the research process there are several paths to follow. In some instances the quickest path will be the appropriate means of research because of pressing time constraints. In other circumstances, when money and human resources are plentiful, the path the research takes may be quite different. Exploration of the various paths of business research decisions is our primary purpose.

Each of the six stages in the research process is briefly described below. (Each stage is discussed in greater depth in later chapters.) Exhibit 4.4 shows the decisions that researchers must make in each stage of the research process. This discussion of the research process begins with problem discovery and definition, because most research projects, albeit at an earlier moment in time, are initiated because of some uncertainty about some aspect of the firm or its environment.

Discovering and Defining the Problem

In Exhibit 4.4 the research process begins with problem discovery, and identifying the problem is the first step toward its solution. The word *problem,* in general usage, suggests that something has gone wrong. Unfortunately, the word *problem* does not connote a business opportunity, such as the chance to expand operations into a foreign country, nor does it connote the need for evaluation of an existing program, such as a professional development program for employees. Actually, the research task may be to clarify a problem, to evaluate a program, or to define an opportunity, and we will discuss *problem discovery and definition* in this broader context. It should be noted that the initial stage is problem *discovery,* rather than *definition.* (The researcher may not have a clear-cut statement of the problem at the outset of the research process.) Often, only symptoms are apparent to begin with. Profits may be declining, but management may not know the exact nature of the problem. Thus, the problem statement is often made only in general terms. What is to be investigated is not yet specifically identified.

A Problem Well Defined

The adage "a problem well defined is a problem half solved" is worth remembering. This adage emphasizes that an orderly definition of the research problem gives a sense of direction to the investigation. Careful attention to

EXHIBIT 4.4 FLOWCHART OF THE RESEARCH PROCESS

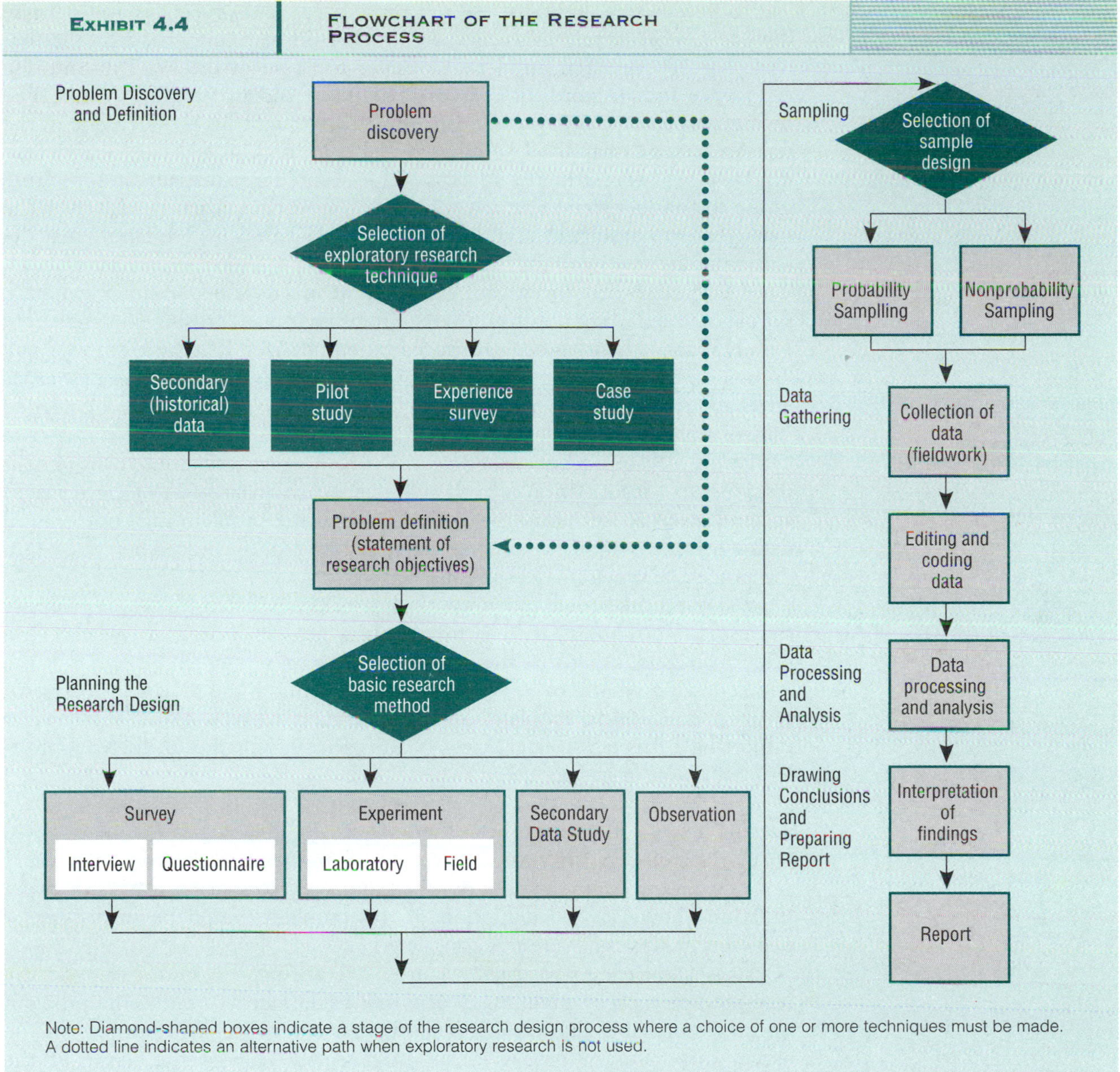

Note: Diamond-shaped boxes indicate a stage of the research design process where a choice of one or more techniques must be made. A dotted line indicates an alternative path when exploratory research is not used.

problem definition
The indication of a specific business decision area that will be clarified by answering some research questions.

problem definition allows a researcher to set the proper research objectives. If the purpose of the research is clear, the chances of collecting the necessary and relevant information—and not collecting surplus information—will be much greater.

It was Albert Einstein who noted that "the formulation of a problem is often more essential than its solution."[10] This is good advice for managers. Too often managers concentrate on finding the right answer rather than asking the right question. Many do not realize that defining a problem may be more difficult than solving it. In business research, if the data are collected before the nature of the business problem is carefully thought out, the data probably will not help solve the problem.

To be efficient, business research must have clear objectives and definite designs. Unfortunately, in many cases little or no planning goes into the formulation of a research problem. Consider the case of the Ha-Pah-Shu-Tse (a Pawnee Indian word for red corn) brand of Indian fried bread mix. The owner of the company, Mr. Ha-Pah-Shu-Tse, thought his product, one of the few American Indian food products available in the United States, wasn't selling because it wasn't highly advertised. He wanted a management consulting group to conduct some research concerning advertising themes. However, the management consultants pointed out to the Ha-Pah-Shu-Tse family that the brand (family) name on the bread mix might be a foremost source of concern. They suggested that investigating the brand image and consumer behavior should be the starting point, rather than focusing on advertising copy research. Family management agreed. (It should be emphasized that we are now using "problem" to refer to the managerial problem, which may be a lack of knowledge about consumers or advertising effectiveness and the lack of needed information.)

Frequently business researchers will not be involved until management discovers that information is needed about a particular aspect of the decision at hand. Even at this point the exact nature of the problem may not be well defined. Once a problem area has been discovered, the researcher can begin the process of precisely defining it.

Although the problem definition stage of the research process is probably the most important stage, it is frequently a neglected area of research. Too often managers forget that the best place to begin a research project is at the end. Knowing what is to be accomplished determines the research process. An error or omission in problem definition is likely to be a costly mistake that cannot be corrected in later stages of the process. (Chapter 6 discusses problem definition in greater detail.)

Exploratory Research

Many research projects with clearly defined problems, such as an annual survey of industry compensation, do not require exploratory research. In many situations, however, the definition of the problem would be inadequate if exploratory research were not conducted.

Exploratory research is usually conducted during the initial stage of the research process. The preliminary activities undertaken to refine the problem into a researchable one need not be formal or precise. The purpose of the exploratory research process is to progressively narrow the scope of the research topic and to transform discovered problems into defined ones, incorporating specific research objectives. By analyzing any existing studies on the subject, by talking with knowledgeable individuals, and by informally investigating the situation, the researchers can progressively sharpen the concepts. After such exploration the researchers should know exactly what data to collect during the formal project and how the project will be conducted. Exhibit 4.4 indicates that managers and researchers must decide whether to use one or more exploratory research techniques. As Exhibit 4.4 indicates, this stage of research is optional.

There are four basic categories of techniques for obtaining insights and gaining a clearer idea of a problem: secondary data analysis, pilot studies, case studies, and experience surveys. These are discussed in detail in Chapter 7. The next two sections briefly discuss secondary data analysis and a very popular type of pilot study, the focus group interview.

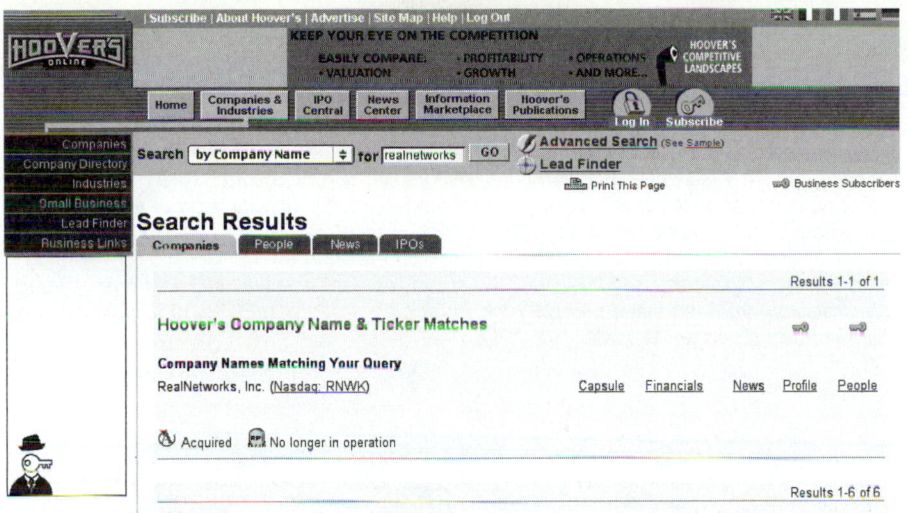

Business researchers find Hoover's Online to be an excellent secondary data source for financial information. Information about IPOs and Securities and Exchange Commission (SEC) data about thousands of companies allow researchers to make comparisons between companies over time and across industries.

secondary data
Data that have been previously collected for some project other than the one at hand.

primary data
Data gathered and assembled specifically for the research project at hand.

Secondary Data **Secondary data,** or historical data, are data previously collected and assembled for some project other than the one at hand. **Primary data** are data gathered and assembled specifically for the project at hand. Secondary data can often be found inside the company, in the library, and on the Internet, or they can be purchased from firms that specialize in providing information, such as economic forecasts, that is useful to organizations. The researcher who assembles data from the *Census of Population* or the *Survey of Current Business* is using secondary sources.

A review of the literature—a survey of published articles and books discussing theories and past empirical studies about a topic—is almost universal in academic research projects. It is also common in many applied research studies. Students who have written term papers should be familiar with the process of checking card catalogs, indexes to published literature, and other library resources to establish a bibliography of past research. Suppose, for example, a bank is interested in determining the best site for additional ATM machines. A logical first step would be to investigate the factors that bankers in other parts of the country consider important. By reading articles in banking journals, the bank management might quickly discover that the best locations are inside supermarkets located in residential areas where people are young, highly educated, and earning higher-than-average incomes. These data might lead the bank to investigate census information to determine where in the city such people live. Reviewing and building on the work already compiled by others are economical starting points for most research.

Secondary data can almost always be gathered faster and more inexpensively than primary data. However, secondary data may be outdated or may not exactly meet the needs of the researcher because they were collected for another purpose. Nevertheless, secondary sources often prove to be of great value in exploratory research. Investigating such sources has saved many a researcher from "reinventing the wheel" in primary data collection.

pilot study
Any small-scale exploratory research technique that uses sampling but does not apply rigorous standards.

Pilot Studies **Pilot studies** collect data from the ultimate subjects of the research project to serve as a guide for the larger study.[12] When the term *pilot study* is used in the context of exploratory research, it refers to a study whose

Jelly Belly brand sells 50 varieties of jelly beans. The company uses applied business research to increase the number of flavors it offers every year. Some of the flavors under development have been suggested by visitors to Jelly Belly's Web site. In return for filling out an interactive questionnaire, visitors get samples sent to them. One question asks for customers' input on new flavors. Jelly Belly gets a great response to this, and marketers take all the suggestions seriously. Researchers categorize them by similar flavors. Some of the ideas are put back on the Web so that people can vote for their favorites. The company has received some really off-the-wall suggestions. Among the strangest are flavors such as Dill Pickle, Tacos, Persimmon Pudding, Blackened Plantain, and Cream of Wheat.[11]

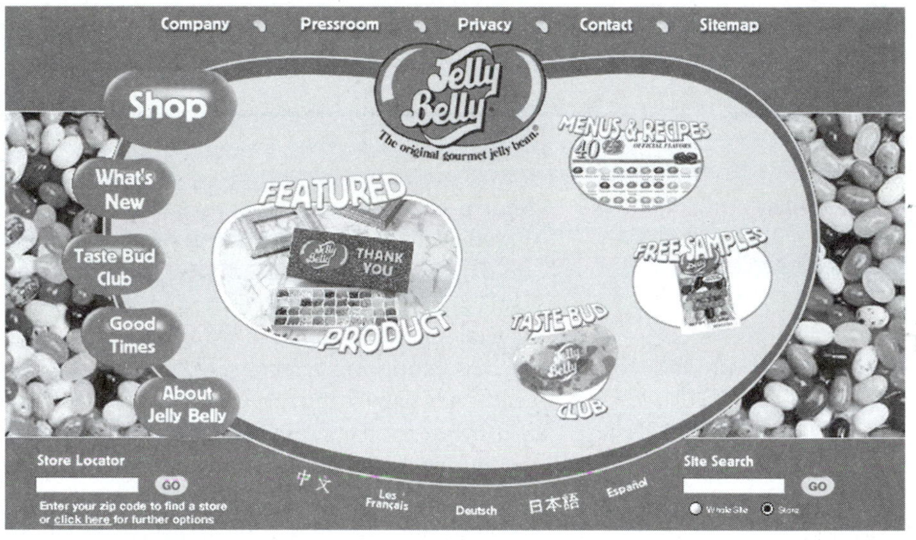

data collection methods are informal and whose findings may lack precision because rigorous standards are relaxed. For instance, a downtown association concerned with revitalization of the city's central business district (CBD) conducted a very flexible survey with questions that were open-ended. The interviewers were given considerable latitude to identify the opinions of local executives (the ultimate subjects) about future requirements in the downtown area. The results of this survey were used to suggest possible topics for formal investigation.

The *focus group interview* is a more elaborate exploratory pilot study. Increasingly popular in recent years, the focus group gathers six to ten people for a group dynamics session. This loosely structured discussion assumes that individuals are more willing to share their ideas when they are able to hear the ideas of others. Qualitative information obtained in these studies serves as a basis for subsequent quantitative study.

For example, the Philadelphia Museum used focus groups to investigate how well its exhibits and shows catered to the public. A local resident who had never visited the museum mentioned that he was not aware of any important artwork there. Another participant in the same focus group voiced the opinion that the museum would be filled with "pictures I would not understand. . . . I've seen art where it looked like kids splashed paint." These findings (confirmed by other research) influenced the museum to reinstate an image of van Gogh's *Sunflowers* on the cover of its brochures.[13]

Four basic types of exploratory research have been identified, but there is no standard design for such research. Since the purposes of exploratory research are to gain insights and to discover new ideas, researchers may use considerable creativity and flexibility. It is common to collect data using several exploratory techniques. Exhausting these sources is generally worth the effort because the expense is relatively low. Further, insights into how and how not to conduct research may be gained from activities during the problem definition stage. If the conclusions made during this stage suggest business opportunities, the researcher is in a position to begin planning a formal, quantitative research project.

Statement of Research Objectives

After identifying and clarifying the problem, with or without exploratory research, researchers should make a formal statement of the problem and the research objectives. A decision must initially be made as to precisely what should be researched, so as to delineate the type of information that should be collected and provide a framework for the scope of the study, or the **research project.**

research project
A specific research investigation; a study that completes or is planned to follow the stages in the research process.

The answers to questions such as "To what extent did the new compensation program achieve its objectives?" are typical research objectives. In this sense the statement of the problem is a research question.

The best expression of a research objective is a well-formed, testable research hypothesis; a *hypothesis* is a statement that can be refuted or supported by empirical data. For example, an exploratory study might lead to the hypothesis that male-dominated unions discriminate against women who want to enter the trades. In basic research, theory is the guide that helps generate hypotheses. Once the hypothesis has been developed, researchers are ready to select a research design.

Planning the Research Design

After the researcher has formulated the research problem, the research design must be developed. A **research design** is a master plan specifying the methods and procedures for collecting and analyzing the needed information. It is a framework or blueprint that plans the action for the research project. The objectives of the study determined during the early stages of the research are included in the design to ensure that the information collected is appropriate for solving the problem. The research investigator must also specify the sources of information, the research method or technique (survey or experiment, for example), the sampling methodology, and the schedule and cost of the research.

research design
A master plan specifying the methods and procedures for collecting and analyzing the needed information.

Selecting the Appropriate Research Design

Again, the researcher must make a decision. Exhibit 4.4 indicates there are four basic research methods for descriptive and causal research: surveys, experiments, secondary data studies, and observation. The objectives of the research methods, the available data sources, the urgency of the decision, and the cost of obtaining the data will determine which method is chosen. The managerial aspects of selecting the research method will be considered later.

You cannot put the same shoe on every foot.

PUBILIUS SYRUS (c. 42 BC)

The Partnership for a Drug Free America is a nonprofit organization that conducts applied business research. Its research indicated that the Partnership should target younger children. As a result, it created a public service announcement called "Big Ol' Bug" to appeal to children ages 6 to 8. The rock music lyrics include the line "I'd rather be a big ol' bug than ever try a stupid drug." The research also led to another public service announcement called "Brain Damaged" to appeal to preteens. Talking in the first person, a funny, likeable brain explains that drugs make a brain slow, confused, and barely able to think.

Surveys The most common method of generating primary data is through surveys. Most people have seen the results of political surveys by Gallup or HarrisInteractive, and some have been respondents (members of a sample that supply answers) to business research questionnaires. A *survey* is a research technique in which information is gathered from a sample of people using a questionnaire. The task of writing a list of questions and designing the exact format of the printed or written questionnaire is an essential aspect of the development of a survey research design.

Research investigators may choose to contact respondents in person, by telephone, by mail, or on the Internet. An advertiser who spends over $2,000,000 for 30 seconds of commercial time during the Super Bowl may telephone people to quickly gather information concerning their response to the advertising. Your congressional representative may mail you a questionnaire to learn how he or she should vote on issues. A mail survey is an inexpensive method of data collection for a member of Congress or any person. A forklift truck manufacturer trying to determine why sales in the wholesale grocery industry are low might choose an Internet questionnaire because the appropriate executives are hard to reach by telephone. In contrast, a computer manufacturer wishing to conduct an organizational survey of employees might need a versatile survey method whereby an interviewer can ask a variety of personal questions in a flexible format. Although personal interviews are expensive, they are valuable because investigators can utilize visual aids and supplement the interview with observations. Each of these survey methods has advantages and disadvantages. The researcher's task is to choose the most appropriate one for collecting the information needed.

Experiments Business experiments hold the greatest potential for establishing cause-and-effect relationships. The use of experimentation allows investigation of changes in one variable, such as productivity, while manipulating one or two other variables, perhaps social rewards or monetary rewards, under controlled conditions. Ideally, experimental control provides a basis for isolating causal factors, because outside (or exogenous) influences do not come into play.

Research Insight

Business Research Solves a Problem

Febreze Fabric Refresher, which can be used on clothing or upholstery, uses a proprietary cleaning formula that penetrates fabrics to eliminate odors, not just cover them up with perfumes.[14] Procter & Gamble began test market experiments for Febreze Fabric Refresher in May 1996 in Phoenix, Boise, and Salt Lake City.

The initial strategy was to position Febreze as a niche product for smokers to use on dry-clean-only clothes. A television commercial showed a woman seated in the smoking section of a restaurant who is frustrated because her blazer smells like cigarette smoke, even though it has just come back from the dry cleaner. The friend she is talking to explains how Febreze neutralizes cigarette odors to bring fabric back to fresh. The research showed that after 6 months this advertising was not broadly relevant or emotional and the focus on cigarette smoke did nothing for the brand.

The researchers focused efforts on what went wrong. The company's researchers began to realize that because they were dealing with a totally new product category, the advertising found it difficult to articulate consumers' need for the innovation. Consumers did not grasp that they had a problem and could not clarify how the product could be improved because they didn't know of any alternative. Consumer studies sometimes took the product team in the wrong direction. Consumers insisted they did not want a product with perfume, but market tests in retail stores showed that the more perfume that was added, the more Febreze sold.

The product was repositioned after research indicated that those who bought Febreze were using it on upholstery and carpeting in addition to clothing. A second ad aimed at pet owners showed a dog sitting on a couch to illustrate how animals can leave odors on upholstery. A woman says that "in a perfect world, my dog Sophie wouldn't get on the furniture—but she does and it smells. I want to get rid of the odor, not Sophie." Consumers found this advertising insensitive and insulting, because it strongly suggested that "your dog smells." Although the ad communicated that Febreze also worked on clothes, it did not do a good job communicating the product's varied uses.

Subsequent survey research indicated the need for consumer education and revealed more about consumers' personal feelings about odors. Researchers learned that odors are an extremely delicate and emotional issue. The company concluded that they had to be careful to communicate with people in a positive manner. This meant putting out a message that said "we can make your clothes smell more pleasant" rather than "you stink," or "this is what your dog is preventing you from doing" instead of "your dog smells."

The finding about the value of consumer education led to an increased use of demonstrations in stores and at community events that included a teaching element explaining how the smell trapped in the fibers was cleaned away. The advertising message was reframed to reduce the negativity. The final test market version showed a mom with five kids. When her firefighter son gets home, "thinking the smoke alarm is going to go off," she sprays Febreze on the couch where he's tossed his fire jacket. Another scene shows her daughter playing in a marching band, and the mom is thinking "it's hot out there and they sweat." The mom solves the problem by spraying Febreze on the band uniform. The message is communicated by illustrating the problems of one family and a mom who understands that Febreze cleans life's smells out of fabrics.

The test market experiments and consumer research lasted 2 years. The marketing effort revamped package size, strength formulations for clothes and household fabrics, and retail prices. The long and expensive process to develop "new product category" innovation paid off: Febreze, with $250 million in retail sales the following year, was an unqualified success. Business research played a major role in its success.

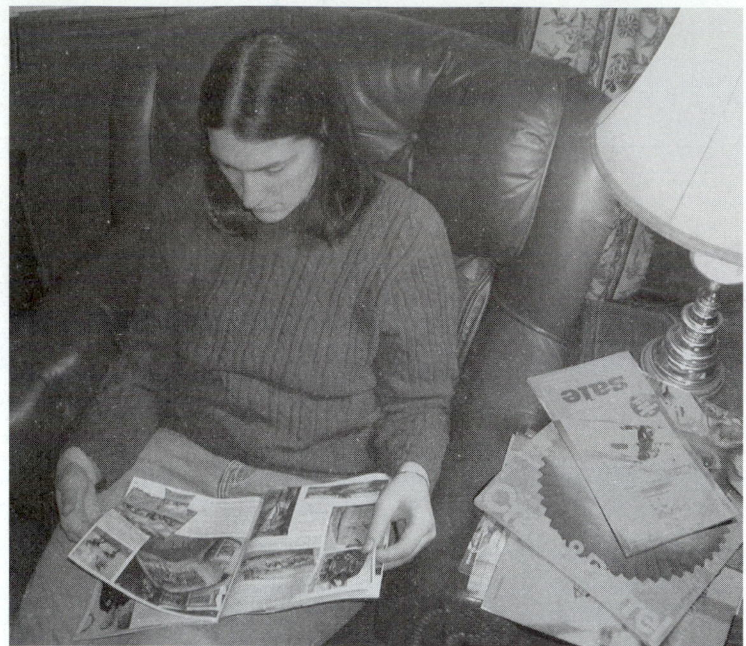

Direct marketers often conduct experiments to determine how to increase response to pamphlets, catalogs, or special offerings. Experiments have shown that the wording of headline copy and prices can greatly influence the success of direct marketing.

Test marketing is a frequent form of business experimentation. The example of Chelsea, Anheuser-Busch's "not-so-soft soft drink," illustrates the usefulness of experiments. Anheuser-Busch first introduced Chelsea as a socially acceptable alternative to beer for adults who didn't want to get intoxicated. Because of the natural flavorings used, Chelsea contained a slight amount of alcohol (less than 0.5 percent)—well within the FDA guidelines for classification as a soft drink. During an experiment to test market the "not-so-soft soft drink" and the "not-so-sweet" concept, a Virginia nurses' association and some religious groups strongly criticized the company and the new product. These critics suggested that Anheuser-Busch had introduced a product that might encourage children to become beer drinkers. They contended that Chelsea was packaged like beer and looked, foamed, and poured like beer. The criticism led the brewery to suspend production, advertising, and promotion of the drink. It later reintroduced the product as a soft drink, with only "a trace of alcohol" and with not-so-sweet and stylish attributes, as a "natural alternative" to other soft drinks. This experiment pointed out to Anheuser-Busch that an extraneous variable—alcohol level—caused an inadvertent miscommunication: Consumers confused the original Chelsea with beer.

An experiment controls conditions so that one or more variables can be manipulated in order to test a hypothesis. In the Chelsea situation there was a trial of a proposed course of action and observation of the effect on sales. This case illustrates that extraneous variables are difficult to control and can influence results. It also portrays a field experiment that led to a deliberate modification of marketing strategy.

Other experiments—laboratory experiments—are deliberate modifications of an environment created for the research itself. Laboratory experiments are often used in basic research to test theories. Consider a laboratory experiment designed as a test of equity theory. Student subjects, hired and paid to code research questionnaires, were separated into two groups. One group was led to believe that it was less qualified than the other workers because it lacked previous experience in coding questionnaires. The group was also told that even though it was less qualified, its pay would be the same as the pay for experienced workers. Thus, the students believed themselves to be overpaid. The other group did not receive any messages about the others' experience and thus was led to believe that the pay was equitable. Both groups coded the questionnaires for 2 hours. The "equitably" paid group was less productive than the group that believed it was overpaid.[15]

Secondary Data Studies Like exploratory research, descriptive and causal studies use previously collected data. (Although the terms *secondary data* and *historical data* are interchangeable, we will use *secondary data*.) An example of a secondary data study is the development of a mathematical model to predict sales on the basis of past sales or on the basis of a correlation with related variables. Manufacturers of digital cameras may find that sales to households are highly correlated with discretionary personal income. To predict future market potential, data concerning projections of disposable personal income may be acquired from the government or from a university. This information can be mathematically manipulated to forecast sales. Formal secondary data studies have benefits and limitations similar to those of exploratory studies that use secondary data. The analysis of secondary data studies, however, generally requires greater quantitative sophistication than does exploratory research.

Observation Techniques In many situations the objective of a research project is merely to record what can be observed—for example, the number of automobiles that pass the proposed site for a gas station. This can be mechanically recorded or observed by any person. The amount of time it takes an employee to perform a task may be observed in a time-and-motion study. Research personnel, known as "mystery shoppers," may act as customers to observe the actions of sales personnel or may do comparison shopping to learn the prices charged at competing outlets.

The main advantage of the observation technique is that it records behavior without relying on reports from respondents. Observational data are often collected unobtrusively and passively without a respondent's direct participation. For instance, the A. C. Nielsen Company's "people meter" is a machine attached to television sets to record the programs being watched by various members of the household. This eliminates the possible bias due to respondents' stating that they watched the president's State of the Union address rather than the situation comedy that was on another channel.

Observation is more complex than mere "nose counting," and the task is more difficult to administer than the inexperienced researcher would imagine. Several things of interest simply cannot be observed. Attitudes, opinions, motivations, and other intangible states of mind cannot be recorded by using the observation method.

Evaluating Research Designs

Researchers argue that there is no one best research design for all situations. There are no hard-and-fast rules for good business research. This does not mean that the researcher, when faced with a problem, is also faced with chaos and confusion. It means that the researcher has many alternative methods for solving the problem. An eminent behavioral researcher has stated this concept quite eloquently:

> There is never a single, standard, correct method of carrying out a piece of research. Do not wait to start your research until you find out the proper approach, because there are many ways to tackle a problem—some good, some bad, but probably several good ways. There is no single perfect design. A research method for a given problem is not like the solution to a problem in algebra. It is more like a recipe for beef Stroganoff; there is no one best recipe.[16]

Knowing how to select the most appropriate research design develops with experience. Inexperienced researchers often jump to the conclusion that the survey method is the best design, because they are most familiar with this method. When Chicago's Museum of Science and Industry wanted to determine the relative popularity of its exhibits, it could have conducted a survey. Instead, a creative researcher, familiar with other research designs, suggested a far less expensive alternative—an unobtrusive observation technique. The researcher suggested that the museum merely keep track of how often the floor tiles in front of the various exhibits had to be replaced—which would indicate where the heaviest traffic occurred. When this was done, it was found that the chick-hatching exhibit was most popular.[17] This method provided the same results as a survey, but at a much lower cost.

Once an appropriate design has been determined, the researcher moves on to the next stage—planning the sample to be used.

Sampling

Although the sampling plan is outlined in the research design, the actual sampling is a separate stage of the research process. However, for convenience, the sample planning and sample generation processes are treated together in this section.

If you take your first bite of a steak and conclude it needs salt, you have just conducted a sample. Sampling involves any procedure that uses a small number of items or a portion of a population to make a conclusion regarding the whole population. In other words, a sample is a subset from a larger population. If certain statistical procedures are followed, it is unnecessary to select every item in a population because the results of a good sample should have the same characteristics as the population as a whole. Of course, when errors are made, samples do not give reliable estimates of the population. A famous example of error due to sample selection is the 1936 *Literary Digest* fiasco. The magazine conducted a survey and predicted that Republican Alf Landon would win over Democrat Franklin D. Roosevelt by a landslide in that year's presidential election. This prediction was wrong—and the error was due to sample selection. The postmortems showed that *Literary Digest* had sampled readers of its magazine and telephone subscribers. In 1936 these people were not a representative cross section of voters, because in those days people who could afford magazine subscriptions and phone service were generally well-to-do—and a disproportionate number of them were Republicans.

This famous example teaches that the first sampling question that must be asked is "Who is to be sampled?" Answering this primary question requires the identification of a target population. Defining the population and determining the sampling units may not be obvious. For example, for answers to image questions, a savings and loan company may survey people who already have accounts. The selected sampling units will not represent potential customers

Surveys should be representative. In 1936, telephone subscribers and subscribers to Literary Digest *were disproportionately Republicans who did not support Roosevelt.*

who do not have accounts with the savings and loan. Specifying the target population is a crucial aspect of the sampling plan.

The next sampling issue concerns sample size. How big should the sample be? Although management may wish to examine every potential buyer of a product, every employee, or every stock traded on an exchange, it is unnecessary (as well as unrealistic) to do so. Typically, large samples are more precise than small samples, but if proper probability sampling is implemented, a small proportion of the total population will give a reliable measure of the whole. (A later discussion will explain how large a sample must be to be truly representative of a universe or population.)

The final sampling decision requires the researcher to choose how the sampling units are to be selected. Students who have taken their first statistics course generally are familiar with simple random sampling, whereby every unit in the population has an equal and known chance of being selected. However, this is only one type of sampling. For example, a cluster sampling procedure may be selected because it may reduce costs and make the data-gathering procedures more efficient. If members of the population are found in close geographic clusters, a sampling procedure that selects area clusters rather than individual units in the population will reduce costs. In other words, rather than selecting 1,000 individuals throughout the United States, it may be more economical to select 25 counties and then sample within those counties. This substantially reduces travel, hiring, and training costs. In determining the appropriate sample plan, the researcher will have to select the most appropriate sampling procedure to meet established study objectives.

There are two basic sampling techniques: probability sampling and nonprobability sampling. A *probability sample* is defined as a sample in which every member of the population has a known, nonzero probability of selection. If sample units are selected on the basis of personal judgment (e.g., a test plant is selected because it appears to be typical), the sample method is a *nonprobability sample.* In actuality, the sampling decision is not a simple choice between two methods. Simple random samples, stratified samples, quota samples, cluster samples, and judgmental samples are some of the many types of samples that may be drawn. (Chapter 16 gives full discussion of these techniques.)

Collecting Data

Once the research design (including the sampling plan) has been formalized, the process of gathering information from respondents may begin. Obviously, because there are many research techniques, there are many methods of data collection. When the survey method is utilized, some form of direct participation by the respondent is necessary during the process. The respondent may participate by filling out a questionnaire or by interacting with an interviewer. If an unobtrusive method of data collection is utilized, the subjects do not actively participate. For instance, a simple count of motorists driving past a proposed franchising location is one kind of data collection. However the data are collected, it is important to minimize errors in the data collection process. For example, it is important that the data collection be consistent in all geographic areas. If an interviewer phrases questions incorrectly or records a respondent's statements inaccurately (not verbatim), this will cause major data collection errors.

Often there are two phases to the process of collecting data: pretesting and the main study. A *pretesting phase,* using a small subsample, may determine whether the data collection plan for the main study is an appropriate procedure. Thus, a small-scale pretest study provides an advance opportunity for the investigator to check the data collection form to minimize errors due to improper design, such as poorly worded or organized questions. There is also the chance to discover confusing interviewing instructions, learn if the questionnaire is too long or too short, and uncover other such field errors. Tabulation of data from the pretests provides the researcher with a format for the knowledge that may be gained from the actual study. If the tabulation of the data and statistical tests do not answer the researcher's questions, the investigator may need to redesign the study.

Processing and Analyzing Data

Editing and Coding

Once the fieldwork has been completed, the data must be converted into a format that will answer the decision maker's questions. Data processing generally begins with the editing and coding of the data. Editing involves checking the data collection forms for omissions, legibility, and consistency in classification. The editing process corrects problems such as interviewer errors (e.g., an answer recorded on the wrong portion of a questionnaire) before the data are transferred to a computer or readied for tabulation.

Before data can be tabulated, meaningful categories and character symbols must be established for groups of responses. The rules for interpreting, categorizing, and recording the data are called *codes.*[18] This coding process facilitates computer or hand tabulation. Of course, if computer analysis is to be utilized, the data are entered into the computer and verified. Computer-assisted (online) interviewing is an example of the impact of technological change on the research process. Telephone interviewers are seated at computer terminals, where survey questions are printed out on the screen. The interviewer asks the questions and then types in the respondents' answers. Thus, answers are collected and processed into the computer at the same time, eliminating intermediate steps where errors could creep in.

Analysis

Analysis is the application of reasoning to understand and interpret the data that have been collected. In simple descriptive research, analysis may involve determining consistent patterns and summarizing the appropriate details revealed in the investigation. The appropriate analytical technique for data analysis will be determined by management's information requirements, the characteristics of the research design, and the nature of the data collected. Statistical analysis may range from portraying a simple frequency distribution to very complex multivariate analysis, such as multiple regression. Later chapters will discuss three general categories of statistical analysis: univariate analysis, bivariate analysis, and multivariate analysis.

Drawing Conclusions and Preparing a Report

As mentioned earlier, most business research is applied research. Hence, the purpose of the research is to make a business decision. An important but often overlooked aspect of the researcher's job is to look at the analysis of the collected information and ask "What does this mean to management?" The final stage in the research process is to interpret the information and draw conclusions relevant to managerial decisions. Making recommendations is often a part of this process.

The research report should communicate the research findings effectively. All too often the report is a complicated statement of the study's technical aspects and sophisticated research methods. Often, management is not interested in detailed reporting of the research design and statistical findings but wants only a summary of the findings. It cannot be overemphasized that if the findings remain unread on the manager's desk, the research study is useless. Research is only as good as the applications made of it. Business researchers must communicate their findings to a managerial audience. The manager's information needs should determine how much detail is provided in the written report. The written report serves another purpose: It is a historical document, a record that may be referred to later if the research is to be repeated or if further research is to be based on what has come before.

Now that we have outlined the research process, note that the order of topics in this book follows the flowchart of the research process presented in Exhibit 4.4. You should keep this flowchart in mind as you read future chapters.

RESEARCH PROJECT VERSUS RESEARCH PROGRAM

Discussion of the business research process began with the assumption that the research investigator wished to gather information to achieve a specific objective. We have emphasized the researcher's need to select specific techniques for solving one-dimensional problems, such as identifying the characteristics of productive employees, selecting the best packaging design, or forecasting bond values.

However, if you think about a firm's strategic activity in a given period of time, perhaps a year, you'll realize that business research is not a one-shot approach. Research is a continuous process. A company may conduct an exploratory research study and then conduct a survey. It is very likely that a specific research project will be conducted for each aspect of a program. If a new product is being developed, the different types of research might include market potential studies, to identify the size and characteristics of the market; product usage testing, which records consumers' reactions to using prototype products; and brand-name and packaging research, to determine the product's symbolic connotations. Ultimately, the new product may go into a test market.

research program
Planning activity that identifies an ongoing series of research projects designed to supply an organization's continuing information needs.

Because research is a continuous process, management should view research at a strategic planning level. A **research program** refers to a firm's overall strategy for utilizing business research. This program is a planning activity that places each research project into the company's strategic plan.

SUMMARY

Decision making is the process of resolving a problem or choosing from alternative opportunities. Decision makers must recognize the nature of the problem/opportunity, identify how much information is available, and recognize what information is needed. Every business decision can be classified on a continuum ranging from complete certainty to absolute ambiguity.

There are three major types of business research projects. Which one is to be used is decided by the clarity with which the research problem is defined. Exploratory research is chosen when management knows only the general problem. It is not conducted to provide conclusive evidence but to clarify problems. Descriptive research is conducted when there is some understanding of the nature of the problem; such research is used to provide a more specific description of the problem. Causal research identifies cause-and-effect relationships when the research problem has been narrowly defined.

The research process proceeds in a series of six interrelated phases. The first is problem definition, which may include exploratory research. Once the problem is defined, the researcher selects a research design, including an appropriate method. The major designs are surveys, experiments, secondary data studies, and observation. Creative selection of the research design can minimize the cost of obtaining reliable results. After the design has been selected, a sampling plan is chosen, using a probability sample, a nonprobability sample, or a combination of the two.

The design is put into action in the data collection phase. This phase may involve a small pretest before the main study is undertaken. In the analysis stage the data are edited and coded, then processed, usually by computer. The results are interpreted in light of the decisions that management must make. Finally, the analysis is presented to decision makers in a written or oral report. This last step is crucial, because an excellent project will not lead to proper action if the results are poorly communicated.

Quite often research projects are conducted as parts of an overall research program. Such programs can involve successive projects that incorporate earlier findings into later research designs.

A major problem facing students of business research is that it is difficult to consider each stage in the research process separately. However, without concentrated emphasis on each stage of the total process, it is difficult to understand the individual stages. Thus, learning business research is like walking a tightrope between too broad an outlook and too narrow a focus.

Key Terms

exploratory research
descriptive research
diagnostic analysis
causal research
forward linkage
backward linkage
problem definition
secondary data
primary data
pilot study
research project
research design
research program

Questions for Review and Critical Thinking

1. For each situation, decide whether the research should be exploratory, descriptive, or causal:
   (a) Establishing the functional relationship between advertising and sales
   (b) Investigating reactions to the idea of a new method of defense budgeting
   (c) Identifying target-market demographics for a shopping center
   (d) Estimating prices for IBM stock 2 years in the future
   (e) Learning how many organizations are actively involved in just-in-time production
   (f) Learning the extent of job satisfaction in a company
2. Describe a research situation that allows the inference of causality.
3. A researcher is interested in knowing the answer to a *why* question, but does not know what sort of answer will be satisfying. Is this exploratory, descriptive, or causal research? Explain.
4. Do the stages in the research process follow the scientific method?
5. Why is the problem definition stage probably the most important stage in the research process?
6. The U.S. Department of the Treasury is considering technological research into creation of a plasticlike substance on which currency notes can be printed. Being printed on this substance would increase the circulation life of low-value currency notes and enhance their utility in vending equipment. What type of research should be conducted?
7. What research design seems appropriate for each of the following studies?
   (a) The manufacturer and marketer of flight simulators and other pilot-training equipment wish to forecast sales volume for the next 5 years.
   (b) A local chapter of the American Lung Association wishes to identify the demographic characteristics of individuals who donate more than $500 per year.
   (c) A manager notices the number of grievances is increasing and wishes to investigate this trend.
   (d) A financial analyst wishes to investigate whether load or no-load mutual funds have higher yields.
   (e) A corporation wishes to evaluate the quality of its college-graduate recruitment program.
   (f) An academic researcher wishes to investigate if the United States is losing its competitive edge in world trade.
   (g) A food company researcher is interested in knowing what types of food are carried in brown-bag lunches to learn if the company can capitalize on this phenomenon.
8. Why is a knowledge of forward and backward linkages in the research process important?
9. Give an example of a program research project in your field of interest.
10. In your field of interest, which research design (surveys, observation, experiments, or secondary data studies) is the most popular?

Exploring the Internet

1. Use a Web browser to go to the Gallup Organization's home page at http://www.gallup.com. The Gallup home page changes regularly. However, it should provide an opportunity to read the results of a political poll. After reading the results of one of Gallup's polls, click on How Polls Are Conducted. List the various stages of the research process and how they were followed in Gallup's project.
2. Use a Web browser to access Lycos (http://www.lycos.com). What keyword topics can be investigated? How might the information you find help you design a research project?

Case Suggestions

Case 3: Tulsa's Central Business District (A)
Video Case 6: Fisher-Price Rescue Heroes
Video Case 12: Burke, Inc.
Video Case 13: Walker Information Group

CHAPTER

5

ETHICAL ISSUES IN BUSINESS RESEARCH

Executives of a firm interested in acquiring information concerning union members' attitudes toward management put a hidden microphone (attached to a tape recorder) in the employees' coffee room so that the union members' conversations might be observed unobtrusively. Is there a moral question involved here?

An accounting researcher who has sampled 100 organizations in a survey on CPA firms' accounting practices believes that a particular CPA firm in the sample is inefficiently managed. He discards its questionnaires, eliminating the firm from the analysis. Is this proper?

A number of West Coast residents believe that national television news networks making early projections about presidential races before local polls close has an impact on voting behavior, especially turnout. Is early projection of election returns an ethical practice?

The personnel manager of a large bank tries to persuade a researcher to undertake a project with "political purposes." Is this in the organization's best interest?

Each of these situations illustrates an ethical issue in business research. Just as there are ethical aspects to all human interaction, there are some ethical questions about business research. This book considers various ethical and moral issues concerning fair business dealings, proper research techniques, and appropriate utilization of research results in other chapters. This chapter addresses the growing concern in recent years about the ethical implications of business research. ■

What you will learn in this chapter

- To explain why ethical questions are philosophical questions.
- To define *societal norms.*
- To describe the three parties involved in most research situations and discuss how the interaction among these parties may identify a series of ethical questions.
- To discuss the rights and obligations of the respondent.
- To discuss the rights and obligations of the researcher.
- To discuss the rights and obligations of the client/sponsor.
- To discuss selected issues such as deception, privacy, and advocacy research from the perspective of each of the three parties.
- To discuss the role of codes of ethics.

ETHICAL QUESTIONS ARE PHILOSOPHICAL QUESTIONS

societal norms
Codes of behavior adopted by a group, suggesting what a member of the group ought to do under given circumstances.

Ethical questions are philosophical questions. There is no general agreement among philosophers about the answers to such questions. However, the rights and obligations of individuals are generally dictated by the norms of society. **Societal norms** are codes of behavior adopted by a group; they suggest what a member of a group ought to do under given circumstances.[1] This chapter reflects the author's perceptions of the norms of our society (and undoubtedly his own values to some extent).[2]

GENERAL RIGHTS AND OBLIGATIONS OF CONCERNED PARTIES

In most research situations, three parties are involved: the *researcher,* the *sponsoring client (user),* and the *respondent (subject).* The interaction of each of these parties with one or both of the other two identifies a series of ethical questions. Consciously or unconsciously, each party expects certain rights and feels certain obligations toward the other parties. Exhibit 5.1 diagrams this relationship. Within any society there is a set of normatively prescribed expectations of behavior (including rights and obligations) associated with a social role, such as researcher, and another, reciprocal role, such as respondent. Certain ethical behaviors may be expected only in certain specific situations, while other expectations may be more generalized. If there are conflicting perspectives about behavioral expectations, ethical problems may arise. For instance, several ethical issues concern the researcher's expected rights versus those of the respondent/subject. A number of questions arise because researchers believe they have the right to seek information, but subjects believe they have a certain right to privacy. A respondent who says "I don't care to answer your question about my income" believes that he or she has the right to refuse to participate. Yet some researchers will persist in trying to get that information. In general, a fieldworker is not expected to overstep the boundary society places on individuals' privacy.

EXHIBIT 5.1 INTERACTION OF RIGHTS AND OBLIGATIONS OF PARTIES IN RESEARCH

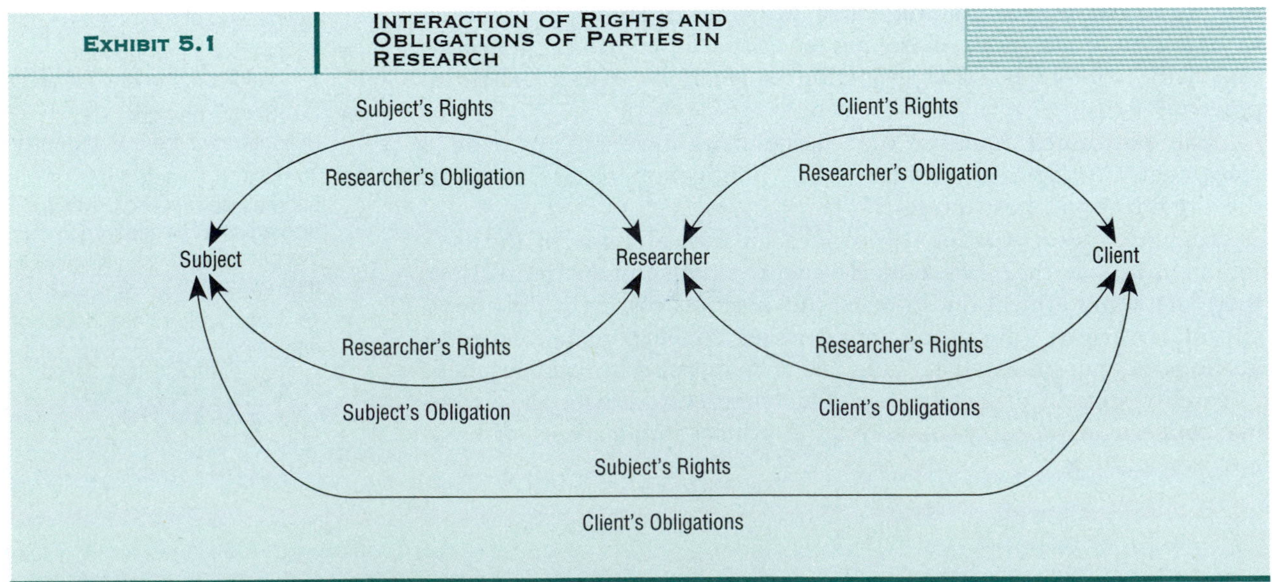

For each of the subject's rights there is a corresponding obligation on the part of the researcher. For example, the individual's right to privacy dictates that the researcher has an obligation to protect the anonymity of the respondent. When a respondent discloses information about personal matters, it is assumed that such information will be guarded from all people other than the researcher.

Rights and Obligations of the Respondent

informed consent
The expressed or implied acknowledgment waiving an individual's right to privacy when he or she agrees to participate in a research study.

The ethical issues vary somewhat, depending on whether the participant has given willing and informed consent. The notion of **informed consent** means that an individual understands the reason for the research and waives his or her right to privacy when he or she agrees to participate in the research study. (The rights of a participant in an unobtrusive observation study differ from a survey respondent's rights because he or she has not willingly consented to be a subject of the research.) In return for being truthful, the survey respondent has the right to expect confidentiality and anonymity. (*Privacy* refers to the issue of whether a respondent chooses to answer a researcher's questions; a person may choose to protect her privacy by not answering. *Confidentiality* refers to the obligation on the part of the researcher not to reveal the identity of an individual research subject. A person who waives her right to privacy by agreeing to answer a researcher's questions nonetheless has a right to expect that her answers and her identity will remain confidential.) Privacy and confidentiality are profound ethical issues in business research.

The Obligation to Be Truthful

When a subject willingly consents to participate, it is generally expected that he or she will provide truthful answers. Honest cooperation is the main obligation of the respondent or subject.

Privacy

Americans relish their privacy. A major polling organization indicated that almost 80 percent of Americans believe that collecting and giving out personal information without their knowledge is a serious violation of their privacy.[3] Hence, the right to privacy is an important question in business research. This issue involves the subject's freedom to choose whether to comply with an investigator's request.[4] Traditionally, researchers have assumed that individuals make an informed choice. However, critics have argued that the old, the poor, the poorly educated, and other underprivileged individuals may not be aware of their right to choose. Further, they have argued that an interviewer may begin with some vague explanation of a survey's purpose, initially ask questions that are relatively innocuous, and then move to questions of a highly personal nature. It has been suggested that subjects be informed of their right to be left alone or to break off the interview at any given time. Researchers should not follow the tendency to "hold on" to busy respondents. However, this view is definitely not universally accepted in the research community.[5]

Another aspect of the privacy issue is illustrated by the question "Is the telephone call that interrupts someone's favorite television program an invasion of privacy?" The answer to this issue—and to most privacy questions—lies in the dilemma of determining where the rights of the individual end and the needs of society for better scientific information on citizen preference take over.[6] Generally, certain standards of common courtesy have been set by interviewing firms—for example, not to interview late in the evening and at

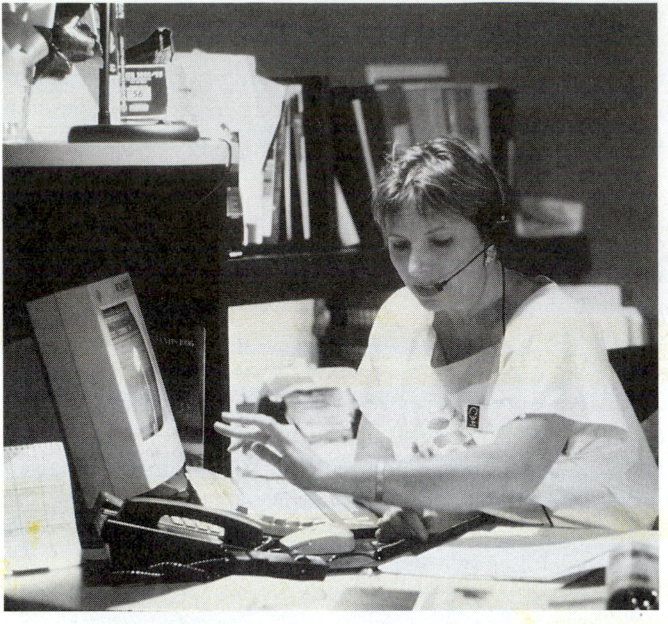

New technologies are making it easier to compile computerized databases that combine survey results with personal records. There is growing public concern about privacy issues as better technology makes it easier for business researchers to link survey respondents' answers to Social Security, tax, and other government records.

other inconvenient times. However, there are several critics who may never be appeased. The computerized interview ("junk phone call") has stimulated increased debate over this aspect of the privacy issue. As a practical matter, respondents may feel more relaxed about privacy issues if they know who is conducting a survey. Thus, it is generally recommended that field interviewers indicate that they are legitimate researchers by passing out business cards, wearing name tags, or in other ways identifying the name of their company.

In an observation study, the major ethical issues concern whether the observed behavior is public or private. Generally it is believed that unobtrusive observation of public behavior in such places as stores, airports, and museums is not a serious invasion of privacy. However, recording private behavior with hidden cameras and the like does represent a violation of this right. For example, in a survey of research directors and executives, the practice of observing women through a one-way mirror as they tried on bras was disapproved of by approximately 80 percent of the executives.[7]

Deception

In a number of situations the researcher creates a false impression by disguising the purpose of the research. The researcher, at least at the outset of the research, is not open and honest. Bluntly stated, to avoid possible biased reactions, the subject is lied to. Deception or concealment may be used if a researcher would otherwise be unable to observe or straightforwardly ask about the phenomena of interest and still hold all other factors constant. Generally, researchers who use deception argue that it is justified under two conditions: (1) No physical danger or psychological harm will be caused by the deception, and (2) the researcher takes personal responsibility for informing the respondent of the concealment or deception after the research project ends.

The issue of deception is interrelated with the subject's right to be informed and with the means-to-an-end philosophical issue. The major question is, Does a small deception substantially increase the value of the research?

Suppose a survey research project must contact busy executives. Pretending to be calling long distance might improve the response rate—but is this a justifiable means to this end?

A distinction has been made between deception and discreet silence. The ethical question concerning the manifest content of a questionnaire versus the true purpose of the research has been cleverly stated as follows:

> Must we really explain, when we ask the respondent to agree or disagree with the statement, "prison is too good for sex criminals; they should be publicly whipped or worse," it is really the authoritarianism of his personality we are investigating, and not the public opinion on crime and punishment?[8]

The Right to Be Informed

It has been argued that subjects have a right to be informed of all aspects of the research, including information about its purpose and sponsorship. The argument for the researcher's obligation to protect this right is based on the academic tradition of informing and enlightening the public.

A pragmatic argument for providing respondents with information about the nature of the study concerns the long-run ability of researchers to gain cooperation from respondents. If the public understands why survey or experimental information has been collected and that the researchers may be trusted with private information, it may be easier in the long run to conduct research. Several research suppliers have suggested that public relations work is needed to sell the public on the benefits of the research industry.

Rights and Obligations of the Researcher

General business ethics should be a standard for business research firms and business research departments. Our concern is not with issues such as bribery or the welfare and safety of one's employees but with ethical issues that are specifically germane to business research practices.

code of ethics
A statement of principles and operating procedures for ethical practice.

More has been written about the ethics of researchers than about those of the other two parties because this group's purpose is clearly identifiable. Exhibit 5.1 illustrated that researchers have obligations to both subjects and clients as well as corresponding rights. A number of professional associations have developed standards and operating procedures for ethical practice by researchers. Exhibit 5.2 is the **code of ethics** for the American Association for Public Opinion Research. This code touches on several major issues that will be further explored in this book. Students contemplating entering business research should check for codes of ethics set out by professional associations.

The Purpose of Research Is Research

It is considered unacceptable to misrepresent a sales tactic as business research. The Federal Trade Commission has indicated that it is illegal to use any plan, scheme, or ruse that misrepresents the true status of the person making the call as a door-opener to gain admission to a prospect's home, office, or other establishment.[9] This sales ploy is considered to be unethical as well as illegal. No research firm should engage in any practice other than scientific investigation.

Objectivity

Ensuring accuracy via objectivity and scientific investigation is stressed throughout this book. Researchers should maintain high standards to ensure

EXHIBIT 5.2 | **CODE OF PROFESSIONAL ETHICS AND PRACTICES: AMERICAN ASSOCIATION FOR PUBLIC OPINION RESEARCH**

We, the members of the American Association for Public Opinion Research, subscribe to the principles expressed in the following Code. Our goals are to support sound and ethical practice in the conduct of public opinion research and in the use of such research for policy and decision making in the public and private sectors, as well as to improve public understanding of opinion research methods and the proper use of opinion research results.

We pledge ourselves to maintain high standards of scientific competence and integrity in conducting, analyzing, and reporting our work and in our relations with survey respondents, with our clients, with those who eventually use the research for decision-making purposes, and with the general public. We further pledge ourselves to reject all tasks or assignments that would require activities inconsistent with the principles of this code.

The Code

I. *Principles of Professional Practice in the Conduct of Our Work*
   A. We shall exercise due care in developing research designs and survey instruments, and in collecting, processing, and analyzing data, taking all reasonable steps to assure the reliability and validity of results.
      1. We shall recommend and employ only those tools and methods of analysis which, in our professional judgment, are well suited to the research problem at hand.
      2. We shall not select research tools and methods of analysis because of their capacity to yield misleading conclusions.
      3. We shall not knowingly make interpretations of research results, nor shall we tacitly permit interpretations that are inconsistent with the data available.
      4. We shall not knowingly imply that interpretations should be accorded greater confidence than the data actually warrant.
   B. We shall describe our methods and findings accurately and in appropriate detail in all research reports, adhering to the standards for minimal disclosure specified in Section III, below.
   C. If any of our work becomes the subject of a formal investigation of an alleged violation of this Code, undertaken with the approval of the AAPOR Executive Council, we shall provide additional information on the survey in such detail that a fellow survey practitioner would be able to conduct a professional evaluation of the survey.

II. *Principles of Professional Responsibility in Our Dealings with People*
   A. *The Public:*
      1. If we become aware of the appearance in public of serious distortions of our research, we shall publicly disclose what is required to correct these distortions, including, as appropriate, a statement to the public media, legislative body, regulatory agency, or other appropriate group, in or before which the distorted findings were presented.
   B. *Clients or Sponsors:*
      1. When undertaking work for a private client, we shall hold confidential all proprietary information obtained about the client and about the conduct and findings of the research undertaken for the client, except when the dissemination of the information is expressly authorized by the client, or when disclosure becomes necessary under terms of Section I-C or II-A of this Code.
      2. We shall be mindful of the limitations of our techniques and capabilities and shall accept only those research assignments which we can reasonably expect to accomplish within these limitations.
   C. *The Profession:*
      1. We recognize our responsibility to contribute to the science of public opinion research and to disseminate as freely as possible the ideas and findings which emerge from our research.
      2. We shall not cite our membership in the Association as evidence of professional competence, since the Association does not so certify any persons or organizations.
   D. *The Respondent:*
      1. We shall strive to avoid the use of practices or methods that may harm, humiliate, or seriously mislead survey respondents.

EXHIBIT 5.2 | **CODE OF PROFESSIONAL ETHICS AND PRACTICES *(CONTINUED)***

2. Unless the respondent waives confidentiality for specified uses, we shall hold as privileged and confidential all information that might identify a respondent with his or her responses. We shall also not disclose or use the names of respondents for nonresearch purposes unless the respondents grant us permission to do so.

III. Standards for Minimal Disclosure

Good professional practice imposes the obligation upon all public opinion researchers to include, in any report of research results, or to make available when that report is released, certain essential information about how the research was conducted. At a minimum, the following items should be disclosed:

1. Who sponsored the survey, and who conducted it.
2. The exact wording of questions asked, including the text of any preceding instruction or explanation to the interviewer or respondent that might reasonably be expected to affect the response.
3. A definition of the population under study, and a description of the sampling frame used to identify this population.
4. A description of the sample selection procedure, giving a clear indication of the method by which the respondents were selected by the researcher, or whether the respondents were entirely self-selected.
5. Size of sample and, if applicable, completion rates and information on eligibility criteria and screening procedures.
6. A discussion of the precision of the findings, including, if appropriate, estimates of sampling error, and a description of any weighting or estimating procedures used.
7. Which results are based on parts of the sample, rather than on the total sample.
8. Method, location, and dates of data collection.

that the data they collect are accurate. Further, they must not intentionally try to prove a particular point for political purposes.

Misrepresentation of Research

Research companies (and clients) should not misrepresent the statistical accuracy of their data, nor should they overstate the significance of the results by altering the findings. Basically, it is assumed that the researcher has the obligation to both the client and the subjects to analyze the data honestly and to report correctly the actual data collection methods. For example, the failure to report a variation from the technically correct probability sampling procedure is ethically questionable. Similarly, any major error that has occurred during the course of the study should not be kept secret from management or the client sponsor. Hiding errors or allowing variations from the proper procedures tends to distort or shade the results. A more blatant breach of the researcher's responsibilities would be the outright distortion of data.

Protecting the Right to Confidentiality of Both Subjects and Clients

A number of clients might be very desirous of a list of favorable organizational prospects generated from a research survey. It is the researcher's responsibility to ensure that the privacy and anonymity of the respondents are preserved. If the respondent's name and address are known, this information should not be forwarded to the sponsoring organization under any circumstances.

Information that a research supplier obtains about a client's general business affairs should not be disseminated to other clients or third parties. The clients (users of business research) have a number of rights and obligations. Their primary right is to expect objective and accurate data from the research supplier. They should also expect that their instructions relating to confidentiality have been carried out.

Dissemination of Faulty Conclusions

Another ethical issue concerns the dissemination of faulty conclusions. After conducting a research project, the researcher or decision maker may disseminate conclusions from the research that are inconsistent with or not warranted by the data. Most research professionals consider this to be improper.

> **TO THE POINT**
>
> *He uses statistics as a drunken man uses a lampost—for support rather than illumination.*
>
> ANDREW LANG

A dramatic example of violation of this principle is an advertisement for cigarettes that cited a study of smokers. The advertisement compared two brands and stated that "of those expressing a preference, over 65 percent preferred" the advertised brand to a competitive brand. The misleading portion of this reported result was that most of the respondents did *not* express a preference; they indicated that both brands tasted about the same. Thus, only a very small percentage of those studied actually revealed a preference, and the results were somewhat misleading. Such shading of the results falls short of the obligation to report accurate findings.

Competing Research Proposals

Consider a client who has solicited several bids for a business research project. The research supplier that wins the bid is asked by the client to appropriate ideas from the proposal of a competing research supplier and include them in the research study to be done for the client. This is generally regarded as unethical.[10]

Rights and Obligations of the Sponsoring Client (User)

Ethics between Buyer and Seller

The general business ethics expected to exist between a purchasing agent and a sales representative should apply in the business research situation. For example, if the purchasing agent has already decided to purchase a product (or research proposal) from a friend, it is generally considered unethical for him to solicit competitive bids that have no chance of being accepted just to fulfill a corporate purchasing policy stating that a bid must be put out to three competitors.

An Open Relationship with Research Suppliers

The sponsoring client has the obligation to encourage the research supplier to seek out the truth objectively. To encourage this objectivity, a full and open statement of the problem, explication of time and money constraints, and any

DILBERT Reprinted by permission of United Features Syndicate, Inc.

Business researchers have certain obligations. The purpose of research should be research.

Research Insight

HERTZ WAS NOT AMUSED

A few years ago, a magazine called *Corporate Travel* published the results of a consumer survey of the travel industry.[11] In the category of rental cars, the magazine declared Avis the winner of what was to be its first annual Alfred Award, named for Alfred Kahn, former chairman of the Civil Aviation Board. Avis, not surprisingly, quickly launched an advertising campaign touting its standing in the poll.

Joseph Russo, vice president for government and public affairs at Avis's archrival, Hertz, was not amused. He called the magazine's editor and asked if he could see a press release and any other material that might explain the survey's results and methodology. "We've won virtually every other poll that's ever been done," said Russo. (Indeed, surveys like these are popularity contests that tend to favor bigger competitors over smaller ones, and they are almost impossible to duplicate or verify.) "So we wanted to see if we were missing the boat."

But Russo said he could not get much information about the survey. "I said, How many people voted in this, was it bigger than a bread basket?"

It turned out that the survey responses had disappeared under mysterious circumstances. The magazine's marketing manager, who had overseen the poll, had left the magazine. "A search of their files has also failed to turn up any statistical tabulation or record of the responses for any category," wrote the president of *Corporate Travel's* parent to Hertz. Meanwhile, said Russo, "We had corporate accounts saying, I see you guys came in after Avis."

Eventually Hertz filed suit against the publisher of the magazine and Avis, charging false advertising. "We said if we allow this to go on, anyone will be able to do anything on the basis of a survey," Russo said. The parties settled, with Avis agreeing to stop calling itself the car rental company of choice among business travelers.

other insights that may help the supplier anticipate costs and problems should be provided.[12] In other words, the research sponsor should encourage efforts to reduce bias and to listen to the voice of the public.

An Open Relationship with Interested Parties

Conclusions should be based on the data. A user of research should not knowingly disseminate conclusions from a given research project or service that are inconsistent with the data or are not warranted by them.[13] Violation of this principle is perhaps the greatest transgression that a client can commit. Justifying a self-serving, political position that is not supported by the data poses serious ethical questions. Indicating that data show something so that a sale can be made is also ethically questionable.

Privacy

The privacy rights of subjects create a privacy obligation on the part of the client. Suppose a database marketing company is offering a mailing list compiled by screening millions of households to obtain brand usage information. The information would be extremely valuable to your firm, but you suspect those individuals who filled out the information forms were misled into thinking they were participating in a survey. Would it be ethical to purchase

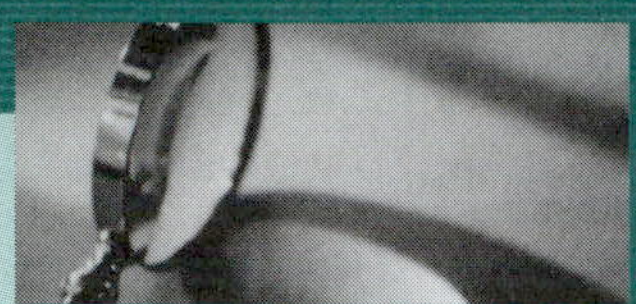

RESEARCH INSIGHT

PUSH POLLING

The question, in the midst of a telephone poll, was as shocking as it was designed to be: Would you still favor Rudy Silbaugh, a Republican candidate for the Wisconsin state assembly, if you knew he voted to give guns back to juveniles who had used them in crimes?[14]

Mr. Silbaugh and other Wisconsin Republicans filed a lawsuit because of that damaging assertion, which the Republican Party said was made recently by a telemarketing firm calling on behalf of Democratic candidates. But they recognized the campaign tactic, having used it themselves.

It's known as "push polling," and it has increasingly become implemented at the last minute of political campaigns when the airwaves have grown saturated with political messages.

For years, campaign pollsters have conducted surveys of a few hundred voters to test the potency of negative information for later use in broad attacks, such as television advertising. What's different about push polling, though not easy to trace, is the use of phone calls as the means of disseminating attacks to thousands of voters at a time. But unlike the case with TV ads or direct-mail brochures, federal law doesn't require congressional campaigns to identify who's paying for the calls.

"If people want to lie, cheat, and steal, they should be held accountable," said Rep. Tom Petri, Republican of Wisconsin, who complains that during an election campaign, anonymous callers told constituents that he was a tool of Japanese auto dealers and responsible for the savings and loan mess.

In Colorado, the campaign of Democratic governor Roy Romer, who was reelected, complained to the state attorney general that opponent Bruce Benson's campaign used push polling in violation of a Colorado statute forbidding anonymous campaigning.

The advocacy in question, according to a script obtained by the governor's aides, asked voters if they'd be more or less likely to support Mr. Romer if they knew that "there have been nearly 1,300 murders in Colorado since Romer was first elected and not one murderer has been put to death." Follow-up questions informed voters that the state parole board "has granted early release to an average of four convicted felons per day every day since Romer took office," that Mr. Romer spent "one out of every four days outside of Colorado" during his four-year term, and that he "is being sued for mismanaging the state's foster-care system."

The attorney general declined to prosecute, but Romer campaign manager Alan Salazar complained that the lack of accountability of push polling, as well as the enhanced credibility of an attack delivered personally to voters, makes the practice worrisome.

the mailing list? If respondents have been deceived about the purpose of a survey and their names subsequently are sold as part of a user mailing list, this practice is certainly unethical. The client as well as the research supplier has the obligation to maintain respondents' privacy.

Consider another example. Sales managers know that a survey of their business-to-business customers' buying intentions includes a means to attach a customer name to each questionnaire. This confidential information could be of benefit to a sales representative calling on a specific customer. A client wishing to be ethical must resist the temptation to identify those accounts (i.e., those respondents) who are the hottest prospects.

Privacy on the Internet

Privacy on the Internet is a controversial issue. A number of groups question whether Web site questionnaires, registration forms, and other means of collecting personal information are legitimate. Many managers argue that their organizations don't need to know who the user is because the individual's name is not important for their purposes. However, they do want to know certain information (such as demographic characteristics or product usage) associated with an anonymous profile. For instance, a Web advertiser could reach a targeted audience without having access to identifying information. Of course, unethical companies may violate the anonymity guideline.

America Online's privacy policy states that AOL will not read customers' e-mail, collect any information about Web site visits, or give key data to other organizations without authorization. AOL will seek parents' written approval to get data from children at sites targeting kids.[15] Research shows that people are more willing to disclose sensitive information if they know a Web site's privacy policy.[16]

For this reason, many high-traffic Web sites such as Yahoo and Lycos have privacy statements that visitors can easily access. Organizations such as the

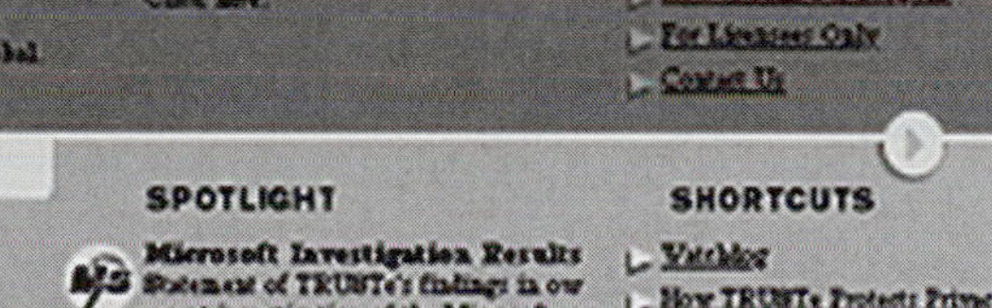

TRUSTe (http://www.Truste.org) is a third-party organization that evaluates Web sites' privacy policies, certifies Web sites, and issues a Seal of Trust to organizations that meet its privacy standards.[17] TRUSTe classifies sites into three categories: "no exchange," sites where no personal user data are collected; "1to1 exchange," sites that collect user data for their own purposes but do not share them with third parties; and "3rd party exchange," sites that share the information with others. "1to1 exchange" sites are permitted to share user data—such as credit card numbers, names, and addresses—with business partners in order to complete transactions as long as the business partners agree not to collect the user data themselves.[18]

Electronic Frontier Foundation and the Online Privacy Alliance are involved in developing privacy guidelines.

Commitment to Research

Some potential clients have been known to request research proposals from a research supplier when there is a low probability that the research will be conducted. A research consultant's opinion may be solicited even though management is not really planning research and funds have not been allocated for the project. For example, obtaining an outsider's opinion of a company problem via a research proposal provides an inexpensive consultation. If the information supports a given manager's position in an ongoing debate within the company, it could be used politically rather than as a basis for research. Because the research supplier must spend considerable effort planning a custom-designed study, most research practitioners believe that the client has the obligation to be serious about considering a project before soliciting proposals.

Pseudo-Pilot Studies

As noted, it is important for clients to be open about the business problem to be investigated. However, there is a special case of this problem that should be explained. Sometimes a client will suggest that a more comprehensive study is in the planning stages and that the proposal the research supplier is bidding on is a pilot study. The client might say something like "I don't want to promise anything, but you should know that this is the first in a very ambitious series of studies we are planning to undertake, and if you sharpen your pencil in estimating cost . . . ."[19] The research consultant is told that if his or her company does a good job during the pilot study stages, there will be an additional major contract down the line. Too often these pilot studies are "come-ons"—the comprehensive study never materializes, and the consultant must absorb a loss.

Advocacy Research

advocacy research
Research undertaken to support a specific claim in a legal action.

Advocacy research—research undertaken to support a specific claim in a legal action—puts a client in a unique situation. Advocacy research, such as a survey conducted to show that a brand name is not a generic name, differs from research that is intended for internal use only.[20] The traditional factors, such as

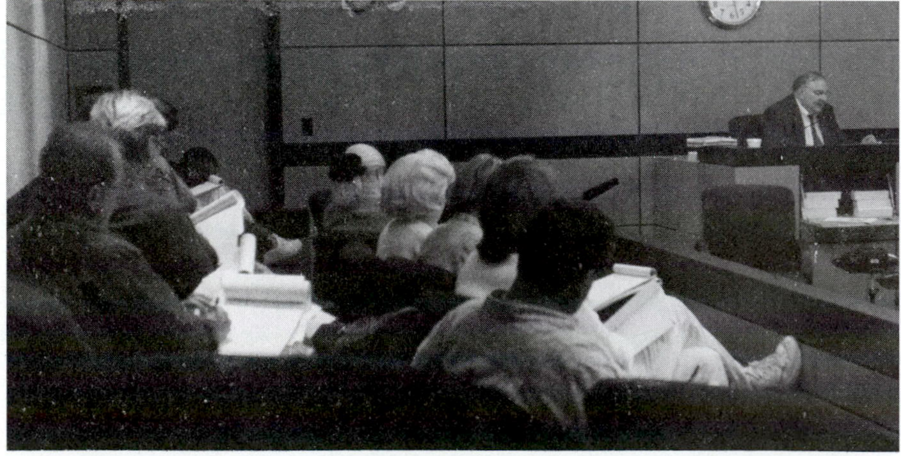

Many lawyers hire jury consultants who use business research methods to help determine what type of person would make a favorable juror. Lawyers also conduct advocacy research to provide evidence from survey findings that support their viewpoints.

sample size, people to be interviewed, and questions to be asked, are weighed against cost when making an internal decision. A court's opinion of the value of advocacy research may be based exclusively on sampling design and validity of the questions asked. Thus, the slightest variation from technically correct sampling procedures may be magnified by an attorney until a standard business research project no longer appears adequate in the judge's eye.

The ethics of advocacy research present a number of serious questions. Consider the following quote:

> Almost never do you see a researcher who appears as an independent witness, quite unbiased. You almost always see a witness appearing either for the FTC or for the industry. You can almost predict what is going to be concluded by the witness for the FTC. And you can almost predict what will be concluded by the witness for industry. That says that research in this setting is not after full truth and it is not dispassionate in nature. And for those of us who consider ourselves to be researchers, that is a serious quandary.[21]

Researchers doing advocacy research do not necessarily bias results intentionally. However, attorneys in an advocacy research trial rarely submit research evidence that does not support the client's position.

The question of advocacy research is one of objectivity: Can the researcher search out the truth when the sponsoring client wishes to support its position at a trial? The ethical question stems from a conflict between legal ethics and research ethics, and perhaps only the individual researcher can resolve this question.

A FINAL NOTE ON ETHICS

There is no question that there are unethical researchers in the world and that shady dealings do occur. But business researchers are no different from other business people—or from people in general, for that matter. One may occasionally run across the case of a researcher who produces a report on fabricated findings, just as there are occasional cases of interviewers who cheat by filling out the questionnaires themselves. (In pre-Castro Cuba there was at least one firm that, for a fee, would provide a handsomely engraved certificate attesting that the Court of Public Opinion held the client or the client's products in whatever kind of high esteem might be desired—with no extra charge for percentages.)[22] Under some circumstances even good researchers take shortcuts, some of which may be ethically questionable. However, like most business people, researchers are generally ethical. Of course, the answer to the question "What is ethical?" is not easy—only one's conscience operates to inhibit any questionable practice.[23]

SUMMARY

There is no general agreement about the answers to ethical questions that surround business research. However, societal norms suggest codes of conduct that are appropriate in given circumstances. There are three concerned parties in business research situations: the researcher, the sponsoring client (user), and the respondent (subject). Each party has certain rights and obligations. The respondent's rights include the right to privacy and the right to be informed about all aspects of the research; his or her main obligation is to give honest answers to research questions. The researcher is expected to adhere to the purpose of the research; maintain objectivity; avoid misrepresenting research findings; protect subjects' and clients' right to confidentiality; and avoid shading research conclusions. The client is obligated to observe general business ethics when dealing with research suppliers; avoid misusing the research findings to support its aims; respect research respondents' privacy; and be open about its intentions to conduct research and about the business problem to be investigated. A serious challenge to objectivity occurs when advocacy research—research conducted to support a specific legal claim—is undertaken.

Key Terms

societal norms
informed consent
code of ethics
advocacy research

Questions for Review and Critical Thinking

1. Why are ethical questions philosophical questions?
2. Identify the rights and obligations of researchers, clients, and subjects of business research.
3. Name some business research practices that are ethically questionable.
4. How might the business research industry take action to ensure that the public believes that research is a legitimate activity and that firms that misrepresent and deceive the public using business research as a sales ploy are not true business researchers?
5. Comment on the ethics of the following situations:
   (a) A researcher plans to code questionnaires in an employee survey using invisible ink.
   (b) A researcher is planning to videotape users' reactions to a new product in a simulated kitchen environment from behind a one-way mirror.
   (c) A food warehouse club advertises "savings up to 30 percent" after a survey showed a range of savings from 2 percent to 30 percent below that of an average shopping trip for selected items.
   (d) A radio station broadcasts the following message during a syndicated rating service's rating period: "Please fill out your diary."
   (e) A researcher pretends to be a member of a business firm's secretarial pool and observes workers without the workers realizing that they are part of a research study.
   (f) A researcher tells a potential respondent that an interview will last 10 minutes rather than the 30 minutes the researcher actually anticipates.
   (g) When you visit your favorite sports team's home page on the Web, you are asked to fill out a registration questionnaire before you enter the site. The team then sells your information (team allegiance, age, address, etc.) to a company that markets sports memorabilia via catalogs and direct mail.
   (h) A regional telephone company contemplates a proposal to telemarket services to its customers with unlisted telephone numbers.
   (i) A drug store chain stopped providing transaction information to a Massachusetts marketing firm that reminded customers to refill prescriptions.
6. Page through your local newspaper to find a story derived from survey research results. Does the newspaper article outline the study's methodology? Could the research have been termed advocacy research?

Exploring the Internet

1. ESOMAR is the World Association of Opinion and Marketing Research Professionals. The organization was founded in 1948 as the European Society for Opinion and Marketing Research. Check out its online ESOMAR Directory of Research Organizations, listing over 1,500 research organizations in 100 countries at http://www.esomar.nl/directory.html.
2. One purpose of the United Kingdom's Market Research Society is to set and enforce the ethical standards to be observed by research practitioners. Go to its Web site at http://www.marketresearch.org.uk/fr-code.htm to view its code of conduct. Visit the Web sites of the Council of American Survey Research Organizations (www.casro.org), the American Marketing Association (www.marketingpower.com), and the Marketing Research Association (www.mra-net.org), and compare their codes of ethics to that of the United Kingdom's Market Research Society.

PART

2

BEGINNING STAGES OF THE RESEARCH PROCESS

CHAPTER

6

PROBLEM DEFINITION AND THE RESEARCH PROPOSAL

What you will learn in this chapter

- To discuss the nature of decision makers' objectives and the role they play in defining the research problem.
- To understand that proper problem definition is essential for effective business research.
- To explain the iceberg principle.
- To understand that identifying key variables is important.
- To discuss how formulation of research questions and hypotheses adds clarity to the problem definition.
- To discuss the influence of the statement of the business problem on the specific research objectives.
- To state research problems in terms of clear and precise research objectives.
- To explain the purpose of the research proposal.
- To outline a research proposal.

Once upon a time a Sea Horse gathered up his seven pieces of eight and cantered out to find his fortune.[1] Before he had traveled very far he met an Eel, who said, "Psst. Hey, bud. Where ya goin'?"

"I'm going out to find my fortune," replied the Sea Horse, proudly.

"You're in luck," said the Eel. "For four pieces of eight you can have this speedy flipper, and then you'll be able to get there a lot faster."

"Gee, that's swell," said the Sea Horse, and paid the money and put on the flipper and slithered off at twice the speed. Soon he came upon a Sponge, who said, "Psst. Hey, bud. Where ya goin'?"

"I'm going out to find my fortune," replied the Sea Horse.

"You're in luck," said the Sponge. "For a small fee I will let you have this jet-propelled scooter so that you will be able to travel a lot faster."

So the Sea Horse bought the scooter with his remaining money and went zooming through the sea five times as fast. Soon he came upon a Shark, who said, "Psst. Hey, bud. Where ya goin'?"

"I'm going out to find my fortune," replied the Sea Horse.

"You're in luck. If you'll take this short cut," said the Shark, pointing to his open mouth, "you'll save yourself a lot of time."

"Gee, thanks," said the Sea Horse, and zoomed off into the interior of the Shark, there to be devoured.

The moral of this fable is that if you're not sure where you're going, you're liable to end up someplace else—and not even know it. ■

Before choosing a research design, managers and researchers need a sense of direction for the investigation. The adage "If you do not know where you are going, any road will take you there" suggests some good advice to managers and researchers: It is extremely important to define the business problem carefully because the definition determines the purpose of the research and, ultimately, the research design.

This chapter explains how to define a business problem and how to prepare a research proposal.

THE NATURE OF THE BUSINESS PROBLEM

Chapter 4 indicated that a decision maker's degree of uncertainty influences decisions about the type of research that will be conducted. This chapter elaborates on the conditions under which decision making occurs and the process managers use to clearly define business problems and opportunities.

Remember that managers may be completely certain about situations they face. For example, a retail store may have been recording and analyzing scanner data for years and know exactly what information its optical scanners need to record every day. Well-tested research techniques are regularly used to investigate routine problems that have already been defined.

At the other extreme, a manager or researcher may face a decision-making situation that is absolutely ambiguous. The nature of the problem to be solved is unclear. The objectives are vague, and the alternatives are difficult to define. This is by far the most difficult decision situation.

Most decision-making situations fall somewhere between these two extremes. Managers often grasp the general nature of the objectives they wish to achieve, but some uncertainty remains about the nature of the problem. They often need more information about important details. Their information is incomplete. They need to clear up ambiguity or uncertainty before making a formal statement of the business problem.

IMPORTANCE OF PROPER PROBLEM DEFINITION

The formal quantitative research process should not begin until the problem has been clearly defined. However, properly and completely defining a business problem is easier said than done. When a problem or opportunity is discovered, managers may have only vague insights about a complex situation. For example, suppose morale is declining at a West Coast television studio, and management does not know the reason. If quantitative research is conducted before learning exactly what issues are important, false conclusions may be drawn from the investigation. The right answer to the wrong question may be absolutely worthless. A decision made on the basis of a solution to the wrong problem may actually be harmful.

Consider what happened in the 1980s when Coca-Cola made the decision to change its formula and introduce "new" Coke. The company's managers decided to investigate consumers' reactions to the taste of reformulated Coke and nothing more. (The company carried out a series of taste tests in shopping malls. No take-home taste tests were conducted.) The results of the taste test led to the introduction of "new" Coke and the withdrawal of regular Coke from the market. As soon as consumers learned the company's original formula was no longer available, there were emotional protests from Coca-Cola loyalists. The consumer protests were so passionate and determined that the original formula was quickly brought back as Coca-Cola Classic. Coke's business research was too narrow in scope, and the problem was not adequately defined. Coca-Cola tested one thing and one thing only. In retrospect we know there was a larger problem. The business research failed to identify consumers' emotional attachment and loyalty to the brand as a problem for investigation. There is a lesson to be learned from the Coca-Cola mistake: Do not ignore investigating the emotional aspects of human behavior.

problem definition
The crucial first stage in the research process—determining the problem to be solved and the objectives of the research.

Just because a problem has been discovered or an opportunity has been recognized does not mean that the problem has been defined. A **problem definition** indicates a specific managerial decision area to be clarified or problem to be solved. It specifies research questions to be answered and the objectives of the research.

THE PROCESS OF PROBLEM DEFINITION

Defining a research problem involves several interrelated steps. As shown in Exhibit 6.1, they are:

1. Ascertain the decision maker's objectives
2. Understand the background of the problem
3. Isolate and identify the problem rather than its symptoms
4. Determine the unit of analysis
5. Determine the relevant variables
6. State the research questions (hypotheses) and research objectives

Ascertain the Decision Maker's Objectives

As a staff person, the research investigator must attempt to satisfy the objectives of the line manager who requests the project. Management theorists suggest that the decision maker should express his or her goals to the researcher in measurable terms. However, expecting a decision maker to follow this recommendation is, unfortunately, somewhat optimistic:

> Despite a popular misconception to the contrary, objectives are seldom clearly articulated and given to the researcher. The decision maker seldom formulates his objectives accurately. He is likely to state his objectives in the form of platitudes which have no operational significance. Consequently, objectives usually have to be extracted by the researcher. In so doing, the researcher may well be performing his most useful service to the decision maker.[2]

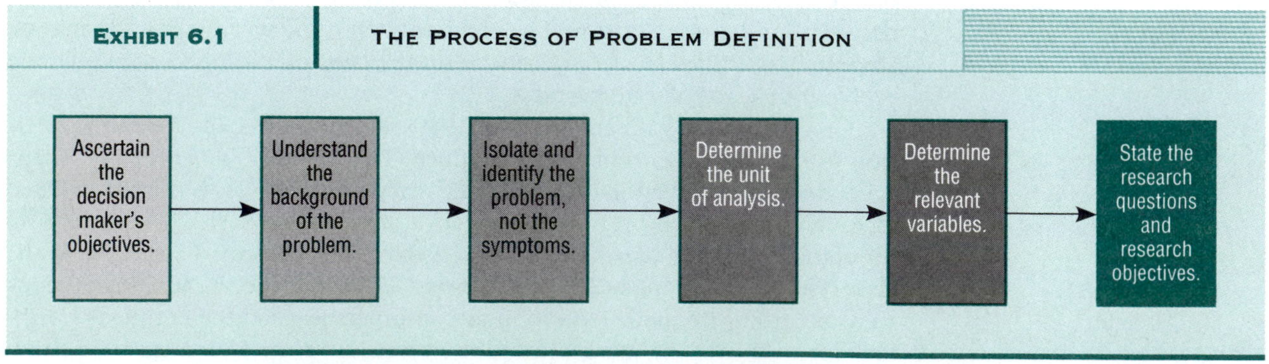
EXHIBIT 6.1
THE PROCESS OF PROBLEM DEFINITION
Ascertain the decision maker's objectives.
Understand the background of the problem.
Isolate and identify the problem, not the symptoms.
Determine the unit of analysis.
Determine the relevant variables.
State the research questions and research objectives.

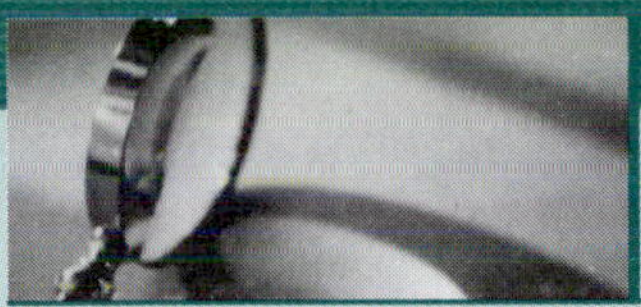

Research Insight

THEY MAY WANT TO STRANGLE YOU!

Hugh Dubberly, a manager with the Times-Mirror Company, advocates a step-by-step process to help clearly define the problem to be solved.[3]

"How do we define the problem? Begin by assembling all the relevant players in a room. Ask each player to describe the unmet need, or in other words, to suggest the cause of the problem. Write down each suggestion. Nothing you will do on the project will be more important. With each suggestion, ask in turn for its cause. And then the cause of the cause. And then the cause of the cause of the cause. Keep at it like a 2-year-old. By the time everyone in the room wants to strangle you, you will very likely have found the root cause of the problem.

After you've developed the problem statement, you need to be sure to gain consensus on it from all the relevant parties. Failure to get 'buy-in' from all the right people at this stage creates the potential for trouble later in the process. Someone who hasn't agreed on the definition up front is likely to want to change it later."

Researchers who must conduct investigations when a line manager wants the information "yesterday" do not usually get a great deal of assistance when they ask, "What are your objectives for this study?" Nevertheless, both parties should attempt to have a clear understanding of the purpose for undertaking the research.

One effective technique for uncovering elusive research objectives is to present the manager with each possible solution to a problem and ask whether he or she would follow that course of action. If the decision maker says "no," further questioning to determine why the course of action is inappropriate usually will help formulate objectives.

Often exploratory research can illuminate the nature of the opportunity or problem and help managers clarify their objectives and decisions.

Iceberg Principle

Why do so many business research projects begin without clear objectives or adequate problem definitions? Managers are logical people, and it seems logical that definition of the problem is the starting point for any enterprise. Frequently researchers and managers cannot discover the actual problem because they lack sufficiently detailed information; the **iceberg principle** serves as a useful analogy. A sailor on the open sea notices only a small part of an iceberg. Only 10 percent of it is above the surface of the water, and 90 percent is submerged. The dangerous part of many business problems, like the submerged portion of the iceberg, is neither visible to nor understood by managers. If the submerged portions of the problem are omitted from the problem definition (and subsequently from the research design), the decisions based on the research may be less than optimal. The example of the new Coke is a case in point. Omission of important information or a faulty assumption about the situation can be extremely costly.

iceberg principle
The idea that the dangerous part of many business problems is neither visible to nor understood by business managers.

Understand the Background of the Problem

Although no textbook outline exists for identifying a business problem, the iceberg principle illustrates that understanding the background of a problem is vital. Often experienced managers know a great deal about a situation and can provide researchers with considerable background information about previous events and why those events occurred. In situations in which the decision maker's objectives are clear, the problem may be diagnosed exclusively by exercising managerial judgment. In other situations, when information about what has happened previously is inadequate or when managers have trouble identifying the problem, a situation analysis is the logical first step in defining the problem. A **situation analysis** involves a preliminary investigation or informal gathering of background information to familiarize researchers or managers with the decision area. Gaining an awareness of organizational or environmental conditions and an appreciation of the situation often requires exploratory research. The many exploratory research techniques that have been developed to help formulate clear definitions of problems will be covered in Chapter 7.

situation analysis
A preliminary investigation or informal gathering of background information to familiarize researchers or managers with the decision area.

Isolate and Identify the Problem, Not the Symptoms

Anticipating all of the dimensions of a problem is impossible for any researcher or executive. For instance, a firm may have a problem with its advertising effectiveness. The possible causes of this problem may be low brand awareness, the wrong brand image, use of the wrong media, or perhaps too small a budget. Management's job is to isolate and identify the most likely causes. Certain occurrences that appear to be "the problem" may be only symptoms of a deeper problem. Exhibit 6.2 illustrates how symptoms may be mistaken for the true problem.

Other problems may be identified only after gathering background information and after conducting exploratory research. How does one ensure that the fundamental problem, rather than symptoms associated with the problem, has been identified? There is no easy or simple answer to this question. Executive judgment and creativity must be exercised. The archeological puzzle in Exhibit 6.3 (page 98) shows that good researchers must be creative in developing problem definitions by investigating situations in new ways.

The real voyage of discovery consists not in seeking new landscapes, but in having new eyes.

MARCEL PROUST

Determine the Unit of Analysis

Defining the problem requires that the researcher determine the unit of analysis for study. The researcher must specify whether the level of investigation will focus on the collection of data about the entire organization, departments, work groups, individuals, or objects. In studies of home buying, for example, the husband–wife dyad rather than the individual typically is the unit of analysis, because the purchase decision is made jointly by husband and wife. In studies of organizational behavior, cross-functional teams rather than individual employees may be selected as the unit of analysis.

Researchers who think carefully and creatively about situations often discover that a problem may be investigated at more than one level of analysis. Determining the unit of analysis, although relatively straightforward in most projects, should not be overlooked during the problem-definition stage of the research. It is a crucial aspect of problem definition.

EXHIBIT 6.2 | **SYMPTOMS CAN BE CONFUSING**

Organization	Symptoms	Problem Definition Based on Symptoms	True Problem
Twenty-year-old neighborhood swimming association in a mid-size town	Membership has been declining for years; new water park with wave pool and water slides moved into town a few years ago.	Neighborhood residents prefer the more expensive water park and have a negative image of the swimming pool.	Demographic changes: Children in the neighborhood have grown up, and older residents no longer swim at all.
Cellular phone manufacturer	Women employees complain that salaries are too low.	Salaries need to be compared to industry averages.	Benefits program is not suited to women's needs (e.g., maternity leave).
Brewery	Consumers prefer taste of competitor's product.	Taste of brewery's product needs to be reformulated.	Old-fashioned package is influencing taste perception.
Television station	Few employees change retirement plan after money market annuity option becomes available.	Attributes of money market annuity program need to be changed.	Except for those close to retirement, most employees are not highly involved in detailed pension-investment decisions; knowledge about plan is minimal.

Determine the Relevant Variables

variable
Anything that may assume different numerical or categorical values.

Another aspect of problem definition is identification of the key variables. The term *variable* is an important one in research. A **variable** is defined as anything that varies or changes in value. Because a variable represents a quality that can exhibit differences in value, usually in magnitude or strength, it may be said that a variable generally is anything that may assume different numerical or categorical values.

Key variables should be identified in the problem definition stage. Attitude toward Internet brokerage firms may be a variable, for example, as people's attitudes may vary from positive to negative. The attitude toward each of the many characteristics of brokerage firms, such as availability of investment advisory services, real-time quotes, toll-free calls, and the like, would be a variable.

categorical variable
Any variable that has a limited number of distinct values.

continuous variable
Any variable that has an infinite number of possible values.

In statistical analysis a variable is identified by a symbol, such as *X*. Categories or numerical values may then be associated with this symbol. The variable "sex" may be categorized as male or female; sex is therefore a **categorical**—or classificatory—**variable** because it has a limited number of distinct values. On the other hand, sales volume may encompass an infinite range of numbers; it is therefore a **continuous variable**—one with an infinite number of possible values.

To address the specific problem, managers and researchers should be careful to identify all of the relevant variables that must be studied. Variables that are superfluous (i.e., not directly relevant to the problem) should not be included.

Exhibit 6.3 | **Look Again**[4]

What language is written on this stone found by archaeologists?

Answer (turn book upside down):

The language is English: TO/TIE/MULES/TO. A great deal of time and effort is spent looking at familiar problems. Managers often do not look at these problems in a new light, however. Too often they see what they want to see or what they expect. They give stereotyped answers to problems. A good researcher creatively develops a hypothesis by looking at problems in a new way.

dependent variable
A criterion or a variable that is to be predicted or explained.

independent variable
A variable that is expected to influence the dependent variable. Its value may be changed or altered independently of any other variable.

In causal research the terms *dependent variable* and *independent variable* are frequently encountered. A **dependent variable** is a criterion or a variable that is to be predicted or explained. An **independent variable** is a variable that is expected to influence the dependent variable. For example, average hourly rate of pay may be a dependent variable that is influenced or can be predicted by an independent variable such as number of years of experience.

These terms are discussed in greater detail in the chapters on experimentation and data analysis.

State the Research Questions and Research Objectives

Both managers and researchers expect problem definition efforts to result in statements of research questions and research objectives. At the end of the problem definition stage of the research process, researchers should prepare a written statement that clarifies any ambiguity about what they hope the research will accomplish.

How Can the Problem Statement Be Clarified?

Formulating a series of research questions and hypotheses can add clarity to the statement of the business problem. For example, a company made the following statement to define a training problem: "The problem is to determine the best ways our company can train existing and potential users of networked personal computers." This problem statement led to the following research questions: "How familiar are employees with the various software applications for personal computers? What attitudes do employees have toward these software packages? How important are the various factors for evaluating the use of a personal computer? How effective are training efforts in increasing knowledge and use of the new applications?"

The inclusion of research questions in the statement of a business problem makes it easier to understand what is perplexing managers and indicates the issues to be resolved. A research question is the researcher's translation of the business problem into a specific need for inquiry. For example, a research question such as "Is advertising copy X better than advertising copy Y?" is vague and too general. Advertising effectiveness can be variously measured—by sales, recall of sales message, brand awareness, intentions to buy, and so on. A more specific research question such as "Which advertisement has a higher day-after recall score?" helps the researcher design a study that will produce pertinent information. The answer to the research question should be a criterion that can be utilized as a standard for selecting alternatives. This stage of the research is obviously related to problem definition. The goal of defining the problem is to state the research questions clearly and to have well-formulated hypotheses.

hypothesis
An unproven proposition or supposition that tentatively explains certain facts or phenomena; a proposition that is empirically testable.

A **hypothesis** is an unproven proposition or possible solution to a problem. Hypothetical statements assert probable answers to research questions. A hypothesis is also a statement about the nature of the world, and in its simplest form it is a guess. A manager may hypothesize that salespersons who show the highest job satisfaction will be the most productive. An organizational researcher may believe that if workers' attitudes toward an organizational climate are changed in a positive direction, there will be an increase in organizational effectiveness among these workers.

Problem statements and hypotheses are similar. Both state relationships, but problem statements are often phrased as questions, whereas hypotheses are declarative. Sometimes they are almost identical in substance. An important difference, however, is that hypotheses are usually more specific than problem statements; they usually more closely reflect the actual research operations and testing.[5] Hypotheses are statements that can be empirically tested.

Formal statements of hypotheses have considerable practical value in planning and designing research. They force researchers to be clear about what they expect to find through the study, and further, the formal statement raises crucial questions about the data that will be required in the analysis stage.[6] When evaluating a hypothesis, researchers should make sure the information collected will be useful in decision making. Notice how the following hypotheses express expected relationships between variables:

> There is a positive relationship between Internet shopping and the presence of younger children in the home.
>
> Voluntary turnover (quitting) will be higher among employees who perceive themselves to be inequitably paid than among employees who perceive themselves to be equitably paid.
>
> Among nonexporters, the degree of perceived importance of overcoming barriers to exporting is related positively to general interest in exporting (export intentions).
>
> Common stocks bought at high dividend yields will afford lower average returns than securities bought at lower dividend yields.
>
> Managers with liberal arts educations will process less accounting data than will those with masters degrees in business administration.
>
> Opinion leaders are more affected by mass media communication sources than are nonleaders.

research objective
The purpose of the research, expressed in measurable terms; the definition of what the research should accomplish.

Decision-Oriented Research Objectives

The **research objective** is the researcher's version of the business problem. Once the research questions and/or hypotheses have been stated, the research project objectives are derived from the problem definition. These objectives

Exhibit 6.4 | **Business Problem Translated into Research Objectives**

Problem/Questions	Research Questions	Research Objectives
Should the organization offer outplacement services?	Are managers aware of outplacement services?	To determine managers' awareness using aided recall
	How concerned are managers about outplacement services?	To measure managers' satisfaction with existing personnel policies
Which of the services should be offered? Severance pay? New employment assistance? Personal counseling? Job contacts?	How do managers evaluate the need for . . . Severance pay? New employment assistance? Personal counseling? Job contacts?	To obtain ratings and rankings of the various outplacement services
Should the services be provided by in-house personnel or outside consultants?	What are the benefits of each outplacement service?	To identify perceived benefits and perceived disadvantages of each outplacement service
	Would managers prefer in-house personnel or outside consultants?	To measure managers' perceptions of the benefits and disadvantages of in-house versus outside consultants
		To measure managers' preferences for these alternatives if discharge occurred
	How much would each alternative cost?	To identify costs associated with each alternative
Do employees with 10 or more years of service have different awareness levels, etc., than employees with fewer than 10 years of service?	Do the answers to the above questions differ by employees' years of service?	To compare, using cross-tabulations, levels of awareness, evaluations, etc., of managers with 10 or more years of service with those of managers with fewer than 10 years of service

Note: For simplification, hypotheses are omitted from the table.

explain the purpose of the research in measurable terms and define standards of what the research should accomplish. In addition to stating the reasons for initiating the research project, the objectives help to ensure that the project will be manageable in size. Exhibit 6.4 illustrates how the business problem of a large organization is translated into research objectives. The organization wants to research the question of whether it should offer outplacement services (e.g., severance pay) to discharged executives.

In some instances the business problem and the research objectives are the same. The objectives must, however, specify the information needed to make a decision. Identifying the information needed may require managers or researchers to be as specific as listing the exact wording of the question in a survey or explaining exactly what behavior might be observed or recorded in an experiment. Statements about the required precision of the information or the source of the information may be required to clearly communicate exactly what information is needed. Many career decisions, for example, are made by both husband and wife. If this is the case, the husband–wife decision-making unit is the unit of analysis. The objective of obtaining *X* information about research questions from this unit should be specifically stated.

It is useful to express the research objective as a managerial action standard. If the criterion to be measured (e.g., absenteeism, sales, or attitude changes) turns out to be higher than some predetermined level, then management will do *A*; if it is not, then management will do *B*. This type of objective leaves no uncertainty about the decision to be made once the research is finished.

The number of research objectives should be limited to a manageable quantity. The fewer the study objectives, the easier it is to ensure that each will be addressed fully.

Exhibit 6.5 shows that the statement of the business problem influences the research objectives. The specific objectives, in turn, are the basis for the research design.

In our earlier example of an organization's research concerning outplacement services, the broad research objective—to determine managers' perceived need for outplacement services in the organization—was translated into specific objectives, namely, to determine ranked preferences for severance pay, new employment assistance, and the like; to compare the needs of employees with more than 10 years of service with those having fewer than 10 years of service; and so on. Therefore, specific objectives influence the research design because they indicate the type of information needed. Once the research is conducted, the results may show an unanticipated aspect of the problem and may suggest that additional research is necessary to satisfy the

EXHIBIT 6.5 **THE STATEMENT OF THE BUSINESS PROBLEM INFLUENCES THE RESEARCH OBJECTIVES AND DESIGN**

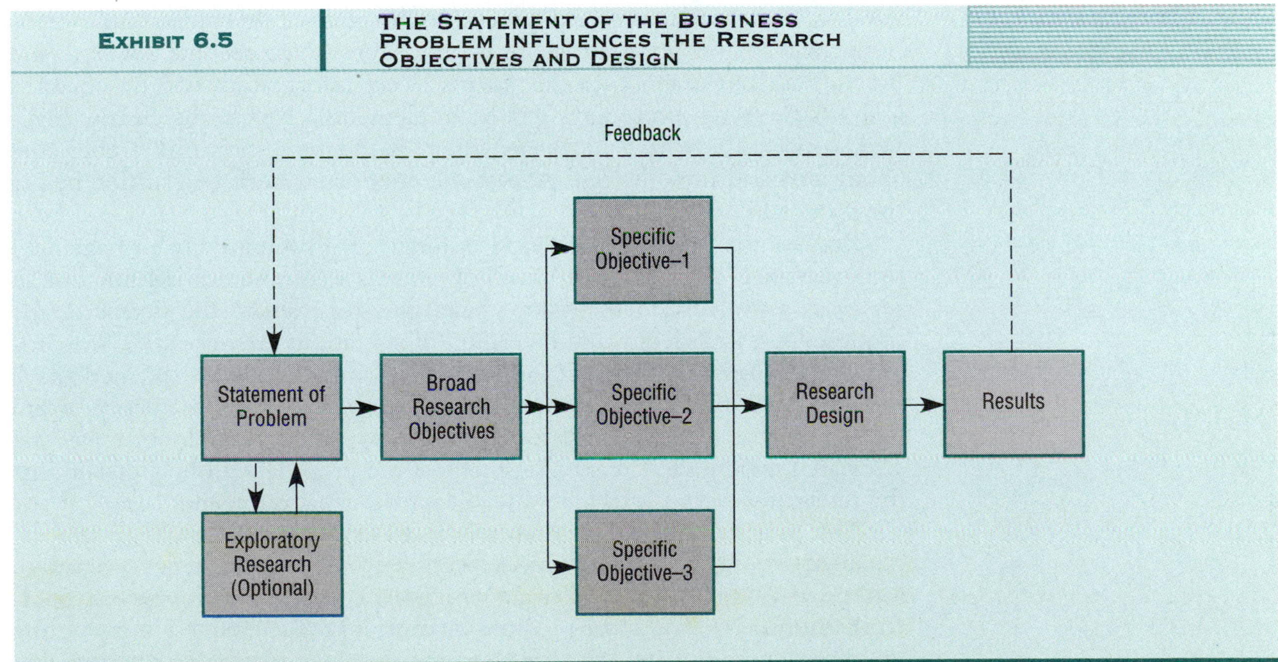

main objective. Exhibit 6.5 also shows that exploratory research may help in the overall definition of the management problem. In routine situations or when managers are quite familiar with background information, however, it is quite likely the problem definition will be based exclusively on the decision maker's objectives.

How Much Time Should Be Spent Defining the Problem?

Budget constraints usually influence the amount of effort that will be spent defining the problem. Most business situations are complex, and numerous variables may have some influence. It is impractical to search for every conceivable cause and minor influence. The importance of the recognized problem will dictate what is a reasonable amount of time and money to spend to determine which explanations or solutions are most likely.

Managers—those responsible for decision making—generally want the problem definition process to proceed quickly, whereas researchers usually take long periods of time to carefully define problems and thereby frequently frustrate managers. Nevertheless, the time spent to identify the correct problem to be researched is time well spent.

THE RESEARCH PROPOSAL

research proposal
A written statement of the research design that includes a statement explaining the purpose of the study and a detailed, systematic outline of a particular research methodology.

The **research proposal** is a written statement of the research design. It always includes an explanation of the purpose of the study (the research objectives) or a definition of the problem. It systematically outlines the particular research methodology and details the procedures that will be utilized at each stage of the research process. Normally a schedule of costs and deadlines is included in the research proposal. Exhibit 6.6 illustrates a short research proposal for an Internal Revenue Service study to explore public attitudes toward a variety of tax-related issues.

Preparation of a research proposal forces the researcher to think critically about each stage of the research process. Vague plans, abstract ideas, and sweeping generalizations about problems or procedures must become concrete and precise statements about specific events. What information will be obtained and what research procedures will be implemented have to be clearly specified so that others may understand their exact implications. All ambiguities about why and how the research will be conducted must be clarified before the proposal is complete.

Because the proposal is a clearly outlined plan submitted to management for acceptance or rejection, it initially performs a communication function; it serves as a mechanism that allows managers to evaluate the details of the proposed research design and determine if alterations are necessary. The proposal helps managers decide if the proper information will be obtained and if the proposed research will accomplish what is desired. If the business problem has not been adequately translated into a set of specific research objectives and a research design, the client's assessment of the proposal will help ensure that the researchers revise it to meet the client's information needs.

The proposal needs to communicate exactly what information will be obtained, where it will be obtained, and how it will be obtained. For this reason, proposals must be explicit about sample selection, measurement, fieldwork, and so on. For instance, most survey proposals include a copy of the proposed questionnaire (or at least some sample questions) to ensure that

Exhibit 6.6 An Abbreviated Version of a Research Proposal for the IRS[7]

Purpose of the Research

The general purpose of this study is to determine the taxpaying public's perceptions of the role of the IRS in administering the tax laws. In defining the limits of this study, the IRS identified study areas to be addressed. A careful review of those question areas led to the development of the following specific research objectives:

1. To identify the extent to which taxpayers cheat on their returns, their reasons for doing so, and approaches that can be taken to deter this behavior
2. To determine taxpayers' experience and satisfaction with various IRS services
3. To determine what services taxpayers need
4. To develop an accurate profile of taxpayers' behavior relative to the preparation of their income tax returns
5. To assess taxpayers' knowledge and opinions about various tax laws and procedures

Research Design

The survey research method will be the basic research design. Each respondent will be interviewed in his or her home. The personal interviews are generally expected to last between 35 and 45 minutes, although the length of the interview will vary depending on the previous tax-related experiences of the respondent. For example, if a respondent has never been audited, questions on audit experience will not be addressed. Or, if a respondent has never contacted the IRS for assistance, certain questions concerning reactions to IRS services will be skipped.

Some sample questions that will be asked are

Did you or your spouse prepare your federal tax return for (year)?

- Self
- Spouse
- Someone else

Did the federal income tax package you received in the mail contain all the forms necessary for you to fill out your return?

- Yes
- No
- Didn't receive one in the mail
- Don't know

If you were calling the IRS for assistance and someone were not able to help you immediately, would you rather get a busy signal or be asked to wait on hold?

- Busy signal
- Wait on hold
- Neither
- Don't know

During the interview a self-administered written questionnaire will be given to the taxpayer. The questionnaire will ask certain sensitive questions; for example, Have you ever claimed a dependent on your tax return that you weren't really entitled to?

- Yes
- No

Sample Design

A survey of approximately 5,000 individuals located in 50 counties throughout the country will provide the database for this study. The sample will be selected on a probability basis from all households in the continental United States.

Eligible respondents will be adults over the age of 18. Within each household an effort will be made to interview the individual who is most familiar with completing the federal tax forms. When there is more than one taxpayer in the household, a random process will be used to select the taxpayer to be interviewed.

Data Gathering

The fieldworkers of a field research organization will conduct the interviews.

Data Processing and Analysis

Standard editing and coding procedures will be utilized. Simple tabulation and cross-tabulations will be utilized to analyze the data.

Report Preparation

A written report will be prepared, and an oral presentation of the findings will be made by the research analyst at the convenience of the IRS.

Budget and Time Schedule

[Any complete research proposal should include (1) a schedule of how long it will take to conduct each stage of the research and (2) a statement of itemized costs.]

managers and researchers agree on the information to be obtained and how questions should be worded.

The format for the IRS research proposal in Exhibit 6.6 follows the six stages in the research process outlined in Exhibit 4.4. At each stage, one or more questions must be answered before the researcher can select one of the various alternatives. For example, before a proposal can be completed, the researcher has to ask "What is to be measured?" Simply answering "market share" may not be enough—market share may be measured by auditing retailers' or wholesalers' sales, by using trade association data, or by asking consumers what brands they buy. The question of what is to be measured is just one of the important questions that must be answered before setting the research process in motion. This issue will be addressed in greater detail in Chapter 13. For now, Exhibit 6.7 presents an overview of some of the basic questions that managers and researchers typically have to answer when planning a research design.

Review the IRS research proposal in Exhibit 6.6 to see how some of the questions in Exhibit 6.7 were answered in a specific situation. The remainder of this book will have to be read before these issues can be fully understood, however.

In business, one often hears the adage "Don't say it, write it." This is wise advice for the researcher who is proposing a research project to management. Misstatements and faulty communication may occur if the parties rely only on each individual's memory of what occurred at a planning meeting. Writing a proposal for a research design, specifying exactly what will be done, creates a record to which everyone can refer and eliminates many problems that might arise after the research has been conducted. With a written proposal, management and researchers alike are less likely to discover after the fact (after the research) that information related to a particular variable was omitted or that the sample size was too small for a particular subgroup. Further, as a statement of agreement between executives and researchers, the formal proposal will reduce the tendency for someone reading the results to say, "Shouldn't we have had a larger sample?" or "Why didn't you do it this way?" As a record of the researcher's obligation, the proposal also provides a standard for determining if the actual research was conducted as originally planned.

When a consultant or an outside research supplier will be conducting the research, the written proposal serves as that person's or company's bid to offer a specific service. Typically, a sponsoring client solicits several competitive proposals, and these written offers help management judge the relative quality of alternative research suppliers.

One final comment needs to be made about the nature of research proposals: Proposals do not all follow the same format. The researcher must adapt his or her proposal to the audience to whom it will be submitted.[8] An extremely brief proposal submitted by an organization's internal research department to its own executives bears little resemblance to a complex proposal submitted by a university professor to an agency of the federal government to test a basic theory about international financial markets.

ANTICIPATING OUTCOMES

The description of the data processing and analysis stage in Exhibit 6.6 is extremely brief because this topic will not be discussed until Chapter 19. However, at this point some advice about data analysis is in order.

EXHIBIT 6.7 BASIC QUESTIONS TYPICALLY ASKED WHEN PLANNING A RESEARCH DESIGN

Decision to Make	Basic Questions
Problem definition	What is the purpose of the study? How much is already known? Is additional background information necessary? What is to be measured? How? Can the data be made available? Should research be conducted? Can a hypothesis be formulated?
Selection of basic research design	What types of questions need to be answered? Are descriptive or causal findings required? What is the source of the data? Can objective answers be obtained by asking people? How quickly is the information needed? How should survey questions be worded? How should experimental manipulations be made?
Selection of sample	Who or what is the source of the data? Can the target population be identified? Is a sample necessary? How accurate must the sample be? Is a probability sample necessary? Is a national sample necessary? How large a sample is necessary? How will the sample be selected?
Data gathering	Who will gather the data? How long will data gathering take? How much supervision is needed? What procedures will data collectors need to follow?
Data analysis and evaluation	Will standardized editing and coding procedures be utilized? How will the data be categorized? Will computer or hand tabulation be utilized? What questions need to be answered? How many variables are to be investigated simultaneously? What are the criteria for evaluation of performance?
Type of report	Who will read the report? Are managerial recommendations requested? How many presentations are required? What will be the format of the written report?
Overall evaluation	How much will the study cost? Is the time frame acceptable? Do we need outside help? Will this research design attain the stated research objectives? When should the research begin?

dummy table
Representation of an actual table that will be in the findings section of the final report; used to provide a better understanding of what the actual outcome of the research will be.

One aspect of problem definition often lacking in research proposals is anticipating the outcome, that is, the statistical findings, of the study. The use of a dummy table in the research proposal often helps the manager gain a better understanding of what the actual outcome of the research will be. **Dummy tables** are representations of the actual tables that will be in the findings section of the final report. They are called *dummy tables* because the researcher fills in, or "dummies up," the tables with likely, but fictitious, data. In other words, the researcher anticipates what the final research report will contain (table by table) before the project begins.

A research analyst can present dummy tables to the decision maker and ask, "Given findings like these, will you be able to make a decision to solve your managerial problem?" If the decision maker says yes, then the proposal may be accepted. However, if the decision maker cannot glean enough information from these dummy tables to make a decision about what the company would do with the hypothetical outcome suggested by the tables, then the decision maker must rethink what outcomes and data analyses are necessary to solve the problem. In other words, the business problem is clarified by deciding on action standards or performance criteria and by recognizing what type of research findings are necessary to make a specific decision.

SUMMARY

The first step in any business research project is to define the problem or opportunity. Decision makers must express their objectives to researchers to avoid getting the right answer to the wrong question. Defining the problem is often complicated in that portions of the problem may be hidden from view. The research must help management isolate and identify the problem to ensure that the real problem, rather than a symptom, is investigated.

A variable is anything that changes in value. Variables may be categorical or continuous. One aspect of problem definition is the identification of the key dependent and independent variables.

Research questions and hypotheses are translations of the business problem into business research terms. A hypothesis is an unproven proposition or a possible solution to the problem. Hypotheses state relationships between variables that can be tested empirically. Research objectives specify information needs. For the research project to be successful, the research problem must be stated in terms of clear and precise research objectives.

The research proposal is a written statement of the research design that will be followed in addressing a specific problem. The research proposal allows managers to evaluate the details of the proposed research and determine if alterations are needed. Most research proposals include the following sections: purpose of the research, research design, sample design, data gathering and/or fieldwork techniques, data processing and analysis, budget, and time schedule.

Key Terms

problem definition
iceberg principle
situation analysis
variable
categorical variable
continuous variable
dependent variable
independent variable
hypothesis
research objective
research proposal
dummy table

Questions for Review and Critical Thinking

1. In its broadest context, what is the task of problem definition?
2. In the nine-dot square below, connect all nine dots using no more than four straight lines and without lifting the pencil from the paper. What analogy can you make between the solution of this problem and the definition of a business problem?

   • • •
   • • •
   • • •

3. What is the iceberg principle?
4. State a problem in your field of interest, and list some variables that might be investigated to solve this problem.
5. Go to the library, find business journals, and record and evaluate some hypotheses that have been investigated in recent years. Identify the key independent and dependent variables.
6. Evaluate the statement of the business problem in each of the following situations:
   (a) *A farm implement manufacturer:* Our objective is to learn the most effective form of capitalization so that we can maximize profits.
   (b) *An employees' credit union:* Our problem is to determine the reasons why employees join the credit union, to determine members' awareness of credit union services, and to measure attitudes and beliefs about how effectively the credit union is operated.
   (c) *The producer of a television show:* We have a problem: The program's ratings are low. We need to learn how to improve our ratings.
   (d) *A soft-drink manufacturer:* The problem is that we do not know if our bottlers are more satisfied with us than our competitors' bottlers are with them.
   (e) *A women's magazine:* Our problem is to document the demographic changes that have occurred in recent decades in the lives of women and to put these changes in historic perspective; to examine several generations of American women through most of this century, tracking their roles as students, workers, wives, and mothers and noting the changes in timing, sequence, and duration of these roles; to examine at what age and for how long a woman enters each of the various stages of her life: school, work, marriage, childbearing, divorce. This documentation will be accomplished by analyzing demographic data over several generations.
   (f) *A manufacturer of fishing boats:* The problem is to determine sales trends over the past 5 years by product category and to determine the seasonality of quarterly unit boat sales by region of the country.
   (g) *The inventor of a tension headache remedy (a cooling pad that is place on the forehead for up to 4 hours):* The purpose of this research is (1) to identify the market potential for the product, (2) to identify what desirable features the product should possess, and (3) to determine possible advertising strategies/channel strategies for the product.
7. What purposes does a research proposal serve?
8. What role should managers play in the development of the research proposal?
9. Comment on the following statements:
   (a) "The best business researchers are prepared to rethink and rewrite their proposals."
   (b) "The client's signature is an essential element of the research proposal."
10. You have been hired by a group of hotel owners, restaurant owners, and other people engaged in businesses that benefit from tourism on South Padre Island, Texas. They wish to learn how they can attract a larger number of college students to their town during spring break. Define the business research problem. (You may substitute a beach town in Florida or California, if you prefer.)
11. The military wishes to understand its image from the public's point of view. Define the business problem.
12. You have solicited research proposals from several firms. The lowest bidder has the best questionnaire and proposal. However, you particularly like one feature from the proposal submitted by a firm that will not receive the job. How should you handle this situation?

Exploring the Internet

1. How could the Internet help in defining a business problem that needs to be researched?
2. Could e-mail be used to solicit research proposals from business research suppliers? What would be the advantages and disadvantages of using this method of solicitation?

Case Suggestions

Case 3: Tulsa's Central Business District (A)
Case 5: Middlemist Precision Tool Company
Case 6: EZ Pass

CHAPTER

7

EXPLORATORY RESEARCH AND QUALITATIVE ANALYSIS

What you will learn in this chapter

- To understand the differences between qualitative research and quantitative research.
- To explain the purposes of exploratory research.
- To identify the four general categories of exploratory research.
- To explain the advantages and disadvantages of experience surveys, case study methods, focus group interviews, projective techniques, depth interviews, and other exploratory research techniques.
- To understand when exploratory techniques are appropriate and to understand their limitations.
- To understand how technology is changing the nature of exploratory research.

It's 5:30 AM in the middle of January.[1] At a trucking terminal in a small town in Pennsylvania a group of ten Teamsters are getting ready to begin their deliveries—but only after they spend about an hour in a makeshift conference room talking about the company to a visitor. Even though the invitation memo spelled it out, the group is not really clear about the purpose of the meeting or whom the visitor represents. The supervisors, who will be in a later group, walk by the still open door to see what's going on. The visitor closes the door and addresses the Teamsters: "Good morning. How many of you have ever been in a focus group?" No one replies.

Welcome to a focus group—an unstructured, free-flowing interview with a small group of people. Forget the image of a focus group as a bunch of middle managers sitting in a plush conference room, eating a catered meal, and spouting the company line, and forget the touchy/feely exercises and unstructured gripe sessions that have passed for focus group interaction in the past.

Designed and conducted properly, focus groups find out what employees throughout the organization have to say about the business and what they can and must contribute to make that business a success. Employees are *not* reluctant to share their thoughts and feelings with management. In fact, managers are often surprised by the level of employee openness. One business researcher at Sibson and Company who is experienced in conducting employee focus groups has learned that employees are happy to participate. "They don't want to choke down cold coffee and Danish at breakfasts with the boss any more than (the bosses) do. They're sick of the symbolism and halfhearted attempts at change. They want (the company) to *do* something." He goes on to say,

> We've conducted focus groups on behalf of senior management for a variety of reasons—strategy implementations, cost-cutting/rightsizing efforts, reorganizations, and employee involvement programs, or simply to find out how employees think the company is doing. We talked to people on the job—on the tarmac, pile driver barge, and manufacturing floor, and in the truck terminal, customer service center, field sales office, and world headquarters office. Afterward, people have often lined up to shake hands or stood up to applaud because, finally, management is doing something.
>
> In fact, just holding a focus group gets a lot of attention. In a focus group at [one airline], one "uninvited" employee was so anxious to hear what was being said in the meeting that he hid in the ceiling crawl space above the makeshift meeting room. The ceiling

panel caved in, and he fell onto the conference table—to the shock of focus group participants. The focus groups we conducted at [this airline] were memorable for other reasons. Despite the difficult situation they experienced, the employees were forthcoming and genuinely concerned about saving their company, and they helped identify operational improvements right up to the end. ■

Focus groups with employees are rapidly gaining acceptance. They do more than uncover issues that concern employees. Successful focus groups generate ideas about potential tactical and strategic issues that need further investigation.

A focus group is just one of the various exploratory techniques used in business research. Exploratory research and qualitative analysis are discussed in this chapter.

EXPLORATORY RESEARCH: WHAT IT IS AND WHAT IT IS NOT

exploratory research
Initial research conducted to clarify and define the nature of a problem.

When a researcher has a limited amount of experience with or knowledge about a research issue, **exploratory research** is a useful preliminary step that helps ensure that a more rigorous, more conclusive future study will not begin with an inadequate understanding of the nature of the management problem. The findings discovered through exploratory research would lead the researchers to emphasize learning more about the particulars of the findings in subsequent conclusive studies. Conclusive research answers questions of fact necessary to determine a course of action. This is never the purpose of exploratory research.

Exploratory researchers can be creative in their search for ideas. Researchers who conduct beeper studies provide consumers or business subjects with a questionnaire and instruct them to record their actions, interactions, moods, stress levels, every time the beeper goes off. Asking subjects to use disposable cameras, video cameras, and tape recorders is a variation of the beeper study.[2]

Much, but certainly not all, exploratory research provides *qualitative* data. Usually, exploratory research provides greater understanding of a concept or crystallizes a problem, rather than providing precise measurement or *quantification*. A researcher may search for numbers to indicate economic trends, but exploratory research does not involve rigorous mathematical analysis. The focus of such qualitative research is not on numbers but on words and observations: stories, visual portrayals, meaningful characterizations, interpretations, and other expressive descriptions. Any source of information may be informally investigated to clarify which qualities or characteristics are associated with an object, situation, or issue.

Alternatively, the purpose of *quantitative* research is to determine the quantity or extent of some phenomenon in the form of numbers. Most exploratory research is *not* quantitative research. This chapter discusses exploratory research under the assumption that its results are qualitative.

Exploratory research may be a single research investigation or a *series* of informal studies intended to provide background information. Researchers must be creative in the choice of information sources to be investigated. They must be flexible enough to investigate all inexpensive sources that may possibly provide information to help understand a problem. This need to be flexible does not mean that researchers do not have to be careful and systematic when designing exploratory research studies. Most of the techniques discussed in this chapter have limitations. Researchers should be keenly aware of the proper and improper uses of the various techniques.

WHY CONDUCT EXPLORATORY RESEARCH?

The purpose of exploratory research is intertwined with the need for a clear and precise statement of the recognized problem. There are three interrelated purposes for exploratory research: (1) diagnosing a situation, (2) screening alternatives, and (3) discovering new ideas.

Diagnosing a Situation

The cure for boredom is curiosity. There is no cure for curiosity.

DOROTHY PARKER

Much has already been said about the need for situation analysis to clarify a problem's nature. Exploratory research helps diagnose the dimensions of problems so that successive research projects will be on target. It helps set priorities for research. In some cases exploratory research provides an orientation for management by gathering information on a topic with which management has little experience. Although a research project has not yet been planned, information about an issue is needed before the appropriate diagnosis of the problem can be developed.

Personnel research managers often conduct exploratory research as a diagnostic tool to point out issues of employee concern or to generate possible explanations for motivational patterns. For example, preliminary interviews with employees may be utilized to learn current "hot" issues, as well as concerns about bread-and-butter issues such as wages, working conditions, career opportunities, and the like.

As another example, when an advertising agency got the account for a new coffee that contained chicory, the firm's researchers began with exploratory research to diagnose the situation. They learned that almost nobody had heard of chicory. It wasn't being used, and users seemed to know nothing about it. This led to the hypothesis that advertising could portray the chicory ingredient any way the client wanted.

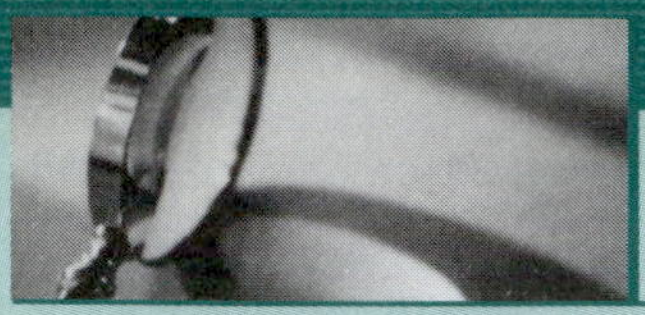

Research Insight

Exploratory Research for New Ideas

A team of researchers from the Management School at the University of Waikato in New Zealand used exploratory research to discover new ideas about "peak performance." The research objective was to identify the essential elements of organizations that maintain leadership over long periods of time (peak performance). The team's contention was that championship sports organizations are the ideal vehicle to study peak performance culture. Among the organizations visited were the Atlanta Braves, the San Francisco 49ers, New Zealand's All Blacks rugby team, Britain's Williams Formula One motor racing team, and Germany's Bayern Munich soccer team.

At the bedrock of the researchers' learning was listening, observing, storytelling, intuition, judgment, and simply "hanging out." In other words, the team conducted an anthropological search for cultural imperatives. What they found is that inside peak performance organizations is an overwhelming passion to win. The team also found a strong practice of "exceeding personal best." They found game-breaking ideas, incremental contributions to the way things are done. In fact, all peak performance organizations have enabled their people to continually push for these new ideas. Finally, the exploratory research identified a peak practice called "the last detail." Without the last detail in place, all else is a waste of time.

Screening Alternatives

When several opportunities arise but the budget precludes investigating all possible options, exploratory research may be used to determine the best alternatives. Perhaps several good investments are available and exploratory research can be used to point to better ones. Or an exploratory look at market data reveals that the market for a planned new product is too small. Although this aspect of exploratory research is not a substitute for conclusive research, certain evaluative information can be acquired in exploratory studies.

concept testing
A form of research that tests something that acts as a proxy for a new or revised program, product, or service.

The need for concept testing is a frequent reason for conducting exploratory research. **Concept testing** is a general term for many different research procedures, all of which have the same purpose: to test something that acts as a proxy for a new or revised program, product, or service. Typically, test subjects are presented with some sort of stimulus or a description of an idea and asked if they would use it, if they like it, and so on. Concept testing is a means of evaluating ideas by providing a "feel" for the merits of an idea prior to the commitment of research and development, manufacturing, or other company resources. Researchers look for trouble signals in evaluations of concepts in order to avoid future problems in business research.

Concept testing may portray the functions, uses, and possible situations for a proposed product. For example, Del Monte conducted a concept test to determine if consumers would accept the idea of shelf-stable yogurt. The plan was scrapped after research showed that buyers refused to accept the idea that yogurt could be kept unrefrigerated. Early investigation indicated that such a concept was viewed as desirable and unique, but the cost of achieving believability was finally judged to be too high.

In other cases, when subjects have expressed reservations about certain aspects of an idea but the general concept has not been evaluated negatively, researchers know that the concept needs to be refined. Exhibit 7.1 presents excellent concept statements for two new seafood products made from squid. The statements portraying the intangibles—brand image, product appearance, name, and price—and a description of the product simulate reality. The idea expressing the nature of the brand is conveyed to the test subjects.

EXHIBIT 7.1 | **CONCEPT STATEMENTS FOR SEAFOOD PRODUCTS**[3]

Squid Concept Alternative 1: CALAMARIOS

CALAMARIOS* are a new and different seafood product made from tender, boneless, North Atlantic squid. The smooth white body (mantle) of the squid is thoroughly cleaned, cut into thin, bite-sized rings, then frozen to seal in their flavor. To cook CALAMARIOS, simply remove them from the package and boil them for only 8 minutes. They are then ready to be used in a variety of recipes.

For example, CALAMARIOS can be combined with noodles, cheese, tomatoes, and onions to make "Baked CALAMARIOS Cacciatore." Or CALAMARIOS can be marinated in olive oil, lemon juice, mint, and garlic and served as a tasty squid salad. CALAMARIOS also are the prime ingredient for "Calamari en Casserole" and "Squid Italienne." You may simply want to steam CALAMARIOS, lightly season them with garlic, and serve dipped in melted butter. This dish brings out the fine flavor of squid. A complete CALAMARIOS recipe book will be available free of charge at your supermarket.

CALAMARIOS are both nutritious and economical. Squid, like other seafood, is an excellent source of protein. CALAMARIOS can be found at your supermarket priced at $6.50 per pound. Each pound you buy is completely cleaned and waste-free.

Because of their convenient versatility, ample nutrition, and competitive price, we hope you will want to make CALAMARIOS a regular item on your shopping list.

Squid Concept Alternative 2: SCLAM CHOWDER

SCLAM CHOWDER is a delicious new seafood soup made from choice New England clams and tasty, young, boneless North Atlantic squid. Small pieces of clam are combined with bite-sized strips of squid and boiled in salted water until they are soft and tender. Sautéed onions, carrots, and celery are then added together with thick, wholesome cream, a dash of white pepper, and sprinkling of fresh parsley. The entire mixture is then cooked to perfection, bringing out a fine, natural taste that will make this chowder a favorite in your household.

SCLAM CHOWDER is available canned in your supermarket. To prepare, simply combine SCLAM CHOWDER with 1½ cups of milk in a saucepan, and bring to a boil. After the chowder has reached a boil, simmer for 5 minutes and then serve. One can makes two to three servings of this hearty, robust seafood treat. Considering its ample nutrition and delicious taste, SCLAM CHOWDER is quite a bargain at $3.99 per can.

Both clams and squid are high in protein, so high in fact that SCLAM CHOWDER makes a healthy meal in itself, perfect for lunches as well as with dinner. Instead of adding milk, some will want to add ⅓ cup of sour cream, and use liquid chowder as an exquisite sauce to be served on rice, topped with grated Parmesan cheese.

However you choose to serve it, you are sure to find SCLAM CHOWDER a tasty, nutritious, and economical seafood dish.

**Calamari* is the Italian word for squid.

Discovering New Ideas

Exploratory research is often used to generate new ideas. Perhaps factory workers have suggestions for increasing production or improving safety. Consumers may suggest new product ideas, or unthought-of problems might be identified.

For example, an automobile manufacturer might have drivers design their dream cars using computerized design software similar to that used by automotive designers. This exploratory research might generate ideas that would never have occurred to the firm's design staff.[4]

CATEGORIES OF EXPLORATORY RESEARCH

There are many techniques for investigating undefined research problems. Several of the most popular qualitative techniques are discussed in this section. However, the *purpose,* rather than the *technique,* determines whether a study is exploratory, descriptive, or causal. For example, telephone surveys (discussed in Chapter 10) are sometimes used for exploratory purposes, although they are used primarily for descriptive research. The versatile techniques discussed in this chapter allow for intensive, in-depth questioning of respondents, and these techniques tend to be used *primarily,* though not exclusively, for exploratory purposes.

A manager may choose from four general categories of exploratory research methods: (1) experience surveys, (2) secondary data analysis, (3) case studies, and (4) pilot studies. Each category provides various alternative ways of gathering information.

Experience Surveys

experience survey
An exploratory research technique in which individuals who are knowledgeable about a particular research problem are surveyed.

In attempting to understand the problems at hand, managers may discuss issues and ideas with top executives and knowledgeable managers who have had personal experience in the field. This constitutes an informal **experience survey.**

For example, a chain saw manufacturer received from its Japanese distributor a recommendation to modify its product with a drilling attachment on the sprocket (replacing the chain and guide bar) so that the chain saw could be used as a mushroom-planting device. The distributor indicated that many such units had been sold in Japan. However, an experience survey with only one individual, the president of the Mushroom Growers Association, indicated the product was not feasible in the United States. Americans mainly consume a white cultured mushroom grown in enclosed areas or caves rather than the variety of mushrooms grown on wood in Japan. The mushroom expert indicated most Americans believe too many old wives' tales about poison mushrooms and would not change their eating habits to include the Japanese variety.

Exploratory research in the form of an experience survey may be quite informal. Discussions with knowledgeable people, both inside and outside the company, may not be much more than conversations. This activity, intended only to get ideas about the problem, may be conducted by the line manager rather than the research department. The financial research analyst may have within an industry many contacts on whom he or she relies for information. Exploratory information from an experience survey is not expected to be conclusive. Often an experience survey consists of interviews with a small number of people who have been carefully selected. Some formal questions may be asked, but the respondents will generally be allowed to discuss the questions with few constraints. Knowledgeable people should be selected for their ability to articulate information; the researcher is not trying to establish a representative probability sample. The purpose of surveying such experts is to help formulate the problem and clarify concepts rather than develop conclusive evidence.

Secondary Data Analysis

secondary data analysis
Preliminary review of data collected for another purpose to clarify issues in the early stages of a research effort.

Another economical and quick source of background information is trade literature. Searching through such material is exploratory research by means of **secondary data analysis.** Basic theoretical research is rarely conducted without extensive reviews of the literature on similar research. Using secondary data may be equally important in applied research. For example, a personnel manager may want to evaluate her company's formal training programs. A short time in a library or on the Web may reveal that in companies with more than 50 employees the average executive receives more than 40 hours of training per year while the average office secretarial worker gets fewer than 20 hours of training per year.[5] Additional information about the types of training, use of computers in training, industry differences in training, and the like may help clarify the issues that need to be researched. If the problem is to determine the reasons for a decline in sales of an existing product, the manager's situational analysis might begin with an analysis of sales records by region and by customer or some other source of internal data.

Investigating data that have been compiled for some purpose other than the project at hand, such as accounting records or trade association data, is one of the most frequent forms of exploratory research. Because this is also a technique for both descriptive and conclusive research, a separate chapter (Chapter 8) is devoted to the investigation of secondary sources.

Once an informal situational analysis using secondary data or experience surveys has been carried out, issues that still need clarification may warrant further exploratory investigation beyond the gathering of background information. At this point a research specialist is needed to design more elaborate exploratory research. The remainder of this chapter presents a number of exploratory and preliminary research techniques that can aid in the definition of the problem.

Case Studies

case study method
An exploratory research technique that intensively investigates one or a few situations similar to the researcher's problem situation.

The purpose of the **case study method** is to obtain information from one or a few situations that are similar to the researcher's problem situation. For example, a bank in Montana may intensively investigate the computer-security activities of an innovative bank in California. An academic researcher, interested in doing a nationwide survey among union workers, may first look at a few union locals to identify the nature of any problems or topics that should be investigated. A business research manager for Schwinn bicycles used observation techniques to conduct an exploratory case study. Here is a description of the situation in his own words:

> We had a very successful dealer on the West Coast. He sold a lot of bicycles. So it occurred to me that we'd go out and find out how he's doing it. We'll use a tape recorder and get in the back room where we'll hear these magic words that he says to people to make them buy bicycles. We'll take that tape back to the factory. We'll have it all typed out. We'll print it in the *Reporter*

> [dealer newsletter]. We'll send it to all the other dealers and everybody can say the same words. And, boy, we'll need another factory! Right? So we go out. The guy's got a nice store out in Van Nuys. We sit in the back room and we listen. The first customers come in, a man and a woman with a boy about nine or ten years old. The dad says, "Which one is it?" The son says, "This one over here." Dad looks at it. He says to the clerk, "How much is it?" The clerk says, "$149.95." The father says, "Okay, we'll take it." It blew the whole bit. So we stand there and we listen to some of these conversations going on like this. Suddenly it dawned on us that it was not what they say, it's the atmosphere of the store. Here was not Joe's old, dirty bike shop—it was a beautiful store on the main street. A big sign was in front, "Valley Cyclery"; inside [were] fluorescent lights, carpeting on the floor, stereo music, air-conditioning, a beautiful display of bicycles. It was like a magnet. People came in. So, maybe this is the catch. We tried to introduce that idea to other dealers. Put a bigger investment into your store and see what happens. Some of them did, and it happened.[6]

This observational case study serendipitously led to a discovery that would change Schwinn's entire channel of distribution strategy. The opportunity was a direct result of being open-minded in the problem-definition stage of business research.

The primary advantage of the case study is that an entire organization or entity can be investigated in depth and with meticulous attention to detail. This highly focused attention enables the researchers to carefully study the order of events as they occur or to concentrate on identifying the relationships among functions, individuals, or entities. A fast-food restaurant may test a new store design, a new operating procedure, or a new menu item in a single location to learn about potential operational problems that could hinder service quality.

Conducting a case study often requires the cooperation of the person whose history is being studied—for example, a franchisee who allows the franchiser access to his or her records and reports. Again, intensive interviews or long discussions with the franchisee and his or her employees may provide an understanding of a complex situation. Researchers, however, have no standard procedures to follow. They must be flexible and attempt to glean information and insights wherever they find them. The freedom to search for whatever data an investigator deems important makes the success of any case study highly dependent on the alertness, creativity, intelligence, and motivation of the individual performing the case analysis.

Like all exploratory research, the results from case studies should be seen as tentative. Generalizing from a few cases can be dangerous, because most situations are atypical in some sense. A bank in Montana may not be in a situation comparable to one in California. But even if situations are not directly comparable, a number of insights can be gained and hypotheses suggested for future research.

Obtaining information about competitors may be very difficult, because they generally like to keep the secrets of success to themselves. The exact formulation of Coca-Cola Classic, for example, is known by only a few top executives in the firm. Confidentiality, they feel, is a definite competitive edge in their product strategy. Thus, researchers may have limited access to information from other firms.

Pilot Studies for Qualitative Analysis

pilot study
Any small-scale exploratory research project that uses sampling but does not apply rigorous standards.

The term *pilot studies* covers a number of diverse research techniques. Within the context of exploratory research, a **pilot study** implies that some aspect of the research (e.g., fieldwork) will be on a small scale. Thus, a pilot study is a research project that involves sampling, but the rigorous standards used to obtain precise, quantitative estimates from large, representative samples are relaxed.

A pilot study generates primary data, usually for qualitative analysis. This characteristic distinguishes pilot studies from secondary data analysis, which gathers background information. The primary data usually are collected from employees, consumers, voters, or other subjects of ultimate concern rather than from a few knowledgeable experts or from a case situation. This distinguishes pilot studies from experience surveys and case studies. The major categories of pilot studies include focus group interviews, projective techniques, and depth interviews.

Focus Group Interview

focus group interview
An unstructured, free-flowing interview with a small group of people.

The focus group interview has become so popular that many research agencies consider it to be the "only" exploratory research tool. A **focus group interview** is an unstructured, free-flowing interview with a small group of people. It is not a rigidly constructed question-and-answer session, but a flexible format that encourages discussion of, say, a labor issue, reactions to a political candidate, or a new-product concept. Participants meet at a central location at a designated time. The group consists of a moderator (interviewer) and six to ten participants who discuss a single topic. The participants may be women talking about maternity leave, petroleum engineers talking about problems in the "oil patch," or patients talking about health care. The moderator introduces the topic and encourages the group members to discuss the subject among themselves. Focus groups allow people to discuss their true feelings, anxieties, and frustrations, and to express the depth of their convictions in their own words. Ideally, the discussion proceeds mostly at the group's initiative.

The primary advantages of focus group interviews are that they are relatively brief, easy to execute, quickly analyzed, and inexpensive. In an emergency situation, three or four group sessions can be conducted, analyzed, and reported in less than a week at a cost substantially lower than that of other attitude-measurement techniques. Remember, however, that a small discussion group will rarely be a representative sample, no matter how carefully it is recruited. Focus group interviews cannot take the place of quantitative studies.

The flexibility of focus group interviews is an advantage, especially when compared with the rigid format of a survey. Numerous topics can be discussed and many insights can be gained, particularly those involving the variations in behavior in different situations. Responses that would be unlikely to emerge in a survey often come out in a group interview. During a focus group interview of people who had never visited the J. Paul Getty Museum, a middle-aged man said, "I've been told there's heavy, very classical type of art, somewhat stuffy and standoffish. It's the kind of place you wouldn't want to take your kids and let them run around." An older woman agreed, saying, "I get the impression it's a little stuffy and has old art." A younger man putting in his two cents' worth added, "I was driving up past Malibu and I saw the sign. I'd never heard of it before. I thought it was a place where they were going to show you how to refine oil or something."[7]

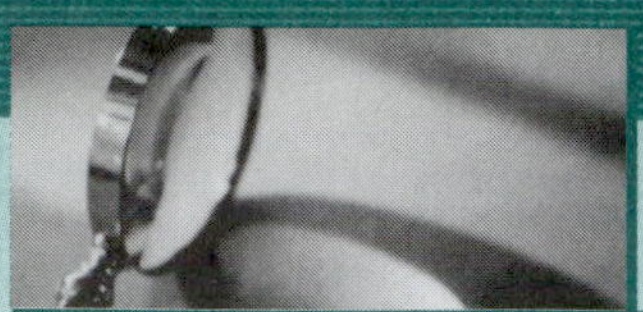

RESEARCH INSIGHT

TGI FRIDAY'S

Because TGI Friday's thought the Navy was an extremely efficient food handler, perhaps more efficient than for-profit companies, the restaurant wanted to understand the sources of that efficiency.[8] Friday's executives concluded that successful imitation of the Navy's food-handling operations might help the firm gain some expertise and lead to increased proficiency in performing its service. This matter was of particular interest to Friday's because the firm's strategy called for building smaller restaurants with almost the same number of seats as were included in the older designs (5,700 square feet with 210 seats, compared to 9,200 square feet with 240 seats). These smaller designs place a premium on handling food efficiently.

To study the Navy's food-based work processes, Friday's CEO spent a day aboard the nuclear submarine USS *West Virginia.* His visit occurred when a crew of 155 was engaged in a 70-day voyage. Because the submarine had a crew on duty 24 hours per day, the Navy served four meals daily in an extremely confined space. A quick calculation shows that four daily meals, for 70 days, for 155 people, is over 43,000 meals.

The Navy was pleased to let Friday's use its operations as a case study. According to one Navy official, "These aren't things we want to keep secret. All of our food service research and development is funded by American tax dollars."

If a researcher is investigating a target group to determine who consumes a particular beverage or why a particular brand is purchased, situational factors must be taken into account. If the researcher does not realize the impact of the occasion on which the particular beverage is consumed or why a product is purchased, the results of the research may be general and not portray the consumers' actual thought process. A focus group can elicit situationally specific responses: "I was driving past Malibu and I saw a sign."

Focus groups are often used for concept screening and refinement. A concept may be continually modified, refined, and retested until management believes that it is acceptable.

The specific advantages of focus group interviews have been categorized as follows:[9]

- Synergy: The combined effort of the group will produce a wider range of information, insights, and ideas than will the cumulation of separately secured responses of a number of individuals.
- Serendipity: It is more often the case in a group than in an individual interview that some idea will drop out of the blue. The group also affords the opportunity to develop the idea to its full significance.
- Snowballing: A bandwagon effect often operates in a group interview situation. A comment by one individual often triggers a chain of responses from the other participants.
- Stimulation: Usually, after a brief introductory period, the respondents want to express their ideas and expose their feelings as the general level of excitement about the topic increases.
- Security: In the well-structured group, the individual can usually find some comfort in the fact that his or her feelings are similar to those of oth-

ers in the group, and that each participant can expose an idea without being obliged to defend it or to follow through and elaborate on it. One is more likely to be candid because the focus is on the group rather than on the individual; the participant soon realizes that the things said are not necessarily being identified with him or her.

- Spontaneity: Since no individual is required to answer any given question in a group interview, the individual's responses can be more spontaneous and less conventional. A spontaneous answer may provide a more accurate picture of the person's position on some issue. In a group interview people speak only when they have definite feelings about a subject, not because a question requires a response.
- Specialization: The group interview allows the use of a more highly trained interviewer (moderator) because there are certain economies of scale when a number of individuals are interviewed simultaneously.
- Scrutiny: The group interview permits closer scrutiny in several ways. First, the session can be observed by several people; this affords some check on the consistency of the interpretations. Second, the session can be tape-recorded or videotaped. Later, detailed examination of the recorded session can offer additional insights and help clear up disagreements about what happened.
- Structure: The group interview affords more control than the individual interview with regard to the topics covered and the depth in which they are treated. The moderator has the opportunity to reopen topics that received too shallow a discussion when initially presented.
- Speed: The group interview permits securing a given number of interviews more quickly than does interviewing individual respondents.

Group Composition The ideal size of the focus group is six to ten individuals. If the group is too small, one or two members may intimidate the others. Groups that are too large may not permit adequate participation by each group member. Homogeneous groups seem to work best. Selecting homogeneous groups allows researchers to concentrate on individuals with similar lifestyles, job classifications, experiences, and communication skills. The session thus does not become confused with too many arguments and different viewpoints stemming from diverse backgrounds of participants. For example, when the Centers for Disease Control and Prevention tested public-service announcements about AIDS through focus groups, it discovered that single-race groups and multicultural groups reacted differently.[10] By conducting separate focus groups, the organization was able to gain important insights about which creative strategies were most appropriate for targeted versus broad audiences.

Researchers who wish to collect information from different types of people should conduct several focus groups. For example, one focus group consisting only of men and another focus group consisting only of women might be conducted. Thus, a diverse sample may be obtained even though each group is homogeneous.

Environmental Conditions The site of the group session may be the research agency, an office conference room, a hotel, or a shopping mall. A "coffee klatch" or "bull session" atmosphere can be established to ensure that the mood of the sessions will be as relaxed and natural as possible.

The Moderator It is the moderator's job to make sure that everyone gets a chance to speak and to ask questions to clarify topics that have been introduced into the discussion. The moderator's job is to develop a rapport with the group and to promote interaction among its members. The combined effort of the group is likely to produce a wider range of information, insights, and ideas than a number of personal interviews would provide.[11] The moderator should be someone who is really interested in people, who listens carefully to what others have to say, and who can readily establish rapport and gain people's confidence and make them feel relaxed and eager to talk. Careful listening by the moderator is especially important, because the group interview's purpose is to stimulate spontaneous responses. The moderator's role is also to focus the discussion on the problem areas of concern. When a topic is no longer generating fresh ideas, the effective moderator changes the flow of the discussion. The moderator does not give the group total control of the discussion, but normally has prepared questions on topics that are of concern to management. However, the timing of these questions and the manner in which they are raised are left to the moderator's discretion. The term *focus group* derives from the moderator's task. He or she starts out by asking for a general discussion but usually focuses in on specific topics during the session.

discussion guide
Written prefatory remarks and an outline of topics/questions that will be addressed in a focus group.

Planning the Focus Group Outline An effective focus group moderator prepares a discussion guide to help ensure that the focus group will cover all topics of interest. The **discussion guide** consists of written prefatory remarks to inform the group about the nature of the focus group and an outline of topics/questions that will be addressed in the group session.

A cancer center that wanted to warn the public about the effects of overexposure to the sun used the discussion guide in Exhibit 7.2. The business researchers had several objectives for this discussion guide:

- The first question, asking participants to describe their feelings about being out in the sun, was intended to elicit the range of views present in the group, given that some individuals might view it as a healthful practice while others would view it as dangerous. It seemed important to have group members see the extent to which others held views different from their own. Furthermore, this was the only question asked of every participant in turn. As no one could fail to be able to answer, it gave each individual a nonthreatening chance to talk and thus "broke the ice."
- The second question, asking whether participants could think of any reason to be warned about exposure to the sun, was simply designed to introduce in question form the idea of a warning.
- Succeeding questions asked, first on an open-ended basis, about possible formats of warnings of danger from the sun. Respondents were asked to react to any formats that participants suggested, on an open-ended basis, then to react to formats the cancer center personnel had in mind.
- Finally, the "bottom line" question asked which format would be most likely to induce participants to take protective measures. Then a "catch-all" question asked for any comments they wanted to pass along to the sponsor, which was revealed as the Houston-based cancer center.[12]

Notice that the researchers who planned the outline established certain objectives for each part of the focus group session. At the outset, the purpose was to break the ice and establish a rapport with the group. The logical flow of the group session then moved from the general discussion about sunbathing to the more focused discussion of the effectiveness of types of warnings about danger from sun exposure.

Exhibit 7.2 | Discussion Guide for Cancer Center Focus Group[13]

Thank you very much for agreeing to help out with this research. We call this a focus group; let me explain how it works, and then please let me know if something isn't clear.

This is a discussion, as though you were sitting around just talking. You can disagree with each other, or just comment. We do ask that just one person talk at a time, because we tape-record the session to save me from having to take notes. Nothing you say will be associated with you or your church—this is just an easy way for us to get some people together.

The subject is health risk warnings. Some of you may remember seeing a chart in a newspaper that gives a pollen count or a pollution count. And you've heard on the radio sometimes a hurricane watch or warning. You've seen warnings on cigarette packages or cigarette advertising, even if you don't smoke.

And today we're going to talk about warnings about the sun. Before we start, does anybody have a question?

1. OK, let's go around and talk about how often you spend time in the sun, and what you're likely to be doing. (FOR PARENTS): What about your kids—do you like them to be out in the sun?

2. OK, can you think of any reason that somebody would give you a warning about exposure to the sun?

(PROBE: IS ANY SUN EXPOSURE BAD, OR ONLY A CERTAIN DEGREE OF EXPOSURE, AND IF SO, WHAT IS IT? OR IS THE SUN GOOD FOR YOU?)

3. What if we had a way to measure the rays of the sun that are associated with skin problems, so that you could find out which times of the day or which days are especially dangerous? How could, say, a radio station tell you that information in a way that would be useful?

4. Now let me ask you about specific ways to measure danger. Suppose somebody said, "We monitored the sun's rays at noon, and a typical fairskinned person with unprotected skin will burn after 40 minutes of direct exposure." What would you think?

5. Now let me ask you about another way to say the same kind of thing. Suppose somebody said, "The sun's rays at noon today measured 10 times the 8 AM baseline level for danger." What would you think?

6. OK, now suppose you heard the same degree of danger expressed this way: "The sun's rays at noon today measured 8 on a sun danger scale that ranges from 1 to 10." What would you think?

7. What if the danger scale wasn't numbers, but words. Suppose you heard, "The sun's rays at noon showed a moderate danger reading," or "The sun's rays showed a high danger reading." What would you think?

8. And here's another possibility: What if you heard "Here's the sun danger reading at noon today—the unprotected skin of a typical fairskinned person will age the equivalent of 1 hour in a 10-minute period."

9. OK, what if somebody said today is a day to wear long sleeves and a hat, or today is a day you need sunscreen and long sleeves. What would you think?

10. OK, here's my last question. There are really three things you can do about sun danger: You can spend less time in the sun, you can go out at less dangerous times of day, like before 10 in the morning or after 4 in the afternoon, and you can cover your skin by wearing a hat, or long sleeves, or using protective sunscreen lotion. Thinking about yourself listening to the radio, what kind of announcement would make you likely to do one or more of those things? (PARENTS: WHAT WOULD MAKE YOU BE SURE THAT YOUR CHILD WAS PROTECTED?)

11. And what would you be most likely to do to protect yourself (YOUR CHILD)?

12. Before we break up, is there anything else you think would be useful for M. D. Anderson's people to know?

OK, thank you *very* much for your help.

Videoconferencing and Streaming Media The videoconferencing industry has grown dramatically in recent years. And as the ability to communicate via telecommunications and videoconferencing links has improved in quality, the number of companies using these systems to conduct focus groups has increased. With traditional focus groups, managers often watch the moderator lead the group from behind one-way mirrors. If the focus group is being conducted out of town, management personnel usually have to spend more time in airplanes, hotels, and taxis than they do watching the group session. With videoconferenced focus groups, managers can stay home.

Focus Vision Network of New York is a business research company that provides videoconferencing equipment and services for clients. The Focus Vision system is modular, which allows it to be wheeled around to capture close-ups of each group member. The system operates via a remote keypad that allows observers in a far-off location to pan the focus group room or zoom in on a particular participant. The system allows executives and managers at remote locations to send messages to the moderator. For example, while new product names were being tested in one focus group, an observing manager had an idea and contacted the moderator, who tested the new name on the spot.[14]

streaming media
Multimedia content, such as audio or video, that can be accessed on the Internet without being downloaded first.

Streaming media consist of multimedia content such as audio or video that is made available in real time over the Internet or a corporate intranet, with no download wait and no file to take up space on a viewer's hard disk.[15] This new technology for digital media delivery allows researchers to "broadcast" focus groups that can be viewed online. The offsite manager uses RealPlayer or Microsoft Media Player to view a focus group on a computer rather than at a remote location. Except for a decrease in quality of the video when there are bandwidth problems, the effect is similar to videoconferencing.

online focus group
A focus group whose members carry on their discussion through an Internet chat room.

Interactive Media and Online Focus Groups The use of the Internet for qualitative exploratory research is growing rapidly. The term **online focus group** refers to a qualitative research effort in which a group of individuals provide unstructured comments by entering their remarks into a computer connected to the Internet. The group participants keyboard their remarks either during a chat room format or when they are alone at their computers. Because respondents enter their comments into the computer, transcripts of verbatim responses are available immediately after the group session. Online groups can be quick and cost-efficient. However, because there is less interaction between participants, group synergy and snowballing of ideas may be diminished.

A research company may set up a private chat room on its company Web site for focus group interviews. Participants in these chat rooms feel that their anonymity is very secure. Often they will make statements or ask questions they would never pose under other circumstances.[16] This can be a major advantage for a company investigating sensitive or embarrassing issues.

Many focus groups using the chat room format involve a sample of participants who are online at the same time, typically for about 60 to 90 minutes. Because participants do not have to be together in the same room, the number of participants in these online focus groups can be much larger than in traditional focus groups. Twenty-five participants or more is not uncommon for the simultaneous chat room format. Participants can be at widely separated locations, even in different time zones, because the Internet does not have geographical restrictions. Of course, a major disadvantage is that only individuals with Internet access can be selected for an online group. (The nature of Internet samples will be discussed in depth in Chapters 10 and 16.)

The job of an online moderator resembles that of an in-person moderator. However, the online moderator should possess fast and accurate keyboard skills or be willing to hire an assistant who does. Ideally, the discussion guide is downloaded directly onto the site so the moderator can, with one click, enter a question into the dialogue stream.[17]

A problem with online focus groups is that the moderator cannot see body language and facial expressions (bewilderment, excitement, interest, etc.) to interpret how people are reacting. Also, the moderator's ability to probe and ask additional questions on the spot is reduced in online focus groups, especially those in which group members are not participating simultaneously.[18] Research that requires focus group members to actually touch something (such as a new easy-opening packaging design) or taste something cannot be performed online.

The complexity of the subject will determine the exact nature and length of an online focus group. For many online projects the group discussion can continue for 24 or 48 hours or even longer. Cross Pen Computing Group tested the appeal of an advertising campaign for a new product called CrossPad with an online brainstorming group that ran for 5 days.[19]

As the session's time expands, so may the number of participants. Some sessions involve quite a large number of participants, perhaps as many as 200. Whether these online chat sessions are true focus groups or not is a matter of some minor debate. However, these online research projects do have their purpose. For example, Nickelodeon uses an online format to learn about a variety of subjects from a group of viewers. These kids use personal computers and the Internet to talk with each other and with network researchers about pets, parents, peeves, and pleasures. Kids post notes on the computer bulletin board whenever they want to. Three times a week they log on for scheduled electronic conferences, during which Nickelodeon researchers lead discussions to answer questions such as "Is this a good scoring methodology for a game show?" or "Do kids understand if we show a sequence of program titles and air times?" On one occasion, the kids told researchers they were confused by the various locations shown in a segment of *The Tomorrow People,* a futuristic series with events occurring around the world. Realizing that the sight of a double-decker bus wasn't enough to allow a modern kid to identify London, the producers wrote the name of the city on the screen.[20]

Although we have not yet discussed Internet surveys, it is important to make a distinction between online focus groups, which provide qualitative information, and Internet surveys, which provide quantitative findings. Chapter 10 discusses technological challenges and how to administer Internet surveys. (Much of that discussion is also relevant for researchers wishing to conduct online focus groups.)

Focus Groups as Diagnostic Tools Researchers predominantly use focus groups to conduct exploratory research. However, the findings from many surveys or other quantitative research studies raise more questions than they answer. Managers who are puzzled about the meaning of survey research results may use focus groups to better understand what consumers have said in surveys. In other words, sometimes researchers use focus groups to diagnose problems suggested by quantitative research. The director of business research at Crown Zellerbach explained it this way: "When done in conjunction with quantitative research [focus groups] can go a long way toward explaining why the numbers come out as they do. Quantitative [research] often is long on *what* but short on *why*."[21]

Shortcomings The shortcomings of focus groups are similar to those of most qualitative research techniques, and they are discussed at the end of this chapter. However, a specific shortcoming of focus groups should be pointed out here. Without a sensitive and effective moderator, a single, self-appointed participant may dominate the session. Sessions that include a dominant participant may be somewhat abnormal. Participants may react negatively toward the dominant member, causing a "halo" effect on attitudes toward the concept or the topic of discussion. In other words, a negative impression of the individual may be projected onto the topic of discussion. Such a situation should be avoided so that a negative impression of an obnoxious person does not inhibit other members from being candid and does not influence the statements that they make.

Projective Techniques

There is an old story about asking one's neighbor why he purchased a Mercedes. If you ask the person directly, he will tell you the car holds its value and does not depreciate much, that it gets better gas mileage than you'd expect, or that it has a comfortable ride. But if you ask that same man why the man down the block purchased a Mercedes, he answers, "Oh, that status seeker!" This story illustrates that individuals may be more likely to give a true answer (consciously or unconsciously) if the question is disguised. The purpose of projective techniques is to discover an individual's attitudes, motivations, defensive reactions, and characteristic ways of responding.

The underlying assumption for these methods is contained in Oscar Wilde's observation: "A man is least himself when he talks in his own person; when he is given a mask he will tell the truth." In other words, advocates of projective techniques assume that when directly questioned, respondents do not express their true feelings because they are embarrassed about answers that reflect poorly on their self-concept. They wish to please the interviewer with the "right" answer, or they cannot reveal unconscious feelings of which they are unaware. However, if respondents are presented with unstructured, ambiguous stimuli, such as cartoons or ink blots, and are allowed considerable freedom to respond, their true feelings will be expressed.

projective technique
An indirect means of questioning that enables a respondent to "project" beliefs and feelings onto a third party, an inanimate object, or a task situation.

A **projective technique** is an indirect means of questioning that enables the respondent to "project" beliefs and feelings onto a third party, an inanimate object, or a task situation. Respondents are not required to provide answers in a structured format. They are encouraged to describe a situation in their own words, with little prompting by the interviewer. Individuals are expected to interpret the situation within the context of their own experiences, attitudes, and personality and to express opinions and emotions that may be hidden from others and, possibly, themselves. The most common projective techniques in business research are word association, sentence completion, the third-person technique, and the Thematic Apperception Test.

word association test
A projective research technique in which the subject is presented with a list of words, one at a time, and asked to respond with the first word that comes to mind.

Word Association During a **word association test** the subject is presented with a list of words, one at a time, and asked to respond with the first word that comes to his or her mind. Both verbal and nonverbal responses (such as hesitation in responding) are recorded. A researcher who reads a list of job tasks to employees expects that the word association technique will reveal

RESEARCH INSIGHT

EMPLOYEE FOCUS GROUPS

Focus groups with employees can be extremely valuable.[22] However, before rushing into a series of focus groups with employees, companies ought to consider some general guidelines. First, focus groups should be made up of randomly selected employees, with one key provision: No employee should participate in the same group with his or her supervisor. Often, random selection is monitored to ensure that specific populations are represented.

Second, employees must understand that the purpose of the focus group is to improve the company and, in so doing, improve the lives of company employees. Although the session may generate some complaining about the company and its management, employees are not let off the hook lightly. For example, a comment like "They [management] don't care about employees" is never left unchallenged. Among the follow-up questions: Who are "they"? What do you expect them to do given current business conditions? What would make you think they care? In other words, in a productive focus group, employees are pressed to provide insight into the problems at hand and to offer solutions.

Third, to be most effective, focus groups must be led by an individual who is not on the company payroll. No matter how open and honest a relationship management thinks it has with employees, employees will *not* offer candid opinions to a senior manager. The credibility of the messenger increases dramatically if employees believe they will still have a job no matter what they tell management.

Contrary to popular belief, employees rarely want to talk about themselves in these groups. Rather, they want to discuss the company and how to make it better. When a major computer company held focus groups to find out what employees thought the company should look like in the future, management was stunned to find that employees had a much different agenda: identifying what was wrong with the company *currently.*

The ever-present hope among employees coming out of focus groups is that "this time it might be different"—that is, that management will actually act on what employees say. Often emotions run high when employees are frustrated by a specific issue that just won't go away or when their formerly high job satisfaction is waning. Employees' gratitude that someone cares about what they have to say can create a halo effect around the focus group process itself.

Make no mistake: Expressing opinions on the job in a focus group is very important to employees. One group in an Oklahoma City–based company included several deaf employees who brought sign language interpreters to the meeting so that their opinions would be heard.

Focus groups are also faster and less expensive, and they yield more insights into the day-to-day lives of employees than an employee attitude survey does. Because they don't rely on structured, rigid questions on a sheet of paper, they're also spontaneous and interactive. The focus group format can be changed on the spot to address a critical employee concern that arises in the discussion.

So what does management think of focus group findings? It depends, although management's reaction to the finding normally falls into three categories:

1. "They said *that?*"
2. "We already know that" (though nothing has been done about it).
3. "Let's do something about what employees are saying."

No matter how management responds initially, the follow-up response must be simple and straightforward: We listened. We understand. We will act. Virtually any other reaction—more analysis paralysis, for example—will dissipate the group's energy and could, in fact, increase employee frustration over management's continued unwillingness to listen and act.

Nabisco's business research shows that cookie consumption is often a form of self-indulgence. The company finds that many brand-loyal women reward themselves with midafternoon gratification. Researchers often use projective techniques when they suspect that true attitudes and motivations, such as controlled guilt about snack food products, will not be divulged if questions are undisguised.

each individual's true feelings about the job task. It is assumed that an employee's first thought is a spontaneous answer because the subject does not have adequate time to think about and avoid making admissions that reflect poorly on himself or herself. This technique is frequently used in testing potential brand names. For example, a liquor manufacturer, attempting to market a clear-colored, light whiskey, tested the brand names Frost, Verve, Ultra, and Master's Choice. Frost was seen as upbeat, modern, clean, and psychologically right. Verve was "too modern," Ultra was "too common," and Master's Choice was "not upbeat enough."

Interpreting word association tests is difficult, and researchers should make sure that they avoid subjective interpretations. When there is considerable agreement in the "free association" process, the researcher assumes that the test has revealed the person's inner feelings about the subject. Word association tests are also analyzed by the amount of elapsed time. For example, if the researcher is investigating sexual harassment, a person's hesitation in responding may indicate that the word arouses some sort of emotion (and the person may be seeking an "acceptable" response). Thus, analysis of projective technique results takes into account not only what people say but what they *do not* say.

Word association tests can also be used to pretest words or ideas to be used in questionnaires. This enables the researcher to know beforehand whether and to what degree the meaning of a word or phrase is understood in the context of a survey.

sentence completion
A projective technique in which respondents are required to complete a number of partial sentences with the first word or phrase that comes to mind.

Sentence Completion **Sentence completion** is another technique based on the assumptions of free association. Respondents are required to complete a number of partial sentences with the first word or phrase that comes to mind. For example:

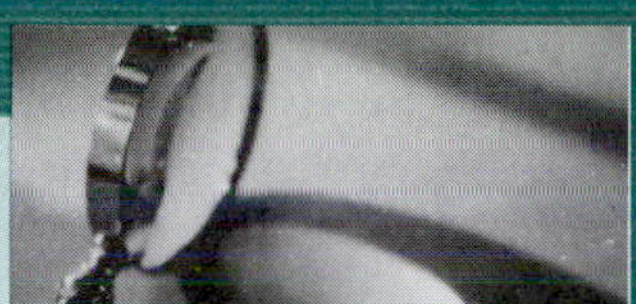

RESEARCH INSIGHT

ANOTHER PROJECTIVE TECHNIQUE

The woman chose a story that she remembered from her childhood.[23] One Christmas she waited in giddy excitement to find out what was in the biggest package under the tree. It had the best wrapping paper. She could hardly imagine what it might be. But after she unwrapped the gift, it turned out to be something so ordinary that she hardly remembers what it was, only the disappointment that it didn't live up to the promise of its package.

The short story, written by a woman who had just finished looking at an early version of the PT Cruiser, was the impetus that prompted designers to take another look at the interior. They redesigned it from standard, fixed seating to the more adaptable, unexpected interior that appears in the production car.

The team studying the design of the PT Cruiser read through hundreds of similar stories, looking for clues they could translate into action. But rather than relying on focus groups as they might have in the past, the team used a different type of qualitative research. Consumers met for 3 hours to look at the vehicle, discuss it, and then write stories. The environment is more relaxed than a focus group, and the goal is not to get people to recommend changes but to get them to tap into less tangible feelings via their creative writing. "Sometimes people just don't know how to say what they really think about a vehicle." Creative writing often draws it out.

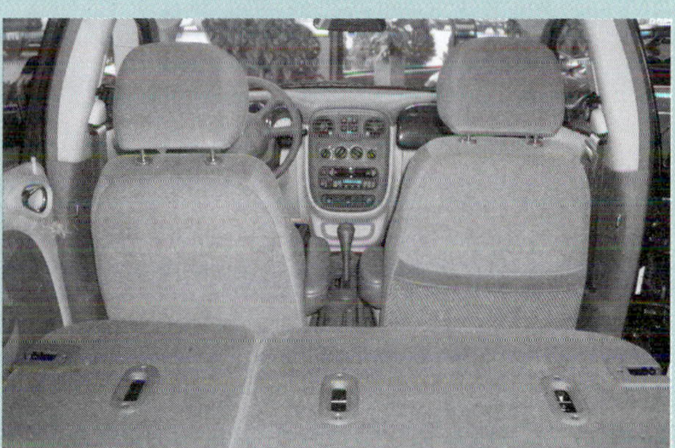

People who work late are ______.
A female manager is most liked by ______.
A boss should not ______.

Answers to sentence completion questions tend to be more extensive than answers to word association tests. The intent of these sentence completion questions is more apparent, however.

third-person technique
A projective technique in which the respondent is asked why a third person does what he or she does or what he or she thinks about an object, event, person, or activity. The respondent is expected to transfer his or her attitudes to the third person.

Third-Person Technique and Role Playing The Iowa Poll asked, "Will you wind up in heaven or hell?" Nearly all Iowans believed they would be saved, but one-third of them described a neighbor as a "sure bet" for hell.[24]

Almost literally, providing a "mask" is the basic idea behind the **third-person technique.** Respondents are asked why a third person (e.g., a neighbor) does what he does or thinks what he thinks about a person, event, or concept. For example, investors might be told: "We are talking to a number of investors like you about this money market fund. Some men and women like it the way it is; others believe that it should be improved. Please think of some of your friends or neighbors and tell us what it is they might find fault with in this new money market fund." Thus, the respondent can transfer his attitudes to his neighbors, to friends, or to people he works with. He is free to agree or disagree with an unknown third party.

The best-known and certainly a classic example of the use of this indirect technique was conducted in 1950 when Nescafé Instant Coffee was new to the market. Two shopping lists, identical except for coffee, were given to two groups of women:

- Pound and a half of hamburger
- 2 loaves of Wonder bread
- Bunch of carrots
- 1 can of Rumford's Baking Powder
- Nescafé Instant Coffee [or Maxwell House Coffee, drip grind]
- 2 cans Del Monte peaches
- 5 pounds potatoes

The instructions were:

> Read the shopping list. Try to project yourself into the situation as far as possible until you can more or less characterize the woman who bought the groceries. Then write a brief description of her personality and character. Whenever possible indicate what factors influenced your judgment.

Forty-eight percent of the housewives who were given the list that included Nescafé described the Nescafé user as lazy and a poor planner. Others indicated that they felt the instant coffee user was not a good wife and spent money carelessly. The Maxwell House user was thought to be practical, frugal, and a good cook.[25]

role playing
A projective technique that requires the subject to act out someone else's behavior in a particular setting.

Role playing is a dynamic reenactment of the third-person technique in a given situation. The role-playing technique requires the subject to act out someone else's behavior in a particular setting. For example, a worker in a role-playing situation who is instructed to perform a supervisor's task projects herself into a supervisor's role. This projective technique can be used to determine a true feeling about a supervisor or work situation. People in role-playing games may become caught up in acting out the roles and thereby reveal their true feelings.

Role playing is particularly useful in investigating situations where interpersonal relationships are the subject of the research, as, for example, salesperson–customer, husband–wife, and worker–supervisor.

thematic apperception test (TAT)
A test consisting of a series of pictures shown to research subjects who are then asked to provide a description of the pictures. The researcher analyzes the content of these descriptions in an effort to clarify a research problem.

Thematic Apperception Test (TAT) A **thematic apperception test (TAT)** consists of a series of pictures or cartoons in which the research topic (co-workers, job task, and the like) is the center of attention. The investigator asks the subject to tell what is happening in the picture and what the people might do next. Hence, themes *(thematic)* are elicited on the basis of the perceptual-interpretive *(apperception)* use of the pictures. The researcher then analyzes the content of the stories that the subjects relate.

The picture or cartoon stimulus must be sufficiently interesting to encourage discussion but sufficiently ambiguous not to disclose the nature of the research project. Clues should not be given to the character's positive or negative predisposition. In a preliminary version of a TAT investigating why men might purchase a chain saw, a picture of a man looking at a very large tree was used in a pretest. The subjects of the research were homeowners and weekend

EXHIBIT 7.3 | **PICTURE FRUSTRATION VERSION OF TAT**

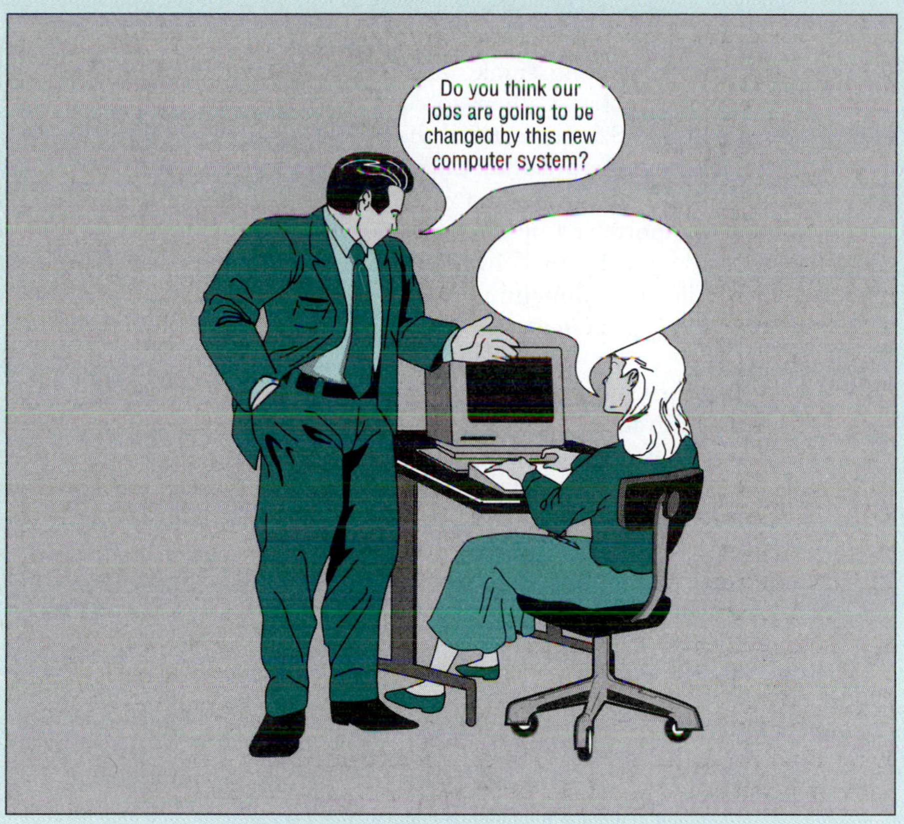

woodcutters. When they were confronted with the picture of the extremely large tree, they almost unanimously said they would get professional help from a tree surgeon. Thus, early in the pretesting process the researchers found that the picture was not sufficiently ambiguous and that the subjects did not identify with the man in the picture. If subjects are to project their views into the situation, the environmental setting should be a well-defined familiar problem, but the "solution" should be ambiguous.

Frequently the test consists of a series of pictures with some continuity so that stories may be constructed in a variety of settings. For example, in the first picture a woman might be working at her desk, and the final picture might show her making a presentation at a conference table.

picture frustration
A version of the Thematic Apperception Test that uses a cartoon drawing for which the respondent suggests dialogue that the cartoon characters might speak.

Picture frustration is a version of the TAT that uses a cartoon drawing in which the respondent suggests dialogue that the cartoon characters might speak. In Exhibit 7.3, a purposely ambiguous illustration of an everyday occurrence, two co-workers are shown in a situation and the respondent is asked what the woman might be saying.

Several other projective techniques apply the logic of the TAT. *Construction techniques* request that respondents draw a picture, construct a collage, or write a short story to express their perceptions or feelings. For example, children hold in their heads many pictures that they are unable to describe in words.

Asking a child to "draw what comes to your mind when you think about going shopping" enables the child to use his or her visual vocabulary to express feelings.[26]

Altoids are a thumbnail-sized breath freshener packaged in a tin. The company's advertising agency did psychological testing with the brand's target market: young, single, urban males. Researchers gave Altoids users ten magazines and asked them to cut out pictures and paste them on paper to make a collage that represented their feelings about Altoids. The researchers' psychological interpretation of the collages suggested that there were three emotional dimensions associated with the brand. One was the feeling of freshness, which was portrayed by open space and outdoor scenes such as waterfalls. A second association was British, which was illustrated with pictures of British royalty. The third dimension was sex appeal, represented by images identified with young male fantasies, such as "hot" women dressed in red.[27]

Depth Interview

depth interview
A relatively unstructured, extensive interview used in the primary stages of the research process.

Motivational researchers, interested in the "why" of organizational or consumer behavior, may use a relatively unstructured, extensive interview during primary stages of the research process. A **depth interview** is similar to a client interview conducted by a clinical psychologist or a psychiatrist. In the interviewing session the researcher asks many questions and probes for elaboration after the subject answers. In depth interviews, in contrast to projective techniques, the subject matter is generally undisguised. The interviewer's role is extremely important. He or she must be a highly skilled individual who can encourage respondents to talk freely without influencing the direction of the conversation. Probing questions, such as "Can you tell me more about that?" "Can you give me an example of that?" "Why do you say that?" are intended to stimulate respondents to elaborate on the topic being discussed. An excerpt from a depth interview is presented in Exhibit 7.4.

International business researchers find that in certain cultures, depth interviews work far better than focus groups. They provide a means to get a quick assessment of buyer behavior in foreign lands.

The depth interview may last more than an hour and it requires an extremely skilled interviewer; thus, it is expensive. In addition, because the topics for discussion are largely at the discretion of the interviewer, the success of the research is dependent on the interviewer's skill. And, as is so often the case, good people are hard to find. A third major problem stems from the necessity of getting both the surface reactions and the subconscious motivations of the respondent. Analysis and interpretation of such data are highly subjective, and it is difficult to determine the "true" interpretation. Finally, for most information, alternative techniques, such as focus groups, may be utilized as a substitute for the depth interview.

A WARNING

Exploratory research cannot take the place of quantitative, conclusive research. Nevertheless, firms often use what should be exploratory studies as final, conclusive research projects. This can lead to incorrect decisions. The most important thing to remember about exploratory research techniques is that they have limitations. Most of them provide qualitative information, and interpretation of the findings is typically judgmental. For example, the findings from projective techniques can be vague. They may produce some interesting, and

EXHIBIT 7.4 | **EXCERPTS FROM A DEPTH INTERVIEW[28]**

An interviewer (I) talks with Marsha (M) about furniture purchases. Marsha indirectly indicates that she delegates the buying responsibility to a trusted antique dealer. She has already said that she and her husband would write the dealer telling him the piece they wanted (e.g., bureau, table). The dealer would then locate a piece he considered appropriate and would ship it to Marsha from his shop in another state.

M. . . . We never actually shopped for furniture since we state what we want and (the antique dealer) picks it out and sends it to us. So we never have to go looking through stores and shops and things.

I. You depend on his [the antique dealer's] judgment?

M. Um, hum. And, uh, he happens to have the sort of taste that we like and he knows what our taste is and always finds something that we're happy with.

I. You'd rather do that than do the shopping?

M. Oh, much rather, because it saves so much time and it would be so confusing for me to go through stores and stores and stores looking for things, looking for furniture. This is so easy and I just am very fortunate.

I. Do you feel that he's a better judge than . . .

M. Much better.

I. Than you are?

M. Yes, and that way I feel confident that what I have is very, very nice because he picked it out and I would be doubtful if I picked it out. I have confidence in him, [the antique dealer] knows *everything* about antiques, I think. If he tells me something—why I know it's true—no matter what I think. I know he is the one that's right.

This excerpt is most revealing of the way in which Marsha could increase her feeling of confidence by relying on the judgment of another person, particularly a person she trusted. Marsha tells us quite plainly that she would be doubtful (i.e., uncertain) about her own judgment, but she "knows" (i.e., is certain) that the antique dealer is a good judge, "no matter what I think." The dealer once sent a chair that, on first inspection, did not appeal to Marsha. She decided, however, that she must be wrong, and the dealer right, and grew to like the chair very much.

occasionally bizarre, hypotheses about what was inside a person's mind, such as the following:

> A woman is very serious when she bakes a cake because unconsciously she is going through the symbolic act of giving birth.
>
> A man buys a convertible as a substitute "mistress."
>
> Men who wear suspenders are reacting to an unresolved castration complex.

Conclusions based on qualitative research may also be subject to considerable interpreter bias.[29]

An example of conflicting claims is illustrated by studies of prunes made by two organizations. One study, using projective techniques, showed that people considered prunes to be shriveled, tasteless, and unappealing in appearance. The research showed that prunes were symbolic of old age and of parental authority (thus, disliked) and associated with hospitals, peculiar people, and the Army. The other study stated that the principal reason people did not like prunes was because of their laxative property.

Findings from focus group interviews may be similarly ambiguous. How should a facial expression or nod of the head be interpreted? Have subjects fully grasped the idea or concept behind a nonexistent product? Have respondents overstated their interest because they tend to like all new products? Because of such problems in interpretation, exploratory findings should be considered preliminary. Another problem with exploratory studies involves the projectibility of the findings. Most exploratory techniques utilize small sample sizes, which may not be representative because they have not been selected on a probability basis. Case studies, for example, may have been selected because they represent extremely good or extremely bad examples of a situation rather than average situations.

Before a scientific decision can be made, a quantitative study with an adequate sample should be conducted to ensure that measurement is precise. This is not to say that exploratory research lacks value; it simply means that such research cannot deliver what it does not promise. The major benefit of exploratory research is that it generates insights and clarifies the business problems for hypothesis testing in future research. One cannot determine the most important attributes of a new program or policy until those attributes have been identified. Thus, exploratory research is extremely useful, but it should be used with caution.

There are some occasions when the research process should stop at the exploratory stage. If, for example, a personnel manager conducted exploratory research to get a better perspective on employees' reaction to eliminating a group dental health insurance plan, and if exploratory findings showed an extreme negative reaction by almost all participants in a focus group, then the personnel manager might decide not to continue the project. Some researchers suggest that the greatest danger of utilizing exploratory research to evaluate alternative programs, new product concepts, and the like is not that a poor idea will be accepted, because successive steps of research will prevent that. The real danger is that a good idea with promise may be rejected because of findings at the exploratory stage. In other situations, when everything looks positive in the exploratory stage, there is the temptation to accept the new idea without further research. What management should do after conducting exploratory research is determine whether the benefits of the additional information would be worth the cost of further research. In most cases when a major commitment of resources is at stake, it is well worth the effort to conduct the quantitative study. Many times good business research only documents the obvious. However, the purpose of a business is to make a profit, and decision makers want to be confident that they have made the correct choice.

SUMMARY

Qualitative research is subjective in nature. It leaves much of the measurement process to the discretion of the researcher. This approach does not use rigorous mathematical analysis. Quantitative research determines the quantity or extent of an outcome in numbers. It provides an exact approach to measurement.

This chapter focused on qualitative exploratory research. Exploratory research may be conducted to diagnose a situation, to screen alternatives, or to discover new ideas. It may take the form of gathering background information through investigating secondary data, conducting experience surveys, scrutinizing case studies, or utilizing a pilot study. The purpose of the research, rather than the technique, determines whether a study is exploratory, descriptive, or causal. Thus, the techniques discussed in this chapter are *primarily* but not exclusively used for exploratory studies. The case study method involves intensive investigation of one particular situation that is similar to the problem under investigation. Focus group interviews are unstructured, free-flowing, group sessions that allow individuals the opportunity to initiate and elaborate on the topics of discussion. There is a synergistic and spontaneous interaction among respondents that has been found to be highly advantageous. Projective techniques are an indirect means of questioning respondents. Some examples are the word association test, the sentence completion test, the third-person technique, role-playing, and the Thematic Apperception Test. Depth interviews are unstructured, extensive interviews that encourage a respondent to talk freely and in depth about an undisguised topic. Although exploratory research has many advantages, it also has several shortcomings and should not take the place of quantitative, conclusive research. Knowing where and how to use exploratory research is important. Many firms make the mistake of using an exploratory study as the final, conclusive research project. This can lead to decisions based on incorrect assumptions. Exploratory research techniques have limitations: The interpretation of the findings is based on judgment, samples are not representative, and these techniques rarely provide precise quantitative measurement. The ability to generalize results is limited.

Key Terms

exploratory research
concept testing
experience survey
secondary data analysis
case study method
pilot study
focus group interview
discussion guide
streaming media
online focus group
projective technique
word association test
sentence completion
third-person technique
role playing
thematic apperception test (TAT)
picture frustration
depth interview

Questions for Review and Critical Thinking

1. What type of exploratory research would you suggest in each of the following situations?
   (a) At an executive meeting a manager suggests the company look into implementing "quality teams" in the factory.
   (b) A bank loan officer wishes to forecast the economy of the state in which the bank operates.
   (c) A product manager suggests that a non-tobacco cigarette, blended from wheat, cocoa, and citrus, be developed.
   (d) A research project has the purpose of identifying the issues of concern to a labor union.
   (e) A manager must determine the best site for a convenience store in an urban area.
2. What benefits can be gained from case studies? What dangers, if any, are there in using them? In what situations are they useful?
3. What is the function of a focus group? What possible application might focus groups have in your particular field of business?
4. What are the advantages and disadvantages of focus groups?
5. A focus group moderator plans to administer a questionnaire before starting the group discussion about several new compensation concepts. Is this a good idea? Explain.
6. Current technology allows researchers to hold focus group sessions by telephone. What advantages and disadvantages do you think this exploratory research technique might have?
7. What are some potential uses of word association tests and sentence completion tests in your particular field of interest?
8. Most projective techniques attempt to discover a respondent's true feelings by asking indirect questions rather than direct questions that give the respondent a good idea about the exact reason the question is being asked. Does the use of this technique constitute deception?

Exploring the Internet

1. How might the following organizations use an Internet chat room for exploratory research?
   (a) A zoo
   (b) A computer software manufacturer
   (c) A video game manufacturer
2. Connect with a special-interest Internet bulletin board such as one for college students. Conduct an online focus group exploring the criteria students use to choose destinations for spring break.
3. The Looking Glass has a state-of-the-art focus group facility. Go to http://www.tlgonline.com to see a video presentation of the layout of the facility.
4. A filmmaker spent a year documenting his son's high school marching band. The film *The Band* provides a crash course in the life and times of the modern teenager. Transcripts of focus group reactions of separate parents and teenage groups can be found at http://www.pbs.org/pov/theband/focus/.
5. To learn about streaming media, go to http://www.realnetworks.com.

Case Suggestions

Case 4: Hamilton Power Tools Corporation (A)
Case 7: Today's Man
Video Case 6: Fisher-Price Rescue Heroes
Video Case 7: Upjohn's Rogaine
Video Case 8: Trading Cards Focus Group

CHAPTER

8

SECONDARY DATA

What you will learn in this chapter

- To explain the differences between secondary and primary data.
- To discuss the advantages and disadvantages of secondary data.
- To give examples of typical types of secondary data analysis conducted by business researchers.
- To understand the nature of model building with secondary data.
- To discuss and give examples of the various internal and proprietary sources of secondary data.
- To discuss the channels of distribution for external sources of secondary data.
- To discuss and give examples of the various external sources of secondary data.

California's 30-year-old ethnic makeover hit a national benchmark at the millennium: the first big state with no racial majority.[1] Census 2000 figures show that California's non-Hispanic white population shrank to 46.7 percent of the state's 33,871,648 residents, while Hispanic and Asian minorities grew at rapid rates. Blacks' share of the population changed little in the 1990s. Since 1970, the state's Hispanic population has more than quadrupled to 10.9 million from 2.4 million. Its share climbed from 12.1 percent of the population to 32.4 percent. Nearly one-third of all Hispanics in the United States live in California.

California also had the highest proportion of people in any large state who said they were of more than one race, 4.7 percent. That's nearly double the national average of 2.4 percent. The multiracial share in the next closest big states were 3.1 percent in New York, 2.5 percent in Texas, 2.4 percent in Florida, and 1.9 percent in Illinois.

The Census Bureau's data show a nation that is less white, more ethnic, more urban and suburban, and Sun Belt–oriented. Those trends are driven home dramatically in California, home of nearly one in eight Americans. They were evident in the 1980s, but they gained greater momentum in the 1990s.

Demographers say the state provides an early glimpse of the United States in the distant future, a time late in the century when some states will still have non-Hispanic white majorities, but most won't. Nationally, non-Hispanic whites will become known as the largest minority.

The Golden State's growing ethnicity and multiracial character make it a melting pot unlike any other place else in the United States, but most of the rest of the country is not moving in the same direction as quickly. Only two much smaller states, Hawaii and New Mexico, have no racial majorities. The Census Bureau projects that by 2010 the United States still will be more than two-thirds non-Hispanic white.

These facts about the population of California and that of the United States illustrate the richness and value of secondary data. They also illustrate that analysis and interpretation are important activities. This chapter discusses how to conduct research with secondary data in a digital age. It examines many of the diverse sources for secondary data. It also includes two appendixes: Appendix 8A, Selected Sources for Secondary Data, and Appendix 8B, Database Searching and Retrieving with Computers. ■

WHAT ARE SECONDARY DATA?

secondary data
Data that have been previously collected for some purpose other than the one at hand.

Secondary data are data gathered and recorded by someone else prior to (and for purposes other than) the current needs of the researcher. Secondary data are usually historical, already assembled, and do not require access to respondents or subjects. For example, there are considerable secondary data concerning financial markets in Standard & Poor's *Market Value Index,* and the Dow Jones Industrial Averages may be found weekly in *Barron's,* daily in the *Wall Street Journal,* and instantaneously on Yahoo. Standard & Poor's *Trade and Security Statistics* contains extensive historical data about financial markets. For instance, a researcher interested in corporate failures can find in this source more than 150 years of secondary data. Market potential is often estimated with secondary data. In many cases exact figures may be published by a trade association or found in another source. However, when the desired information is unavailable, the researcher may estimate market potential by converting different types of secondary data that are available from two or more sources. For example, one source reports a survey finding that 10 percent of all electrical contractors intend to buy a drill. Another source indicates there are 80,000 electrical contractors in the market area. To learn how many drills will be sold to electrical contractors, the researcher multiplies 10 percent times 80,000 to convert the data into an estimate (8,000 drills will be sold to electrical contractors).

ADVANTAGES OF SECONDARY DATA

"Nowhere in science do we start from scratch." The idea expressed in this quote explains the value of secondary data. Researchers are able to build on past research—a "body" of business knowledge. Business researchers use others' experience and data, when these are available, as secondary data. The primary advantage of secondary data is that obtaining secondary data is almost always less expensive than acquiring primary data. In addition, secondary data can usually be obtained rapidly.

TO THE POINT

If I have seen farther than others, it is because I have stood on the shoulders of giants.

ISAAC NEWTON

Consider the money and time saved by researchers who obtained updated population estimates for a town during the interim between the 2000 and 2010 censuses. Instead of doing the fieldwork themselves, researchers could acquire estimates from a firm dealing in demographic information or from sources such as Claritas or PCensus. Many of the activities normally associated with primary data collection (for example, sampling and data processing) are eliminated by using secondary data.

In some instances data cannot be obtained using primary data collection procedures. For example, a manufacturer of farm implements could not duplicate the information in the *Census of Agriculture* because much of the information there (for example, amount of taxes paid) might not be accessible to a private firm.

DISADVANTAGES OF SECONDARY DATA

An inherent disadvantage of secondary data is that they were not designed specifically to meet the researcher's needs. Thus, researchers must ask, "How pertinent are these secondary data?" More specifically, to evaluate secondary data, researchers should ask questions such as these: "Is the subject matter consistent with our problem definition?" "Do the data apply to the population of interest?" "Is the time period consistent with our needs?" "Do the secondary data appear in the correct units of measurement?" "Do they cover the subject of interest in adequate detail?" Consider the following typical situations.

- A researcher interested in forklift trucks finds that the secondary data on the subject are in a broader, less pertinent category, encompassing all industrial trucks and tractors. Furthermore, these data were collected 5 years earlier.
- An investigator wishing to study those who make more than $100,000 per year finds the top category in a secondary study reported at $75,000 or more a year.
- An investor wishing to compare dividends of several industrial robot manufacturers finds that the units of measure differ because of stock splits.
- Every business day the Dow Jones Industrial Average, a stock market indicator series, is reported by the local media. This secondary data source reflects the prices of 30 nonrandomly selected "blue chip" stocks. This readily available and inexpensive source of information may not suit the needs of the individual concerned with the "typical company listed on the New York Stock Exchange."

Each of these situations shows that even when secondary data are available, they may be inadequate. The most common problems are (1) outdated information, (2) variation in definition of terms, (3) different units of measurement, and (4) lack of information to verify the data's accuracy.

Secondary data quickly become outdated in our rapidly changing environment. Since the purpose of most studies is to predict the future, helpful secondary data must be timely. Each primary researcher has the right to define the terms or concepts under investigation. This is little solace to the investigator of black American labor who finds secondary civilian labor force data reported as "12.5 percent nonwhite." Variances in terms or classifications should be scrutinized to determine if differences are important. Units of measurement may cause problems if they are not identical to the researcher's needs. For example, lumber shipments in millions of board feet are quite different from shipments in billions of ton-miles of lumber transported on freight cars. Head-of-household income is not the same unit of measure as total family income. Often the objective of the original, primary study may dictate that the data be summarized, rounded, or reported in such a way that even though the original units of measurement were comparable, these aggregated or adjusted units of measurement are not suitable for the later study.

data conversion
The process of changing the original form of the data to a format suitable to achieve the research objective.

When secondary data are reported in a format that does not exactly meet the researcher's needs, data conversion may be necessary. **Data conversion** (or data transformation) is the process of changing the original form of the data to a format suitable to achieve the research objective. For example, sales for food products may be reported in pounds, cases, or dollars. An estimate of dollars per pound or pounds per case may be used to convert the data reported as dollar volume to pounds or to another suitable format.

Another disadvantage of secondary data is that the user has no control over their accuracy. Even though secondary data may be timely and pertinent to the researcher's requirements, they may be inaccurate. Research conducted by other people may be biased to support the vested interest of the source. For example, media often publish data from surveys to identify the characteristics of their subscribers or viewers, but they will most likely exclude unfavorable data from their reports. If the possibility of bias exists, the secondary data should not be used. Investigators are naturally more prone to accept data from sources such as the U.S. government because of the integrity of the source. Nevertheless, the researcher must assess the reputation of the organization gathering the data and critically assess research design to determine if the research was correctly implemented. Unfortunately, such evaluation may not be possible if the information explaining how the original research was conducted is not available.

cross-check
Comparison of data from one organization with data from another source.

Researchers should verify the accuracy of the data whenever possible. **Cross-checks** of data from multiple sources—that is, comparison of the data from one source with data from another—should be made to determine the similarity of independent projects. When the data are not consistent, researchers should attempt to identify reasons for the differences or to determine which data are most likely to be correct. If the accuracy of the data cannot be established, the researcher must determine if using the data is worth the risk. Exhibit 8.1 presents a series of questions that should be asked to evaluate secondary data.

TYPICAL OBJECTIVES FOR SECONDARY DATA RESEARCH DESIGNS

It would be impossible to identify all possible purposes of business research using secondary data. However, it is useful to illustrate some common business problems that can be addressed with secondary data research. Two general categories of research objectives include fact finding and model building.

Fact Finding

fact finding
A secondary data research objective aimed at collecting descriptive information to support decision making.

The simplest form of secondary data research is **fact finding.** For example, an international business might be interested in knowing what percentage of exports from Canada come from the United States, Japan, and the European Union. Secondary data published by Statistics Canada show that Canada had $422,558 million in exports in 2000: $359,551 million went to the United States, $10,313 million went to Japan, and $22,109 million went to countries in the European Union. These facts would interest a researcher investigating Canadian–American trade relations. Likewise, knowing that the province of Ontario has a higher estimated value of manufactured goods than any other province in Canada is an important fact for organizations that wish to do business in Canada.[2] Of course, fact finding for business research can be much more complex than merely locating a single statistic. A typical research objective might be to uncover all available information about family leave practices in large corporations or to identify labor trends that affect an industry.

Managers watch for trends in the business environment. For example, an investigation of secondary data shows that in 1990, the average major league baseball salary was $578,930.[3] The figure rose to $1,071,029 in 1995, and in 2001 the average player's salary was $2,264,403. Other secondary data show that cola's share of the soft drink market in 1995 was 62.4 percent. It steadily declined each year and was down to 58 percent in 2000.[4]

Almost every corporation routinely investigates brand and product category sales volume using secondary data. This type of analysis typically involves comparisons with competitors' sales or with the company's own sales in other time periods. It also involves making industry comparisons among geographic areas.

Exhibit 8.1 EVALUATING SECONDARY DATA[5]

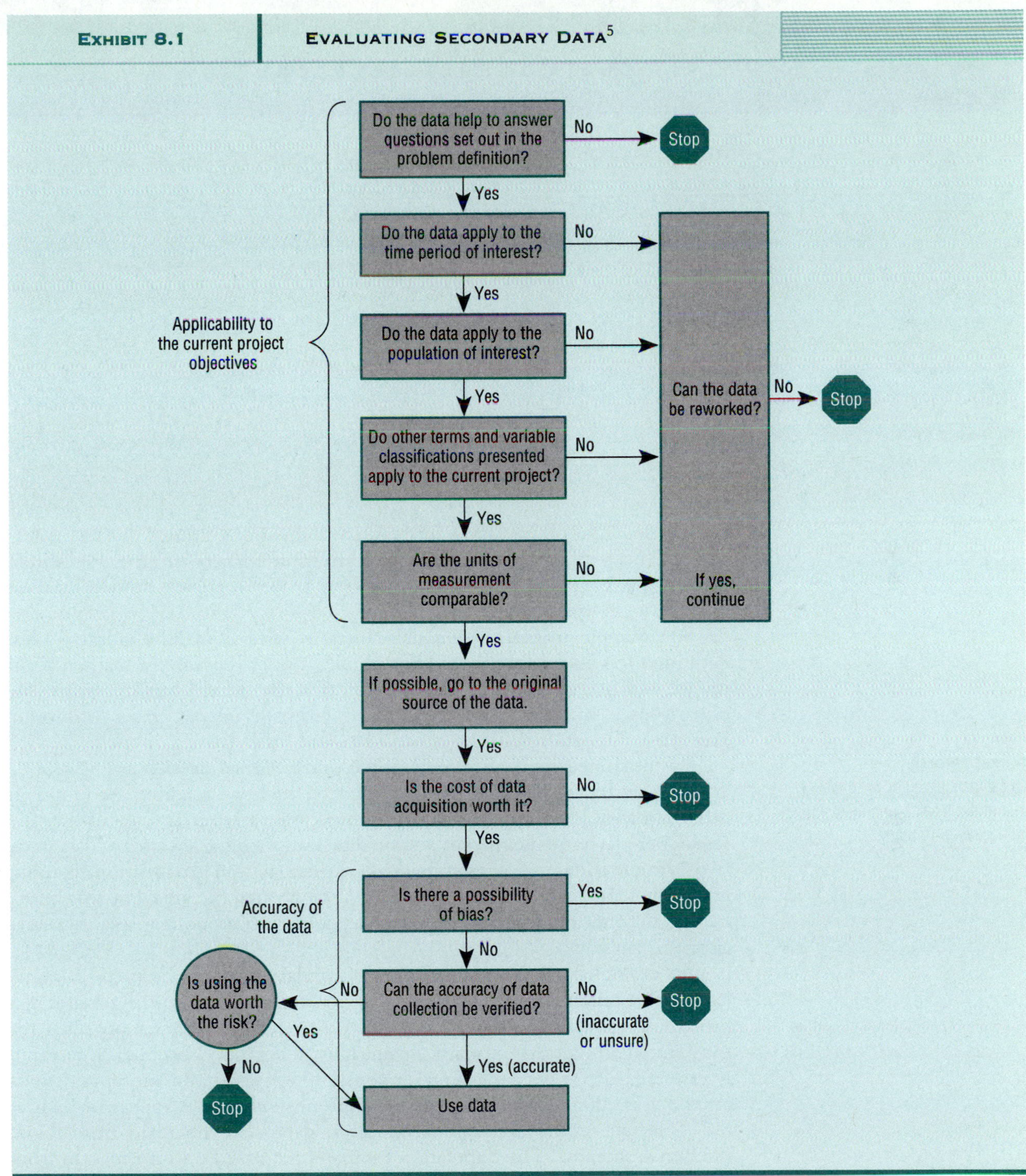

model building
An attempt to specify relationships between variables based on secondary data, sometimes using descriptive or predictive equations.

Model Building

As a general objective for secondary research, **model building** is more complicated than simple fact finding. Model building involves specifying relationships between two or more variables. Although model building can involve

Research Insight

California School Enrollment

In the early 1980s, California used a standard demographic projection method, based on birth and death rates, to predict a decline in the number of children statewide.[6] Forecasts made in 1980 showed that "the California population had fairly stabilized." Schools closed around the state.

Eighteen years later, opening of new classrooms somewhere in California became a regular occurrence. Planners in the state's education department did not foresee the huge wave of immigration from Asia and Latin America that began in the mid-1980s. They did not consider that the immigrants included many young women from countries with high fertility rates, or that baby-boom women would delay childbearing until later in life. Forecasters drew a straight line and predicted that everything would stem from the way things were in the past and the present. It was the equivalent of saying if General Motors is now the largest corporation, it will always remain the largest corporation.

the development of descriptive or predictive equations, it need not be a complicated mathematical process. In fact, decision makers often favor simple models that everyone can readily understand over complex models that are difficult to comprehend.

For example, market share equals company sales divided by industry sales. Although this calculation may seem simple, it does represent a mathematical model. Much economic and financial research uses model building with secondary data. Business researchers often estimate interest rates, economic growth, and inflation with secondary data and mathematical models.

market potential
An estimate based on secondary data of likely sales volume of a given product within a market.

Business researchers also frequently estimate **market potential** using secondary data. Exact figures may be published by trade associations or found in other sources. However, when the desired information is unavailable, the researcher may estimate market potential by transforming secondary data from two or more sources. For example, a manager may find secondary data about market potential for a country or other large geographic area, but this information may not be broken down by state, county, metropolitan area, sales territory, or zip code.

An example will help explain how secondary data can be used to calculate market potential. A manufacturer of crackers is contemplating building a processing plant in Europe. Managers wish to estimate market potential for the United Kingdom, Germany, Spain, Italy, and France. Secondary research uncovered data for per capita cracker consumption and population projections for the year 2005. The data for the five European countries appear in Exhibit 8.2. (The per capita cracker consumption data were obtained from A. C. Nielsen Company.[7] The population estimates are based on information from the CIA *Factbook* database.)

To calculate market potential for Italy in the year 2005, multiply population by per capita cracker consumption.

$$56{,}264 \times 4.33 = 243{,}623$$

In Italy the market potential for crackers is $243,623 thousand, or $243,623,000. Although Germany's population is much higher, it has a much

EXHIBIT 8.2 MARKET POTENTIAL FOR CRACKERS IN EUROPE

Country	(1) Population Projection for 2005 (thousands)	(2) Annual per Capita Cracker Consumption (U.S. $)	(3) Market Potential Estimate (thousands of dollars)
United Kingdom	58,408	9.48	553,708
Germany	82,399	1.91	157,382
Italy	56,264	4.33	243,623
France	59,612	3.56	212,219
Spain	39,225	.62	24,320

lower market potential. The calculated market potentials in Exhibit 8.2 are based on this simple model. The cracker manufacturer might recognize that each country's inflation rate or other variables would influence dollar sales volume. Past inflation rates, also found in secondary data sources, could be included in the calculation to improve the estimate.

Model building and statistical trend analysis using secondary data can be much more advanced than this simple example. Many statistical techniques allow researchers to build complex forecasting models using secondary data. At this point in the text, our objective is to emphasize secondary data rather than statistical analysis. Chapter 23, Bivariate Analysis: Measures of Association, and Chapter 24, Multivariate Analysis, explain more sophisticated statistical model building techniques for forecasting sales. These model building tools often are used for data mining.

DATA MINING

Large corporations' decision support systems often contain millions or even hundreds of millions of records of data. These data volumes are too large and complex to be understood by managers. Consider, for example, a credit card company collecting data on customer purchases. Each customer might make on average ten transactions in a month, or 120 per year. With 3 million customers and 5 years of data, it's easy to see how record counts quickly grow beyond the comfort zone for most humans.[8]

Two points about data volume are important to keep in mind. First, relevant commercial data are often in independent and unrelated files. Second, the number of distinct pieces of information each data record contains is often large. When the number of distinct pieces of information contained in each data record and data volume grow too big, end users don't have the capacity to make sense of it all. Data mining helps clarify the underlying meaning of the data.

data mining
The use of powerful computers to dig through and analyze volumes of data to discover patterns about an organization's customers, products, and activities.

The term **data mining** refers to the use of powerful computers to dig through volumes of data to discover patterns about an organization's customers, products, and activities. It is a broad term that applies to many different forms of analysis. For example, *neural networks* are a form of artificial intelligence in which a computer is programmed to mimic the way in which

The copy for this advertisement for IBM's data mining software says "To our data mining system, they're twins. Because both order milk with their hamburgers."

human brains process information. One computer expert put it this way: "A neural network learns pretty much the way a human being does. Suppose you say 'big' and show a child an elephant, and then you say 'small' and show her a poodle. You repeat this process with a house and a giraffe as examples of 'big' and then a grain of sand and an ant as examples of 'small.' Pretty soon she will figure it out and tell you that a truck is 'big' and a needle is 'small.' Neural networks can similarly generalize by looking at examples."[9]

Wal-Mart uses data mining. Wal-Mart's information system houses more than 7 terabytes of data on point of sale, inventory, products in transit, market statistics, customer demographics, finance, product returns, and supplier performance. The data are mined to develop "personality traits" for each of Wal-Mart's 3,000-plus outlets, which Wal-Mart managers use to determine product mix and presentation for each store. Wal-Mart's data-mining software looks at individual items for individual stores to decide the seasonal sales profile of each item. The data-mining system keeps a year's worth of data on the sales of 100,000 products and predicts which items will be needed in each store.[10]

Market basket analysis is a form of data mining that analyzes anonymous point-of-sale transaction logs to identify coinciding purchases or relationships between products purchased and other retail shopping information.[11] Consider this example about patterns in customer purchases: Osco Drugs mined the databases provided by their checkout scanners and found that when men go to a supermarket to buy diapers in the evening between 6:00 PM and 8:00 PM, they sometimes walk out with a six-pack of beer as well. Knowing this behavioral pattern, it's possible for store managers to lay out their stores so that these items are closer together.[12]

The example of a credit card company with large volumes of data illustrates a data-mining application known as *customer discovery.* The credit card company will probably track information about each customer: age, gender, number of children, job status, income level, past credit history, etc. Very often the data about these factors will be mined to find the patterns that make a particular individual a good or bad credit risk.[13]

When a company knows the identity of the customer who makes repeated purchases from the same organization, an analysis can be made of sequences of purchases. *Sequence discovery,* the use of data mining to detect sequence patterns, is a popular application among direct marketers, such as catalog retailers. A catalog merchant has information for each customer, which reveals sets of products that the customer buys in every purchase order. A sequence discovery function can then be used to discover the set of purchases that frequently precede the purchase of, say, a microwave oven. As another example, sequence discovery used on a set of insurance claims could lead to the identification of frequently occurring medical procedures performed on patients, which in turn could be used to detect cases of medical fraud.

Data mining requires sophisticated computer resources, and it is expensive. That's why companies like DataMind, IBM, Oracle, Information Builders, and Acxiom Corporation offer data-mining services. The customer sends the databases to be analyzed and lets the data-mining company do the "numbers crunching" work.

Now that some of the purposes of secondary data analysis have been addressed, it is appropriate to discuss sources of secondary data.

CLASSIFICATION OF SECONDARY DATA

Chapter 4 classified secondary data as either internal to the organization or external. In the information age this is somewhat simplistic. Some accounting documents are certainly internal records of the organization. Researchers in another organization cannot have access to them. Clearly, a book published by the federal government and located at a public library is external to the company. However, in today's world of electronic data interchange, the data that appear in a book published by the federal government may also be purchased from an online information vendor, accessed instantaneously, and subsequently stored in a company's decision support system, making them internally available.

An organization's internal data can be defined as data that *originated* in the organization. In other words, internal data are data created, recorded, or generated by the organization. Perhaps *internal and proprietary data* is a better term.

Internal and Proprietary Data

Most organizations routinely gather, record, and store internal data to help managers solve future problems. The accounting systems of most firms provide valuable information. Information recorded from routine source documents, such as sales invoices, for external financial reporting can support extensive further analysis. If the data are properly coded into a modular database in the accounting system, a researcher may be able to conduct more detailed analysis using the decision support system.

Sales volumes by product and region can be identified; sales information can be broken down for accounts; information related to orders received, back orders, and unfilled orders can be identified; and sales can be forecast on the basis of past data. Aggregating or disaggregating internal data is a common form of organizational research. Other useful sources of internal data may be files of salespersons' call reports, employee complaints, personnel records—and any other forms or records that a company may keep.

In large organizations consisting of many divisions, it is not unusual for one division to conduct research that proves useful to another division. One department usually does not know what another department is doing or has done, so, to avoid duplicate efforts, researchers should exhaust all sources within the company before searching elsewhere. Too often, secondary data analysis of internal data is ignored because research practitioners are inclined to design a new study every time management is in a quandary.

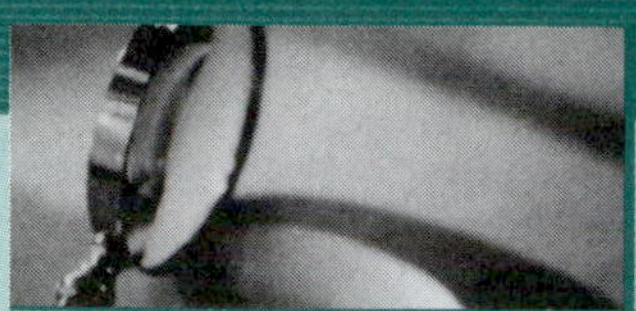

RESEARCH INSIGHT

MARRIOTT VACATION CLUB INTERNATIONAL

Marriott Vacation Club International, the nation's largest seller of vacation time-share condos, has slashed the amount of junk mail it has to send out to get a response.[14] How? With a computer, a database, and some help from Acxiom Corporation, which specializes in processing secondary data.

What Marriott is doing is called data mining. This is the science of combing through digitized customer files to detect patterns. Marriott starts with names, mostly of hotel guests. Digging into a trove of motor vehicle records, property records, warranty cards, and lists of people who have bought by mail, Acxiom enriches the prospect list. It adds such facts as the customers' ages, their children's ages, their estimated income, what cars they drive, and if they golf. Then Marriott uses a complex computer program (a neural network) to figure out who is most likely to respond to a mailed flier.

Using these clues, Marriott is able to cast its net a little more narrowly and catch more fish. Data mining has increased the response rate to Marriott's direct-mail time-share pitches to certain hotel guests from 0.75 percent to 1 percent. . . . That seems like a slim gain, but it makes a big difference to a company that can send out 3 million glossy solicitations at a cost of up to $1.50 each in a year.

Common External Sources of Secondary Data

External data are generated or recorded by an entity other than the researcher's organization. Classifying external sources of secondary data by the nature of the producer of the information yields five basic sources: publishers of books and periodicals, government sources, trade association sources, media sources, and commercial sources. The following sections discuss each external data source.

Books and Periodicals

Books and periodicals found in a library are considered by some researchers to be the quintessential secondary data source. A researcher who finds books on a topic of interest is off to a good start. Professional journals, such as the *Journal of Business Research, Journal of Finance, Journal of Finance and Quantitative Analysis, Financial Analysts Journal, Accounting Review, Journal of Accounting Research, Journal of Marketing Research, Journal of Marketing, Journal of the Academy of Management, Organizational Behavior and Human Performance,* and *Public Opinion Quarterly,* as well as commercial business periodicals such as the *Wall Street Journal, Fortune,* and *Business Week,* contain much useful material. Exhibit 8.3 shows a page from the Complete Economic and Demographic Data Source (CEDDS) by Woods & Poole Economics, which contains forecasts and historical data for all counties and metropolitan statistical areas (MSAs) in the United States. This source can help researchers forecast trends in demographics, labor, and retail activity. To locate data in periodicals, indexing services such as the *Business Periodicals Index* and the *Wall Street Journal Index* are very useful. Several guides to data sources are also helpful—for example, the *American Statistical Index* and *Business Information Source.*

The man who does not read good books has no advantage over the man who cannot read them.

MARK TWAIN

EXHIBIT 8.3 | **SAMPLE MSA DATA FROM CEDDS BY WOODS & POOLE ECONOMICS**[15]

SAMPLE COUNTY DATA TABLE

2001 CEDDS 707

Data Table for every County, State, & MSA in the U.S.

ALAMEDA COUNTY, CALIFORNIA

Historical Data From 1970

Projected Data to 2025

		1970	1980	1990	1998	2000	2001	2002	2005	2010	2015	2020	2025
1	TOTAL POPULATION (in THOUSANDS)	1,073.96	1,108.79	1,305.81	1,397.05	1,427.24	1,439.14	1,451.14	1,486.52	1,544.61	1,604.15	1,665.08	1,727.28
2	UNDER 5 YEARS	[illegible]	73.27	104.29	97.76	94.24	93.96	94.08	95.22	98.30	101.82	104.15	106.10
3	5 to 9 YEARS	[illegible]	70.49	90.99	104.30	101.71	98.71	95.71	90.63	91.76	[illegible]	98.80	101.39
4	10 to 14 YEARS	98.04	79.26	80.47	90.69	95.46	98.78	101.51	101.23	90.46	92.10	95.93	100.21
5	15 to 19 YEARS	94.23	95.65	84.10	92.26	95.05	95.04	94.48	101.51	108.16	96.50	98.39	[illegible]
6	20 to 24 YEARS	112.04	110.83	107.73	94.24	101.28	104.91	108.36	110.97	117.97	124.76	[illegible]	[illegible]
7	25 to 29 YEARS	86.26	110.08	125.30	107.40	103.25	101.42	101.71	107.80	117.06	123.53	[illegible]	[illegible]
8	30 to 34 YEARS	65.83	104.72	128.84	120.88	117.21	116.29	114.98	109.36	113.62	122.55	129.06	[illegible]
9	35 to 39 YEARS	58.06	77.64	116.74	132.11	131.60	129.19	126.17	119.37	111.42	115.68	124.72	[illegible]
10	40 to 44 YEARS	62.13	59.61	104.27	126.70	132.42	134.17	135.15	134.22	121.73	113.64	118.22	127.40
11	45 to 49 YEARS	66.47	53.15	75.13	101.64	108.55	111.66	114.97	121.95	123.89	113.16	106.36	111.21
12	50 to 54 YEARS	58.79	55.94	56.97	77.83	86.46	91.11	91.93	99.89	112.58	115.14	106.42	100.91
13	55 to 59 YEARS	50.65	56.99	47.92	56.71	61.44	62.83	68.18	78.56	91.31	103.41	106.56	99.43
14	60 to 64 YEARS	41.56	46.52	46.52	45.73	48.12	49.35	50.89	57.20	73.15	85.62	97.51	101.29
15	65 to 69 YEARS	32.47	39.01	45.03	41.66	41.50	41.69	42.27	45.73	54.10	69.08	80.94	92.24
16	70 to 74 YEARS	26.80	28.95	34.70	37.50	36.80	36.77	36.56	36.05	39.71	46.98	60.05	70.40
17	75 to 79 YEARS	19.05	21.08	26.59	31.74	32.46	32.32	32.03	31.67	31.28	34.69	41.22	52.89
18	80 to 84 YEARS	12.82	13.72	16.47	19.94	20.70	21.44	22.19	23.52	23.18	23.08	25.86	30.08
19	85 YEARS and OVER	8.61	11.88	13.76	17.96	19.00	19.51	19.99	21.65	24.92	27.36	28.77	31.00
20	WHITE POPULATION	857.40	802.02	843.25	850.27	858.43	858.52	858.66	858.56	858.82	861.60	867.21	873.97
21	BLACK POPULATION	162.19	205.77	247.93	265.41	271.74	274.74	277.77	286.70	300.19	313.09	325.34	336.07
22	OTHER POPULATION	54.37	101.00	214.63	281.37	297.08	305.87	314.72	341.25	385.59	429.46	472.54	517.25
23	HISPANIC POPULATION, ANY RACE	135.02	126.50	192.53	254.56	268.29	272.94	277.40	290.01	307.93	326.54	348.32	373.87
24	POPULATION 0 to 19 YEARS (in THOUSANDS)	373.42	318.66	359.85	385.01	386.46	386.49	385.77	388.59	388.68	385.47	397.26	410.39
25	POPULATION AGE 20 to 64 YEARS	601.80	675.48	809.42	863.23	890.33	900.92	912.33	939.32	982.73	1,017.50	1,030.97	1,039.39
26	POPULATION AGE 65 YEARS and OVER	98.75	114.65	136.54	148.81	150.46	151.73	153.04	158.61	173.20	201.19	236.84	277.50
27	MALE POPULATION (in THOUSANDS)	526.16	539.18	645.97	688.52	704.52	710.62	716.68	734.64	764.47	794.54	824.68	856.03
28	FEMALE POPULATION	547.80	569.61	659.85	708.53	722.73	728.52	734.46	751.88	780.14	809.61	840.39	871.25
29	POPULATION AGE 16 YEARS and OVER	776.05	868.38	1,014.75	1,086.91	1,118.35	1,130.02	1,141.85	1,178.90	1,245.22	1,297.25	1,347.75	1,400.16
30	MEDIAN AGE OF POPULATION (in YEARS)	27.81	30.07	32.30	34.66	35.21	35.43	35.62	36.11	36.62	36.90	37.63	38.20
31	TOTAL EMPLOYMENT (in THOUSANDS of JOBS)	499.79	600.78	759.65	842.93	887.27	904.66	919.85	956.77	1,010.22	1,061.16	1,112.18	1,163.72
32	FARM EMPLOYMENT	3.76	2.14	1.46	1.49	1.47	1.45	1.43	1.37	1.29	1.23	1.17	1.13
33	AGRICULTURAL SERVICES, OTHER	1.85	3.92	5.11e	7.83	8.27	8.39	8.45	8.70	9.21	9.77	10.34	10.91
34	MINING	1.24	0.96	0.84e	0.71	0.70	0.70	0.70	0.69	0.69	0.69	0.71	0.73
35	CONSTRUCTION	21.87	29.17	38.37	44.32	47.58	48.49	49.17	50.61	52.53	54.37	56.24	58.16
36	MANUFACTURING	85.90	87.23	85.23	103.17	103.06	103.04	103.02	103.04	103.28	103.58	103.91	104.31
37	TRANSPORTATION, COMM. & PUBLIC UTILITIES	33.16	34.21	44.58	48.40	50.60	51.50	52.18	53.84	56.26	58.48	60.52	62.34
38	WHOLESALE TRADE	24.39	31.18	43.58	56.45	59.50	61.08	62.48	66.25	72.62	79.35	86.47	93.94
39	RETAIL TRADE	73.02	97.43	122.30	126.01	131.09	133.07	134.78	139.06	144.98	149.98	154.38	158.34
40	FINANCE, INSURANCE & REAL ESTATE	34.44	45.69	50.80	51.78	54.57	55.34	55.90	57.26	59.48	61.48	63.25	64.81
41	SERVICES	92.44	144.43	222.81	282.05	307.20	317.60	327.01	349.65	381.06	410.89	441.31	472.61
42	FEDERAL CIVILIAN GOVERNMENT	27.85	21.76	23.12	12.75	12.28	12.03	11.80	11.14	10.20	9.41	8.74	8.19
43	FEDERAL MILITARY GOVERNMENT	24.91	12.12	19.13	4.49	4.49	4.49	4.49	4.48	4.48	4.48	4.47	4.47
44	STATE AND LOCAL GOVERNMENT	74.94	90.52	102.32	103.47	106.37	107.48	108.42	110.66	114.13	117.46	120.66	123.77
45	TOTAL EARNINGS (in MILLIONS of 1996 $)	$15,448.50	$19,117.10	$25,900.20	$32,735.64	$35,021.29	$36,009.39	$36,928.05	$39,418.45	$43,432.10	$47,537.36	$51,822.47	$56,297.59
46	FARM EARNINGS	77.77	57.10	28.48	11.65	18.35	18.55	18.73	19.20	20.08	21.07	22.19	23.48
47	AGRICULTURAL SERVICES, OTHER	39.94	60.68	106.24e	147.54	157.90	161.71	164.39	173.68	191.83	211.65	232.65	254.67
48	MINING	64.82	98.74	34.26e	40.70	33.02	32.89	32.78	32.55	32.47	32.81	33.61	34.95
49	CONSTRUCTION	990.14	1,315.22	1,840.09	2,111.41	2,293.94	2,351.49	2,398.57	2,510.36	2,673.10	2,830.73	2,987.83	3,144.21
50	MANUFACTURING	3,235.67	3,723.85	3,655.89	5,348.06	5,455.52	5,510.41	5,564.92	5,729.19	6,005.53	6,272.69	6,526.73	6,768.17
51	TRANSPORTATION, COMM. & PUBLIC UTILITIES	1,243.30	1,545.79	2,024.48	2,246.25	2,386.54	2,448.74	2,500.94	2,641.39	2,861.57	3,074.92	3,280.18	3,474.06
52	WHOLESALE TRADE	907.67	1,230.10	1,776.31	2,743.89	2,913.71	3,000.49	3,084.21	3,314.28	3,710.22	4,132.07	4,579.97	5,051.99
53	RETAIL TRADE	1,741.83	2,161.77	2,646.60	2,840.37	2,984.90	3,045.37	3,100.08	3,246.53	3,465.77	3,666.16	3,853.60	4,030.66
54	FINANCE, INSURANCE & REAL ESTATE	655.18	931.41	1,233.28	1,769.45	1,933.75	1,994.45	2,048.60	2,201.66	2,460.91	2,717.59	2,967.24	3,205.81
55	SERVICES	2,191.86	3,494.14	6,636.39	9,723.54	10,883.18	11,406.32	11,904.22	13,247.46	15,386.08	17,621.93	20,043.33	22,666.89
56	FEDERAL CIVILIAN GOVERNMENT	1,090.37	1,048.09	1,139.38	794.61	778.36	768.42	758.82	732.35	695.01	664.06	638.74	618.87
57	FEDERAL MILITARY GOVERNMENT	595.28	337.69	661.93	127.49	●146.47	147.47	148.47	151.49	156.59	161.75	166.97	172.24
58	STATE AND LOCAL GOVERNMENT	2,614.66	3,112.51	4,116.86	4,830.77	5,035.65	5,123.08	5,203.32	5,418.30	5,772.94	6,129.94	6,489.42	6,851.59
59	PERSONAL INCOME (in MILLIONS of 1996 $)	$18,741.29	$24,418.45	$34,970.14	$43,566.29	$46,355.67	$47,570.48	$48,719.76	$51,928.46	$57,229.40	$62,729.00	$68,517.64	$74,611.48
60	WAGES AND SALARIES	13,077.82	15,303.26	20,398.54	26,062.80	27,631.19	28,436.96	29,178.15	31,197.74	34,468.47	37,828.67	41,349.55	45,040.27
61	OTHER LABOR INCOME	1,047.29	2,182.67	3,035.18	3,093.69	3,620.15	3,714.17	3,799.17	4,024.60	4,379.18	4,734.07	5,097.81	[illegible]
62	PROPRIETORS INCOME	1,323.39	1,631.17	2,406.48	3,579.15	3,769.94	3,858.26	3,950.74	4,196.10	4,584.45	4,974.62	5,375.11	[illegible]
63	DIVIDENDS, INTEREST & RENT	2,660.73	4,194.89	6,448.98	7,478.58	7,847.51	8,013.40	8,181.33	8,697.02	9,595.50	10,540.22	11,527.58	[illegible]
64	TRANSFER PAYMENTS TO PERSONS	1,818.64	2,784.38	3,779.99	4,622.36	4,863.17	4,976.95	5,094.06	5,466.64	6,165.65	6,977.42	7,922.71	[illegible]
65	LESS SOCIAL INSURANCE CONTRIBUTIONS	496.71	782.17	1,416.17	1,836.57	1,971.93	2,039.80	2,107.72	2,313.85	2,681.97	3,103.55	3,595.44	[illegible]
66	RESIDENCE ADJUSTMENT	(689.87)	(895.76)	257.15	566.29	595.63	610.53	624.04	660.20	718.13	777.56	840.32	[illegible]
67	INCOME PER CAPITA (in 1996 $)	$17,451	$22,023	$26,780	$31,184	$32,479	$33,055	$33,573	$34,933	$37,051	$39,104	$41,150	[illegible]
68	INCOME PER CAPITA (in CURRENT $)	$4,887	$12,159	$22,932	$32,130	$34,806	$36,241	$37,697	$42,383	$52,174	$64,754	$80,152	$98,967
69	WOODS & POOLE WEALTH INDEX (U.S. = 100)	114.96	116.54	114.08	116.23	116.87	117.22	117.48	117.83	117.68	117.22	116.66	116.03
70	NUMBER OF HOUSEHOLDS (in THOUSANDS)	366.81	428.82	481.16	519.45	532.11	537.92	543.76	560.94	587.77	612.35	633.26	651.24
71	PERSONS PER HOUSEHOLD (in PEOPLE)	2.82	2.52	2.64	2.63	2.62	2.61	2.61	2.59	2.56	2.56	2.56	2.58
72	RETAIL SALES PER HOUSEHOLD (in 1996 $)	$20,447	$21,272	$22,893	$25,634	$27,535	$27,785	$27,996	$28,549	$29,535	$30,615	$31,860	$33,231
73	MEAN HOUSEHOLD INCOME (in 1996 $)	$49,538	$55,784	$71,145	$82,315	$85,495	$86,778	$87,912	$90,806	$95,477	$100,439	$106,053	$112,206
74	MEAN HOUSEHOLD INCOME (in CURRENT $)	$13,872	$30,799	$60,921	$84,811	$91,619	$95,142	$98,710	$110,172	$134,446	$166,321	$206,571	$257,078
75	HOUSEHOLDS with MONEY INCOME (in THOUSANDS)	366.81	428.82	481.16	519.45	532.11	537.92	543.76	560.94	587.77	612.35	633.26	651.24
76	LESS than $10,000 (in 1990 $)	n.a.	n.a.	56.17	50.61	48.98	48.02	47.29	44.81	40.20	36.15	32.34	28.07
77	$10,000 to 19,999	n.a.	n.a.	64.01	57.68	55.82	54.72	53.89	51.06	45.81	41.19	36.85	31.99
78	$20,000 to $29,999	n.a.	n.a.	68.84	62.03	60.03	58.85	57.96	54.92	49.27	44.30	39.63	34.40
79	$30,000 to $39,999	n.a.	n.a.	64.82	58.84	56.94	55.82	54.98	52.09	46.73	42.02	37.59	32.63
80	$40,000 to $49,999	n.a.	n.a.	56.84	68.63	69.59	69.30	68.81	65.40	58.67	52.75	47.19	40.97
81	$50,000 to $59,999	n.a.	n.a.	46.35	60.27	65.46	68.31	70.92	78.84	84.10	77.05	69.74	60.54
82	$60,000 to $74,999	n.a.	n.a.	49.55	64.43	69.98	73.02	75.81	85.36	104.99	126.41	139.90	140.73
83	$75,000 to $99,999	n.a.	n.a.	42.25	54.94	59.67	62.27	64.65	72.78	89.52	108.56	130.33	159.73
84	$100,000 to $124,999	n.a.	n.a.	16.54	21.51	23.36	24.38	25.31	28.49	35.05	42.50	51.03	62.54
85	$125,000 to $149,999	n.a.	n.a.	6.45	8.38	9.11	9.50	9.87	11.11	13.66	16.57	19.89	24.37
86	$150,000 or MORE	n.a.	n.a.	9.33	12.13	13.17	13.74	14.27	16.07	19.76	23.97	28.77	35.26
87	TOTAL RETAIL SALES (in MILLIONS of 1996 $)	$7,500.12	$9,121.71	$11,015.10	$13,315.91	$14,651.51	$14,946.26	$15,223.34	$16,013.90	$17,359.63	$18,747.23	$20,175.54	$21,641.17
88	BUILDING MATERIALS, HARDWARE	227.07	361.43	505.64	706.96	777.20	784.26	793.47	827.53	893.76	972.49	1,055.95	1,139.81
89	GENERAL MERCHANDISE	[illegible]	[illegible]	[illegible]	1,344.63	1,491.05	1,540.49	1,582.56	1,691.70	1,851.61	1,982.01	2,097.55	[illegible]
90	FOOD STORES	[illegible]	[illegible]	[illegible]	2,516.32	2,647.99	2,679.48	2,701.58	2,759.97	2,867.14	2,966.34	3,066.18	[illegible]
91	AUTOMOBILE DEALERS	[illegible]	[illegible]	[illegible]	3,218.27	3,612.15	3,649.68	3,713.56	3,889.29	4,209.64	4,596.31	4,993.28	[illegible]
92	GASOLINE SERVICE STATIONS	[illegible]	[illegible]	[illegible]	671.57	756.11	774.51	788.83	824.51	882.80	[illegible]	[illegible]	[illegible]
93	APPAREL AND ACCESSORIES	[illegible]	[illegible]	[illegible]	502.97	535.32	543.02	549.70	571.44	615.39	663.11	[illegible]	[illegible]
94	FURNITURE, HOME FURNISHINGS	[illegible]	[illegible]	[illegible]	1,001.80	1,080.77	1,100.66	1,111.75	1,167.89	1,265.31	1,382.11	[illegible]	[illegible]
95	EATING AND DRINKING PLACES	661.14	938.19	1,240.80	1,299.89	1,415.06	1,455.00	1,490.57	1,595.92	1,787.74	1,991.92	2,223.76	[illegible]
96	DRUG STORES	387.07	403.99	551.93	562.90	642.15	662.99	680.83	728.42	801.81	865.23	924.55	[illegible]
97	MISCELLANEOUS RETAIL STORES	740.27	1,158.34	1,084.54	1,490.59	1,693.73	1,756.15	1,810.49	1,957.23	2,184.44	2,385.03	2,576.82	[illegible]

Population by Race

Employment by Industry

Household Data

Wealth Index

Households by Income

Retail Sales by Kind of Business

Note: Historical employment, earnings, and income data, 1969-1998, and population data, 1969-1999, is from U.S. Dept. of Commerce (USDoC); retail sales data is historical for '72, '77, '82, '87, '92, and 1997 from USDoC; household data is historical for 1970, 1980, 1985 and 1990 from USDoC; Hispanic data is historical for 1970, 1980, and 1990-1999 from USDoC; all other years of data, 1969-1998, for retail sales, households, and Hispanic population are estimated by Woods & Poole (W&P); "e" indicates withheld employment and earnings data estimated by W&P; all data, 1999-2025 (2000-2025 for population), is projected by W&P; residential population as of July 1; Hispanic population is persons of Spanish origin regardless of race - White, Black, and Other sum to total population; Other is the sum of Asian Americans, Native Americans, and Pacific Islanders; employment in number of jobs includes proprietors and part-time jobs; earnings by industry are earnings of workers - the sum of wages & salaries, proprietors income, and other labor income; historical data on households by money income bracket is for 1990 only (from U.S. Dept. of Commerce) and is not consistent with mean household total personal income data; the projections, 1991-2025, of households by money income bracket (in 1990 $) are based on 1990 data only; please read "Technical Description of the 2001 Regional Projections and Database" (Chapter 2 of this report) for an explanation of data sources, data definitions, and projection methods. HISTORICAL DATA IS SUBJECT TO REVISION; PROJECTIONS ARE UNCERTAIN AND FUTURE DATA MAY DIFFER SUBSTANTIALLY FROM THESE PROJECTIONS. WOODS & POOLE DOES NOT GUARANTEE THE ACCURACY OF THE PROJECTIONS OR HISTORICAL DATA CONTAINED IN THIS TABLE. THIS DATA IS PROVIDED SUBJECT TO ALL TERMS AND CONDITIONS OF THE WOODS & POOLE ECONOMICS, INC. END USER LICENSE AGREEMENT AND IS NOT AUTHORIZED FOR USE IN LEGAL OR FINANCIAL TRANSACTIONS.

Government Sources

Government agencies are prolific in producing data, and most of the data published by the federal government can be counted on for accuracy and high quality of investigation. Most students are familiar with the *Census of Population,* which provides a wealth of data. (Exhibit 8.4 shows some of the geographic areas that are listed in census reports.) Of course, the *Census of Population* is only one of the many resources the federal government provides. Many companies rely heavily on the *Survey of Current Business, Economic Indicators,* and the *Economic Report of the President* for data relating to research on financial and economic conditions. Builders and contractors utilize information in the *Current Housing Report* and *Annual Housing Survey* for their research. The *Statistical Abstract of the United States* is an extremely valuable source for information about the social, economic, and political organization of the United States. Appendix 8A lists and annotates many of these important government documents.

The federal government is a leader in making secondary data available on the Internet. Visit FedWorld (http://www.fedworld.gov) for a central access point and links to many of these important documents. STAT-USA/Internet is another authoritative and comprehensive source of U.S. government information that focuses on economic, financial, and trade data. It contains the following types of information:

- Over 18,000 market research reports on individual countries and markets compiled by foreign trade experts at U.S. embassies
- Economic data series, current and historical, such as GDP, balance of payment, and merchandise trade
- Standard reference works, such as the *Economic Report of the President,* the *Budget of the United States Federal Government,* and the *World Fact Book*
- Worldwide listings of businesses interested in buying U.S. products

Exhibit 8.4 Geographic Building Blocks for Census Data Reporting[16]

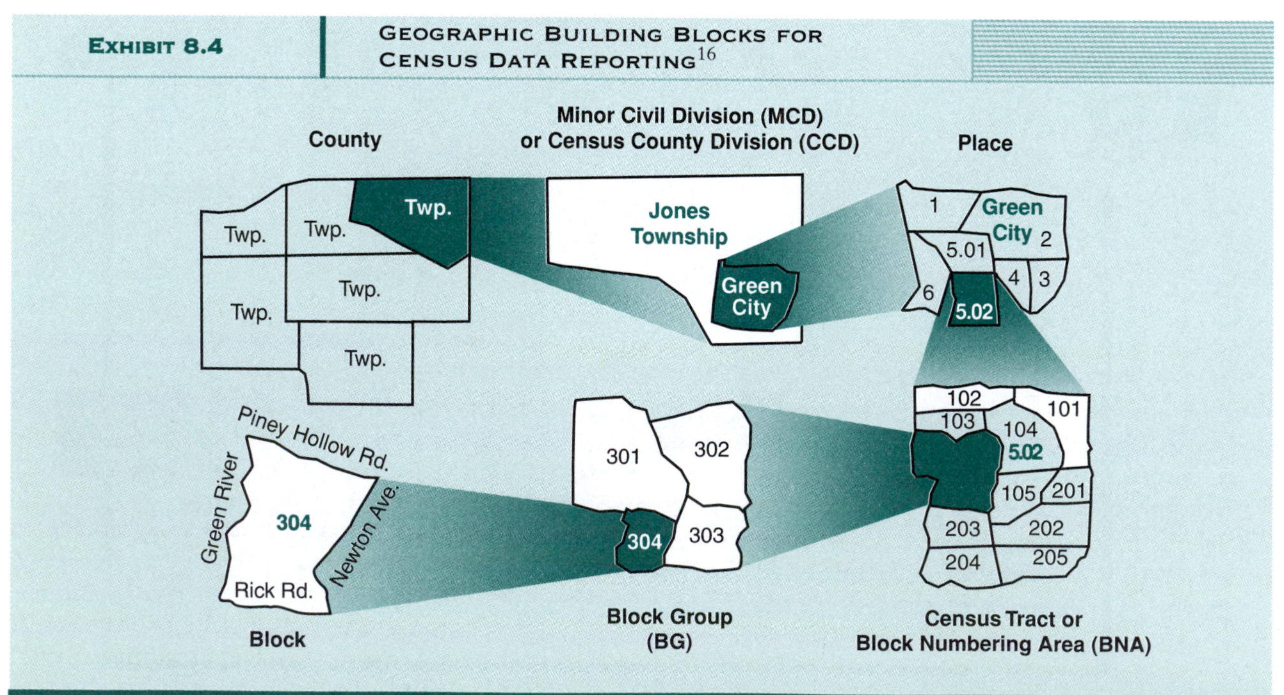

Internal and proprietary secondary data are generated or recorded by the organization. Ryder Truck Rental Inc. uses internal and proprietary secondary data about truck rentals to track consumer migration trends. Ryder has identified a steady trend showing migration from major metropolitan areas to smaller cities with populations of 50,000 to 100,000. Today, many people relocate not for jobs, but in search of more pleasant, less pressured lifestyles.

The STAT-USA/Internet Web address is http://www.stat-usa.gov/. However, only subscribers who pay a subscription fee have access to the service.

Regional Publications

In addition to national material issued by the government, regional data and comments on the economy are published by a number of Federal Reserve banks. The Federal Reserve System is divided into 12 Federal Reserve districts, with a major Federal Reserve bank in each, in the following cities:

Boston	Cleveland	Chicago	Kansas City
New York	Richmond	St. Louis	Dallas
Philadelphia	Atlanta	Minneapolis	San Francisco

Each Federal Reserve district bank has a research department that issues periodic reports. Although most of the publications generated by the various banks differ, monthly reviews, which are available to interested parties, are published by all district banks. In addition to providing descriptive statistics, these reviews typically contain one (or several) articles of interest to those in the region. All Federal Reserve banks have Web sites. The St. Louis Federal Reserve Bank (http://www.stls.frb.org) has a large economic database containing historical federal system and government time series data.

Several large commercial banks, such as Chase Manhattan (New York), prepare weekly or monthly letters that comment on the current and future outlooks. Publications of state, county, and local government agencies can also be useful sources of information. Many states publish state economic models and forecasts. Many cities have metropolitan planning agencies that provide data about their populations, economies, transportation systems, and the like. These data are similar to federal government data but are more current and structured to suit local needs.

Many states publish information on the Internet. Many search engines have directory entries that allow easy navigation to state Web sites. A researcher using Yahoo, for example, needs only to click Regional Information to find numerous paths to information about states.

Media Sources

Information on a broad range of subjects is available from broadcast and print media. The *Wall Street Journal* is a comprehensive source for information on security-market prices. Media frequently commission research studies about various aspects of Americans' lives, such as financial affairs, and make reports of survey findings available to potential advertisers free of charge. *American Woodworker* magazine reports there are nearly 19.6 million woodworkers: 17.2 million of these are amateurs while 2.4 million are professionals. *American Woodworker* also provides demographic information on woodworkers: 84 percent are male, 78 percent are married, the average age is 45, and the average household income is $48,000.[17] Data about the readers of magazines are typically profiled in media kits and advertisements.

Data like these are plentiful. The media like to show that their vehicles are viewed or heard by the advertisers' target markets. These types of data should be evaluated carefully, however, because they often cover only limited aspects of a topic. Nevertheless, they can be quite valuable for research, and they are generally free of charge.

Commercial Sources

Numerous firms specialize in selling and/or publishing information. For example, the Polk Company publishes information on the automotive field, such as average car values and new-car purchase rates by zip code. Many of these organizations offer information in published formats and as CD-ROM or Internet databases. The following discussion of several of these firms provides a sampling of the diverse data that are available.

Market Share Data A number of syndicated services supply either wholesale or retail sales volume data based on product movement. Information Resources, Inc. collects market share data using Universal Product Codes (UPC) and optical scanning at retail store checkouts. Its INFOSCAN is a syndicated store tracking service that collects scanner data weekly from more than 32,000 supermarket, drug, and mass merchandiser outlets across the United States. It also tracks sales in France, Germany, Greece, Italy, the Netherlands, Spain, and the United Kingdom.

Although it is best known for its television rating operations, A. C. Nielsen also has a scanner-based marketing and sales information service called ScanTrack. This service gathers sales and marketing data from a sample of more than 4,800 stores representing more than 800 retailers in 50 major U.S. markets. As part of Nielsen's Retail Measurement Service, auditors visit the stores at regular intervals to track promotions to customers, retail inventories, displays, brand distribution, out-of-stock conditions, and other retail marketing activity. Scanner data allow researchers to monitor sales data before, during, and after changes in advertising frequency, price changes, distribution of free samples, and similar marketing tactics.

Wal-Mart recently introduced its own in-store scanner system called RetailLink. It offers its key suppliers online access to relevant data free of charge.[18]

Many primary data investigations use scanner data to measure the results of experimental manipulations such as altering advertising copy. For example, scanning systems combined with consumer panels are used to create electronic test markets. Systems based on UPC bar codes and similar technology have been implemented in factories, warehouses, and transportation companies to research inventory levels, shipments, and the like.

Demographic and Census Updates A number of firms, such as CACI Marketing Systems and Urban Information Systems, offer computerized U.S. census files and updates of these data broken down by small geographic areas, such as zip codes. Many of these research suppliers provide in-depth information on minority customers and other market segments.

Consumer Attitude and Public Opinion Research Many research firms offer specialized syndicated services that report findings from attitude research and opinion polls. For example, Yankelovich provides custom research, tailored for specific projects, and several syndicated services. Yankelovich's public opinion research studies, such as the voter and public attitude surveys that appear in *Time* and other news magazines, are a source of secondary data. One of the firm's services is the *Yankelovich MONITOR,* a syndicated annual census of changing social values and an analysis of how they can affect consumer marketing. The *MONITOR* charts the growth and spread of new social values, characterizes the types of customers who support the new values and those who continue to support traditional values, and outlines the ways in which people's values affect purchasing behavior.

Harris/Interactive is another public opinion research firm that provides syndicated and custom research for business. One of its services is its ABC News/Harris survey. This survey, released three times per week, monitors the pulse of the American public on topics such as inflation, unemployment, energy, attitudes toward the president, elections, and so on.

Stock Market Sources Numerous firms sell advisory services that supply information on the aggregate market and individual stocks.[19] For example, Standard & Poor's *Corporation Records* is a set of seven volumes, the first six of which contain basic information on corporations, arranged alphabetically. The volumes are updated throughout the year. The seventh volume, a daily news volume, contains recent data on all companies listed in the entire set.

Standard & Poor's *Stock Reports* are comprehensive two-page reports on numerous companies whose stocks are listed on the New York Stock Exchange (NYSE) and the NASDAQ stock exchange, as well as those traded over the counter (OTC). They include the near-term sales and earnings outlook, recent developments, key income-statement and balance-sheet items, and a chart of stock-price movements (in bound volumes by exchange). A sample page is shown in Exhibit 8.5.

Standard & Poor's *Stock Guide* is a monthly publication that contains, in compact form, pertinent financial data on more than 5,000 common and preferred stocks. It is a very useful quick-reference guide for almost all actively traded stocks. A separate section covers over 400 mutual fund issues. For each stock, the guide contains information on price ranges (historical and recent), dividends, earnings, financial position, institutional holdings, and ranking for earnings and dividend stability.

Standard & Poor's *Bond Guide,* also published monthly, contains the most pertinent comparative financial and statistical information on a broad list of bonds, including domestic and foreign bonds (about 3,900 issues), 200 foreign-government bonds, and about 650 convertible bonds.

Moody's Industrial Manual resembles the Standard & Poor's *Corporation Records* service except that it is organized by the type of corporation (i.e., industrial, utility, etc.). It is currently published once a year in two bound volumes. It covers industrial companies listed on the NYSE and the AMEX, as well as those listed on regional exchanges. There is also a section on

Exhibit 8.5 | **A Sample Page from the S & P Stock Reports**[20]

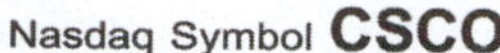

Cisco Systems

Nasdaq Symbol **CSCO**

Stock Reports — **In S&P 500**

09-JUN-01 **Industry:** Computers (Networking)

Summary: Cisco offers a complete line of routers and switching products that connect and manage communications among local and wide area computer networks employing a variety of protocols.

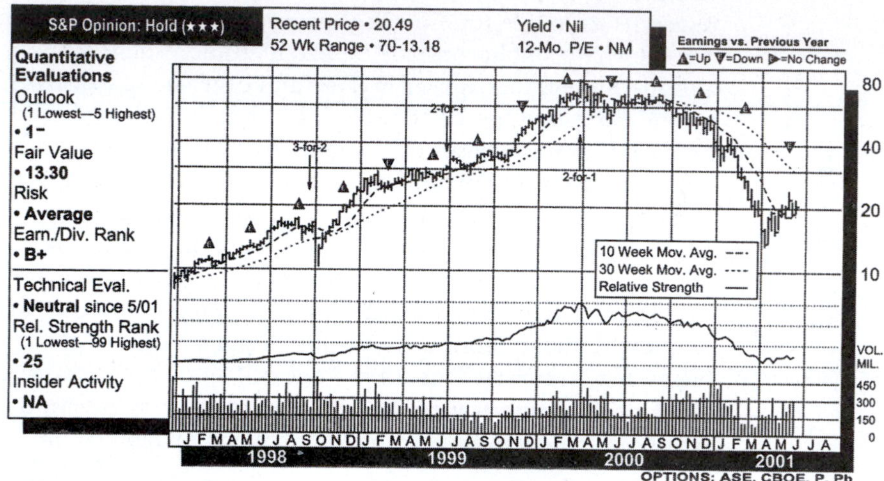

Overview - 10-MAY-01

We project a revenue decline of 6.2% in FY 02 (Jul.), and have lowered our revenue growth projection for FY 01 to 20%. Our prior estimate of 27% had been lowered from 40% and 59% before that. A significant decrease in service provider spending has dampened revenue growth forecasts from prior explosive rates. In addition, this situation has been exacerbated by a weakening of the U.S. economy. We expect gross margin to narrow to less than 60%, from 64.5% in FY 00, reflecting Cisco's success in products for new markets – currently carrying lower margins, the impact of price competition, and the lower unit volumes. We project a gross margin of 56.8% in FY 02. Operating expenses should reflect the benefits of the company's actions to limit discretionary spending, and workforce cutbacks. We forecast EPS of $0.44 for FY 01, before goodwill a[illegible]tization an[illegible] non-recurring items, down from $0.53 [illegible]

Key Stock Statistics

S&P EPS Est. 2001	0.44	Tang. Bk. Value/Share	3.14
P/E on S&P Est. 2001	46.6	Beta	1.84
S&P EPS Est. 2002	0.35	Shareholders	60,150
Dividend Rate/Share	Nil	Market cap. (B)	$149.1
Shs. outstg. (M)	7276.4	Inst. holdings	54%
Avg. daily vol. (M)	56.369		

Value of $10,000 invested 5 years ago: $ 33,004

Fiscal Year Ending Jul. 31

	2001	2000	1999	1998	1997	1996
Revenues (Million $)						
1Q	6,519	3,918	2,588	1,869	1,435	710.2
2Q	6,748	4,357	2,827	2,016	1,592	826.5
3Q	4,728	4,933	3,147	2,184	1,648	985.1
4Q	—	5,720	3,548	2,390	1,765	1,292
Yr.	—	18,928	12,154	[illegible]	6,440	[illegible]

international industrial firms and a news report section that contains items on events that occurred after publication of the basic manual.

Moody's also publishes specialized industry books, such as *Moody's OTC Industrial Manual* (limited to stocks traded in the OTC market), *Moody's Public Utility Manual, Moody's Transportation Manual* (covering railroads, airlines, steamship companies, electric railways, bus and truck lines, oil pipelines, bridge companies, and automobile- and truck-leasing companies), *Moody's Bank and Finance Manual,* and *Moody's Municipal and Government Manual* (data on the U.S. government, all the states, state agencies, municipalities, foreign governments, and international organizations).

The *Value Line Investment Survey* is published in two parts. The first volume contains basic historical information on about 1,700 companies, a number of analytical measures of earnings stability and growth rates, a common-stock safety factor, and a timing-factor rating. It also includes extensive 2-year projections for the given firms and 3-year estimates of performance. The second volume includes a weekly service that provides general investment advice and recommends individual stocks for purchase or sale.

The *Value Line OTC Special Situations Service* is published 24 times a year for the experienced investor who is willing to accept high risk in the hope of realizing exceptional capital gains. Each issue discusses past recommendations and presents eight to ten new stocks for consideration.

Other Financial Sources Financial information about other corporations may be obtained from numerous external sources, such as firms' annual reports, brokerage firm reports, and Securities and Exchange Commission (SEC) reports.

External Data: The Distribution System

The government, newspaper and journal publishers, trade associations, stock exchanges, and many other organizations produce information, and these organizations have always made their data available directly. Traditionally this information has been in published form, and the public library has been a traditional intermediary. Today, however, computerized data archives, the Internet, and electronic data interchange systems make external data as accessible as internal data. Exhibit 8.6 illustrates some traditional and modern ways of distributing information.

Because secondary data have value, these data can be bought and sold in the same way as other products are bought and sold. Many users, such as Fortune 500 corporations, purchase government documents and computerized census data directly from the government. However, many business researchers obtain secondary data from intermediary distributors who are often called *vendors.* Just as a consumer may buy furniture either directly from the factory or through a retailer, researchers can obtain secondary data from an information producer or from a number of distributors or vendors.

In recent years *online vendors* have multiplied rapidly. Vendors such as the Dow Jones News Retrieval Service now allow managers to access thousands of external databases via desktop computers and telecommunications systems.

However, many small companies still study census data at libraries. Traditionally, libraries, being vast storehouses of information, have served as bridges between users and producers of secondary data. The library staff deals directly with the creators of information, such as the federal government, and intermediate distributors of information, such as abstracting and indexing services. Thus, the user needs only to locate the appropriate secondary data on the library shelves. Libraries provide collections of books, journals, newspapers, and so on for reading and reference. They also stock many bibliographies, abstracts, guides, directories, and indexes. Most libraries now also have computers and access to the Internet, as well.

The word *library* typically connotes public or university facilities. However, many major corporations and government agencies also have libraries. A corporate librarian's advice on sources of industry information or a United Nations librarian's help in finding statistics about international markets can be invaluable.

The Internet is, of course, a new source of distribution of much secondary data. Its creation has added an international dimension to the acquisition of secondary data. Earlier in this book we discussed how to access and use the

EXHIBIT 8.6 INFORMATION AS A PRODUCT DISTRIBUTED THROUGH MANY CHANNELS

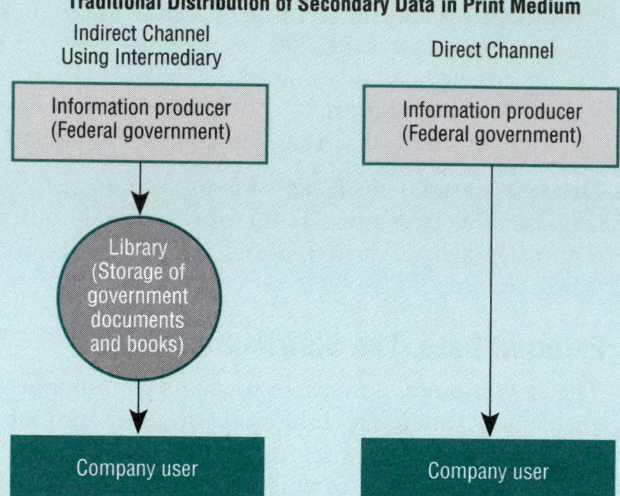
Traditional Distribution of Secondary Data in Print Medium
Indirect Channel
Using Intermediary
Direct Channel
Information producer
(Federal government)
Information producer
(Federal government)
Library
(Storage of
government
documents
and books)
Company user
Company user

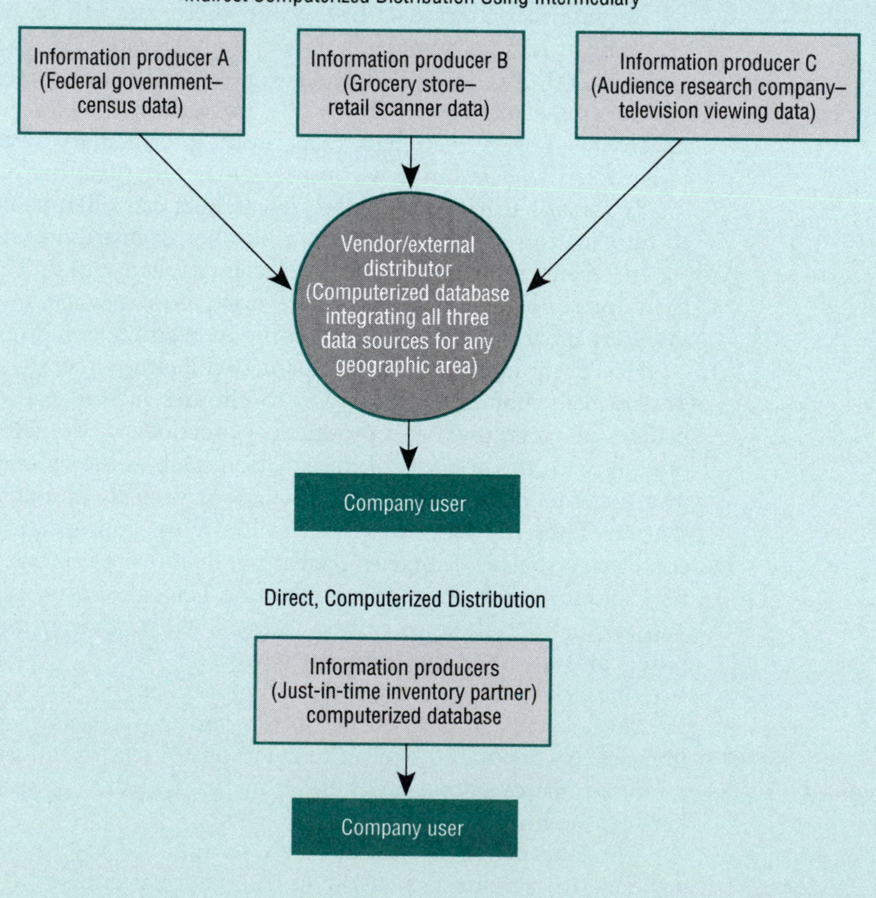
Modern Distribution of Secondary Data
Indirect Computerized Distribution Using Intermediary
Information producer A
(Federal government–
census data)
Information producer B
(Grocery store–
retail scanner data)
Information producer C
(Audience research company–
television viewing data)
Vendor/external
distributor
(Computerized database
integrating all three
data sources for any
geographic area)
Company user
Direct, Computerized Distribution
Information producers
(Just-in-time inventory partner)
computerized database
Company user

EXHIBIT 8.7 | **SELECTED INTERNET SITES THAT PROVIDE FINANCIAL DATA**

Site	URL
New York Stock Exchange	http://www.nyse.com
NASDAQ	http://www.nasdaq.com
Chicago Mercantile Exchange	http://www.cme.com
Chicago Board of Trade	http://www.cbot.com
The Public Register Online Annual Reports Service	http://www.annualreportservice.com/
Securities and Exchange Commission	http://www.sec.gov
United States Treasury Department	http://www.ustreas.gov
Investor's Business Daily	http://www.investors.com
CNN Money	http://money.cnn.com
Yahoo! Finance	http://www.finance.yahoo.com/?u
Quicken's Glossary of Financial Terms	http://www.quicken.com/glossary/

Internet. Exhibit 8.7 lists some Internet addresses where secondary data for financial analysis may be found. It should be understood that this table is just an example. Thousands of Web sites provide useful secondary data for business research. Some are free of charge; others require payment of a subscription fee.

FOCUS ON GLOBAL RESEARCH

As business has become more global, so has the secondary data industry. For example, the Japan Management Association Research Institute is Japan's largest provider of secondary data research to government and industry. The company operates an office in San Diego to help U.S. firms access its enormous store of data about Japan. The institute hopes American firms will use its services to develop and plan their business in Japan. The office in San Diego provides translators and acts as an intermediary between Japanese researchers and U.S. clients.

Secondary data compiled outside the United States have the same limitations as secondary data from within the United States. However, international researchers should watch for certain pitfalls that frequently are associated with foreign data and cross-cultural research. First, desired data may simply be unavailable in certain countries. Second, the accuracy of some data may be questionable. This is especially likely when official statistics are adjusted for the political purposes of foreign governments. Finally, while standardized terms for economic data may be used, various countries use different definitions and accounting/recording practices for many economic concepts. For example, in different countries, figures for disposable personal income may have radically different meanings because of differences in measurement. International researchers should take extra measures to investigate the comparability of data among countries.

The U.S. government and other organizations compile databases that may aid international marketers. For example, *The European Union in the US* (http://www.eurunion.org/) reports on historical and current activity in the European Union. It is a comprehensive reference guide that provides information about laws and regulations, a detailed profile of each European Union member state, investment opportunities, sources of grants and other funding, and other information about business resources. The appendix to this chapter lists many secondary data sources, including some that offer information about countries around the world.

INVESTIGATING GLOBAL MARKETS USING SECONDARY DATA: AN EXAMPLE

The U.S. government offers a wealth of data about foreign countries. *The CIA Factbook* and the *National Trade Data Bank* are especially useful. Both can be accessed using the Internet. This section describes the *National Trade Data Bank* (NTDB), the U.S. government's most comprehensive source of world trade data, to illustrate what is available.

The *National Trade Data Bank* was established by the Omnibus Trade and Competitiveness Act of 1988.[21] Its purpose was to provide "reasonable public access, including electronic access" to an export promotion data system that was centralized, inexpensive, and easy to use.

The U.S. Department of Commerce, which has the responsibility of operating and maintaining the NTDB, works with federal agencies that collect and distribute trade information to keep the NTDB up-to-date. The NTDB has been published monthly on CD-ROM since 1990. Over 1,000 public and university libraries offer access to the NTDB through the Federal Depository Library system.

Within the U.S. Department of Commerce, the organization with primary responsibility for the NTDB is the Economics and Statistics Administration (ESA). STAT-USA is the ESA office that coordinates information from other agencies and produces and fulfills orders for the NTDB over the Internet and on CD-ROM. The National Trade Data Bank consists of 133 separate trade and business-related programs (databases). By using it, small and medium-sized companies get immediate access to information that previously only Fortune 500 companies could afford.

Topics in the NTDB include export opportunities by industry, country, and product; foreign companies or importers looking for specific products; how-to market guides; demographic, political, and socioeconomic conditions in hundreds of countries; and much more. NTDB offers one-stop shopping for trade information from more than 20 federal sources. You do not need to know which federal agency produces the information; all you need to do is consult NTDB.

Some of the specific information that can be obtained from the NTDB is listed in Exhibit 8.8.

SUMMARY

Secondary data are gathered and recorded prior to (and for purposes other than) the current research. Secondary data are usually historical and do not require access to respondents or subjects. Primary data are data gathered for the specific purpose of the current research.

The chief advantage of secondary data is that they are almost always less expensive than primary data. They can generally be obtained rapidly and may provide information not otherwise available to the researcher.

The main disadvantage of secondary data is that they were not designed specifically to meet the researcher's needs. Therefore, the researcher must

Exhibit 8.8 | **Examples of Information Contained in the NTDB**

- Agricultural commodity production and trade
- Basic export information
- Calendars of trade fairs and exhibitions
- Capital markets and export financing
- Country reports on economic and social policies and trade practices
- Energy production, supply, and inventories
- Exchange rates
- Export licensing information
- Guides to doing business in foreign countries
- International trade terms directory
- How-to guides
- International trade regulations/agreements
- Labor, employment, and productivity
- Maritime and shipping information
- Market research reports
- Overseas contacts
- Overseas and domestic industry information
- Price indexes
- Small business information
- State exports
- State trade contacts
- Trade opportunities
- U.S. export regulations
- U.S. import and export statistics by country and commodity
- U.S. international transactions
- *World Fact Book*
- World minerals production

examine secondary data for accuracy, bias, and soundness. One method for doing this is to cross-check different sources of secondary data.

Data conversion is the process of changing the original form of the data to a format suitable to achieving the research objective.

Many common business problems can be addressed with secondary data research. The two general categories of research objectives are fact finding and model building. A typical fact-finding study might seek to uncover all available information about consumption patterns for a particular product category or to identify business trends that affect an industry. Model building is more complicated than simple fact finding because it involves specifying relationships between two or more variables. Model building need not involve complicated mathematics. It can be used for estimating market potential, forecasting sales, selecting sites, and accomplishing many other objectives.

Managers often use internal and proprietary data, such as accounting records, for business research.

External data are generated or recorded by an entity other than the researcher's organization. The government, newspaper and journal publishers, trade associations, and other organizations produce information. Traditionally this information has been distributed in published form either directly from producer to user or indirectly through intermediaries such as public libraries. Modern computerized data archives and the Internet have changed the distribution channels for external data. Because of changes in computer technology, they are now almost as accessible as internal data. Further, the distribution of multiple types of related data by single-source suppliers has radically changed the nature of research using secondary data.

Key Terms

secondary data
data conversion
cross-check
fact finding
model building
market potential
data mining

Questions for Review and Critical Thinking

1. What would be the best source for the following data?
   (a) State population, average income, and state employment rates for Oregon
   (b) Maps of U.S. counties and cities
   (c) Demographic data for Canada and other countries
   (d) Divorce trends in the United States
   (e) Annual sales of the top ten fast-food companies
   (f) Top ten Web sites ranked by number of visitors
2. Suppose you were a business research consultant and a client came to your office and said, "I must have the latest information on the supply of and demand for Maine potatoes within the next 24 hours." What would you do?
3. Find the following data in the *Survey of Current Business* for May 2001:
   (a) U.S. gross domestic product for the first quarter of 2001
   (b) Total exports of goods and services for December 2000
   (c) Total imports of goods and services for December 2000
4. Use the most recent *Sales and Marketing Management's Survey of Buying Power* to find the total population, median age, and total retail sales for (a) your hometown (or county), and (b) the town (or county) in which your school is located.
5. Using secondary sources, what type of information can you find out about American labor unions? What are some current trends in the American labor movement?
6. Provide some examples of model building in your area of business specialization. (Alternatively, develop a model-building hypothesis in your area of interest.)
7. Use secondary data to learn the size of the U.S. golf market and to profile the demographic groups that are most likely to golf.
8. ? A newspaper reporter reads a study that surveyed children and then reports that a high percentage of children recognize Joe Camel, the cigarette spokes-character, but fails to report that the study also found that a much higher percentage of children indicated very negative attitudes toward smoking. Is this a proper use of secondary data?

Exploring the Internet

1. The home page for BRINT (Business Research, Management Research & Information Technology Research) is at http://www.brint.com/. It contains links to hundreds of information-based Web sites. Visit this site and identify several interesting sources you can go to from there.
2. PopClocks estimate the U.S. and world populations. Go to the Census Bureau home page (http://www.census.gov), navigate to the population section, and find today's estimate of the U.S. and world populations.
3. Visit the Small Business Administration's home page at http://www.sbaonline.sba.gov. What type of information can be accessed through this site?
4. Use the Internet to learn what you can about Indonesia
   a. Use your Web browser to go to http://www.asiadragons.com/ and click on Indonesia.
   b. Visit the *CIA World Fact Book* (http://www.cia.gov/cia/publications/factbook/).
   c. Go to Infoseek or Google and use "Indonesia" as a search word. What kinds of information are available from each of these sources?
5. FIND/SVP is a company that provides information about many different industries. Go to the FIND/SVP home page at http://www.findsvp.com. Select an industry. What industry information is available?
6. Go to Statistics Norway at http://www.ssb.no. What data, if any, can you obtain in English?
   a. What languages can be used to search this Web site?
   b. What databases might be of interest to the business researcher?

7. Go to Statistics Canada at http://www.statcan.ca. What languages can be used to search this Web site? What databases might be of interest to the business researcher?
8. *Martindale's Health Science Guide* and *Martindale's The Reference Desk* are hosted by the University of California. They can be found at http://www-sci.lib.uci.edu/HSG/HSGuide.html and at http://www-sci.lib.uci.edu/HSG/Ref.html, respectively. Each provides hyperlinks to a vast amount of information.
9. Go to the University of Michigan library's Web site at http://www.lib.umich.edu/libhome/. What links to secondary data can you find?

Case Suggestions

Case 5: Middlemist Precision Tool Company
Video Case 10: Furniture.com
Video Case 11: The Census Bureau: Census 2000

APPENDIX 8A

SELECTED SOURCES FOR SECONDARY DATA

This appendix briefly describes numerous valuable sources for secondary data. Most are available on CD-ROM and online. Many require subscription fees. However, most college and university libraries allow students to use these sources free of charge.

MAJOR INDEXES

ABI/INFORM Database. A much-used database abstracting by subject significant articles that are published in more than 1,000 leading business and management publications, including over 350 English-language titles from outside of the United States. Full text is available for more than 600 of the most popular and important sources.

Applied Science & Technology Index. (New York: H. W. Wilson Company; monthly except July, with periodic cumulations). Indexes more than 300 journals in applied sciences such as geology and oceanography; technological fields such as petroleum and gas exploration, physics, and plastics; and engineering disciplines, including telecommunications and environmental engineering.

Business Periodicals Index. (New York: H. W. Wilson Company; monthly except July, with periodic cumulations). This is a much-used index of more than 300 U.S. and foreign business/management periodicals, including both scholarly and popular journals. At the end of each issue is an index of business book reviews appearing in the periodicals covered.

General Business File ASAP. (Farmington, MI: Gale Group). This database includes articles on finance, acquisitions and mergers, international trade, money management, new technologies and products, local and regional business trends, and investments and banking. It includes directory listings for over 150,000 companies as well as investment analysts' reports on major companies and industries.

National Newspaper Index. (Foster City, CA: Gale Group) A database that is useful for finding information on current events, lifestyle, biographies, sports, economics, consumer products, world affairs, public health, business trends, entertainment and travel.

PAIS International in Print. (New York: Public Affairs Information Service; monthly with periodic cumulations). A subject index to public policy literature published in 60 countries. Business topics covered emphasize economic factors, industry surveys, and business-societal interactions rather than details of business operations. Besides selectively indexing articles written in English and in five other languages, it covers some books, government publications, and pamphlets.

Reader's Guide to Periodical Literature. (New York: H. W. Wilson Company; published partly monthly and partly semimonthly, with periodic cumulations). Indexes nearly 200 general-interest U.S. and Canadian magazines by subject and author. Does not cover business, academic, or other scholarly magazines, and thus is of greater interest to general audiences.

REFERENCE GUIDES

American Statistics Index. (Bethesda, MD: Congressional Information Service; monthly in two parts, with annual cumulations). CIS publishes three companion guides that describe in detail published statistics from a wide variety of sources. The *American Statistics Index* indexes and abstracts the statistical publications of the federal government, congressional committees, and other federal programs. The tables are indexed by subject and category, commodity or industry, geographic area, title, and report number.

The companion guides are *Statistical Reference Index* and *Index to International Statistics* (both described elsewhere). Yet another monthly index/abstract is *CIS Index,* which is used to identify, evaluate, and obtain information contained in the working papers of the U.S. Congress. It covers hearings, prints, documents, reports, and special publications.

Business Information Sources. 3rd ed. by Lorna M. Daniells. (Berkeley: University of California Press, 1993). An annotated bibliography of books, periodicals, and reference sources in all important areas of business. Of its 21 chapters, three focus on business/economic statistical sources, one on investment sources, and one on marketing (including marketing research, product development, selling, advertising, retailing, and service industries).

Encyclopedia of Business Information Sources. (Detroit: Gale Group Inc.; annual). Identifies sources of information on approximately 1,000 business subjects or industries. For each topic, it lists pertinent abstracts and indexes, bibliographies, directories, online databases, periodicals, statistical sources, and trade and other organizations.

Encyclopedia of Consumer Brands. (Detroit: Gale Group Inc., 1993). The three volumes present the origin, evolution, and current market status of some of the world's most recognizable consumer brands.

Monthly Catalog of United States Government Publications. (Washington, DC: U.S. Government Printing Office; monthly, with semiannual index). Accessible online as *GPO Monthly Catalog;* also on CD-ROM. Describes publications of the U.S. government, arranged by publication number (which is also by issuing agency). Includes subject and title indexes.

The *North American Industry Classification System.* (Washington, DC: U.S. Office of Management and Budget, 1997). Replaced the U.S. Standard Industrial Classification (SIC) system. This reference includes definitions of each industry, tables showing correspondence between 1997 NAICS and 1987 SIC categories, and a comprehensive index. Also available at http://www.census.gov/ epcd/www/naicstab.htm.

Standard Industrial Classification Manual. (Washington, DC: U.S. Office of Management and Budget, 1987). Explains the coding scheme developed by the federal government to make it easier to collect and tabulate statistics on products, industries, or services, especially in the various economic censuses. Commonly called the SIC Code, it (or expanded versions of it) is also used by many commercial sources, such as publishers of directories or indexing/abstracting services, because it offers a logical means of classifying industry data and is so well known. Especially useful for locating industry number statistics on a specific product. The North American Industry Classification System has replaced the SIC system.

Statistical Reference Index. (Bethesda, MD: Congressional Information Service, monthly in two parts, with annual cumulations). SRI is a companion to the *American Statistics Index,* covering U.S. statistical publications published by nongovernment sources, including trade and professional associations, institutes, commercial publishers, businesses, independent research organizations, state governments, and university research centers. This could be especially useful for identifying statistical publications of trade associations covering a specific industry or annual statistical issues of trade journals. Its format is similar to that of the ASI.

Statistics Sources. (Detroit: Gale Research, Inc.; two volumes, annual). A subject guide to statistics on over 20,000 topics, including many business and economic subjects. Arranged alphabetically by very specific subject or geographic location, and indicates where statistics can be found. A companion volume is *State and Local Statistics Sources,* for sources of key data on the state, city, and local levels. For the names of several reference guides to international information, see the section titled "Selected International Sources."

CENSUS DATA

Census statistics can be of great value to marketing researchers because the figures are quoted in such detail, both by subject and by geographic location. The data can be used as a starting point even when they are somewhat out-of-date. The censuses of population and housing are taken every 10 years in the year ending in 0; the other censuses are taken every 5 years in the years ending with 2 and 7. The economic censuses covering manufacturing, retail, wholesale, and services industries are perhaps the most important for statistics on business establishments. These consist of series of reports in an "Industry Series," a "Geographic Area Series" by state, and a specialized "Subject Series." Following are descriptions of major elements of the periodic censuses: Census of Agriculture, Census of Population and Housing, and the Economic Censuses. (The discussion does not cover the Census of Governments or all economic censuses.) For a note about online accessibility of all census reports, go to http://www.census.gov and click on Accessibility.

Census of Agriculture

(http://www.census.gov/econ/overview/ag0100.html) Includes data by state and county on numbers, types, and sizes of farms, land use, irrigation, agricultural products, and value of products. More recent agricultural statistics are published by the U.S. Department of Agriculture, and some agricultural commodity statistics are in the *CRB Commodity Year Book* (see page 161).

Decennial Census

(http://factfinder.census.gov/home/en/decennialdata.html)

Census of Population presents population characteristics of states, counties, MSAs, and towns of 1,000 or more inhabitants. The reports from the 2000 census include the following:

- *General Population Characteristics,* consisting of separate reports by state, each with detailed statistics on age, sex, race, Hispanic origin, marital status, and household relationship characteristics for states, counties, and places of 1,000 or more inhabitants. Separate reports are produced for American Indian and Alaska Native areas, or MSAs and urbanized areas.
- *Social and Economic Characteristics,* focusing on population samples. It also will have separate reports similar to those above.
- *Population Subject Reports,* including 30 reports on particular subjects such as migration, income, and the older population
- *Current Population Reports,* including several useful continuing reports covering statistics on such topics as population characteristics, population estimates and projections, consumer income, and socioeconomic characteristics of individuals, families, and households

Census of Population and Housing. The volumes in the 2000 census include the following:

- *Summary Population and Housing Characteristics,* providing population and housing unit counts as well as summary statistics on age, sex, race, Hispanic origin, household relationship, units in structure, value and rent, number of rooms, tenure, and vacancy characteristics for local governments, including American Indian and Alaska Native areas
- *Population and Housing Unit Counts,* with total population and housing unit counts for 2000 and previous censuses, and data shown for states, counties, minor civil divisions, and towns
- *Population and Housing Characteristics for Census Tracts and Block Numbering Areas,* especially useful for population and housing statistics within MSAs
- *Population and Housing Characteristics for Congressional Districts of the 103rd Congress*
- *Summary Social, Economic, and Housing Characteristics,* with sample data for local governments

Census of Housing. Detailed tabulations of housing conditions and occupancy statistics for states, counties, MSAs, and towns with over 1,000 inhabitants. Volumes published in the 2000 census include the following:

- *General Housing Characteristics,* with detailed statistics for each state on units in structure, value and rent, number of rooms, tenure, and vacancy characteristics. Separate reports are produced for American Indian and Alaska Native areas, MSAs, and urbanized areas.
- *Detailed Housing Characteristics,* which focuses on housing samples. It also has separate reports similar in coverage to those in *General Housing Characteristics.*
- *Housing Subject Reports,* ten special reports on such subjects as space utilization and structural characteristics

Economic Censuses

(http://www.census.gov/mp/www/pub/ind/msind1.html)

The *Economic Census* provides a detailed portrait of the U.S. economy every 5 years, from the national to the local level.

The *1997 Economic Census* (the most recent one) covers nearly all of the U.S. economy in its basic collection of statistics. There are several related programs, including statistics on minority and women-owned businesses. Economic census data are published by industry and by area in well over a thousand reports. Statistics are published primarily in terms of establishments. An establishment is a business or industrial unit at a single location that produces or distributes goods or performs services. The *Economic Census* classifies establishments according to the new North American Industry Classification System (NAICS). NAICS classifies industries using 2-, 3-, 4-, 5-, and 6- digit levels of detail. Sectors, the broadest classifications, are 2-digit codes, while individual industries are represented at the 6-digit code level.

The *Economic Census* provides economy-wide information and information on the following sectors: Mining; Utilities; Construction; Manufacturing; Wholesale Trade; Retail Trade; Transportation and Warehousing; Information; Finance and Insurance; Real Estate and Rental and Leasing; Professional, Scientific, and Technical Services; Management of Companies and Enterprises; Administrative and Support and Waste Management and Remediation Services; Educational Services; Health Care and Social Assistance; Arts, Entertainment, and Recreation; Accommodation and Food Services; Other Services (except Public Administration); and Outlying Areas Services. Some examples of individual reports follow.

- *Census of Construction Industries.* For building and heavy construction contractors, special trade contractors, and land subdividers and developers, this gives detailed statistics on number of construction establishments, number of employees, payroll, hours, value of construction work, cost of materials, rental costs, and capital expenditures.
- *Census of Manufactures.* Useful statistics on each of about 450 manufacturing industries, with reports for specific industries and reports for each state. Figures include number of establishments, inventories, pay-

rolls, production hours worked, value added by manufacture, capital expenditures, and more. *Annual Survey of Manufactures* and *Current Industrial Reports* update some of the statistics between censuses.

- *Census of Mineral Industries.* This specialized census provides statistics (in both industry reports and geographic area reports) on establishments in over 30 industries in metal and coal mining, oil and gas extraction, and mining and quarrying of nonmetallic minerals.
- *Census of Retail Trade.* Presents statistics on retail trade in states, MSAs, Primary Metropolitan Statistical Areas (PMSAs), Consolidated Metropolitan Statistical Areas (CMSAs), counties, and towns. Data include sales, payroll, employees, number of establishments, sales by merchandise lines, and so forth, arranged by Standard Industrial Classification (SIC) code number. Some current statistics based on a sample survey are presented in *Revised Monthly Retail Trade: Sales and Inventories,* which has an annual summary.
- *Census of Wholesale Trade.* Statistics on wholesaling for states, MSAs, and counties cover sales, number of establishments, payrolls, warehouse space, expenses, and so forth, arranged by SIC code number. Some current data are presented in *Revised Monthly Wholesale Trade: Sales and Inventories,* which also has an annual summary.

Bibliography of Census Data

The U.S. Bureau of the Census maintains a descriptive guide to census statistics and reports arranged by broad census subjects such as agriculture and population. Symbols with each item note which are available in digital formats, such as DVD, CD-ROM, diskettes, and tapes. A great deal of the data are accessible via the Internet at the link entitled Catalog at http://www.census.gov/.

STATISTICAL DATA

Business Statistics (Washington, DC: U.S. Bureau of Economic Analysis; biennial). This biennial statistical supplement to the *Survey of Current Business* contains extensive historical tables (annually for 29 years and monthly for the most recent 4 years) for about 1,900 series contained in the monthly *Survey.* An explanatory note for each series describes the series and indicates original sources of data.

County Business Patterns. (Washington, DC: U.S. Bureau of the Census; annual series of reports). For every four-digit SIC industry, this gives statistics on number of establishments, employees, and payroll by employment size class, by state and county. Includes data on financial, insurance, and real estate industries not found in the censuses of retail trade or service industries.

County and City Data Book (Washington, DC: U.S. Bureau of the Census; published irregularly, although at least every 5 years). Provides breakdowns by city and county of statistics on income, population, education, housing, banking, manufacturing, capital expenditures, mineral and agricultural production, retail and wholesale sales, voting records, and other categories. Data are taken from censuses and other government publications and are published as a supplement to the *Statistical Abstract.* The Census Bureau also publishes a *State and Metropolitan Area Data Book* (every 3 years) with similar statistics for metropolitan areas.

CRB Commodity Year Book. (New York: Commodity Research Bureau). Presents statistics on prices, production, exports, stocks, and so forth for about 100 commodities and a few financial futures.

Economic Indicators. (Washington, DC: Council of Economic Advisors; monthly). Current statistics and some charts on prices, wages, money, credit, gross domestic product, federal finance, production, and other series that indicate the country's economic condition.

Economic Report of the President. (Washington, DC: U.S. Government Printing Office; annual). Reviews economic conditions of the United States and economic policy of the administration, taken from the president's yearly address to Congress on the country's economic outlook. Much of this consists of the *Annual Report of the Council of Economic Advisors,* including statistics relating to income, employment, and production.

Federal Reserve Bulletin. (Washington, DC: Board of Governors of the Federal Reserve System; monthly). Current financial and economic statistics, including money, stock, and bank credit, banking institutions, financial markets (including interest rates), federal finance, securities markets and corporate finance, funds flow, economic indicators such as industrial production, and some international statistics.

Historical Statistics of the United States: Colonial Times to 1970. (Washington, DC: U.S. Bureaus of the Census, 1975, two volumes). A supplement to the *Statistical Abstract* (described later), this useful book provides long-term historical trends for basic U.S. statistics. It is arranged in 24 subject sections, and each section contains a short discussion of the sources of the statistics.

Industry Norms & Key Business Ratios, Desk-Top Edition. (New York: Dun & Bradstreet Information Services; annual). Useful for its financial and operating ratios on over 800 lines of business, arranged by industry (four-digit SIC). An alternate source is

Robert Morris Associates' *Annual Statement Studies* (Philadelphia), with ratios for some 360 lines of business, also arranged by four-digit SIC.

Monthly Labor Review. (Washington, DC: U.S. Bureau of Labor Statistics). Contains articles on nationwide labor conditions and trends. Statistics in each issue include labor force data (employment, unemployment, hours), labor compensation and collective bargaining, price data (consumer and producer price indexes), and data on productivity, injury, and illness.

Predicasts Basebook. (Cleveland: Predicasts, Inc.; annual; available online as *PTS U.S. Time Series*). A comprehensive reference providing approximately 27,700 time series for very specific products/industries and for basic economic indicators, arranged by expanded seven-digit SIC numbers. Each record contains about 10 years of data, a calculated growth rate, and the source from which the figures were taken.

Predicasts Forecasts. (Cleveland: Predicasts, Inc.; quarterly with annual cumulations; available also online as *PTS U.S. Forecasts*). Contains both short- and long-range statistical forecasts for products/industries and for the U.S. economy, arranged by expanded seven-digit SIC numbers, taken from journal articles, newspapers, government publications, and other sources. Often has projections for shipments, production, sales, consumption, exports, and so on. Includes the source for each figure. An expensive companion service, covering forecasts for products/industries in foreign countries, is Worldcasts.

Standard & Poor's Statistical Service. (New York: Standard & Poor's Corporation; one loose-leaf volume with monthly supplements). Contains useful historical and current business/economic statistics, arranged in the following sections: banking and finance; production indexes and labor statistics; price indexes (commodities, producer and consumer price indexes, cost of living); income and trade; building and building materials; energy, electric power, and fuels; metals; transportation; textiles, chemicals, paper; agricultural products. Security Price Index Record (the last section) contains long-term trends for S&P's stock price index and Dow Jones averages.

Statistical Abstract of the United States. (Washington, DC: U.S. Bureau of the Census; annual). One of the most valuable statistical reference books, consisting of many social, political, and economic statistical tables, each taken from original government reports. It also serves as a reference for more detailed information because it gives the source of each table and includes guides to statistics, state statistical abstracts, and some foreign statistics at the end. *USA Statistics in Brief* (http:// www.census.gov/statab/www/brief.html) is a supplement to the *Statistical Abstract* and presents national summary data and state population estimates.

Statistics of Income. (Washington, DC: Internal Revenue Service of the U.S. Treasury Department; annual). Income statistics collected by the IRS in two volumes, one based on individual tax returns and the other based on corporate returns. Data for the latter include tables by industry and by asset size. Because publication of these data may be slow, the quarterly *SOI Bulletin* is useful for preliminary statistics on individual and corporate income as well as that of partnerships and sole proprietorships.

Survey of Current Business. (Washington, DC: U.S. Bureau of Economic Analysis; monthly). An important source for current business statistics. Especially noted for its figures on national income, gross domestic product, and personal consumption expenditures, which are presented in each issue and also in more detail in the annual *National Income and Product Accounts* issue (July). Certain issues also contain data on international transactions and foreign direct investments in the United States. Blue pages in each issue cover statistics for general business indicators, commodity prices, construction and real estate, labor/employment earnings, domestic trade, finance, foreign trade, transportation and communication, and 13 major manufacturing industries. Yellow pages give Business Cycle Indicators, monthly estimates for over 250 business cycles, in both table and graph format. As noted earlier, *Business Statistics* is a biennial providing historical statistics from the Survey.

MARKET DATA

The Lifestyle Market Analyst. (Wilmette, IL: Standard Rate & Data Service; annual). A reference guide for consumer market analysis at the local, regional, or national level. Section 1 analyzes each ADI (Area of Dominant Influence) market in terms of demographic characteristics and over 50 lifestyle interests. Sections 2 and 3 provide the same data by specific lifestyle activity and by demographic data.

Market Guide. (New York: Editor & Publisher; annual). Provides market facts on U.S. and Canadian cities where daily newspapers are published, including population, number of households, transportation, climate, retail outlets, principal industries, banks, number of automobiles. It also contains tables somewhat similar to those in the *Survey of Buying Power* covering population, disposable personal income, households, and retail sales (for each of nine retail store groups) by county, newspaper city, and MSA. Ranked tables are at front.

Rand McNally Commercial Atlas & Marketing Guide. (Chicago: Rand McNally; annual). Contains marketing data such as figures from the Survey of Buying Power, population for Rand McNally metropolitan areas, maps of trading areas, MSAs, and zip codes as well as state and large-city maps.

Sourcebook of Zip Code Demographics. (Fairfax, VA: CACI; annual). For researchers needing marketing statistics arranged by U.S. zip code, this annual contains census statistics and other estimates for population and housing (including number of households and a housing profile), demographic figures (percentage by age distribution, race, and median age), socioeconomic statistics (percentage distribution of households by income, education, employment profile), and a purchasing potential index for 13 types of products/services.

Survey of Buying Power. (New York: *Sales & Marketing Management;* annual constitutes an extra August issue of S&MM). *Sales & Marketing Management* publishes three useful extra issues each year, and this is the most important one for researchers interested in geographical variations in population, income, and retail sales. Section C contains current statistical estimates for population (by age groups), households, effective buying income (EBI), and retail sales for six store groups—all for U.S. states, counties, MSAs, and some cities. Section B gives regional and state summaries and metro rankings for the same data.

- Earlier volumes of the *Survey* included statistics for Canadian provinces, counties, and cities; now Canadian tables are prepared separately as *Survey of Buying Power: Canadian Data,* and subscribers to *S&MM* must request it each year from the publisher.
- The extra October issue is *Survey of Media Markets.* This contains media market projection tables showing percentage change over 5 years for population, EBI, and total retail sales for each metro area. It also has Media Market Profiles for each Arbitron ADI market, and a section ranking metro areas for each of ten retail merchandise lines.
- A third extra issue (in June each year) is *Sales Manager's Budget Planner,* intended more for sales managers than for market researchers.

For several sources of international market data, see Selected International Sources at the end of this bibliography.

Marketing Reference Guides

Market Share Reporter. (Detroit: Gale Research, Inc.; annual). An annual compilation of market share data on companies and products that have appeared in periodicals and brokerage reports. It is arranged by two-digit SIC categories and within each chapter by four-digit SICs, and it covers not only brand market share data but also corporate market shares, institutional shares (shares for countries, regions, etc.), and product/commodity/service and facility shares. Data for each usually include brief information on the entry, list of products or companies with number of units sold and percent of group, and name of source. Many entries are taken from the *Investext.*

PTS Marketing and Advertising Reference Service database. This MARS database abstracts articles on marketing and advertising of consumer products. It covers not only specific consumer products but also articles on new products, marketing and advertising strategies, market size/market share information, advertising and promotion campaigns, articles on producer organizations, ad agencies, public relations firms, and much more. Over 140 key publications are scanned for pertinent articles, and many are reproduced in full.

INDUSTRY DATA

Industry Surveys. (New York: Standard & Poor's Corporation; annual with three updates). Separate Basic Analysis surveys for about 20 major U.S. industries, each including comparative statistics for leading companies in that industry. Supplemented by a short Current Analysis with some more recent data (usually two issues per year).

U.S. Industrial Outlook. (Washington, DC: U.S. International Trade Administration of the Department of Commerce; annual). A much-used source of short discussions of recent trends on each of approximately 350 manufacturing and service industries with prospects over the coming 5 years.

There are many other possible sources for information on industries, several of which are listed elsewhere in this appendix. The census, for instance, contains statistics on four-digit industries, as does the annual *County Business Patterns. Predicasts* publications give industry statistics by expanded seven-digit SIC number. Dun & Bradstreet's *Industry Norms & Key Business Ratios* has ratios by four-digit industries. The *Encyclopedia of Business Information Sources* is a good place to start if you do not know what statistics, abstracts, directories, periodicals, and so on are available on an industry/subject. The monthly *Statistical Reference Index* offers one way to locate statistical volumes compiled by various trade associations as well as annual statistical issues sometimes appearing in trade journals such as the *Oil & Gas Journal.* Using a directory of national associations, such as the annual *Encyclopedia of Associations, Volume 1: National Organizations of the U.S.* (Detroit: Gale Research, Inc.), is another way to identify trade associations that may have useful industry statistics or other suggestions for industry information.

Two of the guides noted below offer a means of finding current articles on industries, some of which may be annual statistical issues or articles giving market share or a short-range outlook for the coming year. Researchers who want lists of the major U.S. trade journals in an industry can consult one of several directories, such as the annual *Standard Periodical Directory* or the lesser known (but perhaps more useful for this purpose) *Standard Rate & Data Service: Business Publication Rates and Data* (Wilmette, IL: National Register Publishing Company; monthly). It lists trade journals by industry group and gives subscription and advertising rate information.

Industry Reference Guides

Findex. (Bethesda, MD: Cambridge Scientific Abstracts; annual, with midyear supplement). Available online. A descriptive directory of approximately 13,000 market research reports, studies, and surveys on specific products or industries available from over 500 U.S. and foreign research publishers. They are arranged by subject categories, and for each there is a brief description, publisher, date, paging, and price. Selected company reports are described.

Predicasts F&S Index United States. (Cleveland: Predicasts, Inc.; weekly, with monthly, quarterly, and annual cumulations). Online counterpart is *PTS F&S Indexes.* Useful for identifying current information on products, industries, and companies reported in more than 750 trade and business magazines, newspapers, and special reports. The industry/products section is arranged by expanded seven-digit SIC numbers, and for many industries the data are arranged by subheadings covering topics such as market information, sales, and consumption. The company section lists articles containing recent news and financial and marketing information about each company.

Companion indexes covering Europe and other foreign countries are *Predicasts F&S Index Europe* and *Predicasts F&S Index International* (both are monthly, with quarterly and annual cumulations). These are also online in *PTS F&S Indexes.*

PTS PROMPT Database. PROMPT is an acronym for "Predicasts Overview of Markets and Technology." This database provides quick access to abstracts (and some full text) on industries, companies, products, markets, and applied technology from a wide range of worldwide journals and other sources, such as investment analysts' reports, research studies, and government publications. It can be useful for identifying articles on such subjects as competitive activities, new products and technologies, market size and share, financial trends, mergers and acquisitions, contracts, joint ventures, and new facilities.

There is a print version called *PROMT* (Cleveland: Predicasts, Inc., monthly, with quarterly and annual cumulations).

Gale Group Trade and Industry Index Database. (Foster City, CA: Gale Group). A multi-industry database covering international company, industry, product, and market information, with strong coverage of such areas as management techniques, financial earnings, economic climate, product evaluations, and executive changes. It provides strong coverage of over 65 major international industries, including automotive, defense, chemicals, electronics, advertising and marketing, retailing, telecommunications, insurance, metals, and oil.

CORPORATE DIRECTORIES

Dun's Market Identifiers. (Parsipanny, NJ: Dun & Bradstreet Information Services). The database contains basic information about both public and private U.S. companies of all sizes. The database covers all types of commercial and industrial establishments as well as all product areas. Data on more than 10 million businesses have been gathered via interviews.

Million Dollar Directory: Leading Public and Private Companies. (Parsippany, NJ: Dun & Bradstreet Information Services; five volumes, annual). This is a good directory to start with when seeking brief facts about any of some 160,000 leading U.S. public and private businesses. The first three volumes usually give officers/directors, approximate sales, employees, stock exchange, ticker symbol, SIC code numbers, and more, for each company. Two other volumes index the companies by geographic location and by SIC industry. Some libraries may subscribe to just one volume, *Top 50,000 Companies.*

An alternative directory is *Standard & Poor's Register of Corporations, Directors, and Executives.* (New York: Standard & Poor's Corporation; one volume of three, annual, with cumulated supplements). Accessible online as *Standard & Poor's Register—Corporate,* and on CD-ROM. The other two volumes contain a list of directors and executives, with brief facts about each, and the indexes.

Standard Directory of Advertisers. (Wilmette, IL: National Register Publishing Company; two volumes; annual, with supplements). Volume 1 is a classified directory of some 25,000 U.S. companies that advertise nationally, giving for each not only the usual basic facts but also names of marketing and sales personnel, advertising agencies, sometimes advertising appropriations, and advertising media used. Volume 2 contains indexes, including one for trade names. There is a separate geographic index.

Two companion volumes are the *Standard Directory of International Advertisers & Agencies* (annual), covering foreign companies that advertise and foreign advertising agencies; and the *Standard Directory of Advertising Agencies* (three per year, with supplements), which contains approximate annual billings and names of accounts for each U.S. agency listed.

Thomas Register of American Manufacturers. (New York: Thomas Publishing Company; 26 volumes, annual). Accessible online as Thomas Register Online, and on CD-ROM. Probably the best directory for identifying an American manufacturing company or locating the manufacturer of a particular brand. It lists over 145,000 companies by very specific product, alphabetically and by brand name. For each company it usually gives the address, products made, and asset range. Volumes 17–18 list the companies alphabetically, with Volume 18 including a trade name index; Volumes 19–26 are a catalog file.

The Fortune 500. (annual, in *Fortune,* second issue in April). Each year *Fortune* publishes four ranked lists of largest companies. This one ranks the largest U.S. industrial corporations by sales, assets, profits, and so forth, and also by industry. *Fortune* publishes several other ranked lists:

- *The Fortune Service 500* (first issue in June) with separate rankings for the 100 largest (each) diversified service companies, commercial banks, and diversified financial companies, and the 50 largest (each) savings institutions, life insurance companies, retailing companies, transportation companies, and utilities.
- *The Fortune Global 500* (first issue in July) ranks the largest industrial companies in the world and the largest banks.
- *The Fortune Global 500* (last issue in July), gives separate rankings of worldwide service companies in the same categories as in the U.S. ranked list.

There are many other sources for ranked lists of top companies. See Daniells' *Business Information Sources* (3rd ed., 1993), or use *Business Rankings Annual* (Detroit: Gale Research, Inc.).

Greenbook: International Directory of Marketing Research Companies and Services. (New York Chapter, American Marketing Association; annual). A descriptive list of marketing research companies, arranged alphabetically with four indexes, including one by geographic location.

To identify the numerous published business and industrial directories, buyer's guides, and rosters (both U.S. and foreign), consult a guide such as *Directories in Print* (Detroit: Gale Research, Inc.; annual with supplements) and its companion guide, *City & State Directories in Print.*

INVESTMENT DATA

Corporate Annual Reports and 10-K Reports

Many public and university libraries maintain good microfiche collections of annual reports to stockholders and 10-K reports (annual reports that public corporations are required to file with the Securities and Exchange Commission). Some libraries also have files of reports for leading foreign companies. These are useful sources for up-to-date financial information about public companies, including recent financial and operating statistics. Serious investors find the 10-K reports more useful than the reports to stockholders, because the SEC requires companies to disclose certain information about their operations that might not be in the reports distributed to stockholders. Data from these and other corporate financial documents filed with the SEC can also be accessed online or on CD-ROM, such as Disclosure's *Compact D/SEC.* Reports of an individual company usually can be obtained by writing to the company.

Investment Services and Statistics

Moody's Industrial Manual (two volumes) and *Moody's OTC Industrial Manual.* (New York: Moody's Investors Service; annual, with weekly or semiweekly supplements). Available online and on CD-ROM. Two of eight investment manuals compiled by Moody's. The first gives useful financial information about industrial corporations listed on the NYSE, AMEX, and regional stock exchanges; the second covers industrial companies that are traded over the counter. The amount of information given for each company varies, but "full-coverage" reports usually include a brief financial history, the nature of the business and its products, subsidiaries, officers and directors, CEO's letter to stockholders, 7 years' worth of income and balance sheet statistics, financial and operating data, and more.

The other six manuals are *Moody's Bank & Finance Manual* (four volumes); *Moody's International Manual* (two volumes); *Moody's Municipal & Government Manual* (three volumes); *Moody's OTC Unlisted Manual; Moody's Public Utility Manual* (two volumes); and *Moody's Transportation Manual.*

Standard Corporation Descriptions. (New York: Standard & Poor's Corporation; six looseleaf volumes, with semimonthly supplements). Online counterpart is *Standard & Poor's Corporation Description Online;* also on CD-ROM. This investment manual is an alternative to Moody's, with similar coverage but arranged alphabetically by company in its six volumes rather than in separate services according to type of corporation. Those subscribers who purchase the daily *Current News Edition* receive a seventh volume.

Standard NYSE Stock Reports. (New York: Standard & Poor's Corporation; four looseleaf volumes, with frequent supplementary pages). Useful for researchers who want a concise summary of the nature of a business, important recent developments, current income and balance sheet figures, and revenue, per-share, dividend, and other data. Covers companies listed on the NYSE, with a revised report for each company published at least every 3 months. S&P publishes similar looseleaf services for companies listed on AMEX and companies traded OTC.

Value Line Investment Survey. (New York; looseleaf service in three parts, with weekly supplements). Accessible online as *Value Line DataFile;* also on CD-ROM. This well-known investment advisory service contains one-page statistical profiles of 1,700 companies in about 95 industries and is arranged in 13 sections by industry. Many useful statistics are crammed onto one large page, including a 15-year table for 23 key financial and operating figures and estimates for 3 years into the future, as well as several Value Line ratings, a brief outlook, and investment advice.

CD/Corporate: U.S. Public Companies. (A Lotus One Source CD-ROM). This compact disc is a collection of the more important business/financial data taken from other leading databases, including financial statement figures from SEC filings (Moody's); short reports from OTC and smaller traded companies *(Market Guide);* investment banking firm reports on companies and industries *(Investext);* securities prices (Dow Jones); articles on companies and industries, including marketing strategies, new products, new technologies *(ABI/INFORM and PTS/PROMT);* and biographical facts about key officers and directors (Macmillan). Lotus One Source offers other related CD-ROMs.

Moody's Handbook of Common Stocks. (New York: Moody's Investors Service; quarterly). A popular source for quick access to brief current financial statistics (on one small page) on each of over 900 listed stocks with high investor interest. A companion quarterly covering high-interest NASDAQ stocks is *Moody's Handbook of Nasdaq Stocks.*

The Wall Street Journal. (New York: Dow Jones & Company; every weekday). Accessible online in full text as *Dow Jones News/Retrieval.* This is an indispensable business/financial newspaper arranged in three sections. Section A covers news and feature stories, the economy, international news, politics and policy, and editorial matters. Section B, "Marketplace," focuses on company strategy, marketing, advertising, consumers, technologies, law, and the like. Section C, "Money & Investing," provides useful current stock price quotations; also corporate bonds, government issues, options, futures, mutual fund tables, stock price indexes, foreign exchange rates, and more. People who do not have access to the database can use *The Wall Street Journal Index,* published monthly with annual cumulations.

New York Stock Exchange Fact Book. (New York Stock Exchange, annual). An outstanding source of current and historical data on activity on the NYSE. Also contains comparative data on the AMEX, the OTC market, institutional trading, and investors in general.

AMEX Statistical Review. (New York: American Stock Exchange, annual). Contains pertinent information on the exchange, its membership, listed companies, administration, trading volume, and monthly AMEX market indices. The first issue (entitled AMEX Databook) was published in 1969. The databook was originally published biennially; it is now published annually.

The Dow Jones Investor's Handbook. (New York: Dow Jones and Company; annual). Contains the complete DJIA results for each year, along with earnings and dividends for the series since 1939. Individual reports on common and preferred stocks and bonds listed on the NYSE and AMEX, including high and low prices, volume, dividends, and the year's most active stocks, are also included.

S&P Trade and Security Statistics. (New York: Standard & Poor's Corporation). A service of Standard & Poor's that includes a basic set of historical data on various economic and security price series and a monthly supplement that updates the series for the preceding period. There are two major sets of data: (1) business and finance and (2) security price index record. Within the business and finance section are long-term statistics on trade, banking, industry, prices, agriculture, and financial trends. The security price index record contains historical data for all of the Standard & Poor's indexes. These cover 500 stocks broken down into 88 individual groups, of which the four main groups—industrial composite, rails, utilities, and the 500 composite—are composed. There are also four supplementary group series: capital goods companies, consumer goods companies, high-grade common stocks, and low-priced common stocks. In addition to the stock price series, Standard & Poor's has derived a quarterly series of earnings and dividends for each of the four main groups. The earnings series includes data from 1946 to the present. The booklet also contains data on daily stock sales on the NYSE from 1918 on and historical yields for a number of bond series, both corporate and government.

REFERENCE GUIDES FOR INVESTMENT DATA

Investext database. (Boston: Thomson Financial). A full-text database covering financial research reports on companies and industries prepared by financial analysts at over 385 leading investment banking firms and other research organizations worldwide. These are useful for tracking competitor information, including company analyses, product information, market share, business strategies, emerging technologies, and industry trends.

Nelson's Directory of Investment Research. (Port Chester, NY: Nelson Publications. two volumes; annual). Used to identify investment analysts who cover a particular company, this publication offers a list of worldwide companies citing each analyst and the name of his or her investment firm. Volume 1 covers U.S. companies, and volume 2, international. Each entry includes a short list of financial research reports on the company that appeared during the previous year. There are several indexes, including one listing analysts by industry and one listing companies by geographic location. A supplement, *Nelson's Guide to Institutional Research* (ten issues per year), contains lists of the current year's research reports.

Many other sources for investment information can be found in large public or university libraries with a business/finance department. Most investment texts, for instance, contain useful chapters or sections describing sources of information on investments, such as Chapter 5 of Frank K. Reilly's *Investment Analysis and Portfolio Management,* 4th ed. (Fort Worth, TX: Dryden Press, 1994). Lorna Daniells' *Business Information Sources,* 3d ed. (Berkeley: University of California Press, 1993) also contains a chapter describing basic investment sources.

SELECTED INTERNATIONAL SOURCES

Statistics

Monthly Bulletin of Statistics Online. (Washington, DC: United Nations Statistics Division), http://esa.un.org/unsd/mbs/mbssearch.asp). Presents current monthly economic statistics for most of the countries and areas of the world. Each month a different selection of special tables is presented showing annual and/or quarterly data on a variety of subjects illustrating important long-term economic trends and developments.

OECD Statistics Brief. (Paris: Organization for Economic Cooperation and Development), http://www.oecd.org). Presents important statistical issues to the international community of statisticians, economists, policy makers, and researchers each month.

The 1998 Industrial Commodity Statistics Yearbook. (New York: United Nations Publications). Provides statistics on the production in physical quantities of about 530 industrial commodities by country, geographical region, and economic grouping, and for the world. It includes data for a 10-year period (1989–1998 in the current edition) for about 200 countries.

The World Development Indicators. (Washington, DC: World Bank; annual). Compilation of data about development. WDI 2001 includes approximately 800 indicators organized in six sections: World View, People, Environment, Economy, States and Markets, and Global Links. The data cover 148 economies and 14 country groups, with basic indicators for another 59 economies.

Reference Guides

Europa World Year Book. (London: Europa Publications; two volumes). Important source for brief information about countries, such as recent history, economic statistics, government, political organizations, holidays; also lists important newspapers, periodicals, radio and television stations, banks, insurance companies, trade associations, railroads, and much more. Some data on international organizations are given in volume 1.

European Directory of Marketing Information Sources (biennial) and *International Directory of Marketing Information Sources* (biennial). (London: Euromonitor Plc). These two guides describe the following types of information available for each foreign country: official sources and publications (including statistical publications); libraries and information sources; leading business research companies; information databases; abstracts and indexes; major business and marketing journals; leading business and marketing associations; and European business contacts (such as embassies and chambers of commerce).

Index to International Statistics. (Bethesda, MD: Congressional Information Service; monthly, in two parts, with annual cumulations). A companion service to *American Statistics Index,* this publication abstracts and indexes the statistical publications (in English) published by major international government organizations (IGOs) such as the United Nations and the Organization for Economic Cooperation and Development. It identifies statistics on individual countries but does not cover statistical publications for each country. Some of these latter publications may be found in the previous source.

Corporate Directories and Investment Data

Disclosure/Worldscope: Industrial Company Profiles and *Disclosure/Worldscope: Financial & Service Company Profiles.* (Bridgeport, CT: D/W Partners; eight unnumbered volumes; annual). There are five volumes for the first title. Four volumes contain concise (one-page) statistical profiles for more than 3,000 leading industrial companies in 24 countries and 18 industries. Statistics, usually for a 6-year period, cover financial statement data, financial ratios and growth rate, per-share data, and more. The fifth volume is a users' guide. Two of three volumes of the second title give similar data for over 1,000 major financial, transportation, and utilities companies in 24 countries. The third volume is a user's guide.

Moody's International Manual. (New York: Moody's Investors Service; two volumes, annual, with supplements). A financial manual covering major corporations in some 100 countries and arranged by country. Data given for each corporation usually include a brief financial history, a description of business and property, officers, and financial statement figures, plus more. Center blue pages contain comparative international statistics.

Primary International Businesses. (New York: Dun & Bradstreet Information Services; annual). Directory-type information for approximately 50,000 leading companies in 140 countries; arranged by country, with indexes by SIC industries and by company.

Standard Directory of International Advertisers & Agencies (Wilmette, IL: National Register Publishing Company; annual). Describes both large foreign companies that advertise and foreign advertising agencies. Besides the usual directory information for each company, this directory often gives names of sales personnel, the name of the company's ad agency, advertising appropriations, and media used.

Noted elsewhere in this appendix are two indexes that are good sources for locating current articles and news about foreign companies and industries: *Predicasts F&S Index Europe* and *Predicasts F&S Index International*. Both are accessible online as *PTS F&S Indexes.*

DATABASE SEARCHING AND RETRIEVING WITH COMPUTERS

Developments in information technology have had a major impact on the retrieval and use of published data. Many manual data retrieval methods have been replaced by computerized database retrieval systems.

A large organization might subscribe to the LEXIS system, for example. A business executive could use the computer retrieval system to search for articles related to new laws pertaining to, say, the Internal Revenue Service policy for deductions for an office at home. If the executive needed a broader search to look for material not found in LEXIS, the computer might search all the databases offered by an online vendor such as the Dow Jones News Retrieval Service. Searching more databases is possible, but of course this increases the cost of the research.

A STEP-BY-STEP SEARCH FOR A COMPUTERIZED BIBLIOGRAPHY

To illustrate the database searching process, consider an example of one online information service: ProQuest, which is found in many public and university libraries. ProQuest Direct allows the user to create a computerized bibliography efficiently by collecting information stored in numerous commercial databases. Three examples are described below:

Periodical Abstracts Research II accesses over 1,800 publications covering general reference, health, social sciences, humanities, education, general business, communications, law, general sciences and medicine. Full text is available for over 800 titles.

ABI/INFORM Global accesses nearly 1,500 publications covering accounting, finance, marketing, management, international business, real estate, taxation, investment and banking, business trends, and new technologies and products. Full text is available for over 800 titles.

National and Local Newspapers accesses national newspapers, such as the *New York Times, Washington Post, USA TODAY,* and regional newspapers. Full text is available for most titles.

The typical search begins at the ProQuest Search-by-word screen illustrated in Exhibit 8B.1 and progresses through various screens that present titles of articles. (Before you get to the Search-by-word screen, several simple menu options may have to be turned on or off. However, because the system is menu-driven, advancing to this screen is very simple.) Database searching requires that the researcher initiate either a controlled vocabulary search by entering specific descriptive terms or names, such as a company name, or a subject list search.

An article can be available in any or all of the following five formats.

- *Citation* format displays bibliographic information, such as author, title, source, and date.
- *Abstract* format displays a citation plus a brief summary of the article.
- *Full Text* format displays citation, abstract, and the complete text of the article in ASCII format.
- *Text+Graphics* format displays citation, abstract, and the complete text of the article in ASCII format, plus originally published images in thumbnail size but adjustable for size.
- *Page Image* format displays scanned images of the article as it was originally published. Adobe Acrobat Reader is needed to display an article in Page Image format. (Adobe Acrobat Reader can be downloaded for free from the ProQuest Direct site.)

An onscreen icon indicates the available formats for each article.

Exhibit 8B.2 shows the results of a ProQuest search on "job enrichment."

EXHIBIT 8B.1 | **THE PROQUEST® SEARCH SCREEN**

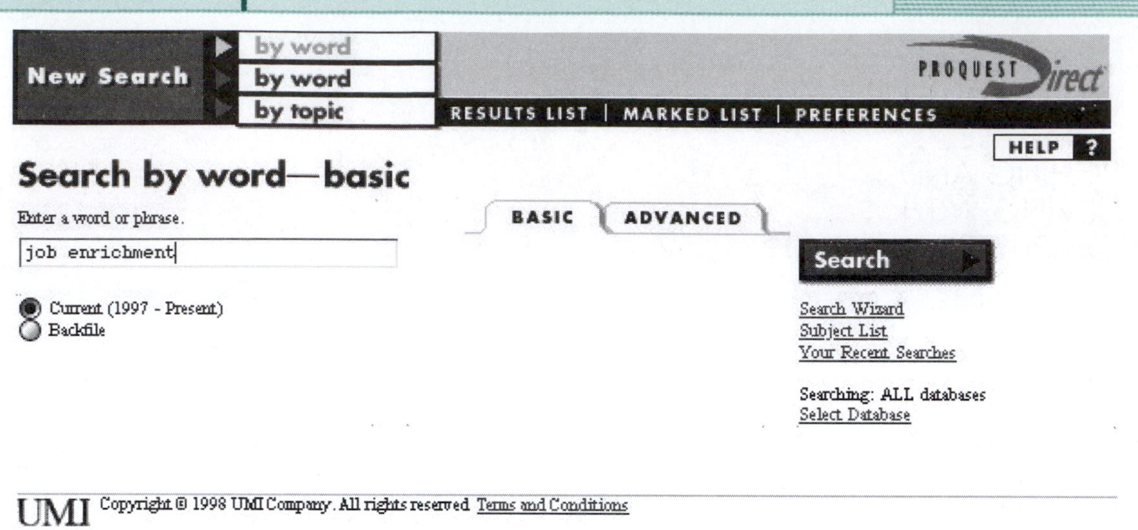

Exhibit 8B.3 shows an abstract obtained in a ProQuest/ABI/INFORM search for an article on "job enrichment."

A controlled vocabulary search relies on standard search terms (specific descriptors or vocabulary code names) in the search list; a free-text search finds matches for user-specified key words. Standard search terms provide a common language for describing key topics in articles. In Exhibit 8B.1, "job enrichment" is a standard search term (vocabulary code) that indicates the primary focus of the article. A free-text search identifies articles on the basis of words in the abstract. Articles that mention job enrichment but do not have it as a primary focus may be found in this way.

Perhaps the major advantage of computerization is the computer's ability to merge or delete references to obtain precisely what is needed. A researcher interested in job enrichment may also use the descriptor "training," which, with a simple change of options in the menu, would restrict the search to articles that discuss training for job enrichment.

Most systems offer several search options, such as an *and* option to merge two descriptive search terms or a *not* option to eliminate certain references. For example, a researcher studying survey research may wish to exclude political polls. The *not* option allows for this. If a search does not retrieve enough abstracted articles, the *or* option can broaden the search, so, for example, instead of the limited search term "cars," a researcher might enter "cars or automobiles." You will have to study the individual search and retrieval system to investigate all the options it offers.

CD-ROM systems provide an alternative technology for storing data and database searching. Large amounts of data (the equivalent of 275,000 printed pages or 1,500 floppy disks) can be stored on a single compact disk that is similar to an audio compact disk. Rather than being stored online in a central computer at another location, the database in a CD-ROM system is stored on a compact disk that can be inserted into a computer at the library or elsewhere. Many libraries have CD-ROMs that contain bibliographic indexes and databases.

CD-ROM systems are also widely used for the storage of financial, statistical, and market databases. For example, *Lotus One Source—CD/Corporate: U.S. Public Companies* is a CD-ROM system that allows access to a wealth of data. *U.S. Public Companies* includes basic business and financial information from Moody's U.S. companies database plus relevant data from Moody's Investors Service, Predicasts, Thomson Financial Networks, UMI/Data Courier, Marquis *Who's Who in Finance and Industry,* Dow Jones News Retrieval Service, Market Guide, and Muller Data Corporation.

EXHIBIT 8B.2 SAMPLE RESULTS FROM A COMPUTERIZED SEARCH FOR ARTICLES ON "JOB ENRICHMENT"

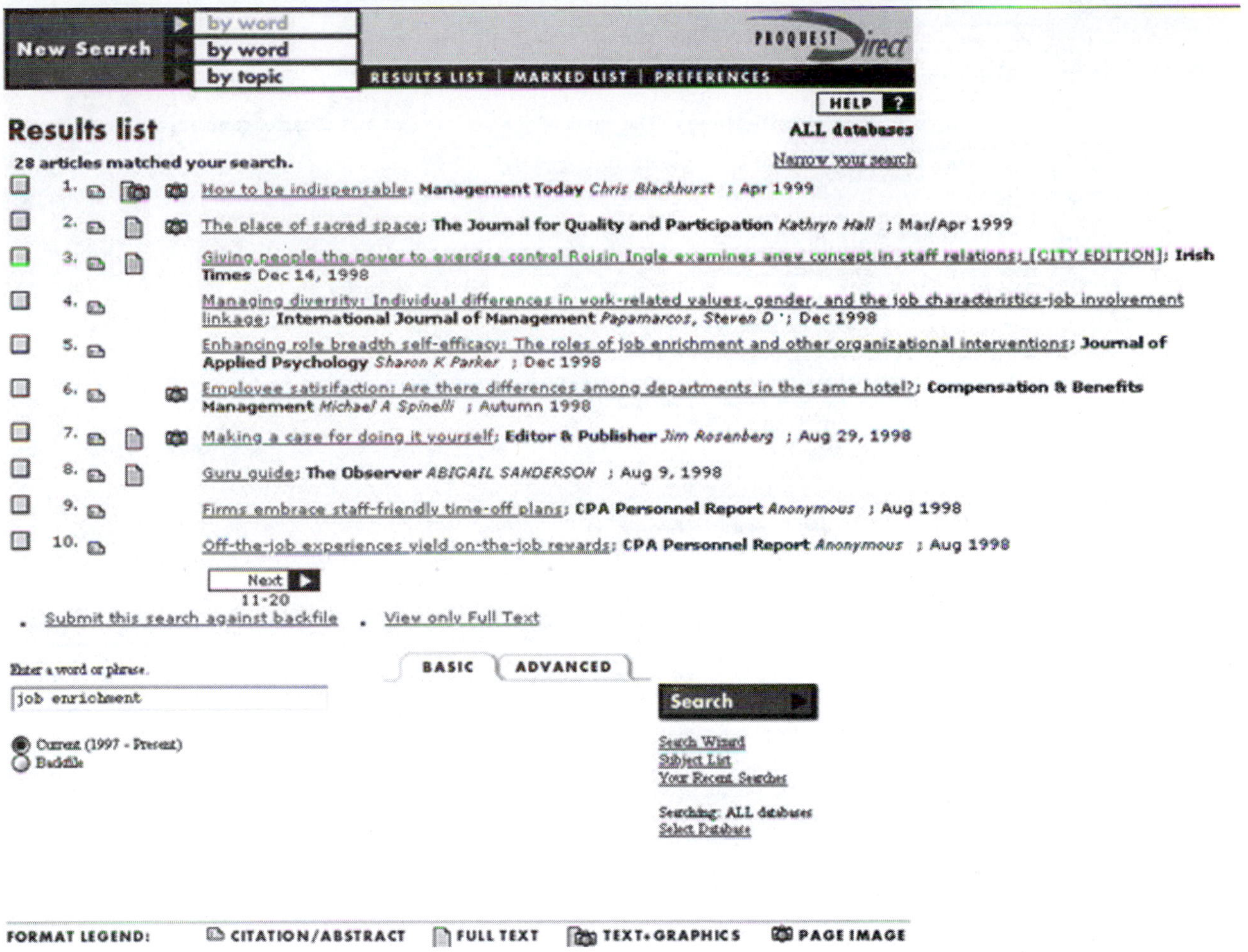

New Search — by word | by word | by topic

PROQUEST Direct

RESULTS LIST | MARKED LIST | PREFERENCES

HELP ?

Results list

ALL databases

28 articles matched your search.

Narrow your search

1. How to be indispensable; **Management Today** *Chris Blackhurst* ; Apr 1999
2. The place of sacred space; **The Journal for Quality and Participation** *Kathryn Hall* ; Mar/Apr 1999
3. Giving people the power to exercise control Roisin Ingle examines anew concept in staff relations; [CITY EDITION]; **Irish Times** Dec 14, 1998
4. Managing diversity: Individual differences in work-related values, gender, and the job characteristics-job involvement linkage; **International Journal of Management** *Papamarcos, Steven D* '; Dec 1998
5. Enhancing role breadth self-efficacy: The roles of job enrichment and other organizational interventions; **Journal of Applied Psychology** *Sharon K Parker* ; Dec 1998
6. Employee satisifaction: Are there differences among departments in the same hotel?; **Compensation & Benefits Management** *Michael A Spinelli* ; Autumn 1998
7. Making a case for doing it yourself; **Editor & Publisher** *Jim Rosenberg* ; Aug 29, 1998
8. Guru guide; **The Observer** *ABIGAIL SANDERSON* ; Aug 9, 1998
9. Firms embrace staff-friendly time-off plans; **CPA Personnel Report** *Anonymous* ; Aug 1998
10. Off-the-job experiences yield on-the-job rewards; **CPA Personnel Report** *Anonymous* ; Aug 1998

Next 11-20

- Submit this search against backfile
- View only Full Text

Enter a word or phrase.

job enrichment

BASIC | ADVANCED

Search

(●) Current (1997 - Present)
( ) Backfile

Search Wizard
Subject List
Your Recent Searches

Searching: ALL databases
Select Database

FORMAT LEGEND: CITATION/ABSTRACT | FULL TEXT | TEXT+GRAPHICS | PAGE IMAGE

EXHIBIT 8B.3 SAMPLE RESULTS OF AN ABSTRACT FROM A COMPUTERIZED SEARCH FOR ARTICLES ON "JOB ENRICHMENT"

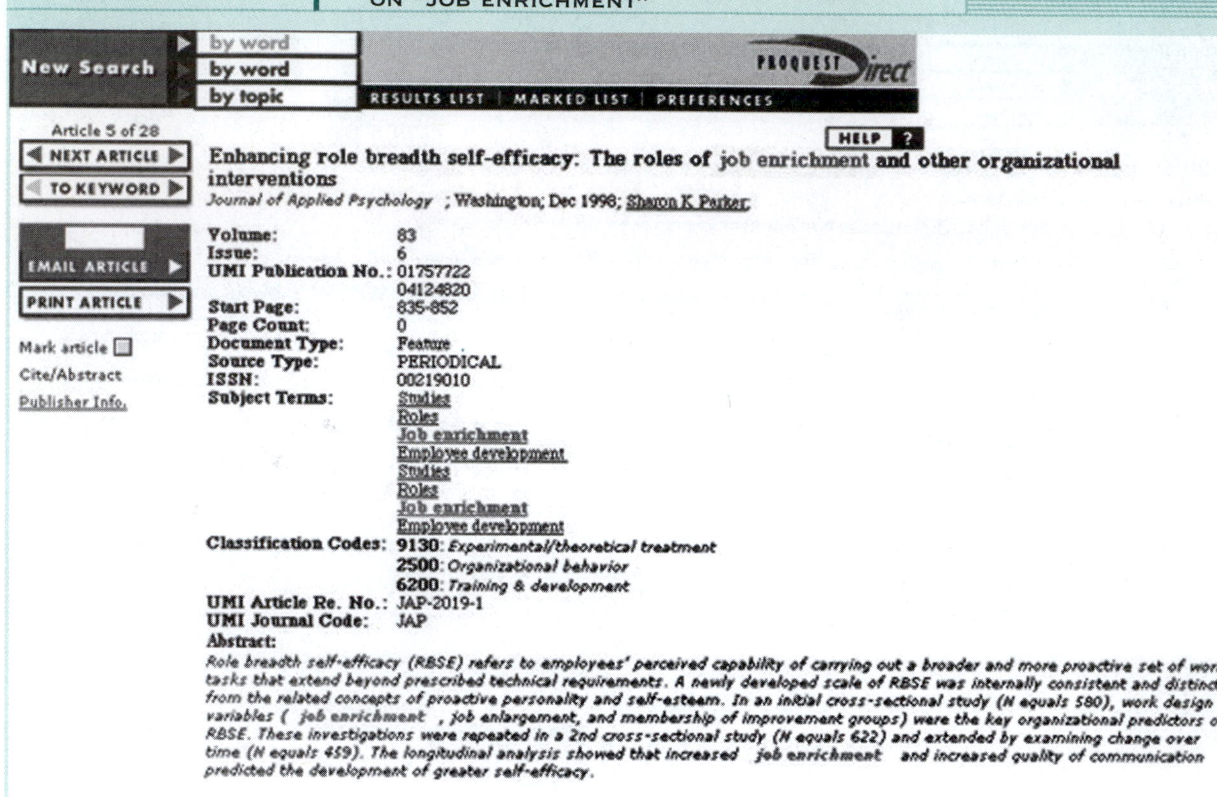
New Search | by word | by word | by topic

PROQUEST Direct

RESULTS LIST | MARKED LIST | PREFERENCES

Article 5 of 28

NEXT ARTICLE

TO KEYWORD

EMAIL ARTICLE

PRINT ARTICLE

Mark article

Cite/Abstract

Publisher Info.

HELP ?

Enhancing role breadth self-efficacy: The roles of job enrichment and other organizational interventions

Journal of Applied Psychology ; Washington; Dec 1998; Sharon K Parker;

Volume:	83
Issue:	6
UMI Publication No.:	01757722 04124820
Start Page:	835-852
Page Count:	0
Document Type:	Feature
Source Type:	PERIODICAL
ISSN:	00219010
Subject Terms:	Studies Roles Job enrichment Employee development Studies Roles Job enrichment Employee development
Classification Codes:	**9130**: *Experimental/theoretical treatment* **2500**: *Organizational behavior* **6200**: *Training & development*
UMI Article Re. No.:	JAP-2019-1
UMI Journal Code:	JAP

Abstract:

Role breadth self-efficacy (RBSE) refers to employees' perceived capability of carrying out a broader and more proactive set of work tasks that extend beyond prescribed technical requirements. A newly developed scale of RBSE was internally consistent and distinct from the related concepts of proactive personality and self-esteem. In an initial cross-sectional study (N equals 580), work design variables (job enrichment , job enlargement, and membership of improvement groups) were the key organizational predictors of RBSE. These investigations were repeated in a 2nd cross-sectional study (N equals 622) and extended by examining change over time (N equals 459). The longitudinal analysis showed that increased job enrichment and increased quality of communication predicted the development of greater self-efficacy.

PART

3

RESEARCH METHODS FOR COLLECTING PRIMARY DATA

CHAPTER

9

SURVEY RESEARCH: An Overview

What you will learn in this chapter

- To understand the terms *survey, sample survey,* and *respondent.*
- To understand the advantage of using surveys.
- To discuss the type of information that may be gathered in a survey.
- To recognize that very few surveys are error-free.
- To distinguish between random sampling error and systematic error.
- To classify the various types of systematic error and give examples of each type.
- To discuss how response error may be an unconscious misrepresentation or a deliberate falsification.
- To classify surveys according to method of communication, according to the degree of structure and disguise in the questionnaires and on a temporal basis.
- To emphasize the importance of survey research to total quality management.

Although KitchenAid is best known for its Stand Mixer, the company markets a full line of small and large kitchen appliances, including dishwashers and refrigerators.[1] A couple of years ago, the counter-top appliance division was doing fine, but sales for the company's larger appliances were declining. The KitchenAid team had to figure out a way to transfer brand equity from its small-appliance division to its large appliances—and they had to do it without increasing their marketing budget.

Researchers started with an analysis of data from 8 years of warranty card surveys for all of KitchenAid's products and with an analysis of the database from the 40,000 households who participate in NFO Worldwide's consumer panel surveys. The KitchenAid researchers learned that across all products, their brand signified "high quality" to customers, but that only their counter-top line of appliances had the reputation for innovation. In a subsequent exploratory research study, researchers discovered consumers weren't interested in the appliance for the appliance's sake. They were interested in what the appliance could do for them—help them to prepare delicious food and be able to entertain friends and family while serving their culinary creations. To confirm and quantify these preliminary findings, KitchenAid conducted a segmentation study. Based on the survey results, management decided to focus on "the culinary-involved," a segment of consumers who were heavy users of kitchen appliances and who believed in having the best products for their homes. These household chefs were passionate about cooking, and most important to KitchenAid, the segment cut across all demographic groups: It wasn't confined to upper-income households.

Past research had shown that consumers actively use magazines to plan their major appliance purchases, often tearing pages out of home and lifestyle magazines to file away for ideas and inspiration, so KitchenAid planned a print-only campaign. One magazine ad featured a picture of lemon soufflé pancakes dominating more than three-quarters of one page. The pancakes are drizzled in a creamy lemon sauce and topped with raspberries. On the page facing the picture, beneath the smaller images of the large and small appliances that helped to prepare the dish, the text invited the reader to visit the company's Web site for the recipe. These ads ran in 59 publications, ranging from *Architectural Digest* to *People.*

What was the payoff of this research and advertising effort? After the first 6 months of 2000, when the campaign started, sales for both countertop and major appliances were showing "double-digit growth." In the first 2 months of the campaign, contacts to KitchenAid's 800 number and its Web site were more than three times what they were over the previous year, and hit rates to the site

were up nearly 60 percent. Most satisfying: The marketing team produced these results using 64 percent of its budget from the previous year—and without use of a television advertising presence. Much of KitchenAid's success can be attributed to the quality of its surveys. ■

The purpose of survey research is to collect primary data—data gathered and assembled specifically for the research project at hand. This chapter, the first of two on survey research, defines the subject. It also discusses typical research objectives that may be accomplished with surveys and the various advantages of the survey method. It explains many potential errors that researchers must be careful to avoid. Finally, it classifies survey research methods.

THE NATURE OF SURVEYS

respondent
The person who answers an interviewer's questions or provides answers to written questions in a self-administered survey.

sample survey
Formal term for survey; it indicates that the purpose of contacting respondents is to obtain a representative sample of the target population.

survey
A research technique in which information is gathered from a sample of people by use of a questionnaire or interview; a method of data collection based on communication with a representative sample of individuals.

primary data
Data gathered and assembled specifically for the research project at hand.

Surveys require asking people, who are called **respondents,** for information, using either verbal or written questions. Questionnaires or interviews are utilized to collect data on the telephone, face-to-face, and through other communication media. The more formal term **sample survey** emphasizes that the purpose of contacting respondents is to obtain a representative sample of the target population. Thus, a **survey** is defined as a method of gathering **primary data** based on communication with a representative sample of individuals.

Survey Objectives: Type of Information Gathered

The type of information gathered in surveys varies considerably, depending on a survey's objectives. Typically, survey investigations attempt to describe what is happening or to learn the reasons for a particular business activity. Most survey research is therefore descriptive research. Some typical survey objectives are to identify characteristics of a particular group, to measure attitudes, and to describe behavioral patterns.

Most surveys have multiple objectives; few gather only a single type of factual information. For example, an organizational researcher might conduct a descriptive survey to determine workers' feelings toward a 4-day work week. Demographic information might also be collected to determine if younger employees' feelings on the subject are different from those of older employees or if men agree with women on the subject.

Although it has been suggested that surveys are conducted to *quantify* certain factual information, certain aspects of surveys may also be *qualitative.* In new-product development surveys, the qualitative objective of a survey is often to test and refine new-product concepts. Stylistic, aesthetic, or functional changes may be made on the basis of respondents' suggestions. Although most surveys are descriptive, they can also be designed to provide causal explanations or to explore ideas.

TO THE POINT

You got to be careful if you don't know where you're going, because you might not get there.
YOGI BERRA

Advantages of Surveys

Surveys provide quick, inexpensive, efficient, and accurate means of assessing information about the population. The examples of surveys earlier in this book illustrate that surveys are quite flexible and, when properly conducted, extremely valuable to managers.

As we discussed in Chapter 1, business research has proliferated in recent years. The growth of survey research is related to the simple idea that to find out what people think, you need to ask them.

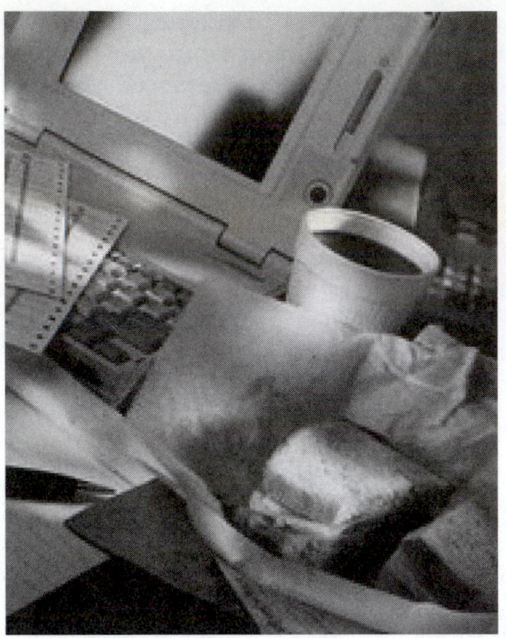

Survey research reveals that the lunch hour isn't what it used to be. Nearly 40 percent of American workers don't break for lunch.[2] Furthermore, one survey by an office-furniture manufacturer showed that even those who do take a break are not doing much more than quickly refueling. The study showed the lunch "hour" averages 36 minutes at or near the employee's regular place of work. The survey revealed even more. Pressed for time in their personal lives, more than half of the workers who take a lunch break don't eat anything at all—they run errands. About 28 percent make personal phone calls, 27 percent go shopping, 6 percent check on their kids in day care, and 1 percent are out looking for another job. About 37 percent read a book or newspaper, and 14 percent jog or work out at a fitness center.

Over the last 50 years, and particularly during the last two decades, survey research techniques and standards have become quite scientific and accurate. When properly conducted, surveys offer managers many advantages. However, survey research can also be used poorly.

> It may be no exaggeration to say that the greater number of surveys conducted today are a waste of time and money. Many are simply bad surveys. Samples are biased; questions are poorly phrased; interviewers are not properly instructed and supervised; and results are misinterpreted. Such surveys are worse than none at all because the sponsor may be misled into a costly area. Even well-planned and neatly executed surveys may be useless if, as often happens, the results come too late to be of value or are converted into a bulky report which no one has time to read.[3]

The disadvantages of specific forms of survey data collection (personal interview, telephone, mail, Internet, etc.) are discussed in Chapter 10. However, this chapter offers a general discussion of errors in surveys.

ERRORS IN SURVEY RESEARCH

A manager evaluating the quality of a survey-based research project must estimate the accuracy of the survey. Exhibit 9.1 outlines the various forms of survey error. The two major sources of survey error are random sampling error and systematic error.

random sampling error
The difference between the result of a sample and the result of a census conducted using identical procedures; a statistical fluctuation that occurs because of chance variation in the elements selected for a sample.

Random Sampling Error

Most surveys try to portray a representative cross-section of a particular target population. Even with technically proper random probability samples, statistical errors will occur because of chance variation in the elements selected for the sample. Unless sample size is increased, these statistical problems are

EXHIBIT 9.1 **TREE DIAGRAM OF TOTAL SURVEY ERROR**

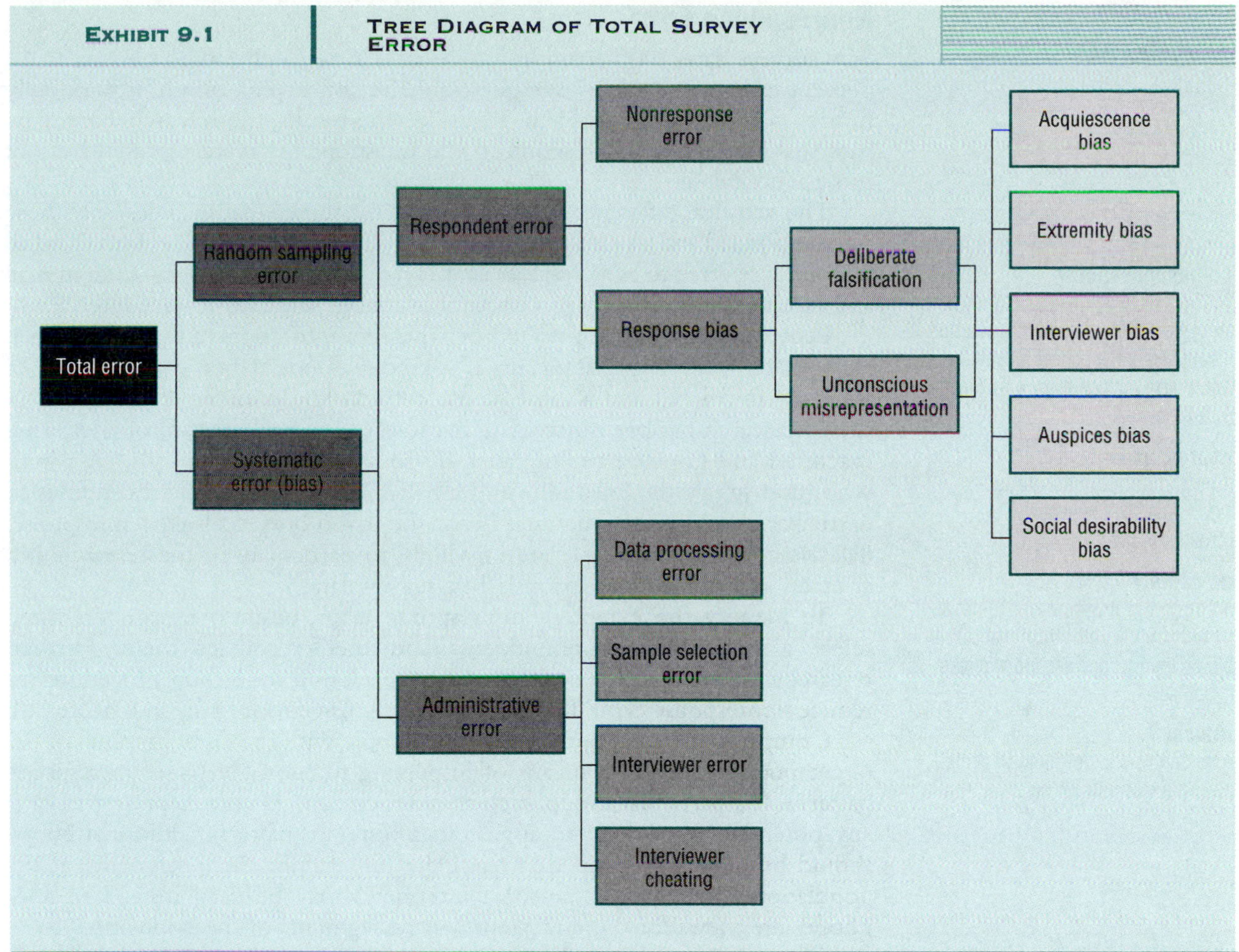

systematic (nonsampling) error
Error resulting from some imperfect aspect of the research design that causes response error or from a mistake in the execution of the research; error arising from sample bias, mistakes in recording responses, or nonresponses from persons not contacted or refusing to participate.

sample bias
A persistent tendency for the results of a sample to deviate in one direction from the true value of the population parameter.

unavoidable. However, such **random sampling errors** can be estimated, and they will be discussed in greater detail in Chapters 16 and 17.

Systematic Error

Systematic error results from some imperfect aspect of the research design or from a mistake in the execution of the research. Because all sources of error other than those introduced by the random sampling procedure are included, these errors or biases are also called *nonsampling errors.* A **sample bias** exists when the results of a sample show a persistent tendency to deviate in one direction from the true value of the population parameter. The many sources of error that in some way systematically influence answers can be classified under two general categories: respondent error and administrative error. These are discussed in the following sections.

RESPONDENT ERROR

Surveys are based on asking people for answers. If respondents cooperate and give truthful answers, a survey will likely accomplish its goal. Two problems that arise if these conditions are not met are nonresponse error and response bias.

Nonresponse Error

Few surveys have 100 percent response rates. A researcher who obtains an 11 percent response to a five-page questionnaire concerning trends in pork belly futures faces a serious problem. To utilize the results, the researcher must be sure that those who *did* respond to the questionnaire were representative of those who *did not.*

The statistical difference in results between a survey that includes only those who responded and a perfect survey that would also include those who failed to respond is referred to as **nonresponse error.** This problem is especially acute in mail and Internet surveys, but it also exists in telephone and face-to-face interviews.

nonresponse error
The statistical difference between a survey that includes only those who responded and a perfect survey that would also include those who failed to respond.

nonrespondent
A person who is not contacted or who refuses to cooperate in a research project.

no contact
A potential respondent who is not at home or who is otherwise inaccessible on the first and second attempts at contact.

refusal
A person who is unwilling to participate in a research project.

People who are not contacted or who refuse to cooperate are called **nonrespondents.** A nonresponse occurs if someone is not at home at the time of both the initial call and a subsequent callback. The number of **no contacts** in survey research has been increasing because of the proliferation of answering machines and growing use of caller ID to screen telephone calls.[4] A parent who must juggle the telephone and a half-diapered child and who refuses to participate in the survey because he or she is too busy is also a nonresponse. **Refusals** occur when people are unwilling to participate in the research. No contacts and refusals can seriously bias survey data.

To identify the extent of nonresponse error, business researchers often select a sample of nonrespondents and then recontact them. Further, researchers have developed systematic callback and follow-up procedures to reduce nonresponse error. These topics are discussed more fully in Chapter 10.

Comparing the demographics of the sample with the demographics of the target population is one means of inspecting for possible biases in response patterns. If a particular group, such as older citizens, is underrepresented or if any potential biases seem to appear in a response pattern, additional efforts should be made to obtain data from the underrepresented segments of the population. For example, personal interviews may be used instead of telephone interviews for the underrepresented segments of the population.

After receiving a refusal from a potential respondent, an interviewer can do nothing except be polite. The respondent who is not at home or who is out of the office when called or visited should be scheduled to be interviewed at a different time of day or on a different day of the week.

self-selection bias
A bias that occurs because people who feel strongly about a subject are more likely to respond to survey questions than people who feel indifferent about that subject.

Within a mail survey the researcher never really knows whether a nonrespondent has refused to participate or is just indifferent. Researchers know that those who are most involved in an issue are more likely to respond to a mail survey. **Self-selection bias** is a problem frequently seen in self-administered questionnaires. A woman who had soup spilled on her at a restaurant, a person who was treated to dinner as a surprise, or others who feel strongly about a restaurant's service are more likely to complete a self-administered questionnaire left at the table than individuals who are indifferent about the restaurant. Self-selection biases a survey because it allows extreme positions to be overrepresented while those who are indifferent are underrepresented. The strategy to increase responses in mail surveys is to encourage respondents to reply. Several techniques for doing so will be discussed in the sections on mail and Internet surveys in the next chapter.

response bias
Survey error that occurs when respondents tend to answer questions in a certain direction. Examples of response bias are acquiescence bias, extremity bias, interviewer bias, auspices bias, and social desirability bias.

Response Bias

A **response bias** occurs when respondents tend to answer in a certain direction, that is, when they consciously or unconsciously misrepresent the truth. If a

Nonresponse error can be high when conducting international business research. People in many other cultures do not share Americans' views about providing information. In Middle Eastern countries many women will refuse to respond to questions from a male interviewer. In Mexico people are often reluctant to provide information over the phone to strangers.

distortion of the measurement occurs because respondents' answers are falsified or misrepresented, either intentionally or inadvertently, the sample bias that occurs is a response bias.

Consider this modern version of the *Literary Digest* study (described in Chapter 4). In a New York City mayoral election, all the polls showed the black candidate leading the white candidate by 12 to 16 percentage points, but the black candidate won by just 2 percentage points. On the same day a black candidate in the Virginia gubernatorial election, who had been 9 to 11 percentage points ahead of the white candidate in the polls, won the Virginia governorship by only 0.3 percentage point.[5] After these elections research experts explained that whites who say that they are undecided in a black–white race nevertheless usually vote overwhelmingly for the white candidate. People who plan to vote against a black candidate, for whatever reason, seem reluctant to admit their true intentions. Perhaps they fear being labeled "racists" or they want the interviewer to think they are socially progressive. But the end result is that in elections with candidates of different races, the survey results are likely to show response bias. Thus, to estimate the true vote, the researchers should include a corrective measure to allow for this response bias.

The results of a study that checked the accuracy of interview techniques among low-income Mexican Americans, low-income white Americans, and middle-income white Americans indicated that the first group tends to distort its beer purchases by reporting no consumption at all, and the second group misrepresents the quantity of beer purchased. Furthermore, all groups systematically overreported the purchases of products with "positive connotations," such as milk.[6]

Deliberate Falsification

Occasionally some people deliberately give false answers. It is difficult to assess why people knowingly misrepresent answers. A response bias may occur when people misrepresent answers in order to appear intelligent, to conceal personal information, to avoid embarrassment, and so on. For example, respondents may be able to remember the total amount of money spent grocery shopping, but they may forget the exact prices of individual items that were purchased. Rather than appear stupid or unconcerned with prices, they may provide their best estimate and not tell the truth—namely, that they can't remember.

Employees may believe that their responses to employee surveys, especially negative responses, may not be confidential. By falsifying their answers, they may believe they are safeguarding their jobs or their chances for advancement. Sometimes employees will not give truthful answers when they think that telling the truth will result in a negative outcome for a supervisor or an organizational unit, ultimately resulting in a less desirable situation for themselves.

Sometimes respondents who become bored with the interview will simply provide answers just to get rid of the interviewer. At other times respondents provide the answers they think are expected of them in order to appear well informed. Sometimes answers are given simply to please the interviewer.

One explanation for conscious and deliberate misrepresentation of facts is the "average man" hypothesis. It may be that individuals prefer to be viewed as average and that they alter their responses to conform more closely to their *perception* of the average person. "Average man effects" have been found to exist in response to questions about topics such as savings account balances, number of hours worked, car prices, voting behavior, and hospitalization.

Unconscious Misrepresentation

Even when a respondent is consciously trying to be truthful and cooperative, response bias can arise from question format, question content, or some other stimulus. For example, bias can be introduced by the situation in which the

National Restaurant Association research shows that when it comes to diet there is considerable response bias. In response to survey questions, Americans say they intend to be virtuous in their eating (fresh fruit and bran muffins) but what they actually eat (many hamburgers) doesn't reflect what they say. McDonald's McLean Deluxe, KFC's skinless fried chicken, and Pizza Hut's low-cal pizza are examples of products whose developers didn't account for response bias in survey research.

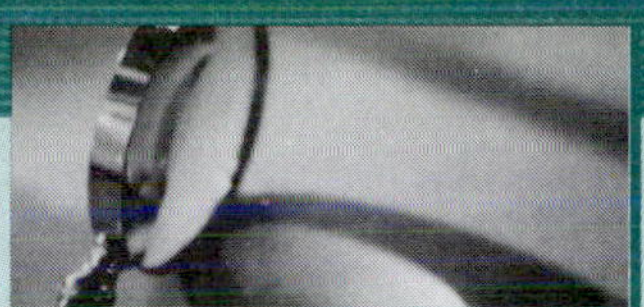

RESEARCH INSIGHT

SEMANTIC CONFUSION

The misunderstanding of questions by respondents often can be humorous.[7] Consider the following misunderstandings.

During advertising research for a disinfectant, the copy showed a housewife referring to the product as a "bathroom sanitizer." The respondent said, "Yes, I'm certainly for that. I think we so need sanity in the bathroom."

In a consumer survey for a new detergent, the question concerned locations of use of detergents within the home. A specific reference was to "germ-ridden areas." "I want a germ-ridden kitchen," one woman said to the interviewer. "What do you mean by that?" dutifully probed the interviewer. "Well, I want to be ridden of all my germs."

An insecticide marketer wished to learn the meaning attached to the term "residual insecticide." Researchers found out that the term meant not only what they always thought it meant, but also:

"has no residual"
"for insects that reside"
"more powerful"
"powdered form"

Research can be fun.

survey is administered. The results of two in-flight surveys concerning aircraft preference illustrate this point. Passengers flying on B-747s preferred B-747s to L-1011s (74 percent versus 19 percent), whereas passengers flying on L-1011s preferred L-1011s to B-747s (56 percent versus 38 percent). The difference in preferences appears to have been largely a function of the aircraft the respondents were flying on when the survey was conducted, although sample differences may have been a factor. A likely influence was the respondent's satisfaction with the plane on which he or she was flying when surveyed. In other words, in the absence of any strong preference, the respondent might simply have identified the aircraft traveled on and indicated that as his or her preference.[8]

Respondents who misunderstand the question may unconsciously provide a biased answer. Other respondents may be willing to answer but unable to do so because they have forgotten the exact details. "When was the last time you received on-the-job training?" may result in a "best guess" estimate because the respondent has forgotten the exact time.

A bias may also occur when a respondent has not thought about the question "sprung" on him or her by an interviewer. Many respondents will answer questions even though they have given them little thought. In most investigations of intentions, the predictability of the intention scales depends on how close the subject is to making a decision. Thus, asking if a respondent intends to change jobs will likely bring a biased response unless the decision is extremely close at hand. In a consumer-purchasing survey, the intentions of respondents who have little knowledge of the brand alternatives being surveyed or the intentions of respondents who have not yet made any purchase plans cannot be expected to predict purchase behavior.

Asking respondents how spicy they like their chili is not likely to produce well-articulated answers. In cases like this, respondents cannot adequately express their feelings in words—there is an unconscious communication breakdown. An international business research survey provides a classic example of unconscious misrepresentation due to a communication breakdown. A survey in the Philippines found that, despite seemingly high toothpaste usage, only a tiny percentage of people responded positively when asked, "Do you use toothpaste?" As it turned out, Colgate is a generic name for toothpaste in the Philippines. The positive response rate soared when researchers returned and asked, "Do you use Colgate?"

As the time between an activity or event and the survey contact increases, there is a tendency to underreport information about that activity or event. Time lapse influences people's ability to properly remember and communicate specific factors. Unconscious misrepresentation bias may also occur because people unconsciously avoid facing the realities of a future situation. For example, housing surveys record that Americans overwhelmingly continue to aspire to owning detached, single-family dwellings (preferably single-level structures requiring two to five times the amount of land per unit required for *attached* homes). However, builders know that *attached* housing purchases by first-time buyers are higher than respondents expect.

Types of Response Bias

There are five specific categories of response bias: acquiescence bias, extremity bias, interviewer bias, auspices bias, and social desirability bias. These categories overlap and are not mutually exclusive. A single biased answer may be distorted for many complex reasons, some deliberate misrepresentations and some unconscious misrepresentations.

acquiescence bias
A category of response bias in which individuals have a tendency to agree with all questions or to indicate a positive connotation to a new idea.

Acquiescence Bias Some respondents are very agreeable. They are "yea sayers" who accept all statements they are asked about. This tendency to agree with all or most questions is known as **acquiescence bias,** and it is particularly prominent in research on new products, new programs, or ideas previously unfamiliar to the respondents. When respondents are faced with a new concept, there is generally some acquiescence bias, since they tend to give positive connotations to most new ideas. Some individuals tend to disagree with all questions, but this is also a form of acquiescence bias. Thus, acquiescence bias is a response bias that arises from respondents' tendency to concur with a particular position.

extremity bias
A category of response bias that results because some individuals tend to use extremes when responding to questions.

Extremity Bias Some individuals tend to use extremes when responding to questions; others always avoid extreme positions and tend to respond neutrally. Response styles vary from person to person, and they may cause an **extremity bias** in the data.[9] This issue is dealt with in Chapter 14 on attitude research.

interviewer bias
Bias in the responses of subjects due to the influence of the interviewer.

Interviewer Bias Response bias may also occur because of an interplay between interviewer and respondent. If an interviewer's presence influences respondents to give untrue or modified answers, the survey is marred by **interviewer bias.** To many retired people or stay-at-home moms, the visit of an interviewer is a welcome break in routine activities; so respondents may give the "right" answers—the ones they believe will please the interviewer rather than the truthful response. Other respondents may wish to appear intelligent and wealthy—of course, they read *Fortune* rather than *Reader's Digest*.

The way the interviewer is dressed, the interviewer's age, gender, tone of voice, facial expressions, or other nonverbal characteristics may have some influence on a respondent's answers. If an interviewer smiles and makes a pos-

In Asia, cultural values about survey research differ from those in the United States. Asians have less patience with the abstract and rational question wording commonly used in the United States. Researchers must be alert for culture-bound sources of response bias in international business research. For example, the Japanese do not wish to contradict others. Thus, there is more acquiescence and yea saying.

itive statement after a respondent's answer, the respondent will be more likely to give similar responses. In a research study on sexual harassment among women, the use of male interviewers might not yield responses as candid as would the same survey conducted by female interviewers.

Most interviewers, contrary to instruction, shorten or rephrase questions to suit their needs. This potential influence on responses can be avoided (to some extent) if interviewers receive training and supervision that emphasizes the necessity of appearing neutral.

If interviews last too long, respondents may feel that their time is being wasted and they may answer as abruptly as possible, without a great deal of forethought.

auspices bias
Bias in the responses of subjects caused by their being influenced by the organization conducting the study.

Auspices Bias If the National Rifle Association is conducting a study on gun control, answers to its survey may be deliberately or subconsciously misrepresented because respondents are influenced by the organization conducting the study. If a national committee on gun control conducted the same study, respondents' answers might vary from those given in a NRA survey because of **auspices bias.**

social desirability bias
Bias in the responses of subjects caused by their desire, either conscious or unconscious, to gain prestige or to appear in a different social role.

Social Desirability Bias A **social desirability bias** in a response may occur, either consciously or unconsciously, because the respondent wishes to create a favorable impression or "save face" in the presence of an interviewer. Surveys of participation rates in outdoor recreation are based on respondent estimates rather than actual measurement of participation. People may overestimate their recreational activities because recreation is perceived as a socially desirable activity. Similarly, answering that one's income is only $40,000 a year might be difficult for someone whose self-concept is that of an upper-middle-class manager "about to make it big." Incomes are inflated, education is overstated, or "respectable" answers are given in order to gain prestige. In contrast, answers to questions that seek factual information or responses that are matters of public knowledge (zip code, number of children, and so on) are usually quite accurate.

An interviewer's presence may increase a respondent's tendency to give an inaccurate answer to sensitive questions such as "Did you vote in the last election?" "Do you have termites or roaches in your home?" or "Have you ever been fired from a job?"

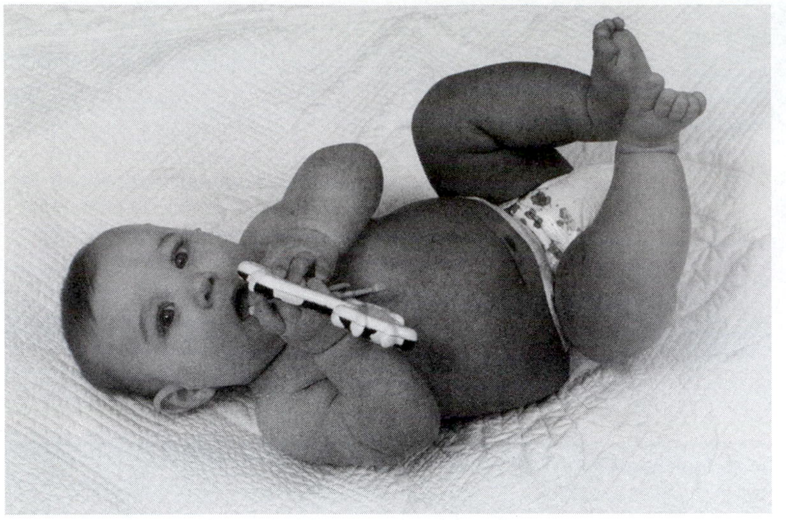

When asked in surveys, parents with children in diapers gave socially desirable answers when they said that they did not want the diapers they used to stereotype their children in male or female roles. However, when one company introduced gender-specific diapers, an American cultural tradition was reaffirmed: Parents bought pink diapers for girls and would not put pink diapers on boys.

ADMINISTRATIVE ERROR

administrative error
An error caused by the improper administration or execution of a research task.

The results of improper administration or execution of the research task are **administrative errors.** Such errors can be caused by carelessness, confusion, neglect, omission, or some other blunder. Four types of administrative error are data-processing error, sample selection error, interviewer error, and interviewer cheating.

Data-Processing Error

data-processing error
A category of administrative error that occurs because of incorrect data entry, incorrect computer programming, or other error during data analysis.

Processing data by computer, like any arithmetic or procedural process, is subject to error, because data must be edited, coded, and entered into the computer by people. The accuracy of data processed by computer depends on correct data entry and programming. **Data-processing error** can be minimized by establishing careful procedures for verifying each step in the data-processing stage.

Sample Selection Error

sample selection error
An administrative error caused by improper selection of a sample.

Executing a sampling plan free of administrative error is difficult. A firm that selects its sample from the telephone book will have some systematic error because unlisted numbers are not included. Stopping respondents during daytime hours in shopping centers excludes working people, who may shop by mail, Internet, or telephone. In other cases the "wrong person" may be interviewed. For example, consider a political pollster who uses random selection of telephone numbers rather than a list of registered voters to select a sample. Unregistered 17-year-olds may be willing to give their opinions, but they are the wrong people to ask because they cannot vote. **Sample selection error** is a systematic error that because of an error in either the sample design or execution of the sampling procedure results in an unrepresentative sample.

Interviewer Error

interviewer error
Administrative error caused by failure of an interviewer to record responses correctly.

Interviewers' abilities vary considerably. **Interviewer error** is introduced when interviewers record answers and check the wrong response or are not able to write fast enough to record answers verbatim. Also, selective perception may cause interviewers to misrecord responses that are not somewhat supportive of their own attitudes and opinions.

Interviewer Cheating

interviewer cheating
The practice of filling in fake answers or falsifying questionnaires while working as an interviewer.

Interviewer cheating occurs when an interviewer falsifies entire questionnaires or fills in the answers to certain questions. To finish interviews as quickly as possible or to avoid asking questions about sensitive topics, an interviewer may intentionally skip questions. To discourage interviewers from cheating, it is wise to let them know that a percentage of respondents will be called on to confirm that the initial interview was actually conducted.

RULE-OF-THUMB ESTIMATES FOR SYSTEMATIC ERROR

Sampling error due to random or chance fluctuations may be estimated by calculating confidence intervals with the statistical tools presented in Chapters 17, 21, 22, and 23.

The techniques for estimating *systematic* or *nonsampling error* are less precise. To estimate systematic error, many researchers have established conservative rules of thumb based on past experience. They have found it useful to have some benchmark figures or standards of comparison in order to understand how much error can be expected. For example, business researchers in the consumer packaged-goods field have a rule of thumb that says that only one-half of those who say they "will definitely buy within the next 3 months" actually do make a purchase. In consumer durables, however, the figures are considerably lower: Only about one-third of those who say they definitely will buy a certain durable within the next 3 months actually do so. Among those who say they "will probably buy," the number who actually purchase the durable is so much lower that it is scarcely worth including it in the early purchase estimates for new durables. Thus, researchers often present actual survey findings *and* their interpretation of estimated purchase response based on estimates of nonsampling error.

WHAT CAN BE DONE TO REDUCE SURVEY ERROR?

Now that the sources of error in surveys have been presented, you may have lost some of your optimism about survey research. Don't be discouraged! The discussion has emphasized the bad news because it is important for managers to realize that surveys are not a panacea. But there are ways of handling and reducing survey errors. For example, Chapter 15, on questionnaire design, discusses the reduction of response bias. Chapters 16 and 17 discuss the reduction of sample selection and random sampling error. Indeed, much of the remainder of this book discusses various techniques for reducing bias in survey research. The good news lies ahead.

CLASSIFYING SURVEY RESEARCH METHODS

Now that we have discussed some advantages and disadvantages of surveys in general, it is appropriate to classify surveys according to several criteria. Surveys may be classified according to the method of communication, the degree of structure and amount of disguise in a questionnaire, and the time frame in which the data are collected (temporal basis).

Classifying surveys according to method of communicating with the respondent, such as personal interviews, telephone interviews, mail surveys, and Internet surveys, is the subject of Chapter 10. The classifications based on structure and disguise and on time frame will be discussed in the remainder of this chapter.

Structured and Disguised Questions

structured question
A question that imposes a limit on the number of allowable responses.

disguised question
An indirect type of question that assumes that the purpose of the study must be hidden from respondents.

In designing a questionnaire (or an *interview schedule*), the researcher must decide how much structure or standardization is needed.[10] A **structured question** limits the number of responses available. For example, the respondent may be instructed to give one alternative response, such as "under 17," "18–35," or "over 35," to indicate his or her age. Unstructured questions do not restrict the answers the respondent is allowed. The open-ended, unstructured question "What do you think are the two most important problems facing your company today?" allows the respondent considerable freedom in answering.

The researcher must also decide whether undisguised or **disguised questions** will be utilized. A straightforward question like "Do you smoke marijuana on the job?" assumes that the respondent is willing to reveal the information. However, researchers know that some questions can threaten a person's ego, prestige, or self-concept. Therefore, they have designed various indirect approaches to questioning to disguise the purpose of the study.

Questionnaires can be categorized by their degree of structure and degree of disguise. For example, interviews in exploratory research might utilize *unstructured-disguised* questionnaires. (The projective techniques discussed in Chapter 7 fall into this category.) Other classifications are *structured-undisguised, unstructured-undisguised,* and *structured-disguised.* This classification system has two limitations. First, the degree of structure and the degree of disguise vary; they are not clear-cut categories. Second, most surveys are hybrids, asking both structured and unstructured questions.

Recognition of the degree of structure and disguise necessary to meet survey objectives will help in the selection of the appropriate communication medium for conducting the survey.

Classifying Surveys on a Temporal Basis

Although most surveys are for individual research projects conducted only once over a short time period, other projects require multiple surveys to be made over a long period of time. Thus, it is possible to classify surveys on a temporal basis.

Cross-Sectional Studies

A nationwide survey was taken to examine the different attitudes of cross-sections of the American public toward the arts, and one aspect of the survey dealt with museums. In general, the public's attitudes toward museums were very positive. Museum preferences varied by demographics or cross-sections of the population: People in towns and rural areas showed greater interest in historical museums, whereas city and suburban residents leaned more heavily toward art museums. The young (16- to 20-year-olds) were more interested than others in art museums and less interested in historical museums.[11]

cross-sectional study
A study in which various segments of a population are sampled at a single point in time.

This study was a **cross-sectional study** because the data were collected at a single point in time. In such a study, various segments of the population are sampled so that relationships among variables may be investigated by cross-tabulation. Most surveys fall into this category.

The typical means of analyzing a cross-sectional survey is to divide the sample into appropriate subgroups. For example, if the National Association of Accountants expects job title or position to influence attitudes toward continuing-education programs, then its survey data are broken down into subgroups based on job title and analyzed to see if there are any similarities or differences among the subgroups.

Longitudinal Studies

longitudinal study
A survey of respondents at different points in time, thus allowing analysis of response continuity and changes over time.

In a **longitudinal study** respondents are questioned at different moments in time. The purpose of longitudinal studies is to examine continuity of response and to observe changes that occur over time. For example, many syndicated polling services, such as Gallup, *New York Times*/CBS News, and Yankelovich Partners, conduct regular polls. In 1999 and again in 2000 the Gallup Poll found that Americans rate the honesty and ethical standards of nurses highest among 26 occupations. Longitudinal research from 1990 to 1998 found pharmacists rated highest for 9 years in a row. The same longitudinal study showed that car salesmen held the dubious honor of finishing dead last, as they have every time since the question was asked in 1977. However, Gallup Poll has found that two newcomers—HMO managers and telemarketers—are giving car salesmen competion at the low end of the spectrum. In 2000, 59 percent of respondents ranked college teacher as an occupation high or very high in honesty and ethics.[12]

Time is but the stream
I go a-fishing in.
HENRY DAVID THOREAU

The *Yankelovich MONITOR* has been tracking American values and attitudes for more than 30 years. It is an example of a longitudinal study that uses successive samples; its researchers survey several different samples at different times. Longitudinal studies of this type are sometimes called *cohort studies,* because similar groups of people (cohorts) are expected to be in each sample.

Studies that monitor voters' attitudes toward issues or their awareness of a candidate when a new political campaign is being launched frequently use successive samples. Having two or more sample groups avoids the problem of response bias that might result from a prior interview. A respondent who had been interviewed in an earlier survey about a certain issue or candidate may become more aware of the issue or pay more attention to the candidate after being interviewed. Using different samples eliminates this problem. Of course, researchers can never be sure whether changes in the variable being measured result from having different people in the sample or reflect an actual change in the variable over time.

panel study
A longitudinal study that involves collecting data from the same sample of individuals or households over time.

Panel Study A longitudinal study that involves collecting data from the same sample of individuals or households over time is called a **panel study.** Consider the researcher who is interested in learning about brand-switching behavior. A consumer panel consisting of a group of people who record their purchasing habits in a diary over time provides continuous information about the brand and product class. Such a longitudinal study enables the researcher to track repeat purchase behavior as well as changes in purchasing habits that occur in response to price changes, special promotions, or other changes in marketing strategy.

Typically, diaries recording a repetitive behavior are completed by the respondents and mailed back to the research organization. In other cases, when panel members have agreed to participate and evaluate a particular topic on a recurring basis (for example, in political polling), telephone interviews are often conducted. In recent years, Internet panels have grown in popularity. The nature of the research problem dictates which type of communication method is utilized.

Panel studies are often conducted by educational organizations and government institutions; examples of such studies include the University of Michigan's Panel Study of Income Dynamics, the Census Bureau's Survey of Income and Program Participation, and the Department of Education's National Longitudinal Study of the Class of 1972. The Survey of Income and Program Participation is one of the largest, with about 30,000 households participating. Because panels are generally expensive to establish and maintain, they are often managed by contractors who offer their services to many organizations. A number of commercial firms, such as NFO Worldwide, specialize in maintaining panels, such as the National Family Opinion Panel, and in collecting information from panel members about many diverse activities and issues. Clients of these firms find that by "sharing the expenses" with other clients, longitudinal data can be acquired at a reasonable cost.

The first questionnaire panel members are asked to complete typically contains general questions about the survey topic and about family members and household demographic characteristics. The purpose of such a questionnaire is to gather behavioral and demographic data that will be used to identify certain types of voters, heavy buyers, difficult-to-reach executives, and the like for future surveys. (Individuals who serve as members of commercial panels are generally compensated with cash, attractive gifts, or the chance to win a sweepstakes.)

TOTAL QUALITY MANAGEMENT AND SATISFACTION SURVEYS

total quality management
A business strategy for integrating customer-driven quality throughout an organization.

As we discussed in Chapter 1, **total quality management** is a business strategy that emphasizes market-driven quality as a top priority. Total quality management involves the process of properly implementing and adjusting business activities to assure customers' satisfaction with the quality of goods or services.

What Is Quality?

Organizations used to define quality by engineering standards. Most companies no longer see quality that way. Some managers say that a quality good or service needs only to conform to consumers' basic requirements; the product must be acceptable. Effective practitioners of total quality management, however, believe that the product's quality must go beyond acceptability for a given price range. Rather than leaving customers pleased that nothing went wrong, a product should give them some delightful surprises or provide unexpected benefits. In other words, quality assurance requires more than just meeting minimum standards.

The level of quality is the degree to which a good or service corresponds to buyers' expectations. Obviously, an S-class Jaguar does not compete with a Nissan Altima. Buyers of these automobiles are in different market segments and their expectations of quality differ widely. Nevertheless, managers at Jaguar and Nissan try to establish the quality levels their target markets expect and then to produce and market products that continually surpass expectations.

Internal and External Customers

Total quality management reaches beyond production operations to involve every employee in the organization. Every employee's job is linked to producing and marketing high-quality, low-cost products that satisfy customers.

Organizations like Arbor, Inc. that have adopted the total quality management philosophy, believe that a focus on customers must include more than external customers. They believe that everyone in the organization has customers:

> Every person, in every department, and at every level, has a customer. The customer is anyone to whom an individual provides service, information, support, or product. The customer may be another employee or department (internal) or [may be someone] outside the company (external).[13]

Thus, companies that have adopted the total quality management strategy view employees as internal customers. In fact, they see a chain of customers within the production/delivery system. An accountant who prepares a report for a sales manager should view the manager as a customer who will use the information to make decisions that will be helpful to external customers who buy the company's products. Every employee should contribute to quality improvement and satisfaction of customer's needs.

Effective total quality management programs work best when every employee knows exactly who his or her customers are and exactly what output internal and external customers expect. It is important to know how customers *perceive* their needs are being met. All too often differences between perceptions and reality are not understood.

IMPLEMENTING TOTAL QUALITY MANAGEMENT

Implementing a total quality management program requires considerable survey research. It involves routinely asking customers to rate a company against its competitors. It involves periodic measuring of employees' knowledge, attitudes, and expectations. It involves monitoring company performance against benchmark standards. It involves determining whether the company provided any delightful surprises or major disappointments. In other words, a total quality management strategy expresses the conviction that to improve quality, the organization must regularly conduct surveys to evaluate quality improvement.

Exhibit 9.2 illustrates the total quality management process. Overall tracking of quality improvement requires longitudinal research. The process begins with a *commitment and exploration stage,* during which management makes a commitment to total quality assurance and business researchers explore the needs and beliefs of external and internal customers. The research must discover what product features are important to customers, what problems customers have with the product, what aspects of the product operation or customer service have disappointed customers, what the company is doing right, and what it is doing wrong.

After internal and external customers' problems and desires have been identified, the *benchmarking stage* begins. Research must establish quantitative measures that can serve as benchmarks, or points of comparison, for evaluating

Exhibit 9.2 LONGITUDINAL RESEARCH FOR TOTAL QUALITY MANAGEMENT

Time	Business Research Activity with External Consumers (Customers)	Management Activity	Business Research Activity with Internal Consumers (Employees)
Time 1 Commitment and Exploration Stage	Exploratory study to determine the quality the customer wants; to discover customer problems; and to identify the importance of specific product attributes	Establish objective that the customer should define quality	Exploratory study to determine if internal customers, such as service employees, are aware of the need for service quality as a major means to achieve customer satisfaction and to determine if they know the quality standards for their jobs. Establish if employees are motivated and trained. Identify roadblocks that get in the way of employees meeting customer needs.
Time 2 Benchmarking Stage	Benchmarking study to measure overall satisfaction and quality ratings of specific attributes	Identify brand's position relative to competitors' satisfaction and quality rating; establish standards for customer satisfaction	Benchmarking to measure employees' actual performance and perceptions about performance
Time 3 Initial Quality Improvement Stage	Tracking wave #1 to measure trends in satisfaction and quality ratings	Improved Quality, Reward Performance	Tracking wave #1 to measure and compare what is actually happening with what is supposed to be happening. Establish if the company is conforming to its quality standards.
Time 4 Continuous Quality Improvement	Tracking wave #2 to measure trends in satisfaction and quality ratings	Improved Quality, Reward Performance	Tracking wave #2 to measure trends in quality improvement

future efforts. The surveys must establish initial measures of overall satisfaction, frequency of customer problems, and quality ratings for specific attributes. It is essential to identify the company's or brand's quality position relative to those of competitors.

During the *initial quality improvement stage,* the firm must establish quality improvement processes within the organization. Managers and employees must translate quality issues into the internal vocabulary of the organization. The company must establish performance standards and expectations for improvement.

For example, Bank One Corporation in Columbus, Ohio, translates customer requirements into specifications and policies. Management specifies quality measures, then sets procedures and objectives in terms of those standards. Bank One insists that everyone in the organization must know what is expected of them if they are to do things correctly on a consistent basis. Bank

RESEARCH INSIGHT

CUSTOMER SURVEYS: DON'T TELL, JUST ASK

You've just dropped your car off at the dealer for service, and a manager politely informs you that you will be asked to answer a quality survey by phone after the work is completed.[14] Or you've just walked out of the supermarket, and a store employee unexpectedly grills you about the convenience and speed of service you just received. In which of the two situations are you likely to be more critical? Hands down: You find more faults at the dealership.

No, not because drivers tend to be skeptical about service pricing at their dealerships. Consumer research shows that when people are told in advance that they will be asked to respond to a survey, they look for problems more actively. Companies want to satisfy their customers, so they are frequently conducting surveys about quality and satisfaction. People who expect to evaluate are decidedly more negative. In fact, merely asking people to state their expectations before they receive service makes them more negative—even though their predispositions may have been quite positive. For example, people who are asked if they think they will like a movie before seeing it will be more negative than people who are not asked beforehand.

One insists that every manager function as a "customer champion" who leads by example. Every service employee must know the quality standards for his or her job because employee awareness of the need for service quality is a major means to achieve customer satisfaction. Thus, managers and employees must be motivated and trained. Employees can face roadblocks that get in the way of meeting customer needs or sometimes they cannot solve problems on their own, so Bank One managers create teams of employees to develop quality improvement projects. The creation of employee teams to analyze and investigate problems and then to develop and implement solutions can lead to significant strides in the improvement of service quality.[15]

After managers and employees have set quality objectives and implemented procedures and standards, the firm then tracks satisfaction and quality ratings in successive waves. The purpose of such tracking is to measure trends in satisfaction and quality ratings. Business researchers determine whether the organization is meeting customer needs as specified by quantitative standards.

The next stage, *continuous quality improvement,* consists of many consecutive waves with the same purpose—to improve over the previous period. Continuous quality improvement requires that management allow employees to initiate problem solving without a lot of red tape. Employees should be able to initiate proactive communications with consumers. In tracking wave 2, results are compared with earlier stages to continue quality improvement management.

Management must reward performance. At Bank One, managers reward performance by recognizing individuals and groups that work diligently toward achieving the standards that have been set. Bank One gives "We Care" awards to individuals who do more than duty requires. They give "Best of the Best" awards to teams and branches with the best performance, and the best bank in the Bank One system receives the "Chairman's Quality Award for Customer Service."[16]

Exhibit 9.2 shows how total quality management programs measure performance against *consumers'* standards—not standards determined by quality engineers within the company. All changes within the organization are oriented toward improvement of consumers' perceptions of quality. The exhibit suggests the complex interrelationships between establishing consumer requirements, quantifying benchmark measures, setting objectives, performing business research studies, and making adjustments in the organization's operations to improve quality. Continuous quality improvement is an ongoing process.

Every Organization Can Use Business Research for TQM

The activities described in Exhibit 9.2 work for organizations that market either goods or services. However, service products and customer services offered along with goods have some distinctive aspects. We will discuss the quality of goods first and then turn to the quality of services.

In general, the marketers of consumer goods and organizational goods track customer satisfaction for quality improvement by measuring perceptions of the product characteristics listed in Exhibit 9.3.[17] These studies measure whether perceptions about product characteristics conform to customers' expectations and how these perceptions change over time. For example, all customer satisfaction surveys will investigate a brand's performance by asking how well the product performs its core function. For example, to determine the quality of a recycling lawn mower, a researcher would ask, "How well does the mower cut grass and eliminate the need for bagging cut grass?" The response may indicate whether the product's performance was a delightful surprise, something well beyond expected performance. Similar questions will be asked about the other major product characteristics.

Time after time, studies have shown large differences between what customers expect during the service encounter and the way frontline personnel deliver the service. Businesses who stress service quality strategies strive to manage the service encounter because the evaluation of service quality is highly dependent on what takes place during that encounter. Service quality involves a comparison of expectations with performance. Consumers who perceive high service quality believe that service providers match their expectations.

In organizations that wish to improve already high levels of service quality, managers identify customer service needs and plan the level of service quality. Managers' analysis and planning lead to specifications for the level of service to be delivered; then frontline personnel are trained and given the responsibility for quality service. Frontline personnel need to be motivated and encouraged to deliver the service according to the specifications planned by managers. Finally, the results of regular surveys of both customers and employees are measured against the standards. Business researchers investigate service quality by measuring satisfaction with the service attributes described in Exhibit 9.3.

The questionnaire in Exhibit 9.4 was used by a brokerage firm to measure its customers' satisfaction with the quality of its services. If service quality is below predetermined standards, adjustments are made.

EXHIBIT 9.3 DIMENSIONS OF QUALITY FOR GOODS AND SERVICES[18]

Quality Dimension	Characteristic	Example
Goods		
Performance	The product performs its core function.	A razor gives a close shave.
Features	The product has auxiliary dimensions that provide secondary benefits.	A motor oil comes in a convenient package.
Conformance with specifications	There is a low incidence of defects.	A vineyard never sells spoiled wine.
Reliability	The product performs consistently.	A lawn mower works properly each time it is used.
Durability	The economic life of the product is within an acceptable range.	A motorcycle runs fine for many years.
Serviceability	The system for servicing the product is efficient, competent, and convenient.	A computer software manufacturer maintains a toll-free phone number staffed by technical people who can answer questions quickly and accurately.
Aesthetic design	The product's design makes it look and feel like a quality product.	A snowmobile is aerodynamic.
Services		
Access	Contact with service personnel is easy.	A visit to the dentist does not involve a long wait.
Communication	The customer is informed and understands the service and how much it will cost.	A computer technician explains needed repairs without using overly technical terms.
Competence	The service providers have the required skills.	A tax accountant has a CPA certification
Courtesy	Personnel are polite and friendly.	Bank tellers smile and wish the customer "good day" at the close of each transaction.
Reliability	The service is performed consistently and personnel are dependable.	Employees of the office cleaning service arrive on schedule every Friday evening after working hours.
Credibility	Service providers have integrity.	The doctor who is performing a heart transplant is trustworthy and believable.

Exhibit 9.4 A Questionnaire to Measure Service Quality of a Full-Service Stock Brokerage

About your trade...

1. How would you rate the service you received from your personal broker/financial consultant *on this particular trade?*

Excellent 5	Good 4	Adequate 3	Not Very Good 2	Poor 1
☐	☐	☐	☐	☐

2. How courteous was the service you received from your personal broker/financial consultant?

Very Courteous 5	Courteous 4	Neutral 3	Not Very Courteous 2	Not at All Courteous 1	Do Not Recall 0
☐	☐	☐	☐	☐	☐

3. A. How satisfied were you with your personal broker/financial consultant's ability to answer your questions? **If you had no questions, skip to #4.**

Completely Satisfied 5	Satisfied 4	Neutral 3	Somewhat Dissatisfied 2	Very Dissatisfied 1	Do Not Recall 0
☐	☐	☐	☐	☐	☐

B. What did your question(s) involve? (You may check more than one box.)

☐ Products and services
☐ Trading requirements
☐ Research
☐ General market information
☐ Other

4. How would you rate the care and attention given to you by your personal broker/financial consultant while handling this trade?

Excellent 5	Good 4	Adequate 3	Not Very Good 2	Poor 1
☐	☐	☐	☐	☐

5. A. How satisfied were you with how quickly you reached your personal broker/financial consultant on the telephone?

Completely Satisfied 5	Satisfied 4	Neutral 3	Somewhat Dissatisfied 2	Very Dissatisfied 1	Do Not Recall 0
☐	☐	☐	☐	☐	☐

B. If you were not satisfied, please indicate why not. (You may check more than one box.)

☐ Phone rang too many times
☐ Put on hold
☐ Transferred too many times
☐ Waited too long listening to the recorded message
☐ Other (please specify) ________________

6. Was the trade completed accurately? If not, please explain.

Yes	No
☐	☐ ________________

7. How satisfied are you with the quality of service you receive from our company?

Completely Satisfied 5	Satisfied 4	Neutral 3	Somewhat Dissatisfied 2	Very Dissatisfied 1
☐	☐	☐	☐	☐

We are committed to providing the best possible service to our customers. A postage-paid envelope is enclosed for your convenience. Your prompt reply is appreciated.

SUMMARY

The survey is a common tool for business research. Surveys can provide a quick, inexpensive, and accurate means to obtain information for a variety of objectives. The typical survey is a descriptive research study that has the objective of measuring awareness, knowledge, behavior, opinions, or the like. The term *sample survey* is often used because a survey is expected to obtain a representative sample of the target population.

There are two major errors common to survey research. The first is random sampling error, caused by chance variation that results in a sample that is not absolutely representative of the target population. These kinds of errors are inevitable, but they can also be predicted by using the statistical methods discussed in the chapters on sampling.

The second major form of error is systematic bias, which takes several forms. Nonresponse error is caused by subjects' failing to respond to a survey. This error can be reduced by comparing the demographics of the sample population with those of the target population and by making added efforts to contact underrepresented groups.

Response bias occurs when a response to a questionnaire is falsified or misrepresented, either intentionally or inadvertently. There are five specific categories of response bias: acquiescence bias, extremity bias, interviewer bias, auspices bias, and social desirability bias. An additional source of survey error comes from administrative problems such as inconsistencies in interviewers' abilities, cheating, or data-processing mistakes.

Surveys may be classified according to the method of communication, by the degrees of structure and disguise in the questionnaire, and by the time frame. Questionnaires may be structured, with limited choices of responses, or unstructured to allow open-ended responses. Disguised questions may be used to probe sensitive subjects.

Surveys may consider the population at a single point in time or may follow trends over a period of time. The first approach, the cross-sectional study, is usually intended as a basis for separating the population into meaningful subgroups. The second type of study, the longitudinal approach, can reveal important population changes over time. Longitudinal studies may involve different sets of respondents or the same ones contacted repeatedly.

One form of longitudinal study is the panel study. Panels are expensive to operate, so they are often conducted by contractors who provide services to many companies, thus spreading the cost over many clients.

Total quality management is the process of properly implementing and adjusting the business strategy to assure customers' satisfaction with the quality of goods or services. Implementing a total quality management program requires considerable survey research, conducted routinely at all stages to ask customers to rate a company against its competitors and to measure employee attitudes. Results allow managers to monitor company performance against benchmark standards. Total quality management is an ongoing process for continuous quality improvement.

Key Terms

respondent
sample survey
survey
primary data
random sampling error
systematic error
sample bias
nonresponse error
nonrespondent

no contact
refusal
self-selection bias
response bias
acquiescence bias
extremity bias
interviewer bias
auspices bias
social desirability bias
administrative error
data-processing error
sample selection error
interviewer error
interviewer cheating
structured question
disguised question
cross-sectional study
longitudinal study
panel study
total quality management

Questions for Review and Critical Thinking

1. Name several nonbusiness applications of survey research.
2. A major petroleum corporation markets its gasoline under a national brand name through a franchise dealer organization. The corporation is considering building a number of company-owned stations with a new brand name to market a low-priced gasoline to compete with the independent dealers. Would survey research be useful? If so, how?
3. What survey research objectives might Ford Motor Company develop to learn about car buyers?
4. Give an example of each type of error listed in Exhibit 9.1.
5. A bank officer is asked what percentage of the time she spends talking on the telephone, in meetings, working on a computer, and working on other on-the-job activities. What types of error might be associated with her responses to such questions?
6. Name some common objectives of cross-sectional surveys.
7. Give an example of a political situation in which longitudinal research might be useful. Do the same for a business situation.
8. What topics about organizational behavior (or consumer behavior) might be too sensitive to question respondents about directly?
9. In a survey conducted by the National Endowment for the Arts, respondents were asked "Have you read a book within the last year?" Can you imagine any possible response bias arising from this question?
10. In what ways might survey results for buying intentions be adjusted for consumer optimism?
11. Is it ethical for a manufacturing company that wishes not to be identified as the sponsor of a mail survey to invent a fictitious research company name and print that name on letterhead paper for the survey? For example, a firm in Ohio wishing to disguise the fact that it is surveying its own distributors might choose a name such as North Central Research Corporation under which to present the survey.

Exploring the Internet

1. The *Washington Post* publishes the results of many of its opinion polls. Go to http://washingtonpost.com/wp-srv/politics/polls/polls.htm or http://washingtonpost.com/wp-srv/politics/polls/vault/vault.htm to find the latest poll or an archive of past polls.
2. Located at the University of Connecticut, the Roper Center is the largest library of public opinion data in the world. An online polling magazine and the methodology and findings of many surveys may be found at http://www.ropercenter.uconn.edu. Report on an article or study of your choice.
3. Go to the Ipsos-ASI Web site (http://www.asiresearch.com) to learn what type of survey research services the firm offers. What links to other survey research services can be accessed through ASI's Web site?
4. The National Longitudinal Surveys (NLS) conducted by the Bureau of Labor Statistics provide data on the labor force experience (current labor force and employment status, work history, and characteristics of current or last job) of five groups of the U.S. population. Go to http://www.bls.gov/nls.home/htm to learn about the objectives and methodology for this study.
5. The Princeton University Survey Research Center is located at http://www.princeton.edu/~abelson/index.html. List three of the numerous survey Web sites it identifies.

Case Suggestions

Case 9: Tulsa's Central Business District (B)
Video Case 12: Burke Inc.
Video Case 13: The Walker Information Group

CHAPTER

10

SURVEY RESEARCH: Basic Methods of Communication with Respondents

What you will learn in this chapter

- To understand when personal interviews, telephone interviews, or self-administered surveys should be conducted.
- To discuss the advantages and disadvantages of personal interviews.
- To explain when door-to-door personal interviews should be used instead of mall intercept interviews.
- To discuss the advantages and disadvantages of telephone surveys.
- To discuss random digit dialing to select telephone numbers for surveys.
- To discuss the advantages and disadvantages of mail, the Internet, and other means of distributing self-administered questionnaires.
- To understand how to increase response rates to mail surveys.
- To select the appropriate survey research design.
- To discuss the importance of pretesting a questionnaire.
- To explain how Internet technology has dramatically changed survey research.

Ford Motor Company conducts research clinics to appraise consumer reactions to exterior and interior styling of new automotive designs. First, fiberglass prototypes or mockups of proposed models are made. Then, respondents are recruited, usually after short telephone interviews, brought to a showroom, and shown the test mockups. Personal interviewers ask about every detail of the car as the prospects pore over it. Ultimately the results are fed back to designers in Detroit. Millions were spent on such surveys during the design of the Ford Taurus and Mercury Sable as well as the new S-type Jaguar.

Chrysler also conducts research to learn consumers' reactions to its cars, both on and off the road.[1] Chrysler researchers give each survey participant a device called a Gridpad to improve the accuracy and speed of data collection. The Gridpad, a flat, 8-by-10-inch box with a penlike wand, looks a little bit like an Etch-a-Sketch, but it is more sophisticated. While the survey respondent inspects new car models, multiple-choice questions are displayed on a screen. To respond, the individual simply touches the appropriate box on the Gridpad with the wand. Another gadget has a computerized touch screen showing a version of the car. Respondents specifically identify sections of the vehicle that they really like, or really hate. The end result is that survey researchers have a computerized map of a car's hot spots. When all the questions have been answered, the information is downloaded into a desktop computer. Previously, survey participants used pencils to fill out the questionnaires, which then had to be sorted, boxed, and shipped to processing centers. The manager of business planning/research for Chrysler estimates that using the Gridpad saves about 100,000 sheets of paper on each research project. ■

Studies of survey research show that approximately three out of four adult Americans have participated in some form of survey in their lives.[2] Survey data are obtained when people respond to questions asked by interviewers (interviews) or to questions they have read (questionnaires). Interviewers may communicate with respondents face-to-face or over the telephone. The use of self-administered questionnaires distributed by mail is a common way to obtain a representative sample for a survey, although there are other means of distribution that are growing in popularity.

Each technique for conducting surveys has its merits and shortcomings. The purpose of this chapter is to explain when different survey methods should be used. The chapter begins with a discussion of the types of media used to communicate with respondents. Then, surveys that use human interviewers—personal interviews and telephone surveys—are explained. Next, the chapter discusses noninteractive self-administered questionnaires with an emphasis on mail questionnaires. It goes on to explain how digital technology and the Internet are dramatically changing survey research.

MEDIA USED TO COMMUNICATE WITH RESPONDENTS

During most of the 20th century, survey data were obtained when individuals responded to questions asked by human interviewers or listed on questionnaires. Interviewers communicated with respondents face-to-face or over the telephone or respondents filled out self-administered paper questionnaires, which were typically distributed by mail. These media for conducting surveys remain popular with business researchers. However, as we mentioned in Chapters 2 and 8, digital technology is having a profound impact on society in general and on business research in particular. Its greatest impact is in the creation of new forms of communications media.

Human Interactive Media and Electronic Interactive Media

human interactive media
Personal forms of communication in which a message is directed at an individual (or small group), who then has the opportunity to interact with the communicator.

electronic interactive media
Communication media that allow an organization and an audience to interact using digital technology (for example, through the Internet).

When two people engage in a conversation, human interaction takes place. **Human interactive media** are personal forms of communication. One human being directs a message to and interacts with another individual (or a small group). When they think of interviewing, most people envision this type of face-to-face dialogue or a conversation on the telephone. **Electronic interactive media** allow organizations to reach a large audience, to personalize individual messages, and to interact with members of the audience using digital technology. To a large extent electronic interactive media are controlled by the users themselves. No other human need be present. In the context of surveys, respondents are not passive audience members. They are actively involved in a two-way communication when electronic interactive media are utilized.

The Internet, a medium that is radically altering many organizations' research strategies, provides a prominent example of the new electronic interactive media. Consumers determine what information they will be exposed to, and for how long they will view or hear it. Electronic interactive media also include CD-ROM and DVD materials, touch-tone telephone systems, interactive kiosks in stores, and other forms of digital technology.

Noninteractive Media

The traditional questionnaire received by mail and completed by the respondent does not allow a dialogue or an exchange of information for immediate feedback. Hence, from our perspective, self-administered questionnaires printed on paper are noninteractive. This does not mean that they are without merit. It only means that this type of survey is not as flexible as surveys using interactive communication media.

PERSONAL INTERVIEWS

Although the history of business research is sketchy, gathering information through face-to-face contact with individuals has a long history. Periodic censuses were used as a basis for tax rates and military conscription in the ancient empires of Egypt and Rome.[3] Later, during the Middle Ages, the merchant families of Fugger and Rothschild prospered in part because their far-flung organizations enabled them to get information before their competitors could.[4] Today it is not uncommon for survey researchers to present themselves on doorsteps throughout the United States and announce, "Good afternoon, my name is ______. I am with ______ Survey Research Company and we are conducting a survey on ______."

personal interview
The gathering of information through face-to-face contact with an individual.

A **personal interview** is a form of direct communication in which an interviewer asks respondents questions in a face-to-face situation. This versatile and flexible method is a two-way conversation between an interviewer and a respondent.

Personal interviews may take place in a factory, in a homeowner's doorway, in an executive's office, in a shopping mall, or in other settings. Our discussion begins by looking at the general characteristics of all types of personal interviews and then taking a separate look at personal interviews conducted in high-traffic locations, such as shopping malls.

Advantages of Personal Interviews

Business researchers find that personal interviews offer many advantages. The face-to-face interaction between interviewer and respondent has several characteristics that help researchers obtain complete and precise information.

Personal interviews are often conducted in a shopping mall or other high-traffic areas. Many visitors who enter Remington Park racetrack participate in a survey. Only one question is asked: "What is your zip code?" As simple as this survey may seem, it provides valuable information about the racetrack's key geographic market segments.

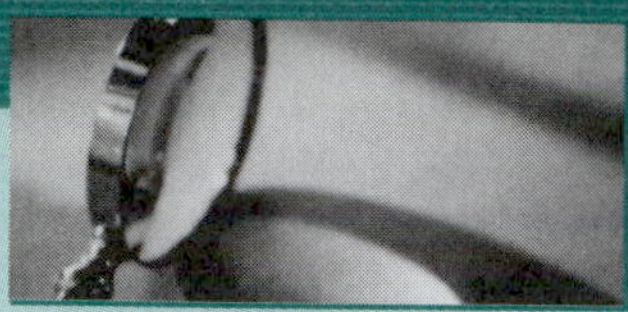

Research Insight

Could Lawyers Do Better?

Many law firms that once paid scant attention to client satisfaction are starting to seek out customers' complaints and even welcome their tirades.[5] Engaging in "relationship talks" is a new way of doing business for lawyers, who were better known not too long ago for their "we're-busy-so-take-it-or-leave-it" approach. But increasing competition for legal work has focused lawyers' attention on keeping clients happy.

Dozens of major law firms are turning to client-satisfaction surveys, generally conducted by outside consultants, to clear the air. So far, clients, who have long grumbled about unreturned phone calls and unintelligible bills, are reveling in the unaccustomed attention. Michael Gilbert, general counsel of KFC Corp., a unit of PepsiCo Inc., called the experience "cathartic. . . . It enabled me to be very candid," he recalls. "It gave me an opportunity to blow steam or express gratification."

Even the law firms involved are calling the surveys useful and not, ultimately, too painful. "One way you can differentiate yourself is if you find out what's important to clients and respond to it," says Luanne Pacer, a nonlawyer manager at Holland & Knight, a 290-lawyer Florida firm that has commissioned surveys. "If you're up against a firm that hasn't done that, you have an edge."

Typically, in such a survey, a law firm retains a management consulting or business research firm to visit a selected group of key clients and conduct personal interviews. The clients' in-house lawyers and other executives are queried about the quality of legal work, billing, and the company's overall relationship with the lawyers. Typically the personal interviews last anywhere from 10 minutes to more than 2 hours. Sometimes telephone interviews or self-administered questionnaires are used, but because of the nature of the clients, the length of the interview, and the need to probe complex answers, personal interviews are often best-suited for the task.

For the law firm, the tab runs between $5,000 and $25,000 depending on the scope of the survey. "It's the kind of thing that any business should be doing, asking its customers what it can do better and then striving to go out and do these things," says Ward Bower, of Altman Weil Pensa Inc., law firm management consultant. "A typical response from clients is, 'I thought they'd never ask.'" Anger over delays in returning phone calls is a recurring theme in client satisfaction surveys. Hinshaw & Culbertson, a 285-lawyer Chicago firm, started surveying its clients . . . when few other law firms had tried it. "It's very interesting to find that there is often a gap between our own perception of our firm and even our really good clients' perception," says Donald Mrozek, the law firm's managing partner. "We've really stressed . . . responsiveness to clients' needs and we generally think we're doing well to be returning phone calls by the end of the business day," Mrozek said. "That's been a big point around here. But we find the clients think that's average. . . . What we think we're doing so darn well at, they think we could do better."

The Opportunity for Feedback

Personal interviews allow for feedback. For example, an employee who is reluctant to provide sensitive information about her workplace may be reassured by the interviewer that her answers will be strictly confidential. The interviewer may also provide feedback in clarifying any questions an employee or any other respondent has about the instructions or questions. Circumstances may dictate that at the conclusion of the interview, the employee or other respondent be given additional information concerning the purpose of the study. This is easily accomplished with the personal interview.

Probing Complex Answers

probing
The verbal prompts made by a fieldworker when the respondent must be motivated to communicate his or her answer more fully. Probing encourages respondents to enlarge on, clarify, or explain answers.

An important characteristic of personal interviews is the opportunity to follow up, by **probing.** If a respondent's answer is brief or unclear, the researcher may ask for a clearer or more comprehensive explanation. Asking "Can you tell me more about what you had in mind?" is an example of probing. (See Chapter 18 on fieldwork for an expanded discussion of probing.) Although interviewers are expected to ask questions exactly as they appear on the questionnaire, probing allows the interviewer some flexibility. Depending on the research purpose, personal interviews vary in the degree to which questions are structured and in the amount of probing required or allowed. The personal interview is especially useful for obtaining unstructured information. Complex questions that cannot easily be asked in telephone or mail surveys can be handled by skillful interviewers.

Length of Interview

If the research objective requires an extremely lengthy questionnaire, personal interviews may be the only alternative. Generally, telephone interviews last fewer than 10 minutes, whereas a personal interview can be much longer, perhaps an hour and a half. A rule of thumb for mail surveys is that they not be longer than six pages.

Complete Questionnaires

item nonresponse
The technical term for an unanswered question on an otherwise complete questionnaire.

The social interaction between a well-trained interviewer and a respondent in a personal interview increases the likelihood that the respondent will answer all items on the questionnaire. The respondent who grows bored with a telephone interview may terminate the interview at his or her discretion simply by hanging up the phone. A respondent's self administration of a mail questionnaire requires more effort. Rather than write a long explanation, the respondent may fail to complete some of the questions on the self-administered questionnaire. **Item nonresponse**—that is, failure to provide an answer to a question—is less likely to occur with an experienced interviewer and a face-to-face interaction.

Props and Visual Aids

Interviewing respondents face to face allows the investigator to show them a new product sample, a sketch of a proposed office or plant layout, or some other visual aid. In a survey to determine whether a "super-lightweight" chain saw should be manufactured, visual props were necessary because the concept of a weight is difficult to imagine. Two small chain saws (already on the market) and a wooden prototype, disguised and weighted to look and feel like the proposed model, were put in the back of a station wagon. Respondents were asked to go to the car, pick up each chain saw, and compare them. This research could not have been done in a telephone interview or mail survey.

High Participation

While some people are reluctant to participate in a survey, the presence of an interviewer generally increases the percentage of people willing to complete the interview. Respondents are generally not required to do any reading or writing—all they have to do is talk. Most people enjoy sharing information and insights with friendly and sympathetic interviewers.

Personal interviews may be conducted at the respondent's home or office or in many other places. The locale for the interview generally influences the participation rate. Increasingly, personal interviews are being conducted in

RESEARCH INSIGHT

INSPECTOR CLOUSEAU OR THE CRUSTY FRENCH LOAF?

Advertising is a hectic business with tight deadlines and rush jobs.[6] When the Leo Burnett advertising agency suggested using an Inspector Clouseau look-alike for Pillsbury's new crusty French loaf, the idea was enthusiastically supported. What could be more perfect for a French bread product than using a spokesperson impersonating the "French" detective character in the Pink Panther movie comedies? Normally, Pillsbury surveys consumer reactions to a "rough" production version of the commercial, featuring either a series of still photographs or live-action videotapes that simulate the finished commercial. But because the timetable was tight, Pillsbury decided to forgo interviews evaluating a rough commercial and instead prepared a finished commercial.

Ultimately, when personal interviews were used to test reactions to the final commercial, the researchers uncovered a problem: *too much* character recognition. The researchers discovered that the Clouseau character was so successful that he overshadowed the product. The viewers tended to register high levels of recognition of Clouseau and forgot about the product. Although the character Clouseau connected very well with French bread, eliminating the research on a rough commercial caused a problem.

shopping malls, even though research has shown that the refusal rate is highest when respondents are shopping in a mall.[7]

Door-to-Door Interviews

door-to-door interview
Personal interview conducted at the respondent's home or place of business.

Door-to-door interviews provide a more representative sample of the population than mail questionnaires. For example, Hispanics, regardless of education, frequently prefer to communicate through the spoken rather than the written word. Response rates to mail surveys are substantially lower among Hispanics, regardless of whether the questionnaire is printed in English or Spanish. People who do not have telephones, who have unlisted telephone numbers, or who are otherwise difficult to contact may be reached through door-to-door interviews.[8] Such interviews can help solve the nonresponse problem; however, they may underrepresent some groups and overrepresent others.

Door-to-door interviews may exclude individuals living in multiple-dwelling units with security systems, such as high-rise apartment dwellers, or executives who are too busy to grant a personal interview during business hours. Telephoning individuals in these subgroups to make an appointment may make the total sample more representative; however, it may be difficult to obtain a representative sample of the security-conscious subgroup based on a listing in the telephone directory.

People who are at home and willing to participate, especially if interviews are conducted in the daytime, are somewhat more likely to be stay-at-home moms or retired people. These and other variables related to respondents' tendencies to stay at home may affect participation.

Intercept Interviews in Malls and Other High-Traffic Areas

mall intercept interviews
Personal interviews conducted in shopping malls.

Personal interviews conducted in shopping malls are referred to as **mall intercept interviews** (or *shopping center sampling*). Interviewers generally stop and attempt to question shoppers at a central point within the mall or at an entrance. The main reason these interviews are conducted at this location is their lower cost. No travel is required to the respondent's home—instead, the respondent comes to the interviewer, and thus many interviews can be carried out quickly. The incidence of refusal is high, however, because individuals may be in a hurry.

In mall intercept interviews the researcher must recognize that he or she should *not* be looking for a representative sample of the total population. Each mall will have its own customer characteristics, and there is likely to be a larger bias than with careful household probability sampling. However, personal interviews in shopping malls may be appropriate when demographic factors are not likely to influence the survey's findings or when the target group is a special population segment, such as the parents of children of bike-riding age. If the respondent indicates that he or she has a child of this age, the parent can then be brought into a rented space and shown several bikes. Or the interviewer may show visual materials, such as a videotape, or give an individual a product to take home and use; the respondent may then be recontacted later by telephone. Mall intercept interviews are also valuable when activities such as cooking and tasting food products must be closely coordinated and timed to follow each other. They may also be appropriate when something must be demonstrated. For example, when videocassette recorders and DVD players were innovations in the prototype stage, the effort and space required to set up and properly display these units ruled out door-to-door testing.

An organization's cafeteria, a primary meeting place at a convention, a college's student union, or another location with high pedestrian traffic may be chosen as a site for conducting personal interviews. In general, what we have said about mall intercept interviewing applies to these other, less common, forms of *high-traffic-area interviewing:* Costs are lower, but samples may not be as representative as with other types of interviewing.

Disadvantages of Personal Interviews

There are numerous advantages to personal interviews, but there are some disadvantages as well. Respondents are not guaranteed anonymity and therefore may be reluctant to provide confidential information to another person. Consider this question that was asked of top executives: "Do you see any major internal instabilities or threats (people, money, material, etc.) to the achievement of your department's objectives?" Many managers may be reluctant to answer this sensitive question honestly in a personal interview where their identity is known.

There is some evidence that the demographic characteristics of the interviewer influence respondents' answers. For example, one research study revealed that male interviewers produced larger variance than female interviewers in a survey where 85 percent of the respondents were female. Older interviewers, interviewing older respondents, produced more variance than other age combinations, whereas younger interviewers, interviewing younger respondents, produced the least variance.[9]

Differential interviewer techniques may be a source of interviewer bias. The rephrasing of a question, the interviewer's tone of voice, and the interviewer's

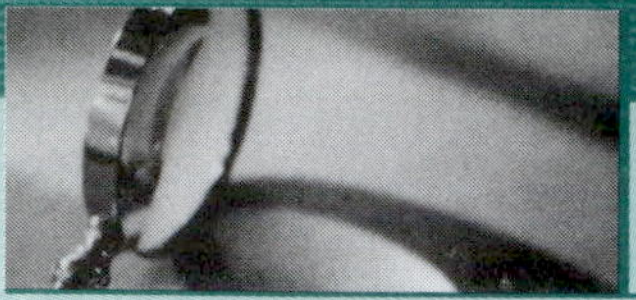

RESEARCH INSIGHT

DO YOU CHEAT ON YOUR INCOME TAX?

During the course of a personal interview concerning taxpayer opinions of the Internal Revenue Service, respondents were asked to provide information on income tax cheating behavior. Needless to say, these are highly sensitive questions. The IRS utilized the locked box technique to ask about tax cheating.

The locked box technique combines two methods of ensuring confidentiality. First, the questionnaire was self-administered. In this way, the respondent was free to reply in a truthful manner without concern about the interviewer's reaction. Second, upon completion of the instrument, the respondent rolled it up, secured it with a rubber band, and placed it in a sealed box (similar to a ballot box). The box was translucent, approximately the size of a shoe box, and designed to hold five or six questionnaires. At all times there was at least one other instrument in the box to further reassure the respondent that his or her response would remain confidential. Once the box was full, the instruments were removed and the box was resealed.

Respondents were read the following instructions and asked ten questions.[10]

Locked Box Instructions

At this point we would like to ask you some specific questions about how you handle your taxes. Because the questions are more personal, and we want you to answer honestly, you are going to fill out this part of the questionnaire privately. Once you are finished, you will drop the questionnaire into this box.

As you can see, the box is sealed, so your questionnaire will not be removed until it is sent to our central office in Virginia. I will never see the questionnaire. There is no identifying information on this questionnaire *(SHOW RESPONDENT QUESTIONNAIRE)*, so your answers will never be identified by name. In fact, we are not interested in individual persons, but in different kinds of people.

Questionnaire

1. Have you ever failed to file a tax return which you think you should have?
   Yes 1   No 2
2. Have you ever purposely listed more deductions than you were entitled to?
   Yes (Go to Q. 3) 1   No (Go to Q. 4) 2
3. About how much was the largest amount?
   Amount: ________
4. Have you ever purposely failed to report some income on your tax return-even just a minor amount?
   Yes (Go to Q. 5) 1   No (Go to Q. 6) 2
5. About how much was the largest amount of income you did not report?
   Amount: ________
6. How honest do you think you were in filling out your tax return for [year]? Circle the point on the line that best describes how honest you think you were.

Absolutely honest	Pretty honest	Somewhat honest	Not at all honest

7. Have you ever claimed a dependent on your tax return that you weren't really entitled to?
   Yes 1   No 2

8. Some people pay fewer taxes than are required by the tax code. Below is a list of ways people have avoided paying all their taxes. Show on the scale how often you use each of these methods by circling the appropriate point.

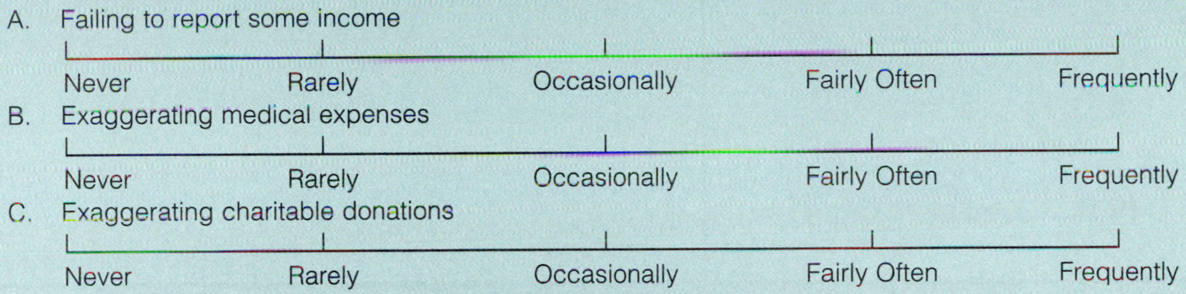

A. Failing to report some income

Never — Rarely — Occasionally — Fairly Often — Frequently

B. Exaggerating medical expenses

Never — Rarely — Occasionally — Fairly Often — Frequently

C. Exaggerating charitable donations

Never — Rarely — Occasionally — Fairly Often — Frequently

9. The following questions ask you about things some people do when filing their tax return. For each one, show on the scale whether your conscience would bother you if you did it. Circle one of the five numbers on the line to show whether your conscience would be bothered.

A. Not filing a return on purpose

1 (Not at all) — 2 — 3 (Some) — 4 — 5 (A lot)

B. Understating your income

1 (Not at all) — 2 — 3 (Some) — 4 — 5 (A lot)

C. Overstating your medical expenses

1 (Not at all) — 2 — 3 (Some) — 4 — 5 (A lot)

D. Claiming an extra dependent

1 (Not at all) — 2 — 3 (Some) — 4 — 5 (A lot)

E. Padding business travel expenses

1 (Not at all) — 2 — 3 (Some) — 4 — 5 (A lot)

F. Not declaring large gambling earnings

1 (Not at all) — 2 — 3 (Some) — 4 — 5 (A lot)

G. Not declaring the value of a service that you traded with someone else

1 (Not at all) — 2 — 3 (Some) — 4 — 5 (A lot)

10. Did you stretch the truth a little in order to pay fewer taxes for [year]?

Yes . . . . 1　　　No 2

Entryware data collection software from Techneos Systems (http://www.techneos.com) can be used on Palm handheld computers to automate personal interviews. Using easy-to-carry handheld computers increases the time efficiency of interviewers and eliminates the need for later data entry.

appearance may influence the respondent's answer. Consider the interviewer who has conducted 100 personal interviews. During the next one the interviewer may lose concentration and either selectively perceive or anticipate the respondent's answer, so that the interpretation of the response may be somewhat different from what the respondent intended.

Typically the public thinks of the person who does business research as a "dedicated scientist." Unfortunately, interviewers who are hired as researchers do not necessarily fit the ideal.[11] Considerable interviewer variability is possible. Cheating is possible. Interviewers may "cut corners" to save time and energy. They may fake parts of their reporting by "dummying up" part or all of the questionnaire. Control over interviewers is important to assure that difficult, embarrassing, and time-consuming questions are handled properly.

Cost

Personal interviews are generally more expensive than mail, Internet, and telephone surveys. The geographic proximity of respondents, the length and complexity of the questionnaire, and the number of people who are nonrespondents because they could not be contacted all influence the cost of the personal interview.

Lack of Anonymity of Respondent

Because a respondent in a personal interview is not anonymous and may be reluctant to provide confidential information to another person, researchers often spend considerable time and effort to phrase sensitive questions so that social desirability bias will not occur. For example, the interviewer might show a respondent a card that lists possible answers and ask him or her to read a category number rather than verbalize sensitive answers.

Necessity for Callbacks

callback
An attempt to recontact an individual selected for the sample.

When a person selected to be in the sample cannot be contacted on the first visit, a systematic procedure is normally initiated to call back at another time. **Callbacks,** or attempts to recontact individuals selected for the sample, are the major means of reducing nonresponse error. Calling back a sampling unit is more expensive than interviewing the person the first time around, because subjects who were initially not at home are generally more widely dispersed geographically than the original sampling units. Callbacks are important because not-at-home individuals (e.g., working women) may systematically vary from those who *are* at home (nonworking women, retired people, and the like).

Global Considerations

Willingness to participate in a personal interview varies dramatically around the world. For example, in many Middle Eastern countries women would never consent to be interviewed by a man. And, in many countries, the idea of discussing grooming behavior and personal-care products with a stranger would be highly offensive. Few would consent to be interviewed on such topics.

TO THE POINT

A man's feet should be planted in his country, but his eyes should survey the world.

GEORGE SANTAYANA

The norms about appropriate business conduct also influence business people's willingness to provide information to interviewers. For example, conducting business-to-business interviews in Japan during business hours is difficult because managers, strongly loyal to their firm, believe that they have an absolute responsibility to oversee employees while on the job. In some cultures when a business person is reluctant to be interviewed, it may be possible to get a reputable third party to intervene so that the interview may take place.

TELEPHONE INTERVIEWS

"Good evening, I'm with a nationwide survey research company. Are you a registered voter?"
"Yes."
"Do you plan to vote in next week's primary election?"

telephone interviewing
Contacting respondents by telephone to gather responses to survey questions.

For several decades **telephone interviewing** has been a mainstay of commercial survey research. The quality of data obtained by telephone may be comparable to that collected in personal interviews. Respondents may even be more willing to provide detailed and reliable information on a variety of personal topics over the telephone than in personal interviews. Telephone surveys can provide representative samples of the general population in most industrialized countries.

Central Location Interviewing

central location interviewing
The practice of conducting telephone interviews from a central location, which allows effective supervision and control of the quality of interviewing.

Research agencies and interviewing services typically conduct all telephone interviews from a central location. WATS (Wide-Area Telecommunications Service) lines, provided by a long-distance telephone service at fixed rates, allow interviewers to make unlimited telephone calls throughout the entire country or within a specific geographic area. Such **central location interviewing** allows firms to hire staffs of professional interviewers and to supervise and control the quality of interviewing more effectively. When telephone interviews are centralized and computerized, the research becomes even more cost-effective.

Computer-Assisted Telephone Interviewing

computer-assisted telephone interviewing (CATI)
A type of telephone interviewing in which the interviewer reads questions from a computer screen and enters the respondent's answers directly into a computer.

Advances in computer technology allow responses to telephone interviews to be entered directly into a computer in a process known as **computer-assisted telephone interviewing (CATI).** Telephone interviewers are seated at computer terminals. A monitor displays the questionnaire, one question at a time, along with precoded possible responses to each question. The interviewer reads each question as it is shown on the screen. When the respondent answers, the interviewer enters the response into the computer, and it is automatically stored in the computer's memory when the computer displays the next question on the screen. A computer-assisted telephone interview requires that answers to questionnaires be highly structured. For instance, if a respondent gives an answer that is not acceptable (i.e., not precoded and programmed), the computer will reject that answer. Computer-assisted telephone interviewing systems include telephone management systems that select telephone numbers, dial numbers automatically, and provide other labor-saving functions. One such system can automatically control sample selection by randomly generating names or fulfilling a sample quota. Another call management feature is automatic callback scheduling. The computer is programmed to time recontact attempts (e.g., recall no-contacts after 2 hours, recall busy numbers after 10 minutes) and allow the interviewer to enter a time slot (a later day and hour) when a busy respondent indicates that he or she can be interviewed. Still another feature supplies daily status reports on the number of completed interviews relative to quotas.

The Strengths and Weaknesses of Telephone Interviews

The advantages and disadvantages of telephone interviews are different from those of personal interviews.

Speed

The speed of data collection is a major advantage of telephone interviewing. For example, union officials who wish to survey members' attitudes toward a strike may conduct a telephone survey during the last few days of the bargaining process. Whereas data collection with mail or personal interviews can take several weeks, hundreds of telephone interviews can be conducted literally overnight. When the interviewer enters the respondents' answers directly into a computerized system, data processing can be done even faster.

Cost

As the cost of personal interviews continues to increase, telephone interviews are becoming relatively inexpensive. It is estimated that the cost of telephone interviews is less than 25 percent of the cost of door-to-door personal interviews. Travel time and costs are eliminated. However, the typical Internet survey is less expensive than a telephone survey.

Absence of Face-to-Face Contact

Telephone interviews are more impersonal than face-to-face interviews. Respondents may answer embarrassing or confidential questions more willingly in a telephone interview than in a personal interview. However, mail surveys, although not perfect, are better media for gathering extremely sensitive information because they are completely anonymous. There is some evidence that people provide information on income and other financial matters only reluctantly, even in telephone interviews. Such questions may be personally threatening for a variety of reasons, and high refusal rates for this type of question occur with each form of survey research.

Although telephone calls may be less threatening because the interviewer is not physically present, the absence of face-to-face contact can also be a liability. The respondent cannot see that the interviewer is still writing down the previous comment and may continue to elaborate on an answer. If the respondent pauses to think about an answer, the interviewer may not realize this and may go on to the next question. Hence, there is a greater tendency for interviewers to record no answers and incomplete answers in telephone interviews than in personal interviews.

Cooperation

In some neighborhoods, people are reluctant to allow a stranger to come inside their homes, or even stop on the doorstep. The same people, however, may be perfectly willing to cooperate with a telephone survey request. Likewise, interviewers may be somewhat reluctant to conduct face-to-face interviews in certain neighborhoods, especially during the evening hours. Telephone interviewing avoids these problems. However, some individuals refuse to participate in telephone interviews, and the researcher should be aware of potential nonresponse bias. Finally, there is some evidence that the likelihood that a call will go unanswered because a respondent is not at home varies by the time of day, the day of the week, and the month.

One trend is very clear. In the last decade, telephone response rates have dropped from 40 percent to around 15 percent.[12] Willingness to cooperate with telephone interviewing has declined over the years. In addition, it is increasingly difficult to establish contact with potential respondents, for three major reasons: (1) the proliferation of telephone numbers dedicated exclusively to fax machines and/or computers, (2) the widespread use of a nondedicated phone line to access the Internet, and (3) the use of call-screening devices to avoid unwanted calls.[13]

Many people who own telephone answering machines will not return a call to help someone conduct a survey. Some researchers argue that leaving the proper message on an answering machine will produce return calls. The message left on the machine should explicitly state that the purpose of the call is not sales related.[14] Others believe no message should be left because researchers will reach respondents when they call back. The logic is based on the fact that answering machines are usually not on 100 percent of the time. Thus, if enough callbacks are made at different times and on different days, most respondents will be reached.[15] Caller ID services can have the same effect as answering machines if respondents do not pick up the phone when the display reads "out of area" or when an unfamiliar survey organization's name and number appear on the display.

Telephone researchers can run into several roadblocks when trying to obtain executives' cooperation at work. Executives may be difficult to reach because secretaries may be hesitant to forward calls. Part of their job may be to minimize the number of telephone interruptions in the boss's day. Voice messaging systems have replaced switchboard operators and secretaries in many organizations. These technologies, which often require the caller to know the manager's extension number, can make telephone access almost impossible. Researchers who leave messages on these systems often must make callbacks.

Callbacks

An unanswered call, a busy signal, or a respondent who is not at home requires a callback. Telephone callbacks are substantially easier and less expensive than personal interview callbacks.

Research Insight

PRIVACY MANAGER

Ameritech's new phone service called Privacy Manager is intended to screen annoying sales calls from telemarketers.[16] However, it is also sure to have an impact on research using telephone surveys.

Ameritech's chief executive says that in product usage tests with 200 customers, reaction to Privacy Manager was off the charts. "We have never had a product test this good," says the CEO, including voice mail and caller ID. "It satisfied a need that consumers have just been pleading to have resolved."

Here's how it works: A customer needs to have a caller ID display box first, and the Privacy Manager service costs $3.95 a month. Calls normally shown on the ID screen with a name and number go right through. But any calls made from phone numbers classified as "private," "blocked," "out of area," "unavailable," or "unknown," are intercepted. A recording comes on and asks outside callers to reveal their identity by speaking their name.

Anyone who doesn't leave a name is automatically disconnected. If the caller leaves a name, the person they attempted to call hears the phone ring, and a recorded message says: "This is Privacy Manager. You have a call from . . ." and then the name of the caller. The customer is given three choices: accept the call, reject it, or play a message that says: "We don't accept telemarketing calls. Please add me to your do-not-call list."

Representative Samples

When an organization's employees are the group of interest, there are few sampling problems in telephone surveys. However, when the group of interest consists of the general population, there are practical difficulties in obtaining a representative sample based on listings in the telephone directory.

Approximately 95 percent of households in the United States have telephones. People without phones are more likely to be poor, aged, or rural. Unlisted phone numbers and numbers obtained too recently to be printed in the directory pose a more significant problem. People have unlisted phone numbers for two reasons: because of mobility and by choice. Individuals whose phone numbers are unlisted because of a recent move differ slightly from those with published numbers. The unlisted group tends to be younger, more urban, and less likely to own a single-family dwelling. Households that maintain unlisted phone numbers by choice tend to have higher incomes. And, as previously mentioned, a number of low-income households are unlisted by circumstance. Researchers conducting surveys in areas where the proportion of unlisted phone numbers is high, such as in California (Sacramento, 71.6 percent; Oakland, 71.4 percent; Los Angeles/Long Beach, 69.8 percent), should be aware of this situation.[17] In other markets, such as Knoxville, Tennessee, where less than 16 percent of phone numbers are unlisted, this may not be a major problem. Nationally, slightly less than 30 percent of phone numbers are unlisted.

random digit dialing
A method of obtaining a representative sample for a telephone interview by using a table of random numbers to generate telephone numbers.

The problem of unlisted telephone numbers can be partially resolved through **random digit dialing.** Random digit dialing eliminates the "counting of names" in a list (e.g., calling every fiftieth name in a column) and subjectively determining whether a directory listing is a business, institution, or household.

In the simplest form of random digit dialing, telephone exchanges (prefixes) for the geographic areas in the sample are obtained; then, using a table of random numbers, the last four digits of the telephone numbers are selected. Telephone directories can be ignored entirely or used in combination with the assignment of one or several random digits. Random digit dialing also helps overcome problems due to new listings and recent changes in numbers.

Lack of Visual Medium

Since visual aids cannot be utilized in telephone interviews, research that requires visual material cannot be conducted by phone. Certain attitude scales and measuring instruments, such as the semantic differential (see Chapter 13), cannot be used easily because they require a graphic scale.

Limited Duration

One disadvantage of the telephone interview is that the length of the interview is limited. Respondents who feel they have spent too much time in the interview will simply hang up. Refusal to cooperate with interviews is directly related to interview length. A major study on survey research found that for interviews of 5 minutes or less, the refusal rate was 21 percent. For interviews of 6–12 minutes, the refusal rate was 41 percent. For interviews of 13 minutes or more, the refusal rate was 47 percent.[18] Thirty minutes is the maximum time most respondents will spend, unless they are highly interested in the survey subject. (In unusual cases a few highly interested respondents may put up with longer interviews.) A good rule of thumb is to plan telephone interviews to be approximately 10 minutes long.

Computerized, Voice-Activated Telephone Interviews

Technological advances have combined computerized telephone dialing and voice-activated computer messages to allow researchers to conduct telephone interviews without human interviewers. However, researchers have found that **computerized, voice-activated telephone interviewing** works best with very short, simple questionnaires. One telephone survey system includes a voice-synthesized module controlled by a microprocessor. With it the sponsor is able to register a caller's single response such as "true/false," "yes/no," "like/dislike," or "for/against." This type of system has been used by television and radio stations to register callers' responses to certain issues. Typically, the interview begins with the announcement that the respondent is listening to a recorded message. Many people are intrigued with the idea of talking to a robot or a computer, so they stay on the line. The computer then asks questions, leaving blank tape in between to record the answers. If the respondent does not answer the first two questions, the computer disconnects and goes to the next telephone number.

computerized, voice-activated telephone interviewing
A form of computer-assisted interviewing in which a voice-synthesized module records a respondent's single-word response in a computer file.

Global Considerations

Different cultures often have different norms about what telephone behavior is proper. For example, business-to-business researchers have learned that Latin American business people will not open up to strangers on the telephone. Hence, these researchers usually find personal interviews more suitable than telephone surveys. In Japan, respondents consider it ill-mannered if telephone interviews last more than 20 minutes.[19]

Exhibit 10.1 Self-Administered Questionnaires Can Be Either Printed or Electronic

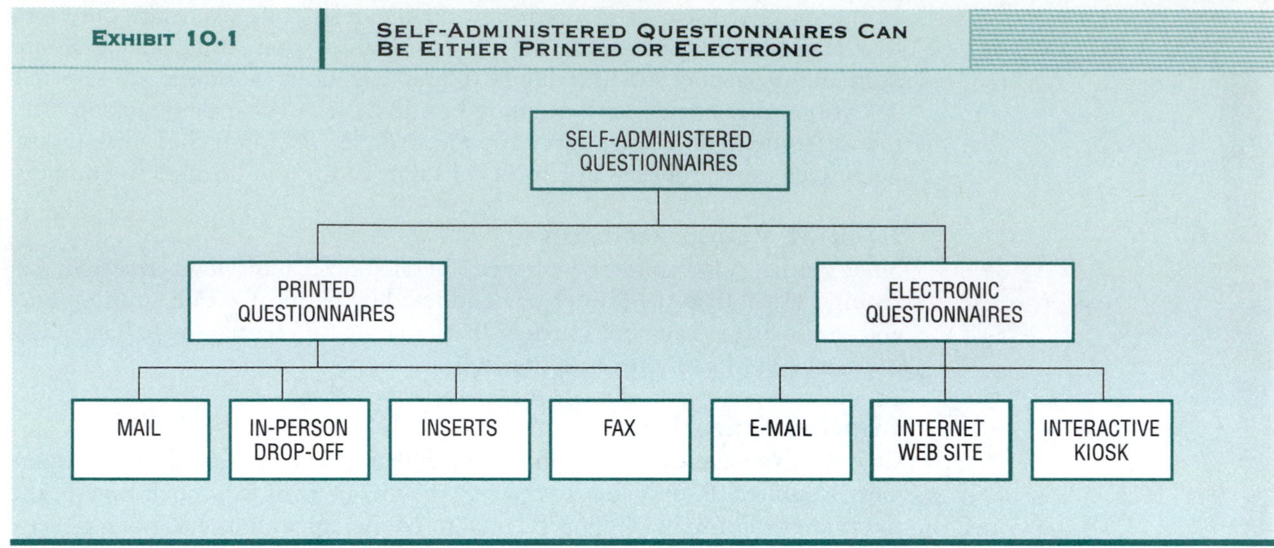

SELF-ADMINISTERED QUESTIONNAIRES

self-administered questionnaire
A questionnaire that is filled in by the respondent rather than by an interviewer.

In many situations an interviewer's presence is not essential. Educational researchers and college professors frequently administer questionnaires to classes of students. Managers call employees together for group sessions where questionnaires are administered. **Self-administered questionnaires** are given to exiting zoo and museum visitors, toll road users, and many other people who use services. Members of Congress regularly mail questionnaires to registered voters.

Business researchers distribute questionnaires to respondents in many other ways. (See Exhibit 10.1). They insert questionnaires in packages and magazines. They may place questionnaires at points of purchase or in high-traffic locations. They may even fax questionnaires to individuals. Questionnaires are usually printed on paper, but they may be posted on the Internet or sent via e-mail. No matter how self-administered questionnaires are distributed, they are different from interviews because the respondent takes responsibility for reading and answering the questions.

Self-administered questionnaires present a challenge to the business researcher because they rely on the clarity of the written word rather than on the skills of the interviewer. The nature of self-administered questionnaires is best illustrated by explaining mail questionnaires.

Mail Questionnaires

mail survey
A self-administered questionnaire sent through the mail to respondents.

A **mail survey** is a self-administered questionnaire sent to respondents through the mail. This paper-and-pencil method has several advantages and disadvantages.

Advantages and Disadvantages

Geographic Flexibility Mail questionnaires can reach a geographically dispersed sample simultaneously and at a relatively low cost because interviewers are not required. Respondents in isolated areas (e.g., farmers) or those who are otherwise difficult to reach (e.g., executives) can be contacted more easily by mail. A pharmaceutical firm may find that doctors are not available

Human resource development managers are concerned with employee motivation. They routinely use self-administered surveys to monitor employee morale and attitudes. The results are reported to the management of the organization. At many companies these employee satisfaction surveys are considered to be so important that the results constitute part of the basis for calculating every manager's annual bonus.

for personal or telephone interviews. Rural and urban doctors, practicing in widely dispersed geographic areas can be reached readily by mail, however.

Self-administered questionnaires can be widely distributed to a large number of employees, so organizational problems may be assessed quickly and inexpensively. Questionnaires may be administered during group meetings, or an hour-long period may be scheduled during the working day so that employees can complete a self-administered questionnaire. These meetings generally allow the researcher to provide basic instructions to a large group (generally fewer than 50 people) and to minimize data collection time. They also give the researcher the opportunity to "debrief" subjects without spending a great deal of time and effort.

Cost Mail questionnaires are relatively inexpensive compared to personal interviews and telephone surveys. However, mail surveys are not cheap. Most include a follow-up mailing, which requires additional postage and the printing of additional questionnaires. And it usually isn't cost-effective to try to minimize costs on printing—questionnaires that are duplicated on poor-quality paper have a greater likelihood of being thrown in the wastebasket than those prepared with more expensive, higher-quality printing.

Respondent Convenience Mail surveys and self-administered questionnaires can be filled out whenever the respondent has time. Thus, there is a better chance that respondents will take time to think about their replies. Many hard-to-reach respondents place a high value on responding to surveys at their own convenience and are best contacted by mail. In some situations, particularly in organizational research, mail questionnaires allow respondents time to collect facts (such as records of absenteeism) that they may not be able to recall without checking. Being able to check information by verifying records or, in the case of household surveys, by consulting with family members should provide more valid, factual information than from either personal or telephone interviews.

Mail order companies utilize mail surveys to estimate sales volume for catalog items by mailing out a "mock" catalog as part of the questionnaire. Respondents are asked to indicate how likely they are to order selected items. Utilizing the mail allows respondents to consult other family members and to make their decisions within a reasonable time span.

Interviewer's Absence Although the absence of an interviewer can induce respondents to reveal sensitive or socially undesirable information, it can also be a disadvantage. Once the respondent receives the questionnaire, the questioning process is beyond the researcher's control. Although the printed stimulus is the same, each respondent will attach a different personal meaning to each question.

Selective perception operates in research as well as in other areas of daily life. The respondent does not have the opportunity to ask questions of an interviewer. Problems that might be clarified in an interview can remain misunderstandings in a mail survey. There is no interviewer who can probe for additional information or clarification of an answer, and the recorded answers must be assumed to be complete.

Standardized Questions Mail questionnaires are highly standardized, and the questions are quite structured. Questions and instructions must be clear-cut and straightforward. If questions or instructions are difficult to comprehend, respondents will make their own interpretations, which may be wrong. Interviewing, on the other hand, allows for feedback from the interviewer regarding the respondent's comprehension of the questionnaire.

An interviewer who notices that the first 50 respondents are having difficulty understanding a question can report this to the research analyst so that revisions can be made. However, once questionnaires are mailed, it is difficult to change the format or questions.

When a respondent self-administers a questionnaire, the entire questionnaire may be read before any answer is given. Thus, questions at the end of a questionnaire may bias answers to earlier questions.

Time Is Money If time is a factor in management's interest in research results or if attitudes are rapidly changing (e.g., toward a political event), mail surveys may not be the best communication medium. A minimum of 2 to 3 weeks is necessary to receive the majority of the responses. Follow-up mailings, which are usually sent when returns begin to trickle in, require an additional 2 or 3 weeks. The time between the first mailing and the cut-off date (when questionnaires will no longer be accepted) is usually 6 to 8 weeks.

In a regional or local study, personal interviews can be conducted more quickly. However, conducting a national study by mail may be substantially faster than conducting personal interviews across the nation.

Length of Mail Questionnaire Mail questionnaires vary considerably in length, ranging from extremely short postcard questionnaires to lengthy, multipage booklets requiring respondents to fill in thousands of answers. As previously mentioned, a general rule of thumb is that a mail questionnaire should not exceed six pages.[20] When a questionnaire requires a respondent to expend a great deal of effort, an incentive is generally required to induce the respondent to return the questionnaire. The following sections discuss several ways to obtain high response rates even when questionnaires are longer than average.

Increasing Response Rates for Mail Surveys

response rate
The number of questionnaires returned or completed, divided by the total number of eligible people who were contacted or asked to participate in the survey.

Response Rates Questionnaires that are boring, unclear, or too complex get thrown in the wastebasket. A poorly designed mail questionnaire may be returned by only 15 percent of those sampled; in other words, it will have a 15 percent response rate. The *basic* calculation for obtaining a **response rate** is to count the number of questionnaires returned or completed, then divide this total by the number of eligible people who were contacted or asked to participate in the survey. Typically, the number in the denominator is adjusted for faulty addresses and similar problems that reduce the number of eligible participants.

The major limitations of mail questionnaires relate to response problems. Respondents who answer the questionnaire may not be typical of all people in the sample. Individuals with a special interest in the topic are more likely to respond to a mail survey than those who are indifferent.

A researcher has no assurance that the intended subject will fill out the questionnaire. The wrong person's answering the questions may be a problem when corporate executives, physicians, and other professionals are surveyed. (A subordinate may be given the mail questionnaire to complete.)

Mail survey respondents tend to be better educated than nonrespondents. If they return the questionnaire at all, poorly educated respondents who cannot read and write well may skip open-ended questions where respondents are required to write out their answers. There is some evidence that cooperation and response rate rise as home value increases.[21] Also, if the sample has a high proportion of retired and well-off householders, response rates will be lower.

Rarely will a mail survey have the response rates of up to 90 percent that can be achieved with personal interviews. However, the use of follow-up mailings and other techniques may increase the response rate to an acceptable percentage. If a mail survey has a low response rate, it should not be considered reliable unless it can be demonstrated with some form of verification that the nonrespondents are similar to the respondents.

Nonresponse error is always a potential problem with mail surveys. Individuals who are interested in the general subject of the survey are more likely to respond than those with less interest or little experience. Thus, people who hold extreme positions on an issue are more likely to respond than individuals who are largely indifferent to the topic. To minimize this bias, researchers have developed a number of techniques to increase the response rate to mail surveys. For example, almost all surveys include postage-paid return envelopes. Forcing respondents to pay their own postage can substantially reduce the response rate. Using a stamped return envelope instead of a bulk rate business reply envelope increases response rates even more.[22] Designing and formatting attractive questionnaires and wording questions so that they are easy to understand also help ensure a good response rate. However, special efforts may be required even with a sound questionnaire. Several of these are discussed in the following subsections.

cover letter
A letter that accompanies the questionnaire in a mail survey. Its purpose is to induce the reader to complete and return the questionnaire.

Cover Letter The **cover letter** that accompanies the questionnaire or is printed on the first page of the questionnaire booklet is an important means of inducing a reader to complete and return the questionnaire. Exhibit 10.2 illustrates a cover letter and some of the points considered by a survey research expert to be important in gaining respondents' attention and cooperation. The first paragraph of the letter explains why the study is important. The basic

EXHIBIT 10.2 | **EXAMPLE OF COVER LETTER FOR HOUSEHOLD SURVEY**[23]

Official letterhead	WASHINGTON STATE UNIVERSITY PULLMAN, WASHINGTON 99968 DEPARTMENT OF RURAL SOCIOLOGY ROOM 23, Wilman Hall
Date mailed	April 19, 20xx
Inside address in matching type	Oliver Jones 2190 Fontane Road Spokane, Washington 99467
What study is about; its social usefulness	Bills have been introduced in Congress and our State Legislature to encourage the growth of rural and small town areas and slow down that of large cities. These bills could greatly affect the quality of life provided in both rural and urban places. However, no one really knows in what kinds of communities people like yourself want to live or what is thought about these proposed programs.
Why recipient is important (and, if needed, who should complete the questionnaire)	Your household is one of a small number in which people are being asked to give their opinion on these matters. It was drawn in a random sample of the entire state. In order that the results will truly represent the thinking of the people of Washington, it is important that each questionnaire be completed and returned. It is also important that we have about the same number of men and women participating in this study. Thus, we would like the questionnaire for your household to be completed by an adult female. If none is present, then it should be completed by an adult male.
Promise of confidentiality; explanation of identification number	You may be assured of complete confidentiality. The questionnaire has an identification number for mailing purposes only. This is so that we may check your name off of the mailing list when your questionnaire is returned. Your name will never be placed on the questionnaire.
Usefulness of study *Token reward for participation*	The results of this research will be made available to officials and representatives in our state's government, members of Congress, and all interested citizens. You may receive a summary of results by writing "copy of results requested" on the back of the returns envelope, and printing your name and address below it. Please do not put this information on your questionnaire itself.
What to do if questions arise	I would be most happy to answer any questions you might have. Please write or call. The telephone number is (509) 335-8623.
Appreciation	Thank you for your assistance.
	Sincerely,
Pressed blue ballpoint signature	
Title	Don A. Dillman Project Director

appeal alludes to the social usefulness of responding. Two other frequently used appeals are asking for help ("Will you do us a favor?") and the egotistical appeal ("Your opinions are important!"). Most cover letters promise confidentiality, invite the recipient to use an enclosed postage-paid reply envelope, describe any incentive or reward for participation, explain that answering the questionnaire will not be difficult and will take only a short time, and describe how the person was scientifically selected for participation.

A personalized letter addressed to a specific individual shows the respondent that he or she is important. Including an individually typed cover letter on letterhead versus a printed form is an important element in increasing the response rate in mail surveys.[24]

Money Helps The respondent's motivation for returning a questionnaire may be increased by offering monetary incentives or premiums. Although pens, lottery tickets, and a variety of premiums have been used, monetary incentives appear to be the most effective and least biasing incentive. Although money may be useful to all respondents, its primary advantage may be that it attracts attention and creates a sense of obligation. It is perhaps for this reason that monetary incentives work for all income categories. Often cover letters try to boost response rates with messages such as "We know that the attached dollar [or coin] cannot compensate you for your time. It is just a token of our appreciation." Response rates increase dramatically when the monetary incentive is to be sent to a charity of the respondent's choice rather than directly to the respondent.

Interesting Questions The topic of the research and thus the point of the questions cannot be manipulated without changing the problem definition. However, certain interesting questions can be added to the questionnaire, perhaps at the beginning, to stimulate respondents' interest and to induce cooperation. Questions that are of little concern to the researchers, but which the respondents want to answer, may provide respondents who are indifferent to the major portion of the questionnaire with a reason for responding.[25]

Follow-Ups Exhibit 10.3 shows graphic plots of cumulative response rates for two mail surveys. The curves are typical of most mail surveys: The response rates start relatively high for the first 2 weeks (as indicated by the steepness of each curve), then gradually taper off.

follow-up
A letter or postcard reminding a respondent to return a questionnaire.

After responses from the first wave of mailings begin to trickle in, most studies use a **follow-up**, a letter or postcard reminder. These request that the questionnaires be returned because a 100 percent return rate is important. A follow-up may include a duplicate questionnaire or may merely be a reminder to return the original questionnaire. Multiple contacts almost always increase response rates. The more attempts made to reach people, the greater the chances of their responding.[26]

EXHIBIT 10.3 PLOT OF ACTUAL RESPONSE PATTERNS FOR TWO COMMERCIAL SURVEYS

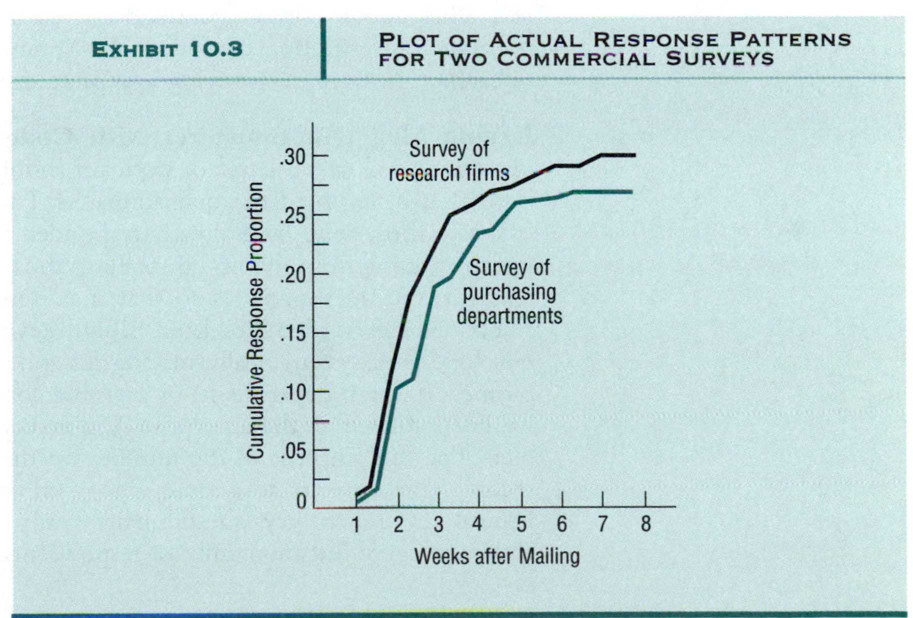

Both of the studies in Exhibit 10.3 used follow-ups. Notice how the cumulative response rates picked up around week four.

Preliminary Notification Advance notification, by either letter or telephone, that a questionnaire will be arriving has been successful in increasing response rates in some situations. For example, this technique helps ensure a high cooperation rate in filling out diaries on television watching or radio listening. Advance notices that go out closer to the questionnaire mailing time produce better results than those sent too far in advance. The optimal lead time for advanced notification is approximately 3 days before the mail survey is to arrive.

Survey Sponsorship It has already been suggested that auspices bias may result from the sponsorship of a survey. One industrial company wished to conduct a survey of its wholesalers to learn their stocking policies and their attitudes concerning competing manufacturers. A mail questionnaire sent on the corporate letterhead very likely would have received a much lower response rate than the questionnaire actually sent, which utilized the letterhead of a commercial survey research firm. Sponsorship by well-known and prestigious organizations, such as universities or government agencies, may also significantly influence response rates. A mail survey sent to members of a longitudinal panel will receive an exceptionally high response rate because panel members have already agreed to cooperate with the organization conducting the survey. For example, well-managed commercial panels can obtain a 75 percent response rate.

Other Techniques Researchers have tried numerous other innovations to increase response rate. For example, variations in the type of postage (regular vs. commemorative stamp), personalization of the cover letter (computer-personalized letters vs. printed), color of the questionnaire, and manipulation of many other aspects of the mechanics of mail surveys have been tried. Each has had at least limited success in certain situations; unfortunately, under other conditions similar techniques have failed to increase response rates significantly. The researcher should always consider the particular situation. For example, a researcher investigating consumers has a much different audience than the researcher involved in surveying corporate executives.

Keying Mail Questionnaires with Codes A survey researcher who is planning a follow-up letter or postcard should not disturb respondents who have already returned the questionnaires. The expense of mailing questionnaires to those who have already responded is usually avoidable. One device for eliminating from follow-up mailings those who have already responded is to mark the questionnaires so that members of the sample who have not responded can be identified later. "Blind" keying of questionnaires on a return envelope (e.g., systematically varying the job number or room number of the business research department) or a visible code number on the questionnaire has been utilized for these purposes. Visible keying is indicated with statements like "The sole purpose of the number on the last page is to avoid sending a second questionnaire to people who complete and return the first one."[27] Ethical researchers key questionnaires only to increase response rates and always preserve the anonymity of respondents.

Global Considerations

Researchers conducting surveys in more than one country must recognize that postal services and cultural circumstances differ around the world. For example, Backer Spielvogel & Bates Worldwide advertising agency conducts its Global Scan survey in 18 countries. In the United States the questionnaire is mailed to individuals selected for the sample. However, in several countries mail is not used. The questionnaire may be personally delivered to respondents because of a fear of letter bombs, unreliable delivery service, or low literacy rates in a particular country.[28]

Self-Administered Questionnaires that Use Other Forms of Distribution

Many forms of self-administered, printed questionnaires are very similar to mail questionnaires. Airlines frequently pass out questionnaires to passengers during flights. Restaurants, hotels, and other service establishments print short questionnaires on cards so that customers can evaluate the service. *Tennis Magazine, Advertising Age, Wired,* and many other publications have used inserted questionnaires to survey current readers inexpensively, and often the results provide material for a magazine article.

Many manufacturers use their warranty or owner registration cards to collect demographic information and data about where and why products were purchased. Using owner registration cards is an extremely economical technique for tracing trends in consumer habits. Again, sampling problems may arise because people who fill out these self-administered questionnaires differ from those who do not.

drop-off method
A survey method that requires the interviewer to travel to the respondent's location to drop off questionnaires that will be picked up later.

Extremely long questionnaires may be dropped off by an interviewer and then picked up later. The **drop-off method** sacrifices some cost savings because it requires traveling to each respondent's location.

Fax Surveys

fax survey
A survey that uses questionnaires distributed and/or returned via fax machines.

With **fax surveys** potential survey respondents receive and/or return questionnaires via fax machines.[29] A questionnaire inserted in a magazine may instruct the respondent to clip out the questionnaire and fax it to a certain phone number. In a mail survey, a prepaid-postage envelope places little burden on the respondent. But faxing a questionnaire to a long-distance number requires that the respondent pay for the transmission of the fax. Thus, a disadvantage of fax surveys is that only respondents with fax machines who are willing to exert the extra effort will return questionnaires. Again, people with extreme opinions will be more likely to respond.

Questionnaires can also be distributed via fax machine. These fax surveys reduce the sender's printing and postage costs and can be delivered and returned faster than traditional mail surveys. Questionnaires distributed via fax can deal with timely issues. Although most households do not have fax machines, when the sample consists of organizations that are likely to have fax machines, the sample coverage may be adequate.

E-Mail Surveys

e-mail survey
A survey that uses questionnaires distributed and returned by e-mail.

Questionnaires can be distributed via e-mail. E-mail is a relatively new method of communication, and many individuals cannot be reached this way. However, certain projects lend themselves to **e-mail surveys,** such as internal surveys of employees or satisfaction surveys of retail buyers who regularly deal with an organization via e-mail. The benefits of incorporating a questionnaire in an e-mail include speed of distribution, lower distribution and processing costs, faster turnaround time, more flexibility, and less handling of paper questionnaires. The speed of e-mail distribution and the quick response time can be major advantages for surveys about time-sensitive issues.

Not much academic research has been conducted on e-mail surveys. Nevertheless, it has been argued that many respondents feel they can be more candid in e-mail than in person or on the telephone, for the same reasons they are candid on other self-administered questionnaires. Nevertheless, in many organizations employees know that their e-mails are not secure, that "eavesdropping" by a supervisor could occur. Further, maintaining respondents' anonymity is difficult, because a reply to an e-mail message typically includes the sender's address. Researchers designing e-mail surveys should assure respondents that their answers will be confidential.

Not all e-mail systems have the same capacity: Some handle color and graphics well; others are limited to text. The extensive differences in the capabilities of respondents' computers and e-mail software limit the types of questions and the layout of the e-mail questionnaire. For example, the display settings for computer screens vary widely, and wrap-around of lines may put the questions and the answer choices into strange and difficult-to-read patterns.[30] Many novice e-mail users find it difficult to mark answers in "brackets" on an e-mail questionnaire and/or to send a completed questionnaire using the e-mail Reply function. For this reason, some researchers give the respondents the option to print out the questionnaire, complete it in writing, and return it via regular mail. Unless the research is an internal organizational survey, this, of course, requires the respondent to pay postage.

In general, the guidelines for printed mail surveys apply to e-mail surveys. However, there are some differences, because the cover letter and the question-

ARE YOU STILL BUYING MARKETING RESEARCH DONE THE OLD-FASHIONED WAY?

Do it better on the Internet with the company that pioneered online marketing research.

Our panel of more than one million consumers from all across the Internet is the largest of its kind. It produces robust samples of any demographic or lifestyle you choose. You'll get richer, more actionable information quicker than you can say dot com.

Join the Research Revolution!™ Contact the world's most experienced Internet marketing research company for studies online, on time, on target and on budget.

www.greenfield.com 888.291.9997

Greenfield Online (http://www.greenfield.com) is a business research company that conducts surveys exclusively online. This advertisement shows that the company offers a variety of services such as concept testing.

naire appear in a single e-mail message. A potential respondent who is not immediately motivated to respond, especially one who considers an unsolicited e-mail survey to be "spam," can quickly hit the Delete button to remove the e-mail. This suggests that e-mail cover letters should be brief and the questionnaires relatively short. The cover letter should explain how the company got the recipient's name. It should include a valid return e-mail address and reveal who is conducting the survey. Also, if the e-mail lists more than one address in the "TO" or "CC" boxes field, all recipients will see the entire list of names. This has the potential to cause response bias and nonresponse error. When possible, the e-mail should be addressed to a single person. (The blind carbon copy, or BCC, box can be used if the same message must be sent to an entire sample.)[31]

E-mail has another important role in survey research. E-mail letters can be used as cover letters asking respondents to participate in an Internet survey. Such e-mails typically provide a password and a link to a unique Web site location that requires a password for access.

Internet Surveys

internet survey
A self-administered questionnaire posted on a web site.

An **Internet survey** is a self-administered questionnaire posted on a Web site. Respondents provide answers to questions displayed on screen by highlighting a phrase, clicking an icon, or keying in an answer. Many survey researchers believe that Internet surveys are the wave of the future. Like every other type of survey, Internet surveys have both advantages and disadvantages.

Speed and Cost Effectiveness Internet surveys allow marketers to reach a large audience (possibly a global one), to personalize individual messages, and to secure confidential answers quickly and cost-effectively. These computer-to-computer self-administered questionnaires eliminate the costs of paper, postage, data entry, and other administrative costs. Once an Internet questionnaire has been developed, the incremental cost of reaching additional respondents is marginal. Hence, samples can be larger than with interviews or other types of self-administered questionnaires. Even with larger samples, surveys that used to take many weeks can be conducted in a week or less.

Visual Appeal and Interactivity Surveys conducted on the Internet can be interactive. The researcher can use more sophisticated lines of questioning based on the respondents' prior answers. Many of these interactive surveys utilize color, sound, and animation, which may help to increase respondents' cooperation and willingness to spend more time answering the questionnaires. The Internet is an excellent medium for the presentation of visual materials, such as photographs or drawings of product prototypes, advertisements, and movie trailers. Innovative measuring instruments that take advantage of the ability to adjust backgrounds, fonts, color, and other features have been designed and applied with considerable success.

Digital Marketing Services' Video E-Val is a proprietary technique combining a CD-ROM that is mailed to potential respondents and Internet software that controls the playing of high-quality video clips from the disc.[32] This technique allows researchers to evaluate television commercials, television programs, and other large video files without being restricted by the small percentage of potentially qualified respondents who have access to broadband communications.

Respondent Participation and Cooperation Participation in some Internet surveys occurs because computer users intentionally navigate to a particular Web site where questions are displayed. For example, a survey of

Technological innovation can change more than the way business is done in an industry—it can change entire cultures. The mechanical clock made regular working hours possible. The invention of railroads and the mass production of automobiles changed the way people thought about distance. Television changed the way we think about news and entertainment. And, because the Internet is the most important communication medium since television, it is having a profound impact on business research. Self-administered polls will increasingly become electronic transactions between people and machines.[33]

over 10,000 visitors to the Ticketmaster Web site helped Ticketmaster better understand its customer purchase patterns and evaluate visitor satisfaction with the site. In some cases individuals expect to encounter a survey at a Web site; in other cases it is totally unexpected. In some instances the visitor cannot venture beyond the survey page without providing information for the organization's "registration" questionnaire. When the computer user does not expect a survey on a Web site and participation is voluntary, response rates are low. And, as with other questionnaires that rely on voluntary self-selection, participants tend to be more interested in or involved with the subject of the research than the average person.

For many other Internet surveys, respondents are initially contacted via e-mail. Often they are members of research panels who have previously indicated their willingness to cooperate. When individuals receive an e-mail invitation to participate, they are given a password or PIN number. The e-mail invitation also provides a link to a URL or instructs a user to visit a certain Web site that contains a welcome screen. Like a cover letter in a mail survey, the **welcome screen** of an Internet survey serves as a means to gain the respondents' cooperation and provides brief instructions. Experienced researchers require a respondent to provide a password or PIN to move from the welcome page to the first question. This prevents access by individuals who are not part of the scientifically selected sample. Assigning a unique password code also allows the researchers to track the responses of each respondent, thereby identifying any respondent who makes an effort to answer the questionnaire more than once.

welcome screen
The first Web page in an Internet survey, which introduces the survey and requests that the respondent enter a password or PIN.

Ideally, the welcome screen contains the name of the research company and information about how to contact the organization if the respondent has

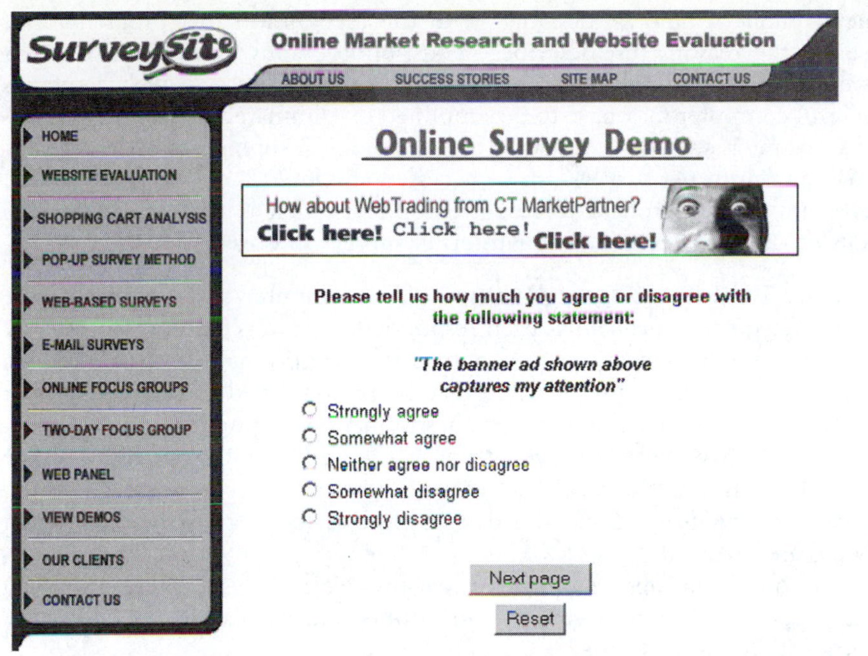

This page from the SurveySite Web site (http://www.surveysite.com/) shows part of an Internet survey to assess consumers' attitudes toward banner advertising. The Internet is an excellent medium for survey research on visual materials, especially those that include animation.

a problem or concern. A typical statement might be: "If you have any concerns or questions about this survey, or if you experience any technical difficulties, please contact [Name of research organization]."

Representative Samples The population to be studied, the purpose of the research, and the sampling methods determine the quality of Internet samples, which varies substantially. If the sample consists merely of those who visit a Web page and voluntarily fill out a questionnaire, it is not likely to be representative of the entire U.S. population, because of self-selection error. However, if the purpose of the research is to evaluate how visitors feel about a Web site, randomly selecting, say, every 100th visitor to fill out a questionnaire may accomplish the study's purpose. Scientifically drawn samples from a research panel or samples randomly generated in other ways can also be representative.[34]

Of course, a major disadvantage of Internet surveys is that many individuals in the general population cannot access the Internet. And, all people with Internet access do not have the same level of technology. Many individuals with low-speed Internet connections (low bandwidth) cannot quickly download high-resolution graphic files. Many lack powerful computers or software that is compatible with advanced features programmed into many Internet questionnaires. Some individuals have minimal computer skills. They may not know how to navigate through and provide answers to an Internet questionnaire. For example, the advanced audio and video streaming technology of RealPlayer or Windows Media Player software can be used to incorporate a television commercial and questions about its effectiveness into an Internet survey. However, some respondents might find downloading the file too slow or even impossible; others might not have the RealPlayer or Windows Media Player software; and others might not know how to use the software to view the commercial.

It appears that for the foreseeable future, Internet surveys sampling the general public should be designed with the recognition that problems may arise for the reasons just described. Thus, photographs, animation, or other cutting-edge technological features created on the researcher's/Web designer's powerful computer may have to be simplified or eliminated so that all respondents can interact at the same level of technological sophistication.

Because Internet surveys can be accessed anytime (24/7) from anywhere, they can reach certain hard-to-reach respondents, such as doctors. Chapter 16 discusses sampling techniques for Internet surveys in greater detail.

Accurate Real-Time Data Capture The computer-to-computer nature of Internet surveys means that each respondent's answers are entered directly into the researcher's computer as soon as the questionnaire is submitted. In addition, the questionnaire software may be programmed to reject improper data entry. For example, on a paper questionnaire a respondent might incorrectly check two responses even though the instructions call for a single answer. In an Internet survey, this mistake can be interactively corrected as the survey is taking place. Thus, the data capture is more accurate than when humans are involved.

Real-time data capture allows for real-time data analysis. A researcher can review up-to-the-minute sample size counts and tabulation data from an Internet survey in real time.

Callbacks When the sample for an Internet survey is drawn from a consumer panel, it is easy to recontact those who have not yet completed the questionnaire. It is often a simple matter of having computer software automatically send e-mail reminders to panel members who did not visit the welcome page. Computer software can also identify the passwords of respondents who completed only a portion of the questionnaire and send those people customized messages. Sometimes such e-mails offer additional incentives to those individuals who comply with the request to finish the questionnaire.

Personalized and Flexible Questioning Computer-interactive Internet surveys are programmed in much the same way as computer-assisted telephone interviews. That is, the software that is used allows questioning to branch off into two or more different lines depending on the respondent's answer to a filtered question. The difference is that there is no interviewer. The respondent interacts directly with software on a Web site. In other words, the computer program asks questions in a sequence determined by a respondent's previous answers. The questions appear on the computer screen, and answers are recorded by simply pressing a key or clicking an icon, thus immediately entering the data into the computer's memory. Of course, these methods avoid labor costs associated with data collection and processing of paper-and-pencil questionnaires.

This ability to sequence questions based on previous responses is a major advantage of computer-assisted surveys. The computer can be programmed to skip from question 6 to question 9 if the answer to question 6 is no. Furthermore, responses to previous questions can lead to questions that can be personalized for individual respondents. (For example, "When you cannot buy your favorite brand, Revlon, what brand of lipstick do you prefer?") Often the respondent's name appears in questions to personalize the questionnaire. Fewer and more relevant questions speed up the response process and increase the respondent's involvement with the survey.

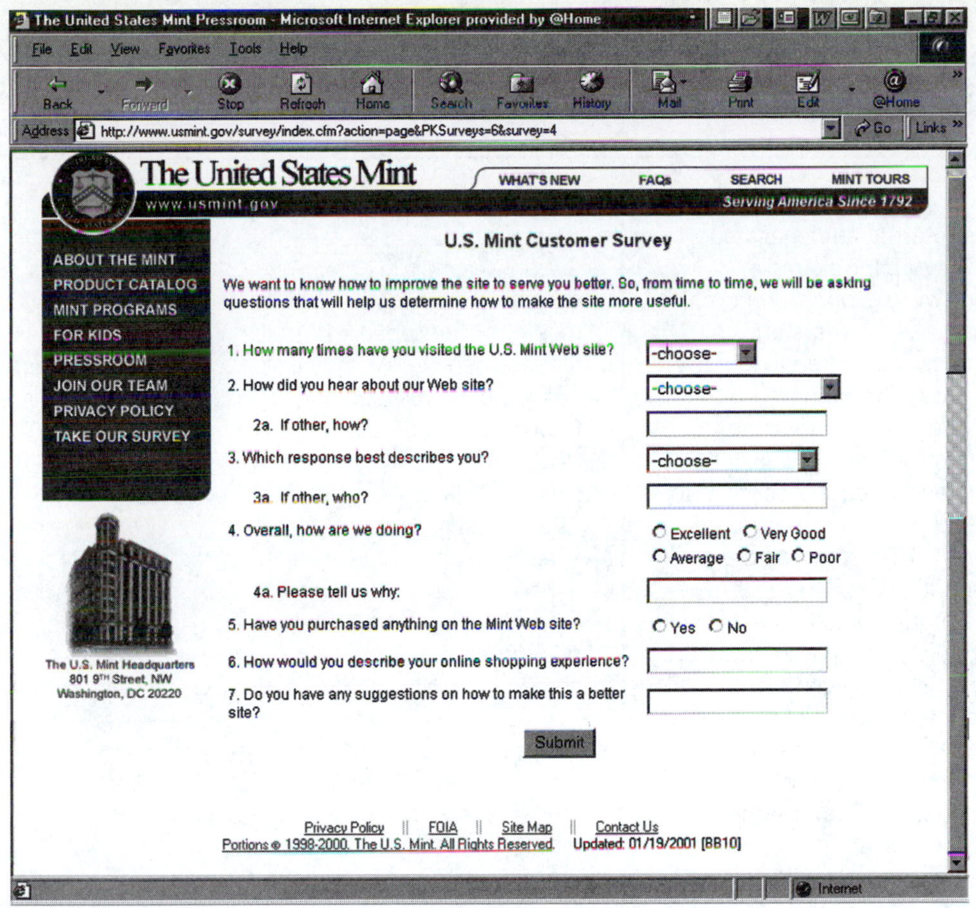

The U.S. Mint has grown into a *Fortune 500* enterprise with more than $3.7 billion in annual revenues and 2,800 employees. A link on the Mint's Web site (http://www.usmint.gov) provides visitors with the opportunity to participate in a survey. Internet surveys use a variety of dialog boxes that prompt respondents to enter information.

dialog box
A window that opens on a computer screen to prompt the user to enter information.

Use of a variety of **dialog boxes** (windows that prompt the respondent to enter information) allows designers of Internet questionnaires to be creative and flexible in the presentation of questions. Chapter 15 discusses software issues, the design of questions, and questionnaire layouts for Internet surveys.

Respondent Anonymity Respondents are more likely to provide sensitive or personal information when they can remain anonymous. The anonymity of the Internet encourages respondents to provide honest answers to sensitive questions.

Most respondents do not find it threatening to enter information into a computer because of the absence of an interviewer. They may be assured that no human will ever see their individual responses. For example, employees may be instructed to navigate to a particular Web site at a convenient time. When an individual logs on to the Web site, an interactive questionnaire may ask about sensitive issues such as a supervisor's effectiveness. If they have been assured that their identities will remain unknown, the employees are more likely to record honest answers.

Response Rates As mentioned earlier, with a password system, people who have not participated in a survey after a pre-determined period of time can be sent a friendly e-mail reminder asking them to participate before the study

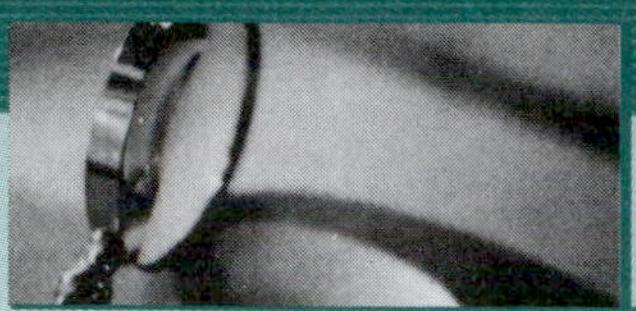

Research Insight

Avon Cuts Costs with Online Panels

Some companies establish online panels for specific audiences, including internal audiences such as their own sales reps.[35] Avon, for example, launched its AvonOpinion (www.avonopinion.com) program for its sales reps nearly 3 years ago. All Avon reps with online access are invited to join the panel, and tens of thousands of them have elected to do so—more are joining every day. Avon sends e-mail messages a minimum of every 2 weeks to randomly selected agents and encourages them to visit the specially encrypted pages on the site and complete the surveys. Certificates for Avon merchandise are given as incentives.

"The goal is to test as many items as we can before we make critical buys," says Beth Landa, product research manager. In any given month Avon speaks to at least a few hundred of its reps. Participants can view pictures—sometimes in the form of slide shows—of the products along with descriptions, and give opinions about how they think the product will sell for them.

Often Avon finds that it can get results immediately with what it dubs its "Quick Clicks." For example, they were able to design a study, post it, invite participation, and tabulate results for a survey all in under 1 week. This online research tool replaces older research tactics where Avon commissioned research with reps in 17 malls. By moving the research online, Avon is able to poll a larger cross-section of its representatives nationwide. Quick Clicks is quicker and more convenient for reps to give feedback.

Avon also sets up monthly surveys on the AvonOpinion home page so that participating panelists who haven't been queried recently don't feel as though they are being overlooked. Here visitors are polled regarding relevant and timely issues. The desired type of information comes from various sources in the company, including the marketing department. For example, a recent survey polled visitors about the company's newspaper, *Representative Times,* about content, clarity, and other issues. Other surveys have been designed to gauge convention feedback.

ends. This kind of follow-up, along with preliminary notification, interesting early questions, and variations of most other techniques for increasing response rates to mail questionnaires, is recommended for Internet surveys.

Unlike mail surveys, Internet surveys do not offer the opportunity to send a physical incentive, such as a dollar bill, to the respondent. Incentives to respond to a survey must be in the form of a promise of a future reward, for example, "As a token of appreciation for completing the survey, the sponsor of the survey will make a sizable contribution to a national charity. You can vote for your preferred charity at the end of the survey." While some researchers have had success with promising incentives, academic research about Internet surveys is sparse, and currently there are few definitive answers about the most effective ways to increase response rates.

Security Concerns Many organizations worry that hackers or competitors may access Web sites in order to discover competitors' new product concepts, new advertising campaigns, and other top-secret ideas. Respondents may worry whether personal information will remain confidential. No system can be 100 percent secure. However, many research service suppliers specializing in Internet surveying have developed password-protected systems that are very secure. One important feature of these systems prevents individuals from filling out a questionnaire over and over again.

Interactive Kiosk Surveys

A computer may be installed in a kiosk at a trade show, at a professional conference, in an airport, or in any other high-traffic location to administer an interactive survey. Because the respondent chooses to interact with an on-site computer, self-selection often is a problem with this type of survey. Computer-literate individuals are most likely to complete these interactive questionnaires. At temporary locations, such as conventions, these surveys often require a fieldworker to be at the location to explain how to use the computer system. This is an obvious disadvantage.

Survey Research That Mixes Modes

For many surveys, research objectives dictate the use of some combination of telephone, mail, e-mail, Internet, and personal interview. For example, the researcher may conduct a short telephone screening interview to determine whether respondents are eligible to participate in a more extensive personal interview. Such a mixed-mode survey combines the advantages of the telephone survey (such as fast screening) and those of the personal interview. A mixed-mode survey can employ any combination of two or more survey methods. Conducting a research study in two or more waves, however, creates the possibility that some respondents will no longer cooperate or will be unavailable for the later parts of the survey.

Several variations of survey research use cable television channels. For example, a telephone interviewer calls a cable subscriber and asks him or her to tune in to a particular channel at a certain time. An appointment is made to interview the respondent shortly after the program or visual material is displayed. NBC uses this type of mixed-mode survey to test the concepts for many proposed new programs.

SELECTING THE APPROPRIATE SURVEY RESEARCH DESIGN

Earlier discussions of research design and problem definition emphasized that many research tasks may lead to similar decision-making information. There is no "best" form of survey. Each has advantages and disadvantages. A researcher who must ask highly confidential questions may conduct a mail survey, thus trading off the speed of data collection to avoid any possibility of interviewer bias. If a researcher must have considerable control over question phrasing, central-location telephone interviewing may be selected.

To determine the appropriate technique, the researcher must ask questions such as "Is the assistance of an interviewer necessary? Are respondents likely to be interested in the issues being investigated? Will cooperation be easily attained? How quickly is the information needed? Will the study require a long and complex questionnaire? How large is the budget?" The criteria—cost, speed, anonymity, and the like—may be different for each project.

Exhibit 10.4 presents a summary of the major advantages and disadvantages of typical door-to-door, high-traffic location, telephone, mail, and Internet surveys. This summary emphasizes the typical survey. For example, it

EXHIBIT 10.4 ADVANTAGES AND DISADVANTAGES OF TYPICAL SURVEY METHODS

	Door-to-Door Personal Interview	Mall Intercept Personal Interview	Telephone Interview	Mail Survey	Internet Survey
Speed of data collection	Moderate	Fast	Very fast	Slow; researcher has no control over return of questionnaire	Instantaneous; 24/7
Geographic flexibility	Limited to moderate	Confined, possible urban bias	High	High	High (worldwide)
Respondent cooperation	Excellent	Moderate to low	Good	Moderate; poorly designed questionnaire will have low response rate	Varies depending on Web site; high from panels
Versatility of questioning	Quite versatile	Extremely versatile	Moderate	Not versatile; requires highly standardized format	Extremely versatile
Questionnaire length	Long	Moderate to long	Moderate	Varies depending on incentive	Moderate; length customized based on answers
Item non-response rate	Low	Medium	Medium	High	Software can assure none
Possibility for respondent misunderstanding	Low	Low	Average	High; no interviewer present for clarification	High
Degree of interviewer influence on answers	High	High	Moderate	None, interviewer absent	None
Supervision of interviewers	Moderate	Moderate to high	High, especially with central-location WATS interviewing	Not applicable	Not applicable
Anonymity of respondent	Low	Low	Moderate	High	Respondent can be either anonymous or known
Ease of callback or follow-up	Difficult	Difficult	Easy	Easy, but takes time	Difficult, unless e-mail address is known
Cost	Highest	Moderate to high	Low to moderate	Lowest	Low
Special features	Visual materials may be shown or demonstrated; extended probing possible	Viewing of video materials possible	Simplified fieldwork and supervision of data collection; quite adaptable to computer technology	Respondent may answer questions at own convenience; has time to reflect on answers	Streaming media software allows use of graphics and animation

is possible that a creative researcher might be able to design highly versatile and flexible mail questionnaires, but most of these have standardized questions. An elaborate mail survey may be far more expensive than a short personal interview, but this is generally not the case.

PRETESTS

A researcher who might have surveyed as many as 3,000 people does not want to find out after questionnaires have been completed or returned that most respondents misunderstood a question, skipped a series of questions, or misinterpreted the instructions for filling out the questionnaire. To avoid problems like these, screening procedures, or *pretests,* are often utilized.

pretest
A trial run with a group of respondents used to screen out problems in the instructions or design of a questionnaire.

Pretests are trial runs with a group of respondents for the purpose of detecting problems in a questionnaire's instructions or design. In a pretest the researcher looks for evidence of ambiguous questions and potential misunderstanding, evidence that the questions mean the same thing to all respondents, the point at which respondent fatigue sets in, and places in a questionnaire where a respondent is likely to terminate. Unfortunately, this stage of research is sometimes eliminated because of cost or time pressure.

Broadly speaking, there are three basic ways to pretest. The first two involve screening the questionnaire with other research professionals; the third—the one most frequently referred to as "pretesting"—is a trial run with a group of respondents. When screening the questionnaire with other research professionals, the investigator asks them to look for such things as difficulties with question wording, problems with leading questions, and bias due to question sequence. An alternative type of screening might be conducted with a client or with the manager who has ordered the research.

Many times managers ask researchers to collect information, but when they read the questionnaire the researcher plans to use, they find it doesn't meet their needs. Only by checking with the individual who requested the questionnaire do researchers know for sure that the questions are going to provide the information needed. Once the researcher has decided on the final questionnaire, data should be collected from a small number of respondents (perhaps 100) to determine whether the questionnaire has to be refined.

TO THE POINT

Practice is the best of all instructors.
PUBLILIUS SYRUS, circa 42 BC

ETHICAL ISSUES IN SURVEY RESEARCH

Chapter 5 presented the code of ethics of the American Association for Public Opinion Research and its principles of professional practice. That discussion covered issues such as the researcher's obligation to protect the public from misrepresentation and to avoid practices that may harm, humiliate, or mislead survey respondents.

Many ethical issues apply especially to survey research, such as respondents' right to privacy; the use of deception; respondents' right to be informed about the purpose of the research; the need for confidentiality; the need for honesty in collecting data; and the need for objectivity in reporting data. You may wish to reexamine Chapter 5's coverage of these issues now that various survey research techniques have been discussed.

SUMMARY

Interviews and self-administered questionnaires are used to collect survey data. Interviews can be categorized based on the medium used to communicate with respondents, such as door-to-door, mall intercept, or telephone interviews. Traditionally interviews have been printed on paper, but survey researchers are increasingly using computers.

Personal interviews give researchers a flexible survey method that allows them to use visual aids and various kinds of props. Door-to-door personal interviews can get high response rates, but they are also more costly to administer than other forms of surveys. The presence of an interviewer may also influence the subjects' responses. When obtaining a sample that is representative of the entire country is not a primary consideration, mall intercept interviews may be conducted to lower costs.

Telephone interviewing has the advantage of providing data fast and at a lower cost per interview. However, not all households have telephones, and not all telephone numbers are listed in directories. This causes problems in obtaining a representative sample. Absence of face-to-face contact and inability to use visual materials also limit telephone interviewing. Computer-assisted telephone interviewing from central locations can improve the efficiency of certain kinds of telephone surveys.

Traditionally, self-administered questionnaires have been distributed by mail. Today, however, self-administered questionnaires may be dropped off to individual respondents, distributed from central locations, or administered via computer. Mail questionnaires generally are less expensive than telephone or personal interviews, but they also introduce a much larger chance of nonresponse error. Several methods can be used to encourage higher response rates. Mail questionnaires must be more structured than other types of surveys and cannot be changed if problems are discovered in the course of data collection.

The Internet and other interactive media provide convenient ways for organizations to conduct surveys. Internet surveys are quick and cost-effective, but not everyone has Internet access. Because the surveys are computerized and interactive, questionnaires can be personalized and data can be captured in real time. There are some privacy and security concerns, but the future of Internet surveys looks promising.

Pretesting a questionnaire on a small sample of respondents is a useful way to discover problems while they can still be corrected.

Key Terms and Concepts

human interactive media
electronic interactive media
personal interview
probing
item nonresponse
door-to-door interview
mall intercept interview
callback
telephone interviewing
central location interviewing
computer-assisted telephone interview (CATI)
random digit dialing
computerized, voice-activated telephone interviewing
self-administered questionnaire
mail survey
response rate
cover letter
follow-up
drop-off method
fax survey
e-mail survey
internet survey
welcome screen
dialog box
pretest

Questions for Review and Critical Thinking

1. What type of communication medium would you utilize to conduct each of the following surveys?
   (a) Survey of achievement motives of industrial engineers
   (b) Survey of satisfaction of rental-car users
   (c) Survey of television advertising awareness
   (d) Survey of top corporate executives
2. A publisher offers college professors one of four best-selling mass-market books as an incentive for filling out a 10-page mail questionnaire about a new textbook. What advantages and disadvantages does this incentive have?
3. "Individuals are less willing to cooperate with surveys today than they were 15 years ago." Comment on this statement.
4. What do you think the maximum length of a self-administered questionnaire should be?
5. Do most surveys utilize a single communication mode (e.g., telephone), as most textbooks suggest?
6. A survey researcher reports that "205 usable questionnaires out of 942 questionnaires delivered in our mail survey converts to a 21.7 percent response rate." What are the subtle implications of this statement?
7. Evaluate the following survey designs:
   (a) A researcher suggests mailing a small safe (a metal file box with a built-in lock) without the lock combination to respondents with a note explaining that respondents will be called in a few days for a telephone interview. During the telephone interview, the respondent is given the combination and the safe may be opened.
   (b) A mall that wishes to evaluate its image places packets including a questionnaire, cover letter, and stamped return envelope in the mall where customers can pick them up if they wish.
   (c) An e-mail message is sent to individuals who own computers, asking them to complete a questionnaire on a Web site. Respondents answer the questions and then have the opportunity to play a slot-machine game on the Web site. Each respondent is guaranteed a monetary incentive but has the option to increase it by playing the slot-machine game.
   (d) A mall intercept interviewing service sets up a room in a regional shopping center for television and movie presentations. Shoppers are used as sampling units. However, mall intercept interviewers recruit additional subjects for television commercial experiments by offering them several complimentary tickets for special sneak previews. Individuals contacted at the mall are allowed to bring up to five guests. In some cases the complimentary tickets are offered through ads in a local newspaper.
   (e) A personnel manager places a packet containing a questionnaire, cover letter, and stamped return envelope in the personnel office where employees can pick it up if they wish.
8. What advantages do Internet surveys have? What disadvantages?
9. A researcher sends out 200 questionnaires, but 50 are returned because the addresses are inaccurate. Of the 150 delivered questionnaires, 50 are mailed back. However, 10 of these respondents wrote that they did not want to participate in the survey. The researcher indicates the response rate was 33.3 percent. Is this correct?

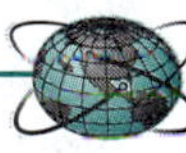

Exploring the Internet

1. Go to the Pew Internet and American Life page at http://www.pewinternet.org/. Several reports based on survey research will be listed. Select one of the reports. What were the research objectives? What were the first three questions on the survey?
2. Go to the Walker Information Web site (http://www.walkerinfo.com), click on Demo Center, and take one of the three surveys. Write a short report about your experience taking an Internet survey.
3. Go to the NPD Group Web site (http://www.npd.com) and click on NPD Store. What types of custom and syndicated survey research services does the company offer?
4. Go to the CASRO (Council of American Survey Research Organizations) home page (http://www.casro.org). Select About CASRO. What are the key aspects of this research organization's mission?
5. Use a search engine such as Yahoo, Excite, or Infoseek to see what you find if you enter "telephone survey" as key words.
6. Surveys Online is located at http://www.surveysonline.com/. What unique service does this company offer?
7. To learn more about customer satisfaction surveys, go to CustomerSat.com at http://www.customersat.com/.

WebSurveyor

Basic Instructions

WebSurveyor (http://www.websurveyor.com) can be used to post Internet surveys online without any hassles. There is no programming required, no need to have a Web site, and no expensive software to buy.

WebSurveyor has two components.

- The *WebSurveyor Desktop* contains software programs that allow you to design, distribute, and analyze Internet surveys.
- *WebSurveyor Server* is a hosting service, or licensed Web server software, that allows you to collect data via the Internet.

The WebSurveyor Desktop software is available to students who purchase new textbooks that contain a WebSurveyor postcard with a serial number. Students with serial numbers should go to http://zikmund.swcollege.com, click on the textbook, click the WebSurveyor button, and follow the steps for registering. Students who need to purchase a serial number should go to http://zikmund.swcollege.com, click on the textbook, click the WebSurveyor button, and follow the steps for purchasing access to the software.

WebSurveyor gives you all the tools you need to assemble, conduct, and analyze Internet surveys.[36] The software focuses on features that make developing Internet surveys easy, but it also includes many tools that will meet the demands of advanced users. Its Survey Wizard walks you through developing each aspect of an online survey. WebSurveyor provides free question libraries, response libraries, and sample questionnaires, all of which make assembling your unique questionnaire easy and fast.

WebSurveyor writes the questionnaire in HTML automatically and enables anyone who has a WebSurveyor account to post the questionnaire to a unique Web address at http://www.WebSurveyor.net.

After the data have been collected, WebSurveyor software analyzes the data and provides tools that automatically graph question responses.

Getting Started[37]

A tutorial explaining how to use WebSurveyor appears at http://zikmund.swcollege.com. Here we offer a brief overview of the WebSurveyor process.

Getting started using WebSurveyor Desktop is quick and easy. The primary steps are

- Creating your survey
- Publishing your survey
- Analyzing your results

Creating Your Survey The quickest way to get your survey started is to use the Survey Builder Wizard. The Wizard will walk you very quickly through the steps in creating a survey using predefined templates. If you want to create your own questionnaire from scratch, you can cancel the Wizard (and even turn that option off if you like) and enter the questions manually. You can add questions to your survey by clicking on the Add button in the Question List. You can also quickly create questions using WebSurveyor's Question Library.

After entering your questions you will want to confirm that your survey Detail information is correct. With those fields properly filled out, you can preview your survey and change the Presentation options to enhance or change the look and feel of the questionnaire.

Once you are satisfied with the look of your survey, you can save it to a WS3 file. A WS3 file is what WebSurveyor uses to hold the definition of your survey. This is a critical file, and you should regularly back up the directory you save this file to.

Publishing Your Survey With the survey saved locally to a WS3 file, you can begin the publishing process. This takes only a matter of minutes.

Analyzing Your Results Once your survey has been published and people have begun to take it, you can begin to pull down the results for analysis. This process is covered in detail in the Analysis section of the Web site's Help system.

WebSurveyor Activities

Run the WebSurveyor Desktop software, and click Example Internet Usage Survey under the heading "Open a sample survey with real data" from the Getting Started Wizard. (If the Getting Started Wizard does not appear, click Tools and then Options from the main menu, make sure "Display the Getting Started Wizard for new surveys" is checked, and then click OK. Next click File and then New from the main menu, and then click Example Internet Usage Survey under the heading "Open a sample survey with real data.")

The software will open the sample survey and prompt you to download the responses. Click the "yes" button. The desktop software will contact the WebSurveyor server and transfer the survey results to your computer. When the transfer is complete, a window will appear with information about the transfer. Click OK, and the results for the first question will automatically appear as a pie chart.

Click Preview under "Survey Editing" to get a look at the questionnaire as it appeared to the survey's respondents. After you have reviewed the questionnaire, click Analysis under "Survey Results" to see the actual results. You can review the results for each question in turn by using the drop-down list or arrow buttons at the top of the graphic display area.

Case Suggestions

Case 9: Tulsa's Central Business District (B)
Case 10: The Greeting Card Study
Case 11: The Evergreen Company
Video Case 12: Burke Inc.

CHAPTER

11

OBSERVATION METHODS

What you will learn in this chapter

- To distinguish between scientific observation and casual observation.
- To discuss what can and cannot be observed.
- To understand when an observation study is the appropriate research design.
- To discuss the characteristics of observation research.
- To give examples of nonverbal behavior that can be observed.
- To discuss the various situations in which direct observation studies may take place.
- To define *response latency.*
- To discuss scientifically contrived observation.
- To define *physical-trace evidence.*
- To define *content analysis.*
- To explain the purposes of content analysis.
- To describe the various types of mechanical observation.
- To discuss the techniques for measuring physiological reactions.

In conversation one day Sherlock Holmes asked Watson how many steps there were to the Baker Street apartment. Watson responded that he did not know. Holmes replied, "Ah, Watson, you see but you do not *observe.*" Although we are constantly looking around in our daily lives, like Dr. Watson we often do not observe in a scientific sense. Holmes, on the other hand, trained himself to systematically observe the environment in order to see what others overlooked.

This chapter discusses how the observation method of data gathering is used in business research. ■

WHEN IS OBSERVATION SCIENTIFIC?

Observation becomes a tool for scientific inquiry when it

- serves a formulated research purpose,
- is planned systematically,
- is recorded systematically and related to general propositions rather than being presented as reflecting a set of interesting curiosities, and
- is subjected to checks or controls on validity and reliability.[1]

scientific observation
The systematic process of recording the behavioral patterns of people, objects, and occurrences as they are witnessed.

Scientific observation is the systematic process of recording the behavioral patterns of people, objects, and occurrences as they are witnessed. No questioning of or communicating with people occurs. The researcher utilizing the observation method of data collection witnesses and records information as events occur or compiles evidence from records of past events. (Although investigation of such secondary data uses observation—see Chapter 8—it is not extensively discussed in this chapter.)

WHAT CAN BE OBSERVED?

A wide variety of information about the behavior of people and objects can be observed. As Exhibit 11.1 indicates, seven kinds of phenomena can be observed: physical actions, such as work patterns or television viewing; verbal behavior, such as office conversations; expressive behavior, such as tone of voice or facial expressions; spatial relations and locations, such as physical distance between workers or traffic patterns; temporal patterns, such as the amount of time spent shopping or time required to perform a work task; physical objects, such as finished goods inventory; and verbal and pictorial records, such as the content of memoranda.

Where observation is concerned, chance favors only the prepared mind.

LOUIS PASTEUR

Although the observation method may be used to describe a wide variety of behaviors, cognitive phenomena, such as attitudes, motivations, expectations, intentions, and preferences, cannot be observed. Another limitation is that the observation period is generally of short duration. Observing behavior patterns over a period of several days or several weeks generally is either too costly or too difficult.

EXHIBIT 11.1 | **WHAT CAN BE OBSERVED?**

Phenomenon	Example
Human behavior or action	Workers' movement patterns in a factory
Verbal behavior	Statements made by airline travelers waiting in line
Expressive behavior	Facial expressions, tone of voice, and other forms of body language
Spatial relations	Proximity of middle managers' offices to the president's office
Temporal patterns	How long workers take to perform a task
Physical objects	How much paper office workers recycle
Verbal and pictorial records	How many illustrations appear in a training booklet

THE NATURE OF OBSERVATION STUDIES

Business researchers can observe people, objects, events, or other phenomena by assigning the task to human observers or by using machines designed for specific observation tasks. Human observers are commonly used when the situation or behavior to be recorded is not easily predictable in advance of the research. Mechanical observation, such as by traffic counters on a factory floor, can be very accurate when the situation or behavior to be recorded is routine, repetitive, or programmatic.

Human or mechanical observation methods may be unobtrusive in that communication with the subjects is not generally necessary. Rather than ask customers how much time they spend shopping in a specific supermarket, the supermarket manager might observe and record shopping time by timing the interval between a shopper's entering and leaving the store. The unobtrusive or nonreactive nature of the observation method often generates data without subjects' knowledge. An observation situation in which the observer's presence is known to the subject is **visible observation.** A situation in which the subject is unaware that observation is taking place is **hidden observation.** Hidden, unobtrusive observation minimizes respondent error. Furthermore, asking subjects to participate in the research is not required when those subjects are unaware that they are being observed. However, hidden observation raises an ethical issue concerning respondents' privacy.

visible observation
Situation in which the observer's presence is known to the subject.

hidden observation
Situation in which the subject is unaware that observation is taking place.

The major advantage of observation studies over surveys, which obtain self-reported data from respondents, is that the data obtained by observation

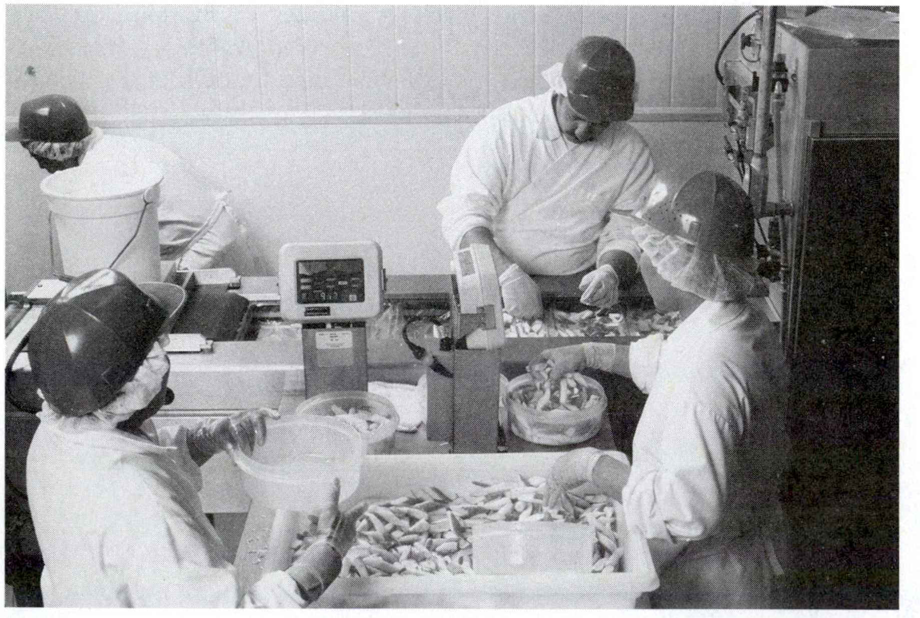

A wide variety of information about human behavior, such as work activity, can be unobtrusively observed. What kinds of nonverbal behaviors might a researcher record in this situation?

are not subject to distortions, inaccuracies, or other response biases due to memory error, social desirability, and so on. The data are recorded when the actual behavior takes place.

OBSERVATION OF HUMAN BEHAVIOR

Surveys emphasize verbal responses, while observation studies emphasize and allow for the systematic recording of nonverbal behavior. A French researcher, who regularly visited his wife's office in the early evening, observed a typical pattern: The married men and single women were working overtime, and nearly all of the single men and married women had gone home. This led to the hypothesis that marriage helps men in their careers and hinders women, because the husband receives family support for job advancement while the married woman does not. This informal observation led to more rigorous quantitative studies.

Toy manufacturers use the observation technique because children often cannot verbally express their reactions to a product. By observing children at play with a proposed toy, doll, or game, business researchers may be able to identify the elements of a potentially successful product. Researchers might observe play with toys to answer the following questions: "How long does the child's attention stay with the toy? Does the child put the toy down after 2 minutes or 20 minutes? Are the child's peers equally interested in the product?"

Behavioral scientists have recognized that *nonverbal behavior* can be a communication process by which meanings are exchanged between individuals. Head nods, smiles, raised eyebrows, and other facial expressions or body movements have been recognized as communication symbols. Observation of nonverbal communication has considerable promise for the business researcher. For example, with regard to customer–salesperson interactions, it has been hypothesized that in low-importance transactions where potential customers are plentiful and easily replaced (e.g., a shoe store), salespersons may show definite nonverbal signs of higher status than the customer. When customers are scarce, as in "big ticket" situations (e.g., real estate sales), the opposite should be true, and a salesperson might show many nonverbal indicators of deference. Observation of the nonverbal communication gestures in Exhibit 11.2 could test this hypothesis.

Of course, verbal behavior is not ignored, and in certain cases verbal responses are very important in observation studies.

SUPPLEMENTARY EVIDENCE

The results of observation studies may amplify the results of other forms of research by providing *complementary* evidence concerning individuals' "true" feelings. Role-playing sessions and focus group interviews are often conducted behind one-way mirrors, so that researchers can observe as well as listen to what is occurring. This allows for the interpretation of such nonverbal behavior as facial expressions or head nods to supplement information from interviews.

For example, in one focus group session concerning hand lotion, researchers observed that the women's hands were *above* the table while they

Exhibit 11.2 | **Nonverbal Communication: Status and Power Gestures**[2]

Behavior	Between People of Equal Status: Intimate	Between People of Equal Status: Nonintimate	Between People of Unequal Status: Used by Superior	Between People of Unequal Status: Used by Subordinate	Between Men and Women: Used by Men	Between Men and Women: Used by Women
Posture	Relaxed	Tense (less relaxed)	Relaxed	Tense	Relaxed	Tense
Personal space	Closeness	Distance	Closeness (optional)	Distance	Closeness	Distance
Touching	Touch	Don't touch	Touch (optional)	Don't touch	Touch	Don't touch
Eye gaze	Establish	Avoid	Stare, ignore	Avert eyes, watch	Stare, ignore	Avert eyes
Demeanor	Informal	Circumspect	Informal	Circumspect	Informal	Circumspect
Emotional expression	Show	Hide	Hide	Show	Hide	Show
Facial expression	Smile	Don't smile	Don't smile	Smile	Don't smile	Smile

casually waited for the session to begin. Seconds after the women were told that the group session was to be about hand lotion, "all hands had been placed under the table or out of sight and the women's faces became tense."[3] This observation, along with the group discussion, revealed the women's anger, guilt, and shame about the condition of their hands. Although the women felt they were expected to have soft and pretty hands, housework requires washing dishes, cleaning floors, and other work that is hard on the hands.

When individual or group behavior is videotaped, observation of nonverbal communication can also add to the researchers' knowledge of the situation.

DIRECT OBSERVATION

direct observation
A straightforward attempt to observe and record what naturally occurs; the investigator does not create an artificial situation.

Direct observation can produce a detailed record of events or what people actually do. The observer plays a passive role; that is, there is no attempt to control or manipulate a situation. The observer merely *records* what occurs.

Many types of data can be obtained more accurately by direct observation than by questioning. For example, records of traffic counts and/or observations of the direction of traffic flows within a factory can be useful when designing workstation layouts. A time-and-motion observation study of workers on a loading dock might attempt to break down tasks into component motions (e.g., grasping, picking up, setting down) so that the efficiency of the work process can be cataloged and evaluated. The observer might use a stopwatch to time each of these discrete motions in the work process. Most respondents, if directly questioned, would be unable to say accurately how much time they spent at each task. With the observation method, determination of the time for each task is not difficult.

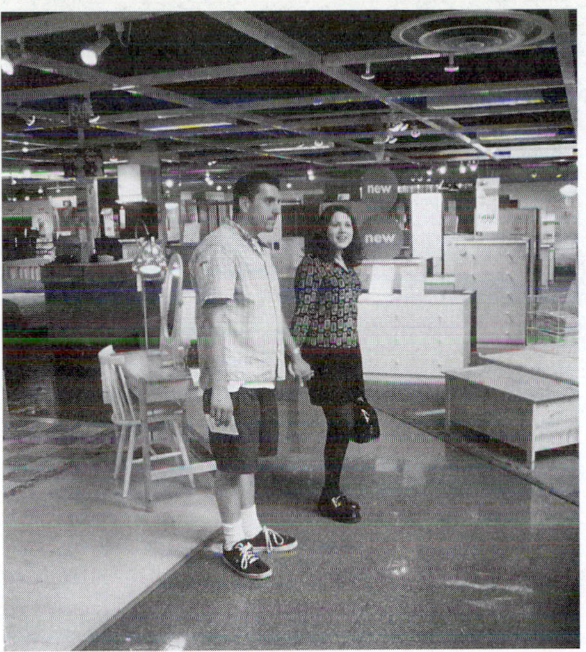

Domain Stores, a chain of 23 furniture stores headquartered in Norwood, Massachusetts, hired Grid II, a business research firm, to videotape consumers in one of its stores. Analysis of the videotapes revealed that people shop for furniture in twos. Of the 1,034 customers who entered the store, 954 came in pairs. In addition, facial expressions and other nonverbal behavior indicated many male customers were visibly ill at ease amid fluffed pillows and floral duvets. "The typical customer needs to be in the store for at least 9 minutes to feel comfortable enough to buy," says the company's CEO. "But if the spouse or boyfriend pulls her away too soon, we lose out on the sale." As a result of the observation research, the company revamped its 23 stores with entertainment centers where sports fans can watch live events via cable.[4]

Researchers using the direct observation method compile data by recording events as they occur. An observation form is often used to help keep the observations consistent and to ensure that all relevant information is recorded. A respondent is not required to recall (perhaps inaccurately) an event after it has occurred. The recording of the observation is instantaneous.

In many cases direct observation is the most straightforward form of data collection (or the only form possible). The produce manager at a Jewel Food Store may periodically gather competitive price information at the Safeway and IGA stores in the neighborhood. In other situations observation is the most economical technique. In a common type of observation study, researchers for a shopping center observe the license numbers on cars in the parking lot. This is an inexpensive means of determining where customers live.

Certain data may be obtained more quickly or easily by direct observation. For example, in a quality-of-life survey, respondents were asked a series of questions that were compiled into an index of well-being. Direct observation was also used by the interviewers because the researchers wanted to investigate whether weather conditions influenced people's answers. The researchers quickly and easily observed and recorded outside weather conditions on the day of the interviews, as well as the temperature and humidity in the building where the interviews were conducted.[5]

Errors Associated with Direct Observation

Although there is no interaction with the subject, direct observation is not error-free; the observer may add subjectivity to the recording. The same visual cues that may influence the interplay between an interviewer and a respondent (e.g., the subject's age or sex) may also come into play in some types of direct observation settings. For example, the observer may subjectively attribute a particular economic status or educational background to the subject. A

RESEARCH INSIGHT

DOCTORS SHOULD EXAMINE THEIR WATCHES

When questioned in a survey, doctors said they spend about nine times as long giving information to patients as they actually do.[6] The physicians who were directly questioned answered [that] they spent about 12 minutes giving information to the average patient, but videotapes of the doctor/patient encounters indicated doctors spent only 1.3 minutes giving information. Further, doctors underestimate how much their patients want to know about their illness. When doctors' answers were compared with patients' answers about how much patients wanted to know, doctors underestimated the amount of information two out of three times.

observer bias
A distortion of measurement resulting from the cognitive behavior or actions of the witnessing observer.

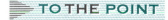

distortion of measurement resulting from the cognitive behavior or actions of the witnessing observer is called **observer bias.** Exhibit 11.3, an excerpt from the observation section of a survey, shows how fieldworkers may be required to rely on their own interpretations of people or situations during the observation process.

If the observer does not record every detail that describes the persons, objects, and events in a given situation, accuracy may suffer. As a general guideline, the observer should record as much detail as possible. However, the pace of events, the observer's memory, the observer's writing speed, and other factors will limit the amount of detail that can be recorded.

What we see depends mainly on what we look for.

SIR JOHN LUBBOCK

Interpretation of observation data is another major source of potential error. Facial expressions and other nonverbal communication may have several meanings. Does a smile always mean happiness? Does the fact that someone is standing or seated in close proximity to the president of a company necessarily indicate the person's status?

Response Latency

response latency
The time it takes to decide between two alternatives; used as a measure of the strength of preference.

The time it takes to decide between two alternatives is a relatively simple, unobtrusive measure known as **response latency.** Response latency is a measure of the strength of the preference between alternatives. It is hypothesized that the longer a decision maker takes to make a choice between two alternatives, the closer the two alternatives are in terms of preference. If a quick decision is made, researchers hypothesize that there is considerable "psychological distance" between alternatives. The response latency measure is growing more popular now that computer-assisted data collection methods are becoming more common (i.e., the computer records the decision time).

Scientifically Contrived Observation

contrived observation
Observation in which the investigator creates an artificial environment in order to test a hypothesis.

Most observation takes place in a natural setting. Observing subjects in an artificial environment in order to test a hypothesis is called **contrived observation.** Contrived observation can increase the frequency of certain behavior patterns. For example, an airline passenger complaining about a meal or poor service from the flight attendant may actually be a researcher recording the flight attendant's reactions. If situations weren't contrived, the research time spent

Exhibit 11.3 An Observation Form[7]

SECTION M: BY OBSERVATION ONLY

M1. IF ANYONE WAS PRESENT DURING THE INTERVIEW OTHER THAN R AND INTERVIEWER GIVE THE FOLLOWING DETAILS FOR EACH:

		PERSON 1	PERSON 2	PERSON 3
M1a.	Age, approximately			
M1b.	Relationship to R			
M1c.	Present for how much of the interview?			
M1d.	How closely was (s)he listening?	1. CLOSELY 2. CASUALLY 3. HARDLY AT ALL	1. CLOSELY 2. CASUALLY 3. HARDLY AT ALL	1. CLOSELY 2. CASUALLY 3. HARDLY AT ALL
M1e.	Did (s)he make any comments on R's answers?			

M2. R's Race? [1. WHITE] [5. BLACK] [OTHER: ______________ (Specify)]

M3. Rate R's physical appearance:

[1. STRIKINGLY HANDSOME OR BEAUTIFUL] [2. GOOD-LOOKING (ABOVE AVERAGE FOR AGE AND SEX)]

[3. AVERAGE LOOKS FOR AGE AND SEX] [4. QUITE PLAIN (BELOW AVERAGE FOR AGE AND SEX)] [5. HOMELY]

M4. How tall would you say R was? ________ FEET ________ INCHES

M5. Rate R's apparent intelligence?

[1. VERY HIGH] [2. ABOVE AVERAGE] [3. AVERAGE] [4. BELOW AVERAGE] [5. VERY LOW]

M6. How suspicious did R seem to be about the study, <u>before</u> the interview?

[1. NOT AT ALL] [3. SOMEWHAT] [5. VERY SUSPICIOUS]

M7. Overall, how great was R's interest in the interview?

[1. VERY HIGH] [2. ABOVE AVERAGE] [3. AVERAGE] [4. BELOW AVERAGE] [5. VERY LOW]

M8. How sincere did R seem to be in his answers, especially to the ones using the CARD 3?

[1. COMPLETELY SINCERE] [2. USUALLY SINCERE] [3. OFTEN SEEMED TO BE INSINCERE]

Note: R = respondent, DU = dwelling unit

EXHIBIT 11.3 | **AN OBSERVATION FORM (CONTINUED)**

M8a. Were there any particular parts of the interview for which you doubted R's sincerity? If so, name them by section or question numbers: ____________________

____

M9. How clean was the interior of the DU?

[1. VERY CLEAN] [2. CLEAN] [3. SO-SO] [4. NOT VERY CLEAN] [5. DIRTY]

M10. How much reading material was visible in the DU?

[1. A LOT] [2. SOME] [3. NONE]

M11. TYPE OF STRUCTURE IN WHICH FAMILY LIVES:

[01. TRAILER]

[02. DETACHED SINGLE FAMILY HOUSE]

[03. 2-FAMILY HOUSE, 2 UNITS SIDE BY SIDE]

[04. 2-FAMILY HOUSE, 2 UNITS ONE ABOVE THE OTHER]

[05. DETACHED 3-4 FAMILY HOUSE]

[06. ROW HOUSE (3 OR MORE UNITS IN AN ATTACHED ROW)]

[07. APARTMENT HOUSE (5 OR MORE UNITS, 3 STORIES OR LESS]

[08. APARTMENT HOUSE (5 OR MORE UNITS, 4 STORIES OR MORE)]

[09. APARTMENT IN A PARTLY COMMERCIAL STRUCTURE]

[10. OTHER] (SPECIFY) ____________________

M12. NUMBER OF STORIES IN THE STRUCTURE, NOT COUNTING BASEMENT:

[1] [2] [3] [MORE THAN 3:] ____________________ (SPECIFY)

M13. NEIGHBORHOOD: Look at 3 structures on each side of DU but not more than 100 yards or so in both directions and check as many boxes as apply, below.

[00. VACANT LAND ONLY]

[01. TRAILER]

[02. DETACHED SINGLE FAMILY HOUSE]

[03. 2-FAMILY HOUSE, 2 UNITS SIDE BY SIDE]

[04. 2-FAMILY HOUSE, 2 UNITS ONE ABOVE THE OTHER]

[05. DETACHED 3-4 FAMILY HOUSE]

[06. ROW HOUSE (3 OR MORE UNITS IN AN ATTACHED ROW)]

[07. APARTMENT HOUSE (5 OR MORE UNITS, 3 STORIES OR LESS)]

[08. APARTMENT HOUSE (5 OR MORE UNITS, 4 STORIES OR MORE)]

[09. APARTMENT IN A PARTLY COMMERCIAL STRUCTURE]

[10. WHOLLY COMMERCIAL OR INDUSTRIAL STRUCTURE]

[11. PARK]

[12. SCHOOL OR OTHER GOVERNMENTAL BUILDING]

[13. OTHER] (Specify) ____________________

waiting and observing situations would expand considerably. The term *mystery shopper* is used by a number of retailers to describe this type of research, in which an observer posing as a shopper comes into a store and pretends to be interested in a particular product or service. After leaving the store, the unknown shopper (observer) evaluates the performance of the salesperson.

OBSERVING SOCIAL SETTINGS

In many situations the purpose of observation is to summarize, systematize, and simplify the activities, meaning, and relationships in a social setting. Often, unstructured methods provide the observer with the greatest flexibility. No restrictive checklist or data collection instruments limit the information recorded in the field notes.[8]

What Should Be Observed?

The definition of the problem will, of course, dictate what information is recorded. However, in general, several elements are of interest in most social settings:

1. *The participants.* The observer wants to know who the participants are. How are they related to one another? How many are there? There are various ways of characterizing the participants, but usually an observer wants to know at least the following about any person who is being observed: age, sex, official function (executive, employee, customer, supplier) in the situation being observed and in the organizational system or the broader social system. An observer also wants to know how the participants are related to one another: Are they strangers or do they know one another? Are they members of some collectivity, and if so, what kind—an informal friendship group, a union, a factory, a retail store? What structures or groupings exist among the participants? Can cliques, focal persons, or isolates be identified by their spatial groupings or patterns of interaction?
2. *The setting.* Social interactions may occur in different settings—a corporate headquarters, a shopping mall, a factory lunchroom, a palatial convention hotel. In addition to noting the appearance of the setting, an observer wants to know what kinds of behavior it encourages, permits, discourages, or prevents. The social characteristics of the setting may also be described in terms of the kinds of behavior that are likely to be perceived as expected or unexpected, approved or disapproved, conforming or deviant.
3. *The purpose.* Is there some official purpose that has brought the participants together, or have they met by chance? If there is an official purpose, what is it—to attend a sales meeting, to compete in a boat race, to participate in an awards ceremony, to meet as a committee, to have fun at a party? How do the participants react to the official purpose of the situation—for example, with acceptance or with rejection? What goals other than the official purpose do the participants seem to be pursuing? Are the goals of the various participants compatible or antagonistic?
4. *The social behavior.* The observer wants to know what actually occurs. What do the participants do? How do they do it? With whom and with what do they do it? With respect to behavior, the observer usually wants to know the following: (a) the stimulus or event that initiated it; (b) its apparent objective; (c) toward whom or what it is directed; (d) what type of behavior it is (talking, word processing, driving a car, gesturing); (e) the

Observation of consumers of juices and juice beverages revealed that many of them poured their beverages from large bottles they had purchased into smaller empty water bottles, the kind with a push-up top. This led to the conclusion that juices packaged in smaller, convenient-to-transport bottles would find a market.[9]

qualities of the behavior (its intensity, persistence, unusualness, appropriateness, duration, affectivity, mannerisms); (f) its effects (for example, the behavior it evokes from others).

5. *Frequency and duration.* The observer wants to know the answer to such questions as these: When did the situation occur? How long did it last? Is it a recurring situation, or is it unique? If it recurs, how frequently does it occur? What are the occasions that give rise to it? How typical of such situations is the one being observed?[10]

Participant Observation

participant observation
Situation in which an observer gains firsthand knowledge by being in or around the social setting being investigated.

Participant observation refers to an observation situation in which an observer gains firsthand knowledge by being in or around the social setting that is being investigated. The individual who joins a management group, for example, may be a known observer or may remain anonymous. In either case the observer generally uses a combination of direct observation and interviewing.

Interview questions may be asked during the course of a conversation or discussion, rather than in any structured format. Long and involved personal interaction with the subjects of the research is the prime advantage of participant observation. Extended contact with the subjects helps them feel comfortable in the participant observer's presence.

The participant observer must develop a system for recording his or her observations. Generally, the observer takes mental notes and jots down field notes where possible. At the end of the day more detailed field notes are recorded to summarize and synthesize the events and activities of the day.

ETHICAL ISSUES IN HUMAN OBSERVATION

Observation methods introduce a number of ethical issues. Hidden observation raises the issue of the subjects' right to privacy. For example, a firm interested in acquiring information about how women put on their bras might persuade some retailers to place one-way mirrors in dressing rooms so that this behavior may be observed unobtrusively. Obviously, there is an ethical question to be resolved in such a situation. Other observation methods, especially contrived observation, raise the possibility of deception of subjects.

Some people might see contrived observation as entrapment. To *entrap* means to deceive or trick into difficulty, which clearly is an abusive action. The problem is one of balancing values. If the researcher obtains permission to observe someone, the subject may not act in a typical manner. Thus, the researcher must determine his or her own view of the ethics involved and decide whether the usefulness of the information is worth telling a "white" lie.

OBSERVATION OF PHYSICAL OBJECTS

physical-trace evidence
A visible mark of some past event or occurrence.

Physical phenomena may be the subject of observation study. **Physical-trace evidence** is a visible mark of some past event or occurrence. For example, the wear on library books indirectly indicates which books are actually read (handled most) when checked out. At Chicago's Museum of Science and Industry, the floor tiles around the hatching-chick exhibit must be replaced every 6 weeks, compared to years between replacement for tiles in other parts of the museum. The rate of wear for the tiles is a measure of the relative popularity of each exhibit.

Clearly, a creative business researcher has many options available for determining the solution to a problem. The story of Charles Coolidge Parlin, generally recognized as one of the founders of commercial business research, counting garbage cans at the turn of the 20th century illustrates another study of physical traces.

> Parlin designed an observation study to persuade Campbell's Soup Company to advertise in the *Saturday Evening Post*. Campbell's was reluctant to advertise because it believed that the *Post* was read primarily by working people who would prefer to make soup from scratch, peeling the potatoes and scraping the carrots, rather than paying 10¢ for a can of soup. To demonstrate that rich people weren't the target market, Parlin selected a sample of Philadelphia garbage routes. Garbage from each specific area of the city that was selected was dumped on the floor of a local National Guard Armory. Parlin had the number of Campbell's soup cans in each pile counted. The results indicated that the garbage from the rich people's homes didn't contain many cans of Campbell's soup. Although they didn't make soup from scratch themselves, their servants did. The garbage piles from the blue-collar area showed a large number of Campbell's soup cans. This observation study was enough evidence for Campbell's. They advertised in the *Saturday Evening Post*.[11]

The method used in this study is also used in a scientific project at the University of Arizona in which aspiring archaeologists sift through modern garbage; they examine soggy cigarette butts, empty milk cartons, and half-eaten Big Macs. Investigation of Arizona household garbage has revealed many interesting findings. For example, in Hispanic households the most popular baby food is squash.[12] It accounts for 38 percent of the baby food vegetables Hispanic babies consume. By contrast, in Anglo households peas account for 29 percent of all baby vegetables; squash ranks only above spinach, which is last. (Squash has been a dietary staple in Mexico and Central America for more than 9,000 years.) Sorting through fast-food restaurants' garbage reveals that wasted food from chicken restaurants (not counting bones) accounts for

RESEARCH INSIGHT

ENVIROSELL

Paco Underhill runs Envirosell, a New York consumer research company that conducts observation research. He became interested in using cameras to analyze the flow of human traffic through public places after hearing a lecture by urban geographer William Whyte. Envirosell's clients include companies such as Quaker Foods, Revlon, Hallmark Cards, and Bloomingdale's. The following is one reporter's account of what he learned about the value of observation research.

Underhill's research in retail settings led him to develop a body of observations he calls "aisle theory."[13] Among his seminal findings is something we'll call the derriere-brush factor, although he calls it by another name. At his offices in New York, he showed me a film-clip shot with a time-lapse camera aimed at a tie display in a narrow, heavily traveled aisle of the Bloomingdale's department store in Manhattan. Such aisles, meant to carry shoppers from store entrances onward into the store, are known in the retail industry as "driveways" or "power aisles."

Shoppers entered and dispersed; most zipped right by the ties. Underhill stopped the projector.

"Stand up," he commanded.

I stood.

"OK, you are standing at a counter. You are looking at ties. One of the most sensitive parts of your anatomy is your tail."

He began brushing my tail with his hand. Derriere-brush factor, he told me, "is simply the idea that the more likely you are to be brushed from the rear while you shop, the less likely you'll be converted from browser to buyer." In retail-speak, the "conversion ratio" of that display or counter will be low.

Underhill's stop-action film showed how few people stopped to examine the ties in the rack. Traffic swept past the few browsers in disconcerting volume.

When Bloomingdale's chairman saw the video, he called the clerk in charge of that department and had him move the tie rack out of the driveway. Later, a Bloomingdale's vice president called Underhill and told him the chairman had personally had the sales tracked from that lone tie rack and discovered that within 6 weeks the increase had paid for Underhill's services. "That told me two things," Underhill said.

35 percent of all food bought. This is substantially greater than the 7 percent of wasted food at fast-food hamburger restaurants.

What is most interesting about the garbage project is the comparison between the results of surveys about food consumption and the contents of respondents' garbage—garbage does not lie.[14] The University of Arizona project indicates that people consistently underreport the quantity of junk food they eat and overreport the amount of fruit and diet soda they consume. Most dramatically, however, studies show that alcohol consumption is underreported by 40 to 60 percent.

Garbage is even more revealing in Buenos Aires, Argentina. The research company Garbage Data Dynamics analyzes discarded containers, newspapers, and other garbage in that city. Because garbage is collected daily in Buenos Aires and people typically dispose of garbage in small bags with grocery store names printed on them, certain types of data that cannot be collected in the United States can be obtained. The results are so specific that they can show what brand of soft drink was consumed with a certain meal.

What would you rather believe? What I say, or what you saw with your own eyes?

GROUCHO MARX

"One, I wasn't charging enough, and two, the markup on ties was even more obscene than I thought."

"He picks up common sense things," said Judith Owens, vice president, marketing, of the National Retail Federation in New York, who periodically invites Underhill to show his stop-action films to the federation's many members. She watched one film of an audio store that drew a mostly teenage clientele, yet placed its racks of CDs so high the kids couldn't reach them. "You watch that happen, then you hear Paco say if you drop your display by 18 inches you'll increase your productivity. Everybody says, my God, I never thought of that."

He showed AT&T that almost 20 percent of the people who came into its Phone Center stores were under 10 years old, and how salespeople spent a lot of their time simply protecting expensive phone systems displayed too close to the ground. His films showed how most people who entered a Revco drugstore failed to pick up a shopping basket and thus were automatically limited to buying only what they could carry.

Early in 1991, the Woolworth Corporation asked Underhill to study several of its Champs Sports stores to help figure out which layouts and designs worked best. Woolworth was planning a huge national expansion of the chain. It knew that sales from the rear section of each store—the "hard goods" section displaying such items as weights and basketballs—lagged far behind sales from other sections, but it didn't know why.

John Shanley, director of research for Woolworth, remembers how Underhill's stop-action film instantly solved the mystery. During peak sales periods, a line of customers would form from the cash register to the opposite wall of the store. "It literally prevented people from going from the front to the back," Shanley recalls. "They walked up to this line, turned and walked away." As a result, all of Champs' 500 stores now feature a checkout area (known in the industry as the "cash-wrap") designed so that lines form along an axis from front to back. "All of a sudden the sales in the back of the store picked up," Shanley recalled.

But, I asked, shouldn't that barrier effect have been obvious without Underhill's help? "The obvious," Shanley answered, "isn't always that apparent."

Counting and recording physical inventories by means of retail or wholesale audits allows researchers to investigate brand sales on regional and national levels, market shares, seasonal purchasing patterns, and so on. Business research suppliers offer audit data at both the retail and the wholesale levels.

An observer can record physical-trace data to discover things that a respondent could not recall accurately. For example, actually measuring the number of ounces of a liquid bleach used during a test provides precise physical-trace evidence without relying on the respondent's memory. The accuracy of respondents' memories is not a problem for the firm that conducts a pantry audit. The pantry audit requires an inventory of the brands, quantities, and package sizes in a consumer's home rather than responses from individuals. The problem of untruthfulness or some other form of response bias is avoided. For example, the pantry audit prevents the possible problem of respondents erroneously claiming to have purchased prestige brands. However, gaining permission to physically check consumers' pantries is not easy, and the fieldwork is expensive. Further, the brand in the pantry may not reflect the brand purchased most often if it was chosen because of a cents-off coupon, because the brand normally purchased was out of stock, or for another reason.

CONTENT ANALYSIS

content analysis
A research technique for the objective, systematic, and quantitative description of the manifest content of communication.

Content analysis obtains data by observing and analyzing the content or message of advertisements, union contracts, reports, letters, and the like. It involves systematic analysis, as well as observation, to identify the specific information content and characteristics of the messages.

Content analysis studies the message itself. Its objective is to obtain a quantitative description of the manifest content of communication. This technique measures the extent of emphasis, or omission of emphasis, on any analytical category. For example, the content of newspaper articles about a company might be investigated with regard to the use of certain words, themes, characters, or space and time relationships. Investigating the frequency and appearance (or "roles") of women, blacks, and other minorities in mass media is a research effort that utilizes content analysis.

Content analysis may ask questions such as: "Do certain advertisers use certain types of themes, appeals, claims, or deceptive practices more than other advertisers?" and "Have recent actions by the Federal Trade Commission influenced the content of advertising?" In order to plan effectively, a cable-television programmer might do a content analysis of network programming to evaluate its competition. For example, sports programs may be analyzed to see how much of the visual material is live action and how much is replay, or how many shots there are of cheerleaders and close-ups of spectators.

Study of the content of communications is more sophisticated than simply counting the items; it requires a system of analysis to secure relevant data. After one employee role-playing session involving "leaders" and "subordinates," videotapes were analyzed to identify categories of verbal behaviors (e.g., positive reward statements, positive comparison statements, and self-evaluation requests). Then trained coders, using a set of specific instructions, recorded and coded the leaders' behavior into specific verbal categories.

MECHANICAL OBSERVATION

mechanical observation
Observation technique that uses video cameras, traffic counters, and other machines to record behavior.

In many situations the primary—and sometimes the sole—means of observation is mechanical rather than human. In **mechanical observation,** videotape cameras, traffic counters, and other machines record behavior.

Some unusual observation studies have used a motion picture camera and time-lapse photography. An early application of this observation technique, photographing train passengers, determined passenger comfort by observing how the passengers sat and moved in their seats. Another time-lapse study, filming traffic flows in an urban "square," resulted in the redesigning of peripheral streets. Similar techniques may be used in research to help design store layouts and to resolve problems in moving people or objects through various spaces over time.

Television Monitoring

Perhaps the best-known business research project involving mechanical observation and computerized data collection is A. C. Nielsen's system for estimating national television audiences. Nielsen uses a consumer panel and a

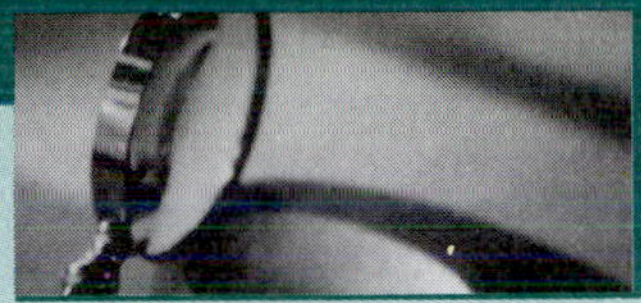

RESEARCH INSIGHT

TEXAS INSTRUMENTS AND E-LAB

E-Lab LLC is a business research and design firm in Chicago that specializes in observing people, identifying patterns in behavior, and developing an understanding of why these patterns exist.[15] The company then uses the knowledge that it gains as a framework in the product development process. Texas Instruments (TI) used E-Lab to investigate the mobility, connectivity, and communications needs of law enforcement officers, which led to ideas for a set of computing and communications products. As part of its product development research, TI's Advanced Integrated Systems Department and E-Lab researchers spent 320 hours shadowing police officers in three Texas police departments. Shadowing involves asking questions while observing. Researchers walked foot patrols, rode in patrol cars, and pedaled with bike patrols. They spent time with crowd control, narcotics, homicide, dispatch, and juvenile teams. They recorded their observations and interviews on paper, digital camera, and video.

A number of interesting findings emerged from all this research. First, police officers are very social, so it was important that any product TI developed should enhance socialization rather than detract from it. For example, an in-car computing and communications device should be able to access a database that lists names and numbers of experts on the force so that officers can call or e-mail the experts directly. Second, police officers are not driven by procedure. That told TI that the procedures for an investigation should reside in the device and that the device should prompt the officer at each step in the process. And third, officers rely on informal information about people and activities on their beats. This information may be kept on scraps of paper, on a spreadsheet back in the office, or in the police officer's head. Business researchers concluded that any device that TI develops should have a place to compile and share informal information.

sophisticated monitoring device called a PeopleMeter to obtain ratings for television programs in 18 countries.[16] Electronic boxes are hooked up to television sets to capture important information on program choices, the length of viewing time, and the identity of the viewer.

Knowing who in the family is watching allows executives to be match television programs with demographic profiles. When the panel household's television set is turned on, a question mark appears on the screen to remind viewers to indicate who is watching. The viewer then uses a handheld electronic device that resembles a television remote control to record who is watching. A device attached to the television automatically sends the observed data—the viewer's age and sex and what programs are being watched—over telephone lines to Nielsen's computers. More than 5,000 households, scientifically selected to be representative of the U.S. population, have agreed to become members of the panel and have meters placed in their homes.

Critics of the PeopleMeter argue that subjects in Nielsen's panel grow bored over time and do not always record when they begin or stop watching television. Nielsen Media Research is working on a unique technology that will allow its PeopleMeters to scan the room, recognize each family member by his or her facial characteristics, and record when they enter or leave the room.

Organizations with a presence on the World Wide Web find that their Web sites are a source of customer data. Researchers can combine a variety of technologies to learn who is visiting their sites. For example, "cookies," which observe and track a Web surfer's movements from page to page, and interactive surveys can be combined to provide consumer profiles of people who are attracted to advertising banners.

Further into the future, as digital television evolves, the current PeopleMeter measurement technologies will become obsolete. For example, Nielsen is working on more sophisticated digital cable technology that uses a set-top box decoding system. The system will "ask" what the set-top box is doing and identify the channel or display on screen. The data, invisible and inaudible to viewers, will be sent to a central processing site during normal data transmission.[17] The TiVo digital television recorder, already on the market but used by only a small percentage of the population, uses similar technology. TiVo records viewing data, such as what commercials people skip by using fast-forward, that is quite valuable to marketers.

Monitoring Web Site Traffic

Most organizations record how many people visit their Web sites. A *hit* occurs when a user clicks on a single page of a Web site. If the visitor clicks on many places to access graphics, or the like, that page receives multiple hits.[18] Organizations with Web sites consisting of multiple pages find it useful to track *page views,* or single, discrete clicks on individual pages. Page views more conservatively indicate how many users visit each individual page on the Web site, and they may also be used to track the path or sequence of pages that each visitor follows. A variety of information technologies are used to measure Web traffic and to maintain access logs.

Jupiter Media Metrix and Nielsen//NetRatings are companies that specialize in monitoring Internet activity. The typical Internet monitoring company installs a special tracking program on the personal computers of a sample of Internet users who agree to participate in the research effort. Nielsen//NetRatings has its software installed on 225,000 computers, in homes and workplaces, in 26 countries. Internet monitoring enables these companies to identify the popularity of Web sites (AOL.com and Yahoo.com are among the most popular), measure the effectiveness of advertising banners, and provide other audience information. For example, a Jupiter Media Metrix study indicated that 63 percent of online shoppers stop short of completing their purchases after shipping charges are computed at the last step, known as the Checkout Line.

Measuring Physiological Reactions

Business researchers have used a number of other mechanical devices to evaluate physical and physiological reactions to various stimuli. There are four major categories of mechanical devices used to measure physiological reactions: (1) eye-tracking monitors, (2) pupilometers, (3) psychogalvanometers, and (4) voice pitch analyzers.

A magazine or newspaper advertiser may wish to grab the reader's attention with a visual scene and then direct it to a package or coupon. Or an advertiser may wish to emphasize selling points identified by measuring "rough" television commercials with an eye-tracking monitor. Eye-tracking equipment records how the subject reads an ad (or views a television commercial) and how much time is spent looking at various stimuli. In physiological terms, the gaze movements of the eye are measured with an *eye camera* or *eye view monitor.*

Eye-tracking monitors measure unconscious eye movements. Originally developed to measure astronauts' eye fatigue, these devices track television viewers' eye movements and focal points through an invisible infrared light beam that "locks" onto subjects' eyes. Modern eye-tracking systems do not require keeping a viewer's head in a stationary position.

Nissan North America in Torrance, California, is putting video cameras and tape recorders in some Nissan cars to learn more about how people behave when they are driving. So far, Nissan has used the tapes to suggest changes in seat design ("Drivers want to feel in touch with the road, while passengers want to be insulated from it"), to include more individual storage space ("People always look uncomfortable when they want to put something away"), and to change the thickness and texture of the steering wheel ("You can tell if someone is touching it like a caress or with revulsion").

The other physiological measurement devices are based on a common principle:

> Physiological research depends on the fact that adrenalin is produced when the body is aroused. When adrenalin goes to work, the heart beats faster and more strongly, and even enlarges.
>
> Blood flows to the extremities and increases capillary dilation at the finger-tips and earlobes. Skin temperature increases, hair follicles stand up, skin pores emit perspiration, and the electrical conductivity of the skin surfaces is affected. Eye pupils dilate, electrical waves in the brain increase in frequency, breathing is faster and deeper, and the chemical composition of expired air is altered. This process offers a choice of about 50 different measures—the question of which measure to use is to some extent irrelevant since they are all measuring arousal.[19]

pupilometer
A device used to observe and record changes in the diameter of the pupils of the eyes.

A **pupilometer** observes and records changes in the diameter of the pupils of the eyes. Subjects are instructed to look at a screen on which an advertisement (or other stimulus) is projected. If the brightness and distance of the stimulus from the subject's eyes are held constant, changes in pupil size may be interpreted as changes in cognitive activity, resulting from the stimulus (rather than from eye dilation and constriction in response to light intensity, distance from

How This Advertisement Was Read

% Noting Each Element

Most Common Starting Point

Most Common Viewing Pattern

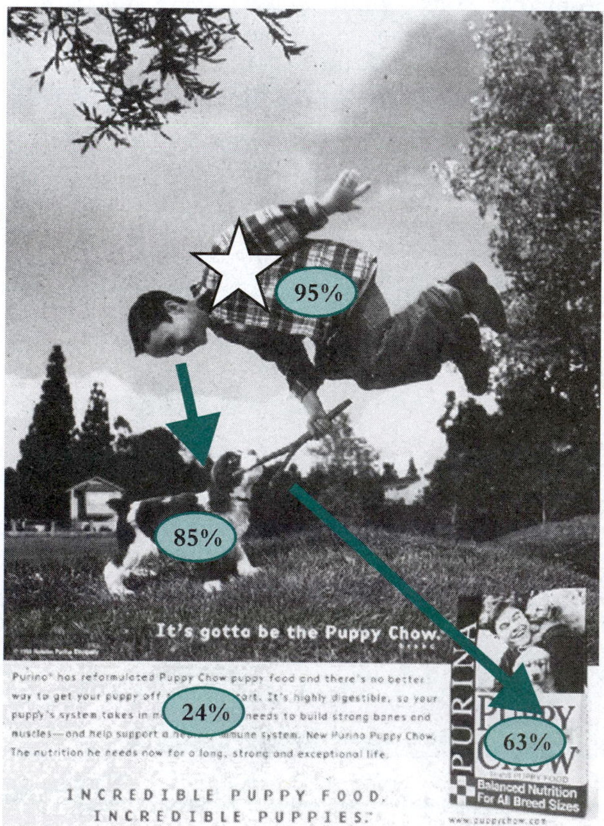

Measurements with an eye-tracking monitor of subjects' responses to this ad for Purina Puppy Chow showed that only 24 percent of consumer viewing time was given to the body copy message and that 95 percent of the viewers started looking at the boy at the top of the ad. The arrows show the most common viewing pattern.

the object, or other physiological reactions to the conditions of observation). This research is based on the assumption that increased pupil size reflects positive attitudes toward and interest in the stimulus.

psychogalvanometer
A device that measures galvanic skin response (GSR), involuntary changes in the electrical resistance of the skin.

A **psychogalvanometer** measures galvanic skin response (GSR), or involuntary changes in the electrical resistance of the skin. Use of this device is based on the assumption that physiological changes, such as increased perspiration, accompany emotional reactions to advertisements, packages, and slogans. Excitement increases the perspiration rate of the body, which increases the electrical resistance of the subject. The test is an indicator of emotional arousal or tension.

Each of these mechanical devices has a limitation in that the subjects it is used with are usually in an artificial setting (watching television in a laboratory rather than at home) and know that they are being observed.

voice pitch analysis
A physiological measurement technique that records abnormal frequencies in the voice that are supposed to reflect emotional reactions to various stimuli.

Voice pitch analysis measures emotional reactions as reflected in physiological changes in a person's voice. Abnormal frequencies in the voice, caused by changes in the autonomic nervous system, are measured with sophisticated audio-adapted computer equipment. This technique does not require subjects to be surrounded by mazes of wires or masses of equipment.

All of the devices described above assume that physiological reactions are associated with persuasiveness or that they predict some cognitive response, but this has not yet been clearly demonstrated. No strong theoretical evidence supports the argument that physiological change is a valid measure of attitude change or behavior change.

Another problem with physiological research relates to the *calibration,* or sensitivity, of measuring devices. Identifying arousal is one thing, but precisely measuring *levels* of arousal is another. In addition, most of these devices are very expensive. However, as a prominent researcher points out, physiological measurement is coincidental: "Physiological measurement isn't an exit interview. It's not dependent on what was remembered later on. It's a live blood, sweat, and tears, moment-by-moment response, synchronous with the stimulus."[20]

Optical Scanners and Bar Codes

Mechanical observation can also be based on optical character recognition or bar code systems such as the universal product code (UPC). Optical scanners in supermarkets provide a wealth of product and brand sales information. Substituting mechanized record keeping for human record keeping has resulted in greater accuracy and more rapid feedback about store activity. Systems based on the UPC bar-code technology have been implemented in factories, warehouses, and transportation companies to research inventory levels, shipments, and the like.

SUMMARY

Observation is the systematic process of recording the behavioral patterns of people, objects, and occurrences as they are witnessed. Questioning or communicating with the individuals under investigation does not need to occur.

Business researchers employ both human observers and machines designed for specific observation tasks. Human observation is commonly used when the situation or behavior to be recorded is not easily predictable in advance of the research. Mechanical observation can be used when the situation or behavior to be recorded is routine, repetitive, or programmatic. Human or mechanical observation may both be unobtrusive. Human observation may suffer from observer bias, however, even though the observer does not interact with the subject.

Seven kinds of phenomena can be observed: physical actions, verbal behavior, expressive behavior, spatial relations and locations, temporal patterns, physical objects, and verbal and pictorial records. Thus, both verbal and nonverbal behavior may be observed. A major disadvantage of the observation technique is that cognitive phenomena such as attitudes, motivations, expectations, intentions, and preferences cannot be observed. Further, only overt behavior of short duration can be observed. Many types of data can be obtained more accurately through direct observation than by questioning respondents. Observation is often the most direct or the only method for collection of certain data.

Observation can sometimes be "contrived" by creating the situations that are to be observed. This is done to reduce the time and expense of obtaining reactions to certain circumstances.

Physical-trace evidence serves as a visible record of past events. Content analysis obtains data by observing and analyzing the content of messages in written and/or spoken communications. Mechanical observation uses a variety of devices to record physiological data.

Key Terms

scientific observation
visible observation
hidden observation
direct observation
observer bias
mechanical observation
pupilometer
response latency
contrived observation
participant observation
physical-trace evidence
content analysis
psychogalvanometer
voice pitch analysis

Questions for Review and Critical Thinking

1. Yogi Berra, former New York Yankee catcher, said, "You can observe a lot just by watching." How does this fit in with the definition of scientific observation?
2. What are the advantages and disadvantages of observation studies compared to surveys?
3. Under what conditions are observation studies most appropriate?
4. Suggest some new uses for observation studies. Be creative.
5. A multinational fast-food corporation plans to locate a restaurant in La Paz, Bolivia. Secondary data for this city are outdated. How might you determine the best location using observation?
6. Discuss how an observation study might be combined with a personal interview.
7. The lost-letter technique has been used to predict voting behavior. Letters addressed to various political groups are spread throughout a city. The "respondent" finds an envelope, reads the address of a group supporting (or opposing) a candidate, and mails back (or throws away) the envelope. It is assumed that the respondent's action indicates a favorable (or unfavorable) attitude toward the organization. Would this technique be appropriate in business research?
8. Outline a research design using observation for each of the following situations:
   (a) A bank wishes to collect data on the frequency of customer use of its various services.
   (b) A state government wishes to determine the driving public's use of seat belts.
   (c) A researcher wishes to know how many women have been featured on *Time* covers over the years.
   (d) A fast-food franchise wishes to determine how long a customer entering a store has to wait for his or her order.

(e) A magazine publisher wishes to determine exactly what people see and what they pass over while reading one of its magazines.
(f) A food manufacturer wishes to determine how people use snack foods in their homes.
(g) An overnight package delivery service wishes to observe delivery workers beginning when they stop the truck, continuing through the delivery of the package, and ending when they return to the truck.

9. Watch the nightly news on a major network for 1 week. Observe how much time is devoted to national news, commercials, and other activity. (Hint: Think carefully about how you will record the contents of the programs.)
10. Comment on the ethics of the following situations:
(a) During the course of telephone calls to investors, a stockbroker records their voices when they are answering sensitive investment questions and then conducts a voice pitch analysis. The respondents do not know that their voices are being recorded.
(b) A researcher plans to invite consumers to be test users in a simulated kitchen located in a shopping mall and then to videotape their reactions to a new microwave dinner from behind a one-way mirror.
(c) A business researcher arranges to purchase the trash from the headquarters of a major competitor. The purpose is to sift through discarded documents to determine the company's strategic plans.

Exploring the Internet

1. The University of Arizona Department of Anthropology houses the Bureau of Applied Research in Anthropology. The garbage project is one of the bureau's research activities. Use a search engine to find the University of Arizona's home page and then navigate to the garbage project. What information is available?
2. If you are interested in content analysis, go to the UCLA Television Violence Monitoring Project at http://www.media-awareness.ca/eng/med/home/resource/ucla.htm or to the National Clearinghouse for Alcohol and Drug Information's project on Substance Use in Popular Prime-Time Television at http://www.health.org/govstudy/tvmediastudy/index.htm.

Case Suggestions

Case 12: Tulsa's Central Business District (C)
Case 13: The Pretesting Company

CHAPTER

12

EXPERIMENTAL RESEARCH

What you will learn in this chapter

- To define *experimentation* and discuss the requirements for making a true experiment.
- To understand the terminology of experimentation.
- To discuss the factors that influence the choice and manipulation of independent variables.
- To evaluate the factors that influence the selection and measurement of dependent variables.
- To understand how test units should be selected and assigned.
- To compare and contrast the two basic types of experimental error.
- To give examples of demand characteristics.
- To discuss how to control extraneous variables in experimental situations.
- To compare and contrast basic and factorial experimental designs.
- To compare and contrast field and laboratory experiments.
- To distinguish between internal and external validity.
- To list the six major factors threatening internal validity and provide examples of each.
- To outline the various quasi-experimental designs and the alternative, better experimental designs.

Does the size of a package influence a person to increase or decrease consumption? A series of tightly controlled laboratory experiments found evidence that larger packages encourage consumers to increase the amount of the product they use.

The hypothesis for one of the experiments was that the larger a package's size, the more a person will use on a given usage occasion.[1] The experiment required altering package size while holding the total supply of the product constant.

The procedure went as follows: The researchers recruited 98 adult women through local parent-teacher associations and donated $6 to the respective organization for each participant. Two different products (Crisco oil and Creamette spaghetti) in two different sizes were selected for the study. In both cases, the larger package held twice as much of the product as the smaller package. The supply of each brand was held constant by leaving the smaller package full and by using only half of the larger package. The volume of each product was determined by the package size in which each was sold.

Each subject was randomly assigned to use either a relatively small or a relatively large package, each holding an identical volume of the product. Two products were used for generalizability, and the pattern of results was expected to be similar for both products.

In individual meetings each subject was told that researchers were collecting some basic "home economics–related" information about two different types of products. The subject was then led to one of four isolated cubicles in which there was one of the two products in one of the two package-size conditions. The research assistant assigned to each cubicle was blind to the purpose of the study. When the subject arrived, the research assistant read a scenario involving the use of the product: for Crisco oil, the scenario was "You are frying a chicken dinner for yourself and another adult"; for Creamette spaghetti, "You are making spaghetti for yourself and another adult." The subject was asked to show how much of the product she would use in this situation, and then asked how much money that use of the product would entail. After the subject left the cubicle, researchers measured the volume of the product the subject intended to use. The procedure was repeated for all subjects.

The dependent measure was the volume of the product each subject indicated she would use. Subjects indicated their use of oil by pouring it into a frying pan; they indictated their use of spaghetti by placing it in a large (dry) pot. The volume of oil they used was measured by pouring the liquid into a narrow beaker. The volume of spaghetti was measured by holding the strands together and

- To discuss the four complex experimental designs: completely randomized, randomized block, factorial, and Latin square.
- To define the interaction effects and main effects in a factorial design.

measuring the circumference with a finely graduated tape measure; this was later translated to an approximation of an individual count.

As was hypothesized, manipulation of package size while holding the supply of each product constant indicated that increases in a package's size are associated with increases in product usage.

Related experiments show that consumers will also use more from a full container than from a half-empty one. Even when a package recommends an amount to use, as household cleaners do, research shows consumers ignore such instructions 70 percent of the time.[2] ■

Experiments like these are a form of business research. The purpose of this chapter is to explore the use of experiments in business research and the various types of experimental designs.

THE NATURE OF EXPERIMENTS

Most students are familiar with the concept of experimentation in the physical sciences. The word *experiment* typically conjures up an image of a chemist surrounded by bubbling test tubes and Bunsen burners. Indeed, behavioral and physical scientists have been far ahead of business researchers in the uses of experimentation. Nevertheless, the purpose of all experimental research is the same.

The purpose of experimental research is to allow the researcher to *control* the research situation so that *causal* relationships among variables may be evaluated. The experimenter therefore manipulates a single variable in an investigation and holds constant all other relevant, extraneous variables. (Events may be controlled in an experiment in a way that is not possible in a survey.) It has even been stated that "the goal of experimental design is the confidence that it gives the researcher that his experimental treatment is the cause of the effect he measures."[3]

experiment
A research method in which conditions are controlled so that one or more variables can be manipulated in order to test a hypothesis. *Experimentation* is a research method that allows evaluation of causal relationships among variables.

Experiments differ from other research methods in terms of degree of control over the research situation. In a typical **experiment** one variable (the *independent variable*) is manipulated and its effect on another variable (the *dependent variable*) is measured, while all other variables that may confound such a relationship are eliminated or controlled. The experimenter either creates an artificial situation or deliberately manipulates a situation.

Once the experimenter manipulates the independent variable, changes in the dependent variable are measured. The essence of a behavioral experiment is to do something to an individual and observe his or her reaction under conditions where this reaction can be measured against a known baseline.

AN ILLUSTRATION: A UNIT-PRICING EXPERIMENT

The concept of experimentation is best illustrated with an extended example concerning unit pricing. Whether or not consumers actually use unit price information is an issue of considerable controversy.[4] The purpose of unit pricing is to help shoppers avoid confusion in attempting to compare prices of comparable products, especially if the products are in different-size packages. There is some evidence that unit pricing has failed to change consumers' purchasing habits. However, much of the research on unit pricing depends on interviewing techniques, question phrasing, and store promotion of unit pricing.

Suppose a researcher argues that unless unit price information is presented in a usable display format, consumers will not use the information. The current form of unit price display is a separate shelf tag for each item. However, presenting the information this way may not facilitate price comparisons. Exhibit 12.1 shows unit prices organized in a single list.

A survey asking respondents if they use the traditional format of unit pricing and if they have any problems with understanding the traditional unit pricing might not yield truthful responses. It may not be socially desirable for respondents to admit they have problems understanding the traditional format, or they may be unwilling to provide truthful responses because they are embarrassed that they do not use a procedure that might reduce their grocery bills. Other limitations of surveys, such as interviewer bias, misunderstanding of the question, and so on, might also cause errors.

In the simplest form of experiment, the researcher's purpose might be to compare the effectiveness of the traditional shelf tag display and the list format, measuring changes toward the purchase of less expensive brands or sizes. The hypothesis would be that a single list of all brands' sizes and their unit prices is an effective arrangement of unit price information. A shift toward the purchase of less expensive items can be measured by average price paid per unit, the dependent variable.

Let us assume researchers conduct the experiment in a supermarket chain in a midwestern city. The supermarket chain has four stores in this city, and none of the stores has previously used unit price information. For a period of 5 weeks, brand purchases for five product categories are recorded in every store to indicate sales over a period of time. During the next 5 weeks, two

EXHIBIT 12.1 UNIT PRICES OF DISHWASHING DETERGENT[5] (ORDER OF INCREASING PRICE PER QUART)

Brand	Price	Unit Price (per Quart)	Unit Price (per Pint)
Par, 48 oz.	$1.08	$0.72	36.0
Par, 32 oz.	0.76	0.76	38.0
Sweetheart, 32 oz.	1.10	1.10	55.0
Brocade, 48 oz.	1.70	1.13	55.0
Sweetheart, 22 oz.	0.78	1.13	56.5
Super 6, 32 oz.	1.18	1.18	59.0
White Magic, 32 oz.	1.18	1.18	59.0
Brocade, 32 oz.	1.26	1.26	63.0
Brocade, 22 oz.	0.90	1.31	65.5
Super 6, 22 oz.	0.90	1.31	65.5
White Magic, 22 oz.	0.90	1.31	65.5
Brocade, 12 oz.	0.54	1.44	72.0
Super 6, 12 oz.	0.58	1.55	77.5
Ivory, 32 oz.	1.60	1.60	80.0
Dove, 22 oz.	1.12	1.63	81.5
Ivory, 22 oz.	1.12	1.63	81.5
Lux, 22 oz.	1.12	1.63	81.5
Palmolive, 32 oz.	1.70	1.70	85.0
Ivory, 12 oz.	0.64	1.71	85.5
Palmolive, 22 oz.	1.20	1.75	87.5
Palmolive, 12 oz.	0.68	1.81	90.5

Exhibit 12.2 | **Unit Price Experiment**

Store	First 5 Weeks	Second 5 Weeks
1	Record sales	Shelf-tag format, record sales
2	Record sales	Shelf-tag format, record sales
3	Record sales	List format, record sales
4	Record sales	List format, record sales

stores may be assigned unit prices on separate shelf tags, and the other two stores display unit price information in the list format (see Exhibit 12.2). This manipulation involves an independent, or experimental, variable.

Exhibit 12.3 shows that for dishwashing detergent the average price paid per unit purchased was 65.0 cents for all stores before the experiment. After the manipulation of the unit price information, the average price paid per unit in the shelf-tag stores was 61.6 cents, and the average price paid per unit in the list-format stores was 60.0 cents. The results indicate that unit price information is effective in shifting purchases toward less expensive items in both the shelf-tag condition and the list condition, as opposed to no unit price information displayed before the experiment. Further, the average price paid per unit is lower in the list-format condition than in the shelf-tag condition, suggesting that the list format is more effective than the tag condition.

It might be argued that some of the influence of shifts in purchases may be due to differences in the stores (for example, the stores with the list of unit prices may have shoppers who are generally more sophisticated than those in other stores). To eliminate or minimize this problem, the researchers could randomly assign the experimental condition of unit-pricing format to the stores. The randomization minimizes the possibility that changes in the variable under study are due to forces other than the unit price format. In our example this randomization process resulted in both the shelf-tag and the list-format stores having equal (65.0 cents) average prices per unit before the experiment began.

This experiment showed that a change in presentation of unit price information (the independent variable) caused a change in average unit price paid (the dependent variable) when other variables were controlled for possible causal effects. For example, store image was held constant because the experiment

Exhibit 12.3 | **Results of Unit Price Experiment: Dishwashing Detergent**

	Average Price Paid per Unit	
Treatment	5 Weeks before Experiment	During Experiment
Shelf-tag format (Stores 1 and 2)	65.0¢	61.6¢
List format (Stores 3 and 4)	65.0	60.0
Total all stores	65.0	61.0

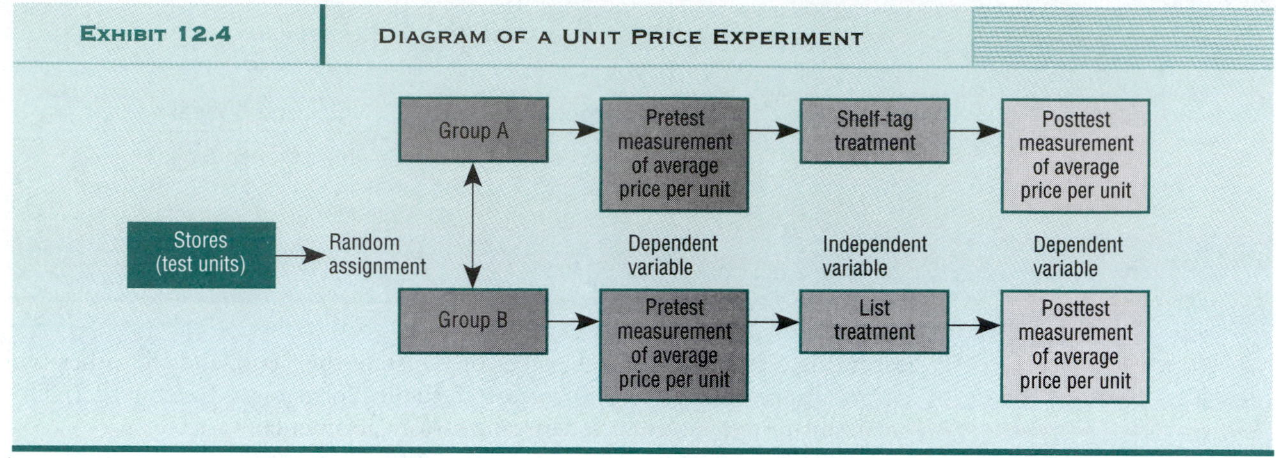

occurred only in stores with the same name. Store image may affect sales, but the researchers controlled for this variable by using only one type of store in one city. They also assumed invariance for certain variables; that is, they did not expect them to vary appreciably. For example, store temperature may affect the amount of time a shopper spends in the store, but researchers assumed (without checking on or controlling this assumption) that all stores are the same for this variable. In other cases researchers assume that some variables are irrelevant. For example, the color of the store managers' eyes may vary, but researchers assume that this does not have any effect on the purchase of products.

This is a simple experiment, intended to introduce some of the concepts of business experimentation. Exhibit 12.4, which diagrams the unit price experiment, can be helpful in understanding pertinent terminology presented in the next section. The remainder of the chapter explores additional aspects of experimental designs.

BASIC ISSUES IN EXPERIMENTAL DESIGN

Decisions must be made about several basic elements of an experiment: (1) manipulation of the independent variable, (2) selection and measurement of the dependent variable, (3) selection and assignment of test units, and (4) control over extraneous variables.[6]

Manipulation of the Independent Variable

independent variable
In an experimental design, the variable that can be manipulated to be whatever the experimenter wishes. Its value may be changed or altered independently of any other variable.

experimental treatment
An alternative manipulation of the independent variable being investigated.

The experimenter has some degree of control over the **independent variable.** The variable is independent because its value can be manipulated by the experimenter to be whatever he or she wishes it to be. Its value may be changed or altered independently of any other variable. The independent variable is hypothesized to be the causal influence.

Experimental treatments are the alternative manipulations of the independent variable being investigated. For example, monthly salaries of $2,200, $2,400, and $2,600 might be the treatments in a personnel experiment.

In business research, the independent variable is often a categorical or classificatory variable, representing some classifiable or qualitative aspects of management strategy. To determine the effects of training, for example, the experimental treatment that represents the independent variable is the training program itself. Alternative financial reporting formats are another example of categorical or classificatory variables. In other situations the independent variable is a *continuous variable.* The researcher must select the appropriate levels of the independent variable for experimental treatments. For example, the number of dollars that can be spent on training employees may be any number of different values.

Experimental and Control Groups

In the simplest type of experiment, only two values of the independent variable are manipulated. For example, consider measuring the influence of a change in the work situation, such as playing music over an intercom during working hours, on employee productivity. In the experimental condition (the treatment administered to the **experimental group**), music is played during working hours. In the control condition (the treatment administered to the **control group**), the work situation remains the same, *without* change. By holding conditions constant in the control group, the researcher controls for potential sources of error in the experiment. Productivity (the dependent variable) in the two treatment groups is compared at the end of the experiment to determine whether playing the music (the independent variable) has had any effect.

experimental group
The group of subjects exposed to an experimental treatment.

control group
A group of subjects who are exposed to the control condition in an experiment—that is, they are subjects not exposed to the experimental treatment.

Several Experimental Treatment Levels

The music/productivity experiment, with one experimental and one control group, may not tell the researcher everything he or she wishes to know about the music/productivity relationship. If the researcher wished to understand the functional nature of the relationship between music and productivity at several treatment levels, additional experimental groups with music played for only 2 hours, only 4 hours, and only 6 hours might be studied. This type of design would allow the experimenter to get a better idea of the impact of music on productivity.

You never know what is enough unless you know what is more than enough.

WILLIAM BLAKE

More Than One Independent Variable

It is possible to assess the effects of more than one independent variable. Perhaps a restaurant chain might wish to investigate the combined effects of increased advertising and a change in prices on sales volume. The more complex experimental designs required for such investigations are discussed later.

Selection and Measurement of the Dependent Variable

The dependent variable is so named because its value is expected to be dependent on the experimenter's manipulation of the independent variable. The **dependent variable** is the criterion or standard by which the results are judged. It is assumed that changes in the dependent variable are a consequence of changes in the independent variable.

dependent variable
The criterion or standard by which the results of an experiment are judged. It is so named because it is expected to be dependent on the experimenter's manipulation of the independent variable.

Selection of the dependent variable is a crucial decision in the design of an experiment. If researchers introduce a new pink-grapefruit tea mix in a test market experiment, sales volume is most likely to be the dependent variable. However, if researchers are evaluating different forms of training programs, defining the dependent variable may be more difficult. For example, measures of turnover, absenteeism, or morale might be alternative choices for the dependent variable, depending on the purpose of the training. In the unit-pricing experiment the dependent variable was the average price per unit. However, the dependent variable might have been preference for the use of pricing information (a cognitive variable); brand-switching behavior, expressed as a percentage of consumers; or attitudes toward the store.

Often the dependent variable selection process, like problem definition, is not as carefully considered by researchers as it should be. The experimenter's choice of a dependent variable determines what type of answer is given to the research question.

In some experiments the amount of time required for the effects to become evident should be considered in choosing a dependent variable. Productivity may be measured several months after the experiment to determine if there were any carryover effects. Changes that are relatively permanent or more long-lasting than changes generated only during the period of the experiment should be considered.

For example, in test market experiments to determine if new products will be successful, it is necessary to think about dependent variables that will identify consumers who initially purchase but do not make repeat purchases over time. In other words, it is necessary to think beyond gross sales or consumers' initial reactions and to select dependent variables that will measure sales behavior over time. Brand awareness, trial purchase, and repeat purchase are all possible dependent variables in such test market experiments. The dependent variable should therefore be carefully considered. Careful problem definition will help researchers select the most important dependent variable(s).

Selection and Assignment of Test Units

test unit
A subject or entity whose responses to experimental treatments are observed and measured.

Test units are the subjects or entities whose responses to the experimental treatment are measured or observed. Individuals, organizational units, sales territories, or other entities may be the test units. People and departments within organizations are the most common test units in most business behavioral experiments. In the unit-pricing example, supermarkets were the test units.

Sample Selection and Random Sampling Error

As in other forms of business research, random sampling errors and sample selection errors may occur in experimentation. For example, experiments sometimes go awry even when a geographic area is specially chosen for a particular investigation. A case in point was the experimental testing of a new lubricant for outboard motors by Dow Chemical Company. The lubricant was tested in Florida and Michigan. Florida was chosen because researchers thought that a warm-weather state, in which the product would have to stand up under continuous use, would prove the most demanding test. In Florida the lubricant was a success, but the story was quite different in Michigan. Although the lubricant sold well and worked well during the summer, the following spring Dow discovered that in the colder northern climate it had congealed, allowing the outboard motors, idle all winter, to rust. The rusting problem, of course, never came to light in Florida where the motors were in year-round use.[8] Thus, some **sample selection error** may occur because of the procedure utilized to assign subjects or test units to either the experimental or the control group.

sample selection error
An administrative procedural error caused by improper selection of a sample, thus introducing bias.

random sampling error
A statistical fluctuation that occurs because of chance variation in the elements for a sample.

Random sampling error may occur if repetitions of the basic experiment sometimes favor one experimental condition and sometimes the other on a chance basis. An experiment dealing with usage of computer monitors and fatigue may require that the people in both the experimental and the control groups be identical with regard to age and experience. However, if subjects are randomly assigned to conditions without consideration of their age or experience, an error resulting from differences in those characteristics will be a random sampling error. Consider another example. Suppose that a potato chip

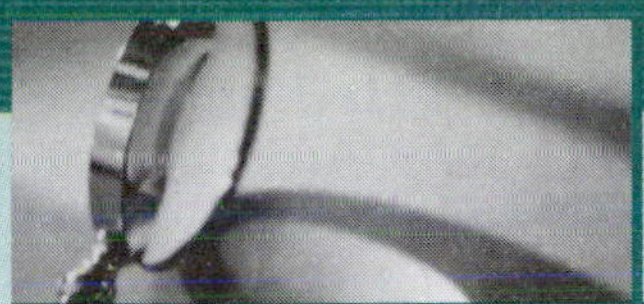

RESEARCH INSIGHT

CAUSALITY

A while back the *New York Herald Tribune* quoted Sir Ronald Fisher, the father of experimental design, on the subject of cigarette smoking and cancer.[7] Fisher pointed out that the only way to establish a causal connection between the two would be to randomly assign a large sample of newborn babies to two groups, those from whom cigarettes would be withheld and those who would be forced to smoke them. Some 70 or 80 years later we *might* have conclusive evidence of the true effects of smoking on death by various causes.

Sir Ronald was simply repeating a lesson that many of us learned in school: To observe a consistent relationship between two variables over time, or over cases at one point in time, does not prove that one causes the other. In its simplest slogan, "Correlation is not causation" or "Correlation is not *necessarily* causation." As the statistician said when he quit smoking, "I know that correlation is not causation, but in this case I'm willing to take a chance."

He put in a nutshell exactly what we do whenever we put a causal interpretation on *any* result, experimental or nonexperimental: We take a chance. Sometimes we express that chance precisely, as in the confidence level at which we reject a hypothesis in a designed experiment; but usually even then, and virtually always in practical business situations, we really have only a subjective estimate of that chance. We have failed to consider sources of error other than random sampling; these must be absent if that confidence level is to be meaningful. Statistics teachers to the contrary, random sampling is not always the main source of error in testing hypotheses, and in many business situations it can be unimportant relative to errors due to bias in sample selection.

manufacturer that wishes to experiment with new advertising appeals wants the experimental and control groups to be identical with respect to advertising awareness, media exposure, and so on. The experimenter must decide how to place subjects in each group and which group should receive which treatment. It is generally agreed that the random assignment of participants to groups and experimental treatments to groups is the best procedure.

Randomization

Random assignment of subjects and treatments is one device for equally distributing, or scattering, the effects of extraneous variables. Thus, the chance of unknown nuisance effects "piling up" in particular experimental groups is identified. The effects of the nuisance variables will not be eliminated, but they will be controlled.

randomization
A procedure in which the assignment of subjects and treatments of groups is based on chance.

Randomization assures the researcher that repetitions of an experiment—under the same conditions—will show the true effects, if they exist.[9] Random assignment of conditions provides "control by chance."[10] Random assignment of subjects allows the researcher to assume that the groups are identical with respect to all variables except for the experimental treatment.

Matching

Random assignment of subjects to the various experimental groups is the most common technique used to prevent test units from differing from each other on key variables; it assumes that all characteristics of these subjects have been similarly randomized. If the experimenter believes that certain extraneous variables may affect the dependent variable, he or she can make sure that the subjects in each group are matched on these characteristics. **Matching** the subjects on the basis of pertinent background information is another technique for controlling assignment errors.

matching
A procedure for the assignment of subjects to groups; it ensures each group of respondents is matched on the basis of pertinent characteristics.

For example, an experiment that deals with performing a work task on a word processor may require that the subjects in both the experimental and the control groups be matched with regard to employment experience and typing ability (speed). Similarly, if income is expected to influence savings behavior, a savings and loan institution that is conducting an experiment may have greater assurance that there are no intersubject differences if the subjects in all experimental conditions are matched on income.

Although matching assures that the subjects in each group are similar on the matched characteristics, the researcher can never be sure that subjects have been matched on all of the characteristics that could be important to the experiment.

Repeated Measures

Experiments in which the same subjects are exposed to all experimental treatments are said to have **repeated measures.** This technique eliminates any problems due to subject differences, but it causes some other problems (to be discussed later).

repeated measures
Experimental technique in which the same subjects are exposed to all experimental treatments in order to eliminate any problems due to subject differences.

Control over Extraneous Variables

The fourth decision about the basic elements of an experiment concerns control over extraneous variables. To understand this issue, it is important to understand the various types of experimental error.

In Chapter 9, total survey error was classified into two basic categories—random sampling error and systematic error. Although this dichotomy applies to all research designs, the terms *random (sampling) error* and *constant (systematic) error* are utilized more frequently when discussing experiments.

Constant Experimental Error

Random error has already been discussed in the context of experimental selection and assignment of test units. **Constant error** (bias) occurs when the extraneous variables or the conditions of administering the experiment are allowed to have an influence on the dependent variables every time the experiment is repeated. When this occurs, the results will be confounded because the extraneous variables have not been controlled or eliminated.

constant error
An error that occurs in the same experimental condition every time the basic experiment is repeated.

For example, if subjects in an experimental group are always administered the treatment in the morning and subjects in the control group are always administered the treatment in the afternoon, this will result in a constant, systematic error. Thus, in such a situation the time of day—an uncontrolled extraneous variable—is a cause of constant error. In a training experiment, other sources of constant error might be the persons who do the training (line managers or external specialists) or whether the training is conducted on the employees' own time or on company time. These and other characteristics of the training may have an impact on the dependent variable and will have to be taken into account:

> The effect of a constant error is to distort the results in a particular direction, so that an erroneous difference masks the true state of affairs. The effect of a random error is not to distort the results in any particular direction, but to

obscure them. Constant error is like a distorting mirror in a fun house; it produces a picture that is clear but incorrect. Random error is like a mirror that has become cloudy with age; it produces a picture that is essentially correct but unclear.[11]

Extraneous Variables

The experiments discussed so far (and indeed most experiments) concern the identification of a single independent variable and the measurement of its effects on the dependent variable. A number of extraneous variables may affect the dependent variable, thereby distorting the experiment.

An illustration shows how extraneous variables may have an impact on results.[12] Suppose a television commercial for Brand Z gasoline shows two automobiles on a highway. The announcer states that one car has used Brand Z *without* the special additive and the other has used Brand Z *with* the special additive. The car without the special additive comes to a stop first, and the car with the special additive comes to a stop 10 to 15 yards beyond it. (We shall assume that both cars used the same quantity of gasoline.) The implication of this commercial is that the special additive (the independent variable) results in extra mileage (the dependent variable). An experimenter concerned with extraneous variables that could affect the result can raise the following questions:

1. Were the *engines* of the same size and type? Were the conditions of the engines the same (tuning and so on)?
2. Were the *cars* of the same condition (gear ratios, fuel injector setting, weight, wear and tear, and so on)?
3. Were the *drivers* different types? Were there differences in acceleration? Were there differences in the drivers' weights?

Because an experimenter does not want extraneous variables to affect the results of an experiment, such variables must be controlled or eliminated.

Demand Characteristics

demand characteristics
Experimental design procedures that unintentionally hint to subjects about the experimenter's hypothesis; situational aspects of an experiment that demand that the participant respond in a particular way.

The term **demand characteristics** refers to experimental design procedures that unintentionally give hints to subjects about the experimenter's hypothesis.[13] Demand characteristics are situational aspects of the experiment that demand that the participant respond in a particular way. Hence, demand characteristics are a source of constant error. If participants recognize the experimenter's expectation or demand, they are likely to act in a manner consistent with the experimental treatment. Even slight nonverbal cues may influence subjects' reactions.

experimenter bias
An effect on an experiment's results caused by the experimenter's presence, actions, or comments.

guinea pig effect
An effect on the results of an experiment caused by subjects changing their normal behavior or attitudes in order to cooperate with an experimenter.

In most experiments, the most prominent demand characteristic is the person who actually administers the experimental procedures. If an experimenter's presence, actions, or comments influence subjects' behavior or influence subjects to slant their answers to cooperate with an experimenter, the experiment has **experimenter bias.**

Subjects in experiments have a tendency to cooperate like guinea pigs and to exhibit behavior that might not be representative of their behavior in the marketplace or workplace. For example, if subjects in a sex discrimination experiment understand that the experimenter is interested in whether they changed their attitudes in accord with a given characteristic of a job applicant, they may answer in the desired direction to please the experimenter. This attitude change reflects a **guinea pig effect** rather than a true experimental treatment effect.

TO THE POINT

We are never deceived, we deceive ourselves.

JOHANN WOLFGANG VON GOETHE

A famous management experiment illustrates a demand characteristic common in many experiments. Researchers were attempting to study the effects on productivity of various working conditions, such as hours of work, rest periods, lighting, and methods of pay at the Western Electric Hawthorne plant in Cicero, Illinois. The researchers found that workers' productivity increased whether the work hours were lengthened or shortened, whether lighting was very bright or very dim, and so on. The surprised investigators realized that the workers' morale was higher because they were aware of being part of a special experimental group. This totally unintended effect is now known as the **Hawthorne effect** because researchers realized that subjects will perform differently when they know they are experimental subjects.[14]

Hawthorne effect
An unintended effect on the results of a research experiment caused by the subjects knowing that they are participants.

If subjects in a laboratory experiment interact (i.e., are not relatively isolated), their conversations may produce "joint" decisions rather than a desired individual decision. Thus, social interaction can be a form of demand characteristic, so, in general, social interaction is restricted in laboratory experiments by isolating subjects.

To reduce demand characteristics, steps are taken to make it difficult for subjects to know what the researcher is trying to find out in the experiment. Experimenters are trained and experimental situations are designed to reduce cues that might serve as demand characteristics. For example, the subjects may be told the purpose of the experiment is one thing when the research's purpose is actually something else. If the purpose of the experiment is disguised, the participant does not know how to be a "good subject" to "help" confirm the hypothesis. Of course, the use of deception (for example, if a lie is told to the subject) presents an ethical question that must be resolved by the researcher.

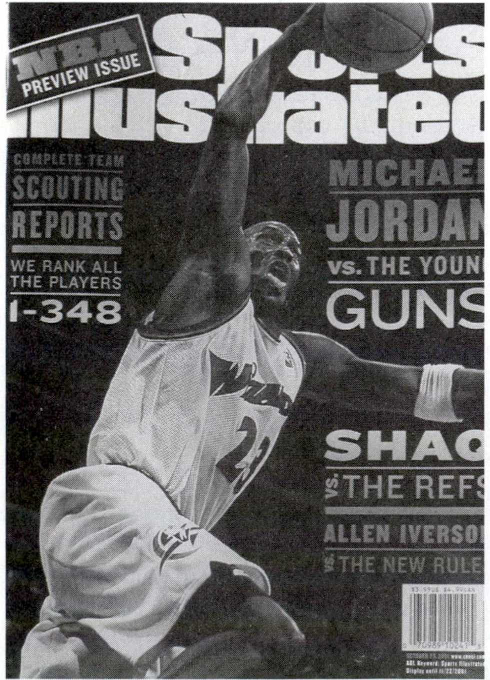

Sports Illustrated *conducts experiments to test its creative strategies and renewal materials to reveal the promotions that generate the highest response rates. For each renewal cycle,* Sports Illustrated *researchers include several control variables—source, price, amount paid, etc.—that are used to test the efficacy of renewal methods. (For example, the payment methods offered—bill me later, credit card, installment, etc.—will each elicit different responses.)*

Establishing Control

The major difference between experimental research and other research is the experimenter's ability to hold certain conditions constant and to manipulate the treatment. To conclude that A causes B, a brewery, experimenting with a "new" red beer's influence on beer drinkers' taste perceptions, must determine the possible extraneous variables that may affect the results and attempt to eliminate or control those variables. Marketers know that brand image and packaging are important factors in beer drinkers' reactions to the products. Wishing to eliminate the effects associated with brand name and packaging, the experimenter may eliminate these two extraneous variables by packaging the test beers in plain white packages without brand identification.

constancy of conditions
A procedure in which subjects in experimental groups are exposed to situations identical except for differing conditions of the independent variable.

When extraneous variables cannot be eliminated, experimenters may strive for **constancy of conditions.**[15] Experimenters want all subjects in each experimental group to be exposed to situations that are exactly alike except for the differing conditions of the independent variable. For example, holding extraneous variables constant might require that all experimental sessions be conducted in the same room at the same time of day.

A supermarket experiment involving four test products shows the care that must be taken to hold all factors constant. The experiment required that all factors other than shelf space were to be kept constant throughout the testing period. In all stores the shelf level (distance above the ground) that existed before the test began was maintained throughout the test period. Only the amount of shelf space (the treatment) was changed. One problem was that store personnel accidentally changed the shelf level when they restocked the test products. This distortion was minimized by auditing each store four times a week. In this way any change in the constancy of conditions could be detected in a minimum amount of time. The experimenter personally stocked as many of the products as possible, and the cooperation of stock clerks also helped lessen treatment deviations.[16]

order of presentation bias
An error in an experiment caused by subjects accumulating experience in the course of responding to multiple experimental treatments.

counterbalancing
A technique to reduce error caused by order of presentation by varying the order of experimental treatments for different groups.

blinding
A technique used to control subjects' knowledge of whether or not they have been given a particular experimental treatment.

double-blind design
A technique in which neither the subjects nor the experimenter knows which are the experimental and which are the controlled conditions.

If the experimental method requires that the same subjects be exposed to two or more experimental treatments, there is a possibility of **order of presentation bias.** An example might be having subjects perform an experimental task that requires a job skill (e.g., assembling a product). Subjects might perform better in a *second* task simply because they acquired experience on the *first* task.

Counterbalancing attempts to eliminate the confounding effects of order of presentation by requiring that half the subjects be exposed first to treatment A and then to treatment B. The other half receives treatment B first and then treatment A.

Blinding is utilized to control subjects' knowledge of whether they have or have not been given a particular experimental treatment. A cola taste test might use two groups of subjects, one group exposed to the new (diet) cola and one group exposed to the regular drink. If all the subjects were "blinded," they may have been told they have *not* been given the diet drink—or that they *have* been given the diet drink. This technique is also used in medical research when subjects who do not receive any medication are given chemically inert pills (placebos).[17]

Blinding may also involve the experimenters. For example, if the researchers do not know which toothpastes are in the tubes marked, say, with triangles, circles, or squares, they will not unconsciously influence the subjects. In such circumstances neither the subjects nor the experimenter knows which are the experimental and which are the controlled conditions. Both parties are "blinded"; hence the term **double-blind design.**

Random assignment of subjects to experimental groups and of experimental treatments to groups is an attempt to control extraneous variations caused by chance. If extraneous variations *cannot* be controlled, it must be assumed that their confounding effects will be present in all experimental conditions and have approximately the same influence. (This assumption may not be made if assignments are not random.) In many experiments, especially laboratory experiments, it is important to eliminate or minimize interpersonal contact between members of the various experimental groups and/or the control group. Thus, after the subjects have been assigned to groups, the various individuals should be kept separated so that discussions about what occurs in a given treatment situation does not become an extraneous variable that contaminates the experiment.

Problems Controlling Extraneous Variables

In business experiments it is not always possible to control everything that should be controlled in order to have the "perfect" experiment. For example, competitors may bring out a new product during the course of an experiment. This form of competitive interference occurred in a Boston test market for Anheuser-Busch's "import" beer, Würzburger Hofbraü, when the Miller Brewing Company introduced its own brand, Munich Oktoberfest, and sent eight salespeople to "blitz" the Boston market.

If a competing firm learns of a test market experiment, it may purposely change its prices or increase its advertising to confuse the test results. This gives the competitor more time to investigate a similar new-product possibility.

Business researchers may also be constrained by management's greater concern with efficiency than with research. In an experiment on the four-day workweek (4 days–40 hours), researchers planned to investigate employee satisfaction, absenteeism, and leisure-time activity *before* implementation of the 4–40 system, *during* the time the system was in effect, and *after* the system was discontinued.[18] The researchers had planned to investigate the effect of the 4–40 schedule over a long period of time, but the organization's management terminated the experiment after 1 month because of "scheduling difficulties."

ETHICAL ISSUES IN EXPERIMENTATION

Experimental researchers must address privacy, confidentiality, deception, accuracy of reporting, and other ethical issues common to other research methods. The question of subjects' right to be informed, however, tends to be very prominent in experimentation. Research codes of conduct often suggest that experimental subjects should be fully informed and receive accurate information. Yet experimental researchers who know that demand characteristics can invalidate an experiment may not give subjects complete information about the nature and purpose of the study. Simply put, experimenters often intentionally hide the true purpose of the experiment from the subjects, perhaps by remaining silent. They then frequently debrief the subjects after the experiment. **Debriefing** is the process of providing subjects with all the pertinent facts about the nature and purpose of the experiment after the experiment has been completed.

debriefing
Providing subjects with all pertinent facts about the nature and purpose of an experiment after its completion.

Debriefing experimental subjects by communicating the purpose of the experiment and the researcher's hypotheses about the nature of worker or consumer behavior is expected to counteract negative effects of deception,

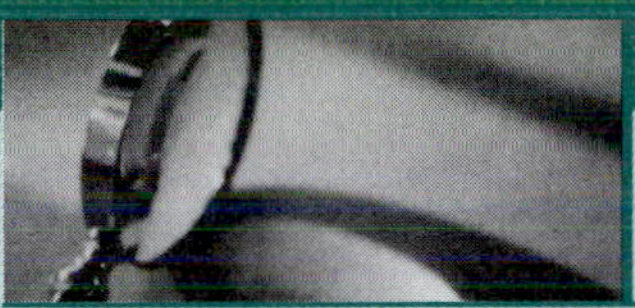

RESEARCH INSIGHT

AN EXTREME EXAMPLE OF LACK OF DEBRIEFING

In an experiment conducted in a natural setting, independent food merchants in a number of Dutch towns were brought together for group meetings, in the course of which they were informed that a large organization was planning to open up a series of supermarkets in the Netherlands.[19] Subjects in the high-threat condition were told that there was a high probability that their town would be selected as a site for such markets, and that the advent of these markets would cause a considerable drop in their business. On the advice of the executives of the shopkeepers' organizations, who had helped to arrange the group meetings, the investigators did not reveal the experimental manipulations to their subjects. I have been worried about these Dutch merchants ever since I heard about this study for the first time. Did some of them go out of business in anticipation of the heavy competition? Do some of them have an anxiety reaction every time they see a bulldozer? Chances are that they soon forgot about this threat (unless, of course, supermarkets actually did move into town) and that it became just one of the many little moments of anxiety that must occur in every shopkeeper's life. Do we have a right, however, to add to life's little anxieties and to risk the possibility of more extensive anxiety purely for the purposes of our experiments, particularly since deception deprives the subject of the opportunity to choose whether or not he wishes to expose himself to the risk that might be entailed?

relieve stress, and provide an educational experience for the subject. It has been suggested that

> . . . proper debriefing allows the subject to save face by uncovering the truth for himself. The experimenter should begin by asking the subject if he has any questions or if he found any part of the experiment odd, confusing, or disturbing. This question provides a check on the subject's suspiciousness and effectiveness of manipulations. The experimenter continues to provide the subject cues to the deception until the subject states that he believes there was more to the experiment than met the eye. At this time the purpose and procedure of the experiment is revealed.[20]

Researchers debrief subjects when there has been clear-cut deception or when they fear subjects may have suffered psychological harm in participating in an experiment (a rarity in business research). However, if the researcher does not foresee potentially harmful consequences in participation, he or she may omit debriefing because of time and cost considerations.

Another issue that may—but typically does not—arise in business experiments is the subject's right to safety from physical and mental harm. Most researchers believe that if the subject's experience may be stressful or cause physical harm, the subject should receive adequate information about this aspect of the experiment *before* agreeing to participate.

FUNDAMENTAL QUESTIONS IN EXPERIMENTATION

Basic versus Factorial Experimental Designs

In *basic experimental designs* a single independent variable is manipulated to observe its effect on a single dependent variable. However, complex dependent variables such as sales, productivity, preference, and so on are influenced by several factors. A simultaneous change in two independent variables such as price and advertising may have a greater influence on sales than if either variable is changed in isolation.

Factorial experimental designs are more sophisticated than basic experimental designs. They allow for investigation of the interaction of two or more independent variables. Factorial experiments are discussed in the section on complex experimental designs later in this chapter.

Field and Laboratory Experiments

laboratory experiment
An experiment conducted in a laboratory or artificial setting to obtain almost complete control over the research setting.

A business experiment can be conducted in a natural setting (field experiment) or in an artificial setting, one contrived for a specific purpose (laboratory experiment). In a **laboratory experiment** the researcher has almost complete control over the research setting. For example, subjects for a laboratory experiment investigating whether increasing the difficulty of performance goals increases productivity are recruited and brought to a university office, a research agency office, or perhaps a mobile unit designed for research purposes. These subjects, who have volunteered to work for 1 hour, are required to perform a task in a setting where they will not be interrupted. Of course, the instructions for the different experimental groups are manipulated by varying the performance goals' level of difficulty.

Let's consider a second example. In a laboratory experiment to measure advertising, subjects are exposed to a television commercial within the context of a program that includes ads for competing products. Then the subjects are allowed to purchase either the advertised product or one of several competing products in a simulated store. Trial purchase measures are thus obtained. A few weeks later the subjects are recontacted to measure satisfaction and to determine repeat purchase intentions. This typical laboratory experiment gives subjects an opportunity to "buy" and "invest." In a short time span, the researcher is able to collect information on decision making.

tachistoscope
A device that controls the amount of time a subject is exposed to a visual image.

Other laboratory experiments may be more controlled or artificial. For example, a **tachistoscope** allows researchers to experiment with the visual impact of advertising, packaging, and so on by controlling the amount of time a subject is exposed to a visual image. Each stimulus (e.g., package design) is projected from a slide to the tachistoscope at varying exposure lengths (1⁄10 of a second, 3⁄10 of a second, etc.). The tachistoscope simulates the split-second duration of a customer's attention to a package in a mass display.

field experiment
An experiment conducted in a natural setting, often for a long period of time.

Field experiments are conducted in natural settings, and they often expose individuals to the treatment for long periods of time. For example, the National Park Service carried out a field experiment with a computerized reservation service in four national parks. The experiment was conducted to measure public reaction to a system that allowed campers to reserve space in the national parks. As another example, McDonald's conducted a field experiment to test market Triple Ripple, a three-flavor ice cream product. The product was dropped because the experiment showed that distribution problems reduced product quality and limited customer acceptance. In the distribution system, the product would freeze, defrost, and refreeze. Solving the problem would have required each McDonald's city to have an ice cream plant with special equipment to roll the three flavors into one. A natural environmental setting for the experiment helped McDonald's executives realize the product was impractical.

EXHIBIT 12.5 ARTIFICIALITY OF LABORATORY VERSUS FIELD EXPERIMENTS

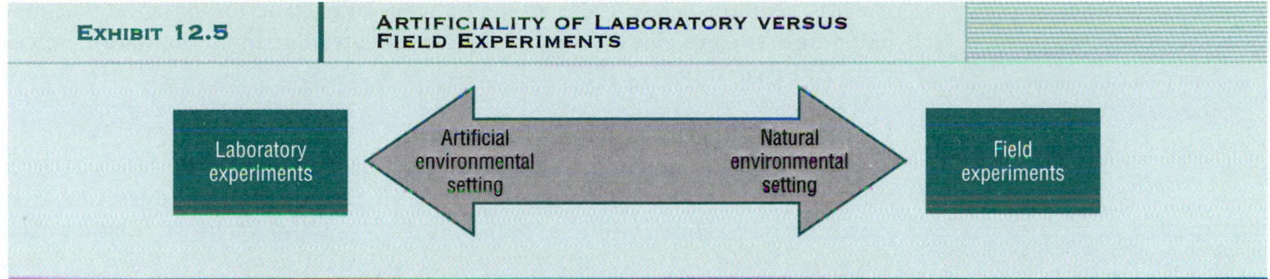

These examples illustrate that experiments vary in degrees of artificiality. As experiments increase in naturalism, they begin to approach the pure field experiment, and as experiments become more artificial, they approach the laboratory type (see Exhibit 12.5). The degree of artificiality in experiments refers to the amount of manipulation and control of the situation that the experimenter creates to ensure that the subjects are exposed to the exact conditions the experimenter desires. In a field experiment the researcher manipulates some of the variables but is not able to control all of the extraneous variables. An example would be NBC's research on new television programs. Viewers who subscribe to a cable television service are asked to watch a cable preview on their home television sets at a certain time on a certain cable channel. However, while the program is being aired, telephone calls from the viewers' friends cannot be controlled. In laboratory tests, on the other hand, researchers can show consumers the same program in a movie theater, where the conditions are the same for all of the subjects, and the realistic interruptions of everyday life are eliminated.

Generally, subjects know when they are participating in a laboratory experiment. Performance of certain tasks, response to questions, or some form of active involvement is characteristic of laboratory experiments. It is common to *debrief* subjects of laboratory experiments to explain the purpose of the research. In some situations only field studies are usable, because it is not feasible to simulate environmental conditions, such as employees' reactions to a new compensation program, in a laboratory.

ISSUES OF EXPERIMENTAL VALIDITY

Experiments are judged by two measures. The first, internal validity, indicates whether the independent variable was the sole cause of the change in the dependent variable. The other, external validity, indicates the extent to which the results of the experiment are applicable in the real world.[21]

Internal Validity

In choosing or evaluating experimental research designs, researchers must determine whether they have internal validity and external validity. The first has to do with interpretation of the cause-and-effect relationship in the experiment. **Internal validity** refers to whether the experimental treatment was the sole cause of observed changes in the dependent variable. If the observed results are influenced by the confounding effects of extraneous factors, the researcher has problems making valid conclusions about the relationship between the experimental treatment and the dependent variable.

internal validity
Validity determined by whether an experimental treatment was the sole cause of changes in a dependent variable.

It is helpful to classify the six major types of extraneous variables that may jeopardize internal validity: history, maturation, testing, instrumentation, selection, and mortality.

History

history effect
A specific event in the external environment occurring between the first and second measurements that is beyond the control of the experimenter and that affects the validity of an experiment.

Suppose a brokerage firm is conducting an experiment. If the stock market takes a steep drop just after the beginning of the experiment, this event may jeopardize the validity of the experiment. This is a history effect. A **history effect** refers to a specific event in the external environment, between the first and second measurements, that is beyond the control of the experimenter. Changes during the course of an organizational behavior field experiment are quite likely. A departmental reorganization, a strike or large layoff, or a change in the economic climate may have an impact on the results of such an experiment.

A special case of the history effect is the *cohort effect*. The cohort effect is a change in the dependent variable that occurs because members of one experimental condition experienced historical situations different from those of members of other experimental conditions. For example, two groups of workers used as subjects may be in different cohorts because one group of workers experienced the turmoil of a long and bitter strike. Another group of workers, hired after the strike, may have experienced a different history and therefore might behave differently in a workplace experiment.

Maturation

maturation effect
An effect on the results of a research experiment caused by changes in the experimental subjects over time.

People change over time; that is, there is a maturing process. During the course of an experiment, subjects may mature or change in some way that will have an impact on the experimental results. The **maturation effect** is an effect on the results of an experiment caused by changes in the experimental subjects over time. It is a function of time rather than a response to a specific event. For example, during a daylong experiment, subjects may grow hungry, tired, or bored. In an experiment over a longer time span, maturation may influence internal validity because subjects grow older, or become more experienced, or change in other ways that may influence the results.

Suppose an experiment was designed to test the impact of a new compensation program on sales productivity. If the new compensation program were tested over a year's time, it is likely that some of the salespeople would mature as a result of more selling experience or increased knowledge. Their sales productivity might improve because of their knowledge and experience, not because of the compensation program.

Testing

testing effect
In a before-and-after study the effect of pretesting, which may sensitize subjects when taking a test for the second time, thus affecting the validity of the experiment.

A **testing effect** is also called a *pretesting effect,* because it is a change in the validity of an experiment that occurs when an initial measurement or test alerts respondents to the nature of the experiment. Thus, respondents may act differently than they would have if no pretest measure had been taken. In a before-and-after study, taking a pretest before the independent variable is manipulated may sensitize respondents when they are taking the test for a second time. For example, students taking achievement and intelligence tests for the second time usually do better than those taking the tests for the first time. Pretesting may increase awareness of socially approved answers, it may increase attention to experimental conditions (i.e., the subject may watch more closely), or it may make the subject more conscious of the dimensions of a problem.

Instrumentation

Measuring the dependent variable in an experiment requires the use of a questionnaire, a test, or other form of measuring instrument. If the identical instrument is used more than once, there may be a testing effect. To avoid the effects of testing, an alternative form of the measuring instrument (for example, a questionnaire or test) may be given as the posttest ("after" measurement). Although this may reduce the testing effect due to a change in the measuring instrument, it may also introduce an instrumentation effect.

instrumentation effect
An effect on the results of an experiment caused by a change in the wording of questions, a change in interviewers, or other changes in procedures to measure the dependent variable.

A change in the wording of questions, a change in interviewers, or a change in other procedures to measure the dependent variable causes an **instrumentation effect,** which may jeopardize internal validity. For example, if the same interviewers are used to ask questions both before and after measurement, some problems may arise. With practice, interviewers may acquire increased skill in interviewing, or they may become bored and decide to reword the questionnaire in their own terms. To avoid this problem, new interviewers are hired, but different individuals are also a source of extraneous variation due to instrumentation variation. There are numerous other sources of instrument decay or variation.

Selection

selection effect
A sample bias resulting in differential selection of respondents for the comparison groups.

The **selection effect** is a sample bias resulting from differential selection of respondents for the comparison groups, or sample selection error, discussed earlier.

Mortality

If an experiment is conducted over a few weeks or more, there may be a sample bias due to *mortality,* or *sample attrition.* Sample attrition occurs when some subjects withdraw from the experiment before it is completed. In an organizational behavior experiment, employee turnover may be a factor.

mortality effect
Sample attrition that occurs when some subjects withdraw from an experiment before it is completed, thus affecting the validity of the experiment.

A **mortality effect** may occur if many subjects drop from one experimental treatment group and not from other treatment or control groups. Consider the example of a training experiment that investigates the effects of close supervision of salespeople (high pressure) versus low supervision (low pressure). The high-pressure condition may misleadingly appear to be superior if those subjects who completed the experiment did very well. If, however, the high-pressure condition caused more subjects to drop out than the other condition, this apparent superiority may be due to a self-selection bias—perhaps only very determined and/or talented salespeople made it through the end of the experiment.

External Validity

external validity
The ability of an experiment to generalize the results to the external environment.

The second type of validity involves the researcher's ability to generalize the results of an experiment to the external environment, such as other corporate offices or the marketplace. **External validity** is the quality of being able to generalize beyond the data of an experiment to other subjects or other groups in the population under study. In essence, determining external validity involves a sampling question: To what extent can the results of a simulated negotiating experiment be transferred to the real world of union–management relations? Will a test market in Fort Wayne, Indiana, be representative of the nationwide market for the product under study? Can one extrapolate the results from a tachistoscope to an in-store shopping situation? Problems of external validity generally relate to the possibility that a specific but limited set of experimental conditions may not deal with the interactions of untested variables in the real world. In other words, the experimental situation may be artificial and it may not represent the true setting and conditions in which the investigated behavior takes place. If the study lacks external validity, it will be difficult to repeat the experiment using different subjects, settings, or time intervals.

Consider a television commercial being pretested by means of personal interviews in a shopping mall. A portable television set simulates an actual program, with the test commercial inserted along with other commercials. Will respondents view the test commercial exactly as they would if they were watching an actual program at home? There probably will be some contamination, but the experiment may still be externally valid if the researchers know how to adjust the results from the artificial setting to the marketplace. Comparative norms may be established, based on similar, previous studies, so that the results can be projected beyond the experiment. Of course, if an experiment lacks internal validity, projecting its results is not possible. Thus, threats to internal validity may also jeopardize external validity.

You cannot create experience. You must undergo it.

ALBERT CAMUS

Student Surrogates

One issue of external validity concerns the use of college students as experimental subjects. Time, money, and a host of other practical considerations often necessitate the use of students as surrogates for other research subjects.[22] This practice is widespread in academic studies.[23] Some evidence shows that students respond similarly to nonstudents, but there is also evidence that students do not provide an accurate prediction of other populations. This is particularly true when students are used as substitutes or surrogates for businesspeople.[24] Any researcher who utilizes student surrogates should be careful to ensure that the student subjects and the "real people" they are to portray are similar. This may not be easy, unless the population under study matches the student population in literacy, alertness, and rationality.

This issue of external validity should be seriously considered because the student population is likely to be atypical. Students are easily accessible but they often are not representative of the total population.

Trade-Offs

Naturalistic field experiments tend to have greater external validity than artificial laboratory experiments. One of the problems facing the business researcher is that often it is necessary to trade off internal validity for external validity. There is more control in a laboratory experiment. The researcher who wishes to test advertising effectiveness via a split-cable experiment has the assurance that the advertisement will be viewed in an externally valid situation—that is, in the respondents' homes. However, the researcher has no assurance that some additional information or a distraction (e.g., a telephone call) won't have some influence that will reduce the internal validity of the experiment. Laboratory experiments with many controlled factors are usually high in internal validity. In general, field experiments have less internal validity but greater external validity.

CLASSIFICATION OF EXPERIMENTAL DESIGNS

The design of an experiment may be compared to an architect's plans for a structure, whether it be a skyscraper or a modest home. The basic requirements for the structure are given to the architect by the prospective owner. It is the architect's task to fill these basic requirements, yet the architect has ample room for exercising ingenuity. Several different plans may be drawn up to meet all the basic requirements. Some plans may be more costly than others. Two plans may have the same cost, but one may offer potential advantages that the second does not.[25]

basic experimental design
An experimental design in which a single independent variable is manipulated in order to observe its effect on a single dependent variable.

There are various types of experimental designs. If only one variable is manipulated, the experiment has a **basic experimental design.** If the experimenter wishes to investigate several levels of the independent variable (e.g., four salary levels) or to investigate the interaction effects of two or more independent variables, then the experiment requires a *complex* experimental design.

Symbolism for Diagramming Experimental Designs

The classic work of Campbell and Stanley has aided many students in understanding the subject of experimental designs.[26] The following symbols will be used in describing the various experimental designs:

X = exposure of a group to an experimental treatment.

O = observation or measurement of the dependent variable. If more than one observation or measurement is taken, subscripts (that is, O_1, O_2, etc.) will be given to indicate temporal order.[27]

[R] = random assignment of test units. [R] symbolizes that individuals selected as subjects for the experiment are randomly assigned to the experimental groups.

The diagrams of experimental designs that follow assume a time flow from left to right. The first of the following three examples of quasi-experimental design will make this clearer.

Three Examples of Quasi-Experimental Design

quasi-experimental design
An experimental design that fails to control adequately for loss of external or internal validity.

Quasi-experimental designs do not qualify as true experimental designs because they do not adequately control for the problems associated with loss of external or internal validity.

One-Shot Design (After-Only Design)

one-shot design
A quasi-experimental design in which a single measure is recorded after the treatment is administered and there is no control group. Also known as an *after-only design.*

The **one-shot** (or *after-only*) **design** is diagrammed as follows:

$$X \quad O_1$$

Suppose an automobile dealer, during a very cold winter, finds himself with a very large inventory of cars. He decides to experiment with a promotional scheme: offering a free trip to New Orleans with every car sold. He experiments with the promotion (X = experimental treatment) and measures his sales (O_1 = measurement of sales after the treatment is administered).

This one-shot design is a case study fraught with problems. In this experiment we do not have any kind of comparison. We have no means of controlling extraneous influences. There should be a measure of what would happen when test units were not exposed to X to compare with the measure when subjects *were* exposed to X.

One-Group Pretest–Posttest Design

Suppose a real estate franchiser wishes to provide a training program for franchisees. If the franchiser measures subjects' knowledge of real estate selling before (O_1) they are exposed to the experimental treatment (X) and then measures their real estate selling knowledge after (O_2) they are exposed to the treatment, the design is as follows:

$$O_1 \quad X \quad O_2$$

one-group pretest–posttest design
A quasi-experimental design in which the subjects in the experimental group are measured before and after the treatment is administered but in which there is no control group.

In this example the researcher is likely to conclude that the difference between O_2 and O_1 ($O_2 - O_1$) is the measure of the influence of the experimental treatment. This **one-group pretest–posttest design** (or *before–after design*) offers a comparison of the same individuals before and after training. Although an improvement over the after-only design, this research still has several weaknesses that may jeopardize internal validity. For example, if the time lapse between O_1 and O_2 was several months, the trainees may have matured (maturation effect) as a result of experience on the job, or the history effect may have had an influence. Some subjects may have dropped out of the training program (mortality effect). The effect of testing may also have confounded the experiment. For example, taking a test on real estate selling may have made subjects more aware of their lack of specific knowledge. Either during the training sessions or on their own, they may have sought to learn material about which, they realized, they were uninformed.

If the second observation or measure (O_2) of salespersons' knowledge was not an identical test, the instrumentation effect may be a problem. If the researcher used an identical test but had different graders for the "before" and "after" measurements, the data may not be directly comparable.

Although this design has a number of weaknesses, it is used frequently in business research. Remember, the cost of the research is a consideration in most business research. Although there may be some problems of internal validity, the researcher must always take into account questions of time and cost.

Static Group Design

static group design
An after-only design in which subjects in the experimental group are measured after being exposed to the experimental treatment, and the control group is measured without having been exposed to the experimental treatment; no pretreatment measure is taken.

In the **static group design**, subjects are identified as either an experimental group or a control group (for example, exposed or not exposed to a fitness program for employees). The experimental group is measured after it has been exposed to the experimental treatment, and the control group is measured without having been exposed to the experimental treatment:

$$\text{Experimental group:} \quad X \quad O_1$$
$$\text{Control group:} \qquad\quad\;\; O_2$$

The results of the static group design are computed by subtracting the observed results in the experimental group from the observed results in the control group ($O_2 - O_1$).

A major weakness of this design is that it provides no assurance that the groups were equal on variables of interest before the experimental group received the treatment. If the groups were selected arbitrarily by the investigator or if entry into either group was voluntary, then there may be systematic differences between the groups that could invalidate the conclusions about the effect of the treatment. For example, suppose a corporation that has a fitness program for employees wishes to determine if there is a significant difference in health insurance claims, absenteeism, personnel turnover, and grievances between the group in the program and the group not in the program. If entry into the groups was voluntary, the research might find that those who volunteered for the fitness program had some reason for choosing that group (for example, atypical numbers of "health nuts"). Sample attrition of experimental-group members who did not like the program might also be a source of error.

On many occasions an after-only design is the only possible design. This is particularly true when "use tests" are conducted for new products or when a new organizational policy is being introduced. Interpretation and recognition of the design's shortcomings may allow this "necessary evil" to be quite valuable. For example, Airwick Industries conducted use tests of Carpet Fresh, a rug cleaner and room deodorizer. Experiments with Carpet Fresh, which was conceived as a granular product to be sprinkled on the carpet before vacuuming, indicated that people were afraid that the granules would lodge under furniture. This research led to changing the texture of the product to a powdery form.

Random assignment of subjects may minimize problems with group differences. If groups can be determined by the experimenter, rather than existing as a function of some other causation, the static-group design is referred to as an *after-only design with control group.*

Three Good Experimental Designs

In a formal, scientific sense, the three designs described above are not true experimental designs. Subjects for the experiments were not selected from a common pool of subjects and randomly assigned to one group or another. In the following discussion of the three basic experimental designs, the symbol [R] to the left of the diagram indicates that the first step in each true experimental design is the randomization of subject assignment.

Pretest–Posttest Control-Group Design (Before–After with Control Group)

pretest–posttest control-group design
A true experimental design in which the experimental group is tested before and after exposure to the treatment, and the control group is tested at the same two times without being exposed to the experimental treatment.

The **pretest–posttest control-group design** (or *before–after with control group design*) is the classic experimental design:

Experimental group:	[R]	O_1	X	O_2
Control group:	[R]	O_3		O_4

As the diagram above indicates, the subjects in the experimental group are tested before and after being exposed to the treatment. The control group is tested twice, at the same times as the experimental group, but these subjects are not exposed to the experimental treatment. This design has the advantages of the before–after design, with the additional advantages gained by having a control group. The effect of the experimental treatment is calculated as follows: $(O_2 - O_1) - (O_4 - O_3)$.

If there is brand awareness among 20 percent of the subjects ($O_1 = 20\%$, $O_3 = 20\%$) before an advertising treatment and 35 percent awareness in the experimental group after exposure to the treatment ($O_2 = 35\%$) and 22 percent awareness in the control group ($O_4 = 22\%$), the treatment effect equals 13 percent:

$$(.35 - .20) - (.22 - .20)$$

or

$$(.15) - (.02) = .13, \text{ or } 13\%$$

It is assumed that the effect of all extraneous variables will be the same on both the experimental and the control groups. For instance, because both groups receive the pretest, no difference between the groups is expected for the pretest effect. This assumption is also made for effects of other events between the before- and after-measurements (history effects), changes within the subjects that occur with the passage of time (maturation effects), testing effects, and instrumentation effects. Of course, in reality there will be some differences in the sources of extraneous variation. In most cases, however, the assumption that the effect is approximately equal for both groups is a sound one.

Nevertheless, a testing effect is possible when subjects are sensitized to the subject of the research. This is analogous to a situation in which people learn a new word: They soon discover that they notice the word much more frequently in what they are reading. In an experiment the combination of being interviewed on a subject and receiving the experimental treatment might be a potential source of error. For example, subjects exposed to a certain television commercial message in an advertising experiment might say, "Ah, there is an ad about the product I was interviewed about yesterday!" The subject pays more attention than normal to the advertisement and may be more prone to change his or her attitude than in a situation where there are no testing effects. This weakness in the before–after with control group design can be corrected (see the next two designs).

Testing the effectiveness of television commercials in movie theaters provides an example of the before–after with control group design. Subjects are selected for the experiments by being told they are going to preview pilot episodes for several new television shows. When the subjects enter the theater, they learn that a drawing for several types of products will be held, and they are asked to complete a brand preference questionnaire (see Exhibit 12.6). A first drawing is then held. The television commercials and television pilots are shown next. Then, the "emcee" announces additional prizes and a second drawing. Finally, subjects fill out the same questionnaire about prizes. The information from the first questionnaire is the "before" measurement and the information from the second questionnaire is the "after" measurement. The control group receives similar treatment, except that on the day they view the pilot television shows, different (or no) television commercials are substituted for the experimental commercials.

Posttest-Only Control Group Design (After-Only with Control Group)

In some situations pretest measurements are impossible. In other situations selection error is not expected to be a problem because the groups are known to be equal. The diagram for the *after-only with control group design* is as follows:

Experimental group:	R	X	O_1
Control group:	R		O_2

The effect of the experimental treatment equals $O_2 - O_1$.

Consider, for example, the manufacturer of an athlete's foot remedy that wishes to demonstrate by experimentation that its product is better than a competing brand. No pretest measure of the effectiveness of the remedy for the fungus is possible. The design is to randomly select subjects, perhaps students, who have contracted athlete's foot and randomly assign them to the experimental or the control group. With only the posttest measurement, testing and instrumentation effects are eliminated. Further, researchers make the

EXHIBIT 12.6 | **PRODUCT PREFERENCE MEASURE IN AN EXPERIMENT**

We are going to give away a series of prizes. If you are selected as one of the winners, which brand from each of the groups listed below would you truly want to win?
Special arrangements will be made for delivery of any product for which bulk, or one-time, delivery is not appropriate.

Indicate your answers by filling in the box like this: ■
Do not "X," check, or circle the boxes please.

Cookies			**Allergy Relief Products**		
(A 3-month supply, pick *ONE*.)			(A year's supply, pick *ONE*.)		
NABISCO OREO	☐	(1)	ALLEREST	☐	(1)
NABISCO OREO DOUBLE STUFF	☐	(2)	BENEDRYL	☐	(2)
NABISCO NUTTER BUTTER	☐	(3)	CONTAC	☐	(3)
NABISCO VANILLA CREMES	☐	(4)	CHLOR-TRIMETON	☐	(4)
HYDROX CHOCOLATE	☐	(5)	DRISTAN	☐	(5)
HYDROX DOUBLES	☐	(6)	NASAL CROM	☐	(6)
NABISCO COOKIE BREAK	☐	(7)	SUDAFED	☐	(7)
NABISCO CHIPS AHOY	☐	(8)	TAVIST-D	☐	(8)
KEEBLER E.L. FUDGE	☐	(9)			
KEEBLER FUDGE CREMES	☐	(10)			
KEEBLER FRENCH VANILLA CREMES	☐	(11)			

same assumptions about extraneous variables described earlier—that is, that they operate equally on both groups, as in the before–after with control group design.

Solomon Four-Group Design

Combining the before–after with control group design and the after-only with control group design, the *Solomon four-group design* provides a means for controlling the testing effect, as well as other sources of extraneous variation. In the diagram below, the two Xs symbolize the same experimental treatment given to each experimental group:

Experimental group 1:	R	O_1	X	O_2
Control group 1:	R	O_3		O_4
Experimental group 2:	R		X	O_5
Control group 2:	R			O_6

Although we will not go through the calculations, it is possible to isolate the effect of the experimental treatment and the effect of testing in this design. Although this design allows for the isolation of the various effects, it is rarely used in business research because of the effort, time, and cost of implementing it. It does point out, however, that there are ways of isolating or controlling most sources of variation.

Compromise Experimental Designs

compromise design
An approximation of an experimental design, which may fall short of the requirements of random assignment of subjects or treatments to groups.

In many instances of business research true experimentation is not possible. The best the researcher can do is *approximate* an experimental design. These **compromise designs** may fall short of the requirements to assign subjects randomly to groups and to assign treatment randomly to groups.[28]

Consider the situation in which a researcher wishes to implement a pretest–posttest control-group design, but it is not possible to assign subjects randomly to the experimental and the control group. Because the researcher does not have the ability to change a workplace situation, one department of an organization is used as the experimental group and another department of the organization is used as the control group. There is no assurance that these naturally occurring groups are equivalent; the researcher has compromised because of the nature of the situation.

The alternative to the compromise design, when random assignment of subjects is not possible, is to conduct the experiment *without* a control group. Generally this is considered a greater weakness than utilizing nonequivalent groups that have already been established.

When the experiment involves a longitudinal study, circumstances usually dictate a compromise with true experimentation.

Time-Series Experimental Designs

time-series design
An experimental design utilized when experiments are conducted over long periods of time. It allows researchers to distinguish between temporary and permanent changes in dependent variables.

Many business experiments may be conducted in short periods of time (a month or less than half a year). However, some business experiments investigate long-term structural change, and these experiments may require **time-series designs.** When experiments are conducted over long periods of time, they are most vulnerable to history effects due to changes in population, attitudes, economic patterns, and the like. Although seasonal patterns and other exogenous influences may be noted, the experimenter can do little to influence these factors when time is a major factor in design. Hence time-series experimental designs are quasi-experimental designs, because they generally do not allow the researcher full control over the treatment exposure or the influence of extraneous variables.

Political polls provide an example. Pollsters normally utilize a series of surveys to track political candidates' popularity. Consider the political candidate who plans a major speech (the experimental treatment) to refocus the political campaign. The simple time-series design can be diagramed as follows:

$$O_1 \quad O_2 \quad O_3 \quad X \quad O_4 \quad O_5 \quad O_6$$

Several observations have been taken before the treatment (X) is administered to identify trends. After the treatment has been administered, several observations are made to determine if the patterns *after* the treatment are similar to the patterns *before* the treatment. Thus, if the longitudinal pattern shifts after the political speech, the researcher may conclude that the treatment had a positive impact on the pattern. Of course, this time-series design cannot give the researcher complete assurance that the treatment caused the change in the trend. Problems of internal validity are greater here than with more tightly controlled before-and-after designs for experiments of shorter duration.

One unique advantage of the time-series design is its ability to distinguish temporary from permanent changes. For example, Exhibit 12.7 shows some possible outcomes in a time-series experiment.

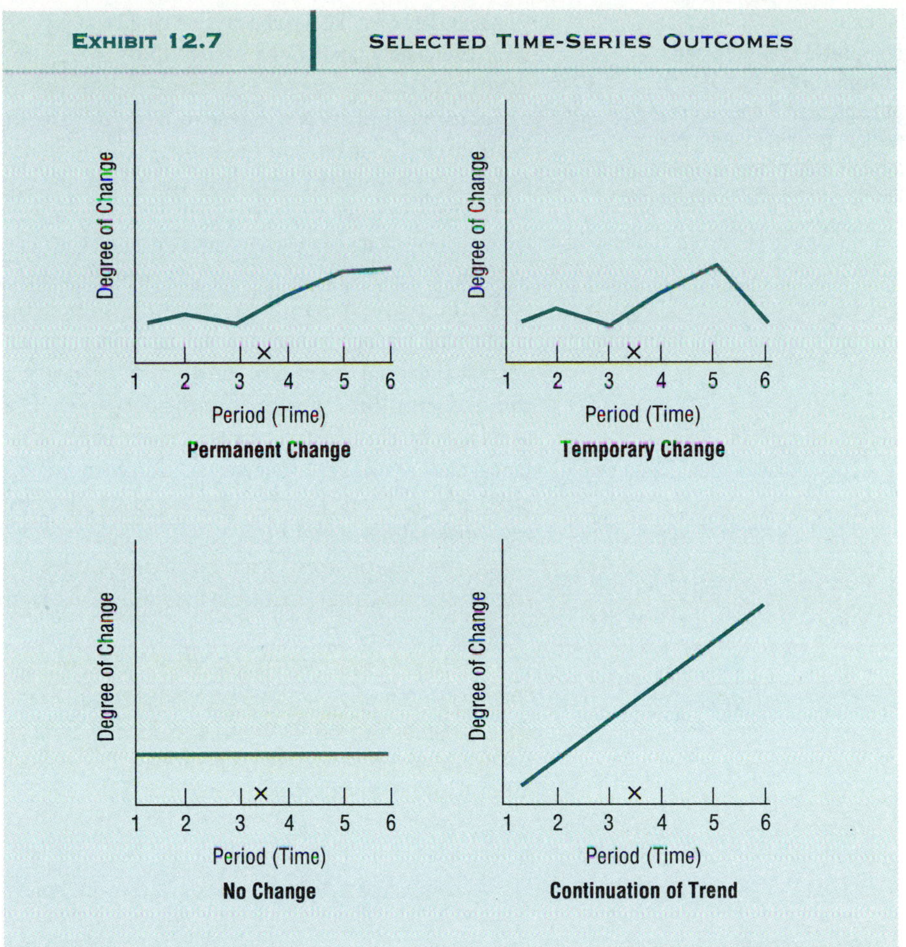

There is another problem in our political campaign example: Political conversions during August may affect the number of political conversions in September, which may in turn influence what happens in October. In time-series designs, there may be carryover effects that cannot be controlled.

An improvement on the basic time-series design is a *time series with control group design.* For example, many test markets utilize different geographic areas, which are similar demographically, as a basis for experimental control. Rarely will geographic areas be identical in any characteristic of interest. Thus control is less than perfect.

Complex Experimental Designs

complex experimental design
An experimental design that uses statistical methods to isolate the effects of extraneous variables or to allow for manipulation of multiple independent variables.

A **complex experimental design** is a statistical design that allows for the isolation of the effects of confounding extraneous variables or allows for manipulation of more than one independent variable in the experiment. *Completely randomized designs, randomized block designs, factorial designs,* and *Latin square designs* are four types of complex experimental design.

completely randomized design (CRD)
An experimental design that uses a random process to assign experimental units to treatments in order to investigate the effects of a single independent variable.

Completely Randomized Design

The **completely randomized design (CRD)** is an experimental design that uses a random process to assign experimental units to treatments. Randomization of experimental units is the researcher's attempt to control all extraneous variables while manipulating a single independent variable, the treatment variable. Several of the experiments previously discussed are completely randomized designs. As an example, consider an experiment to examine the effects of various incentives on response rate in a mail survey (see Exhibit 12.8).[29] Receiving a monetary incentive themselves or having a contribution made to a charity of their choice were the two experimental treatments chosen to provide the incentives. Use of a control group made a total of three treatments: (1) control–no incentive, (2) $1 personal incentive, and (3) $1 charity incentive. Suppose the sample is divided into three groups of 150 people each. Assigning treatments to groups is a relatively simple process. Each treatment is randomly assigned to a group. Exhibit 12.8 shows how we would compare the response rates (dependent variable) of the three treatment groups to determine which method of increasing response rate was the best.

A pretest–posttest with control group(s) that *replicates,* or repeats, the same treatment on different experimental units is another example of a completely randomized design.

Analysis of variance (ANOVA) involves investigating the effects of one treatment variable on an interval-scaled or ratio-scaled dependent variable. In the completely randomized designs, ANOVA is the appropriate form of statistical analysis when the conditions of randomization and replication are met. This topic is discussed in Chapter 22.

EXHIBIT 12.8 | **COMPLETELY RANDOMIZED DESIGN**

	EXPERIMENTAL TREATMENTS		
	Control—No Incentive	**$1 Personal Incentive**	**$1 Charity Incentive**
Response Rate	23.3%	26.0%	41.3%
Number of Observations	150	150	150

Overall response rate: 136/450 = 30.2%

randomized block design (RBD)
An extension of the completely randomized design in which a single extraneous variable that might affect test units' response to the treatment has been identified and the effects of this variable are isolated by being blocked out.

Randomized Block Design

The **randomized block design (RBD)** is an extension of the completely randomized design (CRD). A form of randomization is utilized to control for *most* extraneous variation. In the randomized block design, however, the researcher has identified a single extraneous variable that might affect test units' response to the treatment. The researcher will attempt to isolate the effects of this single variable by blocking out its effects.

The term *randomized block* is derived from agricultural research, where different levels of a treatment variable are applied to each of several blocks of land. Systematic differences in agricultural yields, due to the quality of the blocks of land, may be controlled in the randomized block design.[30] In business research the researcher may wish to isolate block effects such as store size,

Exhibit 12.9 | **Randomized Block Experiment**

	PERCENTAGE WHO PURCHASE PRODUCT			
Treatment	**Mountain**	**North Central West**	**North Central East**	**Mean for Treatments**
Package A	14% (Phoenix)	12% (St. Louis)	7% (Milwaukee)	11%
Package B	16% (Albuquerque)	15% (Kansas City)	10% (Indianapolis)	13.6%
Mean for cities	15%	13.5%	8.5%	

plant location, organization size, and so on. By grouping test units into homogeneous blocks on the basis of some relevant characteristic, one known source of extraneous variation may be separately accounted for.

Suppose a manufacturer of Mexican food is considering two packaging alternatives. It is suspected that geographic region may confound the packaging experiment. The manufacturer has identified three regions of the country where attitudes toward Mexican food may differ. It is assumed that within each region the relevant attitudinal characteristics are relatively homogeneous. In the randomized block design, each block must receive every treatment level. Assigning treatments to each block is a random process. In this example the two treatments are randomly assigned to different cities within each region. Sales results such as those in Exhibit 12.9 might be observed.

The logic behind the randomized block design is similar to the logic underlying the selection of a stratified sample rather than a simple random sample. By isolating the "block effects," one type of extraneous variation is partitioned out and a more efficient experimental design therefore results. This is because experimental error is reduced with a given sample size.

Factorial Designs

Even though the single-factor experiments (considered so far) may have one specific variable blocked and other confounding sources controlled, they are limited. A **factorial design** allows for testing the effects of two or more treatments (factors) at various levels.

factorial design
An experimental design that investigates the interaction of two or more independent variables.

Consider the experimenter who wishes to answer the following questions:

1. What is the effect of varying the salary offered to new business school graduates on the probability of their accepting a job?
2. What is the effect of varying the number of days per week that new business school graduates will spend in job-related travel?
3. Is the effect of varying salary different if there is a great deal of travel on the job versus very little travel on the job? Is there an interaction between the effects of salary and amount of travel on the job?

A factorial design might be used to answer these questions because it allows for the simultaneous manipulation of two or more independent variables at various levels. In this example the independent variables are salary and the number of days spent traveling. Changes in the probability of accepting a job,

RESEARCH INSIGHT

A FACTORIAL EXPERIMENT

A field experiment was undertaken to investigate the possible existence of sex discrimination in the evaluation of job applicants' résumés.[31] Scholastic performance was also manipulated in the experiment. Subjects for the experiment were personnel directors at a sample of corporations listed in the *College Placement* annual as seeking accounting students.

A résumé and an attractive cover letter were sent to each personnel director. The résumé provided a complete description of an actual student's personal history, family background, work experience, degrees (e.g., BS and MS degrees in accounting), etc. The sex variable was manipulated by using the first name of the individual. The initials L. C. were used as a neuter indication, and the name Linda was used to indicate female. The variable concerning academic performance was manipulated by using the GPA of the individual. High academic performance was indicated by a 3.8 GPA (the student's actual GPA). Average academic performance was indicated by a 2.8 GPA.

Each subject was randomly assigned to one of the four treatment groups (N = 25 in each group): initials and high GPA, initials and average GPA, female name and high GPA, and female name and average GPA. Two forms of data that were provided by the personnel directors lent themselves to statistical analysis. The first dependent variable was the number of replies either positive or negative, that is, letters suggesting a personal interview or saying no job was available. A separate analysis was conducted on the number of affirmative responses: those suggesting that the person may have an opportunity for a job at the particular company.

main effect
The influence on a dependent variable by each independent variable (separately).

interaction effect
The influence on a dependent variable by combinations of two or more independent variables.

the dependent variable, attributed to each of these variables, considered separately, are referred to as *main effects.* A **main effect** is the influence on the dependent variable by each independent variable.

The effect of combining these job characteristic variables is the **interaction effect.** A major advantage of the factorial design is its ability to measure the interaction effect, which may be greater than the total of the main effects.[32]

To further explain factorial designs, let us consider an example of a marketer of in-line skates who wished to measure the effect of different prices and packaging designs on consumers' perception of quality of the product. Exhibit 12.10 indicates three treatment levels of price ($60, $75, $95) and two treatment levels of packaging design (gold and red). The exhibit shows that every

EXHIBIT 12.10 FACTORIAL DESIGN FOR STUDY OF IN-LINE SKATES

	PACKAGE DESIGN	
Price	**Red**	**Gold**
$60	Cell 1	Cell 4
$75	Cell 2	Cell 5
$95	Cell 3	Cell 6

combination of treatment levels requires a separate experimental group. In this experiment, with three price levels and two packaging design levels, we have a 3 × 2 (read "three by two") factorial design, because the first factor (variable) is varied in three ways and the second factor is varied in two ways. A 3 × 2 design requires six cells, or six experimental groups (3 × 2 = 6).

The number of treatments (factors) and the number of levels for each treatment identify the factorial design. A 3 × 3 design incorporates two factors, each having three levels. A 2 × 2 × 2 design has three factors, each having two levels. It is not necessary that the treatments have the same number of levels. For example, a 3 × 2 × 4 factorial design is possible. The important idea is that in a factorial experiment, each treatment level is combined with each and every other treatment level. A 2 × 2 experiment requires four different subgroups, or cells. A 3 × 3 experiment requires nine various combinations of subgroups or cells.

In addition to the advantage of investigating two or more independent variables simultaneously, factorial designs have another benefit: They allow researchers to measure the interaction effects. In a 2 × 2 experiment, the interaction is the effect produced by treatments A and B simultaneously, which cannot be accounted for by either treatment alone. If the effect of one treatment is different at different levels of the other treatment, interaction occurs.

To illustrate the value of a factorial design, suppose a researcher is comparing two magazine ads. The researcher is investigating the believability of the ads on a scale from 0 to 100 and wishes to consider the gender of the reader as another factor. The experiment has two independent variables: gender and ads. Each variable (treatment) has two levels. This 2 × 2 factorial experiment permits the experimenter to test three hypotheses. Two hypotheses are about the main effects—which ad is more believable and which gender tends to believe magazine advertising more. However, the primary research question deals with the interaction hypothesis. A high score indicates a highly believable ad. Exhibit 12.11 shows that the mean believability score for both genders is 65. This suggests that there is no main gender effect, because men and women evaluate the advertisements as equally believable. The main effect for ads indicates that ad A is more believable than ad B (70 versus 60). However, if we inspect the data and look within the levels of the factors, we find that men find ad B more believable and women find ad A more believable. This is an interaction effect because the believability score of the advertising factor differs at different values of the other independent variable, gender.

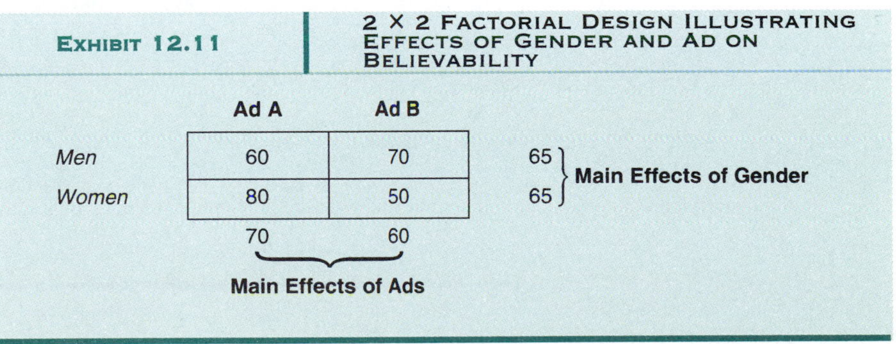

EXHIBIT 12.11 | **2 × 2 FACTORIAL DESIGN ILLUSTRATING EFFECTS OF GENDER AND AD ON BELIEVABILITY**

	Ad A	Ad B	Main Effects of Gender
Men	60	70	65
Women	80	50	65
Main Effects of Ads	70	60	

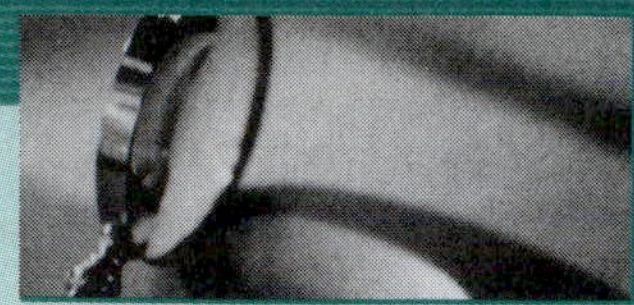

Research Insight

A Lethal Interaction

In pharmacology, the interaction effect is usually called a synergistic effect.[33] An example is the lethal combination of barbiturate sleeping pills and alcohol. Each of these is a drug, and each reduces the number of heartbeats per minute. Their combined effect, however, is a much more severe reduction than one would expect, knowing their individual effects. This is actually a failure of the two treatments to be additive—their combined effect is much more than the sum of their individual effects. Another way of phrasing the synergistic effect is the following: The effect of one treatment differs, depending on the level of the other treatment. That is, the reduction in pulse due to alcohol is different, depending on whether barbiturates are in the person's system or not.

Graphic Interaction

Exhibit 12.12 portrays the results of the believability experiment. The line for men represents the two mean believability scores for the advertising copy for ads A and B. The other line represents the relationship between advertising and believability for women. When there is a difference between the slopes of the two lines, as in this case, such a graph indicates interaction between the two treatment variables. What this means is that the believability of the advertising copy depends on whether a man or a woman is reading the advertisement.

Latin square design
A balanced, two-way classification scheme that attempts to control or block out the effect of two or more extraneous factors by restricting randomization with respect to row and column effects.

Latin Square Design

The **Latin square design** attempts to control or block out the effect of two or more confounding extraneous factors. This design is so named because of the layout of the table that represents the design. A Latin square is a balanced, two-

Exhibit 12.12 Graphic Illustration of Interaction between Gender and Advertising Copy

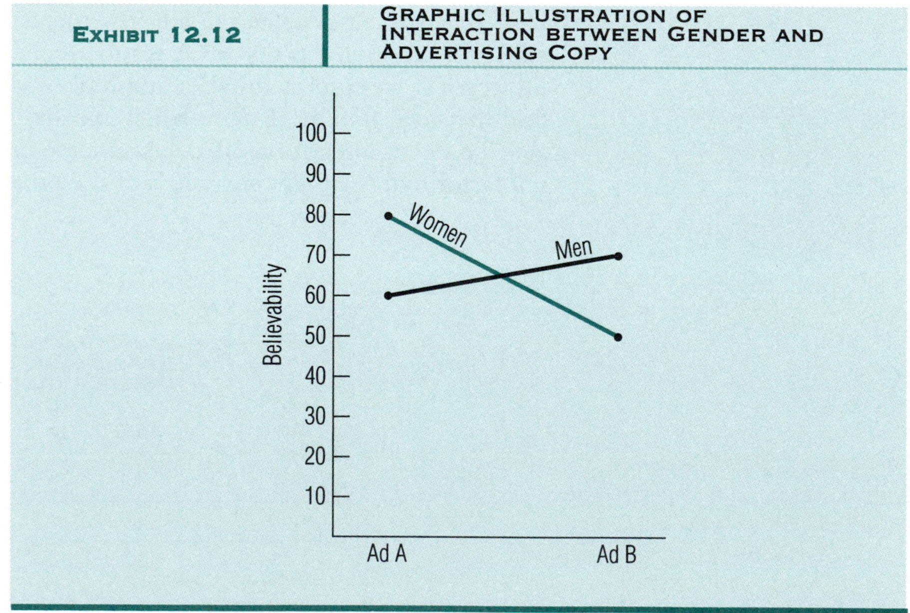

way classification scheme.[34] In the 3 × 3 matrix below, each letter occurs only once in each row and only once in each column:

		Order of Usage		
		1	**2**	**3**
	1	A	B	C
Subject	**2**	B	C	A
	3	C	A	B

The capital letters A, B, and C identify the three treatments. The rows and columns of the table identify the confounding factors. For example, a taste test might be confounded by the order of tasting: The first taste may seem better than the last. The taste test might also be confounded by individual taste preferences. To control for these factors, each subject is exposed to every treatment. If all the subjects receive three tastes and the order in which the subjects taste is randomized, neither individual preference nor order effects can confound the experiment. Thus, the order of treatment may be randomized under the restriction of balance required for the Latin square. The same type of balance is required for the second confounding factor.

The end result of this design is that each treatment will be administered under conditions involving all levels of both confounding factors. In summary, the Latin square design manipulates one independent variable and controls for two additional sources of extraneous variation by restricting randomization with respect to row and column effects.

A major assumption of the Latin square design is that interaction effects are expected to be minimal or nonexistent. Thus, it is assumed that the first subject does not have a strong preference for the first product tasted and the third subject does not have a strong preference for the last product tasted.

A Latin square may have any number of treatments. For example, the matrix for a five-treatment experiment is given below:

	1	**2**	**3**	**4**	**5**
1	A	B	C	D	E
2	B	C	D	E	A
3	C	D	E	A	B
4	D	E	A	B	C
5	E	A	B	C	D

Notice that this 5 × 5 matrix requires 25 cells. This matrix also indicates that the number of treatment levels for confounding factors 1 and 2 must be equal in number. This may present certain problems. For example, suppose a retail grocery chain wishes to control for shelf space and city where a product is sold. The chain may be limited in its experiment because it markets in only three cities, but it wishes to experiment with four levels of shelf spaces.

Having an unequal number of levels for each factor may be a drawback that will eliminate the Latin square design as a possibility. A second limitation is the assumption that there is no interaction effect. Like most other forms of business research, the Latin square design has its disadvantages, but in certain situations it is advantageous to use it.

SUMMARY

The purpose of experimental research is to allow the researcher to control the research situation so that causal relationships among variables may be evaluated. In a basic experiment one variable (the independent variable) is manipulated to determine its effect on another variable (the dependent variable). The alternative manipulations of the independent variable are referred to as *experimental treatments.*

The choice of the dependent variable is crucial, because this determines the kind of answer given to the research problem. In some situations it is difficult to decide on an appropriate operational measure of the dependent variable.

For experiments, random sampling error is especially associated with selection of subjects and their assignment to the treatments. The best solution to this problem is random assignment of subjects to groups and groups to treatments.

Other errors may arise from using unrepresentative populations as a source of samples (for example, college students) or from sample mortality or attrition, when subjects withdraw from the experiment before it is completed. In addition, in business experiments there are often extraneous variables that may affect the dependent variable and obscure the effect of the independent variable. Experiments may also be affected by demand characteristics, when experimenters inadvertently cue desired responses. Also, the guinea pig effect occurs when subjects modify their behavior because they are being observed.

Researchers can control extraneous variables by eliminating them or by holding them constant for all treatments. Some extraneous error may arise from order of presentation. This can be controlled by counterbalancing the order. Blinding can be used, with subjects being ignorant of what treatment they are receiving. Sometimes the blinding is extended to the person administering the test. Finally, random assignment attempts to control extraneous variables by chance.

Two main types of business experiments are field experiments, which are conducted in natural environments (such as test markets), and laboratory experiments, which are conducted in artificial settings contrived for specific purposes. Experiments are judged by two measures of validity. One is internal validity: whether the independent variable was the sole cause of the change in the dependent variable. Six different types of effects may jeopardize internal validity: history, maturation, testing, instrumentation, selection, and mortality. The second type of validity is external validity: the extent to which the results are applicable to the real world. Field experiments are lower in internal validity than laboratory experiments but higher in external validity.

Experimental designs fall into two groups. In basic designs only one variable is manipulated. In complex experimental designs the effects of extraneous variables are isolated or more than one treatment (independent variable) is used. Poor basic designs include the one-shot design, the one-group pretest–posttest design, and the static group design. Good basic designs include the pretest–posttest control-group design, the posttest-only control-group design, and the Solomon four-group design.

Various complex experimental designs are commonly used in business research. These include the completely randomized design, the randomized block design, and various factorial designs. Factorial designs allow for investigation of interaction effects between variables. One variation is the Latin square design, which attempts to block out confounding factors.

Key Terms

experiment
independent variable
experimental treatment
experimental group
control group
dependent variable
test unit
sample selection error
random sampling error
randomization
matching
repeated measures
constant error
demand characteristics
experimenter bias
guinea pig effect
Hawthorne effect
constancy of conditions
order of presentation bias
counterbalancing
blinding
double-blind design
debriefing
laboratory experiment
tachistoscope
field experiment
internal validity
history effect
maturation effect
testing effect
instrumentation effect
selection effect
mortality effect
external validity
basic experimental design
quasi-experimental design
one-shot design
one-group pretest–posttest design
static group design
pretest–posttest control-group design
compromise design
time-series design
complex experimental design
completely randomized design (CRD)
randomized block design (RBD)
factorial design
main effect
interaction effect
Latin square design

Questions for Review and Critical Thinking

1. Name some independent and dependent variables frequently studied in your field of interest.
2. What purpose does the random assignment of subjects serve?
3. In a test of a new coffee, three styrofoam cups labeled A, B, and C are placed before subjects. The subjects are instructed to taste the coffee from each cup. What problems might arise in this situation?
4. What are demand characteristics? Give some examples.
5. Do you think the guinea pig effect is common in experiments? Why or why not?
6. How may an experimenter control for extraneous variation?
7. Provide an example of each of the six major factors influencing internal validity.
8. Consider the following research project conducted by a company investigating a self-contained heating and light source designed to be used during power failures: The product was given to the experimental subjects and they were asked to wait until dark, then turn off their heat and lights, and test the product. A few days later they were telephoned and interviewed about their opinions of the product. Discuss the external and internal validity of this experiment.
9. In a 2 × 2 factorial design there are eight possible patterns of effects. For example, assume independent variable A and independent variable B have significant main effects but there is no interaction between A and B. Another combination might be no effect of variable A but a significant effect of variable B with a significant interaction effect. Try to diagram each of these eight possible effects.
10. Name the type of experiment described in each of the following situations. Evaluate the strengths and weaknesses of each design.
    (a) A major automobile manufacturer is considering a drug-testing program for its assembly workers. It selects an Oklahoma City plant, implements the program, and measures the impact on productivity.
    (b) The data-processing division of a credit card company conducts an experiment to determine if a flexible work time program (employees choosing their own work hours between 6 AM and 7 PM) is better than the traditional working hours (9 AM to 5 PM). Each employee in the San Jose office is asked if he or she would like to be in the experimental group or in the control group. All employees in the La Jolla office remain on the traditional schedule.
    (c) A cigar manufacturer puts the same brand of cigar into two differently labeled packages (wrappers). Each subject in two different groups is given a cigar in a labeled package and asked about the cigar's taste. Subjects in a third group are given unlabeled cigars and asked the same question.
    (d) An advertising agency pretests a television commercial by showing an actual television program with the test commercial inserted along with other commercials to members of a focus group. Following the show there is a group discussion.
    (e) A manufacturer of a new brand of cat food tests product sampling with a trial-size package ver-

sus free sampling and three price levels simultaneously to determine the best market penetration.

11. At a family gathering, Dan Kessler, the manager of an IGA grocery store, got into conversation with his brother-in-law, who supervised a large number of data-entry workers at a public utility company. Kessler's brother-in-law mentioned that his company had recently begun programming background music into the data-entry workers' room with the result that productivity had increased and number of errors had decreased. Kessler thought that playing music in a grocery store might have an impact on customers. Specifically, he thought that customers might stay in the store longer if slow, easy-to-listen-to music were played. After some serious thought, he decided that he should hire a business researcher to design an experiment to test the influence of music tempo on shopper behavior. Operationalize the independent variable "music tempo" (that is, specify some way of measuring the variable). What dependent variables do you think might be important in this study? Develop a hypothesis for each of your dependent variables.

12. Evaluate the ethical and research design implications of the following study:

    Sixty-six willing Australian drinkers helped a Federal Court judge decide that Tooheys didn't engage in misleading or deceptive advertising for its 2.2 beer. The beer contains 2.2% alcohol, compared to 6% for other beers.

    The volunteers were invited to a marathon drinking session after the Aboriginal Legal Service claimed Tooheys' advertising implied beer drinkers could imbibe as much 2.2 as desired without becoming legally intoxicated. Drunken driving laws prohibited anyone with a blood-alcohol level above 0.05 from getting behind the wheel.

    But the task wasn't easy; nor was it all fun. Some couldn't manage to drink in 1 hour the required 10 "middies," an Aussie term for a beer glass of 10 fluid ounces.

    Thirty-six participants could manage only nine glasses. Four threw up and were excluded; another two couldn't manage the "minimum" nine glasses and had to be replaced.

    Justice J. Beaumont observed that consuming enough 2.2 in an hour to reach the 0.05 level was "uncomfortable and therefore an unlikely process." Because none of the ads mentioned such extreme quantities, he ruled they couldn't be found misleading or deceptive.[34]

13. A nighttime cough relief formula contains alcohol. An alternative formulation contains no alcohol. During an experiment subjects are asked to try the products in their homes and are randomly chosen to use each alternative formulation. The instructions to subjects do not mention alcohol. Is this ethical?

14. A mouthwash company learns that a competitor is test-marketing a new lemon-flavored mouthwash in an Arizona city. The head of the company's research division reads the results of the test market, after which the marketing manager is told to lower the price of the company's product to disrupt the test market. Is this ethical?

Exploring the Internet

1. Go to http://www.apa.org/releases/tvviolence.html to find a press release about an experiment dealing with television violence and viewers' memory for advertisements.

2. Learn more about quasi-experimental designs at http://trochim.human.cornell.edu/. Click on Knowledge Base, then Design, and then Quasi-Experimental Designs.

Case Suggestions

Case 14: Professional Recruiters
Case 15: Hamilton Power Tools (B)
Case 16: The Cleveland Clinic Foundation in Jacobs Field

PART

MEASUREMENT CONCEPTS

CHAPTER

13

MEASUREMENT AND SCALING CONCEPTS

What you will learn in this chapter

- To know how a researcher might answer the question "What is to be measured?"
- To define the term *operational definition.*
- To distinguish among nominal, ordinal, interval, and ratio scales.
- To understand the need for index or composite measures.
- To define the three criteria for good measurement.
- To discuss the various methods for determining reliability.
- To discuss the various methods for assessing validity.

BBDO, an advertising agency, has developed a measuring system to evaluate consumers' emotional responses to advertising.[1] Its Emotional Measurement System is a proprietary technique that uses photographs of actors' faces to help consumers choose their reactions to commercials. Researchers at BBDO believe that the process virtually eliminates the inherent bias in traditional copy testing. With the conventional system, consumers often underestimate their emotional responses because they feel "silly" putting them into words, and words are subject to varying interpretations. Thus, traditional copy tests have tended to measure thoughts rather than feelings and therefore have failed to adequately measure emotional responses.

Rather than ask consumers to choose from a simple list or write in their own words, the agency has devised a deck of 53 photos—narrowed from 1,800—representing what BBDO calls the "universe of emotions." Each features one of six actors with different expressions ranging from happy/playful to disgusted/revolted. A total of 26 categories of emotions is covered.

Here's how the system works. In most copy-testing research, participants are shown a single commercial or group of commercials and then are given a questionnaire to test whether they remembered brand names and copy points. At BBDO, the researchers hand out the photos as part of the copy-testing process. Each person is asked to not write or speak about the commercial but to quickly sort through the photos, setting aside any or all that reflect how he or she feels after viewing the commercial.

Innovative techniques such as the Emotional Measurement System using PhotoSort have improved the measurement of business phenomena. This chapter discusses and evaluates the basic forms of measurement used in business research. ■

WHAT IS TO BE MEASURED?

It is possible to measure an object, perhaps your textbook, with either edge of the ruler in Exhibit 13.1. Note that one edge has inches and the other has centimeters; so the scale of measurement will vary, depending on whether the metric edge or the standard edge is used. Many measurement problems in business research are similar to this ruler, with its alternative scales of measurement. The researcher has the opportunity to select a measuring system. Unfortunately, however—unlike the two edges of the ruler—many measurement scales in business research are not directly comparable.

The first question the researcher must answer is "What is to be measured?" This is not as simple a question as it may at first seem. The definition of the problem, based on exploratory research or managerial judgment, indicates the concept to be investigated (for example, sales performance). However, a precise definition of the concept may require a description of how it will be measured, and there is frequently more than one way to measure a particular concept.

For example, if we were conducting research to evaluate what factors influence a sales representative's performance, a number of measures might be used to indicate success. Dollar or unit sales volume or share of accounts lost could be utilized as measures of a salesperson's success. Further, true measurement of concepts requires a process of assigning precise scores or numbers to the attributes of people or objects. The purpose of the assignment of scores or numbers is to convey information about the variable being measured. Hence, the key question becomes "On what basis will scores or numbers be assigned to the concept?"

Suppose the task is to measure the height of a boy named Michael. There are a number of ways to do this.

- We can create five categories:
  (1) Quite tall for his age
  (2) Moderately tall for his age
  (3) About average for his age
  (4) Moderately short for his age
  (5) Quite short for his age
  Then we can measure Michael by saying that, since he is moderately tall for his age, his height measurement is 2.

EXHIBIT 13.1 A TWO-EDGED RULER OFFERS ALTERNATIVE SCALES OF MEASUREMENT

- We can compare Michael to ten other neighborhood children. We give the tallest child the rank of 1 and the shortest child the rank of 11. Michael's height measurement using this procedure is 4, since he is fourth tallest among the 11 neighborhood children.
- We can use some conventional measuring unit such as centimeters and, measuring to the nearest centimeter, designate Michael's height as 137.
- We can define two categories:
  (1) A nice height
  (2) A not so nice height
  Since by our personal standard Michael's height is a nice height, his height measurement is 1.[2]

In each measuring situation a score has been assigned for Michael's height (2, 4, 137, and 1). In scientific research, however, precision is the goal. These various scores have differing precision. The researcher must determine the best way to measure what is to be investigated.

Measurement occurs on campus with girl watching or guy watching. The person who might be a "7" to one person might be a "9" to another. Precise measurement in business research requires a careful conceptual definition, an operational definition, and a system of consistent rules for assigning scores or numbers.

Concepts

concept
A generalized idea about a class of objects, attributes, occurrences, or processes.

Before the measurement process can be initiated, the business researcher must identify the concepts relevant to the problem. A **concept** (or *construct*) is a generalized idea about a class of objects, attributes, occurrences, or processes. Concepts such as age, sex, and number of children are relatively concrete properties, and they present few problems in definition or measurement.[3] Other characteristics of individuals or properties of objects may be more abstract. Concepts such as loyalty, power, job involvement, and the like are more difficult to define and measure. For example, brand loyalty has been measured utilizing the percentage of a person's purchases going to one brand in a given period of time, sequences of brand purchases, the number of different brands purchased, amount of brand deliberation, and various cognitive measures such as attitude toward a brand.

Operational Definitions

operational definition
A definition that gives meaning to a concept by specifying the activities or operations necessary in order to measure it.

A concept must be made operational in order to be measured. An **operational definition** gives meaning to a concept by specifying the activities or operations necessary to measure it.[4] The concept *nutritional consciousness* might be reflected when a shopper reads the nutritional information on a cereal package. Inspecting a nutritional label is not the same as being nutrition conscious, but it is a clue that a person *may* be nutrition conscious.

A concept like *grievances* may be difficult to operationalize, whereas a concept like *personnel turnover* is less difficult. However, *personnel turnover* may be more difficult to operationalize if the researcher is interested in going beyond the simple ratio of new employees to old employees. Are employees with tenure turning over, or is it the recently hired employees who are constantly turning over?

The operational definition specifies what must be done to measure the concept under investigation. If interest in a specific advertisement is to be

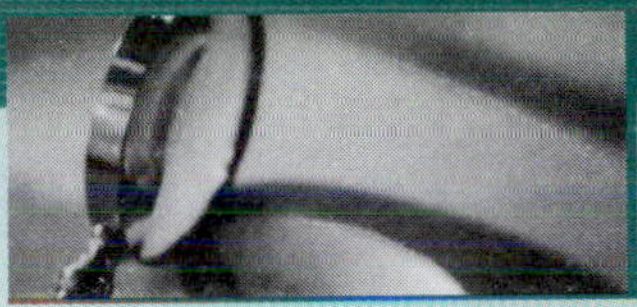

RESEARCH INSIGHT

PUTTING A FACE ON THE BIG BRANDS

Would you belly up to a bar beside a Bud man?[5] The photos below show how American beer drinkers envision the typical consumers of each of the big beer brands. In research commissioned by *Fortune,* ad agency BBDO New York (which handles no beer accounts) interviewed 100 consumers of the type the major brewers target: men, ages 21 to 49, who drink at least six beers weekly. Using a proprietary technique called PhotoSort, BBDO showed each consumer 98 photographs and asked him to match each picture with the brand of beer that the photo subject probably drinks.

As you can see, a Bud drinker, as viewed by the respondents, is not exactly your corporate type: He appears tough, grizzled, blue collar. The Miller drinker, in contrast, comes off as light-blue collar, civilized, and friendly looking. Coors has a somewhat more feminine image—not necessarily a plus in a business where 80 percent of the product gets consumed by men.

Most important, do these user images help or hurt the brands? To find out, BBDO asked the 100 consumers whether they identify positively with the photo subjects whom they assigned to each brand. The more positive the IDs, the higher the "affinity score" for the brand. Budweiser scored 42 percent—not good, since this means that most respondents didn't view the Bud man as likable. Coors's affinity score, 43 percent, is hardly better. Says Karen Olshan, BBDO New York's executive vice president in charge of research: "The Coors drinker was perceived as not a real beer drinker." The most positive user image belongs to Miller. Its affinity score is 66 percent.

Budweiser Prototype

Miller Prototype

Coors Prototype

measured, *interest* may be operationally defined as a certain increase in pupil dilation. Another operational definition of *interest* might rely on direct responses—what people *say* they are interested in. Each operational definition has advantages and disadvantages.

An operational definition is like a manual of instructions or a recipe: Even the truth of a statement like "Gaston Gourmet likes key lime pie" depends on the recipe. Different instructions lead to different results.[6] An operational definition tells the investigator, "Do such-and-such in so-and-so manner."[7] Exhibit 13.2 presents the operational definition from a study on quality of work.

Rules of Measurement

rule of measurement
An instruction to guide assignment of a number or other measurement designation.

A rule is a guide that tells someone what to do.[8] An example of a **rule of measurement** might be "Assign the numerals 1 through 7 to individuals according to how productive they are. If the individual is extremely productive, assign a 7. If the individual is an unproductive worker with little output, assign the numeral 1."

Exhibit 13.2 | **Job Challenge: An Operational Definition**[9]

Concept	Conceptual Definition	Operational Definition
Job challenge	This dimension reflects a worker's desire for stimulation and challenge in his or her job and ability to exercise skills in his or her job.	Please tell me how true each statement is about your job. Is it very true, somewhat true, not very true, or not at all true? 1. The work is interesting. 2. I have an opportunity to develop my own special abilities. 3. I am given a chance to do the things I do best.

Operational definitions help the researcher specify the rules for assigning numbers. If, for example, the purpose of an advertising experiment is to increase the amount of time shoppers spend in a department store, "shopping time" must be operationally defined. Once "shopping time" is defined as the interval between entering the door and receiving the receipt from the clerk, assignment of numbers via stopwatch is facilitated. If a study on office computer systems is not concerned with depth of experience but classifies people as users or nonusers, a 1 for experience with the system and a 0 for no experience with the system can be used.

The values assigned in the measuring process can be manipulated according to certain mathematical rules. The properties of the scale of numbers may allow the researcher to add, subtract, or multiply answers. In certain cases there may be problems with the simple addition of the numbers, or other mathematical manipulations may not be permissible.

TYPES OF SCALES

A *scale* may be defined as any series of items [that] are arranged progressively according to value or magnitude, into which an item can be placed according to its quantification.[10] In other words, a scale is a continuous spectrum or series of categories. The purpose of scaling is to represent, usually quantitatively, an item's, a person's, or an event's place in the spectrum.

In business research there are a great many scales. It is traditional to classify scales of measurement on the basis of the mathematical comparisons that are allowable with these scales. The four types of scales are *nominal, ordinal, interval,* and *ratio.*

Nominal Scale

nominal scale
A scale in which the numbers or letters assigned to objects serve as labels for identification or classification; a measurement scale of the simplest type.

Number 21 on the Chicago Cubs represents Sammy Sosa; Barry Bonds is number 25 on the San Francisco Giants. These numbers nominally identify these superstars. A **nominal scale** is the simplest type of scale. The numbers or letters assigned to objects serve as labels for identification or classification. These are scales "in name only." In Tulsa, Census Tract 25 and Census Tract 87 are merely labels. The number 87 does not imply that this area has more people or a higher income than the number 25. An example of a typical nominal scale in business research is the coding of males as 1 and females as 2.

The first drawing in Exhibit 13.3 depicts the number 7 on a horse's colors. This is merely a label to allow bettors and racing enthusiasts to identify that horse.

Ordinal Scale

ordinal scale
A scale that arranges objects or alternatives according to their magnitudes.

If you've been to the racetrack, you know that when a horse finishes in the "show" position, it has come in third behind the "win" and "place" horses. An **ordinal scale** arranges objects or alternatives according to their magnitude in an ordered relationship. When respondents are asked to *rank order* their investment preferences, they assign ordinal values to them. In our racehorse example, if we assign a 1 to the win position, a 2 to the place position, and a 3 to the show position, we can say that 1 was before 2, and 2 was before 3. However, we cannot say anything about the distance or interval between the win and the show horses or between the show and the place horses.

A typical ordinal scale in business research asks respondents to rate career opportunities, brands, companies, or the like as "excellent," "good," "fair," or "poor." Researchers know "excellent" is higher than "good," but they do not know by how much.

EXHIBIT 13.3 NOMINAL, ORDINAL, INTERVAL, AND RATIO SCALES PROVIDE DIFFERENT INFORMATION

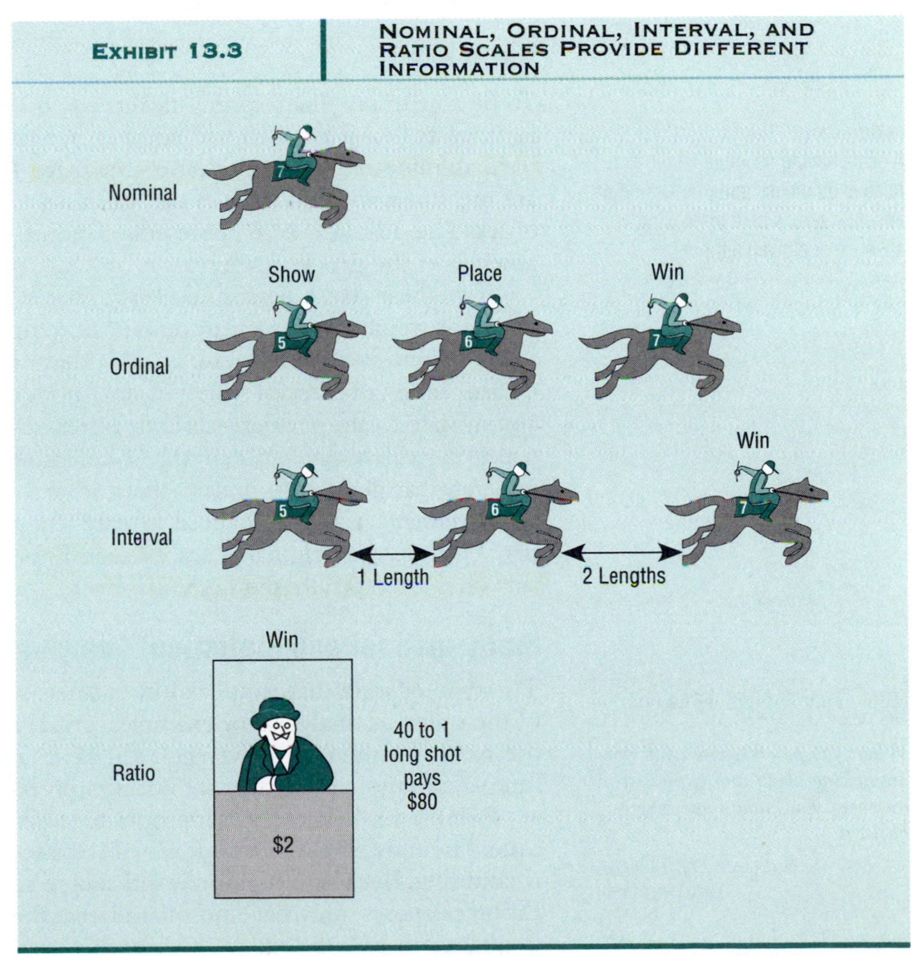

Interval Scale

Exhibit 13.3 depicts a horse race in which the win horse is two lengths ahead of the place horse, which is one length ahead of the show horse. Not only is the order of finish known, but the distance between the horses is known. (The example assumes a standard measure for the term *length*.) **Interval scales** not only indicate order, they also measure order (or distance) in units of equal intervals.

interval scale
A scale that not only arranges objects or alternatives according to their magnitudes but also distinguishes this ordered arrangement in units of equal intervals.

The location of the zero point is arbitrary. In the Consumer Price Index, if the base year is 1983, the price level during 1983 will be set at 100. Although this is an equal-interval measurement scale, the zero point is arbitrary.

The classic example of an interval scale is the Fahrenheit temperature scale. If a temperature is 80°, it cannot be said that it is twice as hot as 40°. The reason for this is that 0° does not represent the lack of temperature, but a relative point on the Fahrenheit scale. Due to the lack of an absolute zero point, the interval scale does not allow the conclusion that 36 is three times as great as the number 12, only that the interval distance is three times greater.

Similarly, when an interval scale is used to measure psychological attributes, the researcher can comment on the magnitude of differences or compare the average differences on attributes that are measured but cannot determine the actual strength of attitudes toward an object. However, changes in concepts over time can be compared if the researcher continues to use the same scale in longitudinal research.

Ratio Scale

To be able to say that winning tickets pay 40 to 1 or that racehorse number 7 is twice as heavy as racehorse number 5, a ratio scale is necessary. **Ratio scales** have absolute rather than relative quantities. For example, money and weight are measured with ratio scales that possess an absolute zero and interval properties. The absolute zero represents a point on the scale where there is an absence of the given attribute.

ratio scale
A scale having absolute rather than relative quantities and possessing an absolute zero, where there is an absence of a given attribute.

If we hear that a person has zero ounces of gold, we understand the zero value for weight. In the measurement of temperature, the Kelvin scale (a ratio scale) begins at absolute zero, a point that corresponds to −273.16° on the Celsius scale (an interval scale). In distribution or logistical research it may be appropriate to think of physical attributes, such as weight or distance, as ratio scales in which the ratio of the scale values is meaningful. Most financial research that deals with dollar values utilizes ratio scales. Because the scale of measurement is ratio, financial researchers are allowed to construct ratios derived from the original scales. However, for most behavioral research, interval scales are typically the highest form of measurement.

Mathematical and Statistical Analysis of Scales

The type of scale that is utilized in business research will determine the form of the statistical analysis. For example, certain operations, such as calculation of the mean (mathematical average), can be conducted only if the scale is of an interval or ratio nature; they are not permissible with nominal or ordinal scales.

TO THE POINT

When you can measure what you are talking about and express it in numbers, you know something about it.

WILLIAM THOMPSON,
LORD KELVIN

Exhibit 13.4 shows the appropriate descriptive statistics for each type of scale. The most sophisticated form of statistical analysis for nominal scale data is counting. Because the numbers in such a scale are merely labels for classification purposes, they have no quantitative meaning. The researcher tallies the frequency in each category and identifies which category contains the high-

Exhibit 13.4 | **Descriptive Statistics for Types of Scales**

Type of Scale	Numerical Operation	Descriptive Statistics
Nominal	Counting	Frequency in each category, percentage in each category, mode
Ordinal	Rank ordering	Median, range, percentile ranking
Interval	Arithmetic operations on intervals between numbers	Mean, standard deviation, variance
Ratio	Arithmetic operations on actual quantities	Geometric mean, coefficient of variation

Note: All statistics that are appropriate for lower-order scales (nominal is the lowest) are appropriate for higher-order scales (ratio is the highest).

est number of observations (individuals, objects, etc.). An ordinal scale provides data that may be rank ordered from lowest to highest. Thus, observations may be associated with a percentile rank such as the median. Because all statistical analysis appropriate for lower-order scales is appropriate for higher-order scales, an interval scale may be used as a nominal scale to uniquely classify or as an ordinal scale to preserve order. In addition, an interval scale's property of equal intervals allows researchers to compare differences between scale values and to perform arithmetic operations such as addition and subtraction. Numbers may be changed, but the numerical operations must preserve order and relative magnitudes of differences. The mean and standard deviation may be calculated when true interval-scale data are obtained. Ratio scales have all the properties of nominal, ordinal, and interval scales. In addition, researchers may make comparisons of absolute magnitude because the scale has an absolute zero point. Arithmetic operations on actual quantities are permissible. The ratios of scale values are meaningful. Chapters 20 through 24 further explore the limitations scales impose on the mathematical analysis of data.

INDEX MEASURES

This chapter has thus far focused on measuring a concept with a single question or a single observation. A researcher measuring awareness, for example, might use one question, such as "Are you aware of ______?" However, measuring more complex concepts may require more than one question because the concept has several attributes. An **attribute** is a single characteristic or fundamental feature of an object, person, situation, or issue. Multi-item instruments used to measure a single concept with several attributes are called **index measures,** or *composite measures.* For example, one index of social class is based on three weighted variables: residence, occupation, and education.

attribute
A single characteristic or fundamental feature of an object, person, situation, or issue.

index (composite) measure
Multi-item instrument constructed to measure a single concept; also called a *composite measure.*

Measures of cognitive phenomena are often composite indexes of a set of variables or scales. Items are combined into a composite measure. For example, a salesperson's morale may be measured by combining questions such as

"How satisfied are you with your job?" "How satisfied are you with your territory?" "How satisfied are you in your personal life?" Measuring a concept by a variety of techniques is one method for increasing precision and accuracy. Asking different questions in order to measure the same thing provides a more accurate cumulative measure than asking a single question.

THREE CRITERIA FOR GOOD MEASUREMENT

There are three major criteria for evaluating measurements: *reliability, validity,* and *sensitivity.*

Reliability

A tailor measuring fabric with a tape measure obtains a "true" value of the fabric's length. If the tailor takes repeated measures of the fabric and each time comes up with the same length, it is assumed that the tape measure is reliable. When the outcome of the measuring process is reproducible, the measuring instrument is reliable.

reliability
The degree to which measures are free from error and therefore yield consistent results.

Reliability applies to a measure when similar results are obtained over time and across situations. Broadly defined, **reliability** is the degree to which measures are free from error and therefore yield consistent results.[11] For example, ordinal measures are reliable if they consistently rank order items in the same manner; reliable interval measures consistently rank order and maintain the same distance between items.

Imperfections in the measuring process that affect the assignment of scores or numbers in different ways each time a measure is taken, such as when a respondent misunderstands a question, are the cause of low reliability. Suppose a respondent understands a question but does not know the real reason for his or her behavior and so cannot give any of several responses with truthfulness. The actual choice between plausible responses may be governed by such transitory factors as mood, whim, or the context set by surrounding questions.[12] Measures of this type will not be error-free and stable over time.

Two dimensions underlie the concept of reliability: one is *repeatability* and the other is *internal consistency.* Assessing the repeatability of a measure is the first aspect of gauging reliability.

test-retest method
The administering of the same scale or measure to the same respondents at two separate points in time in order to test for reliability.

The **test-retest method** of determining reliability involves administering the same scale or measure to the same respondents at two separate times to test for stability. If the measure is stable over time, the test, administered under the same conditions each time, should obtain similar results. For example, suppose a researcher measures job satisfaction and finds that 64 percent of the population is satisfied with their jobs. If the study is repeated a few weeks later under similar conditions, and the researcher again finds that 64 percent of the population is satisfied with their jobs, it appears that the measure has repeatability. The high stability correlation or consistency between the two measures at time 1 and time 2 indicates a high degree of reliability.

At the individual (rather than aggregate) level, assume that a person does not change his or her attitude about the job. If repeated measurements of that individual's attitude toward the job are taken with the same attitude scale, a reliable instrument will produce the same results each time the attitude is measured. When a measuring instrument produces unpredictable results from one testing to the next, the results are said to be unreliable because of error in measurement.

There are two problems with measures of test-retest reliability that are common to all longitudinal studies. First, the premeasure (or first measure) may sensitize the respondents to their participation in a research project and subsequently influence the results of the second measure. Further, if the time between measures is long, there may be attitude change or other maturation of the subjects. Thus, it is possible for a reliable measure to indicate a low or moderate correlation between the first and the second administrations, but this low correlation may be due to an attitude change over time rather than to a lack of reliability.

The second dimension of reliability concerns the homogeneity of the measure. An attempt to measure an attitude may require asking several similar (but not identical) questions or presenting a battery of scale items. The three job-challenge items in Exhibit 13.2 represent a battery of scale items. To measure the *internal consistency* of a multiple-item measure, scores on subsets of the items within the scale are correlated.

The technique of splitting halves is the most basic method for checking internal consistency when a measure contains a large number of items. In the **split-half method** the researcher may take the result obtained from one half of the scale items (e.g., odd-numbered items) and check them against the results from the other half of the items (e.g., even-numbered items).

split-half method
A method of measuring the degree of internal consistency by checking one half of the results of a set of scaled items against the other half.

equivalent-form method
A method of measuring the correlation between alternative instruments, designed to be as equivalent as possible, administered to the same group of subjects.

In the **equivalent-form method** two alternative instruments are designed to be as equivalent as possible. Each of the two measurement scales is administered to the same group of subjects. If there is high correlation between the two forms, the researcher concludes that the scale is reliable. However, there is a problem if there is low correspondence between the two instruments. The researcher will be uncertain whether the measure has intrinsically low reliability or whether a single equivalent form is not similar enough to the other form.[13]

Both the equivalent-form method and the split-half method of measuring reliability assume that the concept being measured is unidimensional. They measure homogeneity, or inter-item consistency, rather than stability over time.

It should be noted that reliability is a necessary condition for validity, but a reliable instrument may not be valid. For example, a voting-intentions measurement technique may consistently indicate that 20 percent of the sample units are willing to vote for a candidate. Whether or not the measure is valid depends on whether 20 percent of the population do indeed vote for this candidate. A reliable but invalid instrument will yield consistently inaccurate results.

Validity

The purpose of measurement is to measure what we intend to measure—but this obvious goal is not as simple as it sounds at first. Consider the student who takes a test (a measurement) in a statistics class. After receiving a poor grade, the student may say, "I really understood that material because I studied hard. The test measured my ability to do arithmetic and to memorize formulas rather than my understanding of statistics." The student's complaint is that the test did not measure her understanding of statistics—what the professor had intended to measure; the test may have measured something else.

For example, consider one method of measuring the intention to buy: the so-called gift method. Respondents are told that a drawing will be held at some future time for a year's supply of a certain product. Respondents report which of several brands they prefer to receive if they win.[14] Do respondents' reports of the brands they prefer to win necessarily constitute a valid measure of the brands they will actually purchase in the marketplace if they don't win the contest? Couldn't there be a systematic bias to identify a brand "I wish I could afford" rather than the brand usually purchased? This is a question affecting validity.

The use of rate of absenteeism to measure morale illustrates another validity issue. It is possible that absenteeism is not a valid measure of morale, because it could reflect either a wave of illness in the community or unsatisfied workers not coming to work.

validity
The ability of a scale or measuring instrument to measure what it is intended to measure.

Researchers want to know if their measure is valid, and the evaluation of validity expresses their concern with accurate measurement. **Validity** is the ability of a measure (for example, an attitude measure) to measure what it is supposed to measure. If it does not measure what it is designated to measure, there will be problems.

Students should be able to empathize with the following validity problem. Consider the controversy about highway patrol officers using radar guns to clock speeders. A "speeder" is clocked at 75 mph in a 55 mph zone, but the same radar gun, aimed at a house, registers 28 mph. (The error occurred because the radar gun picked up impulses from the electrical system in the squad car's idling engine.) The house wasn't speeding—and the test was not valid.

TO THE POINT

Not everything that can be counted counts, and not everything that counts can be counted.

ALBERT EINSTEIN

Researchers have attempted to assess validity in a variety of ways, including asking questions such as "Is there a consensus among my colleagues that my attitude scale measures what it is supposed to measure?" "Does my measure correlate with others' measures of the 'same' concept?" and "Does the behavior expected from my measure predict the actual observed behavior?" Researchers expect the answers to provide some evidence of a measure's validity. This section discusses the three basic approaches to dealing with the evaluation of validity.

face (content) validity
Professional agreement that a scale logically appears to accurately measure what it is intended to measure.

Face validity, or **content validity,** refers to the subjective agreement among professionals that a scale logically appears to reflect accurately what it purports to measure. The content of the scale appears to be adequate. When it appears evident to experts that the measure provides adequate coverage of the concept, a measure has face validity. Clear, understandable questions such as "How many children do you have?" are generally agreed to have face validity. However, in scientific studies researchers generally prefer strong evidence because of the elusive nature of measuring attitudes and other cognitive phenomena. For example, the A. C. Nielsen television-rating system is based on the PeopleMeter, which mechanically records when a sample household's television is engaged and what channel is selected. If one of the viewers moves to another room or falls asleep, the measure is not a valid measure of audience.

Researchers also wish to answer the question "Does my measure correlate with other measures of the 'same' construct?" Consider the physical concept of *length*.[15] It is possible to measure length utilizing tape measures, calipers, odometers, and variations of the ruler. If a new measure of length were developed (for example, through laser technology), finding that the new measure correlated with the other measures of length (the criteria) could provide some assurance that the new measure had **criterion validity.** A researcher wishing to establish criterion validity for a new measure of absenteeism, such as a measure utilizing co-workers' ratings of employee absenteeism, will want to be sure this new measure correlates with other traditional measures of absenteeism, such as total days absent.

criterion validity
The ability of some measure to correlate with other measures of the same construct.

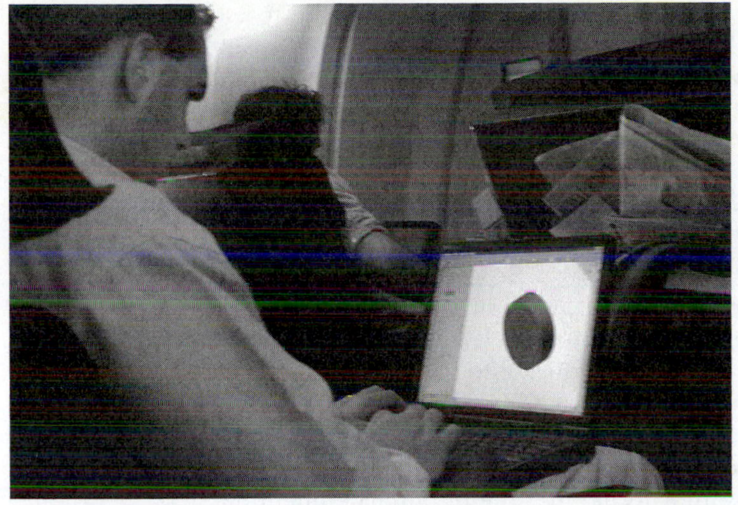

Airline travelers put "space," especially the distance between seat backs and legroom, high on their list of preferences. Space becomes extremely important if a flight is several hours long. Plog Travel Research found that when TWA gave people more legroom, they rated the meals more favorably—even though the meals did not change. In fact, in addition to saying the food tasted better, there was a halo effect influencing the ratings of most other characteristics.[16] Were the measures of food quality and airline characteristics other than legroom valid?

concurrent validity
A type of criterion validity whereby a new measure correlates with a criterion measure taken at the same time.

predictive validity
A type of criterion validity whereby a new measure predicts a future event or correlates with a criterion measure administered at a later time.

Criterion validity may be classified as either *concurrent validity* or *predictive validity*, depending on the time sequence in which the "new" measurement scale and the criterion measure are correlated. If the new measure is taken at the same time as the criterion measure and is shown to be valid, then it has **concurrent validity. Predictive validity** is established when a new measure predicts a future event. The two measures differ only on the basis of a time dimension—that is, the criterion measure is separated in time from the predictor measure. A practical example of predictive validity is illustrated by a commercial research firm's testing of the relationship between a rough commercial's effectiveness (as determined, for example, by recall scores) and a finished commercial's effectiveness (as determined by recall scores). Ad agencies often test animatic rough commercials, photomatic rough commercials, or live-action rough commercials before developing the finished commercial. One research consulting firm suggests that this testing has high predictive validity. Rough commercial recall scores provide correct estimates of the final, finished commercial recall scores more than 80 percent of the time.[17] While face (content) validity is a subjective evaluation, criterion validity provides a more rigorous empirical test.

construct validity
The ability of a measure to confirm a network of related hypotheses generated from a theory based on the concepts.

Construct validity is established by the degree to which a measure confirms a network of related hypotheses generated from a theory based on the concepts. Construct validity is established during the statistical analysis of the data. Construct validity implies that the empirical evidence generated by a measure is consistent with the theoretical logic about the concepts. In its simplest form, if the measure behaves the way it is supposed to, in a pattern of intercorrelation with a variety of other variables, there is evidence for construct validity.[18] For example, a consumer researcher developed a personality scale to measure several interpersonal response traits that management theorists had previously related to occupational preference. Testing the new scale against occupational preference would be a way to establish evidence for construct validity.

To achieve construct validity, a researcher must have already determined the meaning of the measure by establishing what basic researchers call *convergent validity* and *discriminant validity.* Convergent validity is synonymous with criterion validity. The criterion may be a construct that one would logically expect to be associated with the new measure. Thus, to establish validity, the new measure should "converge" with other similar measures; a measure of a theoretical concept has convergent validity when it is highly correlated with different measures of similar constructs. A measure has **discriminant validity** when it has a low correlation with measures of *dissimilar* concepts. This is a complex method of establishing validity and is of less concern to applied researchers than to basic researchers.

discriminant validity
The ability of some measure to have a low correlation with measures of dissimilar concepts.

Reliability and Validity

The concepts of reliability and validity should be compared. A tailor, using a ruler, may obtain the same measurements over time, but it is possible that he is using a bent ruler. A bent ruler, one that does not provide perfect accuracy, is not a valid measurement scale. Thus, reliability, although necessary for validity, is not sufficient by itself. A measure of a subject's physiological reaction to a package (for example, pupil dilation) may be highly reliable, but it does not necessarily constitute a valid measure of purchase intention.

The differences between reliability and validity can be illustrated by the rifle targets in Exhibit 13.5. Suppose an expert sharpshooter fires an equal number of rounds with a century-old rifle and with a modern rifle.[19] The shots from the century-old gun are considerably scattered, but the shots from the new gun are closely clustered. The variability of the old rifle, compared to the new weapon, indicates it is less reliable. The target on the right illustrates the concept of a systematic bias influencing validity. The new rifle is reliable (because it has little variance), but the sharpshooter's vision is hampered by glare from the sun. Although the shots are consistent, the sharpshooter is unable to hit the bull's-eye.

Sensitivity

The sensitivity of a scale is an important measurement concept, particularly when *changes* in attitudes or other hypothetical constructs are under investigation. **Sensitivity** refers to an instrument's ability to accurately measure variability in stimuli or responses. A dichotomous response category, such as "agree or disagree," does not allow the recording of subtle attitude changes. A more sensitive measure, with numerous items on the scale, may be needed. For example,

sensitivity
A measurement instrument's ability to accurately measure variability in stimuli or responses.

EXHIBIT 13.5 RELIABILITY AND VALIDITY ON TARGET

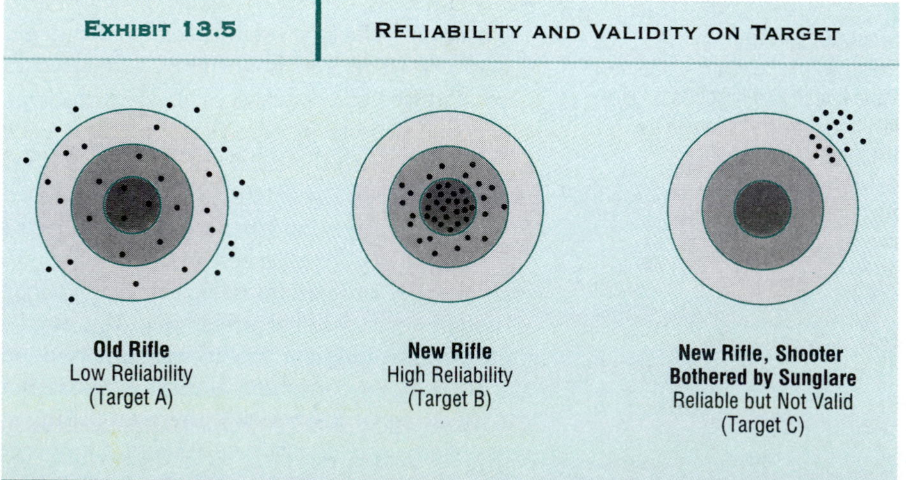

adding "strongly agree," "mildly agree," "neither agree nor disagree," "mildly disagree," and "strongly disagree" as categories increases a scale's sensitivity.

The sensitivity of a scale based on a single question or single item can also be increased by adding additional questions or items. In other words, because index measures allow for a greater range of possible scores, they are more sensitive than single-item scales.

SUMMARY

Business research problems often require the choice of an appropriate measuring system. The concept to be measured must be given an operational definition that specifies how it will be measured. There are four types of measuring scales: Nominal scales assign numbers or letters to objects only for identification or classification. Ordinal scales arrange objects or alternatives according to their magnitude in an ordered relationship. Interval scales measure order (or distance) in units of equal intervals. Ratio scales are absolute scales, starting with absolute zero—total absence of the attribute. The type of scale determines what numerical and statistical operations can be used in analyzing measurements.

Index (composite) measures are often used when measuring complex concepts with several attributes. Asking several questions may yield a more accurate measure than asking a single question.

Measuring instruments are evaluated in terms of reliability, validity, and sensitivity. Reliability refers to the measuring instrument's ability to provide consistent results in repeated uses. Validity refers to the degree to which the instrument measures the concept the researcher wants to measure. Sensitivity is the measuring instrument's ability to accurately measure variability in stimuli or responses.

Reliability may be tested using the test-retest method, the split-half method, or the equivalent-form method. When dealing with evaluation of validity, the three basic approaches are to establish content validity, to establish criterion validity, and to establish construct validity. The sensitivity of a scale can be increased by allowing for a greater range of possible scores.

Key Terms

concept
operational definition
rule of measurement
nominal scale
ordinal scale
interval scale
ratio scale
attribute
index (composite) measure
reliability
test-retest method
split-half method
equivalent-form method
validity
face (content) validity
criterion validity (convergent validity)
concurrent validity
predictive validity
construct validity
discriminant validity
sensitivity

Questions for Review and Critical Thinking

1. What are the appropriate descriptive statistics allowable with nominal, ordinal, and interval scales?
2. Discuss the differences between validity and reliability.
3. What is the difference between a conceptual definition and an operational definition?
4. Why might a researcher wish to utilize more than one question to measure satisfaction with a job?

5. Comment on the validity and reliability of the following:
   (a) A respondent's reporting of an intention to subscribe to *Consumer Reports* is highly reliable. A researcher believes that this self-report constitutes a valid measurement of dissatisfaction with the economic system and alienation from big business.
   (b) A general-interest magazine claimed that it was a better advertising medium than television programs with similar content. Research had indicated that for a soft drink and other test products, recall scores were higher for the magazine ads than for 30-second commercials.
   (c) A respondent's report of frequency of magazine reading consistently indicates that she regularly reads *Good Housekeeping* and *Gourmet* and never reads *Cosmopolitan*.
6. Indicate whether each of the following measures uses a nominal, ordinal, interval, or ratio scale:
   (a) Prices on the stock market
   (b) Marital status, classified as married or never married
   (c) Whether or not a respondent has ever been unemployed
   (d) Professorial rank: assistant professor, associate professor, or professor
7. In the library find out how *Sales and Marketing Management* magazine constructs its buying power index.
8. Define each of the following concepts and then operationally define each concept:
   (a) A good bowler
   (b) A workaholic
   (c) Intent to purchase a new Palm Pilot hand-held computer
   (d) A mentor
   (e) Media skepticism
   (f) The American dream
9. Education is often used as an indicator of a person's socioeconomic status. Historically, the number of years of schooling completed has been recorded in the U.S. Census as a measure of education. Critics say that this measure is no longer accurate as a measure of education. Comment.
10. The number of mixed-race marriages in the United States has increased more than 100 percent since 1980. In the 2000 Census, Americans for the first time were able to identify themselves as belonging to more than one race. Respondents could choose from these categories: white, black (African American or Negro), American Indian or Alaska Native, Asian Indian, Chinese, Filipino, Japanese, Korean, Vietnamese, Native Hawaiian, Guamanian or Chamorro, Samoan, or Other. Multiracial respondents could check all categories that applied. What measurement issues might arise with regard to the responses from multiracial individuals?
11. Many Internet surveys want to know demographic characteristics of their respondents and how technologically sophisticated they are. Create a conceptual definition of "technographics" and operationalize it.
12. Two academic researchers create a scale to measure attitudes toward corporate downsizing/rightsizing. They do not evaluate the reliability or validity of the measuring instrument. Nevertheless, they submit an article about their research using the scale to a scholarly publication for review. Is this ethical?

Exploring the Internet

1. The Office of Scale Research (OSR) is part of the Department of Marketing at Southern Illinois University at Carbondale. The OSR Web site provides a number of technical reports that deal with a wide variety of scaling issues. Go to http://www.siu.edu/departments/coba/mktg/osr/ and select an article from the reading list. What types of scales are listed?
2. A measure of procrastination can be found at http://www.queendom.com/tests/career/procrastination-1.html. Take this "test." Do you think this is a reliable and valid measure?

Case Suggestion

Case 17: Flyaway Airways

CHAPTER

14

ATTITUDE MEASUREMENT

What you will learn in this chapter

- To understand that an attitude is a hypothetical construct.
- To understand the attitude measuring process.
- To discuss the differences among ranking, rating, sorting, and making choices to measure attitudes and preferences.
- To discuss Likert scales, semantic differentials, and many other types of attitude scales.
- To understand how to measure behavioral intentions.
- To understand the issues involved in the decision to select a measurement scale.

Attitude research indicated Lee jeans were way off the cool meter with young consumers.[1] The company didn't want to alienate loyal buyers—women 35 and over—but it had to shed its "mom's jeans" image to appeal to kids. How could Lee Apparel Company connect with 15-to-34-year-olds who think Lee is, like, totally unhip?

Focus groups found that kids under 17 changed their minds daily on what was cool to wear, while adults in their late 20s and early 30s felt comfortable in their broken-in Levi's. The 17-to-22 segment, however, seemed open to new brands, a finding reiterated in an attitude and lifestyle survey. The study divided consumers into 11 psychographic profiles, among them "Fit Me/Fit My Lifestyle." That segment included a number of 17-to-22-year-olds who were style leaders, influential among their peers. If Lee could grab them, their friends would follow.

The study also confirmed that people thought Lees were more durable than other jeans, and that didn't necessarily mean uncool. The success of Timberland and Doc Martens had shown that functional brands could still be fashionable. Additional focus groups revealed that 17-to-22-year-olds wanted their jeans to give them the confidence to do anything, whether it was playing basketball on the court or watching it on TV. Lee needed to connect its durable image with the indestructibility that the target market craved.

A truly break-out advertising campaign needed something that would set Lee apart on the rack. Perhaps, Fallon McElligott, Lee Jeans' advertising agency, suggested, there were icons buried in Lee's archives that would click with today's savvy young consumers—and link unmistakably back to the brand. In interviews with target buyers, three "antiques" grabbed the spotlight. A slogan from the 1940s, "Can't Bust 'Em," had a retro appeal that also suggested strength and quality. The word *dungarees,* resurrected from an earlier line, lent a James Dean authenticity. And then there was the Buddy Lee doll, an all-but-forgotten icon from the 1920s. Buddy Lee reflected the target market's idealized attitudes of that era—and he was cool, like Bart Simpson.

The findings about attitudes toward these icons also influenced product design for the Lee Dungarees line. Researchers had a radical proposal: Dump the signature leather patch and pocket stitching. Kids said the details reminded them of their parents' jeans. Lee leaders gulped, but gave the go-ahead. Tapping into the retro vein, designers incorporated styling similar to jeans circa the 1920s.

Tests of various advertising concepts found that those "Fit Me/Fit My Lifestyle" 17-to-22-year-olds considered themselves cool hunters: They needed to discover Lee Dungarees before everyone else did. A phantom campaign—posters of Buddy Lee, sans type—were plastered around cities like New York and Los Angeles to pique the interest of early adopters. After a run of commercials on cable TV that introduced Buddy Lee, "Man of Action," the pint-size hero hit the mainstream in spots during primetime shows like *Dawson's Creek.*

The payoff of the attitude research and marketing strategy was great. Initial retail orders of Original Straight Leg Dungarees, the line's flagship product, hit 1.3 million units, 300 percent more than anticipated.

Investigating how to measure attitudes—a common business research activity—is the subject of this chapter. ■

ATTITUDE DEFINED

attitude
An enduring disposition to consistently respond in a given manner to various aspects of the world; composed of affective, cognitive, and behavioral components.

affective component
The component of attitude that reflects one's general feelings or emotions toward an object.

cognitive component
The component of attitude that represents one's awareness of and knowledge about an object.

behavioral component
The component of attitude that includes buying intentions and behavioral expectations; reflects a predisposition to action.

There are many definitions for the term *attitude.* An **attitude** is usually viewed as an enduring disposition to respond consistently in a given manner to various aspects of the world, including persons, events, and objects. One conception of attitude is reflected in this brief statement: "Sally loves working at Sam's. She believes it's clean, conveniently located, and has the best wages in town. She intends to work there until she retires." In this short description are three components of attitude: the *affective,* the *cognitive,* and the *behavioral.*

The **affective component** reflects an individual's general feelings or emotions toward an object. Statements such as "I love my job," "I liked that book, *A Corporate Bestiary,*" and "I hate cranberry juice" reflect the emotional character of attitudes.

The way one feels about a product, a person, or an object is usually tied to one's beliefs or cognitions. The **cognitive component** represents one's awareness of and knowledge about an object. A woman might feel happy about her job because she "believes that the pay is great" or because she knows "that my job is the biggest challenge in Arlington."

The third component of an attitude is the **behavioral component.** Intentions and behavioral expectations are included in this component, which therefore reflects a predisposition to action.

ATTITUDE AS A HYPOTHETICAL CONSTRUCT

hypothetical construct
A variable that is not directly observable but is measured through indirect indicators, such as verbal expression or overt behavior.

Many variables that business researchers wish to investigate are psychological variables that cannot be directly observed. For example, someone may have an attitude toward the E-Trade brokerage firm, but we cannot observe this attitude. To measure an attitude, we must infer from the way an individual responds (verbal expression or overt behavior) to some stimulus. The term **hypothetical construct** describes a variable that is not directly observable but is measured through indirect indicators, such as verbal expression or overt behavior.

TECHNIQUES FOR MEASURING ATTITUDES

A remarkable variety of techniques have been devised to measure attitudes. In part, this diversity stems from the lack of consensus about the exact definition of the concept. Further, the affective, cognitive, and behavioral components of an attitude may be measured by different means. For example, sympathetic

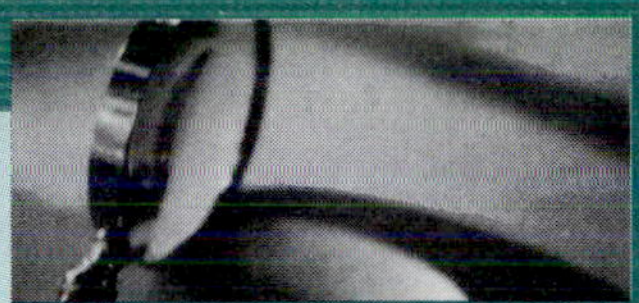

RESEARCH INSIGHT

A HYPOTHETICAL CONSTRUCT IS NEVER HAVING TO SAY YOU'RE SORRY; OR, LOVE IS A FOUR-LETTER WORD

Love is a four-letter word.[2] It is also a hypothetical construct—that is, a term that psychologists use to describe or explain consistent patterns of human behavior. Love, hate, thirst, learning, intelligence—all of these are hypothetical constructs. They are hypothetical in that they do not exist as physical entities; therefore, they cannot be seen, heard, felt, or measured directly. There is no love center in the brain that, if removed, would leave a person incapable of responding positively and affectionately toward other people and things. Love and hate are constructs in that we invent these terms to explain why, for instance, a young man spends all his time with one young woman while completely avoiding another. From a scientific point of view, we might be better off if we said that this young man's behavior suggested that he had a relatively enduring, positive-approach attitude toward the first woman and a negative-avoidance attitude toward the second.

ranking
A measurement task that requires that the respondents rank order a small number of activities, events, or objects on the basis of overall preference or some characteristic of the stimulus.

rating
A measurement task that requires the respondent to estimate the magnitude of a characteristic or quality that an object possesses.

sorting technique
A measurement technique that presents a respondent with several concepts printed on cards and requires the respondent to arrange the cards into a number of piles to classify the concepts.

choice technique
A measurement task that identifies preferences by requiring respondents to choose between two or more alternatives.

nervous system responses may be recorded using physiological measures to measure affect, but they are not good measures of behavioral intentions. Direct verbal statements concerning affect, belief, or behavior are utilized to measure behavioral intent. However, attitudes may also be measured indirectly by using the qualitative, exploratory techniques discussed in Chapter 7. Obtaining verbal statements from respondents generally requires that the respondent perform a task such as ranking, rating, sorting, or making a choice or a comparison.

A **ranking** task requires that the respondents rank order a small number of items on the basis of overall preference or some characteristic of the stimulus. **Rating** asks the respondents to estimate the magnitude of a characteristic or quality that an object possesses. Quantitative scores, along a continuum that has been supplied to the respondents, are used to estimate the strength of the attitude or belief. In other words, the respondents indicate the position, on a scale, where they would rate the object.

A **sorting technique** might present respondents with several product concepts, printed on cards, and require that the respondents arrange the cards into a number of piles or otherwise classify the product concepts. The **choice technique,** choosing one of two or more alternatives, is another type of attitude measurement. If a respondent chooses one object over another, the researcher can assume that the respondent prefers the chosen object over the other.

The most popular techniques for measuring attitudes are presented in this chapter.

PHYSIOLOGICAL MEASURES OF ATTITUDES

Measures of galvanic skin response, blood pressure, and pupil dilation and other physiological measures may be utilized to assess the affective component of attitudes. They provide a means of measuring attitudes without verbally questioning the respondent. In general, they can provide a gross measure of like or dislike, but they are not sensitive measures for identifying gradients of an attitude. (Each of these measures is discussed elsewhere in the text.)

ATTITUDE RATING SCALES

Using rating scales to measure attitudes is perhaps the most common practice in business research. This section discusses many rating scales designed to enable respondents to report the intensity of their attitudes.

Simple Attitude Scales

In its most basic form, attitude scaling requires that an individual agree or disagree with a statement or respond to a single question. For example, respondents in a political poll may be asked whether they agree or disagree with the statement "The president should run for re-election," or an individual might be asked to indicate whether he likes or dislikes labor unions. Because this type of self-rating scale merely classifies respondents into one of two categories, it has only the properties of a nominal scale. This, of course, limits the type of mathematical analysis that may be utilized with this basic scale. Despite the disadvantages, simple attitude scaling may be used when questionnaires are

TO THE POINT

My tastes are very simple. I only want the best.

OSCAR WILDE

Got A Minute?
TELL US HOW WE'RE DOING

Dear Visitor

Thank you for coming and giving us the opportunity of serving you. We know that continued visitor satisfaction is the key to success. With that in mind, we invite your comments and suggestions regarding our SERVICE, CLEANLINESS, ATTITUDE, and EXHIBITS.

We're proud to serve you and we really appreciate your constructive comments. We look forward to serving you again in the very near future.

WE APPRECIATE YOUR OPINION ON THE FOLLOWING

(Please Check boxes below)

	Excl. 1	Good 2	Fair 3	Poor 4	REMARKS
CLEANLINESS					
Grounds					
Galleries					
Rest Rooms					
Exhibits					
SERVICE					
Attitude					
Courtesy					
EXHIBITS					
Appearance					
Information					
Interest					
OVERALL IMPRESSION					

COMMENTS and SUGGESTIONS ____________________

Would you like to be contacted about being a volunteer?
☐ Yes ☐ No

Date ________ Time ________ AM ____ PM ____

Your Name (optional) ____________________

Address ____________________

City ________ State ________ Zip ________

Telephone Number ____________________

FOLD HERE ▶ . . . OR LEAVE IN THE BOX
DROP IN THE MAIL THANK YOU

The Dallas Museum of Natural History and the Dallas Aquarium have their visitors rate attributes such as cleanliness, service, and exhibit appearance. These rating scales provide simple descriptive and evaluative measures of attitudes.

extremely long, when respondents have little education, or for other specific reasons.

A number of simplified scales are merely checklists. A respondent indicates past experience, preference, and the like merely by checking an item. In many cases the items are adjectives that describe a particular object.

The Job Descriptive Index (JDI) is a modified checklist with a large number of items. The Job Descriptive Index measures several dimensions of satisfaction: pay, promotion, co-workers, supervision, and quality of work. A sample item from the JDI appears below.[3]

Directions:
Think of your present work. What is it like most of the time?
Circle YES if it describes your work.
Circle NO if it does NOT describe it.
Circle ? if you cannot decide.

Fascinating	**YES**	**NO**	**?**
Routine	**YES**	**NO**	**?**
Satisfying	**YES**	**NO**	**?**

Most attitude theorists believe that attitudes vary along continua. An early attitude researcher pioneered the view that the task of attitude scaling is to measure the distance from "good" to "bad," "low" to "high," "like" to "dislike," and so on.[4] Thus, the purpose of an attitude scale is to find an individual's position on the continuum. Simple scales do not allow for making fine distinctions in attitudes. Several other scales have been developed to help make more precise measurements.

Category Scales

Some rating scales have only two response categories: agree and disagee. Expanding the response categories provides the respondent more flexibility in the rating task. Even more information is provided if the categories are ordered according to a descriptive or evaluative dimension. Consider the questions below:

How often is your supervisor courteous and friendly to you?
- ☐ **Never**
- ☐ **Rarely**
- ☐ **Sometimes**
- ☐ **Often**
- ☐ **Very often**

If you could choose, how much longer would you stay at your present job?
- ☐ **Less than six months**
- ☐ **Six months to one year**
- ☐ **Longer than one year**

category scale
An attitude scale consisting of several response categories to provide the respondent with alternative ratings.

Each of these **category scales** is a more sensitive measure than a scale with only two response categories. Each provides more information.

Wording is an extremely important factor in the usefulness of these scales. Exhibit 14.1 shows some common wordings for category scales, and question wording is more thoroughly evaluated in Chapter 15.

EXHIBIT 14.1 | **SELECTED CATEGORY SCALES**

Quality				
Excellent	Good	Fair	Poor	
Very good	Fairly good	Neither good nor bad	Not very good	Not good at all
Well above average	Above average	Average	Below average	Well below average
Importance				
Very important	Fairly important	Neutral	Not so important	Not at all important
Interest				
Very interested		Somewhat interested		Not very interested
Satisfaction				
Very satisfied	Somewhat satisfied	Neither satisfied nor dissatisfied	Somewhat dissatisfied	Very dissatisfied
Very satisfied	Quite satisfied	Somewhat satisfied	Not at all satisfied	
Frequency				
All of the time	Very often	Often	Sometimes	Hardly ever
Very often	Often	Sometimes	Rarely	Never
All of the time	Most of the time	Some of the time	Just now and then	
Truth				
Very true	Somewhat true	Not very true	Not at all true	
Definitely true	More true than false	More false than true	Definitely not true	

Summated Ratings Method: The Likert Scale

Likert scale
A measure of attitudes designed to allow respondents to indicate how strongly they agree or disagree with carefully constructed statements that range from very positive to very negative toward an attitudinal object.

Business researchers' adaptation of the summated ratings method, developed by Rensis Likert, is extremely popular for measuring attitudes because the method is simple to administer.[5] With the **Likert scale,** respondents indicate their attitudes by checking how strongly they agree or disagree with carefully constructed statements that range from very positive to very negative toward the attitudinal object. Individuals generally choose from five alternatives: strongly agree, agree, uncertain, disagree, and strongly disagree; but the number of alternatives may range from three to nine.[6]

Consider the following example from a study on mergers and acquisitions:

Mergers and acquisitions provide a faster means of growth than internal expansion.

Strongly Disagree	Disagree	Uncertain	Agree	Strongly Agree
(1)	(2)	(3)	(4)	(5)

To measure the attitude, researchers assign scores or weights to the alternative responses. In this example, weights of 5, 4, 3, 2, and 1 are assigned to the answers. (The weights, shown in parentheses, would not be printed on the questionnaire.) Because the statement used as an example is positive toward the attitude, strong agreement indicates the most favorable attitudes on the statement, and is assigned a weight of 5. If a negative statement toward the object (such as "Your access to copy machines is limited") were given, the weights would be reversed, and "strongly disagree" would be assigned the weight of 5. A single scale item on a summated rating scale is an ordinal scale.

A Likert scale may include several scale items to form an index. Each statement is assumed to represent an aspect of a common attitudinal domain. For example, Exhibit 14.2 shows the items in a Likert scale to measure attitudes toward a management by objectives program. The total score is the summation of the weights assigned to an individual's response.

EXHIBIT 14.2 **LIKERT SCALE TO MEASURE ATTITUDES TOWARD A MANAGEMENT BY OBJECTIVES (MBO) PROGRAM**[7]

Here are some statements that describe how employees might feel about the MBO (management-by-objectives) form of management. Please indicate your agreement or disagreement. For each statement please circle the appropriate number to indicate whether you:

1—STRONGLY AGREE 2—AGREE 3—NEUTRAL 4—DISAGREE 5—STRONGLY DISAGREE

Circle one and only one answer for each statement. There are no right or wrong answers to these questions. Just give your opinion.

	Strongly Agree	Agree	Neutral	Disagree	Strongly Disagree
1. MBO is an effective way of planning and organizing the work for which I am responsible.	1	2	3	4	5
2. MBO provides an effective way of evaluating my work performance.	1	2	3	4	5
3. MBO motivates me to do the very best on my job.	1	2	3	4	5
4. MBO is an effective way of coordinating my work with that of other members of my immediate workgroup.	1	2	3	4	5
5. MBO results in good communication between me and my immediate supervisor.	1	2	3	4	5
6. MBO results in regular cooperation between me and my immediate supervisor.	1	2	3	4	5
7. All things considered, I am satisfied with MBO as it relates to my job.	1	2	3	4	5
8. The MBO program has *reduced* cooperation between divisions of DOT.	1	2	3	4	5
9. The MBO program has helped DOT solve some of its serious problems.	1	2	3	4	5
10. The MBO program has had *little effect* on DOT.	1	2	3	4	5
11. The MBO program has improved communications at DOT.	1	2	3	4	5
12. The MBO program has improved the coordination of efforts between divisions.	1	2	3	4	5

In Likert's original procedure, a large number of statements are generated and then an *item analysis* is performed. The purpose of the item analysis is to ensure that final items evoke a wide response and discriminate among those with positive and negative attitudes. Items that are poor because they lack clarity or elicit mixed response patterns are eliminated from the final statement list. However, many business researchers do not follow the exact procedure prescribed by Likert. Hence, a disadvantage of the Likert-type summated rating method is that it is difficult to know what a single summated score means. Many patterns of response to the various statements can produce the same total score. Thus, identical total scores may reflect different "attitudes" because respondents endorsed different combinations of statements.

Semantic Differential

semantic differential
An attitude measure consisting of a series of seven-point bipolar rating scales allowing response to a concept.

The **semantic differential** is a series of attitude scales. This popular attitude-measurement technique consists of presenting an identification of a company, product, brand, job, or other concept, followed by a series of seven-point bipolar rating scales. Bipolar adjectives, such as "good" and "bad," "modern" and "old-fashioned," or "clean" and "dirty," anchor the beginning and end (or poles) of the scale.

Modern ____ : ____ : ____ : ____ : ____ : ____ : ____ Old-Fashioned

The subject makes repeated judgments of the concept under investigation on each of the scales. For example, Exhibit 14.3 shows a series of scales related to measuring attitudes toward jazz saxophonists' recording styles.[8]

The scoring of the semantic differential can be illustrated by using the scale bounded by the anchors "modern" and "old-fashioned." Respondents are instructed to check the place that indicates the nearest appropriate adjective. From left to right, the scale intervals are interpreted as extremely modern, very modern, slightly modern, both modern and old-fashioned, slightly old-fashioned, very old-fashioned, and extremely old-fashioned. A weight is assigned to each position on the rating scale. Traditionally, scores are 7, 6, 5, 4, 3, 2, 1, or +3, +2, +1, 0, −1, −2, −3.

Many researchers find it desirable to assume that the semantic differential provides interval data. This assumption, although widely accepted, has its critics, who argue that the data have only ordinal properties because the weights are arbitrary. Depending on whether the data are assumed to be interval or

Exhibit 14.3 | **Semantic Differential Scales to Measure Attitudes toward Jazz Saxophonists' Recording Styles**

Fast __ : __ : __ : __ : __ : __ : __ Slow
Intellectual __ : __ : __ : __ : __ : __ : __ Emotional
Contemporary __ : __ : __ : __ : __ : __ : __ Traditional
Composed __ : __ : __ : __ : __ : __ : __ Improvised
Flat __ : __ : __ : __ : __ : __ : __ Sharp
Busy __ : __ : __ : __ : __ : __ : __ Lazy
New __ : __ : __ : __ : __ : __ : __ Old
Progressive __ : __ : __ : __ : __ : __ : __ Regressive

ordinal, the arithmetic mean or the median is utilized to plot the profile of one concept, product, unit, etc., compared with another concept, product, or unit.

The semantic differential technique was originally developed by Charles Osgood and others as a method for measuring the meaning of objects or the "semantic space" of interpersonal experience.[9] Business researchers have found the semantic differential versatile and have modified it for business applications. Replacing the bipolar adjectives with descriptive phrases is a frequent adaptation in image studies.[10] For example, the phrases "aged a long time," "not aged a long time," "not watery looking," and "watery looking" were used in a beer-brand image study. A savings and loan association might use the phrases "low interest on savings," and "favorable interest on savings." These phrases are not polar opposites, but behavioral researchers have found that respondents often are unwilling to use the extreme negative side of a scale. Organizational research with industrial salespeople, for example, found that in rating their own performance, salespeople would not use the negative side of the scale. Hence it was eliminated, and the anchor opposite the positive anchor showed "satisfactory" rather than "extremely poor" performance.

Numerical Scales

numerical scale
An attitude rating scale similar to a semantic differential except that it uses numbers instead of verbal descriptions as response options to identify response positions.

Numerical scales have numbers, rather than "semantic space" or verbal descriptions, as response options, to identify categories (response positions). If the scale items have five response positions, the scale is called a 5-point numerical scale; with seven response positions, it is called a 7-point numerical scale; and so on.

Consider the following numerical scale:

Now that you've had your automobile for about one year, please tell us how satisfied you are with your Ford Taurus.

Extremely Satisfied								Extremely Dissatisfied
	7	6	5	4	3	2	1	

This numerical scale utilizes bipolar adjectives in the same manner as the semantic differential. Exhibit 14.4 shows a measure of leadership effectiveness that combines a semantic differential with an 8-point numerical scale. In practice, researchers have found that for educated populations a scale with numerical labels for intermediate points on the scale is as effective a measure as the "true" semantic differential.

Constant-Sum Scale

Suppose United Parcel Service (UPS) wishes to determine the importance of the attributes of accurate invoicing, delivery as promised, and price to organizations that use its service in business-to-business marketing. Respondents might be asked to divide a constant sum to indicate the relative importance of the attributes.[11] For example:

Divide 100 points among the following characteristics of a delivery service according to how important each characteristic is to you when selecting a delivery company.

Accurate invoicing ______
Delivery as promised ______
Lower price ______

EXHIBIT 14.4 | **LPC: LEAST-PREFERRED CO-WORKER SCALE OF LEADERSHIP EFFECTIVENESS**[12]

Think of the person with whom you work least well, either someone you work with now or someone you knew in the past. The individual does not have to be the person you like the least, but should be the person with whom you have the most difficulty getting a job done. Describe this person as he or she appears to you.

Pleasant	8	7	6	5	4	3	2	1	Unpleasant
Friendly	8	7	6	5	4	3	2	1	Unfriendly
Rejecting	1	2	3	4	5	6	7	8	Accepting
Helpful	8	7	6	5	4	3	2	1	Frustrating
Unenthusiastic	1	2	3	4	5	6	7	8	Enthusiastic
Tense	1	2	3	4	5	6	7	8	Relaxed
Distant	1	2	3	4	5	6	7	8	Close
Cold	8	7	6	5	4	3	2	1	Warm
Cooperative	8	7	6	5	4	3	2	1	Uncooperative
Supportive	8	7	6	5	4	3	2	1	Hostile
Boring	1	2	3	4	5	6	7	8	Interesting
Quarrelsome	1	2	3	4	5	6	7	8	Harmonious
Self-assured	8	7	6	5	4	3	2	1	Hesitant
Efficient	8	7	6	5	4	3	2	1	Inefficient
Gloomy	1	2	3	4	5	6	7	8	Cheerful
Open	8	7	6	5	4	3	2	1	Guarded

constant-sum scale
A measure of attitudes in which respondents are asked to divide a constant sum to indicate the relative importance of attributes.

The **constant-sum scale** works best with respondents with high educational levels. If respondents follow instructions correctly, the results approximate interval measures. As in the paired-comparison method, as the number of stimuli increases this technique becomes more complex.

Preference may be measured by using this technique in a manner similar to the paired comparison method. Organizational researchers who utilize this technique refer to it as the *cafeteria reward system*. For example:

> **Suppose you had $3,000 in benefits per month. How much would you like to allocate to salary, medical insurance, and retirement plan? Divide the $3,000 according to your preference.**
> **Salary** _____
> **Medical insurance** _____
> **Retirement plan** _____

A variant of the constant-sum technique uses physical counters that the respondent is to divide among the items being tested. In an airline study of customer preferences, the following technique could be used:

> **Here is a sheet listing several airlines. Next to the name of each airline is a pocket. Here are ten cards. I would like you to put these cards in the pockets next to the airlines you would prefer to fly on your next trip. Assume that all of the airlines fly to wherever you would choose to travel. You may put as many cards as you want in any pocket, or you may put no cards in any pocket.**

	Cards
American	______
Delta	______
United	______
Southwest	______
Northwest	______

Stapel Scale

Stapel scale
An attitude measure that places a single adjective in the center of an even number of numerical values.

The **Stapel scale** was originally developed in the 1950s to measure the direction and intensity of an attitude simultaneously. Modern versions of the scale use a single adjective as a substitute for the semantic differential when it is difficult to create pairs of bipolar adjectives. The modified Stapel scale places a single adjective in the center of an even number of numerical values (for example, ranging from +3 to −3).[13] It measures how close to or how distant from the adjective a given stimulus is perceived to be. Exhibit 14.5 illustrates a Stapel scale item used in a measurement of attitudes toward a supervisor.

The advantages and disadvantages of the Stapel scale are very similar to those of the semantic differential. However, the Stapel scale is markedly easier to administer, especially over the telephone.[14] Because the Stapel scale does not require bipolar adjectives, as does the semantic differential, the Stapel scale is easier to construct.[15] Research comparing the semantic differential with the Stapel scale indicates that results from the two techniques are largely the same.[16]

Exhibit 14.5 | **A Stapel Scale to Measure Attitudes Toward a Supervisor**[17]

Supervisor's Name

+3
+2
+1
Supportive
−1
−2
−3

Select a *plus* number for words that you think describe the supervisor accurately. The more accurately you think the word describes the supervisor, the larger *plus* number you should choose. Select a *minus* number for words you think do not describe the supervisor accurately. The less accurately you think a word describes the supervisor, the larger the *minus* number you should choose. Therefore, you can select any number from plus 3, for words that you think are very accurate, all the way to minus 3, for words that you think are very inaccurate.

EXHIBIT 14.6	**GRAPHIC RATING SCALE**

Please evaluate each attribute in terms of how important it is to you by placing an "X" at the position on the horizontal line that most reflects your feelings.

Seating comfort	Not Important	________________	Very Important
In-flight meals	Not Important	________________	Very Important
Air fare	Not Important	________________	Very Important

Graphic Rating Scales

graphic rating scale
A measure of attitude consisting of a graphic continuum that allows respondents to rate an object by choosing any point on the continuum.

A **graphic rating scale** presents respondents with a graphic continuum. The respondents are allowed to choose any point on the continuum to indicate their attitudes. Exhibit 14.6 shows a traditional graphic scale, ranging from one extreme position to the opposite position. Typically, a respondent's score is determined by measuring the length (in millimeters) from one end of the graphic continuum to the point marked by the respondent. Many researchers believe scoring in this manner strengthens the assumption that graphic rating scales of this type are interval scales. Alternatively, the researcher may divide the line into predetermined scoring categories (lengths) and record respondents' marks accordingly. In other words, the graphic rating scale has the advantage of allowing the researchers to choose any interval they wish for purposes of scoring. The disadvantage of the graphic rating scale is that there are no standard answers.

Graphic rating scales are not limited to straight lines as sources of visual communication. Picture response options or another type of graphic continuum may be used to enhance communication with respondents. A frequently used variation is the ladder scale, which also includes numerical options:

> **Here is a ladder scale. [Respondent is shown Exhibit 14.7.] It represents the "ladder of life." As you see, it is a ladder with 11 rungs numbered 0 to 10. Let's suppose the top of the ladder represents the best possible life for you as you describe it, and the bottom rung represents the worst possible life for you as you describe it.**
>
> **On which rung of the ladder do you feel your life is today?**
>
> **0 1 2 3 4 5 6 7 8 9 10**

Research investigating children's attitudes has utilized "happy face" scales (see Exhibit 14.8). With the "happy face" scale, children are asked to indicate which face shows how they feel about candy, a toy, or some other concept. Research with the "happy face" scale indicates that children are prone to choose the faces at the ends of the scale. Although this may be because children's attitudes fluctuate more widely than those of adults or because they have stronger feelings both positively and negatively, the tendency to select the extremes is a disadvantage of the scale.

Thurstone Equal-Appearing Interval Scale

In 1927, Louis Thurstone, an early pioneer in attitude research, developed the concept that attitudes vary along continua and should be measured accordingly. Construction of a Thurstone scale is a rather complex process that

EXHIBIT 14.7 | **A LADDER SCALE**

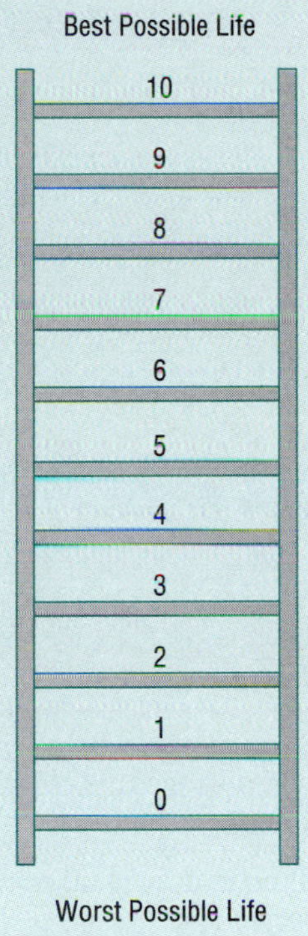

Best Possible Life

10

9

8

7

6

5

4

3

2

1

0

Worst Possible Life

requires two stages. The first stage is a ranking operation, performed by judges, who assign scale values to attitudinal statements. The second stage consists of asking subjects to respond to the attitudinal statements.

The Thurstone method is time-consuming and costly. From a historical perspective it is valuable, but its current popularity is low. Because it is rarely utilized in most applied business research, it will not be discussed further here.

EXHIBIT 14.8 | **GRAPHIC RATING SCALE STRESSING VISUAL COMMUNICATION**

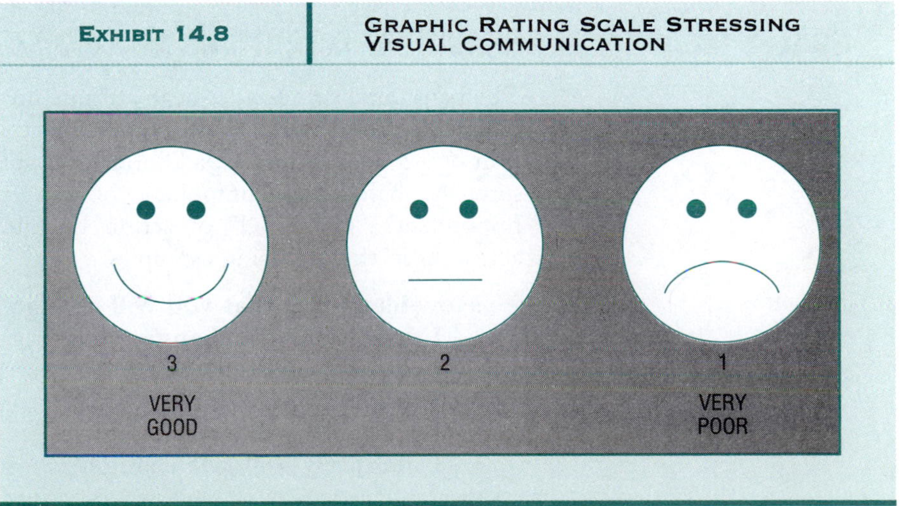

EXHIBIT 14.9 SUMMARY OF THE ADVANTAGES AND DISADVANTAGES OF RATING SCALES

Rating Measure	Subject Must	Advantages	Disadvantages
Category scale	Indicate response category	Flexible, easy to respond to	Items may be ambiguous; with few categories, only gross distinctions can be made
Likert scale	Evaluate statements on a scale that typically contains five alternatives	Easiest scale to construct	Hard to judge what a single score means
Semantic differential and numerical scales	Choose points between bipolar adjectives on relevant dimensions	Easy to construct; norms exist for comparison	Bipolar adjectives must be found; data may be ordinal, not interval
Constant-sum scale	Divide a constant sum among response alternatives	Approximates interval measure	Difficult for respondents with low education levels
Stapel scale	Choose points on a scale with a single adjective in center	Easier to construct than semantic differential, easy to administer	Endpoints are numerical, not verbal, labels
Graphic scale	Choose a point on a continuum	Visual impact, unlimited scale points	No standard answers
Graphic scale with picture response categories	Choose a visual picture	Visual impact	Hard to attach verbal explanation to response

Exhibit 14.9 is a summary of the attitude-rating techniques discussed in this section.

SCALES MEASURING BEHAVIORAL INTENTIONS AND EXPECTATIONS

The behavioral component of an attitude involves the behavioral expectations of an individual toward an attitudinal object. Typically, this represents an intention or a tendency to seek additional information. Category scales that measure the behavioral component of an attitude attempt to determine a respondent's "likelihood" of action or intention to perform some future action, as in the following examples:

How likely is it that you will change jobs in the next six months?
- ☐ **I definitely will change.**
- ☐ **I probably will change.**
- ☐ **I might change.**
- ☐ **I probably will not change.**
- ☐ **I definitely will not change.**

I would write a letter to my congressman or other government official in support of this company if it were in a dispute with government.

☐ **Extremely likely**
☐ **Very likely**
☐ **Somewhat likely**
☐ **Likely, about 50-50 chance**
☐ **Somewhat unlikely**
☐ **Very unlikely**
☐ **Extremely unlikely**

The wording of statements used in these scales often include phrases such as "I would recommend," "I would write," or "I would buy" to indicate action tendencies.

The U.S. Bureau of the Census has used a scale of subjective probabilities, ranging from 100 for absolutely certain to 0 for absolutely no chance, to measure expectations. Management researchers have altered this scale and have used the following subjective probability scale to estimate the chance of job candidates accepting a position:

____ **100% (Absolutely certain) I will accept**
____ **90% (Almost sure) I will accept**
____ **80% (Very big chance) I will accept**
____ **70% (Big chance) I will accept**
____ **60% (Not so big a chance) I will accept**
____ **50% (About even) I will accept**
____ **40% (Smaller chance) I will accept**
____ **30% (Small chance) I will accept**
____ **20% (Very small chance) I will accept**
____ **10% (Almost certainly not) I will accept**
____ **0% (Certainly not) I will accept**

Behavioral Differential

behavioral differential
An instrument developed to measure the behavioral intentions of subjects toward an object or category of objects.

A general instrument, the **behavioral differential**, has been developed to measure the behavioral intentions of subjects toward an object or category of objects. As in the semantic differential, a description of the object to be judged is placed on the top of a sheet, and the subjects indicate their behavioral intentions toward this object on a series of scales. For example, one item might be

A 25-Year-Old Female Commodity Broker
Would ___ : ___ : ___ : ___ : ___ : ___ : ___ : ___ : ___ Would Not
Ask This Person for Advice

RANKING

People often rank order their preferences. An ordinal scale may be developed by asking respondents to rank order (from most preferred to least preferred) a set of objects or attributes. It is not difficult for respondents to understand the task of rank ordering the importance of fringe benefits or arranging a set of job tasks according to preference.

Paired Comparisons

Some time ago a chain-saw manufacturer learned that the competition had introduced a new, lightweight (6½-pound) chain saw. The company's lightest chain saw weighed 9½ pounds. Executives wondered if they needed to introduce a 6-pound chain saw into the product line. The research design was a **paired comparison.** A 6-pound chain saw was designed and a prototype built. To control for color preferences, the competitor's chain saw was painted the same color as the 9½-pound and 6-pound chain saws. Respondents were presented with two chain saws at a time and then asked to pick the one they preferred. Three pairs of comparisons were required to determine the most preferred chain saw.

paired comparison
A measurement technique that involves presenting the respondent with two objects and asking the respondent to pick the preferred object. More than two objects may be presented, but comparisons are made in pairs.

The following question is the typical format for asking about paired comparisons.

I would like to know your overall opinion of two brands of adhesive bandages. They are Curad brand and Band-Aid brand. Overall, which of these two brands—Curad or Band-Aid—do you think is the better one? Or are both the same?
Curad is better ____
Band-Aid is better ____
They are the same ____

If researchers wish to compare four brands of pens on the basis of attractiveness or writing quality, six comparisons $[(n)(n-1)/2]$ are necessary.

Ranking objects with respect to one attribute is not difficult if only a few concepts or items are compared. As the number of items increases, the number of comparisons increases geometrically. If the number of comparisons is too great, respondents may become fatigued and no longer carefully discriminate among them.

SORTING

Sorting tasks require that respondents indicate their attitudes or beliefs by arranging items. Exhibit 14.10 illustrates four cards from a deck of 52 cards used with Bruskin Associates' AIM (Association-Identification-Measurement) technique. Each card reflects an element from advertising for the product being studied, and this omnibus service measures how well customers associate and identify these elements with a particular product, company, or advertising campaign. The following (condensed) interviewer instructions illustrate how sorting is utilized in the AIM survey:

Thoroughly shuffle deck.
Hand respondent deck.
Ask respondent to sort cards into two piles:
Definitely Not Seen or Heard.
Definitely or Possibly Seen or Heard.
Set aside *Definitely Not Seen or Heard* pile.
Hand respondent the *Definitely or Possibly Seen or Heard* pile.
Have respondent identify the item on each card in the *Definitely or Possibly Seen or Heard* pile.
Record on questionnaire.

EXHIBIT 14.10 | **BRUSKIN ASSOCIATES—AIM SYNDICATED SERVICE**[18]

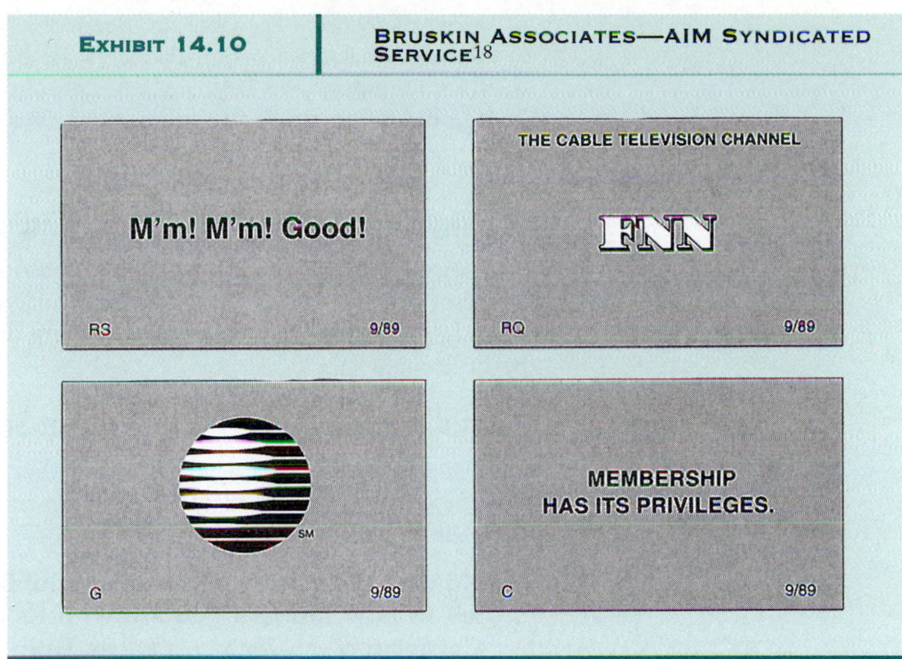

OTHER METHODS OF ATTITUDE MEASUREMENT

Attitudes, as hypothetical constructs, cannot be measured directly. Therefore, measurement of attitudes is, to an extent, subject to the imagination of the researcher. The traditional methods used for attitude measurement have been presented here, but there are several other techniques in the published literature (e.g., the Guttman scale) that can be utilized when a situation dictates. Advanced students will seek out these techniques when the traditional measures do not apply to the investigator's problem. With the growth of computer technology, techniques such as *multidimensional scaling* and *conjoint analysis* are used more frequently. These are complex techniques that require a knowledge of multivariate statistical analysis (see Chapter 24).

SELECTING A MEASUREMENT SCALE: SOME PRACTICAL DECISIONS

Now that we have looked at a number of attitude measurement scales, a natural question arises: "Which is most appropriate?" As in the selection of a basic research design, there is no single best answer that applies to all research projects. The answer to this question is relative, and the choice of scale will be a function of the nature of the attitudinal object to be measured, the manager's problem definition, and the backward and forward linkages to other choices that have already been made (e.g., telephone survey versus mail survey). However, there are several issues that will be helpful to consider when making decisions about the choice of a measurement scale:

1. Is a ranking, sorting, rating, or choice technique best?
2. Should a monadic or a comparative scale be used?
3. What type of category labels, if any, should be used?

4. How many scale positions are needed?
5. Should a balanced or unbalanced scale be chosen?
6. Should respondents be given a forced-choice or a nonforced-choice scale?
7. Should a single measure or an index measure be used?

We will discuss each of these issues.

Is a Ranking, Sorting, Rating, or Choice Technique Best?

The answer to this question is largely determined by the problem definition and especially by the type of statistical analysis that is desired. For example, ranking provides only ordinal data, limiting the statistical techniques that may be utilized.

Should a Monadic or a Comparative Scale Be Used?

If a scale to be used is not a ratio scale, the researcher must make a decision whether to use a standard of comparison in the verbal portion of the scale. Consider the following rating scale:

Now that you've had your automobile for about one year, please tell us how satisfied you are with its engine power and pickup?

Completely Satisfied	Very Satisfied	Fairly Well Satisfied	Somewhat Dissatisfied	Very Dissatisfied

monadic rating scale
Any measure of attitudes that asks respondents about a single concept in isolation.

comparative rating scale
Any measure of attitudes that asks respondents to rate a concept in comparison with a benchmark explicitly used as a frame of reference.

This is a **monadic rating scale,** because it asks about a single concept (the brand of automobile the individual actually purchased) in isolation. The respondent is not given a specific frame of reference. A **comparative rating scale** asks a respondent to rate a concept, such as a specific brand, in comparison with a benchmark—perhaps another similar concept such as a competitive brand—explicitly used as a frame of reference. In many cases the comparative rating scale presents "the ideal situation" as a reference point for comparison with the actual situation. For example:

Please indicate how the amount of authority in your present position compares with the amount of authority that would be ideal for this position.

Too Much	About Right	Too Little

What Type of Category Label, If Any, Will Be Used for the Rating Scale?

We have discussed verbal labels, numerical labels, and unlisted choices. Many rating scales have verbal labels for response categories because researchers believe that these help respondents better understand the response positions. The maturity and educational level of the respondents will influence this decision. The semantic differential, with unlabeled response categories between two bipolar adjectives, and the numerical scale, with numbers to indicate scale positions, are often selected because the researcher wishes to assume interval-scale data.

How Many Scale Categories or Response Positions Are Needed?

Should a category scale have four, five, or seven response positions or categories? Should the researcher utilize a graphic scale that has an infinite number of positions? The original developmental research on the semantic differential indicated that five to eight points were optimal. However, the researcher must determine the number of meaningful positions that is best for the specific project. This issue of identifying how many meaningful distinctions respondents can practically make is basically a matter of sensitivity, but at the operational level rather than the conceptual level.

Should a Balanced or Unbalanced Rating Scale Be Chosen?

balanced rating scale
A fixed-alternative rating scale that has an equal number of positive and negative categories; a neutral or indifference point is at the center of the scale.

The fixed-alternative format may be balanced or unbalanced. For example, the following question, which asks about parent-child decisions relating to television program watching, is a **balanced rating scale:**

Who decides which television programs your children watch?
Child decides all of the time.
Child decides most of the time.
Child and parent decide together.
Parent decides most of the time.
Parent decides all of the time.

unbalanced rating scale
A fixed-alternative rating scale that has more response categories piled up at one end of the scale and an unequal number of positive and negative categories.

This scale is balanced because a neutral point, or point of indifference, is at the center of the scale. In some cases **unbalanced rating scales** are utilized when responses are expected to be distributed at one end of the scale. Unbalanced scales, such as the one below, may eliminate this type of "end piling."

Satisfied
Neither satisfied nor dissatisfied
Quite dissatisfied
Very dissatisfied

The nature of the concept or the researcher's knowledge about attitudes toward the stimulus to be measured generally will determine the choice of a balanced or unbalanced scale.

Should Respondents Be Given a Forced-Choice or a Non-Forced-Choice Scale?

TO THE POINT

Refusing to have an opinion is a way of having one, isn't it?
LUIGI PIRANDELLO

In many situations a respondent has not formed an attitude toward a concept and simply cannot provide an answer. If the respondent is forced to answer, the answer is merely a function of the question. If answers are not forced, the midpoint of the scale may be used by the respondent to indicate unawareness as well as indifference. If many respondents in the sample are expected to be unaware of the attitudinal object under investigation, this problem may be eliminated by utilizing a non-forced-choice scale that provides a "no opinion" category. For example:

How does the Bank of Commerce compare with the First National Bank?
Bank of Commerce is better than First National Bank.
Bank of Commerce is about the same as First National Bank.
Bank of Commerce is worse than First National Bank.
Can't say.

forced-choice scale
A fixed-alternative rating scale that requires respondents to choose one of the fixed alternatives.

Asking this type of question allows the investigator to separate respondents who cannot make an honest comparison from respondents who have had experience with both banks. The argument for **forced-choice scales** is that people really do have attitudes, even if they are unfamiliar with a bank, and they should be required to answer the question. Higher incidences of "no answer" are associated with forced-choice questions.

Should a Single Measure or an Index Measure Be Used?

How complex is the issue to be investigated? How many dimensions are there to the issue? Are individual attributes of the stimulus part of a holistic attitude or are they seen as separate items? The researcher's conceptual definition will be helpful in making this choice.

The researcher has many scaling options. The choice is generally influenced by what is planned for the later stages of the research project. Again, problem definition becomes a determining factor influencing the research design.

SUMMARY

Attitude measurement is particularly important in behavioral research. Attitudes are enduring dispositions to respond consistently, in a given manner, to various aspects of the world, including persons, events, and objects. Three components of attitudes are the affective (emotions or feelings involved), the cognitive (awareness or knowledge), and the behavioral (predisposition to action). Attitudes are hypothetical constructs; that is, they are variables that are not directly observable but must be measured indirectly.

Many methods have been developed to measure attitudes, including ranking, rating, sorting, and choice techniques.

One class of rating scales, category scales, provides several response categories to allow respondents to indicate the intensity of their attitudes. The simplest attitude scale calls for a yes/no or agree/disagree response to a single question. The Likert scale uses a series of statements with which subjects indicate agreement or disagreement. The responses are assigned weights that are summed to indicate the respondents' attitudes.

The semantic differential uses a series of attitude scales anchored by bipolar adjectives. The respondent indicates where his or her attitude falls on the scale between the polar attitudes. Variations on this method, such as numerical scales and the Stapel scale, are also used. The Stapel scale puts a single adjective in the center of numerical values that range from +3 to −3.

Graphic rating scales use continua on which respondents indicate the positions of their attitudes. Constant-sum scales require respondents to divide a constant sum into parts, indicating the weights to be given to various attributes of the item being studied.

Several scales, such as the behavioral differential, have been developed to measure the behavioral component of an attitude.

People often rank order their preferences. Thus, ordinal scales may be developed that ask respondents to rank order a set of objects or attributes. In the paired-comparison technique, two alternatives are paired and respondents are asked to pick the preferred one. Sorting requires respondents to indicate their attitudes by arranging items into piles or categories.

The business researcher can choose from a number of attitude scales. Making a decision among the alternatives requires that the researcher consider several questions, each of which is generally answered by comparing the advantages of each alternative to the problem definition.

A monadic rating scale asks about a single concept. A comparative rating scale asks a respondent to rate a concept in comparison with a benchmark used as a frame of reference.

Scales may be balanced or unbalanced. Unbalanced scales are used to prevent responses from piling up at one end of the scale. Forced-choice scales require the respondent to select an alternative, whereas non-forced-choice scales allow a respondent to indicate inability to select an alternative.

Key Terms

attitude
affective component
cognitive component
behavioral component
hypothetical construct
ranking
rating
sorting technique
choice technique
category scale
Likert scale
semantic differential
numerical scale
constant-sum scale
Stapel scale
graphic rating scale
behavioral differential
paired comparison
monadic rating scale
comparative rating scale
balanced rating scale
unbalanced rating scale
forced-choice scale

Questions for Review and Critical Thinking

1. What is an attitude? Is there consensus concerning its definition?
2. Distinguish between rating and ranking. Which is a better attitude measurement? Why?
3. In what type of situation would the choice technique be most appropriate?
4. In what type of situation would the sorting technique be most appropriate?
5. What advantages do numerical scales have over semantic differential scales?
6. Identify the issues a researcher should consider when making a decision about the choice of a measurement scale.
7. Name some situations in which a semantic differential might be useful.
8. Should a Likert scale ever be treated as if it had ordinal properties?
9. In each of the following indicate the type of scale and evaluate it:
   (a) A U.S. congressman's questionnaire to constituents:
   Do you favor or oppose a Constitutional amendment to balance the budget?
   Favor ☐ Oppose ☐ Don't know ☐
   (b) An academic study on consumer behavior:
   Most people who are important to me think I
   −3 ________________________________ +3
   definitely should not buy — definitely should buy
   (test brand) some time during the next week.
   (c) Psychographic statement:
   I shop a lot for specials.

Strongly Agree	Moderately Agree	Neutral	Moderately Disagree	Strongly Disagree
5	4	3	2	1

   (d) Please distribute 100 points.
   ____ (A) The organization is a very **personal** place. It is like an extended family. People seem to share a lot of themselves.
   ____ (B) The organization is a very **dynamic and entrepreneurial** place. People are willing to stick their necks out and take risks.
   ____ (C) The organization is a very **formalized and structured** place. Bureaucratic procedures generally govern what people do.
   ____ (D) The organization is very **production oriented.** The major concern is with getting the job done. People aren't very personally involved.
   100
   (e) The list below shows a variety of pollutants that can affect the quality of your indoor air. Please indicate which pollutant you are most concerned about affecting the quality of your indoor air by giving this a rank of 1. Please indicate which pollutant you are second most concerned about by giving this a rank of 2, and the one you are third most concerned about by giving a rank of 3. Please rank all pollutants below with a number from 1 to 7.
   ___Animal dander
   ___Dust
   ___Dust mites
   ___Mold spores
   ___Odors
   ___Pollen
   ___Smoke

10. What problems might be involved in attempting to utilize attitude measures to predict specific behavior?
11. If a Likert summated scale has ten scale items, do all ten items have to be phrased as either positive or negative statements, or can both positive and negative statements be used?
12. If a semantic differential has ten scale items, should all the positive adjectives be on the right and all the negative adjectives on the left?
13. A researcher wishes to compare two hotels on the following attributes: convenience of location, friendly personnel, and value for money.
    (a) Design a Likert scale to accomplish this task.
    (b) Design a semantic differential to accomplish this task.
    (c) Design a graphic rating scale to accomplish this task.
14. A researcher has just changed jobs. He kept photocopies of several research reports from his prior employer. One report contains a copyrighted attitude scale that was designed by a consulting company. The researcher finds that this attitude scale could be used on his current project. Should the researcher go ahead and use the attitude scale without hiring the consulting company?

Exploring the Internet

SRI International investigates American consumers by asking questions about their attitudes and values. The company has a Web site so people can VALS-type themselves. To find out your VALS type, go to http://future.sri.com and click on VALS.

WebSurveyor Activities

webSURVEYOR™

Three academic researchers investigated the idea that, in America in sports, there are two segments with opposing views on what constitutes the goal of competition (i.e., winning versus self-actualization) and the acceptable/desirable way of achieving this goal.[19] Persons who believe in "winning at any cost" are proponents of sports success as a product and can be labeled "new school" (NS) individuals. The new school is founded on notions of the player before the team, loyalty to the highest bidder, and high-tech production and consumption of professional sports. On the other hand, persons who value the process of sports and believe that "how you play the game matters" can be labeled "old school" (OS) individuals. The old school emerges from old-fashioned American notions of the team before the player, sportsmanship and loyalty above all else, and competition simply for "love of the game."

The following quotes hint at the difference between new school and old school ideologies:

> "For when the one Great Scorer comes
> To write against your name,
> He marks—not that you won or lost—
> But how you played the game."
> —Grantland Rice, sports commentator

> "Winning isn't everything, it's the only thing,"
> —Vince Lombardi, NFL Hall of Fame coach

> "Serious sport has nothing to do with fair play. It is bound up with hatred, jealousy, boastfulness, disregard of all rules and sadistic pleasure in witnessing violence. In other words, it is war minus the shooting."
> —George Orwell, English novelist and critic

The researcher investigated 17 attitude statements about sports to measure if fans were new school or old school fans. A copy of the survey can be found at http://zikmund.swcollege.com.

Open the survey using the WebSurveyor Desktop software by selecting File, and then Open from the main menu, and select the file named "sports.ws3" from your computer's CD ROM drive.

- Are the attitude measures rating or ranking scales?
- Do the 17 statements seem to adequately measure the concept of *old schoolness*?

The researcher wants old schoolness represented by a low score (1 being the lowest on a single item) and new schoolness represented by a high score (9 being the highest on a single item). Evaluate the first four questions in the survey. Which, if any, should be reverse coded?

Case Suggestion

Case 17: Flyaway Airways

CHAPTER

15

QUESTIONNAIRE DESIGN

What you will learn in this chapter

- To recognize that questionnaire design is not a simple task and that proper wording of relevant questions can contribute immensely to improving the accuracy of surveys.
- To recognize that the type of information needed to answer a manager's questions will substantially influence the structure and content of questionnaires.
- To recognize that decisions about the data collection method (mail, Internet, telephone, or personal interview) will influence question format and questionnaire layout.
- To recognize the difference between open-ended response questions and fixed-alternative questions.
- To understand the guidelines that help to prevent the most common mistakes in questionnaire design.
- To discuss how decisions about the sequence of questions may improve questionnaires.
- To understand how to plan and design a questionnaire layout.
- To understand the importance of pretesting and revising questionnaires.

Results of an early Gallup Poll illustrate that the answer to a question is frequently a function of the question's wording.[1] "People were asked if they owned any stock. A surprisingly high degree of stock ownership turned up in interviews in the Southwest, where respondents were naturally thinking of livestock. The question had to be reworded to make reference to 'securities listed on any stock exchange.' "

Many experts in survey research believe that improving the wording of questions can contribute far more to accuracy than can improvements in sampling. Experiments have shown that the range of error due to vague questions or use of imprecise words may be as high as 20 or 30 percent. Consider the following example, which illustrates the critical importance of selecting the word with the right meaning. The following questions differ only in the use of the words *should, could,* and *might:*

- Do you think anything *should* be done to make it easier for people to pay doctor or hospital bills?
- Do you think anything *could* be done to make it easier for people to pay doctor or hospital bills?
- Do you think anything *might* be done to make it easier for people to pay doctor or hospital bills?[2]

The results from the matched samples: 82 percent replied something *should* be done, 77 percent replied something *could* be done, and 63 percent replied something *might* be done. Thus, a 19 percent difference occurred between the two extremes, *should* and *might.* Ironically, this is the same percentage point error as in the *Literary Digest* Poll, which is a frequently cited example of error associated with sampling. ■

This chapter outlines a procedure for questionnaire design and illustrates that a little bit of research knowledge can be a dangerous thing.

A SURVEY IS ONLY AS GOOD AS THE QUESTIONS IT ASKS

Each stage of the business research process is important because of its interdependence with other stages of the process. However, a survey is only as good as the questions it asks. The importance of wording questions is easily overlooked, but questionnaire design is one of the most critical stages in the survey research process.

"A good questionnaire appears as easy to compose as does a good poem. The end product should look as if effortlessly written by an inspired child—but it is usually the result of long, painstaking work."[3] Business people who are inexperienced in business research frequently believe that constructing a questionnaire is a simple task. Amateur researchers find it easy to prepare a short questionnaire in a matter of hours. Unfortunately, newcomers who naively believe that common sense and good grammar are all that are needed to construct a questionnaire generally learn that their hasty efforts are inadequate.

While common sense and good grammar are important in question writing, more is required in the art of questionnaire design. To assume that people will understand the questions is a common error. People simply may not know what is being asked. They may be unaware of the product or topic of interest, they may confuse the subject with something else, or the question may not mean the same thing to everyone interviewed. Respondents may refuse to answer personal questions. Further, properly wording the questionnaire is crucial, as some problems may be minimized or avoided altogether if a skilled researcher composes the questions.

How often misused words generate misleading thoughts.

HERBERT SPENCER

QUESTIONNAIRE DESIGN: AN OVERVIEW OF THE MAJOR DECISIONS

Relevance and *accuracy* are the two basic criteria a questionnaire must meet if it is to achieve the researcher's purposes.[4] To achieve these ends, a researcher who systematically plans a questionnaire's design will be required to make several decisions—typically, but not necessarily, in the order listed below:

1. What should be asked?
2. How should each question be phrased?
3. In what sequence should the questions be arranged?
4. What questionnaire layout will best serve the research objectives?
5. How should the questionnaire be pretested? Does the questionnaire need to be revised?

WHAT SHOULD BE ASKED?

During the early stages of the research process, certain decisions will have been made that will influence the questionnaire design. The preceding chapters stressed the need to have a good problem definition and clear objectives for the study. The problem definition will indicate which type of information must be collected to answer the manager's questions; different types of questions may be better at obtaining certain types of information than others. Further, the communication medium used for data collection—telephone interview, personal interview, or self-administered survey—will have been determined. This decision is another forward linkage that influences the structure and content of the questionnaire. The specific questions to be asked will be a function of the previous decisions. Later stages of the research process also have an important impact on questionnaire wording. For example, determination of the questions that should be asked will be influenced by the requirements for data analysis. As the questionnaire is being designed, the researcher should be thinking about the types of statistical analysis that will be conducted.

Questionnaire Relevancy

A questionnaire is *relevant* if no unnecessary information is collected and if the information that is needed to solve the business problem is obtained.

Asking the wrong or an irrelevant question is a pitfall to be avoided. If the task is to pinpoint compensation problems, for example, questions asking for general information about morale may be inappropriate. To ensure information relevancy, the researcher must be specific about data needs, and there should be a rationale for each item of information.

After conducting surveys, many disappointed researchers have discovered that some important questions were omitted. Thus, when planning the questionnaire design, it is essential to think about possible omissions. Is information being collected on the relevant demographic and psychographic variables? Are there any questions that might clarify the answers to other questions? Will the results of the study provide the solution to the manager's problem?

Questionnaire Accuracy

Once the researcher has decided what should be asked, the criterion of accuracy becomes the primary concern.

Accuracy means that the information is reliable and valid. While experienced researchers generally believe that one should use simple, understandable, unbiased, unambiguous, nonirritating words, no step-by-step procedure to ensure accuracy in question writing can be generalized across projects. Obtaining accurate answers from respondents is strongly influenced by the researcher's ability to design a questionnaire that facilitates recall and that will motivate the respondent to cooperate.

Respondents tend to be most cooperative when the subject of the research is interesting. Also, if questions are not lengthy, difficult to answer, or ego-threatening, there is a higher probability of obtaining unbiased answers. Question wording and sequence substantially influence accuracy. These topics are treated in subsequent sections of this chapter.

PHRASING QUESTIONS

There are many ways to phrase questions, and many standard question formats have been developed in previous research studies. This section presents a classification of question types and provides some helpful guidelines to researchers who must write questions.

Open-Ended Response versus Fixed-Alternative Questions

open-ended response question
A question that poses some problem and asks the respondent to answer in his or her own words.

Questions may be categorized as either of two basic types, according to the amount of freedom respondents are given in answering them. **Open-ended response questions** pose some problem or topic and ask the respondent to answer in his or her own words. For example:

What things do you like most about your job?
What names of local banks can you think of offhand?
What comes to mind when you look at this advertisement?
Do you think that there are some ways in which life in the United States is getting worse? How is that?

fixed-alternative question
A question in which the respondent is given specific limited-alternative responses and asked to choose the one closest to his or her own viewpoint.

If the question is asked in a personal interview, the interviewer may probe for more information by asking such questions as: Anything else? or Could you tell me more about your thinking on that? Open-ended response questions are free-answer questions. They may be contrasted to the **fixed-alternative question,** sometimes called a "closed question," in which the respondent is given specific, limited-alternative responses and asked to choose the one closest to his or her own viewpoint. For example:

Did you work overtime or at more than one job last week?
Yes ____ No ____

Compared to ten years ago, would you say that the quality of most products made in Japan is higher, about the same, or not as good?
Higher ____ About the same ____ Not as good ____

How much of your shopping for clothes and household items do you do in warehouse club stores? Would you say:
All of it ____
Most of it ____
About half of it ____
About one-quarter of it ____
Less than one-quarter of it ____

In management, is there a useful distinction between what is legal and what is ethical?
Yes ____ No ____

In Aesop's fable "The Ant and the Grasshopper," the ant spent his time working and planning for the future, while the grasshopper lived for the moment and enjoyed himself. Which are you more like?
1. The ant
2. The grasshopper

Open-ended response questions are most beneficial when the researcher is conducting exploratory research, especially if the range of responses is not known. Open-ended questions can be used to learn what words and phrases people spontaneously give to the free-response questions. Respondents are free to answer with whatever is uppermost in their thinking. By gaining free and uninhibited responses, a researcher may find some unanticipated reaction toward the topic. As the responses have the "flavor" of the conversational language that people use in talking about products or jobs, responses to these questions may be a source for effective communication.

Open-ended response questions are especially valuable at the beginning of an interview. They are good first questions because they allow respondents to warm up to the questioning process.

The cost of open-ended response questions is substantially greater than that of fixed-alternative questions, because the job of coding, editing, and analyzing the data is quite extensive. As each respondent's answer is somewhat unique, there is some difficulty in categorizing and summarizing the answers. The process requires an editor to go over a sample of questions to classify the responses into some sort of scheme; then all the answers are reviewed and coded according to the classification scheme.

Another potential disadvantage of the open-ended response question is that interviewer bias may influence the responses. While most instructions state that the interviewer is to record answers verbatim, rarely can even the best interviewer get every word spoken by the respondent. There is a tendency for interviewers to take short cuts in recording answers—but changing even a few of the respondents' words may substantially influence the results. Thus, the final answer often is a combination of the respondent's and the interviewer's ideas rather than the respondent's ideas alone.

Articulate individuals tend to give longer answers to open-ended response questions. These articulate respondents often are better educated and in higher income groups, and thus may not be representative of the entire population, and yet they may give a large share of the responses.

In contrast to open-ended questions, fixed-alternative questions require less interviewer skill, take less time, and are easier for the respondent to answer. This occurs because closed questions require classification of the answer into standardized groupings prior to data collection. Standardizing alternative responses to a question provides comparability of answers, which facilitates coding, tabulating, and, ultimately, interpreting the data.

Earlier in the chapter a variety of fixed-alternative questions were presented. We will now identify and categorize the various types of fixed-alternative questions.

simple-dichotomy question
A fixed-alternative question that requires the respondent to choose one of two alternatives.

The **simple-dichotomy,** or **dichotomous-alternative, question** requires the respondent to choose one of two alternatives. The answer can be a simple "yes" or "no" or a choice between "this" and "that." For example:

Did you make any long-distance calls last week?
☐ **Yes** ☐ **No**

determinant-choice question
A type of fixed-alternative question that requires a respondent to choose one (and only one) response from among several possible alternatives.

Several types of questions provide the respondent with *multiple-choice alternatives.* The **determinant-choice question** requires the respondent to choose one—and only one—response from among several possible alternatives. For example:

Please give us some information about your flight. In which section of the aircraft did you sit?
☐ **First class** ☐ **Business class** ☐ **Coach class**

frequency-determination question
A type of fixed-alternative question that asks for an answer about general frequency of occurrence.

The **frequency-determination question** is a determinant-choice question that asks for an answer about general frequency of occurrence. For example:

How frequently do you watch the MTV television channel?
Every day . . . . ☐
5–6 times a week . . . . ☐
2–4 times a week . . . . ☐
Once a week . . . . ☐
Less than once a week . . . . ☐
Never . . . . ☐

attitude rating scale
Measures used to rate attitudes, such as the Likert scale, semantic differential, and Stapel scale.

Attitude rating scales, such as the Likert scale, semantic differential, and Stapel scale, are also fixed-alternative questions. These were discussed in Chapter 14.

checklist question
A type of fixed-alternative question that allows the respondent to provide multiple answers to a single question.

The **checklist question** allows the respondent to provide multiple answers to a single question. The respondent indicates past experience, preference, and the like merely by checking off an item. In many cases the choices are adjectives that describe a particular object. A typical checklist follows:

Please check which of the following sources of information about investments you regularly use, if any.
- ☐ **Personal advice of your broker(s)**
- ☐ **Brokerage newsletters**
- ☐ **Brokerage research reports**
- ☐ **Investment advisory service(s)**
- ☐ **Conversations with other investors**
- ☐ **Reports on the Internet**
- ☐ **None of these**
- ☐ **Other (please specify)** ____________________

A major problem in developing dichotomous or multiple-choice alternatives is framing the response alternatives. There should be no overlap among categories. Alternatives should be *mutually exclusive;* that is, only one dimension of the issue should be related to that alternative. The following listing of income groups illustrates a common error:

Under $20,000 ____
$20,000–$35,000 ____
$35,000–$60,000 ____
$60,000–$80,000 ____
Over $80,000 ____

How many people with incomes of $35,000 will be in the second group and how many will be in the third group? There is no way to determine the answer. Grouping alternatives without forethought about analysis may cause loss of accuracy.

It should also be noted that few people relish being in the lowest category. Including a category lower than the answers you expect often helps to negate the potential bias caused by respondents' tendency to avoid an extreme category.

When a researcher is unaware of the potential responses to a question, fixed-alternative questions obviously cannot be used. If the researcher assumes what the responses will be, but is in fact wrong, he or she will have no way of knowing the extent to which the assumption was incorrect.

Unanticipated alternatives emerge when respondents think the closed answers do not adequately reflect their feelings. Comments are made to the interviewer or additional answers are written on the questionnaire, indicating that the exploratory research did not yield a complete array of responses. After the fact, not much can be done to correct a closed question that does not provide enough alternatives; therefore, the time spent conducting exploratory research with open-ended response questions is well worth the effort. The researcher should strive to ensure that there are sufficient response choices to include almost all possible answers.

Respondents may check off obvious alternatives, such as price or durability, if they do not see the choice they would prefer. Also, a fixed-alternative question may tempt respondents to check an answer that is untrue but perhaps more prestigious or socially acceptable than the true answer. Rather than stating they do not know why they chose a given product, they may select an alternative among those presented. As a matter of convenience, they may select a given alternative rather than think of the most correct alternative.

Most questionnaires include a mixture of open-ended and closed questions. Each form has unique benefits; in addition, a change of pace can eliminate respondent boredom and fatigue.

Phrasing Questions for Self-Administered, Telephone, and Personal Interview Surveys

The means of data collection (personal interview, telephone, mail, or Internet questionnaire) will influence the question format and question phrasing. In general, questions for mail and telephone surveys must be less complex than those utilized in personal interviews. Questionnaires for telephone and personal interviews should be written in a conversational style. Exhibit 15.1 illustrates how a question may be revised for a different medium.

Consider the following question from a personal interview:

There has been a lot of discussion about the potential health threat to nonsmokers from tobacco smoke in public buildings, restaurants, and business offices. How serious a health threat to you personally is the inhaling of this secondhand smoke, often called passive smoking: Is it a very serious health threat, somewhat serious, not too serious, or not serious at all?

1. **Very serious**
2. **Somewhat serious**
3. **Not too serious**
4. **Not serious at all**
5. **(Don't know)**

Exhibit 15.1 | **Reducing Question Complexity by Providing Fewer Responses**[5]

Mail Form:

How satisfied are you with your community?

1. Very satisfied
2. Quite satisfied
3. Somewhat satisfied
4. Slightly satisfied
5. Neither satisfied nor dissatisfied
6. Slightly dissatisfied
7. Somewhat dissatisfied
8. Quite dissatisfied
9. Very dissatisfied

Revised for Telephone:

How satisfied are you with your community? Would you say you are very satisfied, somewhat satisfied, neither satisfied nor dissatisfied, somewhat dissatisfied, or very dissatisfied?

Very satisfied 1
Somewhat satisfied 2
Neither satisfied nor dissatisfied . . .3
Somewhat dissatisfied 4
Very dissatisfied 5

You probably noticed that the last portion of the question was a listing of the four alternatives that serve as answers. This listing at the end is often used in interviews to remind the respondent of alternatives, because the choices are not presented visually. The fifth alternative (Don't know) is in parentheses because, although the interviewer knows it is an acceptable answer, it is not read because the researcher prefers to "force" the respondent to choose from among the four listed alternatives.

The data collection technique also influences the layout of the questionnaire. Layout will be discussed in a later section of this chapter.

THE ART OF ASKING QUESTIONS

In developing a questionnaire, there are no hard-and-fast rules. Fortunately, however, some guidelines that help to prevent the most common mistakes have been developed from research experience.

Avoid Complexity: Use Simple, Conversational Language

Words used in questionnaires should be readily understandable to all respondents. The researcher usually has the difficult task of adopting the conversational language of people from the lower educational levels without talking down to better-educated respondents. Remember, not all people have the vocabulary of a college student. A substantial number of Americans never go beyond high school.

TO THE POINT

I don't know the rules of grammar. . . . If you're trying to persuade people to do something, or buy something, it seems to me you should use their language, the language they use every day, the language in which they think. We try to write in the vernacular.

DAVID OGILVY

Respondents can probably tell an interviewer whether they are married, single, divorced, separated, or widowed, but providing their "marital status" may present a problem. Also, the technical jargon of corporate executives should be avoided when surveying retailers, factory employees, or industrial users. "Marginal analysis," "decision support systems," and other words from the language of the corporate staff will not have the same meaning to—or be understood by—a store owner-operator in a retail survey. The vocabulary in the following question (from an attitude survey on social problems) is probably confusing for many respondents:

When effluents from a paper mill can be drunk and exhaust from factory smokestacks can be breathed, then humankind will have done a good job in saving the environment. . . . Don't you agree that what we want is zero toxicity: no effluents?

This lengthy question is also a leading question.

Avoid Leading and Loaded Questions

leading question
A question that suggests or implies certain answers.

Leading and loaded questions are a major source of bias in question wording. **Leading questions** suggest or imply certain answers. In a study of the dry-cleaning industry, this question was asked:

Many people are using dry cleaning less because of improved wash-and-wear clothes. How do you feel wash-and-wear clothes have affected your use of dry-cleaning facilities in the past 4 years?

____ Use less ____ No change ____ Use more

The potential "bandwagon effect" implied in this question threatens the study's validity.

loaded question
A question that suggests a socially desirable answer or is emotionally charged.

Loaded questions suggest a socially desirable answer or are emotionally charged. Consider the following:

In light of today's farm crisis, it would be in the public's best interest to have the federal government require labeling of imported meat.

___ Strongly Agree ___ Agree ___ Uncertain ___ Disagree ___ Strongly Disagree

Answers might be different if the loaded portion of the statement, "farm crisis," had another wording suggesting a problem of less magnitude than a crisis.

A television station produced the following 10-second spot asking for viewer feedback:

We are happy when you like programs on Channel 7. We are sad when you dislike programs on Channel 7. Write us and let us know what you think of our programming.

Most people do not wish to make others sad. This question is likely to elicit only positive comments.

Some answers to certain questions are more socially desirable than others. For example, a truthful answer to the following classification question might be painful:

Where did you rank academically in your high school graduating class?

Top quarter 2nd quarter 3rd quarter 4th quarter

When taking personality tests, respondents frequently are able to determine which answers are most socially acceptable, even though those answers do not portray their true feelings. For example, which are the socially desirable answers to the following questions on a self-confidence scale?

I feel capable of handling myself in most social situations.

____ Agree ____ Disagree

I seldom fear my actions will cause others to have a low opinion of me.

____ Agree ____ Disagree

Invoking the status quo is a form of loading that results in bias because the majority of respondents tend to be resistant to change.[6]

An experiment conducted in the early days of polling illustrates the unpopularity of change.[7] Comparable samples of respondents were simultaneously asked two questions about the presidential succession. One sample was asked: **"Would you favor or oppose *adding* a law to the Constitution preventing a president from succeeding himself more than once?"** The other sample was asked: **"Would you favor or oppose *changing* the Constitution in order to prevent a president from succeeding himself more than once?"** To the first question, 50 percent of the respondents answered in the negative; to the second question, 65 percent answered in the negative. Thus the public would rather *add to* than *change* the Constitution.

Partial mention of alternatives is another form of loading.

Building more nuclear power plants, like Three Mile Island, should not be allowed.

How do you generally spend your free time, watching television or what?[8]

Are you familiar with any companies that currently recycle aluminum, such as Coors?

Asking respondents "how often" they use a product or perform a task leads them to generalize about their behavior, because there usually is some variance in their behavior. One is likely to portray one's *ideal* behavior rather than one's average behavior. For instance, all of us should brush our teeth after every meal, but if a person is busy, a brushing or two may be skipped. An introductory statement, or preamble, to a question that reassures the respondent that his embarrassing behavior is not abnormal may yield truthful responses: **"Some people have the time to brush three times daily; others do not. Would you please tell me how often you brushed your teeth yesterday?"**

The question below asked a sample of college professors to record both actual and ideal amounts of time they spend on professional activities. This approach reduces the tendency to idealize the actual amount of time spent in professional activities.

Please indicate (A) your estimate of the actual percentage of time you spend on professional activities during the academic year, and (B) what you consider to be the ideal division of your time as a university professor.

Percentage of Time		
A—Actual	B—Ideal	
		Formal instruction (including preparation, presentation, grading, etc.)
		Informal instruction, advisement, student counseling
		Scholarly research and writing
		Academic administration
		Part-time professional employment outside the university (e.g., private practice, consulting)
		Professional activities outside the university (e.g., speaking, conferences, professional association duties)
100%	100%	

counterbiasing statement
An introductory statement or preface to a question that reduces a respondent's reluctance to answer potentially embarrassing questions.

split-ballot technique
A technique used to control for response bias. Two alternative phrasings of the same questions are utilized for respective halves of the sample to yield a more accurate total response than would be possible if only a single phrasing were utilized.

If a question embarrasses the respondent, it may elicit no answer or a biased response. This is particularly true with regard to personal and classification data such as income and education. The problem may be mitigated by introducing the section of the questionnaire with a **counterbiasing statement** such as: "To help classify your answers, we'd like to ask you a few questions. Again, your answers will be kept in strict confidence."

A question may be leading because it is phrased to reflect either the negative or positive aspects of the issue. To control for this bias, the wording of attitudinal questions may be reversed for 50 percent of the sample. This **split-ballot technique** is utilized with the expectation that two alternative phrasings of the same question will yield a more accurate total response than would be possible with only a single phrasing. A study of small-car-buying behavior, for example, gave one-half of the sample of imported-car purchasers a questionnaire in which they were asked to agree or disagree with the statement **"Small U.S. cars are cheaper to maintain than small imported cars."** The other half of the imported-car owners received a questionnaire in which the statement read **"Small imported cars are cheaper to maintain than small U.S. cars."**

Avoid Ambiguity: Be as Specific as Possible

Items on questionnaires are often ambiguous because they are too general. Consider indefinite words such as *often, occasionally, usually, regularly, frequently, many, good, fair,* and *poor.* Each of these words has many meanings. For one person, *frequent* reading of *Fortune* magazine may be reading six or seven issues a year; for another it may be two issues a year. The word *fair* has a great variety of meanings; the same is true for many indefinite words.

Questions such as the following should be interpreted with care:

How often do you feel that you can consider all of the alternatives before making a decision to follow a specific course of action?
____ Always ____ Fairly often ____ Occasionally ____ Seldom ____ Never

In addition to utilizing words like *occasionally,* this question asks respondents to generalize about their decision-making behavior. The question is not specific. What does *consider* mean? The respondents may have a tendency to provide stereotyped "good" management responses rather than to describe their actual behavior. People's memories are not perfect. We tend to remember the good and forget the bad.

Another example of an ambiguous question is **"Do you usually work alone?"** It would be less ambiguous if the question were restated to something like

Which of the following best describes your working behavior?
I never work alone.
I work alone less than half the time.
I work alone most of the time.

Similarly, although the following question may be important to the researcher, its wording could confuse respondents: **"How difficult is it for you to get the necessary information about divisional or company objectives or goals for decision making?"** The term *necessary information* is highly subjective. It could be interpreted to mean the *minimum* necessary information or the *optimal* necessary information.

Which of the following is ambiguous?

If something happens that puts your immediate supervisor "on the spot," what is he most likely to do?
Should managers be held personally responsible for the wrongdoings of corporations?

As the reader can tell, question ambiguity is a pervasive problem. It is not easily eliminated.

Some scholars have suggested that the rate of diffusion of an innovation is related to the perception of the innovation's attributes, such as divisibility, which

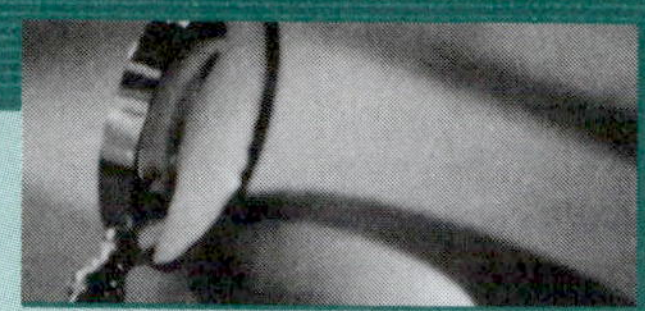

Research Insight

"I Don't Understand the Question"[9]

1. The company should continue its excellent fringe benefit programs.
   a. Yes
   b. No

COMMENT: The fringe benefit programs may not be excellent at all. By answering "yes," the respondent is implying that things are just fine as they are. By answering "no," he implies that the company should discontinue the fringe benefits. Don't place the respondent in that sort of a bind.

BETTER: How satisfied are you with the company's fringe benefit programs?
   a. Very satisfied
   b. Somewhat satisfied
   c. Neither satisfied nor dissatisfied
   d. Somewhat dissatisfied
   e. Very dissatisfied

2. Do you understand and like the company's new hiring policy?
   a. Yes
   b. No

COMMENT: There are really two questions here:
(1) Do you understand the company's new hiring policy?
(2) Do you like it?
The answers to the original question are ambiguous.

BETTER: Do you like the company's new hiring policy?
   a. I don't know what the company policy is.
   b. I don't like it.
   c. I neither like nor dislike it.
   d. I like it.

3. Your supervisor is handling the frequent and serious problems with work quality better now than six months ago.
   a. Strongly disagree
   b. Disagree
   c. Neither agree nor disagree
   d. Agree
   e. Strongly agree

COMMENT: The statement automatically puts respondents in a box, since it assumes that there are frequent, serious problems with their work groups' work quality.

BETTER: Compared with six months ago, how well does your supervisor handle difficult work-related problems?
   a. Much better
   b. Somewhat better
   c. About the same
   d. Somewhat worse
   e. Much worse

4. What makes your job a good one?
   a. The good pay
   b. The opportunity for advancement
   c. A good supervisor
   d. Interesting work

COMMENT: This question assumes that the employee's job is a good one, while the employee may not feel that it is particularly good. There is no provision for selecting one or more than one of the choices. If you really want to find out what the employee likes best about his job, you may want to ask an open-ended question, or you may need to ask a series of questions about different aspects of the job.

BETTER: What do you like best about your job?
   a. The pay
   b. The opportunities for advancement
   c. The working conditions
   d. The people you work with
   e. Your supervisor
   f. The work
   g. The fringe benefits program

refers to the extent to which an innovation may be tried or tested on a limited scale.[10] An empirical attempt to test this theory by using semantic differentials was a disaster. Pretesting found the bipolar adjectives *divisible–not divisible* were impossible for respondents to understand because they did not have the theory in mind as a frame of reference. A revision of the scale used these bipolar adjectives:

Testable (sample use possible) ____ : ____ : ____ : ____ : ____ : ____ : ____ **Not Testable (sample use not possible)**

But the question remained ambiguous because the meaning still was not clear.

A brewing industry study on point-of-purchase displays asked:

What degree of durability do you prefer in your point-of-purchase advertising?
____ Permanent (lasting more than 6 months)
____ Semipermanent (lasting from 1 to 6 months)
____ Temporary (lasting less than 1 month)

Here the researchers clarified the terms *permanent, semipermanent,* and *temporary* by defining them for the respondent. However, the question remains somewhat ambiguous. Beer companies often use a variety of point-of-purchase devices to serve different purposes. Which purpose was the researcher asking about? Furthermore, analysis was difficult because respondents were merely asked to indicate a preference rather than a degree of preference. Thus, the meaning of questions may not be clear because the frame of reference is inadequate for interpreting the context of the question.[11] A student research group asked this question:

What one of these media do you rely on most?
Television ____ Radio ____ Internet ____ Newspapers ____

This question is ambiguous because it does not ask about the content of the media. "Rely on most" for *what*—news, sports, entertainment?

Avoid Double-Barreled Items

double-barreled question
A question that may induce bias because it covers two issues at once.

A question covering several issues at once is referred to as **double-barreled** and should always be avoided. It's easy to make the mistake of asking two questions rather than one. For example, **"Please indicate if you agree or disagree with the following statement: 'I have called in sick or left work to golf.'"** Which reason is it: calling in sick or leaving work (perhaps with permission) to play golf?

When multiple questions are asked in one question, the results may be exceedingly difficult to interpret. For example, consider the following question from a magazine survey entitled "How Do You Feel about Being a Woman?"

Between you and your husband, who does the housework (cleaning, cooking, dishwashing, laundry) over and above that done by any hired help?
I do all of it
I do almost all of it
I do over half of it
We split the work fifty-fifty
My husband does over half of it

The answers to this question do not tell us if the wife cooks and the husband dries the dishes.

Another survey, by a university library, asked:

Research Insight

One or Two Questions?

This study was a part of an ongoing series of "research-on-research" investigations.[12] Its purpose was to establish an accurate means of measuring rate of purchase. Like other such studies, it involved demographically matched samples of households, with each sample receiving a different treatment. Self-administered questionnaires were mailed to female heads of households, and purchase data were obtained for the following products: all-purpose white glue, aspirin, replacement automobile tires, and record albums.

Two different ways of asking the purchase incidence questions were investigated. Alternative A was sent to a sample of 1,000 homes; Alternative B was sent to another sample of 1,000 homes. The samples were closely matched in terms of age, income, geography, and city size. To the right is a sample pair of questions.

The table below lists the percentages of respondents who reported purchasing items in the past 3 months, as revealed by the two forms of the question.

ALTERNATIVE A

Below are listed several products. Please "X" each product you or anyone in your household *bought* in the PAST THREE MONTHS.

ALTERNATIVE B

Below are listed several products. Please "X" each product you or anyone in your household *ever bought*. For each product ever bought, "X" the box that best describes when the product was *purchased most recently:*

- ☐ **Within the past 3 months**
- ☐ **4–6 months ago**
- ☐ **7–12 months ago**
- ☐ **Over 12 months ago**

PURCHASED WITHIN PAST 3 MONTHS

	A 1-Step Question (%)	B 2-Step Question (%)	Percentage Point Difference
White glue	46	32	+14
Aspirin	68	57	+11
Replacement auto tires	32	24	+8

Are you satisfied with the present system of handling "closed-reserve" and "open-reserve" readings? (Are enough copies available? Are the required materials ordered promptly? Are the borrowing regulations adequate for students' use of materials?)
____ Yes   ____ No

Here a respondent may feel torn between a "Yes" to one part of the question and a "No" to another part. The answer to this question does not tell the researchers which problem or combination of problems concerns the library user.

Consider this very appropriate comment about double-barreled questions:

> Generally speaking, it is hard enough to get answers to one idea at a time without complicating the problem by asking what amounts to two questions at once. If two ideas are to be explored, they deserve at least two questions. Since question marks are not rationed, there is little excuse for the needless confusion that results in the double-barreled question.[13]

Avoid Making Assumptions

Consider the following question:

Should Macy's continue its excellent gift-wrapping program?
☐ **Yes** ☐ **No**

This question contains the implicit assumption that people believe the gift-wrapping program is excellent. By answering yes, the respondent implies that the program is, in fact, excellent and that things are just fine as they are. By answering no, he or she implies that the store should discontinue the gift wrapping. The researcher should not place the respondent in that sort of bind by including an implicit assumption in the question.

Another mistake that question writers sometimes make is assuming that the respondent has previously thought about an issue. For example, the following question appeared in a survey concerning Jack-in-the-Box restaurants: **"Do you think Jack-in-the-Box restaurants should consider changing their name?"** It is very unlikely that the respondent has thought about this question before being asked to answer it. Most respondents will answer the question even though they had no prior opinion concerning the name change of Jack-in-the-Box. Research that induces people to express attitudes on subjects they do not ordinarily think about is meaningless.

Avoid Burdensome Questions That May Tax the Respondent's Memory

A simple fact of human life is that people forget. Researchers writing questions about past behavior or events should recognize that certain questions may make serious demands on the respondent's memory. Writing questions about prior events requires a conscientious attempt to minimize the problem associated with forgetting.

In many situations, respondents cannot recall the answer to a question. For example, a telephone survey conducted during the 24-hour period following the airing of the Super Bowl might establish whether the respondent watched the Super Bowl and then ask: **"Do you recall any commercials on that program?"** If the answer is positive, the interviewer might ask: **"What brands were advertised?"** These two questions measure *unaided recall,* because they give the respondent no clue as to the brand of interest.

If the researcher suspects that the respondent forgot the answer to a question, he or she may rewrite the question in an *aided-recall* format—that is, in a format that provides a clue to help jog the respondent's memory. For instance, the question about the advertised beer in an aided-recall format might be: **"Do you recall whether there was a brand of beer advertised on that program?"** or **"I am going to read you a list of beer brand names. Can you pick out the name of the beer that was advertised on the program?"**

While aided recall is not as strong a test of attention or memory as unaided recall, this type of question is less taxing to the respondent's memory.

Telescoping and squishing are two additional consequences of respondents' forgetting the exact details of their behavior. *Telescoping* occurs when respondents believe that past events happened more recently than they actually did. The opposite effect, *squishing,* occurs when respondents think that recent events took place longer ago than they really did. A solution to this problem may be to refer to a specific event that is memorable—for example, **"How often have you gone to a sporting event since the Super Bowl?"**[14] Because forgetting tends to increase over time, the question may concern a recent period: **"How often did you watch Home Box Office on cable television *last week?*"** (During the editing stage, the results can be transposed to the appropriate time period.)

In situations in which "I don't know" or "I can't recall" is a meaningful answer, simply including a "don't know" response category may solve the question writer's problem.

WHAT IS THE BEST QUESTION SEQUENCE?

The order of questions, or the question sequence, may serve several functions for the researcher. If the opening questions are interesting, simple to comprehend, and easy to answer, respondents' cooperation and involvement can be maintained throughout the questionnaire. Asking easy-to-answer questions teaches respondents their role and builds confidence; they know this is a researcher and not another salesperson posing as an interviewer. If respondents' curiosity is not aroused at the outset, they can become disinterested and terminate the interview. A mail research expert reports that a mail survey among department store buyers drew an extremely poor return.[15] However, when some introductory questions related to the advisability of congressional action on pending legislation of great importance to these buyers were placed first on the questionnaire, a substantial improvement in response rate occurred. Respondents completed all the questions, not only those in the opening section.

In their attempts to "warm up" respondents toward the questionnaire, student researchers frequently ask demographic or classification questions at the beginning of the questionnaire. This is generally not advisable, because asking for personal information, such as income level or education, may embarrass or threaten respondents. It is generally better to ask embarrassing questions at the middle or end of the questionnaire, after rapport has been established between respondent and interviewer.

order bias
Bias caused by the influence of earlier questions in a questionnaire or by an answer's position in a set of answers.

Order bias can result from a particular answer's position in a set of answers or from the sequencing of questions. In political elections in which candidates lack high visibility, such as elections for county commissioners and judges, the first name listed on the ballot often receives the highest percentage of votes. For this reason many election boards print several ballots so that each candidate's name appears in every possible position (order) on the ballot.

Order bias can also distort survey results. For example, suppose a questionnaire's purpose is to measure levels of awareness of several charitable organizations. If Big Brothers and Big Sisters is always mentioned first, the Red Cross second, and the American Cancer Society third, Big Brothers and Big Sisters may receive an artificially high awareness rating because respondents are prone to yea-saying (by indicating awareness of the first item in the list).

Sequencing specific questions before asking about broader issues is a common cause of order bias. For example, bias may arise if questions about a specific clothing store are asked prior to those concerning the general criteria for selecting a clothing store. Suppose a respondent who indicates in the first portion of a questionnaire that she shops at a store where parking needs to be improved. Later in the questionnaire, to avoid appearing inconsistent, she may state that parking is less important a factor than she really believes it is. Specific questions may thus influence the more general ones. Therefore, it is advisable to ask general questions before specific questions to obtain the freest of open-ended responses. This procedure, known as the **funnel technique,** allows the researcher to understand the respondent's frame of reference before asking more specific questions about the level of the respondent's information and the intensity of his or her opinions.

funnel technique
Asking general questions before specific questions in order to obtain unbiased responses.

Consider how later answers might be biased by previous questions in this questionnaire on environmental pollution:

Circle the number that best expresses your feelings about the severity of each environmental problem:

Problem	Not a Problem				Very Severe Problem
Air pollution from automobile exhausts	1	2	3	4	5
Air pollution from open burning	1	2	3	4	5
Air pollution from industrial smoke	1	2	3	4	5
Air pollution from foul odors	1	2	3	4	5
Noise pollution from airplanes	1	2	3	4	5
Noise pollution from cars, trucks, motorcycles	1	2	3	4	5
Noise pollution from industry	1	2	3	4	5

Not surprisingly, researchers found that responses to the air pollution questions were highly correlated, almost identical.

Further, when one is using attitude scales, there may be an *anchoring effect.* The first concept measured tends to become a comparison point from which subsequent evaluations are made.[16] Randomization of items on a questionnaire susceptible to the anchoring effect helps minimize order bias.

A related problem is bias caused by the order of the alternatives on closed questions. To avoid this problem, the order of these choices should be rotated if producing alternative forms of the questionnaire is possible. However, business researchers rarely print alternative questionnaires to eliminate problems resulting from order bias. A more common practice is to pencil in Xs or check marks on printed questionnaires to indicate where the interviewer should start a series of repetitive questions. For example, the capitalized phrase and sentence in the following question provide instructions to the interviewer to "rotate" brands, starting with the one checked.

I would like to determine how likely you would be to buy certain brands of candy in the future. Let's start with (X'ED BRAND). (RECORD BELOW UNDER APPROPRIATE BRAND. REPEAT QUESTIONS FOR ALL REMAINING BRANDS.)

START HERE:	( ) Mounds	(X) Almond Joy	( ) York Peppermint Patties
Definitely would buy	−1	−1	−1
Probably would buy	−2	−2	−2
Might or might not buy	−3	−3	−3
Probably would not buy	−4	−4	−4
Definitely would not buy	−5	−5	−5

One advantage of Internet surveys is the ability to reduce order bias by having the computer randomly order questions and/or response alternatives. With complete randomization, question order is random and respondents see response alternatives in random positions. Asking a question that doesn't apply to the respondent or that the respondent is not qualified to answer may be irritating or may cause a biased response because the respondent wishes to please the interviewer or to avoid embarrassment. Including a **filter question** minimizes the chance of asking questions that are inapplicable. Asking **"Where do you generally have check-cashing problems in Springfield?"** may elicit a response even though the respondent has not had any check-cashing problems and may simply wish to please the interviewer with an answer. A filter question such as

filter question
A question in a questionnaire that screens out respondents not qualified to answer a second question.

Do you ever have a problem cashing a check in Springfield?
____ Yes ____ No

would screen out the people who are not qualified to answer. Exhibit 15.2 gives an example of a flowchart plan for a questionnaire that uses filter questions.

Another form of filter question, the **pivot question**, can be used to obtain income information and other data that respondents may be reluctant to provide. For example, a respondent is asked

pivot question
A filter question used to determine which version of a second question will be asked.

"Is your total family income over $50,000?" IF UNDER, ASK, "Is it over or under $25,000?" IF OVER, ASK, "Is it over or under $75,000?"

1. **Under $25,000**
2. **$25,001–$50,000**
3. **$50,001–$75,000**
4. **Over $75,000**

Structuring the order of questions so that they are logical will help to ensure the respondent's cooperation and eliminate confusion or indecision. The researcher maintains legitimacy by making sure that the respondent can comprehend the relationship between a given question (or section of the questionnaire) and the overall purpose of the study. Further, a logical order may aid the individual's memory. Transitional comments explaining the logic of the questionnaire may help guarantee that the respondent continues. Here are some examples:

We have been talking so far about general shopping habits in this city. Now I'd like you to compare two types of department stores—regular department stores and discount department stores.

So that I can combine your answers with those of other farmers who are similar to you, I need some personal information

Exhibit 15.2 FLOW OF QUESTIONS TO DETERMINE THE LEVEL OF PROMPTING REQUIRED TO STIMULATE RECALL[17]

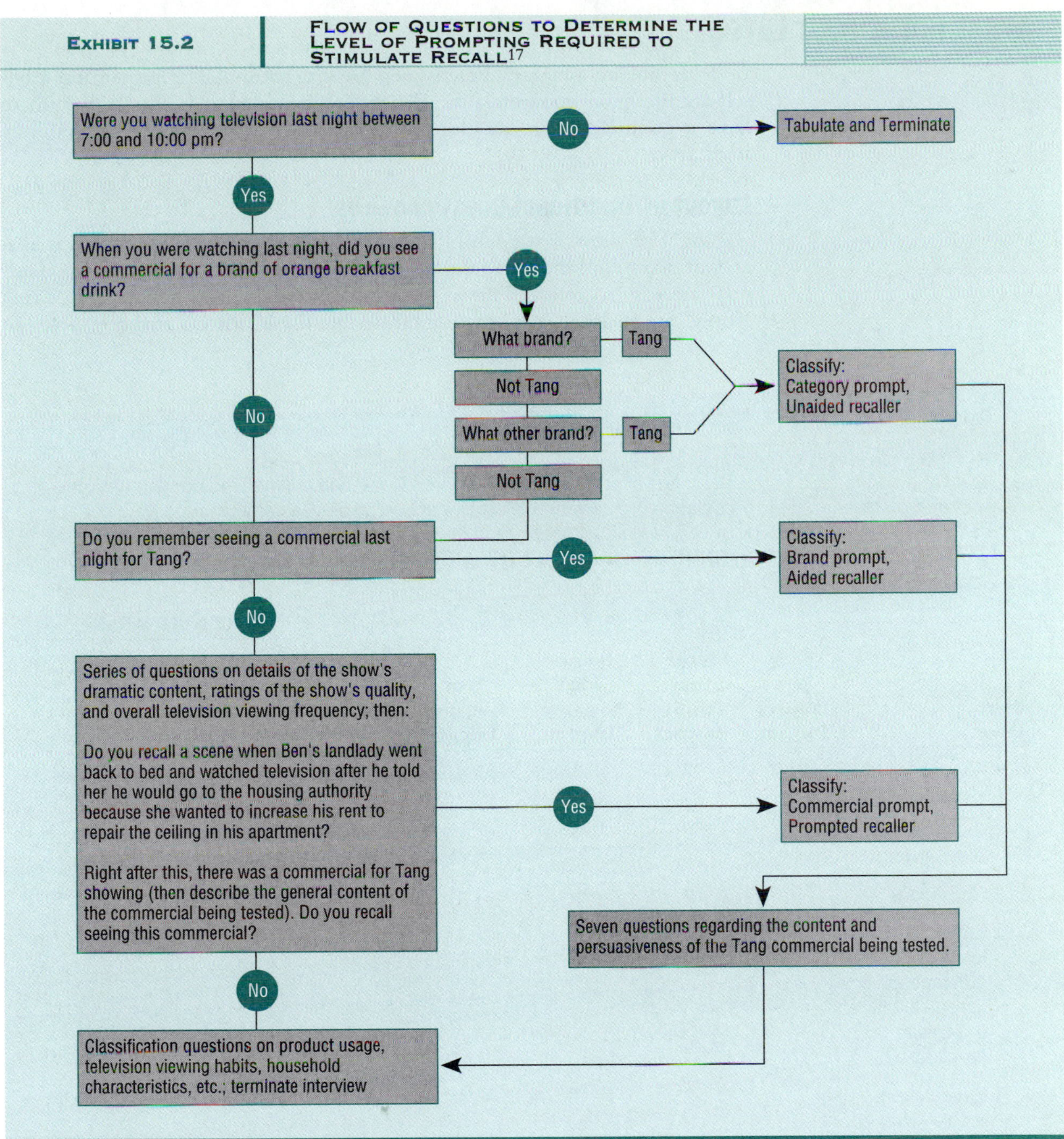

about you. Your answers to these questions—as well as all of the others you've answered—are confidential, and you will never be identified to anyone without your permission.

Thanks for your help so far. If you'll answer the remaining questions, it will help me analyze all your answers.

WHAT IS THE BEST LAYOUT?

Good layout and physical attractiveness are crucial in mail, Internet, and other self-administered questionnaires. For different reasons it is also important to have a good layout in questionnaires designed for personal and telephone interviews.

Layout of Traditional Questionnaires

Exhibit 15.3 shows a page from a telephone questionnaire. The layout is neat and attractive, and the instructions for the interviewer (all boldface capital letters) are easy to follow. The responses "It Depends," "Refused," and "Don't Know" are enclosed in a box to indicate that these answers are acceptable but

EXHIBIT 15.3 | **LAYOUT OF A PAGE FROM A TELEPHONE QUESTIONNAIRE**

5. Now I'm going to read you some types of professions. For each one, please tell me whether you think the work that profession does, on balance, has a very positive impact on society, a somewhat positive impact, a somewhat negative impact, a very negative impact, or not much impact either way on society. First . . . **(START AT X'ED ITEM. CONTINUE DOWN AND UP THE LIST UNTIL ALL ITEMS HAVE BEEN READ AND RATED.)**

Start Here:	Very Positive Impact	Somewhat Positive Impact	Somewhat Negative Impact	Very Negative Impact	Not Much Impact	(DO NOT READ) It Depends	Refused	Don't Know
[ ] Members of Congress	1	2	3	4	5	0	X	Y (24)
[ ] Business executives	1	2	3	4	5	0	X	Y (25)
[ ] Physicians	1	2	3	4	5	0	X	Y (26)
[ ] Political pollsters—that is, people who conduct surveys for public officials or political candidates	1	2	3	4	5	0	X	Y (27)
[ ] Researchers in the media—that is, people in the media such as television, newspapers, magazines and radio, who conduct surveys about issues later reported in the media	1	2	3	4	5	0	X	Y (28)

Exhibit 15.3 LAYOUT OF A PAGE FROM A TELEPHONE QUESTIONNAIRE (CONTINUED)

Start Here:	Very Positive Impact	Somewhat Positive Impact	Somewhat Negative Impact	Very Negative Impact	Not Much Impact	(DO NOT READ) It Depends	Refused	Don't Know
[ ] Telemarketers—that is, people who sell products or services over the phone	1	2	3	4	5	0	X	Y (29)
[ ] Used car salesmen	1	2	3	4	5	0	X	Y (30)
[ ] Market researchers—that is, people who work for commercial research firms who conduct surveys to see what the public thinks about certain kinds of consumer products or services	1	2	3	4	5	0	X	Y (31)
[ ] Biomedical researchers	1	2	3	4	5	0	X	Y (32)
[ ] Public-opinion researchers—that is, people who work for commercial research firms who conduct surveys to see what the public thinks about important social issues	1	2	3	4	5	0	X	Y (33)
[ ] College and university professors	1	2	3	4	5	0	X	Y (34)
[ ] Attorneys	1	2	3	4	5	0	X	Y (35)
[ ] Members of the clergy	1	2	3	4	5	0	X	Y (36)
[ ] Journalists	1	2	3	4	5	0	X	Y (37)

responses from the 5-point scale are preferred. (To see the entire questionnaire, go to the Web site of the Council of American Survey Research Organizations at http://www.casro.org/ and check out their poll about polls.)

Often rate of return can be increased by using money that might have been spent on an incentive to improve the attractiveness and quality of the questionnaire. Mail questionnaires should never be overcrowded. Margins should be of decent size, white space should be used to separate blocks of print, and any unavoidable columns of multiple boxes should be kept to a minimum. Questionnaires should be designed to appear as brief and small as possible. Sometimes it is advisable to use a booklet form of questionnaire, rather than a large number of pages stapled together. In situations where it is necessary to conserve space on the questionnaire or to facilitate entering the data into a computer or tabulating the data, a multiple-grid layout may be used. In this type of layout, a question is followed by corresponding response alternatives arranged in a grid or matrix format. For example:

Airlines often offer special-fare promotions. On a business trip, would you take a connecting flight instead of a nonstop flight if the connecting fare were lower?

	Yes	**No**	**Not Sure**
One hour longer?	☐	☐	☐
Two hours longer?	☐	☐	☐
Three hours longer?	☐	☐	☐

Experienced researchers have found that it pays to phrase the title of the questionnaire carefully. In self-administered and mail questionnaires a carefully constructed title may by itself capture the respondent's interest, underline the importance of the research ("Nationwide Study of Blood Donors"), emphasize the interesting nature of the study ("Study of Internet Usage"), appeal to the respondent's ego ("Survey among Top Executives"), or emphasize the confidential nature of the study ("A Confidential Survey among . . ."). The researcher should take steps to ensure that the wording of the title will not bias the respondent in the same way that a leading question might.

When an interviewer is to administer the questionnaire, the analyst can design the questionnaire to make the job of following interconnected questions much easier by utilizing instructions, directional arrows, special question formats, and other tricks of the trade. Exhibit 15.4 and Exhibit 15.5 (pages 352–353) illustrate portions of telephone and personal interview questionnaires. Note how the layout and easy-to-follow instructions for interviewers in Exhibit 15.4 (e.g., questions 1, 2, and 3) help the interviewer follow the question sequence. The series of questions in Exhibit 15.4 makes use of "skip" questions. Either instructions to skip or an arrow drawn to the next question are provided to help the respondent (or the interviewer) know which question comes next.

Note that Questions 3 and 6 in Exhibit 15.5 instruct the interviewer to hand the respondent a card that bears a list of alternatives. Cards may help respondents to grasp the intended meaning of the question and to help them remember all the brand names or list of items they are being asked about. Also, Questions 2, 3, and 6 instruct the interviewer to start the bank ratings with the bank that has been checked in red pencil on the printed questionnaire. The name of the red-checked bank is not the same on every questionnaire. By rotating the order of the check marks, the researchers attempt to reduce order

Exhibit 15.4 **Telephone Questionnaire with Skip Questions**

1. Did you take the car you had checked to the Standard Auto Repair Center for repairs?
   – 1 Yes **(Skip to Q. 3)** – 2 No

2. **(If no, ask:)** Did you have the repair work done?
   – 1 Yes ↓
   1. Where was the repair work done?
      ____
   2. Why didn't you have the repair work done at the Standard Auto Repair Center?
      ____
      ____
      ____

   – 2 No ↓
   1. Why didn't you have the car repaired?
      ____
      ____
      ____

3. **(If yes to Q. 1, ask:)** How satisfied were you with the repair work? Were you . . .
   – 1 Very satisfied
   – 2 Somewhat satisfied
   – 3 Somewhat dissatisfied
   – 4 Very dissatisfied

   (If somewhat or very dissatisfied:) In what way were you dissatisfied?
   ____
   ____
   ____

4. **(Ask everyone:)** Do you ever buy gas at the 95th Street Standard Center?
   – 1 Yes – 2 No **(Skip to Q. 6)**

5. **(If yes, ask:)** How often do you buy gas there?
   – 1 Always
   – 2 Almost always
   – 3 Most of the time
   – 4 Part of the time
   – 5 Hardly ever

6. Have you ever had your car washed there? – 1 Yes – 2 No

7. Have you ever had an oil change or lubrication done there? – 1 Yes – 2 No

bias caused by respondents' tendency to react more favorably to the first set of questions. To facilitate coding, question responses should be precoded when possible, as in Exhibit 15.4.

Layout is especially important when questionnaires are long or require the respondent to fill in a large amount of information. The use of headings or subtitles to identify groups of questions can help the respondent grasp the scope or nature of the questions to be asked. The respondent can follow the logic of the questionnaire at a glance, because the headings indicate groups of similar questions.

Layout of Internet Questionnaires

Layout is also an important issue for questionnaires appearing on the Internet. A questionnaire on a Web site should be easy to use, flow logically, and have a graphic look and overall feel that motivate the respondent to cooperate from

Exhibit 15.5 | **Personal Interview Questionnaire**[18]

"Hello, my name is ________. I'm a Public Opinion Interviewer with Research Services, Inc. We're making an opinion survey about banks and banking, and I'd like to ask you . . ."

1. What are the names of local banks you can think of offhand? (INTERVIEWER: List names in order mentioned.)
   a. ________
   b. ________
   c. ________
   d. ________
   e. ________
   f. ________
   g. ________

2. Thinking now about the experiences you have had with the different banks here in Boulder, have you ever talked to or done business with . . . (INTERVIEWER: Insert name of bank checked in red below.)
   a. Are you personally acquainted with any of the employees or officers at ________?
   b. (If YES) Who is that?
   c. How long has it been since you have been inside ________?

   (INTERVIEWER: Now go back and repeat 2–2c for all other banks listed.)

	(2) Talked		(2a and 2b) Know Employee or Officer		(2c) Been in Bank in:				
	Yes	**No**	**No**	**Name**	**Last Year**	**1–5**	**5-Plus**	**No**	**DK**
Boulder National Bank	1	2	1	______	1	2	3	4	5
First National Bank	1	2	1	______	1	2	3	4	5
Arapahoe National Bank	1	2	1	______	1	2	3	4	5
Security Bank	1	2	1	______	1	2	3	4	5
United Bank of Boulder	1	2	1	______	1	2	3	4	5
National State Bank	1	2	1	______	1	2	3	4	5

3. (HAND BANK RATING CARD.) On this card there are a number of contrasting phrases or statements—for example, "Large" and "Small." We'd like to know how you rate (NAME OF BANK CHECKED IN RED BELOW) in terms of these statements or phrases. Just for example, let's use the terms "fast service" and "slow service." If you were to rate a bank #1 on this scale, it would mean you find its service "very fast." On the other hand, a #7 rating would indicate you feel its service is "very slow," whereas a #4 rating means you don't think of it as being either "very fast" or "very slow." Are you ready to go ahead? Good! Tell me then how you would rate (NAME OF BANK CHECKED IN RED) in terms of each of the phrases or statements on that card.
   How about (READ NEXT BANK NAME)? (INTERVIEWER: Continue on until respondent has evaluated all six banks.)

	Arapahoe National	**First National**	**Boulder National**	**Security Bank**	**United Bank**	**National State**
a. Service	______	______	______	______	______	______
b. Size	______	______	______	______	______	______
c. Business vs. family	______	______	______	______	______	______
d. Friendliness	______	______	______	______	______	______
e. Big/small business	______	______	______	______	______	______
f. Rate of growth	______	______	______	______	______	______
g. Modernness	______	______	______	______	______	______
h. Leadership	______	______	______	______	______	______
i. Loan ease	______	______	______	______	______	______
j. Location	______	______	______	______	______	______
k. Hours	______	______	______	______	______	______
l. Ownership	______	______	______	______	______	______
m. Community involvement	______	______	______	______	______	______

EXHIBIT 15.5 | **PERSONAL INTERVIEW QUESTIONNAIRE (CONTINUED)**

4. Suppose a friend of yours who has just moved to Boulder asked you to recommend a bank. Which local bank would you recommend? Why would you recommend that particular bank?

   Arapahoe National 1
   First National 2
   Boulder National 3
   Security Bank 4
   United Bank of Boulder 5
   National State Bank 6
   Other (specify) ____________________
   DK/Wouldn't 8

5. Which of the local banks do you think of as: (INTERVIEWER: Read red-checked item first, then read each of the other five.)
   the newcomer's bank? ____________________
   the student's bank? ____________________
   the personal banker bank? ____________________
   the bank where most C.U. faculty and staff bank? ____________________
   the bank most interested in this community? ____________________
   the most progressive bank? ____________________

6. Which of these financial institutions, if any (HAND CARD #2), are you or any member of your immediate family who lives here in this home doing business with now?

   (IF NONE, skip to #19.)

   Bank 1
   Credit union 2
   Finance company 3
   Savings and loan 4
   Industrial bank 5
   None of these 6
   DK/not sure 8

7. If a friend of yours asked you to recommend a place where he could get a loan with which to buy a home, which financial institution would you probably recommend? (INTERVIEWER: Probe for specific name.) Why would you recommend (INSTITUTION NAMED)?

   Would recommend: ____________________
   ____
   Wouldn't 0
   DK/not sure 8

start to finish. Many of the guidelines for layout of paper questionnaires apply to Internet questionnaires. There are, however, some important differences.

With *graphical user interface (GUI)* software, the researcher can exercise control over the background, colors, fonts, and other visual features displayed on the computer screen so as to create an attractive and easy-to-use interface between the computer user and the Internet survey. GUI software allows the researcher to design questionnaires in which respondents click on the appropriate answer rather than having to type answers or codes.

Researchers often use Web publishing software, such as WebSurveyor, FrontPage, or Netscape Composer, to format a questionnaire so that they will know how it should appear online. However, several features of a respondent's computer may influence the appearance of an Internet questionnaire. For example, discrepancies between the designer's and the respondent's computer settings for screen configuration (e.g., 640 x 480 pixels versus 800 x 600 pixels) may result in questions not being fully visible on the respondent's screen, misaligned text, or other visual problems.[19] The possibility that the questionnaire the researcher/designer constructs on his or her computer may look different from the questionnaire that appears on the respondent's computer should always be considered when designing Internet surveys. One sophisticated remedy is to use the first few questions on an Internet survey to ask about operating system, browser software, and other computer configuration issues so that the questionnaire that is delivered is as compatible as possible with the respondent's. A simpler solution is to limit the horizontal width of the questions to 70 characters or less, to decrease the likelihood of wrap-around text.

Layout Issues

Even if the questionnaire designer's computer and the respondents' computers are compatible, there are several layout issues a Web questionnaire designer should consider. The first decision is whether the questionnaire will appear page by page, with individual questions on separate screens (Web pages), or on a scrolling basis, with the entire questionnaire appearing on a single Web page that the respondent scrolls from top to bottom. The *paging layout* (going from screen to screen) greatly facilitates skip patterns. Based on a respondent's answers to filter questions, the computer can automatically insert relevant questions on subsequent pages. If the entire questionnaire appears on one page (the *scrolling layout*) the display should advance smoothly, as if it were a piece of paper being moved up or down. The scrolling layout gives the respondent the ability to read any portion of the questionnaire at any time, but the absence of page boundaries can cause problems. For example, suppose a Likert scale consists of 15 statements in a grid-format layout, with the response categories **Strongly Agree, Agree, Disagree,** and **Strongly Disagree** at the beginning of the questionnaire. Once the respondent has scrolled down beyond the first few statements, he or she may not be able to see both the statements at the end of the list and the response categories at the top of the grid simultaneously. Thus, avoiding the problems associated with splitting questions and response categories may be difficult with scrolling questionnaires.

When a scrolling questionnaire is long, category or section headings are helpful to respondents. It is also a good idea to provide links to the top and bottom parts of each section, so that users can navigate through the questionnaire without having to scroll through the entire document.[20]

push button
On an Internet questionnaire, a small outlined area, such as a rectangle or an arrow, that the respondent clicks on to select an option or perform a function, such as Submit.

Whether an Internet survey is in page-by-page or scrolling format, **push buttons** with labels should clearly describe the actions to be taken. For example, if the respondent is to go to the next page, a large arrow labeled "NEXT" might appear in color at the bottom of the screen.

Decisions must be made about the use of color, graphics, animation, sound, and other special features that the Internet makes possible. One thing to remember is that, although sophisticated graphics are not a problem for people with very powerful computers, many respondents' computers are not powerful enough to deliver complex graphics at a satisfactory speed, if at all. A textured background, colored headings, and small graphics can make a questionnaire more interesting and appealing, but they may present problems for respondents with older computers and/or low-bandwidth Internet connections.

status bar
In an Internet questionnaire, a visual indicator that tells the respondent what portion of the survey he or she has completed.

With a paper questionnaire, the respondent knows how many questions he or she must answer. Because many Internet surveys offer no visual clues about the number of questions to be asked, it is important to provide a **status bar** or some other visual indicator of questionnaire length. For example, including a partially filled rectangular box as a visual symbol and a statement such as "The status bar at top right indicates approximately what portion of the survey you have completed" increases the likelihood that the respondent will finish the entire sequence of questions.

An Internet questionnaire uses windows known as dialog boxes to display questions and record answers. Exhibit 15.6 portrays four common ways of dis-

Exhibit 15.6 Alternative Ways of Displaying Internet Questions

Radio button

Last month, did you purchase products or services over the Internet?

○ Yes

○ No

How familiar are you with Microsoft's X-box video game player?

Know Extremely Well	Know Fairly Well	Know a Little	Know Just Name	Never Heard of
○	○	○	○	○

Drop-down box, closed position

In which country or region do you currently reside?

[Click Here ▼]

Drop-down box, open position

In which country or region do you currently reside?

[Click Here ▼]

Click Here
United States
Asia/Pacific (excluding Hawaii)
Africa
Australia or New Zealand
Canada
Europe
Latin America, South America, or Mexico
Middle East
Other

Check box

From which location(s) do you access the Internet? Select all that apply.

☐ Home
☐ Work
☐ Other Location

Please indicate which of the following Web sites you have ever visited or used. (CHOOSE ALL THAT APPLY.)

☐ E*Trade's Web site
☐ Waterhouse's Web site
☐ Merrill Lynch's Web site
☐ Fidelity's Web site
☐ Schwab's Web site
☐ Powerstreet
☐ Yahoo! Finance
☐ Quicken.com
☐ Lycos Investing
☐ AOL's Personal Finance
☐ None of the above

Open-ended, one-line box

What company do you think is the most visible sponsor of sports?

[ ]

Open-ended, scrolling text box

What can we do to improve our textbook?

[ ]

radio button
In an Internet questionnaire, a circular icon, resembling a button, that activates one response choice and deactivates others when a respondent clicks on it.

drop-down box
In an Internet questionnaire, a space-saving device that reveals responses when they are needed but otherwise hides them from view.

check box
In an Internet questionnaire, a small graphic box, next to an answer, that a respondent clicks on to choose that answer; typically, a check mark or an X appears in the box when the respondent clicks on it.

open-ended box
In an Internet questionnaire, a box where respondents can type in their own answers to open-ended questions.

pop-up boxes
In an Internet questionnaire, boxes that appear at selected points and contain information or instructions for respondents.

playing questions on a computer screen. Many Internet questionnaires require the respondent to activate his or her answer by clicking on a **radio button** for a response. Radio buttons work like push buttons on automobile radios: Clicking on an alternative response deactivates the first choice and replaces it with the new response. A **drop-down box**, such as the one shown in Exhibit 15.6, is a space-saving device that allows the researcher to provide a list of responses that are hidden from view until they are needed. A general statement, such as "Please select" or "Click here" is shown initially. Clicking on the downward-facing arrow makes the full range of choices appear. If the first choice in a list, such as "Strongly Agree," is shown while the other responses are kept hidden, the chance that response bias will occur is increased. Drop-down boxes may present a problem for individuals with minimal computer skills, as they may not know how to reveal responses hidden behind a drop-down menu or how to move from one option to another in a moving-bar menu. However, because a drop-down box only shows permissible alternatives, this question format prevents respondents from entering unacceptable answers.

Checklist questions may be followed by **check boxes**, several, none, or all of which may be checked by the respondent. **Open-ended boxes** are boxes in which respondents type their answers to open-ended questions. Open-ended boxes may be designed as *one-line text boxes* or *scrolling text boxes,* depending on the breadth of the expected answer. Of course, open-ended questions require that respondents have both the skill and the willingness to keyboard lengthy answers on the computer. Some open-ended boxes are designed so that respondents can enter numbers for frequency response, ranking, or rating questions. For example:

> **Below you will see a series of statements that might or might not describe how you feel about your career. Please rate each statement using a scale from 1 to 4, where 4 means "Totally Agree," 3 means "Somewhat Agree," 2 means "Somewhat Disagree," and 1 means "Totally Disagree."**
>
> ***Please enter your numeric answer in the box provided next to each statement.*** **Would you say that . . . ?**
>
> **A lack of business knowledge relevant to my field/career could hurt my career advancement.** [ ]
>
> **My career life is an important part of how I define myself.** [ ]

Pop-up boxes are message boxes that can be used to highlight important information. For example, pop-up boxes may be use to provide a privacy statement, such as the following:

> **IBM would like your help in making our Web site easier to use and more effective.**
>
> **Choose to complete the survey now or not at all.**
>
> [Complete] [No Thank You] [Privacy Statement]

Clicking on Privacy Statement opens the following pop-up box:

Survey Privacy Statement

This overall Privacy Statement verifies that IBM is a member of the TRUSTe program and is in compliance with TRUSTe principles. This survey is strictly for market research purposes. The information you provide will be used only to improve the overall content, navigation, and useability of www.ibm.com.

In some cases, respondents can learn more about how to use a particular scale or get a definition of a term by clicking on a link that generates a pop-up box. One of the most common reasons for using pop-up boxes is *error trapping,* a topic discussed in the next section.

Chapter 14 described graphic rating scales, which present respondents with a graphic continuum. On the Internet, researchers can take advantage of scroll bars or other GUI software features to make these scales easy to use. For example, the graphic continuum may be drawn as a measuring rod with a plus sign on one end and a minus sign on the other. The respondent then moves a small rectangle back and forth between the two ends of the scale to scroll to any point on the continuum. Scoring, as discussed in Chapter 14, is in terms of some measure of the length (millimeters) from one end of the graphic continuum to the point marked by the respondent.

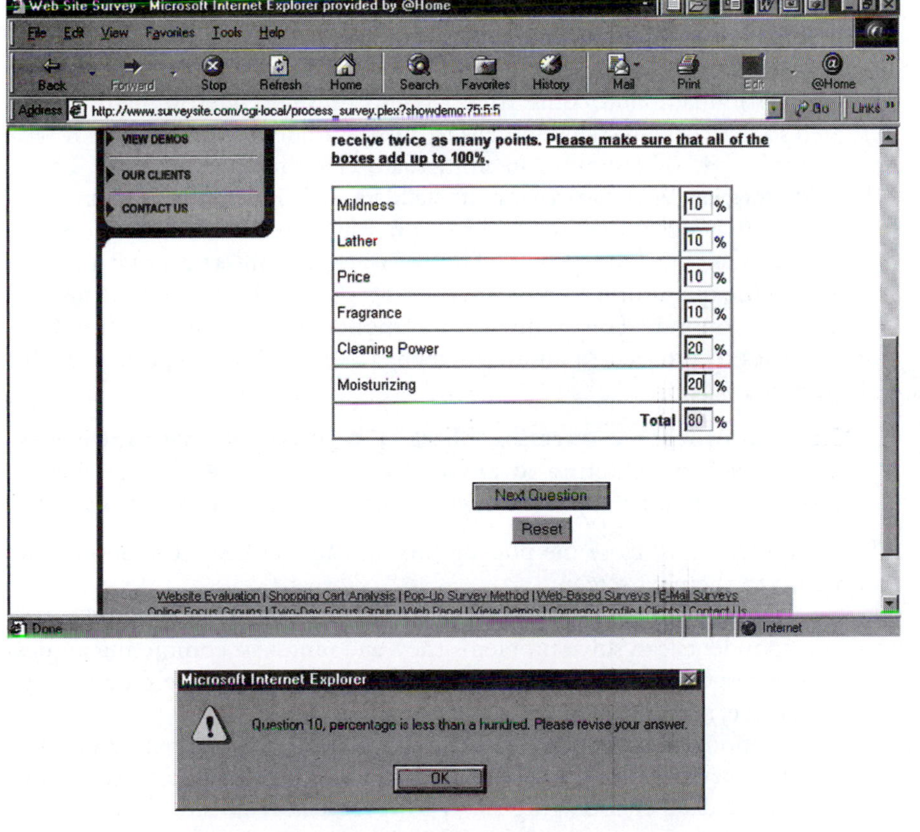

The respondent's answers to this constant-sum scale incorrectly total 80 percent—not the required 100 percent. When mistakes occur, error trapping software may cause a pop-up box to appear, with a message instructing the respondent to adjust his or her answer. With forced answering respondents cannot skip over questions as they do in mail surveys.

Finally, it is a good idea to include a customized thank-you page at the end of an Internet questionnaire, so that a brief thank-you note pops onto their screens when respondents click on the Submit push button.[21]

Software That Makes Questionnaires Interactive

Computer code can be written to make Internet questionnaires interactive and less prone to errors. The writing of software programs is beyond the scope of this discussion. However, several of the interactive functions that software makes possible should be mentioned here.

As discussed in Chapter 10, Internet software allows the branching off of questioning into two or more different lines, depending on a particular respondent's answer, and the skipping or filtering questions. Questionnaire-writing software with Boolean skip and branching logic is readily available. Most of these programs have *hidden skip logic* so that respondents never see any evidence of skips. It is best if the questions the respondent sees flow in numerical sequence.[22] However, some programs number all potential questions in numerical order, and the respondent sees only the numbers on the questions he or she answers. Thus, a respondent may answer questions 1 through 11 and next see a question numbered 15 because of the skip logic.

variable piping software
Software that allows variables to be inserted into an Internet questionnaire as a respondent is completing it.

Software can systematically or randomly manipulate the questions a respondent sees. **Variable piping software** allows variables, such as answers from previous questions, to be inserted into unfolding questions. Other software can randomly rotate the order of questions, blocks of questions, and response alternatives from respondent to respondent.

error trapping
Using software to control the flow of an Internet questionnaire—for example, to prevent respondents from backing up or failing to answer a question.

forced answering software
Software that prevents respondents from continuing with an Internet questionnaire if they fail to answer a question.

Researchers can use software to control the flow of a questionnaire. Respondents can be blocked from backing up, or they can be allowed to stop in mid-questionnaire and come back later to finish. A questionnaire can be designed so that if the respondent fails to answer a question or answers it with an incorrect type of response, an immediate error message appears. This is called **error trapping.** With **forced answering software,** respondents cannot skip over questions as they do in mail surveys. The program will not let them continue if they fail to answer a question.[23] The software may insert a boldface error message on the question screen or insert a pop-up box instructing the respondent how to continue. For example, if a respondent does not answer a question and tries to proceed to another screen, a pop-up box might present the following message:

> **You cannot leave a question blank. On questions without a "Not sure" or "Decline to answer" option, please choose the response that best represents your opinions or experiences.**

The respondent must close the pop-up box and answer the question in order to proceed to the next screen.

interactive help desk
In an Internet questionnaire, a live, real-time support feature that solves problems or answers questions respondents may encounter in completing the questionnaire.

Some designers include **interactive help desks** for their Web questionnaires, so that respondents can solve problems they encounter in completing a questionnaire. A respondent might e-mail questions to the survey help desk or get live, interactive, real-time support via an online help desk.

Some respondents will leave the questionnaire Web site, prematurely terminating the survey. In many cases sending an e-mail message to these respondents at a later date, encouraging them to revisit the Web site, will persuade them to complete the questionnaire. Through the use of software and cookies researchers can ensure that the respondent who revisits the Web site will be able to pick up at the point where he or she left off.

Once an Internet questionnaire has been designed, it is important to pretest it to ensure that it works with Internet Explorer, Netscape, AOL, WebTV, and other browsers. Some general-purpose programming languages, such as Java, do not always work with all browsers. Because different browsers have different peculiarities, a survey that works perfectly well with one may not function at all with another.[24]

HOW MUCH PRETESTING AND REVISING ARE NECESSARY?

Many novelists write, rewrite, and revise certain chapters, paragraphs, and even sentences of their books. The research analyst lives in a similar world. Rarely does one write only a first draft of a questionnaire. Usually, the questionnaire is tried out on a group that is selected on a convenience basis and that is similar in makeup to the one that ultimately will be sampled. Researchers should select a group that is not too divergent from the actual respondents (e.g., business students as surrogates for businesspeople), but it is not necessary to get a statistical sample for pretesting. The pretesting process allows the researchers to determine if the respondents have any difficulty understanding the questionnaire and whether there are any ambiguous or biased questions. This process is exceedingly beneficial. Making a mistake with 25 or 50 subjects can avert the disaster of administering an invalid questionnaire to several hundred individuals.

preliminary tabulation
Tabulation of the results of a pretest.

Tabulating the results of a pretest helps determine whether the questionnaire will meet the objectives of the research. A **preliminary tabulation** often illustrates that although respondents can easily comprehend and answer a given question, it is an inappropriate question because it does not solve the business problem.

Consider the following example from a survey among distributors of powder-actuated tools concerning the percentage of sales to given industries.

Please estimate what percentage of your fastener and load sales go to the following industries:
____ % heating, plumbing, and air-conditioning
____ % carpentry
____ % electrical
____ % maintenance
____ % other (please specify)

____

The researchers were fortunate to learn in pretesting that asking the question in this manner made it virtually impossible to obtain the information actually desired. Most respondents' answers did not total 100 percent. The question had to be revised. Usually a questionnaire goes through several revisions.

Getting respondents to add everything correctly is a problem. Notice how the questions from the survey on secretarial support in Exhibit 15.7 are designed to mitigate this problem. Pretesting difficult questions like this is essential.

What administrative procedures should be implemented to maximize the value of a pretest? Administering a questionnaire exactly as planned in the actual study often is not possible. For example, mailing out a questionnaire might require several weeks. Pretesting a questionnaire in this manner might provide

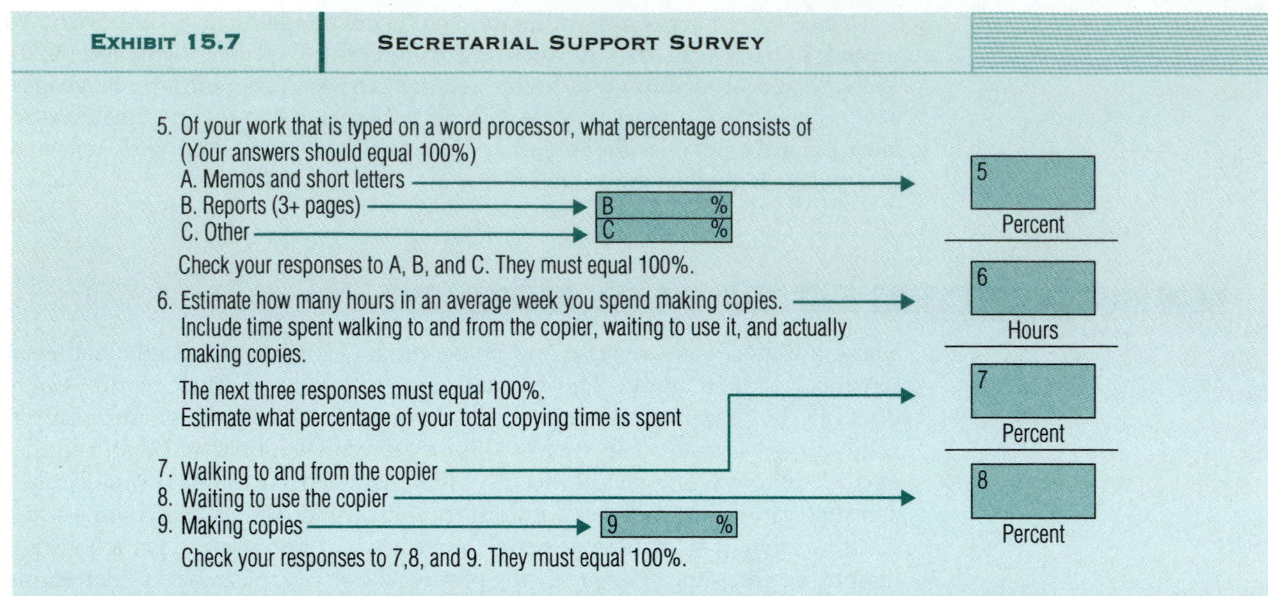

EXHIBIT 15.7 | **SECRETARIAL SUPPORT SURVEY**

5. Of your work that is typed on a word processor, what percentage consists of (Your answers should equal 100%)
   A. Memos and short letters → [5] Percent
   B. Reports (3+ pages) → [B %]
   C. Other → [C %]

   Check your responses to A, B, and C. They must equal 100%.
6. Estimate how many hours in an average week you spend making copies. → [6] Hours
   Include time spent walking to and from the copier, waiting to use it, and actually making copies.

   The next three responses must equal 100%.
   Estimate what percentage of your total copying time is spent
7. Walking to and from the copier → [7] Percent
8. Waiting to use the copier → [8] Percent
9. Making copies → [9 %]

   Check your responses to 7,8, and 9. They must equal 100%.

important information on response rate, but it may not point out why questions were skipped or why respondents found certain questions ambiguous or confusing. The ability of a personal interviewer to record requests for additional explanation and to register comments indicating respondents' difficulty with question sequence or other factors is the primary reason why interviewers are often used for pretest work. Self-administered questionnaires are not reworded to be personal interviews, but interviewers are instructed to observe the person filling out the questionnaire and to ask for the respondent's comments after he or she completes the questionnaire. When pretesting personal or telephone interviews, interviewers may test alternative wordings and question sequences to determine which format is best suited to the respondents.

No matter how the pretest is conducted, the researcher should remember that its purpose is to alert researchers to potential problems that may be caused by the questionnaire. Thus, pretests are typically conducted to answer questions about the questionnaire such as the following:

- Can the questionnaire format be followed by the interviewers?
- Does the questionnaire flow naturally and conversationally?
- Can respondents answer the questions easily?
- Which alternative forms of questions work best?[25]

Pretesting also provides the means to test the sampling procedure. Pretests may determine if interviewers follow the sampling instructions properly and if the procedure is efficient. They also provide estimates of the response rate for mail surveys and the completion rate for telephone surveys.

DESIGNING QUESTIONNAIRES FOR GLOBAL RESEARCH

Now that business research is being conducted around the globe, researchers must take cultural factors into account when designing questionnaires. The most widespread problem involves the translation of a questionnaire into other languages. A questionnaire developed in one country may not easily cross a border because equivalent language concepts do not exist or because of differences in idiom and vernacular. For example, the concepts uncle and aunt are not the same in the United States as in India. In India, the terms *uncle* and *aunt* are different for the maternal and paternal sides of the family.[26] Although Spanish is spoken in both Mexico and Venezuela, one researcher found out that a translation of the English term *retail outlet* worked in Mexico, but not in Venezuela. Venezuelans interpreted the translation to be an electrical outlet, an outlet of a river into an ocean, or the passageway into a patio.

back translation
Taking a questionnaire that has previously been translated into another language and then having a second, independent translator translate it back into the original language.

International business researchers often have questionnaires back translated. **Back translation** is the process of taking a questionnaire that has previously been translated from one language to another and having it translated back into the original language by a second, independent translator. The back translator is often a person whose native tongue is the language that will be used on the questionnaire. Thus, inconsistencies between the English version and the translation can be identified and modified, if necessary. For example, a soft drink company translated its slogan, "Baby, it's cold inside," into Cantonese for research in Hong Kong. The slogan was retranslated as "Small Mosquito, on the inside, it is very cold." (In Hong Kong *small mosquito* is a colloquial expression for a small child.) Clearly, the intended meaning of the advertising message was lost in the translated questionnaire.[27] In another international marketing research project, "out of sight, out of mind" was back translated as "invisible things are insane."[28]

As indicated in Chapter 9, literacy influences the choice between self-administered questionnaires and interviews. This makes knowledge of literacy rates in foreign countries vital, especially for research in countries that are just developing modern economies.

SUMMARY

Good questionnaire design is a key to obtaining good survey results. The specific questions asked will be a function of the type of information needed to answer the manager's questions and of the communication medium for data collection. Relevance and accuracy are the basic criteria for judging questionnaire results. A questionnaire is *relevant* if no unnecessary information is collected and the information necessary for solving the business problem is obtained. *Accuracy* means that the information is reliable and valid.

Knowing how each question should be phrased requires familiarity with the different types of questions. Open-ended response questions present some problem or question and ask the respondent to answer in his or her own words. Fixed-alternative questions require less interviewer skill, take less time, and are easier to answer. In fixed-alternative questions the respondent is given specific limited alternative responses and asked to choose the one closest to his or her own viewpoint. Standardized responses are easier to code, tabulate, and interpret. Care must be taken to formulate the responses so they do not overlap. Respondents whose answers don't fit any of the fixed alternatives may be forced to select alternatives they really don't mean.

Open-ended questions are especially useful in exploratory research or at the beginning of a questionnaire. They make a questionnaire more expensive to analyze because of the uniqueness of the answers. Interviewer bias can also influence the responses to open-ended questions.

Some guidelines to questionnaire construction have emerged from research experience. The language should be simple to allow for variations in educational levels. Researchers should avoid leading or loaded questions, which suggest answers to the respondents, as well as questions that induce them to give socially desirable answers. Respondents have a bias against questions suggesting changes in the status quo. Their reluctance to answer personal questions can be reduced by explaining the need for the questions and by assuring respondents of the confidentiality of their replies. Researchers should be careful to avoid ambiguity in questions. Another common problem is the double-barreled question, which asks two questions at once. Researchers should avoid burdensome questions that may tax the respondent's memory.

Question sequence can be very important to the success of a survey. The opening questions should be designed to interest respondents and keep them involved. Personal questions should be postponed to the middle or end of the questionnaire. General questions should precede specific ones. In a series of attitude scales, the first response may be used as an anchor for comparison to the other responses. The order of alternatives on closed questions can affect the results. Filter questions are useful to avoid unnecessary questions that don't apply to a particular respondent. Such questions may be put into a flowchart for personal or telephone interviewing.

The layout of a mail or other self-administered questionnaire can affect the response rate. An attractive questionnaire encourages a response; a carefully phrased title can also encourage responses. Internet questionnaires present unique design issues. Decisions must be made about the use of color, graphics, animation, sound, and other special layout effects that the Internet makes possible. Pretesting helps reveal errors while they can still be easily corrected.

International business researchers must take cultural factors into account when designing questionnaires. The most widespread problem involves translation into another language. International questionnaires are often back translated.

Key Terms

open-ended response question
fixed-alternative question
leading question
loaded question
counterbiasing statement
split-ballot technique
double-barreled question
order bias
funnel technique
filter question
pivot question
push button
status bar
radio button
drop-down box
check box
open-ended box
pop-up box
variable piping software
error trapping
forced answering software
interactive help desk
preliminary tabulation
back translation

Questions for Review and Critical Thinking

1. Evaluate and comment on the following questions from several different questionnaires:

   (a) A university computer center survey on SPSS usage:

   How often do you use SPSS? Please check one.
   ____ Infrequently (once a semester)
   ____ Occasionally (once a month)
   ____ Frequently (once a week)
   ____ All the time (daily)

   (b) A survey of U.S. congressmen:

   Do you understand and like the current tax laws that allow people who file their federal income tax returns to deduct from their personal income the amount they pay in state and local taxes?
   ____ Yes
   ____ No

(c) A survey on a new, small electric car:

Assuming 90 percent of your driving is in town, would you buy this type of car?
____ Yes
____ No

If this type of electric car had the same initial cost as a current "Big 3" full-sized, fully equipped car but operated at one-half the cost over a 5-year period, would you buy one?
____ Yes
____ No

(d) A student survey:

Since the beginning of this semester approximately what percentage of the time did you get to campus using each of the forms of transportation available to you per week?
Walk ____ Bicycle ____
Public transportation ____
Motor vehicle ____

(e) A survey of employers:

Should the company continue its generous medical insurance program?
____ Yes
____ No

(f) A personnel manager's survey of employees:

In your opinion, are women discriminated against, treated equitably, or given preference in promotion practices?

Discriminated Against	Treated Equitably	Treated Preferentially
☐	☐	☐

(g) A survey of voters:

To make up for past discrimination, do you favor or oppose programs that make special efforts to help minorities get ahead?
☐ Favor
☐ Oppose

(h) A government survey of gasoline retailers:

Suppose the full-service selling price for regular gasoline is 92.8 cents per gallon on the first day of the month. Suppose on the 10th of the month the price is raised to 94.9 cents per gallon; and on the 25th of the month it is reduced to 91.9 cents per gallon. In order to provide the required data, you should list the accumulator reading on the full-service regular gasoline pump when the station opens on the first day, the 10th day, and the 25th day of the month, and when the station closes on the last day of the month.

(i) An antigun-control group's survey:

Do you believe that private citizens have the right to own firearms to defend themselves, their families, and their property from violent criminal attack?
____ Yes
____ No

(j) A survey of the general public:

In the next year, after accounting for inflation, do you think your real personal income will go up or down?

1. Up
2. Stay the same
3. Down
4. (Don't know)

(k) A survey of the general public:

Some people say that companies should be required by law to label all chemicals and substances that the government states are potentially harmful. The label would tell what the chemical or substance is, what dangers it might pose, and what safety procedures should be used in handling the substance. Other people say that such laws would be too strict. They say the law should require labels on only those chemicals and substances that the companies themselves decide are potentially harmful. Such a law, they say, would be less costly for the companies and would permit them to exclude those chemicals and substances they consider to be trade secrets. Which of these views is closest to your own?

1. Require labels on all chemicals and substances that the government states are potentially harmful.
2. (Don't know)
3. Require labels on only those chemicals and substances that companies decide are potentially harmful.

(l) A survey of voters:

Since agriculture is vital to our state's economy, how do you feel about the administration's farm policies?
Strongly favor
Somewhat favor
Somewhat oppose
Strongly oppose
Unsure

2. The following question was asked in an Internet survey:

We are going to ask you to classify the type of fan you consider yourself to be for different sports and sports programs.
Diehard Fan: Watch games, follow up on scores and sports news multiple times a day
Avid Fan: Watch games, follow up on scores and sports news once a day
Casual Fan: Watch games, follow-up on scores and sports news occasionally
Championship Fan: Watch games, follow up on scores and sports news only during championships or playoffs
Non-Fan: Never watch games or follow up on scores
Anti-Fan: Dislike, oppose, or object to a certain sport

Does this question do a good job of avoiding ambiguity?

3. How might the wording of a question asking about income influence the answers of respondents?
4. Design an open-ended response question to measure reactions to a Xerox magazine ad.
5. What is the difference between a leading question and a loaded question?
6. Design a complete questionnaire to evaluate job satisfaction.
7. Design a complete (but short) questionnaire to measure student evaluations of a college course.
8. Develop a checklist of things to consider in questionnaire construction.
9. The Apple Assistance Center offers a hotline to solve problems for users of Macintosh computers and other Apple products. Design a short (postcard-size) questionnaire to evaluate consumer satisfaction/service quality for the Apple Assistance Center.
10. A client tells a researcher that she wants a questionnaire to evaluate the importance of 30 product characteristics and to determine how her firm's brand and 10 competing brands rate on these characteristics. The researcher believes that this questionnaire will induce respondent fatigue because it is far too long. Should the researcher do exactly what the client says or risk losing the business by suggesting a different approach?
11. A lobbying organization designs a short questionnaire about its political position. It also includes a membership solicitation with the questionnaire. Is this approach ethical?

Exploring the Internet

1. Visit the Strategos Institute at http://www.strategos.com/survey/. Evaluate the questions on the questionnaire.
2. Visit Google at http://www.google.com and conduct a search using the key phrase "Questionnaire Design." How many Web sites contain this phrase? Find an interesting Web site and report on your findings.
3. A language translator (English to Spanish, French to English, etc.) can be found at http://babelfish.altavista.com/translate.dyn.

WebSurveyor Activities

Video Games

Run the WebSurveyor Desktop software, and click "From a template" under the heading "Create a new survey" from the Getting Started Wizard. (If the Getting Started Wizard does not appear, click Tools and then Options from the main menu, make sure "Display the Getting Started Wizard for new surveys" is checked, and then click OK. Next click File and then New from the main menu, and then click "From a template" under the heading "Create a new survey.") Use the Survey Builder Wizard and click on the "Marketing Competitive Intelligence" category. Then select the Product Recall Survey template. Identify a product category that interests you (perhaps video games) and identify three or four brands in the product category (perhaps Nintendo Gamecube, Sony PlayStation, and Microsoft Xbox). Create a questionnaire using the standard template. What questions need to be added or deleted to make this questionnaire fit your research objectives?

Starry Nights

The Starry Nights questionnaire was developed using the WebSurveyor's Survey Builder Wizard. The category "Marketing Customer Needs" was chosen and then "Customer Satisfaction—Consumer Service." Some questions were modified. Using the WebSurveyor Desktop software, select File and then Open from the main menu, and then select the file named "StarryNights.ws3." The Question List will appear. Click on "Preview" under Survey Editing to view the questionnaire as a Web page. Do other changes need to be made?

Human Resource Questionnaire

A manager used WebSurveyor's question library to create a questionnaire with 20 attitude scales. Using the WebSurveyor Desktop software, open the survey named "HumanResources.ws3." The Question List will appear. Click on "Preview" under Survey Editing to view the questionnaire as a Web page. Evaluate the questionnaire and, if necessary, create a revised questionnaire.

Designing Your Own Questionnaire

- Using the WebSurveyor Desktop software, design a short but complete questionnaire to measure consumer satisfaction with an airline.
- Using the WebSurveyor Desktop software, design a questionnaire for your local Big Brothers and Big Sisters organization to investigate awareness of and willingness to volunteer time to this organization.

Case Suggestions

Case 20: Canterbury Travels
Case 21: United States Postal Service
Case 22: Schönbrunn Palace in Vienna

PART

5

SAMPLING AND FIELDWORK

CHAPTER

16

SAMPLE DESIGNS AND SAMPLING PROCEDURES

What you will learn in this chapter

- To define the terms *sample, population, population element,* and *census.*
- To explain why a sample rather than a complete census may be taken.
- To discuss the issues concerning the identification of the target population and the selection of a sampling frame.
- To discuss common forms of sampling frames, such as reverse directories, and to discuss sampling frame error.
- To distinguish between random sampling and systematic (nonsampling) errors.
- To explain the various types of systematic (nonsampling) errors resulting from sample selection.
- To discuss the advantages and disadvantages of the various types of probability and nonprobability samples.
- To understand how to choose an appropriate sample design.

We all know it's important to make a good first impression, because, after a sample exposure, people make judgments about what type of people we are. Even a member of the Polar Bear Swimming Club tests the early March water of Lake Michigan with a toe before diving in. Stand in a bookstore and observe the process of sampling. A customer generally picks up a book, looks at the cover, and then samples a few pages to get a feeling for the writing style and the content before deciding whether or not to buy. A high school student who visits a college classroom to listen to a professor's lecture is employing a sampling technique. Selecting a college or university on the basis of one classroom visit may not be scientific sampling, but in a personal situation it may be a practical sampling experience. These examples illustrate the intuitive nature of sampling in everyday usages when it is impossible, inconvenient, or too expensive to measure every item in a population.

Although sampling is commonplace in daily activities, most of these familiar samples are not scientific. The concept of sampling may be intuitive, but the actual process of sampling can be quite complex. Because sampling is a central aspect of business research, it requires in-depth examination.

This chapter explains the nature of sampling and how to determine the appropriate sample design. ■

SAMPLING TERMINOLOGY

The process of **sampling** involves any procedure using a small number of items or parts of the whole population to make conclusions regarding the whole population. A **sample** is a subset, or some part, of a larger population. The purpose of sampling is to enable researchers to estimate some unknown characteristic of the population.

We have defined sampling in terms of the population to be studied. A **population,** or **universe,** is any complete group of people, companies, hospitals, stores, college students, or the like that share some set of characteristics. When a distinction is made between "population" and "universe," it is on the basis of whether the group is finite (population) or infinite (universe). The term **population element** refers to an individual member of the population. A **census** is an investigation of all the individual elements that make up the population: a total enumeration rather than a sample.

WHY SAMPLE?

At a wine-tasting party guests all recognize the impossibility of doing anything but sampling, but in a scientific study, when the objective is to estimate an unknown population value, why should a sample be taken rather than a complete census?

Pragmatic Reasons

Applied business research projects usually have budget and time constraints. If the U.S. government wished to take a census of federal employees' reactions to a proposed retirement program, millions of workers would have to be contacted. Some of these would be inaccessible (for example, out of the country), and it would be impossible to contact all of them within a short time.

Of course, a researcher investigating a population with an extremely small number of population elements may elect to conduct a census rather than a sample because the cost, labor, and time constraints are relatively insignificant. Thus, a company that wants to assess programmers' satisfaction with the computer-networking system may not have any pragmatic reason not to circulate a questionnaire to all 25 of its employees. In most situations, however, there are many pragmatic reasons for sampling. Sampling cuts costs, reduces labor requirements, and gathers vital information quickly.[1] Although these advantages may be sufficient in themselves for using a sample rather than a census, there are other reasons.

Accurate and Reliable Results

Another major reason for sampling is that samples, if properly selected, are sufficiently accurate in most cases. If the elements of a population are quite similar, only a small sample is necessary to accurately portray the characteristic of interest. Most of us have had blood samples taken from the finger, the arm, or another part of the body. The assumption is that because the blood is sufficiently similar throughout the body, the characteristics of the blood can be determined on the basis of a sample.

When the population elements are highly homogeneous, samples are highly representative of the population. Under these circumstances almost any sample is as good as another.[2] Even when populations have considerable

sampling
The process of using a small number of items or parts of a larger population to make conclusions about the whole population.

sample
A subset, or some part, of a larger population.

population (universe)
A complete group of entities sharing some common set of characteristics.

population element
An individual member of a specific population.

census
An investigation of all the individual elements making up a population.

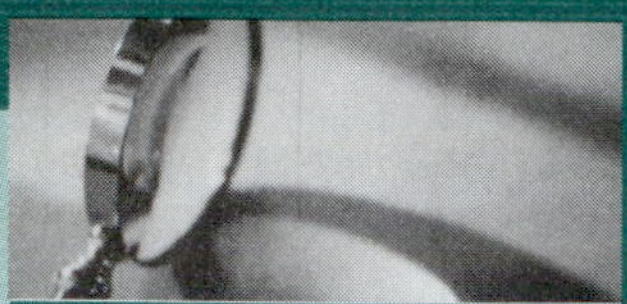

Research Insight

William's Census Was Ahead of Its Time

After William the Conqueror took over England, he wanted to see what his conquest had netted him.[3] Monarchs back then lacked basic information such as the number of estates or livestock in the kingdom. So in 1086, William ordered a unique survey. Every village and fief was counted to the last building, netting detailed data on how much land and wealth each person owned. He used the data to levy taxes. The result was "The Domesday Book," a corruption of "Doomsday," the Day of Judgment. The king's taxes were considered as inescapable as divine judgment. No other king of the Middle Ages conducted such a thorough inventory. Today, governments conduct censuses, keep our names and birthdates on file, and zealously document everything that can be taxed. It's difficult to imagine an age when people were not an entry in the government's books.

heterogeneity, large samples provide data of sufficient precision to make most decisions.

Exhibit 16.1 offers a simple demonstration of how sampling works. The four photographs show how one can take different-size samples and produce a very generalizable conclusion. The first photograph is finely screened and is therefore printed with thousands of dots of ink. Because of the fineness of detail, one might say that this photograph contains nearly all of the detail, or information, that can be provided. In other photographs less detail is provided. Photograph 2 is made up of approximately 2,000 dots. The face is still very clear, but not as much so as in the first photograph; some detail is missing, but the face is still recognizable. Photograph 3 is made up of only 1,000 dots, constituting a sample that is only half as large as that in Photograph 2; the face can still be recognized. In Photograph 4 the sample is down to 250 dots—yet if you look at the picture at a distance you can still make out a face and identify it as the same one shown in Photograph 1. The 250-dot sample is still useful despite the fact that it contains only a small fraction of the number of dots in the other photographs. *Precision* has suffered, but *accuracy* has not. Of course, samples are accurate only when researchers have taken care to draw representative samples properly. More will be said about this later in the chapter.

A sample may be more accurate than a census. In a census of a large population there is a greater likelihood of nonsampling errors. In a survey, mistakes may occur that are unrelated to the selection of people in the study. For example, a response may be coded incorrectly, or the keyboard operator might make a data-entry error. Interviewer mistakes, tabulation errors, and other nonsampling errors may increase during a census because of the increased volume of work. In a sample, increased accuracy is possible because the fieldwork and tabulation of the data can be more closely supervised than would be possible in a census. In a field survey a small, well-trained, closely supervised group may do a more careful and accurate job of collecting information than a large group of nonprofessional interviewers trying to contact everyone. An interesting case in point is the fact that the Bureau of the Census uses samples

EXHIBIT 16.1 A PHOTOGRAPHIC EXAMPLE OF HOW SAMPLING WORKS[4]

Photograph 1
Portrait of young man

Photograph 2
2,000 dots

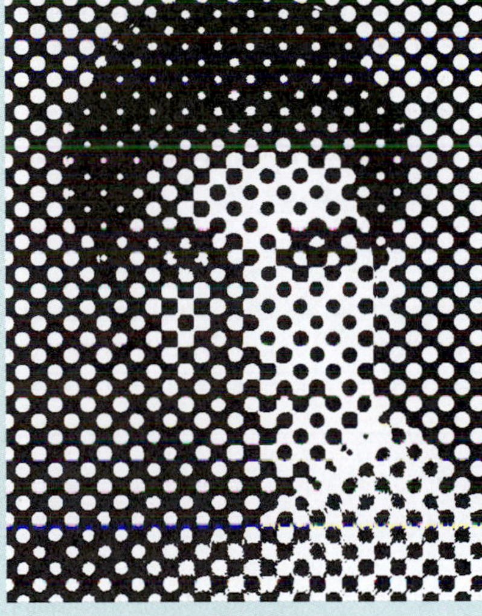
Photograph 3
1,000 dots

Photograph 4
250 dots

to check the accuracy of the U.S. Census. If the sample indicates a possible source of error, the census is redone.

Destruction of Test Units

Many research projects, especially those in quality control testing, require the destruction of the items being tested. If the manufacturer of firecrackers wished to find out whether each product met a specific production standard, there would be no product left after the testing. This is the exact situation in many business field experiments. If an experimental treatment were presented to every potential employee or customer, no employees or potential customers would be left uncontacted after the experiment. In other words, if there is a finite population and everyone in the population participates in the research and cannot be replaced, no population elements remain to be selected as sampling units. The test units have been destroyed.

PRACTICAL SAMPLING CONCEPTS

Researchers must make several decisions before a sample is taken. Exhibit 16.2 presents these decisions as a series of sequential stages, even though the order of decisions does not always follow this particular sequence. These decisions are highly interrelated. The issues associated with each of these stages, except for fieldwork, are discussed in this chapter and in Chapter 17; fieldwork is discussed in Chapter 18.

EXHIBIT 16.2 STAGES IN SELECTION OF A SAMPLE

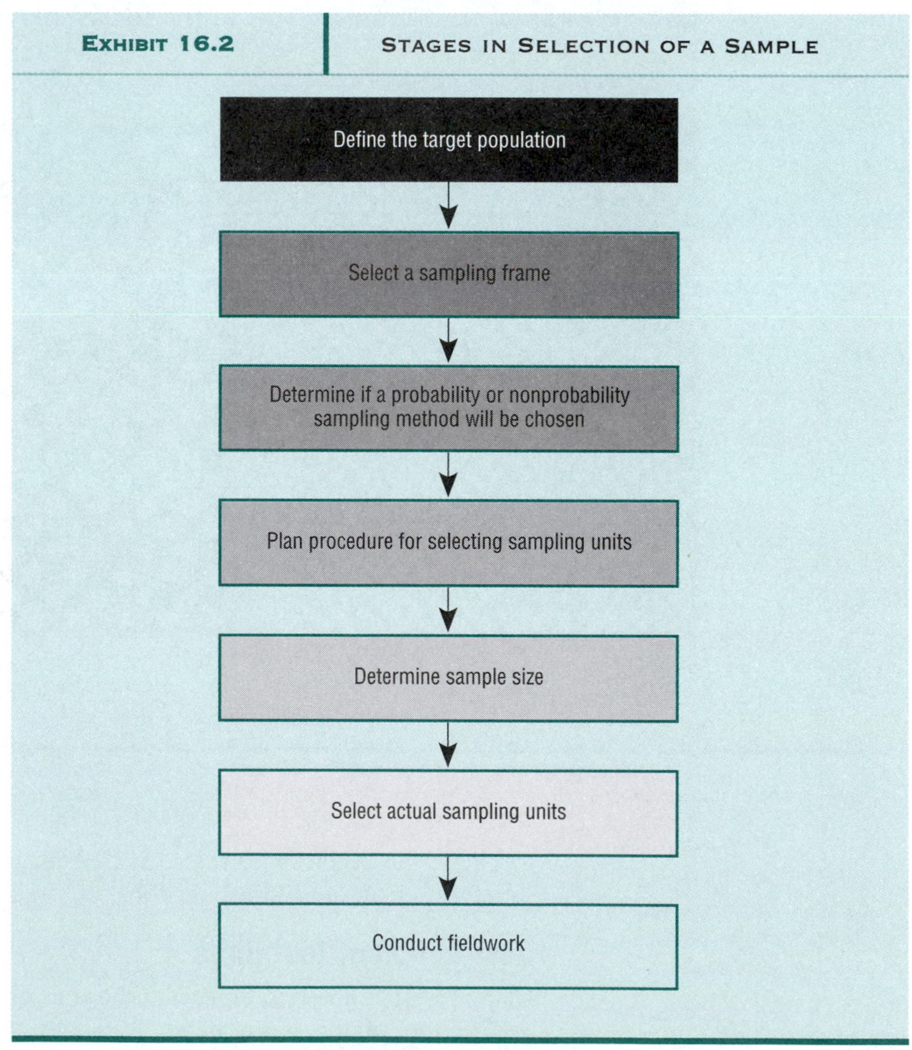
Define the target population
Select a sampling frame
Determine if a probability or nonprobability sampling method will be chosen
Plan procedure for selecting sampling units
Determine sample size
Select actual sampling units
Conduct fieldwork

Defining the Target Population

target population
The specific, complete group relevant to the research project.

Once the decision to sample has been made, the first question related to sampling concerns identifying the **target population,** that is, the complete group of specific population elements relevant to the research project. What is the relevant population? In many cases this is not a difficult question. Registered voters may be clearly identifiable. Similarly, if the 206 employees of a company are the population of concern, there are few definitional problems. In other cases the decision may be difficult. One survey concerning industrial buyer behavior incorrectly defined the population as the purchasing agents whom sales representatives regularly contacted. Investigators discovered, after the survey, that industrial engineers within the customer companies had substantial impact on buying decisions, even though they rarely talked with the salespeople. Frequently, the appropriate population element may be the household or organizational unit rather than the individual member of the household or the employee. This presents some problems, because household lists or lists of population elements may not be available.

At the outset of the sampling process, it is vitally important to carefully define the target population so the proper source from which the data are to be collected can be identified.[5] Answering questions about the critical characteristics of the population is the usual technique for defining the target population. Does the term *comic book reader* include children under six years who do not actually read the words? Does *all persons west of the Mississippi* include people in east-bank metropolitan areas bordering the river, such as East St. Louis, Illinois?

The question "To whom do we want to talk?" must be answered. It may be users, nonusers, recently hired employees, or doctors. To implement the sample in the field, tangible characteristics should be used to define the population. A hospital might define a population as all women who are still capable of bearing children. However, a more specific operational definition would be women between the ages of 12 and 50. While this definition by age may exclude a few women who are capable of childbearing and include some who are not, it is still more explicit and provides a manageable basis for the sample design.[6]

The Sampling Frame

sampling frame
The list of elements from which a sample may be drawn; also called working population.

In actual practice the sample will be drawn from a list of population elements that is often somewhat different from the target population that has been defined. A **sampling frame** is the list of elements from which the sample may be drawn. A simple example of a sampling frame might be a list of all members of the American Banking Association.

It is generally not feasible to compile a list that does not exclude some members of the population. For example, if the student telephone directory is utilized as a sampling frame listing of your university's student population, the sampling frame may exclude those students who registered late, students without phones, or those who have their telephones listed only under their roommates' or pets' name.

The sampling frame is also called the *working population* because it provides the list that can be worked with operationally. If a complete list of population elements is not accessible, materials such as maps or aerial photographs may be utilized as a sampling frame.

EXHIBIT 16.3 | **MAILING LIST DIRECTORY PAGE**[7]

BUSINESSES BY CITY

ABBEVILLE, AL (AREA CODE 334)

COMPANY	ADDRESS	ZIP CODE	PHONE	SIC CODE	CREDIT CODE*	EMP SIZE	EST. SALES
ABBEVILLE, AL				**AREA CODE - 334**			
A W HERNDON OIL CO	100 N Court Square St	36310	585-6424	5983-03	A	F	
ABBEVILLE CHRISTIAN ACADEMY	Eufaula Hwy	36310	585-5100	8211-03	I	D	
ABBEVILLE FOREST PRODUCTS	West Washington	36310	585-5566	2421-01	A	F	F
ABBEVILLE INTERMEDIATE SCHOOL	200 Gilliam St	36310	585-2185	8211-03	I	D	
ABBEVILLE PRIMARY SCHOOL	100 Elm St	36310	585-3679	8211-03	I	D	
BUSTER'S IGA	514 Kirkland St	36310	585-2432	5411-05	B	D	D
CUTLER EGG PRODUCTS INC	104 Industrial Park	36310	585-2268	5144-03	A	F	H
FAMILY PRACTICE CTR	217 Dothan Rd	36310	585-6421	8011-01	B	D	C
FOUR-C TRUCKING	Highway 431 Byp	36310	585-2249	4212-01	C	D	D
FRANKLIN HARDWOODS INC	Singletary Rd	36310	585-5059	2435-01	B	E	E
GREAT SOUTHERN WOOD PRESERVING	Highway 431 N	36310	585-2291	2491-01	B	D	I
GREEN BUSH WOOD PRODUCTS INC	305 W Washington St	36310	585-2253	2499-02	B	D	C
HARDEE'S	650 Ozark Rd	36310	585-6111	5812-08	B	D	C
HENRY COUNTY NURSING HOME	212 Dothan Rd	36310	585-2241	8051-01	A	F	E
HENRY FARM CTR INC	809 Columbia Rd	36310	585-5525	5999-12	B	D	G
MURPHY INDUSTRIES	Hwy 431 S	36310	585-2810	6531-18	B	D	C
MURPHY OIL CO	Highway N 431	36310	585-2863	5172-13	B	D	H
PIGGLY WIGGLY	100 W Washington St	36310	585-2789	5411-05	B	D	D
TELEDYNE CONTROLS	Industrial Park Rd	36310	585-6426	3721-01	A	E	F
TILLIS LAND & TIMBER CO	Highway 27 S	36310	585-2277	2411-98	B	D	E
U S ARMY RESERVE	US Highway 431 N	36310	585-2263	9711-01	I	E	
VALCOM BUSINESS CTR	809 Columbia Rd	36310	585-2239	5734-07	A	F	G
WATFORD LOGGING CO	431 By Pass	36310	585-5588	2411-02	B	D	E
WEST POINT STEVENS INC	Ozark Rd	36310	585-2211	2399-12	A	H	H
ABERNANT, AL				**AREA CODE - 205**			
ALABAMA LAND & MINERAL CORP	Lawsontown Johns Rd & Co Rd 36	35440	302-0870	2999-98	A	F	G
ADAMSVILLE, AL				**AREA CODE - 205**			
ADAMSVILLE CITY HALL	4828 Main St	35005	674-5671	9111-04	I	E	
ADAMSVILLE ELEMENTARY SCHOOL	4600 Hazelwood Rd	35005	674-6481	8211-03	I	E	
ADAMSVILLE FIRE DEPT	4828 Main St	35005	674-5671	9224-04	I	E	
BOTTENFIELD JUNIOR HIGH SCHOOL	400 Hillcrest Rd	35005	674-5605	8211-03	I	E	
BOYD HEATING & AIR	5127 Main St	35005	674-5668	1742-05	B	D	D
BRUNO'S	3980 Adamsville Pkwy	35005	674-9903	5992-01	A	F	E
FLANGE PIPE OF ALABAMA INC	4128 Adamsville Pkwy	35005	674-0960	3498-02	C	D	C
FOOD WORLD	3980 Adamsville Pkwy	35005	674-9903	5411-05	A	E	F
MC CONNELL NIGHT HAWK AGENCY	1630 Wilkinson Dr	35005	674-7742	7381-04	B	D	B
MC DONALD'S	5721 Veterans Memorial Dr	35005	674-7288	5812-08	C	D	B
MINOR HIGH SCHOOL	2285 Minor Pkwy	35005	798-3770	8211-03	I	F	
WINN-DIXIE	5711 Veterans Memorial Dr	35005	674-1922	5411-05	A	E	F
ADDISON, AL				**AREA CODE - 256**			
ADDISON ELEMENTARY SCHOOL	Highway 41	35540	747-1665	8211-03	I	D	
ADDISON FABRICATORS INC	Highway 278	35540	747-1546	1791-03	B	D	D
ADDISON HIGH SCHOOL	Highway 41	35540	747-2286	8211-03	I	E	
CAVALIER HOMES INC	Highway 41 N & Cavalier Rd	35540	747-1575	2452-02	A	I	J
CAVALIER HOMES OF ALABAMA INC	Highway 41 N & Cavalier Rd	35540	747-1575	5039-17	A	H	
CAVALIER HOMES OF ALABAMA INC	Old Saudus Rd	35540	747-1503	5271-02	A	F	G
HYATT'S MARKET	Mc Hann Rd	35540	747-6005	5411-05	B	D	D
LEE'S FURNITURE	Highway 278	35540	747-6518	2599-01	B	E	E
SOUTHERN ENERGY HOMES INC	Highway 41 N	35540	747-8589	2451-01	A	I	I
SOUTHERN LIFE STYLE HOMES	Highway 41 N	35540	747-1509	5039-17	A	F	G
SOUTHERN LIFE STYLE II	Highway 41 S	35540	747-1506	2451-01	A	F	G
WIND-MAR SUPPLY INC	Highway 41 N	35540	747-6013	5211-07	A		
ADGER, AL				**AREA CODE - 205**			

ALEXANDER CITY, AL (AREA CODE 256)

COMPANY	ADDRESS	ZIP CODE	PHONE	SIC CODE	CREDIT CODE*	EMP SIZE	EST. SALES
BIG SPRING LAKE ELEM SCHOOL	257 Country Club Rd	35951	878-7922	8211-03	I	E	
BILLY THRASH LINCOLN-MERCURY	555 Al Highway 75 N	35951	878-7282	5511-02	A	D	F
BOWATER LUMBER CO	660 Industrial Blvd	35950	878-7987	5031-08	A	F	G
BRYANT MANUFACTURING CO	2320 George Wallace Dr	35951	878-3561	2599-01	B	E	E
BURGER KING	103 US Highway 431	35950	878-1193	5812-08	B	E	C
CAPTAIN D'S SEAFOOD RESTAURANT	Highway 431 N	35950	878-0332	5812-08	B	D	B
CATFISH CABIN	8524 US Highway 431	35950	878-8170	5812-08	B	E	C
CHAR-PEN-SHIR HOSIERY INC	1001 Baltimore Ave	35950	878-5278	2252-01	B	E	D
CHARTER COMMUNICATIONS	904 Rose Rd	35951	878-3802	4841-01	B	D	E
CHINET CO	608 Mathis Mill Rd	35951	878-8900	2621-01	A	F	G
COMPASS BANK	300 W Main St	35950	878-5700	6021-01	A	D	
COOK & SONS ACE HARDWARE	7008 US Highway 431	35950	878-2241	5251-04	B	D	C
COOK'S PEST CONTROL INC	175 Highway 75 N	35950	878-5541	7342-01	B	D	C
CORBIN'S HEATING & AIR	455 Al Highway 75 N	35951	878-9138	1711-17	B	D	D
DAIRY QUEEN	8031 US Highway 431	35950	891-4000	5812-08	B	D	B
EMPLOYMENT SERVICE	5920 US Highway 431	35950	878-3031	7361-10	I	D	B
EVANS ELEMENTARY SCHOOL	901 W McKinney Ave	35950	878-7698	8211-03	I	D	
FABCO	1009 Portwood Dr	35951	878-5010	3523-11	A	F	G
FOOD WORLD	5111 US Highway 431	35950	878-9130	5411-05	A	E	F
FOODLAND	313 Sand Mountain Dr SE	35950	891-0390	5411-05	A	F	F
GENESIS MANUFACTURING	521 Baltimore Ave	35950	878-1003	3999-46	B	D	D
GILBERT & BAKER FORD	7394 US Highway 431	35950	891-3000	5511-02	B	D	F
GOLD KIST INC	80 Goldkist St	35950	878-0528	5191-12	A	D	F
GUNTERSVILLE OUTLET	701 Railroad Ave	35951	878-2866	5999-31	A	H	
HARDEE'S	Highway 431	35950	878-7945	5812-08	B	D	B
HINTON MITCHEM TRACTOR INC	4811 US Highway 431	35950	878-1631	5083-04	B	D	E
HOME BANK	7100 US Highway 431	35950	891-1280	6021-01	A	D	
HOSPICE OF MARSHALL COUNTY	8787 US Highway 431	35950	891-7724	8399-98	I	D	
HOUGH INTERNATIONAL	1000 Railroad Ave	35951	878-8254	3523-03	B	E	G
HOWARD BENTLEY PONT GMC JEEP	8048 US Highway 431	35950	878-0992	5511-02	A	D	F
INDUSTRIAL MATERIAL HANDLING	7187 Hustleville Rd	35950	582-1585	3443-05	A	F	F
JUST IN TIME CARTAGE INC	8816 US Highway 431	35950	878-5482	4213-09	B	D	D
K MART	7200 US Highway 431	35950	878-9030	5311-02	A	F	F
KAYLOR'S SCHOOL & OFFICE SUPLS	6325 US Highway 431	35950	878-1200	5112-13	B	E	F
KENDALL HEALTHCARE PRODUCTS CO	127 Textile Ave	35950	878-4401	3842-98	A	G	H
KIRBY CO	5850 US Highway 431	35950	891-3600	5722-16	C	D	D
LABEL MASTERS	651 Railroad Ave	35951	891-4633	5099-05	A	F	H
LIBERTY NATIONAL INSURANCE CO	104 W Alabama Ave # B	35950	878-0981	6411-12	B	D	D
MC CORD AVENUE ELEMENTARY SCHL	303 E McCord Ave	35950	878-6160	8211-03	I	D	
MC DONALD'S	7375 US Highway 431	35950	878-6755	5812-08	B	D	B
MC GRIFF DOWDY & ASSOC	203 S Hambrick St	35950	543-2045	8721-01	B	D	D
MEDICAL CENTER HOME HEALTH	11491 US Highway 431	35950	878-7022	8082-01	B	D	C
MITCHELL GROCERY	550 Railroad Ave	35950	878-4211	5141-05	A	G	I
MOULTRIE NISSAN	9736 US Highway 431	35950	878-4390	5511-02	A	D	F
MUELLER CO	956 Industrial Blvd	35950	878-7930	3321-98	A	G	H
MUNICIPAL UTILITIES BOARD	210 W Main St	35950	878-3761	4941-02	A	E	F
PARAGON PICTURE GALLERY	1605 Progress Dr	35950	593-4700	2499-98	A	F	F
PAUL SMITH CHEVROLET	7710 US Highway 431	35950	878-0281	5511-02	A	D	F
PIGGLY WIGGLY	250 Al Highway 75 N	35951	878-2075	5411-05	B	E	F
PIZZA HUT	6815 US Highway 431	35950	878-7373	5812-08	B	D	B
PLASTICRAFT MFG CO	115 Plasticraft Dr	35951	878-4105	3089-02	A	F	F
PRINTMASTER INC	632 Smith Rd	35951	878-4880	2673-01	A	F	F
PRINTMASTER INC	651 Railroad Ave	35951	878-8880	2673-01	C	E	E
PROGRESS RAIL SVC CORP	1000 Industrial Blvd	35950	878-5849	3743-04	A	H	H
PROGRESS RAIL SVC CORP	1600 Progress Dr	35950	593-1260	3743-04	A		
QUINCY'S FAMILY STEAKHOUSE	501 N Carlisle St	35951	878-8156	5812-08	B	E	C
RAPID CARE INC	9511 US Highway 431	35950	891-7001	8011-04	C	D	D
RAVEN INDUSTRIES INC	709 Railroad Ave	35951	878-6606	3089-02	B	D	C
RE/MAX THE REAL ESTATE GROUP	302 E Main St	35950	878-1000	6531-18	B	D	C
REEVES RUBBER INC	304 Marshall St	35950	878-6810	3053-02	B	E	E
REGIONS BANK ALBERTVILLE	116 Sand Mountain Dr W	35950	878-4616	6021-01	A		
RICK'S ELECTRICAL & PLUMBING	436 Martling Rd	35951	878-6414	1731-01	C	D	D
ROSS-GRADEN LUMBER CO	6737 US Highway 431	35950	878-1461	5211-42	A	D	D
SAND MOUNTAIN FAMILY PRACTICE	5104 US Highway 431	35950	878-8180	8011-01	B	D	C

The discrepancy between the definition of the population and the sampling frame is the first potential source of error associated with selection of a sample. These errors will be discussed later in this chapter.

mailing list
A list of the names, addresses, and phone numbers of specific populations.

Some firms, called *sampling services* or *list brokers,* specialize in providing **mailing lists** or databases that include the names, addresses, phone numbers, and e-mail addresses of specific populations. Exhibit 16.3 shows a page from a mailing list company's offerings. Lists offered by companies such as this one are compiled from subscriptions to professional journals, credit card applications, warranty card registrations, and a variety of other sources. One sampling service obtained its listing of households with children from an ice cream retailer who gave away free ice cream cones on children's birthdays. (The children filled out cards with their names, addresses, and birthdays, which the retailer then sold to the mailing list company.)

reverse directory
A directory similar to a telephone directory in which listings are by city and street address or by telephone numbers rather than alphabetical by last name.

A valuable source of names is Equifax's series of city directories. Equifax City Directory provides complete, comprehensive, and accurate business and residential information. The city directory records the name of each resident over 18 years of age and lists pertinent information about each household. Reverse directory pages offer a unique benefit. A **reverse directory** provides, in a different format, the same information contained in a telephone directory. Listings may be by city and street address or by phone number, rather than alphabetical by last name. Such a directory is particularly useful when a retailer wishes to survey only a certain geographical area of a city or when census tracts are to be selected on the basis of income or another demographic criterion.

sampling frame error
Error that occurs when certain sample elements are not listed or available and are not represented in the sampling frame.

A **sampling frame error** occurs when certain sample elements are excluded or when the entire population is not accurately represented in the sampling frame. One city's manager for community development, in preparation for an upcoming bond issue election, used randomly generated telephone numbers as the basis for a sample survey dealing with attitudes toward capital improvements. When the bond issue failed, consultants pointed out that the appropriate sampling frame would have been a list of registered voters, not adults with phones (since many might not have voted in this type of election). By including respondents who should not have been listed as members of the population, the city manager committed a sampling frame error.

Population elements can also be overrepresented in a sampling frame. A savings and loan association defined its population as all individuals who had savings accounts. However, when it drew a sample from a list of *accounts,* rather than from a list of names of *individuals,* individuals who had multiple accounts were overrepresented in the sample.

Sampling Frames for International Business Research

The availability of sampling frames varies dramatically around the globe. In some countries governments do not conduct censuses of population, telephone directories are incomplete, voter registration lists do not exist, and accurate maps of urban areas are unobtainable.[8] However, in Taiwan, Japan, and other Asian countries, building a sampling frame is relatively easy because the governments release some census information about individuals. If a family moves, updated census information must be reported to a centralized government agency before community services (water, gas, electricity, education, etc.) are made available.[9] This information is then published in the local *Inhabitants' Register.*

Sampling Units

sampling unit
A single element or group of elements subject to selection in the sample.

During the actual sampling process, the elements of the population must be selected according to a certain procedure. The **sampling unit** is a single element or group of elements subject to selection in the sample. For example, if an airline wishes to sample passengers, every 25th name on a complete list of passengers may be taken. In this case the sampling unit is the same as the element. Alternatively, the airline could first select flights as the sampling unit, then select certain passengers on the previously selected flights. In this case defining the sampling unit occurs in two stages.

primary sampling unit (PSU)
A unit selected in the first stage of sampling.

secondary sampling unit
A unit selected in the second stage of sampling.

If the target population has first been divided into units, such as airline flights, additional terminology must be used. The term **primary sampling units (PSUs)** designates units selected in the first stage of sampling. If successive stages of sampling are conducted, sampling units are called **secondary sampling units** or tertiary sampling units (if three stages are necessary).

When there is no list of population elements, the sampling unit is generally something other than the population element. For example, in a random-digit dialing study, the sampling unit will be telephone numbers.

Exhibit 16.4 (page 378) illustrates that defining a sampling unit, such as a member of a household, may not be a simple task.

Research Insight

You Can Learn a Lot from a Few: George Gallup's Nation of Numbers

In the summer of 1932 Iowa Democrats nominated a 60-year-old widow named Ola Babcock Miller as the party's candidate for secretary of state.[10] It was no big deal. No Democrat had carried the state since the Civil War, but it was a nice thing to do, a gesture of respect for her late husband, a small-town newspaper publisher who had spent his life trying, vainly, to bring down Iowa Republicanism.

Mrs. Miller called in the family for help. Her son-in-law, a college professor who had just joined a New York advertising agency, had some ideas. Why not have some people go door to door, using this "scientific" plan he had, and ask voters what they wanted?

The son-in-law's name was George H. Gallup. Mrs. Miller won.

Young George—he was born in 1901—was a go-getter. His father had been a dreamer, a country schoolteacher who tried to develop what he called "a new logic of lateral thinking" and built an eight-sided house on the theory that it would offer better protection against plains windstorms. But George left the octagonal house and the hometown, Jefferson, as soon as he could find his way in a bigger world. The first stop was Iowa City and the State University of Iowa. In 1922, between his junior and senior years, he answered an advertisement for summer employment in St. Louis. The *Post-Dispatch* hired 50 students to survey the city, questioning readers about what they liked and didn't like in the paper.

The students were hired to go to every door in St. Louis—there were 55,000 homes in the city then—and ask the same questions. Gallup, one hot day, knocked on one door too many, got the same answers one time too many, and decided: There's got to be a better way.

"A New Technique for Objective Methods for Measuring Reader Interest in Newspapers" was the way, and the title of Gallup's Ph.D. thesis at Iowa. Working with the Des Moines *Register* and *Tribune* and the 200-year-old statistical theory probabilities of the Swiss mathematician Jakob Bernoulli, Gallup developed "sampling" techniques. You didn't have to talk to everybody, he said, as long as you randomly selected interviews according to a sampling plan that took into account whatever diversity was relevant in the universe of potential respondents—geographic, ethnic, economic.

Although not everybody understood or believed then—or now—this intellectual invention was a big deal. "Guesswork eliminated in new method for determining reader interest" was the lead headline of the February 8, 1930, issue of the newspaper industry's trade journal, *Editor & Publisher.* There

RANDOM SAMPLING ERROR AND NONSAMPLING ERROR

Political pollsters drawing a sample of 1,000 voters to measure if citizens intend to support a bond issue for the construction of a new jail expect the sample to be representative of all voters. However, if there is a difference between the value of a sample statistic of interest (for example, average likelihood of voting for the bond issue) and the value of the corresponding population parameter (again, average likelihood of voting for the bond issue), there has been a *statistical error.*

In Chapter 9 we classified two basic causes of differences between statistics and parameters: random sampling errors and systematic (nonsampling) errors.

random sampling error
The difference between the sample result and the result of a census conducted using identical procedures; a statistical fluctuation that occurs because of chance variation in the elements selected for a sample.

An estimation from a sample is not exactly the same as a census count. **Random sampling error** is the difference between the sample result and the result of a census conducted by identical procedures.[11] Of course, the result of a census is unknown unless one is taken, which is rarely done. Other sources of was a photograph of a big, stolid midwesterner above the caption: "George H. Gallup, instructor, U. of Iowa."

The instructor tried to explain what he was talking about and doing. "Suppose there are seven thousand white beans and three thousand black beans well churned in a barrel," he said then, and again more than 52 years later as we walked together near his office in Princeton, New Jersey. "If you scoop out one hundred of them, you'll get approximately seventy white beans and thirty black in your hand, and the range of your possible error can be computed mathematically. As long as the barrel contains many more beans than your handful, the proportion will remain within that margin of error nine hundred ninety-seven times out of one thousand."

Well, it seemed to work for newspapers, and George Gallup, instructor, was in great demand around the country. He became head of the journalism department at Drake University and then switched to a professorship at Northwestern—all the while doing readership surveys for papers in Chicago, Cleveland, Buffalo, and points east and west. He was hot, and in that summer of '32 a new advertising agency, Young & Rubicam, invited him to New York to create a research department and procedures for evaluating the effectiveness of advertising. He did that too. One of his first Y&R surveys, based on newspaper experience, indicated that the number of readers of advertisements was proportional to the length of the paragraphs in a piece of copy.

And, of course, by the end of that year, 1932, with his mother-in-law's election, Gallup was confident that his methodology was valid not only for beans and newspaper readers but for voters too. As long as you understood the sampling universe—white, black, male, female, rich, poor, urban, rural, Republican, Democratic—you could predict elections or calculate public attitudes on public questions by interviewing a relatively small number of people.

So Gallup went out and formed the grandly titled American Institute of Public Opinion. Keeping his job at Young & Rubicam, he began syndicating surveys to newspapers under the title: "America Speaks: The National Weekly Poll of Public Opinion." The first Gallup Poll, released in October 1935, focused on the question, asked of 3,000 Americans: "Do you think expenditures by the government for relief and recovery are: Too Little? Too Great? About Right?" Three out of five respondents said, "Too Great."

error can also be present. Random sampling error occurs because of chance variation in the scientific selection of sampling units.

The sampling units, even though properly selected according to sampling theory, may not perfectly represent the population, but they are generally reliable estimates. As you'll learn in the discussion of the process of randomization (a procedure designed to give everyone in the population an equal chance of being selected as a sample member), because random sampling errors follow chance variations, they tend to cancel each other out when averaged. This means that samples, properly selected, are generally good approximations of the population.

There is almost always a slight difference between the true population value and the sample value—hence, a small random sampling error. Every once in a while a very unusual sample will be selected, because too many unusual people or companies were included in the sample, and this means there is a large random sampling error.

EXHIBIT 16.4 | **AN OPERATIONAL DEFINITION OF WHO IS TO BE INCLUDED AS A MEMBER OF THE HOUSEHOLD**[12]

Summary Table for Determining Who Is to Be Included as a Member of the Household (Control Card Item 14c)

	Include As Member of Household	
A. PERSONS STAYING IN SAMPLE UNIT AT TIME OF INTERVIEW		
Person is member of family, lodger, servant, visitor, etc.		
1. Ordinarily stays here all the time (sleeps here)	Yes	
2. Here temporarily—no living quarters held for person elsewhere	Yes	
3. Here temporarily—living quarters held for person elsewhere		No
Person is in Armed Forces		
1. Stationed in this locality, usually sleeps here	Yes	
2. Temporarily here on leave—stationed elsewhere		No
Person is a student—Here temporarily attending school—living quarters held for person elsewhere		
1. Not married or not living with own family		No
2. Married and living with own family	Yes	
3. Student nurse living at school	Yes	
B. ABSENT PERSON WHO USUALLY LIVES HERE IN SAMPLE UNIT		
Person is inmate of specified institution—Absent because inmate in a specified institution (see listing in Part C, Table A) regardless of whether or not living quarters held for person here		No
Person is temporarily absent on vacation, in general hospital, etc. (including veterans' facilities that are general hospitals)—Living quarters held here for person	Yes	
Person is absent in connection with job		
1. Living quarters held here for person—temporarily absent while "on the road" in connection with job (e.g., traveling salesperson, railroad person, bus driver)	Yes	
2. Living quarters held here and elsewhere for person but comes here infrequently (e.g., construction engineer)		No
3. Living quarters held here at home for unmarried college student working away from home during summer school vacation	Yes	
Person is in Armed Forces—Was member of this household at time of induction but currently stationed elsewhere		No
Person is a student in school—Away temporarily attending school—living quarters held for person here		
1. Not married or not living with own family	Yes	
2. Married and living with own family		No
3. Attending school overseas		No
4. Student nurse living at school		No
C. EXCEPTIONS AND DOUBTFUL CASES		
Person with two concurrent residences—Determine length of time person has maintained two concurrent residences		
1. Has slept greater part of that time in another locality		No
2. Has slept greater part of that time in sample unit	Yes	
Citizen of foreign country temporarily in the United States		
1. Living on premises of an Embassy, Ministry, Legation, Chancellery, or Consulate		No
2. Not living on premises of an Embassy, Ministry, etc.—		
a. Living here and no usual place of residence elsewhere in the United States	Yes	
b. Visiting or traveling in the United States		No

The theories behind the concept of sample reliability and other fundamental statistical concepts are reviewed in detail in the next chapter. At this point, recognize *random sampling error* or *sampling error* as a technical term that refers *only* to statistical fluctuations that occur because of chance variations in the elements selected for the sample.

Random sampling error is a function of sample size. As sample size increases, sampling error decreases. The resources available, of course, will influence how large a sample may be. (Sample size is covered in the following chapter.) It is possible to estimate the random sampling error that may be expected with various sample sizes. Suppose a survey of approximately 900 employees has been taken to determine the feasibility of moving to a new Sunbelt location. Assume 30 percent of the respondents favor the idea of a new location. The researchers will know, based on the laws of probability, that 95 percent of the time a survey of slightly fewer than 900 people will produce results with an error of approximately plus or minus 3 percent. If the survey were conducted with only 325 people, the margin of error would increase to approximately plus or minus 5 percent.

systematic (nonsampling) error
Error resulting from some imperfect aspect of the research design that causes response error or from a mistake in the execution of the research; error that comes from such sources as sample bias, mistakes in recording responses, and nonresponses from persons who were not contacted or who refused to participate.

Systematic (nonsampling) errors result from nonsampling factors, primarily the nature of a study's design and the correctness of execution. These errors are not due to chance fluctuations. For example, highly educated respondents are more likely to cooperate with mail surveys than poorly educated ones, for whom filling out forms is a more difficult and intimidating task.[13] Sample biases such as these account for a large portion of errors in business research. The term *sample bias* is somewhat unfortunate, because many forms of bias are not related to the selection of the sample.

Nonsampling errors have already been discussed in Chapter 9. Remember that errors due to sample selection problems, such as sampling frame errors, are systematic (nonsampling) errors and should not be classified as random sampling errors.

Less Than Perfectly Representative Samples

Random sampling error and systematic error associated with the sampling process may combine to yield a sample that is less than perfectly representative of the population. Exhibit 16.5 illustrates nonsampling errors (sampling frame error and nonresponse error) related to sample design. The total population is represented by the area of the largest rectangle. *Sampling frame errors* eliminate some potential respondents or include respondents who should not be listed as members of the population. Random sampling error (due exclusively to random, chance fluctuation) may cause an imbalance in the representativeness of the group. Additional errors will occur if individuals refuse to be interviewed or cannot be contacted. This **nonresponse error** may also cause the sample to be less than perfectly representative. Thus, the actual sample is drawn from a population different from (or smaller than) the ideal.

nonresponse error
The statistical difference between a survey that includes only those who responded and a survey that also includes those who failed to respond.

PROBABILITY VERSUS NONPROBABILITY SAMPLING

probability sampling
A sampling technique in which every member of the population has a known, nonzero probability of selection.

There are several alternative ways of taking a sample. The major alternative sampling plans may be grouped into probability techniques and nonprobability techniques. In **probability sampling** every element in the population has a *known nonzero probability* of selection. The simple random sample is the best-known probability sample, in which each member of the population has an equal probability of being selected.

EXHIBIT 16.5 ERRORS ASSOCIATED WITH SAMPLING[13]

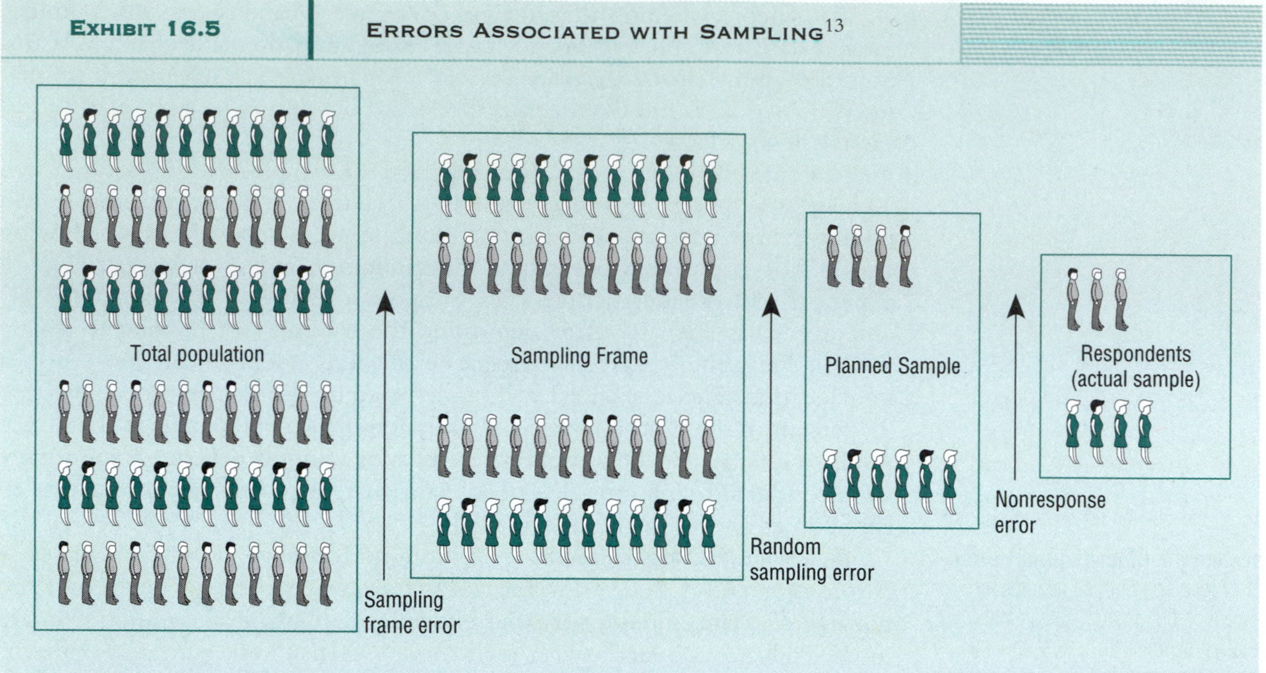

nonprobability sampling
A sampling technique in which units of the sample are selected on the basis of personal judgment or convenience.

In **nonprobability sampling** the probability of any particular member of the population being chosen is unknown. The selection of sampling units in nonprobability sampling is quite arbitrary, as researchers rely heavily on personal judgment. It should be noted that *there are no appropriate statistical techniques for measuring random sampling error from a nonprobability sample. Thus, projecting the data beyond the sample is statistically inappropriate.* Nevertheless, there are occasions when nonprobability samples are best suited for the researcher's purpose.

The various types of nonprobability and probability samples will be explored in the following pages. Although probability sampling is preferred, nonprobability sampling will be discussed first in order to illustrate some potential sources of error and other weaknesses in sampling.

NONPROBABILITY SAMPLING

Convenience Sampling

convenience sampling
The sampling procedure used to obtain those units or people most conveniently available.

Convenience sampling (also called *haphazard* or *accidental sampling*) refers to sampling by obtaining units or people who are most conveniently available. For example, it may be convenient and economical to sample employees in companies in a nearby area. Just before elections, television channels often present person-on-the-street interviews that are presumed to reflect public opinion. (Of course, the television channel often warns that the survey was "unscientific and random.") The college professor who uses students has a captive sample—convenient, but unrepresentative and perhaps unwilling.

A straw vote only shows which way the hot air blows.

O. HENRY

Researchers generally use convenience samples to obtain a large number of completed questionnaires quickly and economically. For example, many Internet surveys are conducted with volunteer respondents who, either intentionally or

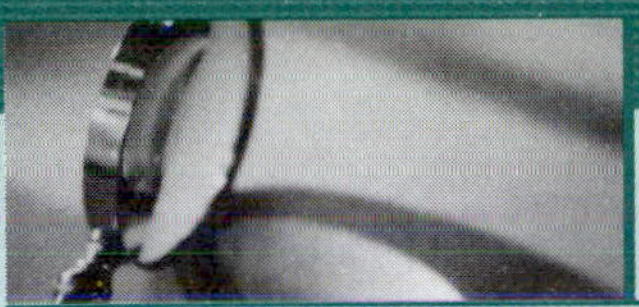

RESEARCH INSIGHT

BUILDING A FORTUNE ON FREE DATA

If you're starting a business yourself, then here's Vinod Gupta, a fellow entrepreneur you'll likely be needing.[15] His American Business Information compiles reams of corporate data, slicing and dicing them so that new businesses have a cheap way to find potential customers, manufacturers, or distributors. The information is available in all kinds of forms, from computer diskettes to telemarketing lists, to pre-printed mailing labels, to 3-by-5 index cards. The newest hot-selling format: CD-ROMs. At $39.95, one contains 70 million U.S. households, listing names, zip codes, and other information useful to marketers. His top-of-the-line CD goes for $2,500. It lists 10 million businesses and tells who owns them and how many are on the payroll. It also gives revenue figures and credit ratings. [ABI's annual sales volume exceeds $75 million and annual profits exceed $12 million.]

Gupta, 48, never imagined such sums as a kid. The child of a doctor practicing in a small village 100 miles from India's capital of New Delhi, he "grew up with no electricity, no roads, no toilets, no TVs, no cars. I didn't know much of what was outside," he recalls. Gupta studied agricultural engineering at the Indian Institute of Technology and won a scholarship to the University of Nebraska at Lincoln, where he earned master's degrees in agricultural engineering and business.

Ironically, this Information Age company started out in the most low-tech way imaginable. Armed with his MBA, Gupta landed a job in Omaha as a marketing executive at Commodore Corp., a maker of mobile homes, which assigned him to put together a list of every dealer in the U.S. for its sales force. To do so, Gupta ordered all 4,800 Yellow Pages directories then available; they duly arrived at his office free of charge because Commodore had WATS lines. "My boss said, 'Vinny, you gotta get these books outta here by five or I'm gonna fire you.' So I hired a moving company and moved them to my garage."

Commodore balked at the $10,000 in labor costs of putting the list together, but allowed Gupta to do it on his own. He defrayed expenses by also selling the list to other dealers. "Starting with $100 of my own, I sent out a mailing to about 1,000 manufacturers to see if they wanted to buy the list. In about three weeks we had orders for about $22,000, and $13,000 in checks." That first year he made an $18,000 profit on revenues of $44,000. Then he quit his day job.

Although he seemingly stumbled upon his niche, it took a keen marketing sense to expand so successfully. With the universe of mobile-home dealers covered, Gupta methodically added other industries. Motorcycle, bicycle, boat, car, tractor, and CB radio dealers were among the first targets. The demand for accurate business-to-business marketing information extended to just about every industry. "I would go to trade shows and work the exhibits, and I would tell them about our lists. People would just say, Yeah, I've been looking for this forever." The key was keeping costs reasonable and providing efficient service. "If somebody wanted a list of ten states and there were 2,000 names," says Gupta, "we would sell it for $160, which was 8 cents a name, in a list form, and send it right away, the same day or the next."

It took 13 years, but in 1986, ABI had the entire Yellow Pages in its databases, ready to be accessed in any form that customers wanted. Gupta had no fear of big data source competitors like Dun & Bradstreet because their corporate customers, like 3M, MCI, or AT&T, want correspondingly large databases and can afford the big guys' average $10,000 charge. "Nobody wanted to mess with the small office equipment dealer worth a $200 order," he says.

Except Gupta, and by continually plowing back the profits, he has built ABI into a business with 400,000 customers and 7,500 industry categories. Some 700 employees make 14 million phone calls a year, verifying, updating, and adding to data that now also include information collected from the White Pages, annual reports, and local chambers of commerce directories.

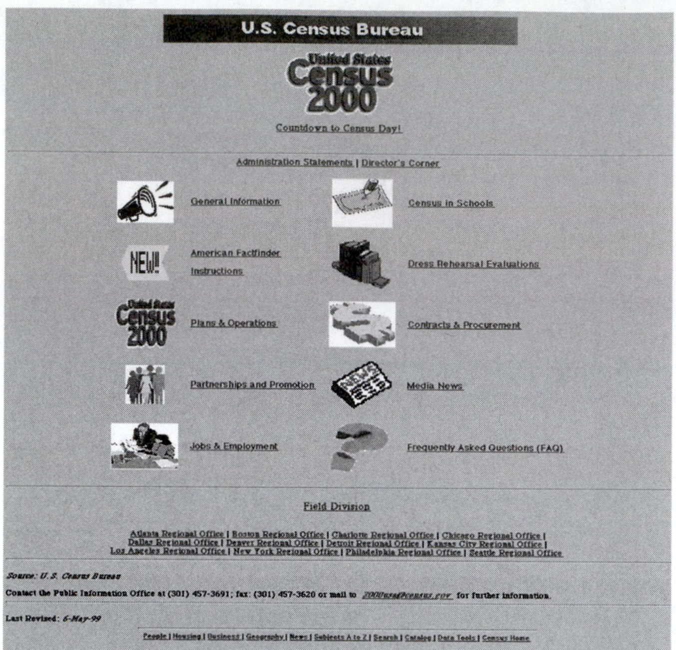

After its 1990 head count, the Census Bureau estimated that it had fallen short of the actual population by about 4 million people, or just below 2 percent. The bureau said unusually high undercounting occurred among blacks, Hispanics, Asians, and American Indians.

To avoid a recurrence of an undercount of hard-to-reach Americans in 2000, the Bureau had planned to use probability sampling and a sampling design incorporating census enumerators' visits to residents who failed to return census forms, and use that information to extrapolate totals for each state. However, in August 1998 the House of Representatives, after an antagonistic debate, voted against allowing probability sampling in the 2000 census.[16]

by happenstance, visit an organization's Web site. Although a large number of responses can be quickly obtained at a low cost, selecting all visitors to a Web site is clearly convenience sampling. Respondents may not be representative because of the haphazard manner by which many of them arrive at the Web site or because of self-selection bias. The user of research based on a convenience sample should remember that projecting the results beyond the specific sample is inappropriate. Convenience samples are best used for exploratory research when additional research will subsequently be conducted with a probability sample.

judgment (purposive) sampling
A nonprobability sampling technique in which an experienced individual selects the sample based upon some appropriate characteristic of the sample members.

Judgment, or **purposive, sampling** is a nonprobability sampling technique in which an experienced individual selects the sample based on his or her judgment about some appropriate characteristic required of the sample members. The researcher selects a sample to serve a specific purpose, even if this makes a sample less than fully representative. The consumer price index (CPI) is based on a judgment sample of market-basket items, housing costs, and other selected goods and services expected to reflect a representative sample of items consumed by most Americans. Test-market cities often are selected because they are viewed as typical cities, with demographic profiles closely matching the national profile. A fashion manufacturer regularly selects a sample of key accounts that it believes are capable of providing the information needed to predict what will sell in the fall; the sample has been selected to satisfy a specific objective.

Judgment sampling is often used in attempts to forecast election results. People often wonder how, say, a television network can predict the results of an election with only 2 percent of the votes reported. Political and sampling experts judge which small voting districts approximate overall state returns from previous election years; then these *bellwether precincts* are selected as the sampling units. Of course, the assumption is that the past voting records of these districts is still representative of the political behavior of the state's population.

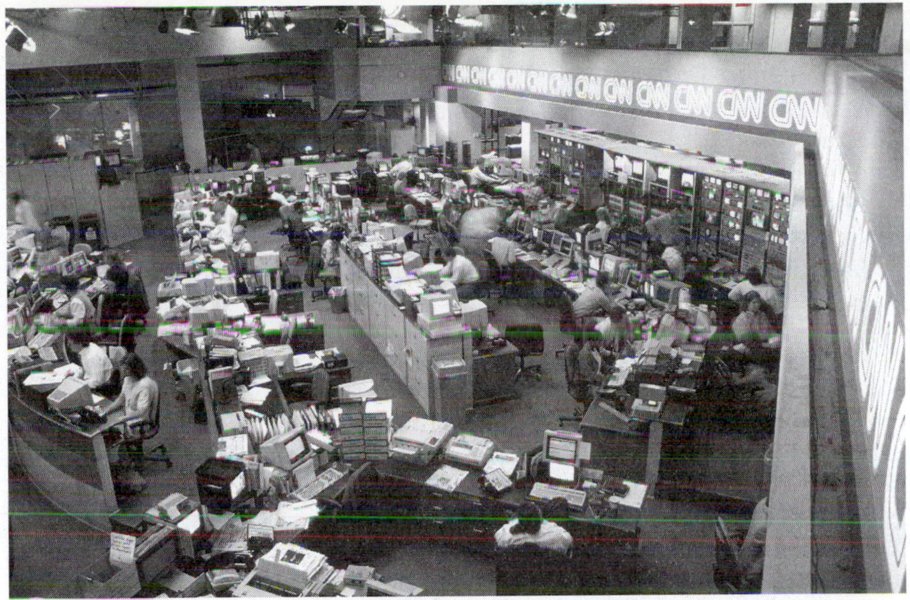

Judgment sampling of bellwether precincts often is used in attempts to forecast election results.

Quota Sampling

quota sampling
A nonprobability sampling procedure that ensures that certain characteristics of a population sample will be represented to the exact extent that the investigator desires.

Suppose a firm wishes to investigate individuals who currently are using the services of a health maintenance organization (HMO). The researchers may wish to ensure that each occupational category is included proportionately in the sample. Strict probability sampling procedures would likely underrepresent certain jobs and overrepresent other jobs. If the selection process were left strictly to chance, some variation would be expected. The purpose of **quota sampling** is to ensure that the various subgroups in a population are represented on pertinent sample characteristics to the exact extent that the investigators desire. Stratified sampling, a probability sampling procedure, also has this objective, and it should not be confused with quota sampling. In quota sampling, the interviewer has a quota to achieve. For example, an interviewer in a particular city may be assigned 100 interviews, 20 of which are with small business owners, 18 with professionals, 10 with managerial employees, 7 with supervisors, and the rest with hourly employees. Aggregating the various interview quotas yields a sample representing the desired proportions of the subgroups.

Possible Sources of Bias

The logic of classifying the population by pertinent subgroups is essentially sound. However, because respondents are selected according to a convenience sampling procedure, rather than on a probability basis (as in stratified sampling), the haphazard selection of subjects may introduce bias. For example, a college professor hired some of his students to conduct a quota sample based on age. When he analyzed the data, it became apparent that almost all of the people in the "under 25 years" category were college educated. Interviewers are human, and they tend to prefer to interview people similar to themselves. Quota samples have a tendency to include people who are easily found, willing to be interviewed, and middle class.

Fieldworkers are given considerable leeway to exercise their judgment concerning selection of respondents. Interviewers often concentrate their interviewing in heavy pedestrian-traffic areas, such as shopping malls, employee lunchrooms, and college campuses. Those who interview door-to-door learn quickly that quota requirements are difficult to meet by interviewing whoever happens to appear at the door. This tends to overrepresent less active people, who tend to stay at home.

One interviewer related a story of working in an upper-middle class neighborhood. After a few blocks it changed into a neighborhood of "mansions." Feeling that most of these people were above his station, the interviewer skipped these houses because he did not feel comfortable knocking on doors that were answered by servants.

Advantages of Quota Samples

Speed of data collection, lower costs, and convenience are the major advantages of quota sampling compared to probability sampling. Although there are many problems with quota sampling, careful supervision of the data collection may provide a representative sample of the various subgroups within a population. A number of laboratory experiments rely on quota sampling because it is difficult to find a sample of the general population willing to visit a laboratory for an experiment.

Snowball Sampling

snowball sampling
A sampling procedure in which initial respondents are selected by probability methods and additional respondents are obtained from information provided by the initial respondents.

Snowball sampling refers to a variety of procedures in which initial respondents are selected by probability methods and additional respondents are then obtained from information provided by initial respondents.[17] This technique is used to locate members of rare populations by referrals.

Suppose a manufacturer of sports equipment is considering marketing a mahogany croquet set for serious adult players. This market is certainly small. An extremely large sample would be necessary in order to find 100 serious adult croquet players. It would be much more economical to survey, say, 300 people and find 15 croquet players and ask them for the names of other players.

Reduced sample sizes and costs are clear advantages of snowball sampling. Bias is likely to enter into the study, however, because a person suggested by someone also in the sample has a higher probability of being similar to the first person. If there are major differences between those who are widely known by others and those who are not, there may be serious problems with snowball sampling.

PROBABILITY SAMPLING

All probability samples are based on chance selection procedures.[18] Because the probability sampling process is random, the bias inherent in the nonprobability sampling procedures is eliminated. Remember that the term *random* refers to the procedure for selecting the sample; it does not describe the data in the sample.[19] Randomness is a characteristic of a procedure whose outcome cannot be predicted because it is dependent on chance.

The procedure of randomization should not be thought of as unplanned or unscientific. It is the basis of all probability sampling techniques.

Simple Random Sampling

simple random sampling
A sampling procedure that assures each element in the population an equal chance of being included in the sample.

Simple random sampling assures that each element in the population has an equal chance of being included in the sample. Drawing names from a hat and selecting the winning raffle ticket from a large drum are typical examples of simple

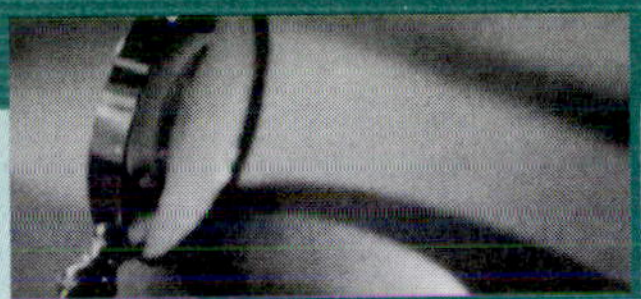

Research Insight

Random Sequences That Don't Look Random

Every basketball player and fan "knows" that players have hot and cold streaks.[20] Players who have hot hands can't seem to miss; those who have cold ones can't find the center of the hoop. When psychologists interviewed members of the Philadelphia 76ers, the players estimated they were about 25 percent more likely to make a shot after they had just made one than after a miss. Nine in ten basketball fans surveyed concurred that a player "has a better chance of making a shot after having just *made* his last two or three shots than he does after having just *missed* his last two or three shots." Believing in shooting streaks, players will feed the ball to a teammate who has just made two or three shots in a row, and many coaches will bench the player who just missed three in a row. When you're hot you're hot.

The only trouble is, it isn't true. When the psychologists studied detailed individual shooting records, they found that the 76ers—and the Boston Celtics, the New Jersey Nets, the New York Knicks, and Cornell University's men's and women's basketball players—were equally likely to score after a miss as after a basket. Fifty percent shooters average 50 percent after just missing three shots, and 50 percent after just making three shots.

Why, then, do players and fans alike believe that players are more likely to score after scoring and miss after missing? In any series of 20 shots by a 50 percent shooter (or twenty flips of a coin), there is a 50-50 chance of four baskets (or heads) in a row, and it is quite possible that one person out of five will have a streak of five or six. Players and fans notice these random streaks and see them as proof of the myth that "when you're hot you're hot."

The same type of thing happens with investors who believe that a mutual fund is more likely to perform well after a string of good years than after a string of bad years. Past performances of mutual funds do not, however, predict their future performances. When funds have streaks of several good or bad years, investors may be fooled into thinking that past success predicts future success.

The moral: Whether watching basketball, choosing stocks, flipping coins, or drawing samples, remember the statistical principle that random sequences often don't look random. Even when the next outcome cannot be predicted from the preceding ones, streaks are to be expected.

random sampling. If the names or raffle tickets are thoroughly stirred, each person (or ticket) should have an equal chance of being selected.

The sampling process is simple because it requires only one stage of sample selection (in contrast to more complex types of probability sampling).

Make everything as simple as possible, but not simpler.

ALBERT EINSTEIN

Drawing names or numbers out of a fish bowl, using a spinner, rolling dice, or turning a roulette wheel may be used to draw a sample from small populations. When populations consist of large numbers of elements, however, tables of random digits (see Table 1 in the Appendix) or computer-generated random numbers are utilized for sample selection.

Selecting a Simple Random Sample

A researcher may be interested in selecting a simple random sample of all presidents of savings and loan associations in New Mexico, Arizona, and Nevada. Each president's name is assigned a number from 1 to 95; then each number is written on a separate piece of paper, and all the slips are placed in a large drum. After the slips of paper have been thoroughly mixed, one is selected for each sampling unit. Thus, if the sample size is to be 45, the selection procedure must be repeated 44 times after the first slip has been selected. Mixing the slips after each selection will ensure that those at the bottom of the bowl will continue to have an equal chance of being selected for the sample.

To use a table of random numbers, a serial number is assigned to each element of the population. Then, assuming the population is 99,999 or less, five-digit numbers may be selected from the table of random numbers merely by reading the numbers in any column or row, moving up, down, left, or right. A random starting point should be selected at the outset. For convenience, we will assume that we have randomly selected the first five digits in columns 1 through 5, row 1, of Table 1 in the Appendix as our starting point. The first number in our sample would be 37751; moving down, our next numbers would be 50915, 99142, and so on.

The random-digit telephone-dialing technique of sample selection requires that researchers identify the exchange or exchanges of interest (the first three numbers) and then use a table of numbers to select the next four numbers.

Systematic Sampling

systematic sampling
A sampling procedure in which an initial starting point is selected by a random process, and then every *n*th number on the list is selected.

Suppose a researcher wants to take a sample of 1,000 from a list consisting of 200,000 names of companies. With **systematic sampling,** every 200th name from the list would be drawn.

sampling interval
The number of population elements between units selected for the sample.

The procedure is extremely simple. An initial starting point is selected by a random process, and then every *n*th number on the list is selected. To take a sample of consumers from a rural telephone directory that does not separate business listings from household listings, for example, every 23rd name might be selected as the **sampling interval.** In the process, it is possible that Mike's Restaurant would be selected. This unit is inappropriate because it is a business listing rather than a consumer listing. Therefore, the next eligible name would be selected as the sampling unit, and the systematic process would continue.

periodicity
A problem that occurs in systematic sampling when the original list has a systematic pattern.

Although this procedure is not actually a random selection procedure, it yields random results if the arrangement of the items in the list is random in character. The problem of **periodicity** occurs if a list has a systematic pattern—that is, if it is not random in character. Collecting retail sales information every seventh day would result in a distorted sample because there would be a systematic pattern of selecting sampling units; sales for only one day of the week, (perhaps Monday) would be sampled. Or, if the first 50 names on a list of contributors to a charity were extremely large donors, periodicity might occur in sampling every 200th name.

Periodicity is rarely a problem for most sampling in business research, but researchers should be aware of the possibility.

Stratified Sampling

stratified sampling
A probability sampling procedure in which simple random subsamples are drawn from within different strata that are more or less equal on some characteristic.

The usefulness of dividing the population into subgroups, or *strata,* whose members are more or less equal on some characteristic was illustrated in our discussion of quota sampling. The first step is the same for both stratified and quota sampling: choosing strata on the basis of existing information, such as classifying retail outlets based on annual sales volume. However, the processes of selecting sampling units within the strata differs substantially. In **stratified sampling** a subsample is drawn utilizing simple random sampling within each stratum. This is not true of quota sampling.

Many business research investigations of organizational activity stratify their samples by industry to ensure that the samples will adequately represent the population's mix of industrial companies.

The reason for taking a stratified sample is to have a more efficient sample than could be taken on the basis of simple random sampling. Suppose, for example, that urban and rural groups differ widely on attitudes toward energy conservation, yet members within each group hold very similar attitudes. Random sampling error will be reduced with the use of stratified sampling, because each group is internally homogeneous but there are comparative differences between groups. More technically, a smaller standard error may result from stratified sampling because the groups are adequately represented when strata are combined.

Another reason for taking a stratified sample is the assurance that the sample will accurately reflect the population on the basis of the criterion or criteria used for stratification. This is a concern because occasionally simple random sampling yields a disproportionate number of one group or another, and the sample ends up being less representative than it could be.

A researcher selecting a stratified sample will proceed as follows: First, a variable (sometimes several variables) is identified as an efficient basis for stratification. The criterion for a stratification variable is that it is a characteristic of the population elements known to be related to the dependent variable or other variables of interest. The variable chosen should increase homogeneity within each stratum and increase heterogeneity between strata. The stratification variable is usually a categorical variable or one easily converted into categories (that is, subgroups). For example, a pharmaceutical company interested in measuring how often physicians prescribe a certain drug might choose physicians' training as a basis for stratification. In this example the mutually exclusive strata are M.D.s (medical doctors) and D.O.s (doctors of osteopathy).

Next, for each separate subgroup or stratum, a list of population elements must be obtained. (If such lists are not available, they can be costly to prepare, and if a complete listing by strata is not available, a true stratified probability sample cannot be selected.) Using a table of random numbers or some other device, a *separate* simple random sample is taken within each stratum. Of course, the researcher must determine how large a sample must be drawn for each stratum.

Proportional versus Disproportional Sampling

proportional stratified sample
A stratified sample in which the number of sampling units drawn from each stratum is in proportion to the population size of that stratum.

If the number of sampling units drawn from each stratum is in proportion to the relative population size of the stratum, the sample is a **proportional stratified sample.** Sometimes, however, a disproportional stratified sample will be selected to ensure an adequate number of sampling units in every stratum. Sampling more heavily in a given stratum than its relative population size warrants is not a problem if the primary purpose of the research is to estimate some characteristic separately for each stratum and if researchers are concerned about assessing the differences among strata.

disproportional stratified sample
A stratified sample in which the sample size for each stratum is allocated according to analytical considerations.

Consider, however, the percentages of retail outlets presented in Exhibit 16.6. A proportional sample would have the same percentages as in the population. Although there is a small percentage of warehouse club stores, the average store size (in dollar volume) for the warehouse club store stratum is quite large and varies substantially from the average store size for the smaller independent stores (again, in dollar volume). To avoid overrepresenting the chain stores and independent stores (with smaller sales volume) in the sample, a disproportional sample is taken. In a **disproportional stratified sample,** sample size for each stratum is not allocated in proportion to the population size, but is dictated by analytical considerations, such as variability in store sales volume. The logic behind this procedure relates to the general argument for sample size: As variability increases, sample size must increase to provide accurate estimates. Thus, the strata that exhibit the greatest variability are sampled more heavily in order to increase sample efficiency—that is, produce smaller random sampling error.

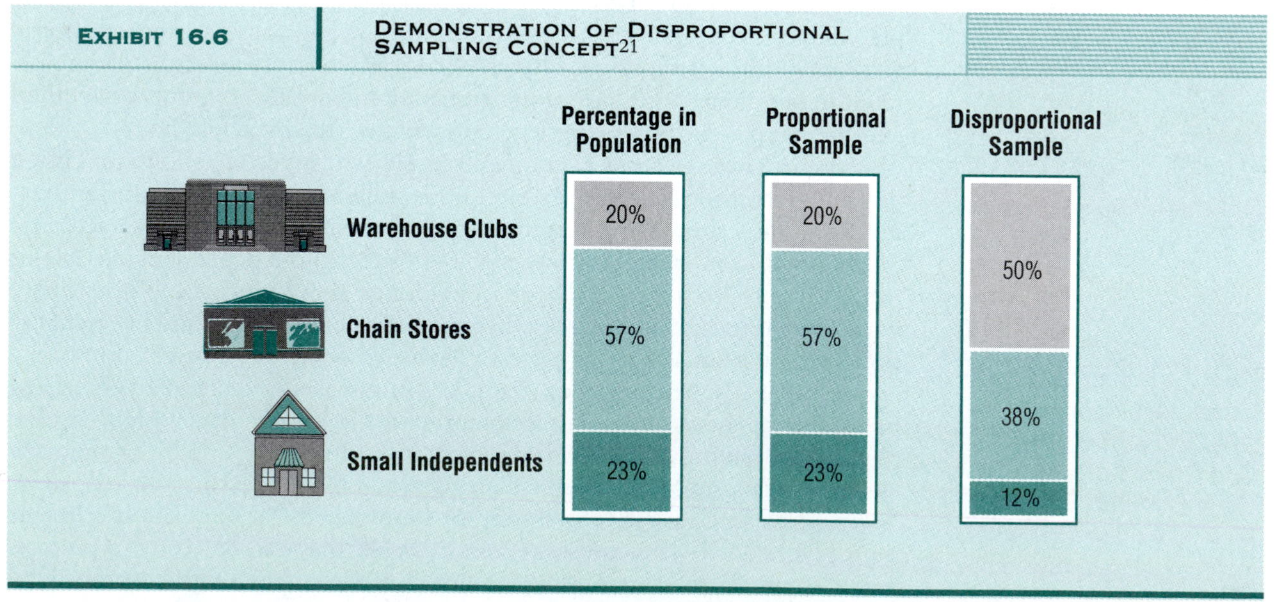

Exhibit 16.6 Demonstration of Disproportional Sampling Concept[21]

Complex formulas (beyond the scope of this book) have been developed to determine the sample size for each stratum. A simplified rule of thumb for understanding the concept of optimal allocation is that stratum sample size increases for strata of larger sizes with the greatest relative variability.

Other complexities arise in determining population estimates. For example, when disproportional stratified sampling is utilized, the estimated mean for each stratum has to be weighted according to the number of elements in each stratum in order to calculate the total population mean.

Cluster Sampling

The purpose of cluster sampling is to sample economically while retaining the characteristics of a probability sample. Consider the researcher who must conduct 500 interviews with individuals scattered throughout the United States. Travel costs are likely to be enormous because the amount of time spent traveling will be substantially greater than the time spent in the interviewing process.

cluster sampling
An economically efficient sampling technique in which the primary sampling unit is not the individual element in the population but a large cluster of elements.

area sample
A cluster sample in which the primary sampling unit is a geographic area.

If an aspirin marketer can assume the product will work as well in Phoenix as it does in Baltimore, or if a pizza restaurant chain can assume employee attitudes toward fringe benefits to be the same in Texas as in Oregon, then **cluster sampling** may be used. In a cluster sample the primary sampling unit is no longer the individual element in the population (e.g., manufacturing firms) but a large cluster of elements (e.g., cities). The **area sample** is the most popular type of cluster sample. A grocery researcher, for example, may randomly choose several geographic areas as the primary sampling units and then interview all, or a sample of, grocery stores within the geographic clusters. Interviews are confined to these clusters; no interviews occur in other clusters. Cluster sampling is classified as a probability sampling technique either because of the random selection of clusters or because of the random selection of elements within each cluster.

Cluster samples are frequently utilized when no lists of the sample population are available. For example, when researchers investigating employees and self-employed workers for a downtown revitalization project found that a list of these people was not available, they decided to take a cluster sample by selecting organizations (business as well as government) as the clusters. A sample of firms within the central business district was developed, using stratified probability sampling to identify clusters. Next, individual workers within the firms (clusters) were selected and interviewed concerning the central business district. Some examples of clusters are listed in Exhibit 16.7.

Ideally a cluster should be as heterogeneous as the population itself—a mirror image of the population. Therefore, a problem may arise with cluster sampling if the characteristics and attitudes of the elements within the cluster are too similar. For example, geographic neighborhoods tend to have residents of the same socioeconomic status; students at a university tend to share similar beliefs. To an extent this problem may be mitigated by constructing clusters that are composed of diverse elements and by selecting a large number of sampled clusters.

Multistage Area Sampling

multistage area sampling
Sampling that involves using a combination of other probability sampling techniques.

We have described two-stage cluster sampling. **Multistage area sampling** involves two or more steps that combine some of the probability techniques already described. Typically, progressively smaller (lower-population) geographic areas are randomly selected in a series of steps. A political pollster investigating an election in Arizona might first choose counties within the state to ensure that

Exhibit 16.7 | **Examples of Kinds of Clusters**

Population Elements	Possible Clusters
U.S. adult population	States Counties Metropolitan statistical areas Localities Census tracts Blocks Households
College seniors Professors	Colleges
Manufacturing firms	Counties Metropolitan statistical areas Localities Plants
Airline travelers	Airports Planes
Hospital patients Doctors	Hospitals
Sports fans	Stadiums Arenas

the different areas are represented in the sample. In the second step, precincts within the selected counties may be chosen. As a final step, blocks (or households) within the precincts could be chosen, then all the blocks (or households) within the geographic area would be interviewed. As many steps as are necessary are taken to achieve a representative sample.

Exhibit 16.8 portrays a multistage area sampling process frequently used by a major academic research center. Progressively smaller geographic areas are selected until a housing unit is selected for interviewing.[22]

The Census Bureau provides maps, population information, demographic characteristics of the population, and so on by regions, states, counties, cities, and several small geographic areas; these may be useful in sampling. Exhibit 16.9 (page 392) shows how census areas may be broken down into progressively smaller geographic areas.

Census classifications of small geographic areas vary depending on the extent of urbanization within metropolitan statistical areas (MSAs) or counties. Exhibit 16.9 illustrates the geographic hierarchy inside and outside urbanized areas.

WHAT IS THE APPROPRIATE SAMPLE DESIGN?

Exhibit 16.10 (pages 392–393) summarizes the advantages and disadvantages of each of the various sampling techniques discussed so far. A researcher who must make a decision concerning the most appropriate sample design for a

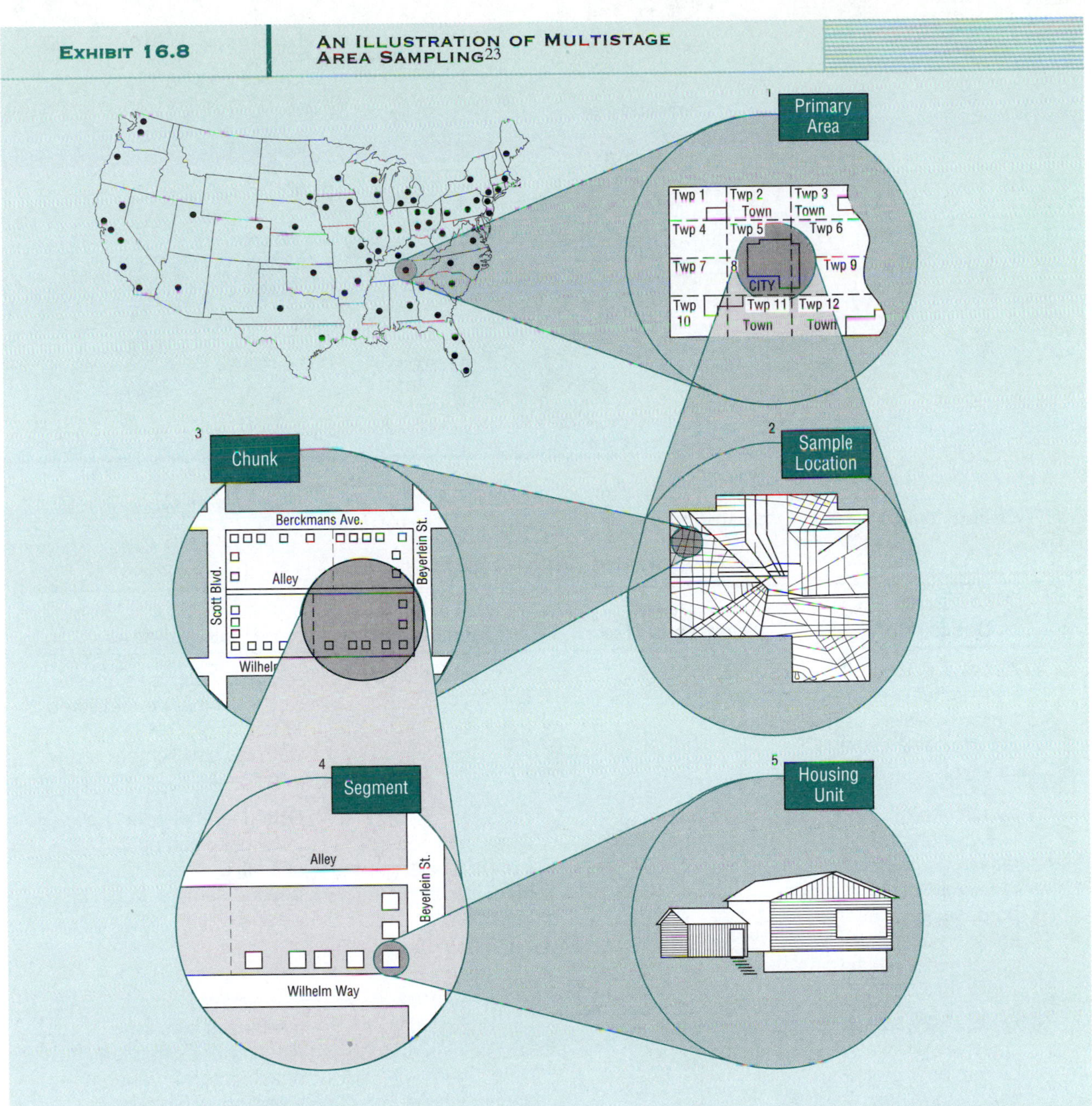

specific project will identify a number of sampling criteria and evaluate the relative importance of each criterion before selecting a sample design. This section outlines and briefly discusses the most common criteria.

Degree of Accuracy

Selecting a representative sample is, of course, important to all researchers. However, the degree of accuracy required or the researcher's tolerance for sampling and nonsampling error may vary from project to project, especially when cost savings or another benefit may be a trade-off for a reduction in accuracy.

Exhibit 16.9 | **Geographic Hierarchy Inside Urbanized Areas**[24]

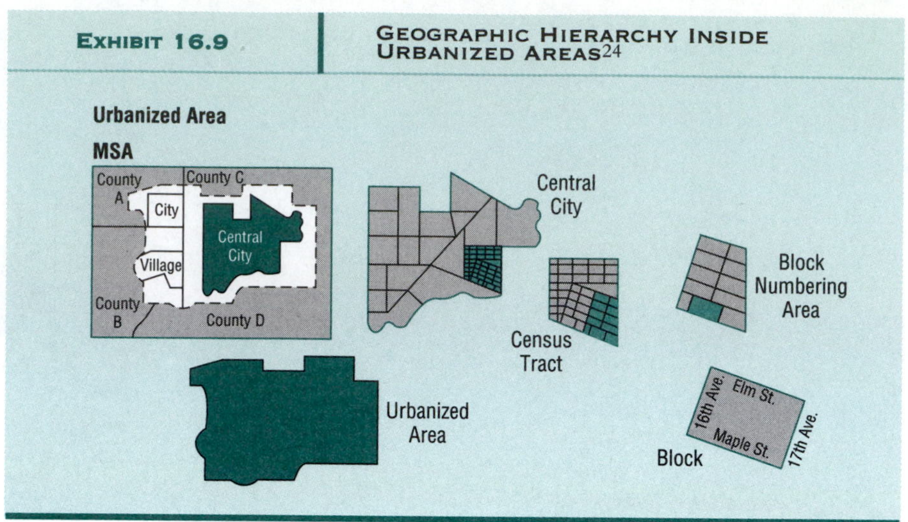

Exhibit 16.10 | **Comparison of Sampling Techniques**

NONPROBABILITY SAMPLES

Description	Cost and Degree of Use	Advantages	Disadvantages
1. *Convenience:* Researcher uses most convenient sample or most economical sample.	Very low cost, extensively used	No need for list of population	Variability and bias of estimates cannot be measured or controlled; projecting data beyond sample is inappropriate
2. *Judgment:* An expert or experienced researcher selects the sample to fulfill a purpose, such as ensuring all members have a certain characteristic.	Moderate cost, average use	Useful for certain types of forecasting; sample guaranteed to meet a specific objective	Bias due to experts' beliefs may make sample unrepresentative; projecting data beyond sample is inappropriate
3. *Quota:* Researcher classifies population by pertinent properties, determines desired proportion of sample from each class, fixes quotas for each interviewer.	Moderate cost, very extensively used	Introduces some stratification of population; requires no list of population	Introduces bias in researcher's classification of subjects; nonrandom selection within classes means error from population cannot be estimated; projecting data beyond sample is inappropriate
4. *Snowball:* Initial respondents are selected by probability samples; additional respondents are obtained by referral from initial respondents.	Low cost, used in special situations	Useful in locating members of rare populations	High bias because sample units are not independent; projecting data beyond sample is inappropriate

Exhibit 16.10 **Comparison of Sampling Techniques (Continued)**

PROBABILITY SAMPLES

Description	Cost and Degree of Use	Advantages	Disadvantages
1. *Simple random:* Researcher assigns each member of the sampling frame a number, then selects sample units by a random method.	High cost, most likely used in random-digit dialing and Internet sampling	Only minimal advance knowledge of population needed; easy to analyze data and compute error	Requires sampling frame to work from; does not use knowledge of population that researcher may have; larger errors for same sample size than with stratified sampling; respondents may be widely dispersed, hence cost may be higher
2. *Systematic:* Researcher uses natural ordering or order of sampling frame, selects an arbitrary starting point, then selects items at a preselected interval.	Moderate cost, moderately used	Simple to draw sample; easy to check	If sampling interval is related to a periodic ordering of the population, may introduce increased variability
3. *Stratified:* Researcher divides the population into groups and randomly selects subsamples from each group. Variations include proportional, disproportional, and optimal allocation of subsample sizes.	High cost, moderately used	Assures representation of all groups in sample; characteristics of each stratum can be estimated and comparisons made; reduces variability for same sample size	Requires accurate information on proportion in each stratum; if stratified lists are not already available, they can be costly to prepare
4. *Cluster:* Researcher selects sampling units at random, then does complete observation of all units in the group.	Low cost, frequently used	If clusters geographically defined, yields lowest field cost; requires listing of all clusters but of individuals only within clusters; can estimate characteristics of clusters as well as of population	Larger error for comparable size than other probability samples; researcher must be able to assign population members to unique cluster or else duplication or omission of individual results
5. *Multistage:* Progressively smaller areas are selected in each stage. Researcher performs some combination of the first four techniques.	High cost, frequently used, especially in nationwide surveys	Depends on techniques combined	Depends on techniques combined

For example, when the sample is being selected for an exploratory research project, a high priority may not be placed on accuracy because a highly representative sample may not be necessary. For other, more conclusive projects, the sample result must be a precise representation of a population's characteristics, and the researcher must be willing to spend the time and money to achieve accuracy.

Resources

The costs associated with the different sampling techniques vary tremendously. If the researcher's financial and human resources are restricted, this limitation of resources will eliminate certain methods. For a graduate student working on a master's thesis, conducting a national survey is almost always out of the question because of limited resources. Managers concerned with the cost of the research versus the value of the information often will opt to save money by using a nonprobability sample design rather than make the decision to conduct no research at all.

Time

Researchers who need to meet a deadline or complete a project quickly will be more likely to select simple, less time-consuming sample designs. A telephone survey utilizing a sample based on random-digit dialing takes considerably less time than a survey using an elaborate disproportionate stratified sample.

Advance Knowledge of the Population

Advance knowledge of population characteristics, such as the availability of lists of population members, is an important criterion. In many cases, however, a list of population elements will not be available to the researcher. This is especially true when the population element is defined by ownership of a particular product or brand, by experience performing a specific job task, or on the basis of a qualitative dimension. A lack of adequate lists may automatically rule out systematic sampling, stratified sampling, or another sampling design, or it may dictate that a preliminary study, such as a short telephone survey utilizing random-digit dialing, be conducted to generate information to build a sampling frame for the study of primary interest. In smaller U.S. towns reverse directories are the exception rather than the rule; thus, researchers planning sample designs will have to work around this limitation.

National versus Local Project

Geographic proximity of population elements will influence sample design. When population elements are unequally distributed geographically, a cluster sampling may become much more attractive.

Need for Statistical Analysis

The need for statistical projections based on the sample is often a criterion. Nonprobability sampling techniques do not allow the researcher to utilize statistical analysis to project the data beyond the sample.

INTERNET SAMPLING IS UNIQUE

Chapter 10 mentioned the rise in the use of Internet surveys that seek information from respondents interacting with software on Web sites. There are some unique problems associated with Internet sampling.

Internet surveys allow researchers to reach a large sample rapidly. This is both an advantage and a disadvantage. Sample size requirements can be met overnight or in some cases almost instantaneously. It is possible, for instance, for a researcher to release a survey during the morning in the Eastern Standard Time zone and have all sample size requirements met before anyone on the West Coast wakes up. If rapid response rates are expected, the sample for an Internet survey should be metered out across all time zones. In addition, people in some populations are more likely to go online during the weekend than on a weekday. If the researcher can anticipate a day-of-the-week effect, the survey should be kept open long enough so that all sample units have the opportunity to participate in the research project.

A major disadvantage of Internet surveys is the lack of computer ownership and Internet access among certain segments of the population. A sample of Internet users is representative only of Internet users, who tend to be younger, better educated, and more affluent than the general U.S. population. This is not to say that all Internet samples are unrepresentative of all target populations. Nevertheless, when using Internet surveys, researchers should be keenly aware of potential sampling problems that can arise because some members of target populations do not have Internet access.

Web Site Visitors

As noted earlier, many Internet surveys are conducted with volunteer respondents who visit an organization's Web site intentionally or by happenstance. These *unrestricted samples* are clearly convenience samples. They may not be representative because of the haphazard manner by which many respondents arrived at a particular Web site or because of self-selection bias.

A better technique for sampling Web site visitors is to randomly select sampling units. SurveySite, a company that specializes in conducting Internet surveys, collects data by using its "pop-up survey" software. The software selects Web visitors at random and "pops up" a small Javascript window asking the person if he or she wants to participate in an evaluation survey. If the person clicks "Yes," then a new window containing the online survey opens up. The person can then browse the site at his or her own pace and switch to the survey at any time to express an opinion.[25]

Randomly selecting Web site visitors can cause a problem. It is possible to overrepresent the more frequent visitors to the site and thus represent site visits rather than visitors. There are several programming techniques and technologies (using cookies, registration data, or prescreening) that can help accomplish more representative sampling based on site traffic.[26] Details of these techniques are beyond the scope of this discussion.

This type of random sampling is most valuable if the target population is defined as visitors to a particular Web site. Evaluation and analysis of visitors' perceptions and experiences of the Web site would be a typical survey objective with this type of sample. Researchers who have broader interests may obtain Internet samples in a variety of other ways.

Panel Samples

Drawing a probability sample from an established consumer panel or other prerecruited membership panel is a popular, scientific, and effective method for creating a sample of Internet users. Typically, sampling from a panel yields a high response rate because panel members have already agreed to cooperate

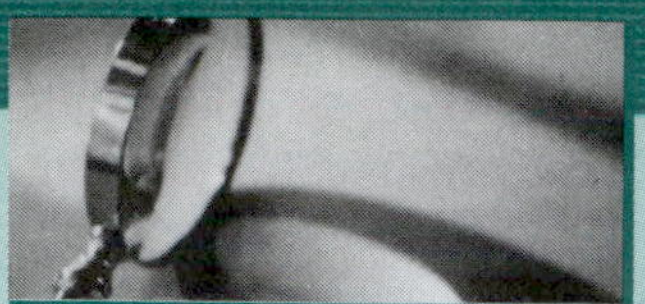

Research Insight

Knowledge Networks

Knowledge Networks (http://www.knowledgenetworks.com) was founded in 1998 by two Stanford University political science professors trying to find a way to conduct Internet surveys with samples that mirrored the U.S. population.[27] They knew the problem was that many households did not own computers or have Internet access. So they decided that the only way to get true representative samples for Internet surveys and political polls was to equip people with interactive TV devices and Internet service. In the summer of 1999, they sent out 40,000 letters, most of them containing $10 bills. The money was the teaser for the big offer: spend 10 minutes each week answering questions over the Internet, and Knowledge Networks would give the household a free Web TV, free Internet access, and a raft of prizes doled out in various contests and raffles. If individuals were uneasy with new technology, the researchers promised not only to give them the TV and the Internet access but also to send an engineer to install the appliances. An astonishing 56 percent of the people they contacted took the offer.

Today, Knowledge Networks is the only Internet survey research company that can reach people whether or not they own computers or have ever used the Internet. By providing a consistent and convenient environment, Knowledge Networks gets consumers to share their opinions in regular multimedia surveys and provide information about the media and their own purchasing behavior.

with the research organization's e-mail or Internet survey. Often panel members are compensated for their time with a sweepstake, small cash incentive, or redeemable points. Further, because the panel has already supplied demographic characteristics and other information from previous questionnaires, researchers are able to select panelists based on product ownership, lifestyle, or other characteristics. A variety of sampling methods and data transformation techniques can be applied to assure that sample results are representative of the general public or a targeted population.

Consider Harris Interactive Inc. The company is an Internet survey research organization that maintains a panel of more than 6.5 million individuals in the United States. In the early 21st century, Harris plans to expand this panel to between 10 million and 15 million and to include an additional 10 million people internationally.[28] A database this large allows the company to draw simple random samples, stratified samples, and quota samples from its panel members.

Because Harris Interactive knows that all demographic groups are not fully accessible via the Internet, it uses a *propensity-weighting* scheme to ensure that survey results are representative. The research company does parallel studies—by phone as well as over the Internet—to test the accuracy of its Internet data-gathering capabilities. Researchers look at the results of the telephone surveys and match those against the Internet-only survey results. Next, they use propensity weighting to adjust the results, taking into account the motivational and behavioral differences between the online and offline populations. (How propensity weighting adjusts for the difference between the Internet population and the general population is beyond the scope of this discussion.)

Recruited Ad Hoc Samples

Another means of obtaining an Internet sample is to obtain or create a sampling frame of e-mail addresses on an *ad hoc* basis. Researchers may create the sampling frame offline or online. Databases containing e-mail addresses can be compiled from many sources including customer/client lists, advertising banners in pop-up windows that recruit survey participants, online sweepstakes, and registration forms that must be filled out in order to gain access to a particular Web site. Researchers may contact respondents by "snail" mail or by telephone to ask for their e-mail addresses and obtain permission for an Internet survey. Using offline techniques, such as random digit dialing and short telephone screening interviews, to recruit respondents can be a very practical way to get a representative sample for an Internet survey. For companies anticipating future Internet research, including e-mail addresses in their customer relationship databases (by inviting customers to provide that information on product registration cards, in telephone interactions, through on-site registration, etc.) can provide a valuable database for sample recruitment.[29]

Opt-In Lists

Survey Sampling Incorporated is a company that specializes in providing sampling frames and scientifically drawn samples. The company offers more than 3,500 lists of high-quality, targeted e-mail addresses of individuals who have given permission to receive e-mail messages related to a particular topic of interest. Survey Sampling Incorporated's database contains over 7 million names of Internet users who have **opted in** for limited participation. An important feature of Survey Sampling Incorporated's database is that the company has each individual confirm and reconfirm interest in communicating about a topic before the person's e-mail address is added to the company's database.[30]

opt in
To give permission to receive selected e-mail, such as questionnaires, from a company with an Internet presence.

By whatever technique the sampling frame is compiled, it is important *not* to send unauthorized e-mail to respondents. If individuals do not opt in to receive e-mail from a particular organization, they may consider unsolicited

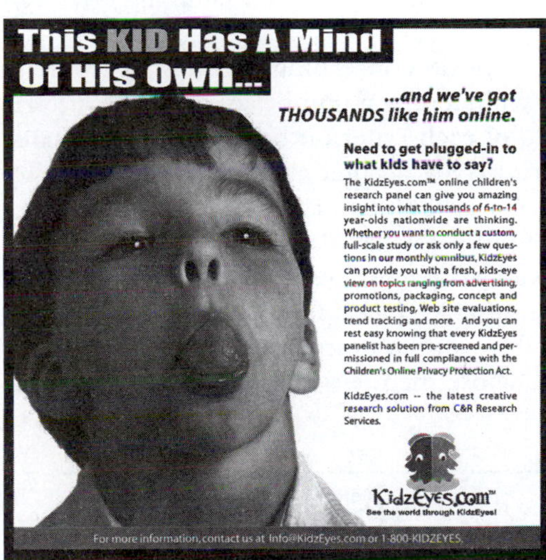

KidzEyes panelists have been prescreened and have given their permission to be surveyed online, in full compliance with the Children's Online Privacy Protection Act. It is very important that members of Internet samples opt in to receive e-mail about survey participation.

survey requests to be spam. A researcher cannot expect high response rates from individuals who have not agreed to be surveyed. Spamming is not tolerated by experienced Internet users, and it can easily backfire, creating a host of problems—the most extreme being complaints to the Internet service provider (ISP), which may shut down the survey site.

SUMMARY

Sampling is a procedure that uses a small number of units of a given population as a basis for drawing conclusions about the whole population. Sampling is often necessary because it would be practically impossible to conduct a census to measure characteristics of all elements of a population. Properly taken, samples lead to accurate portrayals of the whole population. Samples are also needed in cases where measurement involves destruction of the unit measured.

The first problem in sampling is to define the relevant population. Incorrect or vague definition of the population is likely to produce misleading results. A sampling frame is a list of elements, or individual members, of the overall population from which the sample is drawn. A sampling unit is a single element or group of elements subject to selection in the sample.

There are two sources of discrepancy between the sample results and the population parameters. One type of error is random sampling error, arising from chance variations of the sample from the population. Random sampling error is a function of sample size and may be estimated using the central limit theorem, to be discussed in Chapter 17. Systematic (nonsampling) errors come from such sources as sampling frame error, mistakes in recording responses, or nonresponses from persons who are not contacted or who refuse to participate.

The two major sampling methods are probability and nonprobability techniques. The nonprobability techniques include convenience sampling, judgment sampling, quota sampling, and snowball sampling. They are convenient, but there are no statistical techniques to measure their random sampling error. Probability samples are based on chance selection procedures. Some of these procedures are simple random sampling, systematic sampling, stratified sampling, and cluster sampling. With these techniques, random sampling error can be accurately predicted.

A researcher who must make a decision concerning the most appropriate sample design for a specific project will identify a number of sampling criteria and evaluate the relative importance of each criterion before selecting a sampling design. The most common criteria are accuracy requirements, resources available, time constraints, knowledge availability, and analytical requirements.

Internet sampling presents some unique issues. Researchers must be aware that samples may be unrepresentative because not everyone has a computer or access to the Internet. Convenience samples drawn from Web site visitors can create problems. Drawing a probability sample from an established consumer panel or an ad hoc sampling frame whose members opt in can be effective.

Key Terms

sampling
sample
population (universe)
population element
census
target population
sampling frame
mailing list
reverse directory
sampling frame error
sampling unit
primary sampling unit (PSU)

secondary sampling unit
random sampling error
systematic (nonsampling) error
nonresponse error
probability sampling
nonprobability sampling
convenience sampling
judgment (purposive) sampling
quota sampling
snowball sampling
simple random sampling
systematic sampling
sampling interval
periodicity
stratified sampling
proportional stratified sample
disproportional stratified sample
optimal allocation stratified sample
cluster sampling
area sample
multistage area sampling
opt in

Questions

1. If you decide whether to see a new movie or television program on the basis of "coming attractions" or television commercial previews, are you utilizing a sampling technique? A scientific sampling technique? Explain.
2. In what types of situations is conducting a census more appropriate than sampling? When is sampling more appropriate than taking a census?
3. Name some possible sampling frames for the following:
   (a) Electric utilities
   (b) Tennis players
   (c) Dog owners
   (d) McDonald's employees
   (e) Wig and hair-goods retailers
   (f) Minority-owned businesses
   (g) Men over 6 feet tall
4. Describe the difference between a probability sample and a nonprobability sample.
5. Comment on the following sampling designs:
   (a) A citizens group interested in generating public and financial support for a new university basketball arena has published a questionnaire in area newspapers. Readers return the questionnaires by mail.
   (b) A department store that wishes to examine whether it is losing or gaining customers draws a sample from its list of credit card holders by selecting every tenth name.
   (c) A motorcycle manufacturer decided to research consumer characteristics by sending 100 questionnaires to each of its dealers. The dealers would then use their sales records to trace buyers of this brand of motorcycle and distribute the questionnaires to them.
   (d) A research company obtains a sample for a focus group through organized groups such as church groups, clubs, or schools. The organizations are paid for securing respondents, and no individual is directly compensated.
   (e) A banner ad on a business-oriented Web site reads, "Are you a large company Sr. Executive? Qualified execs receive $50 for under 10 minutes of time. Take the survey now!" Is this an appropriate way to select a sample of business executives?
6. When the National Football League planned instant replays to help officiate plays on the field, one television network announced a viewer preference poll. Viewers who thought that the instant replay should be banned could call a particular 900 number to indicate their preference. Those who thought the instant replay should be used could dial another 900 number to register their preference. At the end of the televised announcement of the poll, viewers were told that 50 cents would be added to an individual respondent's phone bill by the telephone company. Evaluate this as a sampling technique.
7. A telephone interviewer asks: "I would like to ask you about race. Are you Native American, Hispanic, black, Oriental, or white?" After the respondent replies, the interviewer says, "We have conducted a large number of surveys with people of your background and we do not need to question you further. Thank you for your cooperation." What type of sampling was utilized?
8. What are the benefits of stratified sampling?
9. What geographic units within a metropolitan area are useful for sampling?
10. Outline the step-by-step procedure you would utilize to select the following:
    (a) A sample of 150 students at your college or university
    (b) A sample of 50 light users and 50 heavy users of beer in a shopping mall intercept sample
    (c) A sample of 50 mechanical engineers, 40 electrical engineers, and 40 civil engineers from the subscriber list of an engineering journal
    (d) A sample of banks, savings and loans, and other financiers of home mortgage loans
    (e) A sample of male and female workers to compare hourly wages of drill press operators
11. Selection for jury duty is supposed to be a totally random process. Comment on the following computer selection procedures and determine if they are indeed random.
    (a) A computer program scans the list of names and

picks names that are next to those from the last scan.

(b) Three-digit numbers are randomly generated to select jurors from a list of licensed drivers. If the weight information listed on the license matches the random number, the person is selected.

(c) The juror source list is obtained by merging a list of registered voters with a list of licensed drivers.

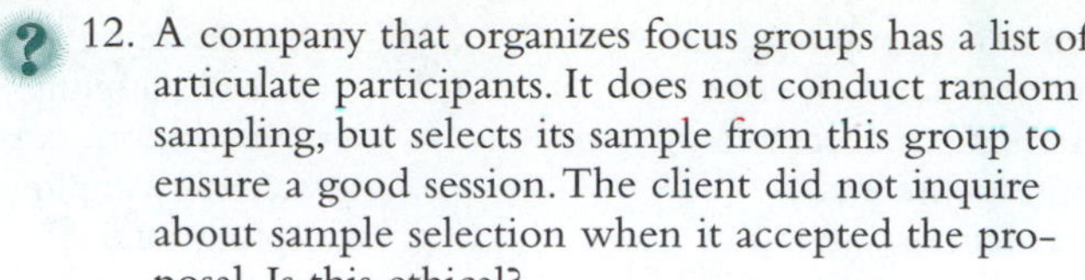

12. A company that organizes focus groups has a list of articulate participants. It does not conduct random sampling, but selects its sample from this group to ensure a good session. The client did not inquire about sample selection when it accepted the proposal. Is this ethical?

Exploring the Internet

1. Visit http://www.prb.org to find a Glossary of Population Terms compiled by the Population Reference Bureau.
2. Go to http://www.reversephonedirectory.com and put in your phone number. How accurate is this database?
3. Go to the U.S. Census Bureau's home page at http://www.census.gov, click on M in Subjects A to Z, and then click on Metropolitan Areas. This will take you to http://www.census.gov/population/www/estimates/metroarea.html, where you can learn about metropolitan statistical areas (MSAs), and view a complete list of MSAs.
4. Use Google to search for ski resorts. At what URL can you find a sampling frame of U.S. ski resorts?
5. Go to http://www.dartmouth.edu/~chance/ to visit the Chance Course. The Chance course is an innovative program to creatively teach introductory materials about probability and statistics. The Chance course is designed to enhance quantitative literacy. Numerous videos can be played online. "Statistical Issues in Census 2000," "To Sample or Not to Sample? Why Is That the Question for Census 2000?" and "Polls" are among numerous lectures that you should find interesting.

Case Suggestions

Case 23: The Business Forms Industry
Video Case 11: The Census Bureau

CHAPTER

17

DETERMINATION OF SAMPLE SIZE: A Review of Statistical Theory

The determination of the appropriate sample size is a crucial aspect of business research. To formally identify the proper sample size requires the use of statistical theory. Unfortunately, statistics has a bad image among students.

The fear of statistics is one of the most universal phobias among college students. "Stat is too difficult; I'll never pass" is a lament often heard on campus. Many students postpone their statistics classes until their last semester. Statistics students are frequently subject to mental blocks. They feel like Saint George who must tame the raging statistical dragon. There is no need, however, for students to have this dread. Statistics can be easily mastered if one learns the tricks of the trade.

Why are there so many myths about statistics? Statisticians, much like lawyers, medical doctors, and computer scientists, have developed their own jargon. Laypeople do not understand the professionals' technical terms. Cynics suspect this ploy is used to impress others and, possibly, to justify higher fees. How many fishermen have you heard say, "Hand me the reticulated lattice joined at the interstices?" Not many, I'll bet. Few fishermen use this terminology when they simply want a net. Then again, compared to professionals who use complex terminology, fishermen don't make much money.[1]

The point is simple: If you don't understand the basics of a language, you'll have problems conversing in that language. Statistics is the language of the researcher. Business researchers use statistics as a means of communication. If administrators and researchers don't speak the same language, there will be a failure to communicate. This chapter explains how to determine sample size and reviews some of the basic terminology of statistical analysis. ■

What you will learn in this chapter

- To explain the difference between descriptive statistics and inferential statistics.
- To discuss the purpose of inferential statistics by explaining the difference between population parameters and sample statistics.
- To organize and summarize data into frequency distributions, proportions, and measurements of central tendency.
- To identify and calculate the various measures of dispersion, such as the standard deviation.
- To identify the characteristics of the normal distribution and to define the standardized normal curve.
- To compute the standardized value, *Z*, and to use the *Z* (standardized normal probability distribution) tables in the appendix of this book.
- To distinguish among population, sample, and sampling distributions and to identify the mean and standard deviation of each.
- To explain the central-limit theorem.
- To compute confidence interval estimates.
- To understand the three factors required for specifying sample size.
- To understand which nonstatistical considerations influence the determination of sample size.
- To understand the three factors required for specifying sample size.
- To estimate the sample size for a simple random sample when the characteristic of interest is a mean and when it is a proportion.

Taming the Statistical Beast

REVIEWING SOME BASIC TERMINOLOGY

The first portion of this chapter summarizes several key statistical concepts necessary for understanding the theory underlying the derivation of sample size. The next 20 pages are intended for students who need to review many of the basic aspects of statistics theory. Even students who received good grades in their elementary statistics classes probably will benefit from a quick review of the basic statistical concepts. Some students will prefer to skim this material and proceed to page 423, where the discussion of the actual determination of sample size begins. Others may need to study this section with care to acquire an understanding of the purpose of statistics for the first time.

Descriptive and Inferential Statistics

descriptive statistics
Statistics used to describe or summarize information about a population or sample.

inferential statistics
Statistics used to make inferences or judgments about a population on the basis of a sample.

The *Statistical Abstract of the United States* presents table after table of figures associated with numbers of births, number of employees of each county of the United States, and other data that the average person calls *statistics.* These are **descriptive statistics.** Another type of statistics, **inferential statistics,** is used to make an inference about a population from a sample. For example, when a firm test markets a new product in Sacramento and Birmingham, it wishes to make an inference from these sample markets to predict what will happen throughout the United States. Thus, there are two applications of statistics: (1) to describe characteristics of a population or sample and (2) to generalize from the sample to the population.

POPULATION PARAMETERS AND SAMPLE STATISTICS

sample statistics
Variables in a sample or measures computed from sample data.

population parameter
Variables in a population or measured characteristics of the population.

The primary purpose of inferential statistics is to make a judgment about the population, or the collection of all elements about which one seeks information. The sample is a subset or relatively small fraction of the total number of elements in the population. It is useful to distinguish between the data computed in the sample and the data or variables in the population. We use the term **sample statistics** to designate variables in the sample or measures computed from the sample data. The term **population parameters** is used to designate variables or measured characteristics of the population. Sample statistics are used to make inferences about population parameters.[2] In our notation, we will generally use Greek lowercase letters (μ or σ, for example) to denote population parameters and we will use English letters ($\bar{X}$ or S, for example) to denote sample statistics.

Frequency Distributions

frequency distribution (table)
A set of data organized by summarizing the number of times a particular value of a variable occurs.

Suppose a telephone survey has been conducted for a savings and loan association. The data on a large number of questionnaires have been recorded. To make the data usable, this information must be organized and summarized. Constructing a **frequency distribution,** or **frequency table,** is one of the most common means of summarizing a set of data. The process begins with recording the number of times a particular value of a variable occurs. This is the frequency of that value. Table 17.1 represents a frequency distribution of respondents' answers to a question from our survey example about how much money customers had deposited in the savings and loan.

TABLE 17.1 | **FREQUENCY DISTRIBUTION OF DEPOSITS**

Amount	Frequency (Number of People Making Deposits In Each Range)
Less than $3,000	499
$3,000–$4,999	530
$5,000–$9,999	562
$10,000–$14,999	718
$15,000 or more	811
	3,120

percentage distribution
A frequency distribution organized into a table (or graph) that summarizes percentage values associated with particular values of a variable.

probability distribution
The organization of probability values associated with particular values of a variable into a table (or graph).

It is also quite simple to construct a distribution of relative frequency, or a **percentage distribution.** In Table 17.2 the frequency of each value in Table 17.1 has been divided by the total number of observations. Multiplying each of the relative class frequencies by 100, we convert them to percentages and obtain a frequency distribution of percentages.

Probability is the long-run relative frequency with which an event will occur. In inferential statistics, we use the concept of a **probability distribution,**

TABLE 17.2 | **PERCENTAGE DISTRIBUTION OF DEPOSITS**

Amount	Percent of People Making Deposits in Each Range
Less than $3,000	16%
$3,000–$4,999	17
$5,000–$9,999	18
$10,000–$14,999	23
$15,000 or more	26
	100%

TABLE 17.3	PROBABILITY DISTRIBUTION OF DEPOSITS
Amount	**Probability**
Less than \$3,000	.16
\$3,000–\$4,999	.17
\$5,000–\$9,999	.18
\$10,000–\$14,999	.23
\$15,000 or more	.26
	1.00

which is conceptually the same as a percentage distribution except that the data have been converted into probabilities (see Table 17.3).

Proportions

proportion
The percentage of population elements that successfully meet some criterion.

When a frequency distribution portrays only a single characteristic in terms of a percentage of the total, it defines the **proportion** of occurrence. A proportion, perhaps the proportion of Hispanic Americans in the workforce, may be expressed as a percentage, a fraction, or a decimal value. A proportion, such as the proportion of tenured faculty at a university, indicates the percentage of population elements that successfully meet some standard with respect to a particular characteristic.

Central Tendency

On a typical day a certain sales manager counts the number of sales calls each of his sales representatives has made. He wishes to inspect the data to find the center or middle area of the frequency distribution. There are three ways to measure this central tendency, and each of these averages has a different meaning.

The Mean

mean
A measure of central tendency; the arithmetic average.

The mean is an average that all of us have been exposed to. The **mean** is simply the arithmetic average, and it is a very common measure of central tendency.

At this point it is appropriate to introduce the summation symbol, the Greek capital letter sigma (Σ). Following is a typical use of this symbol:

$$\sum_{i=1}^{n} X_i$$

This is a shorthand way to write the sum

$$X_1 + X_2 + X_3 + X_4 + X_5 + \ldots + X_n$$

Suppose a sales manager supervises the eight salespeople listed in Table 17.4. Below the Σ is the initial value of an index, usually *i, j,* or *k,* and above it is the final value, in this case *n,* the number of observations. The shorthand expression says to replace *i* in the formula with the values from 1 to 8 and total the observations obtained. Without changing the basic formula, the initial and final index values may be replaced by other values to indicate different starting or stopping points.

TABLE 17.4 | NUMBER OF SALES CALLS PER DAY BY SALESPEOPLE

Salesperson	Number of Sales Calls
Mike	4
Pat	3
Billie	2
Tracy	5
John	3
Frank	3
Anne	1
Samantha	5
Total (sum)	26

To express the sum of the salespersons' calls in Σ notation, we number the salespersons (this number becomes the index number) and associate subscripted variables with their number of calls:

Index		Salesperson	Variable		Calls
1	=	Mike	X_1	=	4
2	=	Pat	X_2	=	3
3	=	Billie	X_3	=	2
4	=	Tracy	X_4	=	5
5	=	John	X_5	=	3
6	=	Frank	X_6	=	3
7	=	Anne	X_7	=	1
8	=	Samantha	X_8	=	5

We then write an appropriate Σ formula and evaluate it:

$$\sum_{i=1}^{8} X_i = X_1 + X_2 + X_3 + X_4 + X_5 + X_6 + X_7 + X_8$$
$$= 4 + 3 + 2 + 5 + 3 + 3 + 1 + 5 = 26$$

The formula for the arithmetic mean is as follows:

$$\text{Mean} = \frac{\sum_{i=1}^{n} X}{n} = \frac{26}{8} = 3.25$$

The sum $\sum_{i=1}^{n} X$ tells us to add all the Xs whose subscripts are between 1 and n inclusive (where n equals the number of observations). The formula shows that the mean number of sales calls in this example is 3.25.

Researchers generally wish to know the population mean, μ (lowercase Greek letter mu), which is calculated as follows:

$$\mu = \frac{\sum_{i=1}^{n} X}{N}$$

where

N = number of observations in the population

Often we will not have enough data to calculate the population mean, μ, so we will calculate a sample mean, $\bar{X}$ (read "X bar"), with the following formula:

$$\bar{X} = \frac{\sum_{i=1}^{n} X}{n}$$

where

n = number of observations in the sample

More likely than not, you already knew how to calculate a mean. However, distinguishing between the symbols Σ, μ, and $\bar{X}$ is necessary for an understanding of statistics. In this introductory discussion of the summation sign (Σ), we have used very detailed notation that included the subscript for the initial index value (i) and the final index value (n). However, from this point on, references to Σ will not include the subscript for the initial index value (i) and the final index value (n) unless there is unique reason to highlight these index values.

median
A measure of central tendency that is the midpoint; the value below which half the values in a sample fall.

The Median

The next measure of central tendency, the **median,** is the midpoint of the distribution, or the 50th percentile. In other words, the median is the value below which half the values in the sample fall. In the sales manager example, 3 is the median, since half the observations are greater than 3 and half are less than 3.

mode
A measure of central tendency; the value that occurs most often.

The Mode

In apparel, *mode* refers to the most popular fashion. In statistics, the **mode** is the measure of central tendency that merely identifies the value that occurs most often. In our example above, Pat, John, and Frank each make three sales calls per day. The value 3 occurs most often, and thus 3 is the mode. The mode is determined by listing each possible value and noting the number of times each value occurs.

Measures of Dispersion

The mean, median, and mode summarize the central tendency of frequency distributions. It is also important to know the tendency of observations to depart from the central tendency. Calculating the dispersion of the data, or how the observations vary from the mean, is another means of summarizing the data. Consider, for instance, the 12-month inventory-level patterns of two products shown in Table 17.5. Both have a mean inventory level of 200 units, but the dispersion of observations for Product B is much greater than for Product A. There are several measures of dispersion.

range
The distance between the smallest and largest values of a frequency distribution.

The Range

The **range** is the simplest measure of dispersion. It is the distance between the smallest and the largest values of a frequency distribution. Thus, for Product A the range is between 196 units and 202 units (6 units), whereas for Product B the range is between 150 units and 261 units (111 units). The range does not take into account all the observations. It merely tells us about the extreme values of the distribution.

TABLE 17.5 INVENTORY LEVELS FOR PRODUCTS A AND B (BOTH AVERAGE 200 UNITS)

	Units Product A	Units Product B
January	196	150
February	198	160
March	199	176
April	200	181
May	200	192
June	200	200
July	200	201
August	201	202
September	201	213
October	201	224
November	202	240
December	202	261

Just as people may be fat or skinny, distributions may be fat or skinny. For example, for Product A the observations are close together and reasonably close to the mean. While we do not expect all observations to be exactly like the mean, in a skinny distribution they will be a short distance from the mean. In a fat distribution the observations will be spread out. Exhibit 17.1 illustrates this concept with two frequency distributions that have identical modes, medians, and means but differing degrees of dispersion.

The *interquartile* range encompasses the middlemost 50 percent of the observations, that is, the range between the bottom quartile (lowest 25 percent) and the top quartile (highest 25 percent).

EXHIBIT 17.1 LOW DISPERSION VERSUS HIGH DISPERSION

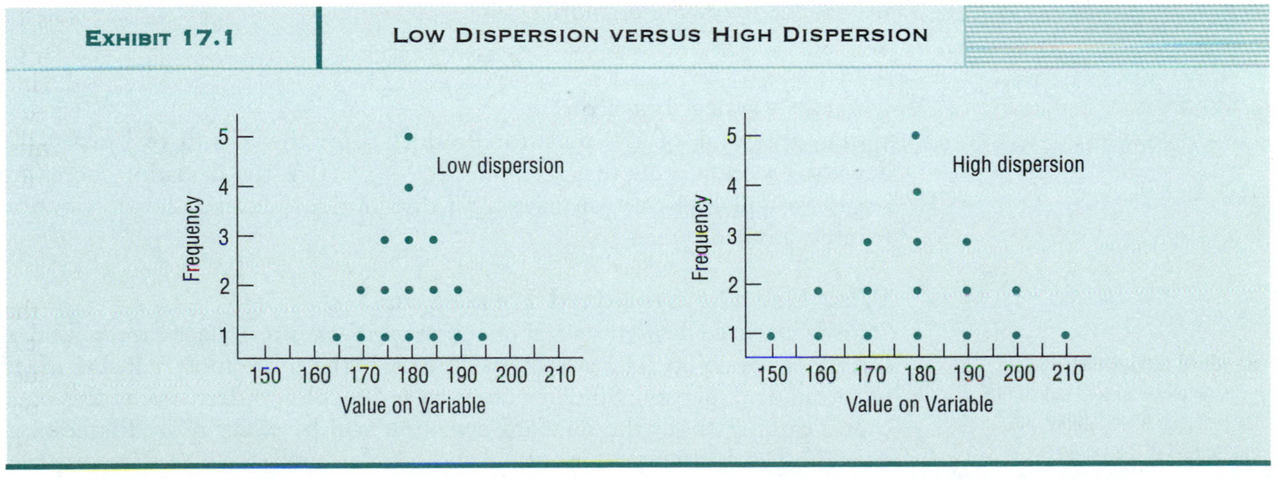

RESEARCH INSIGHT

THE WELL-CHOSEN AVERAGE

When you read an announcement by a corporation executive or a business proprietor that the average pay of the people who work in the establishment is so much, the figure may mean something and it may not.[3] If the average is a median, you can learn something significant from it: Half the employees make more than that; half make less. But if it is a mean (and believe me, it may be that if its nature is unspecified), you may be getting nothing more revealing than the average of one $450,000 income—the proprietor's—and the salaries of a crew of underpaid workers. "Average annual pay of $57,000" may conceal both the $20,000 salaries and the owner's profits taken in the form of a whopping salary.

Let's take a longer look at that one. The table below shows how many people get how much. The boss might like to express the situation as "average annual wage of $57,000"—using that deceptive mean. The mode, however, is more revealing: The most common rate of pay in this business is $20,000 a year. As usual, the median tells more about the situation than any other single figure does; half the people get more than $30,000 and half get less.

Number of People	Title	Salary	
1	Proprietor	$450,000	
1	President	150,000	
2	Vice presidents	100,000	
1	Controller	57,000	← arithmetic average, or mean
3	Directors	50,000	
4	Managers	37,000	
1	Supervisor	30,000	← Median (the one in the middle; 12 values above, 12 below)
12	Workers	20,000	← Mode (occurs most frequently)

Deviation Scores

A method of calculating how far away any observation is from the mean is to calculate individual deviation scores. To calculate a deviation from the mean, we use the following formula:

$$d_i = X_i - \bar{X}$$

where d_i = a deviation score.

For the value of 150 units for Product B for the month of January, the deviation score is -50; that is, $150 - 200 = -50$. If the deviation scores are large, we will find that we have a *fat* distribution, because the distribution exhibits a broad spread.

Why Use the Standard Deviation?

standard deviation
A quantitative index of a distribution's spread or variability; the square root of the variance.

Statisticians have devised several quantitative indexes to reflect a distribution's spread, or variability. The **standard deviation** is perhaps the most valuable index of spread or dispersion. Students often have difficulty understanding this concept. Learning about the standard deviation will be easier if we first look at several other measures of dispersion that may be used. Each of these has certain limitations that the standard deviation does not.

average deviation
A measure of dispersion that is computed by calculating the deviation score of each observation value, summing up the deviation scores, and dividing by the sample size.

First is the average deviation. The **average deviation** is computed by calculating the deviation score of each observation value, (that is, its difference from the mean), summing these scores, then dividing by the sample size (n):

$$\text{Average deviation} = \frac{\Sigma(X_i - \bar{X})}{n}$$

While this method of calculating a measure of spread seems of interest, it is never used. The positive deviation scores are always canceled out by the negative deviation scores, thus leaving an average deviation value of zero. Hence, the average deviation is useless as a measure of spread.

The disadvantage of the average deviation might be corrected by computing the absolute values of the deviations. In other words, we ignore all the positive and negative signs and utilize only the absolute value of each deviation. The formula for the *mean absolute deviation* is

$$\text{Mean absolute deviation} = \frac{\Sigma|X_i - \bar{X}|}{n}$$

While this procedure eliminates the problem of always having a zero score for the deviation measure, it presents some technical mathematical problems that make it less valuable than some other measures. (It is mathematically intractable.)[4]

Variance

There is another means of eliminating the sign problem caused by the negative deviations canceling out the positive deviations. The procedure is to square the deviation scores. The formula below is used to calculate the mean squared deviation:

$$\text{Mean squared deviation} = \frac{\Sigma(X_i - \bar{X})^2}{n}$$

variance
A measure of variability or dispersion. The square root is the standard deviation.

This measure is useful for describing the sample variability. However, we typically wish to make an inference about a population from a sample, and so the divisor $n - 1$ is used (rather than n) in most pragmatic business research problems.[5] This new measure of spread, called the sample **variance**, has the formula

$$\text{Variance, } S^2 = \frac{\Sigma(X_i - \bar{X})^2}{n - 1}$$

The variance is a very good index of the degree of dispersion. The variance, S^2, will be equal to zero if and only if each and every observation in the distribution is the same as the mean. The variance will grow larger as the observations tend to differ increasingly from each other and from the mean.

Standard Deviation

While the variance is frequently used in statistics, it does have one major drawback. The variance reflects a unit of measurement that has been squared. For instance, if measures of sales in a territory are made in dollars, then the mean number is reflected in dollars but the variance will be in squared dollars. Because of this, statisticians take the square root of the variance. The square root of the variance for distribution is called the *standard deviation*. Using the standard deviation eliminates the drawback of having the measure

RESEARCH INSIGHT

THE STATISTICAL DRAGON MEETS THE INTERNET

The World Wide Web provides a new educational medium for teaching statistics. Following are some of the best Web sites providing materials and interactive exercises so students can learn how to use statistics properly.

StatLib
http://lib.stat.cmu.edu/

StatLib is a system for distributing statistical software, data sets, and information by electronic mail, FTP, and the World Wide Web.

SurfStat Australia
http://www.anu.edu.au/nceph/surfstat/surfstat-home/surfstat.html

SurfStat Australia is an on-line text on introductory statistics from the University of Newcastle.

Data and Story Library
http://lib.stat.cmu.edu/DASL/

The Data and Story Library is an online library of data files and stories that illustrate the use of basic statistics methods.

Globally Accessible Statistical Procedures
http://www.stat.sc.edu/rsrch/gasp/

The Globally Accessible Statistical Procedures initiative is designed to make statistical routines easily available via the World Wide Web.

Electronic Encyclopedia of Statistical Examples and Exercises
http://www.stat.ohio-state.edu/~eesee/

The Electronic Encyclopedia of Statistical Examples and Exercises is a resource for the study of statistics that includes real-world examples of the uses and abuses of statistics and statistical inference.

The Rice Virtual Lab in Statistics
http://www.ruf.rice.edu/~lane/rvls.html
http://www.davidmlane.com/hyperstat.index.html

The Rice Virtual Lab in Statistics provides hypertext materials such as HyperStat Online.

Guide to Basic Laboratory Statistics
http://nimitz.mcs.kent.edu/~blewis/stat/scon.html

The Guide to Basic Laboratory Statistics is an informal guide to elementary inferential statistical methods used in the analysis of data from experiments.

WebStat
http://www.stat.sc.edu/webstat/

WebStat is a statistical software package created at the University of South Carolina for statistical analysis via the World Wide Web.

of dispersion in squared units rather than in the original measurement units. The formula for the standard deviation is[6]

$$S = \sqrt{S^2} = \sqrt{\frac{\Sigma(X_i - \bar{X})^2}{n - 1}}$$

Table 17.6 illustrates that the calculation of a standard deviation requires the researcher to first calculate the sample mean. In the example of eight sales-

TABLE 17.6 CALCULATING A STANDARD DEVIATION: NUMBER OF SALES CALLS PER DAY BY SALESPEOPLE

	X	$(X - \bar{X})$	$(X - \bar{X})^2$
	4	(4 − 3.25) = .75	.5625
	3	(3 − 3.25) = −.25	.0625
	2	(2 − 3.25) = −1.25	1.5625
	5	(5 − 3.25) = 1.75	3.0625
	3	(3 − 3.25) = −.25	.0625
	3	(3 − 3.25) = −.25	.0625
	1	(1 − 3.25) = −2.25	5.0625
	5	(5 − 3.25) = 1.75	3.0625
Σ	[a]	[a]	13.5

$$n = 8 \quad \bar{X} = 3.25 \quad S = \sqrt{\frac{\Sigma(X-\bar{X})^2}{n-1}} = \sqrt{\frac{13.5}{8-1}} = \sqrt{\frac{13.5}{7}} = \sqrt{1.9286} = 1.3887$$

[a]The summation of this column is not used in the calculation of the standard deviation.

Order is heaven's first law.
ALEXANDER POPE

persons' sales calls (Table 17.4), we calculated the sample mean to be 3.25. Table 17.6 illustrates how to calculate the standard deviation for these data.

At this point, we can return to thinking about the original purpose for measures of dispersion. We wish to summarize the data from survey research and other forms of business research. Measures of central tendency, such as the mean, help us interpret the data. In addition, we wish to calculate a measure of variability that will give us a quantitative index of the dispersion of the distribution. We have looked at several measures of dispersion and have arrived at two very adequate means of measuring dispersion: the variance and the standard deviation.

At this point we should note that the formula shown above is for the sample standard deviation, S. The formula for the population standard deviation, σ, which is conceptually very similar, has not been given. Nevertheless, you should understand that σ measures the dispersion in the population, while S measures the dispersion in the sample.

These concepts are crucial to understanding statistics. Remember, the student of statistics must learn the language in order to use it in a research project. If you don't understand the language at this point, review the material now.

The Normal Distribution

normal distribution
A symmetrical, bell-shaped distribution that describes the expected probability distribution of many chance occurrences.

One of the most useful probability distributions in statistics is the **normal distribution,** which is also called the *normal curve*. This mathematical and theoretical distribution describes the expected distribution of sample means and many other chance occurrences. The normal curve is bell-shaped, and almost all (99 percent) of its values are within ±3 standard deviations from its mean. An example of a normal curve, the distribution of IQ scores, appears in Exhibit 17.2. In this example, a standard deviation for IQ equals 15. Notice that we can identify the proportion of the curve by measuring a score's distance (in this case, standard deviation) from the mean (100).

EXHIBIT 17.2 THE NORMAL DISTRIBUTION: AN EXAMPLE OF THE DISTRIBUTION OF INTELLIGENCE QUOTIENT (IQ) SCORES

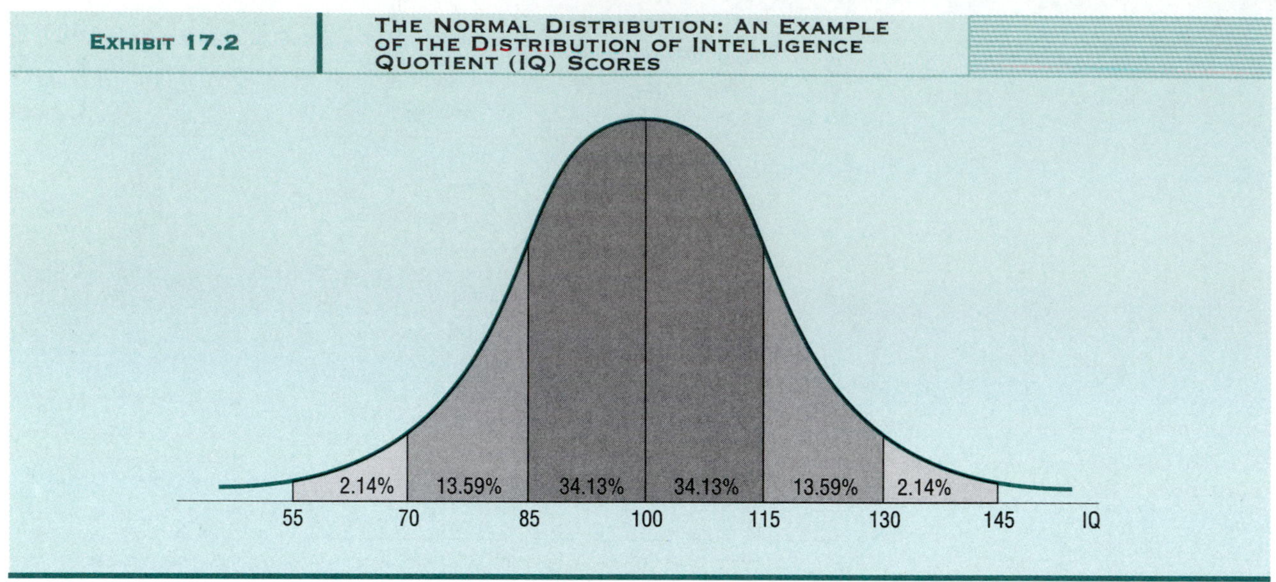

standardized normal distribution
A normal curve with a mean of zero and a standard deviation of one. It is a theoretical probability distribution.

The **standardized normal distribution** is a specific normal curve that has several characteristics: (1) it is symmetrical about its mean; (2) the mean identifies the normal distribution's highest point (the mode) and the vertical line about which this normal curve is symmetrical; (3) the normal distribution has an infinite number of cases (it is a continuous distribution), and the area under the curve has a probability density equal to 1.0; and (4) the standardized normal distribution has a mean of zero and a standard deviation of 1. Exhibit 17.3 illustrates these properties. Table 17.7 is a summary version of the typical standardized normal table found at the end of most statistics textbooks. A more complete table of areas under the standardized normal distribution appears in Table 2 in the Appendix of Statistical Tables at the end of this book.

EXHIBIT 17.3 THE STANDARDIZED NORMAL DISTRIBUTION

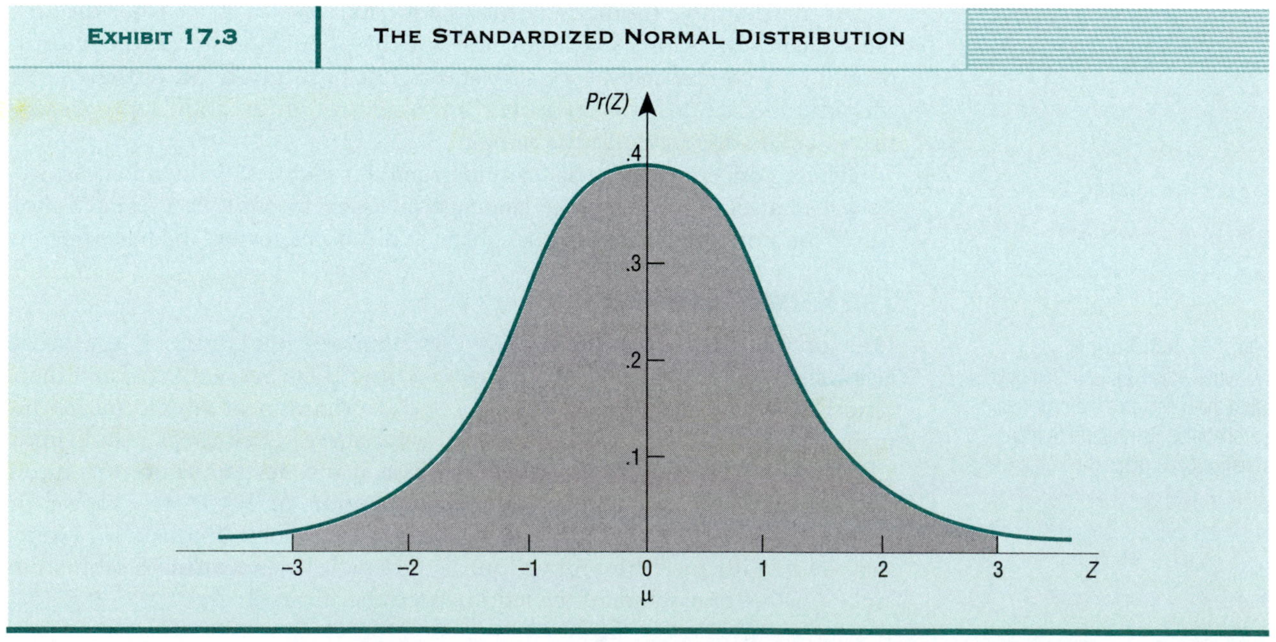

TABLE 17.7 STANDARDIZED NORMAL TABLE: AREA UNDER ONE-HALF OF THE NORMAL CURVE[a]

Standard Deviation from Mean, in Units of Z	STANDARD DEVIATIONS FROM MEAN, IN TENTHS OF UNITS OF Z									
	—.0	—.1	—.2	—.3	—.4	—.5	—.6	—.7	—.8	—.9
0.—	.000	.040	.080	.118	.155	.192	.226	.258	.288	.316
1.—	.341	.364	.385	.403	.419	.433	.445	.445	.464	.471
2.—	.477	.482	.486	.489	.492	.494	.495	.496	.497	.498
3.—	.499	.499	.499	.499	.499	.499	.499	.499	.499	.499

[a]Area under the normal curve in one direction from the mean to the point indicated by each row–column combination. For example, the table shows that about 68 percent of normally distributed observations can be expected to fall within 1.0 standard deviation on either side of the mean (.341 times 2). An interval of almost 2.0 standard deviations around the mean will include 95 percent of all cases.

The standardized normal distribution is a purely theoretical distribution, yet it is the most useful distribution in inferential statistics. Statisticians have spent a great deal of time and effort making it convenient for researchers to find the probability of any portion of the area under the standardized normal curve. All we have to do is transform, or convert, the data from other observed normal distributions to the standardized normal curve. In other words, the standardized normal distribution is extremely valuable because we can translate, or transform, any normal variable, X, into the standardized value Z. Exhibit 17.4 illustrates how we can convert either a *skinny* distribution or a *fat* distribution into the standardized normal distribution. This ability to transform normal variables has many pragmatic implications for the business researcher. The standardized normal table at the back of most statistics and research methods books allows us to evaluate the probability of the occurrence of many events without any difficulty.

Computing the standardized value, Z, of any measurement expressed in original units is simple: Subtract the mean from the value to be transformed and divide by the standard deviation (all expressed in original units). The formula for this procedure and its verbal statement follow. Note that σ, the population standard deviation, is utilized in the formula.[7]

$$Z = \frac{X - \mu}{\sigma}$$

$$\text{Standardized value} = \frac{(\text{Value to be transformed}) - (\text{Mean})}{\text{Standard deviation}}$$

where

$$\mu = \text{hypothesized or expected value of the mean}$$

Suppose that in the past a toy manufacturer has experienced mean sales, μ, of 9,000 units, $\mu = 9{,}000$, and a standard deviation, σ, of 500 units during the month of September. The production manager wishes to know whether wholesalers will demand between 7,500 and 9,625 units during the month of September in the upcoming year. As there are no tables in the back of this book

EXHIBIT 17.4 LINEAR TRANSFORMATION OF ANY NORMAL VARIABLE INTO A STANDARDIZED NORMAL VARIABLE[8]

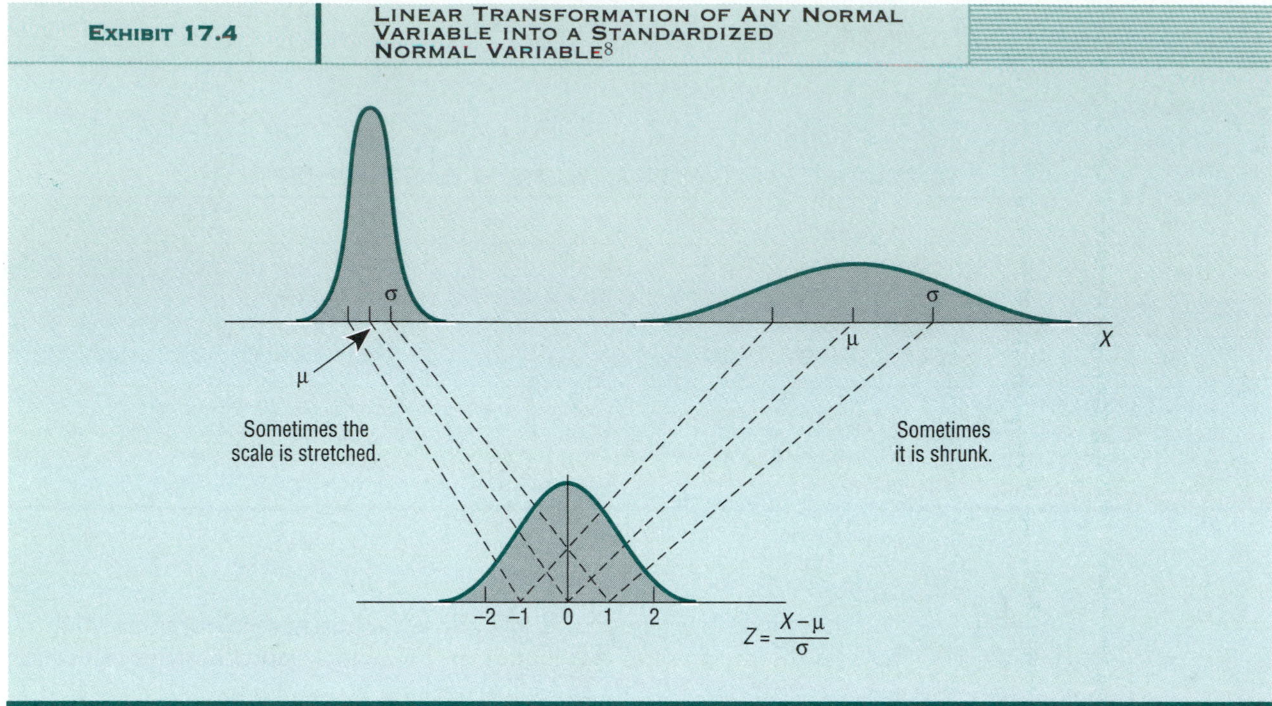

for the distribution whose mean equals 9,000 and whose standard deviation equals 500, we must transform our distribution of sales, X, into the standardized form, utilizing our simple formula. The computation below shows that the probability (Pr) of obtaining sales in this range is probability .893.

$$Z = \frac{X - \mu}{\sigma} = \frac{7{,}500 - 9{,}000}{500} = -3.00$$

and

$$Z = \frac{X - \mu}{\sigma} = \frac{9{,}625 - 9{,}000}{500} = 1.25$$

Using Table 17.7 (or Table 2 in the Appendix), we find that

- When $Z = -3.00$, the area under the curve (probability) equals .499
- When $Z = 1.25$, the area under the curve (probability) equals .394

Thus, the total area under the curve is $.499 + .394 = .893$. The area under the curve corresponding to this computation is the shaded area in Exhibit 17.5. Thus, the sales manager knows there is a .893 probability that sales will be between 7,500 and 9,625.

At this point it is appropriate to reiterate that to understand statistics one must understand the language that statisticians use. Each concept that has been discussed thus far is relatively simple, but a clear-cut command of this terminology is essential for understanding what will be discussed later.

Now that certain basic terminology has been covered, we will outline the technique of statistical inference. Three additional types of distributions must be defined: population distribution, sample distribution, and sampling distribution.

EXHIBIT 17.5 | **STANDARDIZED DISTRIBUTION: TOY EXAMPLE**

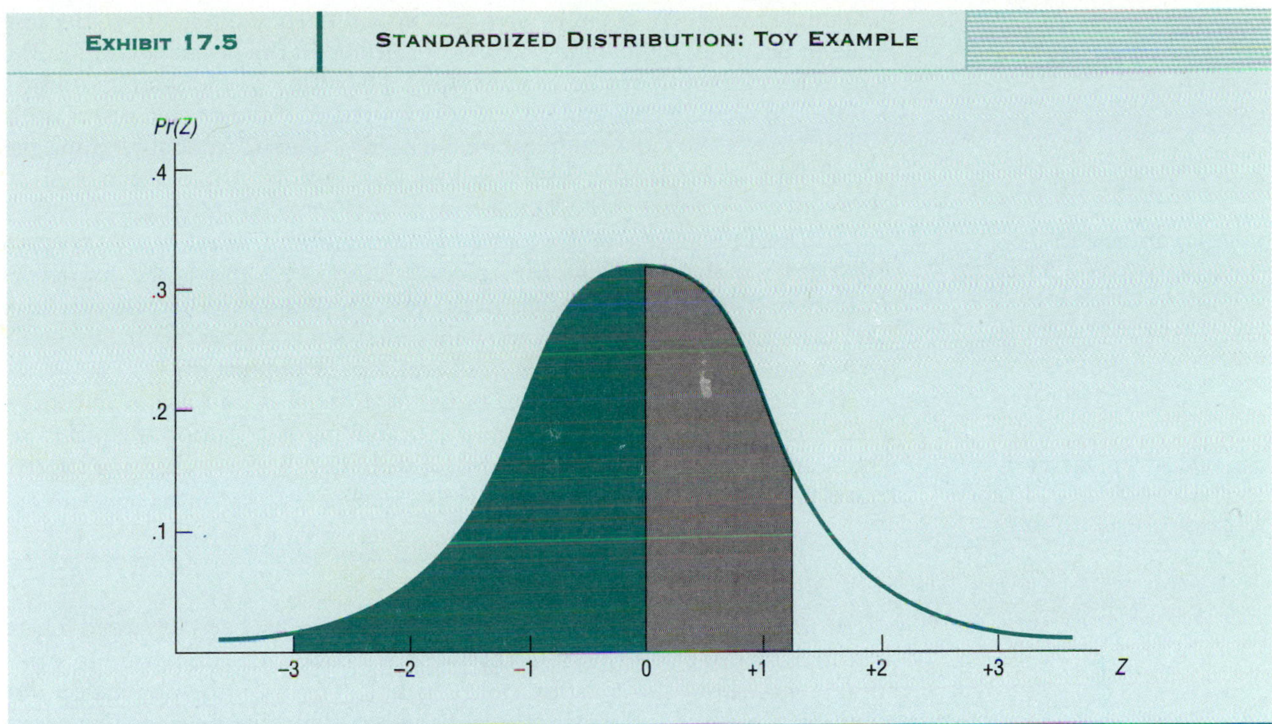

POPULATION DISTRIBUTION, SAMPLE DISTRIBUTION, AND SAMPLING DISTRIBUTION

When conducting a research project or a survey, the researcher's purpose is not to describe the sample of respondents but to make an inference about the population. As defined previously, a population, or universe, is the total set, or collection, of potential units for observation. The sample is a smaller subset of this population.

population distribution
A frequency distribution of the elements of a population.

sample distribution
A frequency distribution of the elements of a sample.

A frequency distribution of the elements of a population is called a **population distribution.** The population distribution has its mean and standard deviation represented by the Greek letters μ and σ. A frequency distribution of the elements of a sample is called a **sample distribution.** The sample mean is designated $\bar{X}$ and the sample standard deviation is designated S.

The concepts of the population distribution and the sample distribution are relatively simple. However, we must now introduce another distribution, the *sampling distribution of the sample mean.* If you forget which distribution is being discussed, you will have some difficulty learning about statistical inference. One must learn the vocabulary to master a new language.

We are now at a crucial point in understanding statistics. Understanding the sampling distribution is the basis for understanding statistics. The sampling distribution is a theoretical probability distribution that in actual practice would never be calculated. Hence, students who are practical and business-oriented have difficulty understanding why the notion of the sampling distribution is even discussed. But statisticians, with their mathematical curiosity, have asked themselves, "What would happen if we were to draw a large number of samples (say 50,000), each having n elements, from a specified population?" Assuming that the large number of samples were randomly selected, the sample means, $\bar{X}$s, could be arranged in a frequency distribution. Because different people or sample units would be selected in the different samples, the sample means would not be exactly equal. The shape of the sampling distribution is of considerable importance to statisticians. If the sample size is sufficiently large and if the samples are randomly drawn, we know from the central-limit theorem that the sampling distribution of the mean will be approximately normally distributed.

sampling distribution
A theoretical probability distribution of all possible samples of a certain size drawn from a particular population.

A formal definition of the sampling distribution is as follows: A **sampling distribution** is a theoretical probability distribution that shows the functional relationship between the possible values of some summary characteristic of *n* cases drawn at random and the probability (density) associated with each value over all possible samples of size *n* from a particular population.[9]

standard error of the mean
The standard deviation of the sampling distribution of the mean.

The sampling distribution's mean is called the *expected value* of the statistic. The expected value of the mean of the sampling distribution is equal to μ. The standard deviation of the sampling distribution of $\bar{X}$ is called the **standard error of the mean** ($S_{\bar{X}}$) and is approximately equal to

$$S_{\bar{X}} = \frac{\sigma}{\sqrt{n}}$$

At this point it is appropriate to review what has just been discussed. There are three important distributions that we must know about if we are to make an inference about a population from a sample. These are the population distribution, the sample distribution, and the sampling distribution. They have the following characteristics:

Distribution	Mean	Standard Deviation
Population distribution	μ	σ
Sample distribution	$\bar{X}$	S
Sampling distribution	$\mu_{\bar{X}} = \mu$	$S_{\bar{X}}$

We now have much of the information that is necessary to understand the concept of statistical inference. To further clarify why the sampling distribution has the characteristic described above, we will elaborate on two concepts: the standard error of the mean and the central-limit theorem. You may be wondering why the standard error of the mean, $S_{\bar{X}}$, is defined as $S_{\bar{X}} = \sigma/\sqrt{n}$. The reason is based on the notion that the variance, or dispersion, within the sampling distribution of the mean will be less if we have a larger sample size for independent samples. Intuitively, we can see that the larger the sample size, the more confident the researcher may be that the sample mean is closer to the population mean. In actual practice the standard error of the mean is estimated by using the sample's standard deviation. Thus, $S_{\bar{X}}$ is estimated by using $S/\sqrt{n}$.

Exhibit 17.6 shows the relationship among a population distribution, the sample distribution, and three sampling distributions of varying sample size. In Part (a) of this exhibit, note that the population distribution is not a normal distribution. In Part (b), note that the sample distribution resembles the distribution of the population; however, there may be some differences. In Part (c), note that each of the sampling distributions is normally distributed and that the means of each of these sampling distributions are the same. We also note that as sample size increases, the spread of the sample means around μ decreases. Thus, with a larger sample size we will have a skinnier sampling distribution.

EXHIBIT 17.6 | **SCHEMATIC OF THE THREE FUNDAMENTAL TYPES OF DISTRIBUTION**[10]

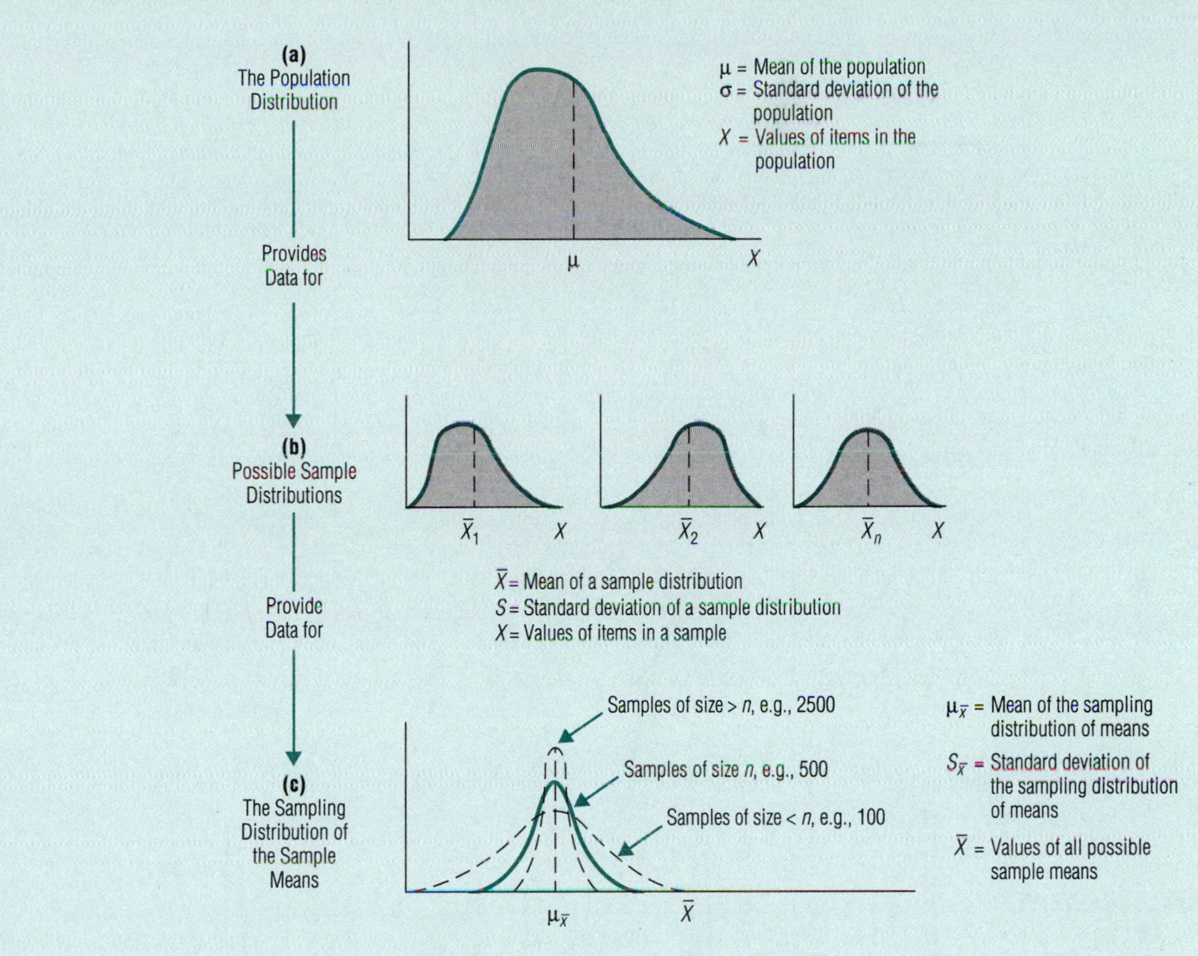

CENTRAL-LIMIT THEOREM

central-limit theorem
The theory stating that as a sample size increases, the distribution of sample means of size *n*, randomly selected, approaches a normal distribution.

Finding that the means of random samples of a sufficiently large size will be approximately normal in form and that the mean of the sampling distribution will approach the population mean is very useful. Mathematically, this is the assertion of the **central-limit theorem**, which states: As the sample size n increases, the distribution of the mean, $\bar{X}$, of a random sample taken from practically any population approaches a normal distribution (with a mean, μ, and a standard deviation, $\sigma/\sqrt{n}$).[11]

The central-limit theorem works regardless of the shape of the original population distribution (see Exhibit 17.7). A simple example will demonstrate the central-limit theorem. Assume that a researcher is interested in the number of dollars children spend on toys each month. Assume further that the population the researcher is investigating is 8-year-old children in a certain private school. In this example the population consists of only six individuals.

Exhibit 17.7 | **Distribution of Sample Means for Samples of Various Sizes and Different Population Distributions**[12]

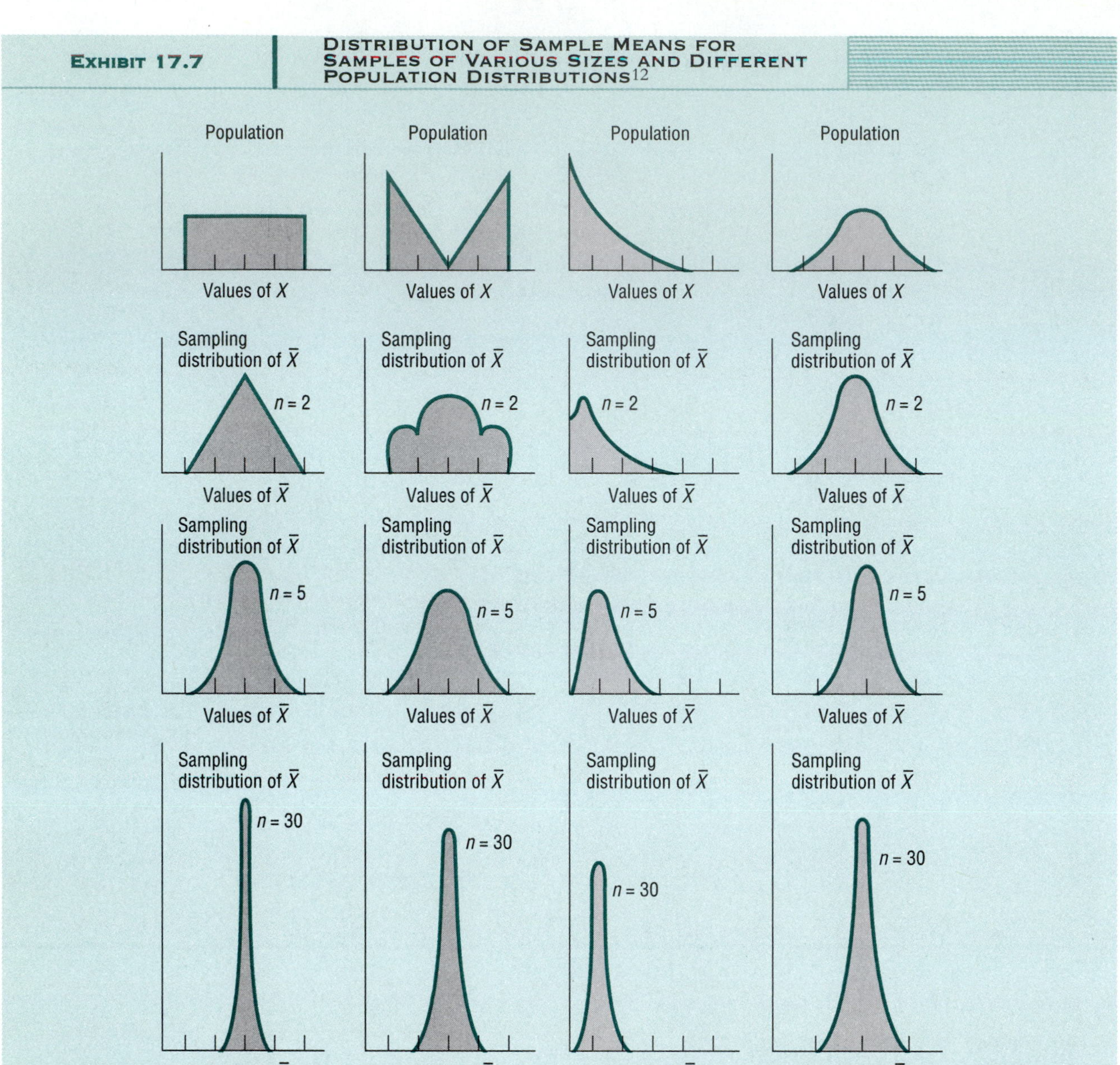

(This is a simple and perhaps somewhat unrealistic example; nevertheless, assume that the population size consists of only six elements.) Table 17.8 shows the frequency distribution of toy expenditures by the six children.

Alice, a relatively deprived child, has only \$1 per month, whereas Fat Freddy, the rich kid, has \$6 to spend. The mean expenditure on toys each month is \$3.50; so the population mean, μ, equals 3.5 (see Table 17.9). Now assume that we do not know everything about the population and we wish to take a sample size of two, to be drawn randomly from the population of six individuals. How many possible samples are there? The answer is 15. They are as follows:

TABLE 17.8 HYPOTHETICAL POPULATION DISTRIBUTION OF TOY EXPENDITURES

Child	Toy Expenditures
Alice	$1.00
Bob	2.00
Chris	3.00
Dana	4.00
George	5.00
Freddy	6.00

TABLE 17.9 CALCULATION OF POPULATION MEAN

	X
	$ 1.00
	2.00
	3.00
	4.00
	5.00
	6.00
Summation	$21.00

Calculation:

$$\mu = \frac{\Sigma X}{N} = \frac{21}{6} = 3.5 = \mu$$

1, 2				
1, 3	2, 3			
1, 4	2, 4	3, 4		
1, 5	2, 5	3, 5	4, 5	
1, 6	2, 6	3, 6	4, 6	5, 6

Table 17.10 (page 420) gives the sample mean of each of the possible 15 samples and shows a frequency distribution of these sample means with their appropriate probabilities. Note that these sample means comprise a sampling distribution of the mean and that the distribution is *approximately* normal. If we increase the sample size to 3, 4, or more, the distribution of sample means would be a closer approximation to a normal distribution. While this simple example is not a proof of the central-limit theorem, it should give you a better understanding of the nature of the sampling distribution of the mean.

This theoretical knowledge about distributions can be used to solve two practical business research problems: estimating parameters and determining sample size. Estimating parameters is dealt with in this chapter because understanding it will help you understand the theory of determining sample size.

ESTIMATION OF PARAMETERS

The Ford Motor Company must have a certain number of workers on an assembly line. Making a proper inference about the number of workers

TABLE 17.10 MEANS OF THE SAMPLES AND THEIR FREQUENCY DISTRIBUTION

Sample	ΣX	$\bar{X}$	Probability
$1,$2	$ 3.00	$1.50	1/15
1, 3	4.00	2.00	1/15
1, 4	5.00	2.50	1/15
1, 5	6.00	3.00	1/15
1, 6	7.00	3.50	1/15
2, 3	5.00	2.50	1/15
2, 4	6.00	3.00	1/15
2, 5	7.00	3.50	1/15
2, 6	8.00	4.00	1/15
3, 4	7.00	3.50	1/15
3, 5	8.00	4.00	1/15
3, 6	9.00	4.50	1/15
4, 5	9.00	4.50	1/15
4, 6	10.00	5.00	1/15
5, 6	11.00	5.50	1/15

Sample Mean ($\bar{X}$)	Frequency	Probability
$1.50	1	1/15
2.00	1	1/15
2.50	2	2/15
3.00	2	2/15
3.50	3	3/15
4.00	2	2/15
4.50	2	2/15
5.00	1	1/15
5.50	1	1/15

expected to show up for work is an important production-planning tool. Statistical analysis of the variance in absenteeism is extremely important.

Suppose that you are a financial analyst and that a planned acquisition is expected to produce cash flows for the next 5 years. These cash flows are not known with certainty. You must make an estimate of cash flows and expected net present value. How could you be sure there were no statistical errors in that estimate? How confident could you be in these figures?[13]

Students often wonder whether statistics are really used in the business world. The two situations outlined above provide examples of the need for statistical estimation of parameters and of the value of statistical techniques as managerial tools.

Point Estimates

Our goal in utilizing statistics is to make an estimate about population parameters. The population mean, μ, and the population standard deviation, σ, are constants, but in most instances of business research they are unknown. To estimate the population values, we are required to sample. As we have discussed, $\bar{X}$ and S are random variables that will vary from sample to sample with a certain probability distribution (sampling distribution).

Our previous example was somewhat unrealistic in that the population had only six individuals. Consider the more realistic example of a prospective racquetball entrepreneur wishing to estimate the average number of days that players participate in this sport each week. When statistical inference is needed, the population mean, μ, is a constant but unknown parameter. To estimate the average number of playing days, we could take a sample of 300 racquetball players throughout the area where our entrepreneur is thinking of building club facilities. If the sample mean, $\bar{X}$, equals 2.6 days per week, we might use this figure as a **point estimate.** This single value, 2.6, would be the best estimate of the population mean. However, we would be extremely lucky if the sample estimate were exactly the same as the population value. A less risky alternative would be to calculate a confidence interval.

point estimate
An estimate of the population mean in the form of a single value, usually the sample mean.

Confidence Intervals

If we specify a range of numbers, or interval, within which a population mean should lie, we can be more confident that our inference is correct. A **confidence interval estimate** is based on the knowledge that $\mu = \bar{X} \pm$ a small sampling error. After calculating an interval estimate, we can determine how probable it is that the population mean will fall within this range of statistical values. In the racquetball project, the researcher, after setting up a confidence interval, would be able to make a statement such as "With 95 percent confidence, I think that the average number of days played is between 2.3 and 2.9 per week." This information can be utilized to estimate market demand because the researcher has a certain confidence that the interval contains the value of the true population mean.

confidence interval estimate
A specified range of numbers within which a population mean is expected to lie; the set of acceptable hypotheses or the level of probability associated with an interval estimate.

Necessity is the mother of taking chances.

MARK TWAIN

The crux of the problem for the researcher is to determine how much random sampling error will be tolerated. In other words, what should the confidence interval be? How much of a gamble should be taken that μ will be included in the range? Do we need to be 80 percent, 90 percent, 99 percent sure? The **confidence level** is a percentage or decimal that indicates the long-run probability that the results will be correct. Traditionally, researchers have utilized the 95 percent confidence level. While there is nothing magical about the 95 percent confidence level, it is useful to select 95 percent confidence level in our examples.

confidence level
A percentage or decimal value that tells how confident a researcher can be about being correct. It states the long-run percentage of the time that a confidence interval will include the true population mean.

As we have mentioned, a point estimate does not give any information about the possible magnitude of random sampling error. The *confidence interval* gives the estimated value of the population parameter, plus or minus an estimate of error. We can express the idea of the confidence interval as follows:

$$\mu = \bar{X} \pm \text{a small sampling error}$$

More formally, assuming the researchers select a large sample (more than 30 observations), the small sampling error is given by

$$\text{Small sampling error} = Z_{\text{c.l.}} S_{\bar{X}}$$

where

$Z_{\text{c.l.}}$ = value of Z, the standardized normal variable, at a specified confidence level (c.l.)

$S_{\bar{X}}$ = standard error of the mean

The precision of our estimate is indicated by the value of $Z_{\text{c.l.}} S_{\bar{X}}$. It is useful to define the **range of possible random error,** E, as follows:

range of possible random error
The potential difference between a population mean and an observed value.

$$E = Z_{\text{c.l.}} S_{\bar{X}}$$

Thus,

$$\mu = \bar{X} \pm E \quad \text{or} \quad \mu = \bar{X} \pm Z_{\text{c.l.}} S_{\bar{X}}$$

where

$\bar{X}$ = sample mean

E = range of sampling error

Note that the confidence interval ($\pm E$) is always stated as one-half of the total confidence interval.

The following is a step-by-step procedure for calculating confidence intervals:

1. Calculate $\bar{X}$ from the sample.
2. Assuming σ is unknown, estimate the population standard deviation by finding S, the sample standard deviation.
3. Estimate the standard error of the mean, utilizing the following formula:

$$S_{\bar{X}} = \frac{S}{\sqrt{n}}$$

4. Determine the Z-value associated with the confidence level desired. The confidence level should be divided by 2 to determine what percentage of the area under the curve must be included on each side of the mean.
5. Calculate the confidence interval.

The following example shows how calculating a confidence interval can be utilized in personnel research. Suppose a personnel manager believes age will be a useful criterion for placement. Successful women at the supervisory level are sampled. As the business researcher, you find that the mean age ($\bar{X}$) of 100 women is 37.5 years, with a standard deviation (S) of 12.0 years. Knowing that it would be extremely coincidental if the point estimate from the sample were exactly the same as the population mean age (μ), you decide to construct a confidence interval around the sample mean, using the steps given above:

1. $\bar{X} = 37.5$ years
2. $S = 12.0$ years
3. $S_{\bar{X}} = \dfrac{12}{\sqrt{100}} = 1.2$
4. Suppose you wish to be 95 percent confident, that is, assured that 95 times out of 100 the estimates from the sample will include the population parameter. Including 95 percent of the area requires that 47.5 percent (half of 95 percent) of the distribution on each side be included. From the Z-table (Table 2 in the Appendix) you find that .475 corresponds to the Z-value 1.96.
5. Substitute the values for $Z_{\text{c.l.}}$ and $S_{\bar{X}}$ into the confidence interval formula:

$$\begin{aligned} \mu &= 37.5 \pm (1.96)\,(1.2) \\ &= 37.5 \pm 2.352 \end{aligned}$$

So you can expect that μ is contained in the range from 35.148 to 39.852 years. Intervals constructed in this manner will contain the true value of μ 95 percent of the time.

Step 3 can be eliminated by using S and n directly in the confidence interval formula:

$$\mu = \bar{X} \pm Z_{\text{c.l.}} \frac{S}{\sqrt{n}}$$

Remember that $S/\sqrt{n}$ represents the standard error of the mean, $S_{\bar{X}}$. Its use is based on the central-limit theorem.

If you wanted to increase the probability that the population mean lies in the confidence interval, you could use the 99 percent confidence level, with a Z-value of 2.57. You may want to calculate the 99 percent confidence interval for the example. The answer will be the range between 34.416 and 40.584.

Recapitulation

We have now presented the basic concepts of inferential statistics. You should understand that sample statistics such as the sample means, $\bar{X}$s, are capable of providing good estimates of population parameters such as μ. You should also realize at this point that there is a certain probability of being in error when you estimate a population parameter from a sample statistic. In other words, there will be a random sampling error that is the difference between the results of a survey and the results of a census of the entire population. If you have a firm understanding of these basic terms and ideas, the rest of statistics will be relatively simple for you. The concepts already discussed are the essence of statistics. Several ramifications of the simple ideas presented so far will permit better decisions about populations based on surveys or experiments.

SAMPLE SIZE

Random Sampling Error and Sample Size

When asked to evaluate a business research project, most people, even those with little research training, will begin by asking "How big was the sample?" Intuitively, we know that the larger the sample, the more accurate the research. This is in fact a statistical truth; that is, random sampling error varies with samples of different sizes. In statistical terms, increasing the sample size decreases the width of the confidence interval at a given confidence level. When the standard deviation of the population is unknown, a confidence interval is calculated by using the following formula:

$$\text{Confidence interval} = \bar{X} \pm Z \frac{S}{\sqrt{n}}$$

Observe that the equation for the plus or minus error factor in the confidence interval includes n, the sample size:

$$E = Z \frac{S}{\sqrt{n}}$$

If n increases, E is reduced. Exhibit 17.8 illustrates that the confidence interval (or magnitude of error) decreases as the sample size, n, increases.

We have already noted that it is not necessary to take a census of all elements of a population to conduct an accurate study. The laws of probability provide investigators with sufficient confidence regarding the accuracy of data collected from a sample. Knowledge of the theory concerning the sampling distribution helps researchers make reasonably precise estimates.

EXHIBIT 17.8 | **RELATIONSHIP BETWEEN SAMPLE SIZE AND ERROR**[14]

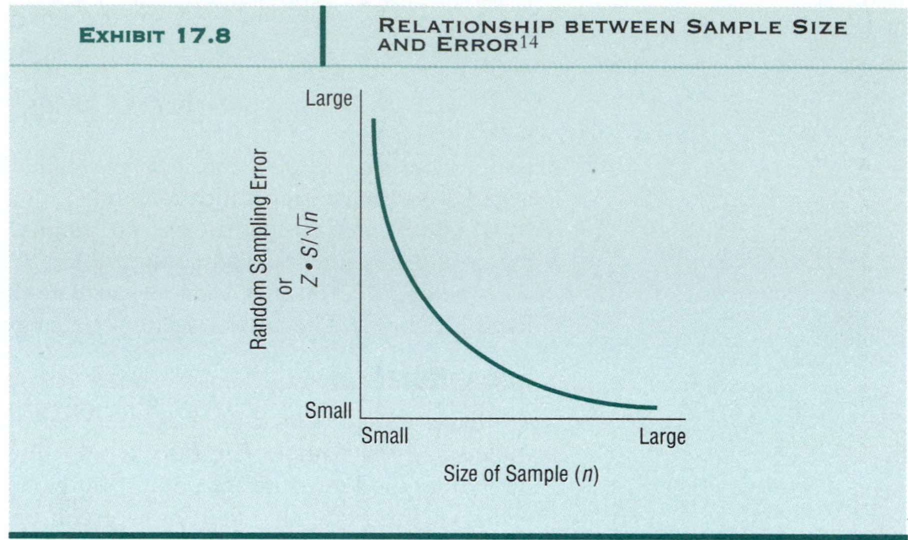

Students familiar with the "law of diminishing returns" in economics will easily grasp the concept that increases in sample size reduce sampling error at a *decreasing rate.* For example, doubling a sample of 1,000 will reduce sampling error by 1 percentage point, but doubling the sample from 2,000 to 4,000 will reduce sampling error by only another ½ percentage point. More technically, random sampling error is inversely proportional to the square root of n. Exhibit 17.8 gives an approximation of the relationship between sample size and error. Thus, the main issue becomes one of determining the optimal sample size.

Factors in Determining Sample Size for Questions Involving Means

Three factors are required to specify sample size:

1. Variance, or heterogeneity, of the population
2. Magnitude of acceptable error
3. Confidence level

Suppose a researcher wishes to find out whether 9-year-old boys are taller than 4-year-old boys. Intuitively, we know that even with a very small sample size, the correct information will probably be obtained. This is based on the fact that the determination of sample size depends on the research question and the variability within the sample.

The *variance,* or *heterogeneity,* of the population is the first necessary bit of information. In statistical terms, this refers to the *standard deviation* of the population parameter. Only a small sample is required if the population is homogeneous. For example, predicting the average age of college students requires a smaller sample size than predicting the average age of people visiting the zoo on a given Sunday afternoon. If we are testing the effectiveness of an acne skin-care product, the sample must be large enough to cover the range of skin types, because as heterogeneity increases, so must sample size.

The magnitude of error, or the confidence interval, is the second necessary bit of information. Defined in statistical terms as E, the *magnitude of error* (range of possible random error) indicates how precise the estimate must be.

Exhibit 17.9 | **Statistical Information Needed to Determine Sample Size**

Variable	Symbol	Typical Source of Information
Standard deviation	S	Pilot study or rule of thumb
Magnitude of error	E	Managerial judgment or calculation ($ZS_{\bar{X}}$)
Confidence level	$Z_{c.l.}$	Managerial judgment

It indicates a certain precision level. From a managerial perspective, the importance of the decision (in terms of profitability) will influence the researcher's specifications of the range of error. If, for example, favorable results from a test market sample will result in the construction of a new plant and unfavorable results will dictate that it not be built, it is likely that the acceptable range of error will be small. The cost of an error is too great to allow much room for sampling errors. In other cases the estimate need not be extremely precise. Allowing an error of ±$1,000 in total family income, instead of $E = \pm\$50$, may be acceptable in most cross-sectional studies.

The third factor of concern is the *confidence level.* In our examples we shall typically use the 95 percent confidence level. This, however, is an arbitrary decision, based on convention. There is nothing sacred about the .05 chance level (i.e., the probability of the true population parameter being incorrectly estimated).[15] Exhibit 17.9 summarizes the information required, to determine sample size.

Estimating Sample Size for Questions Involving Means

sample size
The size of a sample; the number of observations or cases specified by (1) the estimated variance of the population, (2) the magnitude of acceptable error, and (3) the confidence level.

Once the above concepts are understood, determining the actual size for a simple random sample is quite easy. To estimate **sample size,** the researcher does the following:

1. Estimates the standard deviation of the population
2. Makes a judgment about the acceptable magnitude of error
3. Determines a confidence level

The only problem is estimating the standard deviation of the population. Ideally, similar studies conducted in the past can be used as a basis for judging the standard deviation. In practice, researchers without prior information conduct a pilot study for the purpose of estimating the population parameters so that another larger sample, of the appropriate sample size, may be drawn. This procedure is called *sequential sampling* because researchers take an initial look at the pilot study results before deciding on a larger sample that provides more precise information.

A rule of thumb for estimating the value of the standard deviation is to expect it to be one-sixth of the range.[16] In a study on incentive pay, the researcher expected bonus payments to range from $1,000 to $7,000, a $6,000 range. Therefore, a rule-of-thumb estimate for the standard deviation would be $1,000.

For the moment, let us assume that the standard deviation has been estimated in some preliminary work. If our concern is to estimate the mean of a particular population, the formula for sample size is derived from our knowledge that $E = ZS_{\bar{X}}$:

$$n = \left(\frac{ZS}{E}\right)^2$$

where Z = standardized value corresponding to a confidence level

S = sample standard deviation or an estimate of the population standard deviation

E = acceptable magnitude of error, plus or minus an error factor (the range is one-half the total confidence interval)[17]

Suppose a survey researcher studying expenditures on lipstick wishes to have a 95 percent confidence level (Z) and a range of error (E) of less than $2.00. If the estimate of the standard deviation is $29.00, the sample size can be calculated as follows:

$$n = \left(\frac{ZS}{E}\right)^2 = \left[\frac{(1.96)(29.00)}{2.00}\right]^2 = \left[\frac{56.84}{2.00}\right]^2 = (28.42)^2 = 808$$

If a range of error (E) of $4.00 is acceptable, sample size can be reduced:

$$n = \left(\frac{ZS}{E}\right)^2 = \left[\frac{(1.96)(29.00)}{4.00}\right]^2 = \left[\frac{56.84}{4.00}\right]^2 = (14.21)^2 = 202$$

Thus, doubling the range of acceptable error reduces sample size to approximately one-quarter its original size. Stated conversely in a general sense, doubling sample size reduces error by approximately one-quarter.

The Influence of Population Size on Sample Size

The A. C. Nielsen Company conducts television ratings. Throughout the years it has been plagued with questions about how it is possible to rate 100-plus million television homes with such a small sample (approximately 5,000 homes). The answer is, as we have already indicated, it is the variance of the population that has the largest effect on sample size. In most cases the size of the population does not have a major effect on the sample size. However, if the population is very small, population size should be considered so the calculated sample size can be reduced. For a small population, say 5,000 or less, a finite correction factor may be needed to adjust the sample size if the sample size is more than 5 percent of a finite population. If the sample is large relative to the population, the above procedures may overestimate sample size and researchers may need to reduce sample size by a certain percentage. The finite population correction factor is $\sqrt{(N - n)/(N - 1)}$, where N = population size and n = sample size. The resulting percentage is multiplied by the initial sample size.

Factors in Determining Sample Size for Proportions

Researchers are frequently concerned with determining sample size for problems involving estimating population proportions or percentages. When the sample size question involves the estimation of a proportion, the researcher requires some knowledge of the logic for determining a confidence interval around a sample proportion estimation (p) of the population proportion (π). For a confidence interval to be constructed around the sample proportion (p), an estimate of the **standard error of the proportion** (S_p) must be calculated and a confidence level specified.

standard error of the proportion
The standard deviation of the sampling distribution of the proportion.

The precision of the estimate is indicated by the value $Z_{\text{c.l.}}S_p$. Thus, the plus or minus estimate of the population proportion is

$$\text{Confidence interval} = p \pm Z_{\text{c.l.}}S_p$$

If the researcher selects a 95 percent probability for the confidence interval, $Z_{\text{c.l.}}$ will equal 1.96 (see Table 2 in the Appendix).

The formula for S_p is

$$S_p = \sqrt{\frac{pq}{n}} \qquad \text{or} \qquad S_p = \sqrt{\frac{p(1-p)}{n}}$$

where

S_p = estimate of the standard error of the proportion
p = proportion of successes
$q = 1 - p$, or proportion of failures

Suppose that in a sample of 1,200 employees, 20 percent plan to retire in the next 5 years. The proportion of successes (p) equals .2. The proportion of failures (q) equals .8. To estimate the 95 percent confidence interval, we calculate

$$\begin{aligned}\text{Confidence interval} &= p \pm Z_{\text{c.l.}}S_p \\ &= .2 \pm 1.96S_p \\ &= .2 \pm 1.96\sqrt{\frac{p(1-p)}{n}} \\ &= .2 \pm 1.96\sqrt{\frac{(.2)(.8)}{1200}} \\ &= .2 \pm 1.96(.0115) \\ &= .2 \pm .022\end{aligned}$$

Thus, the population proportion of the employees who plan to retire next year is estimated to be included in the interval between .178 and .222, or roughly between 18 percent and 22 percent, with a 95 percent confidence coefficient.

To determine *sample size* for a proportion, the researcher must make a judgment about confidence level and the maximum allowance for random sampling error. Further, the size of the proportion influences random sampling error, thus, an estimate of the expected proportion of successes must be made, based on intuition or prior information. The formula is

$$n = \frac{Z^2_{\text{c.l.}}pq}{E^2}$$

where n = number of items in sample

$Z^2_{\text{c.l.}}$ = square of the confidence level in standard error units

p = estimated proportion of successes

$q = 1 - p$, or estimated proportion of failures

E^2 = square of the maximum allowance for error between the true proportion and the sample proportion, or $Z_{\text{c.l.}}S_p$ squared

Suppose a researcher believes a simple random sample will show that 60 percent of the respondents (p) recognize the name of an industrial corporation. The researcher wishes to estimate with 95 percent confidence ($Z_{c.l.} = 1.96$) that the allowance for sampling error is not greater than 3.5 percentage points (E). Substituting these values into the formula above, the researcher finds

$$
\begin{aligned}
n &= \frac{(1.96)^2(.6)(.4)}{(.035)^2} \\
&= \frac{(3.8416)(.24)}{.001225} \\
&= \frac{.922}{.001225} \\
&= 753
\end{aligned}
$$

Calculating Sample Size for Sample Proportions

A number of tables have been constructed so that sample size may be determined by inspecting the tables. Table 17.11 illustrates a sampling table for problems involving sample proportions (p).

The theoretical principles underlying calculation of sample sizes of proportions are similar to the concepts discussed earlier in this chapter. In the example of corporate name recognition, suppose we wish to take samples of investors in two large cities, New Orleans and Miami. We want no more than 2 percent error and we will be satisfied with a 95 percent confidence level (see Table 17.11). If we assume all other things are equal, then in the New Orleans area, where 15 percent of the investors are aware of the corporation and 85 percent are not aware of it, a sample of 1,222 is needed for results with only 2 percent error. However, in the Miami area, with 30 percent of the investors aware and 70 percent unaware (a less heterogeneous area), a sample size of 2,009 is required for the same sample reliability.

Table 17.12 (page 430) shows a sampling error table that is typical of those that accompany research proposals or reports. Most studies will estimate more than one parameter. Thus, in a survey of 100 people in which 50 percent agree with one statement and 10 percent with another, the sampling error is expected to be 10 percentage points and 6 percentage points of error, respectively.

Determining Sample Size on the Basis of Judgment

Just as sample units may be selected based on the convenience or the judgment of the researcher, sample size may also be determined on the basis of managerial judgment. Using a sample size similar to the sample sizes used in previous studies provides the inexperienced researcher with a comparison of other researchers' judgments.[18]

Another judgmental factor in the determination of sample size is the selection of the appropriate item, question, or characteristic for the sample size calculations. In most studies several characteristics are of concern, and the desired degree of precision may vary for these items. The researcher must exercise judgment to determine which item will be utilized. Often the item that will produce the largest sample size will be utilized to determine the ultimate sample size. However, cost of data collection becomes a major consideration and judgment must be exercised concerning the importance of the item information.

TABLE 17.11 SELECTED TABLES FOR DETERMINING SAMPLE SIZE WHEN THE CHARACTERISTIC OF INTEREST IS A PROPORTION[19]

SAMPLE SIZE FOR A 95 PERCENT CONFIDENCE LEVEL WHEN PARAMETER IN POPULATION IS ASSUMED TO BE OVER 70 PERCENT OR UNDER 30 PERCENT

	Reliability			
Size of Population	±1% Point	±2% Points	±3% Points	±5% Points
1,000	a	a	473	244
2,000	a	a	619	278
3,000	a	1,206	690	291
4,000	a	1,341	732	299
5,000	a	1,437	760	303
10,000	4,465	1,678	823	313
20,000	5,749	1,832	858	318
50,000	6,946	1,939	881	321
100,000	7,465	1,977	888	321
500,000 to ∞	7,939	2,009	895	322

SAMPLE SIZE FOR A 95 PERCENT CONFIDENCE LEVEL WHEN PARAMETER IN POPULATION IS ASSUMED TO BE OVER 85 PERCENT OR UNDER 15 PERCENT

	Reliability			
Size of Population	±1% Point	±2% Points	±3% Points	±5% Points
1,000	a	a	353	235
2,000	a	760	428	266
3,000	a	890	461	278
4,000	a	938	479	284
5,000	a	984	491	289
10,000	3,288	1,091	516	297
20,000	3,935	1,154	530	302
50,000	4,461	1,195	538	304
100,000	4,669	1,210	541	305
500,000 to ∞	4,850	1,222	544	306

[a]In these cases more than 50 percent of the population is required in the sample. Since the normal approximation of the hypergeometric distribution is a poor approximation in such instances, no sample value is given.

Another consideration stems from most analysts' need to analyze the various subgroups within the sample. For example, suppose an analyst wishes to look at a difference in architects' attitudes by geographic region. The analyst will want to make sure that there are an adequate number of sampled architects in the New England region, the Mid-Atlantic region, and the South Atlantic region, to make sure that subgroup comparisons are reliable. There is a judgmental rule of thumb for selecting minimum subgroup sample size. It has been suggested that each subgroup that is to be analyzed separately should have a minimum of 100 units in each category of the major breakdowns.[20] With this procedure, the total sample size is computed by totaling the sample sizes necessary for these subgroups.

TABLE 17.12 ALLOWANCE FOR RANDOM SAMPLING ERROR (PLUS AND MINUS PERCENTAGE POINTS) AT 95 PERCENT CONFIDENCE LEVEL[21]

	SAMPLE SIZE						
Response	2,500	1,500	1,000	500	250	100	50
10 (90)	1.2	1.5	2	3	4	6	8
20 (80)	1.6	2	2.5	4	5	8	11
30 (70)	1.8	2.5	3	4	6	9	13
40 (60)	2	2.5	3	4	6	10	14
50	2	2.5	3	4	6	10	14

Determining Sample Size for Stratified and Other Probability Samples

Stratified sampling involves drawing separate probability samples within the subgroups to make the sample more efficient. With a stratified sample, the sample variances are expected to differ by strata. This makes the determination of sample size more complex. Increased complexity may also characterize the determination of sample size for cluster sampling and other probability sampling methods. The formulas are beyond the scope of this research book. Students interested in these advanced sampling techniques should investigate advanced sampling textbooks.

A REMINDER ABOUT THE LANGUAGE OF STATISTICS

Learning the terms and symbols defined in this chapter will provide you with the basics of the language of statisticians and researchers. In order to learn more about the pragmatic use of statistics in business research, it is essential to master this vocabulary. The speller who forgets "*i* before *e* except after *c*" will have trouble every time he or she must tackle the spelling of a word with the "*i e*" or "*e i*" combination. The same is true for the student who forgets the basics of the "foreign language" of statistics.

SUMMARY

Determination of sample size requires a knowledge of statistics. Statistics is the language of the researcher, and this chapter introduced its vocabulary. Descriptive statistics describe characteristics of a population or sample. Inferential statistics use a sample to draw conclusions about a population.

A frequency distribution summarizes data by showing how frequently each response or classification occurs. A proportion indicates the percentage of a group having a particular characteristic.

Three measures of central tendency are the mean, or arithmetic average; the median, or halfway value; and the mode, or most frequently observed value. These three values may be different, and care must be taken to prevent distortions that may occur when the wrong measure of central tendency is used. Measures of dispersion are used along with the measures of central tendency to describe a distribution. The range is the difference between the largest and smallest values observed. The variance and standard deviation are the most useful measures of dispersion.

The normal distribution fits many observed distributions. It is symmetrical about its mean, with equal mean, median, and mode. Almost all the area of the normal distribution lies within ±3 standard deviations of the mean. Any normal distribution can easily be compared to the standardized normal, or *Z*, distribution, whose mean is 0 and whose standard deviation is 1. This allows easy evaluation of the probability of many occurrences.

The techniques of statistical inference are based on the relationship of the population distribution, the sample distribution, and the sampling distribution. This relationship is expressed in the central-limit theorem.

Estimating a population mean with a single value gives a point estimate. A range of numbers within which the researcher is confident the population mean will lie is a confidence interval estimate. The confidence level is a percentage indicating the long-run probability that the confidence interval estimate is correct.

The statistical determination of sample size requires knowledge of (1) the variance of the population, (2) the magnitude of acceptable error, and (3) the confidence level. Several computational formulas are available for determining sample size. Further, a number of easy-to-use tables have been compiled to help researchers calculate sample size. The main reason a large sample size is desirable is that sample size is related to random sampling error. The smaller the sample, the larger the error one can expect in one's estimates.

Many research problems involve the estimation of proportions. Statistical techniques may be used to determine a confidence interval around a sample proportion. Calculation of sample size for a sample proportion is not difficult. However, most researchers use tables that indicate predetermined sample sizes.

Key Terms

descriptive statistics
inferential statistics
sample statistics
population parameter
frequency distribution (table)
percentage distribution
probability distribution
proportion
mean
median
mode
range
standard deviation
average deviation
variance
normal distribution
standardized normal distribution
population distribution
sample distribution
sampling distribution
standard error of the mean
central-limit theorem
point estimate
confidence interval estimate
confidence level
range of possible random error
sample size
standard error of the proportion

Questions for Review and Critical Thinking

1. What is the difference between descriptive and inferential statistics?
2. The highway speed limits for 13 countries are as follows:

Country	Highway Miles per Hour	Country	Highway Miles per Hour
Italy	87	Denmark	62
France	81	Netherlands	62
Hungary	75	Greece	62
Belgium	75	Japan	62
Portugal	75	Norway	56
Britain	70	Turkey	56
Spain	62		

Calculate the mean, median, and mode for these data.

3. Prepare a frequency distribution for the data in question 2.
4. Why is the standard deviation typically utilized, rather than the average deviation?
5. Calculate the standard deviation for the data in question 2.
6. Draw three distributions that have the same mean value but different standard deviation values. Draw three distributions that have the same standard deviation but different mean values.
7. A manufacturer of DVD players surveyed 100 retail stores in each of its sales regions. An analyst noticed that in the South Atlantic region the average retail price was $165 (mean) and the standard deviation was $30. However, in the Mid-Atlantic region the mean price was $170, with a standard deviation of $15. What do these statistics indicate about these two sales regions?
8. Coastal Star Sales Corporation is a West Coast wholesaler that markets to several manufacturers of leisure products. Coastal Star has an 80-person sales force that sells to wholesalers in a six-state area divided into two sales regions. The table below gives the names from a sample of 11 salespersons, some descriptive information about each salesperson, and the sales performance of each for the past 2 years.

				SALES	
Region	**Salesperson**	**Age**	**Years of Experience**	**Previous Year**	**Current Year**
Northern	Jackson	40	7	$ 412,744	$ 411,007
Northern	Gentry	60	12	1,491,024	1,726,630
Northern	La Forge	26	2	301,421	700,112
Northern	Miller	39	1	401,241	471,001
Northern	Mowen	64	5	448,160	449,261
Southern	Young	51	2	518,897	519,412
Southern	Fisk	34	1	846,222	713,333
Southern	Kincaid	62	10	1,527,124	2,009,041
Southern	Krieger	42	3	921,174	1,030,000
Southern	Manzer	64	5	463,399	422,798
Southern	Weiner	27	2	548,011	422,001

Calculate a mean and a standard deviation for each variable and set a 95 percent confidence interval around the mean for each variable.

9. Calculate the median, mode, and range for each variable in question 8.
10. Organize the data on current year sales in question 8 into a frequency distribution with the following classes: (a) under $500,000, (b) $500,001 to $999,999, and (c) $1,000,000 and over.
11. Organize the data on years of selling experience in question 8 into a frequency distribution consisting of two classes: less than 5 years and 5 or more years.
12. What is a sampling distribution? How does it differ from a sample distribution?
13. What would happen to the sampling distribution of the mean if we increased sample size from 5 to 25?
14. Suppose a fast-food restaurant wishes to estimate average sales volume for a new menu item. The restaurant has observed the sales of the item at a similar outlet and has determined the following results:

$\bar{X} = 500$ (mean daily sales)
$S = 100$ (standard deviation of sample)
$n = 25$ (sample size)

The restaurant manager wants to know into what range the mean daily sales would fall 95 percent of the time. Perform this calculation.

15. In the text example of research on lipstick (page 426) where $E = \$2.00$ and $S = \$29.00$, what sample size would be required if a 99 percent confidence level were desired?
16. Suppose you are planning to sample transportation employees to determine average annual sick days. The following standards have been set: a confidence level of 99 percent and an error of fewer than 5 days. Past research has indicated the standard deviation should be 6 days. What is the required sample size?
17. In a survey of 500, 60 percent responded positively to an attitude question. Calculate a confidence interval at 95 percent to get an interval estimate for a proportion.
18. In a nationwide survey, a researcher expects that 30 percent of the population will agree with an attitude statement. She wishes to have less than 2 percent error and to be 95 percent confident. What sample size is needed?
19. City Opera, a local opera company, wishes to take a sample of its subscribers to learn the average number of years people have been subscribing. The director of research expects the average to be 12 years and believes the standard deviation will be about 2 years (approximately one-sixth of the range). She wishes to be 95 percent confident of her estimate. What is the appropriate sample size?
20. A researcher expects the population proportion of Cubs fans in Chicago to be 80 percent. The researcher wishes to have an error of less than 5 percent and to be 95 percent confident of an estimate to be made from a mail survey. What sample size is required?
21. An automobile dealership plans to conduct a survey to determine what proportion of new-car buyers continue to have their cars serviced at the dealership after the warranty period ends. It estimates that 30 percent of customers do so. It wants the results of its survey to be accurate within 5 percent, and it wants to be 95 percent confident of the results. What sample size is necessary?
22. To understand how sample size is conceptually related to random sampling error, costs, and nonsampling errors, graph these relationships.

23. Using the formulas discussed in this chapter, a researcher determines that at the 95 percent confidence level, a sample of 2,500 is required to satisfy a client's requirements. However, the researcher actually uses a sample of 1,200, because the client has specified a budget cap for the survey. What are the ethical considerations in this situation?

Exploring the Internet

1. Go to http://www.dartmouth.edu/~chance/ to visit the Chance Course. The Chance course is an innovative program to creatively teach introductory materials about probability and statistics. The Chance course is designed to enhance quantitative literacy. Numerous videos can be played online.
2. Go to Lycos at http://www.lycos.com. Enter "population sampling" into the search box and then click on the Go icon. How extensive is the list of sources?
3. A random number generator and other statistical information can be found at The World Wide Web Virtual Library: Random Numbers and Monte Carlo methods, located at http://random.mat.sbg.ac.at/links.
4. The Platonic Realms Interactive Mathematics Encyclopedia is located at http://www.mathacademy.com. It provides many definitions of statistical and mathematical terms.
5. Sample Size Calculators can be found at http://www.surveysystem.com/sscalc.htm and at http://www.svys.com/.
6. Martindale's Calculators On-Line Center at http://www-sci.lib.uci.edu/HSG/RefCalculators.html, and particularly Part IIA: Statistics, http://www-sci.lib.uci.edu/HSG/RefCalculators2A.html, are extremely valuable sites for researchers interested in statistical methods. Visit them and report what you find.

Case Suggestion

Case 23: The Business Forms Industry

CHAPTER

18

FIELDWORK

What you will learn in this chapter

- To recognize that fieldwork can be performed by many different parties.
- To discuss the job requirements of fieldworkers.
- To discuss in-house training for inexperienced interviewers.
- To understand how fieldworkers secure interviews.
- To define foot-in-the-door and door-in-the-face compliance techniques.
- To understand the major principles of asking questions in the field.
- To explain probing and give examples of different interviewers' probes.
- To understand the appropriate procedure for recording responses in surveys.
- To discuss the principles of good interviewing.
- To discuss the activities involved in the management and supervision of fieldworkers.

They stand there, looking for eye contact, sizing up the crowd, looking for the right moment to go up and take a chance.[1] They know more times than not they will be rejected, yet they press on.

You've seen them. Chances are you have walked right past them, even given them the cold shoulder or at worst growled at them that you want to be left alone.

They are interviewers (recruiters), usually women, who prowl outside shops and restaurants looking for volunteers to participate in surveys, with questions ranging from how many beers you drink in a day to what you think of a certain line of clothing or your take on an advertising campaign by a large corporation.

In the business, it's called "mall intercept." It is, on the surface, a thankless task: going up to strangers, clipboard in hand, introducing yourself and trying to convince prospects that you aren't trying to sell them cheap long-distance service, aluminum siding, or the latest debit card. It is a misperceived job. They aren't trying to disrupt a pleasant day of shopping with the family at the mall or stop a harried shopper from getting a last-minute gift. They are, quite simply, doing their job.

Quick Test Inc. has been asking questions at the Hawthorn Center in Vernon Hills, Illinois for 17 years. It is a business whose techniques have changed with the advent of computerized technology but whose image has remained standard for decades. Participants now are asked a few questions in the mall before they move to the Quick Test offices.

Ann Marie Hogan supervises about a dozen employees. They include an assistant manager, a questionnaire editor, and ten full- or part-time interviewers/recruiters. The interviewers are the people who try to persuade shoppers to give up anywhere from 5 to 90 minutes of their time to participate in field research.

Hawthorn Center is an ideal hunting ground because shoppers coming from the surrounding area are basically young and have families, falling into the ideal 25–49 demographic age group.

The company seeking the information remains confidential, and in nearly every case when an interviewer seeks out a shopper, the person being surveyed is not told what company or brand is involved.

In many cases, a recruiter won't even get that far with a prospective interviewee.

It is, in the words of Fern Levin, a market researcher for 30 years, a lesson in accepting rejection.

"I got over it the first day I did it," said Levin. "You have to know that this is a job, and we're out there doing a job. But it's different than it used to be."

Another interviewer says: "It's tough out there, very tough. Many people, most people in fact, are nice about it, but then there are those who aren't, and they think you are selling something. And back when I started, we didn't pay anything except on very rare occasions. People back when I started weren't as money-hungry as they are now."

Interviewers develop special skills to know which customers are more likely to give the coveted "yes." Eye contact is a key: If someone looks away, they aren't good candidates to even be approached.

The advent of computers has, in a sense, made the task a bit easier. Before computers, recruiters would have to sit down, clipboard in hand, and ask a consumer the questions in the middle of the mall with little privacy or comfort.

There are days and times of the week where interviewers will know they face an uphill climb to get anyone to commit. Summer is slow unless it is around a holiday. A good month, Hogan explained, will have 1,200 to 1,300 people interviewed.

"The beginning of the week is slow," Hogan said. "Saturday, that's our big day. Sunday is the worst. You get a lot of people in the mall, but they don't want to stop. They're coming after church, they are with their families, and they just don't want to stop."

A cornerstone of the fieldwork business is the interviewer. This chapter discusses the nature of an effective fieldwork operation and the procedures fieldwork managers follow to minimize errors. ■

THE NATURE OF FIELDWORK

fieldworker
An individual responsible for gathering data in the field; for example, a personal interviewer administering a door-to-door questionnaire.

A personal interviewer administering a questionnaire door to door, a telephone interviewer calling from a central location, an observer counting pedestrians in a shopping mall, and others involved in the collection of data and the supervision of that process are all **fieldworkers.** The activities they perform vary substantially. The supervision of data collection for a mail survey differs from the data collection in an observation study as much as the factory production process for cereal differs from the factory production process for a pair of ski boots. Nevertheless, just as production quality control is basic to each production operation, there are some basic issues in fieldwork. For ease of presentation, this chapter focuses on the interviewing process conducted by personal interviewers. However, many of the issues apply to all fieldworkers, no matter what their specific setting.

WHO CONDUCTS THE FIELDWORK?

Data collection is rarely carried out by the person who designs the research project. However, the data-collecting stage is crucial, because the research project is no better than the data collected in the field. Therefore, it is important that the research administrator select capable people who may be entrusted to collect the data. An irony of business research is that highly educated and trained individuals design the research, but the people who collect the data typically have little research training or experience. Knowing the vital importance of data collected in the field, research administrators must concentrate on carefully selecting fieldworkers.

RESEARCH INSIGHT

A DRESS REHEARSAL OF THE CENSUS

The government made a special effort to do a better job of counting American Indians in the 2000 census.[2] In 1998, the Census Bureau conducted a "dress rehearsal" of the census methodology in Menominee County, Wisconsin, where the Menominee reservation is located and the 1990 population was 3,890 people, 90 percent of whom were Indian. The Census Bureau paid for radio, television, and newspaper advertisements and worked with tribal leaders to promote the dress rehearsal on the Wisconsin reservation.

According to the Census Bureau's Chicago region director, there was a pretty intense campaign to educate people that the census was going on. The tribe held a powwow where tribal members were given free sodas, T-shirts, and trinkets, and the tribal chairman met with students at the school to encourage their families to cooperate with the census. What could go wrong?

As it turned out, plenty. Fewer than 41 percent of the residents returned questionnaires that had been hand-delivered to them. By comparison, the response rate for similar tests in Columbia, South Carolina, and Sacramento, California, was 54 percent. The Census Bureau reported that 60 percent of the reservation households treated the questionnaires as "junk mail." So the Census Bureau had to spend extra money to send a second form.

When the government took the 1990 census, it missed 12 of every 100 American Indians living on reservations. Four percent of blacks and 5 percent of Hispanics weren't counted in 1990. In the dress rehearsal, Census Bureau officials say they eventually got questionnaires filled out by all 2,060 households in Menominee County, but only after workers visited each residence that didn't return the form.

Much fieldwork is conducted by research suppliers who specialize in data collection. When a second party is employed, the job of the study designer at the parent firm is not only to hire a research supplier but also to establish supervisory controls over the field service.

In some cases a third party is employed. For example, a firm may contact a survey research firm, which in turn subcontracts the fieldwork to a field service. Under these circumstances it is still desirable to know the problems that might occur in the field and the managerial practices that can minimize them.

field interviewing service
A research supplier that specializes in gathering data.

There are a number of **field interviewing services** and full-service research agencies that perform door-to-door surveys, central location telephone interviewing, and other forms of fieldwork for a fee. These agencies typically employ field supervisors who oversee and train interviewers, edit questionnaires completed in the field, and confirm that the interviews have been conducted by telephoning or recontacting a certain percentage of respondents.

Whether the research administrator hires in-house interviewers or selects a field interviewing service, it is desirable to have fieldworkers meet certain job requirements. Although the job requirements for different types of surveys vary, normally interviewers should be healthy, outgoing, and of pleasing appearance—that is, well groomed and well dressed. Fieldwork may be strenuous. The interviewer may be walking from house to house or standing in a mall for four or more hours a day. Healthy individuals between 18 and 55 years of age generally seem to have the proper stamina. People who enjoy talking with strangers usually make better interviewers. An essential part of the

The knowledge of the world is only to be acquired in the world and not in the closet.

LORD CHESTERFIELD

interviewing process is establishing rapport with the respondent. Having interviewers who are outgoing helps ensure respondents' full cooperation. Interviewer bias may enter in if the fieldworker's clothing or physical appearance is unattractive or unusual. Suppose that a male interviewer, wearing a dirty T-shirt, interviews subjects in an upper-income neighborhood. Respondents may consider the interviewer slovenly and be less cooperative than they would be with a person dressed more appropriately.

Interviewers and other fieldworkers are generally paid an hourly rate or a per-interview fee. Often interviewers are part-time workers—housewives, graduate students, secondary school teachers—from diverse backgrounds. Primary and secondary school teachers are an excellent source for temporary interviewers during the summer, especially when they conduct interviews outside the school districts where they teach. Teachers' educational backgrounds and experiences with the public make them excellent candidates for fieldwork.

IN-HOUSE TRAINING FOR INEXPERIENCED INTERVIEWERS

After personnel are recruited and selected, they must be trained.[3] Suppose a woman who has just sent her youngest child off to first grade is hired by an interviewing firm. She has decided to become a working mother by becoming a professional interviewer. The training that she will receive after being selected by a company may vary from virtually no training to a 3-day program if she is selected by one of the larger survey research agencies. Almost always there will be a **briefing session** on the particular project. Typically, the recruits will record answers on a practice questionnaire during a simulated **training interview.**

briefing session
A training session to ensure that all interviewers are provided with common information.

training interview
A practice session during which an inexperienced fieldworker records answers on a questionnaire to develop skills and clarify project requirements.

The objective of training is to ensure that the data collection instrument is administered uniformly by all fieldworkers. The goal of training sessions is to ensure that each respondent is provided with common information. If the data are collected in a uniform manner from all respondents, the training session will have been a success.

More extensive training programs are likely to cover the following topics:

1. How to make initial contact with the respondent and secure the interview
2. How to ask survey questions
3. How to probe
4. How to record responses
5. How to terminate the interview

Making Initial Contact and Securing the Interview

Interviewers are trained to make appropriate opening remarks that will convince the person that his or her cooperation is important. For example:

> **Good afternoon, my name is _____ and I'm from a national survey research company. We are conducting a survey concerning _____. I would like to get a few of your ideas.**

For the initial contact in a telephone interview, the introduction might be

> **Good evening, my name is _____. I'm calling from Burke Research in Cincinnati, Ohio.**

By indicating that the telephone call is long distance, interviewers attempt to capitalize on the fact that most people feel a long-distance call is something

The field worker shown here is conducting research on London bus service by interviewing Londoners who emerge from Victoria Station. People who enjoy talking to strangers usually make the best interviewers. Field interviewing services often hire individuals who are healthy, outgoing, and well groomed.

special, unusual, or important. Even though the calls are normally WATS-line calls, identifying them as long-distance calls is a subtle way of impressing the respondent.

Giving one's name personalizes the call. Personal interviewers may carry a letter of identification or an ID card that will indicate that the study is a bona fide research project and not a sales call. The name of the research agency is used to assure the respondent that the caller is trustworthy.

foot-in-the-door compliance technique
Based on foot-in-the-door theory, which attempts to explain compliance with a large or difficult task on the basis of the respondent's prior compliance with a smaller request.

door-in-the-face compliance technique
A two-step method for securing a high response rate. In step 1 an initial request, so large that nearly everyone refuses it, is made. In step 2 a second request is made for a smaller favor; respondents are expected to comply with this more reasonable request.

In its *Interviewer's Manual,* the Survey Research Center at the University of Michigan recommends avoiding questions that ask permission for the interview, such as "May I come in?" and "Would you mind answering some questions?" In some cases the person will refuse to participate or state an objection to being interviewed. Interviewers should be instructed on handling objections. For example, if the respondent says, "I'm too busy right now," the interviewer might be instructed to respond, "Will you be in at 4 o'clock this afternoon? I would be happy to come back then." In other cases client companies will not wish to offend any individual. The interviewers will be instructed to say merely, "Thank you for your time." This might be the case with a telephone company or an oil company that is sensitive to its public image.

The **foot-in-the-door** and the **door-in-the-face compliance techniques** are useful in securing interviews. Foot-in-the-door theory attempts to explain compliance with a large or difficult task on the basis of respondents' earlier compliance with a smaller initial request. The expectation is that respondents' compliance with a minor telephone interview (that is, a small request that few people refuse) will lead to greater compliance with a second, larger request to fill out a long mail questionnaire. With the door-in-the-face technique, the interviewer begins with an initial request so large that nearly everyone refuses it (that is, slams the door in his or her face); the interviewer then requests a small favor, asking the respondent to comply with a "short" survey. Research on the technique presents some interesting considerations for improvement of fieldwork. It also presents an ethical consideration if the respondent is deceived.

Asking the Questions

The purpose of the interview is, of course, to have the interviewer ask questions and record the respondent's answers. Training in the art of stating questions can be extremely beneficial, because interviewer bias can be a source of considerable error in survey research.

There are five major principles for asking questions:

- Ask the questions exactly as they are worded in the questionnaire.
- Read each question very slowly.
- Ask the questions in the order in which they are presented in the questionnaire.
- Ask every question specified in the questionnaire.
- Repeat questions that are misunderstood or misinterpreted.[4]

Although interviewers are generally trained in these procedures, when working in the field many interviewers do not follow them exactly. Inexperienced interviewers may not understand the importance of strict adherence to the instructions. Even professional interviewers take shortcuts when the task becomes monotonous. Interviewers may shorten questions or rephrase unconsciously when they rely on their memory of the question rather than reading the question as it is worded. Even the slightest change in wording can distort the meaning of the question and cause some bias to enter into a study. By reading the question, the interviewer may be reminded to concentrate on avoiding slight variations in tone of voice on particular words or phrases in the question.

If respondents do not understand a question, they will usually ask for some clarification. The recommended procedure is to repeat the question, or if the person does not understand a word, such as *nuclear* in the question "Do you feel nuclear energy is a safe energy alternative?" the interviewer should respond with "Just whatever it means to you." However, interviewers often supply their own personal definitions and ad lib clarifications. Their personal interpretation may include words that are not free from bias. One of the reasons why interviewers do this is that field supervisors have a tendency to reward people for completed questionnaires. They tend to be less tolerant of interviewers who leave questions blank because of alleged misunderstandings.

Often respondents volunteer information relevant to a question that is supposed to be asked at a later point in the interview. In this situation the response should be recorded under the question that deals specifically with that subject. Then, rather than skip the question that was answered out of sequence, the interviewers should be trained to say something like "We have briefly discussed this, but let me ask you . . . ." By asking every question, the

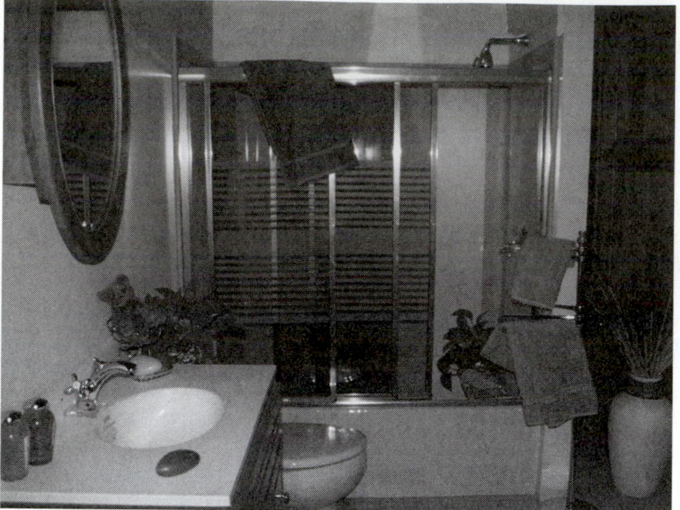

Researchers for a bathroom cleaner kept hearing respondents refer to the surface of a tub or toilet as "shining." When interviewers probed to learn what respondents meant by "shine," they learned that it was a synonym for clean *and* germ-free.

interviewer can be sure that complete answers are recorded. If the partial answer to a question answered out of sequence is recorded on the space reserved for the earlier question and the subsequent question is skipped, an omission error will occur when the data are tabulated.

Probing

probing
The verbal prompts made by a fieldworker when the respondent must be motivated to communicate his or her answer or to enlarge on, clarify, or explain an answer.

General training of interviewers should include instructions on how to *probe* when respondents give no answer, incomplete answers, or answers that require clarification.[5] **Probing** may be needed for two types of situations. First, it is necessary when the respondent must be motivated to enlarge on, clarify, or explain his or her answer. It is the interviewer's job to probe for complete, unambiguous answers. The interviewer must encourage the respondent to clarify or expand on answers by providing a stimulus that will not suggest the interviewer's own ideas or attitudes. The ability to probe with neutral stimuli is the mark of an experienced interviewer. Second, probing may be necessary in situations in which the respondent begins to ramble or lose track of the question. In such cases the respondent must be led to focus on the specific content of the interview and to avoid irrelevant and unnecessary information.

The interviewer has several possible probing tactics to choose from, depending on the situation:

- *Repetition of the question.* The respondent who remains completely silent may not have understood the question or may not have decided how to answer it. Mere repetition may encourage the respondent to answer in such cases. For example, if the question is "What is there that you do not like about your supervisor?" and the respondent does not answer, the interviewer may probe: "Just to check, is there anything you do not like about your supervisor?"
- *An expectant pause.* If the interviewer believes the respondent has more to say, the "silent probe," accompanied by an expectant look, may motivate the respondent to gather his or her thoughts and give a complete response. Of course, the interviewer must be sensitive to the respondent so that the silent probe does not become an embarrassed silence.[6]

Slow and steady wins the race.

AESOP

Exhibit 18.1	Commonly Used Probes and Their Abbreviations[7]

Interviewer's Probe	Standard Abbreviation
Repeat question	(RQ)
Anything else?	(AE or Else?)
Any other reason?	(AO?)
Any others?	(Other?)
How do you mean?	(How mean?)
Could you tell me about your thinking on that?	(Tell more)
Would you tell me what you have in mind?	(What in mind?)
What do you mean?	(What mean?)
Why do you feel that way?	(Why?)
Which would be closer to the way you feel?	(Which closer?)

- *Repetition of the respondent's reply.* As the interviewer records the response, he or she may repeat the respondent's reply verbatim. This may stimulate the respondent to expand on the answer.
- *Neutral questions or comments.* Asking a neutral question may indicate the type of information that the interviewer is seeking. For example, if the interviewer believes that the respondent's motives should be clarified, he or she might ask, "Why do you feel that way?" If the interviewer feels that there is a need to clarify a word or phrase, she might ask, "What do you mean by _____?" Exhibit 18.1 lists some common interviewer probes and the standard abbreviations that are recorded on the questionnaire with the respondent's answer.

The purpose of asking questions as probes is to encourage responses. These probes should be neutral and not leading. They may be general, such as "Anything else?" or they may be questions designed by the interviewer to clarify a statement by the respondent.

Recording the Responses

The analyst who fails to instruct fieldworkers in the techniques of recording answers for one study rarely forgets to do so in the second study. Although the concept of recording an answer seems extremely simple, mistakes can be made in the recording phase of the research. All fieldworkers should use the same mechanics of recording. For example, it may appear insignificant to the interviewer whether she uses a pen or pencil, but to the editor who must erase and rewrite illegible words, using a pencil is extremely important.

The rules for recording responses to closed questionnaires vary with the specific questionnaire. The general rule, however, is to place a check in the box that correctly reflects the respondent's answer. All too often interviewers don't bother recording the answer to a filter question because they believe that the subsequent answer will make the answer to the filter question obvious. However, editors and coders do not know how the respondent actually answered a question.

The general instruction for recording answers to open-ended-response questions is to record the answer verbatim, a task that is difficult for most people. Inexperienced interviewers should be given the opportunity to practice verbatim recording of answers before being sent into the field.

The *Interviewer's Manual* of the Survey Research Center provides detailed instructions on the recording of interviews. Some of its suggestions for recording answers to open-ended-response questions follow:

- Record responses during the interview.
- Use the respondent's own words.
- Do not summarize or paraphrase the respondent's answer.
- Include everything that pertains to the question objectives.
- Include all of your probes.[8]

Exhibit 18.2 shows a completed questionnaire page. Note how the interviewer adds supplementary comments to the answers to fixed-alternative questions and indicates probing questions by placing them in parentheses. The answers have been recorded without paraphrasing. The interviewer has resisted the temptation to conserve time and space by filtering comments. The RQ recorded in Question A4a indicates a repeat-question probe.

Terminating the Interview

The final aspect of training deals with instructing the interviewers on how to close the interview. Fieldworkers should not close the interview before all pertinent information has been secured. The interviewer whose departure is hasty will not be able to record those spontaneous comments respondents sometimes offer after all formal questions have been asked. Recording just one of these comments may result in a new idea or creative solution to some organizational problem. Avoiding hasty departures is also a matter of courtesy.

Fieldworkers should also answer to the best of their ability any questions the respondent has concerning the nature and purpose of the study. Because the fieldworker may be required to reinterview the respondent at some future time, he or she should leave the respondent with a positive feeling about having cooperated in a worthwhile undertaking. It is extremely important to thank the respondent for his or her cooperation.

PRINCIPLES OF GOOD INTERVIEWING

This section presents the principles of good interviewing of one of the nation's top business organizations.[9] These principles apply no matter what the nature of a specific assignment may be; they are universal and represent the essence of sound data collection for business research purposes. For clarity, they have been divided into two categories: (1) *the basics*—the interviewing point of view and (2) *required practices*—standard inquiry premises and procedures.

The Basics

Interviewing is a skilled occupation; not everyone can do it, and even fewer can do it extremely well. A good interviewer observes the following basic principles:

1. *Have integrity and be honest.* This is the cornerstone of all professional inquiry, regardless of its purpose.
2. *Have patience and tact.* Interviewers ask for information from people they do not know. Thus, all the rules of human relations that apply to inquiry situations—patience, tact, and courtesy—apply "in spades" to interview-

Exhibit 18.2 | **Example of Completed Questionnaire Page**[10]

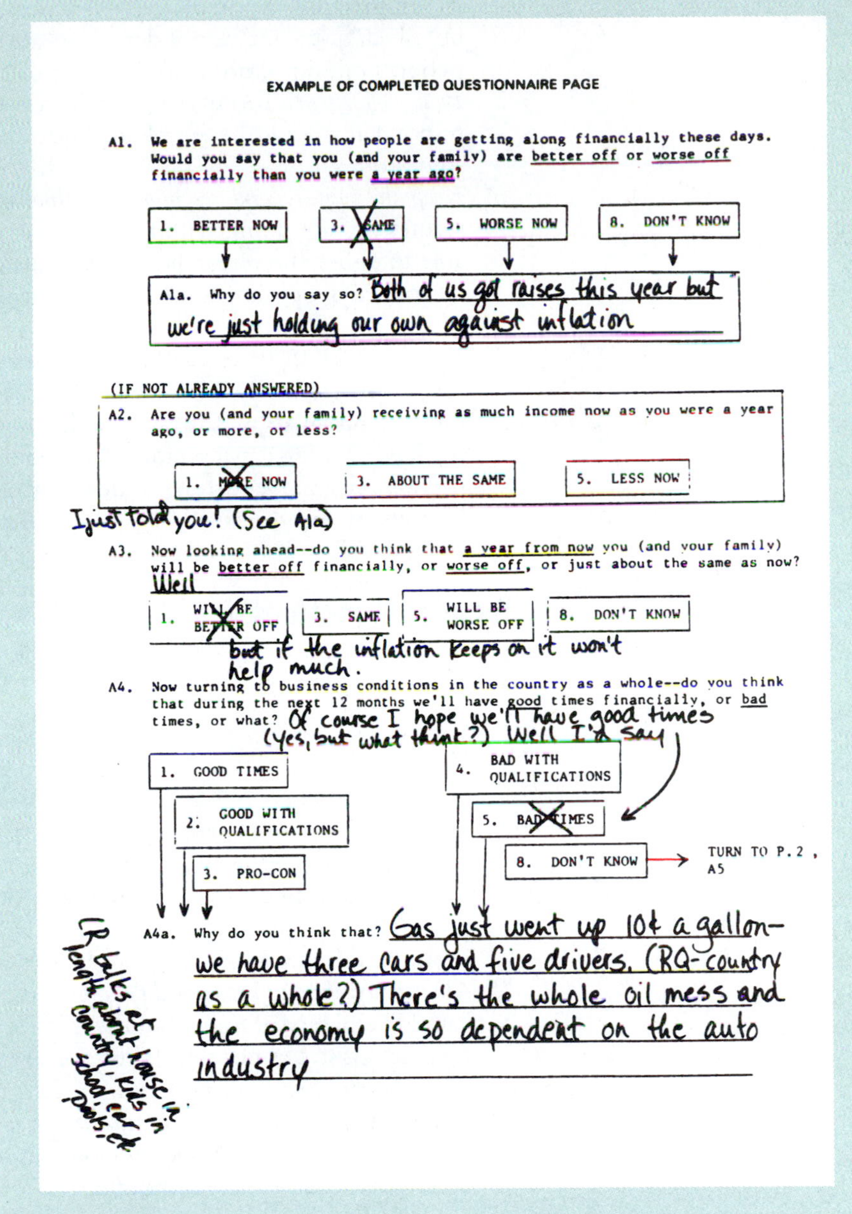

EXAMPLE OF COMPLETED QUESTIONNAIRE PAGE

A1. We are interested in how people are getting along financially these days. Would you say that you (and your family) are better off or worse off financially than you were a year ago?

1. BETTER NOW | 3. SAME [X] | 5. WORSE NOW | 8. DON'T KNOW

A1a. Why do you say so? Both of us got raises this year but we're just holding our own against inflation

(IF NOT ALREADY ANSWERED)

A2. Are you (and your family) receiving as much income now as you were a year ago, or more, or less?

1. MORE NOW [X] | 3. ABOUT THE SAME | 5. LESS NOW

I just told you! (See A1a)

A3. Now looking ahead--do you think that a year from now you (and your family) will be better off financially, or worse off, or just about the same as now?

Well

1. WILL BE BETTER OFF [X] | 3. SAME | 5. WILL BE WORSE OFF | 8. DON'T KNOW

but if the inflation keeps on it won't help much.

A4. Now turning to business conditions in the country as a whole--do you think that during the next 12 months we'll have good times financially, or bad times, or what? Of course I hope we'll have good times (Yes, but what think?) Well I'd say

1. GOOD TIMES | 2. GOOD WITH QUALIFICATIONS | 3. PRO-CON | 4. BAD WITH QUALIFICATIONS | 5. BAD TIMES [X] | 8. DON'T KNOW → TURN TO P.2, A5

A4a. Why do you think that? Gas just went up 10¢ a gallon—we have three cars and five drivers. (RQ-country as a whole?) There's the whole oil mess and the economy is so dependent on the auto industry

(R talks at length about house in country, kids in school, car pools, etc.

ing. Standard business conventions controlling communications and contact are to be observed at all times.

3. *Pay attention to accuracy and detail.* Among the greatest of interviewing "sins" are inaccuracy and superficiality, for the professional analyst can misunderstand, and in turn mislead, a client. A good rule to follow is not to record a response unless you fully understand it yourself. Probe for clarification and detailed, full answers. Record responses verbatim: Never

assume you know what a respondent is thinking or jump to conclusions as to what he or she might have said but did not.

4. *Exhibit a real interest in the inquiry at hand, but keep your own opinions to yourself.* Impartiality is imperative—if your opinions were wanted, you would be asked, not your respondent. You are an asker and a recorder of other people's opinions, not a contributor to the study data.
5. *Be a good listener.* Too many interviewers talk too much, wasting time when respondents could be supplying more pertinent facts or opinions on the study topic.
6. *Keep the inquiry and respondents' responses confidential.* Do not discuss the studies you are doing with relatives, friends, or associates—it is not acceptable to either the research agency or its clients. Above all, *never* quote one respondent's opinion to another—that is the greatest violation of privacy of all.
7. *Respect others' rights.* Survey research depends on the goodwill of others to provide information. There is a "happy medium" path to pursue in obtaining this information. On the one hand is failure to get it all; on the other hand is unnecessary coercion. The middle road is one of clear explanation, friendliness, and courtesy—offered in an interested and persuasive way. Impress on prospective respondents that their cooperation is important and valuable.

Required Practices

Presented below are the practical rules of business research inquiry that are to be followed without exception:

1. *Complete the number of interviews according to the sampling plan assigned to you.* Both are calculated with the utmost precision so that when assignments are returned, the study will benefit from having available the amount and type of information originally specified.
2. *Follow the directions provided.* Remember that there are many other interviewers working on the same study in other places. Lack of uniformity in procedure can spell disaster for later analysis. Each direction has a purpose, even though it may not be completely evident to you.
3. *Make every effort to keep schedules.* Schedules range from "hurry up" to "there should be plenty of time," but there is always a good reason, and you should be as responsive as possible. If you foresee problems, inform your supervisor.
4. *Keep control of each interview you do.* It is up to you to determine the pace of a particular interview, keeping several points in mind:
   a. There is an established *average* length of interview from the time you start to talk to the respondent to the time you finish. It represents a *guideline,* but some interviews will be shorter and some longer.
   b. Always get "the whole story" from the respondent and write it all down in the respondent's own words. Also, remember to keep the interview focused on the subject at hand and not let it wander off into unnecessary small talk.
   c. Avoid offending the respondent by being too talkative yourself.
5. *Complete the questionnaires meticulously.*
   a. Follow exactly all instructions that appear on the questionnaire. Learn in advance what these instructions direct you to do.
   b. Ask the questions from the first to the last in the exact numerical order (unless directed to do otherwise in particular instances). Much

thought and effort go into determining the order of the questioning to avoid bias or to set the stage for subsequent questions.

c. Ask each question exactly as it is written. There is never a justifiable reason for rephrasing a question. The cost of doing so is lack of uniformity—the research agency would never know whether all respondents were replying to the same question or replying to 50 different interviewers' interpretations of the question.

d. Never leave a question blank. It will be difficult to tell whether you failed to ask it, whether the respondent could not answer it because of lack of knowledge or certainty, or whether the respondent refused to answer it for personal reasons. If none of the answer categories provided proves suitable, write in what the respondent said, in his or her own words.

e. Use all the props provided to aid both interviewers and respondents—show cards, pictures, descriptions, sheets of questions for the respondents to answer themselves, and so on. All have a specific interview purpose. Keys to when and how to use them appear on the questionnaire at the point at which they are to be used.

6. *Check over each questionnaire you have completed.* This is best done directly after the questionnaire has been completed. If you find something you have done wrong or omitted, correct it. Often you can call a respondent back, admit you missed something (or are unclear about a particular response), and straighten out the difficulty.
7. *Compare your sample execution and assigned quota with the total number of questionnaires you have completed.* Do not consider your assignments finished until you have done this.
8. *Clear up any questions with the research agency.* If questions arise either at the start or during an assignment for which you can find no explanatory instruction, call the agency to get the matter clarified (many agencies provide toll-free numbers so that there will be no expense to interviewers).

FIELDWORK MANAGEMENT

Managers of the field operation select, train, supervise, and control fieldworkers. Our discussion of fieldwork principles mentioned selection and training. This section investigates the tasks of the fieldwork manager in greater detail.

Briefing Session for Experienced Interviewers

After interviewers have been trained in fundamentals, and even when they have become experienced, it is always necessary to inform workers about the individual project. Both experienced and inexperienced fieldworkers must be instructed on the background of the sponsoring organization, sampling techniques, asking questions, callback procedures, and other matters specific to the project.

If there are special instructions—for example, about using show cards or video equipment or about restricted interviewing times—these should also be covered during the briefing session. Instructions for handling certain key questions are always important. For example, the following fieldworker instructions appeared in a survey of institutional investors who make buy-and-sell decisions about stocks for banks, pension funds, and the like:

Questions 10, 11:

These questions provide verbatim comments for the report to the client. *Probe for more than one- or two-word answers* and record verbatim. Particularly, probe for more information when respondent gives a *general* answer—e.g., "Poor management," "It's in a good industry." Ask: "In what ways is management poor?" "What's good about the industry?" etc.

A briefing session for experienced interviewers might go something like this: All interviewers report to the central office, where the background of the firm and the general aims of the study are briefly explained. Interviewers are not provided with too much information about the purpose of the study, thus ensuring that they will not transmit any preconceived notions to respondents. For example, in a survey about the banks in a community, the interviewers would be told that the research is a banking study, but not the name of the sponsoring bank. To train the interviewers about the questionnaire, a field supervisor conducts an interview with another field supervisor who acts as a respondent. The trainees observe the interviewing process, after which they each interview and record the responses of another field supervisor. Additional instructions are given to the trainees after the practice interview.

Training to Avoid Procedural Errors in Sample Selection

The briefing session also covers the sampling procedure. A number of research projects allow the interviewer to be at least partially responsible for selection of the sample. When the fieldworker has some discretion in the selection of respondents, the potential for selection bias exists. This is obvious in the case of quota sampling, but less obvious in other cases. For example, in probability sampling where every *n*th house is selected, the fieldworker uses his or her discretion in identifying housing units. Avoiding selection error may not be as simple as it sounds. For example, in an older, exclusive neighborhood, a mansion's coach house or servants' quarters may have been converted into an apartment that should be identified as a housing unit. This type of dwelling and other unusual housing units (apartments with alley entrances only, lake cottages, rooming houses) may be overlooked, giving rise to selection error. Errors may also occur in the selection of random-digit dialing samples. Considerable effort should be expended in training and supervisory control to minimize these errors.

Another selection problem is contacting a respondent when and where it is convenient for both parties. Consider the following anecdote from an interviewer:

> Occasionally, getting to the interview is half the challenge and tests the interviewer's ingenuity. Finding your way around a huge steel mill is not easy. Even worse is trying to find a correct turn-off to gravel pit D when it's snowing so hard that most direction signs are obliterated. In arranging an appointment with an executive at a rock quarry outside Kansas City, he told me his office was in "Cave Number 3." It was no joke. To my surprise, I found a luxurious executive office in a cave, which had long ago been hollowed by digging for raw material.[11]

In that case, finding the sample unit was half the battle.

Supervision of Fieldworkers

Although briefing and training interviewers will minimize the probability of their interviewing the wrong households or asking biased questions, there is still considerable potential for errors in the field. Direct supervision of personal interviewers, telephone interviewers, and other fieldworkers is necessary to ensure that the techniques communicated in the training sessions are implemented in the field.

The supervision of interviewers, like other forms of supervision, refers to controlling the efforts of workers. Field supervision of interviewers requires checking to see that field procedures are properly followed. Supervisors check field operations to ensure that the interviewing schedule is being met. They collect questionnaires or other instruments daily and edit them for completeness and legibility. (See Chapter 19 on editing for more detail.) If there are problems, supervisors discuss them with the fieldworkers, providing additional training when necessary.

In addition to quality control, field supervisors may provide continual training. For example, if a telephone supervisor notices that interviewers are allowing the phone to ring more than eight times before considering a call a "no-answer," the supervisor can instruct the interviewer not to do this, as the person who eventually answers is likely to be annoyed.

Sampling Verification

sampling verification
A fieldwork supervision task that requires checking to assure that samples conform to a project's sampling plan.

Another important job of the supervisor is **sampling verification,** which ensures interviews are being conducted according to the sampling plan rather than at households most accessible to the interviewer. An interviewer might be tempted to go to the household next door for an interview rather than record that the sampling unit was not at home, which would require a callback.

Closer supervision of the interviewing procedure can occur in central-location telephone interviewing. The supervisor may be able to listen to the actual interview by switching in to an interviewer's line. This, of course, cannot be done if interviewers make calls from their homes.

Supervisors must also make sure that the right person within the household or sampling unit is being contacted. One research project for a children's cereal required that several cereal products be placed in the home and that children record in a diary their daily consumption of and reactions to each cereal. Although the interviewers were supposed to contact the children to remind them to fill out the diaries, a field supervisor observed that in almost half the cases the mothers filled out the diaries after the children left for school because their children had not done so. The novelty of the research project wore off after a few days; eating a specific cereal each day wasn't fun after the first few times, and the children stopped keeping the diaries.

This situation may also occur with physicians, executives, and other busy people. The interviewer may find it easier to interview a nurse, secretary, or other assistant rather than wait to interview the right person.

Interviewer Cheating

interviewer cheating
The practice by fieldworkers of filling in fake answers or falsifying interviews.

Interviewer cheating in its most blatant form occurs when an interviewer falsifies interviews. The fieldworker merely fills in fake answers rather than contacting respondents. Although this situation does occur, it is not common if the job of selection has been properly accomplished.

However, less obvious forms of interviewer cheating occur with greater frequency. Quota sampling is often seen as time-consuming. Quota sample requirements may be stretched a bit to obtain almost-qualified respondents. In the interviewer's eyes, a young-looking 36-year-old may be the same as a 30-year-old who fits the quota requirement. Thus, checking the under-30 category "isn't really cheating."

Consider the fieldworker who must select only heavy users of a certain brand of hand lotion that the client says is used by 15 percent of the population. If the interviewer finds that only 3 percent of consumers qualify as heavy users, she or he may be tempted to interview an occasional user to stretch the quota somewhat.

Interviewers may fake part of the questionnaire to make it acceptable to the field supervisor. Suppose that in a survey on flex-time, interviewers are requested to ask for five reasons why employees prefer flexible working-hour programs. Finding that most people typically give one or two, perhaps three answers, and even with extensive probing can't think of five reasons, interviewers might be tempted to cheat. If they rarely get people to give five reasons, the interviewers may fill in all five blanks, based on past interviews, rather than have the supervisor think they were being lax about probing.[12] In other cases they may cut corners to save time and energy.

Interviewers may fake answers when they find questions embarrassing or troublesome. Cheating may occur because an interviewer completes most of the questionnaire but leaves out a question or two because she finds it troublesome or time-consuming. For example, in a survey among physicians, an interviewer might find questions about artificial-insemination donor programs embarrassing, skip these questions, and fill in the partial gaps later.

What appears to be interviewer cheating is often caused by improper training or inexperienced fieldworkers. A fieldworker who does not understand the instructions may skip or miss a portion of the questionnaire.

Interviewers may be reluctant to interview sampling units who they feel may be difficult or undesirable to interview. It is the supervisor's function to motivate the interviewers to carefully follow the sampling plan. Sometimes fieldworkers are instructed to say, at the conclusion of each interview, "Thank you for your time—and by the way, my supervisor may call you to ask you about my work. Please say whatever you wish." Not only does this or a similar statement increase the number of respondents who are willing to cooperate with the verification process, it also improves the quality of fieldwork.

Careful recording of the number of completed interviews will help to ensure that the sampling procedure is being conducted correctly.

Verification by Reinterviewing

Supervision for quality control attempts to ensure that the interviewers are following the sampling procedure and to detect interviewers who falsify interviews. Supervisors carry out **verification by reinterviewing** in approximately 15 percent of the interviews. Normally the interview itself is not repeated, but supervisors recontact respondents and ask about the length of the interview and the respondent's reaction to the interviewer; they also collect basic demographic data to check for interviewer cheating. Verification can indicate when the interviewer has falsified interviews without contacting the potential respondents. However, it does not detect the more subtle form of cheating in which only portions of the interview are falsified. Telephone validation and postcard validation checks often remind interviewers to be conscientious in

verification by reinterviewing
A fieldwork supervision task that requires recontacting respondents to assure that interviews were properly conducted.

their work. A validation check may simply point out that an interviewer contacted the proper household but interviewed the wrong individual in that household. This, of course, can be a serious error.

Fieldworkers should be aware of supervisory verification practices. The interviewer who is conducting quota sampling and needs an upper-income Hispanic male will be less tempted to interview a middle-income Hispanic man and to falsify the income data in this situation.

Certain information may allow for partial verification without recontacting the respondent. For example, computer-assisted telephone interviewers often do not know the phone number dialed by the computer or other information about the respondent. Thus, answers to questions added to the end of the telephone interview to identify a respondent's area code, phone number, city, zip code, and so on may be used to verify the interview. The computer can also identify interviewers who cheat by recording every attempted call, the time intervals between calls, and the time required to conduct each completed interview.[13]

SUMMARY

The activities involved in collecting data in the field may be performed by the organization needing information, by research suppliers, or by third-party field service organizations. Proper execution of fieldwork is essential for producing research results without substantial error.

Proper control of fieldwork begins with interviewer selection. Fieldworkers should generally be healthy, outgoing, and well groomed. New fieldworkers must be trained in opening the interview, asking the questions, probing for additional information, recording the responses, and terminating the interview. Experienced fieldworkers are briefed for each new project so that they are familiar with its specific requirements. A particular concern of the briefing session is reminding fieldworkers to adhere closely to the prescribed sampling procedures.

Careful supervision of fieldworkers is also necessary. Supervisors gather and edit questionnaires each day. They check to see that field procedures are properly followed and that interviews are on schedule. They also check to be sure that the proper sampling units are used and that the proper people are responding in the study. Finally, supervisors check for interviewer cheating and verify a portion of the interviews by reinterviewing a certain percentage of each fieldworker's respondents.

Key Terms

fieldworker
field interviewing service
briefing session
training interview
foot-in-the-door compliance technique
door-in-the-face compliance technique
probing
sampling verification
interviewer cheating
verification by reinterviewing

Questions for Review and Critical Thinking

1. What qualities should fieldworkers possess?
2. What impact have changes in women's lifestyles had on fieldwork in the past several decades?
3. What is the proper method for asking questions? What should an interviewer do if a question is misunderstood? What should be done if a respondent answers a question before encountering it in the questionnaire?
4. When should interviewers probe? Give some examples of how probing should be done.

5. How should respondents' answers to open-ended-response questions be recorded?
6. How should the fieldworker terminate the interview?
7. Why is it important to be sure fieldworkers adhere to the sampling procedure specified for a project?
8. What forms can interviewer cheating take? How can such cheating be prevented or detected?
9. Contacting every individual in the United States is a problem for the Census Bureau. List other fieldwork problems that might arise in conducting the U.S. Census. What might be done to mitigate these problems?
10. Comment on the following field situations:
    (a) After conducting a survey with ten respondents, an interviewer noticed that many of the respondents were saying, "Was I right?" after a particular question.
    (b) A questionnaire asking about a new easy-opening can has the following instructions to interviewers: *"(Hand respondent can and matching instruction card.)* Would you please read the instructions on this card and then open this can for me. *(Interviewer: Note any comments respondent makes. Do not under any circumstances help her to open the can or offer any explanation as to how to open it. If she asks for help, tell her that the instructions are on the card. Do not discuss the can or its contents.)"*
    (c) A researcher gives balloons to children of respondents to keep the children occupied during the interview.
    (d) An interviewer tells the supervisor: "With the price of gas, this job isn't paying as well as before!"
    (e) When a respondent asks how much time the survey will take, the interviewer responds that it will take 15 to 20 minutes. The respondent says, "I'm sorry I have to refuse. I can't give you that much time right now."
11. Write interviewer instructions for a telephone survey.
12. A fieldworker conducting a political poll is instructed to interview registered voters. The fieldworker interviews all willing participants who are eligible to vote (who may register in the future) because he feels that allowing their opinions to be recorded is part of his patriotic duty. Is this the right thing to do?
13. An interviewer finds that most potential respondents refuse to cooperate if they are told that a survey will take 15 minutes. The interviewer now tells them it takes 10 minutes and finds that most respondents enjoy answering the questions. Is this the right thing to do?
14. A fieldworker asks respondents if they will answer a few questions. However, the interviewer also observes the respondents' race and approximate age. Is this ethical?

Exploring the Internet

Go to http://www.quirks.com and click on Directories. You will find a Directory of Telephone Interviewing Facilities and a Directory of Mall Interviewing Facilities. What other fieldwork organizations are shown?

PART

6

DATA ANALYSIS AND PRESENTATION

CHAPTER

19

EDITING AND CODING: Beginning To Transform Raw Data Into Information

What you will learn in this chapter

- To define and explain the terms *editing* and *coding.*
- To discuss the purposes of field editing and in-house editing.
- To describe the different tasks performed by an in-house editor.
- To code fixed-alternative questions.
- To code open-ended questions.
- To define the terms *code book* and *production coding.*
- To understand how computerized data processing influences the coding process.

In a managerial survey, respondents were asked:

Relative to other companies in the industry, is your company

☐ **One of the largest**

☐ **About average in size**

☐ **Small**

One respondent checked both the category "one of the largest" and the category "about average in size." Next to the question the respondent wrote "average in retailing, one of the largest in drugstore chains." The editor must make the decision whether the industry should be categorized as "retailing" or "drugstore chain industry" and edit in the appropriate category. A numerical code is then assigned to the answer so that researchers, often with the aid of a computer, may analyze the data.

This chapter discusses how editing and coding transform raw data into a format suitable for analysis. ■

AN OVERVIEW OF THE STAGES OF DATA ANALYSIS

The process of analysis begins after the data have been collected. During the analysis stage several interrelated procedures are performed to summarize and rearrange the data. The research steps related to processing and analysis are presented in Exhibit 19.1. We now turn our attention to this process of data reduction and analysis.

EXHIBIT 19.1 OVERVIEW OF THE STAGES IN DATA ANALYSIS[1]

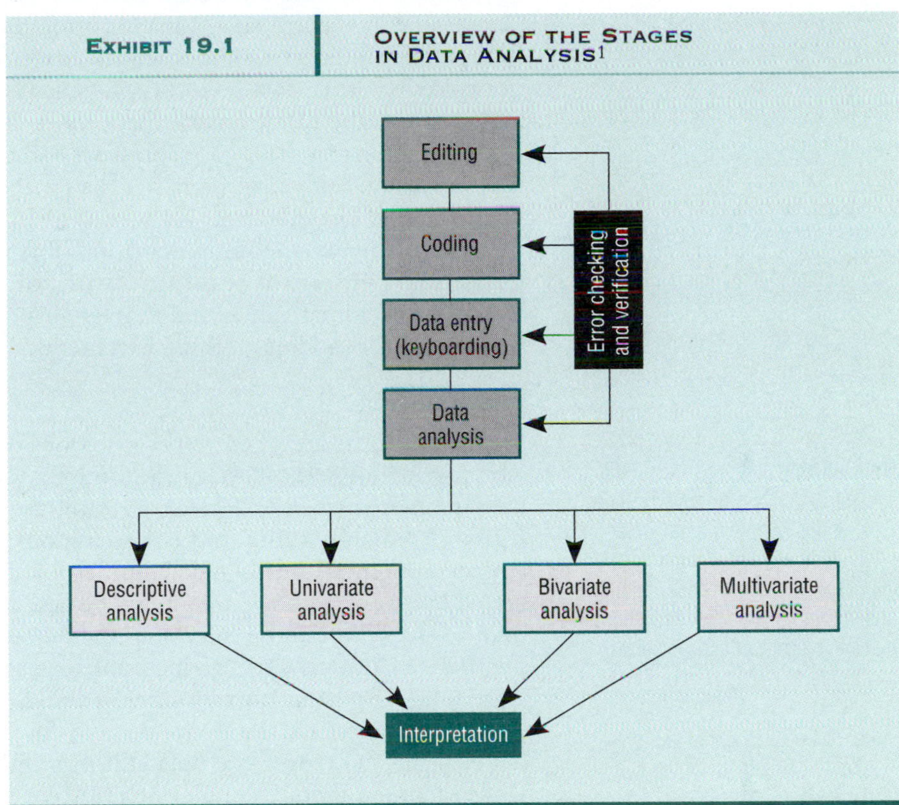

information
A body of facts that are in a format suitable for decision making.

data
Recorded measures of certain phenomena.

The goal of most research is to provide information. There is a difference between raw data and information. **Information** refers to a body of facts that are in a format suitable for decision making, whereas **data** are simply recorded measures of certain phenomena. The raw data collected in the field must be transformed into information that will answer the manager's questions. The conversion of raw data into information requires that the data be edited and coded so that the data may be transferred to a computer or other data storage medium.

If a database is large, there are many advantages to utilizing a computer. Assuming a large database, entering the data into the computer follows the coding procedure.

EDITING

Occasionally, a fieldworker makes a mistake and records an improbable answer (e.g., birth year: 1843) or interviews an ineligible respondent (e.g., someone too young to qualify). Seemingly contradictory answers, such as "no" to automobile ownership but "yes" to an expenditure on automobile insurance, may appear on a questionnaire. There are many problems like these that must be dealt with before the data can be coded. **Editing** procedures are conducted to make the data ready for coding and transfer to data storage. *Editing* is the process of checking and adjusting the data for omissions, legibility, and consistency.

editing
The process of making data ready for coding and transfer to data storage. Its purpose is to ensure the completeness, consistency, and reliability of data.

Editing may be differentiated from *coding,* which is the assignment of numerical scales or classifying symbols to previously edited data. Careful editing makes the coding job easier. The purpose of editing is to ensure the completeness, consistency, and readability of the data to be transferred to data storage.[2] The editor's task is to check for errors and omissions on the questionnaires or other data collection forms. When a problem is discovered, the editor adjusts the data to make them more complete, consistent, or readable.

The editor may have to reconstruct some data. For instance, a respondent may indicate weekly income rather than monthly income, as requested on the questionnaire. The editor must convert the information to monthly data without adding any extraneous information. The process of editing has been compared to the process of restoring a work of art. The editor "should bring to light all the hidden values and extract all possible information from a questionnaire, while adding nothing extraneous."[3]

Field Editing

field editing
Preliminary editing by a field supervisor on the same day as the interview; its purpose is to catch technical omissions, check legibility of handwriting, and clarify responses that are logically or conceptually inconsistent.

Field supervisors are often responsible for conducting preliminary field edits. The purpose of **field editing** on the same day as the interview is to catch technical omissions (such as a blank page on the interview questionnaire), check legibility of handwriting, and clarify responses that are logically or conceptually inconsistent. If a daily field edit is conducted, a supervisor who edits completed questionnaires will frequently be able to question the interviewers, who may be able to recall the interview well enough to correct any problems. The number of "no answers" or incomplete responses can be reduced with the rapid follow-up stimulated by a field edit. The daily field edit also allows fieldworkers to recontact the respondent to fill in omissions before the situation has changed. Moreover, the field edit may indicate the need for further interviewer training if, for example, interviewers did not correctly follow skip patterns or if open-ended responses reflect a lack of probing. When poor interviewing is detected, supervisors may further train the interviewer. Of course, field editing does not occur with mail surveys.

In-House Editing

in-house editing
A rigorous editing job performed by centralized office staff.

Although almost simultaneous editing in the field is highly desirable, in many situations (particularly with mail questionnaires), early reviewing of the data is not always possible. **In-house editing** rigorously investigates the results of data collection. The research supplier or the research department normally has a centralized office staff to perform the editing and coding function.

For example, Arbitron measures radio audiences by having respondents record in diaries their listening behavior—time, station, and place (home or car). After the diaries are returned by mail, in-house editors perform "usability edits" in which they check to make sure the postmarks are after the last day of the survey week, verify the legibility of station call letters (station WXXX could look like WYYY), look for completeness of entries on each day of the week, and perform other editing activities. If the respondent's age or sex are not indicated, the respondent is called to ensure that this information is included.

Excellence is to do a common thing in an uncommon way.

BOOKER T. WASHINGTON

Editing for Consistency

The in-house editor's task is to ensure that inconsistent or contradictory responses are adjusted and that the answers will not be a problem for coders and keyboard operators. Consider the situation in which a telephone interviewer has been instructed to interview only registered voters in a state that requires voters to be 18 years old. If the editor's review of a questionnaire indicates that the respondent was only 17 years of age, the editor's task is to eliminate this obviously incorrect sampling unit. Thus, in this example, the editor's job is to make sure that the sampling unit is consistent with the objectives of the study.

The editor also checks for adherence to the data collection framework. A survey on in-house versus outside training programs might have a question such as the following:

Does your department utilize in-house training or training by outside consultants? Please check the programs in which your employees participated last month.

If a respondent who attended in-house training exclusively accidentally checks a program listed under training by outside consultants, the answer must be edited.

Editing requires checking for logically consistent responses. The in-house editor must determine if the answers given by a respondent to one question are consistent with those given to other, related questions. Many surveys utilize filter questions or skip questions that direct the sequence of questions, depending on the respondent's answer. In some cases the respondent will have answered a sequence of questions that should not have been asked. The editor should adjust these answers, usually to "no answer" or "inapplicable," so that the responses will be consistent. In other cases illogical answers will signal that a recording error has been made. For example, a respondent's salary may be listed at $30,000. This may be inconsistent with the 45-year-old respondent's occupational listing as executive vice president. The editor must use judgment in situations in which he or she finds it highly unlikely that the answers to two questions could both be simultaneously correct.

Editing for Completeness

In some cases the respondent may have answered only the second portion of a two-part question. An in-house editor may have to adjust the answers to the following question for completeness.

Does your organization have more than one Internet Web site?

Yes ____ No ____

If yes, how many?

If a respondent checked neither "yes" nor "no" but indicated three Internet Web sites, the editor may use a colored pencil to check the "yes" to ensure that this answer is not missing from the questionnaire.

item nonresponse
The technical term for an unanswered question on an otherwise complete questionnaire.

Item nonresponse is the technical term for an unanswered question on an otherwise complete questionnaire. Specific decision rules for handling this problem should be meticulously outlined in the editor's instructions. In many situations the decision rule will be to do nothing with the unanswered question: The editor merely indicates an item nonresponse by writing a message instructing the coder to record a "missing value" or a "blank" as the response. However, when

plug value
An answer inserted according to a predetermined decision rule, if an editor finds a missing answer where there can be no missing values.

the relationship between two questions is important, such as one about number of sick days and one about educational level, it may be necessary for the editor to insert a **plug value.** The decision rule may be to "plug in" an average or neutral value in each case of missing data. Another decision rule may be to alternate the choice of the response categories used as plug values (for example, "yes" the first time, "no" the second time, "yes" the third time, and so on). Still another decision rule might be to randomly select an answer. For example, suppose a respondent has indicated as her first compensation preference an "adequate salary" but has given "retirement program" and "insurance benefits" the same second-preference ranking. The editor may randomly select the second and third choices so that data analysis may be performed as planned.

The editor must also decide whether or not an entire questionnaire is "usable." When a questionnaire has too many answers missing, it may not be suitable for the planned data analysis. In such a situation the editor simply records the fact that a particular incomplete questionnaire has been dropped from the sample.[4]

Editing Questions Answered Out of Order

Another situation an editor may face is the need to rearrange the answers to an open-ended response questionnaire. For example, a respondent may have provided the answer to a subsequent question in her answer to an earlier open-ended response question. Because the respondent had already clearly identified her answer, the interviewer may have avoided asking the subsequent question. The interviewer may have wanted to avoid hearing "I already answered that earlier" and to maintain rapport with the respondent and therefore skipped the question. To make the response appear in the same order as on other questionnaires, the editor may move the out-of-order answer to the section related to the skipped question.

Facilitating the Coding Process

While all the previously described editing activities will help coders, several editing procedures are specifically designed to simplify the coding process. For example, the editor checks to make sure every circled response is clearly definable. A response that overlaps two numbers and could be either 3 or 4 is judged by the editor. The editor edits missing information and determines if the answer is "don't know" (DK) or "no answer/not ascertained" (NA). These and other decisions by the editor should not be arbitrary but should be based on a systematic procedure of applying fixed rules for making decisions.

Editing and Tabulating "Don't Know" Answers

In many situations the respondent answers "don't know." On the surface this response seems to indicate that the respondent is not familiar with the individual, object, or situation being asked about or that he or she is uncertain and has not formulated a clear-cut opinion. This *legitimate* "don't know" means the same as "no opinion." However, there may be reasons for this response other than the legitimate "don't know" answer. The *reluctant* "don't know" is given when an individual simply does not want to answer a question and wishes to stop the interviewer from asking more. For example, asking an individual who is not the head of the household about family income may elicit a "don't know" answer meaning "This is personal, and I really do not want to answer the question." If the individual does not understand the question, he or she may give a *confused* "don't know" answer.

In some situations it is possible for the editor to separate the legitimate "don't know" ("no opinion") answers from the other "don't know" answers. The editor may try to identify the meaning of a "don't know" answer from other data provided on the questionnaire. For instance, the approximate value of a home could be derived from a knowledge of the zip code and the average value of homes within that area.

The tabulation of "don't know" answers requires the researcher to make a decision. One alternative is to record all "don't know" answers as a separate category. This provides for all of the actual response categories, but it may cause some problems with percentage calculation. Another alternative is to eliminate the "don't know" answers from the percentage base. The third alternative is to distribute the "don't know" answers among the other categories, usually on a proportionate basis. Although this is a simple procedure, it is criticized because it assumes that people who give "don't know" answers are the same as those who provide actual answers to a question. In many situations this is not the case, and those who give "don't know" responses are actually a highly homogeneous group.

Mechanics of Editing

Frequently, the editor's changes to data are written with a colored pencil. When space on the questionnaire permits, the original data are not erased, to ensure that a subsequent edit can identify the original concepts. In the author's experience, blue or green pencils have been used for editing and red pencils for coding.

Pitfalls of Editing

Subjectivity can easily enter into the editing job. To do a proper editing job, the editor must be intelligent, experienced, and objective. It is highly recommended that a systematic procedure for assessing the questionnaires be developed by the research analysts, so that the editors may follow clearly defined rules.

Pretesting Edit

Editing questionnaires during the pretest stage can prove to be very valuable. For example, certain slight changes in the questionnaire, such as increasing the space for an open-ended answer because respondents' answers in the pretest were longer than anticipated, will be appreciated during the actual analysis. Answers will be more legible because the writers have enough space, answers will be more complete, and answers will be verbatim rather than summarized. Poor instructions or inappropriate question wording on the questionnaire may be identified when editors examine answers to pretests.

CODING

coding
The process of identifying and classifying each answer with a numerical score or other character symbol.

The process of identifying and classifying each answer with a numerical score or other character symbol is called **coding.** Assigning numerical symbols permits the transfer of data from the survey to the computer. Although **codes** are generally considered to be numerical symbols, they are more broadly defined as the rules for interpreting, classifying, and recording data.

Codes allow data to be processed in a computer. Researchers organize coded data into fields, records, and files. A **field** is a collection of characters (a character is a single number, letter of the alphabet, or special symbol such as

Exhibit 19.2 | **A File, Records, and Fields**

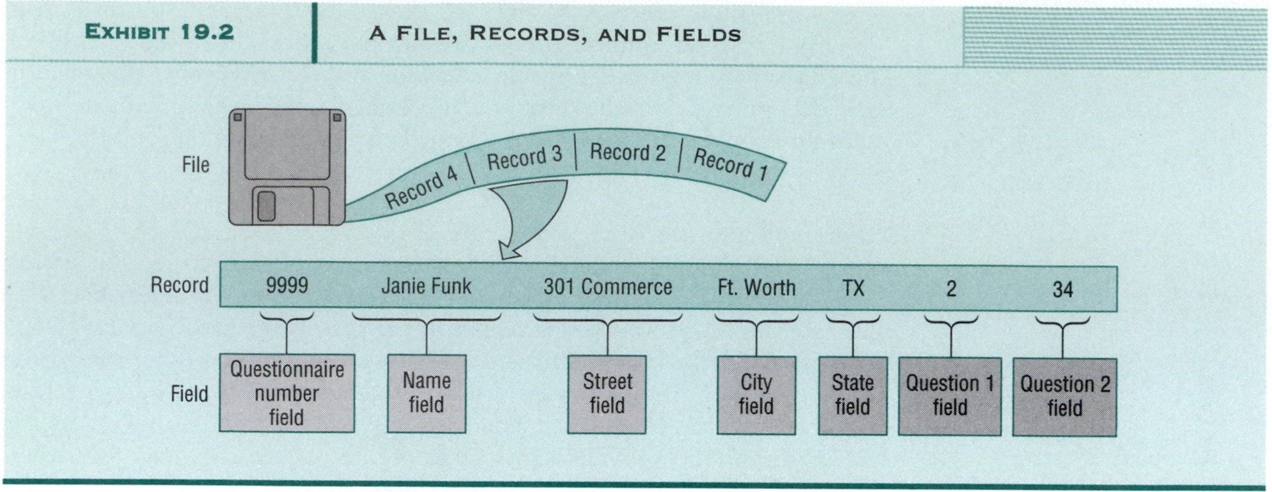

code
A rule used for interpreting, classifying, and recording data in the coding processes; the numerical or other symbol assigned to raw data.

field
A collection of characters that represents a single type of data.

record
A collection of related fields.

file
A collection of related records.

data matrix
A rectangular arrangement of data into rows and columns.

the question mark) that represents a single type of data. A **record** is a collection of related fields. A **file** is a collection of related records. Files, records, and fields are stored on magnetic tapes, floppy disks, or hard drives. Each research study is recorded in a file of all completed questionnaires (see Exhibit 19.2). The file contains a record for each respondent's questionnaire. Each record has a field for various types of information about each respondent and for his or her answers to each question.

The Data Matrix

A **data matrix** is a rectangular arrangement of data in rows and columns. An accountant's spreadsheet on traditional row-and-column accounting paper is one example of a data matrix.

Exhibit 19.3 illustrates a data matrix from a secondary-data study investigating each state's population (in millions), average age of the state's residents, and automobile registrations (per 1,000 residents). Each row in the matrix represents one state. In other words, the rows represent records for individual cases, reflecting the fundamental units of analysis. Each column represents a particular field. In our example the columns correspond to variables that reflect data about each state. The first column contains an abbreviation of the state name. The second column contains the state's population in millions. The third column contains the average age in the state. The fourth column contains the number of automobile registrations per 1,000 residents for each state. The intersection of a row and a column indicates a place to enter a number or other code assigned to a particular state on a particular variable.

direct data entry
The use of a computer terminal as an input device for data storage.

Today data-processing operators performing **direct data entry** on computers is the most common approach to data storage. Nevertheless, the terminology of direct data entry coding systems is based on the long-abandoned terminology of the punch card system.

Code Construction

Exhibit 19.4 shows a typical survey question and its associated codes. When the question has a fixed-alternative (closed) format, the number of categories requiring codes is determined during the questionnaire design stage. The codes 8 and 9 are conventionally given to the "don't know" (DK) and "no

EXHIBIT 19.3 A DATA MATRIX

Records	Row	State Column 1	Population (millions) Column 2	Average Age Column 3	Cars per 1,000 Column 4
		FIELDS			
Alabama	(Row 1)	ALAB	4.0	29.3	543
Alaska	(Row 2)	ALAS	.5	26.1	387
Arizona	(Row 3)	ARIZ	3.6	29.2	485
Arkansas	(Row 4)	ARK	2.4	30.6	442
	•	•	•	•	•
	•	•	•	•	•
	•	•	•	•	•
	•	•	•	•	•
	•	•	•	•	•
	•	•	•	•	•
Wyoming	(Row 50)	WYO	.5	27.1	609

answer" (NA) responses, respectively. However, many computer programs recognize a blank field or a certain character symbol, such as a period (.), as indicating a missing value (no answer). The computer program that will be used should be considered when selecting codes for "no answer" responses.

There are two basic rules for code construction. First, the coding categories should be *exhaustive*—that is, coding categories should be provided for all subjects or objects or responses. With a categorical variable such as sex, making categories exhaustive is not a problem. However, when the response represents a small number of subjects or when responses might be categorized in a class not typically found, there may be a problem. For example, when questioned about automobile ownership, an antique car collector might mention he drives a Packard Clipper. This may present a problem if separate categories have been developed for all possible makes of cars.

Second, the coding categories should also be *mutually exclusive* and *independent*. This means that there should be no overlap between the categories, to ensure that a subject or response can be placed in only one category. This frequently requires that an "other" code category be included, so that the

EXHIBIT 19.4 CODING FOR AN ATTITUDE STATEMENT

Fixed-Alternative Question

In general, self-regulation by business itself is preferable to stricter control of business by the government.

1. Strongly agree
2. Mildly agree
3. Mildly disagree
4. Strongly disagree
8. Don't know
9. No answer

categories are all-inclusive and mutually exclusive. For example, managerial span of control might be coded 1, 2, 3, 4, and "5 or more." The "5 or more" category ensures everyone a place in a category.

When a questionnaire is highly structured, precoding of the categories typically occurs before the data are collected. Exhibit 19.5 shows a questionnaire with the precoded response categories that were determined before the start of data collection.

postcoding
Determination of a framework for classifying responses to questions after editing, because coded categories cannot be established before data collection.

In many cases, such as when researchers are using open-ended response questions to explore an unfamiliar topic, a framework for classifying responses to questions cannot be established before data collection. This situation requires some careful thought concerning the determination of categories after the editing process has been completed. This is called **postcoding,** or simply *coding.*

Precoding Fixed-Alternative Questions

Exhibit 19.5 shows the last page of a questionnaire asking several demographic questions that will be used to classify individuals' scores. Question 29 has three possible answers, and they are precoded 1, 2, 3. Question 30 asks a person to

EXHIBIT 19.5 | **PRECODED, FIXED-ALTERNATIVE RESPONSES**

29. Do you—or does anyone else in your immediate household—belong to a labor union?
 1☐ Yes, I personally belong to a labor union.
 2☐ Yes, another member of my household belongs to a labor union.
 3☐ No, no one in my household belongs to a labor union.

30. Are you the male or female head of the household—that is, the person whose income is the chief source of support of the household?
 1☐ Yes 2☐ No

31. Would you please check the approximate combined yearly income (*before income taxes and any other payroll deductions*) from all sources of all those in your immediate household? *(Please include income from salaries, investments, dividends, rents, royalties, bonuses, commissions, etc.)* Please remember that your individual answers will not be divulged.

1☐ Less than $4,000	7☐ $8,000–$8,999	13☐ $25,000–$29,999
2☐ $4,000–$4,999	8☐ $9,000–$9,999	14☐ $30,000–$39,999
3☐ $5,000–$5,999	9☐ $10,000–$12,499	15☐ $40,000–$49,999
4☐ $6,000–$6,999	10☐ $12,500–$14,999	16☐ $50,000–$74,999
5☐ $7,000–$7,499	11☐ $15,000–$19,999	17☐ $75,000–$99,999
6☐ $7,500–$7,999	12☐ $20,000–$24,999	18☐ $100,000 or more

32a. Do you personally own corporate stocks? 1☐ Yes 2☐ No
b. Do you own stocks in the corporation for which you work?
Do you own them in a corporation for which you do not work?
(Please check as many as apply.)
Own STOCK in:
1☐ Company for which I work 2☐ Other company

THANK YOU VERY MUCH FOR YOUR COOPERATION
If you would like to make any comments on any of the subjects covered in this study, please use the space below:

respond "yes" (1) or "no" (2) to the question "Are you the male or female head of the household?" The small slightly raised numbers to the left of the boxes indicate the codes for each response and will be used by the keyboard operator when entering the data into the computer. For example, a field in the data matrix—say, column 32—will be assigned for the answer to question 30. If the respondent replies "yes," a 1 will be entered. Question 31 will require a larger field because of the large number of possible answers.

The Automarket Research questionnaire in Exhibit 19.6 (page 462) illustrates another form of coding. Question 1a shows that there are five possible answers: completely satisfied, coded 001; very satisfied, coded 002; fairly well satisfied, coded 003; somewhat dissatisfied, coded 004; and very dissatisfied, coded 005. The codes for Question 1b begin with 006 and end with 010. This questionnaire gives each possible answer an individual code number. This system of coding is used when the computer has been programmed to change these codes into traditional codes or categorical answers for each question.

The partial questionnaire in Exhibit 19.7 (page 463) shows a precoding format for a telephone interview. In this situation the interviewer circles the coded numerical score as the answer to the question.

Precoding can be used if the researcher knows what the answer categories will be before data collection occurs. Thus, once the questionnaire has been designed and the structured (or fixed-alternative) answers are identified, coding becomes a routine process. In fact, in some cases the predetermined responses are based on standardized classification schemes. A coding framework that standardizes occupation follows:

What is your occupation? (PROBE: **What kind of work is that?)**

01 Professional, technical, and kindred workers
02 Farmers
03 Managers, officials, and proprietors
04 Clerical and kindred workers
05 Sales workers
06 Craftsmen, foremen, and kindred workers
07 Operatives and kindred workers
08 Service workers
09 Laborers, except farm and mine
10 Retired, widow
11 Student
12 Unemployed, on welfare, laid off
13 Homemaker
14 Other (specify) ______
99 No occupation given

Computer-assisted telephone interviewing (CATI) and Internet surveys require precoding. Changing the coding framework after the interviewing process starts is extremely difficult because it requires changes in the computer programs.

Coding Open-Ended Response Questions

The usual reason for using open-ended response questions is that the researcher has no clear hypotheses regarding the answers, which will be numerous and varied. The purpose of coding such questions is to reduce the large number of individual responses to a few general categories of answers that can be assigned numerical scores. Code construction in these situations necessarily must reflect the judgment of the researcher. A major objective in the code-building process is to accurately transfer the meaning from written

EXHIBIT 19.6 | **A PRECODED, FIXED-ALTERNATIVE QUESTIONNAIRE**[5]

Automarket Research

This questionnaire should be completed by the **principal driver** of the vehicle indicated.
Thank you for taking time to answer these questions.

1. Now that you've had your vehicle for about one year, please tell us how satisfied you are in the following areas.	**Completely satisfied**	**Very satisfied**	**Fairly well satisfied**	**Somewhat dissatisfied**	**Very dissatisfied**
a. Exterior quality of workmanship (fit and finish)?	001 ☐	002 ☐	003 ☐	004 ☐	005 ☐
b. Interior quality of workmanship (fit and finish)?	006 ☐	007 ☐	008 ☐	009 ☐	010 ☐
c. Engine power and pickup?	011 ☐	012 ☐	013 ☐	014 ☐	015 ☐
d. Smoothness of transmission?	016 ☐	017 ☐	018 ☐	019 ☐	020 ☐
e. Riding comfort?	021 ☐	022 ☐	023 ☐	024 ☐	025 ☐
f. Ease of handling?	026 ☐	027 ☐	028 ☐	029 ☐	030 ☐
g. Fuel economy?	031 ☐	032 ☐	033 ☐	034 ☐	035 ☐
h. Quietness?	036 ☐	037 ☐	038 ☐	039 ☐	040 ☐
i. Operation of the accessories (e.g., radio, air conditioner, heater, defroster, etc.)?	041 ☐	042 ☐	043 ☐	044 ☐	045 ☐
j. Overall satisfaction with the vehicle?	046 ☐	047 ☐	048 ☐	049 ☐	050 ☐

2a. Since the time of purchase, have you taken your Ford Motor Company vehicle to your selling dealer for any kind of service, including warranty work or repairs that you paid for? Yes 051 ☐ No 052 ☐ **If no, please skip to question 5.**

2b. If yes, what was the nature of the service? Check those that apply.

053 ☐ Paint/exterior moldings	056 ☐ Brakes/steering	059 ☐ Electrical system	062 ☐ Other (please describe)
054 ☐ Other body	057 ☐ Engine	060 ☐ Wheels/tires	______________
055 ☐ Interior	058 ☐ Transmission	061 ☐ Maintenance service	______________

	Completely satisfied	**Very satisfied**	**Fairly well satisfied**	**Somewhat dissatisfied**	**Very dissatisfied**
2c. How satisfied were you with the service you received?	063 ☐	064 ☐	065 ☐	066 ☐	067 ☐

3. Based on your visit(s) to your selling dealership for service, how satisfied would you say you are with each of the following? Mark one box across.	**Completely satisfied**	**Very satisfied**	**Fairly well satisfied**	**Somewhat dissatisfied**	**Very dissatisfied**
a. The attitude of service department personnel (their interest in you and your problems)	068 ☐	069 ☐	070 ☐	071 ☐	072 ☐
b. Their overall treatment of you as a customer	073 ☐	074 ☐	075 ☐	076 ☐	077 ☐
c. Their promptness in writing up your order	078 ☐	079 ☐	080 ☐	081 ☐	082 ☐
d. Their politeness	083 ☐	084 ☐	085 ☐	086 ☐	087 ☐
e. Their understanding of your problem(s)	088 ☐	089 ☐	090 ☐	091 ☐	092 ☐
f. Convenience of scheduling the work	093 ☐	094 ☐	095 ☐	096 ☐	097 ☐
g. Convenience of service hours	098 ☐	099 ☐	100 ☐	101 ☐	102 ☐
h. Length of time to complete the work	103 ☐	104 ☐	105 ☐	106 ☐	107 ☐
i. Availability of needed parts	108 ☐	109 ☐	110 ☐	111 ☐	112 ☐
j. Their completing all the work you requested	113 ☐	114 ☐	115 ☐	116 ☐	117 ☐
k. The quality of work done (was it fixed right?)	118 ☐	119 ☐	120 ☐	121 ☐	122 ☐
l. Explanation of work and charges (if any)	123 ☐	124 ☐	125 ☐	126 ☐	127 ☐
m. Fairness of prices (if you were charged)	128 ☐	129 ☐	130 ☐	131 ☐	132 ☐
n. Appearance of service department	133 ☐	134 ☐	135 ☐	136 ☐	137 ☐

4. For the most recent service work	**Yes**	**No**	
a. Was the vehicle ready when promised?	138 ☐	139 ☐	
b. Did anyone at the dealership follow up with you after your service visit to see if you were satisfied?	140 ☐	141 ☐	
c. Did the dealership do any repeat work on a problem which they themselves previously tried to but couldn't fix?	142 ☐	143 ☐	**If no, please skip to question 5.**

d. If yes, what was the nature of the service? Check those that apply.

144 ☐ Paint/exterior moldings	147 ☐ Brakes/steering	150 ☐ Electrical system	153 ☐ Other (please describe)
145 ☐ Other body	148 ☐ Engine	151 ☐ Wheels/tires	______________
146 ☐ Interior	149 ☐ Transmission	152 ☐ Maintenance service	______________

(over please)

1

responses to numeric codes. Experienced researchers recognize that the key to this process is basing code building on thoughts, not just words. The end result of code building should be a list, in abbreviated and orderly form, of all comments and thoughts given in answer to each question.

Differentiating categories of answers for the coding of open-ended response questions is more difficult than coding fixed-alternative questions. Developing

Exhibit 19.7 | **Precoded Format for Telephone Interview**

Study #45641 — For office use only
Travel (Telephone Screening) — Respondent # ________
City:
Chicago
Gary
Ft. Wayne
Bloomington

Hello, I'm ____________________ from ________________________, a national survey research company. We are conducting a study and would like to ask you a few questions.

A. Before we begin, do you, or any member of your family, work for . . .
   1 A travel agency   2 An advertising agency   3 A survey research company
   (If "yes" to any of the above, terminate and tally on contact sheet)

B. By the way, have you been interviewed as part of a survey research study within the past month?
   1 Yes—(Terminate and tally on contact sheet)
   2 No—(Continue)

   1. Have you yourself made any trips of over 100 miles within the continental 48 states in the past 3 months?
      1 Yes
      2 No—(Skip to Question 10)
   2. Was the trip for business reasons (paid for by your firm), vacation, or personal reasons?

	Last Trip	Second Last Trip	Other Trips
Business	1	1	1
Vacation	2	2	2
Personal (excluding a vacation)	3	3	3

test tabulation
Tallying of a small sample of the total number of replies to a particular question during the coding process in order to construct coding categories.

an appropriate code from the respondent's exact comments is somewhat of an art. Researchers generally perform a **test tabulation** to identify verbatim responses from approximately 20 percent of respondents' questionnaires and then construct coding categories reflecting the judgment of the person constructing the codes. The test tabulation is a small sample of the total number of replies to a particular question. Its purpose is preliminary identification of the stability and distribution of the answers that will determine how to set up a coding scheme.

The second stage, after tabulating the basic responses, is to determine how many answer categories will be acceptable. This decision will be influenced by the purpose of the study and the limitations of the computer program and plan for data entry. For example, if only one single-digit field is assigned to the particular survey question, the number of possible categories is limited to 10 (0–9). In fact, if an "other" or "miscellaneous" code category appears along with a "don't know/no answer" code category, the code construction will be additionally limited.

Devising the Coding Scheme

A coding scheme should not be too elaborate. The coder's task is to summarize the data. Table 19.1 shows a test tabulation of airport visitors' responses to a question about their experience at the Honolulu airport. A large number of

Table 19.1 **Open-Ended Responses to a Survey about the Honolulu Airport**[6]

	Code Number
Prices high: restaurant/coffee shop/snack bar	90
Dirty–filthy–smelly restrooms/airport	65
Very good/good/excellent/great	59
Need air conditioning	52
Nice/beautiful	45
Gift shops expensive	32
Too warm/too hot	31
Friendly staff/people	25
Airport is awful/bad	23
Long walk between terminal/gates	21
Clean airport	17
Employees rude/unfriendly/poor attitude	16
More signs/maps in lobby/streets	16
Like it	15
Love gardens	11
Need video games/arcade	10
More change machines/different locations	8
More padded benches/comfortable waiting area	8
More security personnel including HPD	8
Replace shuttle with moving walkways	8
Complaint: flight delay	7
Cool place	7
Crowded	7
Provide free carts for carry on	7
Baggage storage inconvenient/need in different location	6
Floor plan confusing	6
Mailbox location not clear/more needed	6
More restaurants and coffee shops/more variety	6
Need a place to nap	6
Polite VIP/friendly/helpful	6
Poor help in gift shops/rude/unfriendly	6
Slow baggage delivery/service	6
Very efficient/organized	6
Excellent food	5
Install chilled water drinking fountains	5
Love Hawaii	5
More TV sets	5
Noisy	5
People at sundries/camera shop rude	5
Shuttle drivers rude	5
Something to do for passengers with long waits	5
Airport too spread out	4
Better information for departing/arriving flights	4
Better parking for employees	4
Better shuttle service needed	4
Cute VIP	4

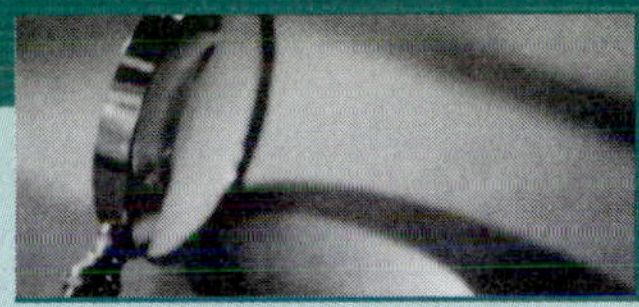

Research Insight

VERBASTAT

Traditional coding of open-ended responses is an expensive, labor-intensive task.[7] For surveys with several open-ended questions, coding can cause the overall cost of research to skyrocket. Verbastat by SPSS provides a fast, reliable way to automate as much of the process as possible—without compromising quality.

Instead of waiting for all questionnaires to come back from the field, researchers can import data while interviewing is in progress. Verbastat leads the coder through the process screen by screen for fast, efficient, and reliable coding. Researchers can reuse code frames to further automate coding—enabling the completion of more surveys in less time, for faster turnaround and lower costs.

Verbastat is not a handwriting recognition scanner or content analysis package; it does not try to decipher the semantic content of sentences and automatically assign values. Rather, it greatly enhances your classification decision-making process by showing you which responses are likely to be classified together. The coder retains control over the process, but Verbastat helps by providing counts, keyword lists, and a user-friendly interface. All decisions are easily reversible, and the entire process is reduced to just three broad steps: data entry, classification, and generation of coded data files that can be used with virtually any analysis package.

answers were given to the question. After the first pass at devising the coding scheme, the researcher must decide if it should be revised and whether the codes are appropriate to answer managerial questions. Preliminary schemes with too many categories can always be collapsed or reduced later in the analysis. If initial coding is too abstract and only a few categories are established, it will be difficult to revise the codes to make more concrete statements unless the raw data were recorded.

In the Honolulu airport example, the many codes in the preliminary tabulation could be reduced to a smaller number of categories. For example, the heading "Friendly/attractive personnel" could include the responses Friendly staff/people, Polite VIP/friendly/helpful, and Cute VIP. Experienced coders group answers under generalized headings that are pertinent to the research question. It is important to make the codes consistent. Individual coders should give the same codes to similar responses. The categories should be sufficiently unambiguous that coders will not classify items in different ways.

Coding open-ended response questions is a very complex issue. Technical treatises on this subject may be referred to if complex problems develop.[8]

Code Book

Up to this point we have assumed that each code's position in the data matrix has already been determined. However, this plan generally is formed only after the coding scheme has been designed for every question.

code book
A book identifying each variable in a study and its position in the data matrix. The book is used to identify a variable's description, code name, and field.

The **code book** gives each variable in the study and its location in the data matrix. With the code book the researcher can identify any variable's description, code name, and field. Exhibit 19.8 illustrates a portion of a code book for the telephone interview illustrated in Exhibit 19.7. Notice that the first few fields record the study number, city, and other information used for identification

EXHIBIT 19.8 | **PORTION OF A CODE BOOK FROM A TRAVEL STUDY**

STUDY #45641
N = 743

Question Number	Field or Column Number	Description and Meaning of Code Values
—	1–5	Study number (45641)
—	6	City 1. Chicago 2. Gary 3. Ft. Wayne 4. Bloomington
—	7–9	Interview number (3 digits on upper left-hand corner of questionnaire)
A	Not entered	Family, work for 1. Travel agency 2. Advertising agency 3. Survey research company
B	Not entered	Interviewed past month 1. Yes 2. No
1.	10	Traveled in past 3 months 1. Yes 2. No
2.	11	Purpose last trip 1. Business 2. Vacation 3. Personal
	12	Purpose second last trip 1. Business 2. Vacation 3. Personal
	13	Purpose other trips 1. Business 2. Vacation 3. Personal

purposes. Researchers commonly identify individual respondents by giving each an identification number or questionnaire number. When each interview is identified with a number entered into each computer record, errors discovered in the tabulation process can be checked on the questionnaire to verify the answer.

production coding
The physical activity of transferring the data from the questionnaire or data collection form after the data have been collected.

Production Coding

Transferring the data from the questionnaire or data collection form after the data have been collected is called **production coding.** Depending on the nature of the data collection form, codes may be written directly on the instrument or

coding sheet
A ruled sheet of paper used to transfer data from questionnaires or data collection forms after data have been collected.

on a special **coding sheet**, which is a facsimile of the data matrix. It is best to have coding done in a central location, where a supervisor may help to solve interpretation problems. The value of training coders should not be overlooked.

> The research staff should prepare one or two practice interviews-questionnaires made up by the research staff in duplicate so that all coders working on the study will be practice-coding the same interviews. The few hours of time invested in training pay off highly in the reduction of coding errors. The objectives of coder training are to demonstrate the consistent and proper application of codes and to encourage the proper use of administrative procedures.[9]

Editing and Coding Combined

Frequently, the person coding the questionnaire performs certain editing functions, such as translating an occupational title given by a respondent into a socioeconomic status. Often a question asking for a description of the job or business is used as a check to make certain there is no problem with classifying the responses. For example, persons who indicate "salesperson" as their occupation might write their job description as "selling shoes in a shoestore" or "selling computer networks to the Defense Department." Generally, coders perform this type of editing function but request the help of a data processing supervisor if questions arise.

Computerized Data Processing

data entry
The process of transferring data from a research project to computers.

optical scanning system
A data processing input device that reads material directly from mark sensed questionnaires.

In most studies with large sample sizes, a computer is used for data processing. The process of transforming data from a research project, such as answers to a survey questionnaire, to computers is referred to as **data entry.** Several alternative means exist for entering data into a computer. In studies involving highly structured paper questionnaires, an **optical scanning system** may be used to read material directly into the computer's memory from *mark sensed questionnaires*. This type of system requires that the computer sense which of several small circles on a special sheet of paper devised for optical scanning has been filled in by the respondent (see Exhibit 19.9). The process is similar to the scanning of answer sheets for exams in large college lecture sections.

In a research study using computer-assisted telephone interviewing or a self-administered Internet questionnaire, responses can be automatically stored and tabulated as they are collected. Direct data capture substantially reduces clerical errors that occur during the editing and coding process. However, respondents taking Internet surveys may make errors, and steps need to be taken to prevent multiple submissions of a respondent's questionnaire. For example, a respondent might click the Submit button at the end of a questionnaire two or more times until there is a response. The data capture software must be written so that respondents are prevented from submitting two or more identical questionnaires. In rare instances, a hacker may enter the survey Web site and try to fill out multiple questionnaires or in some way sabotage the data. If researchers have security concerns, the data collected in an Internet survey should be encrypted and protected behind a firewall.

When data are not optically scanned or entered directly into a computer the moment they are collected, data processing for the computer begins with keyboarding. The data entry process transfers coded data from the questionnaires or coding sheets onto a hard drive or floppy disk. As in every stage of the research process, there is some concern about whether the data entry job

Exhibit 19.9 An Optical Scanning Questionnaire[10]

NCS Trans-Optic® EP01-25394:321 A8404

PIRATES 1887 1987

PITTSBURGH PIRATES FAN SURVEY

In order to help us know you and serve you better, we would appreciate your completing this fan survey. If you wish to be eligible for today's special prize drawing (four club box seats to the game of your choice) please fill in your name and address. For other questions please darken the circle for the appropriate response.

1. GENDER: M F 2. AGE: 6-12 13-18 19-25 26-34 35-49 50+

3. HOUSEHOLD INCOME: $0-9,999 $10,000-19,999 $20,000-34,999 $35,000-49,999 $50,000+

4. HOUSEHOLD SIZE: I live alone I live with 1 2 3 4 5 6+ other persons (including children)

5. Please check your highest level of education: Attended junior high or grade school Attended high school High school graduate Attended college College graduate Post graduate

6. How many years have you been attending Pirate baseball? 1 2 3 4 5 6 7 8 9 10+

7. Please mark the number of Pirate games you attended last season: 0 1 2 3 4 5 6 7 8 9 10 11 12 13 14 15 16 17 18 19 20 21 22 23 24 25 26 27 28 29 30 31 32 33 34 35 36 37 38 39 40 41 42 43 44 45 46 47 48 49 50 51 52 53 54 55 56 57 58 59 60 61 62 63 64 65 66 67 68 69 70 71 72 73 74 75 76 77 78 79 80 81

8. Please mark the number of Pirate games you PLAN to attend this year: 1 2 3 4 5 6 7 8 9 10 11 12 13 14 15 16 17 18 19 20 21 22 23 24 25 26 27 28 29 30 31 32 33 34 35 36 37 38 39 40 41 42 43 44 45 46 47 48 49 50 51 52 53 54 55 56 57 58 59 60 61 62 63 64 65 66 67 68 69 70 71 72 73 74 75 76 77 78 79 80 81

9. Are you a season ticket holder? Yes No If you answered YES, what type of season ticket plan did you buy? Full Season Night (Mon.-Thurs.) Weekend Night (Fri & Sat) Daylight Fan Flex

10. What type of seat did you purchase for today's game? Club Box Mezzanine Box Terrace Box Reserved General Admission

11. With whom did you attend today's game? (You may select more than one.) Family Spouse Date Friend(s) Group Business Associate Alone Other If other, please specify

12. How many days in advance did you buy your tickets for today's game? 0 1 2 3 4 5 6 7 8 9 10 11 12 13 14 15 16 17 18 19 20 21 22 23 24 25 26 27 28 29 30 31 32 33 34 35 36 37 38 39 40 41 42 43 44 45 46 47 48 49 50 51 52 53 54 55 56 57 58 59 60 61 62 63 64 65 66 67 68 69 70 71 72 73 74 75 76 77 78 79 80 81+

13. Where did you travel from for today's game? Home Work Other If other, please specify

14. LOCATION OF WORK: Downtown North South East West Other If other, please specify

15. What was your approximate travel time to today's game? (In minutes) 1 2 3 4 5 6 7 8 9 10 11 12 13 14 15 16 17 18 19 20 21 22 23 24 25 26 27 28 29 30 31 32 33 34 35 36 37 38 39 40 41 42 43 44 45 46 47 48 49 50 51 52 53 54 55 56 57 58 59 60 61+

16. Please indicate the game starting time you prefer.

WEEKDAY NIGHTS (Monday-Thursday)	6:35 p.m.	7:05 p.m.	7:35 p.m.
WEEKEND NIGHTS (Friday-Saturday)	6:35 p.m.	7:05 p.m.	7:35 p.m.

NAME
ADDRESS
CITY STATE
ZIP
PHONE

17. Which TV stations do you watch and approximately how often? (You may mark more than one.)

	EVERY DAY	5-6 TIMES A WEEK	3-4 TIMES A WEEK	1-2 TIMES A WEEK	NEVER
KDKA					
WPXI					
WTAE					
WPGH					
WPTT					
Others-please specify					

18. Which Radio stations do you listen to and approximately how often? (You may mark more than one.)

AM STATIONS	EVERY DAY	5-6 TIMES A WEEK	3-4 TIMES A WEEK	1-2 TIMES A WEEK	NEVER
KDKA					
WTAE					
KQV					
WTKN					
Others-please specify					
FM STATIONS					
B94					
Y97					
WHTX					
WWSW					
WDVE					
Others-please specify					

19. What Newspapers do you read and approximately how often? (You may mark more than one.)

	EVERY DAY	SUN	MON	TUE	WED	THU	FRI	SAT
Pgh. Press								
Pgh. Post Gazette								
Others-please specify								

has been done correctly. Data entry workers, like anyone else, may make errors. To ensure 100 percent accuracy in transferring the codes, the job is *verified* by a second data entry worker, who checks the accuracy of the data entered. If an error has been made, the verifier corrects the data entry. This process of verifying the data is never performed by the same person who entered the original data. A person who misread the coded questionnaire during the keyboarding operation might make the same mistake during the verifying process. The mistake might not be detected if the same person performed both operations.

Data entry workers prefer to have the data on coding sheets so that they do not have to page through the questionnaires to enter the data. However, this usually increases the time and effort required for coding. Coding on the actual questionnaires eliminates the need to transfer the answers to coding sheets. The particular resources of the project will dictate which source is used as input by keyboard operators. Several of the questionnaires illustrated in this chapter indicate how coding may be placed on the questionnaire itself.

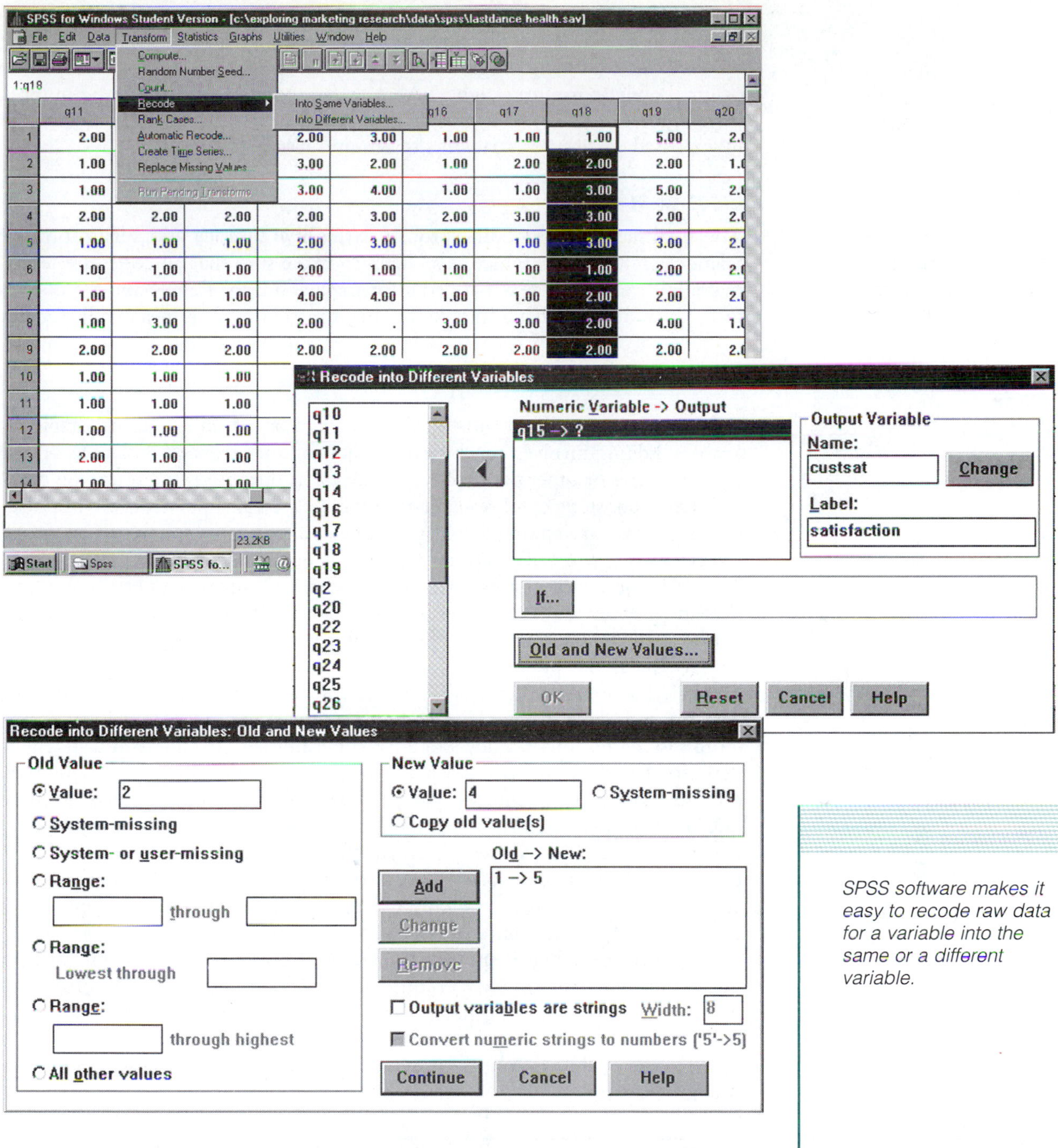

SPSS software makes it easy to recode raw data for a variable into the same or a different variable.

Recoding

It is sometimes easier to enter the raw data into the computer using the precoding on the questionnaire and then program the computer to recode certain data. This often occurs when a researcher measures attitudes with a series of both positive and negative statements. Reversing the order of the codes for negative statements so that their codes reflect the same direction and order or magnitude as the positive statements' codes requires only a simple data transformation. For instance, if a seven-point scale for variable 1 (VAR1) is to be recoded, the following programming statement might be used to subtract the original code score from eight: VAR1 = 8 − VAR1. Collapsing the number of categories or values of a variable or creating new variables (e.g., creating an index based on several variables) also requires **recoding.**

recoding
Changing codes to facilitate analysis.

Error Checking

error checking
The final stage of the coding process, during which codes are verified and corrected as necessary.

The final stage in the coding process is the **error checking** and verification, or "data cleaning," stage, which is a check to make sure that all codes are legitimate. For example, if sex is coded 1 for male and 2 for female and a 3 code is found, it is obvious that a mistake has been made that requires an adjustment.

SUMMARY

Raw data must be edited and coded in order to be put into a form suitable for analysis. Editing involves checking and adjusting for errors or omissions on the questionnaires or other data-collection forms. Its purpose is to ensure the completeness, consistency, and readability of the data. Field supervisors are responsible for preliminary editing. The daily field edit allows rapid follow-up on errors; interviewers may recall responses omitted or be able to recontact respondents. The in-house editor checks for consistency among answers and for completeness and may rearrange responses on an open-ended response questionnaire. The editor's task includes making sure material is ready for coding.

Coding is the process of identifying and classifying each answer with a numerical score or other character symbol. It usually involves entering the data for computer storage. The coding categories should be exhaustive, providing for all responses. They should also be mutually exclusive and independent so that there is no overlap between categories. On highly structured questionnaires, the categories may be precoded. With open-ended response questions, answers are postcoded. This means the categories are assigned after the data have been collected, based on the researcher's judgment. It is better to assign too many categories than too few, as it is easier to collapse several categories into one than to increase the number of categories. A code book identifies each variable and the codes for responses.

Production coding is the actual process of transferring the data from the questionnaire to the storage medium. Data are commonly entered onto a hard drive or disks. However, other possibilities include using computer systems that enter data directly into computer storage as they are collected. Once the raw data are in the computer, programs may be used to recode variables or to check for errors.

Key Terms

information
data
editing
field editing
in-house editing
item nonresponse
plug value
coding
code
field
record
file
data matrix
direct data entry
postcoding
test tabulation
code book
production coding
coding sheet
data entry
optical scanning system
recoding
error checking

Questions for Review and Critical Thinking

1. What is the purpose of editing?
2. Suppose respondents in a political survey were asked if they favored or opposed the Agricultural Trade Act. Edit the following open-ended responses:
   (a) I don't know what it is, so I'll oppose it.
   (b) Favorable, though I don't really know what it is.
   (c) You caught me on that. I don't know, but from the sound of it I favor it.
3. Comment on the coding scheme for this question: "In which of these groups did your total *family* income, from all sources, fall last year—before taxes, that is? Just tell me the code number."

Response	Code	Response	Code
Under $4,000	01	$40,000 to $59,999	07
$4,000 to $9,999	02	$60,000 to $79,999	08
$10,000 to $14,999	03	$80,000 to $99,999	09
$15,000 to $19,999	04	$100,000 or over	10
$20,000 to $29,999	05	Refused to answer	11
$30,000 to $39,999	06	Don't know	98
		No answer	99

4. Suppose information has been gathered about the occupations of several respondents. How would you classify the following respondents' answers in the occupational coding scheme presented in the chapter: plumber, butcher, retail sales, X-ray technician, and veterinarian?
5. A frequently asked question on campus is "What is your major?" Suppose a survey researcher wished to develop a coding scheme for the answer to this question. What would the scheme look like?
6. A researcher asks, "What do you remember about advertising for Gillette Mach3 razors?" How should the code book for this question be structured? What coding problems does the question present?
7. During the month of October a sales manager records the number of days worked, the number of sales calls made, and the actual sales volume for each of his 15 sales representatives. Outline a data matrix for this database.
8. Design a short questionnaire with fewer than five fixed-alternative questions to measure student satisfaction with your college bookstore. Interview five classmates, then arrange the database into a data matrix.
9. A researcher investigating attitudes toward her company notices that one individual answers all image questions at one end of a bipolar scale. Should she throw this questionnaire out and not use it in the data analysis?

Exploring the Internet

1. The Web page of the Research Triangle Institute (http://www.rti.org) describes its coding of survey research data. Go to its Statistics, Health, and Social Policy page (http://www.rti.org/units/shsp/factsheets/B015.cfm) and read the coding factsheet.
2. The University of Michigan's Institute for Social Research (http://www. isr.umich.edu/index.html) houses the Survey Research Center. Go to the Center's Index of Projects (http://www.isr.umich.edu/src/projects. html), and click on Surveys of Consumers (http://athena.sca.isr.umich.edu/scripts/info/info.asp) and then on Questionnaire to see how the questionnaire is coded.
3. Search the Internet to learn what companies offer optical scanning systems and services.

CHAPTER

20

BASIC DATA ANALYSIS: Descriptive Statistics

What you will learn in this chapter

- To understand that analysis consists of summarizing, rearranging, ordering, or manipulating data.
- To define *descriptive analysis.*
- To compute and explain the purposes of simple tabulations and cross-tabulations.
- To discuss how the calculation of percentages helps the researcher understand the nature of relationships.
- To discuss the relationship between two variables with cross-tabulation procedures.
- To elaborate and refine basic cross-tabulations.
- To define and explain *spurious relationships.*
- To understand quadrant analysis.
- To discuss data transformations.
- To calculate an index number.
- To explain some of the computer programs for analyzing descriptive data.
- To explain the purpose of interpretation.

More than half of office workers say that poor lighting in the workplace triggers tired or watery eyes (56 percent).[1] Another 30 percent say they suffer headaches from poor lighting. Moreover, 86 percent believe that making lighting improvements to the workplace would reduce eyestrain and headaches.

How significant are lighting problems in the office? The Steelcase Workplace Index, a semiannual survey that gauges workplace trends in the United States, indicates that eight out of every ten workers report they experience lighting glare. Approximately 38 percent of workers say the light level in their work area is either too dim (22 percent) or too bright (15 percent). And three out of four say they want more control over their lighting.

While lighting is a critical factor in worker health, comfort and productivity, most workers suffer in silence from eye strain. Some workers are taking matters into their own hands. At least three out of ten office workers say they have attempted to change the light levels in the workplace. If the place is too dark, people will either bring in their own lighting from home (15 percent) or obtain lighting from their employer or co-worker (13 percent). If the workplace is too bright, 15 percent of office workers have either removed or blocked the light.

Three out of four office workers indicate improved lighting could help them be more efficient and productive. And two out of every three office workers surveyed reported that improved lighting would help them be more creative.

These interesting findings illustrate the results of a typical descriptive analysis. This chapter explains how to perform descriptive analysis. ■

THE NATURE OF DESCRIPTIVE ANALYSIS

Business researchers edit and code data to provide input that results in tabulated information that will answer research questions. With this input, researchers logically and statistically describe project results. Within this context the term *analysis* is difficult to define because it refers to a variety of activities and processes. One form of analysis is summarizing large quantities of raw data so the results can be interpreted. Categorizing, or separating out the components or relevant parts of the whole data set, is also a form of analysis to make the data easily manageable. Rearranging, ordering, or manipulating data may provide descriptive information that answers questions posed in the problem definition. All forms of analysis attempt to portray consistent patterns in the data so the results may be studied and interpreted in a brief and meaningful way.

descriptive analysis
The transformation of raw data into a form that will make them easy to understand and interpret; rearranging, ordering, manipulating data to provide descriptive information.

Descriptive analysis refers to the transformation of raw data into a form that will make them easy to understand and interpret. Describing responses or observations is typically the first form of analysis. Calculating averages, frequency distributions, and percentage distributions are the most common ways of summarizing data.

As the analysis progresses beyond the descriptive stage, researchers generally apply the tools of inferential statistics. *Univariate analysis,* which is covered in Chapter 21, allows researchers to assess the statistical significance of various hypotheses about a single variable.

In Chapter 13 we saw that the type of measurement scale used determines the permissible arithmetic operations. Exhibit 20.1 outlines the most common descriptive statistics associated with each type of scale. It is important to remember that all descriptive statistics appropriate for a lower-order scale are also appropriate for higher-order scales.

Coca Cola's data analysis shows that the typical resident of Brooklyn, New York, drinks 105 Cokes annually.[2] On Staten Island, however, the average resident drinks a whopping 429 Cokes per year. Descriptive analysis transforms raw data into a form that is easy to understand and interpret.

EXHIBIT 20.1 | **DESCRIPTIVE STATISTICS PERMISSIBLE WITH DIFFERENT TYPES OF MEASUREMENTS**

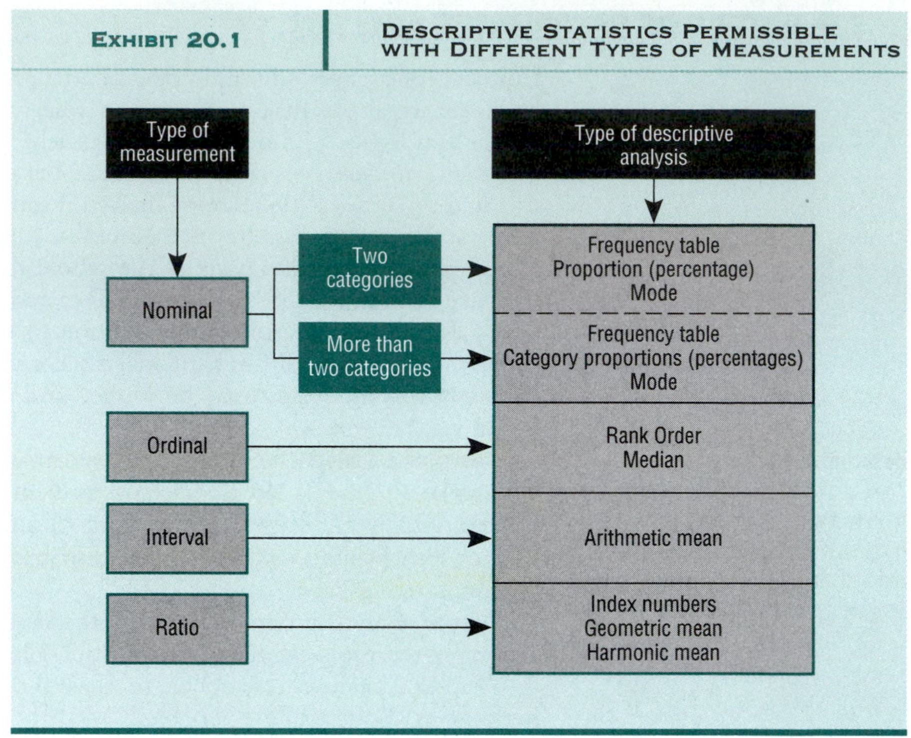

TABULATION

simple tabulation
Counting the number of different responses to a question and arranging them in a frequency distribution.

frequency table
A simple tabulation that indicates the frequency with which respondents give a particular answer.

Tabulation refers to the orderly arrangement of data in a table or other summary format. Counting the number of different responses to a question and putting them in a frequency distribution is a **simple,** or *marginal,* **tabulation.** Simple tabulation of the responses or observations on a question-by-question or item-by-item basis provides the most basic form of information for the researcher and in many cases the most useful information. It tells the researcher how frequently each response occurs. This starting point for analysis requires the counting of responses or observations for each of the categories or codes assigned to a variable. Table 20.1 illustrates a **frequency table.** When this tabulation process is done by hand, it is called *tallying.* Large sample sizes generally require computer tabulation of the data.

TABLE 20.1 | **FREQUENCY TABLE**

DO YOU SHOP AT IGA?

Response	Frequency
Yes	330
No	120
Total	450

TABLE 20.2 | AN ILLUSTRATION OF HOW PERCENTAGES AID IN THE INTERPRETATION OF FREQUENCY DISTRIBUTIONS AND CROSS-TABULATIONS[3]

A: United States Racial and Ethnic Composition (in thousands)

	2000	2010*	Change
Non-Hispanic White	197,061	202,390	5,329
Non-Hispanic Black	33,568	37,466	3,898
Non-Hispanic Asian/Pacific Islander	10,584	14,402	3,818
Non-Hispanic Other	2,054	2,320	266
Hispanic	31,366	41,139	9,773

B: United States Racial and Ethnic Composition (in thousands)

	2000	Percent of Population	2010*	Percent of Population	Change	Percent Change
Non-Hispanic White	197,061	71.8	202,390	68.0	5,329	+2.7
Non-Hispanic Black	33,568	12.2	37,466	12.6	3,898	+11.6
Non-Hispanic Asian/ Pacific Islander	10,584	3.9	14,402	4.8	3,818	+36.1
Non-Hispanic Other	2,054	0.7	2,320	0.8	266	+13.0
Hispanic	31,366	11.4	41,139	13.8	9,773	+31.2

*Projected

Percentages

Whether data are tabulated by computer or by hand, it is useful to have **percentages** and **cumulative percentages** as well as **frequency distributions.** For example, consider Table 20.2. Most people find part B easier to interpret than part A because the percentages are useful for comparing trends over the decades. When discussing percentages, researchers must speak or write with precise language. For example, the difference between 40 percent and 60 percent is not 20 percent, but 20 *percentage points;* this represents an increase of 50 percent.

percentage
A part of a whole expressed in hundredths.

cumulative percentage
A percentage (or percentage distribution) that has increased by successive additions.

frequency distribution
A set of data organized by summarizing the number of times a particular value of a variable occurs.

Measures of Central Tendency

According to Airport Interviewing and Research, Inc. the average number of trips taken annually by a business traveler was 15.[4] This is a measure of central tendency. Describing central tendencies of the distribution with the mean, median, or mode is another basic form of descriptive analysis. Of course, these measures are most useful when the purpose is to identify typical values of a variable or the most common characteristic of a group. If knowing the average or typical performance will satisfy the information need, the measures described in Chapter 17 should be considered.

CROSS-TABULATION

The mere tabulation of data may answer many research questions. In fact, many studies do not go beyond examining the simple tabulation of the question-by-question responses to a survey. On the other hand, although

Table 20.3 CROSS-TABULATION TABLE FROM A SURVEY ON ETHICS IN AMERICA

Activity	Under 50 Years Old	Over 50 Years Old	Men	Women	College Graduate	High School Graduate
	REPORTED BEHAVIOR (PERCENTAGE OF GENERAL PUBLIC WHO HAVE EVER DONE EACH ACTIVITY)					
Taken home work supplies	50	26	47	33	58	21
Called in sick to work when not ill	50	18	Not reported		36	21

Activity	Business Executives	General Public
	REPORTED BEHAVIOR (PERCENTAGE WHO HAVE EVER DONE EACH ACTIVITY)	
Taken home work supplies	74	40
Called in sick to work when not ill	14	31
Used company telephone for personal long-distance calls	78	15
Overstated deductions somewhat on tax forms	35	13
Driven while drunk	80	33
Saw a fellow employee steal something at work and did not report it	7	26

cross-tabulation
Organizing data by groups, categories, or classes to facilitate comparisons; a joint frequency distribution of observations on two or more sets of variables.

frequency counts, percentage distributions, and averages summarize a considerable amount of information, simple tabulation may not yield the full value of the research. Most data can be further organized in a variety of ways. For example, data from a survey that samples both men and women commonly are separated into groups or categories based on gender. Analyzing results by groups, categories, or classes is the technique of **cross-tabulation.**

The purpose of categorization and cross-tabulation is to allow the inspection of differences among groups and to make comparisons. This form of analysis also helps determine the form of relationship between two variables. Cross-tabulating the results of business research helps clarify the research findings as they pertain to industry, market, and organizational segments.

Table 20.3 presents a summary of several cross-tabulations from American citizens' responses to a questionnaire on ethical behavior in the United States. A researcher interested in the relative ethical perspectives of business executives and the general public can inspect this table and easily compare the two groups. The percentage table illustrates the added value of calculating percentages.

Examples of the usefulness of categorization and cross-tabulation can be found in most experiments. It is obvious that the data from the experimental and control groups should be separated or partitioned, because researchers wish to compare the effects of a treatment.

Contingency Table

contingency table
The results of a cross-tabulation of two variables, such as answers to two survey questions.

Part A of Table 20.4 shows how the cross-tabulation of answers to two survey questions (or two variables) results in a **contingency table,** or data matrix. The frequency counts for the question "Do you shop at IGA?" are presented as

TABLE 20.4 POSSIBLE CROSS-TABULATIONS OF ONE QUESTION

A. Cross-Tabulation of Question "Do You Shop at IGA?" by Sex of Respondent

	Yes	No	Total
Men	150	75	225
Women	180	45	225
Total	330	120	450

B. Percentage Cross-Tabulation of Question "Do You Shop at IGA?" by Sex of Respondent, Row Percentage

	Yes	No	Total (Base)
Men	66.7%	33.3%	100% (225)
Women	80.0%	20.0%	100% (225)

C. Percentage Cross-Tabulation of Question "Do You Shop at IGA?" by Sex of Respondent, Column Percentage

	Yes	No
Men	45.5%	62.5%
Women	54.5	37.5
Total	100.0	100.0
(Base)	(330)	(120)

column totals. The total number of men and women in the sample are presented as row totals. These row and column totals are often called *marginals,* because they appear in the table's margins. There are four *cells* within Part A, each representing a specific combination of the two variables. The cell representing women who said they do not shop at IGA has a frequency count of 45.

The contingency table in Part A is referred to as a 2 × 2 table because it has two rows and two columns. Any cross-tabulation table may be classified according to the number of rows by the number of columns (R by C). Thus, a 3 × 4 table is one with three rows and four columns.

Percentage Cross-Tabulations

base (base number)
The number of respondents or observations that indicate a total; used as a basis for computing percentages in each column or row in a cross-tabulation table.

When data from a survey are cross-tabulated, percentages help the researcher understand the nature of the relationship by allowing relative comparison. The total number of respondents or observations may be utilized as a **base** for computing the percentage in each cell. When the objective of the research is to identify a relationship between the answers to two questions (or two variables), it is common to choose one of the questions as the base for determining percentages. For example, look at the data in Parts A, B, and C of Table 20.4. Compare Part B with Part C. Selecting either the row percentages or the column percentages will emphasize a particular comparison or distribution. The nature of the problem the researcher wishes to investigate will determine which marginal total will be used as a base for computing percentages.

Fortunately, there is a conventional rule for determining the direction of percentages if the researcher has identified which variable is the independent variable and which is the dependent variable: The percentages should be computed *in the direction of the independent variable.* That is, the marginal total of the independent variable should be used as the base for computing the percentages. Although survey research does not identify cause-and-effect relationships, one might argue that it would be logical to assume that a variable such as one's gender might predict shopping behavior, in which case independent and dependent variables may be established for the purpose of presenting the most useful information.

Elaboration and Refinement

The *Oxford Universal Dictionary* defines *analysis* as "the resolution of anything complex into its simplest elements." This suggests that once the basic relationship between two variables has been examined, the researcher may wish to investigate this relationship under a variety of different conditions. Typically, a third variable is introduced into the analysis to elaborate and refine the researcher's understanding by specifying the conditions under which the relationship between the first two variables is strongest and weakest.[5] In other words, a more elaborate analysis asks: "Will interpretation of the relationship be modified if other variables are simultaneously considered?"

It is terrible to speak well and be wrong.

SOPHOCLES

elaboration analysis
An analysis of the basic cross-tabulation for each level of a variable not previously considered, perhaps subgroups of the sample.

Performing the basic cross-tabulation within various subgroups of the sample is a common form of **elaboration analysis.** The researcher breaks down the analysis for each level of another variable. For example, if the researcher has cross-tabulated shopping behavior by sex (see Table 20.4) and wishes to investigate another variable (perhaps marital status) that may modify the original relationship, a more elaborate analysis may be conducted. Table 20.5 breaks down the responses to the question "Do you shop at IGA?" by sex and marital status. The data show that marital status does not change the original cross-tabulation relationship among women, but it does change that relationship among men. The analysis suggests that our original conclusion about the relationship between sex and shopping behavior be retained for women; the data confirm the original interpretation. However, the refinements in analysis have pointed out a relationship among men that was not immediately discernible in the two-variable case. It may be concluded that marital status modifies the original relationship among men—that is, that there is an interaction

TABLE 20.5 CROSS-TABULATION OF MARITAL STATUS, SEX, AND RESPONSES TO THE QUESTION "DO YOU SHOP AT IGA?"

	MARRIED		SINGLE	
	Men	Women	Men	Women
"Do you shop at IGA?"				
Yes	55%	80%	86%	80%
No	45	20	14	20

moderator variable
A third variable that, when introduced into an analysis, alters or has a contingent effect on the relationship between an independent variable and a dependent variable.

spurious relationship
An apparent relationship between two variables that is not authentic, but appears authentic because an elaboration analysis with a third variable has not yet been conducted.

effect. In this situation marital status is a moderator variable. A **moderator variable** is a third variable that, when introduced into the analysis, alters or has a contingent effect on the relationship between an independent variable and a dependent variable.

In other situations the adding of a third variable to the analysis may lead us to reject the original conclusion about the relationship. When this occurs, the elaboration analysis will have indicated a **spurious relationship**—an apparent relationship between the original two variables that is not authentic. Our earlier example about high ice cream cone sales and drownings at the beach (Chapter 4) illustrated a spurious relationship. Additional discussion of this topic, dealing with measures of association, appears in Chapter 23.

Elaborating on the basic cross-tabulation is a form of *multivariate analysis,* because more than two variables are simultaneously analyzed to identify complex relationships. When a breakdown of the responses into three or more questions is required, there is usually a multivariate statistical technique for investigating the relationship. Such techniques are discussed in Chapter 24.

How Many Cross-Tabulations?

Surveys may ask dozens of questions. Computer-assisted business researchers often go on "fishing expeditions," cross-tabulating every question on a survey with every other question. Every possible response becomes a possible explanatory variable. All too often this activity provides only reams of extra computer output of no value to management. To avoid this, the number of cross-tabulations should be predetermined when the research objectives are stated.

Quadrant Analysis

quadrant analysis
A variation of the cross-tabulation table in which responses to two rating scale questions are plotted in four quadrants on a two-dimensional table.

Quadrant analysis is a variation of the cross-tabulation table that has grown increasingly popular as a component of total quality management programs. Quadrant analysis plots responses to two rating scale questions into four quadrants on a two-dimensional table. Most quadrant analysis in business research portrays or plots the relationship between the average responses about a product attribute's importance and average ratings of a company's (or brand's) performance with respect to that product feature. Sometimes the term *importance-performance analysis* is used because consumers rate perceived importance of several attributes and then rate the company's brand (and competitors' brands) in relation to that attribute.

Exhibit 20.2 shows a quadrant analysis matrix for a gourmet microwave food product that was evaluated using two seven-point scales.[6] The upper-left quadrant (high importance/low rating) shows importance ratings above 4.0 and performance ratings of 4.0 or below.[7] This exhibit shows that consumers believe a microwave meal should be easy to prepare, but this new product is rated low on this attribute. Consumers know what they want, but they are not getting it. The upper-right quadrant (high importance/high rating) shows importance ratings above 4.0 and performance ratings above 4.0. Microwave meals should taste good, and this product scores high on this attribute. Managers often look to this quadrant for attributes that are "hot buttons" that will be useful in positioning the product. The lower quadrants show attributes of low importance to consumers, with either low or high product ratings. This microwave product could be eaten as a late night snack, but this attribute is not important to consumers.

EXHIBIT 20.2 | **QUADRANT ANALYSIS FOR A MICROWAVE MEAL**

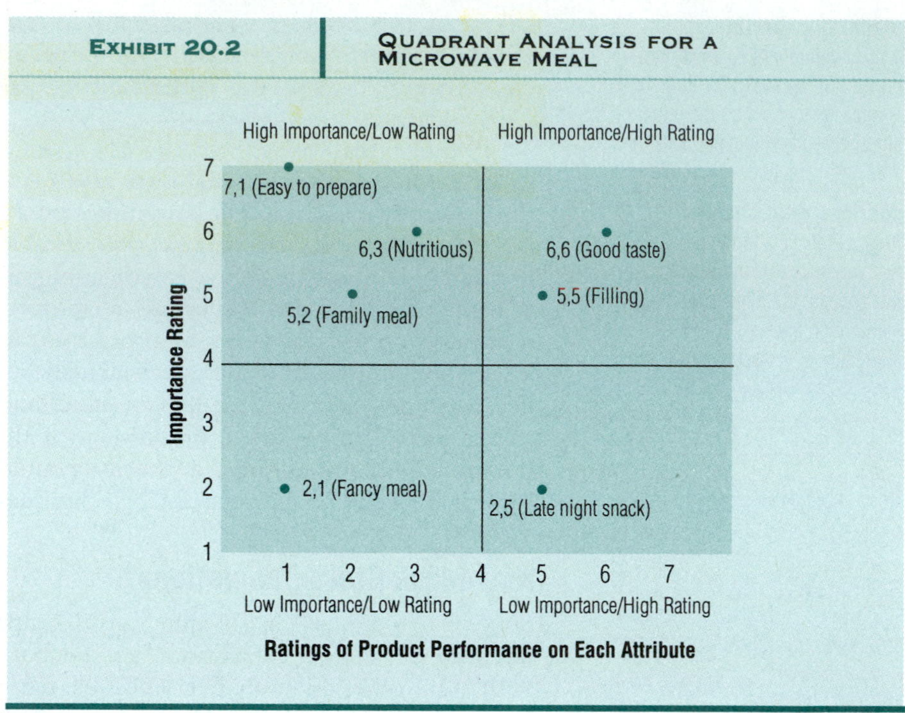

DATA TRANSFORMATION

data transformation
The process of changing data from their original form to a format that better supports data analysis to achieve research objectives. Also called data conversion.

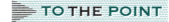

TO THE POINT

All that we do is done with an eye to something else.

ARISTOTLE

Data transformation is the process of changing data from their original form to a format that is more suitable to perform a data analysis that will achieve the research objectives. Researchers often modify the values of scalar data or create new variables. For example, many researchers believe that response bias will be less if interviewers ask consumers for their year of birth rather than their age, even though the objective of the data analysis is to investigate respondents' ages in years. This does not present a problem for the research analyst, because a simple data transformation is possible. The raw data coded as birth year can be easily transformed to age by subtracting the birth year from the current year.

Collapsing or combining adjacent categories of a variable is a common data transformation that reduces the number of categories. Exhibit 20.3 shows an example of a Likert scale item that has been collapsed. The "strongly agree" and the "agree" response categories have been combined. The "strongly disagree" and the "disagree" response categories have also been combined into a single category. The result is the collapsing of the five-category scale down to three.

Creating new variables by respecifying the data with numeric or logical transformations is another important data transformation. For example, Likert summated scales reflect the combination of scores (raw data) from various attitudinal statements. The summative score for an attitude scale with three statements is calculated as follows:

$$\text{Summative Score} = \text{Variable 1} + \text{Variable 2} + \text{Variable 3}$$

This calculation can be accomplished by using simple arithmetic or by programming a computer with a data transformation equation that creates the new variable "summative score."

Exhibit 20.3 | **Collapsing a Five-Category Likert Scale**

Likert Scale as It Appeared on the Questionnaire

Increased foreign investment in the United States poses a threat to our economic independence.

Strongly Agree *Agree* *Neither Agree or Disagree* *Disagree* *Strongly Disagree*

Tabulation of Responses in Original and Collapsed Versions

5-Point Scale	Percentage	Collapsed Scale	Percentage
Strongly Agree	3	Strongly Agree/Agree	15
Agree	12		
Neither Agree nor Disagree	30	Neither Agree nor Disagree	30
Disagree	45	Strongly Disagree/Disagree	55
Strongly Disagree	10		

In many cases, however, the establishment of categories requires careful thought. For example, how does one categorize women on their orientation toward the feminist movement? The first rule for identifying categories, as in other aspects of research, is that the categories should be related to the research problem and purpose.

Index Numbers

index number
Data summary values based on data for some base period to facilitate comparisons over time.

The consumer price index and the wholesale price index are secondary data sources frequently used by business researchers. These price indexes, like other **index numbers,** allow researchers to compare a variable or set of variables in a given time period with another variable or set of variables in another time period. Scores or observations are recalibrated so that they may be related to a certain base period or base number.

Consider the information in Table 20.6 on weekly television viewing (hours:minutes) by household size. Index numbers are computed in the following manner. First, a base number is selected—in this case, the U.S. average of 52 hours and 36 minutes. The index numbers are computed by dividing the

Table 20.6 | **Hours of Television Usage per Week**

Household Size	Hours:Minutes
1	41:01
2	47:58
3+	60:49
Total U.S. average	52:36

score for each category and multiplying by 100. The index shows percentage changes from a base number; for example:

$$\text{1 person:} \quad \frac{41{:}01}{52{:}36} = .7832 \times 100 = 78.32$$

$$\text{2 people:} \quad \frac{47{:}58}{52{:}36} = .9087 \times 100 = 90.87$$

$$\text{3+ people:} \quad \frac{60{:}49}{52{:}36} = 1.1553 \times 100 = 115.53$$

$$\text{Total U.S. average:} \quad \frac{52{:}36}{52{:}36} = 1.0000 \times 100 = 100.00$$

If the data are time-related, a base year is chosen. The index numbers are then computed by dividing each year's activity by the base year activity and multiplying by 100. Index numbers require a ratio scale of measurement.

Calculating Rank Order

Respondents often indicate a rank ordering of brand preference or some other variable of interest to researchers. To summarize these data for all respondents, analysts perform a data transformation by multiplying the frequency times the rank (score) to develop a new scale that represents the summarized rank ordering.

For example, suppose the president of a company had ten executives rank their preferences for "dream destinations" that would be the prize in a productivity contest. Table 20.7 shows how 10 executives ranked each of four locations: Hawaii, Paris, Greece, and China. Table 20.8 tabulates the frequencies of these rankings. To calculate a summary rank ordering, the destination with the first (highest) preference was given the lowest number (1) and the least preferred destination (lowest preference) was given the highest number (4). The summarized rank ordering is obtained with the following calculations:

$$\text{Hawaii:} \quad (3 \times 1) + (5 \times 2) + (1 \times 3) + (1 \times 4) = 20$$

$$\text{Paris:} \quad (3 \times 1) + (1 \times 2) + (3 \times 3) + (3 \times 4) = 26$$

$$\text{Greece:} \quad (2 \times 1) + (2 \times 2) + (4 \times 3) + (2 \times 4) = 26$$

$$\text{China:} \quad (2 \times 1) + (2 \times 2) + (2 \times 3) + (4 \times 4) = 28$$

TABLE 20.7 INDIVIDUAL RANKING OF DREAM DESTINATIONS

Person	Hawaii	Paris	Greece	China
1	1	2	4	3
2	1	3	4	2
3	2	1	3	4
4	2	4	3	1
5	2	1	3	4
6	3	4	1	2
7	2	3	1	4
8	1	4	2	3
9	4	3	2	1
10	2	1	3	4

TABLE 20.8 FREQUENCY TABLE OF DREAM DESTINATION RANKINGS

Destination	PREFERENCE RANKINGS 1st	2nd	3rd	4th
Hawaii	3	5	1	1
Paris	3	1	3	3
Greece	2	2	4	2
China	2	2	2	4

The lowest total score indicates the first (highest) preference ranking. The results show the following rank ordering: (1) Hawaii, (2) Paris, (3) Greece, and (4) China.

TABULAR AND GRAPHIC METHODS OF DISPLAYING DATA

Tables and graphs (pictorial representations of data) may simplify and clarify the research data. Tabular and graphic representations of data may take a number of forms, ranging from computer printouts to elaborate pictographs. The purpose of each table or graph, however, is to facilitate the summarization and communication of the meaning of the data. For example, Table 20.9 illustrates the relationship among education, income, and expenditures on regional airline usage for vacation/pleasure trips. Note that the shaded area emphasizes a

TABLE 20.9 REGIONAL AIRLINE USAGE FOR VACATION/PLEASURE BY INCOME AND EDUCATION

	Total	Under $20,000	$20,000–$39,000	$40,000–$59,000	$60,000 and Over
All Consumers					
Expenditures (%)	100	10	7	16	67
Consumer units (%)	100	42	19	16	23
Index	100	26	36	100	291
Non–High School Grad					
Expenditures (%)	8	1	2	1	4
Consumer units (%)	35	21	6	4	4
Index	21	5	33	25	100
High School Grad					
Expenditures (%)	29	4	2	8	15
Consumer units (%)	30	11	6	6	7
Index	96	36	33	133	214
Attended/graduated College					
Expenditures (%)	63	5	3	7	48
Consumer units (%)	35	10	6	6	13
Index	180	50	50	116	369
				% Pop.	% Expen.
				32 =	78

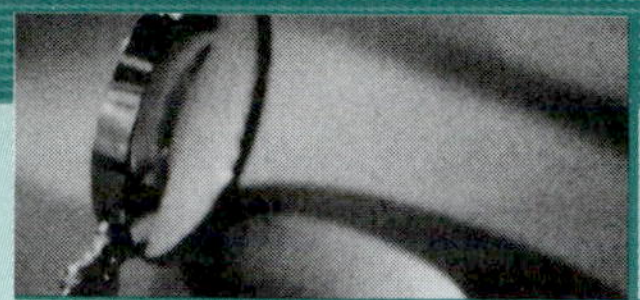

Research Insight

Florence Nightingale: Inventor of the Pie Chart

Florence Nightingale is remembered as a pioneering nurse and hospital reformer.[8] Less well known is her equally pioneering use of statistics. In advocating medical reform Nightingale also promoted statistical description; she developed a uniform procedure for hospitals to report statistical information. She also invented the pie chart, in which proportions are represented as wedges of a circular diagram. Finally, she struggled to get the study of statistics introduced into higher education.

One of Nightingale's analyses compared the peacetime death rates of British soldiers and civilians. She discovered and showed that the soldiers who lived in barracks under unhealthy conditions were twice as likely to die as civilians of the same age and sex. She then used the soldiers' 2 percent death rate to persuade the Queen and the Prime Minister to establish a Royal Commission on the Health of the Army. It is just as criminal, she wrote, for the Army to have a mortality of 20 per 1,000 "as it would be to take 1,100 men per annum out upon Salisbury Plain and shoot them."

key conclusion with respect to market share: The information indicates that 32 percent of the population makes 78 percent of the expenditures. This form of presentation simplifies interpretation.

Although there are a number of standardized forms for presenting data in tables or graphs, the creative researcher can increase the effectiveness of a particular presentation. Bar charts, pie charts, curve diagrams, pictograms, and other graphic forms of presentation create a strong visual impression. (See Chapter 25.)

For example, Exhibit 20.4 shows how a line graph can show comparisons over time. Exhibit 20.5 shows how pie charts and bar charts can enhance information from a survey.

COMPUTER PROGRAMS FOR ANALYSIS

The proliferation of computer technology in businesses and universities has greatly facilitated tabulation and statistical analysis. Commercial statistical packages eliminate the need to write a new program every time you want to tabulate and analyze data with a computer. SAS, Statistical Package for the Social Sciences (SPSS), SYSTAT, and MINITAB are commonly used statistical packages. These user-friendly packages emphasize statistical calculations

EXHIBIT 20.4 LINE GRAPHS HIGHLIGHTING COMPARISONS OVER TIME[9]

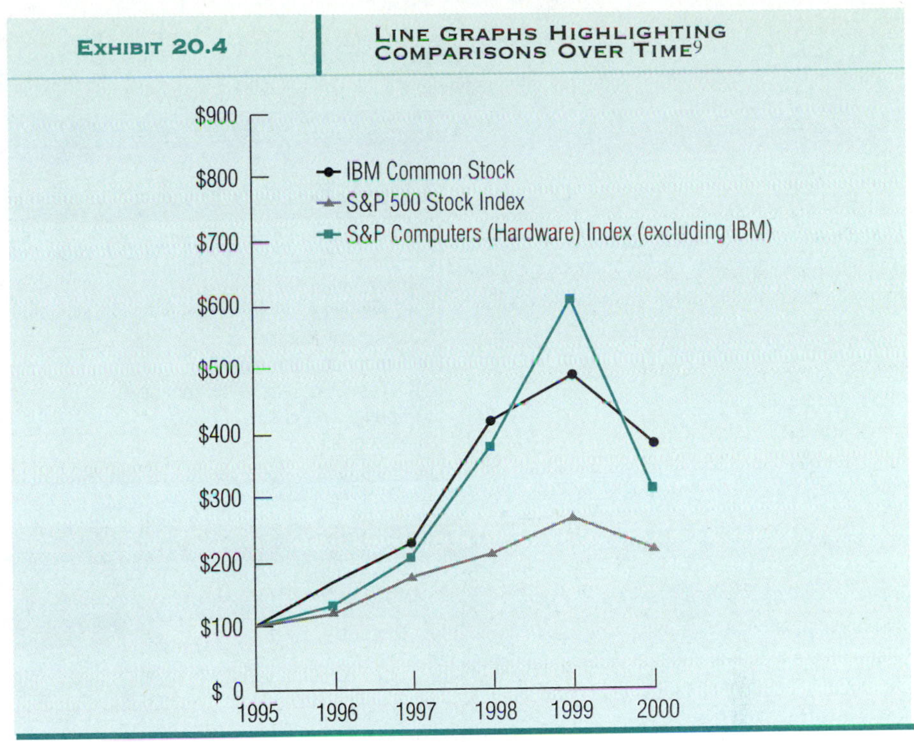

and hypothesis testing for varied types of data. They also provide programs for entering and editing data. Most of these packages contain sizable arrays of programs for descriptive analysis and univariate, bivariate, and multivariate statistical analysis. Several examples will be given in this section to illustrate how easy it is to use these statistical packages.

EXHIBIT 20.5 PIE CHARTS AND BAR GRAPHS ENHANCE VISUAL IMPACT[10]

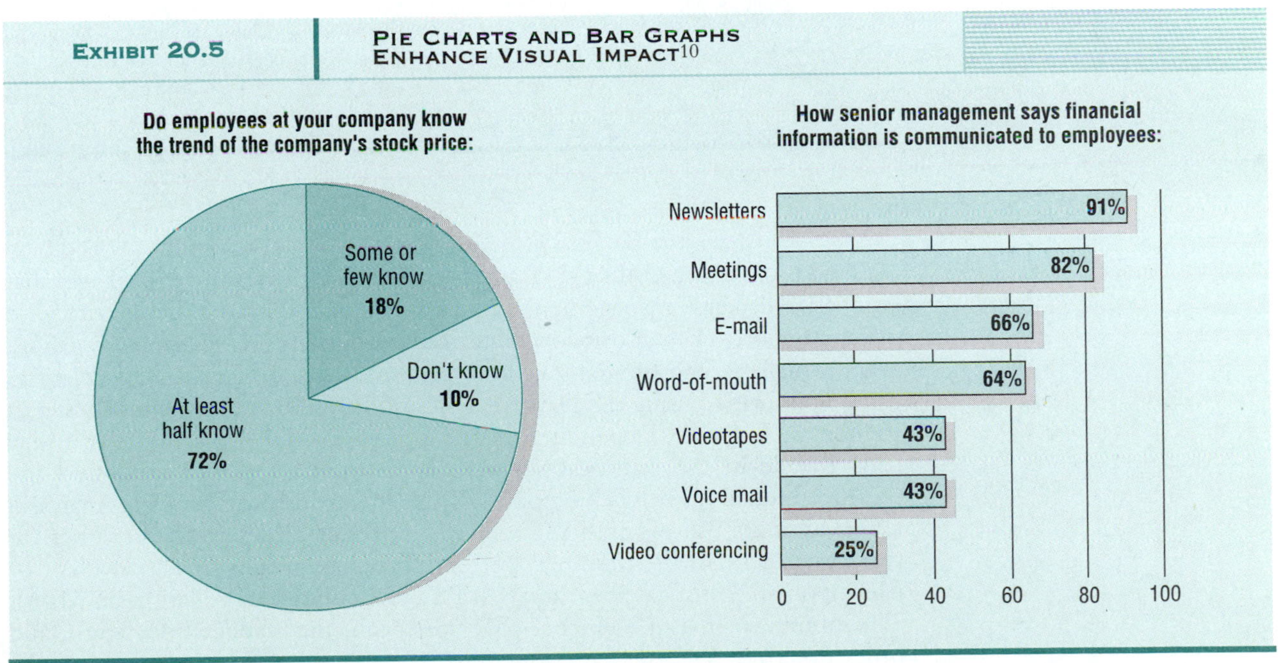

EXHIBIT 20.6 | **EXCEL'S DATA ANALYSIS AND PASTE FUNCTION MENUS FOR STATISTICAL ANALYSIS**

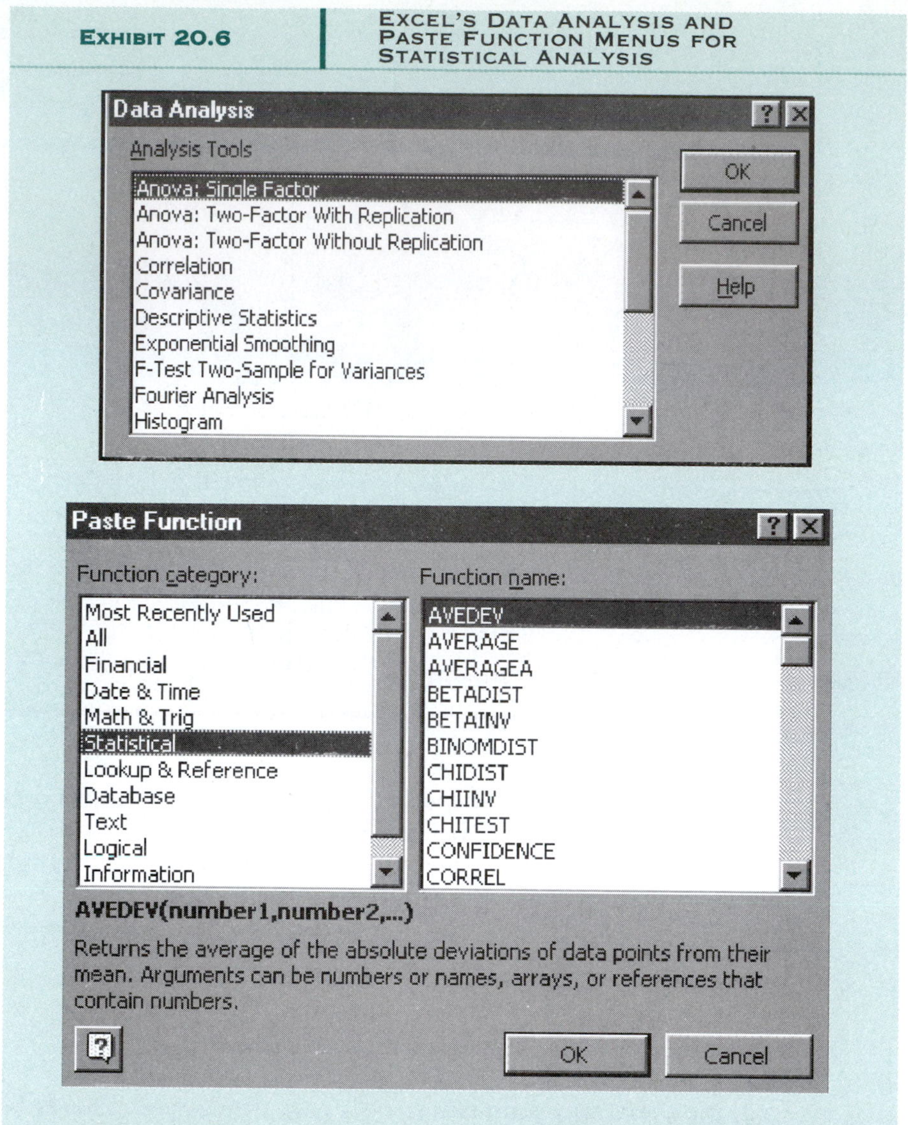

Microsoft Excel, Lotus 1-2-3, and Quatro Pro are spreadsheet packages that emphasize database management and allow a user to enter and edit data with minimal effort. They also incorporate some programs for descriptive analysis, graphic analysis, and limited statistical analysis. In Excel, statistical calculations can be performed using the Data Analysis and Paste Function menus shown in Exhibit 20.6. (Note: Depending on the version of Excel you have, you may have to add-in the statistical software applications. You will then find the enhanced functions by clicking on the Tools menu and then on Data Analysis.)

Exhibit 20.7 shows an SAS computer printout of descriptive statistics for two variables: EMP (number of employees working in an MSA, or Metropolitan Statistical Area) and SALES (sales volume in dollars in an MSA). The numbers of data elements (*N*), the mean, the standard deviation, and other descriptive statistics are displayed.

EXHIBIT 20.7 | **SAS OUTPUT OF DESCRIPTIVE STATISTICS**

State = NY

Variable	**N**	**Mean**	**Standard Deviation**	**Minimum Value**	**Maximum Value**	**STD Error of Mean**	**Sum**	**Variance**	**C.V.**
EMP	10	142.930	232.665	12.8000	788.800	73.575	1429.300	54133.0	162.782
SALES	10	5807.800	11905.127	307.0000	39401.000	3764.732	58078.000	141732049.1	204.985

Key: EMP = Number of employees (000)
SALES = Sales (000)

Exhibit 20.8 presents output from the SPSS package showing the results of a question about confidence in the stock market in a frequency table. This SPSS output gives the absolute frequency of observations, the relative frequency as a percentage of all observations, the valid percentage (the adjusted frequency as a percentage of the number of respondents who provided a recorded answer rather than answering "don't know" or leaving the question blank), and the cumulative percentage.

A histogram is similar to a bar chart. Exhibit 20.9 shows an SPSS histogram plot of purchase price data from a survey. In this histogram, each bar indicates the number of purchasers.

Exhibit 20.10 shows an SPSS cross-tabulation of two variables: gender (GENDER) and satisfaction with daycare (DAYCARE), with the column total used as a basis for percentages.

As you can see, statistical software programs are quite versatile, and they are widely used in business research.

EXHIBIT 20.8 | **SPSS COMPUTER OUTPUT SHOWING FREQUENCIES**

STOCK Confidence in Stock Market

Value Label	Value	Frequency	Percent	Valid Percent	Cum Percent
Yes	1.00	319	59.1	59.4	59.4
No	2.00	218	40.4	40.6	100.0
	.	3	.6	Missing	
	Total	540	100.0	100.0	

Valid cases 537 Missing cases 3

COMPUTER GRAPHICS/COMPUTER MAPPING

Graphic aids prepared by computers are rapidly replacing graphic aids drawn by artists. Computer graphics are extremely useful for descriptive analysis of information stored in databases. Computer-generated graphics and charts may be created inexpensively and quickly with easy-to-use computer software programs such as Power Point or Astound. These software programs are both user-friendly and versatile. Their versatility allows researchers to explore many alternative ways of visually communicating their findings.

EXHIBIT 20.9 | **SPSS HISTOGRAM OUTPUT**[11]

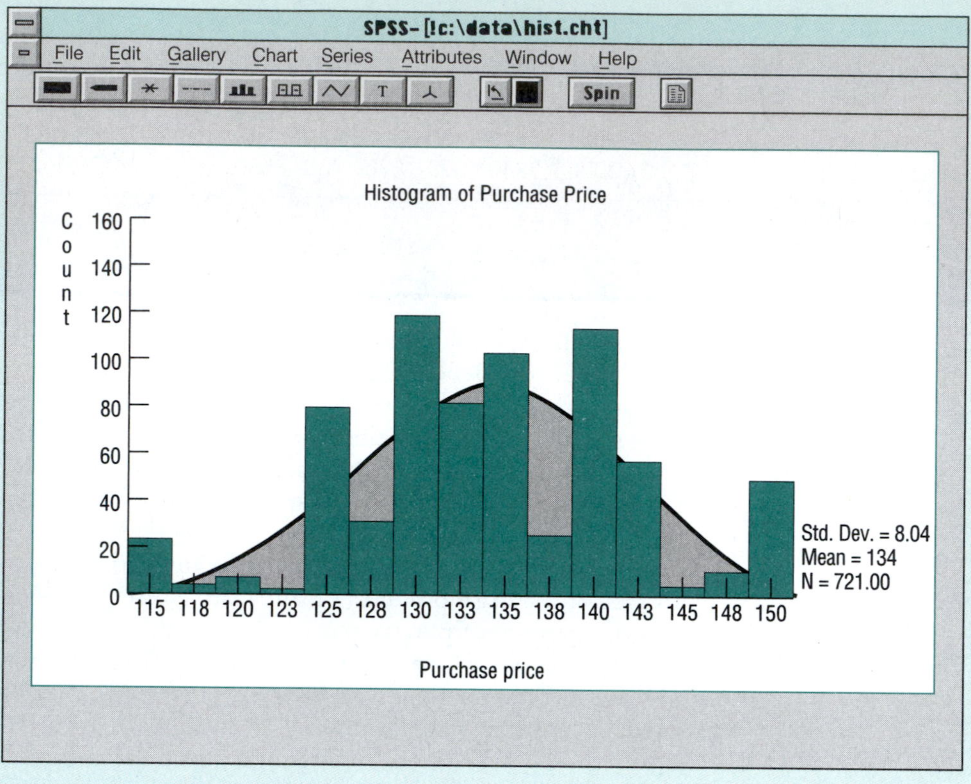

EXHIBIT 20.10 | **SPSS CROSS-TABULATION OUTPUT**

SPSS/PC Cross-Tabulation with Column and Total Percents

Satisfaction with DAYCARE * GENDER Cross-Tabulation

			GENDER		
			women	men	Total
Satisfaction with Daycare	high	Count	9	17	26
		% within GENDER	10.6%	9.2%	9.6%
		% of Total	3.3%	6.3%	9.6%
	low	Count	45	70	115
		% within GENDER	52.9%	37.8%	42.6%
		% of Total	16.7%	25.9%	42.6%
	middle	Count	31	98	129
		% within GENDER	36.5%	53.0%	47.8%
		% of Total	11.5%	36.3%	47.8%
Total		Count	85	185	270
		% within GENDER	100.0%	100.0%	100.0%
		% of Total	31.5%	68.5%	100.0%

computer map
A computer-generated map that portrays a variable, such as demographic data, in two or three dimensions.

Decision support systems can portray data for sales, demographics, lifestyles, production activity, retail activity, and other variables on two- or three-dimensional **computer maps.** For example, in Exhibit 20.11 a computer map displays wiretap surveillance.

Geographic information systems and computer maps have many other uses. When a 911 emergency call comes in, a fire department may use its computer to locate the fire hydrant nearest the fire's location. A city's water department might get a call reporting a water leak near a given intersection and use the geographic information system to map all the water lines and pumps in the area. The information system could also generate a detailed maintenance history on any segment of the water system.[12]

Exhibit 20.11 Computer Graphic Illustrating Wiretap Surveillance Interception by State[13]

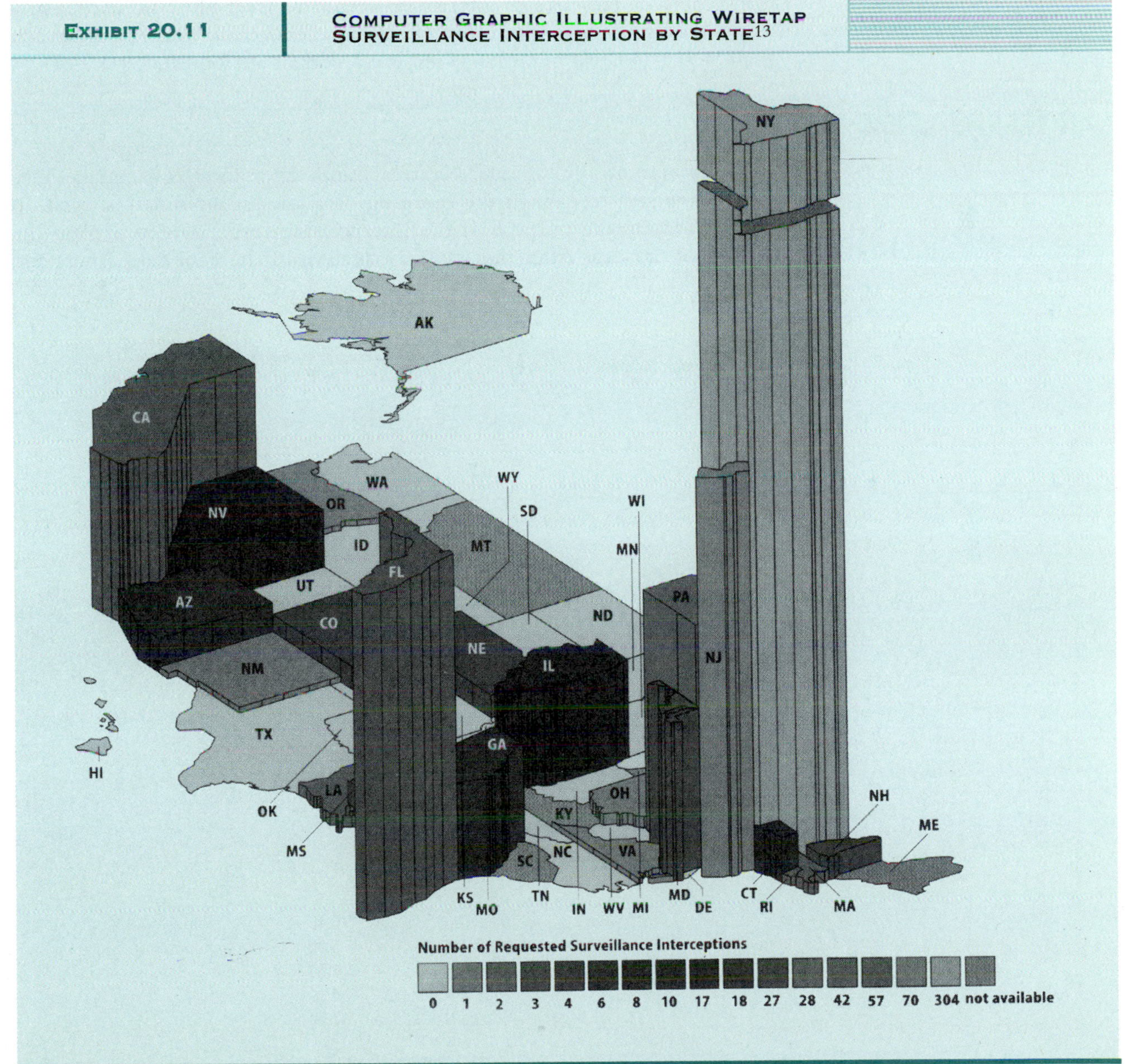

box and whisker plot
A graphic device that represents central tendencies, percentiles, variability, and frequency distributions.

interquartile range
The part of a data distribution between the 25th and 75th percentiles; also called the midspread.

outlier
A value that lies outside the normal range of a set of data.

Many computer programs can draw **box and whisker plots** that graphically represent central tendencies, percentiles, variability, and frequency distributions. Exhibit 20.12 shows a computer-drawn box and whisker plot for 100 responses to a question involving a 10-point scale.[14] The response categories are shown on the vertical axis. The box inside the plot represents 50 percent of the responses; it extends from the 25th percentile to the 75th percentile. This shows a measure of variability sometimes called the **interquartile range,** though the term *midspread* is less complex and more descriptive.[15] The location of the line within the box indicates the median. The dashed lines extending from the top and bottom of the box are the whiskers. Each whisker extends either the length of the box (the midspread in our example is 2 scale points) or to the most extreme observation in that direction. An **outlier** is a value that lies outside the normal range of the data. In Exhibit 20.12, outliers are indicated by either 0s or asterisks. Box and whisker plots are particularly useful for comparing group categories (e.g., men versus women) or several variables (e.g., relative importance levels of product attributes).

INTERPRETATION

An interpreter at the United Nations translates a foreign language into another language to explain the meaning of a foreign diplomat's speech. In business research the purpose of the interpretation process is to explain the meaning of the data. After the statistical analysis of the data, researchers and

EXHIBIT 20.12 COMPUTER-DRAWN BOX AND WHISKER PLOT

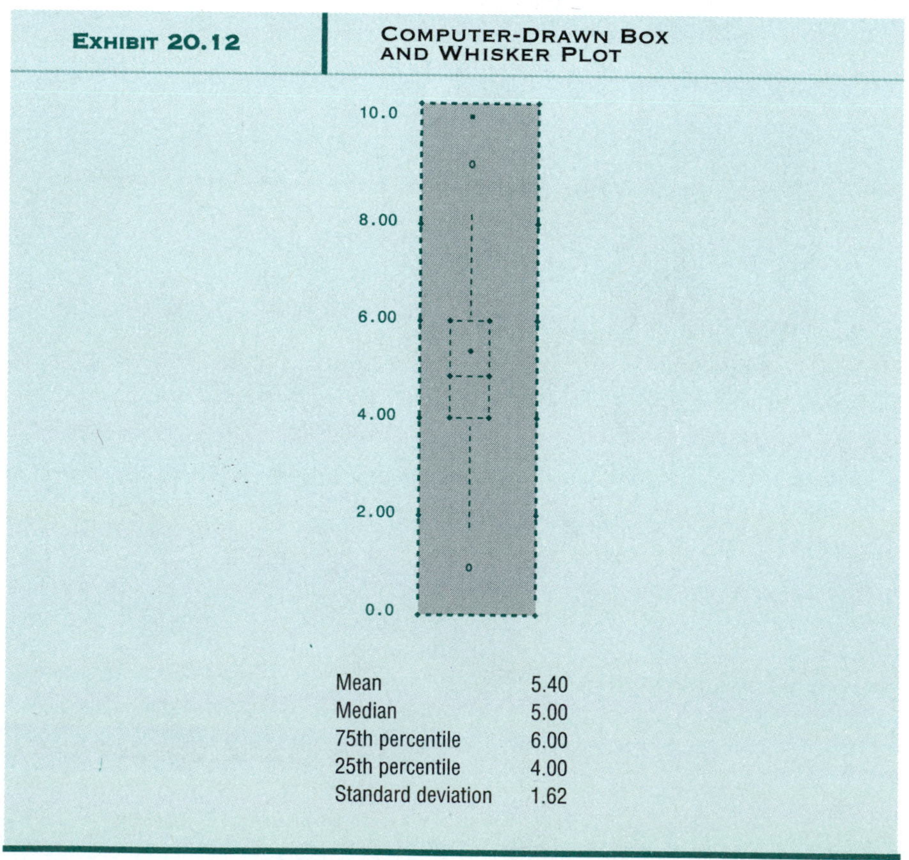

Mean	5.40
Median	5.00
75th percentile	6.00
25th percentile	4.00
Standard deviation	1.62

managers begin to make inferences and formulate conclusions about their meaning.

interpretation
The process of making inferences and drawing conclusions concerning the meaning and implications of a research investigation.

A distinction can be made between *analysis* and *interpretation*. **Interpretation** refers to making inferences pertinent to the meaning and implications of the research investigation and drawing conclusions about the managerial implications of its variables. Of course, the logical interpretation of the data and statistical analysis are closely intertwined. Researchers interpret and analyze at the same time—that is, when a researcher calculates, say, a t-test of two means, he or she almost immediately infers group differences or the existence of a relationship. Almost automatically researchers seek out the significance of the statistical analysis for the research problem as they order, break down, and manipulate the data.[16]

The more we study, the more we discover our ignorance.

PERCY BYSSHE SHELLEY

From a management perspective, however, the qualitative meaning of the data and the managerial implications are important aspects of the interpretation. Consider the crucial role interpretation of the research results played in investigating a new product: a lip stain that could color the lips a desired shade semipermanently and last for a month at a time:

> The lip stain idea, among lipstick wearers, received very high scores on a rating scale ranging from "excellent" to "poor," presumably because it would not wear off. However, it appeared that even among routine wearers of lipstick the idea was being rated highly more for its interesting, even ingenious, nature than for its practical appeal to the consumer's personality. They liked the idea, but for someone else, not themselves. . . . [Careful interpretation of the data] revealed that not being able to remove the stain for that length of time caused most women to consider the idea irrelevant in relation to their own personal needs and desires. Use of the product seems to represent more of a "permanent commitment" than is usually associated with the use of a particular cosmetic. In fact, women attached overtly negative meaning to the product concept, often comparing it with hair dyes instead of a long-lasting lipstick.[17]

This example shows that interpretation is crucial. However, the process is difficult to explain in a textbook because there is no one best way to interpret data. Many possible interpretations of data may be derived from a number of thought processes. Experience with selected cases will help students develop their own interpretative ability.

In all too many instances data are merely reported and not interpreted. Research firms may provide reams of computer output that do not state what the data mean. At the other extreme there are researchers who tend to analyze every possible relationship between each and every variable in the study; they usually have not defined the problem during the earlier stages of research. Researchers who have a clear sense of the purpose of the research do not request statistical analysis of data that may have little or nothing to do with the primary purpose of the research.

SUMMARY

Descriptive analysis refers to the transformation of raw data into an understandable form so that their interpretation will not be difficult. Descriptive information is obtained by summarizing, categorizing, rearranging, and other forms of analysis.

Tabulation refers to the orderly arrangement of data in a table or other summary format. It is useful for indicating percentages and cumulative percentages as well as frequency distributions. The data may be described by measures of central tendency, such as the mean, median, or mode. Cross-tabulation shows how one variable relates to another, revealing differences between groups. Cross-tabulations should be limited to categories related to the research problem and purpose. It is also useful to put the results into percentage form to facilitate intergroup comparisons.

Performing the basic cross-tabulation within various subgroups of the sample is a common form of elaboration analysis. Elaboration analysis often identifies moderator variables or spurious relationships. A moderator variable is a third variable that, when introduced into the analysis, alters or has a contingent effect on the relationship between an independent variable and a dependent variable. A spurious relationship is an apparent relationship between two variables that turns out not to be authentic when a third variable is added to the analysis. Quadrant analysis is a variation of the cross-tabulation table that plots two rating scale questions into four quadrants on a two-dimensional table.

Tables and graphs help to simplify and clarify research data. Computer software greatly facilitates descriptive analysis. Many programs are available that facilitate the construction of graphs and charts. Data transformation is the process of changing data from their original form to a format that is more suitable for data analysis. Index numbers relate data for a particular time period to data for a base year.

Computer mapping portrays demographic, sales, and other data on two- or three-dimensional maps that aid interpretation of descriptive data.

The interpretation of data uses the results of descriptive analysis. Interpretation involves making inferences about the real world and drawing conclusions about the data's managerial implications.

Key Terms

descriptive analysis
simple tabulation
frequency table
percentage
cumulative percentage
frequency distribution
cross-tabulation
contingency table
base (base number)
elaboration analysis
moderator variable
spurious relationship
quadrant analysis
data transformation
index number
computer map
box and whisker plot
interquartile range
outlier
interpretation

Questions for Review and Critical Thinking

1. In a survey respondents were asked to respond to a statement asking if their work was interesting. Interpret the frequency distribution in the SPSS output below.

"My work is interesting."

Category Label	Code	Absolute Frequency	Relative Frequency (Percent)	Adjusted Frequency (Percent)	Cum. Frequency (Percent)
Very true	1	650	23.9	62.4	62.4
Somewhat true	2	303	11.2	29.1	91.5
Not very true	3	61	2.2	5.9	97.3
Not at all true	4	28	1.0	2.7	100.0
		1,673	61.6	Missing	
	Total	2,715	100.0	100.0	

Valid cases 1,042 Missing cases 1,673

2. Use the data in the table below to
   (a) prepare a frequency distribution of respondents' ages and
   (b) cross-tabulate the respondents' genders with cola preference.

Individual	Sex	Age	Cola Preference	Weekly Unit Purchases
John	M	19	Coke	2
Al	M	17	Pepsi	5
Bill	M	20	Pepsi	7
Mary	F	20	Coke	2
Jim	M	18	Coke	4
Bobbie	F	16	Coke	4
Tom	M	17	Pepsi	8
Dawn	F	19	Pepsi	1

3. Data on the average size of a soda (in ounces) at all 30 major league baseball parks are as follows: 14, 18, 20, 16, 16, 12, 14, 16, 14, 16, 16, 16, 14, 14, 16, 20, 12, 16, 20, 12, 16, 16, 24, 16, 16, 14, 14, 12, 14, 20. The results of an Excel Descriptive Statistics analysis of these data are shown on the next page. Interpret the output.

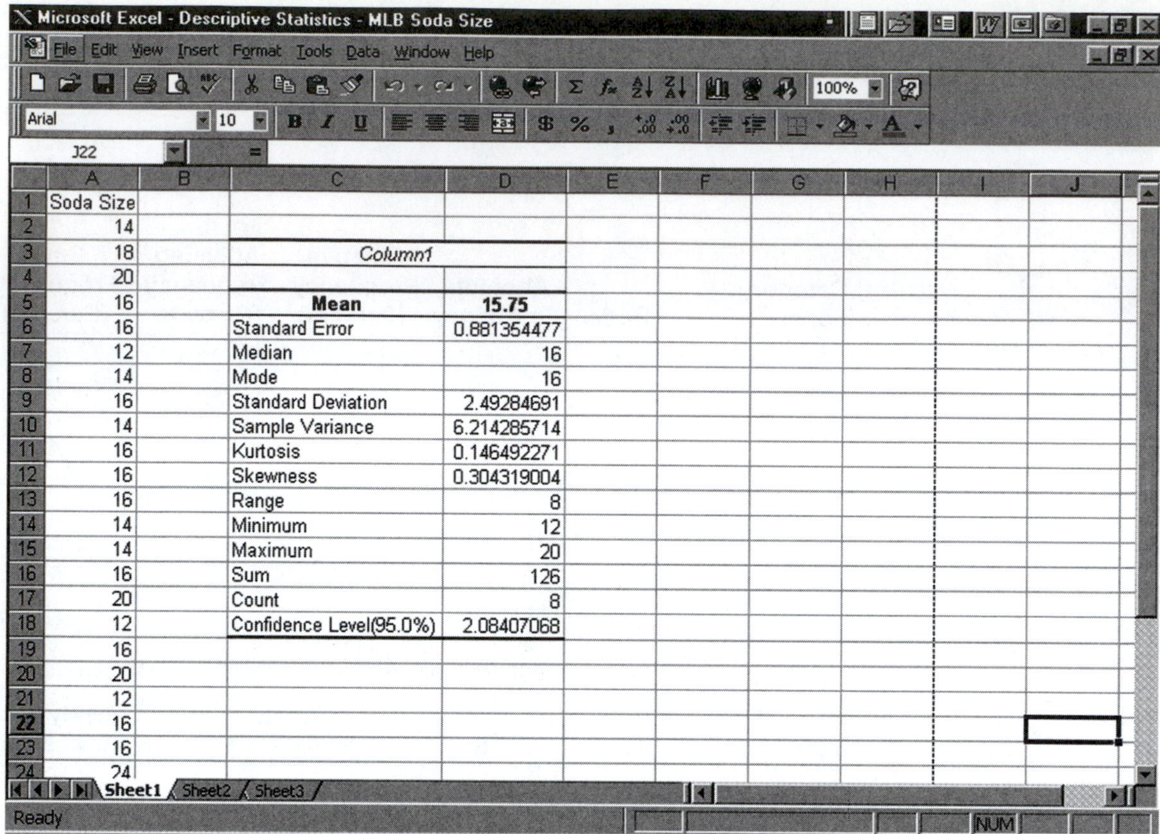
Microsoft Excel - Descriptive Statistics - MLB Soda Size

	A	C	D
1	Soda Size		
2	14		
3	18	*Column1*	
4	20		
5	16	**Mean**	**15.75**
6	16	Standard Error	0.881354477
7	12	Median	16
8	14	Mode	16
9	16	Standard Deviation	2.49284691
10	14	Sample Variance	6.214285714
11	16	Kurtosis	0.146492271
12	16	Skewness	0.304319004
13	16	Range	8
14	14	Minimum	12
15	14	Maximum	20
16	16	Sum	126
17	20	Count	8
18	12	Confidence Level(95.0%)	2.08407068
19	16		
20	20		
21	12		
22	16		
23	16		
24	24		

4. Interpret the following table showing the percentage of individuals on a low-fat or low-cholesterol diet by gender and age.

Age Group	Women	Men	Total
16–24	29%	13%	21%
25–34	43	25	34
35–44	46	28	37
45–54	54	32	43
55+	49	35	43

5. Visit your school's computer center and find out if it has SPSS, SAS, or SYSTAT computer packages.
6. What types of scalar data (that is, nominal, ordinal, interval, or ratio) are typically utilized in cross-tabulation analysis?
7. It has been argued that analysis and interpretation of data are managerial arts. Comment.
8. The data in the following tables are some of the results of an Internal Revenue Service survey of taxpayers. Analyze and interpret the data.

The last year you filed an income tax return, did you get any suggestions or information that was especially helpful to you in filing?

	Absolute Frequency	Relative Frequency (Percent)	Adjusted Frequency (Percent)
Yes	156	29.5	29.8
No	368	69.7	70.2
Don't know	1	.2	Missing
Not ascertained	1	.2	Missing
Blank	2	.4	Missing
	528	100.0	100.0

What kind of information was it?

	Absolute Frequency	Relative Frequency (Percent)	Adjusted Frequency (Percent)
Learned about energy credit	8	1.5	5.4
Learned about another deduction	46	8.7	31.3
Obtained info. about forms to use	9	1.7	6.1
Received pamphlets/forms	40	7.6	27.2
Other	44	8.3	29.9
Don't know	6	1.1	Missing
Not ascertained	2	.4	Missing
Blank	373	70.6	Missing
	528	100.0	100.0

9. A data processing analyst for a research supplier finds that preliminary computer runs of survey results show that consumers love a client's new product. The data processor buys a large block of the client's stock. Is this ethical?

Exploring the Internet

1. The Megapenny Project is located at http://www.kokogiak.com/megapenny/default.asp. Visit this site to get an insight into what large numbers mean.
2. Go to http://www.spss.com and click on Industries and Market Research. What services does the company provide?
3. To see descriptive data analysis in a report on smokeless tobacco, go to the Federal Trade Commission's Bureau of Consumer Protection at http://www.ftc.gov/bcp/reports/smokeless97.htm.
4. Economagic.com's Economic Time Series Page provides links to charts and data for over 68,000 series at http://www.economagic.com.

WebSurveyor Activities

The WebSurveyor Desktop software allows you to control how results are displayed using the Chart Toolbox. Results can be displayed in the following formats: Bar, Horizontal Bar, Pie, Area, Line, Scatter, and Text.

Run the WebSurveyor Desktop software, and click Example Internet Usage Survey under the heading "Open a sample survey with real data" from the Getting Started Wizard. (If the Getting Started Wizard does not appear, click on Tools and then Options from the main menu, make sure "Display the Getting Started Wizard for new surveys" is checked, and then click OK. Next click File and then New from the main menu, and then click Example Internet Usage Survey under the heading "Open a sample survey with real data.")

Using the Chart Toolbox, view the results for question 1 in each format. Which one do you prefer? Why?

Cross Tabulation Analysis

WebSurveyor's cross-tabulation feature allows you to evaluate relationships between responses to two different questions. The Cross Tabs feature of WebSurveyor Desktop is accessed through the Chart Toolbox. First click on Chart Toolbox. You can perform a Cross Tab analysis by selecting a chart type of Text Only on questions of the following types: Select Only One, Select All That Apply, Numeric Values, and Date Values. As soon as you change the chart type to text only, you should see a "Cross Tab" tab appear in the Chart Toolbox.

The Example Internet Usage Survey (Sample3.ws3) was used to create the cross-tabulation shown below.

Using question 1: "How long have you been using the Internet?" from the Example Internet Usage Survey opened above, perform cross-tabulations on gender, marital status, and income.

Filter

Using a filter is a great way to temporarily isolate parts of your data—for example, to view only the responses from those who answered "Male" to the question of gender and "Between 35 and 45" to the question of age.

When a filter is applied, it affects all of the analysis, reports, and data exports. You can create a filter by clicking the Set Filter . . . button in the Analysis window. Use question 6 and view only the female answers. If you understand the operation, use the filter to view the answers of divorced females.

Old School or New School

As mentioned in Chapter 14, three academic researchers investigated the idea that, in America in sports, there are two segments with opposing views on what constitutes the goal of competition (i.e., winning versus self-actualization) and the acceptable/desirable way of achieving this goal.[18] People who believe in "winning at any cost" are proponents of sports success as a product and can be labeled "new school" (NS) individuals. The new school is founded on notions of the player before the team, loyalty to the highest bidder, and high-tech production and consumption of professional sports. On the other hand, people who value the process of sports and believe that "how you play the game matters" can be labeled "old school" (OS) individuals. The old school emerges from old-fashioned American notions of the team before the player, sportsmanship and loyalty above all else, and competition simply for "love of the game." The sample was drawn from attendees at a university spring season football intra-squad scrimmage.

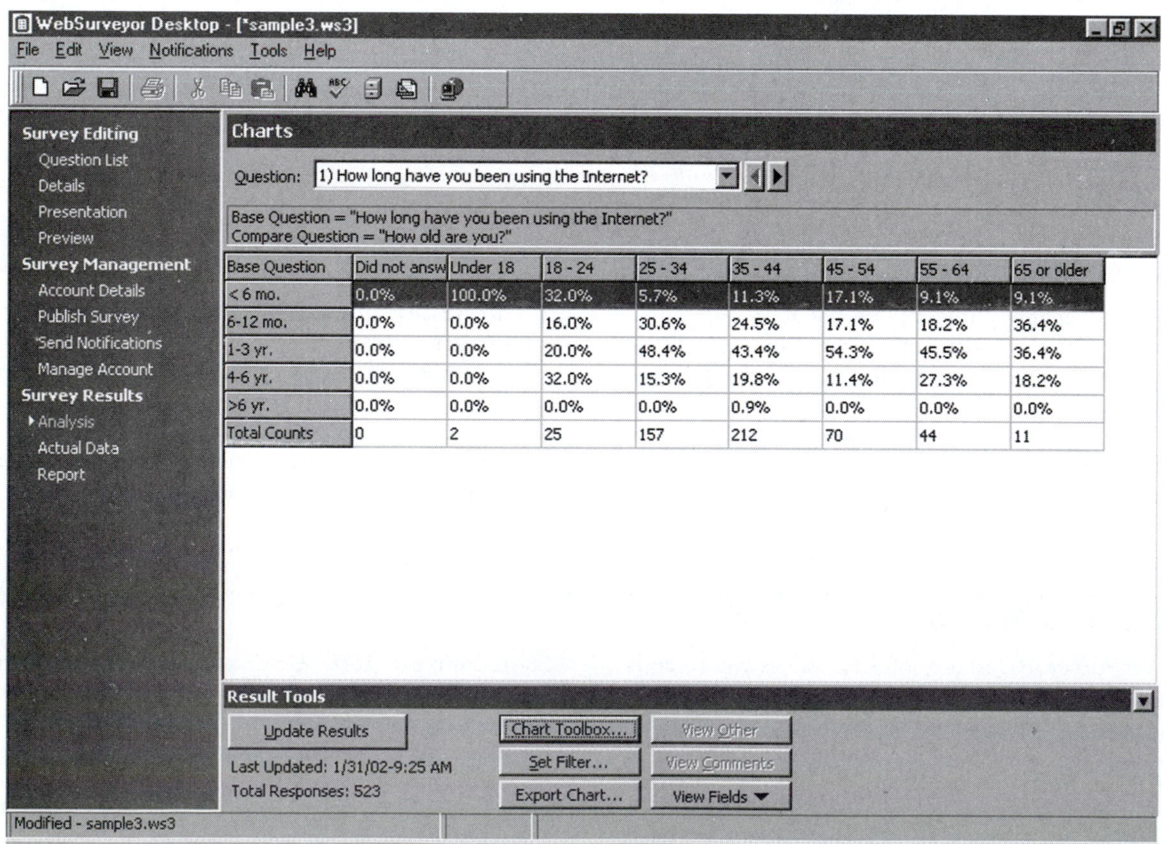

Base Question	Did not answ	Under 18	18 - 24	25 - 34	35 - 44	45 - 54	55 - 64	65 or older
< 6 mo.	0.0%	100.0%	32.0%	5.7%	11.3%	17.1%	9.1%	9.1%
6-12 mo.	0.0%	0.0%	16.0%	30.6%	24.5%	17.1%	18.2%	36.4%
1-3 yr.	0.0%	0.0%	20.0%	48.4%	43.4%	54.3%	45.5%	36.4%
4-6 yr.	0.0%	0.0%	32.0%	15.3%	19.8%	11.4%	27.3%	18.2%
>6 yr.	0.0%	0.0%	0.0%	0.0%	0.9%	0.0%	0.0%	0.0%
Total Counts	0	2	25	157	212	70	44	11

Open the survey using the WebSurveyor Desktop software by selecting File and then Open from the main menu, select the file named "Sports.ws3" and go to Analysis. Select three questions (perhaps "most professional athletes have become too materialistic," "have no sense of loyalty to the team," and "are more interested in making money than playing the game"). Prepare a frequency distribution for each question and write a short report.

2001 Marketing Professionals Salary Survey Open the 2001 Marketing Professionals Salary Survey using the WebSurveyor Desktop software. Click Analysis and go to the question "How did you find your last job?" What conclusions can you draw from the answers to this question?

Case Suggestions

Case 25: The Multiplex Company
Case 26: Survey on Americans and Dietary Supplements
Case 29: LastDance Health Care
Case 30: Sunbelt Energy Corporation
Case 31: Employees Federal Credit Union

CHAPTER

21

UNIVARIATE STATISTICS

What you will learn in this chapter

- To define a statistical hypothesis.
- To define terms such as *null hypothesis, significance level,* and *degrees of freedom.*
- To recognize the statistical notation associated with the null hypothesis and alternative hypothesis.
- To discuss the steps in the hypothesis-testing procedure.
- To compute a hypothesis test about a mean when the sample size is large.
- To distinguish a Type I and a Type II error.
- To describe the factors that influence the choice of which method of statistical analysis to use.
- To distinguish between parametric and nonparametric hypothesis tests.
- To discuss the nature of the *t*-distribution.
- To calculate a hypothesis test about a mean utilizing the *t*-distribution.
- To explain in which situations a univariate chi-square test would be appropriate and how to perform this test.
- To calculate a hypothesis test about a proportion using the *Z*-distribution.

In Chapter 20 we saw that the average annual number of trips taken by a business traveler was 15. This figure is the finding of descriptive analysis. How reliable is this estimate? Suppose a manager at a travel agency assumed the average number of trips was 18. Would this assumption be untenable? Is it reasonable to accept that figure from descriptive analysis? Is it possible to go beyond the simple tabulation of frequencies and the calculation of averages to find some sort of criterion for answering questions about differences between what one expected to find and the actual results of research? This chapter attempts to provide answers to questions such as these.

As we already discussed, for most projects analysis begins with some form of descriptive analysis to reduce the raw data into a summary format. Often researchers wish to go beyond the simple tabulation of frequency distributions and calculation of averages: When the research focuses on *one variable at a time,* they frequently conduct *univariate tests of statistical significance.* The foundation of univariate statistical estimation of parameters involves hypothesis testing. ■

STATING A HYPOTHESIS

What Is a Hypothesis?

hypothesis
An unproven proposition or supposition that tentatively explains certain facts or phenomena; a proposition that is empirically testable.

In statistical theory a **hypothesis** is an unproven proposition or supposition that tentatively explains certain facts or phenomena. A hypothesis is a statement, an assumption about the nature of the world. In its simplest form a hypothesis is a guess. An R&D manager may hypothesize that engineers highest in technical knowledge will be the most productive. A personnel manager may believe that if attitudes toward job security are changed in a positive direction, there will be an increase in employee retention. With statistical techniques we are able to decide whether or not our theoretical hypotheses are confirmed by the empirical evidence.

The Null Hypothesis and the Alternative Hypothesis

null hypothesis
A statement about a status quo asserting that any change from what has been thought to be true will be due entirely to random error.

alternative hypothesis
A statement indicating the opposite of the null hypothesis.

Because scientists should be bold in conjecturing but extremely cautious in testing, statistical hypotheses are generally stated in a null form. A **null hypothesis** is a statement about a status quo. It is a conservative statement that communicates the notion that any change from what has been thought to be true or observed in the past will be due entirely to random error. In fact, the true purpose of setting up the null hypothesis is to provide an opportunity to nullify it. For example, suppose academic researchers expect that highly dogmatic (i.e., closed-minded) individuals will be less likely to try an innovative management technique than less dogmatic individuals. They will generally formulate a conservative null hypothesis. The null hypothesis in this case would be that there is no difference between "high dogmatics" and "low dogmatics" in their willingness to try an innovation. The **alternative hypothesis** would be that there is a difference between high and low dogmatics—that is, it states the opposite of the null hypothesis.

HYPOTHESIS TESTING

We generally assign the symbol H_0 to the null hypothesis and the symbol H_1 to the alternative hypothesis. The purpose of hypothesis testing is to determine which of the two hypotheses is correct. The procedure of hypothesis testing is slightly more complicated than estimating parameters because the decision maker must make a choice between the two hypotheses. However, the student need not worry, because the mathematical calculations are no more difficult than the calculations we have already made.

Hypothesis-Testing Procedure

The process of hypothesis testing goes as follows. First, a statistical hypothesis is determined. We then imagine what the sampling distribution of the mean would be if this hypothesis were a true statement of the nature of the population. Next, we take an actual sample and calculate the sample mean (or appropriate statistic, if we are not concerned about the mean). We know from our previous discussions of the sampling distribution of the mean that obtaining a sample value exactly the same as the population parameter would be highly unlikely. We expect some small difference (although it may be large) between the sample mean and the population mean. We then must determine if the deviation between the obtained value of the sample mean and its

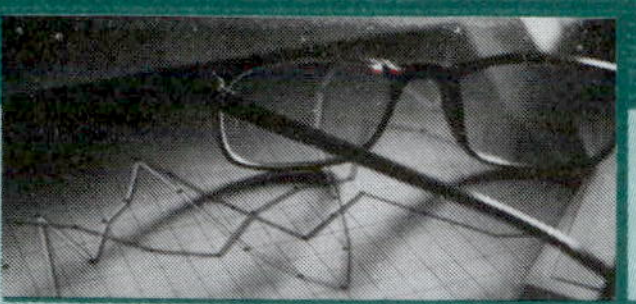

Statistical Tutor

TYPICAL HYPOTHESIS TEST

THE SITUATION:

A hardware franchise has almost 1,000 retail outlets. Monthly sales of a particular tool averaged 612 units for each franchise. The sales manager believed a competitor's new price on a similar item may have an impact on sales. Based on a random sample of 64 franchises, the sales manager wishes to test if the observed sample mean differs from the benchmark figure.

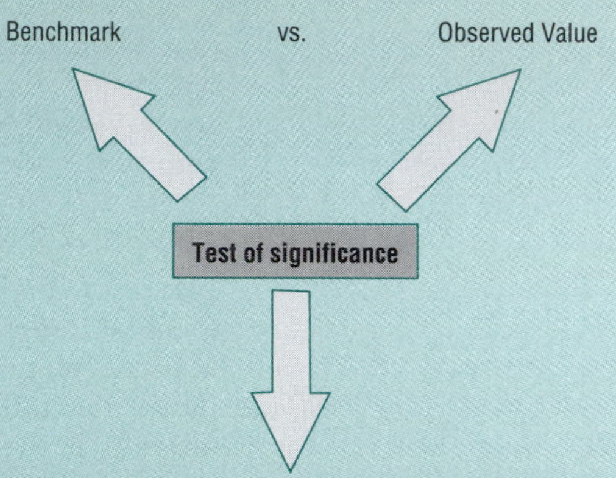

QUESTIONS TO BE ANSWERED:

1. Is the difference between the benchmark and the observed values statistically significant?
2. Does the *magnitude* of the increase (or decrease) in the phenomenon or behavior justify a change in the business strategy?

expected value (based on the statistical hypothesis) would have occurred by chance alone—say 5 times out of 100—if the statistical hypothesis were true.

In other words, we ask the question: "Has the sample mean deviated substantially from the mean of the hypothesized sampling distribution by a large enough value to conclude that this large a deviation would be somewhat rare if the statistical hypothesis were true?" Suppose we observe that the sample value differs from the expected value. Before we can conclude that these results are improbable (or possibly probable), we must have some standard, or *decision rule,* to determine if, in fact, we should reject the null hypothesis and accept the alternative hypothesis. Statisticians have defined the decision criterion as the significance level.

significance level
The critical probability in choosing between the null and alternative hypotheses; the probability level that is too low to warrant support of the null hypothesis.

The **significance level** is a critical probability in choosing between the null hypothesis and the alternative hypothesis. The level of significance determines the probability level—say .05 or .01—that is to be considered too low to warrant support of the null hypothesis. On the assumption that the null hypothesis being tested is true, if the probability of occurrence of the observed data is *smaller* than the level of significance, then the data suggest the null hypothesis should be rejected. In other words, there is evidence to support contradiction of the null hypothesis, which is equivalent to supporting the alternative hypothesis.

The terminology utilized in discussing confidence intervals identifies what we call the *confidence level* or a *confidence coefficient*. The confidence interval may be regarded as the set of acceptable hypotheses or the level of probability associated with an interval estimate. However, when discussing hypothesis testing, statisticians change their terminology and call this the level of significance α (Greek letter alpha).

An Example of Hypothesis Testing

An example should help to clarify the nature of hypothesis testing. Suppose that the Red Lion restaurant is concerned about its image, one aspect of which is the friendliness of the service at the restaurant. In a personal interview customers were asked to indicate their perception of service on a five-point scale, where 1 indicated very unfriendly service and 5 indicated very friendly service. The scale was assumed to be an interval scale, and experience had shown that the previous distribution of this attitudinal measurement for assessing the service dimension was approximately normal. Now suppose that the researcher entertains the hypothesis that customers feel the service at the restaurant is neither friendly nor unfriendly. The researcher formulates the null hypothesis that the mean is equal to 3.0:

$$H_0: \mu = 3.0$$

The alternative hypothesis is that the mean does *not* equal 3.0:

$$H_1: \mu \neq 3.0$$

Next, the researcher must decide on a region of rejection. Exhibit 21.1 shows a sampling distribution of the mean assuming the null hypothesis—that is, assuming $\mu = 3.0$. The darker shaded area shows the region of rejection when $\alpha = .025$ in each tail of the curve. In other words, the *region of rejection* shows those values that are very unlikely to occur if the null hypothesis is true, but relatively probable if the alternative hypothesis is true. The values within the lighter shaded area are called *acceptable at the 95 percent confidence level* (or 5 percent significance level, .05 alpha level), and if we find that our sample mean

EXHIBIT 21.1 A SAMPLING DISTRIBUTION OF THE MEAN ASSUMING $\mu = 3.0$

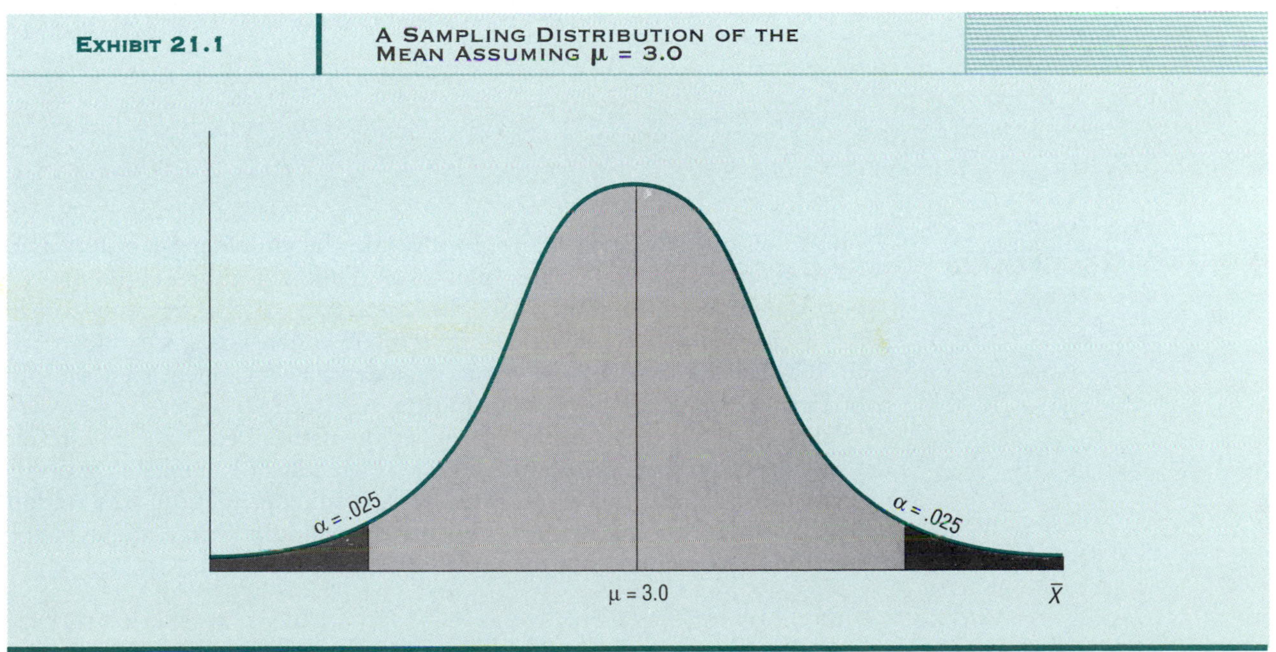

lies within this region of acceptance, we would conclude that the null hypothesis is true. More precisely, we fail to disprove the null hypothesis. In other words, the range of acceptance (1) identifies those acceptable values that reflect a difference from the hypothesized mean in the null hypothesis and (2) shows the range within which any difference is so minuscule that we would conclude that this difference was due to random sampling error rather than to a false null hypothesis.

In our example, the Red Lion restaurant hired research consultants who collected a sample of 225 interviews. The mean score on the five-point scale, $\bar{X}$, equaled 3.78. (If σ is known, it is utilized in the analysis; however, this is rarely true, and was not true in this case.)[1] The sample standard deviation was $S = 1.5$. Now we have enough information to test the hypothesis.

The researchers decided that the decision rule would be to set the significance level at the .05 level. This means that in the long run the probability of making an erroneous decision when H_0 is true will be fewer than 5 times in 100 (.05). From the standardized normal distribution table, the researchers find that the Z-score of 1.96 represented a probability of .025 that a sample mean will lie above 1.96 standard errors from μ. Likewise, the table shows that about .025 of all sample means will fall below -1.96 standard errors from μ.

critical values
The values that lie exactly on the boundary of the region of rejection.

The values that lie exactly on the boundary of the region of rejection are called the **critical values** of μ. Theoretically, the critical values are $Z = -1.96$ and $+1.96$. Now we must transform these critical Z-values to the sampling distribution of the mean for this image study. The critical values are

$$\begin{aligned}\text{Critical value—lower limit} &= \mu - ZS_{\bar{X}} \text{ or } \mu - Z\frac{S}{\sqrt{n}} \\ &= 3.0 - 1.96\left(\frac{1.5}{\sqrt{225}}\right) \\ &= 3.0 - 1.96(.1) \\ &= 3.0 - .196 \\ &= 2.804\end{aligned}$$

$$\begin{aligned}\text{Critical value—upper limit} &= \mu + ZS_{\bar{X}} \text{ or } \mu + Z\frac{S}{\sqrt{n}} \\ &= 3.0 + 1.96\left(\frac{1.5}{\sqrt{225}}\right) \\ &= 3.0 + 1.96(.1) \\ &= 3.0 + .196 \\ &= 3.196\end{aligned}$$

A little inaccuracy sometimes saves a ton of explanation.

H. H. MUNRO (SAKI)

Based on the survey, $\bar{X} = 3.78$. In this case, the sample mean is contained in the region of rejection (see Exhibit 21.2). Thus, since the sample mean is greater than the critical value, 3.196, the researchers say that the sample result is statistically significant beyond the .05 level. In other words, fewer than 5 of each 100 samples would show results that deviate this much from the null hypothesis, when in fact H_0 is actually true.

What does this mean to the management of the Red Lion? The results indicate that customers believe the service is friendly. It is unlikely (probability of less than 5 times in 100) that this result would occur because of random sampling error. This means that the restaurant should worry about factors other than the friendliness of the service personnel.

EXHIBIT 21.2 THE SAMPLING DISTRIBUTION OF X UNDER THE HYPOTHESIS OF $\mu = 3.0$

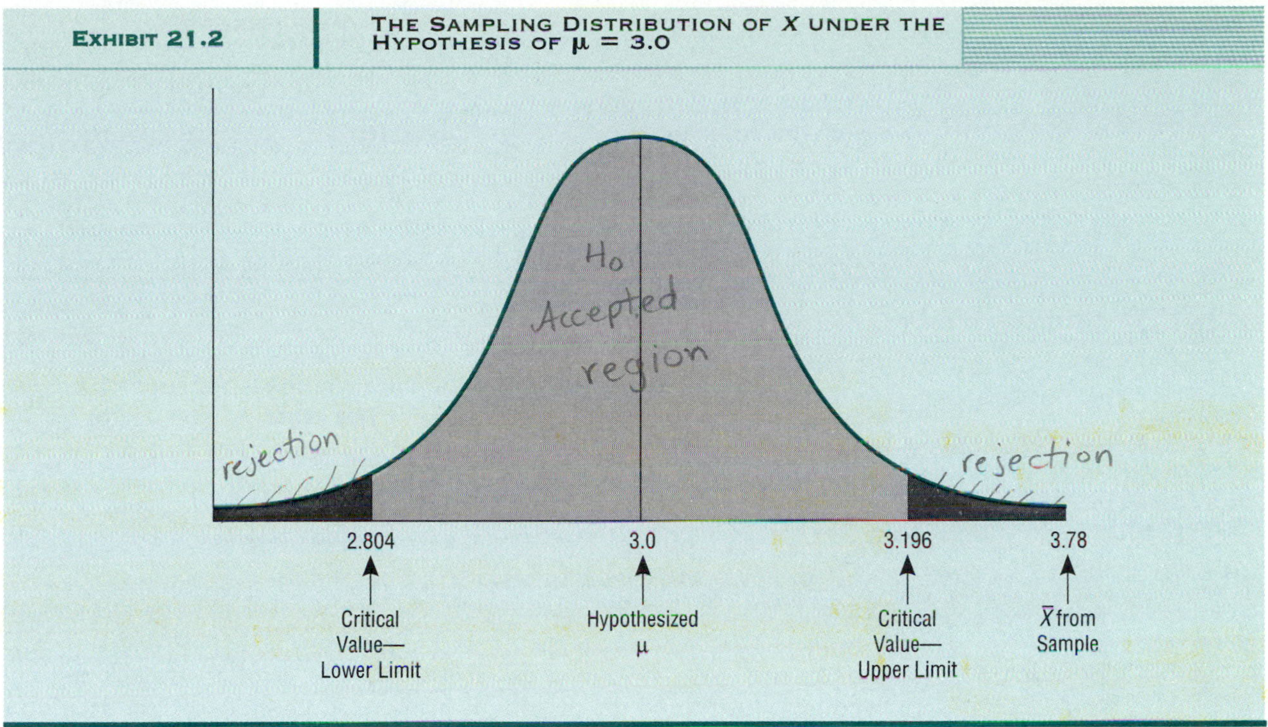

An alternative way of testing the hypothesis is to formulate the decision rule in terms of the Z-statistic. Using the formula below, we can calculate the observed value of the Z-statistic, given a certain sample mean, $\bar{X}$:

$$
\begin{aligned}
Z_{\text{obs}} &= \frac{\bar{X} - \mu}{S_{\bar{X}}} \\
&= \frac{3.78 - \mu}{S_{\bar{X}}} \\
&= \frac{3.78 - 3.0}{.1} = \frac{.78}{.1} = 7.8
\end{aligned}
$$

In this case, the Z-value is 7.8, and we find that we have met the criterion of statistical significance at the .05 level. As a matter of fact, this result is statistically significant at the .000001 level.

Type I and Type II Errors

Hypothesis testing, as we have previously stated, is based on probability theory. Because we cannot make any statement about a sample with complete certainty, there is always the chance that an error will be made. In fact, the researcher runs the risk of committing two types of errors. Exhibit 21.3 summarizes the state of affairs in the population and the nature of Type I and Type II errors. The four possible situations in the table result because the null hypothesis can be either true or false and the statistical decision will be either to accept or to reject the null hypothesis.

EXHIBIT 21.3	TYPE I AND TYPE II ERRORS IN HYPOTHESIS TESTING	
State of Null Hypothesis in the Population	**DECISION**	
	Accept H_0	**Reject H_0**
H_0 is true	Correct—no error	Type I error
H_0 is false	Type II error	Correct—no error

Type I error
An error caused by rejecting the null hypothesis when it is true.

If the decision is made to reject the null hypothesis and, in fact, the null hypothesis is true, we make what is called a **Type I error.** A Type I error has the probability of alpha (α), the level of statistical significance that the decision maker has set up. Simply put, a Type I error occurs when the researcher concludes that there is a statistically significant difference when in reality one does not exist.

Type II error
An error caused by failing to reject the null hypothesis when the alternative hypothesis is true.

If the alternative hypothesis is, in fact, true (and the null hypothesis is actually false) but the decision maker concludes that we should not reject the null hypothesis, then we make what is called a **Type II error.** The probability of making this incorrect decision is called *beta* (β). No error is made if the null hypothesis is true and the decision is made to accept it. A correct decision is also made if the null hypothesis is false and the decision is made to reject the null hypothesis.

Unfortunately, without increasing sample size, the researcher cannot simultaneously reduce Type I and Type II errors, because there is an inverse relationship between these two types of errors. Thus, reducing the probability of a Type II error increases the probability of a Type I error. In business problems, Type I errors are generally more serious than Type II errors, and thus there is greater concern with determining the significance level, alpha, than with determining beta.[2]

CHOOSING THE APPROPRIATE STATISTICAL TECHNIQUE

Now that one statistical technique for hypothesis testing has been illustrated, note that there are a number of statistical techniques to assist the researcher in interpreting data. The choice of the appropriate method of statistical analysis depends on (1) the type of question to be answered, (2) the number of variables, and (3) the scale of measurement.

Type of Question to Be Answered

The type of question the researcher is attempting to answer is a consideration in the choice of statistical technique. For example, a researcher may be concerned about the central tendency of a variable or about the distribution of that variable. Comparison of two divisions' average sales will require a *t*-test of two means, whereas a comparison of the quarterly sales distributions over a year's period will require a chi-square test.

The choice of research design and the type of data to collect should take into consideration the method of statistical analysis. Once the data have been collected, the initial orientation toward analysis of the problem will be reflected in the research design.

univariate data analysis
A type of analysis that assesses the statistical significance of a hypothesis about a single variable.

bivariate data analysis
A type of analysis and hypothesis testing used in the simultaneous investigation of two variables using tests of differences or measures of association between two variables at a time.

multivariate data analysis
Statistical methods that allow the simultaneous investigation of more than two variables.

Number of Variables

The number of variables that will be investigated simultaneously is a primary consideration in the choice of statistical techniques. A researcher who is interested only in the average number of times a prospective home buyer visits financial institutions to shop for interest rates can concentrate on investigating only one variable at a time. **Univariate data analysis** is conducted when the researchers wish to generalize from a sample about one variable at a time.

Statistically describing the relationship between two variables at one time, such as the relationship between gross national product (GNP) and sales volume, requires **bivariate data analysis.** Tests of differences and measuring the association between variables are bivariate topics, discussed in Chapters 22 and 23.

Multivariate data analysis is the simultaneous investigation of more than two variables. Predicting sales volumes on the basis of advertising expenditure and other variables, such as gross national product and number of people in the sales area, is an example of multivariate analysis.

Scale of Measurement

The scale of measurement on which the data are based or the type of measurement reflected in the data determines the permissible statistical techniques and the appropriate empirical operations that may be performed (see Exhibit 21.4). Testing a hypothesis about a mean, as we have just discussed, requires interval- or ratio-scaled data. Suppose a researcher is concerned with a nominal scale that identifies members versus nonmembers of the Teamsters union. Because of the type of scale, the researcher must use the mode as the measure of central tendency.

In other situations, the median may be used as the average, or percentiles may be used as measures of dispersion because the data are measured on an ordinal scale. For example, the ranking of the riskiness of securities generally uses an ordinal scale.

Parametric versus Nonparametric Hypothesis Tests

parametric statistical procedures
Statistical procedures that use interval-scaled or ratio-scaled data and assume populations or sampling distributions with normal distributions.

The terms *parametric statistics* and *nonparametric statistics* refer to the two major groupings of statistical procedures. The major distinction between these two groups of procedures lies in the underlying assumptions about the data to be analyzed.

When the data are interval- or ratio-scaled and the sample size is large, **parametric statistical procedures** are appropriate. These procedures are based on the assumption that the data in the study are drawn from populations with

EXHIBIT 21.4 MEASURES OF CENTRAL TENDENCY AND DISPERSION PERMISSIBLE WITH EACH TYPE OF MEASUREMENT SCALE

Type of Scale	Measure of Central Tendency	Measure of Dispersion
Nominal	Mode	None
Ordinal	Median	Percentile
Interval or ratio	Mean	Standard deviation

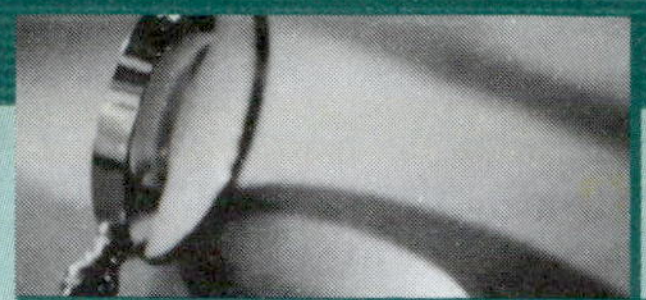

Research Insight

Type I and Type II Errors in the Legal Profession

Although most attorneys and judges do not concern themselves with the statistical terminology of Type I and Type II errors, they do follow this logic. For example, our legal system is based on the concept that a person is innocent until proven guilty. Assume that the null hypothesis is that the person is innocent. If we make a Type I error, we send an innocent person to prison. Our legal system takes many precautions to avoid Type I errors. A person is innocent until proven guilty. A Type II error would occur if a guilty party were set free (the null hypothesis was accepted). Our society places such a high value on avoiding Type I errors that Type II errors are more likely to occur.

normal (bell-shaped) distributions and/or normal sampling distributions. For example, if an investigator has two interval- or ratio-scaled measures, such as gross national product and industry sales volume, it is appropriate to use parametric tests to make a comparison of the intervals. Among the possible statistical tests are *Z*-test (or *t*-test) for a hypothesis about a mean, product-moment correlation analysis, and analysis of variance tests.

nonparametric statistical procedures
Statistical procedures that use nominal- or ordinal-scaled data and make no assumptions about the distribution of the population (or sampling distribution)

When researchers do not make this assumption of normality, it is appropriate to use **nonparametric statistical procedures.** When data are either ordinal or nominal, it is generally inappropriate to make the assumption that the sampling distribution is normal (thus nonparametric statistics are referred to as *distribution-free*).[3] Data analysis of both nominal and ordinal scales typically uses nonparametric statistical tests.

Exhibit 21.5 presents some guidelines for selecting the appropriate univariate statistical method. Although you may not be familiar with most of the statistical tests, the table is meant to illustrate that there are a number of statistical techniques that vary according to the properties of the scale. Similar tables showing examples of the selection of appropriate bivariate and multivariate statistical techniques will be shown in the next three chapters. The appropriate technique will depend both on the properties of the scale and on the number of variables investigated. The actual selection of a univariate statistical test involves many potential choices, because there are more alternatives than illustrated in Exhibit 21.5. A complete discussion of all the relevant techniques is beyond the scope of the discussion at this point.

t-DISTRIBUTION

***t*-distribution**
A family of symmetrical, bell-shaped distributions with a mean of 0 and a standard deviation of 1, used when the population standard deviation is unknown or when testing a hypothesis with a small sample size.

In a number of situations researchers wish to test a hypothesis concerning the population mean with a sample size that is not large enough to be approximated by the normal distribution. In situations where the sample size is small ($n \leq 30$) and the population standard deviation is unknown, we use the *t*-distribution (also called the *student's t-distribution*). The ***t*-distribution,** like the standardized normal distribution, is a symmetrical, bell-shaped distribution with a mean of zero and a standard deviation of 1. When sample size (n) is larger than 30, the *t*-distribution and *Z*-distribution may be considered to be almost identical. Since the *t*-distribution is contingent on sample size, there is a family of

EXHIBIT 21.5 EXAMPLES OF SELECTING THE APPROPRIATE UNIVARIATE STATISTICAL METHOD

Business Problem	Statistical Question to Be Asked	Possible Test of Statistical Significance
Interval or Ratio Scale		
Compare actual and hypothetical values of average salary	Is the sample mean significantly different from the hypothesized population mean?	*Z*-test (if sample is large) *t*-test (if sample is small)
Ordinal Scale		
Compare actual and expected evaluations	Does the distribution of scores on a scale with the categories *excellent, good, fair,* and *poor* differ from the expected distribution?	Chi-square test
Determine ordered preferences for all brands in a product class	Does a set of rank orderings in a sample differ from an expected or hypothetical rank ordering?	Kolmogorov–Smirnov test
Nominal Scale		
Identify sex of key executives	Is the number of female executives equal to the number of male executives?	Chi-square test
Indicate percentage of key executives who are male	Is the proportion of male executives the same as the hypothesized proportion?	*t*-test of a proportion

degrees of freedom (d.f.)
The number of constraints or assumptions needed to calculate a statistical term.

t-distributions. More specifically, the shape of the *t*-distribution is influenced by its **degrees of freedom (d.f.).** Exhibit 21.6 illustrates *t*-distributions for 1, 2, 5, and an infinite number of degrees of freedom. The number of degrees of freedom is equal to the number of observations minus the number of constraints or assumptions needed to calculate a statistical term. Another way of looking at degrees of freedom is to think of adding four numbers together when you know their sum—for example:

$$\begin{array}{c} 4 \\ 2 \\ 1 \\ \underline{X} \\ 10 \end{array}$$

The value of the fourth number has to be 3. In other words, there is a freedom of choice for the first three digits, but the fourth value is not free to vary. In this example there are three degrees of freedom.

Calculation of t closely resembles the calculation of the Z-value. To calculate t, use the formula

$$t = \frac{\bar{X} - \mu}{S_{\bar{X}}}$$

with $n - 1$ degrees of freedom.

The researcher asks two questions to determine whether the Z-distribution or the t-distribution is more appropriate for calculating a confidence interval or conducting a test of statistical significance. The first question is "Is

Exhibit 21.6 *t*-Distributions for Various Degrees of Freedom

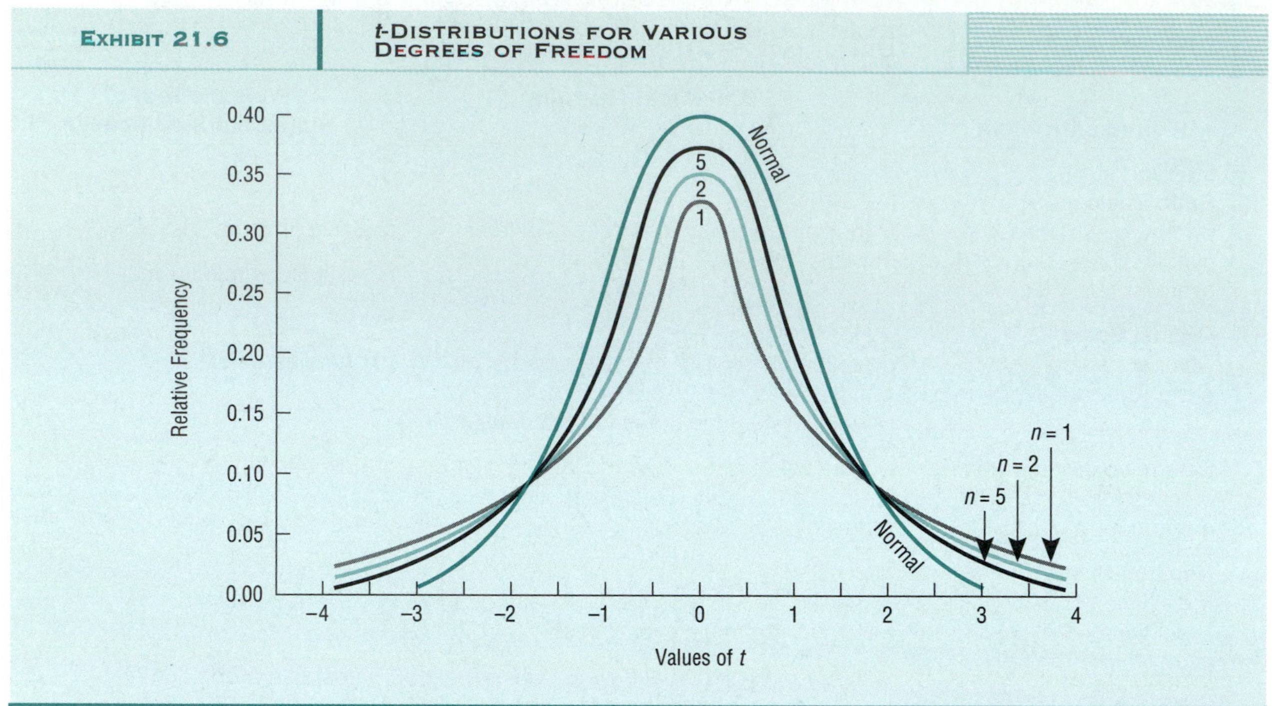

the population standard deviation (σ) known?" If the answer is yes, the Z-distribution is appropriate. When σ is unknown (the situation in most business research studies), a second question is also asked: "Is the sample size greater than 30?" If the answer is no, the t-distribution should be used; if it is yes, the Z-distribution may be used (because as sample size increases, the t-distribution becomes increasingly similar to the Z-distribution).

Calculating a Confidence Interval Estimate Using the *t*-Distribution

Suppose a business organization is interested in finding out how long newly hired MBA graduates remain on their first jobs. On the basis of a small sample of 17 employees with MBAs, the researcher wishes to estimate the population mean with 95 percent confidence. The data from the sample are presented below.

Number of Years on First Job: 3 5 7 1 12 1 2 2 5
4 2 3 1 3 4 2 6

To find the confidence estimate of the population mean for this small sample, we use the formula

$$\mu = \bar{X} \pm t_{\text{c.l.}} S_{\bar{X}}$$

or

$$\text{Upper limit} = \bar{X} + t_{\text{c.l.}}\left(\frac{S}{\sqrt{n}}\right)$$

$$\text{Lower limit} = \bar{X} - t_{\text{c.l.}}\left(\frac{S}{\sqrt{n}}\right)$$

where

$$\mu = \text{population mean}$$
$$\bar{X} = \text{sample mean}$$
$$t_{\text{c.l.}} = \text{critical value of } t \text{ at a specified confidence level}$$
$$S_{\bar{X}} = \text{standard error of the mean}$$
$$S = \text{sample standard deviation}$$
$$n = \text{sample size}$$

More specifically, the step-by-step procedure for calculating the confidence interval is as follows:

1. We calculate $\bar{X}$ from the sample. Summing the data values yields $\Sigma X = 63$, and $\bar{X} = \Sigma X/n = 63/17 = 3.7$.
2. Since σ is unknown, we estimate the population standard deviation by finding S, the sample standard deviation. For our example, $S = 2.66$.
3. We estimate the standard error of the mean using the formula $S_{\bar{X}} = S/\sqrt{n}$. Thus, $S_{\bar{X}} = 2.66/\sqrt{17}$ or $S_{\bar{X}} = .645$.
4. We determine the t-values associated with the confidence level desired. To do this, we go to Table 3 in the Appendix of Statistical Tables. Although the t-table provides information similar to that in the Z-table, it is somewhat different. The t-table format emphasizes the chance of error, or significance level (α), rather than the 95 percent chance of including the population mean in the estimate. Our example is a two-tailed test. Since a 95 percent confidence level has been selected, the significance level equals .05 ($1.00 - .95 = .05$). Once this has been determined, all we have to do to find the t-value is look under the .05 column for *two-tailed tests* at the row in which degrees of freedom (d.f.) equals the appropriate value ($n - 1$). Under 16 degrees of freedom ($n - 1 = 17 - 1 = 16$), the t-value at the 95 percent confidence level (.05 level of significance) is $t = 2.12$.
5. We calculate the confidence interval:

$$\text{Upper limit} = 3.7 + 2.12\left(\frac{2.66}{\sqrt{17}}\right) = 5.07$$

$$\text{Lower limit} = 3.7 - 2.12\left(\frac{2.66}{\sqrt{17}}\right) = 2.33$$

In our hypothetical example it may be concluded with 95 percent confidence that the population mean for the number of years spent on the first job by MBAs is between 5.07 and 2.33.

Univariate Hypothesis Test Using the *t*-Distribution

***t*-test**
A univariate hypothesis test using the *t*-distribution rather than the *Z*-distribution. It is used when the population standard deviation is unknown and the sample size is small.

The step-by-step procedure for a ***t*-test** is conceptually similar to that for hypothesis testing with the Z-distribution. Suppose a production manager believes that the average number of defective assemblies (assemblies not meeting quality standards) produced each day is 20. The factory records the number of defective assemblies for each of the 25 days it was open during a given month.

The first step is to state the null hypothesis and the alternative hypothesis:

$$H_0: \mu = 20$$

$$H_1: \mu \neq 20$$

Next, the researcher calculates a sample mean, $\bar{X} = 22$, and a sample standard deviation, $S = 5$, and then estimates the standard error of the mean ($S_{\bar{X}}$):

$$S_{\bar{X}} = \frac{S}{\sqrt{n}} = \frac{5}{\sqrt{25}} = 1$$

The researcher must then find the t-value associated with the desired level of statistical significance. If a 95 percent confidence level is desired, the significance level is .05. Next, the researcher must formulate a decision rule specifying the critical values by computing the upper and lower limits of the confidence interval to define the region of rejection. This requires determining the value of t. For 24 degrees of freedom ($n - 1 = 25 - 1$), the t-value is 2.064. The critical values are

$$\text{Lower limit} = \mu - t_{\text{c.l.}} S_{\bar{X}} = 20 - 2.064\left(\frac{5}{\sqrt{25}}\right) = 20 - 2.064(1) = 17.936$$

$$\text{Upper limit} = \mu + t_{\text{c.l.}} S_{\bar{X}} = 20 + 2.064\left(\frac{5}{\sqrt{25}}\right) = 20 + 2.064(1) = 22.064$$

Finally, the researcher makes the statistical decision by determining whether the sample mean falls between the critical limits. Based on the sample, $\bar{X} = 22$. In this case the sample mean is *not* included in the region of rejection. Even though the sample result is only slightly less than the critical value at the upper limit, the null hypothesis cannot be rejected. In other words, the production manager's assumption appears to be correct.

As with the Z-test, there is an alternative way of testing a hypothesis with the t-statistic. This is by using the formula

$$t_{\text{obs}} = \frac{\bar{X} - \mu}{S_{\bar{X}}} = \frac{22 - 20}{1} = \frac{2}{1} = 2$$

We can see that the observed t-value is less than the critical t-value of 2.064 at the .05 level when there are $25 - 1 = 24$ degrees of freedom.

CHI-SQUARE TEST FOR GOODNESS OF FIT

Table 21.1 shows the responses to a survey investigating awareness of a particular brand of automobile tire. This frequency distribution, or one-dimensional table from a sample of 100, suggests that the majority of the population (60 percent) is aware of the brand.

chi-square (χ^2) test
A test that statistically determines significance in the analysis of frequency distributions.

The **chi-square (χ^2) test** allows us to test for significance in the analysis of frequency distributions. Thus, categorical data on variables such as sex, education, or dichotomous answers may be analyzed statistically. Suppose, for example, that we wish to test the null hypothesis that the number of consumers

Table 21.1	**One-Way Frequency Table for Brand Awareness**

Awareness of Tire Manufacturer's Brand	Frequency
Aware	60
Unaware	40
	100

aware of a certain tire brand equals the number unaware of the brand. The logic inherent in the χ^2 test allows us to compare the observed frequencies (O_i) with the expected frequencies (E_i) based on our theoretical ideas about the population distribution or our presupposed proportions. In other words, the technique tests whether the data come from a certain probability distribution. It tests the "goodness of fit" of the observed distribution with the expected distribution.

Calculation of the chi-square statistic allows us to determine if the difference between the observed frequency distribution and the expected frequency distribution can be attributed to sampling variation. The steps in this process are as follows:

1. Formulate the null hypothesis and determine the expected frequency of each answer.
2. Determine the appropriate significance level.
3. Calculate the χ^2 value, using the observed frequencies from the sample and the expected frequencies.
4. Make the statistical decision by comparing the calculated χ^2 value with the critical χ^2 value. (It will soon be explained that this value is found in Table 4 in the Appendix.)

To analyze the brand awareness data in Table 21.1, we start with the null hypothesis suggesting that the number of respondents aware of the brand will equal the number of respondents unaware of it. Thus, the expected probability of each answer (aware or unaware) is .5. In a sample of 100, 50 people would be expected to respond yes, or be aware, and 50 would be expected to respond no, or be unaware. After we have determined that the chi-square test is appropriate at the .05 level of significance (or some other probability level), the chi-square statistic may be calculated.

To calculate the chi-square statistic, use the following formula:

$$\chi^2 = \sum \frac{(O_i - E_i)^2}{E_i}$$

where

χ^2 = chi-square statistic
O_i = observed frequency in the ith cell
E_i = expected frequency in the ith cell

We sum the squared differences:

$$\chi^2 = \frac{(O_1 - E_1)^2}{E_1} + \frac{(O_2 - E_2)^2}{E_2}$$

TABLE 21.2 CALCULATING THE CHI-SQUARE STATISTIC

Brand Awareness	Observed Frequency (O_i)	Expected Probability	Expected Frequency (E_i)	$(O_i - E_i)$	$\frac{(O_i - E_i)^2}{E_i}$
Aware	60	.5	50	10	$\frac{100}{50} = 2.0$
Unaware	40	.5	50	−10	$\frac{100}{50} = 2.0$
Total	100	1.0	100	0	$\chi^2 = 4.0$

Thus, we determine that the chi-square value equals 4:

$$\chi^2 = \frac{(60 - 50)^2}{50} + \frac{(40 - 50)^2}{50}$$
$$= 4$$

Table 21.2 shows the detailed calculation of this statistic.

Like many other probability distributions, the χ^2 distribution is not a single probability curve but a family of curves. These curves, although similar, vary according to the number of degrees of freedom ($k - 1$). Thus, we must calculate the number of degrees of freedom. Remember, *degrees of freedom* refers to the number of observations that can be varied without changing the constraints or assumptions associated with a numerical system. We calculate the degrees of freedom as follows:

$$\text{d.f.} = k - 1$$

where

k = the number of cells associated with column or row data[4]

In the brand awareness problem there are only two categorical responses. Thus, degrees of freedom equals 1 (d.f. = 2 − 1 = 1).

Now it is necessary to compare the computed chi-square value with the critical chi-square values associated with the .05 probability level with 1 degree of freedom. In Table 4 of the Appendix, the critical chi-square value is 3.84. Since the calculated chi-square is larger than the tabular chi-square, the null hypothesis—that the observed values are comparable to the expected values—is rejected.[5]

The chi-square test is discussed further in Chapter 22, as it is also frequently utilized in the analysis of contingency tables.

HYPOTHESIS TEST OF A PROPORTION

hypothesis test of a proportion
A statistical test of a hypothesis about a proportion of a population based on data for a sample from the population.

Researchers often test univariate statistical hypotheses about population proportions. The population proportion (π) can be estimated on the basis of the sample proportion (p). The procedure for conducting a **hypothesis test of a proportion** is conceptually similar to hypothesis testing when the mean is the characteristic of interest. However, the formulation of the standard error of the proportion is mathematically different.

Consider the following example. A state legislature is considering a proposed right-to-work law. One legislator has hypothesized that 50 percent of the state's labor force is unionized. In other words, the null hypothesis to be tested is that the proportion of union workers in the state is .5.

The researcher formulates the statistical null hypothesis that the population proportion (π) equals 50 percent (.5):

$$H_0: \pi = .5$$

The alternative hypothesis is that π does not equal .5:

$$H_1: \pi \neq .5$$

Suppose the researcher conducts a survey with a sample of 100 workers and calculates $p = .6$. Even though the population proportion is unknown, a large sample allows the use of the Z-test (rather than the t-test). If the researcher decides that the decision rule will be set at the .01 level of significance, the critical Z-value of 2.57 is used for the hypothesis test. Using the following formula, we can calculate the observed value of Z, given a certain sample proportion:

$$Z_{obs} = \frac{p - \pi}{S_p}$$

where

p = sample proportion
π = hypothesized population proportion
S_p = estimate of the standard error of the proportion

The formula for S_p is

$$S_p = \sqrt{\frac{pq}{n}} \quad \text{or} \quad S_p = \sqrt{\frac{p(1 - p)}{n}}$$

where

S_p = estimate of the standard error of the proportion
p = proportion of successes
$q = 1 - p$, proportion of failures

In our example,

$$S_p = \sqrt{\frac{(.6)(.4)}{100}} = \sqrt{\frac{.24}{100}} = \sqrt{.0024} = .04899$$

Z_{obs} can now be calculated:

$$Z_{obs} = \frac{p - \pi}{S_p} = \frac{.6 - .5}{.04899} = \frac{.1}{.04899} = 2.04$$

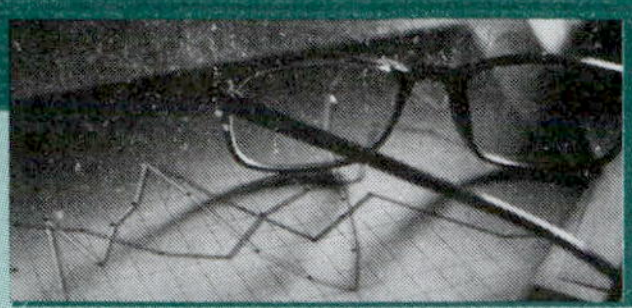

STATISTICAL TUTOR

CHI-SQUARE TEST

THE SITUATION:

A private art museum sponsoring a program of summer art classes for children expects an equal number of boys and girls to be enrolled in its classes. A random sample from its list of students shows that there are more girls than boys.

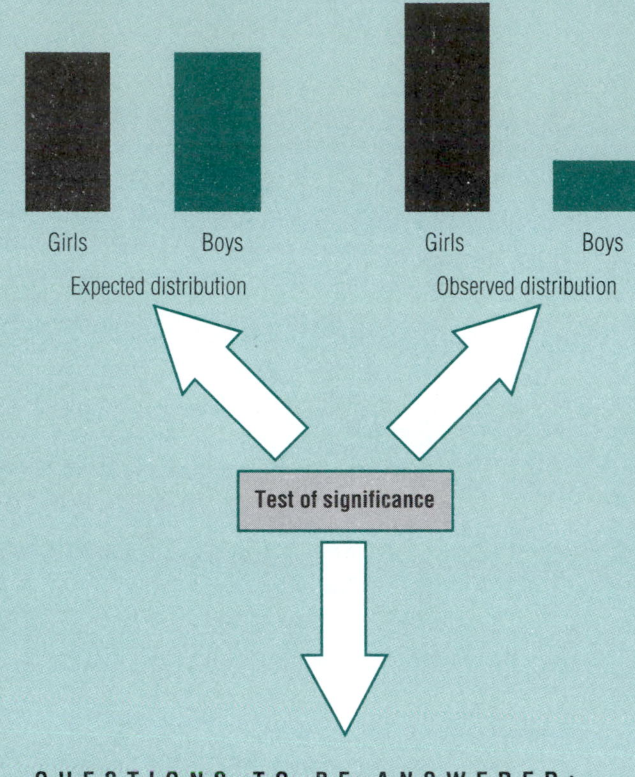

QUESTIONS TO BE ANSWERED:

1. Is the difference between the expected (hypothetical) distribution and the observed distribution statistically significant?
2. If it is statistically significant, is the nature of the difference in distributions of any managerial value?

The Z_{obs} value of 2.04 is less than the critical value of 2.57, so the null hypothesis cannot be rejected.

In our example the researcher drew a large sample and had to estimate the standard error of the proportion. When the sample size is small, the *Z*-test is not appropriate and the *t*-test should be used. The standard rule of thumb for determining if the sample size is too small is to (1) multiply n times π and (2) multiply n by $1 - \pi$. If either product is 5 or below, the sample size is considered to be too small to use the *Z*-test.

ADDITIONAL APPLICATIONS OF HYPOTHESIS TESTING

The discussion of statistical inference in this chapter has been restricted to setting up a confidence interval around the sample mean to estimate the population mean, chi-square tests to test for significance in the analysis of frequency distributions, and *Z*-tests to test hypotheses about sample proportions when the sample sizes are large. As our discussion of the population proportion suggests, there are other hypothesis tests for population parameters estimated from sample statistics. Many of these other tests are no different conceptually in their methods of hypothesis testing. However, the formulas are mathematically different. The purpose of this chapter has been to discuss basic statistical concepts. Once you have learned the basic terminology in this chapter, you should have no problem generalizing to other statistical problems.

As emphasized in Chapter 17, the key to understanding statistics is learning the basics of the language. This chapter has presented verbs, nouns, and some of the rules of the grammar of statistics. It is hoped that some of the myths about statistics have been shattered.

SUMMARY

This chapter discussed univariate statistical procedures for hypothesis testing when the research focuses on one variable. A hypothesis is a statement of assumption about the nature of the world. A null hypothesis is a statement about the status quo. The alternative hypothesis is a statement indicating the opposite of the null hypothesis.

In hypothesis testing a researcher states a null hypothesis about a population mean and then attempts to disprove it. Based on a significance level, the *Z*-test defines critical values on the standardized normal distribution beyond which it is unlikely that the null hypothesis is true. If a sample mean is contained in the region of rejection, the null hypothesis is rejected.

There are two possible types of error in statistical tests: Type I, rejecting a true null hypothesis, and Type II, accepting a false null hypothesis.

A number of appropriate statistical techniques are available to assist the researcher in interpreting data. The choice of method of statistical analysis depends on (1) the type of question to be answered, (2) the number of variables, and (3) the scale of measurement.

Univariate statistical analysis allows the researcher to assess the statistical significance of various hypotheses about a single variable. Bivariate or multivariate analysis is used when two or more variables are to be analyzed. Nonparametric statistical tests are used with nominal and ordinal data, and parametric tests are used for interval or ratio scales. However, if a researcher cannot reasonably assume a normal population or sampling distribution, nonparametric tests should be used.

This chapter presented the technique for using the *t*-distributions in estimating confidence intervals for the mean. Calculation of the confidence interval requires use of the central-limit theorem to estimate a range around the sample mean, which should contain the population mean.

The *t*-distribution is used for hypothesis testing with small samples when the population standard deviation is unknown. The *t*-test is analogous to the *Z*-test. The chi-square test allows the testing of statistical significance in the analysis of frequency distributions: An observed distribution of categorical data from a sample may be compared with an expected distribution for goodness of fit. Conceptually, the hypothesis test of a proportion follows a method similar to the Z-test for a hypothesis about a mean.

Key Terms

hypothesis
null hypothesis
alternative hypothesis
significance level
critical values
Type I error
Type II error
univariate data analysis
bivariate data analysis
multivariate data analysis
parametric statistical procedures
nonparametric statistical procedures
t-distribution
degrees of freedom (d.f.)
t-test
chi-square (χ^2) test
hypothesis test of a proportion

Questions for Review and Critical Thinking

1. What is the purpose of a statistical hypothesis?
2. What is a significance level? How does a researcher choose a significance level?
3. List the steps in the hypothesis-testing procedure.
4. Distinguish between a Type I and a Type II error.
5. What are the factors that determine the choice of the appropriate statistical technique?
6. After a bumper crop, a mushroom grower hypothesizes that mushrooms will remain at the average wholesale price of $1 per pound. State the null hypothesis and the alternative hypothesis.
7. Assume you have the following data: H_0: $\mu = 200$, $S = 30$, $n = 64$, and $\bar{X} = 218$. Conduct a hypothesis test at the .05 significance level.
8. Assume you have the following data: H_0: $\mu = 2{,}450$, $S = 400$, $n = 100$, and $\bar{X} = 2{,}300$. Conduct a hypothesis test at the .01 significance level.
9. If the data in question 8 had been generated with a sample of 25 ($n = 25$), what statistical test would be appropriate?
10. How does the *t*-distribution differ from the *Z*-distribution?
11. The answers to a researcher's question will be nominally scaled. What statistical test is appropriate for comparing the sample data with hypothesized population data?
12. A researcher plans to ask employees if they favor, oppose, or are indifferent to a change in their company's retirement program. Formulate a null hypothesis for a chi-square test and determine the expected frequency for each answer.
13. Give an example of a circumstance in which a Type I error may be more serious than a Type II error.
14. Refer to the brand awareness χ^2 data on pages 511–512. What statistical decisions could be made if the .01 significance level were selected rather than the .05 level?
15. Determine a statistical hypothesis and perform a chi-square test on the following survey data.
    (a) Easy-listening music should be played on the office intercom:

Agree	40
Neutral	35
Disagree	25
	100

    (b) Demographic characteristics of a group indicate

Republicans	100
Democrats	100
	200

16. Quality Motors is an automobile dealership that regularly advertises in its local market area. It claims that a certain make and model of car averages 30 miles to a gallon of gas and mentions that this figure may vary with driving conditions. A local consumer group wishes to verify the advertising claim. To do so, it selects a sample of recent purchasers of this make and model. It asks them to drive their cars until they have used two tanks of gas and to record the mileage. The group then calculates and records the miles per gallon for each car. Following are the results of the tests:

Purchaser	Miles per Gallon	Purchaser	Miles per Gallon
1	30.9	14	27.0
2	24.5	15	26.7
3	31.2	16	31.0
4	28.7	17	23.5
5	35.1	18	29.4
6	29.0	19	26.3
7	28.8	20	27.5
8	23.1	21	28.2
9	31.0	22	28.4
10	30.2	23	29.1
11	28.4	24	21.9
12	29.3	25	30.9
13	24.2		

(a) Formulate a statistical hypothesis that accommodates the consumer group's purpose.

(b) Calculate the mean for miles per gallon. Compute the sample variance and sample standard deviation.

(c) Conduct the appropriate statistical test of your hypothesis, using a .05 statistical significance level.

17. A personnel researcher hypothesizes that 15 percent of employees eligible for early retirement will actually choose to retire early. In a sample of 1,200 employees, 20 percent say they plan to retire early. Perform a hypothesis test.

18. See question 8 in Chapter 17 (page 432) for data about Coastal Star Sales Corporation.
    (a) Develop a hypothesis concerning the average age of the sales force and test the hypothesis.
    (b) Calculate the mean for the previous year's sales and use this as the basis for formulating a hypothesis about current-year sales. Test the hypothesis.

19. A client asks a researcher to conduct a univariate hypothesis test on a single Likert-scaled item. The researcher conducts the analysis even though many researchers say these types of scales are ordinal rather than interval. Is this the right thing to do?

Exploring the Internet

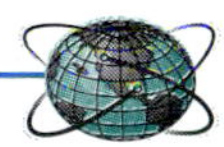

1. The Federal Reserve Bank of St. Louis maintains a database called FRED (Federal Reserve Economic Data). Use a search engine to navigate to the FRED database at http://www.stls.frb.org/fred/index.html. Then find the data on U.S. employment in retail trade. Calculate a mean for the last 5-year period. Then set up a hypothesis for the next 5-year period.
2. The Data and Story Library is an online library of data files and stories that illustrate the use of basic statistics methods. Go to http://lib.stat.cmu.edu/DASL and report what you find.

WebSurveyor Activities

WebSurveyor allows a researcher to download a survey's results to a data file. Exporting data into other applicaitons is handled through CSV (comma separated value) files. Using the sports opinion survey, we have done this for you. The exported files have been converted to Microsoft Excel (Sports.xls) and to SPSS (Sports.sav). Numeric codes are used in these files.

Calculate a mean and construct a confidence interval around the item "There is no harm in showing off after a victory."

Case Suggestions

Case 29: LastDance Health Care
Case 30: Sunbelt Energy Corporation
Case 31: Employees Federal Credit Union

CHAPTER

22

BIVARIATE ANALYSIS: Tests of Differences

FORTUNE Marketing Research and Yankelovich Partners conducted a survey sponsored by Deloitte & Touche.[1] Questionnaires were mailed to 6,000 randomly selected top- and middle management female and 1,000 male *Fortune* subscribers. Respondents were asked for their perceptions of the overall status of women in business, their own career satisfaction, their company's efforts to recruit, develop, and promote women, and about programs or policies they would like to see implemented.

Is there a level playing field? The *Fortune* subscribers polled believe men and women are not judged by the same criteria. Overall, 77 percent of the women believe that they need more experience or a higher level degree than men. Forty-three percent of the men agreed. Fifty-two percent of women over 40 years of age—versus 36 percent of women under 40—feel they have to have a lot more experience or a higher level degree than men.

Do women work harder than men? Fifty-four percent of the female *Fortune* subscribers surveyed say yes. Only 17 percent of men agree. The majority of men, 75 percent, say men and women work equally hard. Older women, those who are not married, and those who earn $75,000 or more annually, are particularly likely to say women work harder than men. Women who are younger, married, and earn less than $75,000 annually are more likely than their counterparts to conclude that the two genders work equally hard. In the survey, respondents were provided with a list of 18 attitudes or situations that could potentially form barriers to women's professional success. The existence of a male- dominated corporate culture was cited by 91 percent of the women and 75 percent of the men as the number-one barrier to the advancement of women. Women also feel that the existence of a glass ceiling (88 percent), their exclusion from informal network communications (86 percent), management's belief that women are less career-oriented than men (84 percent), and the lack of female mentors (78 percent) are among the top five barriers to their advancement. Men listed a difficulty balancing work/family life (71 percent), the lack of female mentors (70 percent), few female bosses to serve as role models (67 percent), and exclusion from informal network communications (66 percent). Among men, existence of a glass ceiling ranks only eighth.

Despite other differences of opinion, men and women are largely motivated by the same factors on the job. Both genders place the highest importance on doing a good job, making an impact on their company or clients, having control of their own destiny, establishing a good work/life balance, and making a difference in the lives of others.

The extent to which individual factors are effective motivators varies by demographic subgroups. While women over 40 get more satisfaction from making a difference in the lives of others, younger

What you will learn in this chapter

- To understand that bivariate statistics deal with the simultaneous investigation of two variables.
- To discuss reasons for conducting tests of differences.
- To understand how the type of measurement scale will influence the bivariate test of difference selected.
- To calculate a chi-square test for a contingency table.
- To understand the difference between observed and expected frequencies and how to calculate the expected frequencies for a chi-square test.
- To calculate a *t*-test for two independent samples to compare differences of means.
- To calculate a *Z*-test for two independent samples to compare differences of proportions.
- To understand the concept of analysis of variance (ANOVA).
- To state a null hypothesis in a test of differences among three or four group means.
- To interpret analysis of variance summary tables.

TO THE POINT

The thing to do is to supply light.
WOODROW WILSON

women are looking for recognition and the possibility of promotion. Women making more than $75,000 annually especially enjoy making an impact on their companies and/or clients. Female employees of small companies are more likely to be motivated by the ability to control their own destiny and have a good work/life balance, and are less likely to be motivated by recognition and the possibility of promotion. ■

Making comparisons such as those above involves bivariate analysis—the topic of this chapter. The purpose of descriptive analysis, as we saw in Chapter 20, is to summarize data. After summarizing the data, the researcher may wish to measure the association between variables or test the difference between groups or objects. The purpose of this chapter is to go beyond univariate statistics, in which the analysis focuses on one variable at a time. Tests of differences and measures of association are in the realm of bivariate statistics, where scores on two variables are of concern to the researcher.

WHAT IS THE APPROPRIATE TEST OF DIFFERENCES?

test of differences
Investigation of a hypothesis that states that two (or more) groups differ with respect to measures on a variable.

bivariate statistics
Tests of differences or measures of association between two variables at a time.

One of the most frequently tested hypotheses states that two groups are different with respect to a certain behavior, characteristic, or attitude. For example, in the classical experimental design, researchers conduct **tests of differences** between subjects assigned to the experimental group and subjects assigned to the control group. Researchers may be interested in determining if males and females perform a task or hold an attitude with the same frequency. In statistical terminology, the null hypothesis is that the two groups are the same.

Exhibit 22.1 illustrates that both the type of measurement and the number of groups to be compared influence the type of test in **bivariate statistics.** Often researchers are interested in testing differences in mean scores between

EXHIBIT 22.1 COMMON BIVARIATE TESTS OF DIFFERENCES

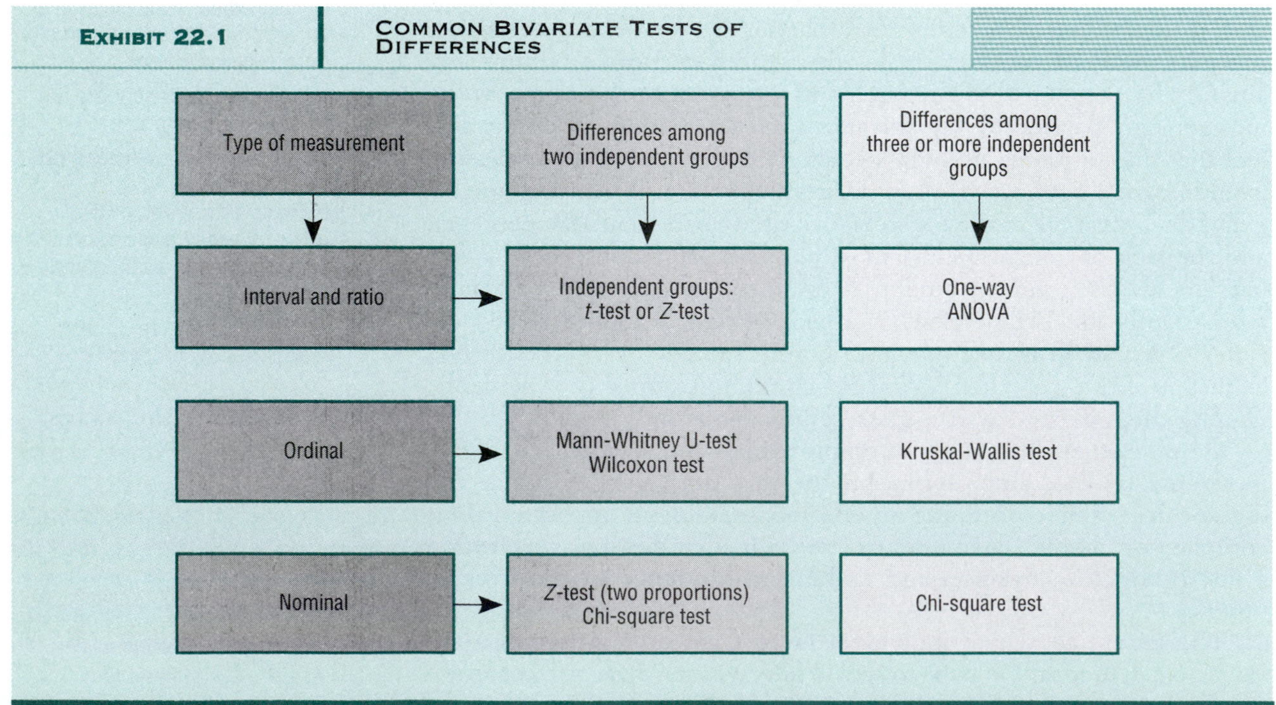

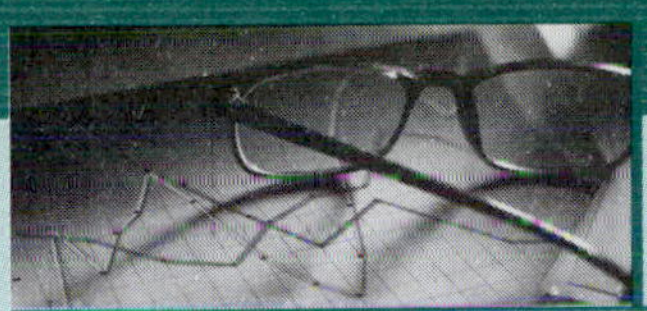

STATISTICAL TUTOR

CHI-SQUARE TEST: DIFFERENCES AMONG GROUPS

THE SITUATION:
A survey among Democrats, Republicans, and Independents asked: "How often do you contribute money to candidates of an opposition party?"

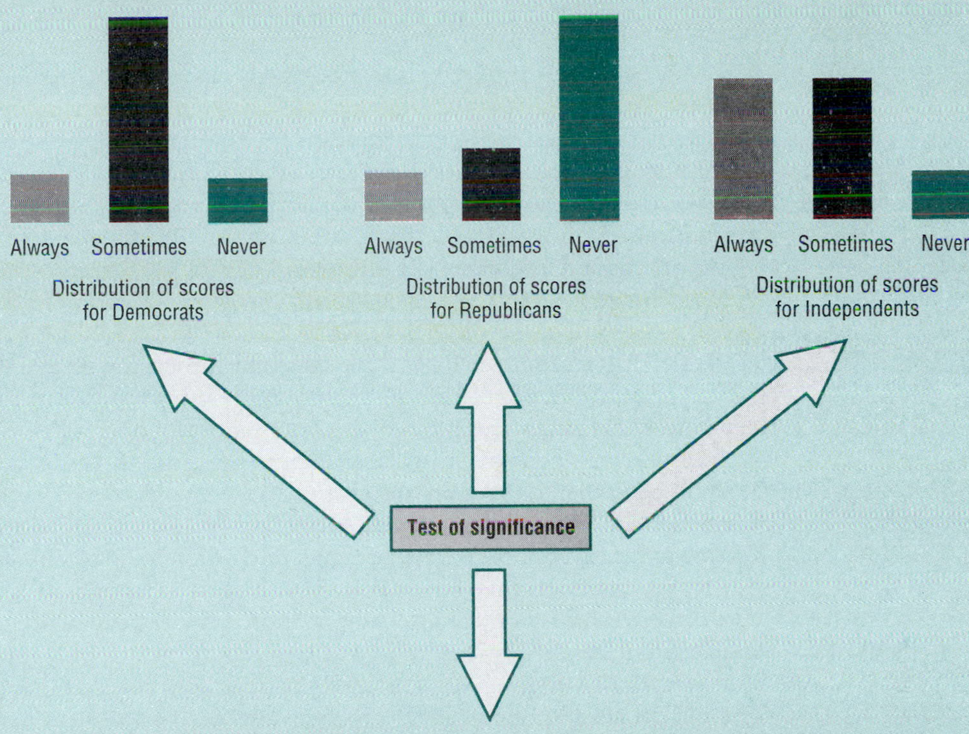

QUESTIONS TO BE ANSWERED:

1. Is the difference among the distributions statistically significant?
2. If it is statistically significant, is the nature of the difference in distributions of any managerial value?

groups or in comparing how two groups' scores are distributed across possible response categories. We will focus our attention on these issues.[2]

Construction of contingency tables and chi-square analysis is a procedure for comparing the distribution of one group with the distribution of another group. This is a good starting point for discussing testing of differences.

CROSS-TABULATION TABLES: THE CHI-SQUARE TEST FOR GOODNESS OF FIT

One of the simplest techniques for describing sets of relationships is the cross-tabulation. A *cross-tabulation,* or *contingency table,* is a joint frequency distribution of observations on two or more sets of variables. This generally means that

Table 22.1	**One-Way Frequency Table for Brand Awareness**

Awareness of Tire Manufacturer's Brand	Frequency
Aware	60
Unaware	40
	100

tabulation of subgroups will be conducted for purposes of comparison. The chi-square distribution provides a means for testing the statistical significance of contingency tables. It allows us to test for differences in two groups' distributions across categories. (Another concern is whether two or more variables are interrelated or associated; this will be discussed in Chapter 23.)

chi-square (χ^2) test
A test that statistically determines significance in the analysis of frequency distributions.

As mentioned in Chapter 21, the **chi-square (χ^2) test** involves comparing the observed frequencies (O_i) with the expected frequencies (E_i). It tests the "goodness of fit" of the observed distribution with the expected distribution.

Table 22.1 reproduces Table 21.1. This one-dimensional table suggests that the majority of the population (60 percent) is aware of the brand. However, if we analyze the data by subgroups based on sex of respondent, as in Table 22.2, we can see the logic of cross-classification procedures. Inspection of Table 22.2 suggests that most men are aware of the brand of tires, whereas most women are not. Thus, from our simple analysis we conclude that there is a difference in brand awareness between men and women. (It might also be stated that brand awareness may be associated with sex of respondent.)

So far we have not discussed the notion of statistical significance. Is the observed difference between men and women the result of chance variation due to random sampling, or is the discrepancy more than sampling variation? The chi-square test allows us to conduct tests for significance in the analysis of an R × C contingency table (where R = row and C = column). The formula for the chi-square statistic is the same as that for one-way frequency tables (see Chapter 20):

$$\chi^2 = \sum \frac{(O_i - E_i)^2}{E_i}$$

Table 22.2	**Contingency Table (Cross-Tabulation) for Brand Awareness by Sex**

Awareness of Tire Manufacturer's Brand	Men	Women	Total
Aware	50	10	60
Unaware	15	25	40
	65	35	100

where

$$\chi^2 = \text{chi-square statistic}$$
$$O_i = \text{observed frequency in the } i\text{th cell}$$
$$E_i = \text{expected frequency in the } i\text{th cell}$$

Again, as in the univariate chi-square test, a frequency count of data that nominally identify or categorically rank groups is acceptable for the chi-square test for contingency tables. Both variables in the contingency table will be categorical variables rather than interval- or ratio-scaled continuous variables.

We begin, as in all hypothesis-testing procedures, by formulating the null hypothesis and selecting the level of statistical significance for the particular problem. Suppose, for the above example, that we wish to test the null hypothesis that an equal number of men and women are aware of the brand and that the hypothesis test will be made at the .05 level of statistical significance.

In managerial terms the research asks whether men and women have different levels of brand awareness. Translated into a statistical question, the problem is "Is brand awareness independent of the respondent's sex?" Table 22.2 is a 2 × 2 (R × C) contingency table that cross-classifies on the basis of answers to the awareness question (rows) and the respondent's sex (columns).

To compute the chi-square value for the 2 × 2 contingency table (Table 22.2), the researcher must first identify an expected distribution for that table. Under the null hypothesis that men and women are equally aware of the tire brand, the same proportion of positive answers (60 percent) should come from both groups. In other words, the proportion of men who are aware of the brand would be the same as the proportion of women who are aware of it. Likewise, the proportion of men who are unaware of the brand would equal the proportion of women who are unaware.

cell
Section of a table representing a specific combination of two variables or a specific value of a variable.

In a contingency table, a **cell** is an intersection of a row and a column that represents a specific combination of two variables or a specific value of a variable. Each box containing a single frequency is a cell. There is an easy way to calculate the expected frequencies for the cells in a cross-tabulation table. To compute an expected number for each cell, use the formula

$$E_{ij} = \frac{R_i C_j}{n}$$

where

$$R_i = \text{total observed frequency in the } i\text{th row}$$
$$C_j = \text{total observed frequency in the } j\text{th column}$$
$$n = \text{sample size}$$

A calculation of the expected values does not utilize the actual observed numbers of respondents in each individual cell—only the total column and total row values are used in this calculation. The expected cell frequencies are calculated as shown in Table 22.3.

To compute a chi-square statistic, we use the same formula as before, except that we calculate degrees of freedom as the number of rows minus one (R − 1) times the number of columns minus one (C − 1):

$$\chi^2 = \sum \frac{(O_i - E_i)^2}{E_i}$$

with (R − 1)(C − 1) degrees of freedom.

TABLE 22.3 CALCULATION OF OBSERVED VERSUS EXPECTED FREQUENCIES FOR BRAND AWARENESS PROBLEM

Awareness of Tire Manufacturer's Brand	Men	Women	Total
Aware	50 (39)	10 (21)	60
Unaware	15 (26)	25 (14)	40
	65	35	100

Note: Expected frequencies are in parentheses. They were calculated as follows:

$$E_{ij} = \frac{R_i C_j}{n} \quad E_{11} = \frac{(60)(65)}{100} = 39 \quad E_{12} = \frac{(60)(35)}{100} = 21 \quad E_{21} = \frac{(40)(65)}{100} = 26 \quad E_{22} = \frac{(40)(35)}{100} = 14$$

Table 22.3 shows the observed versus the expected frequencies for the brand awareness question. Using the data in Table 22.3, we calculate the chi-square statistic as follows:

$$\begin{aligned}\chi^2 &= \frac{(50-39)^2}{39} + \frac{(10-21)^2}{21} + \frac{(15-26)^2}{26} + \frac{(25-14)^2}{14} \\ &= 3.102 + 5.762 + 4.654 + 8.643 \\ &= 22.161\end{aligned}$$

The number of degrees of freedom equals 1:

$$(R - 1)(C - 1) = (2 - 1)(2 - 1) = 1$$

From Table 4 in the Appendix of Statistical Tables at the end of the book, we see that the critical value at the .05 probability level with 1 d.f. is 3.84. Thus, the null hypothesis is rejected, because 22.161 is much greater than 3.84. The brand awareness does not appear to be independent of respondent's sex—in fact, the tabular value for the .001 level is 10.8, and the calculated value of 22.2 far exceeds this critical value.

Proper use of the chi-square test requires that each expected cell frequency (E_{ij}) have a value of at least 5. If this sample size requirement is not met, the researcher should take a larger sample or combine ("collapse") response categories.

t-TEST FOR COMPARING TWO MEANS

_t_-test for difference of means
A technique used to test the hypothesis that the mean scores on some interval-scaled variable are significantly different for two independent samples or groups.

The *t*-test may be used to test a hypothesis stating that the mean scores on some variable will be significantly different for two independent samples or groups. It is used when the number of observations (sample size) is small and the population standard deviation is unknown. To use the ***t*-test for difference of means,** we assume that the two samples are drawn from normal distributions. Because σ is unknown, we assume the variances of the two populations or groups are equal (*homoscedasticity*). Further, we assume interval data.

The null hypothesis about differences between groups is normally stated as $\mu_1 = \mu_2$ or $\mu_1 - \mu_2 = 0$. In most cases comparisons are between two sample means ($\bar{X}_1 - \bar{X}_2$). A verbal expression of the formula for *t* is[3]

$$t = \frac{\text{Mean 1} - \text{Mean 2}}{\text{Variability of random means}}$$

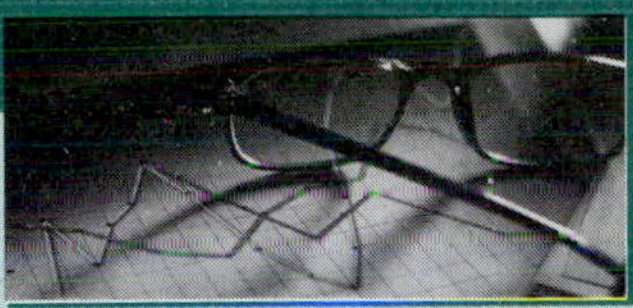

STATISTICAL TUTOR

t-TEST FOR DIFFERENCE OF MEANS

THE SITUATION:

A bank takes a sample to compare the annual salaries (dollars) of professional women employees and those of professional male employees.

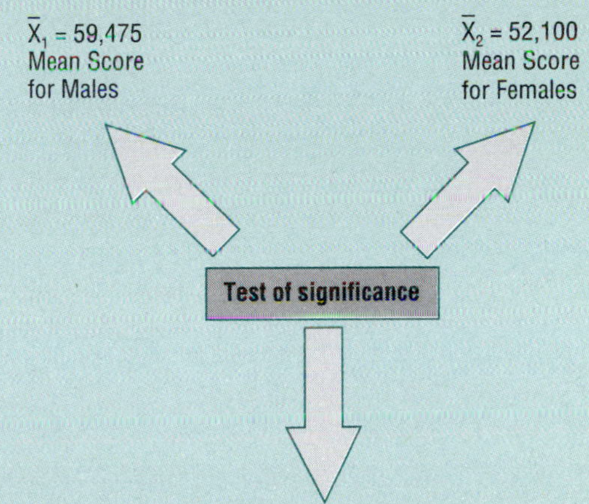

QUESTIONS TO BE ANSWERED:

1. Is the difference between the means of men and women *statistically significant*?
2. Is the magnitude of difference large enough to justify a differential treatment strategy?

Thus, the *t*-value is a ratio with the information about the difference between means (provided by the sample) in the numerator and the random error in the denominator. The question is whether the observed differences have occurred by chance alone. To calculate *t*, the following formula is used:

$$t = \frac{\bar{X}_1 - \bar{X}_2}{S_{\bar{X}_1 - \bar{X}_2}}$$

where

$\bar{X}_1$ = mean for group 1
$\bar{X}_2$ = mean for group 2
$S_{\bar{X}_1 - \bar{X}_2}$ = pooled, or combined, standard error of difference between means

pooled estimate of the standard error
An estimate of the standard error based on the assumption that variances of both groups (populations) are equal.

A **pooled estimate of the standard error** is a better estimate of the standard error than one based on the variance from either sample. It requires the assumption that variances of both groups (populations) are equal. To calculate the pooled standard error of the difference between means of independent samples, use the formula

$$S_{\bar{X}_1 - \bar{X}_2} = \sqrt{\left(\frac{(n_1 - 1)S_1^2 + (n_2 - 1)S_2^2}{n_1 + n_2 - 2}\right)\left(\frac{1}{n_1} + \frac{1}{n_2}\right)}$$

where

$$S_1^2 = \text{variance of group 1}$$
$$S_2^2 = \text{variance of group 2}$$
$$n_1 = \text{sample size of group 1}$$
$$n_2 = \text{sample size of group 2}$$

As an illustration of the *t*-test, suppose a researcher wants to test the difference between sociology majors and business majors on scores on a scale measuring attitudes toward business. We will assume that the attitude scale is an interval scale. The result of the simple random sample of these two groups of college students is presented in Table 22.4. A high score equals a favorable attitude toward business. The null hypothesis is that there is no difference in attitudes toward business (mean score) between the two groups. The relevant data computation is as follows:

$$S_{\bar{X}_1-\bar{X}_2} = \sqrt{\left(\frac{(n_1-1)S_1^2+(n_2-1)S_2^2}{n_1+n_2-2}\right)\left(\frac{1}{n_1}+\frac{1}{n_2}\right)}$$
$$= \sqrt{\left(\frac{(20)(2.1)^2+(13)(2.6)^2}{33}\right)\left(\frac{1}{21}+\frac{1}{14}\right)}$$
$$= .797$$

To calculate the *t*-statistic, use the formula

$$t = \frac{\bar{X}_1-\bar{X}_2}{S_{\bar{X}_1-\bar{X}_2}} = \frac{16.5-12.2}{.797} = \frac{4.3}{.797} = 5.395$$

In a test of two means, degrees of freedom are calculated as follows:

$$\text{d.f.} = n - k$$

where

$$n = n_1 + n_2$$
$$k = \text{number of groups}$$

In our example d.f. equals 33. If the .01 level of significance is selected, reference to Table 3 in the Appendix yields the critical *t*-value. The *t*-value of 2.75 must be surpassed by the observed *t*-value if the hypothesis test is to be statistically significant at the .01 level. The calculated *t* of 5.39 far exceeds the critical value of *t* for statistical significance, so it is significant at $\alpha = .01$. In

TABLE 22.4 COMPARISON OF STUDENT ATTITUDES TOWARD BUSINESS

Business Students	Sociology Students
$\bar{X}_1 = 16.5$	$\bar{X}_2 = 12.2$
$S_1 = 2.1$	$S_2 = 2.6$
$n_1 = 21$	$n_2 = 14$

EXHIBIT 22.2 SAS *t*-TEST OUTPUT, *t*-TEST PROCEDURE VARIABLE: CR SALES

Age	*N*	Mean	Standard Deviation	Standard Error	Minimum	Maximum	Variances	*t*	d.f.	Prob. $>\|t\|$
1	6	61879.33333	22356.20845	9126.88388	41152.00000	103059.0000	Unequal	−0.9758	5.2	0.3729
2	5	86961.80000	53734.45098	24030.77702	42775.00000	172530.0000	Equal	−1.0484	9.0	0.3218

For H_0 variances are equal, $F' = 5.78$ with 4 and 5 d.f., Prob $> F' = 0.0815$.

other words, this research shows that business students' attitude scores are significantly higher than those of sociology students.

As another example, suppose that 11 sales representatives are categorized as either young (1) or old (2) on the basis of their age in years. Exhibit 22.2. presents SAS computer output comparing the mean sales volumes for these two groups.

If σ is known or if σ is unknown but the number of observations in both groups is large, the appropriate test of mean differences between two groups is a *Z*-test rather than a *t*-test. The procedure is conceptually identical to the one just discussed.

Z-TEST FOR COMPARING TWO PROPORTIONS

What type of statistical comparison can be made when the observed statistics are proportions? A researcher may wish to test a hypothesis that the proportion of engineers in a research laboratory who are exposed to a management-by-objectives (MBO) program differs from the proportion of accounting personnel exposed to an MBO program. Testing the null hypothesis that the population proportion for group 1 (π_1) equals the population proportion for group 2 (π_2) is conceptually the same as the *t*-test of two means.

Again, sample size is the appropriate criterion when selecting either a *t*-test or a *Z*-test. This section illustrates a **Z-test for differences of proportions,** which requires a sample size greater than 30.

Z-test for differences of proportions
A technique used to test the hypothesis that proportions are significantly different for two independent samples or groups.

Our hypothesis, which is

$$H_0: \pi_1 = \pi_2$$

may be restated as

$$H_0: \pi_1 - \pi_2 = 0$$

The comparison between the observed *sample proportions* p_1 and p_2 allows the researcher to ask whether the difference between two large random samples occurred due to chance alone. To calculate a *Z*-test statistic, we use the following formula:

$$Z = \frac{(p_1 - p_2) - (\pi_1 - \pi_2)}{S_{p_1 - p_2}}$$

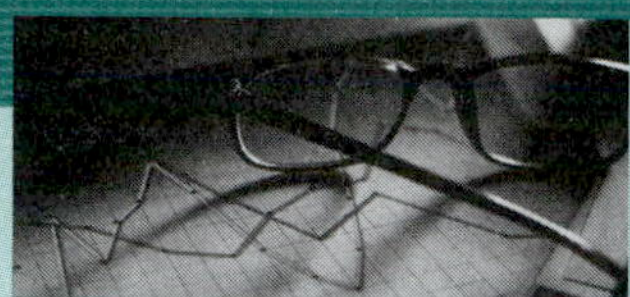

STATISTICAL TUTOR

A Z-TEST FOR DIFFERENCES OF PROPORTIONS

THE SITUATION:

The proportion of respondents in a survey of top executives ($n = 50$) with an annual income of $140,000 or over was 10 percent. A follow-up check of nonrespondents indicated the proportion of nonrespondents with an income over $140,000 was 21 percent.

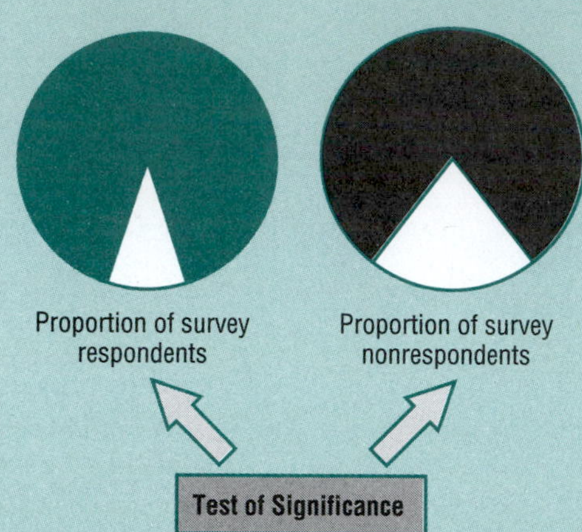

QUESTIONS TO BE ANSWERED:

1. Is the difference in proportion between survey respondents and survey nonrespondents among those with incomes over $140,000 statistically significant?
2. If the difference is statistically significant, is the magnitude of this difference large enough to distort the representativeness of the survey?

where

p_1 = sample proportion of successes in group 1

p_2 = sample proportion of successes in group 2

$(\pi_1 - \pi_2)$ = hypothesized population proportion 1 minus hypothesized population proportion 2

$S_{p_1-p_2}$ = pooled estimate of the standard error of difference of proportions

Normally the value of $(\pi_1 - \pi_2)$ is expected to be 0. So this formula is actually much simpler than it looks at first inspection.

To calculate the standard error of the difference of proportions, use the formula

$$S_{p_1-p_2} = \sqrt{\bar{p}\bar{q}\left(\frac{1}{n_1} + \frac{1}{n_2}\right)}$$

where

$\bar{p}$ = pooled estimate of proportion of successes in a sample of both groups

$\bar{q} = 1 - \bar{p}$, or pooled estimate of proportion of failures in a sample of both groups

n_1 = sample size for group 1

n_2 = sample size for group 2

Because under the null hypothesis π is unknown, a weighted average of the sample proportion ($\bar{p}$) is calculated. To calculate the pooled estimator, $\bar{p}$, use the formula

$$\bar{p} = \frac{n_1 p_1 + n_2 p_2}{n_1 + n_2}$$

Suppose the survey data were as follows:

Engineers	Accountants
$p_1 = .35$	$p_2 = .40$
$n_1 = 100$	$n_2 = 100$

First, the standard error of the difference of proportions is

$$S_{p_1 - p_2} = \sqrt{\bar{p}\bar{q}\left(\frac{1}{n_1} + \frac{1}{n_2}\right)}$$

$$= \sqrt{(.375)(.625)\left(\frac{1}{100} + \frac{1}{100}\right)}$$

$$= .068$$

where

$$\bar{p} = \frac{(100)(.35) + (100)(.4)}{100 + 100} = .375$$

If we wish to test the two-tailed hypothesis of no difference, an observed Z-value must be calculated. Thus,

$$Z = \frac{(p_1 - p_2) - (\pi_1 - \pi_2)}{S_{p_1 - p_2}}$$

$$= \frac{(.35 - .40) - (0)}{.068}$$

$$= -.73$$

So, for this example we will accept the null hypothesis of no difference at the .05 level because the calculated Z-value is less than the absolute critical Z-value of 1.96.

ANALYSIS OF VARIANCE (ANOVA)

analysis of variance (ANOVA) Analysis of the effects of one treatment variable on an interval-scaled or ratio-scaled dependent variable; a technique to determine if statistically significant differences in means occur between two or more groups.

When the means of more than two groups or populations are to be compared, one-way **analysis of variance (ANOVA)** is the appropriate statistical tool. This bivariate statistical technique is referred to as "one-way" because there is only one independent variable (even though there may be several levels of that variable).[4] An example of an ANOVA problem is to compare women who are working full-time outside the home, working part-time outside the home, and not working outside the home on their willingness to purchase a personal computer. Here there is *one* independent variable—working status. The independent variable, working status, is said to have three levels: full-time employment, part-time employment, and no employment outside the home. Because there are three groups (levels), a *t*-test cannot be used to test for statistical significance.

If we have three groups, or levels, of the independent variable, the null hypothesis is stated as follows:

$$\mu_1 = \mu_2 = \mu_3$$

The null hypothesis is that all the means are equal. In the personal computer example, we are concerned with the average purchasing intentions of three different types of women. As the name *analysis of variance* suggests, the problem requires comparing variances to make inferences about the means. The logic of this technique is as follows. The variance of the means of the three groups will be large if these women differ from each other in terms of purchasing intentions. If we calculate this variance within groups and compare it to the variance of the group means about a grand mean, we can determine whether the means are significantly different. This will become clearer as we investigate the *F*-test.

F-Test

_F_-test
A procedure used to determine if there is more variability in the scores of one sample than in the scores of another sample.

The ***F*-test** is a procedure for comparing one sample variance to another sample variance. (The principle is similar to that of the chi-square test, where a sample variance is compared to a population variance.) The *F*-test determines whether there is more variability in the scores of one sample than in the scores of another sample. The key question is whether the two sample variances are different from each other or are from the same population.

The *F*-test utilizes measures of sample variance rather than the sample standard deviation because standard deviations cannot be summed. Summation is allowable with the sample variance.

_F_-statistic
A test statistic that measures the ratio of one sample variance to another sample variance, such as the variance between groups to the variance within groups.

To obtain the ***F*-statistic** (or *F*-ratio), the larger sample variance is divided by the smaller sample variance. To test the null hypothesis of no difference between the sample variances, a table of the *F*-distribution is necessary. Using Table 5 (or Table 6) in the appendix is much like using the tables of the *Z*- and *t*-distributions that we have previously examined. This table portrays the *F*-distribution, which is a probability distribution of the ratios of sample variances. This table of *F*-distributions indicates that the distribution of *F* is actually a family of distributions that change quite drastically with changes in sample sizes. Thus, degrees of freedom must be specified. Inspection of an *F*-table allows the researcher to determine the probability of finding an *F* as large as the calculated *F*.

Identifying and Partitioning the Total Variation

total variance
In analysis of variance, the sum of within-group variance and between-group variance.

within-group variance
Variation of scores within a group due to random error or individual difference.

between-group variance
Variation of scores between groups due either to the manipulation of an independent variable or to characteristics of the independent variable.

In analysis of variance, the basic consideration for the *F*-test is to identify the **total variance.** There will be two forms of variation: (1) variation of scores due to random error or within-group variation due to individual differences and (2) systematic variation of scores between the groups due to the manipulation of an independent variable or due to characteristics of the independent variable. Thus, we can partition total variance into **within-group variance** and **between-group variance.**

Z = 1.96

1 − .4750 = .525 ÷ 2 = .2625

.4750 ÷ 2 = .2375

.05 ÷ 2 = .025

$u = \left(\frac{E}{ZS}\right)$

$\left(\frac{1}{u}\right)\frac{u}{1} = \frac{ZS}{E}$

$\left(\frac{S}{1}\right)\frac{u}{S} = \frac{Z}{E}\left(\frac{S}{1}\right)$

$\left(\frac{Z}{1}\right)\frac{u}{SZ} = E\left(\frac{Z}{1}\right)$

Unicare

PPO

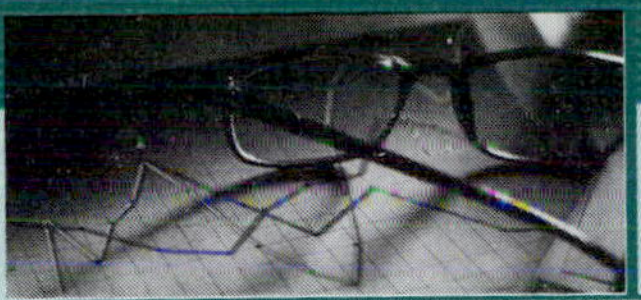

STATISTICAL TUTOR

ANALYSIS OF VARIANCE

THE SITUATION:
An experiment is conducted with four groups. Each group receives a different written instruction for performing a task, and the average productivity for each group is recorded.

QUESTIONS TO BE ANSWERED:
1. Are the differences among the four groups statistically significant?
2. Is the magnitude of difference between group 1 and group 4 large enough to justify a differential strategy?

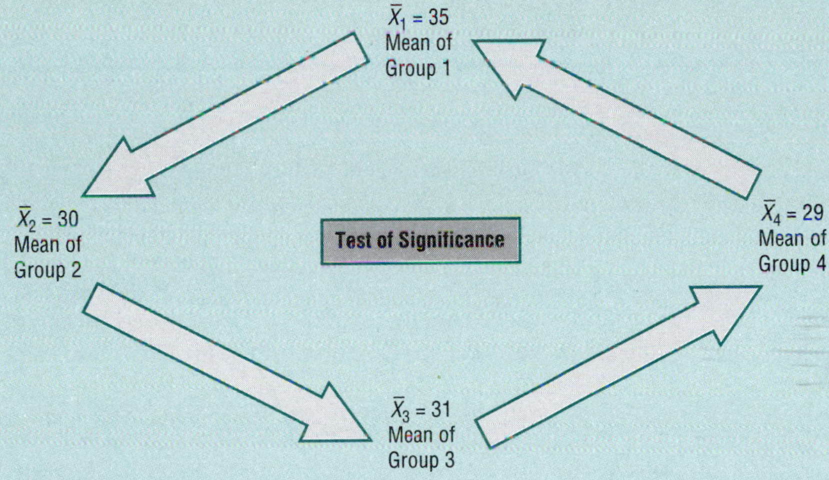

The *F*-distribution is the ratio of these two sources of variances. That is, *F* is defined as

$$F = \frac{\text{Variance between groups}}{\text{Variance within groups}}$$

The larger the ratio of variance between groups to variance within groups, the greater the value of *F*. If the *F*-value is large, it is likely that the results are statistically significant.

Calculating the *F*-Ratio

The data in Table 22.5 are from a hypothetical packaged-goods company's test-market experiment on pricing. Three pricing treatments are administered in four separate test markets (that is, 12 test areas, A–L, were required). These data will be used to illustrate ANOVA.

Terminology for the variance estimates is derived from the calculation procedures; an explanation of the terms used to calculate the *F*-ratio should clarify the meaning of the analysis of variance. The calculation of the *F*-ratio requires that we partition the total variation into two parts:

Table 22.5 A Test Market Experiment on Pricing

	Sales in Units (Thousands)		
	Regular Price $1.59	Reduced Price $1.19	Cents-off Coupon Regular Price
Test market A, B, or C	130	145	153
Test market D, E, or F	118	143	129
Test market G, H, or I	87	120	96
Test market J, K, or L	84	131	99
Mean	$\bar{X}_1 = 104.75$	$\bar{X}_2 = 134.75$	$\bar{X}_3 = 119.25$
Grand mean	$\bar{\bar{X}} = 119.58$		

$$\text{Total sum of squares} = \begin{matrix}\text{Within group}\\\text{sum of squares}\end{matrix} + \begin{matrix}\text{Between group}\\\text{sum of squares}\end{matrix}$$

or

$$SS_{\text{total}} = SS_{\text{within}} + SS_{\text{between}}$$

The total sum of squares, or SS_{total}, is computed by squaring the deviation of each score from the grand mean and summing these squares:[5]

$$SS_{\text{total}} = \sum_{i=1}^{n} \sum_{j=1}^{c} (X_{ij} - \bar{\bar{X}})^2$$

where

X_{ij} = individual score, i.e., the ith observation or test unit in the jth group
$\bar{\bar{X}}$ = grand mean
n = number of all observations or test units in a group
c = number of jth groups (or columns)

In our example,

$$\begin{aligned} SS_{\text{total}} &= (130 - 119.58)^2 + (118 - 119.58)^2 + (87 - 119.58)^2 \\ &\quad + (84 - 119.58)^2 + (145 - 119.58)^2 + (143 - 119.58)^2 \\ &\quad + (120 - 119.58)^2 + (131 - 119.58)^2 + (153 - 119.58)^2 \\ &\quad + (129 - 119.58)^2 + (96 - 119.58)^2 + (99 - 119.58)^2 \\ &= 5{,}948.93 \end{aligned}$$

SS_{within}, the variability that we observe within each group, is calculated by squaring the deviation of each score from its group mean and summing these scores:

$$SS_{\text{within}} = \sum_{i=1}^{n} \sum_{j=1}^{c} (X_{ij} - \bar{X}_j)^2$$

where

X_{ij} = individual score
$\bar{X}_j$ = group mean for the jth group
n = number of observations in a group
c = number of jth groups

In our example,

$$\begin{aligned} SS_{\text{within}} &= (130 - 104.75)^2 + (118 - 104.75)^2 + (87 - 104.75)^2 \\ &\quad + (84 - 104.75)^2 + (145 - 134.75)^2 + (143 - 134.75)^2 \\ &\quad + (120 - 134.75)^2 + (131 - 134.75)^2 + (153 - 119.25)^2 \\ &\quad + (129 - 119.25)^2 + (96 - 119.25)^2 + (99 - 119.25)^2 \\ &= 4{,}148.25 \end{aligned}$$

SS_{between}, the variability of the group means about a grand mean, is calculated by squaring the deviation of each group mean from the grand mean, multiplying by the number of items in the group, and summing these scores:

$$SS_{\text{between}} = \sum_{j=1}^{c} n_j(\bar{X}_j - \bar{\bar{X}})^2$$

where

$\bar{X}_j$ = group mean for the jth group
$\bar{\bar{X}}$ = grand mean
n_j = number of items in the jth group

In our example,

$$\begin{aligned} SS_{\text{between}} &= 4(104.75 - 119.58)^2 + 4(134.75 - 119.58)^2 \\ &\quad + 4(119.25 - 119.58)^2 \\ &= 1{,}800.68 \end{aligned}$$

The next calculation requires dividing the various sums of squares by their appropriate degrees of freedom. These divisions produce the variances, or *mean squares.* To obtain the mean square between groups, SS_{between} is divided by $c - 1$ degrees of freedom:

$$MS_{\text{between}} = \frac{SS_{\text{between}}}{c - 1}$$

In our example,

$$MS_{\text{between}} = \frac{1{,}800.68}{3 - 1} = \frac{1{,}800.68}{2} = 900.34$$

To obtain the mean square within groups, SS_{within} is divided by $cn - c$ degrees of freedom:

$$MS_{\text{within}} = \frac{SS_{\text{within}}}{cn - c}$$

In our example,

$$MS_{\text{within}} = \frac{4{,}148.25}{12 - 3} = \frac{4{,}148.25}{9} = 460.91$$

Finally, the F-ratio is calculated by taking the ratio of the mean square between groups to the mean square within groups. The between-groups mean square is used as the numerator and the within-groups mean square is used as the denominator:

$$F = \frac{MS_{\text{between}}}{MS_{\text{within}}}$$

Table 22.6 **Summary for Analysis of Variance**

Source of Variation	Sum of Squares	Degrees of Freedom	Mean Square	F-Ratio
Between groups	$SS_{\text{between}} = \sum_{j=1}^{c} n_j(\bar{X}_j - \bar{\bar{X}})^2$	$c - 1$	$MS_{\text{between}} = \frac{SS_{\text{between}}}{c - 1}$	—
Within groups	$SS_{\text{within}} = \sum_{i=1}^{n}\sum_{j=1}^{c}(X_{ij} - \bar{X}_j)^2$	$cn - c$	$MS_{\text{within}} = \frac{SS_{\text{within}}}{cn - c}$	$F = \frac{MS_{\text{between}}}{MS_{\text{within}}}$
Total	$SS_{\text{total}} = \sum_{i=1}^{n}\sum_{j=1}^{c}(X_{ij} - \bar{\bar{X}})^2$	$cn - 1$	—	—

where c = number of groups
n = number of observations in a group

In our example,

$$F = \frac{900.34}{460.91} = 1.95$$

There will be $(c - 1)$ degrees of freedom in the numerator and $(cn - c)$ degrees of freedom in the denominator:

$$\frac{c - 1}{cn - c} = \frac{3 - 1}{3(4) - 3} = \frac{2}{9}$$

In Table 5 in the appendix, the critical value of F at the .05 level for 2 and 9 degrees of freedom indicates an F of 4.26 would be required to reject the null hypothesis. In our example we conclude that we cannot reject the null hypothesis. It appears that all the price treatments produce approximately the same sales volume.

The information produced from an analysis of variance is traditionally summarized in table form. Tables 22.6 and 22.7 summarize the formulas and data from our example. Appendix 22B at the end of this chapter provides additional information on analysis of variance in complex experimental designs.

Table 22.7 **Pricing Experiment: ANOVA Table**

Source of Variation	Sum of Squares	Degrees of Freedom	Mean Square	F-Ratio
Between groups	1,800.68	2	900.34	—
Within groups	4,148.25	9	460.91	1.953
Total	5,948.93	11	—	—

SUMMARY

Bivariate statistical techniques analyze scores on two variables at a time. Tests of differences investigate hypotheses stating that two (or more) groups are different with respect to a certain behavior, characteristic, or attitude. Both the type of measurement and the number of groups to be compared influence researchers' choice of statistical tests of differences.

The chi-square statistic allows a researcher to test whether an observed sample distribution fits some given distribution. It can be used to analyze contingency, or cross-tabulation, tables. In this case the test allows us to determine whether two groups are independent. If they are not, then the variables are interrelated. For example, a business researcher may wish to determine if the respondent's sex makes a difference in some observed variable. The *t*-test for two independent samples is used to determine if the means of two independent samples are significantly different. For example, a researcher might compare two populations' characteristics using the same measure of an attribute on samples from both populations.

The *t*-test is appropriate when the population standard deviation is unknown. The *t*-test should be chosen over the *Z*-test if the sample size is small. A *Z*-test for two independent samples is typically used if a large sample has been drawn from each group, because the *t*-distribution approximates the *Z*-distribution when a sample is large. A *Z*-test for two independent samples may be used to determine if two proportions are significantly different.

One-way analysis of variance (ANOVA) compares the means of samples from more than two populations to determine if their differences are statistically significant. The technique is one-way because it deals with only one independent variable, although several levels of that variable may be used. The total variance in the observations is partitioned into two parts, that from within-group variation and that from between-group variation. The ratio of the variance between groups to the variance within groups gives an *F*-statistic. The *F*-distribution is a measure used to determine whether the variability of two samples differs significantly. In ANOVA, if the observed statistic is greater than the test value for some level of significance, the hypothesis that there is no significant difference in the means of the sample groups may be rejected.

Key Terms

test of differences
bivariate statistics
chi-square (χ^2) test
cell
t-test for difference of means
pooled estimate of the standard error
Z-test for differences of proportions
analysis of variance (ANOVA)
F-test
F-statistic
total variance
within-group variance
between-group variance

Questions for Review and Critical Thinking

1. What test of differences is appropriate in each of the following situations?
   (a) Average campaign contributions of Democrats, Republicans, and Independents are to be compared.
   (b) Managers and supervisors have responded "yes," "no," or "not sure" to an attitude question. Their answers are to be compared.
   (c) One-half of a sample receives an incentive in a mail survey. The other half does not. A comparison of response rates is desired.
   (d) Stockbrokers in the East, Midwest, and West were asked their annual incomes. Regional comparisons are to be made.

2. Perform a chi-square test on the following data:
   (a) Regulation is the best way to ensure a safe workplace.

	Managers	Blue-Collar Workers
Agree	58	66
Disagree	34	24
No opinion	8	10
Totals	100	100

   (b) Ownership of residence

	Male	Female
Yes	25	16
No	7	8
Totals	32	24

   (c) Age of shopper

	Store A	Store B
20–34	27	73
35–54	31	82
55 and over	11	93
Totals	69	248

3. Collapse the response categories in the following table so that it meets the assumption of the chi-square test; then perform the test.

	OWNERSHIP	
Education	**Owners**	**Nonowners**
Less than grade 8	0	8
Some high school	5	9
High school graduate	30	25
Some college	10	11
College graduate	12	15
Master's degree	3	6
Ph.D. degree	2	1

4. A personnel manager has a computer-generated list of all employees that indicates that 70 percent are full-time employees, 20 percent are part-time employees, and 10 percent are furloughed or laid-off employees. A sample of 50 employees from the list indicates 40 full-time employees, 6 part-time employees, and 4 furloughed/laid-off employees. Conduct a statistical test to determine if the sample is representative of the population.
5. Interpret the following SPSS computer output for the chi-square test. Variable COMMUTE is "How did you get to work last week?" Variable GENDER is "Are you male or female?"

COMMUTE * GENDER Crosstabulation

			GENDER		Total
			female	male	
COMMUTE	at home	Count	6	10	16
		% within COMMUTE	37.5%	62.5%	100.0%
		% within GENDER	7.0%	17.9%	11.3%
		% of Total	4.2%	7.0%	11.3%
	bus	Count	16	16	32
		% within COMMUTE	50.0%	50.0%	100.0%
		% within GENDER	18.6%	28.6%	22.5%
		% of Total	11.3%	11.3%	22.5%
	drive	Count	32	17	49
		% within COMMUTE	65.3%	34.7%	100.0%
		% within GENDER	37.2%	30.4%	34.5%
		% of Total	22.5%	12.0%	34.5%
	passeng	Count	24	9	33
		% within COMMUTE	72.7%	27.3%	100.0%
		% within GENDER	27.9%	16.1%	23.2%
		% of Total	16.9%	6.3%	23.3%
	walk	Count	8	4	12
		% within COMMUTE	66.7%	33.3%	100.0%
		% within GENDER	9.3%	7.1%	8.5%
		% of Total	5.6%	2.8%	8.5%
Total		Count	86	56	142
		% within COMMUTE	60.6%	39.4%	100.0%
		% within GENDER	100.0%	100.0%	100.0%
		% of Total	60.6%	39.4%	100.0%

Chi-Square Tests

	Value	df	Asymp. Sig. (2-sided)
Pearson Chi-Square	7.751[a]	4	.101
Likelihood Ratio	7.725	4	.102
N of Valid Cases	142		

[a] 1 cells (10.0%) have expected count less than 5. The minimum expected count is 4.73.

6. Test the hypothesis of no differences for average payback period (years) necessary to justify solar heating systems for residences.

Savings and Loans	Other Financiers
$\bar{X}_1 = 8.7$	$\bar{X}_2 = 7.7$
$S_1^2 = .5$	$S_2^2 = .6$
$n_1 = 100$	$n_2 = 64$

7. The managers in a company's East and West regions were rated on the basis of the company's evaluation system. A researcher wishes to conduct a t-test of means to determine if there is a difference between the East and West regions. Perform this calculation.

Region	Manager	Rating	Region	Manager	Rating
West	1	74	East	1	81
West	2	88	East	2	63
West	3	78	East	3	56
West	4	85	East	4	68
West	5	100	East	5	80
West	6	114	East	6	79
West	7	98	East	7	69

8. Given the following data, is there a difference between means?

	Sample 1	Sample 2
Sample mean	324	301
Sample variance	166.41	81
Sample size	44	56

9. A sales force (n = 67) received some management-by-objectives training. Are the before–after mean scores for salespeople's job performance statistically significant at the .05 level?

Skill	Before	After	t
Planning ability	4.84	5.43	4.88
Territory coverage	5.24	5.51	1.89
Activity reporting	5.37	5.42	.27

10. The incomes of owners of trash compactors were compared with the incomes of nonowners. The average incomes were as follows:

	Owners	Nonowners
$\overline{X}$	4.6	3.5

Higher values represent higher levels of income. (Actual scaled average: less than \$7,500 = 1, \$7,500–\$19,999 = 2, \$20,000–\$34,999 = 3, \$35,000–\$49,999 = 4, \$50,000–\$80,000 = 5, over \$80,000 = 6.) Is a t-test appropriate?

11. Test the hypothesis of no difference for the following two groups on credit union usage:

Women under 35	Women 35–54
$P_1 = 13\%$	$P_2 = 23\%$
$S_p = 0.4$	$S_p = 0.4$
$n = 144$	$n = 169$

12. Conduct a Z-test to determine if the following two samples indicate the population proportions are significantly different at the .05 level:

	Sample 1	Sample 2
Sample proportion	.77	.68
Sample size	55	46

13. An Excel Spreadsheet is reprinted below. Interpret the *t*-test results. Are they statistically significant?

Microsoft Excel - MLB t-test

File Edit View Insert Format Tools Data Window Help

Arial 10 100%

D1 =

	A	B	C	D	E	F
1	Beer	Soda				
2	12	14				
3	16	18				
4	20	20		t-Test: Paired Two Sample for Means		
5	20	16				
6	16	16			**Variable 1**	**Variable 2**
7	16	12		Mean	16.83333333	15.8
8	16	14		Variance	10.35057471	7.820689655
9	16	16		Observations	30	30
10	24	14		Pearson Correlation	0.264451682	
11	20	16		Hypothesized Mean Difference	0	
12	16	16		df	29	
13	24	16		t Stat	1.545410551	
14	14	14		P(T<=t) one-tail	0.06654553	
15	14	14		t Critical one-tail	1.699127097	
16	16	16		P(T<=t) two-tail	0.13309106	
17	16	20		t Critical two-tail	2.045230758	
18	16	12				
19	18	16				
20	21	20				
21	16	12				
22	16	16				
23	22	16				
24	20	24				

Sheet1 / Sheet2 / Sheet3

Ready NUM

14. Suppose a researcher has one nominally scaled variable and one interval-scaled variable. The researcher wishes to use a chi-square test. What can be done to make this possible?
15. An organizational researcher conducts an experiment to measure the impact of perception of task difficulty on level of aspiration for performing the task a second time. Group 1 was told the task was very difficult, Group 2 was told the task was somewhat difficult but manageable, and Group 3 was told the task was easy. Perform an ANOVA on the following data:

	SUBJECTS' LEVEL OF ASPIRATION (10-POINT SCALE)		
Subject	**Group 1**	**Group 2**	**Group 3**
1	6	5	5
2	7	4	6
3	5	7	5
4	8	6	4
5	8	7	2
6	6	7	3
Cases	6	6	6

16. A researcher was interested in the characteristics of the clientele at a Hard Rock Cafe at lunchtime and in the evenings. On a Saturday in July the researcher collected the following age data by randomly sampling table numbers at the cafe and then obtaining the age of everyone sitting at the table.

	Lunch		Evening
Table 1	11	Table 1	26
	9		26
	43		27
	39		28
Table 2	40	Table 2	21
	42		23
	13		21
	9		
Table 3	12	Table 3	24
	13		24
	44		23
	47		
Table 4	44	Table 4	24
	10		22
	12		21
	11		24
Table 5	9	Table 5	22
	39		23
	46		27
	11		
Table 6	32	Table 6	22
	9		18
Table 7	39	Table 7	22
	13		19
	11		
Table 8	43	Table 8	23
	5		24
	12		24
Total number of people	28		25

How would you analyze the differences between the evening and the lunchtime clientele? Perform the statistical analysis that you conclude is the best.

17. A researcher finds that 122 respondents have checking accounts at banks, 131 at savings and loans, and 4 at credit unions. The researcher groups the 4 credit union customers in with the savings and loans group so that a bivariate comparison between banks and S&Ls can be made. Is this ethical?

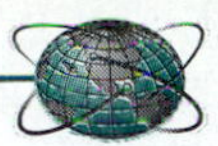

Exploring the Internet

The Federal Reserve Bank of St. Louis maintains a database called FRED (Federal Reserve Economic Data). Navigate to the FRED database at http://www.stls.frb.org/fred/index.html. Randomly select a 5-year period between 1970 and 1995 and then compare average figures for U.S. employment in retail trade with those for U.S. employment in wholesale trade. What statistical tests are appropriate?

WebSurveyor Activities

WebSurveyor allows a researcher to download a survey's results to a data file. Exporting data into other applications is handled through CSV (comma separated value) files. Using the sports opinion survey, we have done this for you. The exported files have been converted to Microsoft Excel (Sports.xls) and to SPSS (Sports.sav). Numeric codes are used in these files.

Using SPSS or Excel, use Gender to conduct a test of difference on several of the old school/new school attitude statements.

Case Suggestions

Case 29: LastDance Health Care
Case 30: Sunbelt Energy Corporation
Case 31: Employees Federal Credit Union

APPENDIX

NONPARAMETRIC STATISTICS FOR TESTS OF DIFFERENCES

For many of the statistical tests you have learned to use, it has been necessary to assume that the population (or sampling distribution) is normally distributed.[6] If it is normal, the error associated with making inferences about the population from sample data can be estimated, but if it is not normal, the error may be large and cannot be estimated. It is therefore valuable to know some tests for which such a strong assumption as normality does not need to be made about the population distribution; these are called *nonparametric* tests. You have already studied one of them: the χ^2 test. There are many others, but only three of them are included here.

The term *nonparametric* is confusing. It was originally applied when no assumption needed to be made about the population distribution (as in the χ^2 tests) and when there was no estimate of a population parameter. Almost always, however, some assumption needs to be made. So *nonparametric* is now used to mean that a less stringent requirement than normality is made for the population distribution. Also, the meaning of the phrase *nonparametric test* has been extended to include any test that uses nominal-scaled or ordinal-scaled data. Thus, a comparison of the heights of two samples of women is made with a nonparametric test if, instead of measuring each person's height, the researcher simple arranges the women in a row in order of height (the two tallest come from Sample 1, the third tallest comes from Sample 2, and so on). Because the data are ranked and not ratio- or interval-scaled, a nonparametric test is used—even if it is known that the heights in both populations from which the samples were chosen are normally distributed.

Nonparametric tests have many advantages: They avoid the error caused by assuming that a population is normally distributed when it is not; the computations that need to be made are often very simple; and the data may be easier to collect (almost certainly so when categorical or ranked rather than ratio- or interval-scaled data are used). Why are nonparametric tests not always used, then? The answer is that you don't get something for nothing. If the population distribution is normal, so that, say, a *t*-test or a nonparametric test may be chosen, the former will generally give a smaller value of β or *Type II* error (i.e., a smaller error) than the latter for a given, fixed level of *Type I* error (value of α). If this is the case, sample size will have to be larger for the nonparametric test if the same limits on α and β are to be attained as with a *t*-test. For the same sample size, then, the *t*-test results usually will be more reliable. Also, the null hypotheses are sometimes more general; rejection may imply that two population distributions are different, but it is not known whether they have different means, different variances, or differently shaped distributions (e.g., one normal and the other not).

WILCOXON MATCHED-PAIRS SIGNED-RANKS TEST

The *Wilcoxon matched-pairs signed-ranks test* is a good measure of differences when a researcher wishes to test the hypothesis $\mu_1 = \mu_2$ and knows that the samples are not independent, or when a researcher wishes to compare magnitudes of differences in ordinal rankings, such as preference ratings between two alternatives. A common situation is the "before/after" experiment, where the same subjects are measured twice.

Suppose a manager wishes to know if a training program will have a positive impact on attitude toward advancement within the organization. Table 22A.1 shows attitude ratings before and after a training program for 11 managers. The Wilcoxon matched-pairs signed-ranks test begins with calculating the signed difference for each matched pair of observations. If the two observations in a pair are the same, this pair is dropped from the analysis. Next, these differences are rank-ordered according to their absolute size. If there are two (or more) pairs with identical absolute-difference values, such as for Manager 2 and Manager 9, an average rank score is given to each of the pairs. Finally, the positive or negative sign is assigned to each rank score, and the scores for the positive and negative groups are separately totaled. The symbol T_p refers to the summed ranks for the positive differences, and the symbol T_n refers to the summed ranks for the negative differences.[7] T represents the *smaller* of T_p or T_n, and for small samples T is the test statistic.

In our example T_n has the smaller value. Thus, the calculated value of T is 17. In the Wilcoxon matched-pairs signed-ranks test, the null hypothesis is rejected if the calculated value of T is *equal to or less than* the critical T-value found in Table 8 in the appendix at the end

Table 22A.1 Training Program Example

Manager	"Before" Score	"After" Score	Sign of Difference	Absolute Difference	Rank	Signed Rank Positive	Signed Rank Negative
1	56	71	+	15	10.0	10.0	
2	46	49	+	3	3.5	3.5	
3	74	73	−	1	1.0		1.0
4	66	72	+	6	8.0	8.0	
5	59	55	−	4	5.5		5.5
6	45	40	−	5	7.0		7.0
7	85	87	+	2	2.0	2.0	
8	63	67	+	4	5.5	5.5	
9	67	64	−	3	3.5		3.5
10	79	79		0	—	—	—
11	70	78	+	8	9.0	9.0	
						$T_p = 38$	$T_n = 17$

of the book. In that table N represents the number of pairs. At $N = 10$ (because the tied pair is discarded from the analysis) the critical T-value is 8 at the .05 level of statistical significance. Because the calculated value of T (17) is greater than 8, we cannot reject the null hypothesis. When the sample size is large, the sampling distribution is approximately normal, and the Z-value may be calculated using the following formula:

$$Z = \frac{T - \dfrac{N(N+1)}{4}}{\sqrt{\dfrac{N(N+1)(2N+1)}{24}}}$$

MANN-WHITNEY TEST

Many tests of group differences concern comparing two sample means to determine if there is a statistically significant difference between the two population means. The Mann-Whitney (or ranked-sum) test allows for testing group differences when the populations are not normally distributed or when it cannot be assumed that the samples are from populations that are equal in variability. It is an alternative to the t-test for two independent samples.

To see how this test is used, consider the following data on the number of minutes needed by two groups of factory workers to learn to assemble a chain saw.[8] Group A received classroom training, whereas Group B received only on-the-job training.

		Average
Group A	35, 39, 51, 63, 48, 31, 29, 41, 55	43.56
Group B	85, 28, 42, 37, 61, 54, 36, 57	50.00

The means for groups A and B are 43.56 and 50, respectively. In this case we wish to decide whether the difference between the means is significant.

The two samples are arranged jointly, as if they were one sample, in order of increasing time, with each value assigned to Group A or to Group B. Then the ranks 1, 2, 3, 4, . . . , 17 are assigned to the scores, as shown.

Time	Group	Rank
28	B	1
29	A	2
31	A	3
35	A	4
36	B	5
37	B	6
39	A	7
41	A	8
42	B	9
48	A	10
51	A	11
54	B	12
55	A	13
57	B	14
61	B	15
63	A	16
85	B	17

Notice that the Group A scores occupy the ranks of 2, 3, 4, 7, 8, 10, 11, 13, and 16. The Group B scores occupy the ranks of 1, 5, 6, 9, 12, 14, 15, and 17. Now we sum the ranks of the group with the smaller sample size (in this case, Group B) and get

$$1 + 5 + 6 + 9 + 12 + 14 + 15 + 17 = 79$$

The sum of the ranks is denoted by R. In this case $R = 79$.

We always let n_1 and n_2 denote the sizes of the two samples, where n_1 represents the smaller of the two sample sizes. Thus, R represents the sum of the ranks of n_1. If both groups are of equal size, then either one is called n, and R represents the sum of the ranks of this group. Statistical theory tells us that if both n_1 and n_2 are large enough (each equal to 8 or more), then the distribution of R can be approximated by a normal distribution. The test statistic is given by the formula

$$Z = \frac{R - \mu_R}{\sigma_R}$$

where

$$\mu_R = \frac{n_1(n_1 + n_2 + 1)}{2}$$

$$\sigma_R = \sqrt{\frac{n_1 n_2(n_1 + n_2 + 1)}{12}}$$

In our case $R = 79$, $n_1 = 8$, and $n_2 = 9$, so

$$\begin{aligned}\mu_R &= \frac{n_1(n_1 + n_2 + 1)}{2} \\ &= \frac{8(8 + 9 + 1)}{2} \\ &= 72\end{aligned}$$

and

$$\begin{aligned}\sigma_R &= \sqrt{\frac{n_1 n_2(n_1 + n_2 + 1)}{12}} \\ &= \sqrt{\frac{8(9)(8 + 9 + 1)}{12}} = \sqrt{108} \\ &= 10.39\end{aligned}$$

The test statistic then becomes

$$Z = \frac{R - \mu_R}{\sigma_R} = \frac{79 - 72}{10.39} = .67$$

Using a .05 level of significance, we reject the null hypothesis of equal means if $Z > 1.96$ or $Z < -1.96$. Since the value of $Z = .67$ falls in the acceptance region, we do not reject the null hypothesis. There is no significant difference between the means of these two groups.

The method just described is called the *Mann-Whitney test.* Statisticians have constructed tables that give the appropriate critical values when both sample sizes, n_1 and n_2, are smaller than 8. The interested reader can find such tables in many books on nonparametric statistics. The corresponding exact statistic is called the *Mann-Whitney U test.*

KRUSKAL-WALLIS TEST FOR SEVERAL INDEPENDENT SAMPLES

When a researcher wishes to compare three or more groups or populations and the data are ordinal, the Kruskal-Wallis test is the appropriate statistical technique. This test may be thought of as a nonparametric equivalent of analysis of variance. However, as with all nonparametric tests, the assumptions are less restricting: The researcher does not have to assume that the underlying populations are normally distributed or that equal variances are shared by each group. If there are three groups, the null hypothesis is that Population 1 equals Population 2, which equals Population 3. In other words, the Kruskal-Wallis test is a technique to determine if the three populations have the same distribution shape and dispersion.

The test requires that the data be ranked from lowest to highest or that the original data be converted so that a numerical rank may be assigned to every observation. If two observations have the same rank (i.e., when ties occur), the mean rank score is assigned to both of the observations. The Kruskal-Wallis test statistic is the H-statistic. As an illustration of the calculation of the H-statistic, consider the following example. An advertising agency employs three different film production companies to produce its television commercials. The advertising agency has taken a sample of five commercials from each of the production houses, and agency executives have ranked the production quality of the commercials from best quality (1) to lowest quality (15). These ranks are shown in Table 22A.2. Notice that the advertising agency considered two commercials to be ranked of equal quality. Hence, rather than being ranked 3 and 4, the two commercials are each ranked 3.5. The H-statistic is calculated as follows:

$$H = \frac{12}{n(n + 1)}\left(\sum \frac{R_i^2}{n_i}\right) - 3(n + 1)$$

where

R_i = sum of the ranks of the ith group
n_i = sample size of the ith group
n = combined sample sizes of all groups

Table 22A.2 Quality Rankings of Television Commercials

RANK		
Production Company 1	Production Company 2	Production Company 3
9	6	1
5	13	7
3.5	10	15
14	2	12
8	3.5	11
$R_1 = 39.5$	$R_2 = 34.5$	$R_3 = 46$

Thus,

$$H = \frac{12}{n(n+1)}\left(\frac{R_1^2}{n_1} + \frac{R_2^2}{n_2} + \frac{R_3^2}{n_3}\right) - 3(n+1)$$

$$= \frac{12}{15(15+1)}\left(\frac{(39.5)^2}{5} + \frac{(34.5)^2}{5} + \frac{(46)^2}{5}\right) - 3(15+1)$$

$$= \frac{12}{240}\left(\frac{1560.25}{5} + \frac{1190.25}{5} + \frac{2116}{5}\right) - 48$$

$$= .05(973.3) - 48$$

$$= 48.665 - 48$$

$$= .665$$

When the sample size (n_i) from each group or population exceeds 4, H is approximately the same as χ^2 with degrees of freedom equal to $K - 1$, where K is the number of groups.

In our example degrees of freedom is $(3 - 1) = 2$. Table 4 in the appendix shows that the critical value at the .05 level with two degrees of freedom is 5.991. Since the calculated H-value is .665, we cannot reject the null hypothesis.

APPENDIX 22B

ANOVA FOR COMPLEX EXPERIMENTAL DESIGNS

ANOVA FOR A RANDOMIZED BLOCK DESIGN

To test for statistical significance in a randomized block design (mentioned in Chapter 12), another version of analysis of variance is utilized. The linear model for the randomized block design for an individual observation is[9]

$$Y_{ij} = \mu + \alpha_j + \beta_i + \epsilon_{ij}$$

where

Y_{ij} = individual observation on the dependent variable
μ = grand mean
α_j = jth treatment effect
β_i = ith block effect
ϵ_{ij} = random error or residual

The statistical objective is to determine if there are significant differences among treatment means and block means. This is done by calculating an F-ratio for each source of effects.

The same logic that applies in single-factor ANOVA—using variance estimates to test for differences among means—applies in ANOVA for randomized block designs. Thus, to conduct the ANOVA, we partition the total sum of squares (SS_{total}) into nonoverlapping components.[10]

$$SS_{total} = SS_{treatments} + SS_{blocks} + SS_{error}$$

The various sources of variance are defined as follows:

- Total sum of squares:

$$SS_{total} = \sum_{i=1}^{r}\sum_{j=1}^{c}(Y_{ij} - \bar{\bar{Y}})^2$$

where

Y_{ij} = individual observation
$\bar{\bar{Y}}$ = grand mean
r = number of blocks (rows)
c = number of treatments (columns)

- Treatment sum of squares:

$$SS_{treatments} = \sum_{i=1}^{r}\sum_{j=1}^{c}(\bar{Y}_j - \bar{\bar{Y}})^2$$

where

$\bar{Y}_j$ = jth treatment mean
$\bar{\bar{Y}}$ = grand mean

- Block sum of squares:

$$SS_{blocks} = \sum_{i=1}^{r}\sum_{j=1}^{c}(\bar{Y}_i - \bar{\bar{Y}})^2$$

where

$\bar{Y}_i$ = ith block mean
$\bar{\bar{Y}}$ = grand mean

- Sum of squares error:

$$SS_{error} = \sum_{i=1}^{r}\sum_{j=1}^{c}(Y_{ij} - \bar{Y}_i - \bar{Y}_j - \bar{\bar{Y}})^2$$

The SS_{error} may also be calculated in the following manner:

$$SS_{error} = SS_{total} - SS_{treatments} - SS_{blocks}$$

The degrees of freedom for $SS_{treatments}$ are equal to $c - 1$ because $SS_{treatments}$ reflects dispersion of treatment means from the grand mean, which is fixed. Degrees of freedom for blocks are $r - 1$ for similar reasons. SS_{error} reflects variations from both treatment and block means; thus, d.f. = $(r - 1)(c - 1)$.

Mean squares are calculated by dividing the appropriate sum of squares by the corresponding degrees of freedom.

Table 22B.1 is an ANOVA table for the randomized block design. It summarizes what has been discussed and illustrates the calculation of mean squares. F-ratios for treatment and block effects are calculated as follows:

$$F_{treatment} = \frac{\text{Mean square treatment}}{\text{Mean square error}}$$

$$F_{blocks} = \frac{\text{Mean square blocks}}{\text{Mean square error}}$$

TABLE 22B.1 ANOVA TABLE FOR RANDOMZIED BLOCK DESIGN

Source of Variation	Sum of Squares	Degrees of Freedom	Mean Squares
Between blocks	SS_{blocks}	$r - 1$	$\frac{SS_{blocks}}{r-1}$
Between treatments	$SS_{treatments}$	$c - 1$	$\frac{SS_{treatments}}{c-1}$
Error	SS_{error}	$(r - 1)(c - 1)$	$\frac{SS_{error}}{(r-1)(c-1)}$
Total	SS_{total}	$rc - 1$	—

FACTORIAL DESIGN

There is considerable similarity between the factorial design (mentioned in Chapter 12) and the one-way analysis of variance. The sum of squares for each of the treatment factors (rows and columns) is similar to the between-groups sum of squares in the single-factor model; that is, each treatment sum of squares is calculated by taking the deviation of the treatment means from the grand mean. Of course, determining the sum of squares for the interaction is a new calculation because this source of variance is not attributable to the treatments sum of squares or the error sum of squares.

ANOVA for a Factorial Experiment

In a two-factor experimental design the linear model for an individual observation is

$$Y_{ijk} = \mu + \beta_i + \alpha_j + I_{ij} + \epsilon_{ijk}$$

where

Y_{ijk} = individual observation on the dependent variable
μ = grand mean
β_i = ith effect of factor B—row treatment
α_j = jth effect of factor A—column treatment
I_{ij} = interaction effect of factors A and B
ϵ_{ijk} = random error or residual

Partitioning the Sum of Squares for a Two-Way ANOVA

Again, the total sum of squares can be allocated into distinct and nonoverlapping portions:

Sum of squares total =
Sum of squares rows (Treatment B)
+ Sum of squares columns (Treatment A)
+ Sum of squares interaction
+ Sum of squares error

or

$$SS_{total} = SSR_{\text{Treatment B}} + SSC_{\text{Treatment A}} + SS_{interaction} + SS_{error}$$

The formulas for calculation are given below.

- Sum of squares total:

$$SS_{total} = \sum_{i=1}^{r} \sum_{j=1}^{c} \sum_{k=1}^{n} (Y_{ijk} - \bar{\bar{Y}})^2$$

where

Y_{ijk} = individual observation on the dependent variable
$\bar{\bar{Y}}$ = grand mean
j = level of factor A
i = level of factor B
k = number of an observation in a particular cell
r = total number of levels of factor B (rows)
c = total number of levels of factor A (columns)
n = total number of observations in the sample

- Sum of squares for the row treatment—factor B:

$$SSR_{\text{Treatment B}} = \sum_{i=1}^{r} (\bar{Y}_i - \bar{\bar{Y}})^2$$

where

$\bar{Y}_i$ = mean of the ith treatment—factor B

- Sum of squares for the column treatment—factor A:

$$SSC_{\text{Treatment A}} = \sum_{j=1}^{c} (\bar{Y}_j - \bar{\bar{Y}})^2$$

where

$\bar{Y}_j$ = mean of the jth treatment—factor A

- Sum of squares interaction:

$$SS_{\text{interaction}} = \sum_{i=1}^{r} \sum_{j=1}^{c} \sum_{k=1}^{n} (\bar{Y}_{ij} - \bar{Y}_i - \bar{Y}_j - \bar{\bar{Y}})^2$$

However, $SS_{\text{interaction}}$ is generally indirectly computed in the following manner:

$$SS_{\text{interaction}} = SS_{\text{total}} - SSR_{\text{Treatment B}} - SSC_{\text{Treatment A}} - SS_{\text{error}}$$

- Sum of squares error:

$$SS_{\text{error}} = \sum_{i=1}^{r} \sum_{j=1}^{c} \sum_{k=1}^{n} (Y_{ijk} - \bar{Y}_{ij})^2$$

where

$\bar{Y}_{ij}$ = mean of the interaction effect

These sums of squares, along with their respective degrees of freedom and mean squares, are summarized in Table 22B.2.

TABLE 22B.2 ANOVA TABLE FOR TWO-FACTOR DESIGN

Source of Variation	Sum of Squares	Degrees of Freedom	Mean Square	*F*-Ratio
Treatment B	$SSR_{\text{Treatment B}}$	$r - 1$	$MSR_{\text{Treatment B}} = \dfrac{SSR_{\text{Treatment B}}}{r - 1}$	$\dfrac{MSR_{\text{Treatment B}}}{MS_{\text{error}}}$
Treatment A	$SSC_{\text{Treatment A}}$	$c - 1$	$MSC_{\text{Treatment A}} = \dfrac{SSC_{\text{Treatment A}}}{c - 1}$	$\dfrac{MSC_{\text{Treatment A}}}{MS_{\text{error}}}$
Interaction	$SS_{\text{interaction}}$	$(r - 1)(c - 1)$	$MS_{\text{interaction}} = \dfrac{SS_{\text{interaction}}}{(r - 1)(c - 1)}$	$\dfrac{MS_{\text{interaction}}}{MS_{\text{error}}}$
Error	SS_{error}	$rc(n - 1)$	$MS_{\text{error}} = \dfrac{SS_{\text{error}}}{rc(n - 1)}$	
Total	SS_{total}	$rcn - 1$		

CHAPTER

23

BIVARIATE ANALYSIS: Measures of Association

If you found a variable that forecast the direction of next year's stock market with an accuracy of better than 80 percent, would you be interested in its prediction? If so, watch the Super Bowl. In 28 out of the 34 years from 1967 to 2000, the market rose by year's end if a team from the original NFL won the championship or fell by year's end if a team from the old American Football League (now the NFL's American Football Conference) won. The value of stock market indexes appears to be associated with the football league winning the Super Bowl. Most likely this is mere coincidence, but many investors still root for teams from the original NFL.

A number of business questions deal with the association between two (or more) variables. Questions such as "Is sales productivity associated with pay incentives?" or "Is socioeconomic status associated with the likelihood of purchasing a recreational vehicle?" or "Does work status relate to attitudes toward the role of women in society?" can be answered by statistically investigating the relationships between the two variables in question. This chapter investigates how to analyze such questions. ■

What you will learn in this chapter

- To give examples of the types of business questions that may be answered by analyzing the association between two variables.
- To list the common procedures for measuring association and to discuss how the measurement scale will influence the selection of statistical tests.
- To discuss the concept of the simple correlation coefficient.
- To calculate a simple correlation coefficient and a coefficient of determination.
- To understand that correlation does not mean causation.
- To interpret a correlation matrix.
- To explain the concept of bivariate linear regression.
- To identify the intercept and slope coefficients.
- To discuss the least-squares method of regression analysis.
- To draw a regression line.
- To test the statistical significance of a least-squares regression.
- To calculate the intercept and slope coefficients in a bivariate linear regression.
- To interpret analysis of variance summary tables for linear regression.

Suppose sales volume is the dependent variable that we wish to predict. The independent variables found to be associated with the dependent variable sales volume may be aspects of the marketing mix, such as price, number of salespeople, amount of advertising, and/or uncontrollable environmental variables such as population or gross national product. For example, most managers would not be surprised to find that sales of baby carriages are associated with the number of babies born a few months prior to the sales period. In this case the dependent variable is the sales volume of baby carriages. The independent variable is the number of babies born.

The mathematical symbol X is commonly used for the independent variable, and Y is typically used for the dependent variable. It is appropriate to label dependent and independent variables only when it is assumed that the independent variable caused the dependent variable.

Exhibit 23.1 compares the Dow Jones industrial average with the long-term interest rate (30-year-bond yield). "Eyeballing" this chart gives the impression that these two financial variables are associated. Specifically, the variables are inversely related: Stock prices are up when interest rates are down. However, we do not have any mathematical measure of the strength of the relationship.

In many situations measures of differences, such as the chi-square test, provide information on whether two or more variables are interrelated, or associated. For example, a chi-square test between a measure of computer literacy and a measure of education provides some information about the independence or interrelationship of the two variables. Although measures such as chi-square are useful sources of information about association, statisticians have developed several other techniques to estimate the strength of association.

EXHIBIT 23.1 **TWO VARIABLES THAT ARE ASSOCIATED: STOCK PRICES AND INTEREST RATES**[1]

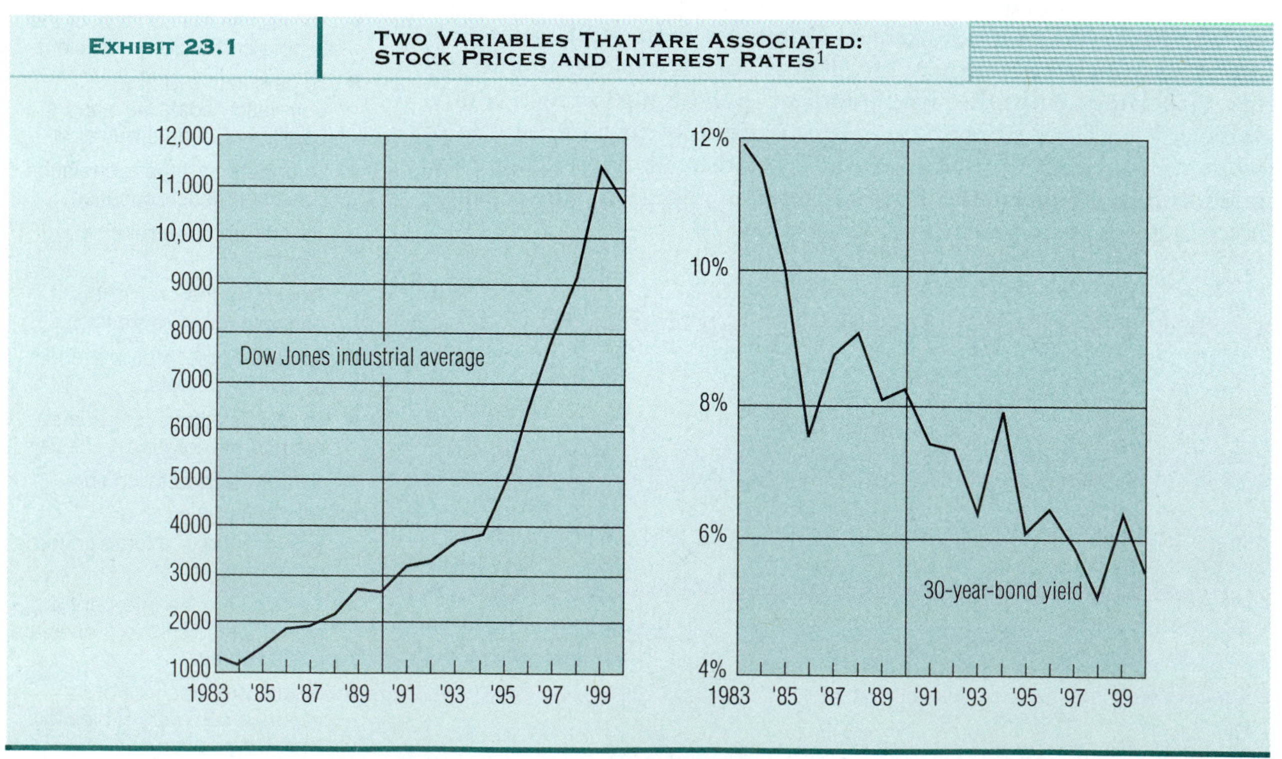

Exhibit 23.2 | **Bivariate Analysis—Common Procedures for Testing Association**

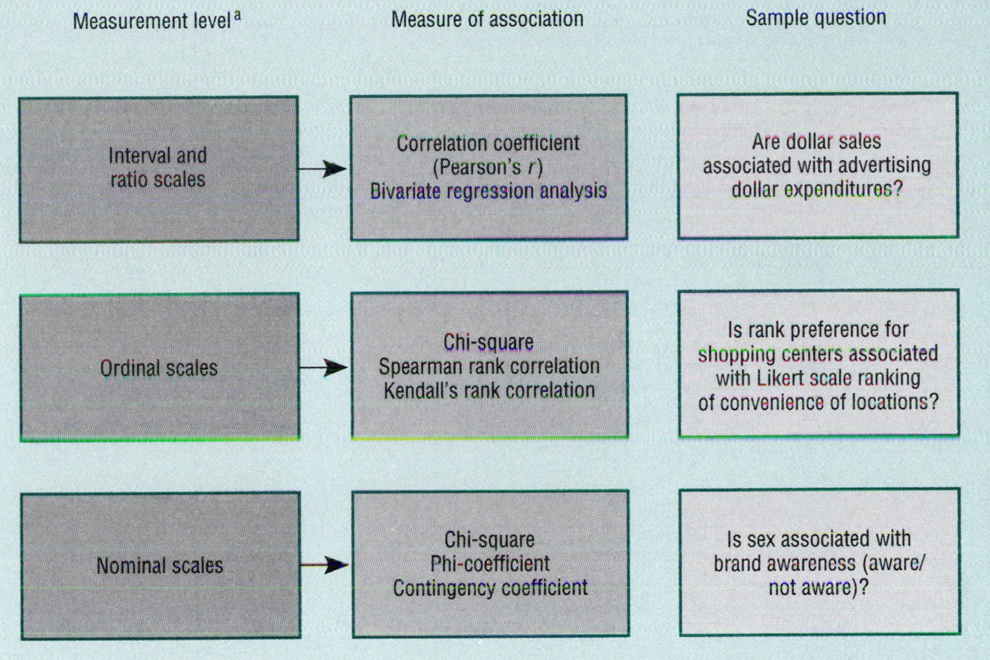

[a] If at least one of the two variables has a given level of measurement, the appropriate procedure is the one with the fewest assumptions about the data.

measures of association
Statistical values designed to represent covariation between variables.

Exhibit 23.2 shows that the type of measures utilized will influence the choice of statistical **measures of association.** This chapter describes simple correlation[2] (Pearson's product-moment correlation coefficient, *r*) and bivariate regression. Both techniques require interval-scaled or ratio-scaled data. The other techniques are for advanced students who have a specific requirement for these tests.[3]

SIMPLE CORRELATION COEFFICIENT

simple correlation coefficient
A statistical measure of the covariation, or association, between two variables.

The most popular technique that indicates the relationship of one variable to another is simple correlation analysis. The **simple correlation coefficient** is a statistical measure of the covariation, or association, between two variables. The correlation coefficient, *r*, ranges from $+1.0$ to -1.0. If the value of *r* is 1.0, there is a perfect positive linear (straight-line) relationship. If the value of *r* is -1.0, there is a perfect negative linear relationship, or a perfect inverse relationship. No correlation is indicated if $r = 0$. A correlation coefficient indicates both the magnitude of the linear relationship and the direction of the relationship. For example, if we find that $r = -.92$, we know we have a relatively strong inverse relationship. That is, the greater the value measured by variable *X*, the less the value measured by variable *Y*.

Medical college of Wisconsin in conjunction with Pull-Ups® training pants. It's an approach to training that has been proven in homes like yours. So take your time as your browse through the three steps we've mapped out for you and your Big Kid...Ready? Out! Coach! Learning to toilet train is like learning any other skill–it takes patience and consistency. Remember, kids train more quickly and easily with a helpful, patient and caring coach around...like you.

Ready?
Actively watch for the signs of readiness.

- Is your child ready?
- What to expect with potty training.
- What is potty training?
- Myths about potty training.
- What stage is your child in?

Out!
Making the big switch out of diapers and into training pants.

- Potty training tools.
- Four "musts" of potty training.

Coach!
Taking an active and positive role in your child's training progress.

- Using Praise and Rewards.
- Consistency is key.
- Keeping your "Big Kid" motivated.
- Celebrating small victories.
- Toilet training on the road.

Kimberly-Clark

For more information about other great Kimberly-Clark brands, visit our Kimberly-Clark Corporation website.

A study in 1997 by the American Academy of Pediatrics found that only 22 percent of children are potty trained by age 2½, compared to 90 percent in 1961. The study found no relationship between the age at which children became potty trained and attendance at daycare, mothers working outside the home, or the presence of siblings.[4]

The formula for calculating the correlation coefficient for two variables X and Y is

$$r_{xy} = r_{yx} = \frac{\Sigma(X_i - \bar{X})(Y_i - \bar{Y})}{\sqrt{\Sigma(X_i - \bar{X})^2 \Sigma(Y_i - \bar{Y})^2}}$$

where the symbols $\bar{X}$ and $\bar{Y}$ represent the sample means of X and Y, respectively.

An alternative way of expressing the correlation formula is

$$r_{xy} = r_{yx} = \frac{\sigma_{xy}}{\sqrt{\sigma_x^2 \sigma_y^2}}$$

where

$$\sigma_x^2 = \text{variance of } X$$

$$\sigma_y^2 = \text{variance of } Y$$

$$\sigma_{xy} = \text{covariance of } X \text{ and } Y$$

with

$$\sigma_{xy} = \frac{\Sigma(X_i - \bar{X})(Y_i - \bar{Y})}{N}$$

If associated values of X_i and Y_i differ from their means in the same direction, then their covariance will be positive. If the values of X_i and Y_i have a tendency to deviate in opposite directions, covariance will be negative.

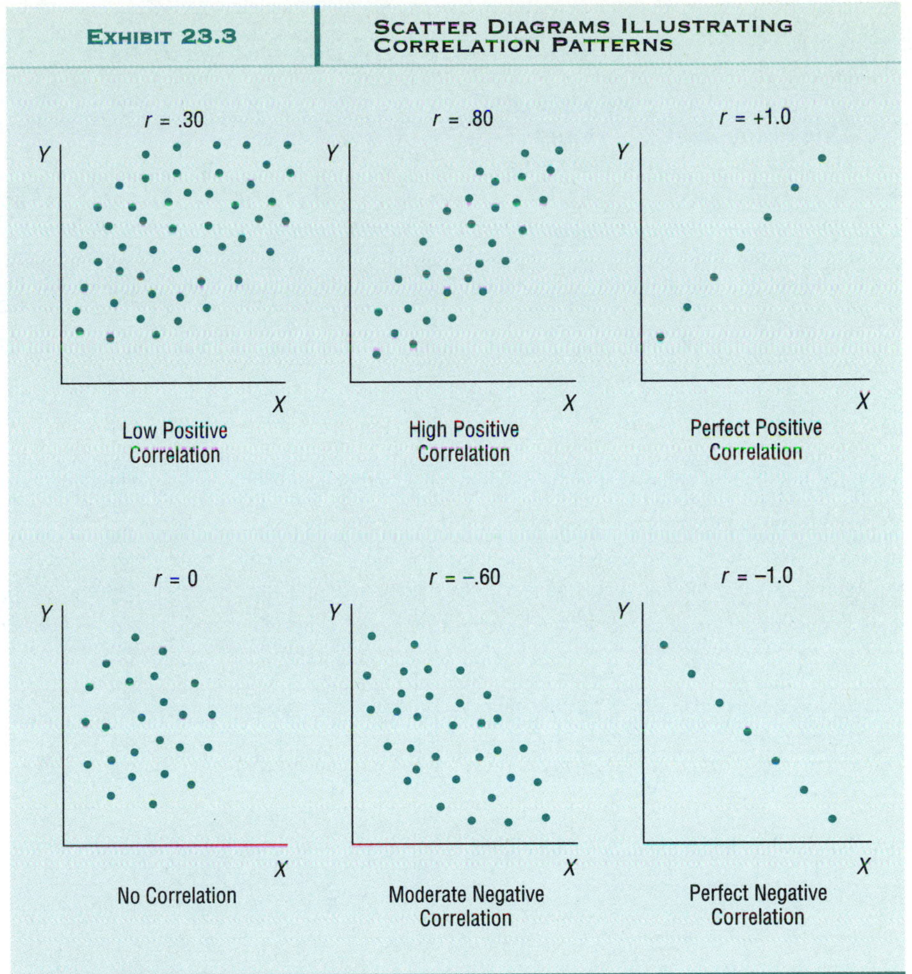

In actuality, the simple correlation coefficient is a standardized measure of covariance. The numerator in the formula represents covariance and the denominator is the square root of the product of the sample variances. Researchers find the correlation coefficient useful because they can compare two correlations without regard to the amount of variation exhibited by each variable separately.

Exhibit 23.3 illustrates the correlation coefficients and scatter diagrams for several sets of data.

An Example

As an illustration of the calculation of the correlation coefficient, consider an investigation made to determine if the average number of hours worked in manufacturing industries is related to unemployment. To determine whether the two variables are associated, a correlation analysis of the data in Table 23.1 is carried out.

The correlation between the two variables is −.635, which indicates an inverse relationship. Thus, when the number of hours worked is high, unemployment is low. This makes intuitive sense. If factories are increasing output, regular workers will typically work more overtime and new employees will be

TABLE 23.1 CORRELATION ANALYSIS OF NUMBER OF HOURS WORKED IN MANUFACTURING INDUSTRIES WITH UNEMPLOYMENT RATE

Unemployment Rate (X_i)	Number of Hours Worked (Y_i)	$X_i - \bar{X}$	$(X_i - \bar{X})^2$	$Y_i - \bar{Y}$	$(Y_i - \bar{Y})^2$	$(X_i - \bar{X})(Y_i - \bar{Y})$
5.5	39.6	.51	.2601	−.71	.5041	−.3621
4.4	40.7	−.59	.3481	.39	.1521	−.2301
4.1	40.4	−.89	.7921	.09	.0081	−.0801
4.3	39.8	−.69	.4761	−.51	.2601	.3519
6.8	39.2	1.81	3.2761	−1.11	1.2321	−2.0091
5.5	40.3	.51	.2601	−.01	.0001	−.0051
5.5	39.7	.51	.2601	−.61	.3721	−.3111
6.7	39.8	1.71	2.9241	−.51	.2601	−.8721
5.5	40.4	.51	.2601	.09	.0081	.0459
5.7	40.5	.71	.5041	.19	.0361	.1349
5.2	40.7	.21	.0441	.39	.1521	.0819
4.5	41.2	−.49	.2401	.89	.7921	−.4361
3.8	41.3	−1.19	1.4161	.99	.9801	−1.1781
3.8	40.6	−1.19	1.4161	.29	.0841	−.3451
3.6	40.7	−1.39	1.9321	.39	.1521	−.5421
3.5	40.6	−1.49	2.2201	.29	.0841	−.4321
4.9	39.8	−.09	.0081	−.51	.2601	.0459
5.9	39.9	.91	.8281	−.41	.1681	−.3731
5.6	40.6	.61	.3721	.29	.0841	.1769

$$\bar{X} = 4.99$$
$$\bar{Y} = 40.31$$
$$\Sigma(X_i - \bar{X})^2 = 17.8379$$
$$\Sigma(Y_i - \bar{Y})^2 = 5.5899$$
$$\Sigma(X_i - \bar{X})(Y_i - \bar{Y}) = -6.3389$$

$$r = \frac{\Sigma(X_i - \bar{X})(Y_i - \bar{Y})}{\sqrt{\Sigma(X_i - \bar{X})^2 \Sigma(Y_i - \bar{Y})^2}}$$
$$= \frac{-6.3389}{\sqrt{(17.8379)(5.5899)}}$$
$$= \frac{-6.3389}{\sqrt{99.712}}$$
$$= -.635$$

hired (reducing the unemployment rate). Both variables are probably related to overall economic conditions.

Correlation and Causation

It is important to remember that correlation does *not* mean causation. No matter how highly correlated the rooster's crow is to the rising of the sun, the rooster does not cause the sun to rise. It has been pointed out that there is a high correlation between teachers' salaries and the consumption of liquor over a period of years. The approximate correlation coefficient is $r = .9$. This high correlation does not indicate that teachers drink, nor does it indicate that the sale of liquor increases teachers' salaries. It is more likely that both teachers' salaries and liquor sales covary because they are both influenced by a third variable, such as long-run growth in national income and/or population.

In this example the relationship between the two variables is apparent but not real. Even though the variables are not *causally* related, they can be *statistically* related because both are caused by a third (or more) factor(s). When this is so, the variables are said to be *spuriously related.*

Coefficient of Determination

coefficient of determination (r^2)
A measure of that portion of the total variance of a variable that is accounted for by knowing the value of another variable.

If we wish to know the proportion of *variance* in Y explained by X (or vice versa), we can calculate the **coefficient of determination** by squaring the correlation coefficient:

$$r^2 = \frac{\text{Explained variance}}{\text{Total variance}}$$

The coefficient of determination, r^2, measures that part of the total variance of Y that is accounted for by knowing the value of X. In the example of the correlation between unemployment and hours worked, $r = -.635$. Therefore, $r^2 = .403$. About 40 percent of the variance in unemployment can be explained by the variance in hours worked, and vice versa.

Correlation Matrix

correlation matrix
The standard form for reporting correlational results.

A **correlation matrix** is the standard form of reporting correlation results. It may be compared to a between-cities mileage table, except that the research variables are substituted for cities and a coefficient of correlation is substituted for mileage. Table 23.2 shows a correlation matrix that relates some measures of sales force performance and satisfaction to characteristics of the sales force, job attitudes from the Role Orientation Index, and a measure of job satisfaction.[5]

Table 23.2 Pearson Product-Moment Correlation Matrix for Sales Force Example[a]

	Variables	S	JS	GE	SE	OD	VI	JT	RA	TP	WL
S	Performance	1.00									
JS	Job satisfaction	.45[b]	1.00								
GE	Generalized self-esteem	.31[b]	.10	1.00							
SE	Specific self-esteem	.61[b]	.28[b]	.36[b]	1.00						
OD	Other-directedness	.05	−.03	−.44[b]	−.24[c]	1.00					
VI	Verbal intelligence	−.36[b]	−.13	−.14	−.11	−.18[d]	1.00				
JT	Job-related tension	−.48[b]	−.56[b]	−.32[b]	−.34[b]	.26[b]	−.02	1.00			
RA	Role ambiguity	−.26[c]	−.24[c]	−.32[b]	−.39[b]	.38[b]	−.05	.44[b]	1.00		
TP	Territory potential	.49[b]	.31[b]	.04	.29[b]	.09	−.09	−.38[b]	−.26[b]	1.00	
WL	Workload	.45[b]	.11	.29[c]	.29[c]	−.04	−.12	−.27[c]	−.22[d]	.49[b]	1.00

[a]Numbers below the diagonal are for the sample. Those above the diagonal are omitted.
[b]$p < .001$.
[c]$p < .01$.
[d]$p < .05$.

You will be faced with this type of matrix on many occasions. Note that the main diagonal in Table 23.2 consists of correlations of 1.00. This will always be the case when a variable is correlated with itself.

The data in this example are from a survey of industrial salespeople selling steel and plastic strapping and seals used in shipping. Performance (*S*) was measured by identifying the salesperson's actual annual sales volume in dollars. Notice that the performance variable has a .45 correlation with the workload variable (*WL*), which was measured by recording the number of accounts in the sales territory. Notice also that the salesperson's perception of job-related tension (*JT*), as measured on an attitude scale, has a −.48 correlation with performance (*S*). Thus when perceived job tension is high, performance is low. Of course, the correlation coefficients in these examples are moderate.

Another question researchers ask concerns statistical significance. The procedure for determining statistical significance is the *t*-test of the significance of a correlation coefficient. Typically it is hypothesized that $r = 0$, and then a *t*-test is performed. The logic behind the test is similar to the significance tests already considered. In a large correlation matrix such as Table 23.2, it is customary to footnote each statistically significant coefficient.[6]

REGRESSION ANALYSIS

Regression is another technique for measuring the linear association between a dependent and an independent variable. Although regression and correlation are mathematically related, regression assumes that the dependent (or criterion) variable, *Y*, is predictively linked to the independent (or predictor) variable, *X*. Regression analysis attempts to predict the values of a continuous, interval-scaled dependent variable from specific values of the independent variable. For example, the amount of external funds required (the dependent variable) might be predicted on the basis of sales growth rates (independent variable). Although there are numerous applications of regression analysis, forecasting sales is by far the most common.

bivariate linear regression
A measure of linear association that investigates straight-line relationships of the type $Y = \alpha + \beta X$, where *Y* is the dependent variable, *X* is the independent variable, and α and β are two constants to be estimated.

intercept
The *Y* intercept; the point at which a regression line intersects the *Y*-axis.

slope
The inclination of a regression line as compared to a base line, rise (vertical distance) over run (horizontal difference).

The discussion here concerns **bivariate linear regression.** This form of regression investigates a *straight-line relationship* of the type $Y = \alpha + \beta X$, where *Y* is the dependent variable, *X* is the independent variable, and α and β are two constants to be estimated. The symbol α represents the *Y* **intercept** and β is the **slope** coefficient. The slope β is the change in *Y* due to a corresponding change of one unit in *X*. The slope may also be thought of as "rise over run" (the rise in units on the *Y* axis divided by the run in units along the *X* axis). (Δ is the notation for "a change in.")

Suppose a researcher is interested in forecasting sales for a construction tools distributor (wholesaler) in Florida. The distributor believes a reasonable association exists between sales and building permits issued by counties. Using bivariate linear regression on the data in Table 23.3, the researcher will be able to estimate sales potential (*Y*) in various counties based on the number of building permits (*X*).

For a better understanding of the data in Table 23.3, we can plot them on a scatter diagram (Exhibit 23.4). In the diagram the vertical axis indicates the value of the dependent variable *Y* and the horizontal axis indicates the value of the independent variable *X*. Each point in the diagram represents an observation of *X* and *Y* at a given point in time—that is, paired values of *Y* and *X*. One way to determine the relationship between *X* and *Y* is to "eyeball," it—

TABLE 23.3 RELATIONSHIP OF SALES POTENTIAL TO BUILDING PERMITS ISSUED

Dealer	Y Dealer's Sales Volume (000)	X Building Permits
1	77	86
2	79	93
3	80	95
4	83	104
5	101	139
6	117	180
7	129	165
8	120	147
9	97	119
10	106	132
11	99	126
12	121	156
13	103	129
14	86	96
15	99	108

that is, draw a straight line through the points in the figure. However, such a line would be subject to human error. As illustrated in Exhibit 23.4, two researchers might draw different lines to describe the same data.

Least-Squares Method of Regression Analysis

least-squares method
A mathematical technique for ensuring that the regression line will best represent the linear relationship between X and Y.

The task of the researcher is to find the best means for fitting a straight line to the data. The **least-squares method** is a relatively simple mathematical technique that ensures that the straight line will best represent the relationship between X and Y. The logic behind the least-squares technique goes as follows. No straight line can completely represent every dot in the scatter diagram. Unless there is a perfect correlation between two variables, there will be a discrepancy between most of the actual scores (the dots) and the predicted score based on the regression line. Simply stated, any straight line that is drawn will generate errors. The method of least squares uses the criterion of attempting to make the least amount of total error in prediction of Y from X. More technically, the procedure used in the least-squares method generates a straight line, which minimizes the sum of squared deviations of the actual values from this predicted regression line. With the symbol e representing the deviations of the dots from the line, the least-squares criterion is:

$$\sum_{i=1}^{n} e_i^2 \text{ is minimum}$$

where

residual
The difference between the actual value of the dependent variable and the estimated value of the dependent variable in the regression equation.

$e_i = Y_i - \hat{Y}_i$ (the **residual**)

Y_i = actual value of the dependent variable

$\hat{Y}_i$ = estimated value of the dependent variable ("Y hat")

n = number of observations

i = number of the particular observation

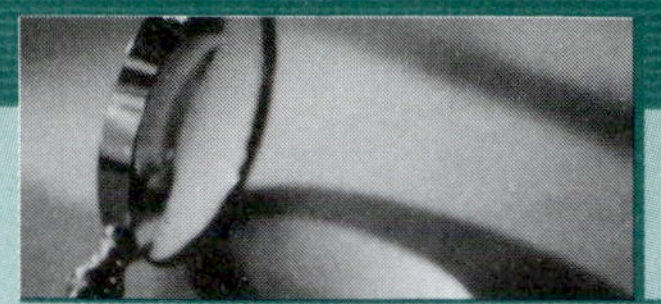

Research Insight

Walkup's First Laws of Statistics

LAW NO. 1
Everything correlates with everything, especially when the same individual defines the variables to be correlated.[7]

LAW NO. 2
It won't help very much to find a good correlation between the variable you are interested in and some other variable that you don't understand any better.

LAW NO. 3
Unless you can think of a logical reason why two variables should be connected as cause and effect, it doesn't help much to find a correlation between them. In Columbus, Ohio, the mean monthly rainfall correlates very nicely with the number of letters in the names of the months!

The general equation of a straight line equals $Y = \alpha + \beta X$. A more appropriate equation includes an allowance for error:

$$Y = \hat{a} + \hat{\beta}X + e$$

Exhibit 23.4 Scatter Diagram and Eyeball Forecast

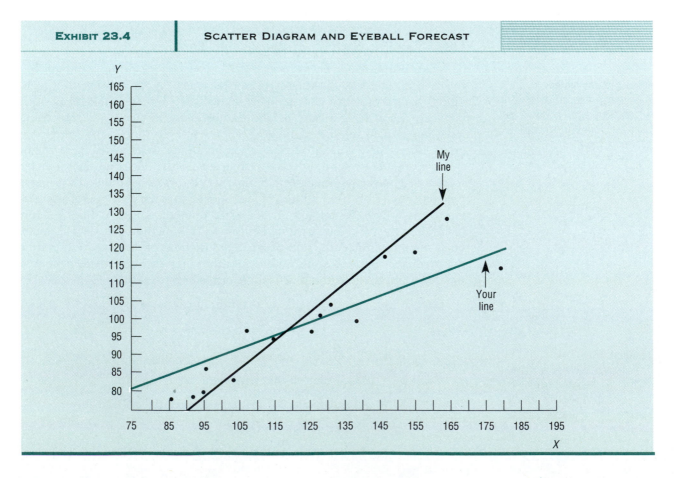

The symbols $\hat{a}$ and $\hat{\beta}$ are utilized when the equation is a regression estimate of the line. Thus, to compute the estimated values of $\hat{a}$ and $\hat{\beta}$, we use the following formulas:

$$\hat{\beta} = \frac{n(\Sigma XY) - (\Sigma X)(\Sigma Y)}{n(\Sigma X^2) - (\Sigma X)^2}$$

and

$$\hat{a} = \bar{Y} - \hat{\beta}\bar{X}$$

where

$\hat{\beta}$ = estimated slope of the line (the regression coefficient)

$\hat{a}$ = estimated intercept of the Y axis

Y = dependent variable

$\bar{Y}$ = mean of the dependent variable

X = independent variable

$\bar{X}$ = mean of the independent variable

n = number of observations

These equations may be solved by simple arithmetic (for the data in Table 23.3; see Table 23.4). To estimate the relationship between the distributor's sales to a dealer and the number of building permits, we perform the following manipulations:

TABLE 23.4 | **LEAST-SQUARES COMPUTATION**

Dealer	Y	Y^2	X	X^2	XY
1	77	5,929	86	7,396	6,622
2	79	6,241	93	8,649	7,347
3	80	6,400	95	9,025	7,600
4	83	6,889	104	10,816	8,632
5	101	10,201	139	19,321	14,039
6	117	13,689	180	32,400	21,060
7	129	16,641	165	27,225	21,285
8	120	14,400	147	21,609	17,640
9	97	9,409	119	14,161	11,543
10	106	11,236	132	17,424	13,992
11	99	9,801	126	15,876	12,474
12	121	14,641	156	24,336	18,876
13	103	10,609	129	16,641	13,287
14	86	7,396	96	9,216	8,256
15	99	9,801	108	11,664	10,692
	$\Sigma Y = 1{,}497$	$\Sigma Y^2 = 153{,}283$	$\Sigma X = 1{,}875$	$\Sigma X^2 = 245{,}759$	$\Sigma XY = 193{,}345$
	$\bar{Y} = 99.8$		$\bar{X} = 125$		

RESEARCH INSIGHT

REGRESSION: ONE STEP BACKWARD

The essence of a dictionary definition of the word *regression* is a going back or moving backward.[8] This notion of regressing, that things "go back to previous conditions," was the source for the original concept of statistical regression. Galton, who first worked out the concept of correlation, got the idea from thinking about "regression toward mediocrity," a phenomenon observed in studies of inheritance.

"Tall men will tend to have shorter sons, and short men taller sons. The sons' heights, then, tend to 'regress to,' or 'go back to,' the mean of the population. Statistically, if we want to predict *Y* and *X* and the correlation between *X* and *Y* is zero, then our best prediction is to the mean." (Incidentally, the symbol *r*, used for the coefficient of correlation, was originally chosen because it stood for "regression.")

$$\begin{aligned}\hat{\beta} &= \frac{n(\Sigma XY) - (\Sigma X)(\Sigma Y)}{n(\Sigma X^2) - (\Sigma X)^2} \\ &= \frac{15(193{,}345) - 2{,}806{,}875}{15(245{,}759) - 3{,}515{,}625} \\ &= \frac{2{,}900{,}175 - 2{,}806{,}875}{3{,}686{,}385 - 3{,}515{,}625} \\ &= \frac{93{,}300}{170{,}760} \\ &= .54638 \\ \hat{a} &= \bar{Y} - \hat{\beta}\bar{X} \\ &= 99.8 - .54638(125) \\ &= 99.8 - 68.3 \\ &= 31.5\end{aligned}$$

The formula $\hat{Y} = 31.5 + 0.546X$ is the regression equation used for the prediction of the dependent variable. Suppose the wholesaler is considering opening a new dealership in an area where the number of building permits equals 89. Sales in this area may be forecast as

$$\begin{aligned}\hat{Y} &= 31.5 + .546(X) \\ &= 31.5 + .546(89) \\ &= 31.5 + 48.6 \\ &= 80.1\end{aligned}$$

Thus, our distributor may expect sales of 80.1 (or $80,100) in this new area.[9]

Calculation of the correlation coefficient gives an indication of how accurate the predictions are. In this example the correlation coefficient is $r = .9356$, and the coefficient of determination is $r^2 = .8754$.

Drawing a Regression Line

Forecasting is like trying to drive a car blindfolded while following directions given by a person who is looking out the back window.

ANONYMOUS

To draw a regression line on a scatter diagram, only two predicted values of Y need to be plotted. For example, if data for Dealer 7 and Dealer 3 are used, we can calculate $\hat{Y}_7$ and $\hat{Y}_3$ as follows:

$$\text{Dealer 7 (actual } Y \text{ value } = 129\text{): } \hat{Y}_7 = 31.5 + .546(165) = 121.6$$

$$\text{Dealer 3 (actual } Y \text{ value } = 80\text{): } \hat{Y}_3 = 31.5 + .546(95) = 83.4$$

Once the two Y values have been predicted, a straight line can be drawn to connect the points $\hat{Y}_7 = 121.6$, $X_7 = 165$ and $\hat{Y}_3 = 83.4$, $X_3 = 95$.

Exhibit 23.5 shows the regression line. If it is desirable to determine the error (residual) of any observation, the predicted value of Y is first calculated. The predicted value is then subtracted from the actual value. For example, the actual observation for Dealer 9 is 97 and the predicted value is 96.5. Thus, only a small margin of error, $e = .5$, is involved in this regression line:

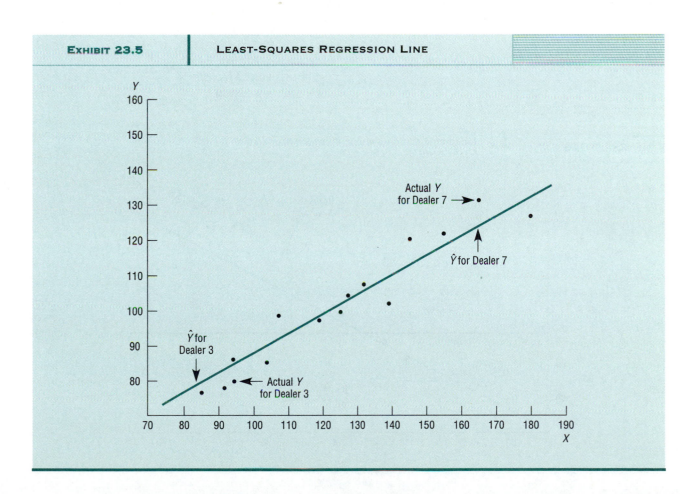

EXHIBIT 23.5 LEAST-SQUARES REGRESSION LINE

$$e_i = Y_9 - \hat{Y}_9$$
$$= 97 - 96.5$$
$$= .5$$

where $\hat{Y}_9 = 31.5 + .546(119)$

Test of Statistical Significance

Now that we have considered the error term, a more detailed look at explained and unexplained variation is possible. Exhibit 23.6 gives some additional information about the fitted regression line. If a researcher wished to predict any dealer's sales volume (Y) without knowing the number of building permits (X), the best prediction would be the average sales volume ($\bar{Y}$) of all dealers. Suppose, for example, a researcher wished to predict Dealer 8's sales without knowing the value of X. The best estimate would be 99.8 ($\bar{Y} = 99.8$). Exhibit 23.6 shows that there would be a large error because Dealer 8's actual sales were 120. Once the regression line has been fitted, it is possible to reduce this error. With the regression equation, Dealer 8's sales are predicted to be 111.8, reducing the error from 20.2 ($Y_i - \bar{Y} = 120 - 99.8$) to 8.2 ($Y_i - \hat{Y} = 120 - 111.8$). Simply stated, error is reduced by using $Y_i - \hat{Y}_i$ rather than $Y_i - \bar{Y}$. The reduction in the error is the "explained" deviation due to the regression; the smaller number, 8.2, is the deviation not explained by the regression.

Thus, the total deviation can be partitioned into two parts:

$$Y_i - \bar{Y} = (\hat{Y}_i - \bar{Y}) + (Y_i - \hat{Y}_i)$$

Total deviation = Deviation explained by the regression + Deviation unexplained by the regression (residual error)

EXHIBIT 23.6 SCATTER DIAGRAM OF EXPLAINED AND UNEXPLAINED VARIATION

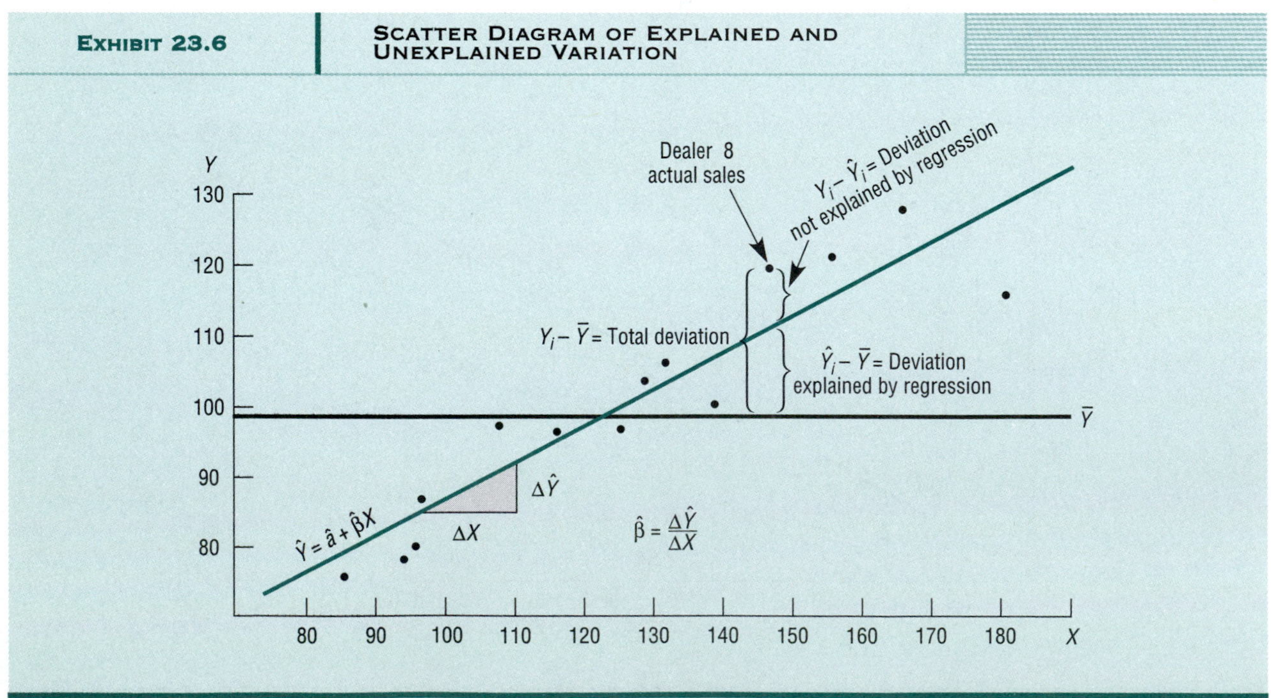

where

$\bar{Y}$ = mean of the total group

$\hat{Y}$ = value predicted with regression equation

Y_i = actual value

For Dealer 8 the total deviation is 120 − 99.8 = 20.2. The deviation explained by the regression is 111.8 − 99.8 = 12, and the deviation unexplained by the regression is 120 −111.8 = 8.2. If these values are summed over all values of Y_i (i.e., all observations) and squared, these deviations provide an estimate of the variation of Y explained by the regression and unexplained by the regression:

$$\Sigma(Y_i - \bar{Y})^2 = \Sigma(\hat{Y}_i - \bar{Y})^2 + \Sigma(Y_i - \hat{Y}_i)^2$$

$$\text{Total variation} = \text{Explained variation} + \text{Unexplained variation (residual)}$$

***F*-test**
A procedure used to determine whether there is more variability in the scores of one sample than in the scores of another sample.

analysis of variance summary table
A table that presents the results of a regression calculation.

We have thus partitioned the total sum of squares, SS_t, into two parts: the regression sum of squares, SS_r, and the error sum of squares, SS_e:

$$SS_t = SS_r + SS_e$$

An ***F*-test,** or an *analysis of variance,* can be applied to a regression to test the relative magnitudes of the SS_r and SS_e with their appropriate degrees of freedom. Table 23.5 shows the technique for conducting the F-test.

For the example on sales forecasting, the **analysis of variance summary table,** comparing relative magnitudes of the mean square, is presented in Table 23.6.

Table 23.5 ANALYSIS OF VARIANCE TABLE FOR BIVARIATE REGRESSION

Source of Variation	Sum of Squares	Degrees of Freedom	Mean Square (Variance)
Explained by regression	$SS_r = \Sigma(\hat{Y}_i - \bar{Y})^2$	$k - 1$	$MS_r = \frac{SS_r}{k-1}$
Unexplained (error)	$SS_e = \Sigma(Y_i - \hat{Y}_i)^2$	$n - k$	$MS_e = \frac{SS_e}{n-k}$

where k = number of estimated parameters (variables)

n = number of observations

Table 23.6 ANALYSIS OF VARIANCE SUMMARY TABLE FOR REGRESSION OF SALES ON BUILDING PERMITS

Source of Variation	Sum of Squares	d.f.	Mean Square	F-Value
Explained by regression	3398.49	1	3398.49	91.30
Unexplained by regression (error)	483.91	13	37.22	
Total	3882.40	14		

Research Insight

The Concept of Beta When Investing in Stocks

Suppose a regression was run using the historic realized rate of return on a particular stock as the dependent variable and the historic realized rate of return on the stock market as the independent variable.[10]

The tendency of a stock to move with the market is reflected in its *beta coefficient,* which is a measure of the stock's *volatility* relative to an average stock. Betas are discussed at an intuitive level in this section.

An *average risk stock* is defined as one that tends to move up and down in step with the general market as measured by some index such as the Dow Jones or the New York Stock Exchange Index. Such a stock will, by definition, have a beta (β) of 1.0, which indicates that, in general, if the market moves up by 10 percent, the stock will also move up by 10 percent, and if the market falls by 10 percent, the stock will likewise fall by 10 percent. A portfolio of such $\beta = 1.0$ stocks will move up and down with the broad market averages and will be just as risky as the averages. If $\beta = 0.5$, the stock is only half as volatile as the market—it will rise and fall only half as much—and a portfolio of such stocks is half as risky as a portfolio of $\beta = 1.0$ stocks. On the other hand, if $\beta = 2.0$, the stock is twice as volatile as an average stock, so a portfolio of such stocks will be twice as risky as an average portfolio.

Betas are calculated and published by Merrill Lynch, Value Line, and numerous other organizations. The beta coefficients of some well-known companies are shown in the table below. Most stocks have betas in the range of 0.75 to 1.50. The average for all stocks is 1.0 by definition.

Stock	Beta
Verisign	2.80
Amazon.com	2.78
Real Networks	2.75
General Electric	1.12
Procter & Gamble	1.22
General Motors	1.11
IBM	.86
McDonald's	.63
Bristol Myers	.31
Cisco Systems	.23
Anheuser-Busch	.00
McDonald's	.63
Mattel	−0.22
Pacific Gas & Electric	−0.29

If a high-beta stock (one whose beta is greater than 1.0) is added to an average risk ($\beta = 1.0$) portfolio, then the beta—and consequently the riskiness—of the portfolio will increase. Conversely, if a low-beta stock (one whose beta is less than 1.0) is added to an average risk portfolio, the portfolio's beta and risk will decline. Thus, *because a stock's beta measures its contribution to the riskiness of the portfolio, beta is the appropriate measure of the stock's riskiness.*

From Table 6 in the appendix we find that the *F*-value of 91.3, with 1 degree of freedom in the numerator and 13 degrees of freedom in the denominator, exceeds the probability level of .01.

The *coefficient of determination,* r^2, reflects the proportion of variation explained by the regression line. The formula for calculating r^2 is

$$r^2 = \frac{SS_r}{SS_t} = 1 - \frac{SS_e}{SS_t}$$

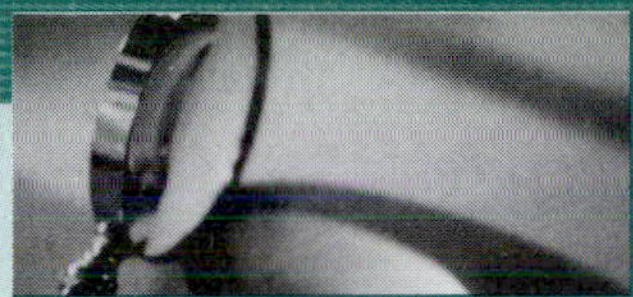

Research Insight

A Note of Caution

The nonstatistical definition of regression—moving backward or reverting to an earlier form—emphasizes the past nature of data and hints that forecasting with statistical regression analysis should be cautiously utilized. Past data may not necessarily reflect future trends. In *Life on the Mississippi,* Mark Twain illustrated this concern about forecasting rather well:

> In the space of one hundred and seventy-six years the Lower Mississippi has shortened itself two hundred and forty-two miles. This is an average of a trifle over one mile and a third per year. Therefore, any calm person, who is not blind or idiotic, can see that in the Old Oölitic Silurian Period, just a million years ago next November, the lower Mississippi River was upward of one million three hundred thousand miles long, and stuck out over the Gulf of Mexico like a fishing-rod. And by the same token any person can see that seven hundred and forty-two years from now the Lower Mississippi will be only a mile and three-quarters long, and Cairo and New Orleans will have joined their streets together, and be plodding comfortably along under a single mayor and a mutual board of aldermen. There is something fascinating about science. One gets such wholesale returns of conjecture out of such a trifling investment of fact.[11]

In our example, r^2 is .875:

$$r^2 = \frac{3{,}398.49}{3{,}882.40} = .875$$

The coefficient of determination may be interpreted to mean that 87 percent of the variation in sales was explained by associating the variable with building permits.

SUMMARY

In many situations two variables are interrelated, or associated. Many bivariate statistical techniques can be used to measure association. Researchers select the appropriate technique on the basis of each variable's scale of measurement.

The correlation coefficient (r), a statistical measure of association between two variables, ranges from $r = +1.0$ for a perfect positive correlation to $r = -1.0$ for a perfect negative correlation. No correlation is indicated for $r = 0$. Simple correlation is the measure of the relationship of one variable to another. The correlation coefficient indicates the strength of the association of two variables and the direction of that association. It is important to remember that correlation does not prove causation, as variables other than those being measured may be involved. The coefficient of determination (r^2) measures the amount of the total variance in the dependent variable that is accounted for by knowing the value of the independent variable. The results of correlation computations are often presented in a correlation matrix.

Bivariate linear regression investigates a straight-line relationship between one dependent variable and one independent variable. The regression can be done intuitively by plotting a scatter diagram of the X and Y points and drawing a line to fit the observed relationship. The least-squares method mathematically determines the best-fitting regression line for the observed data. The line determined by this method may be used to forecast values of the dependent variable, given a value for the independent variable. The goodness of the line's fit may be evaluated by a variant of the ANOVA (analysis of variance) technique or by calculating the coefficient of determination.

Key Terms

measures of association
simple correlation coefficient
coefficient of determination (r^2)
correlation matrix
bivariate linear regression
intercept
slope
least-squares method
residual
F-test
analysis of variance summary table

Questions for Review and Critical Thinking

1. The discussion in this chapter is limited to linear relationships. Try to diagram some nonlinear relationships that would show an r of zero, using the tests shown in the text.
2. Suppose Abraham Lincoln had answered a survey questionnaire in which he indicated that he had not received a grade school diploma. The researcher found that Lincoln's educational score did not correlate highly with the expected variables. What was wrong?
3. The management of a regional bus line thought its cost of gas might be correlated with its passenger/mile ratio. Comment on the data and correlation matrix below.

Avg. Wholesale Cost of Gas	Passenger/Mile Ratio
56.5	8.37
59.4	8.93
63.0	9.15
65.6	9.79
89.0	11.20

Correlation Coefficients/Probability > |R| under H0: RHO = 0/N = 5

	Year	Price	Mile
Year	1.00000	.87016	.95127
	.0000	.0551	.0128
Price	.87016	1.00000	.97309
	.0551	.0000	.0053
Mile	.95127	.97309	1.0000
	.0128	.0053	.00000

4. A correlation matrix (correlation coefficients and probability level under the hypothesis rho = 0) for a company's sales force (age, years of service, and current sales) is given below. Comment.

	Age	Years of Service	Current Sales
Age	1.00000	.68185	.21652
	.0000	.0208	.5225
Years of service	.68185	1.00000	.64499
	.0208	.0000	.0321
Current sales	.21652	.64499	1.00000
	.5225	.0321	.00000

5. Interpret the following:
   (a) $\hat{Y} = \hat{a} + \hat{\beta}X$; $\hat{Y} = 3.5 + .7X$, where $\hat{Y}$ = likelihood of buying a new car and X = total family income.
   (b) $\hat{Y} = \hat{a} + \hat{\beta}X$; $\hat{Y} = 3.5 - .4X$, where $\hat{Y}$ = likelihood of buying tickets to a rock concert and X = age.
6. The ANOVA summary table below is the result of a regression of sales on year of sales. Is the relationship statistically significant at .05? Comment.

Source of Variation	Sum of Squares	d.f.	Mean Square	*F*-Value
Explained by regression	605,370,750	1	605,370,750	3.12
Unexplained by regression	1,551,381,712	8	193,922,714	
Total error		9		

7. A metropolitan economist is attempting to predict the average total budget of retired couples in Phoenix, based on average U.S. urban retired couples' total budget. An r^2 of .7824 is obtained. Will the regression be a good predictive model?
8. A football team's season ticket sales, percentage of games won, and number of active alumni for the years 1992–2000 are given below:

Year	Season Ticket Sales	Percentage of Games Won	Number of Active Alumni
1992	4,995	40	NA
1993	8,599	54	NA
1994	8,479	55	NA
1995	8,419	58	NA
1996	10,253	63	NA
1997	12,457	75	6,315
1998	13,285	36	6,860
1999	14,177	27	8,423
2000	15,730	63	9,000

   (a) Interpret the correlation between each set of variables.
   (b) Calculate: Regression sales = Percentage of games won.
   (c) Calculate: Regression sales = Number of active alumni.

9. Are the different forms of consumer installment credit in the table below highly correlated? Explain.

	Debt Outstanding (millions of dollars)					
Year	Gas Cards	Travel and Entertainment Cards	Bank Credit Cards	Retail Cards	Total Credit Cards	Total Installment Credit
1	$ 939	$ 61	$ 828	$ 9,400	$11,228	$ 79,428
2	1,119	76	1,312	10,200	12,707	87,745
3	1,298	110	2,639	10,900	14,947	98,105
4	1,650	122	3,792	11,500	17,064	102,064
5	1,804	132	4,490	13,925	20,351	111,295
6	1,762	164	5,408	14,763	22,097	127,332
7	1,832	191	6,838	16,395	25,256	147,437
8	1,823	238	8,281	17,933	28,275	156,124
9	1,893	273	9,501	18,002	29,669	164,955
10	1,981	238	11,351	19,052	32,622	185,489
11	2,074	284	14,262	21,082	37,702	216,572

10. A manufacturer of disposable washcloths/wipes told a retailer that sales for this product category closely correlated with the sales of disposable diapers. The retailer thought he would check this out for his own sales-forecasting purposes. Where might a researcher find data to make this forecast?

11. The Springfield Electric Company manufactures electric pencil sharpeners. The company believes that sales are correlated with the number of workers employed in specific geographical areas. The following table presents Springfield's sales of electric pencil sharpeners and the total number of employees in 17 Metropolitan Statistical Areas (MSAs) in New York State and New Jersey. Calculate and interpret the correlation coefficient data in the table.

MSA: New York	Number of Employees (000)	Sales	MSA: New Jersey	Number of Employees (000)	Sales
Albany-Schenectady-Troy	58.3	3,749	Allentown–Bethlehem–Easton	110.7	6,123
Binghamton	37.0	2,695	Atlantic City	8.7	2,666
Buffalo	135.6	4,926	Jersey City	74.2	3,210
Elmira	12.8	2,808	Long Branch–Asbury Park	22.8	2,078
Nassau–Suffolk	149.0	7,423	New Brunswick–Perth Amboy–Sayreville	78.9	2,894
New York	788.8	43,401	Newark	252.1	14,989
Poughkeepsie	24.3	3,254	Paterson–Clifton–Passaic	60.1	3,806
Rochester	139.1	8,924			
Syracuse	53.6	13,119			
Utica–Rome	30.8	3,151			

12. Using the data in question 11, estimate the regression equation coefficients for the data (assuming sales is the independent variable).

13. Using the regression equation from question 12, forecast sales for the MSAs in the table on the next page:

MSA: Washington	Number of Employees (000)	MSA: Oregon	Number of Employees (000)	MSA: California	Number of Employees (000)
Richland–Kennewick	7.8	Eugene-Springfield	18.2	Anaheim–Santa Ana–Garden Grove	149.0
Seattle–Everett	123.6	Portland	90.5	Bakersfield	7.1
Spokane	11.1	Salem	12.5	Fresno	20.5
Tacoma	18.7			Los Angeles–Long Beach	750.3
Yakima	8.8			Modesto	18.7
				Oxnard–Simi Valley–Ventura	14.9
				Riverside–San Bernardino–Ontario	51.8
				Sacramento	20.5
				Salinas–Seaside–Monterey	8.0

14. A researcher has a series of Likert-scaled items and a measure of frequency of absenteeism. He uses each of the Likert-scaled items in a separate bivariate correlation with absenteeism without testing for the assumptions of linear relationships. Is this ethical?

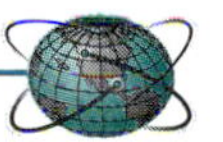

Exploring the Internet

1. Go to the Chance Web site at http://www dartmouth.edu/~chance/ChanceLecture/AudioVideo.html and view the very interesting streaming video "Streaks in Sports."
2. The Federal Reserve Bank of St. Louis maintains a database called FRED (Federal Reserve Economic Data). Navigate to the FRED database at http://www.stls.frb.org/fred/index.html. Randomly select a 5-year period between 1970 and 1995 and then find the correlation between average U.S. employment in retail trade and U.S. employment in wholesale trade. What statistical test is appropriate?

WebSurveyor Activities

WebSurveyor allows a researcher to download a survey's results to a data file. Exporting data into other applications is handled through CSV (comma separated value) files. Using the sports opinion survey, we have done this for you. The exported files have been converted to Microsoft Excel (sports.xls) and to SPSS (sports.sav). Numeric codes are used in these files.

Using SPSS or Excel, run a correlation analysis between the following items:

1. "Professional athletes should bear the responsibility of being role models."
2. "These days professional athletes have no sense of loyalty to the team."
3. "There's no harm done if an athlete argues with an official about a call he/she doesn't like."
4. "Winning isn't everything; it's the only thing."

Are the results statistically significant? Interpret the correlation coefficients.

Case Suggestions

Case 29: LastDance Health Care
Case 30: Sunbelt Energy Corporation
Case 31: Employees Federal Credit Union

APPENDIX

NONPARAMETRIC MEASURES OF ASSOCIATION

In situations in which it cannot be assumed that data are metric (interval- or ratio-scaled), a nonparametric correlation technique may be utilized as a substitute for the Pearson correlation technique.[12] A group of correlation measures deals with rank-order data. Suppose two groups of consumers are asked to rank, in order of preference, the brands of a product class. The researcher wishes to determine the agreement, or correlation, between the two groups. Two possible statistics can be computed to accomplish this purpose: the Spearman rank-order correlation coefficient, r_s (rho), and the Kendall rank correlation coefficient, τ (tau).

The *Spearman rank-order correlation coefficient* is computed as follows:

$$r_s = 1 - \frac{6\sum_{i=1}^{n} d_i^2}{n^3 - n}$$

where d_i is the difference between the ranks given to the ith brand by each group. Thus, if Brand B were ranked first by Group 1 and sixth by Group 2, d_b^2 would be equal to $(1 - 6)^2$, or 25. In some cases two brands may be given equal scores by a group or be tied for a certain rank. If the number of ties is not large, their effect is small, and we simply assign the average of the ranks that would have been assigned had no ties occurred. We then calculate r_s as before. If the number of ties is large, however, a correction factor can be introduced to offset their effect on r_s.

TABLE 23A.1 EXAMPLE OF SPEARMAN RANK-ORDER CORRELATION

	RAW DATA		RANKING VALUES		DIFFERENCES	
Employee	Sales Aptitude Rating (X)	Years of Service (Y)	Rank of X (X_r)	Rank of Y (Y_r)	d_i ($X_r - Y_r$)	d_i^2
1	3	5	3.5	4.5	−1.0	1.00
2	5	11	6.5	9	−2.5	6.25
3	1	1	1	1	.0	.00
4	4	3	5	2	3.0	9.00
5	8	5	10	4.5	5.5	30.25
6	3	4	3.5	3	.5	.25
7	6	13	8	10	−2.0	4.00
8	2	6	2.0	6.0	4.0	16.00
9	5	9	6.5	7.0	.5	.25
10	7	10	9	8	1.0	1.00
						$\Sigma d^2 = 68$

Consider the relationship between a sales manager's ratings of employees' sales aptitude and their years of service with the organization. The data are portrayed in Table 23A.1, where the highest rating is given the highest ranking (10). For our example, r_s is calculated as follows:

$$r_s = 1 - \frac{6\sum_{i=1}^{n} d_i^2}{n^3 - n} = 1 - \frac{6(68)}{(10)^3 - 10} = 1 - .412 = .588$$

The answer $r_s = .588$ is interpreted in a manner similar to that used to interpret the Pearson correlation coefficient.

The Kendall rank correlation coefficient, *Kendall's tau,* is useful for the same type of situation as is appropriate for the Spearman coefficient, but its computation is not quite so straightforward and may best be explained by an example. Suppose two groups have ranked Brands A, B, C, and D in the following way:

	Brand A	Brand B	Brand C	Brand D
Group I	3	4	2	1
Group II	3	1	4	2

Rearranging the items so that Group I's ranks appear in order, we have the following:

	Brand D	Brand C	Brand A	Brand B
Group I	1	2	3	4
Group II	2	4	3	1

To determine the degree of consistency between the two rankings, we examine Group II's rankings to see how many are in the correct order vis-à-vis one another. The first pair, D and C, are in natural order; that is, 2 (for D) comes before 4 (for C), so we assign a score of +1 to this pair. We proceed to compare the rank for Brand D with the ranks of the other brands. The second pair, D and A, is assigned a score of +1, while the pair D and B is assigned a score of −1 because Groups I and II do not agree. The total so far is +1. Each rank in turn is compared similarly, with the resulting final total of −2. (Rank of C versus A = −1, C versus B = −1, A versus B = −1, yielding a final real value of −2.) The next step is to compare this actual total with the maximum possible total. The maximum value would occur if Group II rankings were identical to those of Group I. This maximum is found by taking four things two at a time

$$\binom{N}{2} = \binom{4}{2} = \frac{4!}{2!(4-2)!} = 6$$

Tau is therefore equal to the ratio of the actual total to the maximum possible total:

$$\tau = \frac{\text{Actual total score}}{\binom{N}{2}} = \frac{-2}{6} = -.33$$

This is the measure of correlation between the two ranks. Tied observations are treated in the same way as for the Spearman coefficient. Values obtained for r_s and t from the same data will not be equal and are not comparable to each other.

These measures of correlation can be subjected to tests of significance to determine whether the correlations are sufficiently different from chance expectations and thus are not due to random sampling error alone. However, the types of tests to be utilized and the rules governing their use are beyond the scope of this appendix. The reader should refer to specialized statistics texts for the appropriate tests.[13]

The *contingency coefficient* is intended to measure association of nominal data recorded in bivariate contingency tables.[14] It is the only correlation coefficient appropriate for use with nominal data, with the possible exception of the phi coefficient, which is limited to 2 × 2 tables. There is no restriction on the number of categories, provided the number of measures is quite large.

The magnitude of a chi-square statistic calculated from a contingency table is a function of the relationship between the row and column variables. This fact is utilized to develop a formula for the calculation of the contingency coefficient:

$$C = \frac{\chi^2}{n + \chi^2}$$

where

C = contingency coefficient
χ^2 = calculated chi-square value
n = sample size or total number of observations

The test for statistical significance is the same as in the chi-square test of independence.

Unfortunately, the size of the contingency coefficient is a function of the number of cells in the table, and under no circumstances is it possible for the coefficient to be unity, even though a perfect relationship may exist. The maximum value of the contingency coefficient for a 2 × 2 table is .707, for a 3 × 3 table is .816, and for a 4 × 4 table is .866.

CHAPTER

24

MULTIVARIATE ANALYSIS

What you will learn in this chapter

- To distinguish among univariate analysis, bivariate analysis, and multivariate analysis.
- To distinguish between the two basic groups in multivariate analysis; dependence methods and interdependence methods.
- To discuss the concept of multiple regression analysis.
- To define the coefficient of partial regression and the coefficient of multiple determination.
- To interpret the statistical results of multiple regression analysis.
- To define and discuss discriminant analysis.
- To define and discuss canonical correlation.
- To define and discuss multivariate analysis of variance.
- To define and discuss factor analysis.
- To define and discuss cluster analysis.
- To define and discuss multidimensional scaling.

Business executives are a great vacation market.[1] Each year, they average four vacations of at least three days and two nights. Shorter vacations don't mean that they spend less money: Three in four executives agree that they would rather take a shorter vacation at a luxury hotel than a longer vacation at a budget hotel. However, are all executive vacationers alike? Do they have the same attitudes toward vacations? Are there demographic variables that identify different market segments?

Attitude surveys that include demographic variables are often utilized as a basis for market cluster analysis. Business researchers for Hyatt Hotels measured executives' attitudes toward vacations and used multivariate analysis to identify five distinct segments.

The largest segment, called "Fugitives" (25 percent), are overstressed and looking for an escape. Once on vacation, they forget their diets, drink more, and are less sexually inhibited. But they do not stop worrying about their jobs, the cost of the vacation, and the homes, children, and pets they leave behind. Fugitives are dominated by female baby-boomers: 57 percent of Fugitives are between the agers of 25 and 44, and 60 percent are women.

"Power Players" and "Stress Fighters" each represents 21 percent of executive vacationers. Stress Fighters make it their mission to relax on vacation. Because of their extreme health orientation, they aggressively pursue athletics and refrain from eating and drinking excessively. Fifty-three percent of Stress Fighters are baby boomers, and half are women. Eighty-four percent are married, and 77 percent have children.

Power Players know how to mix business with pleasure. They stay in touch with the office but say that this doesn't interfere with their vacations. Their habits don't change significantly while they are away from the office, which may be why they don't experience a significant improvement in job performance when they get back. Power Players are calm, cool, and confident people who are likely to be seen at poolside talking on a cell phone. The group is older and more male-dominated than the other segments; 74 percent are aged 45 or older, and 68 percent are men.

Nineteen percent of vacationing executives are "Schedulers" who have as much fun planning their vacations as actually taking them. Schedulers are quintessential tourists. They enjoy sightseeing and absorbing the local culture. They don't keep in touch with the office and feel that their job performance improves when they return. Fifty-eight percent of Schedulers are 45 or older, and half are women.

Thirteen percent of executive vacationers are "Fun Worshipers." Nearly 70 percent are women, 60 percent are aged 25 to 44, and only 40 percent have children. They concentrate on leaving their worries behind and having a good time. While on vacation, FunWorshipers become more athletic, outgoing, and romantic. They return to their jobs reinvigorated.

This study using multivariate analysis with data on attitudes and demographic variables helped Hyatt Hotels visualize target markets as real people with real concerns and real attitudes about products.

The purpose of this chapter is to explore how multivariate analysis can benefit managerial decision making. ■

THE NATURE OF MULTIVARIATE ANALYSIS

Most business problems are inherently multidimensional. Corporations can be described along a wide variety of dimensions. The price of domestic crude oil can be simultaneously influenced by rate of inflation, political instability, and the balance of payments. Individuals can evaluate various investments on the basis of many different attributes. As researchers increasingly become aware of the multidimensional nature of their problems, they will increasingly utilize multivariate analysis to help them solve complex problems.

As discussed earlier, the investigation of one variable at a time is referred to as *univariate analysis.* Investigation of the relationship between two variables is *bivariate analysis.* When problems are multidimensional and three or more variables are involved, we utilize *multivariate analysis.* Multivariate statistical methods allow the effects of more than one variable to be considered at one time. For example, suppose a forecaster wished to estimate oil consumption for the next five years. While consumption might be predicted by past oil consumption records alone, adding additional variables such as average number of miles driven per year, coal production, and nuclear plants under construction is likely to give greater insight into the determinants of oil consumption.

TO THE POINT

The essence of mathematics is not to make simple things complicated, but to make complicated things simple.

S. GUDDER

To evaluate the probability of corporate bankruptcy, a researcher may select multiple financial ratios, such as current ratio, debt/assets ratio, and return on assets. Consumers, evaluating grocery stores, may be concerned with distance to each store, perceived cleanliness, price levels, and many other attributes of these stores. To understand problems like these, researchers need multivariate analysis.

This chapter presents a nontechnical description of some multivariate methods. Computational formulas are not presented.

CLASSIFYING MULTIVARIATE TECHNIQUES

multivariate data analysis
Statistical methods that allow the simultaneous investigation of more than two variables.

A useful classification of most **multivariate data analysis** techniques is presented in Exhibit 24.1.[2] Two basic groups of multivariate techniques are *dependence methods* and *interdependence methods.*

Analysis of Dependence

If a multivariate technique attempts to explain or predict the dependent variable(s) on the basis of two or more independent variables, then we are attempting to analyze dependence. The common judgment "Is a person a

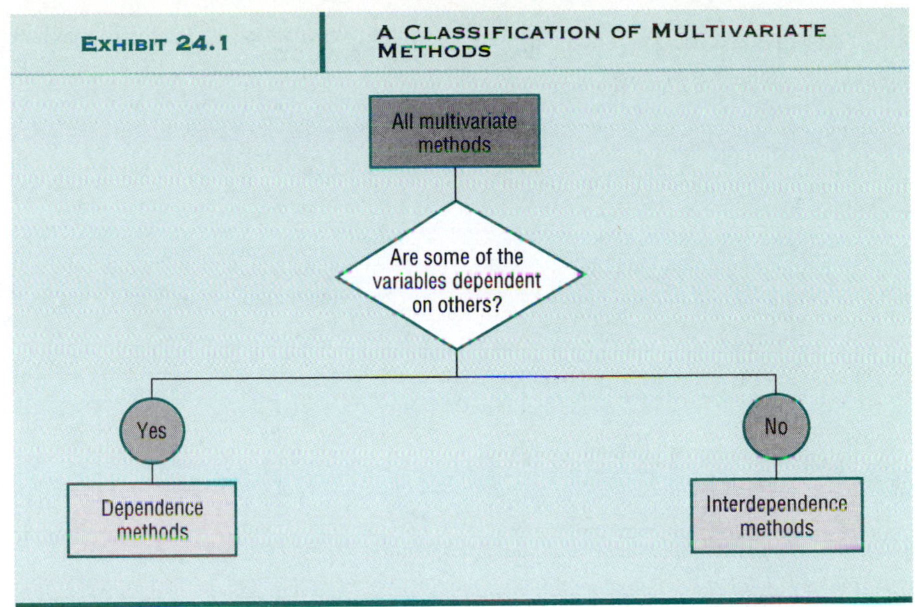

Exhibit 24.1 A Classification of Multivariate Methods

good or a poor credit risk based on age, income, and marital status?" illustrates an instance where the researcher is interested in specifying a relationship between one dependent variable and several independent variables. Another example of the **analysis of dependence** would be forecasting the dependent variable "sales" on the basis of numerous independent variables. *Multiple regression analysis, multiple discriminant analysis, multivariate analysis of variance,* and *canonical correlation analysis* are all dependence methods.

analysis of dependence
A collective term to describe any multivariate statistical technique that attempts to explain or predict the dependent variable on the basis of two or more independent variables.

Analysis of Interdependence

The goal of interdependence methods is to give meaning to a set of variables or to seek to group things together. No one variable or variable subset is to be predicted from the others or explained by them. The most common of these methods for **analysis of interdependence** are *factor analysis, cluster analysis,* and *multidimensional scaling.* A manager might utilize these techniques to identify profitable market segments or market clusters. Hyatt's clustering of business executives into vacation clusters is an example of this type of research. Another researcher might use interdependence techniques to identify and classify similar cities on the basis of population size, income distribution, race and ethnic distribution, and consumption of a manufacturer's product so as to select comparable test markets.

analysis of interdependence
A collective term to describe any multivariate statistical technique that attempts to give meaning to a set of variables or seeks to group things together.

Influence of Measurement Scales

As in other forms of data analysis, the nature of the measurement scales will determine which multivariate technique is appropriate for the data. Exhibit 24.2 and Exhibit 24.3 (page 577) show that selection of a multivariate technique requires consideration of the types of measures used for both independent and dependent sets of variables. For ease of diagraming, Exhibits 24.2 and 24.3 refer to nominal and ordinal scales as *nonmetric* and interval and ratio scales as *metric.* Exhibit 24.2 assumes that the independent variable is metric.

Exhibit 24.2 | **Multivariate Analysis: Classification of Dependence Methods**

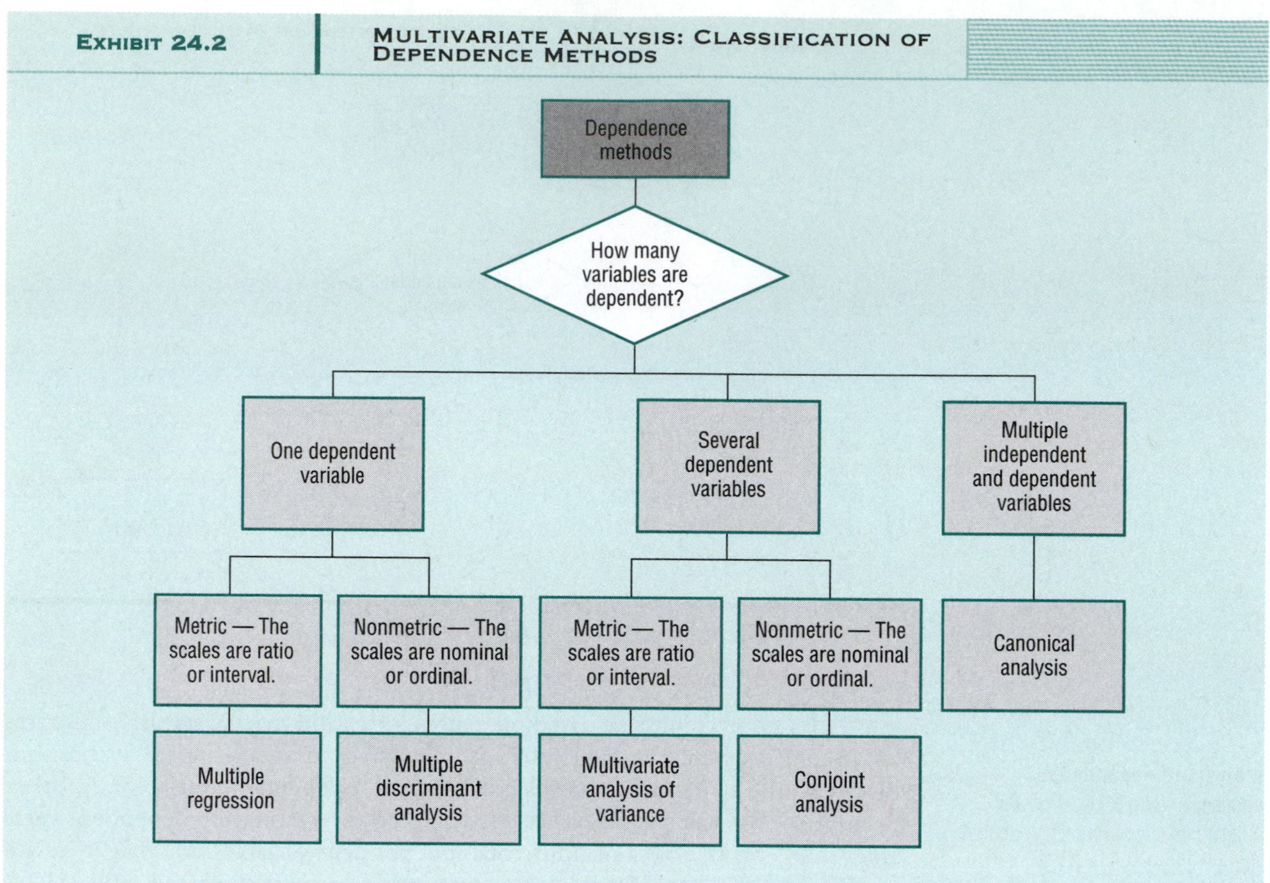

ANALYSIS OF DEPENDENCE

Multiple Regression Analysis

multiple regression analysis
An analysis of association in which the effects of two or more independent variables on a single, interval-scaled or ratio-scaled dependent variable are investigated simultaneously.

Multiple regression analysis is an extension of bivariate regression analysis, which allows for the simultaneous investigation of the effect of two or more independent variables on a single interval-scaled dependent variable. Chapter 23 illustrated bivariate linear regression analysis with an example concerning a construction tools dealer's sales volume. In this bivariate regression example, variations in the dependent variable were attributed to changes in a single independent variable. Yet reality suggests that several factors are likely to affect such a dependent variable. For example, sales volume might be hypothesized to depend not only on the number of building permits but also on price levels, amount of advertising, and the incomes of families in the area. Thus, the problem requires identification of a linear relationship with multiple regression analysis. The multiple regression equation is

$$Y = a + \beta_1 X_1 + \beta_2 X_2 + \beta_3 X_3 + \cdots + \beta_n X_n$$

Another forecasting example is useful in illustrating multiple regression. Assume a toy manufacturer wishes to forecast sales by sales territory. It is thought that competitors' sales, the presence or absence of a company salesperson in the territory (a binary variable), and grammar school enrollment are

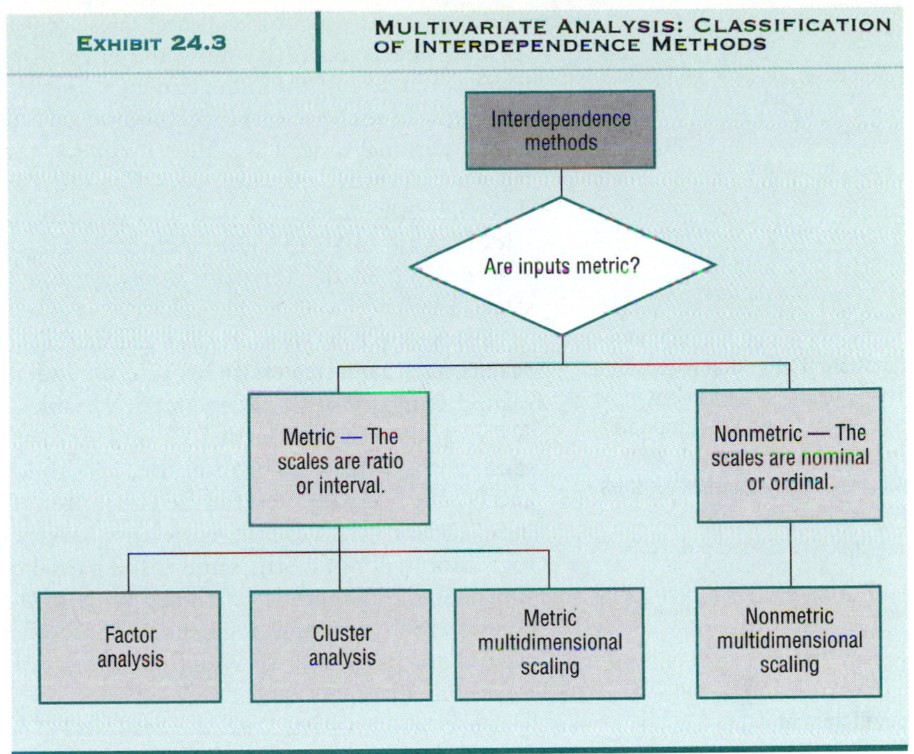

the independent variables that might explain the variation in the sales of a toy. The data appear in Table 24.1. Following are the statistical results from the multiple regression after mathematical computations have been made.

Regression equation: $Y = 102.18 + .387X_1 + 115.2X_2 + 6.73X_3$
Coefficient of determination (R^2): .845
F-value: 14.6

TABLE 24.1 DATA FOR A MULTIPLE REGRESSION PROBLEM

Y Sales (000)	X_1 Competitors' Sales (000)	X_2 Salesperson (1) or Agent (0)	X_3 Grammar School Enrollment (000)
222	106	0	23
304	213	0	18
218	201	0	22
501	378	1	20
542	488	0	21
790	509	1	31
523	644	0	17
667	888	1	25
700	941	1	32
869	1066	1	36
444	307	0	30
479	312	1	22

The regression equation indicates sales are positively related to X_1 and X_2 and X_3. The coefficients (βs) show the effects on the dependent variable of unit increases in any of the independent variables. The value of $\beta_2 = 115.2$ indicates that an increase of $115,200 (000 included) in toy sales is expected with each additional unit of X_2. Thus, it appears that adding a company salesperson has a very positive effect on sales. Grammar school enrollments also help predict sales. An increase of one unit of enrollment (1,000 students) indicates a sales increase of $6,730 (000 included). A 1-unit increase in competitors' sales volume (X_1) in the territory does not add much to the toy manufacturer's sales. ($387).

coefficient of partial regression
The percentage of the variance in the dependent variable that is explained by a single independent variable, with the other independent variables held constant.

In multiple regression the coefficients β_1, β_2, and so on are called **coefficients of partial regression** because the independent variables are usually correlated with the other independent variables. The correlation between Y and X_1, with the correlation that X_1 and X_2 have in common with Y held constant, is the partial correlation. Because the partial correlation between sales and X_1 has been adjusted for the effect produced by variation in X_2 (and other independent variables), the correlation coefficient obtained from the bivariate regression will not be the same as the partial coefficient in the multiple regression. Stated differently, the original value of β is the simple bivariate regression coefficient. In multiple regression the coefficient β_1 is defined as the partial regression coefficient for which the effects of other independent variables are held constant.

coefficient of multiple determination
In multiple regression, the percentage of the variance in the dependent variable that is explained by the variation in the independent variables.

As in the bivariate case, the **coefficient of multiple determination,** or the *multiple index of determination,* indicates the percentage of variation in Y explained by the variation in the independent variables. $R^2 = .845$ in our example tells us that the variation in the independent variables accounted for 84.5 percent of the variance in the dependent variable. Typically, adding additional independent variables in the regression equation explains more of the variation in Y than it is possible to explain with fewer variables. In other words, the amount of variation explained by two independent variables in the same equation is usually greater than the variation in Y explained by either one separately.

To test for statistical significance, an F-test comparing the different sources of variation is necessary. The F-test allows for testing of the relative magnitudes of the sum of squares due to the regression (SS_r) and the error sum of squares (SS_e), with their appropriate degrees of freedom:

$$F = \frac{(SS_r)/k}{(SS_e)/(n - k - 1)}$$

where

k = number of independent variables
n = number of respondents or observations

Table 5 in the Appendix of Statistical Tables at the end of the book shows the F-distributions for hypothesis testing at the .05 significance level. For our example the F-ratio equals 14.6. Degrees of freedom (d.f.) are calculated as follows:

$$\text{d.f. for the numerator} = k$$
$$\text{d.f. for the denominator} = n - k - 1$$

For this example,

$$\text{d.f. (numerator)} = 3$$
$$\text{d.f. (denominator)} = 12 - 3 - 1 = 8$$

Table 5 in the appendix indicates that an F-value of 4.07 or more is necessary to reject the null hypothesis at the .05 level of statistical significance. Thus, it can be concluded that the estimated functional relationship is not due to chance or random variation. There does appear to be an association between the dependent variable and the independent variables other than random variation in the data.

A continuous, interval-scaled dependent variable is required in multiple regression, as it is in bivariate regression. Interval scaling is also a requirement for the independent variables; however, *dummy variables,* such as the binary variable in our example, may be utilized. A dummy variable is a variable that has two (or more) distinct levels, which are coded 0 and 1.

There are several other assumptions needed for multiple regression (and other multivariate techniques) that require advanced study. Several excellent technical books deal with this topic.[3] The growing availability of user-friendly software allows the researcher to compute multiple regressions without a great deal of effort. Managers should be aware of the limitations of these software packages, however.

Discriminant Analysis

In a myriad of situations the researcher's purpose is to classify objects, by a set of independent variables, into two or more mutually exclusive categories. A physician might record a person's blood pressure, weight, and blood cholesterol level and then categorize that person as having a high probability of a heart attack or a low probability. Researchers interested in small-business failures might be able to group firms as to whether they eventually failed or did not fail on the basis of independent variables—location, financial ratios, management changes. A bank might want to be able to discriminate between potentially successful and unsuccessful sites for small branch offices. A personnel manager might want to distinguish between applicants to hire and those not to hire. The challenge is to find the discriminating variables to be utilized in a predictive equation that will produce better than chance assignment of the individuals to the two groups.

multiple discriminant analysis
A statistical technique for predicting the probability that an object will belong in one of two or more mutually exclusive categories (dependent variable), based on several independent variables.

The prediction of a categorical variable (rather than a continuous, interval-scaled variable, as in multiple regression) is the purpose of **multiple discriminant analysis.** In each of the above problems the researcher must determine which variables are associated with the probability of an object's falling into one of several groups or categories. In a statistical sense, the problem of studying the direction of group differences is a problem of finding a linear combination of independent variables, the discriminant function, that shows large differences in group means. *Discriminant analysis* is a statistical tool for determining such linear combinations. Deriving the coefficients of the discriminant function (a straight line) is the task of the researcher.

We will consider a two-group discriminant analysis problem where the dependent variable, Y, is measured on a nominal scale. (Note that n-way discriminant analysis is possible, but it is beyond the scope of this discussion.) Suppose a personnel manager for an electrical equipment wholesaler has been keeping records on successful versus unsuccessful sales employees. The personnel manager believes it is possible to predict whether an applicant will be successful on the basis of age, sales aptitude test scores, and mechanical ability test scores. As stated at the outset, the problem is to find a linear function of the independent variables that shows large differences in group means. The first task is to estimate the coefficients of the individual applicant's discriminant function. To calculate the individuals' discriminant scores, the following linear function is used:

$$Z_i = b_1 X_{1i} + b_2 X_{2i} + \cdots + b_n X_{ni}$$

where

X_{ni} = applicant's value on the *n*th independent variable
b_n = discriminant coefficient for the *n*th variable
Z_i = *i*th applicant's discriminant score

Using scores for all the individuals in the sample, a discriminant function is determined based on the criterion that the groups be maximally differentiated on the set of independent variables.

Returning to the example with three independent variables, suppose the personnel manager calculates the standardized weights in the equation to be

$$\begin{aligned} Z &= b_1 X_1 + b_2 X_2 + b_3 X_3 \\ &= .069 X_1 + .013 X_2 + .0007 X_3 \end{aligned}$$

This means that age (X_1) is much more important than sales aptitude test scores (X_2). Mechanical ability (X_3) has relatively minor discriminating power.

In the computation of the linear discriminant function, weights are assigned to the variables such that the ratio of the difference between the means of the two groups to the standard deviation within groups is maximized. The standardized discriminant coefficients, or weights, provide information about the relative importance of each of these variables in discriminating between the two groups.

An important goal of discriminant analysis is to perform a classification function. The object of classification in our example is to predict which applicants will be successful and which will be unsuccessful, and to group them accordingly. To determine if discriminant analysis can be used as a good predictor, information provided in the "confusion matrix" is utilized. Suppose the personnel manager has 40 successful and 45 unsuccessful employees in the sample. The confusion matrix in Table 24.2 shows that the number of cor-

TABLE 24.2 CONFUSION MATRIX

	PREDICTED GROUP		
Actual Group	**Successful**	**Unsuccessful**	
Successful	34	6	40
Unsuccessful	7	38	45

rectly classified employees (76 percent) in the example is much higher than would be expected by chance. Tests can be performed to determine if the rate of correct classification is statistically significant.

A second example will allow us to portray discriminant analysis from a graphic perspective.[4] Suppose a bank loan officer wants to segregate corporate loan applicants into those likely to default and those likely not to default. Assume that data for some past period are available on a group of firms that went bankrupt and on another group that did not. For simplicity, we assume that only the current ratio and the debt/assets ratio are analyzed. These ratios for our sample of firms are given in Columns 2 and 3 of Table 24.3.

The data in Table 24.3 are plotted in Exhibit 24.4. The *X*s represent firms that went bankrupt and the dots represent firms that remained solvent. For

TABLE 24.3 DATA ON BANKRUPT AND SOLVENT FIRMS

Firm Number (1)	Current Ratio (2)	Debt/Assets Ratio (Percent) (3)	Did Firm Go Bankrupt? (4)	Z-Score (5)	Probability of Bankruptcy (6)
1	3.6	60%	No	−.780	17.2%
2	3.0	20	No	−2.451	.8
3	3.0	60	No	−.135	42.0
4	3.0	76	Yes	.791	81.2
5	2.8	44	No	−.847	15.5
6	2.6	56	Yes	.062	51.5
7	2.6	68	Yes	.757	80.2
8	2.4	40	Yes[a]	−.649	21.1
9	2.4	60	No[a]	.509	71.5
10	2.2	28	No	−1.129	9.6
11	2.0	40	No	−.220	38.1
12	2.0	48	No[a]	.244	60.1
13	1.8	60	Yes	1.153	89.7
14	1.6	20	No	−.948	13.1
15	1.6	44	Yes	.441	68.8
16	1.2	44	Yes	.871	83.5
17	1.0	24	No	−.072	45.0
18	1.0	32	Yes	.391	66.7
19	1.0	60	Yes	2.012	97.9

[a]Denotes a misclassification. Firm 8 had $Z = -.649$, so multiple discriminant analysis predicted no bankruptcy, but the firm *did* go bankrupt. Similarly, multiple discriminant analysis predicted bankruptcy for Firms 9 and 12, but they did *not* go bankrupt. The following tabulation shows bankruptcy and solvency predictions and actual results:

	Z Positive: Multiple Discriminant Analysis Predicts Bankruptcy	*Z* Negative: Multiple Discriminant Analysis Predicts Solvency
Went bankrupt	8	1
Remained solvent	2	8

Had the multiple discriminant analysis been "perfect" as a bankruptcy predictor, all the firms would have fallen in the diagonal cells of a confusion matrix. The model did not perform perfectly, as two predicted bankrupts remained solvent while one firm that was expected to remain solvent went bankrupt. Thus, the model misclassified 3 out of 19 firms, or 16 percent of the sample.

Exhibit 24.4 | **Discriminant Boundary between Bankrupt and Solvent Firms, Based on Current and Debt Ratios**[5]

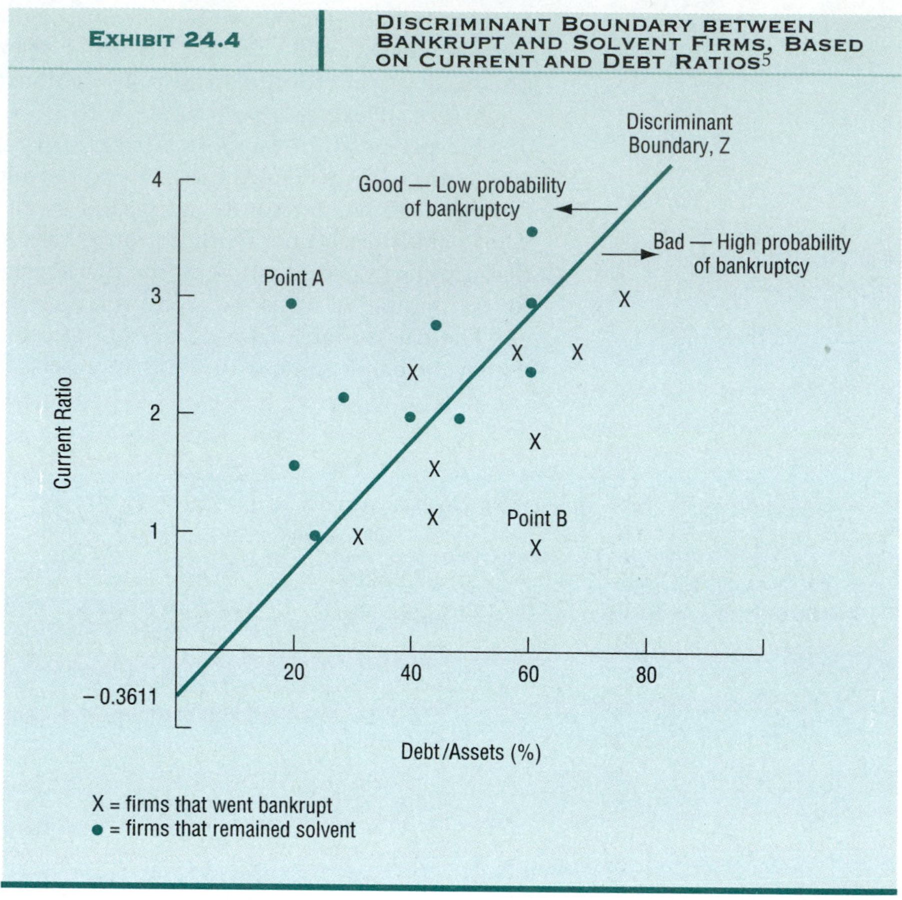

example, Point A in the upper left section is the point for Firm 2, which had a current ratio of 3.0 and a debt/assets ratio of 20 percent. The dot at Point A indicates that the firm did not go bankrupt. Point B, in the lower right section, represents Firm 19, which had a current ratio of 1.0 and a debt/assets ratio of 60 percent. It *did* go bankrupt. From a graphic perspective, we construct a boundary line (the discriminant function) through the graph such that if a firm is to the left of the line, it is not likely to become insolvent. In our example the line takes this form:

$$Z = a + b_1(\text{current ratio}) + b_2(\text{debt/assets ratio})$$

Here a is a constant term and b_1 and b_2 indicate the effect that the current ratio and the debt/assets ratio have on the probability of a firm's going bankrupt.

The following discriminant function is obtained:

$$Z = -.3877 - 1.0736(\text{current ratio}) + .0579(\text{debt/assets ratio})$$

This equation may be plotted in Exhibit 24.4 as the locus of points for which $Z = 0$. All combinations of current ratio and debt/assets ratio shown on the line result in $Z = 0$.[6] Companies that lie to the left of the line are not likely to go bankrupt, while those to the right are likely to fail. You can see from the graph that one X, indicating a failed company, lies to the left of the line, while two dots, indicating nonbankrupt companies, lie to the right of the line. Thus, the discriminant analysis failed to properly classify three companies.

Once we have determined the parameters of the discriminant function, we can calculate the *Z*-score for other companies—say, loan applicants at a bank. The *Z*-scores for our hypothetical companies are given in Column 5 of Table 24.3, and they may be interpreted as follows:

$Z = 0$: 50–50 probability of future bankruptcy (say, within 2 years). The company lies on the boundary line.

$Z < 0$: If *Z* is negative, there is less than a 50 percent probability of bankruptcy. The smaller the *Z*-score, the lower the probability of bankruptcy (shown in Column 6 of Table 24.3).

$Z > 0$: If *Z* is positive, the probability of bankruptcy is greater than 50 percent. The larger *Z* is, the greater the probability of bankruptcy.

The mean *Z*-score of the companies that did not go bankrupt is −.583, while that for the bankrupt firms is +.648. These means, along with approximations of the *Z*-score probability distributions of the two groups, are graphed in Exhibit 24.5. We may interpret this graph as indicating that if *Z* is less than about −.3, there is a very small probability that a firm will turn out to be in the bankrupt group, while if *Z* is greater than +.3, there is only a small probability that it will remain solvent. If *Z* is in the range ±.3, we are highly uncertain about how the firm should be classified. This range is called *the zone of ignorance.*

The signs of the coefficients of the discriminant function are logical. Since its coefficient is negative, the larger the current ratio, the lower a company's *Z*-score, and the lower the *Z*-score, the smaller the probability of failure. Similarly, high debt ratios produce high *Z*-scores, which can be directly translated into a higher probability of bankruptcy.

The discriminant function we have been discussing has only two variables, but other characteristics could be introduced. For example, we could add such variables as the rate of return on assets (ROA), the times-interest-earned ratio, the quick ratio, and so forth.[7] If we introduced return on assets, we might find that Firm 8 (which failed) had a low ROA, while Firm 9 (which did not fail) had a high ROA. A new discriminant function would be calculated:

$$Z = a + b_1(\text{current ratio}) + b_2(\text{D/A}) + b_3(\text{ROA})$$

EXHIBIT 24.5 | **PROBABILITY DISTRIBUTIONS OF Z SCORES**[8]

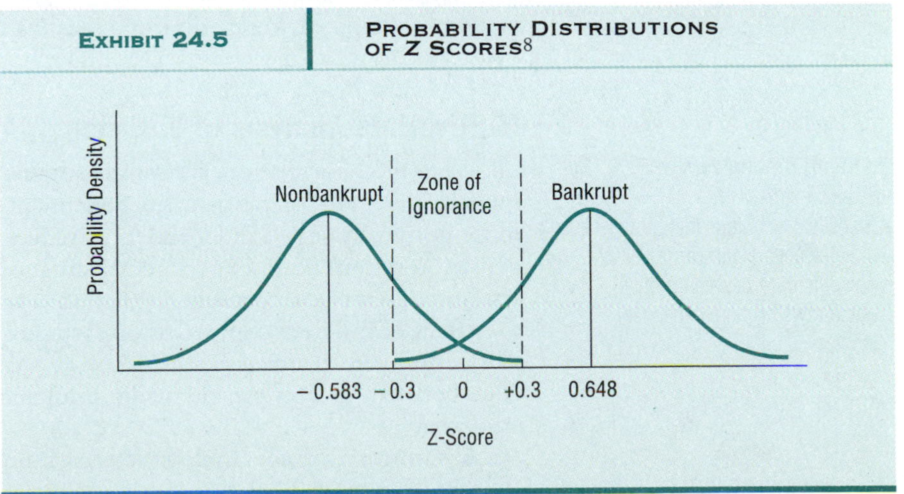

Firm 8 might now have a positive Z, while Firm 9's Z might become negative. Thus, it is quite possible that by adding more characteristics we could improve the accuracy of our bankruptcy forecasts.

In terms of Exhibit 24.5, introducing more characteristics would spread the probability distributions apart and narrow the zone of ignorance; in terms of the confusion matrix in Table 24.2, more firms would fall on the diagonal and fewer in the off-diagonal cells.

Canonical Correlation

canonical correlation analysis
A technique used to determine the degree of linear association between two sets of variables, each consisting of several variables.

Canonical correlation is a very complex statistical technique that is not extensively used, but we will briefly examine it here. When the research analyst has two or more criterion variables (dependent variables) and multiple predictor variables (independent variables), canonical correlation analysis is an appropriate statistical technique. Multiple regression analysis investigates the linear relationship between a single dependent, or criterion, variable and multiple independent variables. **Canonical correlation analysis** is an extension of multiple regression that focuses on the relationship between two sets of interval-scaled variables.

Suppose a researcher wishes to specify the correlation between a set of shopping behavior variables (the criterion set) and some personality variables (the predictor set). The researcher is interested in knowing how several personality traits influence various grocery shopping behaviors, such as list preparation, use of store coupons, number of stores visited, and number of trips per week. The researcher is attempting to find personality profiles that tend to be associated with various shopping patterns.

Canonical correlation maximizes the correlation between two linear combinations. For example, the linear combinations for shopping behavior might be

$$Z = a_1X_1 + a_2X_2 + \cdots + a_nX_n$$

and the linear combination for the personality variables might be

$$W = b_1Y_1 + b_2Y_2 + \cdots + b_nY_n$$

As in regression analysis, a set of canonical coefficients, or weights, is identified for the predictor set of variables. Another set of canonical coefficients, or weights, is identified for the criterion set. To interpret the canonical analysis, the researcher examines the relative magnitude and the signs of the several weights defining each equation, and sees if a meaningful interpretation can be given.

Multivariate Analysis of Variance (MANOVA)

multivariate analysis of variance (MANOVA)
A statistical technique that provides a simultaneous significance test of mean difference between groups, made for two or more dependent variables.

Like canonical correlation, **multivariate analysis of variance** is used when there are multiple interval- or ratio-scaled dependent variables. There may be one or more nominally scaled independent variables. By manipulating the sales compensation system in an experimental situation and holding the compensation system constant in a controlled situation, a researcher may be able to identify the effect of the new compensation system on sales volume, as well as on job satisfaction and turnover. With MANOVA a significance test of mean difference between groups can be made simultaneously for two or more dependent variables.

A summary of the multivariate techniques for analysis of dependence appears in Exhibit 24.6.

EXHIBIT 24.6 SUMMARY OF MULTIVARIATE TECHNIQUES FOR THE ANALYSIS OF DEPENDENCE

Technique	Purpose	Number of Dependent Variables	Number of Independent Variables	TYPE OF MEASUREMENT: Dependent	TYPE OF MEASUREMENT: Independent
Multiple regression	To simultaneously investigate the effects of several independent variables on a dependent variable	1	2 or more	Interval or ratio	Interval or ratio
Discriminant analysis	To predict the probability that an object or individual will belong in one of two or more mutually exclusive categories, based on several independent variables	1	2 or more	Nominal	Interval or ratio
Canonical correlation	To determine the degree of linear association between two sets of variables, each consisting of several variables	2 or more	2 or more	Interval or ratio	Interval or ratio
MANOVA	To determine if statistically significant differences of means of several variables occur simultaneously between two levels of a variable	2 or more	1	Interval or ratio	Nominal

ANALYSIS OF INTERDEPENDENCE

We now turn our attention to the analysis of interdependence. Rather than attempting to predict a variable or set of variables from a set of independent variables, the purpose of techniques such as factor analysis, cluster analysis, and multidimensional scaling is to further understand the structure of a set of variables or objects.

Factor Analysis

Suppose that we measure the heights, weights, occupations, educations, and sources of income for 50 men. The results of a factor analysis might indicate that height and weight may be summarized by the underlying dimension of size. The variables occupation, education, and source of income may be summarized by the underlying concept of social status. In this example, two new variables, or *factors,* explain the five variables at a more generalized level (see Exhibit 24.7).

EXHIBIT 24.7 | **FACTOR ANALYSIS EXAMPLE**

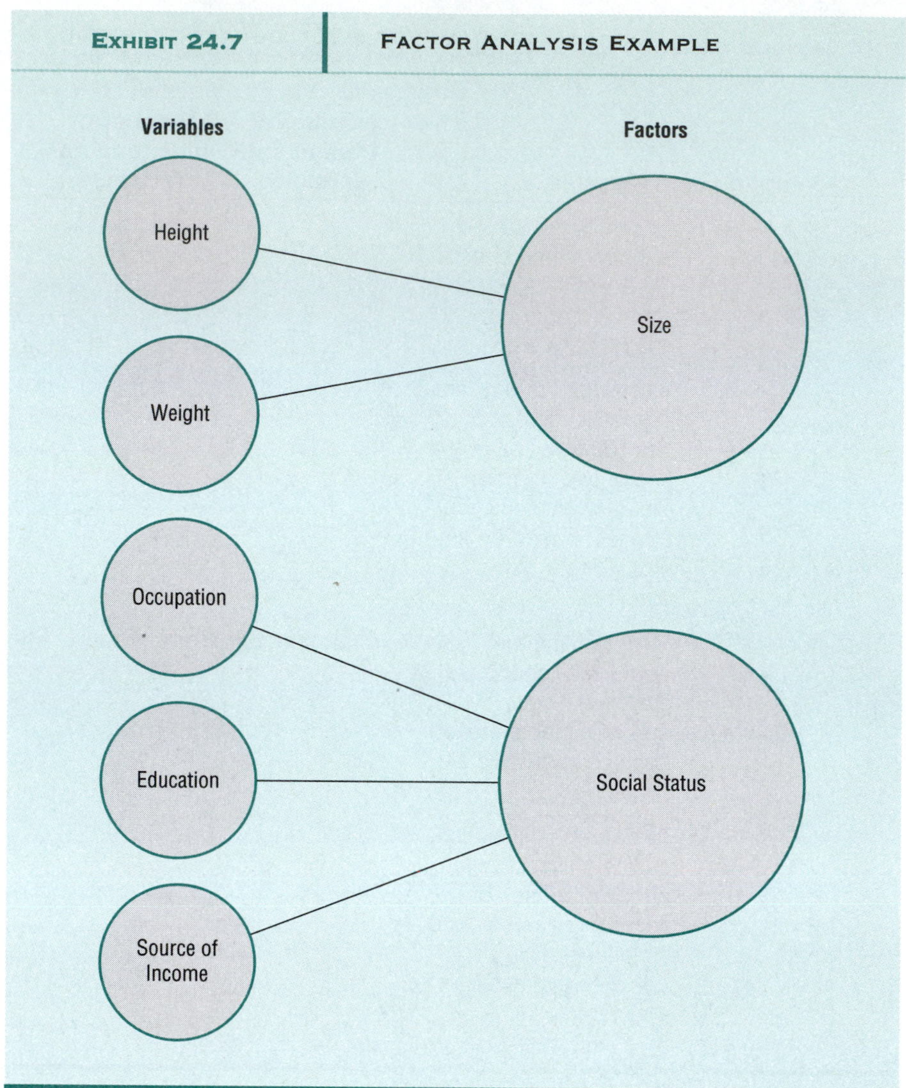

factor analysis
A type of analysis used to discern the underlying dimensions or regularity in phenomena. Its general purpose is to summarize the information contained in a large number of variables into a smaller number of factors. There are a number of factor-analytical techniques.

The general purpose of **factor analysis** is to summarize the information contained in a large number of variables into a smaller number of factors. Factor analysis refers to a number of diverse techniques used to discern the underlying dimensions or regularity in phenomena.[9]

If a researcher has a set of variables and suspects that these variables are interrelated in a complex fashion, then factor analysis may be used to untangle the linear relationships into their separate patterns. The statistical purpose of factor analysis is to determine linear combinations of variables that aid in investigating the interrelationships. For example, suppose a researcher collects a variety of data on intermediaries' attitudes toward their working relationship with a manufacturer. Numerous questions about delivery, pricing arrangements, discounts, sales personnel, repair service, and other relevant issues are asked. The researcher, however, wants to reduce the large number of variables to certain underlying constructs, or dimensions, that will summarize the important information contained in the variables. Thus, the researcher's purpose is to discover the basic structure of a domain and to add substantive interpretation to the underlying dimensions. Factor analysis accomplishes this by combining the questions to create new, more abstract variables called *factors.* In general, the goal of factor analysis is parsimony: to reduce a large number of variables to as few dimensions or constructs as possible.

Interpreting Factor Results

How factor analysis can be used to reduce a large number of variables to a few interpretable dimensions is illustrated in the following consumer behavior example in a health-care setting. With advances in medical science, there has been an increased demand for nonregenerative body parts, such as kidneys, and regenerative body parts, such as blood. The researchers were attempting to investigate whether willingness to donate body parts was a unidimensional domain. Based on factor analysis (Table 24.4), there appear to be three separate underlying dimensions of willingness to donate: Factor 1, blood, skin, and marrow donations; Factor 2, death (cadaver) donation; and Factor 3, kidney donation.

TABLE 24.4 FACTOR ANALYSIS WITH VARIMAX ROTATION—TEN WILLINGNESS-TO-DONATE VARIABLES[10]

Variable and Factor Descriptions	Factor Loadings[a]		
	Factor 1	Factor 2	Factor 3
Blood, Skin, Marrow			
I would be willing to donate *blood* at least once every two months.	[.3807][b]	.1646	.2009
If I witnessed a traffic accident, I would not be willing to donate *blood* to a victim.	[−.4244]	−.0304	−.1503
If needed, I am willing to give *blood* to a relative or close friend.	[.6339]	.0988	.0517
I would give a piece of my *skin* to a relative who has been seriously burnt.	[.4556]	.1405	.1356
If necessary, I would donate some *bone marrow* to be extracted from my breastbone to a relative.	[.5377]	.3440	.2681
Death Donation			
I am willing to donate both my eyes to a stranger upon my *death.*	.1412	[.7944]	.2946
I am willing to arrange an agreement to donate my heart or any other vital organ for use after my *death.*	.2410	[.7582]	.1664
Kidney Donation			
I would never donate one of my *kidneys* to someone outside of my family, not even to a close friend.	−.1669	−.2544	[−.6770]
If needed, I would donate one of my *kidneys* to a stranger at this very moment.	.1641	.1486	[.6584]
If at this moment I learned that a relative desperately needed a *kidney* to survive, I would not donate one of mine.	−.3814	−.1596	[−.5272]
Explained Variance per Factor	36.9%	12.2%	10.2%
Cumulative	36.9	49.1	59.3

[a]377 respondents
[b][ ] indicates the highest loading in each row.

factor loading
A measure of the importance of a variable in measuring a factor; a means for interpreting and labeling a factor.

Factor Loadings. The factor loadings in Table 24.4 are roughly analogous to the correlation (or a set of the correlations) of the original variable with the factor. Each **factor loading** is a measure of the importance of the variable in measuring each factor. The statement "If needed, I am willing to give blood to a relative or close friend" has a high factor loading (.6339) on the first factor and a relatively low loading on Factors 2 and 3. Inspection of the table indicates that for each of the variables loading on the blood, skin, marrow factor (Factor 1), the loading is much higher on Factor 1 than on Factors 2 and 3. Factor loadings provide a means for interpreting and labeling the factors.

Total Variance Explained. In addition to the factor loadings, Table 24.4 shows a percentage of total variance of the original variables explained by each factor. The first factor summarizes 36.9 percent of the variance, and the second factor summarizes 12.2 percent of the variance. Together the two factors summarize 49.1 percent of the total variance. This explanation of variance is equivalent to R^2 in multiple regression.

factor score
A number that represents each observation's calculated value on each factor in a factor analysis.

Factor Scores. Each individual observation has a score, or value, associated with each of the original variables. Factor analysis procedures derive **factor scores** that represent each observation's calculated value, or score, on each of the factors. The factor score will represent an individual's combined response to the several variables representing the factor.

The factor scores may be used in subsequent analysis. When the factors are to represent a new set of variables that may predict or be dependent on some phenomenon, the new input may be factor scores.

In addition to reducing a large number of variables to a manageable number of dimensions, factor analysis may also reduce the problem of *multicollinearity* in multiple regression.[11] If several independent variables are highly correlated, conducting a factor analysis as a preliminary step prior to regression analysis and use of factor scores may reduce the problem of having several intercorrelated independent variables. Thus, factor analysis may be utilized to meet the statistical assumptions of various models.

communality
In factor analysis, a measure of the percentage of a variable's variation that is explained by the factors.

Communality. A researcher may wish to know how much a variable has in common with all factors. **Communality** is a measure of the percentage of a variable's variation that is explained by the factors. A relatively high communality indicates that a variable has much in common with the other variables taken as a group.

How Many Factors?

This discussion has concentrated on summarizing the patterns in the variables with a reduced number of factors. The question arises, "How many factors will be in the problem's solution?" This question requires a lengthy, complex answer. It is complex because there can be more than one possible solution to any factor analysis problem, depending on factor rotation. The technical aspects of the concept of factor rotation are beyond the scope of this book. However, the term *rotation* is important in factor analysis and should be briefly explained. Solutions to factor analysis problems may be portrayed by geometrically plotting the values of each variable for all respondents or observations. Geometric axes may be drawn to represent each factor. New solutions are represented geometrically, by rotation of these axes. Hence a new solution with fewer or more factors is called a **rotation.**

rotation
In factor analysis, changing of geometric axes that represent the factors so as to contemplate a new problem solution having fewer or more factors.

Exhibit 24.8 Clusters of Individuals on Two Dimensions

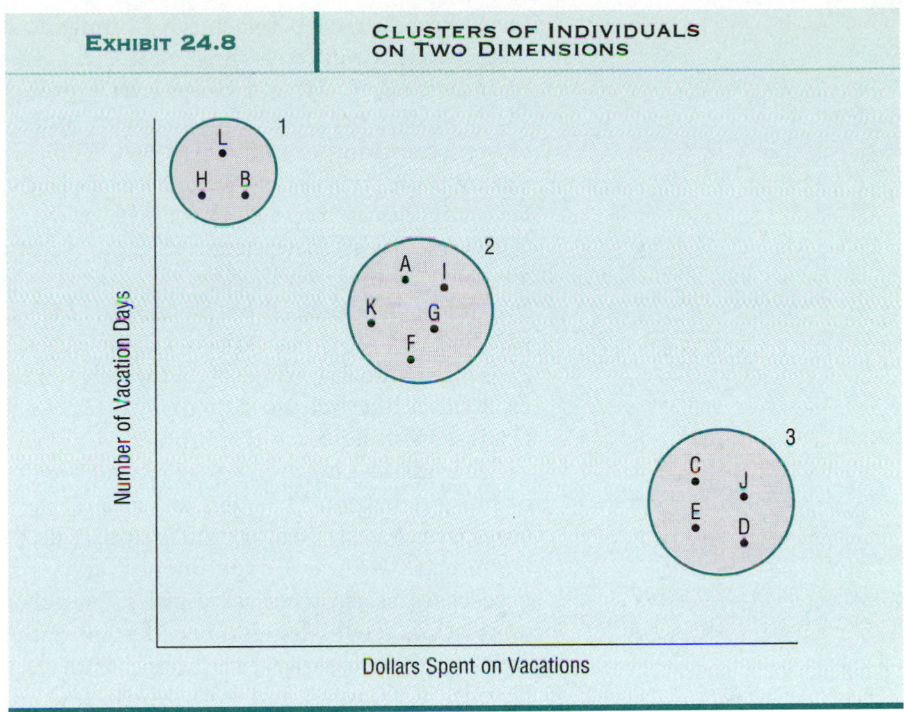

Although the concept of factor analysis is relatively easy to grasp, the technical vocabulary of factor analysis includes a number of unusual terms, such as *eigenvalues, rotated matrix,* and *orthogonal.* Because this is a simplified introduction to the topic of multivariate statistics, we will not define these terms. Competent statisticians should be consulted when working on problems involving factor analysis.

Cluster Analysis

cluster analysis
An analysis that classifies individuals or objects into a small number of mutually exclusive groups, ensuring that there will be as much likeness within groups and as much difference among groups as possible.

Cluster analysis is a term given to a body of techniques used to identify objects or individuals that are similar with respect to some criterion. The purpose of cluster analysis is to classify individuals or objects into a small number of mutually exclusive and exhaustive groups. The researcher's focus is to determine how objects or individuals should be assigned to groups to ensure that there will be as much likeness within groups and as much difference among groups as possible. The cluster should have high internal (within-cluster) homogeneity and high external (between-cluster) heterogeneity.

A typical use of cluster analysis is to facilitate market segmentation by identifying subjects or individuals who have similar needs, lifestyles, or responses to marketing strategies. Clusters, or subgroups, of recreational vehicle owners may be identified on the basis of their similarity of usage of and benefits sought from recreational vehicles. Alternatively, the researcher might use demographic variables or lifestyle variables to group individuals into clusters identified as market segments.

TO THE POINT

The ability to simplify means to eliminate the unnecessary so that the necessary may speak.
HANS HOFFMAN

We will illustrate cluster analysis with a hypothetical example relating to the types of vacations taken by 12 individuals. Vacation behavior is represented on two dimensions: number of vacation days and dollar expenditures on vacations during a given year. Exhibit 24.8 is a scatter diagram that represents the geometric distance between the 12 individuals in two-dimensional space. The scatter diagram portrays three clear-cut clusters. The first subgroup, consisting of individuals L, H, and B, suggests a group of individuals who have many vacation days but do not spend much money on their vacations. The second cluster, consisting of individuals A, I, K, G, and F, represents intermediate values on both variables: an average number of vacation days and an average dollar expenditure on vacations. The third group consists of a cluster of individuals who have relatively few vacation days but who spend large amounts on these outings.

In this hypothetical example individuals are grouped on the basis of their similarity or proximity to other individuals. The logic of cluster analysis is to group individuals or objects on the bases of their similarity to or distance from each other. The actual mathematical procedures for deriving clusters will not be dealt with here, as our purpose is only to introduce the technique.

A study investigating test markets provides a pragmatic example of the use of cluster analysis. Managers are frequently interested in finding test-market cities that are sufficiently similar so that no extraneous variation causes a difference between the experimental and control markets. In this study the objects to be clustered were cities. The characteristics of the cities, such as population, retail sales, number of retail outlets, and percentage of nonwhites, were used to identify the groups. Cities such as Omaha, Oklahoma City, Dayton, Columbus, and Fort Worth and cities such as Newark, Pittsburgh, Cleveland, Buffalo, and Baltimore were similar, but individual cities in each group of cities were dissimilar. See Exhibit 24.9.

This example should clarify the difference between factor analysis and cluster analysis. In factor analysis the researcher might search for constructs underlying the variables (population, retail sales, number of retail outlets); in cluster analysis the researcher searches for constructs underlying the objects (cities).

Cluster analysis differs from multiple discriminant analysis in that the groups are not predefined. The purpose of cluster analysis is to determine how many distinct groups exist and to define their composition. It describes a sample of objects after examining only a sample. It does not predict relationships.

Multidimensional Scaling

multidimensional scaling
A technique that measures attitudes about objects in multidimensional space on the basis of respondents' judgments of similarity of objects.

Multidimensional scaling provides a means for measuring objects in multidimensional space on the basis of respondents' judgments of the similarity of objects. The perceptual difference among objects is reflected in the relative distance between objects in multidimensional space.

Traditionally, attitudes have been measured by using a scale to measure each component of an attitude and then combining the individual scores into an aggregate score. In the most common form of multidimensional scaling, the subject is asked to evaluate an object's similarity to other objects. For example, in a career orientation study the respondent may be asked to rate the similarity of a certified public accountant to a management consultant. The analyst then attempts to explain the differences between the objects on the basis of the components of attitudes. The unfolding of the attitude components aids in an understanding of why objects are judged to be similar or dissimilar.

An illustration of the ways that MBA students perceive six graduate schools of business also helps to explain multidimensional scaling. The students were asked to provide their perceptions of relative similarities among the set of graduate schools. Next, the overall similarity scores for all possible pairs of

Exhibit 24.9 | **Cluster Analysis of Test-Market Cities**[12]

Cluster Number	City	Cluster Number	City	Cluster Number	City
1	Omaha	7	Sacramento	13	Allentown
	Oklahoma City		San Bernardino		Providence
	Dayton		San Jose		Jersey City
	Columbus		Phoenix		York
	Fort Worth		Tucson		Louisville
2	Peoria	8	Gary	14	Paterson
	Davenport		Nashville		Milwaukee
	Binghamton		Jacksonville		Cincinnati
	Harrisburg		San Antonio		Miami
	Worcester		Knoxville		Seattle
3	Canton	9	Indianapolis	15	San Diego
	Youngstown		Kansas City		Tacoma
	Toledo		Dallas		Norfolk
	Springfield		Atlanta		Charleston
	Albany		Houston		Ft. Lauderdale
4	Bridgeport	10	Mobile	16	New Orleans
	Rochester		Shreveport		Richmond
	Hartford		Birmingham		Tampa
	New Haven		Memphis		Lancaster
	Syracuse		Chattanooga		Minneapolis
5	Wilmington	11	Newark	17	San Francisco
	Orlando		Cleveland		Detroit
	Tulsa		Pittsburgh		Boston
	Wichita		Buffalo		Philadelphia
	Grand Rapids		Baltimore	18	Washington
6	Bakersfield	12	Albuquerque		St. Louis
	Fresno		Salt Lake City		
	Flint		Denver		
	El Paso		Charlotte		
	Beaumont		Portland		

objects were aggregated for all individual respondents and arranged in a matrix. With the aid of a complex computer program, the similarity judgments were statistically transformed into distances by placing the graduate schools of business into a specified multidimensional space. The distance between similar objects on the perceptual map is small; dissimilar objects are farther apart.

Exhibit 24.10 is a perceptual map in two-dimensional space. Inspection of the map illustrates that Harvard and Stanford were perceived to be quite similar to each other, and that MIT and Carnegie were perceived to be very similar. However, MIT and Chicago were perceived to be dissimilar. The researchers identified the two axes as "quantitative versus qualitative curriculum" and "less versus more prestige." The labeling of the dimension axes is a task of interpretation for the researcher and is not statistically determined. As with other multivariate techniques in the analysis of interdependence, there are several alternative mathematical techniques for multidimensional scaling.

Exhibit 24.10 | **Perceptual Map of Six Graduate Business Schools—Simple Space**[13]

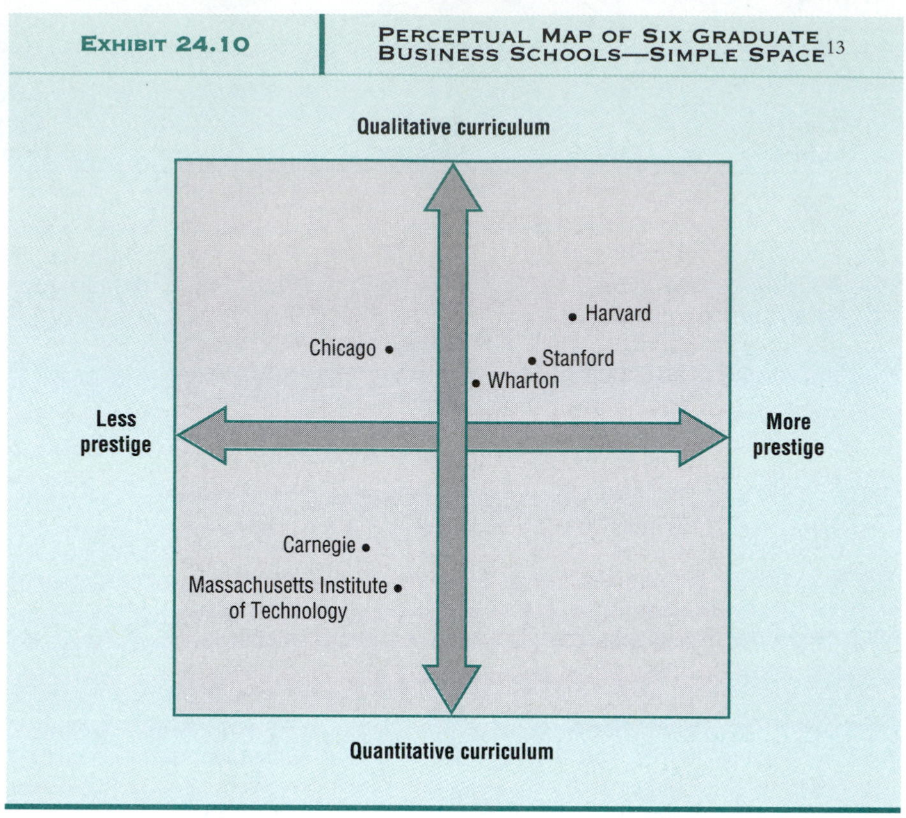

Chi-Square Automatic Interaction Detection (CHAID)

chi-square automatic interaction detection (CHAID)
A clustering method used to investigate the interaction of a large set of independent variables; a method of breaking a large heterogeneous group into various homogeneous subgroups.

Chi-square automatic interaction detection (CHAID) is a multivariate technique that investigates the relationship between a dependent variable and a series of predictor variables. CHAID, which may be utilized as a clustering method, was originally developed to investigate the interaction of a large set of independent variables. The computer-assisted analysis begins with a total group. The objective is to form subgroups through a number of sequentially generated binary splits. The procedure begins when the researcher selects a dependent variable. The CHAID program then "tears down" the groups by searching through the various categorical independent variables to obtain a split on a single independent variable that will account for the largest variation in the dependent variable.

Exhibit 24.11 shows an example of CHAID analysis in the savings and loan industry. "Average savings account balance" was selected as the dependent variable. Thus, the analysis will attempt to explain the shared characteristics of the major segments associated with "average savings account balance."[14] In the box labeled "Base group," the average savings account balance for all customers observed ($\bar{Y}$) is 9.906, or approximately $35,000 per account. The CHAID algorithm searches all of the independent variables and attempts to find the variables that have the largest difference in terms of mean value and sum of squares. It picks as the first variable of the split the variable that contributes most to the splitting. In our example, the first binary split is based on age. The first split is between people under 55 and people over 55 years of age. People under 55 have a mean balance value of 8.014 and people over 55 have a different mean balance of 11.530. Hence it appears that older individuals have larger savings and loan balances.

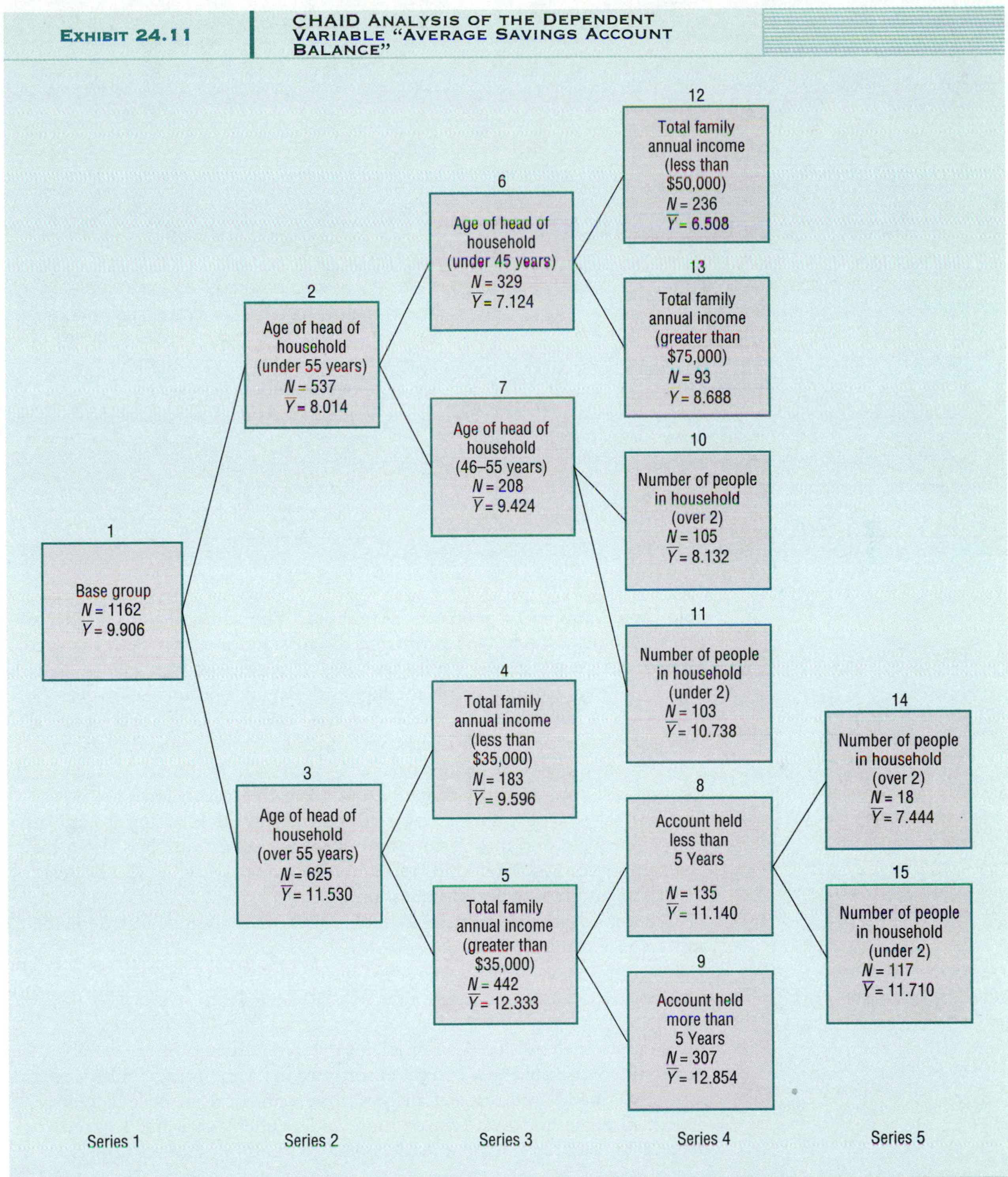

As the sequence progresses to the next split, the group of individuals over 55 is split into two subgroups. This splitting is based on differences in the mean of the dependent variable for income level. Further splits in the CHAID tree are based on the two other independent variables, "years account has been

Research Insight

SEVEN COMMANDMENTS FOR USERS OF MULTIVARIATE METHODS

1. Do not be technique oriented—focus on management's needs, then choose an appropriate analytical tool.[15]
2. Consider multivariate models as information for management—multivariate models (equations, or perceptual maps) are an aid to, not a substitute for, managerial judgment.
3. Do not substitute multivariate methods for researcher skill and imagination—statistics do not assure causality and are not substitutes for common sense.
4. Develop communication skill—management seldom accepts findings based on methods [it doesn't] understand.
5. Avoid making statistical inferences about the parameters of multivariate models—because of nonsampling and measurement errors, we are seldom certain of the distribution of a population.
6. Guard against the danger of making inferences about the market realities when such inferences may reflect the peculiarities of the method—be sure the statistical findings are consistent with sound theory and common sense.
7. Exploit the complementary relationship between functional and structural methods—use one method to support another.

held" and "number of people in household." The value of the CHAID program becomes evident by scrutinizing the interaction effect with the predictor variable "total annual family income." It appears at first glance that the higher the total family income, the higher the savings balance. However, closer inspection of Exhibit 24.11 reveals that the "over $35,000" mark is prevalent only for people who are 55 years and older. For younger savers the income requirement for greater savings balance is at the $75,000 mark, as seen by the splitting of Group 6 into Groups 12 and 13 in the fourth series.

CHAID is a very interesting and logical way of breaking a large nonhomogeneous group into various homogeneous subgroups. It is also a logical first step in doing several kinds of multivariate analysis when the homogeneity of the sample is in serious question.

A summary of the multivariate techniques for analysis of interdependence appears in Exhibit 24.12.

SUMMARY

Multivariate analysis is used for problems involving three or more variables. The availability of user-friendly computer software that can process multivariate statistics has made multivariate analysis more practical in recent years. The dependence method uses two or more independent variables to predict the dependent variable(s). The interdependence method groups subsets of the variables.

A common dependence method is multiple regression. It is an extension of bivariate linear regression using more than one independent variable. The coefficients of partial regression obtained in multiple regression are based on holding all other independent variables constant, and thus they are not identical to the corresponding simple regression coefficients. The coefficient of

EXHIBIT 24.12 | **SUMMARY OF MULTIVARIATE TECHNIQUES FOR ANALYSIS OF INTERDEPENDENCE**

Technique	Purpose	Type of Measurement
Factor analysis	To summarize into a reduced number of factors the information contained in a large number of variables	Interval or ratio
Cluster analysis	To classify individuals or objects into a smaller number of mutually exclusive and exhaustive groups, ensuring that there will be as much likeness within groups and as much difference between groups as possible	Interval or ratio
Multidimensional scaling	To measure objects in multidimensional space on the basis of respondents' judgments of their similarity	Varies depending on technique

multiple determination (R^2) represents the portion of the variance in the dependent variable accounted for by the model. An F-test can be used to determine statistical significance.

Another dependence technique is discriminant analysis. It uses independent variables to classify observations into one of a set of mutually exclusive categories.

Canonical correlation and multivariate analysis of variance are more complex dependence techniques. Canonical correlation uses two or more criterion variables (dependent variables) and multiple predictor variables (independent variables). Multivariate analysis of variance, or MANOVA, allows significance tests of mean differences between groups for two or more dependent variables.

One interdependence method is factor analysis. It is used to summarize the information contained in a large number of variables into a smaller number of factors. A second method is cluster analysis, which classifies observations into a small number of mutually exclusive and exhaustive groups. These should have as much likeness within groups and as much difference between groups as possible. In cluster analysis the groups are not predefined. A third interdependence method is multidimensional scaling. It measures objects in multidimensional space, based on respondents' judgments of their similarity. The procedure explains the perceived relationships by unfolding the attitude components making up the judgments.

The purpose of CHAID (chi-square automatic interaction detection) analysis is to form subgroups by searching through the various categorical independent variables to obtain a split on a single independent variable that will account for the largest variation in the dependent variable.

Key Terms and Concepts

multivariate data analysis
analysis of dependence
analysis of interdependence
multiple regression analysis
coefficient of partial regression
coefficient of multiple determination
multiple discriminant analysis
canonical correlation analysis
multivariate analysis of variance (MANOVA)
factor analysis
factor loading
factor score
communality
rotation
cluster analysis
multidimensional scaling
chi-square automatic interaction detection (CHAID)

Questions for Review and Critical Thinking

1. How do multivariate statistical methods differ from univariate and bivariate methods?
2. What is the distinction between dependence methods and interdependence methods?
3. What is the aim of multiple linear regression? Discriminant analysis? Canonical correlation? Multivariate analysis of variance?
4. Give an example of a situation in which each of the techniques mentioned in question 3 might be used.
5. What is the aim of factor analysis? Cluster analysis? Multidimensional scaling?
6. Give an example of a situation in which each of the techniques mentioned in question 5 might be used.
7. Why have computer software programs increased the use of multivariate analysis?
8. Why might a researcher want to use multivariate analysis rather than a univariate or bivariate analysis technique?
9. Using the data from Question 8 in Chapter 17, answer the following questions:
   (a) Calculate all bivariate regression equations that will predict current sales. Which is the best one?
   (b) Using multiple regression, find a model that will help explain current sales.
   (c) Conduct a multiple discriminant analysis to see if you can predict the region in which a salesperson works.
   (d) Use cluster analysis to see if there are any natural groupings among the salespeople.
10. A researcher uses multiple regression to predict a client's sales volume based on gross domestic product, personal income, disposable personal income, unemployment, and the consumer price index. What should the researcher be obligated to tell the client about this multiple regression model?
11. A researcher is in a hurry to prepare a report for a client. The researcher conducts multiple regression analysis but does not take the time to verify that the statistical assumptions of the model have been met. Is this the right thing to do?

Exploring the Internet

1. The American Statistical Association home page is located at http://www.amstat.org/. Select the CareerCenter option to learn what a career in statistics might have to offer.
2. Go to http://www-psych.nmsu.edu/regression/home.html to find the Multiple Regression with Ren & Stimpy! Web site. Take the tutorial.
3. The Federal Reserve Bank of St. Louis maintains a database called FRED (Federal Reserve Economic Data). Navigate to the FRED database at http://www.stls.frb.org/fred/index.html. Select a variable to be the dependent variable in a multiple regression analysis. What variables might be utilized in a multiple regression to predict this variable?

WebSurveyor Activities

WebSurveyor allows a researcher to download a survey's results to a data file. Exporting data into other applications is handled through CSV (comma separated value) files. Using the sports opinion survey, we have done this for you. The exported files have been converted to Microsoft Excel (sports.xls) and to SPSS (sports.sav). Numeric codes are used in these files.

Using SPSS or Excel, conduct a factor analysis using the first 17 items.

Case Suggestions

Case 29: LastDance Health Care
Case 30: Sunbelt Energy
Case 31: Employees Federal Credit Union

CHAPTER

25

COMMUNICATING RESEARCH RESULTS: Report, Presentation, and Follow-Up

What you will learn in this chapter

- To explain how the research report is the crucial means for communicating the whole research project.
- To discuss the research report from a communications model perspective.
- To define the term *research report.*
- To outline the research report format and its parts.
- To discuss the importance of using graphics in research reporting.
- To explain how tables and charts are useful for presenting numerical information and how to interpret the various portions of tables and charts.
- To identify the various types of research charts.
- To discuss how an oral presentation may be the most efficient means of supplementing the written report.
- To understand the importance of the research follow-up.

After spending days, weeks, or even months working on a project, a researcher is likely to feel that preparation of a report on that project is an anticlimactic formality. After all, it seems the real work has all been done; it just has to be put on paper. This attitude can be disastrous. The project may have been well designed, the data carefully obtained and analyzed by sophisticated statistical methods, and important conclusions reached, but if the project is not effectively reported, all the preceding effort has been wasted. Many times the research report is the only part of the project that others ever see. Users of the report cannot separate the *content* of the project from the *form* in which it is presented. If people who need to use the research results have to wade through a disorganized presentation, or are detoured by technical jargon they don't understand, or find sloppiness of language or thought, they will probably discount the report and make decisions without it—just as if the project had never been done. Thus, the research report is the crucial means for communicating the whole project—the medium by which it makes an impact on decisions. ■

This chapter explains how research reports, oral presentations, and follow-up conversations help communicate research results.[1]

INSIGHTS FROM THE COMMUNICATIONS MODEL

communication process
The process by which one person or source sends a message to an audience or receiver and then receives feedback about the message.

Some insights from the theory of communications help clarify the importance of the research report. Exhibit 25.1 illustrates one view of the **communication process.** Several elements enter into successful communication:

1. The *communicator,* the source or sender of the message (the writer of the report)
2. The *message,* the set of meanings being sent to or received by the audience (the findings of the research project)
3. The *medium,* the means by which the message is carried or delivered to the audience (the oral or written report itself)
4. The *audience,* the receiver or destination of the message (the manager who will make a decision based, we hope, on the report findings)
5. *Feedback,* communication also involving a message and channel, that flows in the reverse direction (from the audience to the original communicator) and which may be used to modify subsequent communications (the manager's response to the report)

It is a luxury to be understood.
RALPH WALDO EMERSON

This model of communication overstates the case, though. It implies that the message flows smoothly along from the writer to the reader, who in turn promptly provides the writer with feedback. Actually, things are more complex, and Exhibit 25.2 illustrates one of the difficulties. The communicator and the audience each have individual fields of experience. These overlap to some extent; otherwise, no communication would be possible. Nevertheless, there is much experience that is not common to both parties. As communicators send a message, they code it in terms that make sense to them, based on their fields of experience. As the audience receives the message, individuals decode it, based on their own fields of experience. The message is successfully

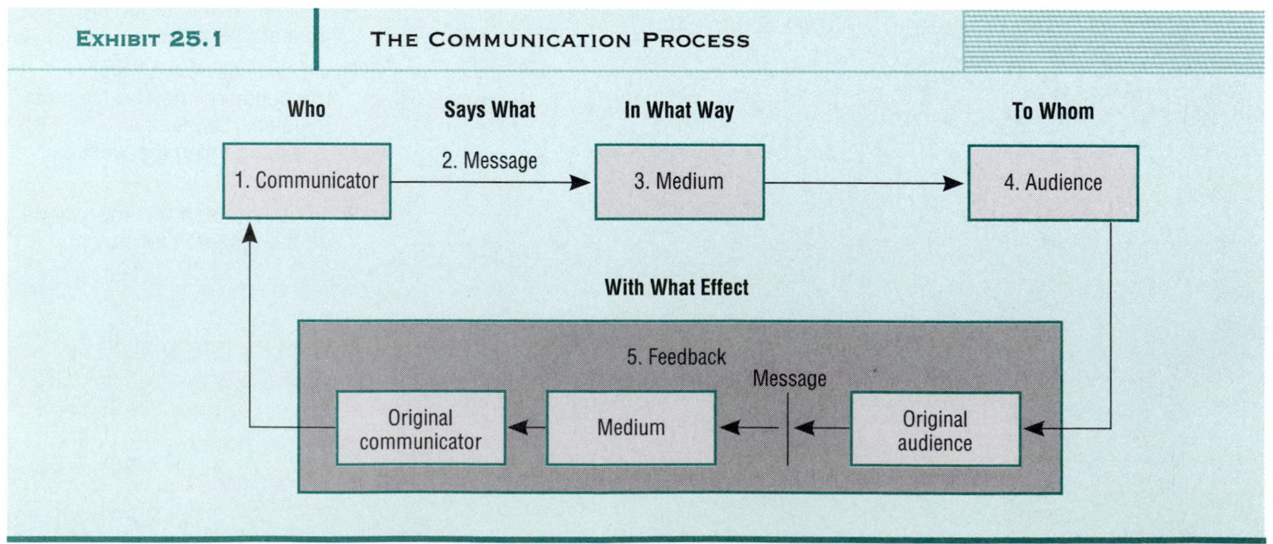

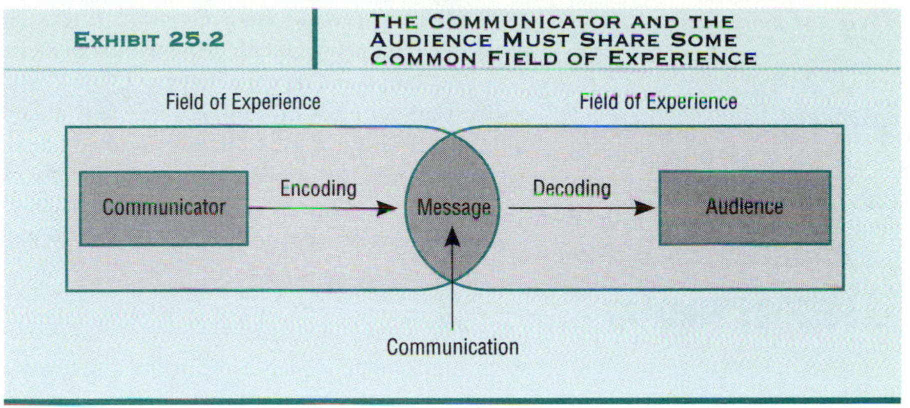

Exhibit 25.2 The Communicator and the Audience Must Share Some Common Field of Experience

communicated only if there is enough common experience that it may be encoded, transmitted, and decoded with roughly the same meaning.

In the research setting there is a communicator (the researcher) who has spent a great deal of time studying a problem. The researcher has looked at secondary sources, gathered primary data, used statistical techniques to analyze the data, and reached conclusions. When the report on the project is written, all this "baggage" affects its content. Researchers may assume the reader has a lot of background information on the project. The researchers produce pages of unexplained tables, assuming the reader will dig out from them the same patterns they have observed. The report may use technical terms, such as *parameter, F-distribution, hypothesis test, correlation,* or *eigenvalue,* on the assumption that the reader will understand them. On the other hand, the report may go overboard, explaining everything in sixth-grade terms to make sure the reader is not lost, insulting the reader in the process.

In reality, when the reader receives the report, he or she usually hasn't thought much about the project. The reader may or may not know anything about statistics. In addition, the reader may have many other responsibilities, and if the report can't be understood quickly, it may be added to the stack of things to do "someday."

Under these circumstances, which are certainly not unusual, simply delivering the report to an audience is not sufficient to ensure that it gets attention. The report needs to be written so as to draw on the area of common experience between the researcher and the reader. And drawing on that common zone of experience is the responsibility of the writer, not the reader. Unless the report is really crucial, a busy reader will not spend time and effort struggling through an inadequate report.

THE REPORT IN CONTEXT

research report
A presentation of research findings directed to a specific audience to accomplish a specific purpose.

A **research report** is an oral presentation and/or a written statement that has the purpose of communicating research findings, recommendations for courses of action, other findings to management or other specific audiences. Although this chapter deals primarily with the final *written report,* with one section on the oral presentation of the research findings, remember that the final report may not be the only kind prepared. For a small project, a short oral or written report on the results may be all that is needed. On the other hand, extensive projects may involve many written documents, interim reports, and a long, final, written report, with several oral presentations.[2]

The emphasis in this chapter on the final report should not be taken to mean that other communications, such as progress reports, during the project are any less important to its eventual success. The chapter's suggestions can be easily adapted to apply to shorter, less formal reports. An appendix on the writing process appears at the end of this chapter, where several principles for organizing, writing, and rewriting are discussed in detail.

REPORT FORMAT

Although every research report is custom-made for the project it represents, some conventions of report format are universal. These conventions have developed over a long period of time, and they represent a consensus about what parts are necessary to a good research report and how they should be ordered. The consensus is not inviolable law, though. Each report-writing book suggests its own unique format, and every report writer has to pick and choose the parts and the order that work best for the project at hand. Many companies and universities also have in-house, suggested report formats or writing guides that researchers should be aware of. Thus, the format suggested here is the basis for the discussion in this chapter, and a beginning point from which the writer can shape his or her own appropriate format.[3] The **report format** is listed here and shown graphically in Exhibits 25.3 and 25.4:

report format
The general plan of organization for the parts of a written or oral research report.

1. Title page (sometimes preceded by title fly page)
2. Letter of transmittal
3. Letter of authorization
4. Table of contents (and lists of figures and tables)

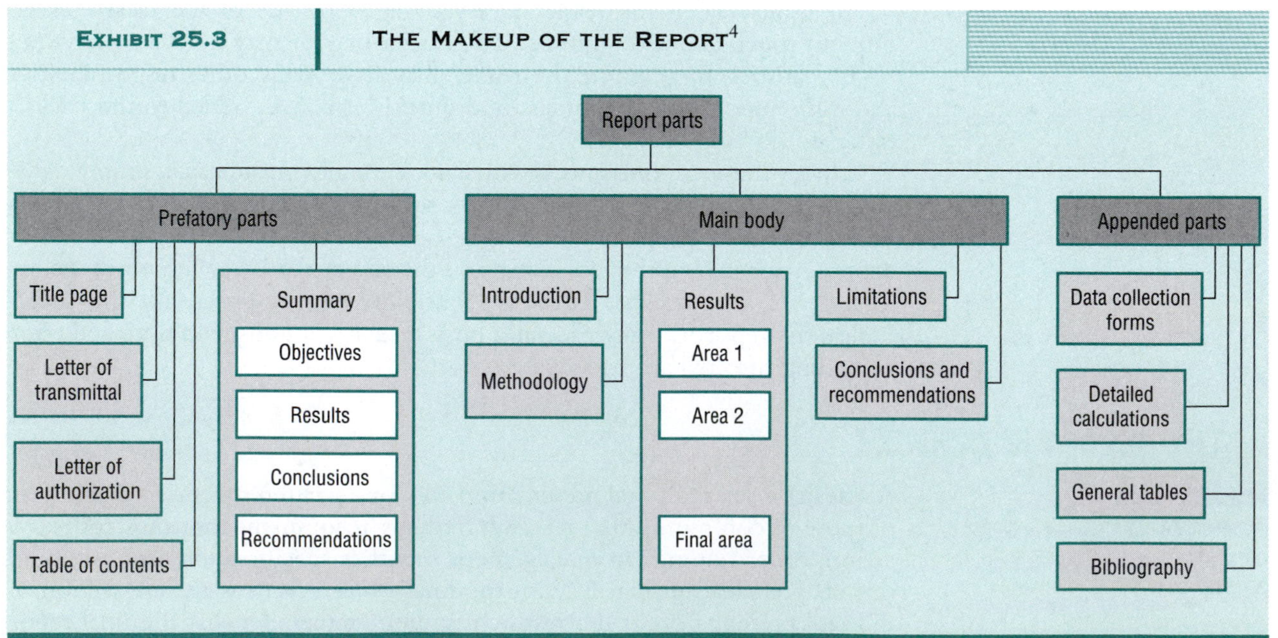

EXHIBIT 25.3 THE MAKEUP OF THE REPORT[4]

EXHIBIT 25.4 | **THE REPORT FORMAT**[5]

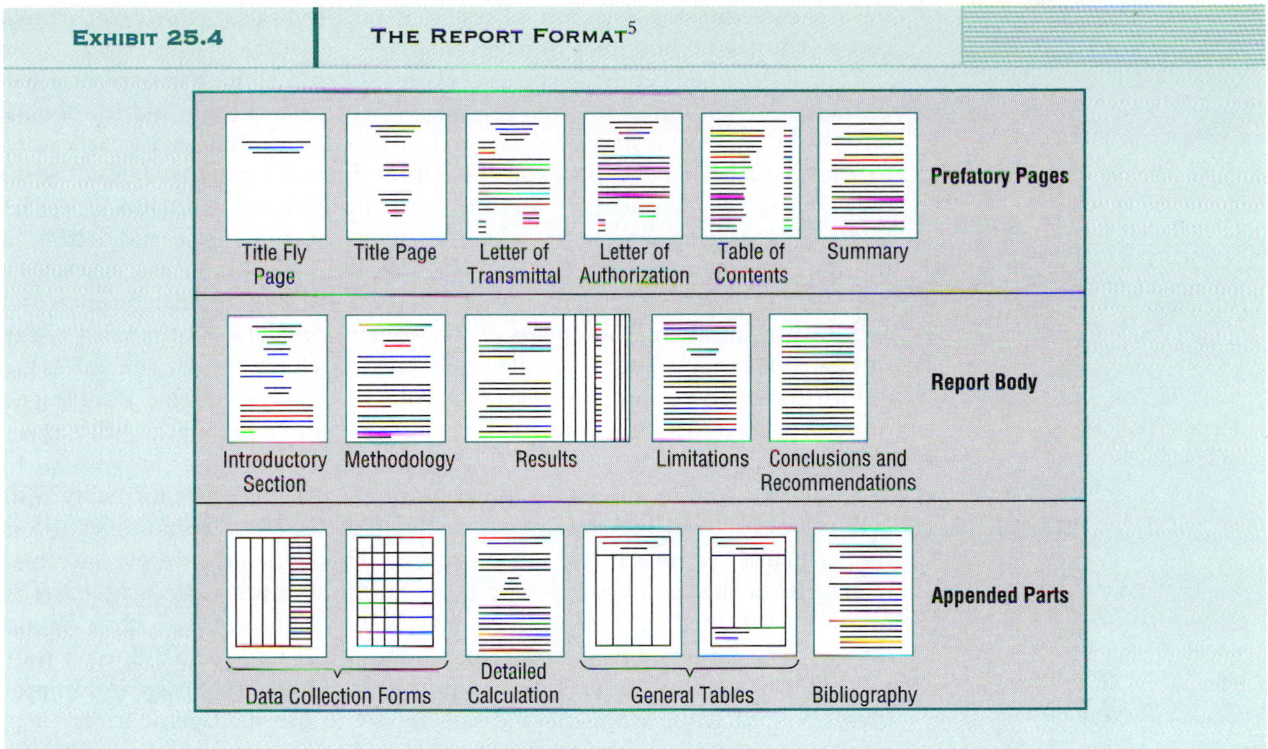

5. Summary
    5.1 Objectives
    5.2 Results
    5.3 Conclusions
    5.4 Recommendations
6. Body
    6.1 Introduction
        6.11 Background
        6.12 Objectives
    6.2 Methodology
    6.3 Results
    6.4 Limitations
    6.5 Conclusions and recommendations
7. Appendix
    7.1 Data collection forms
    7.2 Detailed calculations
    7.3 General tables
    7.4 Bibliography
    7.5 Other support material

Tailoring the Format to the Project

The format of a research report may need adjustment for two reasons: (1) to obtain the proper level of formality and (2) to decrease the complexity of the report. The format given here is for the most formal type, such as a report for a large project done within an organization or one done by a research agency for a client company. This sort of report is usually bound with a permanent cover and may be hundreds of pages long.

For less formal reports, each part is shorter, and some parts are omitted. Exhibit 25.5 illustrates how the format is adapted to shorter and less formal reports. The situation may be compared to the way clothing varies according to the formality of the occasion. The most formal report is dressed, so to speak, in white tie and tails (or long evening gown).[6] It includes the full assortment of prefatory parts—the title fly page, title page, and letters of transmittal and authorization.

The next level of formality would correspond to a regular business suit and involves dropping those parts of the prefatory material not needed in this situation and reducing the complexity of the body material. In general, as the report moves down through the sport coat, slacks, and then blue jeans stages, more prefatory parts are dropped and the complexity and length of the report body are reduced.

How does the researcher decide on the appropriate level of formality? The general rule is to include all the parts needed for effective communication in the particular circumstances, and no more.[7] This depends on how far up in management the report is expected to go and how routine the matter is. The researcher's immediate supervisor doesn't need a 100-page "full-dress" report on a routine project. On the other hand, the board of directors doesn't want a 1-page "blue jeans" report on a big project backing a major expansion program. Note that the white-tie-and-tails report to top management may later be stripped of some of the prefatory parts (and thus reduced in formality) for wider circulation on the company intranet.

EXHIBIT 25.5 ADAPTING FORMAT TO LEVEL OF FORMALITY[8]

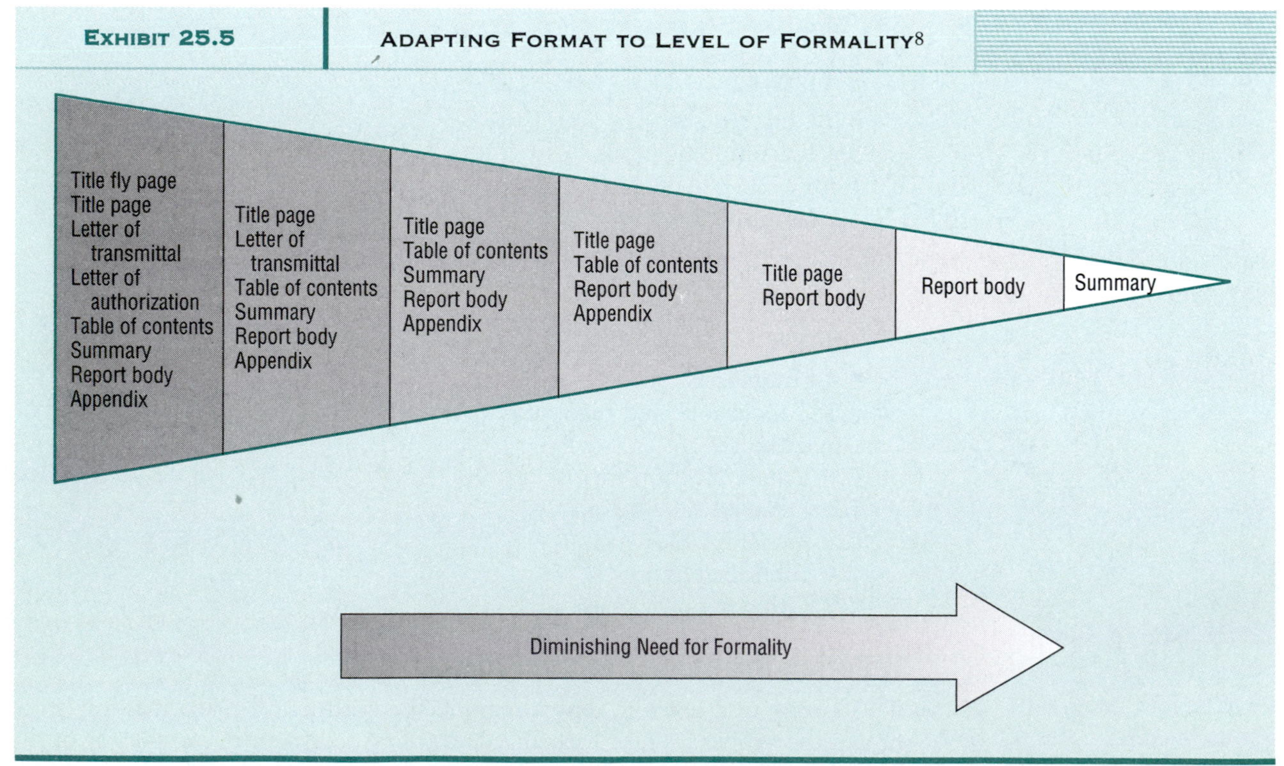

Parts of the Report

Title Page

The title page includes the title of the report, the name(s) of the person(s) for whom the report was prepared, the name(s) of the person(s) who prepared it, and the date of release or presentation. The title should be chosen to give a brief but complete indication of the purpose of the research project. Addresses and titles of the preparer and recipient may also be included. On reports of a confidential nature a list of the people to whom it should be circulated may be supplied. For the most formal reports, a title fly page precedes the title page. Only the title appears on this page.

Letter of Transmittal

This element is included in relatively formal and very formal reports. Its purpose is to release or deliver the report to the recipient. It also serves to establish some rapport between the reader and the writer. This is the one part of the formal report where a personal, or even a slightly informal, tone should be used. The transmittal should not dive into report findings except in the broadest terms.

A sample letter of transmittal is shown in Exhibit 25.6. Note that the opening paragraph releases the report and briefly identifies the factors of authorization. The letter comments generally on findings and matters of interest about the research. The closing section expresses the writer's personal interest in the project just completed and in doing additional, related work.[9]

Letter of Authorization

This is a letter to the researcher approving the project, detailing who has responsibility for the project and indicating what resources are available to support it. Because the researcher would not write this letter personally, writing guidelines will not be discussed here.[10] In many situations, referring to the authorization in the letter of transmittal is sufficient. If so, the letter of authorization need not be included in the report. In some cases, though, the readers may be unfamiliar with the authorization or may need detailed information about the authorization factors. In such cases the letter should be included, preferably an exact copy of the original.

Table of Contents

A table of contents is essential to any report more than a few pages long. It should list the divisions and subdivisions of the report with page references. The table of contents is based on the final outline of the report, but it should include only the first-level subdivisions. For short reports it is sufficient to include only the main divisions. If the report includes many figures or tables, lists of these should immediately follow the table of contents.

Summary

The summary briefly tells why the research project was conducted, what aspects of the problem were considered, what the outcome was, and what should be done. It is a vital part of the report. Studies have indicated that most managers always read a report's summary, whereas only a minority read the rest of the report.[11] Thus, the only chance a writer may have to make an impact may be in the summary.

Exhibit 25.6 | **Sample Letter of Transmittal**[12]

SOFTPROOF LEATHER PRODUCTS COMPANY, INC.
KENT, OHIO 44240

December 1, 20XX

Mr. Carl M. Wheeler
Vice President for Marketing
Home Office

Subject: Presentation of Report on Study of Small-Volume Customers

Dear Mr. Wheeler:

Here is my report on the study of small-volume customers. This report, the subject of our conference today, was prepared according to your authorization memorandum dated April 21, 20XX.

As we suspected would be the case when we started the study, the report recommends that we take a very careful new look at our present attitude toward serving customers whose volumes are less than $20,000 per year. Some of the experienced sales representatives whom we contacted in personal interviews gave us some excellent suggestions about what our new attitude should be.

The returns from our mail survey of small-volume customers were not as high as we wanted them to be. We do believe, though, that the questionnaires returned are representative of the customers involved in the study. The follow-up survey of a sample of customers who did not return the first questionnaire was most reassuring on this point.

As is perhaps typical of a research department, we discovered during this study another problem area which might bear investigation. This area is that of redefining the boundaries of our sales territories. We are now doing some preliminary thinking about this problem. Should we decide research is warranted, we later will make our recommendations to you.

We are grateful to you, Mr. Wheeler, for your cooperation in this important study. Your keeping the president informally up to date on our progress should pave the way toward his accepting the recommendations made in the report.

Sincerely,

Harold M. Johnson

Harold M. Johnson
Associate Analyst
Sales Analysis Section

Approved:
December 1, 20XX

T. T. Landham
Director and Senior Analyst
Sales Analysis Section

The summary should be written only after the rest of the report is completed. It represents the essence of the report. It should be one page long (or at most two pages), so the writer must carefully sort out what is important enough to appear in it. As Exhibit 25.7 illustrates, several pages of the full report may have to be condensed into one summary sentence. Note that different parts of the report may be condensed more than others—the number of words in the summary will not be in proportion to the relative lengths of the sections. The summary should be written to be self-sufficient. In fact, it is not uncommon for a summary to be detached from the report and circulated by itself.

The summary contains four elements. First, the objectives of the report are stated, including the most important background and the specific purposes of the project. The major results are then presented. The key results regarding each purpose should be included. Next come the conclusions. These are opin-

EXHIBIT 25.7 | **CONDENSING FULL REPORT INTO SUMMARY**[13]

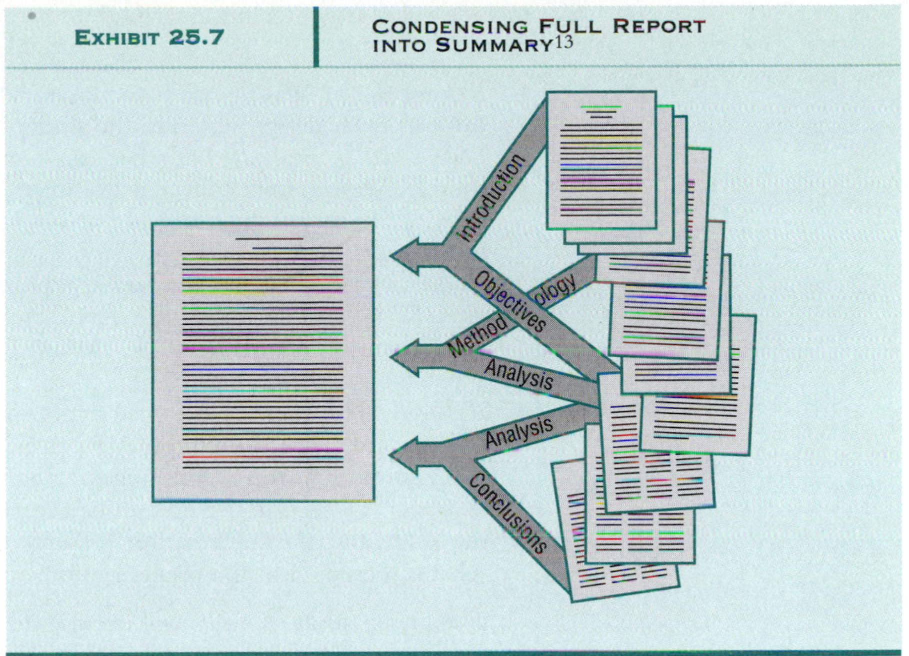

ions, based on the results, and constitute an interpretation of what the results say. Finally come recommendations, or suggestions for action, based on the conclusions. In many cases managers prefer not to have recommendations included in the report or summary. Whether or not recommendations are to be included should be clear from the particular context of the report.

Body

The body constitutes the bulk of the report. It begins with an introduction that sets out both the background factors that make the project necessary and the objectives of the report. It continues with discussions of the methodology, results, and limitations of the study. It finishes with conclusions and recommendations based on the results.

The introduction section explains why the project was undertaken and what it aimed to discover. It should include the basic authorization and submittal data. The relevant background should come next. There should be enough background to explain why the project was worth doing, but nonessential historical factors should be omitted. The question of how much is enough should be answered by considering the needs of the audience. A government report that will be made widely available requires more background than a company's internal report on employee satisfaction. The last part of the introduction explains just what this particular project tried to discover. It discusses the statement of the problem and research questions as they were stated in the research proposal. Each purpose presented here should have a corresponding results section later in the report.

The second part of the body explains the research methodology. This part is a challenge to write, because technical procedures must be explained in a manner appropriate for the audience. It may be useful to supplement the material in this section with more detailed explanations in the appendix, or to include a glossary of technical terms. This part of the report should address five topics:

1. *Research design.* Was the study exploratory, descriptive, or causal? Why was this particular design suited to the study?
2. *Data collection methods.* Did the data come from primary or secondary sources? Were results collected by survey, observation, or experiment? A copy of the survey questionnaire or observation form should be included in the appendix.
3. *Sample design.* What was the target population? What sampling frame was used? What sample units were used? How were they selected? Detailed computations supporting these explanations should be reserved for the appendix.
4. *Fieldwork.* How many and what types of fieldworkers were used? What training and supervision did they receive? Was the work verified? This section is important for establishing the degree of accuracy of the results.
5. *Analysis.* This section should outline the general statistical methods used in the study, but the information presented here should not overlap with what is presented in the results section.

The presentation of *results* will occupy the bulk of the report. This section presents in some logical order those findings of the project that bear on the objectives. The results should be organized as a continuous narrative, designed to be convincing but not to oversell the project. Summary tables and charts should be used to aid the discussion. Tables and charts may serve as points of reference to the data being discussed and free the prose from an excess of facts and figures. Comprehensive or detailed charts should be reserved for the appendix.

The covers of this book are too far apart.

AMBROSE BIERCE

No report is perfect, so it is important to indicate a report's limitations. If there were problems with nonresponse error or sampling procedures, they should be discussed. The discussion of limitations should avoid overemphasizing the weaknesses, though. Its aim should be to provide a realistic basis for assessing the results.

The last part of the body of the report presents the conclusions and recommendations based on the results. As was mentioned, conclusions are opinions based on the results, whereas recommendations are suggestions for action. The conclusions and recommendations are presented here in more detail than in the summary, with whatever justification is needed.

Appendix

The appendix presents the "too . . . " material. Any material that is too technical or too detailed to go in the body should appear in the appendix. This includes materials of interest only to some readers, or subsidiary materials not directly related to the objectives. Some examples of appendix material are data collection forms, detailed calculations, discussions of highly technical questions, detailed or comprehensive tables of results, and a bibliography (if appropriate).

EFFECTIVE USE OF GRAPHIC AIDS

The person who first said "a picture is worth a thousand words" probably had graphic aids in mind. Used properly, **graphic (visual) aids** can clarify complex points or emphasize a message, but if used improperly or sloppily, graphics can

graphic (visual) aid
A picture or diagram used to clarify a complex point or to emphasize a message.

be distracting or misleading. The key to effective use of graphic aids is to make them an integral part of the text. The graphics should always be interpreted in the text. This doesn't mean that the writer should exhaustively explain an obvious chart or table. It *does* mean that the text should point out the key elements of any graphic aid and relate them to the discussion in progress in the text.

Several types of graphic aids may be useful in research reports, such as tables, charts, maps, and diagrams. The discussion below will briefly cover the most common ones—tables and various sorts of charts. The writer interested in other types should consult more specialized sources.

Tables

table
A graphic aid generally used for presenting numerical information, especially when such information can be arranged in rows and columns.

Tables are most useful for presenting numerical information, especially when several pieces of information have been gathered about each item discussed. For example, consider how hard it would be to follow all the information in Table 25.1[14] if it were presented in narrative form. Using tables allows the writer to point out significant features without getting bogged down in detail. Only relatively short summary tables should be included in the body of the report. Comprehensive tables should be reserved for the appendix.

Each table should include the following:

1. *Table number.* A table number allows for simple reference from the text to the table. If there are many tables, a list of tables should be included just after the table of contents.
2. *Title.* The title should indicate the contents of the table and be complete enough to be intelligible without the text. The table number and title are generally placed at the top, since the table is read from top down.
3. *Bannerheads and stubheads.* The bannerheads (or boxheads) contain the captions for the columns of the table, the stubheads contain those for the rows.
4. *Footnotes.* Any explanations or qualifications for particular table entries or sections should be given in footnotes.
5. *Source.* If a table is based on material from a secondary source, not on new data generated by the project, the source should be acknowledged, usually below the table following the footnotes.

Table 25.2 illustrates a typical table from a survey research report. It shows a cross-tabulation of demographics with survey responses. Table 25.3 shows how data from a statistical test might be reported in table format.

Charts

chart
A graphic aid used to translate numerical information into visual form so that relationships may be easily understood.

Charts translate numerical information into visual form so that relationships may be easily grasped. The accuracy of the numbers is reduced to gain this advantage. Each chart should include the following:

1. *Figure number.* Charts (and other illustrative material) should be numbered in a series separate from tables. The number allows for easy reference from the text. If there are many figures, a list of them should be included after the table of contents.
2. *Title.* The title should indicate the contents of the chart and be independent of the text explanation. The figure number and title may be placed at the top or bottom of the figure.

TABLE 25.1 | **PARTS OF A TABLE**

Table number → Title →

No. 768. Consumer Price Index (CPI) by Major Groups: 1980–1999

[1982–84 = 100. Represents annual averages of monthly figures. Reflects buying patterns of all urban consumers. Minus sign (−) indicates decrease. See text, this section]

← Bannerheads

Year	All items	Commodities	Energy	Food	Shelter	Apparel and upkeep	Transportation	Medical care	Fuel oil	Electricity	Utility (piped) gas	Telephone services
1980	82.4	86.0	86.0	86.8	81.0	90.9	83.1	74.9	87.7	75.8	65.7	77.7
1985	107.6	105.4	101.6	105.6	109.8	105.0	106.4	113.5	94.6	108.9	104.8	111.7
1986	109.6	104.4	88.2	109.0	115.8	105.9	102.3	122.0	74.1	110.4	99.7	117.2
1987	113.6	107.7	88.6	113.5	121.3	110.6	105.4	130.1	75.8	110.0	95.1	116.5
1988	118.3	111.5	89.3	118.2	127.1	115.4	108.7	138.6	75.8	111.5	94.5	116.0
1989	124.0	116.7	94.3	125.1	132.8	118.6	114.1	149.3	80.3	114.7	97.1	117.2
1990	130.7	122.8	102.1	132.4	140.0	124.1	120.5	162.8	98.6	117.4	97.3	117.7
1991	136.2	126.6	102.5	136.3	146.3	128.7	123.8	177.0	92.4	121.8	98.5	119.7
1992	140.3	129.1	103.0	137.9	151.2	131.9	126.5	190.1	88.0	124.2	100.3	120.4
1993	144.5	131.5	104.2	140.9	155.7	133.7	130.4	201.4	87.2	126.7	106.5	121.2
1994	148.2	133.8	104.6	144.3	160.5	133.4	134.3	211.0	85.6	126.7	108.5	123.1
1995	152.4	136.4	105.2	148.4	165.7	132.0	139.1	220.5	84.8	129.6	102.9	124.0
1996	156.9	139.9	110.1	153.3	171.0	131.7	143.0	228.2	97.0	131.8	107.2	125.9
1997	160.5	141.8	111.5	157.3	176.3	132.9	144.3	234.6	96.9	132.5	114.6	127.7
1998	163.0	141.9	102.9	160.7	182.1	133.0	141.6	242.1	84.8	127.4	112.4	100.7
1999	166.6	144.4	106.6	164.1	187.3	131.3	144.4	250.6	86.6	126.5	113.0	100.1
	PERCENT CHANGE[1]											
1980	13.5	12.3	30.9	8.6	17.6	7.1	17.9	11.0	39.0	15.5	19.2	2.5
1985	3.6	2.1	0.7	2.3	5.6	2.8	2.6	6.3	−4.0	3.4	−0.7	3.9
1986	1.9	−0.9	−13.2	3.2	5.5	0.9	−3.9	7.5	−21.7	1.4	−4.9	4.9
1987	3.6	3.2	0.5	4.1	4.7	4.4	3.0	6.6	2.3	−0.4	−4.6	−0.6
1988	4.1	3.5	0.8	4.1	4.8	4.3	3.1	6.5	—	1.4	−0.6	−0.4
1989	4.8	4.7	5.6	5.8	4.5	2.8	5.0	7.7	5.9	2.9	2.8	1.0
1990	5.4	5.2	8.3	5.8	5.4	4.6	5.6	9.0	22.8	2.4	0.2	0.4
1991	4.2	3.1	0.4	2.9	4.5	3.7	2.7	8.7	−6.3	3.7	1.2	1.7
1992	3.0	2.0	0.5	1.2	3.3	2.5	2.2	7.4	−4.8	2.0	1.8	0.6
1993	3.0	1.9	1.2	2.2	3.0	1.4	3.1	5.9	−0.9	2.0	6.2	0.7
1994	2.6	1.7	0.4	2.4	3.1	−0.2	3.0	4.8	−1.9	0.0	1.9	1.6
1995	2.8	1.9	0.6	2.8	3.2	−1.0	3.6	4.5	−0.9	2.3	−5.2	0.7
1996	3.0	2.6	4.7	3.3	3.2	−0.2	2.8	3.5	14.4	1.7	4.2	1.5
1997	2.3	1.4	1.3	2.6	3.1	0.9	0.9	2.8	−0.1	0.5	6.9	1.4
1998	1.6	0.1	−7.7	2.2	3.3	0.1	−1.9	3.2	−12.5	−3.8	−1.9	—
1999	2.2	1.8	3.6	2.1	2.9	−1.3	2.0	3.5	2.1	−0.7	0.5	−0.6

Stubheads

Footnotes

— Represents zero. [1]Change from prior year.

Source: Bureau of Labor Statistics, *Monthly Labor Review and Handbook of Labor Statistics*, periodic.

Source

3. *Explanatory legends.* Enough explanation should be put on the chart to guide the reader without reference to the accompanying text. Such explanations could include labels for axes, scale numbers, a key to the different quantities being graphed, and so on.
4. *Source and footnotes.* Any secondary source for the data should be acknowl-

TABLE 25.2 REPORT FORMAT FOR TYPICAL SURVEY CROSS-TABULATION[15]

Would you say you are enjoying your work more, less, or about the same as you were five years ago?

	Overall	Professionals/ Managers	Technicians	Sales/Adminis- trative Workers	Blue-Collar Workers
More	52%	60%	55%	51%	44%
Less	19	14	18	22	24
About the same	27	24	26	26	31
Don't know/ no answer	2	2	1	1	1

edged. If footnotes are needed to explain items, they may also be used, although they are less common for charts than for tables.

Charts are subject to distortion, whether unintentional or deliberate. Exhibit 25.8 shows how altering the scale changes the reader's impression of the data. A particularly severe type of distortion comes from treating unequal intervals as if they were equal. This generally results from a deliberate attempt to distort data. Exhibit 25.9 shows this sort of distortion, where someone attempted to make the rise on the chart more dramatic by compressing the portion where there is little change.

Another common way of introducing distortion is to begin the vertical scale at some value larger than zero. Note in Exhibit 25.10 (page 611) how this exaggerates the amount of change in the period covered. This kind of broken scale is often used in published reports of stock price movements. In this case it is assumed that the readers are mostly interested in the changes and are aware of the exaggeration of a broken scale. For most research reports this will not be the case. Graphs should start at zero on the vertical axis.

Pie Charts

pie chart
A graphic aid that shows the composition of some total quantity at a particular time; each angle, or "slice," is proportional to its percentage of the whole.

One of the most useful kinds of charts is the **pie chart.** It shows the composition of some total quantity at a particular time. Each angle, or "slice," is proportional to its percentage of the whole, and it should be labeled with its description and percentage of the whole. Do not try to include too many small slices (as in Exhibit 25.11, page 611)—about six slices is the usual maximum. Pie charts are commonly used by organizations to show the sources of

TABLE 25.3 REPORTING FORMAT FOR A STATISTICAL TEST

Will investors be more cautious about buying stock in companies with questionable advertising?

	Executives	Management
Yes	57%	46%
No	27	35
Not sure	16	19
	n = 177	n = 154

$\chi^2 = 4.933$ d.f. = 2 $p < .08$

Exhibit 25.8 **Distortion by Alternating Scales**[16]

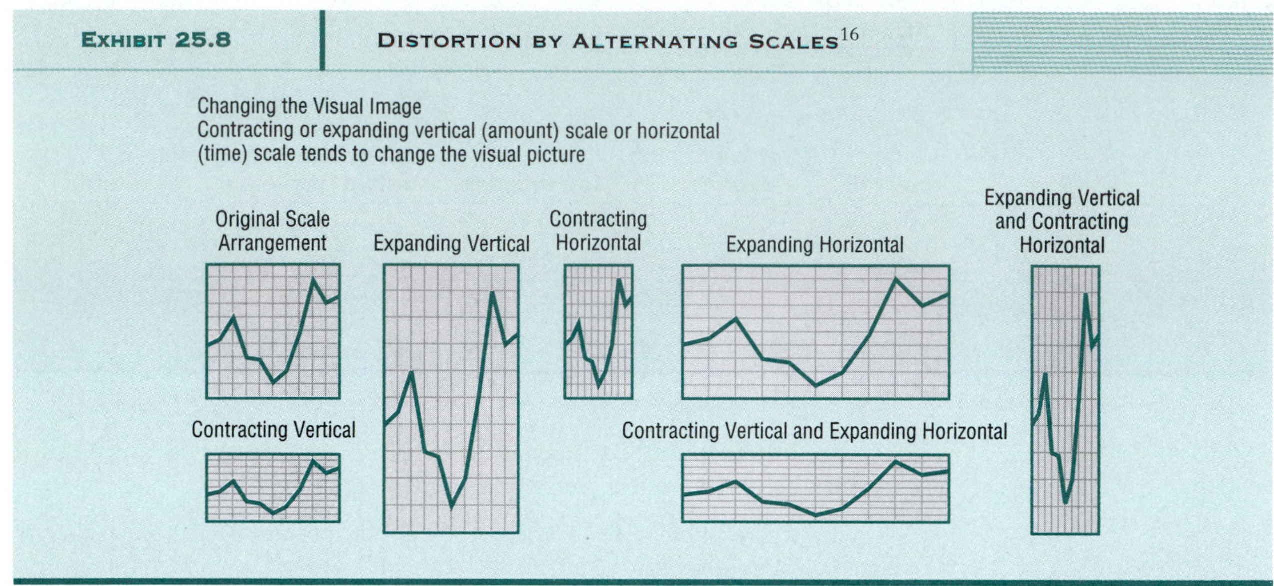

their income and how their revenues have been used, what assets they hold, or the composition of their sales.

line graph
A graphic aid showing the relationship of one variable to another. The dependent variable is generally shown on the vertical axis and the independent variable on the horizontal axis.

Line Graphs

A **line graph** is used to show the relationship of one variable to another. The dependent variable is generally shown on the vertical axis, and the independent variable is shown on the horizontal axis. The most common independent variable for such charts is time, but it is by no means the only one. Exhibit 25.12 (page 612) depicts a simple line graph. Other variants of line graphs are also useful. A multiple-line graph (Exhibit 25.13, page 613) shows the

Exhibit 25.9 **Distortion of Time Intervals**

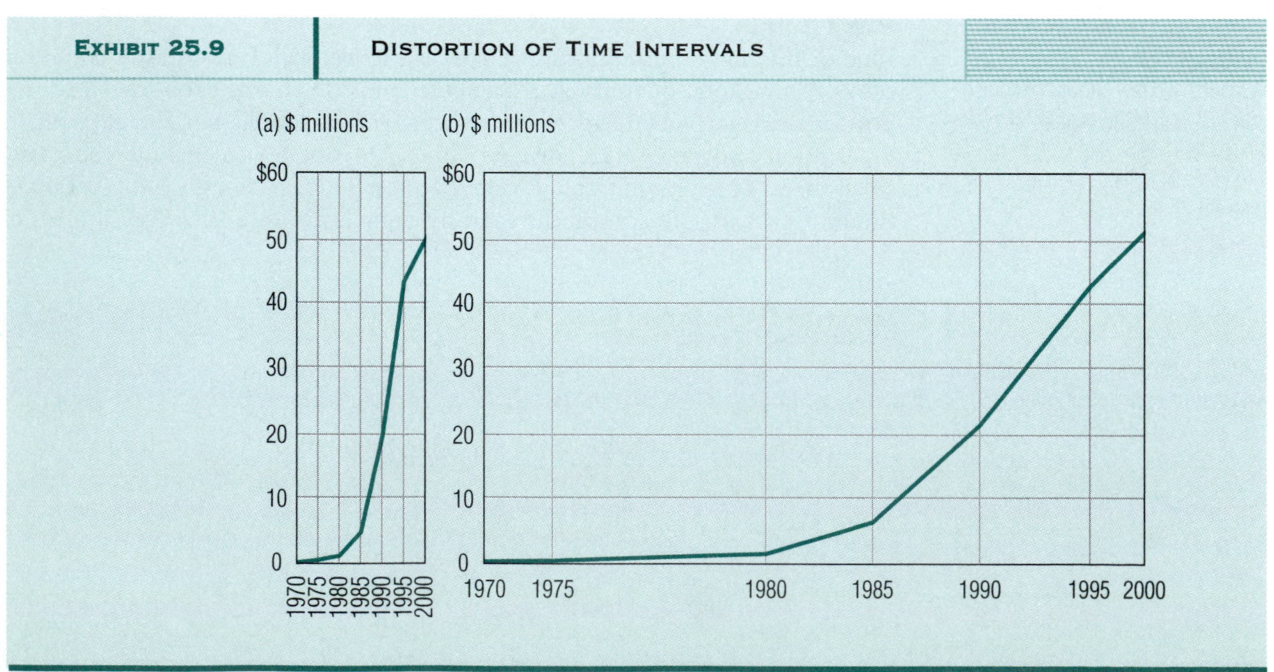

EXHIBIT 25.10 **DISTORTION FROM BROKEN VERTICAL LINES**

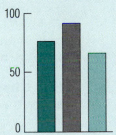

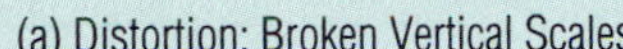

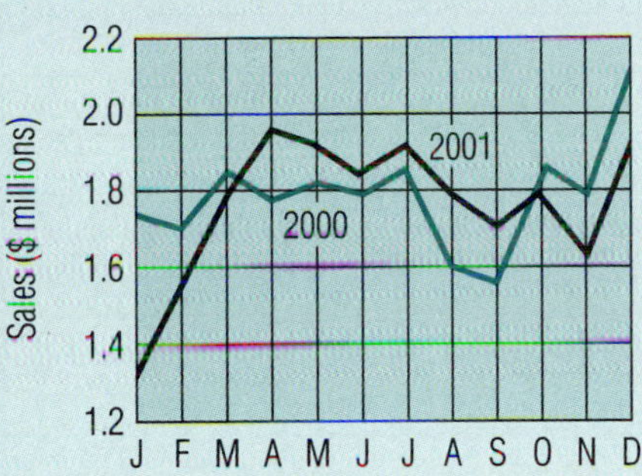

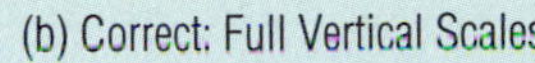

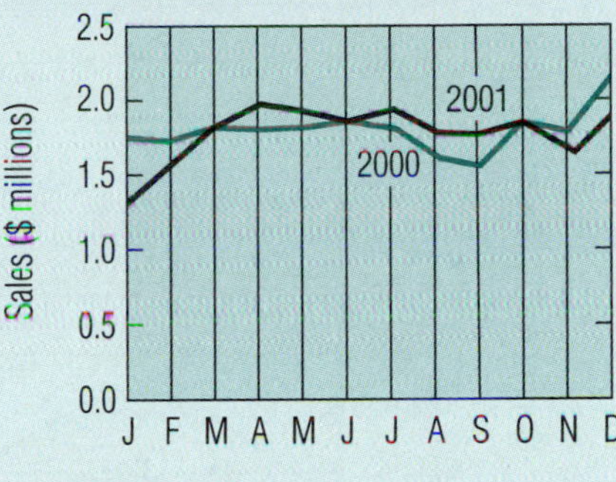

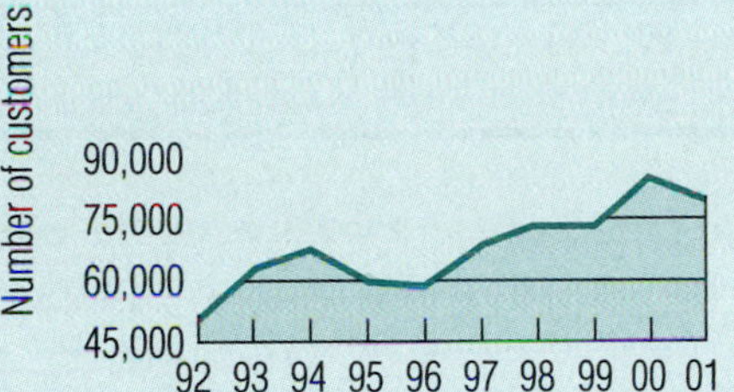

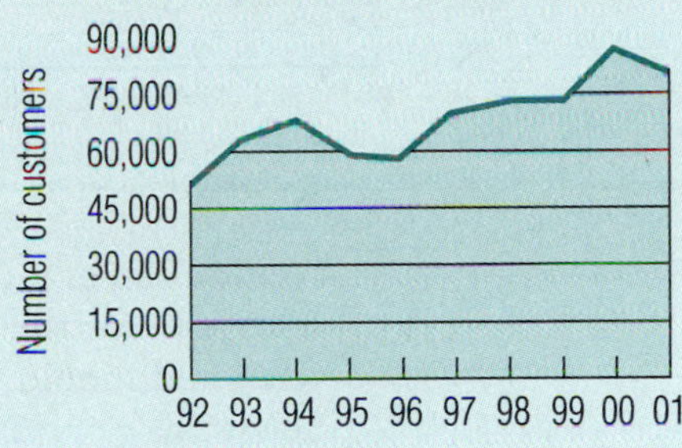

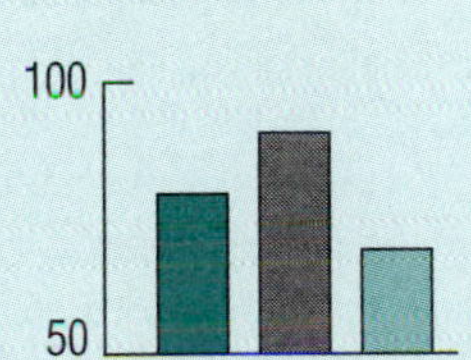

EXHIBIT 25.11 **A PIE CHART WITH TOO MANY SLICES LOSES ITS EFFECTIVENESS**[17]

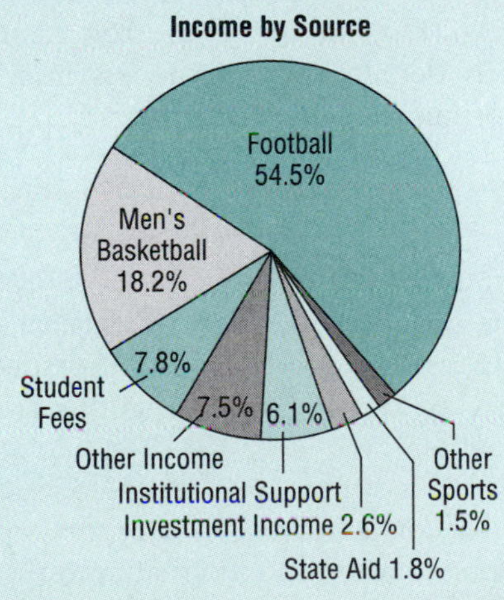

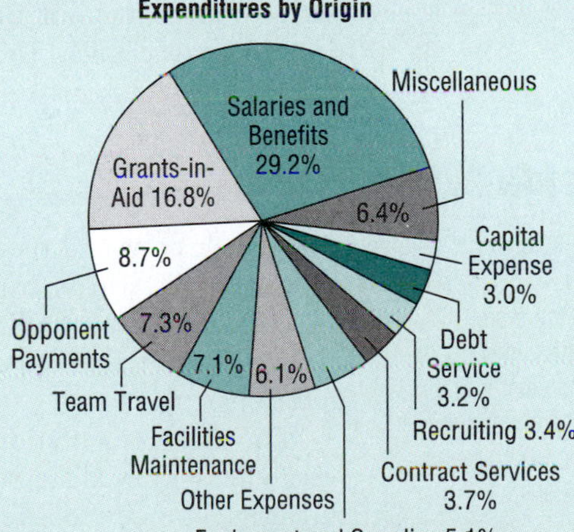

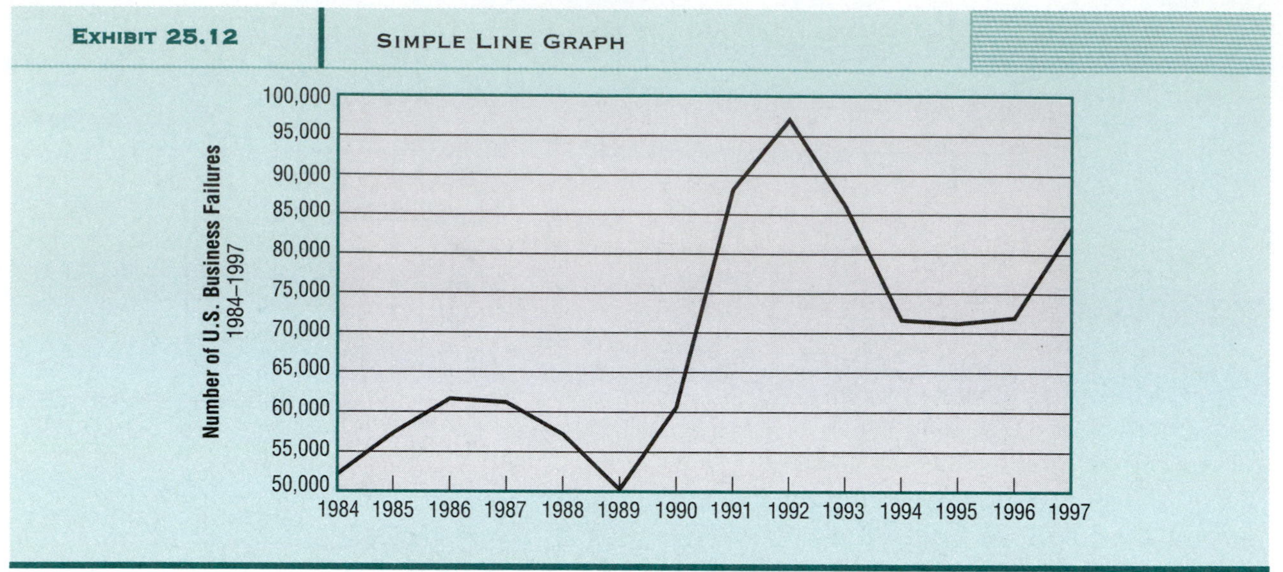

relationship of more than one dependent variable to the independent variable. The lines for the dependent variables should be in contrasting colors or patterns and should be clearly labeled. Do not try to squeeze in too many variables; this can quickly lead to confusion, not clarification. A second variation is the stratum chart (Exhibit 25.14, page 614), which shows how the composition of a total quantity changes as the independent variable changes. The same cautions mentioned in connection with multiple-line graphs should also apply to stratum charts.

Bar Charts

bar chart
A graphic aid that shows changes in a variable at discrete intervals.

Bar charts show changes in the value of a dependent variable (plotted on the vertical axis) at discrete intervals of the independent variable (horizontal axis). A simple bar chart is shown in Exhibit 25.15 (page 615). A common variant is the subdivided bar chart (Exhibit 25.16, page 616). It is much like a stratum chart, showing the composition of the whole quantity. Bar charts may be horizontal as well as vertical. A multiple-bar chart shows how multiple variables are related to the primary variable. Each variable needs to be clearly identified with a different color or pattern. Do not try to use too many divisions or dependent variables. Too much detail obscures the essential advantage of charts, which is to make relationships easy to visualize.

THE ORAL PRESENTATION

oral presentation
A spoken summary of the major findings, conclusions, and recommendations, given to clients or line managers to provide them with the opportunity to clarify any ambiguous issues by asking questions.

The conclusions and recommendations of most research reports are presented orally as well as in writing. The purpose of an **oral presentation** is to highlight the most important findings of a research project and to provide clients or line managers with the opportunity to clarify any ambiguous issues by asking questions.

The oral presentation may be as simple as a short conference with the researcher's immediate supervisor, or as formal as a report to the board of directors. The key to effective presentation in either situation is preparation.

Communication specialists often suggest that a person preparing an oral presentation should begin at the end. In other words, the researcher should

EXHIBIT 25.13

MULTIPLE-LINE GRAPH[18]

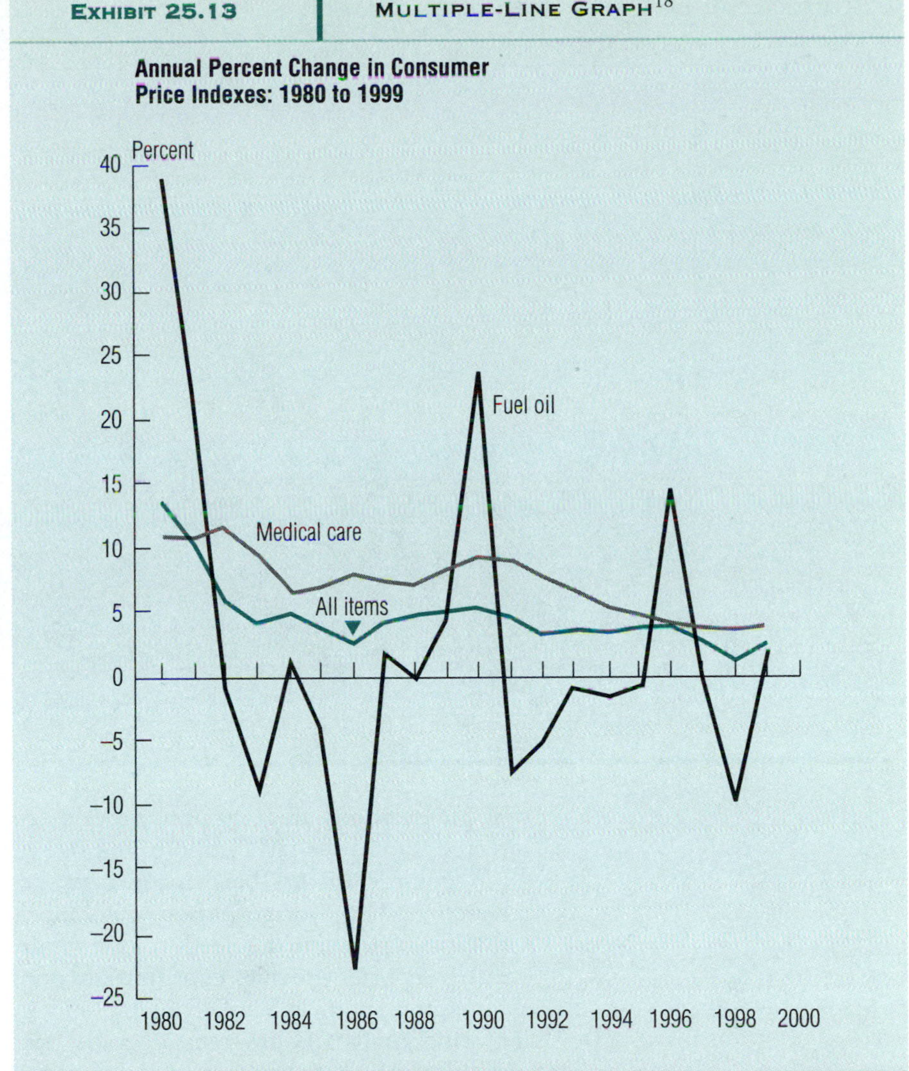

think about what he or she wants the client to know at the end of the presentation. The researcher should keep these desired outcomes in mind as he or she prepares the presentation. The researcher should select the three or four most important findings for emphasis and should rely on the written report for a full summary. The researcher needs to be ready to defend the results. This is not the same as being defensive. Rather, it means being prepared to deal in a confident, competent manner with the questions that will arise. Remember that even the most reliable, valid research project is worthless if the managers who must act on its results are not convinced of its importance.

As with the written report, a key to an effective oral presentation is adaptation to the audience. Delivering an hour-long formal speech when a ten-minute discussion is called for (or vice versa) reflects poorly on both the presenter and the report. Many business researchers view themselves as technicians whose purpose is to generate numbers using sophisticated research designs and statistical techniques. As a result, unfortunately, some researchers'

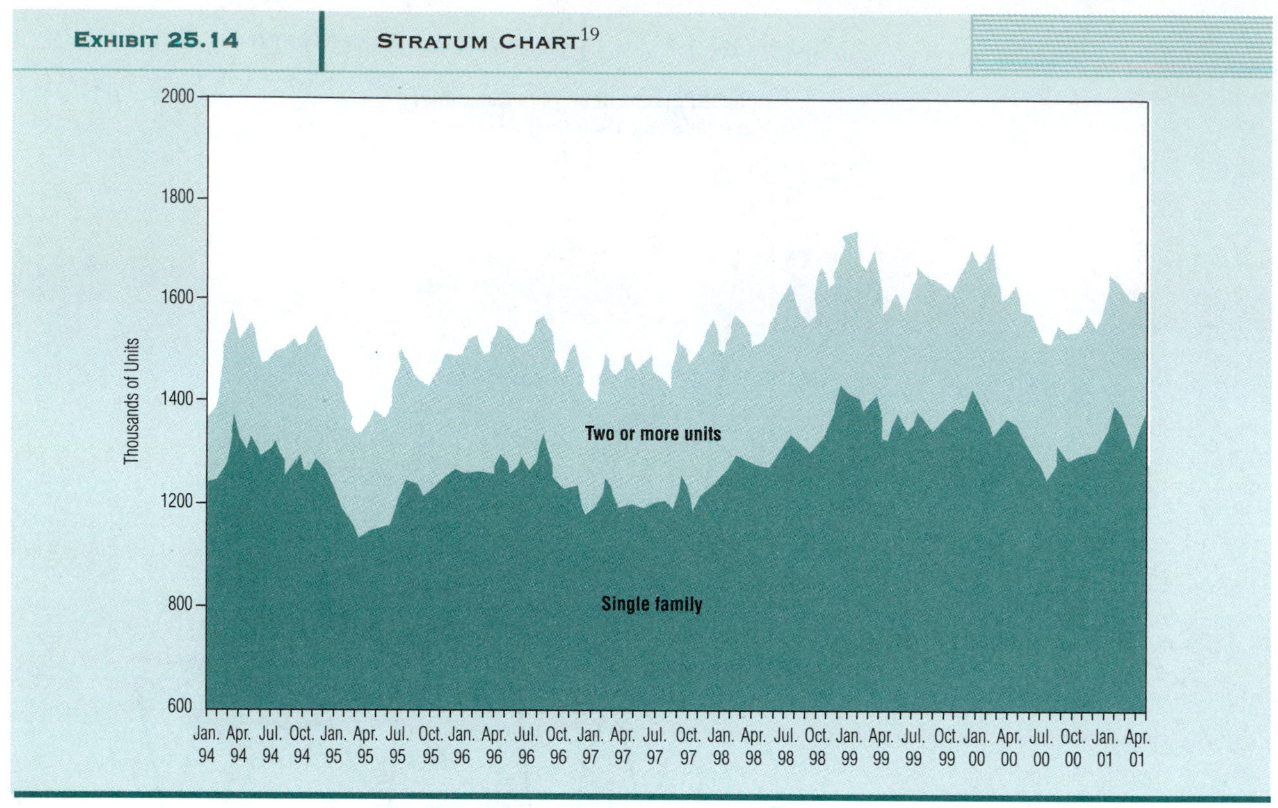

oral presentations are organized around technical details rather than being directed toward the satisfaction of management's or the client's needs.

A comparison has been made between weather reporters and business researchers. The average person watching a TV weather reporter wants to know whether he or she needs to take an umbrella to work the next day. The weather reporter provides enormous amounts of information: It's snowing in Washington, sunny in San Diego, and raining in Texas. Maps full of lines showing fronts, high- and low-pressure areas, and other weather facts are extraneous information to the person who merely wants to avoid getting wet. Fortunately, most weather reporters eventually let us know if rain is forecasted. In a similar vein, if the client only wants an executive summary, the oral presentation should emphasize material that one would expect to be contained in the summary section of the written report. Managers can always ask for additional detail about the methodology or clarification of the data analysis.

The principles of good speech making apply when making a research presentation. Lecturing or reading to the audience is sure to impede communication at any level of formality. The presenter should avoid reading his material word for word by relying on brief notes, being familiar with the subject, and rehearsing as much as the occasion calls for. The presenter should avoid research jargon and should use short, simple words. The speaker should maintain eye contact and should repeat the main points. Because the audience cannot go back and replay what the speaker has said, oral presentations are often organized around the adage "Tell them what you are going to tell them, tell them, then tell them what you just told them."

Graphic and other visual aids can be as useful in an oral presentation as in a written one. Again, the presenter needs to interpret these aids for the audi-

Exhibit 25.15 | **Simple Bar Chart**[20]

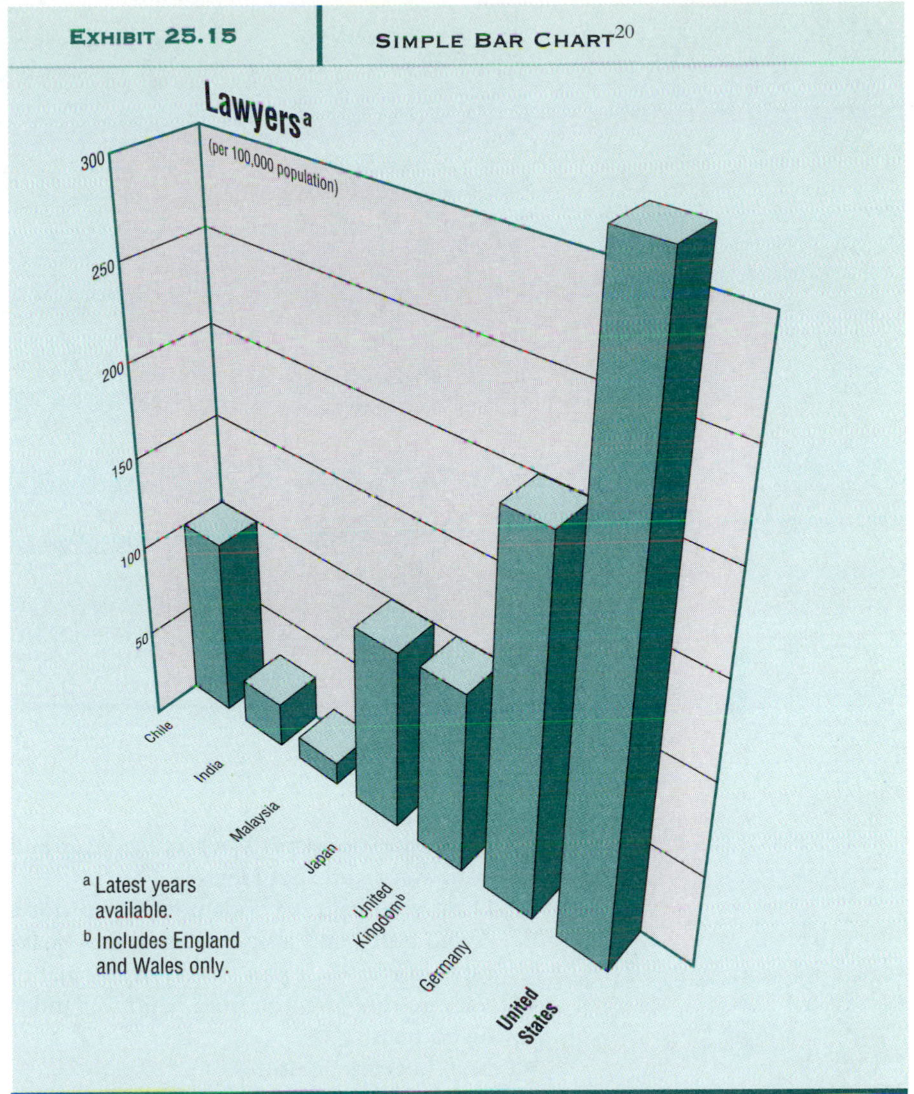

ence by pointing out the key elements that are related to the discussion. There are a variety of media for presenting research results in an oral presentation. Presentation graphics on a computer or overhead projector acetates will be useful for large audiences or formal presentations. For smaller audiences the researcher may put the visual aids on posters or flip charts. Another possibility is to duplicate copies of the charts for each participant and perhaps supplement these with one of the other forms of graphic presentation.

Whatever medium is chosen, the visual aids should be designed to convey a simple, attention-getting message that supports a point on which the audience should focus its thinking. The best slides are easily read and quickly interpreted. Large typeface, multiple colors, highlighting bullets, and other artistic devices should be considered as means to enhance the readability of charts and other graphics.

Using gestures when presenting can also help convey the message and make the presentation more interesting. Here are some tips on how to gesture:[21]

EXHIBIT 25.16 | **SUBDIVIDED BAR CHART**[22]

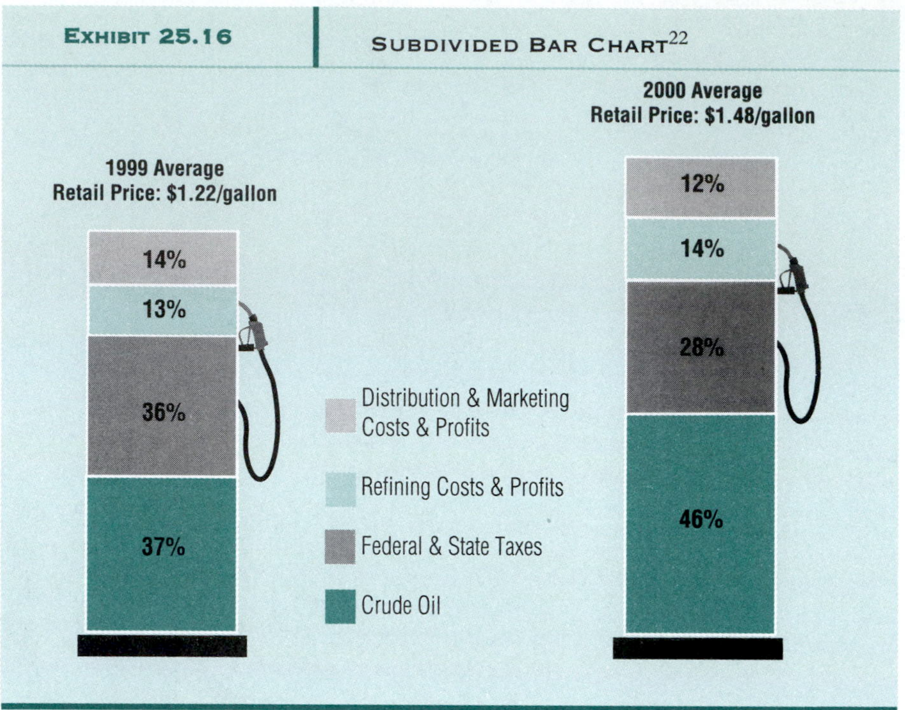

- Open up your arms to embrace your audience. Keep your arms between your waist and shoulders.
- Drop your arms to your sides when not using them.
- Avoid quick and jerky gestures; they make you appear nervous. Hold gestures longer than you would in normal conversation.
- Vary gestures. Switch from hand to hand and at other times use both hands or no hands.
- Don't overuse gestures.

REPORTS ON THE INTERNET

Many clients want numerous employees to have access to research findings. One easy way to share data is to have executive summaries and reports available on a company intranet. Or, a company can use information technology on the Internet to design questionnaires, administer surveys, analyze data, and share the results in a presentation-ready format. Real-time data capture allows for beginning-to-end reporting. A number of companies offer fully Web-based research management systems—for example, WebSurveyor's online solution for capturing and reporting research findings.

THE RESEARCH FOLLOW-UP

Research reports and oral presentations should communicate the research findings in a manner that will allow managers to make a business decision. In many cases the manager who receives the research report is unable to interpret the information and draw conclusions relevant to his or her managerial

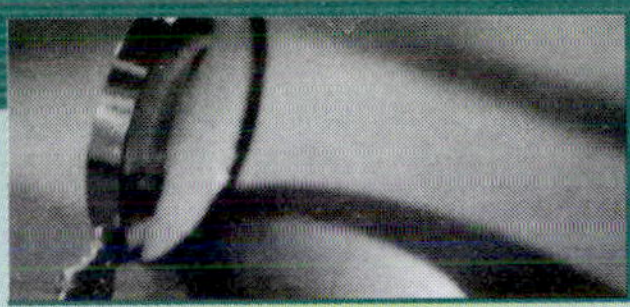

RESEARCH INSIGHT

NOAH'S LAW OF OVERHEAD TRANSPARENCIES

During oral presentations of research reports, many presenters use transparencies that viewers in the back row cannot read.[23] In fact, some presenters use transparencies that viewers in the front row cannot read.

All viewers would be much happier if all presenters were to follow Noah's Law of Overhead Transparencies. Noah's Law says: Never, ever, under any circumstances whatsoever, put more than 40 words on a transparency. A number counts as a word. Noah's Law is called Noah's Law because, when God made it rain for 40 days and 40 nights, he flooded the whole world, and no presenter should attempt that with one overhead.

Note that, in Noah's Law, 40 is the absolute upper limit. Twenty is a good average. Seven is even better. If seven words look lonely, presenters can always MAKE THE LETTERS BIGGER.

Advertising legend David Ogilvy was a devout follower of Noah's Law. He thought so highly of it that he invented and enforced Ogilvy's Corollary. Ogilvy's Corollary says: Never put anything on a transparency (or a slide or a chart) that you don't intend to read out loud to your audience word for word. He reasoned that, when one message comes in on the visual channel while another comes in on the auditory channel, the audience will probably neglect one message or the other.

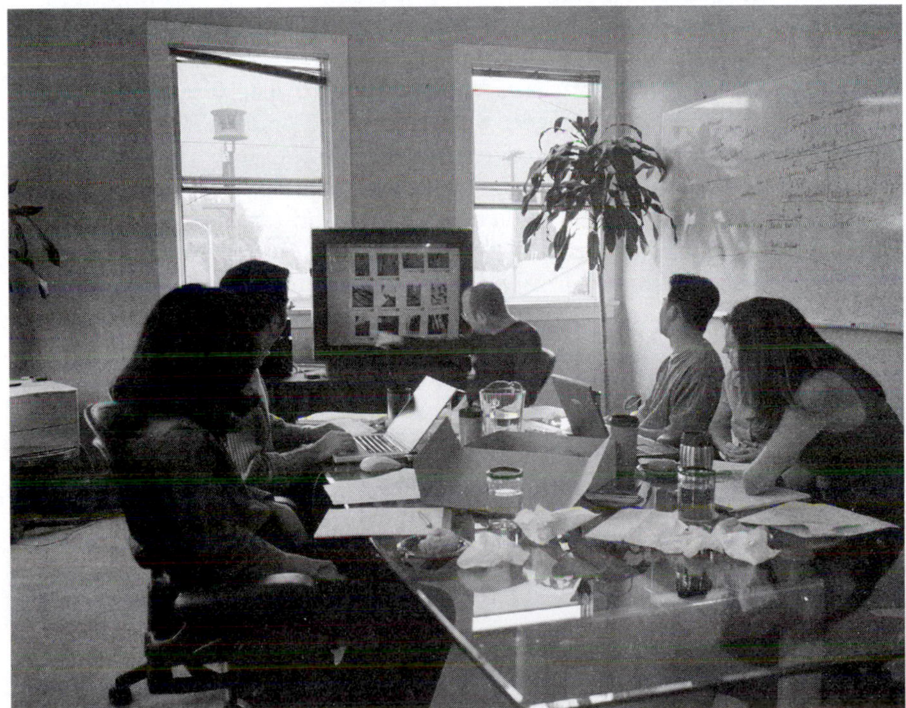

Computer presentation software packages are extremely useful aids to oral presentations. They allow the researcher to convey a simple, attention-getting message.

research follow-up
Recontacting decision makers and/or clients after they have had a chance to read a research report.

decision. For this reason effective researchers do not see the report as the end of the research process. The **research follow-up** involves recontacting of decision makers and/or clients after they have had a chance to read over the research report. Its purpose is to determine if the researchers need to provide additional information or clarify issues of concern to management.

SUMMARY

Report preparation is the final stage of the research project. It is a key stage because the project can guide management decisions only if it is effectively communicated. The theory of communication emphasizes that the writer (communicator) must tailor the report (message) so that it will be understood by the manager (audience) who has a different field of experience. A research report is an oral or written presentation of research findings directed to a specific audience to accomplish a specific purpose.

The generally accepted format for research reports includes certain prefatory parts, the body of the report, and appended parts. The report format should be adapted to suit the level of formality of the particular report situation.

The prefatory parts of a formal report include a title page, letters of transmittal and authorization, a table of contents, and a summary. The summary is the part of a report most often read, and it should include a brief statement of the objectives, results, conclusions, and, depending on the research situation, recommendations. The report body includes an introduction that gives the background and objectives, a statement of methodology, a discussion of the results, their limitations, and appropriate conclusions and recommendations. The appendix includes various materials too specialized to appear in the body of the report.

Effective use of graphic aids enhances a presentation. Tables present large amounts of numerical information in a concise manner. Charts present numerical data in a way that highlights their relationships. Pie charts, line graphs, and bar charts are useful forms of charts, with variants for special purposes.

Because most research projects will be reported orally as well as in writing, the researcher needs to prepare an oral presentation. The preparation should defend the results without being defensive. It is vital to tailor the presentation to the situation and audience. Graphic aids are also useful supplements to the oral report.

The research follow-up involves recontacting decision makers after the report has been submitted so that any issues of concern to management may be clarified.

Key Terms

communication process
research report
report format
graphic (visual) aid
table
chart
pie chart
line graph
bar chart
oral presentation
research follow-up

Questions for Review and Critical Thinking

1. Why is it important to view the research report from a communications perspective?
2. As a manager, what degree of formality would you like from your research department?
3. What type of tables might be used to describe some of the various statistical tests discussed in previous chapters?
4. What do you believe will be the impact of computer graphics on the research report-writing format? Explain.
5. Find some research reports in your library. How do they meet the standards set forth in this chapter?
6. How does the oral presentation of research results differ from the written research report?
7. What ethical concerns arise when you prepare (or read) a research report?

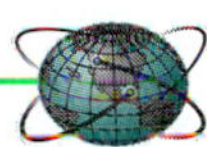

Exploring the Internet

Go to Burke Interactive's Digital Dashboard demo at http://report.burke.com/dd_demo/welcome.asp. The site contains an online customer satisfaction report for JCN Computers, a fictional personal-computer manufacturer. Evaluate the format of the online research report.

WebSurveyor Activities

Using the WebSurveyor desktop software, select "Open a Sample Survey with Real Data" and select the file named "Internet Usage Survey." Write a report on the results of this survey.

Case Suggestions

Case 26: Survey on Americans and Dietary Supplements
Case 29: LastDance Health Care
Case 30: Sunbelt Energy Corporation
Case 31: Employees Federal Credit Union

APPENDIX

THE WRITING PROCESS

ORGANIZING THE REPORT

The writing process is outlined in Exhibit 25A.1. The first step in writing a research report is to organize the way the material is to be presented. To a large degree, the organization flows from the earlier stages of the project. This is especially true of a well-organized project. If, in a major project, the researcher moved from exploratory and secondary research to a clear statement of the objectives of the main project and then designed a study specifically to meet them, he or she will have a considerable organizational advantage when it comes time to report on the project. Suppose, on the other hand, that a researcher never did the preliminary work needed to clarify the research problems, but instead sent out questionnaires in the hope of getting some sort of results. This approach will certainly cause difficulty in analyzing the results; it will also be a barrier to finding a coherent framework for reporting results.

Writing a report even for the best-run project calls for consideration of how to organize the presentation effectively. The major sections are usually determined by what is customary in the discipline or by organizational practice (see the report format in Exhibit 25.4). The writer's job is to make these blocks a coherent whole—a piece of writing that is unified from the first page to the last. "The readers should be able to read the objectives, turn to the conclusions section, and find specific conclusions relative to each objective." They should also be able to turn to the results section, or the methodology section, or the letter of authorization—in fact, to any part of the report—and see the whole tied together by concern with one problem, stated in terms of a small number of interrelated objectives.

A unified theme helps the reader understand what has been accomplished. A report with the results section organized one way and the conclusions a different way, and neither relating back to the objectives, is like a disassembled color television set. All the parts may be there, but until they are put together they will never be capable of showing a football game or soap opera. Of course, during a project researchers often encounter dead ends and detours and must reassess what is and is not important. These aspects of the project should not be obscured in the report. If the research did not produce a conclusion on a point, the writer should say so. Since the report is written after the fact, it can take all these factors into consideration and show how they are interrelated.

Good organization is achieved by outlining. Many people resist using outlines for various reasons. Some may have had teachers who insisted on a detailed outline when it wasn't needed. Others may have found that no matter how they outlined, they ended up altering the outline in the course of writing. However, a research report is a long and complex piece of writing. Even someone who has been connected with the project from the start finds it hard to sit down and produce a well-structured account of the project without planning. The writer may leave out important parts and realize it later, or talk in circles, or repeat things over and over, or give undue emphasis to minor matters. If, on the other hand, the writer plans ahead, looking at the relationship of ideas and the order in which they should be presented, the report will usually be better organized. A better plan might yet be discovered halfway through the first draft, but more often it will be discovered in the original outlining process.

The Outline

An outline has two main functions: (1) to show the order of presentation and (2) to show the way the parts relate to each other—particularly how small parts go together to form larger ones. The first function is accomplished by listing topics in order on the page, the second by indenting subordinate parts.

There are also two major sorts of outline notation. The traditional method alternates letters and numbers to show levels of subordination, whereas the newer method uses a decimal system, with successive places to the right of the decimal showing successively lower levels of subordination:

Traditional Form

I. Main division
  A. First-level subdivision
    1. Second-level subdivision
      a. Third-level subdivision
      b. Third-level subdivision
    2. Second-level subdivision
  B. First-level subdivision

EXHIBIT 25A.1 THE WRITING PROCESS

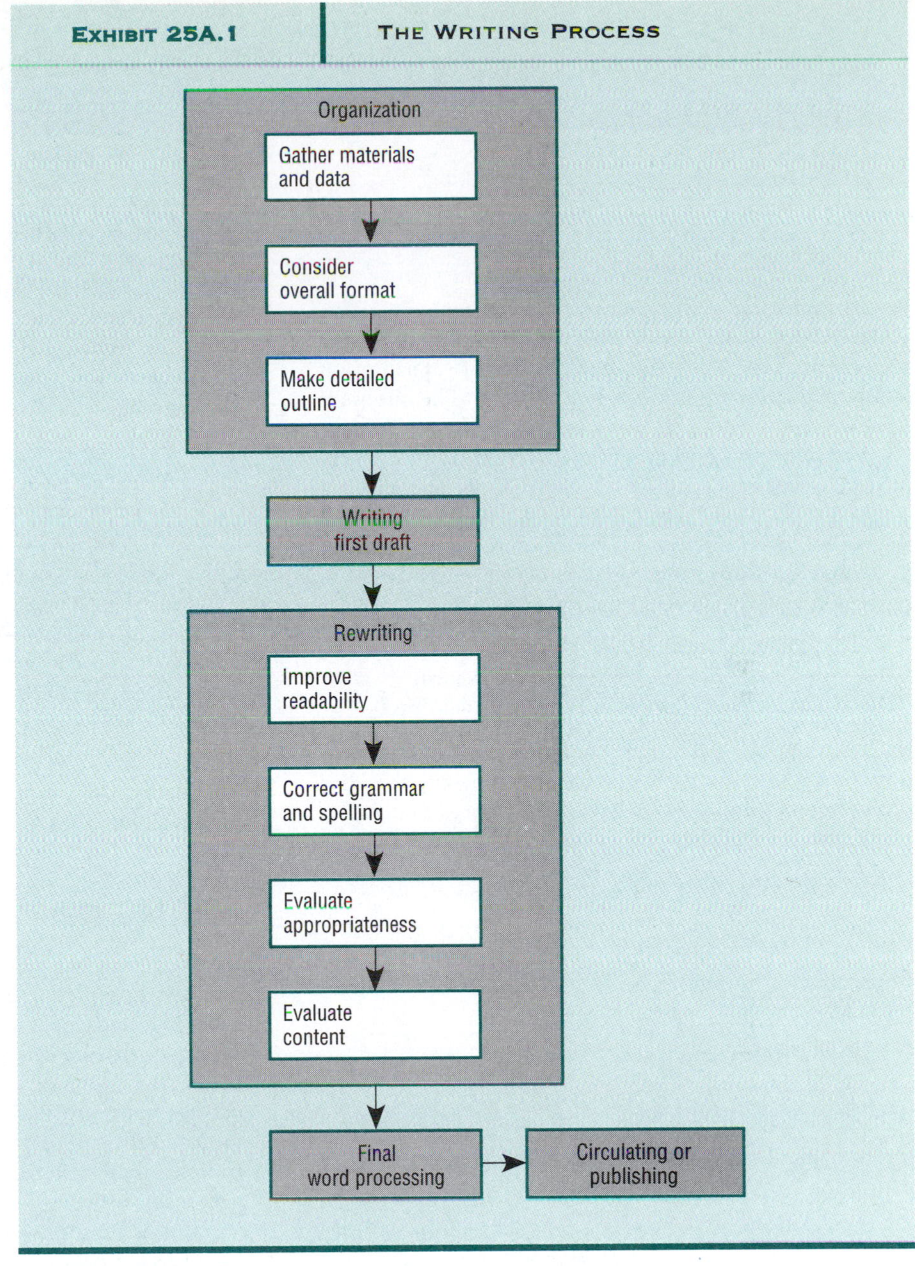

II. Second main division
etc.

Decimal Form

I. Main division
  1.1 First-level subdivision
    1.11 Second-level subdivision
      1.111 Third-level subdivision
      1.112 Third-level subdivision
    1.12 Second-level subdivision
  1.2 First-level subdivision

II. Second main division
etc.

Three levels of subordination are all that will be needed for most reports. Note that there should not be any single subdivisions. A subdivision implies that an idea is being broken into parts. When there is only one subsidiary point you want to make about a segment of the report, rewrite the segment caption to include it. For example:

2.31 Costs
    2.311 Cost overruns

could be recast as

2.31 Costs and cost overruns

or

2.31 Costs
    2.311 High basic cost
    2.312 Cost overruns

In preparing a working outline for your own use, you need not worry about whether the outline is a topic or sentence type. Also, the conventions of capitalization and punctuation are not overly important. The outline is a means to the end. It is not a goal in itself.

Attention to good practices in classification is useful in developing good outlines. First, use only one basis for organization at each level. This basis should include all the topics to be discussed. The following is an example of a mixed classification for part of a business research report on an experimental shampoo formula.

I. Exploratory studies (*type of study*)
II. New York City survey (*geographic location*)
III. Characteristics (*attributes of subject studied*)

Each of the three parts uses a different basis of classification. As a result, the parts don't seem to belong together in a coherent whole. Instead, the basis of organization for classification could be type of study:

I. Exploratory studies
II. City surveys
III. Consumer usage study

Alternatively, the report could be organized geographically:

I. New York City survey
II. Chicago survey
III. Los Angeles survey

Or it could be classified by the characteristics of the shampoo:

I. Cleaning
II. Physical form
    A. Color
    B. Odor
    C. Package

Of course, none of these schemes is comprehensive. Each includes points the others leave out. A full outline could employ all three classifications, but each on a different level:

I. Exploratory studies (*type of study*)
II. City surveys (*type of study*)
    A. New York City
    B. Chicago
    C. Los Angeles
    } (*geographic location*)
III. Consumer usage study (*type of study*)
    A. Cleaning
    B. Physical form
        1. Color
        2. Odor
        3. Package
        } (*attributes of shampoo*)

The writer must decide which classification principle to use at which level. The above example might be appropriate if the writer wanted to report the results of the three different studies. Suppose instead the writer wanted to stress the characteristics of the product rather than the individual studies. The shampoo attributes could be promoted to the first level of classification, and the type of study demoted to a subordinate level:

I. Cleaning (*attributes of shampoo*)
    A. Exploratory studies
    B. City surveys
    C. Consumer usage study
    } (*type of study*)
II. Physical form (*attributes of shampoo*)
    A. Color
        1. Exploratory studies
        2. City surveys
        3. Consumer usage studies
        } (*type of study*)
    B. Odor
    etc.

For further discussion of outlining, consult a good basic composition book.

WRITING THE FIRST DRAFT

Joe B. Researcher, who works for Bigg Enterprises Inc., has just completed a research project. It is Monday morning, and Joe's boss wants to have the report on Friday so that he can read it over the weekend, before a major staff conference early next week. Joe feels his project has come up with good results, and he has already prepared the outline for the report. He tells his secretary to hold all calls, then gets out a yellow pad and a pen and gets ready to write.

But as he looks at the empty pad, Joe can't decide how to start. All the bright ideas in his head seem to disappear as he puts his pen to the paper. Finally, he writes a sentence, then looks at it, rips the page off, crumples it up, and tosses it at the wastebasket (he misses). He glances at the clock and sees that, somehow, it's already 10 o'clock—time for coffee break! When he goes on break, a couple of his staff need to talk to him, so he doesn't get back to the office for an hour. When he is back, there are a dozen phone calls he needs to return. The whole afternoon is scheduled with meetings, and Joe knows no writing will get done that day.

That's the way it goes the whole week. Joe can't get to his report on Tuesday. Wednesday he tries writing at home, but the kids keep making noise. On Thursday

Joe's secretary asks when the report will be ready to type and Joe snaps, "How should I know!" As 5 o'clock rolls around, Joe calls his wife, telling her he'll be very late because he still has to get the (censored) report written. By the time the sun comes up the next morning, Joe has finally gotten most of the report done, impelled by sheer desperation. As he looks at it, he knows it is not his best work. It is incoherent in places, includes unexplained technical language in a couple of spots, and has several redundancies. Joe knows that a lot of the language and sentence structure should be reworked for better clarity, but the job is finally done, and Joe stretches out on his office couch to get an hour of sleep before the workday starts again.

This example is a bit exaggerated, but it's not too far from what many writers do. Some of them, unlike Joe, look at the mess they've just produced with indulgent eyes. They overlook all the problems and take any criticism personally. However, a first draft can almost always be improved. Often it needs major work, but doing that work is much easier than writing the draft in the first place. Every research writer, indeed every writer, should memorize two maxims: "Easy writing is hard reading" and "Good writing comes from good rewriting."

Why is this so? Trying to produce a perfect job on the first draft means combining creation and criticism. It's bound to be hard to write anything when you're continually crossing it out in your head before it gets on paper. Trying to create and criticize simultaneously makes it almost impossible to write anything. What seems clear in thought evaporates into vagueness the moment the pen touches the paper. All the underlying assumptions and experiences have to be made explicit on paper. The only chance the writer of a report has to clarify is in rewriting, before the reader ever sees the report—and rewriting a first draft is almost always easier than getting the first draft down to begin with. (The next section deals with some of the "hows" of effective rewriting. The discussion here concerns ways to overcome the difficulties of writing the first draft.)

The key to getting the first draft down, before that last-minute desperation, is suppressing the critical "internal editor" and releasing your creative side. Some suggestions:

1. Consolidate your time. There is usually wasted motion in getting started. Once you get started, don't stop prematurely. Most writers accomplish more in two hours of uninterrupted work than in four half-hour sessions spread over a day or week.
2. If you have trouble getting started, set your pen on the paper and keep it going, writing anything that comes into your mind—connected or not. You may have to write "I can't think, I hate writing," and so on for a few minutes before you relax enough to move into your subject. Later, you can cross out the irrelevant. The job now is *to get started*.
3. The introduction is one of the hardest parts to write, but that's where many writers start. Instead, try writing a later section that you're very sure of. If you move from the sections that are easy for you to the others, you have the reassurance that you are making progress. This suggestion assumes you have an outline, so that you know how all the sections "look" together. If you use this technique, pay special attention to transitions between sections as you are rewriting.
4. Don't keep shifting gears from writing to revising. You may make some false starts that have to be crossed out, but don't take the time for extensive revision or rewriting during the first draft. You may want to make marginal notes to yourself to use in revision, but don't stop now or valuable thoughts may escape.
5. Many writers find it easier to "talk" the first draft into a tape recorder. Most people speak more easily than they write, and the result may be more natural. This approach will also overcome the tendency to stop and revise while creation is in progress. When revising, you need to pay special attention to phrasings that are appropriate for speech but not for writing. That doesn't mean, however, that you write in stilted, straitjacketed, polysyllabic prose.

CRITICIZING AND REWRITING

The professional writer who doesn't make extensive revisions is a rarity. As an authority on business communications points out, "All good writers revise diligently; many great ones revised almost endlessly. Victor Hugo, for example, revised one novel 11 times; Hemingway rewrote the final page of *A Farewell to Arms* 39 times; Thomas Jefferson spent 18 days writing and rewriting the Declaration of Independence; and Voltaire frequently spent an entire night laboring over a single sentence." When we read these writers' works, they seem to fit together naturally, but the "naturalness" is the end product of careful rewriting. The report writer's aim is different from the novelist's, poet's, or statesman's, but the tools of revision in shaping rough work into a final product are just as useful.

The key to effective revision is objectivity. In writing the first draft, the challenge is to suppress the critical side and be creative. In revision the task is to look at the work as a self-editor. Thoughts such as "it's mine, and to change it is a slap in my face" or "I'll never get any sense out of this mess" get in the way. One of the best ways to achieve objectivity is to put the first draft aside for a while before revising it. A day or two is good, but even an hour or two will help you to gain a critical distance from the work. Another suggestion is to let someone else look at what you've written and to encourage that person not to withhold suggestions for fear of offending you.

A Revision Inventory

How do you go about revising? What do you watch for? The best way to learn is to become sensitive to the qualities of good and bad writing you encounter, imitating the good and purging the bad in your own writing. Even so, writers on writing invariably say, "Be concise, be clear, be forceful." Often the person who reads such advice doesn't find it very helpful. It's like being told, "Be brave, be beautiful, be happy." No one questions the desirability of these attributes, but if writers knew how to realize them, they probably wouldn't need the advice.

The revision inventory in Exhibit 25A.2 can help a writer overcome the problem of vagueness. It presents details to check in a framework of four general criteria: readability, correctness, appropriateness, and thought. These criteria may be considered one at a time in suc-

EXHIBIT 25A.2 | **A REVISION INVENTORY**[24]

READABILITY

Reader's Level

- ☐ Too specialized in approach
- ☐ Assumes too great a knowledge of research topic
- ☐ So underestimates the reader that it belabors the obvious

Familiarity of Words

- ☐ Too much jargon
- ☐ Pompous language
- ☐ Unnecessarily abstract

Sentence Construction

- ☐ Unnecessarily long and complex
- ☐ Subject-verb-object word order too rarely used
- ☐ Choppy, overly simple style (in simple material)

Paragraph Construction

- ☐ Lack of topic sentences
- ☐ Too many ideas in single paragraph
- ☐ Too long

Reader Direction

- ☐ Lack of "framing" (i.e., failure to set up the purpose and direction of forthcoming discussion)
- ☐ Inadequate transitions between paragraphs
- ☐ Absence of subconclusions to summarize reader's progress at end of divisions in the discussion

Focus

- ☐ Unclear as to subject of communication
- ☐ Unclear as to purpose of message

CORRECTNESS

Mechanics

- ☐ Questionable grammar
- ☐ Improper punctuation
- ☐ Serious or abundant spelling errors

Format

- ☐ Sloppy appearance of documents
- ☐ Failure to use customary company form

Coherence

- ☐ Sentences seem awkward owing to illogical and ungrammatical coupling of unrelated ideas
- ☐ Failure to develop a logical progression of ideas through coherent, logically juxtaposed paragraphs

APPROPRIATENESS

A. Internal Reports (Researcher to Superior)

Tact

- ☐ Failure to recognize differences in position between writer and receiver
- ☐ Impolite or even brusque, argumentative, or insulting tone

Attitude

- ☐ Too obvious a desire to please superior
- ☐ Too defensive in the face of authority
- ☐ Too fearful to be able to do best work

B. External Reports (Researcher to Client)

Customer Orientation

- ☐ Failure to recognize that messages shape corporate image
- ☐ Failure to recognize needs and rights of client
- ☐ Failure to adopt managerial decision-oriented perspective—narrowly technical viewpoint

Attitude

- ☐ Unfavorable results slanted or suppressed to gain favor of recipient
- ☐ Too defensive about technical purity of study
- ☐ Obviously attempting to use this report to gain further assignments from client

C. Common to Both

Supporting Detail

- ☐ Inadequate support for statements
- ☐ Too much undigested detail for busy reader

Opinion

- ☐ Adequate research but too great an insertion of personal opinion
- ☐ Too few facts (and too little research) to entitle drawing of conclusions
- ☐ Presence of unasked for but clearly implied recommendations

THOUGHT

Preparation

- ☐ Inadequate thought given to purpose of communication prior to its final completion
- ☐ Inadequate preparation or use of data known to be available

Competence

- ☐ Subject beyond intellectual capabilities of writer
- ☐ Subject beyond experience of writer

Analysis

- ☐ Superficial examination of data leading to unconscious overlooking of important pieces of evidence
- ☐ Failure to draw obvious conclusions from data presented
- ☐ Presentation of conclusions unjustified by evidence
- ☐ Failure to qualify tenuous assertions
- ☐ Failure to identify and justify assumptions used
- ☐ Bias, conscious or unconscious, which leads to distorted interpretation of data

Persuasiveness

- ☐ Seems more convincing than facts warrant
- ☐ Seems less convincing than facts warrant
- ☐ Too obvious an attempt to sell ideas
- ☐ Lacks action-orientation and managerial viewpoint
- ☐ Too blunt an approach where subtlety and finesse called for

cessive reviews of the report or all together, depending on what the individual writer finds most effective. Note that the criteria are related to the communications model presented earlier in Chapter 25.

The readability criterion refers to factors that facilitate or block the transition from the writer's field of experience to the reader's. The correctness criterion refers to the way the message has been put into the code of the medium—written English. The appropriateness criterion emphasizes consideration of the audience. Finally, the thought criterion refers to the message itself, the set of meanings the report is to convey.

Revising for Readability

The readability criterion concerns the clarity of the writing. The writing style of a research report should be transparent, making the content clear and never calling attention to itself. Whenever readers give their attention to the *way* something is said, they are no longer concentrating on *what* is being said. The first elements listed in Exhibit 25A.2 refer to tailoring the report to the reader's field of experience. First, the report should be aimed at the reader's level of understanding. It should not insult the reader by talking down to him or her, belaboring the obvious. Nor should it assume too much. The reader usually has less technical background in the field being reported on than does the writer. The language employed must be appropriate.

The hardest of the three listed language problems to overcome is improper use of jargon. Jargon amounts to "shop talk," and among those who understand it, it speeds and clarifies communication. When spoken or written to an outsider, however, jargon hinders comprehension. If a report is aimed at an audience without the proper technical background, technical words should be translated or used only after they have been clearly defined.

Next come the elements of sentence and paragraph construction. The sentence part refers to the choice among appropriate grammatical structures, not to grammatical correctness itself (which is considered in the next criterion). The aim should be an appropriate variety of long and short, of simple, compound, and complex sentences. The average sentence length should be reduced in difficult, technical passages and increased in less difficult ones. Also watch out for overuse of the passive voice ("The report *was prepared* by Melissa Acuña") and "there" or "it" constructions ("*There* was no real need for the report," "*It* could be seen that the report was pointless"). These add wasteful words and invert the normal sentence order, forcing the reader to search for the meaning.

In revising paragraphs, aim for unity. Each paragraph should have only one topic. Stating the topic in the first sentence will help the writer focus the paragraph and will help the reader grasp the main idea. Keep the paragraphs to a reasonable length. The reader will be daunted by paragraphs that go on for pages. Long paragraphs usually contain too many main ideas and lack unity.

Finally, *reader direction* and *focus* refer to showing the report's goal and how the writer is moving toward that goal. The introduction should state the aim of the report and how it will be reached. The body should follow the plan laid out in the introduction, and the conclusion should show that the aim has been reached. It is like giving the reader a road map at the beginning of the report, then putting in mileposts and directional signs through it, and showing the reader the destination has been reached as the report closes.

Revising for Correctness

Correctness is necessary for a report to be acceptable, but it is not sufficient to ensure that it will be acceptable. Even the best report, one that meets the other criteria, will not be received well if it is full of grammatical, punctuation, or spelling errors. These mechanical errors indicate that the writer has approached the work casually. Every writer should have (and use) a good English handbook and a standard college dictionary.

Proper format is another ingredient of correctness. Many companies and universities have a standard report format. In such cases, the writer should follow the format or adapt it to the individual report. Another consideration here is the "correctness" of such elements as margins, section heading format, figure and table titles, and so on. Such factors as neat and accurate typing are also included here. Many writers dismiss these things as not their responsibility, expecting their secretaries, typists, or spell checkers to handle them. Typists and secretaries are indispensable, of course, but the writer also needs to pay attention to these factors in preparing the draft for final typing, giving directions, proofreading, and inspecting the final product. After all, the writer's name is on the report—not the secretary's.

The final element of correctness is less cut-and-dried. Coherence comes from putting related sentences and paragraphs together and making clear the transitions between unrelated ideas.

Revising for Appropriateness

The appropriateness criterion refers to the "tone" of the report, which reflects the writer's attitude toward the report and the person for whom it is written. Research reports usually are written either for a superior in the writer's organization or for a client in another organization. In either case the report should balance detail and generalization and focus on facts, not opinions. The report should not include recommendations, unless they were requested in the assignment; rather, it should present conclusions that are reasonable, given the facts assembled.

In reports to superiors the writer needs to strike a balance between too much familiarity and too much deference to the boss. Either extreme will reduce the credibility of the report and lead the reader to question its objectivity. In reports to outside clients the writer needs to be aware that the report represents the organization as well as the writer. The report should be oriented to the needs of the client, to the decisions to be made, not to the technical questions with which the writer is probably most familiar. Attitude can also be a problem here: The findings must be presented objectively, not slanted toward what the writer thinks the client wants to hear.

Evaluation of Thought

The final criterion turns from a concentration on form to a concentration on content. Remember that the two are really inseparable: The only way that a reader can grasp the "content" is through the "form." We artificially separate the two here only for convenience. A report will miss the mark if it is based on inadequate preparation, if the project was beyond the researcher's competence, if the report doesn't fulfill the assignment, or if it reflects too little analysis or an improper persuasiveness. Many of these problems arise during stages of the project itself, long before the report is prepared. If the project hasn't been done properly, it will be too late to make up the lack in the report.

SUMMARY

The report-writing process begins with making sure that the material to be presented is effectively organized. Organization helps develop consistency throughout the report. The first stage in the writing process is outlining, which shows the order of presentation and the subordination of subdivisions to major sections. The second stage is writing the first draft. At this point the key is to suppress the "internal editor" and get an initial version of the report in writing. Finally, the first draft is rewritten, possibly several times, to produce the final draft.

The key to rewriting is objectivity. A revision inventory is presented as an aid to effective revision. It covers the evaluation of readability, correctness, appropriateness, and thought.

A FINAL NOTE ON BUSINESS RESEARCH

Business research is not a panacea or a substitute for judgment—it is only a tool. Yet business research, properly conducted and utilized by management, can play an indispensible role in improving decision making. It is hoped that you have gained a greater appreciation of the diverse nature of business research from reading this book. Business research is not a black-and-white area in which there is always a correct technique for solving a given problem. It is a gray area that in many cases requires considerable experience, a bit of skill, and the touch of an artist. It is further hoped that you will be interested in exploration of the more complex aspects of business research now that you have mastered the basics.

VIDEO CASE

POLAROID I-ZONE

"Where will you stick it?"[1] If you hear those words from a young teen brandishing a brightly colored camera, relax. You aren't being attacked or insulted. To the contrary, your friend probably just wants to take your picture. "Where will you stick it?" is Polaroid's slogan for its new I-Zone pocket camera, the firm's first consumer-product introduction in more than 20 years. The product is also aimed at a new target market for a Polaroid product: teens. Polaroid, famous for its instantly developing film, has come up with a new filmstrip with a sticky back that turns tiny photos into instant stickers. Kids can snap a photo, pull out the strip, wait a few seconds for the picture to develop, then peel it off the strip and stick it anywhere—on a notebook, on a jacket or hat, on a key chain, on a purse, or on a bicycle. Within months of its launch, the I-Zone became the No. 1–selling camera in the United States.

How did the I-Zone zoom to the top of the charts so quickly? Polaroid made a commitment to integrated marketing communications in researching the market, getting the product to the right consumers, and promoting it. First, they did the research and discovered that teens now have more spending power than any other generation of teens before them. "Polaroid decided to enter the kids market because the kids market right now is the biggest it's ever been in history," says Mary Courville, an I-Zone marketing executive. Second, they divided the market further, into preteens—tweens—and older teenagers. Girls seem to be most interested in taking pictures, so the Polaroid team focused there. Third, they thought "outside the box" about different uses for a camera. For instance, the younger girls actually view the camera as a fashion accessory—so a sleek design in fashionable bright colors was important. By thinking creatively, the team came up with whole new ways to use a camera. "It's not about taking pictures to put in a photo album," explains Courville. This is "a cool camera that allows kids to be creative and have fun. It's about play and doing what you want to do." The I-Zone's sticky film lets young photographers become artists. They can take their camera anywhere and stick their pictures anywhere.

Courville stresses that Polaroid couldn't have come up with either the product or the promotion that followed without integrated communications among the marketing, public relations, advertising, and promotion staff. "We're a very tight group," she says. "We're always together." They conducted focus groups and field tests together. They met with the advertising agency together. "We are just always talking to each other," she says. "Always, always, always." Not only does this increase the efficiency with which the product is launched, it keeps the message to the consumer consistent. The consumer sees the same message through television commercials, magazine or Internet ads, and various promotions.

What exactly is the message? For Polaroid in general, says Courville, it's about instant gratification. "Only Polaroid can give you that photograph instantly. Only Polaroid can enliven your time, your party, right then. Polaroid is the only one that allows you to capture the moment instantly." I-Zone takes it a step farther by giving kids instant pictures that they can use to transform and personalize something else—a backpack, a belt buckle, a baseball cap.

In addition to advertising in traditional media as well as over the Internet, Polaroid decided to hook up with the popular teen group the Backstreet Boys, becoming a sponsor of their "Into the Millennium" tour. "Sponsorship allowed us wonderful promotional opportunities," comments Courville. Since the group's biggest fans are girls age 14 to 17, the match was perfect. The Backstreet Boys actually used the I-Zone cameras during their concerts, and girls were invited on stage to have their pictures taken with band members, with I-Zone cameras, of course. Polaroid distributed cameras to fans at concerts so that they could take pictures of each other and the band. Results were so positive that Polaroid decided to sponsor another pop singer, Britney Spears, the following year. "This sponsorship is the perfect combination of music, fun, and friendship—all key aspects of our target consumers' lifestyle. Polaroid is committed to giving teens and tweens exactly what they want." Even the stars themselves seem hooked on I-Zone. "I'm psyched to be working with Polaroid," says Spears. "The I-Zone is the coolest way for me and my fans to have fun taking pictures. We can stick them everywhere." That's just what Polaroid has in mind.

Questions

1. What are the key elements of the I-Zone marketing mix?
2. What aspects of the I-Zone marketing mix might have been influenced by or developed based on business research?
3. What role should business research play in a consumer products organization such as Polaroid?

VIDEO CASE 2

WBRU

WBRU, an independent radio station based in Providence, Rhode Island, plays a variety of formats and appeals to a diverse group of listeners. Student volunteers play jazz in the very early morning, modern rock during the day, and retro music at noon. Every Friday at midnight, listeners experience the best in techno, big beat, drum 'n' bass, and remixes. Weekdays at 3, WBRU hands over the reins to its listeners—they pick the music. Every Wednesday night at 10, the station's "Breaking and Entering" broadcasts 4 hours of new music. Contests and sweepstakes with many free prizes are included in the programming.

WBRU is not a large corporate station with a large budget; it sees itself as a cool, fun station. Much time is spent seeking creative ways to please both listeners and advertisers.

Questions

1. Does a small independent station like WBRU need business research information, or is creative marketing enough?
2. What type of business research might WBRU find useful?

VIDEO CASE

BEN & JERRY'S

Ben & Jerry's Homemade, Inc., the Vermont-based manufacturer of ice cream, frozen yogurt, and sorbet, was founded in 1978 in a renovated gas station in Burlington, Vermont, by childhood friends Ben Cohen and Jerry Greenfield, with a $12,000 investment ($4,000 of which was borrowed).[2] They soon became popular for their innovative flavors, made from fresh Vermont milk and cream. The company currently distributes ice cream, low-fat ice cream, frozen yogurt, sorbet, and novelty products nationwide, as well as in selected foreign countries, in supermarkets, grocery stores, convenience stores, franchised Ben & Jerry's scoop shops, restaurants, and other venues.

Ben & Jerry's product strategy is to differentiate its super premium brand from other ice cream brands. The brand image reflects high quality, uniqueness, and a bit of amusement. Its all-natural flavors have unique names. For example, "Chubby Hubby" has chunks of chocolate-covered peanut-butter-filled pretzels in a rich vanilla malt ice cream with deep ripples of fudge and peanut butter. Other names in the company's line of ice creams include Cherry Garcia, Bovinity Divinity, Dilbert Totally Nuts, New York Super Fudge Chunk, Chunky Monkey, and From Russia with Buzz.

The new product development process and flavor naming process are a top priority at Ben & Jerry's. For example, Phish Food ice cream was developed as a unique product with a fun name associated with the band Phish. Ben Cohen had been a neighbor of members of Phish since the band's early years as favorites on the local music scene. When Ben & Jerry's suggested mixing up a Phish ice cream to celebrate their shared Vermont roots, the band agreed. So Ben & Jerry's concocted a chocolate ice cream with chewy marshmallow nougat, a thick caramel swirl, and a school of fudge fish in very pint. Most marshmallow variegates disappear into nothingness. The company took great pains to make sure that the marshmallow was the way it was meant to be. With Phish Food you can see, taste, and feel the white streaks of marshmallow. The Phish Food package is a departure from Ben & Jerry's traditional graphics. The pint container is designed with images from Phish's concert light show, featuring Phish band members Trey Anastasio, Mike Gordon, Jon Fishman, and Page McConnell on the pint lid along with Ben and Jerry.

Question

What role does business research play in new product development and brand name development for a company like Ben & Jerry's?

VIDEO CASE

FOSSIL—A WATCH FOR EVERY WRIST

When Fossil recently opened the doors on its chain of specialty stores, it created the perfect place to showcase its ever-growing product line.[3] "This is Fossil in a box. Really, for us to be able to communicate the essence of the brand, we had to be in a retail setting where it was all together in one place—where you could walk into this environment and it's very readily communicated what our brand image [is] from a product perspective," says Vice President of Image Tim Hale.

At the retail store, surrounded by Fossil's trademark salute to 1950s' nostalgia, shoppers can choose from hundreds of different Fossil products. Although Fossil is best known for its fashion-savvy watches, the company's trendy eye wear, leather goods, sports caps, and even boxer shorts are becoming hot fashion accessories around the world. While the majority of its products are manufactured in Hong Kong, Fossil designs its products at its corporate headquarters in Richardson, Texas.

Stephanie Thatcher, director of marketing, says, "For each product division that we have—watches, sunglasses, leather goods—we have a design team. That design team spends a lot of time overseas researching trends and seeing what's new and happening. They spend a lot of time in Europe and in Hong Kong really finding out what's going on in those markets and then adapting them to our market and to our customers."

Whether it's in a Fossil kiosk in Hong Kong or at the flagship Fossil store in Dallas, Fossil employs a universal product strategy. "We have a business system that works, and that system is that you buy at least 85 percent of your product from a core assortment that we have identified as our best-selling product. We still do realize there are some cultural differences. Some parts of the world like a little more gold than silver, some areas sell more blue dials than yellow dials, and we allow a 15 percent tweak factor for regional differences in taste levels," says Gary Bolinger, senior vice president of international sales and marketing.

Questions

1. Does a company that focuses on a retro image of the 1950s need business research?
2. How do the information needs of an entrepreneurial company change as it begins to market its product through its own retail stores rather than through a traditional channel of distribution?
3. How can a company use business research to determine the best products to sell in global markets?
4. How can business research help a firm that focuses on high fashion watches?

VIDEO CASE

5

IBM: ENTERPRISE RESOURCE PLANNING

By centralizing information and making it more widely available, IBM's ERP (Enterprise Resource Planning) system has the potential to make companies much more competitive and responsive.[4] Here is what IBM says about ERP:

> ERP solutions are effective at streamlining business processes that cut across the functional areas of your business. ERP brings together fragmented operations, often replacing a multiplicity of legacy systems. By sharing common information across an integrated set of application modules, ERP can speed up transactions. For instance, ERP can consolidate financial records, allowing you to close the books faster and more accurately.
>
> ERP can help you better manage your inventory, driving dramatic cost savings. ERP can map customer orders to your production plans, helping to improve the cycle time to respond to customer demand. And ERP can help eliminate process duplication, wait times, and information errors, yielding productivity improvements for your professionals. In addition, the regimen of an ERP implementation forces you to look at how you run your business—your processes, practices, and procedures. ERP implementations are a great opportunity to institutionalize a number of changes, many of which you may have been considering for some time.
>
> While ERP is very good at driving improvements, its focus is inward, within your own enterprise. However, if your company's top challenges involve relationships with your customers or trading partnerships with your suppliers, you may want to consider other solutions—either implemented individually or together with an ERP solution. Also, given the time it takes to fully deploy an ERP solution, you may want to consider a phased approach that includes these additional areas. This will ensure that the solution you implement meets your needs for the coming years, not just your immediate problem.
>
> IBM offers industry expertise to know what it takes to differentiate your business. Plus, IBM offers solution expertise spanning ERP, e-commerce, supply chain, customer relationship management, business intelligence, and more, to help you decide the combination that's best for your business.

Question

Different companies use different terminology for global information systems and decision support systems. After viewing the video, explain how IBM's ERP system parallels the book's definition and explanation of global information systems and decision support systems.

VIDEO CASE 6

FISHER-PRICE RESCUE HEROES

Fisher-Price's action-figure collection Rescue Heroes, as well as the CBS TV show with the same name, is popular with boys age 3 and up. The Rescue Heroes characters' mission is to help and rescue with courage, perseverance, resourcefulness, and nonviolent problem solving. The product line consists of action figures (such as Jake Justice Police Officer, Wendy Waters Firefighter, and Rocky Canyon Mountain Ranger), vehicles (for example, Rescue Heroes Quick Response Helicopter), and command centers.

Fisher-Price uses business research extensively in its new product development process. Rescue Heroes went from an identified need to a commercial product line with the help of a multistage research program. Through exploratory research, the company learned that there was a gap in toys available for preschool and early elementary school boys. Little boys liked the idea of action figures that their older brothers and friends played with, but those toys were difficult for them to understand and handle. The findings led Fisher-Price to coin the term KAGO—"Kids Are Getting Older"—meaning younger children want more grown-up toys.

Research with moms indicated their toy preferences. The moms liked the idea of imaginative play with action figures, but they clearly did not want their young children playing with toys that had violent overtones. As a result of these research findings and creative thinking, Fisher-Price came up with the idea of age-appropriate action figures. After much business research, the company learned that young boys had trouble with the figures toppling over. The product concept was refined so that the new action figures would have wide feet for stability.

During the business research process, Fisher-Price's researchers conduct focus group interviews to test new toy concepts. They interview both kids and moms in search of ideas for toys that have play value—the tangible features and intangible allure that entice a child to interact with and have fun with a toy. Fisher-Price tried versions of the action figure line in its play laboratory, a large nursery overflowing with toys. However, it is different from ordinary nurseries because there is a wall of one-way mirrors and microphones dangle from the ceiling so that researchers can observe how children are using the toys.

Fisher-Price conducted extensive in-home testing around the country. After the boys played with the toys at home, researchers interviewed the parents about price and asked if they would buy the toys.

Questions

1. Using the flowchart in Exhibit 4.4 (page 61), outline the steps in the research process that you would recommend Fisher-Price take in evaluating an idea for a new toy.
2. What type of outcome might Fisher-Price expect from its exploratory research efforts?
3. Describe the program strategy for Rescue Heroes. How did the early research projects influence subsequent research objectives?

7 VIDEO CASE

UPJOHN'S ROGAINE

The Upjohn Company, based in Kalamazoo, Michigan, manufactures and markets pharmaceuticals and health-related products. With more than 19,000 employees and distribution in over 30 countries from Australia to Zaire, the company's annual sales top $1 billion. Upjohn is constantly developing and marketing new products. One example is Rogaine.

Originally developed as an antihypertension drug, Rogaine was shown in clinical tests to encourage moderate hair growth on some balding male volunteers. Thereafter, Upjohn quickly applied to the U.S. Food & Drug Administration (FDA) for the right to market the drug as a hair-growth product in the United States.

Questions

1. Define Rogaine's marketing problem from a business research perspective.
2. What type of exploratory business research should Upjohn conduct?

VIDEO CASE

TRADING CARDS FOCUS GROUP

A manufacturer of baseball cards, football cards, and other sport and novelty cards had never conducted business research with its customers. The president of the company decided that the company needed to learn more about its customers. He instructed his business research department to conduct a focus group with some boys in the fourth grade.

Questions

1. Outline what you would like to learn in the focus group.
2. What particular problems might be involved when conducting a focus group with children?

9 VIDEO CASE

V8

V8 is a 100-percent vegetable juice drink produced and marketed by the Campbell Soup Company. The juice drink, made from concentrate with added ingredients, provides a full serving of vegetables and is a natural source of beta carotene. V8's ingredients include tomato juice from concentrate; reconstituted vegetable juice blend, made from water and concentrated juices of carrots, celery, beets, parsley, lettuce, watercress, and spinach; salt; vitamin C (ascorbic acid); flavoring; and citric acid. The drink contains no fat or cholesterol, and it is a good source of vitamins A and C.

V8 has for many years had a large share of the tomato and vegetable juice market. However, sales had begun to slip, so the company decided it needed to conduct consumer research that would enable it to develop a new advertising campaign.

Questions

1. What research objectives should marketers at V8 establish?
2. What research methods would be most appropriate to accomplish these objectives?

10 VIDEO CASE

FURNITURE.COM

"Decorating one's home is an extremely personal and information-intensive decision," says Andrew L. Brooks, president and CEO of Furniture.com.[5] Decorating in general, and furniture shopping in particular, can be a frustrating, time-consuming, and intimidating experience for many people. Few people relish dragging spouses or kids from furniture store to furniture store to sit on sofas and order swatches. And many consumers are just plain afraid to make a decision—what if the color or style is "wrong"? What if the dining room table is too big for the room? Furniture.com is determined to change all that.

Unlike other Internet businesses. Furniture.com is not an online start-up company. The idea to sell furniture on the Web actually began with the owner of a brick-and-mortar furniture store called Empire Furniture Showroom in downtown Worcester, Massachusetts. Steven Rothschild and his partner, Misha Katz, launched the first version of the online company from the Worcester store in the late 1990s. Rothschild is now company chairman and Katz is vice president of new technology. Throughout the changes the company has undergone, however, it has maintained a clear mission, as articulated by Brooks: "To take a shopping experience in the traditional world, which is not particularly easy, to re-create it, and to make it fun, easy, and accessible to everybody."

Rothschild and Katz recognized an opportunity. "The traditional brick-and-mortar environment hasn't been very good to furniture consumers," explains Brooks. "The average consumer needs to go to five or six retail establishments. That potentially ruins five or six weekend days with kids in tow, trying to find the perfect place. That is often a frustrating exercise." With more and more consumers flocking to the Internet to do their shopping, Furniture.com took advantage of a strategic window to attract customers early and keep them coming back for more. The company offers over 50,000 items from 140 manufacturers through its site, and it provides free delivery and setup. Most brick-and-mortar stores offer only 4,000 to 10,000 items, and many charge for delivery beyond a few miles.

Connecting all these pieces of furniture with the right customers requires strategic and tactical planning. Perhaps the company's most important strategy is considering the impact of every decision its managers make on the consumer. "Examples of that include multiple ways to search," explains Brooks. "You can search on our site by room, by piece, and by very specific criteria. . . . What sets us apart is the extent to which we have identified real consumer needs. We then found technology that can provide solutions as opposed to technology for technology's sake." To that end, customers can build their own virtual showroom at the Web site, filled with their favorite pieces of furniture to see what the finished product will look like. The Room Planner, Style Guide, Furniture Finder, and Personal Shopper features of Furniture.com's site are all implementations of the overall strategy.

Furniture.com's strengths include the following:

- Its huge selection—as already mentioned, the company offers over 50,000 items, much more than competitors
- Its service—customer service is open around the clock, by phone, live Internet chat, or e-mail, and sales reps contact customers after delivery to make certain the right items arrived on time
- Its freedom from having to hold inventory—most items are shipped directly from manufacturers.

Its one major weakness is the fact that currently the company does not offer cash refunds; instead, customers receive an exchange or store credit. Since furniture is a major purchase for most consumers, having $500 or $1,000 tied up in store credit could be a problem. However, Furniture.com does have a "no questions asked" return policy, and the company pays return shipping fees.

Looking toward future growth, Furniture.com has entered into several strategic alliances with other organizations. The company now has online advertising agreements with MSN Internet service, Yahoo!, and Lycos as part of a move to strengthen its position in the e-commerce marketplace. Indeed, Furniture.com's position is already at the head of its class. In review after review, the company receives high marks for selection and service. *Entertainment Weekly* calls the site "best of breed." *Access* rates the company with four stars, and *PC Magazine* reports, "The smartest furniture shoppers are heading to Furniture.com." That's a satisfying image for Furniture.com's founders: smart shoppers buying products from a smart company.

Questions

1. Doing business on the Internet is entering into unchartered waters for most companies. How useful is business research when most people have little or no experience with a new type of shopping?
2. What type of research objectives might Furniture.com be able to satisfy by using secondary data?
3. Suggest some external data sources and the channel of distribution Furniture.com might use to obtain data from these sources.

VIDEO CASE 11

THE CENSUS BUREAU: CENSUS 2000

Fact-finding is one of America's oldest activities.[6] In the early 17th century, a census was taken in Virginia, and people were counted in nearly all of the British colonies that became the United States. Following independence, there was an almost immediate need for a census of the entire nation. The first census was taken in 1790. The census counted 3.9 million inhabitants. Down through the years, the nation's needs and interests evolved and have become more complex. Today there is a need for statistics to help people understand what is happening and to form a basis for planning.

The Census Bureau is part of the U.S. Department of Commerce. Its mission is to be the preeminent collector and provider of timely, relevant, and quality data about the people and economy of the United States.

The censuses of population and housing are taken every 10 years in the year ending in 0. The census of population reports on population characteristics by geographical areas and provides detailed statistics on age, sex, race, Hispanic origin, marital status, and household relationship characteristics for states, counties, and places of 1,000 or more inhabitants. The economic censuses, covering manufacturing, retail, wholesale, and services industries, are taken every 5 years in the years ending with 2 and 7.

Questions

1. Why do we need a census of population? What good does it do the average person?
2. What is the population undercount? Is it equal among all demographic groups?
3. What types of marketing efforts might help the Census Bureau increase citizen participation in the census?

VIDEO CASE 12

BURKE, INC.

Burke, Inc. provides a number of management consulting services to clients around the world. Burke has four business units: Burke Marketing Research, Burke Customer Satisfaction Associates, Burke Strategic Consulting Group, and the Training and Development Center.

Burke Marketing Research provides full-service custom marketing research, analysis, and consulting for consumer and business-to-business product and service companies to help them understand marketplace dynamics worldwide. Services include product testing, brand equity research, pricing research, market segmentation, image and positioning studies, and a wide range of other marketing research services. Burke has been providing marketing research services to Blue Chip companies since 1931. Burke has tremendous depth of experience in all forms of research designs, including telephone, Internet, mail, and mall intercept.

Burke Marketing Research procedures are typical of those of suppliers of custom research studies. A client may come to Burke indicating it has a marketing "problem." Burke will spend some time investigating the problem and then submit a research proposal to the client. If the client approves the proposal, Burke conducts the fieldwork and prepares a research report.

Questions

1. Outline the steps in the survey research process.
2. How might a company like Burke help a client in each step of the survey research process?

VIDEO CASE

THE WALKER INFORMATION GROUP

The Walker Information Group is one of the 20 largest marketing research companies in the world. The Walker Group's total revenue tops that of such well-known names as J. D. Power & Associates, Roper, and Yankelovich Partners. Walker's clients include many Fortune 500 and Blue Chip industry leaders such as Cummins Engine Company, LensCrafters, Continental Cablevision, Florida Power & Light, and Oglethorpe Power Corporation.

The Indianapolis-based company was founded in 1939 as a field interviewing service by Tommie Walker, mother of Frank Walker, the current chairman and chief executive officer of the organization.

In the 1920s Tommie Walker's late husband worked for a bank that was considering sponsoring an Indianapolis radio show featuring classical music. The bank wanted to know who was listening to this show. Tommie was hired to do the interviewing, and she threw herself into the work. After that, referrals brought her more interviewing work for surveys. During an interview with a woman whose husband was a district sales manager for A&P, she learned that the grocery chain was looking for a surveyor in the midwest. A&P's sales manager liked Tommie but wouldn't hire anyone without a formal company, a field staff, and insurance. Tommie founded Walker Marketing Research on October 20, 1939, and her business with A&P lasted 17 years.

Today, the Walker Information Group specializes in business, healthcare, and consumer research, as well as database marketing. The company is organized into six strategic business units.

Walker Market Research and Analysis conducts traditional market research services ranging from questionnaire design and data collection to advanced analysis and consultation. Walker has expertise in helping companies measure how their actions are perceived by the audiences most important to them and how these perceptions affect their image, reputation, corporate citizenship, recruiting, sales, and more.

Data Source is a business unit that primarily is concerned with data collection and processing. It specializes in telephone data collection.

Customer Satisfaction Measurement (CSM), as the name implies, specializes in measuring customer satisfaction and helping clients improve their relationships with customers.

CSM Worldwide Network spans more than 50 countries. It is the first international network of professional research and consulting businesses dedicated to customer satisfaction measurement and management. The CSM Worldwide Network assures that multi-country customer satisfaction research is consistent by taking into account local conditions and cultural norms. Network members are trained to use consistent methods that allow information to be standardized and compared from country to country.

Walker Direct designs, develops databases for, and implements direct marketing programs that help generate leads for businesses and raise funds for nonprofit organizations. Walker Clinical is a health-care product-use research company. Walker helps pharmaceutical, medical-device, and consumer-product manufacturers test how well new products work and how customers like them.

Questions

1. What type of custom survey research projects might Walker Market Research and Analysis conduct for its clients?
2. What stages are involved in conducting a survey? For which stages might a client company require research from Walker Market Research and Analysis? From Data Source?
3. What is the purpose of customer satisfaction measurement?
4. What measures, other than findings from surveys, might a company use to evaluate the effectiveness of a total quality management program?

THE ATLANTA BRAVES

A visit to Turner Field, the Atlanta Braves' $242.5 million, state-of-the-art ballpark, feels like a trip back to the future.[7] The stadium has been described as "20th century tradition meets 21st century technology."

The Braves' marketing campaign reflects the charm and nostalgia of baseball's past, but it has a futuristic slogan: "Turner Field: Not just baseball. A baseball theme park."

Fans love the fact that they're closer to the action at Turner Field. It's only 45 feet from first and third base to the dugouts. On top of that, there's a Braves Museum and Hall of Fame with more than 200 artifacts. Cybernauts will find Turner Field awesome because it's a ballpark that makes them a part of the action. At the stadium, built for the 1996 Olympics and converted for baseball use since the Games, there are interactive games to test fans' hitting and pitching skills, as well as their knowledge of baseball trivia; electronic kiosks with touch screens and data banks filled with scouting reports on 300 past and present Braves, along with the Braves' Internet home page; a dozen 27-inch television monitors mounted above the Braves' Clubhouse Store, broadcasting all the other major league games in progress, with a video ticker-tape screen underneath spitting out up-to-the-minute scores and stats; a sophisticated BellSouth communications system, with four miles of fiber-optic cable underneath the playing field that will allow World Series games to be simulcast around the globe, as well as special black boxes placed throughout the stadium to allow as many as 5,500 cell-phone calls an hour.

The marketing of Turner Field is aimed at many types of fans. It is not enough just to provide nine innings of baseball.

Turner Field's theme-park concept was the brainchild of Braves President Stan Kasten. In the early 1990s, as the Braves grew into one of the best teams in baseball, Kasten increasingly became frustrated while watching fans flock to Atlanta–Fulton County Stadium a few hours before games, with little to do but eat overcooked hot dogs and watch batting practice.

As Kasten saw it, they spent too much time milling on the club-level concourse and too little time spending money. What if he could find a way for families to make an outing of it, bring the amenities of the city to Hank Aaron Drive and create a neighborhood feel in a main plaza at the ballpark? "I wanted to broaden fans' experience at the ballpark and broaden our fan base," Kasten says. "People have no problem spending money when they're getting value. We have one of the highest payrolls in baseball, and I needed to find new ways to sustain our revenues."

Turner Field's main entry plaza opens 3 hours before games—compared to 2 hours for the rest of the ballpark—and stays open for about 2 hours after games. On weekends, there is live music.

Everyone's invited—$1 "skyline seats" are available for each game—and that buck gets you anywhere, from the open-air porch at the Chop House restaurant (which specializes in barbecue, bison dogs, Moon Pies, and Tomahawk lager) to the grassy roof at Coke's Sky Field, where fans can keep cool under a mist machine.

Interactive games in Scouts Alley range from $1 to $4, and the chroma-key studios in the East and West Pavilions, where fans can have their picture inserted into a baseball card or into a photo of a great moment in Braves history, cost $10–$20. Admission to the museum is $2. And it should come as no surprise that there are seven ATMs located throughout the ballpark.

One of the Braves' key marketing objectives is to help build a new generation of baseball fans. The stadium was planned so that fans will find something to love and learn at every turn. The minute a fan's ticket is torn, that person becomes part of what's happening at Turner Field.

Questions

1. What are the key elements of the Turner Field marketing effort?
2. What aspects of the Atlanta Braves marketing mix might have been influenced by or developed based on business research?
3. What role should business research play in a sporting organization such as the Atlanta Braves?

CASE 2

HARVARD COOPERATIVE SOCIETY

From his office window overlooking the main floor of the Harvard Cooperative Society, CEO Jerry Murphy can glance down and see customers shopping.[8] They make their way through the narrow aisles of the crowded department store, picking up a sweatshirt here, trying on a baseball cap there, checking out the endless array of merchandise that bears the Harvard University insignia.

Watching Murphy, you can well imagine the Coop's founders, who started the store in 1882, peering through the tiny windowpanes to keep an eye on the shop floor. Was the Harvard Square store attracting steady traffic? Were the college students buying enough books and supplies for the Coop to make a profit? Back then, it was tough to answer those questions precisely. The owners had to watch and wait, relying only on their gut feelings to know how things were going from minute to minute.

Now, more than a hundred years later, Murphy can tell you, down to the last stockkeeping unit, how he's doing at any given moment. His window on the business is the PC that sits on his desk. All day long it delivers up-to-the-minute, easy-to-read electronic reports on what's selling and what's not, which items are running low in inventory and which have fallen short of forecast. In a matter of seconds, the computer can report gross margins for any product or supplier, and Murphy can decide whether the margins are fat enough to justify keeping the supplier or product on board. "We were in the 1800s, and we had to move ahead," he says of the $55 million business.

Questions

1. What is a decision support system? What advantages does a decision support system have for a small business like the Harvard Cooperative Society?
2. How would the decision support system of a small business like the Harvard Cooperative Society differ from that of a major corporation?
3. Briefly outline the components of the Harvard Cooperative Society's decision support system.

CASE 3

TULSA'S CENTRAL BUSINESS DISTRICT (A): Developing a Research Project

When Bob Griffin, vice president of Williams Realty Corporation, asked the Metropolitan Tulsa Chamber of Commerce to meet with him, he had spent much time thinking how downtown Tulsa was changing. Only a year before, construction had begun on a $2.6 million central pedestrian mall system. Mayor Robert LaFortune said that the carrying out of the downtown revitalization project reflected a solid "partnership of public and private interests. . . . We have to see great things emerge both in private development and in general use of this facility by all Tulsans."

The project called for improving Main Street from Third to Sixth Streets and Fifth Street from Boston to Denver, including landscaping, a multilevel fountain at Fifth and Main, and brick paving. Throughout the mall there would be rest areas, drinking fountains, and other facilities, such as telephone booths and a postal service center. The concept of the central pedestrian system was expected to strengthen the Main Street segment as the prime rental area in downtown Tulsa.

NEW WILLIAMS CENTER COMPLEX

One of the most obvious symbols of what was happening downtown was the 52-story Bank of Oklahoma (BOK) Tower, the focal point of the new Tulsa skyline. The Williams Companies had constructed the $18 million tower, the state's tallest building, and office space was beginning to be leased. This was the first of several Williams Center projects to be completed.

The Williams Center was planned as a $50 million complex located in the heart of downtown, consisting of a 52-story office building, a hotel, a shopping center, and a performing arts center.

Twenty-five thousand square feet would be given over to food service establishments. There would be a cafeteria and several fast-food places on the first floor; on the second floor, overlooking a skating rink from the west end, would be a restaurant that would likely specialize in crepes. A first-rate restaurant would be on the third, or plaza, level—the same level as Bank of Oklahoma's main banking facilities.

In addition to casual shoppers, the retail area was expected to draw from 7,000 people working in the BOK Tower plus 500 guests of the hotel.

PLANNING FOR REVITALIZATION

Bob Griffin was responsible for the development of the Williams Center. He had asked two members of the Metropolitan Tulsa Chamber of Commerce—Don Wolfe, manager of community relations, and John Piercey, manager of research—to meet with him in his office.

The Williams Company was incorporated on February 3, 1949, as the Williams Brothers Company, the successor to an oil-related business established in 1908. Its headquarters were in Tulsa. The company was primarily engaged in the chemical fertilizer, energy, and metals businesses. In its chemical fertilizer business, the company manufactured and marketed chemical fertilizer materials worldwide (Agrico Chemical Company). Its energy-related activities included operating the largest independently owned pipeline system in the United States (Williams Pipeline Company), retailing and wholesaling liquefied petroleum gas (Williams Energy Company), exploring for and developing oil and gas properties (Williams Exploration Company), and operating an intrastate natural gas pipeline in Louisiana. In its metals business the company purchased, processed, and distributed steel and other metals, principally on the East Coast (Edgecomb Steel Company) and in the Midwest (Steel Sales Corporation). The company's activities also included investing in short-term paper, marketable securities, and equity interests. The Williams Realty Corporation's primary purpose was to develop a major area of downtown Tulsa.

The company had a rich history. In 1908 two young brothers were sent by their employer, a Kansas City contractor, to begin a highway paving job. When the bond issue for this project was delayed, the contractor decided to move on—but not David R. and S. Miller Williams, Jr. The brothers persuaded their employer to accept their note for the equipment and supplies and agreed to complete the city's project piecemeal as funds permitted. Thus the Williams Brothers Company was founded.

The company's first pipeline venture, in 1915, established Williams Brothers as the principal builder in this new field. Ever since, the name Williams has been synonymous with pipelines.

Williams Brothers expanded beyond Canada and the United States in the late 1930s. An important milestone occurred when the company purchased the assets of the 6,200-mile Great Lakes Pipe Line Company in 1966 and subsequently expanded this system to provide more complete coverage of its upper Midwest distribution area.

The Williams Companies consisted of the founding organization, Williams Pipeline, Williams Energy, Williams Exploration Company, Agrico Fertilizer Company, and Williams Realty.

WILLIAMS REALTY WORKS WITH THE CHAMBER OF COMMERCE

Bob Griffin's chief responsibility as vice president of Williams Realty was to sell the idea that downtown Tulsa was revitalizing and the Williams Center in particular would be a good place to locate offices and a shopping center.

After the usual informal chitchat about goings-on in the city, Griffin addressed the group. "I've found out many things since the Williams Companies made the decision to develop the Williams Center. One is that we need to know more about the central business district. As I speak to prospective occupants of our space, one question almost universally asked is "How many people work in the downtown area?" I have been able to do some rough computations by estimating the average number of workers per square foot and then multiplying that figure times our estimate of the square footage in the downtown area. That is the answer I give people. Nevertheless, we do not have a reliable estimate of how many people work in the downtown area. Knowing how many people work here is only the tip of the information iceberg. There are a number of other things I'd like to know about the downtown area."

John Piercey commented, "You know, Bob, the future of Tulsa's central business district has been a topic of concern for many years. Its present conditions and its future are perceived to be an indication of the vitality and future of the entire city. Just a few years ago, Tulsa's CBD was in a state of decline. At that time there was every indication that Tulsa's downtown was going the way of those in so many other cities. But the Chamber of Commerce and Downtown Tulsa Unlimited started revitalization plans, hoping to reverse the declining trend. Many major private investments have been made in the last few years. But most of these efforts have been made on the basis of intuitive feelings about the CBD. I think you're right. The lack of timely information is hampering industrial decision making and commercial marketing efforts in the downtown area. If the Chamber of Commerce is going to help the central business district, we have to eliminate the information gap about the central business district. We need information on (1) the quantity and nature of the downtown population, (2) commercial enterprise (and vacancy) inventory, (3) business's opinions about the CBD, and (4) shoppers' opinions about the CBD."

Don Wolfe suggested that many downtown firms might be interested in the type of information that the Williams Companies desired. He said, "I believe the Chamber of Commerce should develop a statement of information needs and determine our research objectives; then we can see if any of the firms in the central business district would be willing to support some research."

John Piercey added, "I think this is going to be an extremely big task. The chamber's research department is not going to be able to collect such massive amounts of data. Perhaps we can utilize the services of an outside consultant, perhaps one of the universities in the area."

Don Wolfe said, "Yes, I believe we need someone who could help us out substantially in defining our research objectives and collection of the data."

Bob Griffin said, "Fine, gentlemen, I think we've made an important decision."

The Chamber of Commerce decided that the project would require extensive fieldwork in four interrelated areas:

1. A survey of the central business district employers and employees (characteristics, work habits, and attitudes).
2. A survey of commercial establishments and off-street parking facilities (type, size, and location).
3. A survey of commercial vacancies (concentrating on ground-floor space, but with some consideration given to multistory commercial buildings).
4. An on-the-street *sample* survey of shopping attitudes and preferences (which would also address attitudes toward working and living downtown).

Questions

1. Do you agree with the Chamber of Commerce's research objectives and proposed methods of data collection? Why or why not?
2. Briefly outline a research proposal by listing the appropriate techniques for collection of these data.

CASE 4

HAMILTON POWER TOOLS (A)

On July 13, 1997, Mr. Campagna, the marketing manager for Hamilton Power Tools, was anxiously awaiting his meeting with the business research firm. He felt the findings from the business research would change Hamilton from a sales-oriented company to a firm that would adopt the consumer-oriented philosophy of the marketing concept.

For more than 55 years Hamilton Power Tools had been marketing industrial products by catering to the construction and industrial tool markets. Its construction product lines included power trowels, concrete vibrators, generators, and powder-actuated tools. Its industrial products were primarily pneumatic tools: drills, screwdrivers, and the like. One of its products, the gasoline-powered chain saw, was somewhat different from traditional construction and industrial tools. The chain saw line had been added in 1949, when John Hamilton, Sr., had the opportunity to acquire a small chain saw manufacturer. Hamilton believed that construction workers would have a need for gasoline-powered chain saws. He acquired the business in order to diversify the company into other markets.

During the late 1970s and early 1980s the chain saw market was rapidly changing, and Hamilton Power Tool executives began to realize they needed some expert marketing advice. Mr. Campagna felt that a major change in the company's direction was on the horizon. Campagna had been in the chain saw business for 15 years. Reports from trade publications, statistics from the Chain Saw Manufacturers Association, and personal experience had led him to believe that the current chain saw industry was composed of roughly the following markets: professionals (lumberjacks), farmers, institutions, and casual users (home or estate owners with many trees on their lots). The casual user segment was considered to be the future growth market. Campagna wished to ensure that Hamilton would not make any mistakes in marketing its product to this segment of "weekend woodcutters" who once or twice a year used a chain saw to cut firewood or to prune trees in the backyard.

In March 1997, when chain saw sales began to slow down because of the seasonal nature of the business, Campagna and Ray Johnson, the chain saw sales manager, had a meeting with John Hamilton, Sr. Although Hamilton believed they had been doing well enough in chain saw sales over the past decade, Campagna and Johnson were able to persuade the aging executive that some consumer research was necessary. After talking with several business research firms, Hamilton Power Tools hired Consumer Metrics of Chicago to conduct two research projects. The first was a thematic apperception test (TAT).

The TAT research was completed in the first week of July. Campagna arranged for a meeting with the business research firm the following week. As Dale Conway and Frank Baggins made their presentation of the results of the survey of chain saw users, Campagna thought back to the day Consumer Metrics had originally suggested the idea of a TAT to John Hamilton. Conway had sold him on the idea with his argument that motivational research was widely used in consumer studies to uncover people's buying motives. Conway had mentioned that Consumer Metrics had recently hired a young, bright MBA. This MBA—Baggins, as it turned out—had specialized in consumer psychology and business research at a major state university. Conway had thought that Baggins was one of the best-qualified people to work on this type of project. Since Hamilton Power Tools had had no experience in consumer research, Campagna had been eager to proceed with the in-depth thematic apperception test.

Conway told Campagna, Hamilton, and Johnson that in the TAT respondents are shown a series of pictures and are asked to express their feelings about the people in the pictures. He told Campagna that although the present study was exploratory, it could be used to gain insights into the reasons people make certain purchases. He also suggested that the test would be a means of gaining the flavor of the language people use in talking about chain saws, and it could be a source of new ideas for copywriting.

Campagna remembered that at one time he had thought this project wouldn't be very worthwhile; however, he also realized he did not know that much about the consumer market. During the initial meeting with the research firm, it had been proposed that an exploratory research project be conducted within the states of Illinois and Wisconsin to obtain some indication of the attitudes of potential casual users toward chain saws. The researcher had suggested a TAT. Campagna had not known much about this type of research and needed time to think. After a week's deliberation, he called Conway and told the researchers to go ahead with the project. Case Exhibit 4.1 shows the TAT used by the researchers.

At the meeting, Conway and Baggins carefully presented the research results. They pointed out that in the TAT study several screening questions were asked at the beginning of the interview. The findings of this study were based on those respondents who either planned to purchase a chain saw in the next 12 months, already owned a chain saw, or had used a chain saw in the past. The presentation closely followed the written report submitted to Campagna. The findings were as follows.

The first picture (Exhibit A in Case Exhibit 4.1) shown to the respondent was of a man standing looking at a tree. The interviewer asked the respondent the following question:

> I have a problem which you may find interesting. Here's a picture of a man who is thinking about the purchase of a chain saw. Suppose that such a man is your neighbor. What do you suppose he is thinking about?

After the respondent's initial answer, the following probing question was asked:

> Now, if he came to you for advice and you really wanted to help him, what would you tell him to do? Why do you think this would be the best thing for him to do?

Initial responses seemed to center around what the man would do with the tree. Many respondents expressed an interest in the tree and were concerned with preservation. It seemed that pride in having a tree that beautified the owner's property was important to some respondents. Some of the typical responses were as follows:

> He's thinking about cutting the tree down.
> Why cut a whole tree when you can save part of it?
> He could trim out part of those trees and save some of them.
> We lose trees due to disease and storm damage.
> Trees beautify property and make it more valuable.
> I don't like to destroy trees.

Considering the alternatives to buying a chain saw was the next step many of the respondents took. Basically, the ultimate consumer sees the alternatives to the purchase of a chain saw as

1. Using a hand saw
2. Hiring a tree surgeon
3. Renting or borrowing a chain saw

These alternatives were in the respondents' minds partly because they were concerned about the cost of doing the job. They seemed to be worried about the investment in a chain saw, about whether it paid to buy one for a small, one-time job. (Another reason for the alternatives came out in responses to a later picture.) Some quotations illustrate these points:

> He's thinking how to go about it. He will use his hand saw.
> He doesn't have to invest in a chain saw for only one tree.

CASE EXHIBIT 4.1 **HAMILTON TAT STUDY**

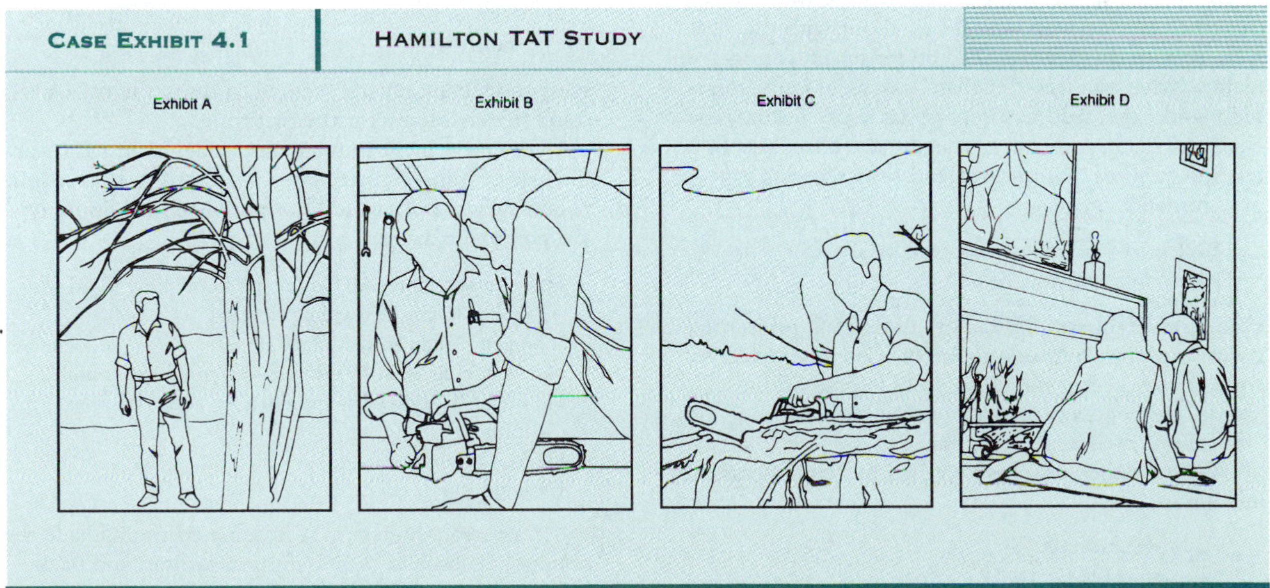

He's thinking about how to get the tree down—the cost of doing it himself versus having someone else do it. Have him cut it down himself, it's not too big a tree. He'll save the cost.

He's thinking whether it pays for a couple of trees. If it would be worth it. How much longer with an axe.

He's thinking whether he should do it himself or get someone else to do it for him. Get someone who knows what he is doing.

He's thinking he'll rent a chain saw for a small area and would buy one for a large area.

The best way to get a job done. Chain saw is faster, but a hand saw is cheaper. Depends on how much work he has to do.

An interesting comment made by two respondents was "He's thinking about Dutch elm disease." The area had recently been hit by that disease. The respondents were projecting their situations into the TAT pictures.

Other statements were made concerning the ease and speed of using a chain saw. Some questions regarding the characteristic performance of a chain saw were raised in response to this question; however, Exhibit B covered this area more adequately. This picture showed two men standing in a chain saw store looking at a chain saw. The question asked went as follows:

Here is a picture of the same man in a chain saw store. Suppose he's a friend of yours—your next-door neighbor, perhaps. Tell me what you think he will talk about with the chain saw clerk.

The issue most frequently raised was how the chain saw worked. An equal number of respondents wanted to know first how much it cost. Weight (lightness) was the next most frequently raised issue. Horsepower was of concern to many of the respondents. Other subjects they thought the man would talk about with the clerk were maintenance and availability of repair, performance (what size tree the chain saw would cut), durability and expected life, safety (what safety features the chain saw had), and ease of starting the chain saw. In relation to price, respondents had the following types of comments:

Well, price is the most important, of course.

He's wondering how he will pay for it.

One respondent said, "He's not considering price; price means nothing compared to safety." One individual was concerned whether the chain would come off the "blade" (respondents referred to the guide bar as a "blade" rather than a "guide bar").

Various other issues were raised by respondents, including:

Ease of handling
Length of blade
Which was the best brand
Whether it had direct drive
Whether it had a gas protector
Self-lubrication
The warranty (guarantee)
Ease of controls
Specifications
Availability of credit
Possibility of mixing oil and gas

Exhibit C showed a man cutting a felled tree with the chain saw. Respondents were asked:

The man in the picture is the same man as in the last picture. He purchased the chain saw he was looking at. Knowing that he purchased the chain saw, what can you tell me about him? Can you tell me anything about the character and personality of this man?

A follow-up question was

What do you suppose this man is thinking about while he's using his chain saw?

A common response was that the man was satisfied. Typical responses were "He's pleased," "He's happy he bought the chain saw," "Lots of time saved," and "He's happy with the chain saw; he made the right decision." Many favorable overtones to using a chain saw were given, for example:

Sure beats bucking with an axe.

He's thinking about speed of getting through, time saved.

How much easier it is to cut a tree down with a chain saw than a hand saw.

He seems to be saying, "Why didn't I buy a chain saw sooner?"

Respondents in general seemed to think the man was using the chain saw for the first time.

Very prominent in many respondents' answers was the fear of using a chain saw—it seemed to be a major reason why people would not purchase one. Some typical comments were

He's a little frightened. He doesn't know how to go about it, but he's willing to learn.

If he gets caught in that blade . . .

He's watching what he's doing—he could lose a limb.

He might be somewhat apprehensive about the use of it.

He looks scared of it.

He better think safety.

In general, the test, as it is designed to do, made the respondents project their own personalities and backgrounds onto the character of the man in the pictures. Respondents described the man in a variety of ways. He was described as a blue-collar worker, an office worker laboring after hours and on weekends, a somewhat wealthy man able to afford a chain saw, and a homeowner. A number of responses indicated that he was a do-it-yourselfer, a man who liked to "do his own thing." "Farmer" was another more than scattered response. Associations with an outdoorsman, a man who liked to keep in shape, were also indicated. One quotation seems to sum it all up:

> This seems to be his first job. He seems to be happy about it. He seems to think the chain saw will lighten his work load. He looks like he has not owned many power tools. He looks excited. He seems like he will be able to do a lot of cleanup work that he would not have been able to do without the chain saw. The chain saw is sure an improvement over the hand saw. It's faster, easier to use.

The fourth picture (Exhibit D) showed a man and woman seated before a fireplace. The question read,

> Here's a picture of the same man as in the previous pictures, sitting and talking with a woman. What do you suppose they're talking about?

An analysis of the fourth picture in the projection test showed that respondents felt the man and woman in the picture were happy, content, cozy, and enjoying the fireplace. The man was "enjoying the fruits of his labor." It came out very strongly that a man who uses a chain saw is proud of himself after he cuts the wood; he thinks his cutting of wood with a chain saw is a job well done. Some typical comments:

> He's very happy to cut his own wood for his fireplace—real proud of himself.
>
> He's telling her how much he saved by cutting it himself.
>
> They're talking about the logs, how pleased he is with himself.
>
> He's thinking about the beauty of the fire, fire logs he himself sawed from their property.

The people projecting their feelings into the picture seemed to think that because the job was well done, purchasing a chain saw was worthwhile:

> The man in the picture is saying, "The chain saw pays for itself. There's a $200 job, and you will be able to use the chain saw afterwards."
>
> Work's done, and there's enough for winter, and he has trees for winters to come.
>
> What a good buy that chain saw was. Cut wood costs, save money.

The woman in the picture was also very happy; she was satisfied and probably thinking about the future, but most of all she was very proud of her husband. This came out very strongly. For example,

> The woman is looking to the enjoyment of the fireside and of the money saved because they cut their own wood. She might have questioned the investment before this, before sitting in front of the fireplace.
>
> She is proud of her husband.
>
> She is pleased the tree is down.
>
> The woman is probably proud of the fireplace and starting the fire. He's probably thinking about the wood he sawed.
>
> The man and woman are congratulating each other on finally getting around to buying a chain saw and cutting firewood.
>
> She is complimenting him on his ability and on how handy it is to have a man around the house. She is also thinking that possibly it was easier for her husband to use a chain saw.

The woman didn't care about the chain saw, but she was satisfied. The husband's concern over his wife's approval of this investment was also brought out by this picture—evidently men were worried that their wives would not see the value of a chain saw purchase. Also, there were implications that the man should be tired after using the chain saw—"and he had to work hard in the afternoon to get the logs for the fireplace."

After the presentation, Campagna was reasonably impressed. He asked Hamilton what his opinion was. Hamilton said, "This is all very interesting, but I don't see how it can lead to greater profits in our chain saw division."

Questions

1. How should Conway and Baggins respond to Hamilton's comment?
2. Is Hamilton investigating the casual-user market segment correctly?
3. What conclusions would you draw from the thematic apperception test? Do you feel this is a valid and reliable test?
4. What specific recommendations would you make to Campagna concerning the casual-user chain saw market?

CASE 5

MIDDLEMIST PRECISION TOOL COMPANY

Dennis Middlemist was a weekend do-it-yourselfer. A hobby he particularly enjoyed was building furniture for his own home. After many years of frustration with trial-and-error adjustment of his radial arm saw (using a T square and trial cuts), Middlemist decided that he needed to invent an alignment device.

It wasn't long thereafter that Middlemist had designed a solution. A custom prototype was built at a local engineering shop. When Middlemist tested the device, it seemed to work perfectly for his needs. The proud inventor sought out an attorney to patent the device, and it looked as if a patent would be available. At this point Middlemist started to dream about the possibility of the Middlemist Precision Tool Company and the vast empire he would leave to his children. In reality, however, he did not know much about marketing and wondered what market information he would need before getting serious about manufacturing the device, such as what the market potential would be. He thought the best place to start would be to determine how many radial arm saws there were in the United States and how many prospective customers there might be for his invention.

Questions

1. If you were a research consultant called in to help Middlemist define his business problem, what information do you think would be most important to him?
2. Middlemist has decided to see what information about the radial arm saw market can be found in secondary data sources. Go to your library and find what you can on radial arm saws and/or any related information that might be of value to Middlemist.

CASE 6

EZPASS

In the 1990s, a task force was formed among executives of seven regional transportation agencies in the New York–New Jersey area.[9] The mission of the task force was to investigate the feasibility and desirability of adopting electronic toll collection (ETC) for the interregional roadways of the area. Electronic toll collection is accomplished by providing commuters with small transceivers (tags) that emit a tuned radio signal. Receivers placed at toll booths are able to receive the radio signal and identify the commuter associated with the particular signal. Commuters establish ETC accounts that are debited for each use of a toll road or facility, thus eliminating the need for the commuter to pay by cash or token. Because the radio signal can be read from a car in motion, ETC can reduce traffic jams at toll plazas by allowing tag holders to pass through at moderate speeds.

At the time the New York–New Jersey agencies were studying the service, electronic toll collection was already being used successfully in Texas and Louisiana. Even though several of the agencies had individually considered implementing ETC, they recognized that independent adoption would fall far short of the potential benefits achievable with an integrated interregional system.

The task force was most interested in identifying the ideal configuration of service attributes for each agency's commuters, and determining how similar or different these configurations might be across agencies. The task force identified a lengthy list of attributes that was ultimately culled to seven questions:

- How many accounts are necessary and what statements will be received?
- How and where does one pay for EZPass?
- What lanes are available for use and how they are controlled?
- Is the tag transferable to other vehicles?
- What is the price of the tag and possible service charge?
- What is the price of the toll with an EZPass tag?
- What are other possible uses for the EZPass tag (airport parking, gasoline purchases)?

From a business researcher's perspective, it also seemed important to assess commuter demand for the service. However, the task force was not convinced that it needed a projection of demand, because it was committed to implementing ETC regardless of initial commuter acceptance. The task force considered its principal role to be investigating commuters' preferences for how the service should be configured ideally.

Questions

1. Evaluate the problem definition. Has the problem been defined adequately?
2. What type of research design would you recommend for this project?

CASE

TODAY'S MAN

David Feld, founder of Today's Man, a $204 million retailer based in Moorestown, New Jersey, guessed that many men equated buying clothes with going to the dentist, but he didn't know why.[10] Feld paid for focus groups to uncover the truth. But he never met a focus group he trusted.

Finally, Feld's advertising agency recommended he talk to a company of professional hypnotists based in New York. Feld was skeptical, but he was desperate and curious enough to commission a study focused on why men feel uncomfortable in clothing stores. "The results really shook us up," Feld reports. The comments the men made under hypnosis had the ring of authenticity he had been searching for.

Hypnotized men revealed that they often hated the way their clothes fit but didn't know how to complain. "One guy told us that the last time he bought a suit, it didn't fit right—but he didn't say anything," Feld says. "He then told the hypnotist how insecure and dopey he felt when he wore that suit." Further, some of the groggy men admitted to a sense of powerlessness—they felt ganged up on by both their wives and pushy salespeople. "We had never gotten that answer before," Feld says.

Questions

1. Evaluate the research methods used by Today's Man.
2. Would you recommend any additional research?

CASE 8

BEHAVIORAL SCIENCE RESEARCH OF CORAL GABLES, FLORIDA

Lawyers use focus groups and surveys to find out what wins in the courtroom.[11] Their research shows that demographics and values affect the way juries see evidence. It also shows that trial arguments, like advertising copy, often succeed or fail on the turn of a phrase. Jury research gives lawyers an edge when the case is close, the facts are controversial, and the jury pool is diverse.

"We know that various demographic groups and people with various types of jobs will respond differently to the same facts," says Robert Ladner, president of Behavioral Science Research in Coral Gables, Florida. "A high school teacher has different responses to arguments than an elementary school teacher or a college professor does."

Ladner has developed PercepTrac, a juror database that operates like the databases used by television researchers. PercepTrac has a handheld device that mock jurors use to gauge their positive or negative responses to facts presented in a trial. During the attorneys' opening statements, for example, mock jurors twist a knob on the device to register the degree of positive or negative feelings about each statement. Ladner typically shows the trial to 30 "jurors" equipped with the device, just as an advertising agency would run a campaign past a focus group.

"I can track the responses of those 30 people according to their age, income, and psychographic profile. I can track responses minute by minute for everything that goes on in the mock trial," Ladner says. Watching the resulting data "is like looking at an electrocardiogram."

Ladner was hired by a Florida city that had to condemn some land for a new road. "We had to evaluate two elements: the perception that the acquisition by condemnation was unfair and the perception that the damages paid were not sufficient," he says.

Ladner first conducted a survey to find out the "core attitudes" of people in the jury pool. His goal was to learn who was most likely to be sympathetic to the government and who was most likely to favor the property owner. He found that non-Hispanic whites were the ethnic group most sympathetic to the Department of Transportation's need to widen roads, but they were also more sympathetic to property owners than were blacks or Hispanics. A majority of blacks (56 percent) felt that the DOT was unfair in taking the property, compared with 23 percent of whites; and 78 percent of blacks felt that property owners are greedy, compared with 41 percent of whites.

Next, the city's attorney presented his case to a mock jury equipped with PercepTrac. He lost the mock trial, but the device showed a small point that had alienated the jury and eroded the credibility of the municipality's case. That small point was a legal term used in condemnation proceedings: a "taking."

"To Joe Lunchbucket on the jury, the word 'taking' has enormous negative connotations," says Ladner. In the actual trial, the city's attorney described his case in everyday language and won.

Mock juries also show how nonfactual things, such as mannerisms, may alienate or attract jurors. "For years, this was considered voodoo litigation," Ladner says. "But not only does it work, it also gives trial attorneys a sense of confidence in their preparation. They know what to look out for, and they can prepare targeted arguments rather than guess which ones are going to work."

The effectiveness of jury research is easy to test, and Ladner says that PercepTrac juries predict the actual verdict 80 percent of the time. "Your stuff has to be bulletproof," Ladner says. "You have to know these people as if you are living inside their bodies and brains and are seeing with their eyes."

Questions

1. Does this survey fall into the traditional categories of surveys discussed in the book? What are the advantages of this type of survey?
2. What sources of survey error are most likely to occur in a study of this type?
3. Is this type of research ethical?

CASE 9

TULSA'S CENTRAL BUSINESS DISTRICT (B)

In Case 3, Tulsa's Central Business District (A), the Metropolitan Tulsa Chamber of Commerce had recognized that there was an absence of timely information about the Central Business District (CBD). There was a great need for information for investment decision making, commercial efforts, and continued revitalization of the downtown area. One of the research projects was a survey of chief executives of business firms in the CBD. The purpose of this survey was to gather information concerning the number of employees working in downtown Tulsa, employees' salary distributions, proposed future investment in downtown Tulsa, and executive's attitudes toward a variety of dimensions of the downtown area.

For the purposes of this research, downtown Tulsa was defined as coinciding with Census Tract 25 and the inner dispersal loop (a system of expressways).

A mail survey of the chief executives of business firms within the inner dispersal loop was conducted. The questionnaire appears in Case Exhibit 9.1.

In order to ensure a representative picture of executives' opinions of downtown Tulsa, each firm within the CBD was given the opportunity to be selected in the sample. However, as the larger firms were expected to have a greater impact on the future of downtown, a stratified sample was selected. Prior to sampling, these larger firms were identified on the basis of information gleaned from the Oklahoma Employment Security Commission and a proprietary source listing the square footage of firms in the CBD. Several additional firms were included after researchers consulted with the Metropolitan Tulsa Chamber of Commerce. The stratum of larger firms consisted of 154 major firms within the inner dispersal loop. This stratum was broken into two parts: *key firms,* including the largest 40 firms, and *other major firms,* including the remaining 114 firms of major importance in the CBD. Every firm on this list of major firms was sent a questionnaire. The other stratum consisted of all other firms in the CBD.

A systematic random sample of the firms in the second stratum was selected from *Polk's City of Tulsa Directory* (a reverse directory). The sample size for this stratum was 218. Together, then, the total sample had 372 elements.

Of the 372 questionnaires sent out, 11 were undeliverable or otherwise unusable, leaving a true sample size of 361. Two hundred nineteen of the 361 remaining questionnaires were filled out and returned. Thus, the survey yielded approximately a 61 percent response rate. Case Table 9.1 indicates the pattern of responses according to pretest, main test, and follow-up. Case Table 9.2 indicates the composition of the respondents according to designation by stratum.

To ensure a high response rate, researchers sent an advance notification letter to all firms selected in the sample, then a cover letter from the president of the Chamber of Commerce was included with a questionnaire (see Case Exhibit 9.1). A follow-up letter (with second questionnaire included) was sent to those firms that did not respond after three weeks had elapsed. Researchers made telephone calls to certain key firms that did not respond after six weeks had elapsed, asking if the questionnaires had been received and if they could be completed and returned.

Questions

1. Is a mail survey the best way to contact business executives in this situation?
2. Evaluate the sampling design in this case.
3. Does the questionnaire appear to satisfy the research objective? Why or why not?

CASE EXHIBIT 9.1 | **SURVEY OF TULSA EXECUTIVES**

INSTRUCTIONS

This is a survey concerning firms in *Tulsa's Central Business District (CBD).* Technically, we are referring to the area within the *inner dispersal loop* and not "suburban" Tulsa. As you respond to this questionnaire, answer only about your firm's *Central Business District (downtown)* operations.

Is the person to whom this letter was addressed the "right" person to answer the questionnaire?
If not, will you please give the letter and questionnaire to the person who is best able to respond to the questions and ask him or her to complete the questionnaire for us?

Case Exhibit 9.1 | **Survey of Tulsa Executives (Continued)**

EXECUTIVE OPINION SURVEY

First, we would like to ask you some *general* questions about Tulsa's Central Business District (CBD). Please check (✔) your answer.

1. Overall, how would you rate business conditions in Tulsa's Central Business District?
   ☐ Excellent ☐ Good ☐ Fair ☐ Poor ☐ Very poor
2. Would you say Tulsa's Central Business District is more or less suitable for your business now than it was five years ago? (If not in operation five years ago, use the date when you started your business.)
   ☐ More suitable ☐ Same ☐ Less suitable ☐ No opinion
3. If past trends continue, would you predict there will be fewer, more, or the same number of firms in Tulsa's Central Business District next year?
   ☐ Fewer ☐ More ☐ Same

The following statements are things that some businesspeople have said about Tulsa's Central Business District.

Please indicate your degree of agreement with the statement below. Please *circle* if you strongly agree, mildly agree, neither agree nor disagree, mildly disagree, or strongly disagree.

4. Tulsa's Central Business District is an active retail center (shopping complex).
   Strongly Agree | Mildly Agree | Neither Agree nor Disagree | Mildly Disagree | Strongly Disagree
5. The future of Tulsa's Central Business District looks very bright.
   Strongly Agree | Mildly Agree | Neither Agree nor Disagree | Mildly Disagree | Strongly Disagree
6. One major problem in the Tulsa Central Business District is an increasing crime rate.
   Strongly Agree | Mildly Agree | Neither Agree nor Disagree | Mildly Disagree | Strongly Disagree
7. In the next five years there will be a decreasing emphasis on the Tulsa Central Business District as a retail shopping complex.
   Strongly Agree | Mildly Agree | Neither Agree nor Disagree | Mildly Disagree | Strongly Disagree
8. Occupying an office in the Central Business District rather than elsewhere in the city has more advantages than disadvantages.
   Strongly Agree | Mildly Agree | Neither Agree nor Disagree | Mildly Disagree | Strongly Disagree
9. Off-street parking in the Tulsa Central Business District is inadequate.
   Strongly Agree | Mildly Agree | Neither Agree nor Disagree | Mildly Disagree | Strongly Disagree
10. In the next five years the Central Business District will lose its share of occupied office space to other parts of the city.
    Strongly Agree | Mildly Agree | Neither Agree nor Disagree | Mildly Disagree | Strongly Disagree
11. The new Williams Center will be a major stimulus to downtown Tulsa and its financial future.
    Strongly Agree | Mildly Agree | Neither Agree nor Disagree | Mildly Disagree | Strongly Disagree
12. In the next five years our business will move out of Tulsa's Central Business District.
    Strongly Agree | Mildly Agree | Neither Agree nor Disagree | Mildly Disagree | Strongly Disagree
13. The Tulsa city government is very willing to respond to problems in Tulsa's Central Business District.
    Strongly Agree | Mildly Agree | Neither Agree nor Disagree | Mildly Disagree | Strongly Disagree

CASE EXHIBIT 9.1 | **SURVEY OF TULSA EXECUTIVES (CONTINUED)**

We would now like to ask you about your firm's business activity in the *Central Business District*.

If your company has offices, warehouses, factories, etc. at other locations, please provide *only* the information about your operation in the *Tulsa Central Business District*.

To determine what actions are needed to improve business conditions in your business district, it is essential that we know more about the current level of business activity in Tulsa's CBD. The remaining questions are similar to those asked by the Bureau of the Census.

Responses will be kept CONFIDENTIAL and used only to analyze the entire business area and for classification purposes (e.g., small vs. large firms). The data will NOT be used in any way that will allow determination of individual firms or the competitive position of your type of firm.

14. What is your primary business activity?
    - ☐ Manufacturing
    - ☐ Retail trade
    - ☐ Wholesale trade
    - ☐ Finance, insurance, real estate
    - ☐ Services
    - ☐ Construction
    - ☐ Agriculture, forestry, fishing
    - ☐ Mining
    - ☐ Transportation and public utilities
    - ☐ Other (please specify) ______________________

15. What was your average number of paid *full-time* employees in the Tulsa Central Business District last year?
    ____

16. Please estimate how many of these employees are managerial and how many are nonmanagerial.
    ____________ Number of managerial employees
    ____________ Number of nonmanagerial employees

17. What was your *average monthly payroll* for the firm (before deductions) in the Tulsa Central Business District last year? ______________________

18. What was the distribution of your firm's payroll to *full-time* employees in the Central Business District?

Annual Salary/Wage Range	Number of Employees
Under $20,000	________
$20,000–$39,999	________
$40,000–$59,999	________
$60,000–$89,999	________
$90,000 or over	________

19. Approximately how much *office space* does your company or business organization *occupy* in the Tulsa Central Business District?
    ____________ Office space in square feet
    ____________ Other space in square feet

20. Does your business operation in the Tulsa Central Business District generate sales revenue from customers buying *within* the Central Business District?
    - ☐ Yes (Go to Question 21)
    - ☐ No (Go to Question 22)

21. If yes, please estimate your dollar sales volume for the last fiscal year from customers buying within Tulsa's Central Business District.
    $______________

22. In what year did you start operating your business in the Tulsa Central Business District?
    ____

23. Do you intend to invest in capital improvement for expansion or remodeling of your Central Business District facility in the next five years?
    ____________ Yes (Go to Question 24)
    ____________ No (Thank you for completing the questionnaire.)
    ____________ Uncertain (Thank you for completing the questionnaire.)

24. If yes, approximately how much do you intend to invest?
    $______________

Thank you very much for your cooperation. Please return the completed questionnaire in the postage-paid envelope at your earliest convenience.

Case Table 9.1 | **Response Patterns**

	Number Sent Out	Number Returned	Percentage of Number Sent Out	Percentage of Total Number Returned
Pretest	36	24	66.7%	11.0%
Main test[a]	325	144	44.3	65.7
Follow-up	181	51	28.2	23.3
Total	361	219	60.7	100.0

[a]Excluding 11 undeliverable.

Case Table 9.2 | **Response Patterns by Stratum**

	Number Returned	Percentage of Number Sent Out	Percentage of Respondents
Stratum 1: "Major" firms	101	63.125%	46.119%
Stratum 2: "Random" firms	118	55.660	53.881
Total	219		100.000

CASE 10

THE GREETING CARD STUDY

Selected adult members of a consumer panel were sent the following cover letter and a questionnaire referred to as a *purchase diary* (the purchase diary form is not shown here).

> We are presently conducting a study for a greeting card manufacturer who, in order to be able to provide the "right card for the right person," would like to know the type of cards being purchased now—and to whom they are being sent. We are asking our members to participate in this project by keeping a record of the greeting cards they purchase and receive during the next month.
>
> As a participant, here is what we would like you to do.
>
> 1. Please record all purchases of greeting cards made by you and members of your household in the green purchase diary form provided for July. It is most important for this study that we have the information on ALL cards purchased by EVERYONE in your

household. Please make it known that as soon as someone in your household purchases a greeting card, he or she should either show you the card or give you the appropriate information so that you can make the diary entry as soon after the purchase as possible.

Section 1 is for entries of individual greeting cards; Section 2 is to record the purchase of boxes or packages of cards.

2. Here is the very unusual part of this study. Please save all of the greeting cards you and other members of your household receive during the month of July and follow "Instructions for Cards Received" (blue page).

Accurate reporting is very important, so please read the instruction page for each form carefully.

Your report will be for the month of July, so on July 31st—or as soon after as possible—please return the appropriate materials. (We've enclosed a postage-paid envelope for your convenience.)

Your cooperation is deeply appreciated. We are sending you a dollar bill, as a token of our sincere thanks for your time and effort. Thank you very much!

Questions

1. Evaluate the cover letter. What type of appeal is used? Does the format of the cover letter follow the pattern indicated in the book?
2. In your opinion, will respondents comply with the researcher's request? Why or why not?
3. What sources of survey error are most likely in a study of this type?

CASE 11

THE EVERGREEN COMPANY

A married woman working at the Evergreen Company put the following note in the company's suggestion box:

> It would make life a lot easier for employees with children if our company had an on-site day care center.

Many members of the executive committee that reviewed employee suggestions favored further study of the idea of locating a day care center at the company headquarters and plant. A committee member suggested conducting an employee survey.

Questions

1. What are the primary information needs of the Evergreen Company?
2. What type of survey research design should be used in this study?
3. Design a questionnaire to satisfy the Evergreen Company's information needs.

CASE

TULSA'S CENTRAL BUSINESS DISTRICT (C)

The Metropolitan Tulsa Chamber of Commerce recognized that there was a critical gap between the timely information available about the central business district (CBD) and the information needed for investment decision making, commercial marketing efforts, and the continued pursuit of the goal of downtown revitalization. The Chamber of Commerce undertook four separate research projects to gather information about the CBD. One project was a physical inventory of the existing downtown commercial base. The objectives of the study were to determine what types of establishments were operating in the CBD and the number of vacancies there and to generally profile the commercial geography of the CBD. The researchers found that the CBD was based on the U.S. Bureau of the Census classification scheme. The CBD was identified as the area encompassed by the inner dispersal loop (a system of expressways), which corresponded identically with Census Tract 25 (see Case Exhibit 12.1).

A team of ten pedestrian fieldworkers covered each block in the inner dispersal loop. Fieldworkers utilized the observation form in Case Exhibit 12.2 to record the company name, address, primary business activity, estimated frontage, and other relevant information about each building site or office. Fieldworkers recorded Standard Industrial Classification (SIC) codes

CASE EXHIBIT 12.1 CENSUS BLOCKS IN CENSUS TRACT 25

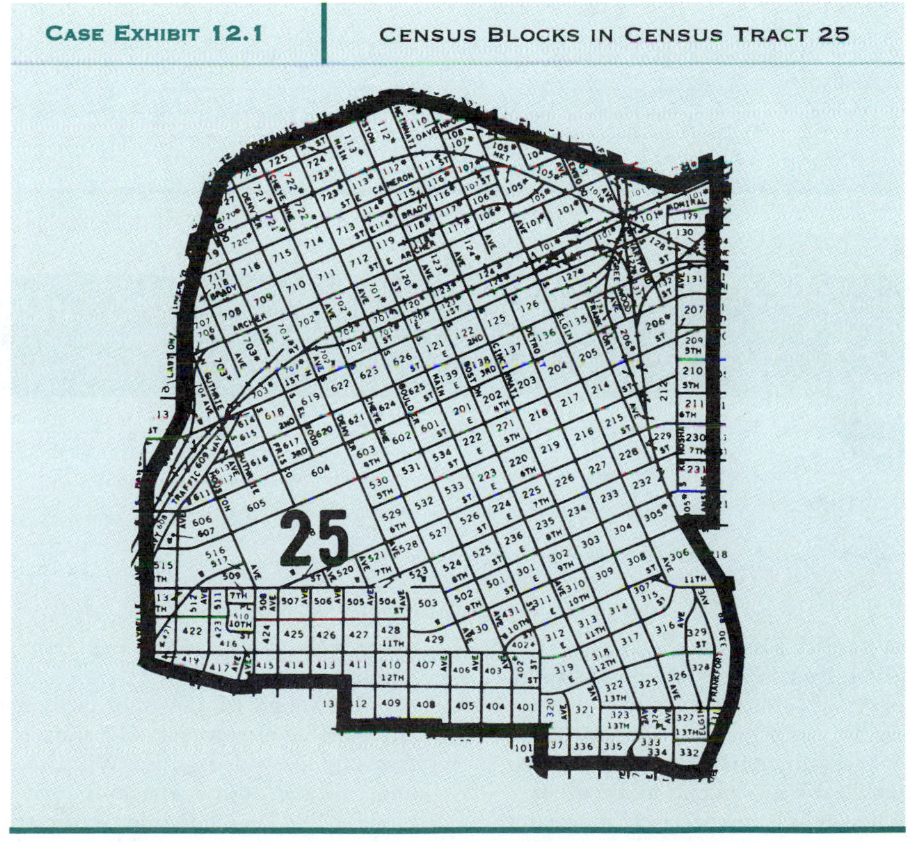

for retailers. SIC codes for all other establishments were recorded by research assistants after the data were collected. All the data were identified by census block.

Questions

1. Evaluate the research design in this case.
2. What changes, if any, would you make in the observation form?
3. What problems would you expect in the data collection stage?
4. What techniques would you use to analyze the data?

CASE EXHIBIT 12.2 | **OBSERVATION STUDY QUESTIONNAIRE**

Company Name ____________________

Address ____________________
____
____
Tulsa, Oklahoma

Activities: ___1 Vacant ___2 Retail ___3 Wholesale ___4 Manufacturing
___5 Service ___6 Other (Specify) ________

Retail SIC ___52 ___53 ___54 ___55 ___56 ___57 ___58
___59 ___60

Other activities (describe) ____________________
____

Is the building: ___1 For sale?
___2 For rent?

Leasable space ____________________
Realtor's name ____________________
Realtor's phone ____________________
Rent (per sq. foot) ____________________

Is the building being: ___1 Restored?
___2 Remodeled?

Estimated frontage (feet) ____________________
Estimated number of stories ____________________

Comments ____________________
____
____

CASE 13

THE PRETESTING COMPANY

Basically it looks like a desk lamp with a chunky smoked-glass body.[12] In fact, it is Lee Weinblatt's People Reader, a device designed to surreptitiously monitor the way people react to magazine advertising. Behind the smoked glass are two tiny, remote-controlled video cameras, one that tracks eye movements and another that monitors which page is being perused. In a nearby office, technicians measure each dismissive glance and longing gaze.

Will a high school senior unconsciously dwell on an Air Force recruitment ad featuring computer screens that look like video games? Will a middle-aged man linger over an automobile ad featuring leggy female models? The People Reader was intended to answer questions like these for companies that spend millions of dollars on advertising and, in the past, have had to depend on the accuracy of a test subject's memory.

Mr. Weinblatt, 43 years old, is founder of the Pretesting Company, a 15-year-old concern in Englewood, New Jersey, that has become the leader in sleight-of-hand advertising research. He has developed an extensive bag of tricks, some of them incorporating technology originally developed for espionage. The People Reader is one; another is a mock car radio that plays prerecorded material and measures the speed with which a driver silences a commercial. There is also a television system that measures the tendency of viewers armed with remote-control devices to "zap" a particular commercial and a computer-simulated supermarket to measure the allure of a new package. Mr. Weinblatt has hidden video cameras in a fake bar of Ivory soap, in a box of cereal ("old hat" now, he says), and in a ceiling sprinkler.

The unifying theme of Mr. Weinblatt's technology is eliciting responses consumers may not be aware of. Typically, people being tested are given only a limited idea—and often the wrong one—about what is actually being measured.

Since starting his company in 1985, Mr. Weinblatt has acquired an impressive list of clients, including Ralston Purina, RJR Nabisco's Planter's peanuts, S. C. Johnson's Raid insecticide, *Sports Illustrated,* and *The New Yorker.* Although Pretesting remains small, with revenues of $5.5 million, clients say Mr. Weinblatt offers them insights unlike those generated by any other advertising researchers. "I've recommended his tests many times," said Sue Le Barron, a project manager for pet food marketing research at Ralston Purina.

Traditionally, advertising research has been based on fairly overt approaches. To test a proposed television ad, for example, companies arrange to transmit the commercials to television sets of test subjects during normal programming and then interview them the next day on their ability to remember the ad and on their reactions. Similarly, the traditional method of pretesting a new package or design is to expose it to a "focus group" of consumers who examine and react to it. Mr. Weinblatt argues that such techniques provide at best a murky picture, often failing to measure the impact of subliminal messages or, in the case of focus groups, prompting judgments in situations that don't mirror real life.

"Diagnostic research can be very useful for understanding what the problem is with a product, but it can never tell you what people are going to do in the real world," said Mr. Weinblatt. "Do people read *Newsweek* from the front or the back? How do you time the sequence of television ads? How does print stack up against TV? The questions have been piling up."

Mr. Weinblatt has been tinkering with attention-measuring devices since 1971. Armed with a master's degree in industrial psychology (and, later, in photography), he started out with the research subsidiary of the Interpublic Group of Companies Inc., which owns several major advertising agencies.

At the time, many advertising researchers were experimenting with "pupilmetrics," the measurement of pupil dilation, by filming people who were strapped into chairs and whose heads were anchored into wax molds. Mr. Weinblatt designed equipment that was less intrusive. His first assignment came from Philip Morris, which, he said, wanted to find the least noticeable place to mount warning labels required by the Surgeon General on a pack of cigarettes. "We found out that it didn't make any difference," said Mr. Weinblatt. "Smokers don't want to see."

In 1976, Mr. Weinblatt started Telcom Research, a manufacturer of portable eye movement recorders, which he sold in 1982, just before it was about to go bankrupt. He continued inventing increasingly unobtrusive measurement devices and founded the Pretesting Company in 1985. Today he holds 28 patents.

To measure the chances that consumers will be attracted to a new package on crowded supermarket shelves, Mr. Weinblatt developed a computer-simulated shopping spree. Researchers evaluating a new line of dog food, for example, begin by recreating a supermarket rack in the dog food section that contains the new package. They then photograph the shelf as a whole and take close-ups of each quadrant of the shelf. This material is mixed in with similar sequences depicting the store entrance and several other supermarket sections.

People being tested are then told to "walk" through the store by reviewing slides of these images on a screen. Pressing buttons on a controller, they can move forward or backward between shelves and move in for closeups. At each section they are asked to pick out what, if anything, they would like to buy. Their answers, however, constitute only a small part of the test. The key measurements, according to Mr. Weinblatt, are based on the way they move through the slides. Unknown to the customers, a computer linked to the controller logs the amount of time spent at each picture and provides an instant tabulation of how long a person lingered at the dog food rack and at the particular part of it containing the new product. Those data, in turn, can be compared with data for the rest of the supermarket and for competing products.

Mr. Weinblatt concedes there have been instances in which he incorrectly predicted that a commercial would fail. Nevertheless, he argues, his measurements offer crucial information in a world of cluttered store shelves, where nine out of ten new products fail. "The typical person spends 22 minutes shopping in a supermarket that contains 18,000 products," said Mr. Weinblatt. "What we're saying is, before you bet all that money on a new product, let's do the ideal and see if people are even going to notice it."

Question

Evaluate each observation technique used by the Pretesting Company. What possible applications might each technique have?

CASE 14

PROFESSIONAL RECRUITERS

Professional Recruiters, a consulting firm that specializes in helping large corporations improve their recruiting efforts among college students, decided it needed sound information about job-rating criteria used by MBA students. More specifically, the firm wanted to examine selected evaluation criteria utilized by college graduates when considering jobs and job offers encountered in the recruiting process. What are students looking for when they consider their future careers? What really motivates acceptance of a job offer?

In particular, the consulting firm hypothesized that there was an increased interest among college students in the place of business in society. Professional Recruiters questioned whether the social responsibility exhibited by a firm could be a significant influence in the job selection process. They wanted to know if corporate recruiters should stress salary or their firms' social responsibility. After reviewing some academic literature in the organizational behavior field, Professional Recruiters concluded that the nature of the work, opportunity for advancement, and salary, in that order, are the major factors influencing students as they make their job selections.

The researchers noted that past research dealing with the factors influencing job selection had been based primarily on findings from survey research. They thought that using a research format that merely asks students which factors are important in job selection may be biased by the social desirability of certain answers. For example, rating a firm's social responsibility as an important job determinant factor has some potential for response bias because of the obvious desirability of positive answers. The researchers chose to utilize an experimental method to provide better control of the variables influencing job selection and to secure information on relationships among selected factors expected to influence job selection.

The subjects for the experiment were 36 male MBA students at a prestigious state university. The sample was selected because researching MBA students offers the best chance of comparing experimental results with past findings. Only MBA students then currently interviewing for positions in anticipation of graduation at the conclusion of the spring or summer term were included in the study.

Each subject participated in four separate experiments. The subjects were presented with a series of job offers to which they indicated their probability of acceptance. In each situation two of the variables of interest were paired.

The four situational pairings were salary/interesting work, salary/social responsibility, interesting work/social responsibility, and interesting work/opportunity for advancement. Three levels of monthly salary (\$3,450, \$4,000, and \$4,450) and two values (high and low) of interesting work, opportunity for advancement, and social responsibility were utilized.

Thus, the design produced a 3 × 2 matrix when salary was one of the paired variables. In other cases, because all other variables had two values, a 2 × 2 matrix resulted. Six subjects were placed in each cell of the 3 × 2 matrix and nine subjects in each cell of the 2 × 2 matrix. For example, a student might be asked to respond to a situation in which the work was *interesting* but the company was *low in social responsibility:*

> You have been offered a position with a well-known company in your area of academic specialization or interest. The salary appears to be competitive. From the interview you have gained some impressions about what your future activities would consist of. It appears that the job will be challenging and the nature of your proposed future activities appeals to you. After the interview you discussed the job with one of your friends, who had also interviewed with

this company. He has informed you that the company has recently been in the news because it is being sued for water and air pollution.

The MBA students were then asked to indicate their estimate of the chance of their accepting a position:

_____ 100% (Certain) I will accept
_____ 90% (Almost sure) I will accept
_____ 80% (Very big chance) I will accept
_____ 70% (Big chance) I will accept
_____ 60% (Not so big a chance) I will accept
_____ 50% (About even) I will accept
_____ 40% (Smaller chance) I will accept
_____ 30% (Small chance) I will accept
_____ 20% (Very small chance) I will accept
_____ 10% (Almost certainly not) I will accept
_____ 0% (Certainly not) I will accept

Descriptions of job offers for several other situational pairings are given below.

Low Salary/Low Interesting Work:

You have been offered a position in your area of academic specialization or interest at a starting salary of $3,450 per month with a well-known company. Before your interview with the company, you looked into the organization and found that it was well established in its industrial classification and all indications were that it would actually be expanding its activities in the future. During the interview itself, you got the impression from both the job description and the discussion with the company's representative that your particular job does not appear to be a great challenge and the nature of the work does not really appeal to you.

High Salary/High Social Responsibility:

A well-known company has offered you a job at a salary of $4,450 per month in your area of academic specialization or interest. Because of your recent interest in the company, you have noticed a series of articles in newspapers covering its activities. The company seems assured of stability in the near future because of good consumer acceptance of its most recent product line. You have also noticed that the company has a good record of social responsibility and has actively led civic campaigns to clean up the environment.

High Opportunity for Advancement/
Low Interesting Work:

A well-known company has offered you a position in your area of academic specialization or interest. The salary is competitive. At the campus interview, you got the impression that the opportunity for advancement is high and you are assured of moving up the ladder quickly. From the interview it also appears that the job is not challenging and your proposed future activities do not appeal to you.

Questions

1. What type of experimental design is this?
2. Evaluate the research design in this case.
3. What type of statistical analysis would be required to analyze the data obtained from this experiment?

CASE 15

HAMILTON POWER TOOLS (B)

Hamilton Power Tools, like many organizations, generated a large percentage of its profits from new products. In its chain saw division the company was increasingly focusing attention on the casual-user market segment's need for chain saws [see Case 4: Hamilton Power Tools (A)].

Because of a competitor's actions, Bill Campagna, marketing manager, had to make a decision. Recently a major competitor, McCulloch, had introduced a six-pound chain saw. Prior to this, Hamilton's 9-pound chain saw was the world's lightest chain saw. Campagna believed this competitive move took away a substantial promotional advantage because it eliminated Hamilton's ability to say that all other chain saws were heavier than its HL-9 model. Reacting to McCulloch's strategy, Hamilton's engineers produced a prototype of a 6-pound chain saw made of wood and existing chain saw parts. It looked almost exactly like a real chain saw.

A business research study was conducted to gain insights into whether consumers preferred the experimental six-pound chain saw (the HL-6) over Hamilton's existing HL-9 chain saw and over McCulloch's 6-pound chain saw. The basic research design was a personal interview asking consumers to compare the various models. (The McCulloch, originally painted yellow, was painted red and white to avoid any color bias. Thus, all three experimental chain saws were red and white.)

The basic assumption underlying the research was that all these chain saws would be marketed to male homeowners and not to professional, institutional, or farm users of chain saws. It was also assumed that the prices of the three chain saws would be comparable.

Hamilton's headquarters were in northern Illinois. To reduce costs, the study used cluster sampling within Illinois and Wisconsin. Each county within these states had an equal chance of being selected as a cluster. Researchers consulted secondary data to determine the number of households with annual incomes of $100,000 or more within each county selected as a cluster. Then a judgmental proportion of all households in the county was selected. Where street maps of the counties were available, smaller areas were randomly selected and interviews were conducted at every third house on every block within each area. In rural areas for which street maps were not available, individual towns were randomly selected and interviewing took place at every third house until the quota was reached.

Personal interviews were used to collect the data at respondents' homes. As it was assumed that the researchers were concerned primarily with the opinions of men already familiar with chain saws, the first few questions of the survey asked for information to qualify respondents by either ownership of a chain saw, previous use, or plans for future purchase. Only men familiar with chain saws were interviewed.

In the remainder of the interview, each respondent was asked to choose between a pair of unidentified chain saws and state his preference for one or the other. A total of three pairs of chain saws were shown to each respondent. Thus, after indicating a preference from the first pair of chain saws, the respondent was asked to choose between that chain saw and another one that had not been previously shown. Finally, the third pair of chain saws shown to the respondent consisted of the "losing" chain saw from the first comparison and the chain saw with which it had not yet been paired (either the losing chain saw from the second comparison if the same chain saw was preferred in both the first and the second comparisons or the chain saw selected in the second comparison if different from the first choice). The chain saws shown in the first pair were randomly rotated to avoid any bias caused by the presentation of any pair of chain saws first.

Questions

1. Evaluate this research design.
2. Is this an experiment? Why or why not?

CASE 16

THE CLEVELAND CLINIC FOUNDATION IN JACOBS FIELD

In 1995, Jacobs Field, a new downtown ballpark, opened as the home of the Cleveland Indians American League baseball club.[13] The research department of the Cleveland Clinic Foundation (CCF) had the responsibility of evaluating the foundation's advertising signage (billboards) in the stadium.

In its arrangement with the Cleveland Indians, CCF had two signs: (1) a large mural in the lower level concourse along which spectators walked to reach their seats and buy food and souvenirs and (2) a sign in the upper right-hand corner of the large main scoreboard behind center field. The latter was a revolving sign, rotating repeatedly at several-minute intervals throughout each game and alternating between CCF's bright green-and-gold display and ads for Ford and McDonald's.

STRIKING OUT

The purpose of the study was to develop an initial empirical determination of the level of awareness and image association provided by the signage at Jacobs Field as measures of effectiveness of billboard advertising at a sports stadium.

Originally, the researchers selected a panel of respondents on the basis of demographic and geographic distribution of members of the population who typically visit Jacobs Field. A sample of respondents was contacted about the image of organizations in Cleveland as a pretest of awareness.

Respondents then were given two tickets to a specific Cleveland Indians game to be played in August. The plan was to follow up after the game with individuals who attended to measure their awareness of the advertising compared to the pretest results.

Unfortunately, the baseball players' strike that year made this methodology impossible to carry out. The research team, however, was able to modify the design when the strike prevented the original sample from attending games in late August.

PINCH HITTING

As an alternative methodology, the researchers used a local market research firm to conduct a survey of 300 respondents. This approach replaced the before/after results sought in the initial methodology.

The sample was drawn using a random-digit-dialing technique called "plus-one." Respondents were screened to ensure that neither they nor any member of their household worked for an ad agency or a market research firm. Trained interviewers then administered a structured questionnaire during day and evening hours to ensure that both employed and unemployed consumers were represented. The sample contained nonattendees (no games), infrequent attendees (1–3 games), and frequent attendees (4+ games).

After careful examination of the results provided by the market research firm, the researchers determined that the 25–34 age group was disproportionately represented in the "frequent attendance" group, and the 65+ age group was disproportionately represented in the "no attendance" group. A subsample ($n = 179$) of respondents between the ages of 35 and 64 was drawn from the original sample to create a more evenly distributed sample. The breakdown of nonattendees and attendees by these three age groups is shown in Case Exhibit 16.1.

The demographic characteristics of this subsample included

- An even distribution of male and female respondents (46% and 54%, respectively).
- A normal distribution with respect to education and income levels, with the larger percentages occurring in the middle categories of "some college to college graduate (49%)."
- Earnings of $35,000–$74,900 per year (53%).

In the questionnaire, respondents were asked several questions to tap their (unaided) awareness of "well-managed companies or organizations in Northeastern Ohio." Of all the companies named, CCF ranked fifth in number of mentions. When asked to name the medical facility or hospital that first came to mind in Northeastern Ohio, CCF was mentioned first by 45% of the total sample. Of the total mentions of awareness of medical facilities in Northeastern Ohio, CCF was mentioned by 80 percent of respondents (see Case Exhibit 16.2).

Respondents who said they attended 1–3 games or 4+ games were asked which companies came to mind when they thought of companies advertising at Jacobs Field. Unaided awareness of CCF's signage increased with number of games attended, as did total awareness.

Unaided recall of CCF signage at the ballpark was relatively low (7% of the total sample; 10% of those attending 4+ games). However, total awareness was moderate; more than one-third of the respondents who had been to the ballpark remembered seeing CCF's advertising.

As the frequency of attendance at the ballpark increased, so did the likelihood of recall. Only 30 percent of those who saw 1–3 games remembered the sign, whereas 40 percent of those seeing 4+ games recalled it.

Respondents who remembered seeing the advertising recalled obvious characteristics such as the CCF name and the location of the ad on the scoreboard. Frequent attendees were more likely to remember other items, such as the gold-and-green coloring, the logo, and the fact that the ad was not stationary.

Finally, and possibly most noteworthy, those respondents who had been to Jacobs Field were more likely to select CCF as a well-managed company and more likely to say they would use CCF if they required medical care within the next 12 months.

Several recent studies have examined the effectiveness of outdoor, or billboard, advertising. These studies conclude that the effectiveness of this type of advertising is dependent on the viewer's recall, retention, and actual usage of the product or service being advertised. For example, researchers have investigated the independent factors that influence aided and unaided recall of outdoor advertising—factors such as type of product, brand differentiation, type of appeal, size and position of signage, color, number of words, legibility, the subject's experience with the product or service, and attitudes toward advertising. Some factors may be controlled, such as the creativity and illustration of the product.

The business press has reported on new display technology and the general impressions made by billboard advertising during sporting events, but none of the reports has focused on systematic investigations of specific variables related to the effectiveness of such signage.

One common theme has been the size of the audience that local and international network television can bring to stadium signage. With continuing advances in technology and communication networks, sport stadium and arena billboard advertising in one city might be seen simultaneously around the world. "High-tech" advertising includes such signage as AdTime, the rotating signage located in 14 National Basketball Association arenas, and perimeter billboards used during the televised coverage of the 52 World Cup soccer matches.

Billboards in baseball stadiums are located anywhere from peripheral locations on left- and right-field walls or behind the foul line to more obvious spots on the scoreboard and behind home plate.

Questions

1. What type of research design was originally planned? What are the strengths and weaknesses of this design?
2. What type of research design was actually conducted? What are the strengths and weaknesses of this design?
3. What conclusions can be drawn from the findings?

Case Exhibit 16.1 Age by Number of Visits to Jacobs Field

	No Games	1–3 Games	4+ Games	Total
35–44 years	29	28	25	82
	48%	46%	43%	46%
45–54 years	19	25	24	68
	32%	41%	41%	38%
55–64 years	12	8	9	29
	20%	13%	16%	16%
Total	**60**	**61**	**58**	**179**

Case Exhibit 16.2 Awareness and Impression by Number of Games Attended

	No Games	1–3 Games	4+ Games	Total
Unaided awareness of medical facilities in Northeast Ohio (First mention = CCF)	42%	44%	50%	45%
Unaided awareness of medical facilities in Northeast Ohio (CCF total mentions)	80%	80%	81%	80%
If you needed a medical facility in the next 12 months, how likely would you be to use CCF? (% very likely)	42%	55%	53%	50%
Unaided awareness of CCF advertising at Jacobs Field	—	3%	10%	7%
Total awareness of CCF advertising at Jacobs Field	—	30%	40%	34%
(n = 179)				

CASE

17

FLYAWAY AIRWAYS

Wesley Shocker, research analyst for FlyAway Airways, has been asked by the director of research to make recommendations regarding the best approach for monitoring the quality of service provided by the airline.[14] FlyAway Airways is a national air carrier that has a comprehensive route structure consisting of long-haul, coast-to-coast routes and direct, nonstop routes between short-haul metropolitan areas. Current competitors include Midway and Alaska Airlines.

FlyAway Airways is poised to surpass the billion-dollar revenue level required to be designated as a major airline. This change in status brings a new set of competitors. To prepare for this move up in competitive status, Shocker has been asked to review the options available for monitoring the quality of FlyAway Airways service and the service of its competitors. Such monitoring would involve better understanding the nature of service quality and the ways in which quality can be tracked for airlines.

After some investigation, Shocker discovered two basic approaches to measuring quality of airline service that can produce similar ranking results. His report must outline the important aspects to consider in measuring quality as well as the critical points of difference and similarities between the two approaches to measuring quality.

SOME BACKGROUND ON QUALITY

In today's competitive airline industry, it's crucial that an airline do all it can to attract and retain customers. One of the best ways to do this is by offering quality service to consumers. Perceptions of service quality vary from person to person, but an enduring element of service quality is the consistent achievement of customer satisfaction. For customers to perceive an airline as a valued, quality service, they must be satisfied, and that usually means receiving a service outcome that is equal to or greater than what they expected.

An airline consumer usually is concerned most with issues of schedule, destination, and price when choosing an airline. Given that most airlines have competition in each of these areas, other factors that relate to quality become important to the customer when making a choice between airlines. Both subjective aspects of quality (i.e., food, pleasant employees) and objective aspects (i.e., on-time performance, safety, lost baggage) have real meaning to consumers. These secondary factors may not be as critical as schedule, destination, and price, but they do affect a customer's quality judgments.

There are many possible combinations of subjective and objective aspects that could influence a customer's perception of quality at different times. Fortunately, since 1988 consumers of airline services have had access to objective information from the Department of Transportation regarding service performance in some basic categories. Unfortunately, the average consumer is most likely unaware of or uninterested in these data on performance; instead, consumers rely on personal experience and subjective opinion to judge quality of service. Periodic surveys of subjective consumer opinion regarding airline service experience are available through several sources. These efforts rely on contact with a sample of consumers who may or may not have an informed opinion regarding the quality of airline service for all airlines being compared.

CONSUMER SURVEYS

In his research, Shocker discovered a large study conducted to identify favorite airlines of frequent flyers. This study is typical of the survey-based, infrequent (usually only annually), subjective research efforts conducted to assess airline quality. A New York firm, Research & Forecasts, Inc., published results of a consumer survey of frequent flyers that used several criteria to rate domestic and international airlines. Criteria included comfort, service, reliability, quality of food, cost, delays, routes served, safety, and frequent flyer plans. The survey was sent to 25,000 frequent flyers.

The 4,462 people who responded were characterized as predominantly male (59 percent) professional managers (66 percent) whose average age was 45 and who traveled an average of at least 43 nights a year for both business and pleasure. This group indicated that the most important factors in choosing an airline were: (1) route structure (46 percent); (2) price (42 percent); (3) reliability (41 percent); (4) service (33 percent);

(5) safety (33 percent); (6) frequent-flyer plans (33 percent); and (7) food (12 percent). When asked to rate twenty airlines, respondents provided the following rankings:

1. American
2. United
3. Delta
4. TWA
5. SwissAir
6. Singapore
7. British Airways
8. Continental
9. Air France
10. Pan Am
11. Lufthansa
12. USAir
13. KLM
14. America West
15. JAL
16. Alaska
17. Qantas
18. Midway
19. Southwest
20. SAS

WEIGHTED-AVERAGE RANKINGS

Besides the survey, Shocker also discovered a newer, more objective approach to measuring airline quality in a study recently published by the National Institute for Aviation Research at the Wichita State University in Wichita, Kansas. The Airline Quality Rating (AQR) is a weighted average of 19 factors that have relevance when judging the quality of airline services (see Case Exhibit 17.1). The AQR is based on data that are readily obtainable (most of the data are updated monthly) from published sources for each major airline operating in the United States. Regularly published data on such factors as consumer complaints, on-time performance, accidents, number of aircraft, and financial performance are available from the Department of Transportation, the National Transportation Safety Board, Moody's Bond Record, industry trade publications, and annual reports of individual airlines.

To establish the 19 weighted factors, an opinion survey was conducted with a group of 65 experts in the aviation field. These experts included representatives of most major airlines, air travel experts, FAA representatives, academic researchers, airline manufacturing and support firms, and individual consumers. Each expert was asked to rate the importance that each individual factor might have to a consumer of airline services, using a scale of 0 (no importance) to 10 (great importance). The average importance ratings for each of the 19 factors was then used as the weight for that factor in the AQR. Case Exhibit 17.1 shows the factors included in the Airline Quality Rating, the weight associated with each factor and whether the factor has a positive or negative impact on quality from the consumer's perspective.

Using the Airline Quality Rating formula and recent data gives the following AQR scores and rankings for the ten major U.S. airlines:

Rank Score	Airline	AQR
1	American	+.328
2	Southwest	+.254
3	Delta	+.209
4	United	+.119
5	USAir	+.054
6	Pan Am	+.003
7	Northwest	−.063
8	Continental	−.346
9	America West	−.377
10	TWA	−.439

WHAT COURSE TO CHART?

Shocker has discovered what appear to be two different approaches to measuring quality of airlines. One relies on direct consumer opinion and is mostly subjective in its approach to quality and the elements considered. The other relies on performance data that are available through public sources and appear to be more objective. Both approaches incorporate pertinent elements that could be used by consumers to judge the quality of an airline. Shocker's recommendation must consider the comprehensiveness and usefulness of the approach for FlyAway Airways as the firm moves into a more competitive environment. What course of action should he recommend?

Questions

1. How comparable are the two methods? In what ways are they similar? In what ways are they different?
2. What positive and negative aspects of each approach should Shocker consider before recommending a course of action for FlyAway Airways?
3. What aspects of service quality does each approach address well and not so well?
4. Considering the two methods outlined, what types of validity would you consider to be demonstrated by the two approaches to measuring quality? Defend your position.
5. Which of the methods should Shocker recommend? Why?

CASE EXHIBIT 17.1 | **FACTORS INCLUDED IN THE AIRLINE QUALITY RATING (AQR)[a]**

Factor	Weight
1. Average age of fleet	−5.85
2. Number of aircraft	+4.54
3. On-time performance	+8.63
4. Load factor	−6.98
5. Pilot deviations	−8.03
6. Number of accidents	−8.38
7. Frequent flyer awards	−7.35
8. Flight problems[b]	−8.05
9. Denied boardings[b]	−8.03
10. Mishandled baggage[b]	−7.92
11. Fares[b]	−7.60
12. Customer service[b]	−7.20
13. Refunds[b]	−7.32
14. Ticketing/boarding[b]	−7.08
15. Advertising[b]	−6.82
16. Credit[b]	−5.94
17. Other[b]	−7.34
18. Financial stability	+6.52
19. Average seat-mile cost	−4.49

$$AQR = \frac{w_1F1 - w_2F2 + w_3F3 + \cdots - w_{19}F19}{w_1 + w_2 + w_3 + \cdots + w_{19}}$$

[a]The 19-item rating has a reliability coefficient (Cronbach's Alpha) of 0.87.
[b]Data for these factors come from consumer complaints registered with the Department of Transportation.

CASE 18

THE *WALL STREET JOURNAL*/ HARRIS INTERACTIVE BUSINESS SCHOOL SURVEY

The *Wall Street Journal*/Harris Interactive Business School Survey is based on the opinions of 1,600 M.B.A. recruiters.[15] All interviews were conducted online between August 23 and December 15, 2000. The 1,600 recruiters, all of whom were asked to rate schools with which they were familiar, provided a total of 2,687 school ratings. A total of 50 business schools are rated and ranked in this survey. Each school has been rated by a minimum of 20 M.B.A. recruiters (range = 20 to 109). Each school rating is based on perceptions of the school and the school's students (80%) and on the school's "mass appeal" (20%), as defined by the total number of recruiters rating that school. The final ratings in this survey range from a low of 55.3 to a high of 81.2.

The initial universe of U.S.-based schools identified for inclusion in the survey consisted of the 344 U.S. business schools accredited as of March 2000 by the International Association for Management Education. The initial universe of foreign schools identified for inclusion was the result of meetings and discussions with experts in the field of M.B.A. recruiting, including business-school deans, business-school associations, recruiters, and career-services directors.

The *Wall Street Journal*/Harris Interactive Business School Survey focuses on the opinions of recruiters who recruit full-time business-school graduates, and schools with fewer than 50 full-time graduates in their Class of 2000 were eliminated. (Although that requirement was relaxed for some schools outside the United States, all 50 schools that are rated and ranked in this survey did meet the requirement.) The final sample of business schools eligible and available for rating included 188 U.S. schools and 56 foreign schools.

THE SURVEY

The content of the recruiter survey was the result of more than a year of consultation with business-school representatives, corporate recruiters, students, search firms, independent consultants, and members of relevant associations. The goal was to identify school and student characteristics that recruiters consider most important when they make decisions about which schools to recruit from and which students to recruit.

THE RECRUITERS

Recruiters invited to take part in The *Wall Street Journal*/Harris Interactive Business School Survey were contacted by the *Wall Street Journal* and Harris Interactive via e-mail and regular mail, using contact information provided directly by the business schools from which they recruit. In addition to receiving general information about the project in the invitation, each recruiter received the URL to access the recruiter survey online and a unique password to ensure that he or she did not take the survey more than once. Each recruiter was invited to rate as many as three schools (59% rated one school, 14% rated two schools, and 27% rated three schools) and was instructed to rate only schools with which he or she had recruiting experience in the previous 2 years. Although the business schools provided the recruiter contact information and/or contacted their recruiters directly, they did not have control over which schools the recruiters chose to rate.

In addition to school ratings, recruiters were asked to provide information about their overall recruiting efforts. To maximize the likelihood that only qualified recruiters had obtained access to the survey, an audit was done on the information supplied by recruiters and any suspicious respondents and their data were removed. A total of 1,600 recruiters took part in and qualified for the survey.

CALCULATING THE RATINGS

To be rated and ranked in The *Wall Street Journal*/Harris Interactive Survey, a school had to be rated by a minimum of 20 recruiters. A school rating was calculated for all schools reaching that minimum. Each rating was based on three components:

- Perception A: The perceptions of the school on the 12 school and 13 student attributes
- Perception B: The perceptions of the school on the two overall attributes
- Mass Appeal: The number of recruiters rating the school

Calculating Perception A

Perception A (75% of overall rating) is based on recruiter ratings of each school on the 12 school and the 13 student attributes. Each recruiter was asked to rate the school using a 10-point scale where 1 = "poor performance, does not meet your needs" and 10 = "excellent performance, meets your needs very well."

1. Each individual recruiter's rating (from 1 to 10) on each of the 25 individual attributes was multiplied by the importance that recruiter gave that attribute (from 1 = "not at all important" to 4 = "very important").
2. For each individual recruiter, the sum across the 25 attributes (importance rating multiplied by the rating of school on that attribute) was divided by the total score possible. The total score possible is the total number of attributes answered (maximum of 25) multiplied by 10 (the maximum rating possible) multiplied by 4 (the maximum importance that could have been given to an attribute).
3. The final Perception A rating for each school was calculated by summing the Perception A ratings from all recruiters rating that school, dividing by the total number of recruiters for that school, and multiplying by 75 (to reflect the 75% contribution of Perception A to the overall school rating).

Calculating Perception B

The Perception B rating (5% of overall rating) consists of the two "overall" attributes—"ability to meet your overall recruiting needs in terms of the number and quality of students" and "overall value for the money invested in the recruiting effort." Individual recruiters' ratings (from 1 to 10) on the two overall attributes were summed (with a maximum possible score of 20) and divided by 4 (reflecting the 5% contribution made by this component to the overall school rating). In cases where recruiters rated only one of the two overall attributes, their rating on the answered attribute was divided by 2 (again to reflect a maximum possible rating of 5 for the Perception B component). If both overall attributes were left unrated for a particular school, no Perception B rating was contributed by that recruiter for that school.

Calculating Mass Appeal

The total number of recruiters rating each school was divided by 109 (the highest number of recruiters rating any one school) and multiplied by 20 (to reflect the 20% contribution of the Mass Appeal component to the overall school rating).

Calculating the Final Score

The final school rating is based on the sum of Perception A, Perception B, and Mass Appeal (with a maximum possible score of 100).

Recruiter ratings for each school were examined individually and outlier ratings were removed so as to prevent individual recruiters from exerting an extreme positive or negative influence on a school's overall rating. All schools with at least 20 recruiter ratings were rank-ordered based on their overall school rating. The 50 schools ranked in The *Wall Street Journal*/Harris Interactive Survey represent the 50 schools with the highest ratings overall.

Results may be found in the e-book "The Wall Street Journal Guide to Business Schools" (available at WSJbooks.com) or on the *Wall Street Journal's* Web site at http://www.careerjournal.com/specialreports/bschoolguide/20010430-alsop-thewinner.html.

Questions

1. Evaluate the survey design.
2. Is the measurement scale nominal, ordinal, interval, or ratio?
3. Do you believe this measure is reliable? Do you believe this measure is valid? Please explain.

CASE 19

OMAR'S FAST FREIGHT

Omar's Fast Freight, a regional truck transportation company, had eight offices and accompanying truck docks located in a four-state area.[16] Trucks arrived daily with inbound freight that had to be unloaded onto the truck dock and then reloaded onto smaller trucks for city delivery. The process for outbound freight was similar: The city trucks picked up the local freight that had to be unloaded onto the truck dock and then loaded onto outbound trucks going to the other cities served by Omar's Fast Freight. The nature of the transportation business required Omar's Fast Freight to operate its truck docks around the clock. Dock workers worked rotating shifts. There were three shifts:

- Day (8:00 A.M. to 3:30 P.M.)
- Evening (3:30 P.M. to midnight)
- Night (midnight to 8:00 A.M.)

Mr. Weslow, the personnel manager, had heard of some grumblings about shift work from the dock workers. He wanted to learn what the workers thought about working the rotating shift, so he decided to conduct a survey. The questionnaire used in his survey appears in Case Exhibit 19.1.

Weslow personally designed the questionnaire items concerning the rotating shift. He also thought it would be a good idea to ask some questions concerning job satisfaction. He went to the library to learn about this subject.

During his library research he found an apparently valid and reliable eight-question scale on identification with the work organization. Because he didn't want to make the questionnaire too long, he selected only three of the best questions to include in his survey.

Because Weslow also thought that some of the workers might be drinking on the job, he decided that some questions concerning the consumption of alcohol would be of value. He suspected that direct questions about whether workers drank on the job wouldn't get truthful answers. He disguised the questions by asking if individuals knew someone else who frequently consumed alcohol on the job.

Weslow wanted to impress the workers that it was important to complete the questionnaire. Therefore he personally handed out the questionnaires at the end of the evening and night shifts, asking the workers to return them the following day.

Questions

1. Evaluate the research design in this case.
2. Could any improvements be made in the questionnaire?

CASE EXHIBIT 19.1 | **SURVEY OF EMPLOYEES**

QUESTIONNAIRE

1. What part of your rotating shift are you working this week? Please check below.
   Day ______
   Evening ______
   Night ______

2. Compared to working steady days, do you feel that shift work is in conflict with your activities and responsibilities as a husband (accompanying wife in her activities, protecting her at home, etc.) such that you decide not to go on job that day?

Evening:	Very often	Often	Occasionally	Rarely	Never
Night:	Very often	Often	Occasionally	Rarely	Never

3. Compared to working steady days, do you feel that shift work is in conflict with your activities as a friend (enjoying the company of your friends, attending weddings, reunions of family and/or friends, and other get-togethers) such that you decide not to go on job that day?

Evening:	Very often	Often	Occasionally	Rarely	Never
Night:	Very often	Often	Occasionally	Rarely	Never

4. Compared to working steady days, do you feel that shift work is in conflict with your activities and responsibilities as a father (teaching your children, spending time with them, taking them to children's programs, etc.) such that you decide not to go on job that day?

Evening:	Very often	Often	Occasionally	Rarely	Never
Night:	Very often	Often	Occasionally	Rarely	Never

5. Compared to working steady days, do you feel that shift work is in conflict with your activities as a member of social organizations (attending meetings, sports events, etc.) such that you decide not to go on job that day?

Evening:	Very often	Often	Occasionally	Rarely	Never
Night:	Very often	Often	Occasionally	Rarely	Never

Now we would like to ask some questions about the psychological and physical effects of shift work.

Psychological: related to your esteem, ego status, anxiety over shift work, etc.

Physical: related to your health and bodily functions.

In Questions 6 and 7 two shift workers are expressing their views about shift work. Read both views, evaluate your position regarding them, and then check the appropriate box.

6.

Tom	Dick
Shift workers are not only out of sight but also out of mind of management. In shifts we lose our visibility to management and thus chances of growth. Working in shifts makes me feel that I am a part of a rotating machine and completely divorced from my status as a social being. One way to show my dissatisfaction with shifts is to be absent more often.	Our work is always visible to our assessors and being constantly evaluated. Good performance and regularity improve our chances of growth. Shift staff is very important to the plant and as such enjoys a special status. I try to be regular in my job for my good and for the good of the company.

Check one box:

I am like Tom.	I am more like Tom than Dick.	I am halfway between Tom and Dick.	I am more like Dick than Tom.	I am like Dick.

Case Exhibit 19.1 Survey of Employees (Continued)

7.

Bob	Pat
Shift work offers more problems than it solves. It is damaging rather than adding to our social status. On occasions (for example, at a party) I do not like people to know that I have an abnormal life routine. On such occasions I prefer skipping the job to show that shifts are no limitation on my social life.	I like shift work. It facilitates me more than it hinders my activities. Although it makes life routine somewhat abnormal, people have a clear recognition and appreciation of the contribution we are making to national growth. As such I am not facing any psychological problems in shift work.

Check one box:

I am like Bob.	I am more like Bob than Pat.	I am halfway between Bob and Pat.	I am more like Pat than Bob.	I am like Pat.

8. Compared to working steady days, while working in shifts, how often does getting proper sleep or rest become so difficult that you decide not to go on the job that day?

Evening:	Very often	Often	Occasionally	Rarely	Never
Night:	Very often	Often	Occasionally	Rarely	Never

9. Compared to working steady days, while working in shifts, how often do you feel sufficiently unwell physically (stomach upsets, bowel problems, loss of appetite) that you decide not to go on job that day?

Evening:	Very often	Often	Occasionally	Rarely	Never
Night:	Very often	Often	Occasionally	Rarely	Never

10. How satisfied are you with your work schedule, that is, with the present arrangement of your hours for work? Check one.
______ Completely satisfied with my schedule.
______ Very well satisfied.
______ I do not care what my working hours are.
______ Dissatisfied a little.
______ Very dissatisfied with my schedule.

11. If you could begin working over again in the same occupation that you are in now, how likely would you be to choose Omar's as a place to work? Check one.
(1) ______ Definitely would choose another place over Omar's.
(2) ______ Probably would choose another place over Omar's.
(3) ______ Wouldn't care much whether it was Omar's or some other place.
(4) ______ Probably would choose Omar's over another place.
(5) ______ Definitely would choose Omar's over another place.

12. How do you feel when you hear (or read about) someone criticizing Omar's or comparing Omar's unfavorably to other trucking companies? Check one.
(1) ______ It doesn't really bother me; I don't care much what other people think of Omar's.
(2) ______ It bothers me a little.
(3) ______ It bothers me quite a bit; I'm anxious to have people think well of Omar's.
(4) ______ I never hear or read such criticism.

13. How often do you leave the truck dock during lunch break?
Always ______ Very often ______ Occasionally ______ Never ______

CASE EXHIBIT 19.1 | **SURVEY OF EMPLOYEES (CONTINUED)**

14. Have you worked around someone who frequently consumed alcohol on the job?
    Yes ______ No ______
15. If yes, do you ever worry about your safety?
    Always ______ Sometimes ______ Never ______
16. How would you try to deal with employees drinking on the job?
    ____
    ____
    ____
17. In your opinion, which one of these suggestions would be most appropriate for dealing with the situation?
    ______ Employees should not be permitted to leave the plant during lunch break unless authorized.
    ______ More employee awareness through educational programs.
    ______ Adoption of stricter rules in dealing with the problem.
18. How satisfied are you with your earnings?
    ____
    ____
    ____
19. What is your age? ______
20. What is your marital status? ______________
21. Name of respondent ______________
22. Job position ______________

CASE 20

CANTERBURY TRAVELS

Hometown, located in the northcentral United States, has a population of about 50,000. There were two travel agencies in Hometown before Canterbury Travels opened its doors.

Canterbury Travels was in its second month of operation. Roxanne Freeman had expected to have more business than she actually had. She decided that she needed to conduct a survey to determine how much business there was in Hometown. She also wanted to learn if people were aware of Canterbury Travels; she thought that this survey would determine the effectiveness of her advertising.

The questionnaire that Roxanne Freeman designed is shown in Case Exhibit 20.1.

Questions

1. Critically evaluate the questionnaire.
2. Will Canterbury Travels have the information that it needs once the survey has been conducted?

Case Exhibit 20.1 | **Travel Questionnaire**

QUESTIONNAIRE

The following questionnaire pertains to a project being conducted by a local travel agency. The intent of the study is to better understand the needs and attitudes of Hometown residents toward travel agencies. The questionnaire will take only 10 to 15 minutes to fill out at your convenience. Your name will in no way be connected with the questionnaire.

1. Have you traveled out of state?
   ___ Yes ___ No
2. If yes, do you travel for:
   ___ Business
   ___ Pleasure
   ___ Both
3. How often do you travel for the above?
   ___ 0–1 times per month
   ___ 2–3 times per month
   ___ 4–5 times per month
   ___ 6 or more times per month
   ___ 0–1 times per year
   ___ 2–3 times per year
   ___ 4–5 times per year
   ___ 6 or more times per year
4. How do you make your travel arrangements?
   ___ Airline
   ___ Travel agency
   ___ Other (please specify) ______________________________
5. Did you know that travel agencies do not charge the customer for their services?
   ___ Yes ___ No
6. Please rate the following qualities that would be most important to you in the selection of a travel agency:

	Good				Bad
Free services (reservations, advice, and delivery of tickets and literature)	___	___	___	___	___
Convenient location	___	___	___	___	___
Knowledgeable personnel	___	___	___	___	___
Friendly personnel	___	___	___	___	___
Casual atmosphere	___	___	___	___	___
Revolving charge account	___	___	___	___	___
Reputation	___	___	___	___	___
Personal sales calls	___	___	___	___	___

7. Are you satisfied with your present travel agency?

	Very Satisfied				Very Dissatisfied
Holiday Travel	___	___	___	___	___
Leisure Tours	___	___	___	___	___
Canterbury Travels	___	___	___	___	___
Other	___	___	___	___	___

8. If not, what are you dissatisfied with about your travel agency?

	Good				Bad
Free services (reservations, advice, and delivery of tickets and literature)	___	___	___	___	___
Convenient location	___	___	___	___	___
Knowledgeable personnel	___	___	___	___	___
Friendly personnel	___	___	___	___	___
Casual atmosphere	___	___	___	___	___
Revolving charge account	___	___	___	___	___
Reputation	___	___	___	___	___
Personal sales calls	___	___	___	___	___

9. Did you know that there is a new travel agency in Hometown?
   ___ Yes ___ No

CASE EXHIBIT 20.1 | **TRAVEL QUESTIONNAIRE (CONTINUED)**

10. Can you list the travel agencies in Hometown and their locations?
____
____
____

11. Do you use the same travel agency repeatedly?

	0–1 times per month	2–3 times per month	4–5 times per month	6 or more times per month	0–1 times per year	2–3 times per year	4–5 times per year	6 or more times per year
Holiday Travel								
Leisure Tours								
Canterbury Travels								
Other (please specify)								

12. Have you visited the new travel agency in Hometown?
___ Yes ___ No

13. If yes, what is its name? ______________________________

14. How do you pay for your travel expenses?
___ Cash ___ Company charge
___ Check ___ Personal charge
___ Credit card ___ Other

15. Which of these have you seen advertising for?
___ Holiday Travel
___ Leisure Tours
___ Canterbury Travels
___ Other ______________________________

16. If yes, where have you seen or heard this advertisement?

17. Would you consider changing travel agencies?
___ Yes ___ No

The following are some personal questions about you that will be used for statistical purposes only. Your answers will be held in the strictest confidence.

18. What is your age?
___ 19–25 ___ 46–55
___ 26–35 ___ 56–65
___ 36–45 ___ Over 65

19. What is your sex?
___ Male ___ Female

20. What is your marital status?
___ Single ___ Divorced
___ Married ___ Widowed

21. How long have you lived in Hometown?
___ 0–6 months ___ 5–10 years
___ 7–12 months ___ 11–15 years
___ 1–4 years ___ Over 15 years

CASE EXHIBIT 20.1 | **TRAVEL QUESTIONNAIRE (CONTINUED)**

22. What is your present occupation?
    ___ Business and professional
    ___ Salaried and semiprofessional
    ___ Skilled worker
    ___ Laborer
    ___ Student
23. What is the highest level of education you have completed?
    ___ Elementary school
    ___ Junior high school
    ___ Senior high school
    ___ Trade or vocational school
    ___ 1–2 years of college
    ___ 3–4 years of college
    ___ More than 4 years of college
24. What is your yearly household income?
    ___ $0–$5,000
    ___ $5,001–$10,000
    ___ $10,001–$20,000
    ___ $20,001–$30,000
    ___ $30,001–$45,000
    ___ $45,001–$70,000
    ___ $70,000 and above

CASE 21

UNITED STATES POSTAL SERVICE

Case Exhibit 21.1 reproduces a questionnaire that was used by the United States Postal Service to measure employee morale and satisfaction with working conditions.

Question

Evaluate the questionnaire.

CASE EXHIBIT 21.1 | **UNITED STATES POSTAL SERVICE EMPLOYEE OPINION SURVEY**

See your supervisor regarding the best time and place to complete this survey. Completion of this survey is voluntary and must be done on the clock. Please return your survey in the enclosed envelope by November 27.

1. Overall, how would you rate the Postal Service as a place to work compared with other organizations you know about? (Mark one)
   ☐ One of the best
   ☐ Above average
   ☐ Average
   ☐ Below average
   ☐ One of the worst
2. How do you rate the Postal Service as a place to work today compared with the way it was when you first started working here? (Mark one)
   ☐ It's better now
   ☐ It's about the same
   ☐ It's not as good now
   ☐ I don't know/I haven't been here long enough to judge
3. How would you rate the Postal Service on each of the following, considering your experience here as well as what you know of other organizations?

Case Exhibit 21.1 — **United States Postal Service Employee Opinion Survey (Continued)**

(Mark one response for each item):

	Very Good	Good	Average	Poor	Very Poor
Your employee benefits	☐	☐	☐	☐	☐
Your pay	☐	☐	☐	☐	☐
Your opportunity for advancement	☐	☐	☐	☐	☐
Your job security	☐	☐	☐	☐	☐
The physical working conditions	☐	☐	☐	☐	☐
Providing training so that you can handle your present job properly	☐	☐	☐	☐	☐
Providing training to help you qualify for a better job	☐	☐	☐	☐	☐
Cooperation between employees in different functional areas	☐	☐	☐	☐	☐
Treating employees with respect and dignity as individuals	☐	☐	☐	☐	☐
Taking employee interests into account when making important decisions	☐	☐	☐	☐	☐

4. Please read the following phrases carefully and indicate how much opportunity you feel your present job provides on each of these:

   (Mark one response for each item):

	Great Deal	Above Average Amount	Average Amount	Limited Amount	Hardly Any
A chance to have your ideas adopted and put into use	☐	☐	☐	☐	☐
A chance to do challenging and interesting work	☐	☐	☐	☐	☐

5. How strongly do you agree or disagree with the following statements?

   (Mark one response for each statement):

	Strongly Agree	Tend to Agree	Hard to Decide	Tend to Disagree	Strongly Disagree
I have enough authority to carry out my job effectively	☐	☐	☐	☐	☐
I often experience a high degree of stress in my job	☐	☐	☐	☐	☐
I like the kind of work I do	☐	☐	☐	☐	☐
Poor employee performance is usually not tolerated	☐	☐	☐	☐	☐
The work flow is well-organized	☐	☐	☐	☐	☐
Overall, I am satisfied with my job	☐	☐	☐	☐	☐
Management's words and actions are often not consistent	☐	☐	☐	☐	☐
Decisions currently made at a high level could be better made at lower levels	☐	☐	☐	☐	☐
The Postal Service's actions show a sincere commitment to safety	☐	☐	☐	☐	☐
I am kept informed about important matters by management	☐	☐	☐	☐	☐
Generally, union and management work well together	☐	☐	☐	☐	☐
Union and management can trust each other to act in good faith	☐	☐	☐	☐	☐
Over the past five years, relationships between employees and management have deteriorated at my work location *(Leave blank if you have been employed with the Postal Service less than five years)*	☐	☐	☐	☐	☐
Supervisors consistently follow the provisions of the national agreements	☐	☐	☐	☐	☐
Too many changes of supervisors have caused problems in my work group	☐	☐	☐	☐	☐
I have been penalized for taking sick leave when I was actually sick	☐	☐	☐	☐	☐
Supervisors/managers often make personnel decisions based on favoritism	☐	☐	☐	☐	☐
Many supervisors have given up trying to discipline employees	☐	☐	☐	☐	☐
It is nearly impossible to fire an employee who should be terminated	☐	☐	☐	☐	☐
The Postal Service is committed to providing equal opportunity for all employees	☐	☐	☐	☐	☐
When assigned new work, I am given sufficient instructions and training to do it properly	☐	☐	☐	☐	☐

	Strongly Agree	Tend to Agree	Hard to Decide	Tend to Disagree	Strongly Disagree
The applicants who are promoted to supervisor or manager positions are the most qualified	☐	☐	☐	☐	☐
Sexual discrimination is not a problem where I work	☐	☐	☐	☐	☐
Racial discrimination is not a problem where I work	☐	☐	☐	☐	☐
Sexual harassment is not a problem where I work	☐	☐	☐	☐	☐
Increasing revenue is just as important to the Postal Service as decreasing costs	☐	☐	☐	☐	☐
As an organization, we do a good job of choosing where to cut costs	☐	☐	☐	☐	☐
Pay should be based more on performance than it is at present	☐	☐	☐	☐	☐
Formal postal communications (e.g., Frank Talk, Postal Life, division and MSC newsletters) are effective	☐	☐	☐	☐	☐
I can usually believe the information I get from the Postal Service	☐	☐	☐	☐	☐

6. When things go well on the job, how often is your contribution recognized? (Mark one)

- ☐ Always
- ☐ Frequently
- ☐ Occasionally
- ☐ Rarely
- ☐ Never

7. How would you rate your immediate supervisor on the following? (If you report to more than one supervisor, please rate the person who supervises you most often.)
(Mark one response for each item).

	Very Good	Good	Average	Poor	Very Poor
Knowing his or her job	☐	☐	☐	☐	☐
Dealing fairly with everyone—playing no favorites	☐	☐	☐	☐	☐
Listening to your problems, complaints, or ideas	☐	☐	☐	☐	☐
Encouraging teamwork in getting the job done	☐	☐	☐	☐	☐
Letting you know what kind of job you are doing	☐	☐	☐	☐	☐
Giving you the information you need to do a good job	☐	☐	☐	☐	☐
Taking action on your problems, complaints, or ideas	☐	☐	☐	☐	☐
Being trustworthy	☐	☐	☐	☐	☐

8. In your opinion, what is the quality of service provided by the Postal Service to the American people? (Mark one)

- ☐ Very good quality
- ☐ Good quality
- ☐ Average quality
- ☐ Poor quality
- ☐ Very poor quality
- ☐ I don't know

9. In your opinion, what is the quality of service provided by the Postal Service to the American people now, compared to two years ago? (Mark one)

- ☐ It's better now
- ☐ It's about the same
- ☐ It's not as good now
- ☐ I don't know

10. How strongly do you agree or disagree with the following statements?
(Mark one response for each statement):

	Strongly Agree	Tend to Agree	Hard to Decide	Tend to Disagree	Strongly Disagree
I know how my work impacts customer satisfaction	☐	☐	☐	☐	☐
The Postal Service is serious about quality work	☐	☐	☐	☐	☐
Performing well just gets you extra work	☐	☐	☐	☐	☐
We spend more time on "quick fixes" than on solving the underlying problems	☐	☐	☐	☐	☐
I put as much effort into my job as I possibly can	☐	☐	☐	☐	☐
Productivity goals are achieved at the expense of customer service	☐	☐	☐	☐	☐
In my area, some people do most of the work while others do just enough to get by	☐	☐	☐	☐	☐
The Postal Service continuously strives to improve its products and services	☐	☐	☐	☐	☐
I am encouraged to come up with new and better ways of doing things	☐	☐	☐	☐	☐

Case Exhibit 21.1 — **United States Postal Service Employee Opinion Survey (Continued)**

	Strongly Agree	Tend to Agree	Hard to Decide	Tend to Disagree	Strongly Disagree
At the Postal Service, taking a calculated risk and failing is better than not taking a risk at all	☐	☐	☐	☐	☐
I get rewarded for high levels of performance	☐	☐	☐	☐	☐
Work groups are rewarded for cooperating with each other	☐	☐	☐	☐	☐
The Postal Service is doing a good job of implementing automation	☐	☐	☐	☐	☐
I am concerned that automation may harm my job situation	☐	☐	☐	☐	☐
Automation is critical to keeping the Postal Service competitive	☐	☐	☐	☐	☐
Competition presents a serious threat to the Postal Service	☐	☐	☐	☐	☐
I am proud to work for the Postal Service	☐	☐	☐	☐	☐
Employees are reluctant to reveal problems or errors to management	☐	☐	☐	☐	☐
I am committed to the success of the Postal Service	☐	☐	☐	☐	☐
Alcohol abuse among employees is a problem where I work	☐	☐	☐	☐	☐
Drug abuse among employees is a problem where I work	☐	☐	☐	☐	☐
My work group places emphasis on doing the job right the first time	☐	☐	☐	☐	☐
Something will be done about the problems uncovered in this survey	☐	☐	☐	☐	☐
The Postal Service does a good job of managing change	☐	☐	☐	☐	☐
If I had to start my career again, I would choose the Postal Service	☐	☐	☐	☐	☐

11. Please rate the U.S. Postal Service on . . .

Its overall performance:

(Poor—Fair) Good (Very Good—Excellent) Don't Know

1 2 3 4 5 6 7 8

Providing services that are a good value for the price:

(Poor—Fair) Good (Very Good—Excellent) Don't Know

1 2 3 4 5 6 7 8

THE FOLLOWING QUESTIONS ARE FOR MANAGERS AND SUPERVISORS. ALL OTHER EMPLOYEES GO ON TO ITEM I IN THE NEXT COLUMN.

12. To what extent do you agree or disagree with the following items? (Mark one response for each statement):

	Strongly Agree	Tend to Agree	Hard to Decide	Tend to Disagree	Strongly Disagree
My performance goals are realistic and attainable	☐	☐	☐	☐	☐
Formal management training I have received is useful considering the realities of my job	☐	☐	☐	☐	☐
Management goals don't promote cooperation among functional areas	☐	☐	☐	☐	☐
Management is supportive when a supervisor, following the procedures of the national agreements, issues discipline	☐	☐	☐	☐	☐

13. How useful was your most recent performance evaluation in helping you improve your performance? (Mark one)

☐ Very useful ☐ Somewhat useful ☐ Not very useful Not at all useful

The following items will help us understand how groups of employees view things. In order to protect your confidentiality, results will not be released to management for your group or any employee group in which there are fewer than 10 employees.

I. Please indicate your type of job. (Mark one)

BARGAINING EMPLOYEES

☐ City Carrier
☐ Clerk, Clerical, and Secretarial
☐ Facility and Equipment Maintenance

☐ Mail Handler
☐ Rural Carrier
☐ Bargaining position not listed above

NONBARGAINING EMPLOYEES

☐ Clerical/Administrative
☐ Professional Staff (Field/Region)
☐ First-Line Supervisor
☐ Manager/Superintendent/Supervisor (Above First-Line)
☐ Postmaster
☐ PCES Executive (Field/Regional/MSC Director)
☐ Headquarters—Professional Staff/Program Manager
☐ Headquarters—PCES Executive/EAS Manager
☐ Nonbargaining position not listed above

II. Please indicate how long you have worked for the U.S. Postal Service. (Mark one)

☐ Less than 6 years
☐ 6–10 years
☐ 11–15 years
☐ 16–20 years
☐ 21–25 years
☐ More than 25 years

III. Are you a part-time flexible employee?

☐ Yes
☐ No

IV. Please indicate your age. (Mark one)

☐ 20 years or under
☐ 21–30
☐ 31–40
☐ 41–50
☐ 51–60
☐ 61 and over

V. Please indicate your sex.

☐ Male
☐ Female

VI. Please indicate the group with which you most closely identify yourself. (Mark one)

☐ American Indian
☐ Asian or Pacific Islander
☐ Black (not of Hispanic origin)
☐ Hispanic
☐ White (not of Hispanic origin)

VII. Please use the space below for any additional comments you may wish to make about any topic, regardless of whether it was covered in the questionnaire. A random sample of the responses will be read by the Postmaster General and senior management.

TO ALL EMPLOYEES: THANK YOU FOR SHARING YOUR OPINIONS AND OBSERVATIONS WITH US. THEY WILL GREATLY CONTRIBUTE TO THE SUCCESS OF THIS SURVEY PROCESS.

PLEASE RETURN YOUR SURVEY IN THE ENCLOSED ENVELOPE BY NOVEMBER 27.

CASE

SCHÖNBRUNN PALACE IN VIENNA

The Schönbrunn Palace in Vienna was constructed in the 18th century during the reign of the Hapsburgs. Today this former summer residence of the imperial family is one of Austria's top tourist attractions.

The questions in Case Exhibit 22.1 about a visit to the Schönbrunn Palace originally appeared in German. They were translated into English and printed on another questionnaire.

Questions

1. What is the typical process for developing questionnaires for markets where consumers speak a different language?
2. Find someone who speaks German and have the person back translate the questions that appear in the case. Are these German questions adequate?

Case Exhibit 22.1 | QUESTIONNAIRE FROM SCHÖNBRUNN PALACE, VIENNA

Befragung der Besucher **Schloß Schönbrunn**

Land/Staat ____________________ **Bundesland (nur für Ö)** ____________

Alter _______ Jahre **Geschlecht** ¤ männlich ¤ weiblich

Heutiges Datum ___ . ___ . 199__ **Uhrzeit** _________

- **Waren Sie heute zum ersten Mal im Schloß Schönbrunn?**
  ¤ ja ¤ nein, zum ___. Mal
- **Welche Tour haben Sie gemacht?**
  ¤ *Grand Tour* (40 Räume)
  ¤ *Imperial Tour* (22 Räume)
- **Welche Art von Führung haben Sie gewählt?**
  ¤ *Schönbrunn Führung (Angebot des Schlosses)*
  ¤ *eigener Reiseführer (Reisegruppe, Fremdenführer)*
  ¤ *Tonbandführer (Audioguide) in* ______________________ *Sprache*
  ¤ *keinerlei Führung*
- **Falls Sie an einer Führung teilgenommen haben:**
  Wie finden Sie Ihren Führer bzw. Ihre Führerin?
  ¤ sehr freundlich ¤ eher freundlich ¤ eher unfreundlich ¤ sehr unfreundlich
  weil ... ____

Case Exhibit 22.1 | **Questionnaire from Schönbrunn Palace, Vienna (continued)**

- **Bei Verwendung eines Tonbandführers (Audioguide):**
  Wie finden Sie die angebotenen Audioguides?
  ¤ sehr gut ¤ eher gut ¤ eher schlecht ¤ sehr schlecht
  weil ... ____________________

- **Wie ist Ihr Gesamteindruck vom Schloß Schönbrunn alles in allem?**
  ¤ sehr gut ¤ eher gut ¤ eher schlecht ¤ sehr schlecht
  weil ... ____________________

- **Wie ist Ihr Eindruck vom Personal im Schloß?**
  ¤ sehr gut ¤ eher gut ¤ eher schlecht ¤ sehr schlecht
  weil ... ____________________

- **Wie gut finden Sie sich im Schloß Schönbrunn/Park zurecht (Hinweisschilder, kennt man sich gut aus, findet man die Kassen, Toiletten, den Ausgang, etc.)?**
  ¤ sehr gut ¤ eher gut ¤ eher schlecht ¤ sehr schlecht
  weil ... ____________________

- **Fühlten Sie sich nach dem Besuch gut informiert über das Schloß und seine Geschichte?**
  ¤ sehr gut ¤ eher gut ¤ eher schlecht ¤ sehr schlecht

- **Wurden Sie bei der Besichtigung gestört?**
  durch (andere) Gruppen:
  ¤ sehr stark ¤ etwas ¤ kaum ¤ gar nicht
  durch Einzelbesucher:
  ¤ sehr stark ¤ etwas ¤ kaum ¤ gar nicht

- **Wie finden Sie die Art, wie die Räume dargestellt werden (Einrichtung, Möblierung, Beleuchtung, Dekoration, etc.)?**
  ¤ sehr gut ¤ eher gut ¤ eher schlecht ¤ sehr schlecht
  weil ... ____________________

- **Haben Sie nach dem Besuch im Schloß Schönbrunn eine lebendige Vorstellung vom einstigen Leben bei Hof?**
  ¤ ja ¤ etwas ¤ kaum ¤ nein
  weil ... ____________________

- **Was würden Sie noch gerne über das Schloß erfahren?**
  ____

- **Wie finden Sie die Eintrittspreise?**
  ¤ viel zu teuer ¤ etwas zu teuer ¤ angemessen ¤ günstig

- **Wie finden Sie das Angebot im Museumshop?**
  ¤ sehr gut ¤ eher gut ¤ eher schlecht ¤ sehr schlecht
  weil ... ____________________

Case Exhibit 22.1 | **Questionnaire from Schönbrunn Palace, Vienna (continued)**

• **Was könnte Ihrer Meinung nach noch verbessert werden?**

____

____

____

____

Vielen Dank für Ihren Besuch und Ihre Anregungen!

CASE 23

THE BUSINESS FORMS INDUSTRY

The business forms industry is heavily dependent on personal selling.[17] Case Exhibit 23.1 shows a sampling frame containing a list of 200 salespeople in the business forms industry.

The first column is an identification number associated with the salesperson whose name is listed in Column 2. Column 3 indicates the salesperson's gender. Column 4 indicates the number of sales calls the salesperson made during the previous month. Column 5 gives the name of the company where the salesperson works. The last column is used for snowball sampling. During the snowball sampling procedure, the researcher must select a first-stage sample of nominators. The nominators then point out the salespeople whom they know, and these elements are also included in the sample. For example, T. Montz (I.D. number 14) knows four respondents—I.D. number 1, A. Abbott; I.D. number 170, C. R. Gemelli; I.D. number 194, S. T. Siwula; and I.D. number 200, J. Zorilla.

A sales manager wishes to determine the mean number of sales calls made per month.

Download the data sets for this case from http://zikmund.swcollege.com or request them from your instructor.

ADDITIONAL INFORMATION

The data from this case are stored in a computerized database. Your instructor will provide information about obtaining the Business Forms data set if this material is part of the case assignment.

Questions

1. Using a table of random numbers, draw a simple random sample (number of observations = 15). Discuss the step-by-step procedure you used to draw the simple random sample. For the number of sales calls, calculate the sample mean and standard deviation for your sample. Calculate the proportion of women in the industry.
2. Using the results from question 1, determine what sample size would be necessary if the researcher wanted to be 95 percent confident and have a range of error no larger than two sales calls.
3. Draw a systematic sample of the sample size that you calculated in question 2. Calculate the sample

mean and a 95 percent confidence interval for the mean.

4. Draw a snowball sample ($n = 20$) using a random numbers table to determine the nominators.
5. Draw a two-stage cluster sample ($n = 20$) using each company as a single cluster. At the first stage randomly select one of the clusters (or companies). At the second stage use a random numbers table to select four elements (or salespeople) from each of the five clusters selected at Stage 1. Calculate the sample mean at a 95 percent confidence interval.

CASE EXHIBIT 23.1 **SAMPLING FRAME**

Identification Number	Salesperson Name	Gender	Number of Sales Calls	Company	Snowball Referral
1	Abbot, A.	M	42	Formcraft	14, 34, 47, 48, 154
2	Barton, R.	M	20	Formcraft	199, 186, 82
3	Brinson, C.	F	30	Formcraft	13, 35, 168
4	Butler, D.	M	41	Formcraft	12
5	Chafin, J.	M	24	Formcraft	150, 151, 197, 18
6	Ciliberti, R.	F	42	Formcraft	7, 93, 106, 167
7	Dunn, P.	M	37	Formcraft	6, 169, 180, 197
8	Gallin, F.	M	37	Formcraft	9, 180, 76, 91, 110
9	Hicks, G.	F	39	Formcraft	8, 188, 95, 96, 106
10	Howard, C.	M	42	Formcraft	108, 116, 119, 130
11	Knoclel, D.	M	40	Formcraft	None
12	Leverick, W.	M	23	Formcraft	4, 146
13	Mahon, J.	F	40	Formcraft	3, 139, 175
14	Montz, T.	M	40	Formcraft	1, 170, 194, 200
15	Nelson, P.	M	40	Formcraft	17, 29, 44
16	Porras, F.	M	39	Formcraft	26, 38, 72, 60
17	Riddell, G.	F	41	Formcraft	15, 68, 74, 89
18	Stevens, W.	F	40	Formcraft	28, 83, 89, 136
19	Traweek, S.	F	30	Formcraft	20, 135, 149, 164, 194
20	Young, B.	M	37	Formcraft	19, 151
21	Aaron, A.	M	37	Western Business Forms	39, 43, 79
22	Abud, M.	M	39	Western Business Forms	None
23	Atkinson, O. R.	F	41	Western Business Forms	85
24	Barnett, J. J.	M	41	Western Business Forms	27, 111
25	Battels, L.	M	38	Western Business Forms	38, 59, 134
26	Chen, S.	M	37	Western Business Forms	16, 27, 141
27	Craft, T.	M	38	Western Business Forms	24, 158, 161, 179
28	Davis, A.	M	39	Western Business Forms	18, 36, 45
29	Floyd, P.	F	39	Western Business Forms	15, 181, 182
30	Gentry, D.	M	41	Western Business Forms	25, 31, 48, 181
31	Holmes, S.	F	33	Western Business Forms	30, 186
32	Jones, C.	F	39	Western Business Forms	42, 43, 198, 49, 58
33	Lee, K.	M	41	Western Business Forms	41, 53, 62, 87
34	Lyon, D.	M	41	Western Business Forms	84
35	Olm, K.	M	38	Western Business Forms	3, 40, 90
36	Rawlings, D.	M	13	Western Business Forms	4, 28, 108, 136
37	Salazar, A.	M	33	Western Business Forms	None
38	Ullman, L.	M	40	Western Business Forms	16, 143, 152, 200
39	Wood, F.	M	33	Western Business Forms	21, 44, 138, 145, 149
40	Zapalac, J.	M	40	Western Business Forms	35, 158, 161
41	Allen, M.	M	41	McGregor Printing	33, 57, 70, 71

CASE EXHIBIT 23.1 | **SAMPLING FRAME (CONTINUED)**

Identification Number	Salesperson Name	Gender	Number of Sales Calls	Company	Snowball Referral
42	Bell, R.	F	37	McGregor Printing	32, 80, 81
43	Branch, K.	F	34	McGregor Printing	21, 32
44	Diaz, A.	M	38	McGregor Printing	15, 39, 98, 165
45	Ellis, J.	M	31	McGregor Printing	28, 47, 56, 65
46	Fagan, D.	F	34	McGregor Printing	None
47	Gonzalez, E.	M	40	McGregor Printing	1, 45, 195
48	Hestings, O.	M	34	McGregor Printing	1, 30, 46, 66
49	Lang, D.	F	40	McGregor Printing	50, 51, 52, 53
50	Lorenz, K.	F	42	McGregor Printing	49, 64, 77, 100, 114, 140, 172
51	Meek, J.	M	28	McGregor Printing	52, 49
52	Morris, N.	F	42	McGregor Printing	55, 67, 101, 102
53	Newman, P.	M	25	McGregor Printing	33, 49, 54, 71
54	Parker, L.	M	38	McGregor Printing	53, 110
55	Potter, H.	M	38	McGregor Printing	52, 56, 109, 111
56	Roy, M.	F	34	McGregor Printing	45, 55, 167
57	Scott, D.	F	31	McGregor Printing	41, 195
58	Stone, M.	M	37	McGregor Printing	32, 172, 173
59	Trimble, L.	F	39	McGregor Printing	25, 61, 73, 112
60	Williams, W.	F	25	McGregor Printing	16, 63, 69, 108
61	Antill, J.	M	40	Control Business Forms	59, 118, 183
62	Ashley, K.	F	41	Control Business Forms	33, 184
63	Berker, L.	F	41	Control Business Forms	60, 74, 184, 197
64	Burton, S.	M	41	Control Business Forms	50, 69, 187
65	Carter, J.	M	40	Control Business Forms	45, 185
66	Edwards, K.	M	32	Control Business Forms	48
67	Finger, T.	M	37	Control Business Forms	52, 189, 190, 191
68	Ganesh, G.	M	38	Control Business Forms	17, 193
69	Green, W.	F	38	Control Business Forms	64, 192, 193, 196
70	Ivey, T.	M	33	Control Business Forms	41, 78
71	Johnson, C.	F	34	Control Business Forms	53, 86, 92, 93
72	Jones, F.	M	41	Control Business Forms	16, 88, 89, 136, 143
73	Landry, T.	M	36	Control Business Forms	59, 63, 82
74	Lewis, C.	F	34	Control Business Forms	17, 89, 90, 104
75	Matthews, M.	M	38	Control Business Forms	None
76	O'Neil, J.	F	41	Control Business Forms	8, 77, 138
77	Rice, J.	F	38	Control Business Forms	50, 76, 94, 137
78	Sanchez, M.	F	38	Control Business Forms	70, 1, 82
79	Welch, B.	M	33	Control Business Forms	21
80	Zeff, S.	M	42	Control Business Forms	42, 142, 143, 144, 145
81	Bishop, N.	F	39	Brunswick Press	42, 115, 140
82	Bryan, W.	M	37	Brunswick Press	2, 73, 144
83	Cloud, P.	M	40	Brunswick Press	18, 7, 117
84	Dyer, P.	F	36	Brunswick Press	34
85	Elliott, G.	M	36	Brunswick Press	23, 11, 147, 155, 156
86	Gray, J.	M	38	Brunswick Press	71, 157, 163, 187
87	Hale, K.	M	41	Brunswick Press	33, 88

Identification Number	Salesperson Name	Gender	Number of Sales Calls	Company	Snowball Referral
88	Keller, J.	F	41	Brunswick Press	72, 87, 89
89	Kramer, C.	F	38	Brunswick Press	18, 74, 90, 91
90	Love, S.	M	32	Brunswick Press	35, 89, 91
91	Morse, H.	M	41	Brunswick Press	8, 89, 90, 196
92	Palmer, G.	M	36	Brunswick Press	71, 104, 105, 120
93	Pyle, G.	M	39	Brunswick Press	6, 71, 121, 133, 147, 148
94	Riley, T.	M	29	Brunswick Press	77, 123
95	Summer, V.	M	32	Brunswick Press	9, 122, 123, 132, 146
96	Thompson, L.	M	34	Brunswick Press	9, 98, 104
97	Trahan, J. R.	F	32	Brunswick Press	None
98	White, E.	M	37	Brunswick Press	44, 96, 106, 9, 104, 195
99	Wilson, F. A.	M	40	Brunswick Press	None
100	York, H.	F	39	Brunswick Press	50
101	Bizek, R.	M	32	Arnold Corporation	52, 102
102	Blais, D. R.	M	40	Arnold Corporation	52, 103, 101
103	Harp, V.	M	41	Arnold Corporation	192
104	Hines, A.	M	40	Arnold Corporation	74, 92, 126, 127
105	Moore, A. A.	F	38	Arnold Corporation	92, 107, 119
106	Payne, R. L.	M	36	Arnold Corporation	6, 9, 98, 17, 107
107	Payne, W.	M	30	Arnold Corporation	105, 106, 128
108	Peters, B.	M	37	Arnold Corporation	60, 128, 115, 116
109	Peters, L. R.	M	33	Arnold Corporation	55, 129
110	Raines, C.	M	24	Arnold Corporation	54, 159, 170
111	Richards, A. L.	M	39	Arnold Corporation	55, 112
112	Rogers, R.	M	36	Arnold Corporation	59, 111
113	Samad, I.	M	36	Arnold Corporation	24, 174, 176, 184
114	Scruggs, J.	M	36	Arnold Corporation	50, 117, 130
115	Simmons, E. M.	F	41	Arnold Corporation	81, 108, 139, 140
116	Smith, R. J.	M	36	Arnold Corporation	10, 108
117	Starks, T. W.	M	36	Arnold Corporation	83, 114, 6, 182
118	Tomey, E. L.	M	36	Arnold Corporation	61, 131, 141, 142, 184
119	Vail, M.	M	40	Arnold Corporation	10, 105
120	Walker, K. L.	F	36	Arnold Corporation	92, 121, 134, 191
121	Abbott, J.	F	39	Moore Business Forms	93, 120, 134, 191, 192
122	Author, R. L.	F	36	Moore Business Forms	95, 142, 143
123	Bough, M.	F	36	Moore Business Forms	94, 124, 149, 152
124	Coleman, W.	M	35	Moore Business Forms	24, 123, 149, 152, 161
125	Collins, O. L.	F	35	Moore Business Forms	None
126	Eades, A. M.	M	35	Moore Business Forms	104, 127
127	Enloe, S. D.	M	35	Moore Business Forms	104, 126, 128
128	Fisher, N.	M	41	Moore Business Forms	107, 106, 170
129	Holifield, W. B.	F	35	Moore Business Forms	109
130	Lott, M.	M	35	Moore Business Forms	10, 114, 176, 131, 118

Case Exhibit 23.1 | **Sampling Frame (Continued)**

Identification Number	Salesperson Name	Gender	Number of Sales Calls	Company	Snowball Referral
131	Love, A. J.	M	35	Moore Business Forms	118, 130, 139, 3
132	Lucas, D.	F	39	Moore Business Forms	95, 80, 118, 141, 122, 133, 93, 17
133	Norris, L. A.	F	35	Moore Business Forms	93, 132, 122, 118
134	Rouse, J.	F	38	Moore Business Forms	24, 120, 121, 142, 80
135	Rouwalk, C.	M	38	Moore Business Forms	19, 142, 148, 151, 152
136	Taynor, S. A.	M	38	Moore Business Forms	72, 137, 77, 153
137	Teel, B.	M	38	Moore Business Forms	77, 136, 72, 167, 6, 7, 93
138	Waters, J.	M	42	Moore Business Forms	39, 115, 166, 167
139	White, K.	M	42	Moore Business Forms	3, 140, 50
140	Willis, R.	M	40	Moore Business Forms	50, 139, 6, 56, 137
141	Argo, M.	F	42	Taylor-Made Forms	26, 118, 142, 80, 122
142	Aris, B.	M	42	Taylor-Made Forms	80, 118, 141, 122, 134, 135, 143
143	Baird, R. S.	M	42	Taylor-Made Forms	80, 142, 95, 142
144	Balinski, J.	F	39	Taylor-Made Forms	82, 142, 146
145	Brancheau, C. C.	F	39	Taylor-Made Forms	80, 169, 147, 148
146	Brown, S.	M	39	Taylor-Made Forms	4, 95
147	Brugnoli, G. A.	M	34	Taylor-Made Forms	85, 145
148	Brunt, R.	M	34	Taylor-Made Forms	93, 145
149	Bybee, W. D.	F	42	Taylor-Made Forms	19, 123, 124, 150
150	Cupps, T.	M	40	Taylor-Made Forms	5, 149
151	Gurun, L.	F	14	Taylor-Made Forms	20
152	Kondelka, F.	F	15	Taylor-Made Forms	136
153	Kovalcik, A.	F	16	Taylor-Made Forms	136, 152, 159, 154, 1, 142
154	Kowis, M.	F	40	Taylor-Made Forms	1, 142, 153, 155
155	McZeal, E.	F	42	Taylor-Made Forms	85, 145, 153, 154, 180
156	Meduris, C. A.	M	27	Taylor-Made Forms	85, 145
157	Peters, W.	M	31	Taylor-Made Forms	86, 163, 189, 190
158	Searl, S.	F	42	Taylor-Made Forms	27, 35, 40
159	Teziano, E.	M	39	Taylor-Made Forms	110, 54, 145, 153, 164, 174
160	Thiede, C.	M	42	Taylor-Made Forms	145
161	Avalos, H.	F	37	Key Printing	27, 40, 163, 86
162	Awl, J. N.	F	37	Key Printing	145
163	Baird, D.	F	37	Key Printing	86, 157, 161, 40
164	Balderas, O. L.	M	37	Key Printing	19, 159, 16, 165
165	Bekins, J. B.	M	37	Key Printing	44, 145, 164, 19
166	Bivin, W.	M	37	Key Printing	138, 167, 145, 168
167	Breda, H.	M	42	Key Printing	6, 56, 137
168	Freeman, J. F.	M	35	Key Printing	3, 145, 176
169	Gekeler, D.	M	35	Key Printing	7, 145, 176
170	Gemelli, C. R.	M	42	Key Printing	14, 110, 193, 68

Case Exhibit 23.1 | Sampling Frame (Continued)

Identification Number	Salesperson Name	Gender	Number of Sales Calls	Company	Snowball Referral
171	Goss, E.	M	33	Key Printing	142
172	Gulick, R. W.	M	41	Key Printing	58, 173
173	Hansen, C.	M	41	Key Printing	58, 172, 178
174	Kostelic, P. P.	M	33	Key Printing	113, 180, 181, 8
175	Nowacki, D.	F	40	Key Printing	13, 142
176	Pesl, J. V.	M	42	Key Printing	142, 145, 169, 178, 173
177	Smith, R. A.	M	42	Key Printing	None
178	Tomey, T. S.	M	42	Key Printing	173, 145, 176, 142
179	Usrey, B.	M	42	Key Printing	27, 145
180	Vader, L.	F	42	Key Printing	8, 174, 181, 196
181	Blake, P.	M	19	Form Tech	29, 174, 180, 182, 117
182	Brechtel, W. J.	M	39	Form Tech	29, 117, 181, 188, 8, 189
183	Burks, R.	M	35	Form Tech	61, 145, 184, 62, 113
184	Chirco, S. J.	M	35	Form Tech	62, 113, 183
185	Distefano, E.	M	36	Form Tech	None
186	Duong, C. V.	M	36	Form Tech	30, 198, 26
187	Dupka, A.	M	41	Form Tech	86, 142, 192, 13
188	Fournier, P.	M	32	Form Tech	8, 67, 189
189	Gomez, J. G.	M	33	Form Tech	67, 157, 182, 8
190	Harlar, C.	M	34	Form Tech	67, 189, 157, 194
191	Lomax, J.	M	35	Form Tech	192, 134, 121, 142, 186, 187
192	Manos, E. P.	F	42	Form Tech	86, 142, 187
193	McAdoo, R. O.	F	37	Form Tech	68, 145, 170, 14, 110
194	Siwula, S. T.	F	38	Form Tech	14, 145, 190, 67
195	Stanzel, J. Z.	M	39	Form Tech	41
196	Stubbs, D.	M	40	Form Tech	91, 180, 197, 5, 7
197	Wacpeng, L.	M	41	Form Tech	5, 7, 142
198	Wu, A.	F	42	Form Tech	32, 145, 187, 199, 2
199	Young, P. P.	M	39	Form Tech	2, 145, 189, 32, 186
200	Zorilla, J.	M	21	Form Tech	14, 142

CASE 24

ZAGORSKI FIELD SERVICES

Margaret Murphy O'Hara was fatigued. As she wiped the perspiration from her brow, she felt that the Massachusetts summer sun was playing a trick on her. It was her first day at work, and the weather was hot. She had no idea that being a field interviewer required so much stamina. Even though she was tired, she was happy with her new job. She didn't yet have the knack of holding her purse, questionnaires, and clipboard while administering the show cards, but she knew she'd get the hang of it. The balancing act can be learned, she thought.

When she met her supervisor, Mary Zagorski, at the end of her first day, Margaret described her day. Margaret said she thought the questionnaire was a bit too long. She laughed, saying that an elderly lady had fallen asleep after about 20 minutes of interviewing.

Margaret mentioned that a number of people had asked why they were selected. Margaret told Mary that when somebody asked, "Why did you pick me?" Margaret did not know exactly what to say.

She said that the nicest person she had interviewed was a man whose wife wasn't home to be surveyed. He was very friendly and didn't balk at being asked about his income and age like some of the other people she had interviewed.

She said she had one problem that she needed some help with. Four or five people refused to grant the interview. Margaret explained that one woman answered the door and said she was too busy because her son, an army private, was leaving the country. The woman was throwing a little party for him before he went off to the airport. Margaret didn't want to spoil their fun with the survey. Another lady said that she was too busy and really didn't know anything about the subject anyway. However, she did suggest Bill Jerpe, her next-door neighbor, who was very interested in the subject. Margaret was able to interview this person to make up for the lost interview. It actually went quite well.

Margaret said another woman wouldn't be interviewed because she didn't know anything about the Zagorski interviewing service and Margaret didn't know quite what to tell her. Finally, she couldn't make one interview because she didn't understand the address: 9615 South Francisco Rear. Margaret told Mary it was quite a day, and she looked forward to tomorrow.

Questions

1. Is Margaret going to be a good professional interviewer?
2. What should Mary Zagorski tell Margaret?

CASE 25

THE MULTIPLEX COMPANY

Multiplex Inc. is a St. Louis manufacturer of automatic beverage dispensers with 150 employees. The company's chief executive officer, J. W. Kisling, decided to conduct a survey of the company's 80 factory workers. Kisling based his questionnaire on one published by the National Association of Manufacturers. It posed 52 questions dealing with nine categories of information: attitude toward top management, work and safety conditions, supervisory effectiveness, pay and employee benefits, communication and recognition, job security and promotion, attitude toward fellow workers, quality, and attitude toward the survey. The questions were randomly ordered on the questionnaire.

Case Exhibit 25.1 shows the frequency distributions for some of the questions. Case Exhibit 25.2 collapses the categories "Strongly agree" and "Somewhat agree" to provide a percentage agreement score. It shows agreement with several statements for selected categories along with the national norms provided by the National Association of Manufacturers.

Questions

1. How important is it for Multiplex to conduct a survey of this nature?
2. Based on a descriptive analysis, how do you interpret the results of the data that appear in Case Exhibits 25.1 and 25.2?

CASE EXHIBIT 25.1 RESPONSES TO SELECTED QUESTIONS FROM MULTIPLEX QUESTIONNAIRE[18]

	Strongly Agree	Somewhat Agree	No Opinion	Somewhat Disagree	Strongly Disagree	Percentage Agreement
1. I always feel free to speak to anyone in top management.	20	19	1	6	6	39/75%[a]
2. Our top management tries to make Multiplex Company a good place to work.	16	19	4	11	2	35/67
3. Starting and quitting times are satisfactory.	30	15	2	1	3	45/89
4. Management tries to make this a safe place to work.	21	20	2	6	3	41/79
5. My supervisor gives praise where praise is due.	14	13	6	12	6	27/53
6. Good cooperation exists between departments.	11	18	2	8	15	29/54
7. Our insurance plan provides good coverage.	16	18	3	8	6	34/66

Case Exhibit 25.1 **Responses to Selected Questions from Multiplex Questionnaire (Continued)**

	Strongly Agree	Somewhat Agree	No Opinion	Somewhat Disagree	Strongly Disagree	Percentage Agreement
8. My performance is recognized by this company.	6	18	11	6	9	24/48
9. Our management keeps us informed about new plans and developments.	20	19	4	4	4	39/76
10. I would recommend employment at Multiplex to my friends.	20	20	4	3	2	42/82
11. I believe the quality at Multiplex is better now than a year ago.	20	16	6	4	5	36/70
12. Multiplex Company is a good place to work.	24	21	3	3	0	35/68
13. Things at Multiplex are better than they were a year ago.	3	13	10	6	8	26/52
⋮						
24. The longer I work here the more I enjoy it.	9	20	13	6	4	29/55
25. We are given little or no information about the company.	4	8	2	20	17	37/72
26. My supervisor generally gives me clear instructions.	30	16	2	2	2	46/88

[a]Read as 39 respondents agreed with the statement, which corresponded to 75 percent of the sample.

Case Exhibit 25.2 **Agreement with Selected Statements Compared to National Norm**

	Percentage Agreement	National Norm
Attitude toward Top Management		
1. I always feel free to speak to anyone in top management.	75%	65%
2. Our top management tries to make this company a good place to work.	67	71
17. Many times, top management here does not have my interest in mind.	34	43
40. Top management here is not friendly toward the employees.	56	66
41. In my opinion, top management here could operate the company more efficiently.	54	28
46. Top management here does not supply me with the necessary equipment to do a good job.	64	62

Case Exhibit 25.2 AGREEMENT WITH SELECTED STATEMENTS COMPARED TO NATIONAL NORM (CONTINUED)

	Percentage Agreement	National Norm
Work and Safety Conditions		
3. Starting and quitting times are satisfactory.	89	87
4. Management tries to make this a safe place to work.	79	79
21. I am never bored with my job.	43	61
22. Our washrooms are adequate and they are kept clean.	54	60
30. My work is pleasant—I am not pushed for more than I can do.	68	56
Supervisory Effectiveness		
5. My supervisor gives praise where praise is due.	53	55
14. Often, my supervisor doesn't keep promises.	50	65
16. I have been well-trained on all jobs to which I have been assigned.	82	64
Pay and Employee Benefits		
7. Our insurance plan provides good coverage.	66	66
11. My rate of pay is fair and equitable for the job I am doing.	70	39
42. I understand the company insurance plan.	65	65
Communication and Recognition		
8. My performance is recognized by this company.	48	—
9. Our management keeps us informed about new plans and developments.	76	56
25. We are given little or no information about the company.	72	56
27. We are encouraged to make suggestions for improvements in our work.	74	62
35. We are never informed about changes, even those that affect us personally.	51	62
39. Consideration and attention are shown to me when I use good judgment and initiative.	59	57
51. I feel my family receives worthwhile information about Multiplex from the News Dispenser.	71	—
Job Security and Promotion		
18. My abilities and skills are used by this company.	68	58
12. Multiplex is a good place to work.	68	—
13. Things at Multiplex are better than they were a year ago.	52	—
Attitude toward Fellow Workers, etc.		
6. Good cooperation exists between departments.	54	45
10. I would recommend employment in this company to my friends.	82	—
15. My co-workers are cooperative and work well together.	61	69
19. Frequently I am sorry that I work here.	56	67
24. The longer I work here, the more I enjoy it.	55	67
28. I am pleased to tell others where I work.	88	71
37. Some of my co-workers think they run the company.	67	47
44. Too many problems exist here between co-workers.	58	54

CASE 26

SURVEY ON AMERICANS AND DIETARY SUPPLEMENTS

The NPR/Kaiser/Kennedy School Poll is a project of National Public Radio, the Henry J. Kaiser Family Foundation, and Harvard University's Kennedy School of Government.[19] These organizations collaborated to conduct a Survey on Americans and Dietary Supplements. The results of this survey are based on telephone interviews conducted between February 19 and February 25, 1999, with 1,200 adults 18 years or older nationwide.

Case Exhibits 26.1 through 26.6 summarize some of the results of this survey.

Question

Analyze these data and write a report on your conclusions.

CASE EXHIBIT 26.1 KNOWLEDGE OF AND ATTITUDES ABOUT DIETARY SUPPLEMENTS BY FREQUENCY OF USE

		FREQUENCY OF USE		
	Total	Regularly	Sometimes	Hardly Ever/Never
Follow news reports about dietary supplements very/fairly closely	35%	56%	49%	27%
Very/somewhat familiar with supplements	55%	88%	83%	40%
Give supplements to kids (have kids < 18)	18%	42%	40%	8%
Important to have access to supplements	60%	91%	84%	46%
Good for health/well-being	52%	85%	76%	38%
Supplements can help people with at least 4 of 6 illnesses	36%	57%	47%	27%
Supplements are inadequately tested	48%	39%	44%	52%
Many supplements don't do what ads claim	49%	29%	36%	58%
Boosting immune system means:				
Prevents illness	64%	73%	63%	62%
Helps people when sick	43%	48%	45%	41%
People who use supplements are hurt/sick often/sometimes	47%	38%	45%	50%
Know that government doesn't regulate supplements	53%	58%	46%	54%
Should be more government regulation of:				
Safety	59%	55%	55%	62%
Purity/dosage	60%	55%	58%	62%
Ad claims	63%	62%	62%	65%
Extra regulation for supplements produced for children	77%	78%	77%	77%
If government said supplements were ineffective, would continue to use	72%	71%	72%	NA

Case Exhibit 26.2 | **Knowledge of and Attitudes about Dietary Supplements by Age**

	Total	18–29	Sum 30+	30–49	50–64	65+
Very/somewhat familiar with supplements	55%	63%	53%	58%	57%	37%
Know that government doesn't regulate supplements	53%	45%	56%	58%	57%	47%
Use supplements regularly	18%	16%	19%	15%	24%	22%
Good for health/well-being	52%	56%	51%	53%	54%	43%
Supplements can help people with at least 4 of 6 illnesses	36%	35%	36%	38%	37%	29%
Supplements are inadequately tested	48%	43%	50%	51%	53%	45%
Many supplements don't do what ads claim	49%	44%	50%	50%	56%	44%
Extra regulation for supplements produced for children	77%	82%	76%	79%	73%	70%

Case Exhibit 26.3 | **Knowledge of and Attitudes about Dietary Supplements by Education**

	Total	College Graduate	Some College	High School Graduate or Less
Follow news reports very/fairly closely	35%	46%	39%	30%
Very/somewhat familiar with supplements	55%	64%	64%	49%
Know that government doesn't regulate supplements	53%	67%	56%	46%
Supplements are inadequately tested	48%	62%	49%	43%
Many supplements don't do what ads claim	49%	55%	47%	47%
Boosting immune system means:				
Prevents illness	64%	68%	69%	60%
Helps people when sick	43%	42%	43%	43%
Should be more government regulation of:				
Safety	59%	62%	61%	58%
Purity/dosage	60%	65%	64%	57%
Ad claims	63%	68%	63%	62%
Use supplements regularly	18%	22%	20%	16%
Good for health/well-being	52%	53%	59%	49%
Supplements can help people with at least 4 of 6 illnesses	36%	37%	38%	34%

Case Exhibit 26.4 | **Demographic Profile of Regular Users of Dietary Supplements**

This table gives the percent of regular users who are in each category.

Men	46%
Women	55%
18–29	20%
30–49	34%
50–64	25%
65+	19%
Household income:	
<$20K	20%
$20–29.9K	16%
$30–49.9K	15%
$50–74.9K	13%
$75K+	10%
Refused	20%
Don't Know	5%
Education:	
< High-School Graduate	4%
High-School Graduate	27%
Some College	32%
College Graduate	27%
Region:	
East	22%
Midwest	20%
South	32%
West	26%
Urban/rural:	
Urban	31%
Suburban	48%
Rural	21%
Party ID:	
Republican	24%
Democrat	27%
Independent	42%
Think they promote health:	
Yes	85%
No	3%
Belief in their health benefits:	
High	57%
Medium	34%
Low	9%

Case Exhibit 26.5 | **Regular Users of Dietary Supplements**

This table gives the percent of each specific group who are regular users.

National	18%
By gender:	
Men	18%
Women	19%
By age:	
18–29	16%
30–49	15%
50–64	24%
65+	22%
By race/ethnicity:	
White (non-Hispanic)	20%
Black (non-Hispanic)	8%
Hispanic	14%
By household income:	
<$20K	20%
$20–29.9K	20%
$30–49.9K	16%
$50–74.9K	17%
$75K+	16%
By education:	
<High-School Graduate	16%
High-School Graduate	17%
Some College	20%
College Graduate	22%
By region:	
East	20%
Midwest	15%
South	17%
West	23%
By urban/rural:	
Urban	18%
Suburban	19%
Rural	18%
By party ID:	
Republican	17%
Democrat	16%
Independent	21%
By think they promote health:	
Yes	30%
No	3%
By belief in their health benefits:	
High	30%
Medium	14%
Low	8%

Case Exhibit 26.6 | **Believers in Benefits of Dietary Supplements**

This table gives the percent of each group who believe dietary supplements are good for people's health and well-being.

National	52%
By gender:	
Men	51%
Women	53%
By age:	
18–29	56%
30–49	53%
50–64	54%
65+	43%
By race/ethnicity:	
White (non-Hispanic)	53%
Black (non-Hispanic)	40%
Hispanic	57%
By household income:	
<$20K	54%
$20–29.9K	56%
$30–49.9K	53%
$50–74.9K	58%
$75K+	45%
By education:	
<High-School Graduate	46%
High-School Graduate	50%
Some College	59%
College Graduate	53%
By region:	
East	54%
Midwest	51%
South	49%
West	56%
By urban/rural:	
Urban	49%
Suburban	52%
Rural	56%
By party ID:	
Republican	54%
Democrat	48%
Independent	54%
By use of supplements:	
Regular	85%
Sometimes	76%
Hardly ever/never	38%

CASE 27

OLD SCHOOL VERSUS NEW SCHOOL SPORTS FANS

Download the data sets for this case from http://zikmund.swcollege.com or request them from your instructor.

Three academic researchers investigated the idea that in America in sports, there are two segments with opposing views of the goal of competition (i.e., winning versus self-actualization) and the acceptable/desirable way of achieving this goal.[20] Persons who believe in "winning at any cost" are proponents of sports success as a product and can be labeled new school (NS) individuals. The new school is founded on notions of the player before the team, loyalty to the highest bidder, and high-tech production and consumption of professional sports. On the other hand, persons who value the process of sports and believe that "how you play the game matters" can be labeled old school (OS) individuals. The old school emerges from old-fashioned American notions of the team before the player, sportsmanship and loyalty above all else, and competition simply for "love of the game."

New School/Old School was measured by asking agreement with 10 attitude statements. The scores on these statements were summed. Higher scores represent an orientation toward old school values. For purposes of this case study, individuals who did not answer every question were eliminated from the analysis. Based on their summated scores, respondents were grouped into low score, middle score, and high score groups. Case Exhibit 27.1 shows the SPSS computer output of a cross-tabulation to relate the gender of the respondent (GENDER) with the New School/Old School grouping (OLDSKOOL).

Questions

1. Is this form of analysis appropriate?
2. Interpret the computer output.

Advanced Question

3. Obtain the data set associated with this case (Excel and SPSS formats are available) and perform additional bivariate analysis.

Case Exhibit 27.1 | **SPSS Output**

OLDSKOOL * GENDER Crosstabulation

			GENDER		
			women	men	Total
OLDSKOOL	high	Count	9	17	26
		% within OLDSKOOL	34.6%	65.4%	100.0%
		% within GENDER	10.6%	9.2%	9.6%
		% of Total	3.3%	6.3%	9.6%
	low	Count	45	70	115
		% within OLDSKOOL	39.1%	60.9%	100.0%
		% within GENDER	52.9%	37.8%	42.6%
		% of Total	16.7%	25.9%	42.6%
	middle	Count	31	98	129
		% within OLDSKOOL	24.0%	76.0%	100.0%
		% within GENDER	36.5%	53.0%	47.8%
		% of Total	11.5%	36.3%	47.8%
Total		Count	85	185	270
		% within OLDSKOOL	31.5%	68.5%	100.0%
		% within GENDER	100.0%	100.0%	100.0%
		% of Total	31.5%	68.5%	100.0%

Chi-Square Tests

	Value	df	Asymp. Sig. (2-sided)
Pearson Chi-Square	6.557[a]	2	.038
Likelihood Ratio	6.608	2	.037
N of Valid Cases	270		

[a] 0 cells (.0%) have expected count less than 5. The minimum expected count is 8.19.

CASE 28

FIDELITY INVESTMENTS

A Fidelity Investments newsletter for its IRA shareholders reported the following information from a survey by the Public Agenda Foundation.[21]

> Should you be saving more for your retirement? If the answer is "yes," take heart. You're certainly not alone.
>
> According to recent findings of the Public Agenda Foundation, a non-profit agency that gauges public sentiment on major policy issues, almost a third of all Americans have saved very little (if anything) for retirement. Nor is this problem confined to the lower income brackets: Public Agenda found that

23% of those surveyed with incomes between $40,000 and $60,000 have saved less than $10,000. Among the groups most at risk are "baby boomers" and employees of small companies.

Why are people not saving enough? Public Agenda identified several key hurdles to adequately preparing for retirement. For some, it is simply the fact that they do not earn enough. But for many others the reasons are more complex. The need for retirement planning is too far in the future or too easily overshadowed by more immediate daily financial pressures—or clouded by a lack of knowledge about retirement basics.

Over 60% of those surveyed do not know how much personal savings they will need to maintain a similar standard of living during retirement. And many said they steered clear of stocks, preferring instead an overly conservative approach to retirement investing. In fact, over half of the survey's respondents did not know that the stock market has historically earned higher returns than a CD or savings account.

Another hurdle identified by Public Agenda was an individual's own "savings personality." According to their findings, there are four distinct personality patterns that influence a person's ability to save for retirement.

Strugglers try to save, but have too little income to build a sufficient nest egg.

Deniers refuse to worry about the future, believing it will take care of itself.

Impulsives display a "live for today" mentality and are less willing to cut back on discretionary spending in order to save.

Planners save regularly, enjoy planning their retirement saving strategy, and are well on their way to a comfortable retirement.

Only an estimated 21% of Americans are "planners." By contributing regularly to an IRA, you are most likely to be one of them.

In its conclusions, Public Agenda suggests that Americans should try to save more regularly for retirement, seek out unbiased advice on retirement planning, and avoid playing it too safe with their investments.

Questions

1. What aspects of this report reflect sound principles for the effective communication of research results?
2. Would graphical presentation of the findings enhance the report?
3. Would any additional information be of value in this report?
4. Suppose you had to present the results of this study in a longer, more formal report. Outline the nature of this report.

CASE

LASTDANCE HEALTH CARE SYSTEMS

Download the data sets for this case from http://zikmund.swcollege.com or request them from your instructor.

Senior citizens have different health care needs than the rest of the population.[22] Today there are more seniors living in the United States than ever before. As baby boomers grow older, it is anticipated that the baby boomer generation will have higher standards of quality in healthcare and higher customer service expectations than previous generations. LastDance is a managed care provider in the North Central region of the country. LastDance managers want to be prepared for any changes in expectations so that they can increase their customer service levels and retain their image as a top-quality managed care provider. The company conducted a survey of consumer service expectations of seniors age 65 and over and current LastDance customers under the age of 65. The major survey objectives were as follows:

- To identify health care delivery and service expectations of consumers aged 55 and older
- To compare the expectations of consumers age 55–64 with those of consumers age 65 and older

METHODOLOGY

One thousand questionnaires were mailed to each group—under 65 and 65 and over. The mailing list for the 65 and over group was purchased from a commercial mailing list provider; the mailing list for the 55–64 group was compiled from LastDance's internal decision support system. Each envelope contained a cover letter, a questionnaire, and a return envelope. No monetary incentive was included. The questionnaire consisted of 35 items, with 4 classification questions, 30 questions regarding consumer expectation levels, and 1 numbered instruction. Case Exhibit 29.1 shows the questionnaire and the associated codes. A list of variables appears in Case Exhibit 29.2.

ADDITIONAL INSTRUCTIONS

Several of the questions will require the use of a computerized database. Your instructor will provide information about obtaining the LastDance data set if this material is part of the case assignment. (The data are available in SPSS or Excel format.)

Questions

1. Evaluate the survey's methodology. Are the study's objectives clear? Is the research design sound?
2. Using the computerized database, profile the survey respondents.
3. Identify three questions from the survey and prepare three hypotheses for research investigation.
4. Using the computerized database, prepare a descriptive research report.

CASE EXHIBIT 29.1 | **SURVEY INSTRUMENT**

Health Care Services Improvement

Thank you very much for participating in our research study. Please read each question thoroughly and answer to the best of your knowledge. Simply mark an "X" in the box next to your response.

A. Appointments

The first few questions are about your appointments with your primary care physician.

1. How long is reasonable to wait for an appointment to see your primary care doctor for a minor illness (such as a cold or the flu)?

☐ Same day (1) ☐ 1–3 days (2) ☐ 4–7 days (3)
☐ 8–14 days (4) ☐ 15–30 days (5) ☐ 31–60 days (6) ☐ More than 60 days (7)

B. Physician Specialist

A specialist is a doctor who focuses on a certain field of medicine (e.g., a heart specialist).

2. How long is reasonable for you to wait for a referral from your primary care doctor to see a specialist for non-emergency care?

☐ Same day (1) ☐ 1–3 days (2) ☐ 4–7 days (3)
☐ 8–14 days (4) ☐ 15–30 days (5) ☐ 31–60 days (6) ☐ More than 60 days (7)

C. Doctor's Office and Waiting Room

3. How much time do you consider acceptable to drive to your primary care doctor's office from your home?

☐ Less than 10 minutes (1) ☐ 10 to 15 minutes (2) ☐ 16 to 30 minutes (3)
☐ 31 to 45 minutes (4) ☐ 46 minutes to 1 hour (5) ☐ More than 1 hour (6)

4. How long would you expect to wait from the time you arrive at a physician's office until you are taken to the exam room?

☐ Less than 10 minutes (1) ☐ 10 to 15 minutes (2) ☐ 16 to 30 minutes (3)
☐ 31 to 45 minutes (4) ☐ 46 minutes to 1 hour (5) ☐ More than 1 hour (6)

5. I believe a comfortable waiting room is important during a visit to the doctor's office.

☐ Strongly agree (1) ☐ Agree (2) ☐ Uncertain (3)
☐ Disagree (4) ☐ Strongly disagree (5) ☐ Don't know (6)

Case Exhibit 29.1 | **Survey Instrument (Continued)**

D. Exam Room

6. How long would you expect to be in the exam room until the doctor sees you?

☐ Less than 10 minutes (1) ☐ 10 to 15 minutes (2) ☐ 16 to 30 minutes (3)
☐ 31 to 45 minutes (4) ☐ 46 minutes to 1 hour (5) ☐ More than 1 hour (6)

E. Doctors

The following questions are designed to measure your expectations of your doctor. Please check one box for each question.

7. I expect to be able to select my primary care doctor from a large number of choices.

☐ Strongly agree (1) ☐ Agree (2) ☐ Uncertain (3)
☐ Disagree (4) ☐ Strongly disagree (5) ☐ Don't know (6)

8. I expect to see a doctor rather than a physician's assistant during my visit.

☐ Strongly agree (1) ☐ Agree (2) ☐ Uncertain (3)
☐ Disagree (4) ☐ Strongly disagree (5) ☐ Don't know (6)

9. I expect to see the same doctor every visit.

☐ Strongly agree (1) ☐ Agree (2) ☐ Uncertain (3)
☐ Disagree (4) ☐ Strongly disagree (5) ☐ Don't know (6)

10. I expect to know my doctor's background (education, training, etc.) before my first visit.

☐ Strongly agree (1) ☐ Agree (2) ☐ Uncertain (3)
☐ Disagree (4) ☐ Strongly disagree (5) ☐ Don't know (6)

11. I expect my doctor to be board certified in his/her specialty.

☐ Strongly agree (1) ☐ Agree (2) ☐ Uncertain (3)
☐ Disagree (4) ☐ Strongly disagree (5) ☐ Don't know (6)

12. It is important that my doctor listen carefully to me.

☐ Strongly agree (1) ☐ Agree (2) ☐ Uncertain (3)
☐ Disagree (4) ☐ Strongly disagree (5) ☐ Don't know (6)

13. It is important that my doctor answer all my questions in terms that I can understand.

☐ Strongly agree (1) ☐ Agree (2) ☐ Uncertain (3)
☐ Disagree (4) ☐ Strongly disagree (5) ☐ Don't know (6)

14. I expect my doctor to call me at home after my office appointment to follow up on treatment.

☐ Strongly agree (1) ☐ Agree (2) ☐ Uncertain (3)
☐ Disagree (4) ☐ Strongly disagree (5) ☐ Don't know (6)

15. If my doctor left the health plan that I currently belong to, I would try to follow him/her.

☐ Strongly agree (1) ☐ Agree (2) ☐ Uncertain (3)
☐ Disagree (4) ☐ Strongly disagree (5) ☐ Don't know (6)

F. Doctor's Office

16. I expect a polite receptionist in the doctor's office.

☐ Strongly agree (1) ☐ Agree (2) ☐ Uncertain (3)
☐ Disagree (4) ☐ Strongly disagree (5) ☐ Don't know (6)

17. I expect the phones in my doctor's office to be answered by a person rather than an automated voice system.

☐ Strongly agree (1) ☐ Agree (2) ☐ Uncertain (3)
☐ Disagree (4) ☐ Strongly disagree (5) ☐ Don't know (6)

18. I expect the phones in my doctor's office to be answered within three rings.

☐ Strongly agree (1) ☐ Agree (2) ☐ Uncertain (3)
☐ Disagree (4) ☐ Strongly disagree (5) ☐ Don't know (6)

19. I expect a medically knowledgeable receptionist in the doctor's office.

☐ Strongly agree (1) ☐ Agree (2) ☐ Uncertain (3)
☐ Disagree (4) ☐ Strongly disagree (5) ☐ Don't know (6)

G. Managed Care

20. Which best describes your type of health plan (check one)?

☐ A. **Traditional Insurance:** You receive care from physicians in their private offices. You may seek care from any physician. You must submit claim forms and the insurance company or Medicare pays the doctor. You may be responsible for a percentage of the doctor's bill.
☐ B. **HMO:** You can only go to a clinic or health care center for the physician care you receive. You may have to pay a copay ($5–$10), but you do not have to submit claim forms for payment. X-ray, laboratory, and pharmacy services are provided in the clinic. You may be referred to other physicians if needed.
☐ C. **PPO:** You receive care from physicians in their private offices. You may seek care from any physicians but the plan has an approved list of physicians, who provide you care at less expense. You must generally go elsewhere for X-ray, laboratory, and pharmacy services.
☐ D. **IPA:** You receive care only from physicians on the plan's approved list in their private practice offices. You may seek care from any hospital or doctor not on the list, but you are fully responsible to pay for your care in that case. You must generally go elsewhere for X-ray, laboratory, and pharmacy services.
☐ E. **OTHER:** please specify ______________________________

21. If you checked plan type A in question 20 above, go to question 27, otherwise please continue with question 22.

22. I understand how to use my managed care health plan to receive care.

☐ Strongly agree (1) ☐ Agree (2) ☐ Uncertain (3)
☐ Disagree (4) ☐ Strongly disagree (5) ☐ Don't know (6)

23. The quality of care provided by managed care is at least as good as that provided in other health insurance arrangements.

☐ Strongly agree (1) ☐ Agree (2) ☐ Uncertain (3)
☐ Disagree (4) ☐ Strongly disagree (5) ☐ Don't know (6)

24. I believe that all managed care organizations are similar in terms of the benefits that they provide.

☐ Strongly agree (1) ☐ Agree (2) ☐ Uncertain (3)
☐ Disagree (4) ☐ Strongly disagree (5) ☐ Don't know (6)

25. I believe that all managed care organizations are similar in terms of the quality of doctors that they provide.

☐ Strongly agree (1) ☐ Agree (2) ☐ Uncertain (3)
☐ Disagree (4) ☐ Strongly disagree (5) ☐ Don't know (6)

26. I believe that all managed care organizations provide the same level of customer services to members.

☐ Strongly agree (1) ☐ Agree (2) ☐ Uncertain (3)
☐ Disagree (4) ☐ Strongly disagree (5) ☐ Don't know (6)

27. I am satisfied with my current health care plan.

☐ Strongly agree (1) ☐ Agree (2) ☐ Uncertain (3)
☐ Disagree (4) ☐ Strongly disagree (5) ☐ Don't know (6)

28. In a managed care plan, I would expect to have free membership to a health club.

☐ Strongly agree (1) ☐ Agree (2) ☐ Uncertain (3)
☐ Disagree (4) ☐ Strongly disagree (5) ☐ Don't know (6)

29. In a managed care plan, I would expect to have free transportation to my doctor's office.

☐ Strongly agree (1) ☐ Agree (2) ☐ Uncertain (3)
☐ Disagree (4) ☐ Strongly disagree (5) ☐ Don't know (6)

30. In a managed care plan, I would expect my primary care doctor's office to be within 15 minutes driving time of my home.

☐ Strongly agree (1) ☐ Agree (2) ☐ Uncertain (3)
☐ Disagree (4) ☐ Strongly disagree (5) ☐ Don't know (6)

31. In a managed care plan, I would expect to be offered health awareness classes provided by my managed care organization.

☐ Strongly agree (1) ☐ Agree (2) ☐ Uncertain (3)
☐ Disagree (4) ☐ Strongly disagree (5) ☐ Don't know (6)

32. I expect a managed care plan to help me live a healthier lifestyle.

☐ Strongly agree (1) ☐ Agree (2) ☐ Uncertain (3)
☐ Disagree (4) ☐ Strongly disagree (5) ☐ Don't know (6)

I. Demographics

The last few questions are for classification purposes only.

33. What is your age?

☐ Under 55 (1) ☐ 55–59 (2) ☐ 60–64 (3) ☐ 65–69 (4)
☐ 70–74 (5) ☐ 75–79 (6) ☐ 80–84 (7) ☐ 85 or older (8)

34. What is your gender?

☐ Male (1) ☐ Female (2)

35. Which of the following best describes your ethnic background?

☐ Hispanic (1) ☐ Native American (5)
☐ Black or African American (2) ☐ Other (6)
☐ Asian (3) ☐ Refused (7)
☐ White or Caucasian (4)

Thank you for taking the time to complete this survey.

Case Exhibit 29.2	Variable Names
ID Q1–Q32 Questions in the order they appear on the questionnaire in Case Exhibit 28.1. Age Gender Race	

CASE

SUNBELT ENERGY CORPORATION

Download the data sets for this case from http://zikmund.swcollege.com or request them from your instructor.

Sunbelt Energy Corporation is a diversified petroleum company engaged in producing and marketing gasoline, motor oil, and petrochemicals, as well as a number of other energy-related activities such as coal mining, uranium extraction, and atomic-power generation.[23] Sunbelt markets its petroleum products though its own retail outlets and independent suppliers in a 25-state area within the continental United States. The firm's company-owned service stations are the latest in station design and automation. Sunbelt's retail marketing strategy emphasizes modern station designs, and the firm continually works to improve the appearance of both its company-owned and its independent retail outlets.

A research study to investigate consumers' reaction to a new method of payment was conducted in a single town in which the company owns all stations. The company investigated the use of automated teller machines (using the same technology as automated teller machines used by banks) and gasoline credit cards to pay for gas and services.

The specific objectives of the research were to determine the following:

1. The overall percentage of customers who use the automated teller machines.
2. What features of the automated teller machines people like.
3. What improvements to the machine could be made to assist current users of these machines.
4. What improvements to the automated teller machine could be made to cause nonusers to use them.
5. The percentage of people who not only purchase gasoline but also purchase something else at the station.
6. The percentage of people who pay using cash, a Sunbelt credit card, or a bank credit card.

The research was conducted in a southwestern town where the company owns all retail outlets and each station has automated teller machines. Respondents were interviewed as they filled their cars with gasoline. The personal interview lasted only a few minutes, because most people wish to purchase gasoline and leave as quickly as possible. This time frame restricted the number of questions that could be asked. All questions were short and to the point.

Four stations in the town had automated teller machines.

- Station Number 1—Limestone
- Station Number 2—Boulevard
- Station Number 3—Performance Plaza
- Station Number 4—Madison Convenience Store

Fifty interviews were conducted at each station for a total of 200 personal interviews.

SAMPLING

Every automobile that entered the service station in the self-service lanes was considered a member of the sampling frame. After a car arrived, the interviewer waited until the customer got out of his or her car and made a selection at the pump. As the gasoline was being pumped, interviewers introduced themselves and conducted the interviews. Only one individual refused to grant an interview. The questionnaire is shown in Case Exhibit 30.1.

ADDITIONAL INFORMATION

Several of the questions below require the use of a computerized database. Your instructor will provide information about obtaining the Sunbelt data if this material is part of the case assignment. Case Exhibit 30.2 lists the variable names. (The data are available in SPSS or Excel format.)

Questions

1. Evaluate the research objectives.
2. Evaluate the research design in light of the stated research objectives.
3. Using the computerized database, obtain simple frequencies for the answers to each question (the answers to the open-ended questions are not included on the database).
4. Perform the appropriate cross-tabulations.
5. Perform the appropriate univariate and bivariate statistical tests after you develop hypotheses for these particular tests.

CASE EXHIBIT 30.1 | PERSONAL INTERVIEW QUESTIONNAIRE

"Hello, my name is ____________________. In cooperation with Sunbelt, I am conducting a survey on how Sunbelt can better serve you. I'd like to ask you a few short questions."

Question 1
To start off, did you know that this station has an automated teller machine?
Yes _____ No _____

Question 2
In addition to a gasoline purchase, are you planning to purchase anything else, such as a soft drink, motor oil, or cigarettes?
Yes _____ No _____

Question 3
For today's purchase, are you planning to pay using the automated teller machine, or are you planning to go inside and pay the station attendant?
Go inside and pay attendant _____ (Skip to Question 9)
Use the automated teller machine _____ (Proceed to Questions 4, 5, 6, 7, and 8)

Question 4
Have you ever used the automated teller machine to pay for your gasoline purchase?
Yes _____ (Proceed to next question)
No _____ (Go to Question 8)

Question 5
What features of the automated teller machine do you like?
____
____
____
____
____

Question 6
What features of the automated teller machine do you dislike?
____
____
____
____
____

Question 7
From your viewpoint, are there any improvements that could be made to make it easier to use the automated teller machine?
____
____
____
____
____

Case Exhibit 30.1 | **Personal Interview Questionnaire (Continued)**

Question 8
Up to today, what features of the automated teller machine have caused you not to use it?

___
___
___
___
___

(Skip to the observation section)

Question 9
Will you be paying for your purchase in cash, or will you be using a credit card?
Pay with cash _____ (Skip to observation part)
Pay with a credit card _____ (Proceed to Question 10)

Question 10
Will you use a Sunbelt credit card, or will you use a Visa or MasterCard for payment?
Sunbelt card _____ (Proceed to Question 11)
Use other type _____ (Skip to observation section)

Question 11
Have you ever used the automated teller machine for your purchase?
Yes _____ (Proceed to Questions 12, 13, and 14)
No _____ (Skip to Question 15)

Question 12
What features of the automated teller machine do you like?

___
___
___
___
___

Question 13
What features of the automated teller machine do you dislike?

___
___
___
___
___

Question 14
From your viewpoint, are there any improvements that could be made to make it easier to use the automated teller machine?

___
___
___
___
___

(Skip to observation section)

Question 15
What features of the automated teller machine have caused you not to use it?

___
___
___
___
___

Observation Section

On behalf of Sunbelt, I thank you for your time and comments.

Is the driver of the vehicle male or female?	Male _____	Female _____
Is the driver under or over 40?	Under _____	Over _____
Are there any passengers in the vehicle?	Yes _____	No _____
Does the vehicle have Washington County tags?	Yes _____	No _____

Case Exhibit 30.2 | **Variable Names in the Sunbelt Database**

Variable Name	Label
ATM	Auto teller knowledge
ELSE	Purchase anything else
USE	Use ATM to pay
USEGAS	Use ATM to pay for gas
CASH	Pay with cash or credit card
SUNBELT	Use Sunbelt credit card
EVER	Ever use ATM for purchase
SEX	Male or female
AGE	Under or over 40
PASS	Passengers: yes or no
TAGS	Washington county tags

CASE 31

EMPLOYEES FEDERAL CREDIT UNION

Download the data sets for this case from http://zikmund.swcollege.com or request them from your instructor.

Employees Federal Credit Union (EFCU) is the credit union for a Fortune 500 firm.[24] Any employee of the organization is eligible for membership in the credit union.

Over the past few years the Employees Federal Credit Union has accumulated a large amount of surplus funds, which have been invested in certificates of deposit. It has also experienced a lower loan/share ratio than other credit unions of similar size. Because of these factors, the credit union's average earnings on its investments have slowly declined and its profit margins are being squeezed. The EFCU board of directors decided that a research project should be conducted to determine why its members are not borrowing money from the credit union. More specifically, the research project was mandated to answer the question of why the members are borrowing money from other alternative sources instead of from the credit union.

In addition to the above, the EFCU board of directors expressed its desire to determine what the members' attitudes were toward the overall management and operations of the credit union. Also, it was determined that the following questions should be addressed:

- How informed is the membership about the services provided by the credit union?
- Are there any differences in opinion toward borrowing funds and the services provided by the credit union between members who live in the area of the firm's headquarters and members who live outside of the area?

RESEARCH OBJECTIVES

To respond to the questions raised by the board, researchers developed the following objectives. The research design was formulated to address each of the objectives stated below:

- To determine the reasons why people join the Credit Union.
- To determine the reasons why members use other financial institutions when they need to borrow funds.
- To measure member attitudes and beliefs about the proficiencies of credit union employees.
- To determine whether there are any perceived differences between members who live in the area of the firm's headquarters and members who live elsewhere.
- To determine member awareness of the services offered by the credit union.

- To measure member attitudes and beliefs about how effectively the credit union is operated.

RESEARCH DESIGN AND DATA COLLECTION METHOD

The research data were collected by a mail questionnaire survey. This technique was determined to be the best method for collecting the research data for the following reasons:

- The credit union membership is widely dispersed geographically.
- The board wanted to minimize the cost of conducting the research.
- Several of the questions asked in the questionnaire are of a sensitive nature.
- The board had the flexibility of being able to wait for the survey results before taking any actions.

A copy of the questionnaire used to gather the research data is provided in Case Exhibit 31.1. Most of the questions were designed as structured questions because of the variation in the educational backgrounds, job functions, and interests of the members surveyed. However, the respondents were given the flexibility to answer several key questions in an unstructured format. The Likert scale was principally used where attitude measurements were requested.

SAMPLING PROCEDURES

The population of the EFCU is well defined; consequently, a simple random sample of the membership was selected. A sample size of 300 was calculated using the estimated population standard deviation based on the responses from 15 members to Question 37 of the questionnaire. Question 37 was used because it capsulized the essence of the research project.

The random numbers used in making the selection of the sampling units were generated with the help of a personal computer. The sampling frame used was the January 31 trial balance listing of the EFCU membership. According to the sampling frame, the EFCU had 3,531 members on that date. As a result, the 300 random numbers were generated within the range of 1 to 3,531. Each random number was matched to a corresponding number in the sampling frame, and those individuals were selected to receive copies of the survey questionnaire.

FIELDWORK

Most of the fieldwork for the research project, including all of the editing and coding of the survey data, was performed by the supervisory committee chairperson. The following is a list of the (much appreciated) assistance received during the field procedures:

- Bob Perkins obtained a copy of the most currently available listing of the membership of the EFCU.
- The payroll department prepared mailing labels for all the members in the sample who were having withholding for the credit union taken out of their payroll checks.
- The credit union clerks obtained the addresses and prepared mailing labels for all the remaining individuals selected in the sample.
- Administrative assistants helped copy and collate the survey questionnaires and prepare them for mailing.
- Ron Walker mailed all of the survey questionnaires.

The survey data from the structured questions were coded based on classifications established by the researcher. The codes were input into a series of databases using an IBM personal computer and a statistical software package.

Of the 125 returned questionnaires, two were not included in the survey results. One of the questionnaires was returned without the first two pages attached, and the other questionnaire appeared to have been deliberately falsified; not only were all the responses on this questionnaire at the extremes, but a number of contradictions were noted as well.

ADDITIONAL INFORMATION

Several of the questions below require the use of a computerized database. Your instructor will provide information about obtaining the EFCU data set if this material is part of the case assignment. (The data are available in SPSS or Excel format.) Each variable name is coded by its question number. Q1 is the variable name for question 1, "Are you a member of the Employees Federal Credit Union?" Q2 is the variable name for question 2, and so on. Exhibit 31.2 presents the coding.

Questions

1. Evaluate the research objectives.
2. Evaluate the research design in light of the stated research objectives.
3. Using the computerized database, obtain simple frequencies for the answers to each question (the answers to the open-ended questions are not included on the database).
4. Perform the appropriate cross-tabulations.
5. Perform the appropriate univariate and bivariate statistical tests after you develop hypotheses for these particular tests.

Case Exhibit 31.1 — EFCU Member Opinion Survey

1. Are you currently a member of the Employees Federal Credit Union (EFCU)?
   Yes ( ) No ( )
   If no, please have the member of your household who is a member of the EFCU complete the questionnaire. If no one in your household is a member, please return the questionnaire in the enclosed prepaid envelope.

2. Why did you join the Credit Union? (Check as many answers as are applicable.)
   _____ Convenience
   _____ Higher interest rates on my savings than other financial institutions pay
   _____ More personal than other facilities
   _____ Wanted a readily available source for borrowing money
   _____ Advertisements prompted me to join
   _____ Other—please explain:
   ____
   ____

Statements 3 through 6 ask for your opinion of the Credit Union employees. Check the response that best describes your rating of the Credit Union employees in each category. Please check only one response for each statement.

3. The Credit Union employees are courteous.

Strongly disagree	Disagree	Uncertain	Agree	Strongly agree
( )	( )	( )	( )	( )

4. The Credit Union employees are helpful.

Strongly disagree	Disagree	Uncertain	Agree	Strongly agree
( )	( )	( )	( )	( )

5. The Credit Union employees are professional.

Strongly disagree	Disagree	Uncertain	Agree	Strongly agree
( )	( )	( )	( )	( )

6. The Credit Union employees are always available.

Strongly disagree	Disagree	Uncertain	Agree	Strongly agree
( )	( )	( )	( )	( )

7. What is your opinion about the rates the Credit Union is paying on its share (members/savings) accounts?
   A. Very high _____ B. High _____ C. Average _____
   D. Low _____ E. Very low _____ F. No opinion _____

8. What is your opinion about the rates the Credit Union is charging its members to borrow funds?
   A. Very high _____ B. High _____ C. Average _____
   D. Low _____ E. Very low _____ F. No opinion _____

9. How often do you receive a financial statement of your account activity?

Too often	Very often	About right	Not often enough	Never
( )	( )	( )	( )	( )

10. How would you rate the accuracy of your statements?

Excellent	Good	Fair	Poor
( )	( )	( )	( )

11. Are they easy to understand?
    Yes ( ) No ( )

12. Do you feel that the Credit Union maintains your account information in a confidential manner?
    Yes ( ) No ( )

CASE EXHIBIT 31.1 | **EFCU MEMBER OPINION SURVEY (CONTINUED)**

The questions in the next section are important in determining how effective the Credit Union has been in communicating its different services to the members. Please answer each question honestly—remember, there are no right or wrong answers.

Circle the response that best describes your awareness of the services offered by the Credit Union.

Circle 1—If you were aware of the service and have used it.
Circle 2—If you were aware of the service but have not used it.
Circle 3—If you did not know this service was offered by the Credit Union.

	Aware and Have Used	Aware but Have Not Used	Unaware of Service
13. Regular share accounts	1	2	3
14. Special subaccounts	1	2	3
15. Christmas club accounts	1	2	3
16. Individual retirement accounts	1	2	3
17. MasterCard credit cards	1	2	3
18. Signature loans	1	2	3
19. New car loans	1	2	3
20. Late model car loans	1	2	3
21. Older model car loans	1	2	3
22. Household goods/appliance loans	1	2	3
23. Recreational loans	1	2	3
24. Share collateralized loans	1	2	3
25. IRA loans	1	2	3
26. Line of credit loans	1	2	3

27. Do you currently have a loan with the Credit Union?
    Yes ( )   No ( )

28. During the past year, have you borrowed money from a bank or other lending source other than the Credit Union?
    Yes ( )   No ( )
    If no, go to Question 30.

29. Why did you go to a source other than the Credit Union?
    _____ My loan application at the Credit Union was not approved.
    _____ The Credit Union did not offer this type of credit.
    _____ I found better loan rates elsewhere.
    _____ I have an established credit line elsewhere.
    _____ I prefer to use a local financial institution.
    _____ Other: ______________________________
    ____

For Statements 30 through 34, check the response that best describes your feelings about the statements. Check only one response for each statement given.

30. The Credit Union's loan rates are lower than those offered by other institutions.

Strongly disagree	Disagree	Uncertain	Agree	Strongly agree
( )	( )	( )	( )	( )

Case Exhibit 31.1 | **EFCU Member Opinion Survey (Continued)**

31. The Credit Union personnel will keep my personal financial information confidential.

Strongly disagree	Disagree	Uncertain	Agree	Strongly agree
( )	( )	( )	( )	( )

32. The Credit Union is prompt in processing loan applications.

Strongly disagree	Disagree	Uncertain	Agree	Strongly agree
( )	( )	( )	( )	( )

33. The current financial services provided by the Credit Union meet the needs of its members.

Strongly disagree	Disagree	Uncertain	Agree	Strongly agree
( )	( )	( )	( )	( )

34. The loan applications used by the Credit Union are simple and easy to complete.

Strongly disagree	Disagree	Uncertain	Agree	Strongly agree
( )	( )	( )	( )	( )

35. Which of the services provided by the Credit Union do you like best?

____

36. Which of the services provided by the Credit Union do you like least?

____

37. Overall, how do you feel the Credit Union is being managed and operated?
A. Excellent ____ B. Good ____ C. Average ____
D. Poor ____ E. Very poor ____ F. No opinion ____

38. Do you live in the headquarters area?
Yes ( ) No ( )
If yes, go to Question 40.

39. Do you feel the Credit Union meets your needs as well as those of members who live in the headquarters area?
Yes ( ) No ( )
If no, please explain:

____

____

40. If you were managing the Credit Union, what changes would you make and what additional services, if any, would you provide?

____

____

____

____

We sincerely appreciate the time and effort you made in completing this questionnaire. Thank you for your help.

Case Exhibit 31.2 | **Codes for Questionnaire**

strongly disagree = 1, strongly agree = 5
very high = 1, very low = 5, no opinion = 6
too often = 1, never = 5
excellent = 1, poor = 4
excellent = 1, very poor = 5, no answer = 6
yes = 1, no = 2, no answer = 3
aware and have used = 1, unaware = 3

CASE 32

VALUES AND THE AUTOMOBILE MARKET

Download the data sets for this case from http://zikmund.swcollege.com or request them from your instructor.

In the last decade, the luxury car segment became one of the most competitive in the automobile market.[25] Many American consumers who purchase luxury cars prefer imports from Germany and Japan.

A marketing vice president with General Motors once commented, "Import-committed buyers have been frustrating to us." This type of thinking has led industry analysts to argue that to successfully compete in the luxury car segment, U.S. carmakers need to develop a better understanding of the consumers so that they can better segment the market and better position their products via more effective advertising. Insight into the foreign-domestic luxury car choice may result from examining owners' personal values in addition to their evaluations of car attributes, because luxury cars, like many other conspicuously consumed luxury products, may be purchased mainly for value-expressive reasons.

Industry analysts believe it would be important to assess whether personal values of consumers could be used to explain ownership of American, German, and Japanese luxury cars. Further, they believe they should also assess whether knowledge of owners' personal values provides any additional information useful in explaining ownership of American, German, and Japanese luxury cars beyond that obtained from their evaluations of the car's attributes.

Personal values are likely to provide insights into reasons for ownership of luxury cars for at least two reasons. First, Americans have always had a very personal relationship with their cars and have used them as symbols of their self-concept. For instance, people who value a *sense of accomplishment* are quite likely to desire a luxury car that they feel is an appropriate symbol of their achievement, whereas people who value *fun, enjoyment,* and *excitement* are likely to desire a luxury car that they perceive as fun and exciting to drive. An advertiser trying to persuade the former segment to purchase a luxury car should position the car as a status symbol that will help its owners demonstrate their accomplishments to others. Similarly, an advertiser trying to persuade the latter segment to purchase a luxury car should position the car as a fun and exciting car to drive. In other words, effective advertising shows consumers how purchasing a given product will help them achieve their valued state, because brands tied to values will be perceived more favorably than brands that deliver more mundane benefits.

Second, when a market is overcrowded with competing brands offering very similar options—as is the case with the luxury car market—consumers are quite likely to choose between brands on the basis of value-expressive considerations.

METHOD

Data were collected via a mail survey sent to 498 consumers chosen at random from a list obtained from a syndicated research company located in an affluent county in a southern state. The list contained names of people who had purchased either a luxury American car (Cadillac or Lincoln Mercury), a luxury German car (Mercedes or BMW), or a luxury Japanese car (Infiniti or Lexus) within the last year. A cover letter explained that the survey was part of an academic research project. People were asked to return the questionnaires anonymously to a university address (a postage-paid envelope was provided with each survey). Beyond an appeal to help the researchers, respondents were not offered any other incentive to complete the surveys. Of the 498 surveys originally sent, 17 were returned by the post office as undeliverable. One hundred fifty-five completed surveys were received, for a response rate of 32.2 percent [155/(498 − 17)].

The Survey Instrument

The survey included questions on (1) various issues that people consider when purchasing new cars, (2) importance of car attributes, (3) importance of different values, and (4) demographics (sex, age, education, and family income). Questions relating to the issues that people consider when purchasing new cars were developed through initial interviews with consumers and were measured with a 7-point Likert scale with end anchors of "strongly agree" and "strongly disagree."

(See Case Exhibit 32.1.) A list of 12 car attributes was developed from the initial interviews with consumers and by consulting *Consumer Reports.* (See Case Exhibit 32.2.) The importance of each attribute was measured with a 7-point numerical scale with end points labeled "very important" and "very unimportant." For measuring the importance of values, the List of Values (LOV) scale was used to measure the importance of values. (See Case Exhibit 32.3.) Respondents were asked to rate each of the eight values (we combined fun, enjoyment, and excitement into one value) on a 7-point numerical scale with end points labeled "very important" and "very unimportant."

The Sample

Of the 155 respondents in the sample, 58 (37.4 percent) owned an American luxury car, 38 (24.5 percent) owned a European luxury car, and 59 (38.1 percent) owned a Japanese luxury car. The majority of the sample consisted of consumers who were older (85 percent were 35 years of age or above), more educated (64 percent were college graduates), and economically well-off (87.2 percent earned $65,000 or more).

The Code Book

Case Exhibit 32.4 lists the SPSS variable names and identifies codes for these variables. (Note that this data set is also available in Microsoft Excel.)

ADDITIONAL INFORMATION

Several of the questions will require the use of a computerized database. Your instructor will provide information about obtaining the VALUES data set if the material is part of the case assignment. (The data are available in SPSS or Excel format.)

Questions

1. Is the sampling method adequate? Is the attitude measuring scale sound? Explain.
2. Using the computerized database with a statistical software package, calculate the means of the three automotive groups for the values variable. Do any of the values variables show significant differences among American, Japanese, and European car owners?
3. Are there any significant differences on importance of attributes?
4. Write a short statement interpreting the results of this research.

Advanced Questions

5. Are any of the value scale items highly correlated?
6. Should multivariate analysis be used to understand the data?

CASE EXHIBIT 32.1 ISSUES THAT CONSUMERS CONSIDER WHEN BUYING LUXURY AUTOMOBILES

Codes	Issues
Having a luxury car is a major part of my fun and excitement.*	Issue 1
Owning a luxury car is a part of "being good to myself."	Issue 2
When I was able to buy my first luxury car, I felt a sense of accomplishment.	Issue 3
I enjoy giving my friends advice about luxury cars.	Issue 4
Getting a good deal when I buy a luxury car makes me feel better about myself.	Issue 5
I seek novelty and I am willing to try new innovations in cars.	Issue 6
I tend to buy the same brand of the car several times in a row.	Issue 7
I tend to buy from the same dealer several times in a row.	Issue 8
I usually use sources of information such as *Consumer Reports* in deciding on a car.	Issue 9
I usually visit three or more dealerships before I buy a car.	Issue 10
I would read a brochure or watch a video about defensive driving.	Issue 11
When buying a new luxury car, my family's opinion is very important to me.	Issue 12
My family usually accompanies me when I am shopping for a new luxury car.	Issue 13
I usually rely upon ads and salespersons for information on cars.	Issue 14
I usually rely upon friends and acquaintances for information on cars.	Issue 15
When shopping for a car, it is important that the car dealer make me feel at ease.	Issue 16
Most of my friends drive luxury import cars.	Issue 17
Most of my friends drive luxury domestic cars.	Issue 18
I think celebrity endorsers in ads influence people's choices of luxury cars.	Issue 19
I would not buy a luxury car if I felt that my debt level is higher than usual.	Issue 20

*Note: Subjects' responses were measured with 1 as "strongly agree" and 7 as "strongly disagree."

CASE EXHIBIT 32.2 | **CAR ATTRIBUTES**

Attribute	Code	Attribute	Code
Comfort	Comfort	Low maintenance cost	Lowmc
Safety	Safety	Reliability	Rely
Power	Power	Warranty	Warrant
Speed	Speed	Nonpolluting	Nonpol
Styling	Styling	High gas mileage	Gasmle
Durability	Durabil	Speed of repairs	Repairs

CASE EXHIBIT 32.3 | **LIST OF VALUES**

Value	Code	Value	Code
Fun–Enjoyment–Excitement	Fun	Sense of accomplishment	Accomp
Sense of belonging	Belong	Warm relationship	Warm
Being well respected	Respect	Security	Security
Self-fulfillment	Selfful	Self-respect	Selfres

CASE EXHIBIT 32.4 | **LIST OF VARIABLES AND COMPUTER CODES**

ID—Identification number
Age (categories are 2 = < 35 yrs, 3 = 36–45 yrs, 4 = 46–55 yrs, 5 = 56–65 yrs, 6 = 65+ yrs)
Sex (1 = male, 0 = female)
Education (1 = less than high school, 2 = high-school grad, 3 = some college, 4 = college graduate, 5 = graduate degree)
Income (1 = less than or equal to $35,000, 2 = $35–50,000, 3 = $50–65,000, 4 = $65,000+)
Car—Type of luxury car (American, European, Japanese)
Issues—The sequence of issues listed in Case Exhibit 32.1. (Strongly agree = 1; strongly disagree = 7)
Attributes—The sequence of car attributes listed in Case Exhibit 32.2. (Very important to you = 1; very unimportant to you = 7)
Values—The sequence of values listed in Case Exhibit 32.3. (Very important = 1; very unimportant = 7)

APPENDIX: STATISTICAL TABLES

TABLE 1 **RANDOM DIGITS**

37751	04998	66038	63480	98442	22245	83538	62351	74514	90497
50915	64152	82981	15796	27102	71635	34470	13608	26360	76285
99142	35021	01032	57907	80545	54112	15150	36856	03247	40392
70720	10033	25191	62358	03784	74377	88150	25567	87457	49512
18460	64947	32958	08752	96366	89092	23597	74308	00881	88976
65763	41133	60950	35372	06782	81451	78764	52645	19841	50083
83769	52570	60133	25211	87384	90182	84990	26400	39128	97043
58900	78420	98579	33665	10718	39342	46346	14401	13503	46525
54746	71115	78219	64314	11227	41702	54517	87676	14078	45317
56819	27340	07200	52663	57864	85159	15460	97564	29637	27742
34990	62122	38223	28526	37006	22774	46026	15981	87291	56946
02269	22795	87593	81830	95383	67823	20196	54850	46779	64519
43042	53600	45738	00261	31100	67239	02004	70698	53597	62617
92565	12211	06868	87786	59576	61382	33972	13161	47208	96604
67424	32620	60841	86848	85000	04835	48576	33884	10101	84129
04015	77148	09535	10743	97871	55919	45274	38304	93125	91847
85226	19763	46105	25289	26714	73253	85922	21785	42624	92741
03360	07457	75131	41209	50451	23472	07438	08375	29312	62264
72460	99682	27970	25632	34096	17656	12736	27476	21938	67305
66960	55780	71778	52629	51692	71442	36130	70425	39874	62035
14824	95631	00697	65462	24815	13930	02938	54619	28909	53950
34001	05618	41900	23303	19928	60755	61404	56947	91441	19299
77718	83830	29781	72917	10840	74182	08293	62588	99625	22088
60930	05091	35726	07414	49211	69586	20226	08274	28167	65279
94180	62151	08112	26646	07617	42954	22521	09395	43561	45692
81073	85543	47650	93830	07377	87995	35084	39386	93141	88309
18467	39689	60801	46828	38670	88243	89042	78452	08032	72566
60643	59399	79740	17295	50094	66436	92677	68345	24025	36489
73372	61697	85728	90779	13235	83114	70728	32093	74306	08325
18395	18482	83245	54942	51905	09534	70839	91073	42193	81199
07261	28720	71244	05064	84873	68020	39037	68981	00670	86291
61679	81529	83725	33269	45958	74265	87460	60525	42539	25605
11815	48679	00556	96871	39835	83055	84949	11681	51687	55896
99007	35050	86440	44280	20320	97527	28138	01088	49037	85430
06446	65608	79291	16624	06135	30622	56133	33998	32308	29434
37913	83900	49166	00249	53178	72307	72190	75931	77613	20172
89444	98195	46733	37201	71901	55023	54570	83126	09462	93979
12582	41940	36060	56756	07999	64138	06492	25815	19518	86938
50494	80008	64774	51382	08059	66448	16437	91579	39197	43798
78301	66128	12840	22254	15193	81210	95747	47344	33660	41707
79457	31686	94486	27386	41641	72199	67265	51794	81521	01556
49337	10475	49588	79338	32156	47732	29464	92835	09498	81902
92540	56528	21200	87462	08924	56993	57330	85069	10903	80904
17729	61914	74616	20433	59474	21270	96406	13090	94308	02072
24003	80475	19793	71578	52010	72216	15692	96689	80452	46312
16129	49245	21693	20946	60873	82451	32516	23823	30046	06870
05453	03060	83621	43443	17082	04401	15299	64642	73497	88426
67711	70526	46700	00171	55077	11440	95932	91116	17259	19645
76306	39287	31026	49379	30267	68885	98147	70311	43856	37376
81300	17782	76403	00972	12558	46140	19818	20440	83967	61036

TABLE 2 AREA UNDER THE NORMAL CURVE

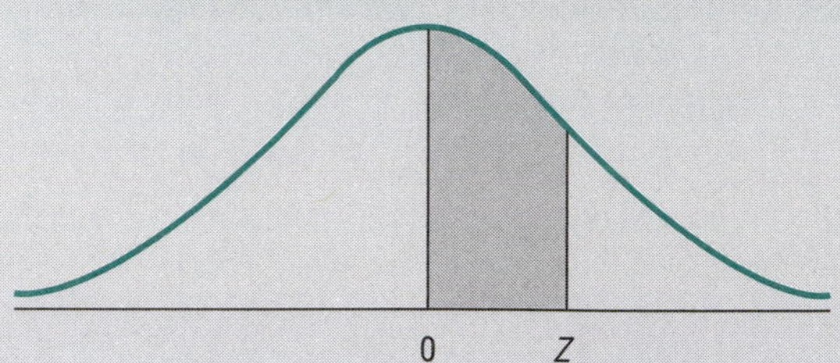

z	.00	.01	.02	.03	.04	.05	.06	.07	.08	.09
0.0	.0000	.0040	.0080	.0120	.0160	.0199	.0239	.0279	.0319	.0359
0.1	.0398	.0438	.0478	.0517	.0557	.0596	.0636	.0675	.0714	.0753
0.2	.0793	.0832	.0871	.0910	.0948	.0987	.1026	.1064	.1103	.1141
0.3	.1179	.1217	.1255	.1293	.1331	.1368	.1406	.1443	.1480	.1517
0.4	.1554	.1591	.1628	.1664	.1700	.1736	.1772	.1808	.1844	.1879
0.5	.1915	.1950	.1985	.2019	.2054	.2088	.2123	.2157	.2190	.2224
0.6	.2257	.2291	.2324	.2357	.2389	.2422	.2454	.2486	.2518	.2549
0.7	.2580	.2612	.2642	.2673	.2704	.2734	.2764	.2794	.2823	.2852
0.8	.2881	.2910	.2939	.2967	.2995	.3023	.3051	.3078	.3106	.3133
0.9	.3159	.3186	.3212	.3238	.3264	.3289	.3315	.3340	.3365	.3389
1.0	.3413	.3438	.3461	.3485	.3508	.3531	.3554	.3577	.3599	.3621
1.1	.3643	.3665	.3686	.3708	.3729	.3749	.3770	.3790	.3810	.3830
1.2	.3849	.3869	.3888	.3907	.3925	.3944	.3962	.3980	.3997	.4015
1.3	.4032	.4049	.4066	.4082	.4099	.4115	.4131	.4147	.4162	.4177
1.4	.4192	.4207	.4222	.4236	.4251	.4265	.4279	.4292	.4306	.4319
1.5	.4332	.4345	.4357	.4370	.4382	.4394	.4406	.4418	.4429	.4441
1.6	.4452	.4463	.4474	.4484	.4495	.4505	.4515	.4525	.4535	.4545
1.7	.4554	.4564	.4573	.4582	.4591	.4599	.4608	.4616	.4625	.4633
1.8	.4641	.4649	.4656	.4664	.4671	.4678	.4686	.4693	.4699	.4706
1.9	.4713	.4719	.4726	.4732	.4738	.4744	.4750	.4756	.4761	.4767
2.0	.4772	.4778	.4783	.4788	.4793	.4798	.4803	.4808	.4812	.4817
2.1	.4821	.4826	.4830	.4834	.4838	.4842	.4846	.4850	.4854	.4857
2.2	.4861	.4864	.4868	.4871	.4875	.4878	.4881	.4884	.4887	.4890
2.3	.4893	.4896	.4898	.4901	.4904	.4906	.4909	.4911	.4913	.4916
2.4	.4918	.4920	.4922	.4925	.4927	.4929	.4931	.4932	.4934	.4936
2.5	.4938	.4940	.4941	.4943	.4945	.4946	.4948	.4949	.4951	.4952
2.6	.4953	.4955	.4956	.4957	.4959	.4960	.4961	.4962	.4963	.4964
2.7	.4965	.4966	.4967	.4968	.4969	.4970	.4971	.4972	.4973	.4974
2.8	.4974	.4975	.4976	.4977	.4977	.4978	.4979	.4979	.4980	.4981
2.9	.4981	.4982	.4982	.4983	.4984	.4984	.4985	.4985	.4986	.4986
3.0	.49865	.4987	.4987	.4988	.4988	.4989	.4989	.4989	.4990	.4990
4.0	.49997									

TABLE 3 Distribution of *t* for Given Probability Levels

	Level of significance for one-tailed test					
	.10	.05	.025	.01	.005	.0005
	Level of significance for two-tailed test					
d.f.	**.20**	**.10**	**.05**	**.02**	**.01**	**.001**
1	3.078	6.314	12.706	31.821	63.657	636.619
2	1.886	2.920	4.303	6.965	9.925	31.598
3	1.638	2.353	3.182	4.541	5.841	12.941
4	1.533	2.132	2.776	3.747	4.604	8.610
5	1.476	2.015	2.571	3.365	4.032	6.859
6	1.440	1.943	2.447	3.143	3.707	5.959
7	1.415	1.895	2.365	2.998	3.499	5.405
8	1.397	1.860	2.306	2.896	3.355	5.041
9	1.383	1.833	2.262	2.821	3.250	4.781
10	1.372	1.812	2.228	2.764	3.169	4.587
11	1.363	1.796	2.201	2.718	3.106	4.437
12	1.356	1.782	2.179	2.681	3.055	4.318
13	1.350	1.771	2.160	2.650	3.012	4.221
14	1.345	1.761	2.145	2.624	2.977	4.140
15	1.341	1.753	2.131	2.602	2.947	4.073
16	1.337	1.746	2.120	2.583	2.921	4.015
17	1.333	1.740	2.110	2.567	2.898	3.965
18	1.330	1.734	2.101	2.552	2.878	3.922
19	1.328	1.729	2.093	2.539	2.861	3.883
20	1.325	1.725	2.086	2.528	2.845	3.850
21	1.323	1.721	2.080	2.518	2.831	3.819
22	1.321	1.717	2.074	2.508	2.819	3.792
23	1.319	1.714	2.069	2.500	2.807	3.767
24	1.318	1.711	2.064	2.492	2.797	3.745
25	1.316	1.708	2.060	2.485	2.787	3.725
26	1.315	1.706	2.056	2.479	2.779	3.707
27	1.314	1.703	2.052	2.473	2.771	3.690
28	1.313	1.701	2.048	2.467	2.763	3.674
29	1.311	1.699	2.045	2.462	2.756	3.659
30	1.310	1.697	2.042	2.457	2.750	3.646
40	1.303	1.684	2.021	2.423	2.704	3.551
60	1.296	1.671	2.000	2.390	2.660	3.460
120	1.289	1.658	1.980	2.358	2.617	3.373
∞	1.282	1.645	1.960	2.326	2.576	3.291

TABLE 4

CHI-SQUARE DISTRIBUTION

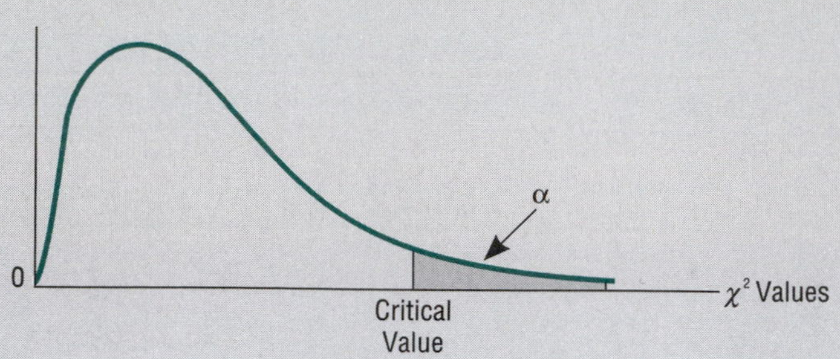

Degrees of Freedom (d.f.)	AREA IN SHADED RIGHT TAIL (α)		
	.10	.05	.01
1	2.706	3.841	6.635
2	4.605	5.991	9.210
3	6.251	7.815	11.345
4	7.779	9.488	13.277
5	9.236	11.070	15.086
6	10.645	12.592	16.812
7	12.017	14.067	18.475
8	13.362	15.507	20.090
9	14.684	16.919	21.666
10	15.987	18.307	23.209
11	17.275	19.675	24.725
12	18.549	21.026	26.217
13	19.812	22.362	27.688
14	21.064	23.685	29.141
15	22.307	24.996	30.578
16	23.542	26.296	32.000
17	24.769	27.587	33.409
18	25.989	28.869	34.805
19	27.204	30.144	36.191
20	28.412	31.410	37.566
21	29.615	32.671	38.932
22	30.813	33.924	40.289
23	32.007	35.172	41.638
24	33.196	36.415	42.980
25	34.382	37.652	44.314
26	35.563	38.885	45.642
27	36.741	40.113	46.963
28	37.916	41.337	48.278
29	39.087	42.557	49.588
30	40.256	43.773	50.892

Table 5 Critical Values of F_{ν_1, ν_2} for $\alpha = .05$

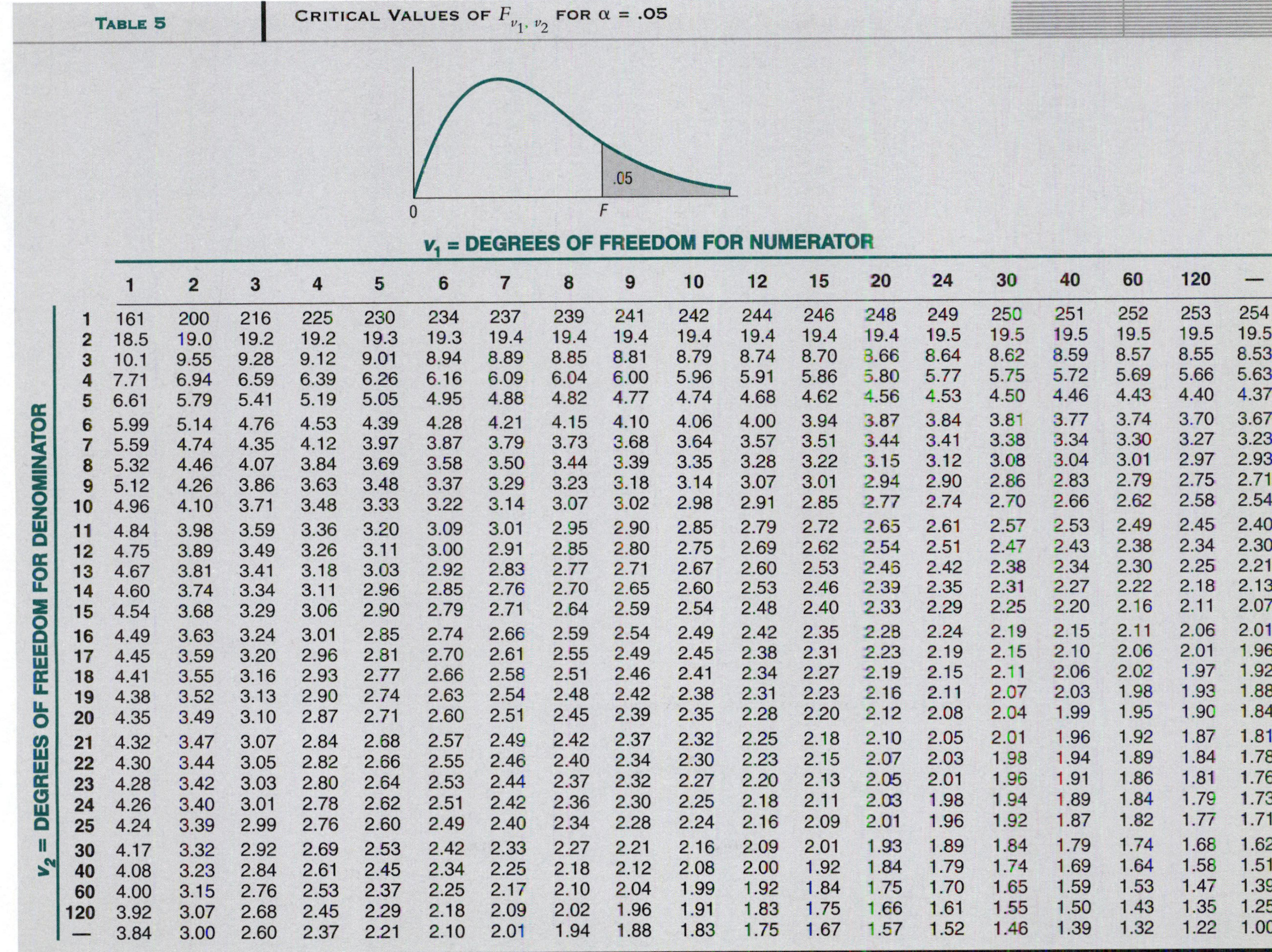

ν_1 = DEGREES OF FREEDOM FOR NUMERATOR

ν_2 = DEGREES OF FREEDOM FOR DENOMINATOR	1	2	3	4	5	6	7	8	9	10	12	15	20	24	30	40	60	120	—
1	161	200	216	225	230	234	237	239	241	242	244	246	248	249	250	251	252	253	254
2	18.5	19.0	19.2	19.2	19.3	19.3	19.4	19.4	19.4	19.4	19.4	19.4	19.4	19.5	19.5	19.5	19.5	19.5	19.5
3	10.1	9.55	9.28	9.12	9.01	8.94	8.89	8.85	8.81	8.79	8.74	8.70	8.66	8.64	8.62	8.59	8.57	8.55	8.53
4	7.71	6.94	6.59	6.39	6.26	6.16	6.09	6.04	6.00	5.96	5.91	5.86	5.80	5.77	5.75	5.72	5.69	5.66	5.63
5	6.61	5.79	5.41	5.19	5.05	4.95	4.88	4.82	4.77	4.74	4.68	4.62	4.56	4.53	4.50	4.46	4.43	4.40	4.37
6	5.99	5.14	4.76	4.53	4.39	4.28	4.21	4.15	4.10	4.06	4.00	3.94	3.87	3.84	3.81	3.77	3.74	3.70	3.67
7	5.59	4.74	4.35	4.12	3.97	3.87	3.79	3.73	3.68	3.64	3.57	3.51	3.44	3.41	3.38	3.34	3.30	3.27	3.23
8	5.32	4.46	4.07	3.84	3.69	3.58	3.50	3.44	3.39	3.35	3.28	3.22	3.15	3.12	3.08	3.04	3.01	2.97	2.93
9	5.12	4.26	3.86	3.63	3.48	3.37	3.29	3.23	3.18	3.14	3.07	3.01	2.94	2.90	2.86	2.83	2.79	2.75	2.71
10	4.96	4.10	3.71	3.48	3.33	3.22	3.14	3.07	3.02	2.98	2.91	2.85	2.77	2.74	2.70	2.66	2.62	2.58	2.54
11	4.84	3.98	3.59	3.36	3.20	3.09	3.01	2.95	2.90	2.85	2.79	2.72	2.65	2.61	2.57	2.53	2.49	2.45	2.40
12	4.75	3.89	3.49	3.26	3.11	3.00	2.91	2.85	2.80	2.75	2.69	2.62	2.54	2.51	2.47	2.43	2.38	2.34	2.30
13	4.67	3.81	3.41	3.18	3.03	2.92	2.83	2.77	2.71	2.67	2.60	2.53	2.46	2.42	2.38	2.34	2.30	2.25	2.21
14	4.60	3.74	3.34	3.11	2.96	2.85	2.76	2.70	2.65	2.60	2.53	2.46	2.39	2.35	2.31	2.27	2.22	2.18	2.13
15	4.54	3.68	3.29	3.06	2.90	2.79	2.71	2.64	2.59	2.54	2.48	2.40	2.33	2.29	2.25	2.20	2.16	2.11	2.07
16	4.49	3.63	3.24	3.01	2.85	2.74	2.66	2.59	2.54	2.49	2.42	2.35	2.28	2.24	2.19	2.15	2.11	2.06	2.01
17	4.45	3.59	3.20	2.96	2.81	2.70	2.61	2.55	2.49	2.45	2.38	2.31	2.23	2.19	2.15	2.10	2.06	2.01	1.96
18	4.41	3.55	3.16	2.93	2.77	2.66	2.58	2.51	2.46	2.41	2.34	2.27	2.19	2.15	2.11	2.06	2.02	1.97	1.92
19	4.38	3.52	3.13	2.90	2.74	2.63	2.54	2.48	2.42	2.38	2.31	2.23	2.16	2.11	2.07	2.03	1.98	1.93	1.88
20	4.35	3.49	3.10	2.87	2.71	2.60	2.51	2.45	2.39	2.35	2.28	2.20	2.12	2.08	2.04	1.99	1.95	1.90	1.84
21	4.32	3.47	3.07	2.84	2.68	2.57	2.49	2.42	2.37	2.32	2.25	2.18	2.10	2.05	2.01	1.96	1.92	1.87	1.81
22	4.30	3.44	3.05	2.82	2.66	2.55	2.46	2.40	2.34	2.30	2.23	2.15	2.07	2.03	1.98	1.94	1.89	1.84	1.78
23	4.28	3.42	3.03	2.80	2.64	2.53	2.44	2.37	2.32	2.27	2.20	2.13	2.05	2.01	1.96	1.91	1.86	1.81	1.76
24	4.26	3.40	3.01	2.78	2.62	2.51	2.42	2.36	2.30	2.25	2.18	2.11	2.03	1.98	1.94	1.89	1.84	1.79	1.73
25	4.24	3.39	2.99	2.76	2.60	2.49	2.40	2.34	2.28	2.24	2.16	2.09	2.01	1.96	1.92	1.87	1.82	1.77	1.71
30	4.17	3.32	2.92	2.69	2.53	2.42	2.33	2.27	2.21	2.16	2.09	2.01	1.93	1.89	1.84	1.79	1.74	1.68	1.62
40	4.08	3.23	2.84	2.61	2.45	2.34	2.25	2.18	2.12	2.08	2.00	1.92	1.84	1.79	1.74	1.69	1.64	1.58	1.51
60	4.00	3.15	2.76	2.53	2.37	2.25	2.17	2.10	2.04	1.99	1.92	1.84	1.75	1.70	1.65	1.59	1.53	1.47	1.39
120	3.92	3.07	2.68	2.45	2.29	2.18	2.09	2.02	1.96	1.91	1.83	1.75	1.66	1.61	1.55	1.50	1.43	1.35	1.25
—	3.84	3.00	2.60	2.37	2.21	2.10	2.01	1.94	1.88	1.83	1.75	1.67	1.57	1.52	1.46	1.39	1.32	1.22	1.00

Table 6 Critical Values of F_{ν_1, ν_2} for $\alpha = .01$

ν_1 = DEGREES OF FREEDOM FOR NUMERATOR

ν_2 = Degrees of Freedom for Denominator	1	2	3	4	5	6	7	8	9	10	12	15	20	24	30	40	60	120	—
1	4,052	5,000	5,403	5,625	5,764	5,859	5,928	5,982	6,023	6,056	6,106	6,157	6,209	6,235	6,261	6,287	6,313	6,339	6,366
2	98.5	99.0	99.2	99.2	99.3	99.3	99.4	99.4	99.4	99.4	99.4	99.4	99.4	99.5	99.5	99.5	99.5	99.5	99.5
3	34.1	30.8	29.5	28.7	28.2	27.9	27.7	27.5	27.3	27.2	27.1	26.9	26.7	26.6	26.5	26.4	26.3	26.2	26.1
4	21.2	18.0	16.7	16.0	15.5	15.2	15.0	14.8	14.7	14.5	14.4	14.2	14.0	13.9	13.8	13.7	13.7	13.6	13.5
5	16.3	13.3	12.1	11.4	11.0	10.7	10.5	10.3	10.2	10.1	9.89	9.72	9.55	9.47	9.38	9.29	9.20	9.11	9.02
6	13.7	10.9	9.78	9.15	8.75	8.47	8.26	8.10	7.98	7.87	7.72	7.56	7.40	7.31	7.23	7.14	7.06	6.97	6.88
7	12.2	9.55	8.45	7.85	7.46	7.19	6.99	6.84	6.72	6.62	6.47	6.31	6.16	6.07	5.99	5.91	5.82	5.74	5.65
8	11.3	8.65	7.59	7.01	6.63	6.37	6.18	6.03	5.91	5.81	5.67	5.52	5.36	5.28	5.20	5.12	5.03	4.95	4.86
9	10.6	8.02	6.99	6.42	6.06	5.80	5.61	5.47	5.35	5.26	5.11	4.96	4.81	4.73	4.65	4.57	4.48	4.40	4.31
10	10.0	7.56	6.55	5.99	5.64	5.39	5.20	5.06	4.94	4.85	4.71	4.56	4.41	4.33	4.25	4.17	4.08	4.00	3.91
11	9.65	7.21	6.22	5.67	5.32	5.07	4.89	4.74	4.63	4.54	4.40	4.25	4.10	4.02	3.94	3.86	3.78	3.69	3.60
12	9.33	6.93	5.95	5.41	5.06	4.82	4.64	4.50	4.39	4.30	4.16	4.01	3.86	3.78	3.70	3.62	3.54	3.45	3.36
13	9.07	6.70	5.74	5.21	4.86	4.62	4.44	4.30	4.19	4.10	3.96	3.82	3.66	3.59	3.51	3.43	3.34	3.25	3.17
14	8.86	6.51	5.56	5.04	4.70	4.46	4.28	4.14	4.03	3.94	3.80	3.66	3.51	3.43	3.35	3.27	3.18	3.09	3.00
15	8.68	6.36	5.42	4.89	4.56	4.32	4.14	4.00	3.89	3.80	3.67	3.52	3.37	3.29	3.21	3.13	3.05	2.96	2.87
16	8.53	6.23	5.29	4.77	4.44	4.20	4.03	3.89	3.78	3.69	3.55	3.41	3.26	3.18	3.10	3.02	2.93	2.84	2.75
17	8.40	6.11	5.19	4.67	4.34	4.10	3.93	3.79	3.68	3.59	3.46	3.31	3.16	3.08	3.00	2.92	2.83	2.75	2.65
18	8.29	6.01	5.09	4.58	4.25	4.01	3.84	3.71	3.60	3.51	3.37	3.23	3.08	3.00	2.92	2.84	2.75	2.66	2.57
19	8.19	5.93	5.01	4.50	4.17	3.94	3.77	3.63	3.52	3.43	3.30	3.15	3.00	2.92	2.84	2.76	2.67	2.58	2.49
20	8.10	5.85	4.94	4.43	4.10	3.87	3.70	3.56	3.46	3.37	3.23	3.09	2.94	2.86	2.78	2.69	2.61	2.52	2.42
21	8.02	5.78	4.87	4.37	4.04	3.81	3.64	3.51	3.40	3.31	3.17	3.03	2.88	2.80	2.72	2.64	2.55	2.46	2.36
22	7.96	5.72	4.82	4.31	3.99	3.76	3.59	3.45	3.35	3.26	3.12	2.98	2.83	2.75	2.67	2.58	2.50	2.40	2.31
23	7.88	5.66	4.76	4.26	3.94	3.71	3.54	3.41	3.30	3.21	3.07	2.93	2.78	2.70	2.62	2.54	2.45	2.35	2.26
24	7.82	5.61	4.72	4.22	3.90	3.67	3.50	3.36	3.26	3.17	3.03	2.89	2.74	2.66	2.58	2.49	2.40	2.31	2.21
25	7.77	5.57	4.68	4.18	3.86	3.63	3.46	3.32	3.22	3.13	2.99	2.85	2.70	2.62	2.53	2.45	2.36	2.27	2.17
30	7.58	5.39	4.51	4.02	3.70	3.47	3.30	3.17	3.07	2.98	2.84	2.70	2.55	2.47	2.39	2.30	2.21	2.11	2.01
40	7.31	5.18	4.31	3.83	3.51	3.29	3.12	2.99	2.89	2.80	2.66	2.52	2.37	2.29	2.20	2.11	2.02	1.92	1.80
60	7.08	4.98	4.13	3.65	3.34	3.12	2.95	2.82	2.72	2.63	2.50	2.35	2.20	2.12	2.03	1.94	1.84	1.73	1.60
120	6.85	4.79	3.95	3.48	3.17	2.96	2.79	2.66	2.56	2.47	2.34	2.19	2.03	1.95	1.86	1.76	1.66	1.53	1.38
—	6.63	4.61	3.78	3.32	3.02	2.80	2.64	2.51	2.41	2.32	2.18	2.04	1.88	1.79	1.70	1.59	1.47	1.32	1.00

Table 7	**Critical Values of the Pearson Correlation Coefficient**			
	Level of Significance for One-Tailed Test			
	.05	**.025**	**.01**	**.005**
	Level of Significance for Two-Tailed Test			
d.f.	**.10**	**.05**	**.02**	**.01**
1	.988	.997	.9995	.9999
2	.900	.950	.980	.990
3	.805	.878	.934	.959
4	.729	.811	.882	.917
5	.669	.754	.833	.874
6	.622	.707	.789	.834
7	.582	.666	.750	.798
8	.549	.632	.716	.765
9	.521	.602	.685	.735
10	.497	.576	.658	.708
11	.476	.553	.634	.684
12	.458	.532	.612	.661
13	.441	.514	.592	.641
14	.426	.497	.574	.623
15	.412	.482	.558	.606
16	.400	.468	.542	.590
17	.389	.456	.528	.575
18	.378	.444	.516	.561
19	.369	.433	.503	.549
20	.360	.423	.492	.537
21	.352	.413	.482	.526
22	.344	.404	.472	.515
23	.337	.396	.462	.505
24	.330	.388	.453	.496
25	.323	.381	.445	.487
26	.317	.374	.437	.479
27	.311	.367	.430	.471
28	.306	.361	.423	.463
29	.301	.355	.416	.456
30	.296	.349	.409	.449
35	.275	.325	.381	.418
40	.257	.304	.358	.393
45	.243	.288	.338	.372
50	.231	.273	.322	.354
60	.211	.250	.295	.325
70	.195	.232	.274	.303
80	.183	.217	.256	.283
90	.173	.205	.242	.267
100	.164	.195	.230	.254

Table 8 — Critical Values of *T* in the Wilcoxon Matched-Pairs Signed-Ranks Test

N	Level of Significance for Two-Tailed Test		
	.05	.02	.01
6	1	—	—
7	2	0	—
8	4	2	0
9	6	3	2
10	8	5	3
11	11	7	5
12	14	10	7
13	17	13	10
14	21	16	13
15	25	20	16
16	30	24	19
17	35	28	23
18	40	33	28
19	46	38	32
20	52	43	37
21	59	49	43
22	66	56	49
23	73	62	55
24	81	69	61
25	90	77	68

ENDNOTES AND PHOTO CREDITS

CHAPTER 1

1. Adapted from "DuPont Employee Survey Finds Eldercare Emerging as Key Work/Life Issue," *PR Newswire,* January 2, 2001, p. 4993.

2. Ian P. Murphy, "Aided by Research, Harley Goes Whole Hog," *Marketing News,* December 2, 1996, p. 16.

3. Justin Martin, "Ignore Your Customer," *Fortune,* May 1, 1995, p. 126.

4. Adapted with permission from NUA Internet Surveys, http://www.nua.ie/surveys/index.cgi?f=VS&art_id=905356229&rel=true, downloaded March 31, 2001.

5. "Cyber Dialogue: Doctors Keep Work Offline," NUA Internet Surveys, December 11, 2000, http://www.nua.ie/surveys/index.cgi?f=VS&art_id=905356229&rel=true, downloaded March 31, 2001.

6. http://stats.bls.gov/oco/ocos010.htm. Downloaded March 31, 2001.

7. Peter Larson, "Keep Those Employees Satisfied; There's a Link Between Keeping Customers and Employees Happy," *Montreal Gazette,* July 6, 1992, p. T15.

8. Stephanie Thompson, "Food for What Ails You," *Brandweek,* May 4, 1998, p. 38.

9. Louise Kramer, "Pepsi Moves New Storm into Broad Battlefield," *Advertising Age,* July 13, 1998, pp. 1, 40.

10. "The U.S. Mint Reports to Congress on the Success of the Golden Dollar after the First Year," Press Release, U.S. Mint, April 2, 2001.

11. Mike Beirne, "Exploring New Waters," *BrandWeek,* January 1, 2000, pp. 1, 6, and http://www.royalcaribbean.com/

12. From "No Deodorant? No Sweat!" *Tulsa World,* December 18, 1991, p. A-1. Adapted with permission from Associated Press.

13. Adapted with permission from Gerry Khermouch, "Sticking Their Neck Out," *Brandweek,* November 9, 1998, pp. 25–34. © 1998–1999 VNU Business Media Inc. Used with permission.

14. Jack Honomichi, "Growth Stunt," *Marketing News,* June 4, 2001, p. H4.

15. "You Say Tomato, I Say Tomahto," *Express Magazine,* Spring 1992, p. 19.

16. William G. Zikmund and Michael d'Amico, *Effective Marketing* (Cincinnati: South-Western, 2002), p. xxxii.

CHAPTER 2

1. Reprinted from *PC Magazine,* February 20, 2001 with permission. Copyright © 2001 Ziff-Davis Media. All rights reserved.

2. Anne Stuart, "Five Uneasy Pieces, Part 2," *CIO Magazine,* June 1, 1996.

3. Thomas H. Davenport and Laurence Prusak, *Working Knowledge: How Organizations Manage What They Know* (Boston: Harvard Business School Press, 1998).

4. *Trends in Knowledge Management: A Qualitative Study of CEOs and CIOs.* Conducted by Venture Forward, November 1997. Ellen M. Knapp, "Knowledge Management," *Business and Economic Review,* July-September 1998, pp. 3–6. http://research.moore.sc.edu/research/bereview/be44_4/Knapp.htm, downloaded November 9, 2001.

5. http://www.cio.com/forums/knowledge/

6. See Thomas G. Exter, "The Next Step Is Called GIS," *American Demographics Desk Reference,* May 1992, p. 2.

7. Adapted from Ralph H. Sprague Jr. and Hugh J. Watson, *Decision Support Systems: Putting Theory into Practice,* 3rd Ed., p. viii. © 1993 Prentice-Hall, Inc., Upper Saddle River, New Jersey.

8. Stewart Deck, "What Is CRM?" *Darwin Online,* May 16, 2001, http://www.darwinmag.com/learn/curve/column.html?ArticleID=104, downloaded June 5, 2001.

9. whatis.com, http://whatis.techtarget.com/definition/0,289893,sid9_gci213567,00.html.

10. Excerpt from Regis McKenna, *Real Time* (Boston: Harvard Business School Press, 1997), pp. 3–4.

11. For an extensive listing of databases, see the annual *Gale Directory of Databases* (Detroit: Gale Research, Inc., two volumes).

12. H. G. Wells, "The Brain: Organization of the Modern World," 1940.

13. Nielsen//NetRatings. http://www.eratings.com/news/20000907.htm. Downloaded May 16, 2001.

14. Patrick A. Moore and Ronald E. Milliman, "Application of the Internet in Marketing Education." Paper presented to the Southwest Marketing Association, Houston, Texas, 1995.

15. Nicholas Negroponte, *Being Digital* (New York: Knopf, 1995), p. 6.

16. Adapted with permission from Miryam Williams, "Getting to Know You," *WebMaster Magazine,* September 1996; p. 30: Courtesy of CXO Media Inc.

17. Donald E. L. Johnson, "Knowledge Management Is New Competitive Edge," *Health Care Strategic Management,* July 1998, pp. 2–3.

18. Charles S. Parker, *Understanding Computers Today and Tomorrow* (Ft. Worth, TX: Dryden Press, 1998), p. 69.

CHAPTER 3

1. Fred N. Kerlinger, *Behavioral Research: A Conceptual Approach* (New York: Holt, Rinehart and Winston, 1979), p. 3.

2. Robert Dubin, *Theory Building* (New York: Free Press, 1969), p. 9.

3. Reavis Cox, Wroe Alderson, and Stanley J. Shapiro, *Theory in Marketing* (Chicago: American Marketing Association, 1964), p. 20.

4. Kerlinger, *Behavioral Research,* p. 42.

5. Robert Bartels, *Marketing Theory and Metatheory* (Chicago: American Marketing Association, 1970), p. 6.

6. R. B. Braithwaite, *Scientific Explanation* (London: Cambridge University Press, 1968), p. 9.

7. Clark L. Hull, *A Behavioral System,* (New York: John Wiley & Sons, 1952), p. 6.

8. Hull, *A Behavioral System,* p. 1.

9. Based on Ellen J. Jackofsky, "Turnover and Job Performance: An Integrated Process Model," *Academy of Management Review 9,* No. 1 (1984), p. 78; and Paul Solomon, "Reducing Unwanted Staff Turnovers in Public Accounting: An Action Plan," *Northern California*

Executive Review (Spring 1986), pp. 22–25.

10. George Schultz, quoted in "Another Professor with Power," *Time,* February 26, 1973, p. 80.

11. Gerald Zaltman and Philip C. Burger, *Marketing Research* (Hinsdale, IL: Dryden Press, 1975), p. 28.

12. Stephen Jay Gould, "Evolution as Fact and Theory," *Discover,* May 1981, p. 35.

13. From W. T. Tucker, *Foundation for a Theory of Consumer Behavior* (New York: Holt, Rinehart and Winston, 1967), pp. v–vii.

14. Gerald Zaltman, Christian Pinson, and Reinhart Angelmar, *Metatheory and Consumer Research* (New York: Holt, Rinehart and Winston, 1972), pp. 12–13.

15. From Robert M. Pirsig, *Zen and the Art of Motorcycle Maintenance,* © 1974 by Robert M. Pirsig, pp. 107–111.

CHAPTER 4

1. Adapted from Ruth Wageman, "Interdependence and Group Effectiveness," *Administrative Science Quarterly,* March 1, 1995.

2. This section is based on Richard Daft, *Management* (Fort Worth, TX: Dryden Press, 1990), pp. 180–193; and John R. Schermehrhorn, Jr., James G. Hunt, and Richard N. Osborn, *Managing Organizational Behavior* (New York: John Wiley & Sons, 1991), pp. 364–366.

3. Becky Ebenkamp, "For Whom the Bell Tolls," *BrandWeek,* May 7, 2001, p. 22.

4. Barry Janoff, "Brands of the Land," *BrandWeek,* April 20, 2001, p. 28.

5. "PepsiCo Foods International to Introduce Lay's Potato Chips to Consumers Worldwide," *PR Newswire,* November 30, 1995.

6. Claire Selltiz, Lawrence S. Wrightsman, and Stuart W. Cook, *Research Methods in Social Relations* (New York: Holt, Rinehart and Winston, 1976), pp. 114–115.

7. Paul E. Green, Donald S. Tull, and Gerald Albaum, *Research for Marketing Decisions* (Englewood Cliffs, NJ: Prentice-Hall, 1988), pp. 105–110.

8. Donald P. Warwick and Charles A. Lininger, *The Sample Survey: Theory and Practice* (New York: McGraw-Hill, 1975), pp. 20–21.

9. Philip J. Runkel and Joseph E. McGrath, *Research on Human Behavior: A Systematic Guide to Method* (New York: Holt, Rinehart and Winston, 1972), p. 2.

10. A. Einstein and L. Infeld, *The Evolution of Physics* (New York: Simon & Schuster, 1942), p. 95.

11. Michelle Keyo, "Web Site of the Week: Jelly Belly: Using Sampling to Build a Customer Database," *Inc. Online,* December 9, 1996, http://www.inc.com.

12. Pretests of full-blown surveys and experiments are also called pilot studies. These smaller versions of the formal studies generally are utilized for refining techniques rather than for problem definition and clarification of the hypothesis.

13. Carol Vogel, "Dear Museumgoer: What Do You Think?" *New York Times,* December 20, 1992, pp. 1H, 32H.

14. Jamie Egazti, "Fresh Breeze at P&G," Marketers of the Year, *BrandWeek,* October 11, 1999, pp. M50–M56. © 1998–1999 VNU Business Media Inc. Used with permission; and "P&G Tests Febreze," *Advertising Age,* May 9, 1996.

15. R. D. Middlemist and R. B. Peterson, "Test of Equity Theory by Controlling for Comparison Co-Workers' Efforts," *Organizational Behavior and Human Performance 15* (1976), pp. 335–354; and R. Dennis Middlemist and Michael A. Hitt, *Organizational Behavior: Applied Concepts* (Chicago: Science Research Associates, 1981), p. 33.

16. Julian Simon, *Basic Research Methods in Social Science: The Art of Empirical Investigation* (New York: Random House, 1969), p. 4.

17. Stewart H. Britt, "Marketing Research: Why It Works and Why It Doesn't Work," Chicago Chapter, American Marketing Association, Conference on Marketing Research, 1972.

18. John A. Sonquist and William C. Dunkelberg, *Survey and Opinion Research: Procedures for Processing and Analysis* (Englewood Cliffs, NJ: Prentice-Hall, 1977), p. 9.

CHAPTER 5

1. Don Martindale, *The Nature and Types of Sociological Theory* (Boston: Houghton Mifflin, 1960), pp. 478–480.

2. For an alternative perspective, see Kenneth C. Schneider's excellent article "Marketing Research Industry Isn't Moving toward Professionalism," *Marketing Educator* (Winter 1984), pp. 1, 6.

3. Lawrence D. Wiseman, "The Present Value of Future Studies," speech to the Advertising Research Foundation, March 1980.

4. Alice M. Tybout and Gerald Zaltman, "Ethics in Marketing Research: Their Practical Relevance," *Journal of Marketing Research* (November 1974), pp. 357–368.

5. Robert L. Day, "A Comment on Ethics in Marketing Research," *Journal of Marketing Research* (May 1975), pp. 232–233.

6. Robert O. Carlson, "The Issue of Privacy in Public Opinion Research," *Public Opinion Quarterly* (Spring 1967), pp. 1–8.

7. C. Merle Crawford, "Attitudes of Marketing Executives toward Ethics in Marketing Research," *Journal of Marketing* (April 1970), pp. 46–52.

8. Leo Bogart, "The Researcher's Dilemma," *Journal of Marketing* (January 1962), pp. 6-11.

9. C. J. Frey and T. C. Kinnear, "Legal Constraints in Marketing Research: Review and Call to Action," *Journal of Marketing Research* (August 1979), p. 259.

10. Sidney Hollander, Jr., "Ethics in Marketing Research," in *Handbook of Marketing Research,* Robert Ferber, Ed. (New York: McGraw-Hill, 1974), pp. 1–11.

11. Excerpt from Cynthia Crossen, *Tainted Truth* (New York: Simon and Schuster, 1994). p. 95.

12. Lawrence D. Gibson, "Use of Marketing Research Contractors," in *Handbook of Marketing Research,* Robert Ferber, Ed. (New York: McGraw-Hill, 1974), p. 129.

13. Marketing Research Standards Committee, *Marketing Research Code of Ethics* (Chicago: American Marketing Association, 1972).

14. Adapted from *The Wall Street Journal Europe,* © 1994 Dow Jones & Company, Inc. All Rights Reserved Worldwide.

15. "Consumer Demand, Not New Laws, Will Protect Web Privacy," *USA Today,* July 7, 1998, p. 12A.

16. *USA Today,* July 7, 1998.

17. Kim M. Bayne, "Privacy Still Burning Web Issue," *Advertising Age,* June 29, 1998, p. 37.

18. Rick Bruner, "TRUSTe Pitches Its Seal of Approval," *Advertising Age,* June 9, 1997.

19. Robert Bezilla, Joel B. Haynes, and Clifford Elliot, "Ethics in Marketing Research," *Business Horizons* (April 1976), pp. 83–86.

20. "New Market Research Guides Urged," *Advertising Age,* April 30, 1979, p. 54.

21. H. Keith Hunt, "The Ethics of Research in the Consumer Interest: Panel Summary," *Proceedings of the American Council of Consumer Interests Conference,* Norleen M. Ackerman, Ed., 1979, p. 152.

22. Bogart, "The Researcher's Dilemma."

23. Crawford, "Attitudes of Marketing Executives"; and Shelby D.

Hunt, Lawrence B. Chonko, and James D. Wilcox, "Ethical Problems of Marketing Researchers," *Journal of Marketing Research* (August 1984), pp. 309–324.

CHAPTER 6

1. From *Preparing Instructional Objectives* by Robert F. Mager. Copyright © 1984 by David S. Lake Publishers, Belmont, CA 94002.

2. Russell L. Ackoff, *Scientific Method* (New York: John Wiley & Sons, 1962), p. 71.

3. Adapted from *Communication Arts* (January/February 1995), pp. 138, 140.

4. Adapted from Robert Ferber, Donald F. Blankertz, and Sidney Hollander, Jr., *Marketing Research* (New York: Ronald Press, 1964), p. 157.

5. Fred N. Kerlinger, *Behavioral Research: A Conceptual Approach* (New York: Holt, Rinehart and Winston, 1979), p. 34.

6. Donald T. Warwick and Charles A. Lininger, *The Sample Survey: Theory and Practice* (New York: McGraw-Hill, 1975), p. 51.

7. Adapted from *A General Taxpayer Opinion Survey,* Office of Planning and Research, Internal Revenue Service (March 1980). (Note: Because of space restrictions, this exhibit presents an abbreviated research proposal. Often, entire questionnaires appear as exhibits in proposals.)

8. Students interested in additional information on writing a research proposal should review Appendix 25A: The Writing Process.

CHAPTER 7

1. Adapted with permission from Richard A. Moran and George Bailey, "Postcards from Employees," Sibson and Company, Inc. *Perspectives,* Vol. IV, No. 3, pp. 44–46.

2. Bruce Rayner, "Product Development—Now Hear This!" *Electronic Business,* August 1997.

3. Glen L. Urban and John R. Hauser, *Design and Marketing of New Products,* pp. 35–37. © 1980, Prentice-Hall, Inc., Upper Saddle River, New Jersey.

4. Gary Hamel and C. K. Prahalad, "Corporate Imagination and Expeditionary Marketing," *Harvard Business Review,* July–August 1991, p. 85.

5. Dale Fever, "Where the Dollars Go," *Training* (October 1985), p. 46.

6. Excerpt adapted from Ray Burch, "Marketing Research: Why It Works, Why It Doesn't Work," speech to the Chicago chapter of the American Marketing Association, 1973.

7. Carol Vogel, "Dear Museumgoer: What Do You Think?" *New York Times,* December 20, 1992, p. H-1.

8. Adapted from Michael A. Hitt, R. Duane Ireland, and Robert E. Huskisson, *Strategic Management: Competitiveness and Globalization Concepts* (St. Paul, MN: West Publishing, 1995), p. 82.

9. John M. Hess, "Group Interviewing," in *New Science of Planning,* R. L. King, Ed. (Chicago: American Marketing Association, 1968), p. 194. The general advantages of the focus group interview are based on this source.

10. Steve Rabin, "How to Sell across Cultures," *American Demographics,* March 1, 1994, p. 56.

11. William D. Wells, "Group Interviewing," in *Handbook of Marketing Research,* Robert Ferber, Ed., (New York: McGraw-Hill, 1977), pp. 2–133.

12. Excerpt reprinted with the permission of the American Marketing Association from Betsy D. Gelb and Michael P. Eriksen, "Market Research May Help Prevent Cancer," *Marketing Research,* September 1991, pp. 41–42.

13. Betsy D. Gelb and Michael P. Eriksen, "Market Research May Help Prevent Cancer," *Marketing Research,* September 1991, p. 46. Published by the American Marketing Association. Reprinted with permission.

14. Rebecca Piirto Heather, "Future Focus Groups," *American Demographics,* January 1, 1994, p. 6.

15. http://www.realnetworks.com/getstarted/index.html, downloaded June 30, 2001.

16. Nicholas Negroponte, "Being Anonymous," *Wired,* October 1998, p. 216.

17. Casey Sweet, "Anatomy of an Online Focus Group," *Quirks Marketing Research Review,* December, 1999, Article Number 0548.

18. Kate Maddox, "Virtual Panels Add Real Insights for Marketers," *Advertising Age,* June 29, 1998, p. 34.

19. Jon Rubin, "Online Marketing Research Comes of Age," *BrandWeek,* October 30, 2000, p. 28.

20. Adapted from Tibbett Speer, "Nickelodeon Puts Kids Online," *American Demographics,* January 1, 1994, p. 16.

21. "Qualitative Research Is Marketing Research Because It Aids Decision Makers," *Marketing News,* January 22, 1982, pp. 2–8.

22. Adapted with permission from Richard A. Moran and George Bailey, "Postcards from Employees," Sibson Company *Perspectives* Vol. IV No. 3, pp. 44–46.

23. Reprinted from Jeff Green, "The PT Cruiser's Storied History," *BrandWeek,* October 16, 2000, pp. M68–M70. © 1998–1999 VNU Business Media Inc. Used with permission.

24. The Iowa Poll, August 1977.

25. Mason Haire, "Projective Techniques in Marketing Research," *Journal of Marketing* (April 1950), pp. 649–652.

26. James McNeal, *The Kids Market: Myths and Realities,* (Ithaca, NY: Paramount Market Publishers, 1999), p. 245.

27. Brian Sternthal and Alice M. Tybout, "Segmentation and Targeting," in *Kellogg on Marketing,* Dawn Iacobucci, Ed. (New York: John Wiley and Sons, 2001), p. 21.

28. Donald F. Cox, *Risk Taking and Information Handling in Consumer Behavior* (Boston: Division of Research, Harvard Business School, 1967), pp. 65–66. Copyright © 1967 by the President and Fellows of Harvard College. Reprinted by permission of Harvard Business School Press.

29. Philip Kotler, "Behavioral Models for Analyzing Buyers," *Journal of Marketing* (October 1965), pp. 37–45.

CHAPTER 8

1. Excerpts from John Ritter, "Calif. Racial Data Shifts: Becomes the First Big State with No Ethnic Majority," *USA TODAY,* March 30, 2001, p. 1A. Copyright 2001, *USA TODAY.* Reprinted with permission.

2. Statistics Canada, http://www.statcan.ca/english/Pgdb/Economy/International/gblec02a.htm, downloaded July 13, 2001.

3. *Sporting News,* April 4, 2001, http://tsn.sportingnews.com/baseball/articles/20010404/307767.html, downloaded July 13, 2001.

4. Theresa Howard, "Coca-Cola Hopes Taking New Path Leads to Success," *USA TODAY,* March 6, 2001, p. 6b.

5. Adapted from Robert W. Joselyn, *Designing the Marketing Research Project* (New York: Petrocelli/Charter, 1977), p. 54. Copyright © 1977 by Petrocelli/Charter Company. Reprinted by permission of Van Nostrand Reinhold.

6. Adapted with permission from Dan Fost, "How to Think About the Future," *American Demographics,* February 1998.

7. As reported in "Datawatch," *Advertising Age,* January 18, 1993, p. 1–12.

8. Based on material from DataMind's home page at http://www.datamindcorp.com.

9. Srikumar S. Rao, "Technology: the Hot Zone," *Forbes,* November 18, 1996.

10. John Foley, "Squeezing More Value from Data," *Information Week,* December 9, 1996, downloaded from http://www.informationweek.com; Copyright © 1996, CMP Media Inc.

11. IBM Business Intelligence Data Mining Product Discovery, http://www.ibm.com.

12. Todd Wasserman, Gerry Khermouch, and Jeff Green, "Mining Everyone's Business," *Brandweek,* February 28, 2000, p. 34; and Ira Sager, "Big Blue Wants to Mine Your Data," *Business Week,* June 3, 1996.

13. Based on materials from DataMind's home page at http://www.datamindcorp.com.

14. Excerpt from Janet Novack. "The Data Miners," *Forbes,* February 1998. Reprinted by permission of Forbes Magzine. © 2002 Forbes Inc.

15. Woods and Poole Economics, Inc., Washington: D.C.

16. U. S. Department of Commerce, Bureau of the Census.

17. "Going with the Grain," *Advertising Age,* September 11, 1995, p. 3.

18. Jack Neff, "Wal-Mart Takes Stock in RetailLink System," *Advertising Age,* May 21, 2001, p. 6.

19. This section is adapted from Frank K. Reilly and Keith C. Brown, *Investment Analysis and Portfolio Management* (Ft. Worth, TX: The Dryden Press, 1997).

20. Used with permission of Standard & Poor's Reports.

21. This section is based on information that can be accessed from the NTDB home page at http://www.stat-usa.gov/tradtest.nsf.

CHAPTER 9

1. Adapted from Sara Eckel and Alison Stein Wellner, "For Wannabe Chefs, Pictures Speak Louder Than Words," *American Demographics,* March 2001, p. S15.

2. Sheree R. Curry, "Lunch Ain't What It Used to Be," *Fortune,* November 10, 1997, p. 286.

3. Paul B. Sheatsley, "Survey Design," in *Handbook of Marketing Research,* Robert Ferber, Ed. (New York: McGraw-Hill, 1974), pp. 2–67.

4. Peter Tuckel and Harry O'Neill, "The Vanishing Respondent in Telephone Surveys," a paper presented at the 56th annual conference of the American Association of Public Opinion Research (AAPOR) in Montreal, May 17–20, 2001.

5. Adam Clymer, "Election Day Shows What the Opinion Polls Can't Do," *New York Times,* November 12, 1989, p. E-4.

6. William Rathje and Cullen Murphy, *Rubbish!: The Archaeology of Garbage* (Harper Perennial, 1993).

7. From Lee Adler, "Confessions of an Interview Reader," *Journal of Marketing Research,* May 1996, pp. 194–195. Published by the American Marketing Association. Reprinted with permission.

8. Douglas Aircraft Corp., *Consumer Research* (undated), p. 13.

9. For an interesting study of extremity bias, see Hans Baumgartner and Jan-Benedict E. M. Steekamp, "Response Styles in Marketing Research: A Cross-National Investigation," *Journal of Marketing Research,* May 2001, pp. 143–156.

10. The term *questionnaire* technically refers only to mail and self-administered surveys, and the term *interview schedule* is used for telephone and face-to-face interviews. However, in this book, *questionnaire* is used for all forms of communication.

11. *Americans and the Arts: Highlights from a Survey of Public Opinion,* National Research Center of the Arts (undated), p. 14.

12. Darren K. Carlson, "Nurses Remain at Top of Honesty and Ethics Poll; Car Salesmen Still Seen as Least Honest and Ethical," Gallup News Service, November 27, 2000; and Leslie McAneny, "Nurses Displace Pharmacists at Top of Expanded Honesty and Ethics Poll," Gallup News Service, November 16, 1999.

13. *Profiles in Quality: Blueprints for Action from 50 Leading Companies* (Boston: Allyn and Bacon, 1991), p. 113.

14. Adapted from Barbara Buell, "The Effect of Expecting to Evaluate on Quality and Satisfaction Evaluations," *Stanford Business,* May 2000, Volume 68, Number 3. The research was based on Chezy Ofir and Itamar Simonson, GSB Research Paper #1608, Stanford University Graduate School of Business, July 1999.

15. Based on material in *Profiles in Quality,* pp. 97–98.

16. *Profiles in Quality,* pp. 97–98.

17. David A. Garvin, "Competing on the Eight Dimensions of Quality," *Harvard Business Review,* November-December 1987, pp. 101–108.

18. Adapted from David A. Aaker, *Managing Brand Equity* (New York: Macmillan, 1991), pp. 90–95; David Gavin, "Product Quality: An Important Strategic Weapon," *Business Horizons* (May-June 1984), pp. 40–43; and A. Parasuraman, Valarie A. Zeithaml, and Leonard L. Berry, "A Conceptual Model of Service Quality and Its Implications for Future Research," *Journal of Marketing* (Fall 1985), pp. 41–50.

CHAPTER 10

1. Jeff Green, "The PT Cruiser's Storied History," *BrandWeek,* October 16, 2000, pp. M68–M70.

2. *Industry Image Study: Research on Research* (Indianapolis: Walker Marketing Research, 1988).

3. Donald T. Warwick and Charles A. Lininger, *The Sample Survey: Theory and Practice* (New York: McGraw-Hill, 1975), p. 2.

4. L. C. Lockley, "Notes on the History of Marketing Research," *Journal of Marketing* (April 1950), p. 733.

5. Ellen Joan Pollock, "Competition Forces Law Firms to Heed Clients' Criticism," *The Wall Street Journal,* © 1992 Dow Jones and Company, Inc. All Rights Reserved Worldwide. Used with permission.

6. "Revised Pillsbury Spot in the Pink," *Advertising Age,* February 13, 1986, p. 15.

7. *Your Opinion Counts: 1986 Refusal Rate Study* (Indianapolis: Walker Marketing Research, 1986), p. 14.

8. For an interesting study, see Sigfredo A. Hernandes and Carol J. Kaufman, "Marketing Research in Hispanic Barrios: A Guide to Survey Research," *Marketing Research: A Magazine of Management and Applications* (March 1990), pp. 11–27.

9. John Frieman and Edgar Butler, "Some Sources of Interviewer Variance in Surveys," *Public Opinion Quarterly* (Spring 1976), pp. 79–81.

10. From *A General Taxpayer Opinion Survey,* Office of Planning and Research, Internal Revenue Service, 1980, pp. A-1, A-2.

11. Naghi Namakforoosh, "Data Collection Methods Hold Key to Research in Mexico," *Marketing News,* August 29, 1994, p. 28.

12. Jon Rubin, "Online Marketing Research Comes of Age," *BrandWeek,* October 30, 2000, p. 28; and Michael Lewis, "The Two-Bucks-a-Minute Democracy," *New York Times* Magazine, November 5, 2000, p. 65.

13. Peter Tuckel and Harry O'Neill, "The Vanishing Respondent in Telephone Surveys," a paper presented at the 56th annual conference of the American Association of Public Opinion Research (AAPOR) in Montreal on May 17–20, 2001.

14. Peter Tuckel and Trish Shukers, "The Answering Machine Dilemma," *Marketing Research* (Fall 1997), pp. 5–9.

15. P. S. Tuckel and B. M. Finberg, "The Answering Machine Poses Many Questions for Telephone Survey Research," *Public Opinion Quarterly* (Summer 1991).

16. Adapted with permission from Sally Beatty, "Ameritech's New Phone Service Aims to Keep Telemarketers at Bay," *The Wall Street Journal,* September 23, 1998, p. B-10.

17. "Sacramento Is Most Unlisted," *The Frame,* (March 1997) a quarterly newsletter published by Survey Sampling Inc., http://www.worldopinion.com/the_frame/index.html.

18. *Your Opinion Counts.* See also J. M. Struebbe, J. B. Kernan, and T. J. Grogan, "The Refusal Problem in Telephone Surveys," *Journal of Advertising Research* (June/July 1986), pp. 284–287; and M. J. Walters and J. Ferrante-Wallace, "Lessons from Nonresponse in a Consumer Survey," *Journal of Health Care Marketing* (Winter 1985), pp. 17–28.

19. "Some Things We've Learned about Global Research," Research International, New York.

20. Under certain circumstances questionnaire length can affect response rate. For an interesting article, see Andrew G. Bean and Michael J. Roszkowski, "The Long and the Short of It: When Does Questionnaire Length Affect Response Rate?" *Marketing Research* (Winter 1995), pp. 21–32.

21. Valentine Appel and Julian Baim, "Correcting Response Rate Problems," paper presented to the Advertising Research Foundation, April 1991; and "Who Slammed the Door on Research?" *American Demographics,* September 1991, p. 14.

22. Don A. Dillman, *Mail and Internet Surveys: The Tailored Design Method* (New York: John Wiley and Sons, 2000), p. 173.

23. Courtesy of Washington State University and Don A. Dillman, *Mail and Telephone Surveys: The Total Design Method* (New York: John Wiley and Sons, 1978), p. 169.

24. David R. Schaefer and Don A. Dillman, "Development of a Standard E-Mail Methodology: Results of an Experiment," *Public Opinion Quarterly,* Fall 1998, p. 378.

25. For an interesting article dealing with this issue, see Michael Geurts and David Whitlark, "A Little Inducement Goes a Long Way," *Marketing Research: A Magazine of Management and Applications,* (Summer 1994), pp. 13–15.

26. Schaefer and Dillman, "Development of a Standard E-Mail Methodology."

27. Paul L. Erdos and James Regier, "Visible vs. Disguised Keying on Questionnaires," *Journal of Advertising Research* (February 1977), p. 15.

28. Lewis C. Winters, "International Psychographics," *Marketing Research: A Magazine of Management and Application,* September 1992, p. 48.

29. For a complete discussion of fax surveys, see the excellent article by John P. Dickson and Douglas L. Maclachlan, "Fax Surveys: Return Patterns and Comparison with Mail Surveys," *Journal of Marketing Research* (February 1996), pp. 108–113.

30. Dillman, *Mail and Internet Surveys,* pp. 369–372.

31. http://www.websurveyor.com/learn_howto.asp, downloaded May 14, 2001.

32. http://www.dmsdallas.com/, downloaded April 23, 2001.

33. Neil Postman, *Technology: The Surrender of Culture to Technology* (New York: Vintage Books, 1993), pp. 6–15, and James P. Ronda, "Thomas Moran and the Eastern Railroads," *The Gilcrease Journal* (Spring/Summer) 1997, p. 38.

34. "Recent Research Confirms Online Surveys are a Viable Means of Reaching General Population." Digital Marketing Services, Inc, September 17, 1998, http://www.dmsdallas.com/press_room.html, downloaded April 24, 2001.

35. Richard Cross and Mollie Neal, "Real-Time and Online Research Is Paying Off," *Direct Marketing,* May 2000, p. 58. Copyright 2000 Hoke Communications, Inc.

36. http:://www.websurveyor.com/prod_features.asp, downloaded July 26, 2001.

37. This section is reprinted from the Help box on WebSurveyor. Copyright © 2001, WebSurveyor Corporation. All rights reserved.

CHAPTER 11

1. Claire Selltiz, Lawrence S. Wrightsman, and Stuart W. Cook, *Research Methods in Social Relations,* 3rd ed. (New York: Holt, Rinehart and Winston, 1976), p. 251.

2. Nancy M. Henley, *Body Politics: Power, Sex, and Nonverbal Communication* (New York: Simon & Schuster, 1977), p. 181.

3. Glen L. Urban and John R. Hauser, *Design and Marketing of New Products* (Englewood Cliffs, NJ: Prentice-Hall, 1980), p. 129.

4. Joshua Macht, "The New Market Research," *Inc.,* July 1998, pp. 92–93.

5. Angus Campbell, Philip E. Converse, and Willard L. Rodgers, *The Quality of American Life* (New York: Russell Sage Foundation, 1976), p. 112. Although weather conditions did not correlate with perceived quality of life, the comfort variable did show a relationship with the index of well-being. This association might be confounded by the fact that absence of ventilation and/or air conditioning is more likely to be found in less affluent homes. Income was previously found to correlate with quality of life.

6. From Howard B. Waitzkin, "Information Giving and Medical Care," *Journal of Health and Social Behavior,* 26,1995), pp. 81–101; and *USA TODAY,* February 10, 1987, p. D-1.

7. Campbell, Converse, and Rogers, *The Quality of American Life.*

8. Selltiz, Wrightsman, and Cook, *Research Methods in Social Relations,* pp. 269–272.

9. Bill Abrams, *The Observational Research Handbook* (Chicago: NTC Business Books, 2000), p. 14.

10. Adapted from Selltiz, Wrightsman, and Cook, *Research Methods in Social Relations,* p. 272.

11. Adapted from the April 30, 1980 issue of *Advertising Age.* Copyright © 1980 by Crain Communications, Inc.

12. William Rathje and Cullen Murphy, "Garbage Demographics," *American Demographics,* May 1992, pp. 50 53, William Rathje and Cullen Murphy, *Rubbish!: The Archaeology of Garbage* (Harper Perennial, 1993).

13. Adapted from Erik Larson, "Attention Shoppers: Don't Look Now But You Are Being Tailed," Copyright 1993 by Erik Larson.

14. Witold Rybczynski, "We Are What We Throw Away," *New York Times Book Review,* July 5, 1992, pp. 5–6.

15. Adapted with permission from Bruce Raytner, "Product Development: Now Hear This!" *Electronic Business,* August 1997.

16. http://www.acnielsen.com, downloaded July 5, 2001.

17. Press release, "A.C. Nielsen Unveils 'Future-Proofing' Technologies; TV Ratings System Revamped for Digital Era." March 10, 1999. http://acnielsen.com/news/asiapacific/au/1999/19990310.htm, downloaded July 5, 2001.

18. http://www.mra-net.org/docs/resources/technology/buzzwords.cfm, downloaded April 24, 2001.

19. "Live Simultaneous Study of Stimulus Response Is Physiological Measurement's Greatest Virtue," *Marketing News,* May 15, 1981, pp. 1, 20.

20. Herbert B. Krugman, as quoted in "Live Simultaneous Study," p. 1.

CHAPTER 12

1. Adapted with permission from Brian Wansink, "How and Why a Package's Size Influences Usage Volume," Trace Discussion Paper TI 95-1, Timbergen Instituet, Amsterdam-Rotterdam, The Netherlands.

2. Anne G. Perkins, "Package Size: When Bigger Is Better," *Harvard Business Review,* March-April 1995, p. 14.

3. Seymour Banks, "Designing Marketing Research to Increase Validity," *Journal of Marketing* (October 1964), pp. 32–40.

4. See J. Edward Russo, "The Value of Unit Price Information," *Journal of Marketing Research* (May 1977), pp. 193–201; and J. Edward Russo, Gene Krieser, and Sally Miyashita, "An Effective Display of Unit Price Information," *Journal of Marketing* (April 1975), pp. 11–19. The example in this section is hypothetical, based on the experiments and material in these two articles.

5. Russo, Krieser, and Miyashita, "An Effective Display of Unit Price Information," reprinted from *Journal of Marketing* (April 1975), p. 14, published by the American Marketing Association.

6. Vernon Ellingstad and Norman W. Heimstra, *Methods in the Study of Human Behavior* (Belmont, CA: Brooks/Cole Publishing, 1973), pp. 61–62.

7. From Charles Ramond, *The Art of Using Science in Marketing* (New York: Harper & Row, 1974), pp. 20–21.

8. "The Most Dangerous Game in Marketing," *Dun's Business Month* (formerly *Dun's Review*), June 1967. Dun & Bradstreet Publications Corp.

9. William L. Hays, *Statistics* (New York: Holt, Rinehart and Winston, 1963), p. 450.

10. Barry F. Anderson, *The Psychological Experiment: An Introduction to the Scientific Method* (Belmont, CA: Brooks/Cole Publishing, 1971), p. 28.

11. Anderson, *The Psychological Experiment,* pp. 42–44.

12. M. Venkatesan and Robert T. Holloway, *An Introduction to Marketing Experimentation: Methods, Applications, and Problems* (New York: Free Press, 1971), p. 14.

13. For an excellent discussion of demand characteristics, see Alan G. Sawyer, "Demand Artifacts in Laboratory Experiments in Consumer Research," *Journal of Consumer Research* 1 (March 1975), pp. 20–30; and Alan G. Sawyer, Parker Worthing, and Paul E. Sendak, "The Role of Laboratory Experiments to Test Marketing Strategies," *Journal of Marketing* (Summer 1979), pp. 60–67.

14. See F. J. Roethlisberger and W. J. Dickson, *Management and the Worker* (Cambridge, MA: Harvard University Press, 1939).

15. Venkatesan and Holloway, *Introduction to Marketing Experimentation,* p. 36.

16. Keith K. Cox, *The Relationship between Shelf Space and Product Sales in Supermarkets* (Austin: Bureau of Business Research, University of Texas, 1964), p. 20.

17. Anderson, *Psychological Experiment,* p. 54.

18. W. Millard, Diane L. Lockwood, and Fred Luthans, "The Impact of a Four-Day Work Week on Employees," *MSU Business Topics* (Spring 1980), p. 33.

19. From Herbert L. Kelman, "Human Use of Human Subjects: The Problem of Deception in Social Psychological Experiments," *Psychological Bulletin* (January 1967), pp. 1–11.

20. Alice M. Tybout and Gerald Zaltman, "Ethics in Marketing Research: Their Practical Relevance," *Journal of Marketing Research* (November 1974), pp. 357–368.

21. This section is based on Donald T. Campbell and Julian C. Stanley, *Experimental and Quasi-Experimental Designs for Research* (Chicago: Rand McNally, 1966), pp. 5–9. Published by the American Educational Research Association, Washington, DC.

22. Donald E. Vinson and William J. Lundstrom, "The Use of Students as Experimental Subjects in Marketing Research," *Journal of the Academy of Marketing Sciences* (Winter 1978), pp. 114–125.

23. William H. Cunningham, Thomas W. Anderson, Jr., and John H. Murphy, "Are Students Real People?" *Journal of Business* (July 1974), pp. 399–409; and Ben M. Enis, Keith K. Cox, and James E. Stafford, "Students as Subjects in Consumer Behavior Experiments," *Journal of Marketing Research* (February 1972), pp. 72–74.

24. Fred W. Morgan, Jr., "Students in Marketing Research: Surrogates vs. Role-Players," *Journal of the Academy of Marketing Science* (Summer 1979), pp. 255–264.

25. B. J. Winer, *Statistical Principles in Experimental Design* (New York: McGraw-Hill, 1971), p. 1.

26. This section is based largely on Campbell and Stanley, *Experimental and Quasi-Experimental Designs,* pp. 13–25.

27. *Observation* is used in the most general way. Although most business experiments will use some other form of measurement rather than the direct observation of some dependent variable in an experiment, the terminology used by Campbell and Stanley is utilized here because of its traditional nature.

28. Marjorie B. Platt, "Naturally Occurring Groups Aid Choice of Marketing Mix," *Journal of Business Forecasting Methods and Systems* (Fall 1984), pp. 14–18; and Fred N. Kerlinger, *Foundations of Behavioral Research,* 2d ed. (New York: Holt, Rinehart and Winston, 1973), p. 341.

29. Dan H. Robertson and Danny N. Bellenger, "A New Method of Increasing Mail Survey Responses: Contributions to Charity," *Journal of Marketing Research* (November 1978), p. 633.

30. Ya-Lun Chou, *Statistical Analysis with Business and Economic Applications* (New York: Holt, Rinehart and Winston, 1975), p. 355.

31. Adapted from William G. Zikmund, Michael A. Hitt, and Beverly Pickins, "Influence of Sex and Scholastic Performance on Reactions to Job Applicants' Résumés," *Journal of Applied Psychology,* 63, No. 2, 1978, pp. 252–253. Copyright © 1978 by American Psychological Association.

32. For an interesting study related to this issue see U. N. Umesh, Robert A. Peterson, Michelle McCann-Nelson, and Rajiv Vaidyanathan, "Type IV Error in Marketing Research: The Investigation of ANOVA Interactions," *Journal of the Academy of Marketing Science,* Winter 1996, pp. 17–26.

33. From Ya-Lun Chou, *Statistical Analysis with Business and Economic Applications,* p. 365.

34. Winer, *Statistical Principles in Experimental Design,* p. 685.

CHAPTER 13

1. Gary Levin, "Emotion Guides BBDO's Ad Tests," *Advertising Age,* January 29, 1990, p. 12.

2. Sarah M. Dinham, *Exploring Statistics: An Introduction for Psychology and Education* (Belmont, CA: Brooks/Cole Publishing Co./Wadsworth, Inc., 1976), p. 3.

3. Donald P. Warwick and Charles A. Lininger, *The Sample Survey: Theory and Practice* (New York: McGraw-Hill, 1975), p. 27.

4. This definition is adapted from Fred N. Kerlinger, *Foundations of Behavioral Research* (New York: Holt, Rinehart and Winston, 1973), p. 31.

5. From "Putting a Face on the Big Brands," *Fortune,* September 19, 1994, p. 80.

6. Barry F. Anderson, *The Psychology Experiment* (Belmont, CA: Brooks/Cole Publishing, 1971), p. 26.

7. Fred N. Kerlinger, *Behavioral Research: A Conceptual Approach* (New York: Holt, Rinehart and Winston, 1979), p. 41.

8. Kerlinger, *Foundations of Behavioral Research,* p. 428.

9. Based on Angus Campbell, Philip E. Converse, and Willard L. Rodgers, *The Quality of American Life* (New York: Russell Sage Foundation, 1976), 297–298.

10. Benjamin B. Wolman, ed., *Dictionary of Behavioral Science* (New York: Van Nostrand Reinhold, 1973), p. 333.

11. See J. Paul Peter, "Reliability: A Review of Psychometric Basis and Recent Marketing Practices," *Journal of Marketing Research* (February 1979), pp. 6–17, for an excellent review of advanced techniques concerning reliability.

12. Campbell, Converse, and Rodgers, *The Quality of American Life,* p. 45.

13. Philip J. Runkel and Joseph E. McGrath, *Research on Human Behavior* (New York: Holt, Rinehart and Winston, 1972), p. 155.

14. L. J. Rothman, "Foundation of an Index of Propensity to Buy," *Journal of Marketing Research* 1 (1964), pp. 21-25.

15. Runkel and McGrath, *Research on Human Behavior,* pp. 158-161.

16. Cathy Lynn Grossman, "Passenger-Jet Designers Ponder Pie-in-the-Sky Idea," *USA TODAY,* April 18, 1995, p. 3D.

17. Burke Marketing Research, *Rough Commercial Recall Testing* (Cincinnati, OH, undated).

18. John A. Sonquist and William C. Dunkelburg, *Survey and Opinion Research: Procedures for Processing and Analysis* (Englewood Cliffs, N.J.: Prentice-Hall, 1977), p. 335.

19. Keith K. Cox and Ben M. Enis, *The Marketing Research Process* (Goodyear Publishing, Scott, Foresman and Company, 1972), pp. 335–355; and Kerlinger, *Foundations of Behavioral Research,* p. 44.

CHAPTER 14

1. Adapted from Jennifer Lach, "Hip Check," *American Demographics,* March 1999.

2. *Psychology Today: An Introduction* (Del Mar, CA: CRM Books, 1970), p. 613.

3. P. C. Smith, L. M. Kendall, and C. L. Hulin, *The Measurement of Satisfaction in Work and Retirement* (Chicago: Rand McNally, 1969).

4. Louis L. Thurstone, "Law of Comparative Judgment," *Psychological Review* 34 (1927), pp. 273–278.

5. Rensis Likert, "A Technique for the Measurement of Attitudes," *Archives of Psychology 19* (1932), pp. 44–53.

6. See Jacob Jacoby and Michael S. Matell, "Three-Point Likert Scales Are Good Enough," *Journal of Marketing Research* (November 1971), pp. 495-506; and Roger Best, Del I. Hawkins, and Gerald Albaum, "The Effect of Varying Response Intervals on the Stability of Factor Solutions of Rating Scale Data," in *Advances in Consumer Research,* vol. 7, Jerry Olson, Ed. (San Francisco: ACR, 1979), pp. 539–554.

7. Dow Scott, "The Causal Relationship between Trust and the Assessed Value of Management by Objectives," *Journal of Management,* 6, No. 2 (1980), p. 166.

8. Joel Huber and Morris B. Holbrook, "Using Attribute Ratings for Product Positioning: Some Distinctions among Compositional Approaches," *Journal of Marketing Research,* November 1979, p. 510. Reprinted by permission of the American Marketing Association.

9. Charles Osgood, George Suci, and Percy Tannenbaum, *The Measurement of Meaning* (Urbana: University of Illinois Press, 1957).

10. William A. Mindak, "Fitting the Semantic Differential to the Marketing Problem," *Journal of Marketing* (April 1961), pp. 29–33.

11. G. David Hughes, "The Measurement of Beliefs and Attitudes," in *Handbook of Marketing Research,* Robert Ferber, Ed. (New York: McGraw-Hill, 1974), pp. 30–31.

12. Fred E. Friedler, *A Theory of Leadership Effectiveness* (New York: McGraw-Hill, 1967), pp. 40–41.

13. Crespi, "Use of a Scaling Technique."

14. D. I. Hawkins, G. Albaum, and R. Best, "Stapel Scale or Semantic Differential in Marketing Research?" *Journal of Marketing Research* (August 1972), pp. 318–322.

15. Dennis Menezes and Norbert F. Elbert, "Alternate Semantic Scaling Formats for Measuring Store Image: An Evaluation," *Journal of Marketing Research* (February 1979), pp. 80–87.

16. Menezes and Elbert, "Alternate Semantic Scaling Formats"; and Hawkins, Albaum, and Best, "Stapel Scale or Semantic Differential in Marketing Research?"

17. Based on Irving Crespi, "Use of a Scaling Technique and Surveys, *Journal of Marketing* (July 1961), pp. 69–72. Published by the American Marketing Association.

18. Courtesy of Bruskin Associates Market Research.

19. This material was created by Ajay Sukhdial, Oklahoma State University; Damon Aiken, Butler University; and Lynn Kahle, University of Oregon. Additional details can be found in "Are You Old School? A Scale for Measuring Sports Fans' Old-School Orientation," *Journal of Advertising Research,* in press. The data have been modified for this activity.

CHAPTER 15

1. Charles W. Roll, Jr., and Albert H. Cantril, *Polls: Their Use and Misuse in Politics* (New York: Basic Books, 1972), p. 106.

2. Stanley L. Payne, *The Art of Asking Questions* (Princeton, NJ: Princeton University Press, 1951), pp. 8–9. The reader who wishes a more detailed account of question wording is referred to this classic book.

3. Paul L. Erdos, *Professional Mail Surveys* (New York: McGraw-Hill, 1970), p. 37.

4. Donald P. Warwick and Charles A. Lininger, *The Sample Survey: Theory and Practice* (New York: McGraw-Hill, 1975), p. 127.

5. Don A. Dillman, *Mail and Telephone Surveys: The Total Design Method* (New York: John Wiley & Sons, 1978), p. 209.

6. Payne, *The Art of Asking Questions,* p. 185.

7. Roll and Cantril, *Polls,* pp. 106–107.

8. Warwick and Lininger, *The Sample Survey,* p. 143.

9. Gloria E. Wheeler, "'Yes; No; All of the Above:' Before You Conduct a Survey," *Exchange* (Spring–Summer 1979), p. 21.

10. The other attributes are relative advantage, compatibility, complexity, and communicability. See Thomas S. Robertson, *Innovative Behavior and Communication* (New York: Holt, Rinehart and Winston, 1971), pp. 46–47.

11. Warwick and Lininger, *The Sample Survey,* p. 141.

12. Omar J. Bendikas, "One-step Questionnaire May Overstate Response; Two-step Questionnaires Hike Involvement, Accuracy," *Marketing News,* May 18, 1979, p. 9. Reprinted with permission of the American Marketing Association.

13. Payne, *The Art of Asking Questions,* pp. 102–103.

14. Richard F. Yalch, "Book Review of Hans J. Hippler, Norbert Schwartz, and Seymore Sudman's *Social Information Processing Methodology," Journal of Marketing Research,* February 1989, p. 127.

15. Erdos, *Professional Mail Surveys,* p. 59.

16. E. Laird Landon, Jr., "Order Bias, the Ideal Rating, and the Semantic Differential," *Journal of Marketing Research, 8,* August 1971, pp. 375–378.

17. F. Steward DeBruicker and Scott Ward, *Cases in Consumer Behavior* (Englewood Cliffs, NJ: Prentice-Hall, 1980), p. 217.

18. Research Services, Inc., Denver, Colorado, and the United Bank of Boulder, Boulder, Colorado.

19. Dillman, *Mail and Internet Surveys: The Tailored Design Method* (New York: John Wiley and Sons, 2000), pp. 357–361.

20. Sarah J. Young and Craig M. Ross, "Web Questionnaires: A Glimpse of Survey Research in the Future," *Parks & Recreation,* Vol. 35, No. 6 (June 2000), p. 30.

21. Young and Ross, "Web Questionnaires."

22. http://www.decisionanalyst.com/online/surtech.htm, downloaded February 6, 2001.

23. http://www.decisionanalyst.com/online/surtech.htm, downloaded February 6, 2001.

24. Matt Michel, "Controversy Redux," *CASRO Journal,* http://www.decisionanalyst.com/publ_art/contredux.htm, downloaded February 8, 2001.

25. Jeffrey L. Pope, *Practical Marketing Research* (New York: AMACOM, 1981), p. 78.

26. Philip R. Cateora, *International Marketing* (Homewood, IL: Richard D. Irwin, 1990), pp. 387–389.

27. Cateora, *International Marketing.*

28. Subhash C. Jain, *International Marketing Management* (Boston: PWS Kent, 1990), p. 338.

CHAPTER 16

1. Morris James Slonim, *Sampling in a Nutshell* (New York: Simon and Schuster, 1960), p. 3.

2. Donald P. Warwick and Charles A. Lininger, *The Sample Survey: Theory and Practice* (New York: McGraw-Hill, 1975), p. 70.

3. Reprinted from "Millennium Milestones: William's Census Was Ahead of Its Time," *Tulsa World,* March 27, 1998, p. A-3, Associated Press.

4. A. D. Fletcher and T. A. Bowers, *Fundamentals of Advertising Research* (Columbus, OH: Grid Publishing, 1983), pp. 60–61.

5. Seymour Sudman, *Applied Sampling* (New York: Academic Press, 1976), pp. 12–13.

6. Sudman, *Applied Sampling,* p. 14.

7. Provided by InfoUSA/American Business Information, Inc.

8. Philip R. Cateora, *International Marketing* (Homewood, IL: Richard D. Irwin, 1990), pp. 384–385.

9. Sabra E. Brock, "Marketing Research in Asia: Problems, Opportunities, and Lessons," *Marketing Research,* September 1989, p. 47.

10. Richard Reeves, "George Gallup's Nation of Numbers," *Esquire,* December 1983, pp. 91–92.

11. This discussion follows Ya-Lun Chou, *Statistical Analysis* (New York: Holt, Rinehart and Winston, 1975), pp. 390–391.

12. U. S. Department of Commerce, Bureau of the Census, *Current Population Survey, 1982,* Interviewer's Information Card Booklet, p. 3.

13. Sudman, *Applied Sampling,* p. 17.

14. Adapted by permission from Keith K. Cos and Ben M. Enis, *The Marketing Research Process* (Pacific Palisades, CA: Goodyear/Scott, Foresman and Company, 1972), pp. 377–379; and Danny N. Bellenger and Barnet A. Greenberg, *Marketing Research: A Management Information Approach* (Homewood, IL: Richard D. Irwin, 1978), pp. 154–155.

15. Jacqueline M. Graves, "Building a Fortune on Free Data," *Fortune,* February 6, 1995, p. 31. Copyright © Time, Inc. All Rights Reserved.

16. Alan Fram, "GOP Says No to Statistical Sampling" and "House Nixes Census Plan," *Tulsa World,* August 6, 1998, p. a7, Associated Press.

17. Sudman, *Applied Sampling,* pp. 210–212.

18. Slonim, *Sampling in a Nutshell,* p. 7.

19. Ya-Lun, *Statistical Analysis,* p. 393.

20. From David G. Meyers, *Exploring Psychology* (New York: Worth Publishers, 1990), p. 471.

21. This is a hypothetical example.

22. For additional details see *Interviewer's Manual,* rev. ed. (Ann Arbor, MI: Survey Research Center, Institute for Social Research, University of Michigan, 1976, pp. 35–37. Reprinted by permission.

23. *Interviewer's Manual,* rev. ed., p. 36. Reprinted by permission.

24. "Census Geography—Concepts and Product," *U. S. Census—Factfinder for the Nation,* August 1985, p. 3.

25. http://www.surveysite.com.

26. "Frequently Asked Questions about Conducting Online Research: New Methodologies for Traditional Techniques," Council of American Survey Research Organizations, http://www.casro.org/faq.cfm, February 8, 2001.

27. Michael Lewis, "The Two-Bucks-a-Minute Democracy," *New York Times Magazine,* November 5, 2000, p. 65; and http://www.knowledgenetworks.com.

28. Gloria Mellinger, "Harris Interactive Inc.," *WorldOpinion Research Profiles,* July 18, 2000.

29. "Frequently Asked Questions about Conducting Online Research: New Methodologies for Traditional Techniques."

30. http://www.ssisamples.com, January 3, 2001.

CHAPTER 17

1. Morris James Slonim, *Sampling in a Nutshell* (New York: Simon & Schuster, 1960), pp. 1–2.

2. Most of the statistical material in this book assumes that population parameters are unknown, which is the typical situation in most applied research projects.

3. Adapted from Darrell Huff and Irving Geis, *How to Lie with Statistics* (New York: Norton, 1954), p. 33.

4. For a discussion of this problem, see Thomas H. Wonnacott and Ronald J. Wonnacott, *Introductory Statistics* (New York: John Wiley & Sons, 1969), pp. 6–7.

5. The reasons for this are related to the concept of degrees of freedom, which will be explained later. At this point, disregard the intuitive notion of division by n, because it produces a biased estimate of the population variance.

6. An alternative version of this formula is easier to use in computation:

$$S = \sqrt{\frac{\sum_{i=1}^{n} X_i^2 - \frac{\left(\sum_{i=1}^{n} X_i\right)^2}{n}}{n-1}}$$

Rather than computing each deviation and summing, one can find the sum and sum of squares of the observations, substitute them into the formula, and evaluate. Many pocket calculators have features that make it easy to accumulate $\sum_{i=1}^{n} X_i$ and $\sum_{i=1}^{n} X_i^2$ at the same time.

7. In practice, most survey researchers do not utilize this exact formula. A modified version of the formula, $Z = (X - \mu)/S$, utilizing the sample standard deviation in an adjusted form, is frequently used.

8. Wonnacott and Wonnacott, *Introductory Statistics* p. 70.

9. William L. Hayes, *Statistics* (New York: Holt, Rinehart and Winston, 1963), p. 193.

10. D. H. Sanders, A. F. Murphy, and R. J. Eng, *Statistics: A Fresh Approach,* p. 123. © 1980 McGraw-Hill.

11. Wonnacott and Wonnacott, *Introductory Statistics,* p. 125.

12. Ernest Kurnow, Gerald J. Glasser, and Frederick R. Ottman, *Statistics for Business Decisions* (Homewood, IL: Richard D. Irwin, 1959), pp. 182–183. Reprinted with permission.

13. James H. Bowman, "Test Marketing Remains the Ol' Standby," *Advertising Age,* February 19, 1979, pp. 24–25.

14. Fred N. Kerlinger, *Foundations of Behavioral Research* (New York: Holt, Rinehart and Winston, 1973).

15. See, for example, James K. Skipper, J. R. Anthony Guenther, and Gilbert Mass, "The Sacredness of .05 Levels of Significance in Social Science," *American Sociologist* 2 (1967), pp. 16–18.

16. Walter B. Wentz, *Marketing Research: Management and Methods* (New York: Harper & Row, 1972), p. 145.

17. Note that the derivation of this formula is (1) $E = ZS_{\bar{X}}$, (2) $E = ZS/\sqrt{n}$, (3) $\sqrt{n}\ ZS/E$, (4) $n = (ZS/E)^2$.

18. Seymour Sudman, *Applied Sampling* (New York: Academic Press, 1976), pp. 86–87.

19. Nan Lin, *Foundations of Social Research* (New York: McGraw-Hill), p. 447. © 1976 McGraw-Hill.

20. Sudman, *Applied Sampling,* p. 30.

21. Lin, *Foundations of Social Research.*

CHAPTER 18

1. Excerpts adapted with permission from Randy Minkoff, "Matters of Opinon: Foot Soldiers of Marketing Research Battle for a Moment of Your Time in the Mall," *Chicago Tribune,* July 5, 1998.

2. Reprinted with permission of the Associated Press from "Census to Target American Indians," August 6, 1998.

3. This section relies heavily on the work of the Survey Research Center, Institute for Social Research, at the University of Michigan. For an excellent treatment of fieldwork procedures, see Survey Research Center, *Interviewer's Manual,* rev. ed. (Ann Arbor: Institute for Social Research, The University of Michigan, 1976).

4. *Interviewer's Manual,* rev. ed., p. 11.

5. For an extensive treatment of probing, see *Interviewer's Manual,* rev. ed. pp. 15–19.

6. Donald P. Warwick and Charles A. Lininger, *The Sample Survey: Theory and Practice* (New York: McGraw-Hill, 1975), p. 213.

7. *Interviewer's Manual,* rev. ed., p. 16. Reprinted with permission.

8. *Interviewer's Manual,* rev. ed., pp. 19–21.

9. This section is adapted from Yankelovich, Skelly and White, Inc., *Interviewing Handbook for Senior Council Interviewers.*

10. *Interviewer's Manual,* rev. ed., p. 26.

11. G. Birch Ripley, "Confessions of an Industrial Marketing Research Executive Interviewer," *Marketing News,* September 10, 1976, p. 20.

12. Based on Julius A. Roth, "Hired Hand Research," *American Sociologist* (August 1966), pp. 190–196.

13. Alan Dutka, *AMA Handbook for Customer Satisfaction* (Lincolnwood, IL: NTC Books, 1993), p. 108.

CHAPTER 19

1. Adapted from John A. Sonquist and William C. Dunkelberg, *Survey and Opinion Research: Procedures for Processing and Analysis* © 1977, p. 8.

2. Sonquist and Dunkelberg, *Survey and Opinion Research,* pp. 41–72. This is an excellent source for information about the data processing of survey data.

3. Paul L. Erdos, *Professional Mail Surveys* (New York: McGraw-Hill, 1970), p. 176.

4. D. W. Stewart, "Filling the Gap: A Review of the Missing Data Problem," in Bruce J. Walker et al., *An Assessment of Marketing Thought and Practice* (Chicago: American Marketing Association, 1982), pp. 395–399.

5. A. R. Automarket Research.

6. State of Hawaii, Department of Transportation.

7. Adapted from http://www.spss.com/spssmr/products/coding/FAQs.htm#how, downloaded June 26, 2001.

8. Philip S. Sibel, "Coding," in *Handbook of Marketing Research,* ed. by Robert Ferber (New York: McGraw-Hill, 1974), p. 181.

9. Sonquist and Dunkelberg, *Survey and Opinion Research,* p. 9.

10. Courtesy of the Pittsburgh Pirates.

CHAPTER 20

1. Adapted from "The Eyes Have It! Soreness, Fatigue, Strain, You Name It, According to Worker Survey," *Business Wire,* January 10, 2000, p. 1146, Article BP58502136.

2. Bruce Horovitz, "Coke's New Marketing Chief Really Knows the Business," *USA TODAY,* July 13, 1998, p. 4B.

3. *American Demographics,* June 2000, p. 72.

4. "Mobility Index," *Inc.,* April 1999, p. 22.

5. Herman J. Loether and Donald G. McTavish, *Descriptive Statistics for Sociologists: An Introduction* (Boston: Allyn & Bacon, 1974), pp. 265–266.

6. Adapted from David Schwartz, *Concept Testing* (New York: AMACOM, 1987), pp. 80–81.

7. Alternative methods may be used to determine the quadrants. They will not be discussed here.

8. David G. Meyers, *Exploring Psychology* (New York: Worth Publishers, 1990), p. 464.

9. Reprinted with permission from IBM, *Notice of 2001 Annual Meeting* and *Proxy Statement,* p. 31.

10. "Keeping Employees in the Know," *USA TODAY,* December 14, 1995, p. 2B.

11. From *Real Stats, Real Easy, SPSS for Windows.* Copyright 1992 by SPSS Inc.

12. Peter H. Lewis, "When Maps Are Tied to Data Bases," *New York Times,* May 28, 1989, p. 10.

13. Graphic from "Wiretap Nation," by Todd Lappin, *Wired,* August 1998, p. 88. Copyright © 1999 by Condé Nast Publications Inc. All rights reserved.

14. "Graphic Displays of Data: Box and Whisker Plots," Report No. 17 from Market Facts, Inc.

15. Frederick Hartwig with Brian E. Dearing, *Exploratory Data Analysis* (Beverly Hills, CA: Sage Publications, 1979), p. 21.

16. Fred N. Kerlinger, *Foundations of Behavioral Research,* 2nd ed. (New York: Holt, Rinehart and Winston, 1973), pp. 134–135.

17. Bill Iuso, "Concept Testing: An Appropriate Approach," *Journal of Marketing Research* (May 1975), p. 230, published by the American Marketing Association.

18. This material was created by Ajay Sukhdial, Oklahoma State University; Damon Aiken, Butler University; and Lynn Kahle, University of Oregon. Additional details can be found in "Are You Old School? A Scale for Measuring Sports Fans' Old-School Orientation," *Journal of Advertising Research,* in press.

CHAPTER 21

1. Technically the *t*-distribution should be used when the population variance is unknown and the standard deviation is estimated from sample data. However, with large samples it is convenient to use the *Z*-distribution, because the *t*-distribution approximates the *Z*-distribution.

2. A complete discussion of this topic is beyond the scope of this book. See almost any statistics textbook for a more detailed discussion of Type I and Type II errors.

3. A more complete discussion of the differences between parametric and nonparametric statistics is given in Appendix 22A.

4. The reader with an extensive statistics background will recognize that there are a few rare cases in which the degrees of freedom are not equal to $k - 1$. These cases are infrequently encountered by readers of this level of book, and to present them would only complicate the presentation offered here.

5. An example of how to use the chi-square table is given in Table 4 of the Appendix of Statistical Tables.

CHAPTER 22

1. Excerpts reprinted from an advertisement for "Women at Work," a special report on the status and satisfaction of working women and initiatives for their advancement, conducted by Fortune Marketing Research for Deloitte & Touche LLP.

2. Three nonparametric tests (the Wilcoxon matched-pairs signed-ranks test, the Kruskal-Wallis test, and the Mann-Whitney *U* test) and ANOVA for complex experimental designs are covered in the appendixes to this chapter.

3. Fred N. Kerlinger, *Behavioral Research: A Conceptual Approach* (New York: Holt, Rinehart and Winston, 1979), p. 313.

4. A one-way analysis of variance may also be referred to as a *single-factor analysis of variance* because only one variable (factor) is manipulated.

5. At first, $\sum_{i=1}^{n} \sum_{j=1}^{c}$ looks complicated. Our example shows that the procedure is not difficult, but it does require that all observations within a group (*n*) be summed up, then these totals be summed for all groups (*c*).

6. This section is reprinted with minor adaptations from Norma Gilbert, *Statistics* (Philadelphia: Saunders College Publishing, 1981), pp. 380–381.

7. If a completely random relationship between the observations in each pair exists, the values of T_p and T_n are expected to be equal.

8. This example is modified from Joseph Newmark, *Statistics and Probability in Modern Life,* 2nd ed. (New York: Holt, Rinehart and Winston, Inc., 1977), pp. 434–436.

9. We assume no interaction effect between treatments and blocks.

10. In the ANOVA table it is conventional to place the treatments in columns and the blocks in rows. Because of this convention, $SS_{\text{treatment}}$ may be referred to as SS_{columns} and SS_{blocks} may be referred to as SS_{rows} in some research reports.

CHAPTER 23

1. Susan E. Kuhn, "How Crazy Is the Market?" *Fortune,* April 15, 1996, p. 80. Updated with data from http://www.djindexes.com/jsp/uiHistoricalIndexRep.jsp and www.economagic.com.

2. The symbol of the correlation coefficient of a population is the Greek letter rho.

3. For a discussion of the other measures of association, see the appendix to this chapter and Jean Dickinson Gibbons, *Nonparametric Methods for Quantitative Analysis* (New York: Holt, Rinehart and Winston, 1976).

4. Jack Neff, "Kids Take Longer to Train; Diaper Business Swells," *Advertising Age,* July 20, 1998, p. 3.

5. See Richard P. Bagozzi, "Salesforce Performance and Satisfaction as a Function of Individual Difference, Interpersonal and Situational Factors," *Journal of Marketing Research* (November 1978), pp. 517–531.

6. To calculate a *t*-test under the null hypothesis rho = 0, *t* is distributed with d.f. = $n - 2$:

$$t = \frac{r}{s_r}, \text{ where } s_r = \sqrt{\frac{1 - r^2}{n - r}}$$

Table 7 in the Appendix of Statistical Tables at the back of the book provides the critical values of *r* for the Pearson correlation coefficient to test the null hypothesis that rho equals zero.

7. From Lewis E. Walkup, "Walkup's First Five Laws of Statistics," *The Bent,* a publication of Tau Beta Pi, Summer 1974, p. 43, as quoted in Robert W. Joselyn, *Designing the Research Project* (New York: Petrocelli/Charter, 1977), p. 175.

8. Frederick Kerlinger, *Foundations of Behavioral Research,* 2nd ed. (New York: Holt, Rinehart and Winston, 1985), p. 528.

9. This is a point estimate. It is possible to calculate a confidence interval for this sales estimate; however, the topic is beyond the scope of this book.

10. From Eugene F. Brigham and Louis C. Gapenski, *Financial Management: Theory and Practice,* 5th ed., pp. 189–191. Copyright ©1988 by The Dryden Press.

11. From *Life on the Mississippi,* by Mark Twain (Samuel Clemens).

12. Portions of this section are reprinted, with adaptations, from Gerald Zaltman and Philip Burger, *Marketing Research* (Hinsdale, IL.: Dryden Press, 1976), pp. 488–449.

13. For more detail see Gibbons, *Nonparametric Methods for Quantitative Analysis.*

14. This material is based on John T. Roscoe, *Fundamental Research for Behavioral Science* (New York: Holt, Rinehart and Winston, 1975), pp. 260–261.

CHAPTER 24

1. Adapted with permission from Judith Waldrop, "Executive Downtime," *American Demographics,* August 1, 1993, p. 4.

2. For excellent discussions of multivariate analysis, see Joseph F. Hair, Jr., Rolph E. Anderson, and Ronald L. Tatham, *Multivariate Data Analysis with Readings,* 2nd ed. (New York: Macmillan, 1987).

3. Hair, Anderson, and Tatham, *Multivariate Data Analysis with Readings.*

4. This example is adapted from Eugene F. Brigham and Louis C. Gapenski, *Financial Management: Theory and Practice,* 5th ed. (Hinsdale, IL: Dryden Press, 1988), pp. 801–805.

5. Brigham and Gapenski, *Financial Management: Theory and Practice,* 7th ed. Copyright © 1994 Dryden Press.

6. To plot the boundary line, let D/A = 0% and 80%, then find the current ratio that forces $Z = 0$, for example, at D/A = 0.

$$Z = -.3877 - 1.0736(\text{current ratio}) + .0579(0) = 0$$
$$0 = -.3877 - 1.0736(\text{current ratio})$$
$$-1.0736(\text{current ratio}) = .3877$$
$$\text{Current ratio} = .3877/-1.0736 = -.3611$$

Thus, −0.3611 is the vertical axis intercept. Similarly, the current ratio at D/A = 80% is found to be 3.3633. Plotting these two points in Exhibit 24.4 and then connecting them provides the discriminant boundary line. It is the line that best partitions the companies into bankrupt and nonbankrupt. Note that nonlinear discriminant functions may also be used.

7. With more than two variables, it is difficult to graph the function, but this presents no problem in actual usage because graphs are only used to explain multiple discriminant analysis.

8. Brigham and Gapenski, *Financial Management.*

9. The purpose of this section is to discuss factor-analytic techniques at an intuitive level. The discussion is not complicated by the various mathematically complex differences between the techniques. An excellent discussion of the mathematical aspects of factor analysis can be found in R. J. Rummel, "Understanding Factor Analysis," *Journal of Conflict Resolution 11,* no. 4, pp. 444–480.

10. Edgar A. Pessemier, Albert C. Bemmaor, and Dominique M. Hanssens, "Willingness to Supply Human Body Parts: Some Empirical Results," *Journal of Consumer Research 4,* no. 3 (December 1977), pp. 131–140. Reprinted by permission of the University of Chicago Press.

11. The multiple regression model assumes the independent variables are independent of each other. *Multicollinearity* is the technical term used when some of the predictor variables are correlated with each other. For example, the consumer price index and the federal mortgage rate both show a similar historical trend. Thus, it would be difficult to appraise their individual influence on a dependent variable, as opposed to their joint influence.

12. Paul E. Green, Ronald E. Grank, and Patrick J. Robinson, "Cluster Analysis in Test Market Selection," *Management Science 13* (April 1967), p. B393 (Table 2). Copyright 1967 by The Institute of Management Science.

13. F. J. Carmone, and P. J. Robertson, "Nonmetric Scaling Methods: An Exposition and Overview," *Wharton Quarterly* 2 (1968), pp. 159–173.

14. This discussion follows the logic of Gerald Zaltman and Philip Berger, *Marketing Research* (Hinsdale, IL: Dryden Press, 1973), pp. 511–512. The example is adapted from James Richard Darnaby, "Bank Marketing: Market Segmentation Aimed at Increasing Consumer Profitability," pp. 31–34. (Master's thesis, Oklahoma State University, July 1979)

15. Jagdish N. Sheth, "Seven Commandments for Users of Multivariate Methods," in *Multivariate Methods for Market and Survey Research,* 1977, pp. 333–335, edited by Jagdish N. Sheth. Reprinted by permission.

CHAPTER 25

1. Harper W. Boyd, Jr., Ralph Westfall, and Stanley F. Stasch, *Marketing Research: Text and Cases,* 4th ed. (Homewood, IL: Irwin, 1977), p. 546.

2. John C. Hodges and Mary E. Whitten, *Harbrace College Handbook* (New York: Harcourt Brace Jovanovich, 1977), pp. 336–350; or Frederick Crews, *The Random House Handbook* (New York: Random House, 1977), pp. 35–44; or a business writing book, such as William J. Gallagher, *Report Writing for Management* (Reading, MA: Addison-Wesley, 1969), pp. 60–68; or David M. Robinson, *Writing Reports for Management Decisions* (Columbus, OH: Merrill, 1969), pp. 212–217.

3. This section gives some suggestions from Gallagher, *Report Writing for Management,* pp. 69–74. People particularly afflicted with writer's block should see James W. Miller, Jr., *Word, Self, Reality: The Rhetoric of Imagination* (New York: Dodd, Mead, 1972). This book deals with the flow of language, not with rules and restrictions, and offers numerous exercises useful in learning to let out the words locked within one's head.

4. Adapted from Jessamon Dawe and William Jackson Lord, Jr., *Functional Business Communication,* 2nd ed., p. 195. ©1974, Prentice-Hall Inc., Englewood Cliffs, NJ.

5. Gallagher, *Report Writing for Management,* p. 84.

6. Adapted from Robinson, *Writing Reports for Management Decisions,* p. 301. Reprinted with permission.

7 Dawe and Lord, *Functional Business Communication,* p. 495.

8. Adapted from Robinson, *Writing Reports for Management Decisions,* p. 295.

9. The following discussion is indebted to John Fielden, "What Do You Mean I Can't Write?" *Harvard Business Review* (May–June 1964).

10. Dawe and Lord, *Functional Business Communication,* Chapters 10 and 11; see also Robinson, *Writing Reports for Management Decisions,* pp. 302–312.

11. This section has been adapted and does not refer to division of the report into categories for upward and downward communications. The interested reader may want to refer to the original inventory, by Fielden, in "What Do You Mean I Can't Write?" p. 147.

12. Adapted from Robinson, *Writing Reports for Management Decisions,* p. 340.

13. Adapted from Robinson, *Writing Reports for Management Decisions,* p. 204.

14. http://www.census.gov/prod/2001pubs/statab/sec15.pdf

15. "Can You Satisfy All the People All the Time?" *Inc.,* November 1992, p. 102. Copyright 1992 by Goldhirsch Group, Inc.

16. Adapted from Mary Eleanor Spear, *Practical Charting Techniques* (New York: McGraw-Hill, 1969), p. 56.

17. *The New York Times,* August 13, 1989, p. Y-29. Copyright © 1989 by The New York Times Company. Reprinted by permission.

18. *Statistical Abstract of the United States,* http://www.census.gov/prod/2001pubs/statab/sec15.pdf.

19. U.S. Bureau of the Census, http://www.census.gov/briefrm/esbr/www/esbr020.html.

20. "The Lawsuit Industry," *Forbes,* September 14, 1992, p. 304. Reprinted by permission of Forbes magazine. © 1992 Forbes, Inc.

21. Adapted from Marjorie Brody, president, Brody Communications, 1200 Melrose Ave., Melrose Park, PA 19126, as it appeared in "How to Gesture When Speaking," *Communication Briefings* 14(11). p. 4.

22. National Energy Information Center, http://www.eia.doe.gov/pub/oil_gas/petroleum/analysis_publications/primer_on_gasoline_prices/html/petbro.html, downloaded January 5, 2002.

23. Adapted from William D. Wells, University of Minnesota, "Noah's Law of Overhead Transparencies," *ACR Newsletter,* June 1993, p. 10. Published by the Association for Consumer Research.

24 Adapted from Fielden, "What Do You Mean I Can't Write?" *Harvard Business Review,* May–June 1964, p. 147.

VIDEO CASES AND CRITICAL THINKING CASES

1. Reprinted from Louis E. Boone and David L. Kurtz, *Contemporary Marketing,* 10th edition (Ft. Worth: Harcourt, 2001), pp. vc1–vc18.

2. Information from Ben & Jerry's Web page at http://www.benjerry.com; LearNet's video *Ben & Jerry's,* and a press release from Ben & Jerry's, February 20, 1997.

3. Adapted from Louis E. Boone and David L. Kurtz, *Contemporary Business,* 9th edition (Fort Worth, TX: Dryden Press, 1999), p. 407.

4. Excerpt reprinted from http://houns54clearlake. ibm.com/solutions/erp/erppub.nsf/detailcontacts/stage_1_ERP/Lifecycle_Solution_inquirywhat, downloaded June 21, 2001.

5. Reprinted from Louis E. Boone and David L. Kurtz, *Contemporary Marketing,* 10th edition (Ft. Worth: Harcourt, 2001), pp. vc7–vc8.

6. This historical material and additional details may be found at http://www.census.gov/acsd/www/history.html.

7. Adapted from Jill Lieber, "Braves Bank on Future: Converted Olympic Stadium Incorporates Latest Technology," *USA TODAY,* April 3, 1997, p. 3C. Copyright 1997, *USA TODAY.*

8. Adapted from Jennifer deJony, "View from the Top," *Inc. Technology 1,* 1995, downloaded from the Internet July 3, 1998.

9. Excerpt reprinted with permission from Paul E. Green, Abba M. Krieger, and Terry G. Varra, "Evaluating New Products," *Marketing Research: A Magazine of Management and Applications* (Winter 1997), pp. 17–18.

10. Adapted from Mike Hoffman, "Hocus Pocus Focus," *Inc.,* July, 1998, p. 90.

11. Excerpts reprinted from Joe Schwartz, "Marketing the Verdict (Advantages of Jury Research)," *American Demographics,* February 1, 1993, p. 52.

12. Edmund L. Andrews, "Delving into the Consumer Unconscious," *New York Times,* July 22, 1990, p. F-9. Copyright © 1990 by the New York Times Company. Reprinted by permission.

13. Adapted from Peter L. Miller and William R. Gombeski, Jr., "Research in the Strike Zone," *Marketing Research,* Winter 1995, pp. 28–33. American Marketing Association.

14. Dean E. Headley, Brent D. Bowen, and Jacqueline R. Luedtke prepared this case.

15. Reprinted from About the Survey, http://www.careerjournal.com/specialreports/bschoolguide/aboutsurvey.html, downloaded May 7, 2001.

16. M. Patchen, *Some Questionnaire Measures of Employee Motivation and Morale: A Report on the Reliability and Validity* (Ann Arbor: University of Michigan, Institute for Social Research, 1965).

17. This case is based on materials supplied by Scott Burton, Louisiana State University, and George M. Zinkham, Conn Professor of Marketing, University of Houston.

18. Terri Lammers, "The Essential Employee Survey" (table), *Inc.* magazine, December 1992, pp. 159–161. Goldhirsch Group, Inc., 38 Commercial Wharf, Boston, MA 02110.

19. This case is from the NPR/Kaiser/Kennedy School Poll, a project of National Public Radio, the Henry J. Kaiser Family Foundation, and Harvard University's Kennedy School of Government. http://www.npr.org/programs/specials/survey/front.html.

20. This material was created by Ajay Sukhdial, Oklahoma State University; Damon Aiken, Butler University; and Lynn Kahle, University of Oregon. Additional details can be found in "Are You Old School? A Scale for Measuring Sports Fans' Old School Orientation," *Journal of Advertising Research,* forthcoming.

21. Excerpts reprinted from "New Report Shows How Americans View Retirement Savings," *Research Insights,* Fidelity Investments, January 1995.

22. Case prepared by Tobin Zikmund.

23. Based on research by George L. Bazin II. The company name is fictitious in order to protect confidentiality. The data are adjusted slightly for the same purpose. Reprinted with permission.

24. This case was prepared by John H. Walkup. Reprinted with permission.

25. This case was prepared by Ajay S. Sukdial and Goutam Chakroborty, Oklahoma State University.

STATISTICAL TABLES

Table 1: Source: *A Million Random Digits with 100,000 Normal Deviates.* Copyright © The Rand Corporation.

Table 2: Chaiho Kim, *Statistical Analysis for Induction and Decision.* Copyright © 1973 by the Dryden Press.

Table 3: Abridged from Table III of R. A. Fisher and F. Yates, *Statistical Tables for Biological, Agricultural, and Medical Research,* published by Longman Group, Ltd., London (previously published by Oliver & Boyd, Ltd., Edinburgh).

Table 4: Abridged from Table IV of Fisher and Yates, *Statistical Tables for Biological, Agricultural, and Medical Research.*

Table 5: Maxine Merrington and Catherine M. Thompson, "Table of the Percentage Points of the Inverted *F*-Distribution." *Biometrica 33* (1943), pp. 73–78.

Table 6: Merrington and Thompson, "Table of the Percentage Points of the Inverted *F*-Distribution."

Table 7: Abridged from Table IV of Fisher and Yates, *Statistical Tables for Biological, Agricultural, and Medical Research.*

Table 8: Adapted from Table 2 of Frank Wilcoxon and Roberta A. Wilcoxon, 1964, *Some Rapid Approximate Statistical Procedures.* New York: American Cyanamid Company, p. 28.

PHOTO CREDITS

p. 4, © Michael Newman/PhotoEdit; p. 6, Courtesy, U.S. Mint; p. 9, © AP/Wide World Photos; p. 17, © Richard Alcorn/Colgate-Palmolive Company; p. 21, © Mark Windom/Index Stock Imagery; p. 30, © 2002, Chicago Mercantile Exchange. Reprinted with permission; p. 34, top, middle, Screen shots courtesy of YAHOO!. Copyright ©1999 YAHOO!; p. 34, bottom, By permission from Merriam-Webster OnLine, www.merriam-webster.com, © 2002 by Merriam-Webster; p. 35 top, middle, Google, Inc.; p. 35, bottom, By Permission Clio Awards; p. 36, © 2002 zeroknowledge. com; p. 54, © Susan Van Etten; p. 63, © Hoover's OnLine, Reprinted with permission; p. 64, Courtesy of Jelly Belly Candy Company; p. 66, Courtesy, Partnership for a Drug Free America; p. 68, © Susan Van Etten; p. 71, © *Literary Digest;* p. 80, © Spencer Grant/PhotoEdit; p. 84, DILBERT reprinted by permission of United Features Syndicate, Inc.; p. 87, Screen Shot Courtesy of TRUSTe. Copyright © 1999 TRUSTe; p. 88, © AP/Wide World Photos; p. 110, © Susan Van Etten; p. 119, © Susan Van Etten; p. 126, © Susan Van Etten; p. 127, © Susan Van Etten; p. 142, Courtesy, © IBM; p. 147, © Spencer Grant/PhotoEdit; pp. 170, 171, 172, Proquest Screen Shot Courtesy of Proquest Direct, © Bell & Howell; p. 176, © Eric Camp/Index Stock Imagery; p. 179, © David Hiser/CORBIS; p. 180, © David Burch/Index Stock Imagery; p. 183, © Charles Gupton/CORBIS; p. 184, © Laura Wright/CORBIS; p. 199, © Spencer Grant/StockBoston; p. 206, Courtesy, © Techneos Systems; p. 213, © PhotoDisc, Inc.; p. 220, © Greenfield OnLine; p. 222 top, © Prisma Dia/Index Stock Imagery; p. 222 bottom left and right, © Don Couch Photography; p. 223, © SurveySite.com; p. 225, Courtesy, U.S. Mint; p. 236, © PhotoDisc, Inc.; p. 239, © Don Couch Photography; p. 244, © Susan Van Etten; p. 250, © Susan Van Etten; p. 251, © Susan Van Etten; p. 252, Courtesy, Perception Research Services, Inc.; p. 266, Photo by Susan Van Etten/Cover © Sports Illustrated, 10/29/2001; p. 295, From "Putting a Face on the Big Brands," *Fortune,* September 19, 1994, p. 80; p. 303, © Susan Van Etten; p. 371, © Wallace Garrison/Index Stock Imagery; p. 382, Courtesy, U.S. Census Bureau; p. 383, © Mark E. Gibson/CORBIS; p. 387, © EyeWire; p. 397, © ™KidzEyes, Inc.; p. 402, Cartoon by Tony Hall. From Sarah M. Dinham, EXPLORING STATISTICS: AN INTRODUCTION TO PSYCHOLOGY & EDUCATION, © 1970 by Wadsworth, Inc. Reprinted by permission of Brooks/Cole Publishing, Monterey, CA; p. 438, © John Coletti/Index Stock Imagery; p. 440, © Susan Van Etten; p. 473, © Susan Van Etten; p. 484, © Bettmann/CORBIS; p. 552, Copyright © Kimberly-Clark Corporation; p. 617, © Patrick Giardino/CORBIS

GLOSSARY OF FREQUENTLY USED SYMBOLS

GREEK LETTERS

α **(alpha)** level of significance or probability of a Type I error
β **(beta)** probability of a Type II error or the slope of the regression line
μ **(mu)** population mean
ρ **(rho)** population Pearson correlation coefficient
Σ **(summation)** take the sum of
π **(pi)** population proportion
σ **(sigma)** population standard deviation
χ^2 chi-square statistic

ENGLISH LETTERS

d.f.	number of degrees of freedom
F	F-statistic
n	sample size
p	sample proportion
Pr( )	probability of the outcome in the parentheses
r	sample Pearson correlation coefficient
r^2	coefficient of determination (squared correlation coefficient)
S	sample standard deviation (inferential statistics)
$S_{\bar{X}}$	estimated standard error of the mean
S_p	estimated standard error of the proportion
S^2	sample variance (inferential statistics)
t	t-statistic
X	a variable or any unspecified observation
$\bar{X}$	sample mean
Y	any unspecified observation on a second variable, usually the dependent variable
$\hat{Y}$	predicted score
Z	standardized score (descriptive statistics) or Z-statistic

GLOSSARY OF TERMS

abstract level In theory development, the level of knowledge expressing a concept that exists only as an idea or a quality apart from an object.
acquiescence bias A category of response bias in which individuals have a tendency to agree with all questions or to indicate a positive connotation to a new idea.
administrative error An error caused by the improper administration or execution of a research task.
advocacy research Research undertaken to support a specific claim in a legal action.
affective component The component of attitude that reflects one's general feelings or emotions toward an object.
alternative hypothesis A statement indicating the opposite of the null hypothesis.
analysis of dependence A collective term to describe any multivariate statistical technique that attempts to explain or predict the dependent variable on the basis of two or more independent variables.
analysis of interdependence A collective term to describe any multivariate statistical technique that attempts to give meaning to a set of variables or seeks to group things together.
analysis of variance (ANOVA) Analysis of the effects of one treatment variable on an interval-scaled or ratio-scaled dependent variable; a technique to determine if statistically significant differences in means occur between two or more groups.
analysis of variance summary table A table that presents the results of a regression calculation.
applied research Research undertaken to answer questions about specific problems or to make decisions about a particular course of action or policy decision.
area sample A cluster sample in which the primary sampling unit is a geographic area.
attitude An enduring disposition to consistently respond in a given manner to various aspects of the world; composed of affective, cognitive, and behavioral components.
attitude rating scale Measures used to rate attitudes, such as the Likert scale, semantic differential, and Stapel scale.
attribute A single characteristic or fundamental feature of an object, person, situation, or issue.
auspices bias Bias in the responses of subjects caused by their being influenced by the organization conducting the study.
automatic interaction detection See *Chi-square automatic interaction detection (CHAID).*
average deviation A measure of dispersion that is computed by calculating the deviation score of each observation value, summing up the deviation scores, and dividing by the sample size.

back translation Taking a questionnaire that has previously been translated into another language and then having a second, independent translator translate it back into the original language.
backward linkage A term implying that the late stages of the research process will have an influence on the early stages.
balanced rating scale A fixed-alternative rating scale that has an equal number of positive and negative categories; a neutral or indifference point is at the center of the scale.
bar chart A graphic aid that shows changes in a variable at discrete intervals.
base (base number) The number of respondents or observations that indicate a total; used as a basis for computing percentages in each column or row in a cross-tabulation table.
basic experimental design An experimental design in which a single independent variable is manipulated in order to observe its effect on a single dependent variable.
basic (pure) research Research that is intended to expand the boundaries of knowledge itself; or to verify the acceptability of a given theory.
behavioral component The component of attitude that includes buying intentions and behavioral expectations; reflects a predisposition to action.
behavioral differential An instrument developed to measure the behavioral intentions of subjects toward an object or category of objects.
between-group variance Variation of scores between groups due either to the manipulation of an independent variable or to characteristics of the independent variable.
bivariate data analysis A type of data analysis and hypothesis used in the testing when the investigation concerns simultaneous investigation of two variables using tests of differences or measures of association between two variables at a time.
bivariate linear regression A measure of linear association that investigates straight-line relationships of the type $Y = \alpha + \beta X$, where Y is the dependent variable, X is the independent variable, and a and b are two constants to be estimated.
bivariate statistics Tests of differences or measures of association between two variables at a time.
blinding A technique used to control subjects' knowledge of whether or not they have been given a particular experimental treatment.
box and whisker plot A graphic device that represents central tendencies, percentiles, variability, and frequency distributions.
briefing session A training session to ensure that all interviewers are provided with common information.
business intelligence software Computer programs that permit managers to restructure and analyze data in extensive data warehouses to discover significant patterns and relationships.
business research The systematic and objective process of gathering, recording, and analyzing data for aid in making business decisions.

callback An attempt to recontact an individual selected for the sample.
canonical correlation analysis A technique used to determine the degree of linear association between two sets of variables, each consisting of several variables.
case study method An exploratory research technique that intensively investigates one or a few situations similar to the researcher's problem situation.
categorical variable Any variable that has a limited number of distinct values.
category scale An attitude scale consisting of several response categories to provide the respondent with alternative ratings.
causal research Research conducted to identify cause-and-effect relationships among variables when the research problem has already been narrowly defined.
cell Section of a table representing a specific combination of two variables or a specific value of a variable.
census An investigation of all the individual elements making up a population.
central-limit theorem The theory stating that as a sample size increases, the distribution of sample means of size n, randomly selected, approaches a normal distribution.
central location interviewing The practice of conducting telephone interviews from a central location, which allows effective supervision and control of the quality of interviewing.
chart A graphic aid used to translate numerical information into visual form so that relationships may be easily understood.

check box In an Internet questionnaire, a small graphic box, next to an answer, that a respondent clicks on to choose that answer; typically, a check mark or an X appears in the box when the respondent clicks on it.
checklist question A type of fixed-alternative question that allows the respondent to provide multiple answers to a single question.
chi-square automatic interaction detection (CHAID) A clustering method used to investigate the interaction of a large set of independent variables; a method of breaking a large heterogeneous group into various homogeneous subgroups.
chi-square (χ^2) test A test that statistically determines significance in the analysis of frequency distributions.
choice technique A measurement task that identifies preferences by requiring respondents to choose between two or more alternatives.
classificatory variable See *Categorical variable.*
cluster analysis An analysis that classifies individuals or objects into a small number of mutually exclusive groups, ensuring that there will be as much likeness within groups and as much difference among groups as possible.
cluster sampling An economically efficient sampling technique in which the primary sampling unit is not the individual element in the population but a large cluster of elements.
code A rule used for interpreting, classifying, and recording data in the coding processes; the actual numerical or other character symbol assigned to raw data.
code book A book identifying each variable in a study and its position in the data matrix. The book is used to identify a variable's description, code name, and field.
code of ethics A statement of principles and operating procedures for ethical practice.
coding The process of identifying and classifying each answer with a numerical score or other character symbol.
coding sheet A ruled sheet of paper used to transfer data from questionnaires or data collection forms after data have been collected.
coefficient of correlation See *Simple correlation coefficient.*
coefficient of determination (r^2) A measure of that portion of the total variance of a variable that is accounted for by knowing the value of another variable.
coefficient of multiple determination In multiple regression, the percentage of the variance in the dependent variable that is explained by the variation in the independent variables.
coefficient of partial regression The percentage of the variance in the dependent variable that is explained by a single independent variable, with the other independent variables held constant.
cognitive component The component of attitude that represents one's awareness of and knowledge about an object.
cohort effect A change in the dependent variable resulting from subjects in one experimental condition experiencing historical situations different from those of subjects in other experimental conditions.
communality In factor analysis, a measure of the percentage of a variable's variation that is explained by the factors.
communication process The process by which one person or source sends a message to an audience or receiver and then receives feedback about the message.
comparative rating scale Any measure of attitudes that asks respondents to rate a concept in comparison with a benchmark explicitly used as a frame of reference.
completely randomized design (CRD) An experimental design that uses a random process to assign experimental units to treatments in order to investigate the effects of a single independent variable.
complex experimental design An experimental design that uses statistical methods to isolate the effects of extraneous variables or to allow for manipulation of multiple independent variables.
compromise design An approximation of an experimental design, which may fall short of the requirements of random assignment of subjects or treatments to groups.
computer-assisted telephone interviewing (CATI) A type of telephone interviewing in which the interviewer reads questions from a computer screen and enters the respondent's answers directly into a computer.
computer interactive survey A survey in which a respondent completes a self-administered questionnaire displayed on a computer monitor. The computer is programmed to ask questions in a sequence determined by respondents' previous answers.
computer map A computer-generated map that portrays a variable, such as demographic data, in two or three dimensions.
computerized, voice-activated telephone interviewing A form of computer-assisted interviewing in which a voice-synthesized module records a respondent's single-word response in a computer file.
concept A generalized idea about a class of objects, attributes, occurrences, or processes; an abstraction of reality that is the basic unit for theory development.
concept testing A form of research that tests something that acts as a proxy for a new or revised program, product, or service.
conceptual definition A verbal explanation of the meaning of a concept. It defines the domain of the concept, and it may explain what the concept is not.
concomitant variation The variation of two phenomena or events together.
concurrent validity A type of criterion validity whereby a new measure correlates with a criterion measure taken at the same time.
confidence interval estimate A specified range of numbers within which a population mean is expected to lie; the set of acceptable hypotheses or the level of probability associated with an interval estimate.
confidence level A percentage or decimal value that tells how confident a researcher can be about being correct. It states the long-run percentage of the time that a confidence interval will include the true population mean.
constancy of conditions A procedure in which subjects in experimental groups are exposed to situations identical except for differing conditions of the independent variable.
constant error An error that occurs in the same experimental condition every time the basic experiment is repeated.
constant-sum scale A measure of attitudes in which respondents are asked to divide a constant sum to indicate the relative importance of attributes.
construct validity The ability of a measure to confirm a network of related hypotheses generated from a theory based on the concepts.
consumer panel A sample of individuals or households that record their attitudes, behavior, or purchasing habits in a diary over time.
content analysis A research technique for the objective, systematic, and quantitative description of the manifest content of communication.
contingency table The results of a cross-tabulation of two variables, such as answers to two survey questions.
continuous variable Any variable that has an infinite number of possible values.
contrived observation Observation in which the investigator creates an artificial environment in order to test a hypothesis.
control group A group of subjects who are exposed to the control condition in an experiment—that is, they are subjects not exposed to the experimental treatment.
convenience sampling The sampling procedure used to obtain those units or people most conveniently available.
cookies Small computer files inserted by a content provider into the computer of a visitor to a Web site; a cookie allows the content provider to track the user's visits to other Web sites and store that information.
correlation coefficient See *Simple correlation coefficient.*
correlation matrix The standard form for reporting correlational results.
counterbalancing A technique to reduce error caused by order of presentation by varying the order of experimental treatments for different groups.
counterbiasing statement An introductory statement or preface to a question that reduces a respondent's reluctance to answer potentially embarrassing questions.
cover letter A letter that accompanies the questionnaire in a mail survey. Its purpose is to induce the reader to complete and return the questionnaire.

criterion validity The ability of some measure to correlate with other measures of the same construct.
critical values The values that lie exactly on the boundary of the region of rejection.
cross-check Comparison of data from one organization with data from another source.
cross-functional teams Teams of people from various departments within a company, who work together to accomplish a common goal.
cross-sectional study A study in which various segments of a population are sampled at a single point in time.
cross-tabulation Organizing data by groups, categories, or classes to facilitate comparisons; a joint frequency distribution of observations on two or more sets of variables.
cumulative percentage A percentage (or percentage distribution) that has increased by successive additions.
customer relationship management (CRM) A decision support system that brings together numerous pieces of information about customers and their relationship with the company.

data Recorded measures of certain phenomena.
data conversion The process of changing the original form of the data to a format suitable to achieve the research objective.
data entry The process of transferring data from a research project to computers.
data matrix A rectangular arrangement of data into rows and columns.
data mining The use of powerful computers to dig through and analyze volumes of data to discover patterns about an organization's customers, products, and activities.
data-processing error A category of administrative error that occurs because of incorrect data entry, incorrect computer programming, or other error during data analysis.
data transformation The process of changing data from their original form to a format that better supports data analysis to achieve research objectives. Also called data conversion.
database A collection of raw data or information arranged in a logical manner and organized in a form that can be stored and processed by a computer.
database search and retrieval system A computerized system that allows a user to find and retrieve data.
debriefing Providing subjects with all pertinent facts about the nature and purpose of an experiment after its completion.
decision support system A computer-based system that helps decision makers confront problems through direct interaction with databases and analytical software.
deductive reasoning The logical process of deriving a conclusion about a specific instance based on a known general premise or something known to be true.
degrees of freedom (d.f.) The number of constraints or assumptions needed to calculate a statistical term.
demand characteristics Experimental design procedures that unintentionally hint to subjects about the experimenter's hypothesis; situational aspects of an experiment that demand that the participant respond in a particular way.
dependence method Any multivariate statistical technique used to explain the behavior of one or more dependent variables on the basis of two or more independent variables. Multiple regression analysis is a dependence method.
dependent variable A criterion or a variable that is to be predicted or explained. The criterion or standard by which the results of an experiment are judged. It is so named because it is expected to be dependent on the experimenter's manipulation of the independent variable.
depth interview A relatively unstructured, extensive interview used in the primary stages of the research process.
descriptive analysis The transformation of raw data into a form that will make them easy to understand and interpret; rearranging, ordering, manipulating data to provide descriptive information.
descriptive research Research designed to describe characteristics of a population or a phenomenon.
descriptive statistics Statistics used to describe or summarize information about a population or sample.
determinant-choice question A type of fixed-alternative question that requires a respondent to choose one (and only one) response from among several possible alternatives.
diagnostic analysis Analysis used to clarify research findings, such as explanations respondents give for a behavior or attitude.
dialog box A window that opens on a computer screen to prompt the user to enter information.
direct data entry The use of a computer terminal as an input device for data storage.
direct observation A straightforward attempt to observe and record what naturally occurs; the investigator does not create an artificial situation.
discriminant analysis A statistical tool for determining linear combinations of independent variables that show large differences in group means. The intent is to predict the probability of objects belonging in two or more mutually exclusive categories based on several independent variables.
discriminant validity The ability of some measure to have a low correlation with measures of dissimilar concepts.
discussion guide Written prefatory remarks and an outline of topics/questions that will be addressed in a focus group.
disguised question An indirect type of question that assumes that the purpose of the study must be hidden from respondents.
disproportional stratified sample A stratified sample in which the sample size for each stratum is allocated according to analytical considerations.
door-in-the-face compliance technique A two-step method for securing a high response rate. In step 1 an initial request, so large that nearly everyone refuses it, is made. In step 2 a second request is made for a smaller favor; respondents are expected to comply with this more reasonable request.
door-to-door interview Personal interview conducted at the respondent's home or place of business.
double-barreled question A question that may induce bias because it covers two issues at once.
double-blind design A technique in which neither the subjects nor the experimenter knows which are the experimental and which are the controlled conditions.
drop-down box In an Internet questionnaire, a space-saving device that reveals responses when they are needed but otherwise hides them from view.
drop-off method A survey method that requires the interviewer to travel to the respondent's location to drop off questionnaires that will be picked up later.
dummy table Representation of an actual table that will be in the findings section of the final report; used to provide a better understanding of what the actual outcome of the research will be.

e-mail survey A survey that uses questionnaires distributed and returned by e-mail.
editing The process of making data ready for coding and transfer to data storage. Its purpose is to ensure the completeness, consistency, and reliability of data.
elaboration analysis An analysis of the basic cross-tabulation for each level of a variable not previously considered, perhaps subgroups of the sample.
electronic data exchange (EDI) The linking of two or more companies' computer systems.
electronic interactive media Communication media that allow an organization and an audience to interact using digital technology (for example, through the Internet).
empirical level Level of knowledge that is verifiable by experience or observation.
environmental scanning Information gathering designed to detect indications of environmental changes in their initial stages of development.
equivalent-form method A method of measuring the correlation between alternative instruments, designed to be as equivalent as possible, administered to the same group of subjects.
error checking The final stage of the coding process, during which codes are verified and corrected as necessary.
error trapping Using software to control the flow of an Internet questionnaire—for

example, to prevent respondents from backing up or failing to answer a question.
evaluation research The formal, objective measurement and appraisal of the extent to which a given activity, project, or program has achieved its objectives.
experience survey An exploratory research technique in which individuals who are knowledgeable about a particular research problem are surveyed.
experiment A research method in which conditions are controlled so that one or more variable can be manipulated in order to test a hypothesis and experimentation is a research method that, by manipulating only one variable, allows evaluation of causal relationships among the variables.
experimental group The group of subjects exposed to an experimental treatment.
experimental treatment An alternative manipulation of the independent variable being investigated.
experimenter bias An effect on an experiment's results caused by the experimenter's presence, actions, or comments.
exploratory research Initial research conducted to clarify and define the nature of a problem.
external validity The ability of an experiment to generalize the results to the external environment.
extremity bias A category of response bias that results because some individuals tend to use extremes when responding to questions.
eye-tracking equipment Any of a number of devices that record how a subject views a stimulus, such as an advertisement, and how much time is spent looking at the various parts of the stimulus.

***F*-statistic** A test statistic that measures the ratio of one sample variance to another sample variance, such as the variance between groups to the variance within groups.
***F*-test** A procedure used to determine if there is more variability in the scores of one sample than in the scores of another sample.
face (content) validity Professional agreement that a scale logically appears to accurately measure what it is intended to measure.
fact finding A secondary data research objective aimed at collecting descriptive information to support decision making.
factor analysis A type of analysis used to discern the underlying dimensions or regularity in phenomena. Its general purpose is to summarize the information contained in a large number of variables into a smaller number of factors. There are a number of factor-analytical techniques.
factor loading A measure of the importance of a variable in measuring a factor; a means for interpreting and labeling a factor.
factor score A number that represents each observation's calculated value on each factor in a factor analysis.
factorial design An experimental design that investigates the interaction of two or more independent variables.
fax survey A survey that uses questionnaires distributed and/or returned via fax machines.
feedback A reverse flow of communication that may be used to modify subsequent communication.
field A collection of characters that represent a single type of data.
field editing Preliminary editing by a field supervisor on the same day as the interview; its purpose is to catch technical omissions, check legibility of handwriting, and clarify responses that are logically or conceptually inconsistent.
field experiment An experiment conducted in a natural setting, often for a long period of time.
field interviewing service A research supplier that specializes in gathering data.
fieldworker An individual responsible for gathering data in the field; for example, a personal interviewer administering a door-to-door questionnaire.
file A collection of related records.
file server An Internet server that contains documents and programs that can be accessed and downloaded via the host to a user's own computer.
file transfer protocol (ftp) A software program that allows users to establish an interactive file transfer session with a remote host's computer system so that the user can read and download full-text versions of files from the remote system.
filter question A question in a questionnaire that screens out respondents not qualified to answer a second question.
fixed-alternative question A question in which the respondent is given specific limited alternative responses and asked to choose the one closest to his or her own viewpoint.
focus group interview An unstructured, free-flowing interview with a small group of people.
follow-up A letter or postcard reminding a respondent to return a questionnaire.
foot-in-the-door compliance technique Based on foot-in-the-door theory, which attempts to explain compliance with a large or difficult task on the basis of the respondent's prior compliance with a smaller request.
forced answering software Software that prevents respondents from continuing with an Internet questionnaire if they fail to answer a question.
forced-choice scale A fixed-alternative rating scale that requires respondents to choose one of the fixed alternatives.
forecasting An effort to predict future business activity using secondary data and statistical techniques.
forward linkage A term implying that the early stages of the research process will influence the design of the later stages.
frequency-determination question A type of fixed-alternative question that asks for an answer about general frequency of occurrence.
frequency distribution A set of data organized by summarizing the number of times a particular value of a variable occurs.
frequency table A simple tabulation that indicates the frequency with which respondents give a particular answer.
funnel technique Asking general questions before specific questions in order to obtain unbiased responses.

global information system An organized collection of computer hardware and software, data, and personnel designed to capture, store, update, manipulate, analyze, and immediately display information about worldwide business activity.
graphic (visual) aid A picture or diagram used to clarify a complex point or to emphasize a message.
graphic rating scale A measure of attitude consisting of a graphic continuum that allows respondents to rate an object by choosing any point on the continuum.
guinea pig effect An effect on the results of an experiment caused by subjects changing their normal behavior or attitudes in order to cooperate with an experimenter.

Hawthorne effect An unintended effect on the results of a research experiment caused by the subjects knowing that they are participants.
hidden observation Situation in which the subject is unaware that observation is taking place.
history effect A specific event in the external environment occurring between the first and second measurements that is beyond the control of the experimenter and that affects the validity of an experiment.
host Any computer that has access to other computers on the Internet. One or more people may log on to a host computer through their personal computers.
human interactive media Personal forms of communication in which a message is directed at an individual (or small group), who then has the opportunity to interact with the communicator.
hypothesis An unproven proposition or supposition that tentatively explains certain facts or phenomena; a proposition that is empirically testable.
hypothesis test of a proportion A statistical test of a hypothesis about a proportion of a population based on data for a sample from the population.
hypothetical construct A variable that is not directly observable but is measured through an indirect indicators, such as verbal expression or overt behavior.

iceberg principle The idea that the dangerous part of many business problems is neither visible to nor understood by business managers.
in-house editing A rigorous editing job performed by centralized office staff.
in-house interviewer A fieldworker who is employed by the company that will be

using the survey data rather than by a research supplier.

independent variable A variable that is expected to influence the dependent variable. Its value may be changed or altered independently of any other variable. In an experimental design, the variable that can be manipulated to be whatever the experimenter wishes.

index (composite) measure Multi-item instrument constructed to measure a single concept; also called a composite measure.

index number Data summary values based on data for some base period to facilitate comparisons over time.

inductive reasoning The logical process of establishing a general proposition on the basis of observation of particular facts.

inferential statistics Statistics used to make inferences or judgments about a population on the basis of a sample.

information A body of facts that are in a format suitable for decision making.

informed consent The expressed or implied acknowledgment waiving an individual's right to privacy when he or she agrees to participate in a research study.

instrument A data collection form such as a questionnaire or other measuring device.

instrumentation effect An effect on the results of an experiment caused by a change in the wording of questions, a change in interviewers, or other changes in procedures to measure the dependent variable.

interaction effect The influence on a dependent variable by combinations of two or more independent variables.

interactive help desk In an Internet questionnaire, a live, real-time support feature that solves problems or answers questions respondents may encounter in completing the questionnaire.

intercept An intercepted segment of a line. The point at which a regression line intersects the *Y*-axis.

internal and proprietary data Secondary data that are created, recorded, or generated by the organization.

internal records and reports system A data collection and retrieval system that establishes orderly procedures to ensure that data on costs, shipments, inventory, sales, and other recurrent data are routinely collected, entered, and stored in a computer.

internal source Source of secondary data that is found inside the organization. The data are often referred to as internal and proprietary.

internal validity Validity determined by whether an experimental treatment was the sole cause of changes in a dependent variable.

Internet A worldwide network of computers that allows access to information and documents from distant sources; a combination of a worldwide communication system and the world's largest public library, containing seemingly endless range of information.

Internet survey A self-administered questionnaire posted on a Web site.

interpretation The process of making inferences and drawing conclusions concerning the meaning and implications of a research investigation.

interquartile range The part of a data distribution between the 25th and 75th percentiles; also called the midspread.

interval scale A scale that not only arranges objects or alternatives according to their magnitudes but also distinguishes this ordered arrangement in units of equal intervals.

interviewer bias Bias in the responses of subjects due to the influence of the interviewer.

interviewer cheating The practice of filling in fake answers or falsifying questionnaires while working as an interviewer.

interviewer error Administrative error caused by failure of an interviewer to record response correctly.

intranet A company's private data network that uses Internet standards and technology.

intuitive decision making Decision making based on impressions or experience, without evident rational thought or inference.

item nonresponse The technical term for an unanswered question on an otherwise complete questionnaire.

judgment (purposive) sampling A nonprobability sampling technique in which an experienced researcher selects the sample based upon some appropriate characteristic of the sample members.

knowledge A blend of information, experience, and insights that provides a framework that can be thoughtfully applied when assessing new information or evaluating relevant situations.

knowledge management The process of creating an inclusive, comprehensive, easily accessible organizational memory, which is often called the organization's intellectual capital.

laboratory experiment An experiment conducted in a laboratory or artificial setting to obtain almost complete control over the research setting.

ladder of abstraction Organization of concepts in sequence from the most concrete and individual to the most general.

Latin square design A balanced, two-way classification scheme that attempts to control or block out the effect of two or more extraneous factors by restricting randomization with respect to row and column effects.

leading question A question that suggests or implies certain answers.

least-squares method A mathematical technique for ensuring that the regression line will best represent the linear relationship between *X* and *Y*.

Likert scale A measure of attitudes designed to allow respondents to indicate how strongly they agree or disagree with carefully constructed statements that range from very positive to very negative toward an attitudinal object.

line graph A graphic aid showing the relationship of one variable to another. The dependent variable is generally shown on the vertical axis and the independent variable on the horizontal axis.

list server An Internet server that permits subscribers to join a mailing list and communicate with others around the globe.

loaded question A question that suggests a socially desirable answer or is emotionally charged.

longitudinal study A survey of respondents at different points in time, thus allowing analysis of response continuity and changes over time.

magnitude of error A value from a confidence interval that indicates how precise an estimate must be.

mail survey A self-administered questionnaire sent through the mail to respondents.

mailing list A list of the names, addresses, and phone numbers of specific populations.

main effect The influence on a dependent variable by each independent variable (separately).

mall intercept interviews Personal interviews conducted in shopping malls.

marginals Row and column totals in a contingency table.

market potential An estimate based on secondary data of likely sales volume of a given product within a market.

market tracking The observation and analysis of trends in industry volume and brand share over time.

matching A procedure for the assignment of subjects to groups; it ensures each group of respondents is matched on the basis of pertinent characteristics.

maturation effect An effect on the results of a research experiment caused by changes in the experimental subjects over time.

mean A measure of central tendency; the arithmetic average.

measures of association Statistical values designed to represent covariation between variables.

mechanical observation Observation technique that uses video cameras, traffic counters, and other machines to record behavior.

median A measure of central tendency that is the midpoint; the value below which half the values in a sample fall.

mode A measure of central tendency; the value that occurs most often.

model A representation of a system or a process.

model building An attempt to specify relationships between variables based on secondary data, sometimes using descriptive or predictive equations.

moderator variable A third variable that, when introduced into an analysis, alters or has a contingent effect on the relationship between an independent variable and a dependent variable.

monadic rating scale Any measure of attitudes that asks respondents about a single concept in isolation.

mortality effect Sample attrition that occurs when some subjects withdraw from an experiment before it is completed, thus affecting the validity of the experiment.

multidimensional scaling A technique that measures attitudes about objects in multidimensional space on the basis of respondents' judgments of similarity of objects.

multiple discriminant analysis A statistical technique for predicting the probability that an object will belong in one of two or more mutually exclusive categories (dependent variable), based on several independent variables.

multiple regression analysis An analysis of association in which the effects of two or more independent variables on a single, interval-scaled or ratio-scaled dependent variable are investigated simultaneously.

multistage area sampling Sampling that involves using a combination of other probability sampling techniques.

multivariate analysis of variance (MANOVA) A statistical technique that provides a simultaneous significance test of mean difference between groups, made for two or more dependent variables.

multivariate data analysis Statistical methods that allow the simultaneous investigation of more than two variables.

nominal scale A scale in which the numbers or letters assigned to objects serve as labels for identification or classification; a measurement scale of the simplest type.

nonforced-choice scale A fixed-alternative rating scale that provides a no-opinion category or that allows respondents to indicate that they cannot say which alternative is their choice.

nonparametric statistics Statistical procedures that use nominal- or ordinal-scaled data and make no assumptions about the distribution of the population (or sampling distribution).

nonprobability sampling A sampling technique in which units of the sample are selected on the basis of personal judgment or convenience.

nonrespondent A person who is not contacted or who refuses to cooperate in a research project.

nonresponse error The statistical difference between a survey that includes only those who responded and a perfect survey that would also include those who failed to respond.

normal distribution A symmetrical, bell-shaped distribution that describes the expected probability distribution of many chance occurrences.

not-at-home contact A potential respondent who is not at home or who is otherwise inaccessible on the first and second attempts at contact.

null hypothesis A statement about a status quo asserting that any change from what has been thought to be true will be due entirely to random error.

numerical scale An attitude rating scale similar to a semantic differential except that it uses numbers instead of verbal descriptions as response options to identify response positions.

observation The systematic recording of nonverbal as well as verbal behavior and communication.

observer bias A distortion of measurement resulting from the cognitive behavior or actions of the witnessing observer.

one-group pretest–posttest design A quasi-experimental design in which the subjects in the experimental group are measured before and after the treatment is administered but in which there is no control group.

one-shot design A quasi-experimental design in which a single measure is recorded after the treatment is administered and there is no control group. Also known as an after-only design.

online focus group A focus group whose members carry on their discussion through an Internet chat room.

open-ended box In an Internet questionnaire, a box where respondents can type in their own answers to open-ended questions.

open-ended response question A question that poses some problem and asks the respondent to answer in his or her own words.

operational definition A definition that gives meaning to a concept by specifying the activities or operations necessary in order to measure it.

opt in To give permission to receive selected e-mail, such as questionnaires, from a company with an Internet presence.

optical scanning system A data processing input device that reads material directly from mark sensed questionnaires.

optimal allocation stratified sample A sampling procedure in which both the size and the variation of each stratum are considered when determining sample size for each stratum.

oral presentation A spoken summary of the major findings, conclusions, and recommendations, given to clients or line managers to provide them with the opportunity to clarify any ambiguous issues by asking questions.

order bias Bias caused by the influence of earlier questions in a questionnaire or by an answer's position in a set of answers.

order of presentation bias An error in an experiment caused by subjects accumulating experience in the course of responding to multiple experimental treatments.

ordinal scale A scale that arranges objects or alternatives according to their magnitudes.

outlier A value that lies outside the normal range of a set of data.

paired comparison A measurement technique that involves presenting the respondent with two objects and asking the respondent to pick the preferred object. More than two objects may be presented, but comparisons are made in pairs.

panel study A longitudinal study that involves collecting data from the same sample of individuals or households over time.

parametric statistical procedures Statistical procedures that use interval-scaled or ratio-scaled data and assume populations or sampling distributions with normal distributions.

participant observation Situation in which an observer gains firsthand knowledge by being in or around the social setting being investigated.

percentage A part of a whole expressed in hundredths.

percentage distribution A frequency distribution into a table (or graph) that summarizes percentage values associated with particular values of a variable.

performance-monitoring research Research that regularly provides feedback for evaluation and control of business activity.

periodicity A problem that occurs in systematic sampling when the original list has a systematic pattern.

personal interview The gathering of information through face-to-face contact with an individual.

physical-trace evidence A visible mark of some past event or occurrence.

picture frustration A version of the Thematic Apperception Test that uses a cartoon drawing for which the respondent suggests dialogue that the cartoon characters might speak.

pie chart A graphic aid that shows the composition of some total quantity at a particular time; each angle, or "slice," is proportional to its percentage of the whole.

pilot study Any small-scale exploratory research technique that uses sampling but does not apply rigorous standards.

pivot question A filter question used to determine which version of a second question will be asked.

plug value An answer inserted according to a predetermined decision rule, if an editor finds a missing answer where there can be no missing values.

point estimate An estimate of the population mean in the form of a single value, usually the sample mean.

pooled estimate of the standard error An estimate of the standard error based on the assumption that variances of both groups (populations) are equal.

pop-up boxes In an Internet questionnaire, boxes that appear at selected points and contain information or instructions for respondents.

population (universe) A complete group of entities sharing some common set of characteristics.

population distribution A frequency distribution of the elements of a population.

population element An individual member of a specific population.
population parameter Variables in a population or measured characteristics of the population.
postcoding Determination of a framework for classifying responses to questions after editing, because coded categories cannot be established before data collection.
posttest-only control group design An after-only design in which the experimental group is tested after exposure to the treatment, and the control group is tested at the same time without having been exposed to the treatment; no premeasure is taken.
predictive validity A type of criterion validity whereby a new measure predicts a future event or correlates with a criterion measure administered at a later time.
preliminary tabulation Tabulation of the results of a pretest.
pretest A trial run with a group of respondents used to screen out problems in the instructions or design of a questionnaire.
pretest–posttest control-group design A true experimental design in which the experimental group is tested before and after exposure to the treatment, and the control group is tested at the same two times without being exposed to the experimental treatment.
pretesting The administration of a questionnaire to a small group of respondents in order to detect ambiguity or bias in the questions.
primary data Data gathered and assembled specifically for the research project at hand.
primary sampling unit (PSU) A unit selected in the first stage of sampling.
probability distribution The organization of probability values associated with particular values of a variable into a table (or graph).
probability sampling A sampling technique in which every member of the population has a known, nonzero probability of selection.
probing The verbal prompts made by a fieldworker when the respondent must be motivated to communicate his or her answer more fully. Probing encourages respondents to enlarge on, clarify, or explain answers.
problem definition The crucial first stage in the research process—determining the problem to be solved and the objectives of the research. The indication of a specific business decision area that will be clarified by answering some research questions.
production coding The physical activity of transferring the data from the questionnaire or data collection form after the data have been collected.
program strategy The overall plan to utilize a series of business research projects; a planning activity that places each project into the company's business plan.
projective technique An indirect means of questioning that enables a respondent to "project" beliefs and feelings onto a third party, an inanimate object, or a task situation.
proportion The percentage of population elements that successfully meet some criterion.
proportional stratified sample A stratified sample in which the number of sampling units drawn from each stratum is in proportion to the population size of that stratum.
proposition A statement concerned with the relationships among concepts; an assertion of a universal connection between events that have certain properties.
pseudo-research Research conducted for the purpose of organizational politics rather than to gather objective information for business decisions.
psychogalvanometer A device that measures galvanic skin response (GSR), involuntary changes in the electrical resistance of the skin.
psychographics A basis for market segmentation stressing consumer life-style characteristics and buying patterns in pursuit of life goals.
pupilometer A device used to observe and record changes in the diameter of the pupils of the eyes.
push button In a dialog box on an Internet questionnaire, a small outlined area, such as a rectangle or an arrow, that the respondent clicks on to select an option or perform a function, such as Submit.
push technology An information technology that delivers content to the viewer's desktop (using computer software known as smart agents or intelligent agents to find information) without the user's having to do the searching, or that stores entire Web sites on a user's computer for later viewing.

quadrant analysis A variation of the cross-tabulation table in which responses to two rating scale questions are plotted in four quadrants on a two-dimensional table.
quasi-experimental design An experimental design that fails to control adequately for loss of external or internal validity.
quota sampling A nonprobability sampling procedure that ensures that certain characteristics of a population sample will be represented to the exact extent that the investigator desires.

radio button In an Internet questionnaire, a circular icon, resembling a button, that activates one response choice and deactivates others when a respondent clicks on it.
random digit dialing A method of obtaining a representative sample for a telephone interview by using a table of random numbers to generate telephone numbers.
random error An error in which repetitions of the basic experiment sometimes favor one experimental condition and sometimes the other on a chance basis. See also *Random sampling error.*
random sampling error The difference between the result of a sample and the result of a census conducted using identical procedures; a statistical fluctuation that occurs because of chance variation in the elements selected for a sample.
randomization A procedure in which the assignment of subjects and treatments of groups is based on chance.
randomized block design (RBD) An extension of the completely randomized design in which a single extraneous variable that might affect test units' response to the treatment has been identified and the effects of this variable are isolated by being blocked out.
randomized response questions A research procedure for dealing with sensitive topics that uses a random procedure to determine which of two questions a respondent will be asked.
range The distance between the smallest and largest values of a frequency distribution.
range of possible random error The potential difference between a population mean and an observed value.
ranking A measurement task that requires that the respondents rank order a small number of activities, events, or objects on the basis of overall preference or some characteristic of the stimulus.
rating A measurement task that requires the respondent to estimate the magnitude of a characteristic or quality that an object possesses.
ratio scale A scale having absolute rather than relative quantities and possessing an absolute zero, where there is an absence of a given attribute.
recoding Changing codes to facilitate analysis.
record A collection of related fields.
refusal A person who is unwilling to participate in a research project.
region of rejection An area under a curve with values that are very unlikely to occur if the null hypothesis is true but relatively probable if the alternative hypothesis is true.
regression (bivariate) analysis A technique that attempts to predict the values of a continuous, interval-scaled or ratio-scaled dependent variable from the specific values of the independent variable.
reliability The degree to which measures are free from error and therefore yield consistent results.
repeat purchase rate Percentage of purchasers making a second or repeat purchase.
repeated measures Experimental technique in which the same subjects are exposed to all experimental treatments in order to eliminate any problems due to subject differences.
report format The general plan of organization for the parts of a written or oral research report.
research design A master plan specifying the methods and procedures for collecting and analyzing the needed information.
research follow-up Recontacting of decision makers and/or clients after they have had a chance to read a research report.

research methodology A discussion within the body of a research report of the research design, data collection methods, sampling techniques, fieldwork procedures, and data analysis efforts.

research objective The purpose of the research, expressed in measurable terms; the definition of what the research should accomplish.

research program Planning activity that identifies an ongoing series of research projects designed to supply an organization's continuing information needs.

research project A specific research investigation; a study that completes or is planned to follow the stages in the research process.

research proposal A written statement of the research design that includes a statement explaining the purpose of the study and a detailed, systematic outline of a particular research methodology.

research report A presentation of research findings directed to a specific audience to accomplish a specific purpose.

research supplier A commercial business research service that conducts business research activity for clients. The research supplier may be thought of as a business research consulting company.

residual The difference between the actual value of the dependent variable and the estimated value of the dependent variable in the regression equation.

respondent The person who answers an interviewer's questions or provides answers to written questions in a self-administered survey.

respondent error A classification of sample biases resulting from some respondent action or inaction, such as nonresponse or response bias.

response bias Survey error that occurs when respondents tend to answer questions in a certain direction. Examples of response bias are acquiescence bias, extremity bias, interviewer bias, auspices bias, and social desirability bias.

response latency The time it takes to decide between two alternatives; used as a measure of the strength of preference.

response rate The number of questionnaires returned or completed, divided by the total number of eligible people who were contacted or asked to participate in the survey.

reverse directory A directory similar to a telephone directory in which listings are by city and street address or by telephone numbers rather than alphabetical by last name.

role playing A projective research technique that requires the subject to act out someone else's behavior in a particular setting.

rotation In factor analysis, changing of geometric axes that represent the factors so as to contemplate a new problem solution having fewer or more factors.

rule of measurement An instruction to guide assignment of a number or other measurement designation.

sample A subset, or some part, of a larger population.

sample bias A persistent tendency for the results of a sample to deviate in one direction from the true value of the population parameter.

sample distribution A frequency distribution of the elements of a sample.

sample selection error An administrative procedural error caused by improper selection of a sample, thus introducing bias.

sample size The size of a sample; the number of observations or cases specified by (1) the estimated variance of the population, (2) the magnitude of acceptable error, and (3) the confidence level.

sample statistics Variables in a sample or measures computed from sample data.

sample survey Formal term for survey; it indicates that the purpose of contacting respondents is to obtain a representative sample of the target population.

sampling The process of using a small number of items or parts of a larger population to make conclusions about the whole population.

sampling distribution A theoretical probability distribution of all possible samples of a certain size drawn from a particular population.

sampling error See *Random sampling error.*

sampling frame The list of elements from which a sample may be drawn; also called working population.

sampling frame error Error that occurs when certain sample elements are not listed or available and are not represented in the sampling frame.

sampling interval The number of population elements between units selected for the sample.

sampling unit A single element or group of elements subject to selection in the sample.

sampling verification A fieldwork supervision task that requires checking to assure that samples conform to a project's sampling plan.

scale Any series of items that are progressively arranged according to value or magnitude; a series into which an item can be placed according to its quantification.

scanner data Product and brand sales data collected through optical character-recognition systems.

scientific method Techniques or procedures used to analyze empirical evidence in an attempt to confirm or disprove prior conceptions.

scientific observation The systematic process of recording the behavioral patterns of people, objects, and occurrences as they are witnessed.

search engine A computerized directory that allows anyone to search the World Wide Web for information in a particular way. Some search titles or headers of documents, others search the documents themselves, and still others search other indexes or directories.

secondary data Data that have been previously collected for some purpose other than the one at hand.

secondary data analysis Preliminary review of data collected for another purpose to clarify issues in the early stages of a research effort.

secondary sampling unit A unit selected in the second stage of sampling.

selection effect A sample bias resulting in differential selection of respondents for the comparison groups.

self-administered questionnaire A questionnaire that is filled in by the respondent rather than by an interviewer.

self-selection bias A bias that occurs because people who feel strongly about a subject are more likely to respond to survey questions than people who feel indifferent about that subject.

semantic differential An attitude measure consisting of a series of seven-point bipolar rating scales allowing response to a concept.

sensitivity A measurement instrument's ability to accurately measure variability in stimuli or responses.

sentence completion A projective technique in which respondents are required to complete a number of partial sentences with the first word or phrase that comes to mind.

server A computer that provides services on the Internet. A *file server* is an Internet server containing documents and programs that can be accessed and downloaded via the host to the user's own computer. A *list server* is an Internet server that admits subscribers to a mailing list to communicate with each other around the globe.

significance level The critical probability in choosing between the null and alternative hypotheses; the probability level that is too low to warrant support of the null hypothesis.

simple correlation coefficient A statistical measure of the covariation, or association, between two variables.

simple-dichotomy question A fixed-alternative question that requires the respondent to choose one of two alternatives.

simple random sampling A sampling procedure that assures each element in the population an equal chance of being included in the sample.

simple tabulation Counting the number of different responses to a question and arranging them in a frequency distribution.

situation analysis A preliminary investigation or informal gathering of background information to familiarize researchers or managers with the decision area.

slope The inclination of a regression line as compared to a base line, rise (vertical distance) over run (horizontal difference).

smart agent software Software that learns preferences and finds information without the user's having to search for it.

snowball sampling A sampling procedure in which initial respondents are selected by probability methods and additional respondents are obtained from information provided by the initial respondents.

social desirability bias Bias in the responses of subjects caused by their desire, either conscious or unconscious, to gain prestige or to appear in a different social role.

societal norms Codes of behavior adopted by a group, suggesting what a member of the group ought to do under given circumstances.

Solomon four-group design A true experimental design that combines both the pretest-posttest with control group and the posttest-only with control group designs, thereby providing a means for controlling the interactive testing effect and other sources of extraneous variation.

sorting technique A measurement technique that presents a respondent with several concepts printed on cards and requires the respondent to arrange the cards into a number of piles to classify the concepts.

split-ballot technique A technique used to control for response bias. Two alternative phrasings of the same questions are utilized for respective halves of the sample to yield a more accurate total response than would be possible if only a single phrasing were utilized.

split-half method A method of measuring the degree of internal consistency by checking one half of the results of a set of scaled items against the other half.

spurious relationship An apparent relationship between two variables that is not authentic, but appears authentic because an elaboration analysis with a third variable has not yet been conducted.

standard deviation A quantitative index of a distribution's spread or variability; the square root of the variance.

standard error of the mean The standard deviation of the sampling distribution of the mean.

standard error of the proportion The standard deviation of the sampling distribution of the proportion.

standardized normal distribution A normal curve with a mean of zero and a standard deviation of one. It is a theoretical probability distribution.

Stapel scale An attitude measure that places a single adjective in the center of an even number of numerical values.

static group design An after-only design in which subjects in the experimental group are measured after being exposed to the experimental treatment, and the control group is measured without having been exposed to the experimental treatment; no pretreatment measure is taken.

status bar In an Internet questionnaire, a visual indicator that tells the respondent what portion of the survey he or she has completed.

stratified sampling A probability sampling procedure in which subsamples are drawn from simple random within different strata that are more or less equal on some characteristic.

streaming media Multimedia content, such as audio or video, that can be accessed on the Internet without being downloaded first.

structured question A question that imposes a limit on the number of allowable responses.

survey A research technique in which information is gathered from a sample of people by use of a questionnaire or interview; a method of data collection based on communication with a representative sample of individuals.

syndicated service A business research supplier that provides standardized information for many clients, such as, for example, the A. C. Nielsen Retail Index.

systematic (nonsampling) error Error resulting from some imperfect aspect of the research design that causes response error or from a mistake in the execution of the research; error arising from sample bias, mistakes in recording responses, or nonresponses from persons who were not contacted or who refused to participate.

systematic sampling A sampling procedure in which an initial starting point is selected by a random process, and then every nth number on the list is selected.

***t*-distribution** A family of symmetrical, bell-shaped distributions with a mean of 0 and a standard deviation of 1, used when the population standard deviation is unknown or when testing a hypothesis with a small sample size.

***t*-test** A univariate hypothesis test using the t-distribution rather than the *Z*-distribution. It is used when the population standard deviation is unknown and the sample size is small.

***t*-test for difference of means** A technique used to test the hypothesis that the mean scores on some interval-scaled variable are significantly different for two independent samples or groups.

table A graphic aid generally used for presenting numerical information, especially when such information can be arranged in rows and columns.

tabulation The orderly arrangement of data in a frequency table or other summary format.

tachistoscope A device that controls the amount of time a subject is exposed to a visual image.

target population The specific, complete group relevant to the research project.

telephone interviewing Contacting respondents by telephone to gather responses to survey questions.

telephone survey The data collection method that uses telephone interviewing to collect the data.

test of differences Investigation of a hypothesis that states that two (or more) groups differ with respect to measures on a variable.

test marketing The scientific testing and controlled experimental procedure that provides an opportunity to test a new product or a new marketing plan under realistic marketing conditions to obtain a measure of sales or profit potentials.

test-retest method The administering of the same scale or measure to the same respondents at two separate points in time in order to test for reliability.

test tabulation Tallying of a small sample of the total number of replies to a particular question during the coding process in order to construct coding categories.

test unit A subject or entity whose responses to experimental treatments are observed and measured.

testing effect In a before-and-after study the effect of pretesting, which may sensitize subjects when taking a test for the second time, thus affecting the validity of the experiment.

thematic apperception test (TAT) A test consisting of a series of pictures shown to research subjects who are then asked to provide a description of the pictures. The researcher analyzes the content of these descriptions in an effort to clarify a research problem.

theory A coherent set of general propositions used to explain the apparent relationships among certain observed phenomena. Theories allow generalizations beyond individual facts or situations.

third-person technique A projective technique in which the respondent is asked why a third person does what he or she does or what he or she thinks about an object, event, person, or activity. The respondent is expected to transfer his or her attitudes to the third person.

Thurstone scale An attitude measure in which judges assign scale values to attitudinal statements and then subjects are asked to respond to these statements.

time-series design An experimental design utilized when experiments are conducted over long periods of time. It allows researchers to distinguish between temporary and permanent changes in dependent variables.

total quality management (TQM) A business philosophy that focuses on integrating customer-driven quality throughout the organization.

total variance In analysis of variance, the sum of within-group variance and between-group variance.

training interview A practice session during which an inexperienced fieldworker records answers on a questionnaire to develop skills and clarify project requirements.

Type I error An error caused by rejecting the null hypothesis when it is true.

Type II error An error caused by failing to reject the null hypothesis when the alternative hypothesis is true.

unbalanced rating scale A fixed-alternative rating scale that has more response categories piled up at one end of the scale and an unequal number of positive and negative categories.

undisguised question A straightforward question that assumes the respondent is willing to reveal the answer.

univariate data analysis A type of analysis that assesses the statistical significance of a hypothesis about a single variable.

universal product code (UPC) A system that records product and brand sales information in bar codes that can be read by optical scanners.

unstructured question A question that does not restrict the respondent's answers.

user interaction system Computer software that manages the interface between the user and the system.

validity The ability of a scale or measuring instrument to measure what it is intended to measure.

variable Anything that may assume different numerical or categorical values.

variable piping software Software that allows variables to be inserted into an Internet questionnaire as a respondent is completing it.

variance A measure of variability or dispersion. The square root is the standard deviation.

verification The quality control procedures used in fieldwork to ensure that interviewers are following the sampling procedures; the method used to determine if interviewers are falsifying interviews.

verification by reinterviewing A fieldwork supervision task that requires recontacting respondents to assure that interviews were properly conducted.

visible observation Situation in which the observer's presence is known to the subject.

voice pitch analysis A physiological measurement technique that records abnormal frequencies in the voice that are supposed to reflect emotional reactions to various stimuli.

welcome screen The first Web page in an Internet survey, which introduces the survey and requests that the respondent enter a password or PIN.

within-group variance Variation of scores within a group due to random error or individual difference.

word association test A projective research technique in which the subject is presented with a list of words, one at a time, and asked to respond with the first word that comes to mind.

World Wide Web (WWW) A portion of the Internet that is a system of computer servers that organize information into documents called Web pages.

***Z*-test** A univariate hypothesis test using the standardized normal distribution, which is the distribution of Z.

***Z*-test for differences of proportions** A technique is used to test the hypothesis that proportions are significantly different for two independent samples or groups.

INDEX

E

F

G

H

I

J

S

T